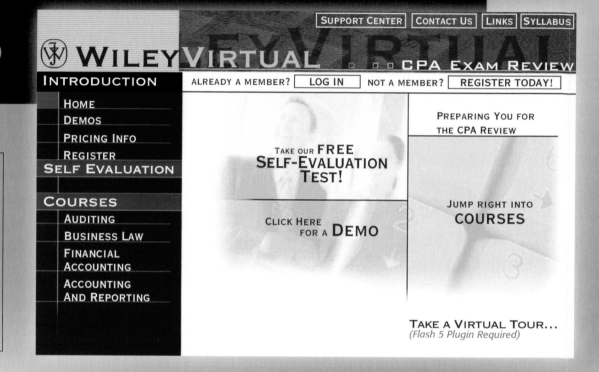

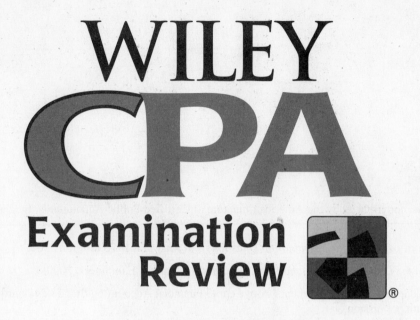

WILEY
CPA
Examination Review

2003

Financial Accounting and Reporting
BUSINESS ENTERPRISES

O. Ray Whittington, CPA, PhD   **Patrick R. Delaney,** CPA, PhD

John Wiley & Sons, Inc.

CONTENTS

[1] *As explained in Chapter 1, this book is organized into 12 modules (manageable study units). The numbering of the modules commences with number 22 to correspond with the numbering system used in our two-volume set.*

PREFACE

Passing the CPA exam upon your first attempt is possible! The *Wiley CPA Examination Review* preparation materials provide you with the necessary materials (visit our website at www.wiley.com/cpa for more information). It's up to you to add the hard work and commitment. Together we can beat the first-time pass rate of less than 20%. All Wiley CPA products are continuously updated to provide you with the most comprehensive and complete knowledge base. Choose your products from the Wiley preparation materials and you can proceed confidently. You can select support materials that are exam-based and user-friendly. You can select products that will help you pass!

Remaining current is one of the keys to examination success. Here is a list of what's new in this edition of the *Wiley CPA Examination Review Financial Accounting and Reporting* **text.**

- The latest AICPA Content Specification Outline for Financial Accounting and Reporting
- Revised, up-to-date information, especially on accounting for business combinations and goodwill and other intangibles
- Revisions and additions to the Financial Accounting Standards Board's Standards, Concepts, and Interpretations, especially in the areas of

  - Statement of Financial Accounting Standard 145, *Rescission of FASB Statements No. 4, 44, and 64, Amendment of FASB Statement No. 13*
  - Statement of Financial Accounting Standard 146, *Accounting for Costs Associated with Exit or Disposal Activities*

The objective of this work is to provide you with the knowledge to pass the Financial Accounting and Reporting portion of the Uniform Certified Public Accounting (CPA) Exam. The text is divided up into fifteen areas of study called modules. Each module contains written text with discussion, examples, and demonstrations of the key exam concepts. Following each text area, actual American Institute of Certified Public Accountants (AICPA) unofficial questions and answers are presented to test your knowledge. We are indebted to the AICPA for permission to reproduce and adapt examination materials from past examinations. Author constructed questions are provided for new areas or areas that require updating. All author constructed questions are modeled after AICPA question formats. The multiple-choice questions are grouped into topical areas, giving candidates a chance to assess their areas of strength and weakness. Selection and inclusion of topical content is based upon current AICPA Content Specification Outlines. Only testable topics are presented. If the CPA exam does not test it, this text does not present it.

The CPA exam is one of the toughest exams you will ever take. It will not be easy. But if you follow our guidelines and focus on your goal, you will be thrilled with what you can accomplish.

Ray Whittington
November 2002

**Don't forget to visit our website at www.wiley.com/cpa
for supplements and updates.**

ABOUT THE AUTHORS

Patrick R. Delaney was the Arthur Andersen LLP Alumni Professor of Accountancy and Department Chair at Northern Illinois University. He received his PhD in Accountancy from the University of Illinois. He had public accounting experience with Arthur Andersen LLP and was coauthor of *GAAP: Interpretation and Application*, also published by John Wiley & Sons, Inc. He served as Vice President and a member of the Illinois CPA Society's Board of Directors, and was Chairman of its Accounting Principles Committee; was a past president of the Rockford Chapter, Institute of Management Accountants; and had served on numerous other professional committees. He was a member of the American Accounting Association, American Institute of Certified Public Accountants, and Institute of Management Accountants. Professor Delaney was published in *The Accounting Review* and was a recipient of the Illinois CPA Society's Outstanding Educator Award, NIU's Excellence in Teaching Award, and Lewis University's Distinguished Alumnus Award. He was involved in NIU's CPA Review Course as director and instructor.

Ray Whittington, PhD, CPA, CMA, CIA, is the Ledger & Quill Director of the School of Accountancy at DePaul University. Prior to joining the faculty at DePaul, Professor Whittington was the Director of Accountancy at San Diego State University. From 1989 through 1991, he was the Director of Auditing Research for the American Institute of Certified Public Accountants (AICPA), and he previously was on the audit staff of KPMG. He previously served as a member of the Auditing Standards Board of the AICPA and as a member of the Accounting and Review Services Committee and the Board of Regents of the Institute of Internal Auditors. Professor Whittington has published numerous textbooks, articles, monographs, and continuing education courses.

ABOUT THE CONTRIBUTORS

Richard E. Baker, PhD, CPA, is the Ernst and Young Professor of Accountancy and University Presidential Teaching Professor at Northern Illinois University and teaches in the NIU CPA Review Course. Professor Baker prepared the Business Combinations and Consolidations Module. He has received several teaching awards at NIU.

John C. Borke, MAS, CPA, is an Associate Professor of Accounting at the University of Wisconsin-Platteville. He received the UW-Platteville Excellence in Teaching Award, and has worked as a staff auditor with KPMG Peat Marwick. Professor Borke prepared several other sections in Financial Accounting including the section in Chapter 5 on the Conceptual Framework.

John McDougald, MAS, CPA, is an Instructor in the College of Business at Northern Illinois University. He has extensive industry experience having spent 28 years in management positions with Ameritech. Mr. McDougald prepared the Derivatives section of Module 32.

W. Max Rexroad, PhD, CPA, is Professor of Accounting at Illinois State University. He has received the Distinguished Teaching Award from the College of Business at ISU as well as other teaching awards. He has taught numerous CPE courses for the Illinois CPA Society and other state societies. He prepared a revision of the Pensions section in Module 26.

John R. Simon, PhD, CPA, is the Coopers and Lybrand LLP Professor of Accountancy and a Presidential Teaching Professor at Northern Illinois University. He has taught in NIU's CPA Review Course for the past 24 years and was the director of the course for 10 years. He is a recipient of NIU's Excellence in Teaching Award. Professor Simon prepared the Earnings Per Share section of the Stockholders' Equity Module, the Foreign Currency Translation Module, and expanded topical coverage in several other modules in Chapter 5.

Susan Smith, MA, CAS (English), CPA, Garvey International, Inc. Ms. Smith has taught rhetoric and technical writing at Northern Illinois University. She prepared material for "Improving Your Writing" in Chapter 3.

1 BEGINNING YOUR CPA REVIEW PROGRAM

To maximize the efficiency of your review program, begin by studying (not merely reading) this chapter and the next three chapters of this volume. They have been carefully organized and written to provide you with important information to assist you in successfully completing the Financial Accounting and Reporting section of the CPA exam. Beyond providing a comprehensive outline to help you organize the material tested on the Financial Accounting and Reporting section of the exam, Chapter 1 will assist you in organizing a study program to prepare for the Financial Accounting and Reporting portion. Self-discipline is essential.

GENERAL COMMENTS ON THE EXAMINATION

Successful completion of the Uniform CPA Examination in Financial Accounting and Reporting is an attainable goal. Keep this point foremost in your mind as you study the first four chapters in this volume and develop your study plan.

Purpose of the Examination[1]

The CPA examination is designed to measure the wide range of knowledge and skills that entry-level CPAs are expected to possess. The examination assesses candidates' knowledge and skills at three different levels of increasing difficulty.

1. Understanding—The ability to recognize or recall learned materials and grasp the meaning.
2. Application—The ability to use learned materials in new situations.
3. Evaluation—The ability to draw conclusions, make decisions, and communicate judgments.

Presently, at least 60% of each examination section assesses candidates' knowledge and skills at the application and evaluation levels. As the majority of the exam is testing at these higher levels of comprehension, **it is crucial that candidates know the material rather than merely being familiar with the material**.

The CPA examination is one of many screening devices to assure the competence of those licensed to perform the attest function and to render professional accounting services. Other screening devices include educational requirements, ethics examinations, and work experience.

---

[1] *The following general comments are largely adapted from* **Information for Uniform CPA Examination Candidates,** *published by the American Institute of Certified Public Accountants.* **Information for Uniform CPA Examination Candidates** *is usually sent to CPA candidates by their State Board of Accountancy as they apply to sit for the CPA Examination. If you will not be immediately applying to your State Board of Accountancy to sit for the exam, you may purchase the latest edition by contacting the AICPA order department at 888-777-7077. You can find some of the information on the web at www.aicpa.org/edu/index.htm.*

The examination appears to test the material covered in accounting programs of the better business schools. It also appears to be based upon the body of knowledge essential for the practice of public accounting and the audit of a medium-sized client. Since the examination is primarily a textbook or academic examination, you should plan on taking it as soon as possible after completing your accounting education.

Examination Content

Guidance concerning topical content of the Financial Accounting and Reporting part of the CPA exam can be found in a document prepared by the Board of Examiners of the AICPA entitled *Content Specification Outlines for the Uniform Certified Public Accountant Examination*. We have included the content outlines for Financial Accounting and Reporting in Chapter 5. Although the exam is now nondisclosed, these outlines should be used as an indication of the topics' relative importance on past exams.

The Board's objective in preparing this detailed listing of topics tested on the exam is to help "in assuring the continuing validity and reliability of the Uniform CPA Examination." These outlines are an excellent source of guidance concerning the areas and the emphasis to be given each area on future exams.

The AICPA Board of Examiners issued revised Content Specification Outlines in May 2000. These are provided to each candidate in *Information for Uniform CPA Examination Candidates* along with the Examination application or may be purchases by contacting the AICPA order department at 888-777-7077.

New accounting and auditing pronouncements, including those in the governmental and not-for-profit areas, are tested six months after the pronouncement's *effective* date. If early application is permitted, a pronouncement is tested six months after the *issuance* date; candidates are also responsible for the old pronouncement until it is superseded. The exam covers the Internal Revenue Code and federal tax regulations in effect six months before the date of the exam. For the Business Law and Professional Responsibilities section, federal laws are tested six months following their *effective* date and of uniform acts one year after their adoption by a simple majority of jurisdictions. The AICPA posts content changes regularly on its Internet site. The address is www.aicpa.org.

Nondisclosure of Examination Questions and Answers

Beginning May 1996, the Uniform CPA Examination became nondisclosed. For each exam section, candidates are required to sign a *Statement of Confidentiality,* which states that they will not divulge the nature and content of any exam question. Candidates no longer retain or receive their question booklets after the exam. Complete examination questions and answers are no longer published. The AICPA does, however, periodically release selected questions and answers. The released questions are no longer used on actual exams, but they are representative of questions appearing on future exams.

Schedule of Examinations

The two-day Uniform Certified Public Accountant Examination is given twice a year, usually on the first consecutive Wednesday-Thursday in May and November. The subject and time schedules are

CPA EXAM SCHEDULE AND FORMAT

			FORMAT	
SECTION	TIME PERIOD	MC	OOAF	FRE/P
Business Law and Professional Responsibilities	Wed. 9:00 - Noon	50-60%	20-30%	20-30%
Auditing	Wed. 1:30 - 6:00	50-60%	20-30%	20-30%
Accounting and Reporting (Taxation; Managerial; and Governmental and Not-for-Profit Organizations)	Thurs. 8:30 - Noon	50-60%	40-50%	--
Financial Accounting and Reporting (Business Enterprises)	Thurs. 1:30 - 6:00	50-60%	20-30%	20-30%
TOTAL	15.5 hours			
MC = Multiple-Choice; OOAF = Other Objective Answer Format; FRE/P = Free Response Essay/Problem				

The above schedule presents three basic questions formats.

1. Multiple-Choice
2. Other Objective Answer Format
3. Free Response Essay/Problem

See the beginning of Chapter 5 for a table of contents of question formats by module and topic. The exact number of multiple-choice, other objective answer format, and essay questions that appear on the exam is unknown. Approximately 10 to 15% of the multiple-choice questions are considered to be "pretest" questions. Pretesting means that some questions are not counted in the tabulation of the candidate's final grade. The pretest questions are used to help the AICPA develop future examination test question databases.

The AICPA no longer lists suggested time limits. In order to avoid the possibility of running out of time, it is imperative that today's candidate utilize some form of time management. See Chapter 4, Allocation of Time, for suggested time management techniques.

The following chart lists upcoming examination administrations and the corresponding uniform mailing dates (dates grades will be mailed by the state boards).

Examination Administration	*Uniform Mailing Date*
May 7 and 8, 2003	August 4, 2003
November 5 and 6, 2003	February 2, 2004

In 2004, the AICPA plans to begin using a computerized Uniform CPA Examination. As of the publication date of this text, very little information has been released. We will post more detailed information as it become available on the CPA Examination Review Wiley website at www.wiley.com/cpa.

State Boards of Accountancy

The right to practice public accounting as a CPA is governed by individual state statutes. While some rules regarding the practice of public accounting vary from state to state, all State Boards of Accountancy use the Uniform CPA Examination and AICPA advisory grading service as one of the requirements to practice public accounting. Every candidate should contact the applicable State Board of Accountancy to determine the requirements to sit for the exam (e.g., education, filing dates, references, and fees). A frequent problem candidates encounter is failure to apply by the deadline. **Apply to sit for the examination early. Also, you should use extreme care in filling out the application and mailing the required materials to your State Board of Accountancy.** If possible, have a friend review your completed application before mailing with check, photo, etc. Candidates can be turned down for a particular CPA examination simply because of minor technical details that were overlooked (checks not signed, photos not enclosed, question not answered on application, etc.). **Because of the very high volume of applications received in the more populous states, the administrative staff does not have time to call or write to correct minor details and will simply reject your application.** This can be extremely disappointing particularly after spending many hours preparing to sit for a particular exam.

The various state boards, their addresses, and telephone numbers are listed on the following page. Be sure to inquire to your state board for specific and current requirements.

It is possible for candidates to sit for the examination in another state as an out-of-state candidate. Candidates desiring to do so should contact the State Board of Accountancy in their home state.

ATTRIBUTES OF EXAMINATION SUCCESS

Your primary objective in preparing for the Financial Accounting and Reporting part of the CPA exam is to pass. Other objectives such as learning new and reviewing old material should be considered secondary. The six attributes of examination success discussed below are **essential**. You should study the attributes and work toward achieving/developing each of them **before** taking the examination.

1. **Knowledge of Material**

   Two points are relevant to "knowledge of material" as an attribute of examination success. **First,** there is a distinct difference between being familiar with material and knowing the material. Frequently candidates confuse familiarity with knowledge. Can you remember when you just could not answer an examination question or did poorly on an examination, but maintained to yourself or your instructor that you knew the material? You probably were only familiar with the material. On the CPA examination, familiarity is insufficient; you must know the material. For example, you may be familiar with the concepts in accounting for leases (SFAS 13), but can you compute the present value of an annuity due under a lease agreement and record entries for the lessee and lessor? Once again, a major concern must be to know the material rather than just being familiar with it. Knowledgeable discussion of the material is required on the CPA examination. **Second,** the Financial Accounting and Reporting exam tests a literally overwhelming amount of material at a rigorous level. From an undergraduate point of view, the CPA examination in Financial Accounting and Reporting includes material from the following courses.

   Intermediate Financial (usually two semesters)
   Advanced Financial

	STATE BOARD ADDRESS	TELEPHONE #
AK	Dept. of Comm. and Econ. Dev. Div. of Occ. Licensing • P.O. Box 110806 • Juneau, AK • 99811-0806	(907) 465-3811
AL	P.O. Box 300375 • Montgomery, AL • 36130-0375	(334) 242-5700
AR	101 E. Capitol • STE 430 • Little Rock, AR • 72201	(501) 682-1520
AZ	3877 N. 7th St. • STE 106 • Phoenix, AZ • 85014	(602) 255-3648
CA	2000 Evergreen St.• STE 250 • Sacramento, CA • 95815-3832	(916) 263-3680
CO	1560 Broadway • STE 1340 • Denver, CO • 80202	(303) 894-7800
CT	Secretary of State • 30 Trinity Street • PO Box 150470 • Hartford, CT • 06115	(860) 509-6179
DC	941 North Capital St., NE • Rm. 7200 • Washington, DC • 20002	(202) 442-4461
DE	Cannon Bldg. • STE 203 • 861 Silver Lake Blvd.• Dover, DE • 19904	(302) 744-4500
FL	240 NW 76 Dr. • STE A • Gainesville, FL • 32607	(352) 333-2500
GA	237 Coliseum Drive • Macon, GA • 31217-3858	(478) 207-1400
GU	GCIC Bldg 414 W. Soledad Ave., STE 508 • Hagatua, Guam • 96910-5014	(671) 477-1050
HI	Dept. of Commerce & Consumer Affairs • P.O. Box 3469 • Honolulu, HI • 96801-3469	(808) 586-2696
IA	1918 S.E. Hulsizer Ave. • Ankeny, IA • 50021-3941	(515) 281-4126
ID	P.O. Box 83720 • Boise, ID • 83720-0002	(208) 334-2490
IL	505 E. Green St. • Room 216 • Champaign, IL • 61820-5723	(217) 333-1565
IN	302 W. Washington St. • Rm E034 • Indianapolis, IN • 46204-2246	(317) 232-5987
KS	900 S.W. Jackson Street • STE 556 • Topeka, KS • 66612-1239	(785) 296-2162
KY	332 W. Broadway • STE 310 • Louisville, KY • 40202-2115	(502) 595-3037
LA	Pan-American Life Center • 601 Poydras St. • STE 1770 • New Orleans, LA • 70139	(504) 566-1244
MA	239 Causeway St. • STE 450 • Boston, MA • 02114	(617) 727-1806
MD	500 N. Calvert St. • 3rd Floor • Baltimore, MD • 21202-3651	(410) 333-6322
ME	Dept. of Prof. & Fin. Reg. • #35 State House Station • Augusta, ME • 04333	(207) 624-8603
MI	Dept. of Consumer & Industry Services • P.O. Box 30018 • Lansing, MI • 48909-7518	(517) 241-9249
MN	85 E. 7th Pl. • STE 125 • St. Paul, MN • 55101	(651) 296-7938
MO	P.O. Box 613 • Jefferson City, MO • 65102	(573) 751-0012
MS	653 N. State St. • Jackson, MS • 39202-3304	(601) 354-7320
MT	301 S. Park • P.O. Box 200513 • Helena, MT • 59620-0513	(406) 841-2389
NC	1101 Oberlin Rd. • STE 104 • P.O. Box 12827 • Raleigh, NC • 27605-2827	(919) 733-4222
ND	2701 S. Columbia Rd. • Grand Forks, ND • 58201-6029	(701) 775-7100
NE	P.O. Box 94725 • Lincoln, NE • 68509-4725	(402) 471-3595
NH	6 Chenell Dr. • STE 220 • Concord, NH • 03301	(603) 271-3286
NJ	P.O. Box 45000 • Newark, NJ • 07101	(973) 504-6380
NM	1650 University N.E. • STE 400A • Albuquerque, NM • 87102	(505) 841-9108
NV	200 S. Virginia St. • STE 670 • Reno, NV • 89501-2408	(775) 786-0231
NY	Div. of Pro. Lic. Ser. • 89 Washington Ave. • 2nd Fl. E. Mezz. • Albany, NY • 12230	(518) 474-3817
OH	77 S. High St. • 18th Floor. • Columbus, OH • 43266	(614) 466-4135
OK	4545 Lincoln Blvd. • STE 165 • Oklahoma City, OK • 73105-3413	(405) 521-2397
OR	3218 Pringle Rd SE #110 • Salem, OR • 97302-6307	(503) 378-4181
PA	124 Pine St. • 1st Floor • Harrisburg, PA • 17101-2649	(717) 783-1404
PR	Box 9023271 • Old San Juan Station • San Juan, PR • 00902-3271	(787) 722-4816
RI	Dept. of Bus. Reg. • 233 Richmond St. • STE 236 • Providence, RI • 02903-4236	(401) 222-3185
SC	P.O. Box 11329 • Columbia, SC • 29211	(803) 896-4492
SD	301 E. 14th St. • STE 200 • Sioux Falls, SD • 57104	(605) 367-5770
TN	500 James Robertson Prkwy. • 2nd Floor. • Nashville, TN • 37243-1141	(615) 741-2550
TX	333 Guadalupe Tower 3 • STE 900 • Austin, TX • 78701-3900	(512) 305-7800
UT	P.O. Box 146741 • Salt Lake City, UT • 84114-6741	(801) 530-6720
VA	3600 West Broad Street • STE 696 • Richmond, VA • 23230-4917	(804) 367-8505
VI	Office of Boards & Comm. • Golden Rock Shopping Center • Christiansted • St. Croix, VI • 00822	(340) 773-4305
VT	26 Terrace St. • Drawer 09 • Montpelier, VT • 05609-1106	(802) 828-2191
WA	Box 9131 • Olympia, WA • 98507-9131	(360) 753-2585
WI	1400 E. Washington Ave. • P.O. Box 8935 • Madison, WI • 53708-8935	(608) 266-5511
WV	122 Capitol St. • Charleston, WV • 25301	(304) 558-3557
WY	2020 Carey Ave. • Cheyenne, WY • 82002-0610	(307) 777-7551

NOTE: The publisher does not assume responsibility for errors in the above information. You should request information concerning requirements in your state at least six months in advance of the exam dates.

Furthermore, as noted earlier, the CPA exam will test new material sometimes as early as six months after issuance. In other words, you are not only responsible for material in the above courses, but also for all new developments in each of these areas.

This text contains outlines of accounting topics from FASB pronouncements, financial accounting courses, etc. Return to the original material (e.g., FASB, your accounting textbooks, etc.) only if the outlines do not reinforce material you already know.

2. **Commitment to Exam Preparation**

Your preparation for the CPA exam should begin at least three to four months prior to your scheduled exam date. Over the course of your preparation, you will experience many peaks and valleys. There will be days when you feel completely prepared and there will also be days when you feel totally overwhelmed. This is not unusual and, in fact, should be expected.

The CPA exam is a very difficult and challenging exam. How many times in your college career did you study months for an exam? Probably not too many. Therefore, candidates need to remain focused on the objective--succeeding on the CPA exam.

Develop a personal study plan so that you are reviewing material daily. Of course, you should schedule an occasional study break to help you relax, but don't schedule too many breaks. Candidates who dedicate themselves to studying have a much greater chance of going through this process one time. On the other hand, a lack of focus and piecemeal preparation will only extend the process over several exams.

3. **Solutions Approach**

The solutions approach is a systematic approach to solving the problems found on the CPA examination. Many candidates know the material fairly well when they sit for the CPA exam, but they do not know how to take the examination. Candidates generally neither work nor answer problems efficiently in terms of time or grades. The solutions approach permits you to avoid drawing "blanks" on CPA exam problems; using the solutions approach coupled with grader orientation (see below) allows you to pick up a sizable number of points on questions testing material with which you are not familiar. Chapter 3 outlines the solutions approach for problem/essay questions, multiple-choice questions, and other objective questions. Example problems are worked as well as explained.

4. **Grader Orientation**

Your score on each section of the exam is determined by the sum of points assigned to individual questions. Thus, you must attempt to maximize your points on each individual question. The name of the game is to satisfy the grader, as s/he is the one who awards you points. Your answer and the grading guide (which conforms closely to the unofficial answer) are the basis for the assignment of points.

This text helps you develop grader orientation by analyzing AICPA grading procedures and grading guides (this is explained further in Chapter 2). The author believes that the solutions approach and grader orientation, properly developed, are worth at least 10 to 15 points on each section to most candidates.

5. **Examination Strategy**

Prior to sitting for the examination, it is important to develop an examination strategy (i.e., a preliminary inventory of the questions, the order in which to work questions, etc.). Your ability to cope successfully with the 4 1/2 hours of examination in Financial Accounting and Reporting can be improved by

a. Recognizing the importance and usefulness of an examination strategy
b. Using Chapter 4 "Taking the Examination" and previous examination experience to develop a "personal strategy" for the exam
c. Testing your "personal strategy" on previous CPA questions under examination conditions (using no reference material and with a time limit)

6. **Examination Confidence**

You need confidence to endure the physical and mental demands of 4 1/2 hours of problem solving under tremendous pressure. Examination confidence results from proper preparation for the exam, which includes mastering the first five attributes of examination success. Examination confidence is necessary to enable you to overcome the initial frustration with problems for which you may not be specifically prepared.

This study manual, when properly used, contributes to your examination confidence. Build confidence by completing the questions contained herein.

Common Candidate Mistakes

The CPA Exam is a formidable hurdle in your accounting career. With a first-time pass rate of less than 20%, the level of difficulty is obvious. The good news, though, is that about 20% of all candidates (first-time and re-exam) sitting for each examination eventually pass. The authors believe that the first-time pass rate could be higher if candidates would be more careful. Seven common mistakes that many candidates make are

1. Failure to understand the exam question requirements
2. Misunderstanding the supporting text of the problem
3. Lack of knowledge of material tested, especially recently issued pronouncements
4. Inability to apply the solutions approach
5. Lack of an exam strategy (e.g., allocation of time)
6. Sloppiness and computational errors
7. Failure to proofread and edit

These mistakes are not mutually exclusive. Candidates may commit one or more of the above items. Remind yourself that when you decrease the number of common mistakes, you increase your chances of successfully becoming a CPA. Take the time to read carefully the exam question requirements. Don't jump into a quick start, only to later find out that you didn't understand what information the examiners were asking for. Read slowly and carefully. Take time to recall your knowledge. Respond to the question asked. Apply an exam strategy such as allocating your time among all question formats. Don't spend too much time on the multiple-choice questions, leaving no time to spend on preparing your essay responses. Write neatly and label all answer sections. Upon completion of the essays, proofread and edit your answer. Answer questions quickly but precisely, avoid common mistakes, and increase your score.

PURPOSE AND ORGANIZATION OF THIS REVIEW TEXTBOOK

This book is designed to help you prepare adequately for the Financial Accounting and Reporting examination. There is no easy way to prepare for the successful completion of the CPA Examination; however, through the use of this manual, your approach will be systematic and logical.

The objective of this book is to provide study materials supportive to CPA candidates. While no guarantees are made concerning the success of those using this text, this book promotes efficient preparation by

1. Explaining how to **"satisfy the grader"** through analysis of examination grading and illustration of the solutions approach.
2. **Defining areas tested** through the use of the content specification outlines. Note that predictions of future exams are not made. You should prepare yourself for all possible topics rather than gambling on the appearance of certain questions.
3. **Organizing your study program** by comprehensively outlining all of the subject matter tested on the examination in 12 easy-to-use study modules. Each study module is a manageable task which facilitates your exam preparation. Turn to the Chapter 5 and peruse the contents to get a feel for the organization of this book.
4. **Providing CPA candidates with previous examination problems** organized by topic (e.g., consolidations, inventory, etc.) Questions have also been developed for new areas.
5. **Explaining the AICPA unofficial answers** to the examination questions included in this text. The AICPA publishes unofficial answers for all questions from exams administered prior to 1996 and for any released questions from exams administered on or after May 1996. However, no explanation is made of the approach that should have been applied to the examination questions to obtain these unofficial answers. Relatedly, the AICPA unofficial answers to multiple-choice and other objective questions provide no justification and/or explanation.

As you read the next few paragraphs which describe the contents of this book, flip through the chapters to gain a general familiarity with the book's organization and contents. Chapters 2, 3, and 4 are to help you "satisfy the grader."

     Chapter 2   Examination Grading and Grader Orientation
     Chapter 3   The Solutions Approach
     Chapter 4   Taking the Examination

Chapters 2, 3, and 4 contain material that should be kept in mind throughout your study program. Refer back to them frequently. Reread them for a final time just before you sit for the exam.

Chapter 5, Financial Accounting and Reporting, outlines and discusses the coverage of the Financial Accounting and Reporting section of the CPA examination. It also contains the AICPA Content Specification Outlines for all the Financial Accounting and Reporting topics tested in this part of the exam.

Chapter 5 (Financial Accounting and Reporting Modules) contains:

1. AICPA Content Specification Outlines of the material tested on the Financial Accounting and Reporting part of the exam
2. Multiple-choice questions
3. Other objective questions
4. Practice problems and/or essay questions
5. AICPA unofficial answers with the author's explanations for the multiple-choice questions
6. AICPA unofficial answers with the author's explanations for the other objective questions
7. AICPA unofficial answers prefaced by the author's solution guides for the problems
8. AICPA unofficial answers prefaced by the author's answer outlines for the essay questions

Also included at the end of this text is a complete Sample Financial Accounting and Reporting CPA Examination. The sample exam is included to enable candidates to gain experience in taking a "realistic" exam. While studying the modules, the candidate can become accustomed to concentrating on fairly narrow topics. By working through the sample examination near the end of their study programs, candidates will be better prepared for taking the actual examination. The selection of multiple-choice and essay questions/practice problems was based on a statistical analysis of recent exams.

Other Textbooks

This text is a comprehensive compilation of study guides and outlines; it should not be necessary to supplement them with accounting textbooks and other materials for most topics. You probably already have some of these texts or earlier editions of them. In such a case, you must make the decision whether to replace them and trade familiarity (including notes therein, etc.), with the cost and inconvenience of obtaining the newer texts containing a more updated presentation.

Before spending time and money acquiring new texts, begin your study program with *CPA EXAMINATION REVIEW: FINANCIAL ACCOUNTING AND REPORTING* to determine your need for supplemental texts.

Ordering Other Textual Materials

You probably already have intermediate and advanced texts for financial accounting and reporting. If you cannot order desired texts through a local bookstore, write the publisher directly.

If you want to order AICPA materials, locate an AICPA educator member to order your materials, since educator members are entitled to a 30% discount and may place telephone orders. The backlog at the order department is substantial; telephone orders decrease delivery time.

Telephone: 888-777-7077   Address: Order Department
                                                      American Institute of Certified
                                                      Public Accountants
                                                      P.O. Box 2209
                                                      Jersey City, NJ 07303-2209

A variety of supplemental CPA products are available from John Wiley & Sons, Inc. By using a variety of learning techniques, such as software, computer-based learning, and audio CDs, the candidate is more likely to remain focused during the study process and to retain information for a longer period of time. Visit our website at **www.wiley.com/cpa** for other products, supplements, and updates.

Working CPA Questions

The AICPA Content Outlines, study outlines, etc., will be used to acquire and assimilate the knowledge tested on the examination. This, however, should be only **one-half** of your preparation program. The other half should be spent practicing how to work problems. Some candidates probably spend over 90% of their time reviewing material tested on the CPA exam. Much more time should be allocated to working previous examination problems **under exam conditions**. Working previous examination problems (including essay questions) serves two functions. First, it helps you develop a solutions approach as well as solutions that will satisfy the grader. Second, it provides the best test of your knowledge of the material. At a minimum, candidates should work one of the more complex and difficult problems (e.g., pensions, statement of cash flows, consolidated financial statement worksheet) in each area or module.

The multiple-choice questions and answers can be used in many ways. First, they may be used as a diagnostic evaluation of your knowledge. For example, before beginning to review deferred taxes you may wish to answer 10 to 15 multiple-choice questions to determine your ability to answer CPA examination questions on deferred taxes. The apparent difficulty of the questions and the correctness of your answers will allow you to determine the necessary breadth and depth of your review. Additionally, exposure to examination questions prior to review and study of the material should provide motivation. You will develop a feel for your level of proficiency and an understanding of the scope and difficulty of past examination questions. Moreover, your review materials will explain concepts encountered in the diagnostic multiple-choice questions.

Second, the multiple-choice questions can be used as a poststudy or postreview evaluation. You should attempt to understand all concepts mentioned (even in incorrect answers) as you answer the questions. Refer to the explanation of the answer for discussion of the alternatives even though you selected the correct response. Thus, you should read the explanation of the unofficial answer unless you completely understand the question and all of the alternative answers.

Third, you may wish to use the multiple-choice questions as a primary study vehicle. This is probably the quickest but least thorough approach in preparing for the exam. Make a sincere effort to understand the question and to select the correct response before referring to the unofficial answer and explanation. In many cases, the explanations will appear inadequate because of your unfamiliarity with the topic. Always refer back to an appropriate study source, such as the outlines and text in this volume, your accounting textbooks, FASB pronouncements, etc.

The multiple-choice questions outnumber the essay questions/practice problems by greater than 10 to 1 in this book. This is similar to recent CPA exams. One problem with so many multiple-choice questions is that you may overemphasize them. Candidates generally prefer to work multiple-choice questions because they are

1. Shorter and less time-consuming
2. Solvable with less effort
3. Less frustrating than essay questions and practice problems

Another problem with the large number of multiple-choice questions is that you may tend to become overly familiar with the questions. The result may be that you begin reading the facts and assumptions of previously studied questions into the questions on your examination. Guard against this potential problem by reading each multiple-choice question with **extra** care.

Beginning with the May 1992 examination, the AICPA began testing with other objective formats. The other objective format questions that were given on previous exams and others prepared by the author are incorporated in the modules to which they pertain. (See the listing of question and problem material at the beginning of Chapter 5.)

Essay questions require the ability to organize and compose a solution, as well as knowledge of the subject matter. Remember, working essay questions/practice problems is just as important as, if not more important than, working multiple-choice questions. The essay questions and unofficial answers may also be used for study purposes without preparation of answers. Before turning to the unofficial answers, study the question and outline the solution (either mentally or in the margin of the book). Look at our answer outline preceding the unofficial answer for each question and compare it to your own. Next, read the unofficial answer, underlining keywords and phrases. The underlining should reinforce your study of the answer's content and also assist you in learning how to structure your solutions. Answer outlines representing the major concepts found in the unofficial answer are provided for each Financial Accounting and Reporting question. These will facilitate your study of essay questions.

Remember! The AICPA does **not** accept solutions in outline form. **The AICPA expects the grading concepts to be explained in clear, concise, well-organized sentences.** However, you may prepare answers in list form as long as the listed items complete a sentence that begins with a lead-in phrase.

The questions and solutions in this volume provide you with an opportunity to diagnose and correct any exam-taking weaknesses prior to sitting for the examination. Continually analyze your incorrect solutions to determine the cause of the error(s) during your preparation for the exam. Treat each incorrect solution as a mistake that will not be repeated (especially on the examination). Also attempt to generalize your weaknesses so that you may change, reinforce, or develop new approaches to exam preparation and exam taking.

After you have finished reviewing for the Financial Accounting and Reporting exam, work the complete sample exam provided in Appendix A.

SELF-STUDY PROGRAM

CPA candidates generally find it difficult to organize and to complete their own self-study programs. A major problem is determining **what** and **how** to study. Another major problem is developing the self-discipline to stick to a study program. Relatedly, it is often difficult for CPA candidates to determine how much to study (i.e., determining when they are sufficiently prepared).

The following suggestions will assist you in developing a **systematic, comprehensive,** and **successful** self-study program to help you complete the Financial Accounting and Reporting exam.

Remember that these are only suggestions. You should modify them to suit your personality, available study time, and other constraints. Some of the suggestions may appear trivial, but CPA candidates generally need all the assistance they can get to systemize their study programs.

Study Facilities and Available Time

Locate study facilities that will be conducive to concentrated study. Factors that you should consider include

1. Noise distraction
2. Interruptions
3. Lighting
4. Availability (e.g., a local library is not available at 5:00 A.M.)
5. Accessibility (e.g., your kitchen table vs. your local library)
6. Desk or table space

You will probably find different study facilities optimal for different times (e.g., your kitchen table during early morning hours and local libraries during early evening hours).

Next review your personal and professional commitments from now until the exam to determine regularly available study time. Formalize a schedule to which you can reasonably commit yourself. At the end of this chapter, you will find a detailed approach to managing your time available for the exam preparation program.

Self-Evaluation

The *CPA EXAMINATION REVIEW: FINANCIAL ACCOUNTING AND REPORTING* self-study program is partitioned into 12 topics or modules. Since each module is clearly defined and should be studied separately, you have the task of preparing for the Financial Accounting and Reporting section of the CPA exam by tackling 12 manageable tasks. Partitioning the overall project into 12 modules makes preparation psychologically easier, since you sense yourself completing one small step at a time rather than seemingly never completing one or a few large steps.

By completing the following "Preliminary Estimate of Your Knowledge of Subject" inventory, organized by the 12 modules in this program, you will tabulate your strong and weak areas at the beginning of your study program. This will help you budget your limited study time. Note that you should begin studying the material in each module by answering up to 1/4 of the total multiple-choice questions covering that module's topics (see instruction 4.A. in the next section). This "mini-exam" should constitute a diagnostic evaluation as to the amount of review and study you need.

PRELIMINARY ESTIMATE OF YOUR PRESENT KNOWLEDGE OF SUBJECT*

No.	Module	Proficient	Fairly proficient	Generally familiar	Not familiar
22	Basic Theory and Financial Reporting				
23	Inventory				
24	Fixed Assets				
25	Monetary Current Assets and Current Liabilities				
26	Present Value				
27	Deferred Taxes				
28	Stockholders' Equity				
29	Investments				
30	Statement of Cash Flows				
31	Business Combinations and Consolidations				
32	Derivative Instruments and Hedging Activities				
33	Miscellaneous				

The number of modules in this text commences with number 22 to correspond with the numbering system used in our two-volume set.

Time Allocation

The study program below entails an average of 80 hours (Step 5. below) of study time. The breakdown of total hours is indicated in the left margin.

[2 1/2 hrs.]   1. Study Chapters 2-4 in this volume. These chapters are essential to your efficient preparation program. Time estimate includes candidate's review of the examples of the solutions approach in Chapters 2 and 3.

[1/2 hr.]   2. Begin FINANCIAL ACCOUNTING AND REPORTING by studying Chapter 5.

                 3. Study one module at a time. The modules are listed above in the self-evaluation section.

                 4. For each module

[10 hrs.]   A. Work 1/4 of the multiple-choice questions (e.g., if there are 40 multiple-choice questions in a module, you should work every 4th question). Score yourself. This diagnostic routine will provide you with an index of your proficiency and familiarity with the type and difficulty of questions.
                         Time estimate: 3 minutes each, not to exceed 1 hour total.

[20 hrs.]   B. Study the outlines and illustrations. Refer to outlines of authoritative pronouncements per instructions. Also refer to your accounting textbooks and original authoritative pronouncements (this will occur more frequently for topics in which you have a weak background).
                         Time estimate: 1 hour minimum per module, with more time devoted to topics less familiar to you.

[20 hrs.]   C. Work the remaining multiple-choice questions. Study the explanations of the multiple-choice questions you missed or had trouble answering.
                         Time estimate: 3 minutes to answer each question and 2 minutes to study the answer explanation of each question missed.

[5 hrs.]   D. Work the other objective format questions.
                         Time estimate: 20 minutes for each other objective question and 10 minutes to study the answer explanations for each item missed.

[16 hrs.]   E. Under exam conditions, work at least 2 essay questions and/or practice problems. Work additional essay/problems as time permits.
                         Time estimate: 20 minutes for each essay question, 45 minutes for each practice problem, and 10 minutes to review the unofficial answer and solution guide for each problem worked.

[6 hrs.]   F. Work through the sample CPA examination presented at the end of this text. The exam should be taken in one sitting.

                         Take the examination under simulated exam conditions (i.e., in a strange place with other people present [e.g., your local municipal library]). Apply your solutions approach to each problem and your exam strategy to the overall exam.

                         You should limit yourself to the time that you will have when taking the actual CPA exam section (4.5 hours for the Financial Accounting and Reporting section). Spend time afterwards grading your work and reviewing your effort. It might be helpful to do this with other CPA candidates. Another person looking over your exam might be more objective and notice things such as clarity of essays, logic of problem presentations, etc.

                         Time estimate: 5-6 hours to take the exam and review it later.

                 5. The total suggested time of 80 hours is only an average. Allocation of time will vary candidate by candidate. Time requirements vary due to the diverse backgrounds and abilities of CPA candidates.

                     Allocate your time so you gain the most proficiency in the least time. Remember that while 80 hours will be required, you should break the overall project down into 12 more manageable tasks. Do not study more than one module during each study session.

Using Notecards

Below are one candidate's notecards on financial accounting and reporting topics which illustrate how key definitions, formulas, lists, etc. can be summarized on index cards for quick review. Since candidates can take these anywhere they go, they are a very efficient review tool.

<table>
<tr><td>

Business Combinations

Purchase: FMV, differential may have goodwill & NI from date of combination

Pooling: BV, capital mix no goodwill
No longer acceptable

</td><td>

Accounting Changes

	Cum. effect	Pro forma	Restate FS
Δ in estimate	N	N	N
Δ in principle	Y	Y	N
Δ in reporting entity	N	N	Y

</td></tr>
</table>

Prepared by Greg Graber, CPA, former student, Northern Illinois University

Levels of Proficiency Required

What level of proficiency must you develop with respect to each of the topics to pass the exam? You should work toward a minimum correct rate on the multiple-choice questions of 80%. Working towards these correct rates or higher ones for Financial Accounting and Reporting will allow for a margin.

Warning: Disproportional study time devoted to multiple-choice and other objective questions (relative to essay questions/problems) can be disastrous on the exam. You should work a substantial number of essay questions and problems under exam conditions, even though multiple-choice questions are easier to work and are used to gauge your proficiency. The authors believe that practicing essay questions and problems will also improve your proficiency on the multiple-choice questions.

Multiple-Choice Feedback

One of the benefits of working through previous exam questions is that it helps you to identify your weak areas. Once you have graded your answers, your strong areas and weak areas should be clearly evident. Yet, the important point here is that you should not stop at a simple percentage evaluation. The percentage only provides general feedback about your knowledge of the material contained within that particular module. The percentage **does not** give you any specific feedback regarding the concepts which were tested. In order to get this feedback, you should look at the questions missed on an individual basis because this will help you gain a better understanding of **why** you missed the question.

This feedback process has been facilitated by the fact that within each module where the multiple-choice answer key appears, two blank lines have been inserted next to the multiple-choice answers. As you grade the multiple-choice questions, mark those questions which you have missed. However, instead of just marking the questions right and wrong, you should now focus on marking the questions in a manner which identifies **why** you missed the question. As an example, a candidate could mark the questions in the following manner: ✓ for math mistakes, x for conceptual mistakes, and ? for areas which the candidate was unfamiliar with. The candidate should then correct these mistakes by reworking through the marked questions.

The objective of this marking technique is to help you identify your weak areas and thus, the concepts which you should be focusing on. While it is still important for you to get between 75% and 80% correct when working multiple-choice questions, it is more important for you to understand the concepts. This understanding applies to both the questions answered correctly and those answered incorrectly. Remember, questions on the CPA exam will be different from the questions in the book, however, the concepts will be the same. Therefore, your preparation should focus on understanding concepts, not just getting the correct answer.

Conditional Candidates

If you have received conditional status on the examination, you must concentrate on the remaining part(s). Unfortunately, many candidates do not study after conditioning the exam, relying on luck to get them through the remaining part(s). Conditional candidates will find that material contained in Chapters 1-4 and the information contained in the appropriate modules will benefit them in preparing for the remaining part(s) of the examination.

PLANNING FOR THE EXAMINATION

Overall Strategy

An overriding concern should be an orderly, systematic approach toward both your preparation program and your examination strategy. A major objective should be to avoid any surprises or anything else that would rattle you during the examination. In other words, you want to be in complete control as much as possible. Control is of paramount importance from both positive and negative viewpoints. The presence of control on your part will add to your confidence and your ability to prepare for and take the exam. Moreover, the presence of control will make your preparation program more enjoyable (or at least less distasteful). On the other hand, a lack of organization will result in inefficiency in preparing and taking the examination, with a highly predictable outcome. Likewise, distractions during the examination (e.g., inadequate lodging, long drive) are generally disastrous.

In summary, establishing a systematic, orderly approach to taking the examination is of paramount importance. Follow these six steps:

1. Develop an overall strategy at the beginning of your preparation program (see below)
2. Supplement your overall strategy with outlines of material tested on the Financial Accounting and Reporting exam (see Chapter 5)
3. Supplement your overall strategy with an explicitly stated set of problem-solving procedures--the solutions approach
4. Supplement your overall strategy with an explicitly stated approach to each examination session (see Chapter 4)
5. Evaluate your preparation progress on a regular basis and prepare lists of things "to do" (see Weekly Review of Preparation Program Progress on following page)
6. RELAX: You can pass the exam. About 10,000 candidates successfully complete the exam each sitting. You will be one of them if you complete an efficient preparation program and execute well (i.e., use your solutions approach and exam strategy) while writing the exam.

The following outline is designed to provide you with a general framework of the tasks before you. You should tailor the outline to your needs by adding specific items and comments.

A. Preparation Program (refer to Self-Study Program discussed previously)

1. Obtain and organize study materials
2. Locate facilities conducive for studying and block out study time
3. Develop your solutions approach (including solving essay questions and practice problems as well as multiple-choice questions)
4. Prepare an examination strategy
5. Study the material tested recently and prepare answers to actual exam questions on these topics under examination conditions
6. Periodically evaluate your progress

B. Physical Arrangements

1. Apply to and obtain acceptance from your state board
2. Reserve lodging for examination nights

C. Taking the Examination (covered in detail in Chapter 4)

1. Become familiar with exam facilities and procedures
2. Implement examination strategies and the solutions approach

Weekly Review of Preparation Program Progress

The following pages contain a hypothetical weekly review of program progress. You should prepare a similar progress chart. This procedure, which takes only about 5 minutes per week, will help you proceed through a more efficient, complete preparation program.

Make notes of materials and topics

1. That you have studied
2. That you have completed
3. That need additional study

Weeks to go	Comments on progress, "to do" items, etc.

12
1) Read Basic Theory and Financial Reporting Module
2) Made notecards
3) Worked the MC and Other Objective Questions
4) Need to work Problems using the solutions approach

11
1) Read Fixed Assets and Stockholders' Equity Modules
2) Made notecards
3) Read the SFAS and APB outlines that correspond to these topics
4) Briefly looked over the MC for both modules

10
1) Read Monetary Current Assets and Current Liabilities Module
2) Made notecards
3) Read the corresponding SFAS/APB outlines
4) Worked the MC and Other Objective Questions for Fixed Assets, Stockholders' Equity, and Monetary CA/CL

9
1) Read the Inventory and Statement of Cash Flows Modules
2) Made notecards
3) Skimmed the SFAS and APB outlines, taking notes of important areas
4) Worked the MC and Other Objective Questions

8
1) Read the Present Value Module
2) Made notecards
3) Studied the SFASs and APBs on leases and pensions
4) Completed the MC and Other Objective Questions
5) Need to work Problems for leases and pensions

7
1) Read Deferred Taxes Module
2) Made notecards
3) Read the corresponding SFAS and APB outlines
4) Worked the MC and Other Objective Questions
5) Worked some Essays/Problems for all modules studied thus far

6
1) Read the Derivative Instruments and Hedging Activities and Miscellaneous Modules
2) Made notecards
3) Read the corresponding SFAS and APB outlines
4) Worked the MC and Problems for these modules
5) Confident with these mods; only need a quick review

5	1) Read Investments Module
	2) Made notecards
	3) Read the corresponding SFAS and APB outlines
	4) Worked the MC and Other Objective Questions

4	1) Read the Business Combinations and Consolidations Module
	2) Reviewed consolidations in an advanced accounting textbook
	3) Made notecards
	4) Worked the MC and Other Objective Questions

3	1) Worked some Essays/Problems for all modules studied in weeks 6-4
	2) Took Financial Accounting and Reporting Sample Exam
	3) Worked lease, pension, and purchase and pooling problems. Am now confident in those areas.

2	1) Reviewed all prior topics, picking out a few MC for each topic and working them out
	2) Did a statement of cash flows
	3) Completed all Essays/Problems

| 1 | 1) Reviewed notecards and SFAS and APB outlines |
| | 2) Worked MC from Deferred Taxes and Stockholders' Equity Modules |

| 0 | 1) Tried to relax and review topics |

Time Management of Your Preparation

As you begin your CPA exam preparation, you obviously realize that there is a large amount of material to cover over the course of the next three to four months. Therefore, it is very important for you to organize your calendar, and maybe even your daily routine, so that you can allocate sufficient time to studying. An organized approach to your preparation is much more effective than a last week cram session. An organized approach also builds up the confidence necessary to succeed on the CPA exam.

An approach which we have already suggested, is to develop weekly "to do" lists. This technique helps you to establish intermediate objectives and goals as you progress through your study plan. You can then focus your efforts on small tasks and not feel overwhelmed by the entire process. And as you accomplish these tasks you will see yourself moving one step closer to realizing the overall goal, succeeding on the CPA exam.

Note, however, that the underlying assumption of this approach is that you have found the time during the week to study and thus accomplish the different tasks. Although this is an obvious step, it is still a very important step. Your exam preparation should be of a continuous nature and not one that jumps around the calendar. Therefore, you should strive to find available study time within your daily schedule, which can be utilized on a consistent basis. For example, everyone has certain hours of the day which are already committed for activities such as jobs, classes, and, of course, sleep. There is also going to be the time you spend relaxing because CPA candidates should try to maintain some balance in their lives. Sometimes too much studying can be counterproductive. But there will be some time available to you for studying and working through the questions. Block off this available time and use it only for exam prep. Use the time to accomplish your weekly tasks and to keep yourself committed to the process. After awhile your preparation will develop into a habit and the preparation will not seem as overwhelming as it once did.

NOW IS THE TIME
TO MAKE YOUR COMMITMENT

2 EXAMINATION GRADING AND GRADER ORIENTATION

All State Boards of Accountancy use the AICPA advisory grading service. As your grade is to be determined by this process, it is very important that you understand the AICPA grading process and its **implications for your preparation program and for the solution techniques you will use during the examination**.

The AICPA has a full-time staff of CPA examination personnel whose responsibilities include

1. Preparing questions for the examination
2. Working with outside consultants who prepare questions
3. Preparing grading guides and unofficial answers
4. Supervising and reviewing the work of examination graders

The AICPA examination staff is under the supervision of the AICPA Board of Examiners, which has the responsibility for the CPA examination.

This chapter contains a description of the AICPA grading process, including a determination of the passing standard and a description of AICPA grading in *Information for Uniform CPA Examination Candidates*.

Setting the Passing Standard of the Uniform CPA Examination

Until May 1997, the passing standard for the CPA examination was based on the policy that all candidates who achieved a raw score of 75% on each section would pass; however, if nationally fewer than 30% of the candidates achieved this standard, candidates' raw scores were bumped up to 75 or higher; this policy passed the top 30% on each section for every examination administration. Consequently, if a group of candidates were particularly well prepared or not, the top 30% would pass, regardless.

Today, the 30% criterion no longer exists, since neither the Board of Examiners (BOE) nor the state boards were comfortable with it. The passing standard for each section of the Uniform CPA Examination is currently based on the Angoff passing standard studies which were held during 1996. The procedure, known as a modified Angoff standard-setting method, generally involves convening a panel of judges familiar with the work of entry-level professionals, who evaluate each question of each section of an examination. Each panelist's task is to estimate the probability that a "borderline" or "minimally qualified" professional would answer each question correctly. For the May 1996 exam, the panelists were given the questions and official answers for the specific sections they were assigned. They were instructed to read each question and assign a minimum pass level (MPL). The individual MPLs were tallied and the panelists were provided with a summary of the range of MPLs they had assigned. Then the panelists were given the statistics on actual candidate performance. They were then instructed to rate each question again. The second set of MPLs for all questions were tallied to arrive at the "initial passing score" that, in the judgment of the panelists, was needed for the minimally qualified candidate to pass that section of the examination.

The BOE uses a method called "equating" to determine if one examination is more or less difficult than another examination and to test for evidence that the candidate pools are significantly different. Examinations are "equated" by imbedding questions from earlier examinations into later ones. If the candidate pools are equal in ability, they should perform equally well on the equating questions. If the candidates perform significantly better or worse on the equating questions, it is assumed the candidate pools were different.

Grading the Examination

The AICPA exercises very tight control over all of the examination papers during the grading process and prior to their return to individual State Boards of Accountancy.

Multiple-choice and other objective questions are graded electronically. Only the candidates' responses are graded. No consideration is given to any comments or explanations. **The AICPA has begun to pretest**

multiple-choice questions on the exam; approximately 10-15% of the questions in each section of the exam are pretest questions that are not included in the candidate's grade. Different versions of each exam section contain different pretest questions. Essay and problem answers are graded individually on the basis of grading guides. Grading guides consist of **grading concepts,** which are ideas, constructs, principles, etc., that can be clearly defined.

While tentative grading guides (answers) are prepared prior to the examination, the final grading guides are based upon a test grading of samples of actual examinations. Objective questions are analyzed to determine whether a significant number of candidates selected an answer other than the one identified as the best answer by the AICPA. If an alternative answer is determined to be valid, the Grading Subcommittee may accept both answers. Other acceptable concepts may be added to the grading guide as a result of the test grading process. Additionally alternative interpretations and approaches to essay and problem solutions may result in changes in the grading guides. Once grading guides are fully developed, "production graders" perform the first grading of the examination. The "production graders" are practicing CPAs, university professors, attorneys, etc., commissioned by the AICPA on a per diem basis to grade the examination. These graders specialize in a single essay or problem answer, and grade answers to that question for about 6 weeks.

In this process examination papers move from grader to grader. Attached to each essay/problem is a grading guide similar to the "Hypothetical Grading Guide" on page 21. The objective at this stage is to separate candidates' papers into three categories: obvious pass, marginal, and obvious failures.

A **first review** is performed by highly experienced graders. Essay or problem answers that receive this review fall in the 65-79 range. Quality control is obtained in this process because the reviewer examines the work of individual graders to make sure that the grading guides are being applied correctly. Grading errors are corrected in this process.

Upon completion of the first review for all sections of the exam, a **second review** is done by a grading supervisor or a reviewer who did not perform the first review. To qualify for a second review, the candidates' papers must earn grades from 72 through 74 on the sections of the exam failed. According to the *Information for Uniform CPA Examination Candidates*, as amended, the second review consists of

1. Manual verification of the accuracy of the objective answer grade.
2. Independent verification of the accuracy of the essay and problem grading by a reviewer who did not perform the first review.

Based on this review, candidate grades are adjusted to reflect any scoring inconsistencies. Second reviews are also given to failing papers of candidates who need to meet a minimum grade requirement in their state in order to condition the exam.

The examination grades are returned to the individual state boards several weeks prior to the official grade release date. The grade release date is usually at the beginning of February for the November exam, and at the beginning of August for the May exam.

Multiple-Choice Grading

Each multiple-choice question is worth one point (excluding pretest questions) and grades are based on an overall curve using a combined difficulty adjustment for all types of questions for the Financial Accounting and Reporting section of the exam. Thus, candidates should do their best regardless of the difficulty of the questions. Perfect and use the "multiple-choice question solutions approach" discussed in Chapter 3. If you are unsure about a particular question, you should make an educated guess (i.e., pick the "best" answer). Your grade will be based on your total correct answers since no penalty exists for incorrect answers. The grading procedure for multiple-choice questions is explained in the instructions at the beginning of each section of the exam. As mentioned earlier, 10-15% of the multiple-choice questions are pretest items that are not included in the candidate's grade. The importance of carefully reading and following these and all other instructions cannot be overemphasized.

Other Objective Question Grading

These questions are also graded electronically. The weight for each item will depend on the number of points assigned to the question. For example, if a question that has been assigned 10 points contains 13 items, each correct response would be worth .77 (10/13) of a point. Again, do not be discouraged by your performance; the Financial Accounting and Reporting section is curved on an overall basis.

Essay Grading

To illustrate the grading of essay questions, we have included an essay question from the Financial Accounting and Reporting Examination. Following the question are the AICPA Unofficial Answer and a hypothetical grading guide.

ESSAY QUESTION

At December 31, 2001, Niki Co. reviewed the following situations to consider their impact on its 2001 financial statements:

- In December 2001, Niki became aware of a safety hazard related to one of its products. Estimates of the probable costs resulting from the hazard include highest, most likely, and lowest amounts.
- During 2001, Niki received a note for goods sold to a customer. The note was sold to a bank with recourse. The customer filed for bankruptcy in December 2001, before the note's 2002 due date.
- In 1997, Niki moved and assigned the remaining 10 years of its old lease to Pro Co., an unrelated third party. Pro agreed to make all payments due on the assigned lease, but Niki has prime responsibility for the lease to the lessor. At December 31, 2001, it is reasonably possible that Pro will be unable to make all payments due on the assigned lease.
- On November 30, 2001, Niki received goods with a cost denominated in pounds. During December 2001, the dollar's value declined relative to the pound. Niki believes that the original exchange rate will be restored by the time payment is due in 2002.

Required:

For each of the following occurrences, state how Niki should report the impact, if any, on its 2001 financial statements, and explain why the reporting is appropriate.

a. The safety hazard.

b. The customer's filing for bankruptcy.

c. Pro's reasonably possible inability to make all payments due on the assigned lease.

d. Changes in the exchange rate of the dollar and the pound.

UNOFFICIAL ANSWER

a. For the safety hazard, Niki should accrue for a loss and a liability equal to the most likely cost. The most likely loss is the best estimate of the expected loss. Accrual of a loss is appropriate because the loss is both probable and can be reasonably estimated. In addition, Niki should separately disclose in the notes to the 2001 financial statements the nature of the hazard and the range of possible loss.

b. Niki should accrue for a loss and a liability for the note sold to a bank. The accrual should equal the amount due on the note plus related costs and less any expected settlement from the bankruptcy. Accrual is appropriate because it is probable that a loss has occurred, as evidenced by the bankruptcy filing, even though this note is not yet due.

c. Niki should disclose the possible loss on the assigned lease in notes to the 2001 financial statements. Disclosures should include details of the assigned lease and the amounts due, estimates of any revenues that might be earned on the property, and any amounts recoverable from Pro. Although disclosure is appropriate for the financial statements not to be misleading, accrual of a loss is inappropriate because the loss is only reasonably possible.

d. Niki should report a foreign exchange loss on its 2001 income statement, and an increase in the account payable to reflect the exchange rate at December 31, 2001. Reporting a foreign exchange loss is appropriate because, consistent with accrual accounting, the exchange rate on December 31, 2001, should be used to value the contract. Niki's beliefs as to future exchange movements are excluded from the financial statements.

Essay questions are generally graded based on the number of **grading concepts** in the candidate's solution. The grading guide is a list of the grading concepts and raw point(s) assigned to each concept. It is necessary for candidates to identify all concepts listed in the AICPA Unofficial Answer to receive all available points. A hypothetical grading guide for the preceding accounting theory question appears below. Note that there are 17 grading concepts. The maximum points for the entire question is 10 points.

To assure full credit, however, candidates should be very careful to organize their answers to meet the question requirements; you should answer requirement **a.** in answer **a.**, answer requirement **b.** in answer **b.**, etc. Additionally, the efficient use of time is of the utmost importance. If you have included grading concepts in one part of a question that are applicable to another part of the same question, **do not repeat them**. Simply refer the grader to your previous answer.

Two common misconceptions about the AICPA grading of essay questions have cost candidates points in recent years. First, answers should **not** consist of a listing (or outline) of **keywords**. Answers should be set forth in short, concise sentences, organized per the requirements of the question. Second, a candidate should **not** answer only one or two parts of a question very thoroughly and leave the remaining parts blank. Maximize your points by attempting all question requirements.

The examiners will grade two samples from essay questions (e.g., requirement c. from one essay and requirement b. from another essay) in the Financial Accounting and Reporting section for writing skills. Five percent of the points available on this section is allocated to writing skills. The samples are graded according to the following characteristics:

1. Coherent organization
2. Conciseness
3. Clarity
4. Use of standard English
5. Responsiveness to the requirements of the question
6. Appropriateness for the reader

The "holistic" grading process will provide for the same graders who grade for content to assign 0-5 points based on their overall evaluation of the six characteristics as follows:

0	1	2	3	4	5
	Less than competent		Competent	More than competent	

Prior to the actual grading, writing consultants will grade a sample of papers and assign points as shown above. The content graders then use the consultants' evaluations as a guide.

The grading guide might be thought of as a brief outline on the unofficial answer. Note the similarities between the grading guide and the unofficial answer shown with question Number 5. In the above grading guide, note that each grading concept is summarized in a **keyword**. Graders undoubtedly scan for these **keywords** during the first grading. Note that if one of the writing samples, worth 2 points, were taken from the above essay, then each concept would be worth .47 points [(10 total points - 2 writing points) ÷ 17 concepts mentioned]. If the candidate received a 4 (out of 5 available writing points) on the writing sample from this question, 1.6 (4/5 x 2) points would be added to the points received for the concepts portion of the question. However, the number of points allocated to writing skills will not be specified in the candidate's grade.

Problem Grading

Problem grading guides are more structured than the grading guides for essay questions, because essay questions have an open-ended nature. Although some alternative calculations may be acceptable for problems, relatively little latitude is available in the problem solutions. Problem grading guides consist of check figures from throughout the unofficial answer. The grading of a practice problem is illustrated in the next chapter, The Solutions Approach.

HYPOTHETICAL GRADING GUIDE[1]

Grading Concepts	Grading Concepts Mentioned
a. Probable that liability incurred	◯
Amount of loss can be reasonably estimated	◯
Accrue most likely amount (best estimate)	◯
Disclose nature of hazard	◯
Disclose range of possible loss in FS notes	◯
b. Probable that liability incurred	◯
Amount of loss can be reasonably estimated	◯
Accrue amount equal to amount due on note plus related costs minus any expected settlement	◯
c. Loss only reasonably possible--no accrual	◯
Disclose possible loss in notes to FS	◯
Include:	
Details of assigned lease	◯
Estimates of revenue that may be earned	◯
Amounts recoverable from Pro	◯
d. Report foreign exchange loss on IS	◯
Report increase in AP	◯
Spot rate should be used to value contract	◯
Consistent with accrual accounting	◯
Grading Concepts Mentioned	═

---

[1] *The AICPA Board of Examiners does not release the grading guides used for scoring essay questions and practice problems. The grading guide above was prepared by the authors to illustrate the manner in which points are allocated to grading concepts.*

The conversion scale below converts the number of concepts mentioned to the grade on the question.

CONVERSION SCALE

Concepts Mentioned	17	16	15	14	13	12	11	10	9	8	7	6	5	4	3	2	1	0
Grade	10	9.4	8.9	8.3	7.7	7.1	6.5	5.9	5.3	4.7	4.1	3.5	3	2.4	1.8	1.2	.6	0

Overall Grade

A hypothetical example appears below to indicate how a candidate's grade is determined for the Financial Accounting and Reporting section of the exam. The example presents one possibility for the format and point assignment on this section of the exam. Candidates should remember that the point distribution of the exam consists of 50-60% multiple-choice, 20-30% other objective answer format, and 20-30% essay/problem.

Type Question	Question Number	Points Allocated	Earned Points
Multiple-Choice	1	60*	43.1
Other Objective Answer Format	2	10	5.3
	3	10	7.2
Essay/Problem	4	10	6.8**
	5	10	8.2**
		100	70.6
Rounding adjustment***			.4
			71.0
Angoff adjustment			7.0
Grade reported to candidate			78.0

      * *Excluding pretested questions*
    ** *Including writing skill points*
  *** *Rounded up*

Allocation of Points to Questions

Candidates should be concerned with point allocations for the purpose of allocating their time on the exam. When answering each question, candidates should allocate the total examination time in proportion to the question's point value. For more information, see "Allocation of Time" in Chapter 4.

Grading Implications for CPA Candidates

Analysis of the grading process helps you to understand what graders are looking for and how you can present solutions to "satisfy the grader." Before turning to Chapter 3 for a discussion of how to prepare solutions, consider the following conclusions derived from the foregoing grading analysis.

1. Present your solution in a neat and organized manner to maximize points earned
2. Allocate your time based on point value
3. Do your best on every question, no matter how difficult

   a. Remember that the exam is graded on a relative basis
   b. If a question is difficult for you, it probably is difficult for others also
   c. Develop a "solutions approach" to assist you

4. No supporting notes or computations are required for the multiple-choice questions; however, you may use the margins of the Examination Booklet to perform computations, etc. The multiple-choice answers are machine-graded, and any related work on the Examination Booklet is ignored.

   a. Conversely, supplementary computation sheets should be prepared for problems for submission to the grader

5. Essay solutions should be numbered and organized according to the problem requirements (e.g., a., b.1., b.2., c.1., c.2., c.3.).

   a. Start your solution to each question at the top of a new page
   b. Label your solutions parallel to the requirements
   c. Emphasize keywords
   d. Separate grading concepts into individual sentences or short paragraphs

      (1) Do not bury grading concepts in lengthy paragraphs that might be missed by the grader. Include as many **sensible** grading concepts as possible.

      (2) Use short, uncomplicated sentence structure

      (3) Do not present your answer in outline format

  e. Do not omit any requirements

6. Problem solutions should also be numbered and organized according to the requirements of the problem

  a. Solutions should be complete because of the finite number of grading concepts

  b. Label solutions neatly to help the grader find the required grading concepts (check figures)

      (1) Headings should be prepared for all schedules and statements

      (2) Assumptions should be briefly stated indicating knowledge of alternative treatments

  c. All supporting calculations should be prepared on answer sheets or computational sheets

      (1) Reasonable abbreviations are fine (e.g., AP for accounts payable)

      (2) All such supporting calculations and schedules should be labeled

      (3) In your answer, you should use references such as "See schedule A" or simply place numbers in parentheses alongside the amounts that correspond to subschedules of the required financial statements or main schedules

In summary, **satisfy the grader**. You need neat, readable solutions organized according to the requirements, which will also be the organization of the grading guides. Remember that a legible, well-organized solution gives a professional appearance. Additionally, recognize the plight of the grader having to decipher one mess after another, day after day. Give him/her a break with a neat, orderly solution. The "halo" effect will be rewarded by additional consideration (and hopefully points!).

Candidate Diagnostic Report

State Boards may include a "Candidate Diagnostic Report" along with the candidates' scores. A sample of the Financial Accounting and Reporting report appears below.

JURISDICTION ILLINOIS			CANDIDATE NUMBER 1-09-000426		EXAMINATION DATE MAY 2000					
SECTION	GRADE		CONTENT AREAS AND PERCENT COVERAGE		PERCENTAGE OF AREA EARNED					
					≤50	51-60	61-70	71-80	81-90	>90
FARE	85	I	Concepts and Standards for Financial Statements	20%					*	
		II	Typical Items in Financial Statements	40%					*	
		III	Specific Transactions and Events in Financial Statements	40%				*		
				100%						

3 THE SOLUTIONS APPROACH

The solutions approach is a systematic problem-solving methodology. The purpose is to assure efficient, complete solutions to CPA exam problems, some of which are complex and confusing relative to most undergraduate accounting problems. Unfortunately, there appears to be a widespread lack of emphasis on problem-solving techniques in accounting courses. Most accounting books and courses merely provide solutions to specific types of problems. Memorization of these solutions for examinations and preparation of homework problems from examples is "cookbooking." "Cookbooking" is perhaps a necessary step in the learning process, but it is certainly not sufficient training for the complexities of the business world. Professional accountants need to be adaptive to a rapidly changing, complex environment. For example, CPAs have been called on to interpret and issue reports on new concepts such as price controls, energy allocations, and new taxes. These CPAs rely on their problem-solving expertise to understand these problems and to formulate solutions to them.

The steps outlined below represent only one of many possible series of solution steps. Admittedly, the procedures suggested are **very** structured; thus, you should adapt the suggestions to your needs. You may find that some steps are occasionally unnecessary, or that certain additional procedures increase your problem-solving efficiency. Whatever the case, substantial time should be allocated to developing an efficient solutions approach before taking the examination. You should develop your solutions approach by working problems.

Note that the steps below relate to any specific question or problem; overall examination strategies are discussed in Chapter 4.

Multiple-Choice Questions Solutions Approach Algorithm

1. **Work individual questions in order.**

   a. If a question appears lengthy or difficult, skip it until you can determine that extra time is available. Put a big question mark in the margin to remind you to return to questions you have skipped or need to review.

2. **Cover the choices before reading each question.**

   a. The answers are sometimes misleading and may cause you to misread or misinterpret the question.

3. **Read each question *carefully* to determine the topical area.**

   a. Study the requirements **first** so you know which data are important.
   b. Underline keywords and important data.
   c. Identify pertinent information with notations in the margin of the exam.
   d. Be especially careful to note when the requirement is an **exception** (e.g., "Which of the following is **not** an accounting change handled by the cumulative effect method?").
   e. If a set of data is the basis for two or more questions, read the requirements of each of the questions before beginning to work the first question (sometimes it is more efficient to work the questions out of order or simultaneously).
   f. Be alert to read questions as they are, not as you would like them to be. You may encounter a familiar looking item; don't jump to the conclusion that you know what the answer is without reading the question completely.
   g. For comprehensive questions, prepare intermediary solutions as you read the question.

4. **Anticipate the answer before looking at the alternative answers.**

   a. Recall the applicable principle (e.g., change in estimate) or the applicable model (e.g., net present value).
   b. If a question deals with a complex area like earnings per share, set up full-blown diagrams in the margins of the Examination Booklet, if necessary, using abbreviations that enable you to follow your work (remember that these multiple-choice questions are machine-graded).

5. **Read the answers and select the *best* alternative.**

   a. If the answer you have computed is not among the choices, quickly check your math and the logic of your solution. If you don't arrive at one of the given answers in the time you have allotted for that particular problem, make an educated guess.

6. **Mark the correct answer (or your educated guess) on the examination booklet itself.**
7. **After completing all of the individual questions in an overall question, transfer the answers to the machine gradable answer sheet with extreme care.**

   a. Be very careful not to fall out of sequence with the answer sheet. A mistake would cause most of your answers to be wrong. **Since the AICPA uses answer sheets with varying formats, it would be very easy to go across the sheet instead of down or vice versa.** Note the format of your answer sheet carefully!
   b. Review to check that you have transferred the answers correctly.
   c. Do not leave this step until the end of the exam as you may find yourself with too little time to transfer your answers to the answer sheet. **The exam proctors are not permitted to give you extra time to transfer your answers.**

   EXAMPLE: The following is an example of the manner in which the answer sheet should be marked for a multiple-choice question. A No. 2 pencil should be used to blacken the appropriate oval(s) on the Objective Answer Sheet to indicate the answer

Item	Select One			
19	(A)	●	(C)	(D)
20	(A)	(B)	(C)	●

Multiple-Choice Question Solutions Approach Example

A good example of the multiple-choice solutions approach follows, using an actual multiple-choice question from a previous Financial Accounting and Reporting Exam.

Step 3:

Topical area? Bad debt expense

Allowance for uncollectible accounts--1/1/02	$ 30,000
Uncollectible accounts written off during 2002	18,000
Uncollectible accounts recovered during 2002	2,000
Accounts receivable at 12/31/02	350,000

Step 4A:

Principle? Recognize that uncollectible accounts are debited to the allowance account

Inge Co. determined that the net value of its accounts receivable at December 31, 2002, based on an aging of the receivables, was $325,000. Additional information is as follows:

For 2002, what would be Inge's uncollectible accounts expense?

a. $ 5,000
b. $11,000
c. $15,000
d. $21,000

Currently, all multiple-choice questions are scored based on the number correct (i.e., there is no penalty for guessing). The rationale is that a "good guess" indicates knowledge. Thus, you should answer all multiple-choice questions.

Other Objective Questions Solutions Approach Algorithm

The following types of other objective questions have been tested previously on the Financial Accounting and Reporting section:

a) Matching

b) Yes/No or True/False

c) Numerical computations with answers presented in a list of choices

d) Fill-in-the-numbers (no longer used)

The following solutions approach is suggested for answering other objective questions:

1. **Glance over the entire problem.** Scan the problem in order to get a feel for the topical area and related concepts that are being tested. Even though the format of the question may vary, the exam continues to test your understanding of applicable principles or concepts. Relax, take a deep breath, and determine your strategy for conquering the problem.

2. **Identify the requirements of the problem.** This step will help you focus in more quickly on the solution(s) without wasting time reading irrelevant material.

3. **Study the items to be answered.** As you do this and become familiar with the topical area being tested, you should review the concepts of that area. This will help you organize your thoughts so that you can relate logically the requirements of the question with the applicable concepts.

4. **Answer each item one at a time.** The type of OOAF question determines how the candidate should accomplish this step. For instance, when the answer choices are presented in a matching question, the candidate must first understand how the answer choices apply to the question items. The candidate will then be able to differentiate among the answer choices in order to select the appropriate answer for each question. You may want to work backwards from the answers to the questions. Don't be afraid to answer questions out of order. Just be careful to place your selected answer next to the appropriate item number in your Booklet.

5. **Use journal entries, T-accounts, time lines, schedules, etc. as appropriate.** The use of these items helps to lay out the information in a logical manner to avoid silly mistakes.

6. **Mark your selected answer on the examination booklet itself.** Once the candidate has selected an answer it should be clearly marked on the examination booklet before moving on to the next question.

7. **After completing all of the items, carefully transfer the answers to the answer sheet.** Be careful to follow the instructions given for the correct placement of zeros. It is very important that all items be recorded on the objective answer sheet, as they cannot be graded if they are not.

EXAMPLE: The following is an example of the manner in which the Objective Answer Sheet should be marked.

Other Objective Questions Solutions Approach Examples

Problem 2

This problem consists of 5 items. Use a No. 2 pencil to indicate your answers on the Objective Answer Sheet. These items require numerical answers and selection of the proper cash flow category. **Answer all items.** Your grade will be based on the total number of correct answers.

Following are selected balance sheet accounts of Zach Corp. at December 31, 2002 and 2001, and the increases or decreases in each account from 2001 to 2002. Also presented is selected income statement information for the year ended December 31, 2002, and additional information.

Selected balance sheet accounts	2002	2001	Increase (Decrease)
Assets			
Op. Accounts receivable	$ 34,000	$ 24,000	$10,000
Inv. Property, plant, and equipment	277,000	247,000	30,000
Accumulated depreciation	(178,000)	(167,000)	(11,000)
Liabilities and stockholders' equity			
Bonds payable	49,000	46,000	3,000
Dividends payable	8,000	5,000	3,000
Fin. Common stock, $1 par	22,000	19,000	3,000
Additional paid-in capital	9,000	3,000	6,000
Retained earnings	104,000	91,000	13,000
Selected income statement information for the year ended December 31, 2002			
Op. Sales revenue	$155,000		
Inv. Depreciation	33,000		
Gain on sale of equipment	13,000		
Net income	28,000		

Additional information

Inv. • During 2002, equipment costing $40,000 was sold for cash.

Op. • Accounts receivable relate to sales of merchandise.

Fin. • During 2002, $20,000 of bonds payable were issued in exchange for property, plant, and equipment. There was no amortization of bond discount or premium.

AD   ?
Cash   ?
Equipment   40,000
Gain   13,000

PPE   20,000
BP   20,000   } *Noncash*

Required:

Items 101 through 105 represent activities that will be reported in Zach's statement of cash flows for the year ended December 31, 2002. The following two responses are required for each item:

• Determine the amount that should be reported in Zach's 2002 statement of cash flows.
• Using the list below, determine the category in which the amount should be reported in the statement of cash flows and blacken the corresponding oval on the Objective Answer Sheet.

    O. Operating activity
    I.   Investing activity
    F. Financing activity

Items to be answered

Op. **101.** Cash collections from customers (direct method).
Inv. **102.** Payments for purchase of property, plant, and equipment.
Inv. **103.** Proceeds from sale of equipment.
Fin. **104.** Cash dividends paid.
Fin. **105.** Redemption of bonds payable.

AR

Beg.	24	*x = collections*
Sales	155	
End	34	

PPE

Beg.	247	*40 sold*
Exch.	20	
Purch. =	*x*	
End	277	

ANSWER NUMBER 2

101. ($145,000, O)   The solutions approach is to set up a T-account for accounts receivable.

	Accounts receivable	
12/31/01	24,000	
Sales revenue	155,000	? Collections
12/31/02	34,000	

Collections = $ 24,000 + $155,000 - $34,000
         = $145,000

Per SFAS 95, operating activities generally involve delivering or producing goods for sale and providing services. Cash collections from customers are specifically identified as an operating activity.

102.   ($50,000, I)   The solutions approach is to prepare a T-account for property, plant, and equipment.

	Property, plant & equipment	
12/31/01	247,000	
Equipment from exchange of B/P	20,000	
Payments for purchase of PP&E	?	40,000 Equipment sold
12/31/02	277,000	

Payments = $277,000 + $40,000 - $247,000 - $20,000
         = $50,000

SFAS 95 states that investing activities include the acquisition and disposition of long-term productive assets. Accordingly, the purchase of property, plant, and equipment is an investing activity. Note that the acquisition of property, plant, and equipment in exchange for bonds payable would be disclosed as a noncash investing and financing activity.

103.   ($31,000, I)   The solutions approach is to set up a T-account for accumulated depreciation.

Accumulated depreciation			
		167,000	12/31/01
Equipment sold	?	33,000	Depreciation expense
		178,000	12/31/02

Accumulated depreciation on equipment sold $= \$167,000 + \$33,000 - \$178,000$
$= \$\underline{\ 22,000}$

The entry to reflect the sale of equipment is

Cash (proceeds from sale of equipment)	31,000 (plug)	
Accumulated depreciation	22,000	
Property, plant, and equipment		40,000 (given)
Gain on sale of equipment		13,000

The proceeds from the sale of equipment of $31,000 is considered an investing activity. Investing activities include the acquisition and disposition of long-term productive assets.

104. ($12,000, F)   The cash dividends paid can be determined by analyzing T-accounts for retained earnings and dividends payable.

Retained earnings			
		91,000	12/31/01
Dividends declared	?	28,000	Net income
		104,000	12/31/02

Dividends declared $= \$91,000 + \$28,000 - \$104,000$
$= \$\underline{15,000}$

Dividends payable			
		5,000	12/31/01
Cash dividends paid	?	15,000	Dividends declared
		8,000	12/31/02

Cash dividends paid $= \$\ 5,000 + \$15,000 - \$8,000$
$= \$\underline{12,000}$

Financing activities include all cash flows involving liabilities and equity other than operating items. Payment of cash dividends is thus a financing activity.

105. ($17,000, F)   The redemption of bonds payable amount is determined by setting up a T-account.

Bonds payable			
		46,000	12/31/01
Redemption of B/P	?	20,000	Issuance of B/P for PP&E
		49,000	12/31/02

The problem states that there was no amortization of bond premium or discount; thus, the redemption of bonds payable is the only change not accounted for.

Redemption of bonds payable $= \$46,000 + \$20,000 - \$49,000$
$= \$\underline{17,000}$

Financing activities include all cash flows involving liabilities and equity other than operating items. Therefore, redemption of bonds payable is considered a financing activity.

Problem 3   (15 to 25 minutes)[1]

This question consists of 11 items. Select the **best** answer for each item. Use a No. 2 pencil to blacken the appropriate ovals on the Objective Answer Sheet to indicate your answers. **Answer all items.** Your grade will be based on the total number of correct answers.

Edge Co., a toy manufacturer, is in the process of preparing its financial statements for the year ended December 31, 2002. Edge expects to issue its 2002 financial statements on March 1, 2003.

---

[1]   *Estimated time is no longer provided on the Uniform CPA Examination. See "Allocation of Time" in Chapter 4.*

Required: *Step 2:*

Items 106 through 116 represent various information that has not been reflected in the financial statements. For each item, the following two responses are required:

a. Determine if an adjustment is required and select the appropriate amount, if any, from the list below.

b. Determine (Y/N) if additional disclosure is **required**, either on the face of the financial statements or in the notes to the financial statements.

Blacken the corresponding ovals on the Objective Answer Sheet.

<u>Adjustment amounts</u>

A.	No adjustment is required	D.	$250,000
B.	$100,000	E.	$400,000
C.	$150,000	F.	$500,000

Items to be answered   *Step 4:*   *Step 6:*

106. Edge owns a small warehouse located on the banks of a river, in which it stores inventory worth approximately $500,000. Edge is not insured against flood losses. The river last overflowed its banks 20 years ago.   *A, N*

   No impairment or liability incurred.

107. During 2002, Edge began offering certain health care benefits to its eligible retired employees. Edge's actuaries have determined that the discounted expected cost of these benefits for current employees is $150,000.   *C, Y*

   Probable and reasonably estimable = Accrue, disclose details in notes.

108. Edge offers an unconditional warranty on its toys. Based on past experience, Edge estimates its warranty expense to be 1% of sales. Sales during 2002 were $10,000,000. *Probable & Reasonably estimable*   *B, N*

   $10,000,000 x .01 = $100,000. No additional disclosure

109. On October 30, 2002, a safety hazard related to one of Edge's toy products was discovered. It is considered probable that Edge will be liable for an amount in the range of $100,000 to $500,000.
   Probable and reasonably estimable - Accrue low amount; disclose high   *B, Y*

110. On November 22, 2002, Edge initiated a lawsuit seeking $250,000 in damages from patent infringement.
   Gain contingency   *A, N*

111. On December 17, 2002, a former employee filed a lawsuit seeking $100,000 for unlawful dismissal. Edge's attorneys believe the suit is without merit. No court date has been set.
   Remote   *A, N*

112. On December 15, 2002, Edge guaranteed a bank loan of $100,000 for its president's personal use.   *A, Y*
   Guarantee of indebtedness of others

113. On January 5, 2003, a warehouse containing a substantial portion of Edge's inventory was destroyed by fire. Edge expects to recover the entire loss, except for a $250,000 deductible, from insurance.   *A, Y*
   Subsequent event—Condition did not exist at balance sheet date = Disclose

114. On January 24, 2003, inventory purchased FOB shipping point from a foreign country was detained at that country's border because of political unrest. The shipment is valued at $150,000. Edge's attorneys have stated that it is probable that Edge will be able to obtain the shipment.
   Possibility of loss is remote   *A, N*

115. On January 30, 2003, Edge issued $10,000,000 bonds at a premium of $500,000.
   Subsequent event—Did not exist at balance sheet date = Disclose   *A, Y*

116. On February 4, 2003, the IRS assessed Edge an additional $400,000 for the 2001 tax year. Edge's tax attorneys and tax accountants have stated that it is likely that the IRS will agree to a $100,000 settlement.   *B, Y*
   Subsequent event about conditions which existed at balance sheet date = Adjustment, use best estimate Disclose range

ANSWER NUMBER 3

106.   **(A, N)**   This situation is a nonevent. In other words, there has been no impairment of an asset or incurrence of a liability (i.e., no flood has occurred). Therefore, no adjustment or disclosure is required.

107.   **(C, Y)**   In this situation, the contingency is probable and reasonably estimable. Therefore, an adjustment of $150,000 is required to the financial statements. The detail of the postretirement benefit and actuarial assumptions would be required in notes to the financial statements.

108.   **(B, N)**   Per SFAS 5, a loss contingency should be accrued if it is probable that a liability has been incurred at the balance sheet date and the amount of the loss is reasonably estimable. In this situation, the warranty liability is probable and reasonably estimable. Therefore, $100,000 (10,000,000 x 1%) should be accrued for warranty liability. No additional disclosure is required.

109.   **(B, Y)**   In this situation, the loss is both probable and reasonably estimable. FASB Interpretation 14 requires that when some amount within an estimated range is a better estimate than any other amount in the range, that amount is accrued. If no amount within the range is a better estimate than any other amount, the amount at the low end of the range is accrued and the amount at the high end is disclosed. Therefore, a loss of $100,000 should be accrued.

110.   **(A, N)**   This situation involves a gain contingency. According to SFAS 5, contingencies that might result in gains usually are not reflected in the accounts since to do so might be to recognize revenue prior to its realization. Therefore, no adjustment is required. SFAS 5 also states that adequate disclosure shall be made of contingencies that might result in gains, but care should be exercised to avoid misleading implications as to the likelihood of realization. Consequently, unless the probability of collection is **extremely high**, it is not necessary to disclose the gain contingency.

111.   **(A, N)**   In this situation, the possibility of loss is **remote.** Accordingly, no adjustment or disclosure is required.

112.   **(A, Y)**   Per SFAS 5, contingencies such as the guarantee of indebtedness of others should be disclosed in the financial statements even though the possibility of loss may be remote. Therefore, no adjustment is required but disclosure is required.

113.   **(A, Y)**   In this situation, the fire loss is a subsequent event. Subsequent events can be defined as events or transactions having a material effect on the financial statements that occur subsequent to the balance sheet date, but prior to issuance of the financial statements and auditor's report. There are two types of subsequent events.

    a.   **Type I subsequent events**--Those events that provide additional evidence about **conditions that existed** at the date of the balance sheet and affect the estimates used in preparing financial statements.

    b.   **Type II subsequent events**--Those events that provide evidence with respect to **conditions that did not exist** at the date of the balance sheet being reported on, but arose after that date.

Type I subsequent events require an adjustment to the financial statements. Type II subsequent events require disclosure in notes to the financial statements. Since the fire loss was not a condition which existed at the balance sheet date, it is a type II subsequent event which only requires disclosure.

114.   **(A, N)**   In this situation, the possibility of loss is **remote.** Therefore, no adjustment or disclosure is required.

115.   **(A, Y)**   This event is a type II subsequent event. Therefore, no adjustment is required but disclosure is required.

116.   **(B, Y)**   Since this condition existed at the date of the financial statements, it is a Type I subsequent event which requires an adjustment to the financial statements. FASB Interpretation 14 requires that when some amount within an estimated range is a better estimate than any other amount in the range, that amount is accrued. In this situation, the $100,000 would be accrued since it is the best estimate. Disclosure of the range is required.

Problem Solutions Approach Algorithm

1.   **Glance over the problem.** Only scan the problem. Get a feel for the type or category of problem. Do not read it. Until you understand the requirements, you cannot discriminate important data from irrelevant data.

2.   **Study the requirements.** "Study" as differentiated from "read." Candidates continually lose points due to misunderstanding the requirements. Underline key phrases and words.

2a.   **Visualize the solution format.** Determine the expected format of the required solution. Develop an awareness of "schedule and statement format." Put headings on the required statements and schedules. Often a single requirement will require two or more statements, schedules, etc. A common example is a question followed by "why" or "explain." Explicitly recognize multiple requirements by numbering or lettering them on your examination booklet, expanding on the letters already assigned to problem parts.

3.   **Outline the required procedures mentally.** Interrelate any data (e.g., a trial balance or comparative balance sheets) given in the problem to the expected solution format, mentally formulating a "to do" list. Determine what it is you are going to do before you begin doing it. You should usually work through the requirements in order. However, be watchful for problems with interrelated requirements (e.g., each paragraph of information given in the problem is needed to solve more than one requirement). An alternative solutions approach for these types of problems is to make all required computations for each item of information at one time. By using this time-saving approach, you will solve a part of each requirement as each item of information is covered, but not necessarily in the same order as given on the exam.

3a. **Review applicable principles, knowledge.** Before immersing yourself in the details of the problem, quickly (30-60 seconds) review and organize your knowledge of the principles applicable to the problem. Jot down any acronyms, formulas, or other memory aids relevant to the topic of the question. Otherwise, the details of the problem may confuse and overshadow your previous knowledge of the applicable principles.

4. **Study the text of the problem.** Read the problem carefully. With the requirements in mind, you can now begin to sort relevant data from irrelevant data. Underline and circle important data. The data necessary for answering each requirement may be scattered throughout the problem. As you study the text, use arrows, etc. to connect data pertaining to a common requirement. List the requirements (a., b., etc.) in the margin alongside the data to which they pertain. Use a bright colored pen to mark up the problem. Heavy colored underlining and comments are attention-getting and give you confidence.

4a. **Prepare intermediary solutions as you study the problem.** For example, calculate goodwill, reconstruct accounts, prepare time diagrams, etc. You are able to perceive these required intermediary solutions because you already understand the problem requirements. These intermediary solutions, along with your underlining and your notes in the text of the problem, will drastically decrease rereading time.

5. **Prepare the solution.** You now are in a position to write a neat, complete, organized, labeled solution. Label computations, intermediary solutions, assumptions made, etc., in your answer booklet. Make any notes that you do **not** want the grader to see in your question booklet.

6. **Proofread and edit.** Do not underestimate the utility of this step. Just recall all of the "silly" mistakes you made on undergraduate examinations. Corrections of errors and completion of oversights during this step can easily make the difference between passing and failing.

7. **Review the requirements.** Assure yourself that you have answered them all.

Schedule layout. Many candidates are concerned with how to "lay out" schedules and "set up" problems. As you visualize the solution formats, prepare the statement and schedule headings. This will help you understand the requirements and develop the necessary intermediary solutions, analyses, etc. Put the headed answer sheets aside until you have worked through the entire problem and are ready to write up your final solution.

In preparation for the examination, you should continually be concerned with schedule and statement formats. As you study topics (e.g., consolidations, leases, inventory, etc.) and work CPA exam problems, always note the schedule and statement formats. To assist you, numerous formats are illustrated throughout this text. Recognize that there generally are several acceptable formats for most presentations. Become comfortable with the alternate presentations by comparing and contrasting unfamiliar formats to the format(s) with which you are familiar.

It is not necessary to memorize the format to be able to solve many financial accounting problems because the necessary components are often listed in the requirements. For example, assume a problem has the following requirement:

a. Prepare a schedule analyzing the changes in each of the plant asset accounts during 2002. This schedule should include columns for beginning balances, increase, decrease and ending balances for each of the plant asset accounts.

Analysis: The requirement is to prepare a schedule with four columns as follows:

Cord Company
ANALYSIS OF CHANGES IN PLANT ASSETS
For the Year Ended December 31, 2002

Balance 12/31/01	*Increase*	*Decrease*	*Balance 12/31/02*

Diagrams are very important to help you understand interrelationships within a problem setting. You should practice using diagrams to analyze problems. For example, if the Sterling Company has investments in Turner, Grotex, and Scott Companies, this may be diagrammed as

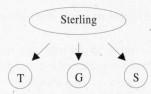

A very important form of diagram is the time diagram or time line as shown below. Time diagrams are frequently helpful to sort out a series of transactions occurring over several time periods.

Diagrams are recommended for three reasons. First, diagrams help to organize your analysis of the information in the problem. Second, diagrams create a firmer impression in your mind so as to prevent confusion while you are working the problem. A simple diagram, such as 0 ————▸ S indicating that Operating Corp. invested in Service Corp., will often aid your solution. Third, time diagrams promote preparation of solutions in chronological order, which tends to make them more orderly and complete.

T-accounts (representing ledger accounts) are extremely useful to reconstruct account balances and to depict the flow of information from account to account. One example of information flows is drawn from revenue recognition when the installment sales method is used. The gross profit on the installment sales is deferred to future periods and then recognized proportionately to collection of the receivables.

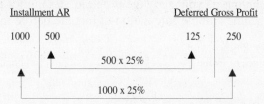

An example of T-account analysis to reconstruct ledger accounts is inherent in the solution to the multiple-choice question below.

> With certain products, Hite Foods, Inc. includes coupons having no expiration date which are redeemable in merchandise. In the Company's experience, 40% of such coupons are redeemed. The liability for unredeemed coupons at December 31, 2001, was $9,000. During 2002, coupons worth $18,000 were issued and merchandise worth $8,000 was distributed in exchange for coupons redeemed. The December 31, 2002 balance sheet should include a liability of
> a. $ 7,600.
> b. $ 8,200. (correct per the T-account below)
> c. $ 9,800.
> d. $13,000.

	Liability	
Beginning		9,000
40% of Issued		7,200
Redeemed	8,000	
Ending		8,200

Journal entries. Journal entries are often a "solutions approach" in themselves. When you do not understand a transaction (e.g., amount of profit on a combined sale-financing lease), prepare the journal entries. Furthermore, journal entries can constitute a solutions approach even though they are not explicitly required in the solution, as in the preparation of consolidated worksheets. Many candidates have trouble with journal entries. When you come upon a seemingly difficult entry, diagram the economic event that occurred. Most economic events are transactions with third parties. Therefore, ask yourself, "What did we give up?" and "What did we receive?" Also, always start with the easy elements of a journal entry. If we sold something for cash, debit cash and then focus on the credit. This is particularly important with compound/complex entries.

Problem Solutions Approach Example

We have selected a problem from a previous CPA exam to demonstrate the solutions approach. It appears on the following pages. Following this solution guide is the AICPA Unofficial Answer.

First, glance over the problem, noting that it requires the preparation of an income statement from a condensed trial balance.

Second, study the requirements. Notice that a multiple-step income statement is required. As the requirements specifically request earnings per share information and supporting computations for current and deferred income taxes, emphasis should be placed on providing this information. Underline these key words and phrases in order to draw attention to them later.

Next, visualize the solution format. Recall the format for a multiple-step income statement. Begin the statement by putting down the proper heading for Probe Co.'s income statement for the year ended December 31, 2002.

Third, outline the required procedures mentally. Identify which accounts on the trial balance are to be included in the income statement. Identify items which would be included as other income/expense or as extraordinary items. Determine what information will be used in calculating current and deferred income taxes.

Next, review applicable principles and knowledge. Jot down any acronyms, formulas, or other memory aids that relate to the problem. If you do not remember the outline for a multiple-step income statement, write down the portions you do remember. Write down anything that would help you determine what should be reported net of tax. Write out the formulas for income taxes as well as earnings per share.

Fourth, study the text of the problem. Read through the problem carefully. Circle important dates and numbers. Underline relevant words and phrases. Feel free to use arrows to connect information that pertains to a common requirement, such as the computation of deferred taxes.

Next, prepare intermediary solutions as you study the problem. Examples of intermediary solutions would be the computation of operating income and the calculation of income before tax and extraordinary items.

Number 4 (Estimated time--30 to 40 minutes)*

The following condensed trial balance of Probe Co., a publicly held company, has been adjusted except for income tax expense.

Probe Co.
CONDENSED TRIAL BALANCE**

	12/31/02 Balances Dr. (Cr.)	12/31/01 Balances Dr. (Cr.)	Net change Dr. (Cr.)
Cash	$ 473,000	$ 817,000	$(344,000)
Accounts receivable, net	670,000	610,000	60,000
Property, plant, and equipment	1,070,000	995,000	75,000
Accumulated depreciation	(345,000)	(280,000)	(65,000)
Dividends payable	(25,000)	(10,000)	(15,000)
Income taxes payable	35,000	(150,000)	185,000
Deferred income tax liability	(42,000)	(42,000)	--
Bonds payable	(500,000)	(1,000,000)	500,000
Unamortized premium on bonds	(71,000)	(150,000)	79,000
Common stock	(350,000)	(150,000)	(200,000)
Additional paid-in capital	(430,000)	(375,000)	(55,000)
Retained earnings	(185,000)	(265,000)	80,000
Sales	(2,420,000)		
Cost of sales	1,863,000		
Selling and administrative expenses	220,000		
Interest income	(14,000)		*Other income/Expense*
Interest expense	46,000		
Depreciation	88,000		
Loss on sale of equipment	7,000	*Extraordinary --Show net of tax*	
Gain on extinguishment of bonds	(90,000)		
	$ 0	$ 0	$300,000

* *Estimated time is no longer provided on the Uniform CPA Examination. See "Allocation of Time" in Chapter 4.*

** *The reason that this problem contains comparative trial balances with net changes is because Number 3 on the same FARE Exam, which was a SCF, OOAF format, used the same information (see Module 30, Other Objective Questions, Problem 1).*

Additional information

- During 2002 equipment with an original cost of $50,000 was sold for cash, and equipment costing $125,000 was purchased.   → *Loss of $7,000. Given*
- On January 1, 2002, bonds with a par value of $500,000 and related premium of $75,000 were redeemed. The $1,000 face value, 10% par bonds had been issued on January 1, 1990, to yield 8%. Interest is payable annually every December 31 through 2011 .   *Net gain = [$90,000 - ($90,000 x 30%)]* ←
- Probe's tax payments during 2002 were debited to Income Taxes Payable. For the year ended December 31, 2001, Probe had recorded a deferred income tax liability of $42,000 based on temporary differences of $120,000 and an enacted tax rate of 35%. Probe's 2002 financial statement income before income taxes was greater than its 2002 taxable income, due entirely to temporary differences, by $60,000. Probe's cumulative net taxable temporary differences at December 31, 2002, were $180,000. Probe's enacted tax rate for the current and future years is 30%.
- 60,000 shares of common stock, $2.50 par, were outstanding on December 31, 2001. Probe issued an additional 80,000 shares on April 1, 2002.   *60,000 sh. o/s 3 months,   140,000 sh. o/s 9 months*
- There were no changes to retained earnings other than dividends declared.

Required:

Prepare Probe Co.'s multiple-step income statement for the year ended December 31, 2002, with earnings per share information and supporting computations for current and deferred income tax expense.

SOLUTION
Number 4

1.   The requirement is to prepare a multiple-step income statement with earnings per share information and all components of income tax appropriately shown.

2.   The basic outline for a formal multiple-step income statement is presented below.

    Net sales
–   Cost of sales
    Gross profit
–   Operating expenses
    Operating income
±   Other income (expense)
    Income from continuing operations before income
      taxes
–   Income taxes
    Income from continuing operations
±   Discontinued operations (net of tax)
    Income before extraordinary items and cumula-
      tive effect of accounting change
±   Extraordinary items (net of tax)
±   Cumulative effect of change in
     accounting principle (net of tax)
    Net income
    Per share data

3.   Once the revenue and expense items have been identified on the trial balance, the top half of the income statement can be prepared. Probe had no unusual or infrequent items during 2002.

3.1   The sales, cost of sales, and operating expense figures are given in the problem. Operating income equals $249,000, calculated as:

Sales	$2,420,000
CGS	(1,863,000)
S&A exp.	(220,000)
Depr. exp.	(88,000)
Operating inc.	$ 249,000

3.2   Interest income and interest expense are not related to the principal operations of the firm and should be reported as other income (expense). Likewise, the

$7,000 loss on sale of equipment (given) is reported as other expense.

Operating inc.	$249,000
Interest inc.	14,000
Interest exp.	(46,000)
Loss on sale of equipment	(7,000)
Income before income tax and extraordinary item	$210,000

4.   The only item to be shown net of tax on Probe's income statement is the gain on extinguishment of debt, which is an extraordinary item. Thus two sections of the income statement will disclose income tax expense. Additionally, income taxes on income before income tax and extraordinary item will consist of both current and deferred taxes.

4.1   Since pretax financial statement income exceeded taxable income by $60,000 (given), this amount is subtracted from income before income tax and extraordinary item to determine the amount of income subject to tax. ($210,000 – $60,000 = $150,000 taxable income.) The $60,000 represents temporary differences (no permanent differences occurred in 2002). The current portion of income tax expense equals 30% of taxable income ($150,000 x 30% = $45,000 current tax expense).

4.2   The amount of deferred income tax expense to be reported in 2002 equals the change in Probe's deferred tax liability during the year. Probe's cumulative temporary differences as of 12/31/02 ($180,000, given) multiplied by Probe's tax rate in 2002 (30%) yields the deferred tax liability at year-end ($180,000 x 30% = $54,000 deferred tax liability). Subtracting from this the deferred tax liability as of 12/31/01 ($42,000, given) results in the deferred tax expense for 2002 ($54,000 – $42,000 = $12,000 deferred tax expense).

5.   In 2002, Probe realized a $90,000 gain on extinguishment of debt. Per SFAS 4, gains and losses from debt extinguishment are classified as extraordinary items to be reported separately and net of tax. Thus, Probe's gain is reported after income before extraordinary item at $63,000 [$90,000 – ($90,000 x 30%)].

6.   Earnings per share data must be presented on the face of the income statement because Probe is a publicly held company.

6.1   The weighted-average number of shares outstanding for 2002 must be calculated. 60,000 common shares were outstanding for the first 3 months of the year, and 140,000 (60,000 + 80,000 newly issued) for the remaining 9 months. Thus, weighted-average shares are calculated as:

$$\frac{(60{,}000 \times 3) + (140{,}000 \times 9)}{12} = 120{,}000$$

6.2   Earnings per share information must be shown on the face of the income statement for the following items:

- Income before extraordinary item(s)
- Net income

Reporting a gain or loss per share due to extraordinary items may appear on the face of the statement or in the footnotes.. The three earnings per share amounts are calculated by dividing the respective income amounts by the weighted-average common shares outstanding. Income before extraordinary item equals $153,000 [$210,000 – ($45,000 current + $12,000 deferred tax)], or $1.275 per share. $0.525 per share was earned on the $63,000 extraordinary gain. Net income equals $216,000 ($153,000 + $63,000 extraordinary gain), or $1.80 per share.

Fifth, prepare the solution (see following pages). You now should be ready to prepare a multiple-step income statement. Make sure the statement is organized, neat, and well labeled. Be sure that all earnings per share data and tax computations are included.

Sixth, proofread and edit.

Seventh, review later if time permits.

UNOFFICIAL ANSWER
Number 4

Probe Co.
INCOME STATEMENT
For the Year Ended December 31, 2002

Sales		$2,420,000
Cost of sales		1,863,000
Gross profit		557,000
Selling and administrative expenses	$220,000	
Depreciation	88,000	308,000
Operating income		249,000
Other income (expenses):		
Interest income	14,000	
Interest expense	(46,000)	
Loss on sale of equipment	(7,000)	(39,000)
Income before income tax and extraordinary item		210,000
Income tax:		
Current	45,000 [1]	
Deferred	12,000 [2]	57,000
Income before extraordinary item		153,000
Extraordinary item:		
Gain on extinguishment of debt, net of income taxes of $27,000		63,000
Net income		$ 216,000
Earnings per share		
Earnings before extraordinary item		$1.275 [3]
Extraordinary item		.525
Net income		$1.800

[1]   Current income tax expense:

Income before income tax and extraordinary item	$ 210,000
Differences between financial statement and taxable income	(60,000)
Income subject to tax	150,000
Income tax rate	x 30%
Income tax excluding extraordinary item	$ 45,000

[2]   Deferred income tax expense:

Cumulative temporary differences--12/31/02	$ 180,000
Income tax rate	x 30%
Deferred tax liability--12/31/02	54,000
Deferred tax liability--12/31/01	42,000
Deferred tax expense for 2002	$ 12,000

[3]   Earnings per share:
Weighted-average number of shares outstanding for 2002:

January thru March	60,000 x 3	180,000
April thru December	140,000 x 9	1,260,000
Total		1,440,000
		÷ 12
		120,000
Income before extraordinary item		153,000
Earnings per share	(153,000 ÷ 120,000)	1.275

The hypothetical grading guide below is a schedule of key solution figures showing the "raw" grading points assigned to these key figures.

Hypothetical Grading Guide[2]

Grading concepts mentioned

Probe Co.
INCOME STATEMENT
For the Year Ended December 31, 2002
○

			Concepts
Sales		$2,420,000	○
Cost of sales		1,863,000	○
Gross profit		557,000	○
Selling and administrative expenses	$220,000		○
Depreciation	88,000	308,000	○
Operating income		249,000	○
Other income (expenses):			○
Interest income	14,000		○
Interest expense	(46,000)		○
Loss on sale of equipment	(7,000)	(39,000)	○
Income before income tax and extraordinary item		210,000	○
Income tax:			○
Current	45,000		○○○
Deferred	12,000	57,000	○○○
Income before extraordinary item		153,000	○
Extraordinary item:			○
Gain on extinguishment of debt, net of income taxes of $27,000		63,000	○○○
Net income		$ 216,000	○
Earnings per share			○
Earnings before extraordinary item		$1.275	○○○
Extraordinary item		.525	Optional
Net income		$1.800	○

Grade for the Problem

Grade = # of concepts mentioned x .33 (10 points ÷ 30 concepts) per concept

NOTE: Credit would be given for aggregate numbers listed for each category such as for other income (expense) even if only two of the three items were listed. For items like deferred income taxes partial credit would be given on a second grading.

Essay Question Solutions Approach Algorithm

1. **Glance over the question.** Scan the question to get a feel for the topical area addressed. Do not read it. Until you understand the requirements, you cannot discriminate important data from irrelevant data.

2. **Study the requirements.** "Study" as differentiated from "read." Candidates continually lose points due to misunderstanding the requirements. Underline key phrases and words.

2a. **Visualize the solution format.** Determine the expected format of the required solution. As you would expect, the usual format for the solution to essay questions will be the paragraph format. However, there will be occasions where the requirements of the question may be answered by a list of items. Also, a single question may contain two or more requirements. Explicitly recognize multiple requirements (e.g., a, b, c) by numbering or lettering them on your examination booklet, expanding on the letters already assigned to the question (e.g., a.1, a.2, a.3, b.1, b.2, etc.).

3. **Outline the required procedures mentally.** Interrelate the background data given in the question to the expected solution format, mentally noting a "to do" list. Determine what it is you are going to do before you begin doing it. You should work through the requirements in order but be alert for questions with interrelated requirements.

3a. **Review applicable principles, knowledge.** Before immersing yourself in the details of the essay, quickly (30-60 seconds) review and organize your knowledge of the principles applicable to the question. Jot down any acronyms, formulas, or other memory aids relevant to the topics of the question. Otherwise, the details of the question may confuse and overshadow your previous knowledge of the applicable principles.

---

[2] *The AICPA Board of Examiners does not release the grading guides used for scoring essay questions and problems. The grading guide above was prepared by the author to illustrate to candidates the manner in which points are allocated to grading concepts.*

4. **Study the text of the question.** Read the question carefully. With the requirements in mind, you can now begin to sort out relevant from irrelevant data. Underline and circle important data. The data necessary for answering each requirement may be scattered throughout the question. List the requirements in the margin alongside the data to which they pertain. Remember--this is your exam and you should use whatever technique you find effective to highlight important data and concepts.

4a. **Write down keywords (concepts).** Jot down a list of keywords (grading concepts) in the margin of the examination or on the lined paper. Some candidates may want to organize the list of keywords into a solutions outline.

5. **Prepare the solution.** You are now in a position to write a neat, complete, and organized solution. Remember that 5% of your score on each section comes from the grading of your writing skills. Therefore, it is very important that you write something for each requirement of the question and take the time to develop a clear and organized essay for the reader/grader.

6. **Proofread and edit.** Do not underestimate the benefits of this step. Just recall all of the "silly" mistakes you made on undergraduate exams. Corrections of errors and completion of oversights during this step can easily be the difference between passing and failing.

7. **Review the requirements.** Assure yourself that you have answered them all.

Turn back to the essay question, unofficial answer, and hypothetical grading guide presented in Chapter 2. You should read this section and then practice the solutions approach on the essay question provided in Chapter 2. The major difference between the solutions approach for problems and the one for essay questions is the use of a **keyword** outline. The **keyword** outline in the essay solutions approach takes the place of the intermediary solution in the problem solutions approach.

Highlights of the Solutions Approach to Essay Questions

After studying the requirements and visualizing the format of the unofficial answer, study the text of the question, making notes and preparing a **keyword** outline. After the keyword outline has been prepared, a basic distinction must be made as to the type of essay question presented. The first type of essay question contains one fact situation from which two or more requirements cover the **same** or similar accounting rules. The proper method of answering this type of question is to handle the requirements simultaneously. In other words, apply each step in the solutions approach to all of the requirements before moving on to the next step.

The second type of essay question contains one fact situation from which two or more requirements cover **different** topics or rules. The proper method of answering this type of question is to handle the requirements independently, following each step of the solutions approach separately for each requirement. Thus, after the first requirement is completed, repeat the solutions approach for each remaining requirement. The benefit to handling the requirements independently lies in keeping the different topics or rules separate in your mind, which allows you to complete one requirement before moving on to another requirement and mentally "changing gears."

When you have identified the type of question involved, reorganize the keyword outline for the entire answer. Make sure that you have answered each requirement completely, but be careful not to preempt an answer to another requirement. The **keyword** outline for the example question should be similar to the grading guide in Chapter 2. Next, write your solution and edit as needed. Revisions may be made in the margin of your answer sheet, or, you might use only 3/4 of each page to write your solution. The remaining 1/4 can then be used to add material or to make revisions which can be keyed to the text with asterisks. Alternatively, write on every other line. The solution will thus be easier for the grader to read, and also easier for you to proofread and edit. Remember, there is no limit on the number of answer sheets you may use. If you have time later, review your solution again.

NOTE: You **must** write out the answers to the essay questions. **Keyword** outlines are not sufficient. The AICPA requires you to show an understanding of the grading concepts, not merely a listing of grading concepts. However, you may prepare answers in list form as long as the listed items are in sentence format. Prepare brief paragraphs consisting of several concise sentences about each grading concept. The paragraphs may be numbered in an outline format similar to that of the unofficial answers.

The examiners grade candidates on their writing skills. Samples will be taken from each section of the exam (e.g., requirement **c.** from one essay and requirement **b.** from another essay). Candidates will not be told which responses will be evaluated. Writing skills will be assessed by the same individuals who grade the essay responses for technical content. Five percent of the total points available on the Financial Accounting and

Reporting section will be based on writing skills. However, candidates' scores with respect to writing skills will not be disclosed separately in the candidate diagnostic report.

Candidates' writing skills will be graded according to the following six characteristics:

1. **Coherent organization**

    Candidates should organize their responses in a manner that is logical and easy to follow. Jumbled paragraphs and disorderly sentences will only confuse the grader and make his/her job more difficult. The following techniques will help improve written coherence.[3]

    - Use short paragraphs composed of short sentences
    - Indent paragraphs to set off lists, equations, key ideas, etc. when appropriate
    - Maintain coherence **within** paragraphs

        - Use a topic sentence at the beginning of each paragraph
        - Develop and support this topic throughout the rest of the paragraph
        - Present old or given information before discussing new information
        - Discuss ideas in chronological order
        - Use parallel grammatical structure
        - Be consistent in person, verb tense, and number
        - Substitute pronouns or synonyms for previously used keywords
        - Use transitions (e.g., therefore, finally)

    - Maintain coherence **between** paragraphs

        - Repeat keywords from previous paragraph
        - Use transitions

    As discussed above, candidates are strongly advised to keyword outline their responses **before** writing their essays. This technique helps the candidate to focus on the flow of ideas s/he wants to convey before starting the actual writing task.

2. **Conciseness**

    Candidates should express themselves in as few words as possible. Complex, wordy sentences are hard to understand. Conciseness can be improved using the following guidelines.

    - Write in short sentences
    - Use a simple word instead of a long word if it serves the same purpose
    - Avoid passive constructions (e.g., **was** evaluated)
    - Use words instead of phrases
    - Combine sentences, if possible
    - Avoid empty fillers (e.g., **it is** apparent; **there seems to be**)
    - Avoid multiple negatives (e.g., **no** reason for **not** using)

3. **Clarity**

    Written responses should leave no doubt in the reader's mind as to the meaning intended. Clarity can be improved as follows:

    - Do **not** use abbreviations
    - Use correct terminology
    - Use words with specific and precise meanings
    - Write in short, well-constructed sentences
    - Make sure subjects and verbs agree in number
    - Make sure pronouns and their antecedents agree in number (e.g., the partnership must decide how **it** (not **they**) wants to split profits.)
    - Avoid unclear reference to a pronoun's antecedent (e.g., the comptroller should inform the staff accountant that **he** must compute depreciation. -- Who does "he" refer to?)

4. **Use of standard English**

    Spelling, punctuation, and word usage should follow the norm used in most books, newspapers, and magazines. Note the following common mistakes:

    ---

    [3] *Adapted from **Writing for Accountants** by Aletha S. Hendrickson (Cincinnati, OH: Southwestern Publishing Co., 1993) pp.128-209.*

- Confusion of its/it's
  *The firm issued **its** stock.*
  ***It's** (it is) the stock of that firm.*

- Confusion of there/their/they're
  ***There** will be a dividend declaration.*
  ***Their** dividend was declared last week.*
  ***They're** (they are) declaring a dividend.*

- Spelling errors
  *Separate **not** seperate*
  *Receivable **not** recievable*

5. **Responsiveness to the question's requirements**

   Candidates should respond directly to the question being asked. No more information should be given than necessary. Broad expositions on the general topic demonstrate an inability to focus and organize writing to fulfill a specific purpose. Avoid irrelevance by following your keyword outline.

6. **Appropriateness for the reader**

   Essay questions may ask the candidate to prepare a document for a certain reader (e.g., a memorandum for a client). Writing that is appropriate for the reader will take into account the reader's background, knowledge of the subject, interests, and concerns. (When the intended reader is not specified, the candidate should write for a knowledgeable CPA.)

   Intended readers may include those who are unfamiliar with most terms and concepts, and who seek financial information because of self-interest (i.e., clients, stockholders). Try the following techniques for these readers:

   - Avoid jargon, if possible (i.e., GAAP, etc.)
   - Use parenthetical definitions
     - *unearned revenues (advance payments by customers)*
     - *marketable equity securities (short-term investments in stock)*
   - Set off definitions as appositives
     For example: The lag, the time between the receipt and deposit of cash, needs to be shortened.
   - Incorporate a "you" attitude

   The requirement of a question may also specify that the response should be directed to professionals who are knowledgeable of most terms and concepts. Employ the following techniques with these readers:

   - Use jargon
   - Refer to authoritative sources (i.e., FASB pronouncements)
   - Incorporate a "we" attitude

   Again, preparing a keyword outline will assist you in meeting many of these requirements. You should also reread each written answer in its entirety. Writing errors are common during the exam, so it is well worth your time to proofread and edit your answers.

Methods for Improving Your Writing Skills

1. **Organization**

   In preparing to answer a CPA exam essay, read the question carefully, determining the exact requirements of the question. Reread the question, underlining main points and noting them in the margin of your exam booklet. (This is the keyword approach.) Once you have identified the keywords, take a few minutes to organize these ideas in a logical manner.

   For example, if the question requires a discussion of the equity and cost adjusted for fair value methods of accounting for an investment in another company, you might consider these main points: recording of the investment, recognition of income, recognition of dividends, and disposition of the investment. This question lends itself to comparison/contrast type development. Thus, you would arrange your keywords to reflect that type of organization. Your first body paragraph(s) might discuss how to account for an investment under the cost adjusted for fair value method, detailing how the investment is first recorded, how dividends are treated, and how the investment is taken off the books when it is disposed of. Your next paragraph(s) would discuss the above points as they relate to the equity method.

Sometimes, a long narrative is provided prior to the actual questions. This narrative exists to facilitate your answer; it provides data to work with so that you do not have to make up all your own examples. If this type of narrative exists, read through it, searching for accounting issues and examples; these will come in handy when actually writing your response.

2. **Development**

Frequently, the CPA exam essays merely require you to recite a list of main points in an essay format. The graders are looking more for how many points you have covered than the depth with which you covered any one of them. Unfortunately, putting together a number of semirelated facts into a coherent essay may prove to be a more difficult task than coming up with the facts to begin with.

In this situation, try to see if you can group your points into categories. These categories may be thematic, chronological, or descriptive. If you are able to group the points, then each category can be discussed in one paragraph. If not, you may have to unify your answer with a topic sentence that indicates the many facets of the problem about which you are writing. This type of sentence sets up your essay for listing these facets.

Regardless of how you begin, do not simply list your points--this becomes monotonous. Rather, list, explain, and provide an example. Move from general to specific: provide the general concept, explain it in more specific terms, and provide a very pointed example. In addition, do not forget to use sequential connectors such as "first," "second," "next," etc.

3. **Syntax, grammar, and style**

By the time you sit for the CPA exam, you have at your disposal various grammatical constructs from which you may form sentences. Believe it or not, you know quite a bit of English grammar; if you did not, you would never have made it this far in your studies. So in terms of your grammar, relax! You already know it.

A frequent problem with writing occurs with the syntactic structure of sentences. Although the Board of Examiners does not expect the rhetoric of Cicero, it does expect to read and understand your answer. The way in which the graders will assess writing skills further indicates that they are looking more for writing skills at the micro level (sentence level) than at the macro level (organizational level).

a. Basic syntactic structure (transitive and intransitive action verbs)

Most English sentences are based on this simple dynamic: that someone or something (the subject) does some action (the predicate). These sentences involve action verbs and are grouped in the following categories:

(1)   Subject-Verb

The CONSTRUCTION COMPANY WAITED until the contract was complete to record any revenue.

(2)   Subject-Verb-Direct Object (The object receives the action of the verb.)

The ACCOUNTANT CALCULATED an AGING SCHEDULE.

(3)   Subject-Verb-Indirect Object-Direct Object (The direct object receives the action of the verb, but the indirect object is also affected by this action, though not in the same way as the direct object.)

The INVESTEE GAVE US our DIVIDEND soon after the date of declaration.

b. Syntactic structure (linking verbs)

Linking verbs are verbs which, rather than expressing action, say something about the subject's state of being. In sentences with linking verbs, the subject is linked to a word which describes it or renames it.

(1)   Subject-Linking Verb-Nominative (The nominative renames the subject.)

In the field of Accounting, the FASB IS the standard-setting BOARD.

(2)   Subject-Linking Verb-Adjective (The adjective describes the subject.)

An amortization SCHEDULE IS always HELPFUL in determining interest payments.

c. Subordinate clauses

(1) Adverbial clauses (subordinating connector + sentence). These clauses modify the action of the main clause.

When a related-party transaction occurs, it must be disclosed in the footnotes to the financial statements.

(2) Noun clauses (nominal connectors + sentence). These clauses function as nouns in the main sentence.

In pension accounting, we know that excessive unrecognized gains and losses must be amortized.

(3) Adjective clauses [relative pronoun + verb + (object/nominative/adjective)]. These clauses function as noun modifiers.

The depreciation methods which show the greatest amount of depreciation in the first year are the accelerated methods.

d. The above are patterns which form basic clauses (both dependent and independent). In addition, numerous phrases may function as modifiers of the basic sentence elements.

(1) Prepositional (a preposition + an object)

of the FASB
on the data
about a new type of depreciation

(2) Verbal

(a) Verb + ing + a modifier (noun, verb, adverb, prepositional phrase)

i] Used as an adjective

the discount requiring amortization
the option maximizing operating income

ii] Used as a noun (gerund)

Consolidating the balance sheets of an entity's subsidiaries is difficult and time-consuming.

(b) Verb + ed + modifier (noun, adverb, prepositional phrase)

i] Used as an adjective

The method of depreciation used to depreciate a group of assets as a single unit is the composite method.

(c) Infinitive (to + verb + object)

i] Used as a noun

The company needs to depreciate that asset over 5 years.

4. **Sentence clarity**

a. When constructing your sentences, do not separate basic sentence elements with too many phrases:

The amortization of unrecognized gains and losses falling outside of a predetermined corridor value is another component of pension cost.

Better: *One component of pension cost is the amortization of unrecognized gains and losses which fall outside a predetermined corridor value.*

b. Refrain from lumping prepositional and infinitive phrases together:

The exposure draft by the FASB on the accounting for the restructuring of an entity due to troubled debt is very recent.

Better: *Accounting for troubled debt restructuring is the topic of the most recent FASB Exposure Draft.*

c. Make sure that your pronouns have a clear and obvious referent.

When accountants prepare notes to the financial statements, they serve a special function.

Better: *The notes to the financial statements serve a special function.*

d. Make sure that any adjectival verbal phrase clearly modifies a noun stated in the sentence.

To reach this decision, each investment's market value was compared to its purchase price.

Better: *To reach this decision, we compared each investment's market value to its purchase price.*

Time Requirements for the Solutions Approach

Many candidates bypass the solutions approach because they feel it is too time-consuming. Actually, the solutions approach is a time-saver, and more importantly, it helps you prepare better solutions to all problems.

Without committing yourself to using the solutions approach, try it step-by-step on several essay questions and problems. After you conscientiously go through the step-by-step routine a few times, you will begin to adopt and modify aspects of the technique which will benefit you. Subsequent usage will become subconscious and painless. The important point is that you must try the solutions approach several times to accrue any benefits.

Efficiency of the Solutions Approach

The mark of an inefficient solution is one wherein the candidate immediately begins to write an essay/ problem solution. Remember, the final solution is one of the last steps in the solutions approach. You should have the solution under complete control (with the **keyword** outline or intermediary solutions) before you begin your final solution.

While the large amount of intermediary work in the solutions approach may appear burdensome and time-consuming, this technique results in more complete solutions in less time than do haphazard approaches. Moreover, the solutions approach really allows you to work out problems that you feel unfamiliar with at first reading. The solutions approach, however, must be mastered prior to sitting for the CPA examination. In other words, the candidate must be willing to invest a reasonable amount of time into perfecting his/her own solutions approach.

In summary, the solutions approach may appear foreign and somewhat cumbersome. At the same time, if you have worked through the material in this chapter, you should have some appreciation for it. Develop the solutions approach by writing down the seven steps in the solutions approach algorithm at the beginning of this chapter, and keep them before you as you work previous CPA exam problems. Remember that even though the suggested procedures appear **very structured** and **time-consuming,** integration of these procedures into your own style of problem solving will help improve **your** solutions approach. The next chapter discusses strategies for the overall examination.

**NOW IS THE TIME
TO MAKE YOUR COMMITMENT**

4 TAKING THE EXAMINATION

This chapter is concerned with developing an examination strategy (e.g., how to cope with the environment at the examination site, the order in which to work problems, etc.).

EXAMINATION STRATEGIES

Your performance during the 2-day examination is final and not subject to revision. While you may sit for the examination again if you are unsuccessful, the majority of your preparation will have to be repeated, requiring substantial, additional amounts of time. Thus, examination strategies (discussed in this chapter) that maximize your exam-taking efficiency are very important.

Getting "Psyched Up"

The CPA exam is quite challenging and worthy of your best effort. Explicitly develop your own psychological strategy to get yourself "up" for the exam. Pace your study program such that you will be able to operate at peak performance when you are actually taking the exam. Many candidates give up because they have a bad day or encounter a rough problem. Do the best you can; the other candidates are probably no better prepared than you.

Examination Supplies

The AICPA recommends that candidates prepare their solutions in pencil. As you practice your solutions approach, experiment with pencils, lead types, erasers, etc., that are comfortable to use and that also result in good copy for the grader.

In addition to an adequate supply of pencils and erasers, it is very important to take a watch to the examination. Also, take refreshments (as permitted) that are conducive to your exam efficiency. Finally, dress to assure your comfort during the exam. Layered clothing is recommended for possible variations in temperature at the examination site.

Do **not** take study materials to the examination room. You will not be able to use them. They will only muddle your mind and get you "uptight." Finally, **do not** carry notes or crib sheets upon your person—this can only result in the gravest of problems. Do not risk being expelled from the exam.

Lodging, Meals, Exercise

Make advance reservations for comfortable lodging convenient to the examination facilities. Do not stay with friends, relatives, etc. Both uninterrupted sleep and total concentration on the exam are a must. Consider the following in making your lodging plans:

1. Proximity to exam facilities
2. Lodging and exam parking facilities
3. Availability of meals and snacks
4. Recreational facilities

Plan your meal schedule to provide maximum energy and alertness during the day and maximum rest at night. Do not experiment with new foods, drinks, etc., during the examination time period. Within reasonable limits, observe your normal eating and drinking habits. Recognize that overconsumption of coffee during the exam could lead to a hyperactive state and disaster. Likewise, overindulgence in alcohol to overcome nervousness and to induce sleep the night before might contribute to other difficulties the following morning.

Tenseness should be expected before and during the examination. Rely on a regular exercise program to unwind at the end of the day. As you select your lodging for the examination, try to accommodate your exercise pleasure (e.g., running, swimming, etc.). Continue to indulge in your exercise program on the days of the examination.

To relieve tension or stress while studying, try breathing or stretching exercises. Use these exercises before and during the examination to start and to keep your adrenaline flowing. Do not hesitate to attract attention by doing pushups, jumping jacks, etc., in a lobby outside of the examination room if it will improve your exam efficiency. Remain determined not to go through another examination to obtain your certificate.

A problem you will probably experience during the exam related to general fatigue and tenseness is writer's cramp. Experiment with alternate methods of holding your pencil, rubbing your hand, etc., during your preparation program.

In summary, the examination is likely to be both rigorous and fatiguing. Expect it and prepare for it by getting in shape, planning methods of relaxation during the exam and exam evenings, and finally building the confidence and competence to successfully complete the exam.

Examination Facilities and Procedures

Visit the examination facilities at least the evening before the examination to assure knowledge of the location. Remember: no surprises. Having a general familiarity with the facilities will lessen anxiety prior to the examination. Talking to a recent veteran of the examination will give you background for the general examination procedures, such as

1. Procedure for distributing exam booklets, papers, etc.
2. Accessibility of restrooms
3. Availability of beverages and snacks at exam location
4. Admissibility of beverages and snacks in the exam room
5. Peculiar problems of exam facilities (e.g., noise, lighting, temperature, etc.)
6. Permissibility of early departure from exam
7. Experience in taking the exam
8. Other important information

As you can see, it is important to talk with someone who recently sat for the examination at the same location where you intend to sit. The objective is to reduce your anxiety just prior to the examination and to minimize any possible distractions. Finally, if you have any remaining questions regarding examination procedure, call or write your state board.

On a related point, do not be distracted by other candidates who show up at the examination completely relaxed and greet others with confidence. These are most likely candidates who have been there before. Probably the only thing they are confident of is a few days' vacation from work. Also, do not become distracted when candidates leave early. A candidate's early departure may mean s/he is giving up.

Arrive at the Examination Early

On the day of the exam, be sure to get to the examination site at least 30 minutes early to reduce tension and to get yourself situated. Most states have assigned seating. If this is the case, you will be seated by your candidate ID number. However, if you have a choice, it is probably wise to sit away from the door and the administration table to avoid being distracted by candidates who arrive late, leave early, ask questions, etc., and by proctors who occasionally converse. **Avoid all possible distractions. Stay away from friends.** Find a seat that will be comfortable; consider sunlight, interior lighting, heating/air conditioning, pedestrian traffic, etc.

Usually the proctors open the sealed boxes of exams and distribute the Examination Question Booklets to candidates ten minutes before the scheduled beginning of the examination. Shown below are the cover sheets for the Examination Question Booklet and the Examination Answer Booklet from the November 1995 Financial Accounting and Reporting exam, the last disclosed exam. Now, candidates receive only one booklet that contains both the questions and the answer sheets. Record your 7-digit candidate number in the boxes provided at the upper right-hand corner of the front cover of the Examination Booklet. You are not permitted to open the booklet until the starting signal is given, but you should study the instructions printed on the front cover. The instructions generally explain

1. How to turn in examination papers
2. Handling of Examination Question and Answer Booklet
3. Examiners' consideration of the candidate's ability to express him/herself in acceptable written language

The Examination Answer Booklet is divided into four sections:

1. An Attendance Record and Statement of Confidentiality
2. Examination Questions
3. An Objective Answer Sheet
4. Essay/Problem Answer Ruled/Columnar Paper

Prior to the start of the exam, you will be instructed to complete and detach the Attendance Record and to sign a Statement of Confidentiality, which will be retained by the State Boards of Accountancy. You should record your 7-digit candidate number on this record and on all other papers you submit. You are also permitted to record your 7-digit candidate number in the upper right-hand corner and blacken the corresponding oval below each box on the front and back covers of your booklet.

The Objective Answer Sheet contained in the booklet will be used to record answers to both the multiple-choice section of the exam and other objective format questions. In some states, you will be asked to detach the Objective Answer Sheet and turn it in separately; however, in other states the Objective Answer Sheet is to remain attached to the booklet. Follow the instructions of your state board. Also, record your candidate number where indicated.

The AICPA is now using a "generic" two-sided objective answer sheet (shown below). The multiple-choice answers should be entered on side 1, and the other objective answers should be entered on side 2. The information and numbering for each side is as follows:

- **Side 1:   Multiple-choice** answers contain spaces to answer question numbers **1 to 100,** with letter **choices "a" through "d."** Use only what you need. For example, the Law exam usually contains 60 multiple-choice questions (excluding pretest). In this case, the remaining numbers up to 100 will be left blank. The Auditing exam might contain 90 multiple-choice questions (excluding pretest). Again, use only what you need. **Then, turn over the answer sheet to side 2 to use for the other objective questions.**
- **Side 2:   Other objective** answers contain spaces to answer questions numbers **101 to 165,** with letter **choices "a" through "z."** Again, use only what you need. For example, if the other objective questions end at number 150, leave numbers 151 through 165 blank.

It is very important to turn the answer sheet over and always begin the other objective answers with question number 101. Take your time, darkening an oval for each answer, one question at a time.

Two different versions of the Objective Answer Sheet from the November 1995 Financial Accounting and Reporting Exam are shown below. **Candidates should be aware that different versions of the answer sheet have different arrangements for the multiple-choice questions. The answer sheet may be organized vertically, horizontally, or a combination of the two. The candidate, therefore, must be sure to correctly transfer all answers to the answer sheet.**

The essay/problem answer ruled/columnar paper will be used for answering the essay questions/problems. Record your candidate number on the ruled paper where indicated. As you proceed through the exam, you will write, in the upper left-hand corner the essay question or problem number which is being answered. Always begin the start of an answer to a question on top of a new page. Additional ruled paper is available if needed and should be enclosed in the booklet when turning it in. If you do not want the grader to grade a particular page, place a large "X" over the page.

Inventory of the Examination Content

When you receive your booklet, carefully read the instructions. The objective is to review the standard instructions, to note any new or special items, and to comply with examination procedures. After reviewing the instructions on the front of your booklet, make note of the number of questions/problems and the point value of each. Immediately after receiving permission to open the booklet, glance over each of the questions sufficiently and jot down the topics next to the question number on the front of the booklet. This will give you an overview of the ensuing 4 1/2 hours of work. You may find it to your advantage to write down keywords, acronyms, etc. on the front of the booklet **before** you forget them, but only **after** you have been told to begin the examination.

E X A M I N A T I O N   Q U E S T I O N S

CANDIDATE NUMBER

Record your 7-digit candidate number in the boxes.

Print your **STATE** name here.

UNIFORM CERTIFIED PUBLIC ACCOUNTANT EXAMINATION

Financial Accounting & Reporting—Business Enterprises

The point values for each question, and estimated time allotments based primarily on point value, are as follows:

	Point Value	Estimated Minutes Minimum	Maximum
No. 1	60	130	140
No. 2	10	15	25
No. 3	10	15	25
No. 4	10	30	40
No. 5	10	30	40
Totals	100	220	270

FARE

November 2, 1995; 1:30 P.M. to 6:00 P.M.

INSTRUCTIONS TO CANDIDATES *Failure to follow these instructions may have an adverse effect on your Examination grade.*

1. Do not break the seal around the *Examination Questions* (pages 3 through 26) until you are told to do so.

2. Question Numbers 1, 2, and 3 should be answered on the *Objective Answer Sheet*, which is pages 35 and 36. You should attempt to answer all objective items. There is no penalty for incorrect responses. Work space to solve the objective questions is provided in the *Examination Questions* on pages 5 through 21. Since the objective items are computer-graded, your comments and calculations associated with them are not considered. Be certain that you have entered your answers on the *Objective Answer Sheet* before the examination time is up. The objective portion of your examination will not be graded if you fail to record your answers on the *Objective Answer Sheet*. You will not be given additional time to record your answers.

3. Question Numbers 4 and 5 should be answered beginning on page 27. Support all answers with properly labeled and legible calculations that can be identified as sources of amounts used to derive your final answer. If you have not completed answering a question on a page, fill in the appropriate spaces in the wording on the bottom of the page "QUESTION NUMBER ⎯⎯ CONTINUES ON PAGE ⎯⎯." If you have completed answering a question, fill in the appropriate space in the wording on the bottom of the page "QUESTION NUMBER ⎯⎯ ENDS ON THIS PAGE." Always begin the start of an answer to a question on the top of a new page (which may be the reverse side of a sheet of paper). Use the entire width of the page to answer requirements of a noncomputational nature. To answer requirements of a computational nature, you may wish to use the three vertical columns provided on the right side of each page.

4. Although the primary purpose of the examination is to test your knowledge and application of the subject matter, selected essay responses will be graded for writing skills.

5. You are required to turn in by the end of each session:
   a. Attendance Record and Calculator Sign-off Record Form, page 1;
   b. *Examination Questions*, pages 3 through 26;
   c. *Essay Ruled Paper*, pages 27 through 34;
   d. *Objective Answer Sheet*, pages 35 and 36;
   e. Calculator; and
   f. All unused examination materials.
   Your examination will not be graded unless the above listed items are handed in before leaving the examination room.

Prepared by the Board of Examiners of the American Institute of Certified Public Accountants and adopted by the examining boards of all states, the District of Columbia, Guam, Puerto Rico, and the Virgin Islands of the United States.

Copyright © 1995 by the American Institute of Certified Public Accountants, Inc.

Examination Questions Booklet No.

3 07331 Q

over 3

E X A M I N A T I O N   Q U E S T I O N   A N D   A N S W E R   B O O K L E T

ATTENDANCE RECORD
(To Be Retained by State Board)

CANDIDATE NUMBER

Record your 7-digit candidate number in the boxes.

Print your **STATE** name here.

Name (please print)

Home Address

City _____ State _____ Zip Code _____

CALCULATOR SIGN-OFF RECORD
Test Calculations

Keystroke				Display
CA 53000	+	47600	=	100600
CA 125000.	−	98300	=	26700
CA 5000	×	1.667	=	8335
CA 39000	÷	1300	=	30

I hereby certify that the calculator I received was tested by me and performed all test functions accurately.

Signature _____   Date _____

FARE   VERSION 2

UNIFORM CERTIFIED PUBLIC ACCOUNTANT EXAMINATION
Financial Accounting & Reporting—Business Enterprises

November 2, 1995; 1:30 P.M. to 6:00 P.M.

INSTRUCTIONS TO CANDIDATES

(This *Examination Question and Answer Booklet* contains an *Attendance Record and Calculator Sign-Off Record*, *Examination Questions*, *Essay Ruled Paper*, and *Objective Answer Sheet*)

1. Do not begin writing on this *Booklet* until you are told to do so.

2. Complete the *Attendance Record* and *Calculator Sign-off Record*, and your 7-digit candidate number above. Detach the page at the perforation so it can be collected and retained by the State Board.

3. Test your calculator and sign the *Calculator Sign-off Record*. Press CA once to turn the calculator on. The display will read "0". Perform the *test calculations*. The calculator automatically turns itself off approximately 8 minutes after the last entry. Instructions on how to use the calculator are on pages 2 and 4.

4. Turn the *Booklet* over and record your 7-digit candidate number and state on the *Objective Answer Sheet*.

5. The *Objective Answer Sheet* is on pages 35 and 36. The objective portion of your examination will not be graded if you fail to record your answers on the *Objective Answer Sheet*.

6. In order to grade your *Objective Answer Sheet* and essay answers, the Booklet No. above must be identical to the Booklet Nos. on pages 3, 27, and 36.

over 1

307331 S

Attendance Record Booklet No.

OBJECTIVE ANSWER SHEET

CANDIDATE NUMBER

- Record your 7-digit candidate number in the boxes on the right, then blacken completely the oval for each digit you have recorded.
- Use a Number 2 pencil.
- Erase clearly any marks you wish to change. Make no stray marks on this sheet.
- INCORRECT MARKS   CORRECT MARK

Print your STATE name here.

For Proctor Use Only

UNIFORM CERTIFIED PUBLIC ACCOUNTANT EXAMINATION
Financial Accounting & Reporting—Business Enterprises

FARE
VERSION 2

November 2, 1995; 1:30 P.M. to 6:00 P.M.

Objective Answer Sheets may vary from examination to examination. Be certain that your answer corresponds directly in number with the examination item.

QUESTION 1

307331 S

Objective Answer Sheet Booklet No.

QUESTION NUMBERS 2 AND 3 ARE ON PAGE 35

end

36

DesignExpert™ by NCS   Printed in U.S.A.   Mark Reflex® EM-159596-2:654321

OBJECTIVE ANSWER SHEET

CANDIDATE NUMBER

- Record your 7-digit candidate number in the boxes on the right, then blacken completely the oval for each digit you have recorded.
- Use a Number 2 pencil.
- Erase clearly any marks you wish to change. Make no stray marks on this sheet.
- INCORRECT MARKS   CORRECT MARK

Print your STATE name here.

For Proctor Use Only

UNIFORM CERTIFIED PUBLIC ACCOUNTANT EXAMINATION
Financial Accounting & Reporting—Business Enterprises

FARE
VERSION 1

November 2, 1995; 1:30 P.M. to 6:00 P.M.

Objective Answer Sheets may vary from examination to examination. Be certain that your answer corresponds directly in number with the examination item.

QUESTION 1

307330 S

Objective Answer Sheet Booklet No.

QUESTION NUMBERS 2 AND 3 ARE ON PAGE 35

end

36

DesignExpert™ by NCS   Printed in U.S.A.   Mark Reflex® EM-159596-2:654321

101	Ⓐ Ⓑ	Ⓒ Ⓓ	Ⓔ Ⓕ	Ⓖ Ⓗ	Ⓘ Ⓙ	Ⓚ Ⓛ	Ⓜ Ⓝ	Ⓞ Ⓟ	Ⓠ Ⓡ	Ⓢ Ⓣ	Ⓤ Ⓥ	Ⓦ Ⓧ	Ⓨ Ⓩ
102	Ⓐ Ⓑ	Ⓒ Ⓓ	Ⓔ Ⓕ	Ⓖ Ⓗ	Ⓘ Ⓙ	Ⓚ Ⓛ	Ⓜ Ⓝ	Ⓞ Ⓟ	Ⓠ Ⓡ	Ⓢ Ⓣ	Ⓤ Ⓥ	Ⓦ Ⓧ	Ⓨ Ⓩ
103	Ⓐ Ⓑ	Ⓒ Ⓓ	Ⓔ Ⓕ	Ⓖ Ⓗ	Ⓘ Ⓙ	Ⓚ Ⓛ	Ⓜ Ⓝ	Ⓞ Ⓟ	Ⓠ Ⓡ	Ⓢ Ⓣ	Ⓤ Ⓥ	Ⓦ Ⓧ	Ⓨ Ⓩ
104	Ⓐ Ⓑ	Ⓒ Ⓓ	Ⓔ Ⓕ	Ⓖ Ⓗ	Ⓘ Ⓙ	Ⓚ Ⓛ	Ⓜ Ⓝ	Ⓞ Ⓟ	Ⓠ Ⓡ	Ⓢ Ⓣ	Ⓤ Ⓥ	Ⓦ Ⓧ	Ⓨ Ⓩ
105	Ⓐ Ⓑ	Ⓒ Ⓓ	Ⓔ Ⓕ	Ⓖ Ⓗ	Ⓘ Ⓙ	Ⓚ Ⓛ	Ⓜ Ⓝ	Ⓞ Ⓟ	Ⓠ Ⓡ	Ⓢ Ⓣ	Ⓤ Ⓥ	Ⓦ Ⓧ	Ⓨ Ⓩ
106	Ⓐ Ⓑ	Ⓒ Ⓓ	Ⓔ Ⓕ	Ⓖ Ⓗ	Ⓘ Ⓙ	Ⓚ Ⓛ	Ⓜ Ⓝ	Ⓞ Ⓟ	Ⓠ Ⓡ	Ⓢ Ⓣ	Ⓤ Ⓥ	Ⓦ Ⓧ	Ⓨ Ⓩ
107	Ⓐ Ⓑ	Ⓒ Ⓓ	Ⓔ Ⓕ	Ⓖ Ⓗ	Ⓘ Ⓙ	Ⓚ Ⓛ	Ⓜ Ⓝ	Ⓞ Ⓟ	Ⓠ Ⓡ	Ⓢ Ⓣ	Ⓤ Ⓥ	Ⓦ Ⓧ	Ⓨ Ⓩ
108	Ⓐ Ⓑ	Ⓒ Ⓓ	Ⓔ Ⓕ	Ⓖ Ⓗ	Ⓘ Ⓙ	Ⓚ Ⓛ	Ⓜ Ⓝ	Ⓞ Ⓟ	Ⓠ Ⓡ	Ⓢ Ⓣ	Ⓤ Ⓥ	Ⓦ Ⓧ	Ⓨ Ⓩ
109	Ⓐ Ⓑ	Ⓒ Ⓓ	Ⓔ Ⓕ	Ⓖ Ⓗ	Ⓘ Ⓙ	Ⓚ Ⓛ	Ⓜ Ⓝ	Ⓞ Ⓟ	Ⓠ Ⓡ	Ⓢ Ⓣ	Ⓤ Ⓥ	Ⓦ Ⓧ	Ⓨ Ⓩ
110	Ⓐ Ⓑ	Ⓒ Ⓓ	Ⓔ Ⓕ	Ⓖ Ⓗ	Ⓘ Ⓙ	Ⓚ Ⓛ	Ⓜ Ⓝ	Ⓞ Ⓟ	Ⓠ Ⓡ	Ⓢ Ⓣ	Ⓤ Ⓥ	Ⓦ Ⓧ	Ⓨ Ⓩ
111	Ⓐ Ⓑ	Ⓒ Ⓓ	Ⓔ Ⓕ	Ⓖ Ⓗ	Ⓘ Ⓙ	Ⓚ Ⓛ	Ⓜ Ⓝ	Ⓞ Ⓟ	Ⓠ Ⓡ	Ⓢ Ⓣ	Ⓤ Ⓥ	Ⓦ Ⓧ	Ⓨ Ⓩ
112	Ⓐ Ⓑ	Ⓒ Ⓓ	Ⓔ Ⓕ	Ⓖ Ⓗ	Ⓘ Ⓙ	Ⓚ Ⓛ	Ⓜ Ⓝ	Ⓞ Ⓟ	Ⓠ Ⓡ	Ⓢ Ⓣ	Ⓤ Ⓥ	Ⓦ Ⓧ	Ⓨ Ⓩ
113	Ⓐ Ⓑ	Ⓒ Ⓓ	Ⓔ Ⓕ	Ⓖ Ⓗ	Ⓘ Ⓙ	Ⓚ Ⓛ	Ⓜ Ⓝ	Ⓞ Ⓟ	Ⓠ Ⓡ	Ⓢ Ⓣ	Ⓤ Ⓥ	Ⓦ Ⓧ	Ⓨ Ⓩ
114	Ⓐ Ⓑ	Ⓒ Ⓓ	Ⓔ Ⓕ	Ⓖ Ⓗ	Ⓘ Ⓙ	Ⓚ Ⓛ	Ⓜ Ⓝ	Ⓞ Ⓟ	Ⓠ Ⓡ	Ⓢ Ⓣ	Ⓤ Ⓥ	Ⓦ Ⓧ	Ⓨ Ⓩ
115	Ⓐ Ⓑ	Ⓒ Ⓓ	Ⓔ Ⓕ	Ⓖ Ⓗ	Ⓘ Ⓙ	Ⓚ Ⓛ	Ⓜ Ⓝ	Ⓞ Ⓟ	Ⓠ Ⓡ	Ⓢ Ⓣ	Ⓤ Ⓥ	Ⓦ Ⓧ	Ⓨ Ⓩ
116	Ⓐ Ⓑ	Ⓒ Ⓓ	Ⓔ Ⓕ	Ⓖ Ⓗ	Ⓘ Ⓙ	Ⓚ Ⓛ	Ⓜ Ⓝ	Ⓞ Ⓟ	Ⓠ Ⓡ	Ⓢ Ⓣ	Ⓤ Ⓥ	Ⓦ Ⓧ	Ⓨ Ⓩ
117	Ⓐ Ⓑ	Ⓒ Ⓓ	Ⓔ Ⓕ	Ⓖ Ⓗ	Ⓘ Ⓙ	Ⓚ Ⓛ	Ⓜ Ⓝ	Ⓞ Ⓟ	Ⓠ Ⓡ	Ⓢ Ⓣ	Ⓤ Ⓥ	Ⓦ Ⓧ	Ⓨ Ⓩ
118	Ⓐ Ⓑ	Ⓒ Ⓓ	Ⓔ Ⓕ	Ⓖ Ⓗ	Ⓘ Ⓙ	Ⓚ Ⓛ	Ⓜ Ⓝ	Ⓞ Ⓟ	Ⓠ Ⓡ	Ⓢ Ⓣ	Ⓤ Ⓥ	Ⓦ Ⓧ	Ⓨ Ⓩ
119	Ⓐ Ⓑ	Ⓒ Ⓓ	Ⓔ Ⓕ	Ⓖ Ⓗ	Ⓘ Ⓙ	Ⓚ Ⓛ	Ⓜ Ⓝ	Ⓞ Ⓟ	Ⓠ Ⓡ	Ⓢ Ⓣ	Ⓤ Ⓥ	Ⓦ Ⓧ	Ⓨ Ⓩ
120	Ⓐ Ⓑ	Ⓒ Ⓓ	Ⓔ Ⓕ	Ⓖ Ⓗ	Ⓘ Ⓙ	Ⓚ Ⓛ	Ⓜ Ⓝ	Ⓞ Ⓟ	Ⓠ Ⓡ	Ⓢ Ⓣ	Ⓤ Ⓥ	Ⓦ Ⓧ	Ⓨ Ⓩ
121	Ⓐ Ⓑ	Ⓒ Ⓓ	Ⓔ Ⓕ	Ⓖ Ⓗ	Ⓘ Ⓙ	Ⓚ Ⓛ	Ⓜ Ⓝ	Ⓞ Ⓟ	Ⓠ Ⓡ	Ⓢ Ⓣ	Ⓤ Ⓥ	Ⓦ Ⓧ	Ⓨ Ⓩ
122	Ⓐ Ⓑ	Ⓒ Ⓓ	Ⓔ Ⓕ	Ⓖ Ⓗ	Ⓘ Ⓙ	Ⓚ Ⓛ	Ⓜ Ⓝ	Ⓞ Ⓟ	Ⓠ Ⓡ	Ⓢ Ⓣ	Ⓤ Ⓥ	Ⓦ Ⓧ	Ⓨ Ⓩ
123	Ⓐ Ⓑ	Ⓒ Ⓓ	Ⓔ Ⓕ	Ⓖ Ⓗ	Ⓘ Ⓙ	Ⓚ Ⓛ	Ⓜ Ⓝ	Ⓞ Ⓟ	Ⓠ Ⓡ	Ⓢ Ⓣ	Ⓤ Ⓥ	Ⓦ Ⓧ	Ⓨ Ⓩ
124	Ⓐ Ⓑ	Ⓒ Ⓓ	Ⓔ Ⓕ	Ⓖ Ⓗ	Ⓘ Ⓙ	Ⓚ Ⓛ	Ⓜ Ⓝ	Ⓞ Ⓟ	Ⓠ Ⓡ	Ⓢ Ⓣ	Ⓤ Ⓥ	Ⓦ Ⓧ	Ⓨ Ⓩ
125	Ⓐ Ⓑ	Ⓒ Ⓓ	Ⓔ Ⓕ	Ⓖ Ⓗ	Ⓘ Ⓙ	Ⓚ Ⓛ	Ⓜ Ⓝ	Ⓞ Ⓟ	Ⓠ Ⓡ	Ⓢ Ⓣ	Ⓤ Ⓥ	Ⓦ Ⓧ	Ⓨ Ⓩ
126	Ⓐ Ⓑ	Ⓒ Ⓓ	Ⓔ Ⓕ	Ⓖ Ⓗ	Ⓘ Ⓙ	Ⓚ Ⓛ	Ⓜ Ⓝ	Ⓞ Ⓟ	Ⓠ Ⓡ	Ⓢ Ⓣ	Ⓤ Ⓥ	Ⓦ Ⓧ	Ⓨ Ⓩ
127	Ⓐ Ⓑ	Ⓒ Ⓓ	Ⓔ Ⓕ	Ⓖ Ⓗ	Ⓘ Ⓙ	Ⓚ Ⓛ	Ⓜ Ⓝ	Ⓞ Ⓟ	Ⓠ Ⓡ	Ⓢ Ⓣ	Ⓤ Ⓥ	Ⓦ Ⓧ	Ⓨ Ⓩ
128	Ⓐ Ⓑ	Ⓒ Ⓓ	Ⓔ Ⓕ	Ⓖ Ⓗ	Ⓘ Ⓙ	Ⓚ Ⓛ	Ⓜ Ⓝ	Ⓞ Ⓟ	Ⓠ Ⓡ	Ⓢ Ⓣ	Ⓤ Ⓥ	Ⓦ Ⓧ	Ⓨ Ⓩ
129	Ⓐ Ⓑ	Ⓒ Ⓓ	Ⓔ Ⓕ	Ⓖ Ⓗ	Ⓘ Ⓙ	Ⓚ Ⓛ	Ⓜ Ⓝ	Ⓞ Ⓟ	Ⓠ Ⓡ	Ⓢ Ⓣ	Ⓤ Ⓥ	Ⓦ Ⓧ	Ⓨ Ⓩ
130	Ⓐ Ⓑ	Ⓒ Ⓓ	Ⓔ Ⓕ	Ⓖ Ⓗ	Ⓘ Ⓙ	Ⓚ Ⓛ	Ⓜ Ⓝ	Ⓞ Ⓟ	Ⓠ Ⓡ	Ⓢ Ⓣ	Ⓤ Ⓥ	Ⓦ Ⓧ	Ⓨ Ⓩ
131	Ⓐ Ⓑ	Ⓒ Ⓓ	Ⓔ Ⓕ	Ⓖ Ⓗ	Ⓘ Ⓙ	Ⓚ Ⓛ	Ⓜ Ⓝ	Ⓞ Ⓟ	Ⓠ Ⓡ	Ⓢ Ⓣ	Ⓤ Ⓥ	Ⓦ Ⓧ	Ⓨ Ⓩ
132	Ⓐ Ⓑ	Ⓒ Ⓓ	Ⓔ Ⓕ	Ⓖ Ⓗ	Ⓘ Ⓙ	Ⓚ Ⓛ	Ⓜ Ⓝ	Ⓞ Ⓟ	Ⓠ Ⓡ	Ⓢ Ⓣ	Ⓤ Ⓥ	Ⓦ Ⓧ	Ⓨ Ⓩ
133	Ⓐ Ⓑ	Ⓒ Ⓓ	Ⓔ Ⓕ	Ⓖ Ⓗ	Ⓘ Ⓙ	Ⓚ Ⓛ	Ⓜ Ⓝ	Ⓞ Ⓟ	Ⓠ Ⓡ	Ⓢ Ⓣ	Ⓤ Ⓥ	Ⓦ Ⓧ	Ⓨ Ⓩ
134	Ⓐ Ⓑ	Ⓒ Ⓓ	Ⓔ Ⓕ	Ⓖ Ⓗ	Ⓘ Ⓙ	Ⓚ Ⓛ	Ⓜ Ⓝ	Ⓞ Ⓟ	Ⓠ Ⓡ	Ⓢ Ⓣ	Ⓤ Ⓥ	Ⓦ Ⓧ	Ⓨ Ⓩ
135	Ⓐ Ⓑ	Ⓒ Ⓓ	Ⓔ Ⓕ	Ⓖ Ⓗ	Ⓘ Ⓙ	Ⓚ Ⓛ	Ⓜ Ⓝ	Ⓞ Ⓟ	Ⓠ Ⓡ	Ⓢ Ⓣ	Ⓤ Ⓥ	Ⓦ Ⓧ	Ⓨ Ⓩ
136	Ⓐ Ⓑ	Ⓒ Ⓓ	Ⓔ Ⓕ	Ⓖ Ⓗ	Ⓘ Ⓙ	Ⓚ Ⓛ	Ⓜ Ⓝ	Ⓞ Ⓟ	Ⓠ Ⓡ	Ⓢ Ⓣ	Ⓤ Ⓥ	Ⓦ Ⓧ	Ⓨ Ⓩ
137	Ⓐ Ⓑ	Ⓒ Ⓓ	Ⓔ Ⓕ	Ⓖ Ⓗ	Ⓘ Ⓙ	Ⓚ Ⓛ	Ⓜ Ⓝ	Ⓞ Ⓟ	Ⓠ Ⓡ	Ⓢ Ⓣ	Ⓤ Ⓥ	Ⓦ Ⓧ	Ⓨ Ⓩ
138	Ⓐ Ⓑ	Ⓒ Ⓓ	Ⓔ Ⓕ	Ⓖ Ⓗ	Ⓘ Ⓙ	Ⓚ Ⓛ	Ⓜ Ⓝ	Ⓞ Ⓟ	Ⓠ Ⓡ	Ⓢ Ⓣ	Ⓤ Ⓥ	Ⓦ Ⓧ	Ⓨ Ⓩ
139	Ⓐ Ⓑ	Ⓒ Ⓓ	Ⓔ Ⓕ	Ⓖ Ⓗ	Ⓘ Ⓙ	Ⓚ Ⓛ	Ⓜ Ⓝ	Ⓞ Ⓟ	Ⓠ Ⓡ	Ⓢ Ⓣ	Ⓤ Ⓥ	Ⓦ Ⓧ	Ⓨ Ⓩ
140	Ⓐ Ⓑ	Ⓒ Ⓓ	Ⓔ Ⓕ	Ⓖ Ⓗ	Ⓘ Ⓙ	Ⓚ Ⓛ	Ⓜ Ⓝ	Ⓞ Ⓟ	Ⓠ Ⓡ	Ⓢ Ⓣ	Ⓤ Ⓥ	Ⓦ Ⓧ	Ⓨ Ⓩ
141	Ⓐ Ⓑ	Ⓒ Ⓓ	Ⓔ Ⓕ	Ⓖ Ⓗ	Ⓘ Ⓙ	Ⓚ Ⓛ	Ⓜ Ⓝ	Ⓞ Ⓟ	Ⓠ Ⓡ	Ⓢ Ⓣ	Ⓤ Ⓥ	Ⓦ Ⓧ	Ⓨ Ⓩ
142	Ⓐ Ⓑ	Ⓒ Ⓓ	Ⓔ Ⓕ	Ⓖ Ⓗ	Ⓘ Ⓙ	Ⓚ Ⓛ	Ⓜ Ⓝ	Ⓞ Ⓟ	Ⓠ Ⓡ	Ⓢ Ⓣ	Ⓤ Ⓥ	Ⓦ Ⓧ	Ⓨ Ⓩ
143	Ⓐ Ⓑ	Ⓒ Ⓓ	Ⓔ Ⓕ	Ⓖ Ⓗ	Ⓘ Ⓙ	Ⓚ Ⓛ	Ⓜ Ⓝ	Ⓞ Ⓟ	Ⓠ Ⓡ	Ⓢ Ⓣ	Ⓤ Ⓥ	Ⓦ Ⓧ	Ⓨ Ⓩ
144	Ⓐ Ⓑ	Ⓒ Ⓓ	Ⓔ Ⓕ	Ⓖ Ⓗ	Ⓘ Ⓙ	Ⓚ Ⓛ	Ⓜ Ⓝ	Ⓞ Ⓟ	Ⓠ Ⓡ	Ⓢ Ⓣ	Ⓤ Ⓥ	Ⓦ Ⓧ	Ⓨ Ⓩ
145	Ⓐ Ⓑ	Ⓒ Ⓓ	Ⓔ Ⓕ	Ⓖ Ⓗ	Ⓘ Ⓙ	Ⓚ Ⓛ	Ⓜ Ⓝ	Ⓞ Ⓟ	Ⓠ Ⓡ	Ⓢ Ⓣ	Ⓤ Ⓥ	Ⓦ Ⓧ	Ⓨ Ⓩ
146	Ⓐ Ⓑ	Ⓒ Ⓓ	Ⓔ Ⓕ	Ⓖ Ⓗ	Ⓘ Ⓙ	Ⓚ Ⓛ	Ⓜ Ⓝ	Ⓞ Ⓟ	Ⓠ Ⓡ	Ⓢ Ⓣ	Ⓤ Ⓥ	Ⓦ Ⓧ	Ⓨ Ⓩ
147	Ⓐ Ⓑ	Ⓒ Ⓓ	Ⓔ Ⓕ	Ⓖ Ⓗ	Ⓘ Ⓙ	Ⓚ Ⓛ	Ⓜ Ⓝ	Ⓞ Ⓟ	Ⓠ Ⓡ	Ⓢ Ⓣ	Ⓤ Ⓥ	Ⓦ Ⓧ	Ⓨ Ⓩ
148	Ⓐ Ⓑ	Ⓒ Ⓓ	Ⓔ Ⓕ	Ⓖ Ⓗ	Ⓘ Ⓙ	Ⓚ Ⓛ	Ⓜ Ⓝ	Ⓞ Ⓟ	Ⓠ Ⓡ	Ⓢ Ⓣ	Ⓤ Ⓥ	Ⓦ Ⓧ	Ⓨ Ⓩ
149	Ⓐ Ⓑ	Ⓒ Ⓓ	Ⓔ Ⓕ	Ⓖ Ⓗ	Ⓘ Ⓙ	Ⓚ Ⓛ	Ⓜ Ⓝ	Ⓞ Ⓟ	Ⓠ Ⓡ	Ⓢ Ⓣ	Ⓤ Ⓥ	Ⓦ Ⓧ	Ⓨ Ⓩ
150	Ⓐ Ⓑ	Ⓒ Ⓓ	Ⓔ Ⓕ	Ⓖ Ⓗ	Ⓘ Ⓙ	Ⓚ Ⓛ	Ⓜ Ⓝ	Ⓞ Ⓟ	Ⓠ Ⓡ	Ⓢ Ⓣ	Ⓤ Ⓥ	Ⓦ Ⓧ	Ⓨ Ⓩ
151	Ⓐ Ⓑ	Ⓒ Ⓓ	Ⓔ Ⓕ	Ⓖ Ⓗ	Ⓘ Ⓙ	Ⓚ Ⓛ	Ⓜ Ⓝ	Ⓞ Ⓟ	Ⓠ Ⓡ	Ⓢ Ⓣ	Ⓤ Ⓥ	Ⓦ Ⓧ	Ⓨ Ⓩ
152	Ⓐ Ⓑ	Ⓒ Ⓓ	Ⓔ Ⓕ	Ⓖ Ⓗ	Ⓘ Ⓙ	Ⓚ Ⓛ	Ⓜ Ⓝ	Ⓞ Ⓟ	Ⓠ Ⓡ	Ⓢ Ⓣ	Ⓤ Ⓥ	Ⓦ Ⓧ	Ⓨ Ⓩ
153	Ⓐ Ⓑ	Ⓒ Ⓓ	Ⓔ Ⓕ	Ⓖ Ⓗ	Ⓘ Ⓙ	Ⓚ Ⓛ	Ⓜ Ⓝ	Ⓞ Ⓟ	Ⓠ Ⓡ	Ⓢ Ⓣ	Ⓤ Ⓥ	Ⓦ Ⓧ	Ⓨ Ⓩ
154	Ⓐ Ⓑ	Ⓒ Ⓓ	Ⓔ Ⓕ	Ⓖ Ⓗ	Ⓘ Ⓙ	Ⓚ Ⓛ	Ⓜ Ⓝ	Ⓞ Ⓟ	Ⓠ Ⓡ	Ⓢ Ⓣ	Ⓤ Ⓥ	Ⓦ Ⓧ	Ⓨ Ⓩ
155	Ⓐ Ⓑ	Ⓒ Ⓓ	Ⓔ Ⓕ	Ⓖ Ⓗ	Ⓘ Ⓙ	Ⓚ Ⓛ	Ⓜ Ⓝ	Ⓞ Ⓟ	Ⓠ Ⓡ	Ⓢ Ⓣ	Ⓤ Ⓥ	Ⓦ Ⓧ	Ⓨ Ⓩ
156	Ⓐ Ⓑ	Ⓒ Ⓓ	Ⓔ Ⓕ	Ⓖ Ⓗ	Ⓘ Ⓙ	Ⓚ Ⓛ	Ⓜ Ⓝ	Ⓞ Ⓟ	Ⓠ Ⓡ	Ⓢ Ⓣ	Ⓤ Ⓥ	Ⓦ Ⓧ	Ⓨ Ⓩ
157	Ⓐ Ⓑ	Ⓒ Ⓓ	Ⓔ Ⓕ	Ⓖ Ⓗ	Ⓘ Ⓙ	Ⓚ Ⓛ	Ⓜ Ⓝ	Ⓞ Ⓟ	Ⓠ Ⓡ	Ⓢ Ⓣ	Ⓤ Ⓥ	Ⓦ Ⓧ	Ⓨ Ⓩ
158	Ⓐ Ⓑ	Ⓒ Ⓓ	Ⓔ Ⓕ	Ⓖ Ⓗ	Ⓘ Ⓙ	Ⓚ Ⓛ	Ⓜ Ⓝ	Ⓞ Ⓟ	Ⓠ Ⓡ	Ⓢ Ⓣ	Ⓤ Ⓥ	Ⓦ Ⓧ	Ⓨ Ⓩ
159	Ⓐ Ⓑ	Ⓒ Ⓓ	Ⓔ Ⓕ	Ⓖ Ⓗ	Ⓘ Ⓙ	Ⓚ Ⓛ	Ⓜ Ⓝ	Ⓞ Ⓟ	Ⓠ Ⓡ	Ⓢ Ⓣ	Ⓤ Ⓥ	Ⓦ Ⓧ	Ⓨ Ⓩ
160	Ⓐ Ⓑ	Ⓒ Ⓓ	Ⓔ Ⓕ	Ⓖ Ⓗ	Ⓘ Ⓙ	Ⓚ Ⓛ	Ⓜ Ⓝ	Ⓞ Ⓟ	Ⓠ Ⓡ	Ⓢ Ⓣ	Ⓤ Ⓥ	Ⓦ Ⓧ	Ⓨ Ⓩ
161	Ⓐ Ⓑ	Ⓒ Ⓓ	Ⓔ Ⓕ	Ⓖ Ⓗ	Ⓘ Ⓙ	Ⓚ Ⓛ	Ⓜ Ⓝ	Ⓞ Ⓟ	Ⓠ Ⓡ	Ⓢ Ⓣ	Ⓤ Ⓥ	Ⓦ Ⓧ	Ⓨ Ⓩ
162	Ⓐ Ⓑ	Ⓒ Ⓓ	Ⓔ Ⓕ	Ⓖ Ⓗ	Ⓘ Ⓙ	Ⓚ Ⓛ	Ⓜ Ⓝ	Ⓞ Ⓟ	Ⓠ Ⓡ	Ⓢ Ⓣ	Ⓤ Ⓥ	Ⓦ Ⓧ	Ⓨ Ⓩ
163	Ⓐ Ⓑ	Ⓒ Ⓓ	Ⓔ Ⓕ	Ⓖ Ⓗ	Ⓘ Ⓙ	Ⓚ Ⓛ	Ⓜ Ⓝ	Ⓞ Ⓟ	Ⓠ Ⓡ	Ⓢ Ⓣ	Ⓤ Ⓥ	Ⓦ Ⓧ	Ⓨ Ⓩ
164	Ⓐ Ⓑ	Ⓒ Ⓓ	Ⓔ Ⓕ	Ⓖ Ⓗ	Ⓘ Ⓙ	Ⓚ Ⓛ	Ⓜ Ⓝ	Ⓞ Ⓟ	Ⓠ Ⓡ	Ⓢ Ⓣ	Ⓤ Ⓥ	Ⓦ Ⓧ	Ⓨ Ⓩ
165	Ⓐ Ⓑ	Ⓒ Ⓓ	Ⓔ Ⓕ	Ⓖ Ⓗ	Ⓘ Ⓙ	Ⓚ Ⓛ	Ⓜ Ⓝ	Ⓞ Ⓟ	Ⓠ Ⓡ	Ⓢ Ⓣ	Ⓤ Ⓥ	Ⓦ Ⓧ	Ⓨ Ⓩ

Allocation of Time

Budget your time. Time should be carefully allocated in an attempt to maximize points per minute. While you must develop your own strategy with respect to time allocation, some suggestions may be useful. First, consider the Financial Accounting and Reporting examination, which is 270 minutes long. Allocate 5 minutes to reading the instructions and to taking an inventory, jotting the topics tested by question on the front cover. Assuming 60 (66-69 with pretest questions) individual multiple-choice and 4 essay/other objective questions, you should spend about 10 minutes **keyword** outlining each of the 2 or 3 essay questions.

Budget your time based on the points allocated to each question. The FARE exam is a 4 1/2 hour (270 minutes) exam which could have points allocated as follows:

Hypothetical Time Budget (4 1/2 hour exam)

Question	*Type*	*Point Value*	*Calculated Maximum Time*
No. 1	Multiple-Choice	60	60/100 x 270 min. = 160 min.
No. 2	OOAF	10	10/100 x 270 min. = 27 min.
No. 3	OOAF	10	10/100 x 270 min. = 27 min.
No. 4	Essay	10	10/100 x 270 min. = 27 min.
No. 5	Essay	10	10/100 x 270 min. = 27 min.
Total		100	268 min.

Note that this budget can be done easily with a calculator, which is provided for the FARE exam. It is your responsibility to be ready at the start of the session and to stop writing when told to do so. Take control of the exam from the very start.

Plan on spending about 2 to 2 1/2 minutes working each of the individual multiple-choice questions. Next, work the other objective answer format questions. (Do not prepare the final solutions to the essay questions until you work all of the objective questions. Frequently, objective questions will jog your memory about additional grading concepts for the essays.) Then complete the objective question answer sheet by **carefully** transferring your answers from the question booklet to the machine gradable form. This should take about 5 minutes. The answers must be transferred before the exam session ends. **The proctors are not allowed to give you extra time to do this.**

After completing these tasks, you now have spent 3 1/3 to 3 2/3 hours and have substantially completed both the objective questions and essay questions. Revise the **keyword** outline and prepare the final solutions of the essay questions one at a time. Allocate about 15 minutes to each solution. Recognize that you can write all the grader will care to read in 15 minutes from a well-developed outline. This time should include proofreading and editing.

Techniques for Time Management

The Financial Accounting and Reporting exam has historically had about 60 multiple-choice questions (excluding pretest questions). Referring to the above hypothetical time budget, note that the maximum time you should take to complete a group of 10 questions is about 25 minutes per group. Remember that you alone control watching your progress towards successfully completing this exam. One possible way of monitoring your progress is to write check times throughout the exam. For example, if you begin the multiple-choice at 1:30 p.m. go to question number 12 and write 2:00. By question number 24, write 2:30, and by question number 36, write 3:00. By question number 48, write 3:30. Now you have benchmarks to check your time against as you proceed through the exam. If you complete the multiple-choice questions by 3:50 p.m., you have successfully banked 10 minutes to use when answering the other objective and essay questions.

Order of Working Questions

Select the question that you are going to work first from the notes you made on the front of your examination. Some will select the question that appears easiest to get started and build confidence. Others will begin with the question they feel is most difficult to get it out of the way. Objective questions generally should not be worked first on the Financial Accounting and Reporting exam, since each question may contain 4 or 5 grading concepts (for possible inclusion in your essay solutions) as alternate answers. You should therefore work through the objective questions only after you have **keyword** outlined all of the essay questions (but before you write your final solutions). This way, when doing the objective questions, you may pick up a grading concept or keyword which you had not included in your initial keyword outline.

Once you select a question, you should apply the solutions approach. Comprehensive problems should be worked through to the final stage, and all calculations and schedules should be labeled before leaving the problem. If you start another problem before completing one, you will have to rework (or at a minimum, waste time becoming familiar again with) the unfinished problem.

You should, however, leave a problem if you get stuck, rather than just "spinning your wheels." Later, when you come back and retool the problem, you may be able to think of a new approach to "unlock" the solution. Likewise, proofreading and editing should be undertaken after working on one or more other problems, so you have a fresh perspective as you evaluate your own solution.

On the other hand, essay questions should be worked only through the **keyword** outline prior to moving on to the next question. Recall that essay questions are generally graded with an open-ended grading guide. Thus, you want to include as many grading concepts as possible in your solution. Waiting to write your essay solution until after all other questions have been dealt with will force you to take a fresh look at the question. As a result, additional grading concepts are often found. As you recognize grading concepts applicable to other questions, turn to the respective question and jot down the **keywords** (remember that the **keyword** outlines should be prepared in the margin of your exam booklet).

Candidates should allocate more time to the questions which are troublesome. The natural tendency is to write on and on for questions with which you are conversant. Remember to do the opposite—spend more time where more points are available (i.e., you may already have earned the maximum allowable on the question familiar to you).

Never, but never, leave a question blank, as this almost certainly precludes a passing grade on that section. Some candidates talk about "giving certain types of questions to the AICPA," (i.e., no answer). The only thing being given to the AICPA is grading time since the grader will not have to read a solution. Expect a couple of "far out" or seemingly insurmountable questions/problems. Apply the solutions approach—imagine yourself having to make a similar decision, computation, explanation, etc., in an actual situation—and come up with as much as possible to answer the question.

Calculator Use

Candidates are provided with calculators at the examination sites for use on the Accounting and Reporting—Taxation, Managerial, and Governmental and Not-for-Profit Organizations, and the Financial Accounting and Reporting sections.

Candidates should only need to use the calculators' four primary functions—add, subtract, multiply, and divide. However, the calculators also have function keys for square root, percentage, and memory. Candidates are given an opportunity to test the calculators to ensure that the calculators are functioning properly. **It is the candidate's responsibility to notify one of the proctors immediately in the event of a malfunction.** Replacement calculators are available. Test calculations are printed in the examination booklets.

To turn the calculator on press ⓒ·ᶜᴱ. The display will read "0." The calculator automatically turns itself off approximately 8 minutes after the last entry. All data in the calculator will be lost once the calculator is off. When you complete a calculation, we recommend that after you press ⟨=⟩, you press ⓒ·ᶜᴱ before beginning a new calculation. The basic key descriptions are as follows:

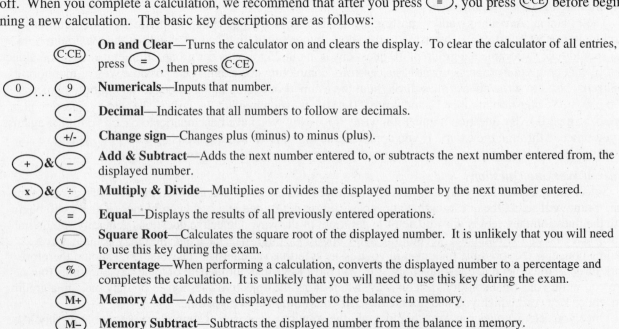

On and Clear—Turns the calculator on and clears the display. To clear the calculator of all entries, press ⟨=⟩, then press ⓒ·ᶜᴱ.

Numericals—Inputs that number.

Decimal—Indicates that all numbers to follow are decimals.

Change sign—Changes plus (minus) to minus (plus).

Add & Subtract—Adds the next number entered to, or subtracts the next number entered from, the displayed number.

Multiply & Divide—Multiplies or divides the displayed number by the next number entered.

Equal—Displays the results of all previously entered operations.

Square Root—Calculates the square root of the displayed number. It is unlikely that you will need to use this key during the exam.

Percentage—When performing a calculation, converts the displayed number to a percentage and completes the calculation. It is unlikely that you will need to use this key during the exam.

Memory Add—Adds the displayed number to the balance in memory.

Memory Subtract—Subtracts the displayed number from the balance in memory.

Recall/Clear Memory—Pressed once, displays the balance in memory. Pressed twice in a row, eliminates the balance in memory but not the displayed number.

Since each AICPA calculator provided has these basic functions, the only difference between calculators is in the placement of the keys. While it may be helpful to have the exact calculator that you are familiar with, this is not essential to your examination success. AICPA calculators may be purchased by contacting the AICPA order department at 888-777-7077.

Test Calculations

Keystroke							*Display*
C·CE	53000	+	47600	=	100600
C·CE	125000	−	98300	=	26700
C·CE	5000	x	1.667	=	8335
C·CE	39000	÷	1300	=	30

Pitfalls of Calculator Use

The use of calculators is designed to save candidates time on performing and verifying manual calculations. However, there are some pitfalls that the candidate must remain aware of throughout the entire exam. For instance, how many times have you simply hit the wrong key (e.g., a six instead of a nine)? Or, how many times have you forgotten to clear the calculator before beginning a new calculation? Both of these mistakes are simple errors that everyone makes at one time or another. Yet, these simple mistakes could be the difference between a candidate receiving a passing grade or a failing grade. In order to guard against these errors, candidates should avoid rushing through the questions. Accuracy is just as important, if not more so, as speed. Candidates should work each section of the exam with a time budget in mind to avoid any last-minute panic attacks. There are no points given for finishing first, and so, candidates should concentrate on working accurately, by using the calculator carefully to ensure such accuracy.

The candidate should also guard against using the calculator as a crutch. For example, there should be no need to multiply an amount by 10%. This calculation simply distracts the candidate from the real issue of solving the problem.

In addition, candidates should avoid the urge to overcalculate. While the calculator may give you some extra time, there is no benefit to number crunching all the different possibilities. The focus of the exam remains understanding and applying the basic concepts of accounting. A candidate will not be able to successfully pass the exam simply by using the calculator to back into the answer.

Postmortem of Your Performance

Don't do it and especially don't do it until Thursday evening. Do not speak to other candidates about the exam after completing sections on Wednesday noon, Wednesday evening, and Thursday noon. Exam postmortem will only upset, confuse, and frustrate you. Besides, the other candidates probably will not be as well prepared as you, and they certainly cannot influence your grade. Often, those candidates who seem very confident have overlooked an important requirement(s) or fact(s). As you leave the exam room after each session, think only ahead to achieve the best possible performance on each of the remaining sections.

AICPA GENERAL RULES GOVERNING EXAMINATION[1]

Rules for Examination Day

The examination is a closed-book examination and no reference materials are permitted to be taken to an examination site. Candidates are not permitted to bring calculators, computers, other electronic data storage devices, or communication devices into the examination room.

At the examination site, candidates are provided with an Examination Question and Answer Booklet for each section they are taking. In addition, for the Accounting & Reporting—Taxation, Managerial, and Governmental and Not-for-Profit Organizations, and Financial Accounting & Reporting sections, candidates are provided with official AICPA calculators identified for the specific examination. Candidates should bring adequate supplies of Number 2 pencils and erasers. Rulers are not allowed.

The general candidate instructions are as follows:

---

[1] *Information for Uniform CPA Examination Candidates*, Sixteenth Edition, AICPA, 2000, p. 44.

1. Prior to the start of the examination, you will be required to sign a *Statement of Confidentiality* which states:

   I hereby attest that I will not divulge the nature or content of any question or answer to any individual or entity, and I will report to the board of accountancy any solicitations and disclosures of which I become aware. I will not remove, or attempt to remove, any Uniform CPA Examination materials, notes, or other unauthorized materials from the examination room. I understand that failure to comply with this attestation may result in invalidation of my grades, disqualification from future examinations, and possible civil and criminal penalties.

2. The only aids you are allowed to take to the examination tables are pens, No. 2 pencils, and erasers.

3. You will receive a prenumbered identification card (or admission notice) with your 7-digit candidate number on it. The prenumbered identification card must be available for inspection by the proctors throughout the examination.

4. Any reference during the examination to books or other materials or the exchange of information with other persons shall be considered misconduct sufficient to bar you from further participation in the examination.

   Penalties will be imposed on any candidate who is caught cheating before, during, or after the examination. These penalties may include expulsion from the examination, denial of applications for future examinations, and civil or criminal penalties.

5. You must observe the fixed time for each session. It is your responsibility to be ready at the start of the session and to stop writing when told to do so.

6. The following is an example of point values for each question as they might appear in the *Examination Questions* portion of the *Examination Question and Answer Booklet (Booklet)*.

	Point value
No. 1	60
No. 2	10
No. 3	10
No. 4	10
No. 5	<u>10</u>
Total	<u>100</u>

   When answering each question, you should allocate the total examination time in proportion to the question's point value.

7. The *Booklet* will be distributed shortly before each session begins. Do not break the seal around the *Examination Questions* portion of the *Booklet* until you are told to do so.

   Prior to the start of the examination, you are permitted to complete page 1 of the *Booklet* by recording your 7-digit candidate number in the boxes provided in the upper right-hand corner of the page and by filling out and signing the *Attendance Record*. You are also permitted to turn the *Booklet* over and record your 7-digit candidate number and State on the *Objective Answer Sheet* portion of the *Booklet*.

   You must also check the booklet numbers on the *Attendance Record, Examination Questions, Objective Answer Sheet*, and *Essay Paper*. Notify the proctor if any of these numbers do not match.

   You must also review the *Examination Questions* (after you are told to break the seal), *Objective Answer Sheet*, and *Essay Paper* for any possible defects, such as missing pages, blurred printing, or stray marks (*Objective Answer Sheet* only). If any defects are found, request an entirely new *Booklet* from a proctor before you answer any questions.

8. For the Business Law and Professional Responsibilities (LPR), Auditing (AUDIT), and Financial Accounting and Reporting (FARE) sections, your answers to the essay questions or problems must be written on the paper provided in the *Essay Paper* portion of the *Booklet*. After the start of the examination, you should record your 7-digit candidate number, state, and question number on the first page of the *Essay Paper* portion of the *Booklet* and on the other pages where indicated.

9. For the ARE and FARE examination sections, you will be given a calculator. You should test the calculator in accordance with the instructions on the cover page of the *Booklet*. Inform your proctor if your calculator is defective. Calculators will not be provided for the LPR and AUDIT examination sections because the number of questions requiring calculations is minimal and the calculations are simple.

10. All amounts are to be considered material unless otherwise stated.

11. Answer all objective items on the *Objective Answer Sheet* provided. Use a No. 2 pencil only. You should attempt to answer all objective items, as there is no penalty for incorrect responses. Since the objective items are scanned optically, your comments and calculations associated with them are not considered. You should blacken the ovals as darkly as possible and erase clearly any marks you wish to change. You should make no stray marks.

   Approximately 10-15% of the multiple-choice items are included for pretesting only and are not included in your final grade.

12. It is important to pay strict attention to the manner in which your *Objective Answer Sheet* is structured. As you proceed with the examination, be certain that you blacken the oval that corresponds exactly with the item number in the *Examination Questions* portion of your *Booklet*. If you mark your answers in the *Examination Questions* portion of your *Booklet*, be certain that you transfer them to the *Objective Answer Sheet* before the session ends. Your examination paper will not be graded if you fail to record your answers on the *Objective Answer Sheet*. You

will not be given additional time to record your answers.

13. Answer all essay questions and problems on the *Essay Paper* provided. Always begin your answer to a question on the top of a new page (which may be the reverse side of a sheet of paper). Cross out anything that you do not want graded.

14. Selected essay responses will be graded for writing skills.

15. Include all computations to the problems in the FARE section. This may assist the graders in understanding your answers.

16. You may not leave the examination room with any examination materials, nor may you take notes about the examination with you from the examination room. You are required to turn in by the end of each session:

   a. *Attendance Record* and *Statement of Confidentiality*
   b. *Examination Questions*
   c. *Essay Paper* (for LPR, AUDIT, and FARE). Do not remove unused pages.
   d. *Objective Answer Sheet*
   e. Calculator (for ARE and FARE)

   f. All unused examination materials
   g. Prenumbered Identification Card (or Admission Notice) at the last examination section for which you sit (if required by your examining jurisdiction)

Your examination will not be graded unless you hand in these items before you leave the examination room.

17. If you believe one or more questions contain errors and want your concerns evaluated, you must fax your comments to the AICPA (201-938-3443). The fax should include the precise nature of any error; your rationale; and, if possible, references. The fax should include your 7-digit candidate identification number and must be received by the AICPA within 4 days of the completion of the examination administration. This will ensure that all comments are reviewed before the grading bases for the Uniform CPA Examination are confirmed. Although the AICPA cannot respond directly to each fax, it will investigate all comments received within the 4-day period.

18. Contact your board of accountancy for information regarding any other applicable rules.

In addition to the above general rules, oral instructions will be given by the examination supervisor shortly before the start of each session. They should include the location and/or rules concerning

   a. Storage of briefcases, handbags, books, personal belongings, etc.
   b. Food and beverages
   c. Smoking (usually not permited)
   d. Rest rooms
   e. Telephone calls and messages
   f. Requirements (if any) that candidates must take all parts not previously passed each time they sit for the examination. Minimum grades (if any) needed on parts failed to get credit on parts passed.
   g. Official clock, if any
   h. Additional supplies
   i. Assembly, turn-in, inspection, and stapling of solutions

The next section provides a detailed listing (mind-jogger) of things to do for your last-minute preparation. It also contains a list of strategies for the exam.

CPA EXAM CHECKLIST

One week before exam

__ 1. Look over major topical areas, concentrating on schedule formats and the information flow of the formats.
For example:
Accounting Changes and Error Correction
Income Statement Format
Long-Term Construction Accounting
Inventory Methods
Investments
Lessee-Lessor Accounting
Statement of Cash Flows
Purchase, Pooling, Consolidation Methods

__ 2. If time permits, work through a few questions in your weakest areas so that techniques/concepts are fresh in your mind.

__ 3. Assemble notecards and key outlines of major topical areas into a manageable "last review" notebook to be taken with you to the exam.

What to bring

__ 1. *Registration material*—for the CPA exam. You will save time at the examination site by filling out ahead of time the survey that you received with your registration materials.

__ 2. *Hotel confirmation.*

___ 3. *Cash*—payment for anything by personal check is rarely accepted.

___ 4. *Major credit card*—American Express, Master Card, Visa, etc.

___ 5. *Alarm clock*—this is too important an event to trust to a hotel wake-up call that might be overlooked.

___ 6. *Food*—candidates should carefully review the instructions provided by their State Board Examiners regarding policies about food at the exam.

___ 7. *Clothing*—should be comfortable and layered to suit the temperature range over the 2-day period and the examination room conditions.

___ 8. *Watch*—it is imperative that you be aware of the time remaining for each session.

___ 9. *Earplugs*—even though an examination is being given, there is constant activity in the examination room (e.g., proctors walking around, rustling of paper, people coughing, etc.). The use of earplugs may block out some of this distraction and help you concentrate better.

___ 10. *Other*—"last review" materials, pencils, erasers, leads, sharpeners, pens, etc.

While waiting for the exam to begin

1. Put your ID card on the table for ready reference to your number. The front page of your Examination Booklet contains an Attendance Record and Statement of Confidentiality. When told to do so, complete this information so the proctor can collect it prior to the start of the exam.

2. Realize that proctors will be constantly circulating throughout each exam session. You need only raise your hand to receive more paper at any time.

3. Take a few deep breaths and compose yourself. Resolve to do your very best and to go after every point you can get!

Before leaving for exam each day

1. Put your ID card in your wallet, purse, or on your person for entry to take the exam. This is your official entrance permit that allows you to participate in all sections of the exam.

2. Remember your hotel room key.

3. Pack snack items and lunch (optional).

4. Limit consumption of liquids.

5. Realize that on Thursday morning you must check out and arrange for storage of your luggage (most hotels have such a service) **prior to** departing for the exam to prevent late charges on your hotel bill.

Evenings before exams

1. Reviewing the evenings before the exams could earn you the extra points needed to pass a section. Just keep this last-minute effort in perspective and **do not panic** yourself into staying up all night trying to cover every possible point. This could lead to disaster by sapping your body of the endurance needed to attack questions creatively during the next 7-8 hour day.

2. Before the Financial Accounting and Reporting session, scan the general schedule formats to imprint the *flow* of information on your mind (e.g., income statement, statement of cash flows, and lease formats, etc.).

3. Read over **key** notecards or the most important outlines on topics in which you feel deficient.

4. Go over mnemonics and acronyms you have developed as study aids. Test yourself by writing out the letters on paper while verbally giving a brief explanation of what the letters stand for.

5. Scan outlines of SFAC 1, 2, 5, 6, 7 and any other notes pertinent to answering conceptual questions to imprint keywords.

6. Avoid postmortems during the examination period. Nothing you can do will affect your grade on sections of the exam you have already completed. Concentrate only on the work ahead in remaining sections.

7. **Set your alarm and get a good night's rest!** Being well rested will permit you to meet each day's challenge with a fresh burst of creative energy.

Exam taking strategy

1. Open the exam booklet, noting the number of objective questions and the areas they cover.

2. Scan the "required" sections of all problems to get a feel for the nature of the topics covered, making a mental note of the points allotted to each problem (exam point allotments parallel time allocation). Also note whether the problems require schedules or FS or numerical responses. Remember to divide allotted time per question proportionately over **all** parts of a question (parts are often unrelated, so don't forget that if 40-50 minutes are allowed for Problem 5, that much time must be divided among all required parts). Knowing the nature of these problems that you will tackle later allows your subconscious to sort out needed facts for solving them as you work the objective questions.

3. Reconcile the problem numbers with the questions listed on the front of the exam booklet and check consecutive page numbers in your booklet to reassure yourself that it is complete, that no pages are stuck together, etc.

4. Recognize that you may be feeling a little "burned out" by Thursday afternoon, so fight to stay sharp and go after the available points!

5. Begin working the multiple-choice questions, noting the time begun at the start of each set. Realize that you have approximately 2 to 2 1/2 minutes per computational-type multiple-choice question and approximately 1 2/3 minutes per concept-type multiple-choice question. Use the area marked "work space" in the Examination Booklet for the computations. Do not waste time labeling computations because the grader will not use objective question computation sheets. It is wise to number your computations for your own use if you wish to come back to a question, however.

6. Read each question **carefully!** Dates are extremely important! (For example, a long-term contract problem using the percentage-of-completion method may give information for a contract begun in 20**X1** but ask for income recognized for the year ended Dec. 31, 20**X2**.)

7. If you are struggling with problems beyond your time limit, use the strategy of dividing objective questions into two categories.

   a. Questions for which you **know** you lack knowledge to answer: Drawing from any resources you have, narrow answers down to as few as possible; then make an **educated guess**.
   b. Questions for which you feel you should be getting correct answer: Put "?" by the question on your Booklet and label your computations so you can return to them later. Your mental block may clear, or you may spot a simple math error that now can be corrected, thus giving you extra points.

8. Remember: **never** change a first impulse objective question answer later unless you are **absolutely certain** you are right. It is a proven fact that your subconscious often guides you to the correct answer.

9. Work problems that you consider easiest first, noting time begun and time allotted. Your goal is to pick up extra time to allocate to problems you are weaker on.

10. Read the "required" section, underlining and noting **every** requirement that you are asked for.

11. Read the information given, underlining key facts, circling percentages and interest rates that you plan to use, crossing out extraneous information, etc.

12. Draw time lines, visualize schedule headings, schedule formats, etc., that will help you respond to requirements. Do not forget to put a heading on each schedule or statement.

13. Computations should be made on columnar paper contained in your Examination Booklet which **will** be used by the grader as an "audit trail" to support your work. Label and cross-reference to schedules and worksheets as necessary. (For example, when asked to show comparative balance sheets for 20X1 and 20X2 with the correct valuation of Investment in Subsidiary, show supporting computations by stating "See Schedule A on page ....")

14. Write legibly; be neat and organized. Leave space on schedules, etc., to add information that you might think of later. Remember: A legible, well-organized, grammatically correct answer—containing as many keywords as possible—gives a professional appearance.

15. For essays/problems, format, organization, technique, disclosure, etc., are of critical importance.

16. Constantly compare your progress with the time remaining. **Never** spend more than the maximum allotted time on any problem until **all** problems are answered and time remains. Fight the urge to **complete** one problem at the expense of another problem. Remember that there are more gradable points in the **beginning** stages of problems than toward the end (the law of diminishing returns applies!). Once you feel you have answered sufficiently, **move on!**

17. As each problem is completed, quickly reread the "required" section again to make sure you have responded to each requirement. Organize any additional pages used to answer each question and set them aside for final assembly before handing in.

18. Each test will include a problem or question for which you may feel unprepared. Accept the challenge and go after the points! Draw from all your resources. Ask yourself how GAAP would be applied to similar situations, scan the objective questions for clues, look for relationships in **all** the available information given in the problem, try "backing into" the problem from another angle, etc. Every problem (no matter how impossible it may look at first glance) contains some points that are yours for the taking. Make your best effort. You may be on the right track and not even know it!

19. The cardinal rule is **never,** but **never,** leave an answer blank.

20. When you see alternate routes to take in problem solving, explain to the grader any assumptions you are making and why. Should you run out of time on a problem that you know how to complete, write a note to the grader briefly describing what you would have done had time permitted.

21. The most important technique to use for **all** essay questions is to constantly remind yourself that the grader assumes you know nothing (s/he cannot read your mind). As a candidate for a professional designation, you must convince him/her of your knowledge of the subject matter under question. **Never omit the obvious!**

22. If time permits, go back to any objective question that you "guessed" on.

23. Double-check to make certain you have answered **all** parts of **every** problem to the best of your ability. You've come too far to end the exam early, just because it's the last part and you feel you've written enough. Stick it out until they call for the exams.

24. Transfer objective question answers to the form provided in your Examination Booklet. Be especially careful to follow the numbers exactly, because number patterns differ on each answer form! Don't wait until it's too late. The proctors are not authorized to give you extra time for this.

25. Assemble any additional answer sheets in the correct order.

26. Take your Examination Booklet to the front of the exam room. Staple the additional answer sheets to the Booklet.

HAVE YOU MADE YOUR
COMMITMENT?

5 FINANCIAL ACCOUNTING AND REPORTING

Module 22/Basic Theory and Financial Reporting (TREP)

Module 24/Fixed Assets (FA)

		Page no.			Page no.
A.	Acquisition Cost	195	J.	Goodwill and Other Intangible Assets (SFAS 142)	206
B.	Capitalization of Interest	195			
C.	Nonmonetary Exchanges	196	K.	Reporting on the Costs of Start-up Activities	208
D.	Purchase of Groups of Fixed Assets	201			
E.	Capital vs. Revenue Expenditures	201	L.	Research and Development Costs (SFAS 2)	209
F.	Depreciation	202			
G.	Disposals and Impairment of Value	205	M.	Computer Software Costs	209
H.	Depletion	206	N.	Development Stage Enterprises (SFAS 7)	210
I.	Insurance	206			

	No. of minutes	Problem	Answer
		Page no.	
77 Multiple-Choice		211	222
1 Other Objective		219	230
5 Essay Questions			
1 Practice Problem			
1. Replacement of Components; Accelerated Depreciation; Inventory Method of Depreciation	15-25	220	232
2. Selection of Depreciation Method, Nonmonetary Exchange, and Composite Depreciation Method	15-25	220	232
3. Impairment of Fixed Assets	15-25	220	233
4. Intangible Assets	30-40	220	234
5. Impairment of Goodwill	15-20	220	235
6. R&D Costs	15-25	221	235

Module 25/Monetary Current Assets and Current Liabilities (CACL)

		Page no.			Page no.
A.	Cash	237	C.	Current Liabilities	246
B.	Receivables	238	D.	Ratios	251

	No. of minutes	Problem	Answer
		Page no.	
108 Multiple-Choice		252	268
2 Other Objective		264	280
5 Essay Questions			
1 Practice Problem			
1. AR Factored, Noninterest NR, Bad Debts	15-25	266	281
2. Schedule to Calculate Provision and Allowance for Bad Debts	20-25	266	281
3. Notes Receivable: Valuation, Discounting and Estimating Losses	15-25	266	282
4. Receivable Transfers	15-25	266	283
5. Contingencies	15-25	266	283
6. Contingencies	15-25	267	283

Module 26/Present Value (PV)

		Page no.			Page no.
A.	Fundamentals	285	D.	Pensions	332
B.	Bonds	203	E.	Leases	358
C.	Debt Restructure	325			

	No. of minutes	Problem	Answer
		Page no.	
A. Fundamentals			
22 Multiple-Choice		293	298
1 Other Objective		296	301
1 Practice Problem			
1. Notes Receivable	45-55	297	302
B. Bonds			
42 Multiple-Choice		310	316
2 Other Objective		314	321
3 Essay Questions			
1. Issuance of Bonds	15-25	315	323
2. Effective Interest Method; Effect of Using SL vs. Effective Interest Method; Extinguishment of Debt in IS and SCF	15-25	315	323
3. Convertible Debt and EPS	10-15	315	324

Module 27/Deferred Taxes (DETX)

Module 28/Stockholders' Equity (STK)

Module 29/Investments (IVES)

Module 30/Statement of Cash Flows (SCF)

Module 31/Business Combinations and Consolidations (BCC)

INTRODUCTION

This chapter is written to help you review intermediate and advanced accounting (financial accounting) for the Financial Accounting and Reporting section of the exam. The AICPA Content Specification Outline of financial accounting coverage appears on the following page.

Although the time devoted to financial accounting on the CPA exam since May 1994 is only 55% of the time previously devoted to this area, the scope of coverage has not been reduced. Additionally, the depth of coverage has not changed under reduced coverage.

The chapter is organized along the lines of the traditional intermediate and advanced accounting texts. The topics are arranged per the twelve financial modules (on the previous pages). The objective is to provide you with the basic concepts, journal entries, and formulas for each topic and subtopic. Hopefully you will be able to expand, adapt, and apply the basics to specific problem situations as presented in multiple-choice questions, other objective-type questions, essay questions, and problems appearing on the exam. Keep in mind the importance of working all four types of questions under exam conditions as you study the basics set forth in this chapter. Refer to the multiple-choice questions, other objective-type questions, essay questions, and problems on each of the financial accounting topics.

As you work through this chapter, remember that there are many possible series of journal entries and account titles that can be used in accounting for a specific type of economic transaction (e.g., long-term construction contracts). Reconcile the approach illustrated in the chapter with the approach you studied as an undergraduate per your intermediate or advanced text.

In this chapter, you will be referred frequently to the outlines of authoritative pronouncements at the end of the financial accounting modules in this chapter on the particular topic being discussed. These outlines can be located easily by referring to the headings identifying the pronouncements which appear at the top of each page at the end of this chapter. At first consideration, the presentation might appear more comprehensive if the outlines of APB, SFAS, etc., were integrated in this chapter rather than presented separately. Separate presentation, however, allows separate study of the pronouncements which is particularly beneficial as a last minute review. Please note that you **do not need to know** the numbers of these pronouncements for the exam.

AICPA Content Specification Outline

The AICPA Content Specification Outline of the coverage of Financial Accounting and Reporting appears on the following page. This outline was issued by the AICPA, effective for November 2000.

AICPA CONTENT SPECIFICATION OUTLINE: FINANCIAL ACCOUNTING AND REPORTING

I. Concepts and Standards for Financial Statements (**20%**)

  A. Financial Accounting Concepts

  B. Financial Accounting Standards for Presentation and Disclosure in General Purpose Financial Statements

    1. Consolidated and Combined Financial Statements

    2. Balance Sheet

    3. Statement(s) of Income, Comprehensive Income, and Changes in Equity Accounts

    4. Statement of Cash Flows

    5. Accounting Policies and Other Notes to Financial Statements

  C. Other Presentations of Financial Data

    1. Financial Statements Prepared in Conformity with Comprehensive Bases of Accounting other than Generally Accepted Accounting Principles

    2. Personal Financial Statements

    3. Prospective Financial Information

  D. Financial Statement Analysis

II. Recognition, Measurement, Valuation, and Presentation of Typical Items in Financial Statements in Conformity with Generally Accepted Accounting Principles (**40%**)

  A. Cash, Cash Equivalents, and Marketable Securities

  B. Receivables

  C. Inventories

  D. Property, Plant, and Equipment

  E. Investments

  F. Intangible and Other Assets

  G. Payables and Accruals

  H. Deferred Revenues

  I. Notes and Bonds Payable

  J. Other Liabilities

  K. Equity Accounts

  L. Revenue, Cost, and Expense Accounts

III. Recognition, Measurement, Valuation, and Presentation of Specific Types of Transactions and Events in Financial Statements in Conformity with Generally Accepted Accounting Principles (**40%**)

  A. Accounting Changes and Corrections of Errors

  B. Business Combinations

  C. Cash Flow Components—Financing, Investing, and Operating

  D. Contingent Liabilities and Commitments

  E. Discontinued Operations

  F. Earnings Per Share

  G. Employee Benefits

  H. Extraordinary Items

  I. Financial Instruments

  J. Foreign Currency Transactions and Translation

  K. Income Taxes

  L. Interest Costs

  M. Interim Financial Reporting

N. Leases
O. Nonmonetary Transactions
P. Quasi Reorganizations, Reorganizations, and
   Changes in Entity

Q. Related Parties
R. Research and Development Costs
S. Segment Reporting

PREPARING FOR FINANCIAL ACCOUNTING AND REPORTING

This section of the exam includes financial accounting theory and its practical application (problem-solving). Candidates can expect to see multiple-choice questions (both concept and computational), other objective format questions, essays, and problems. Therefore, in order to be thoroughly prepared for this section of the exam, candidates will need to master the material covered in Modules 22-33. Refer to Appendix B for a summary of past exam coverage on the Financial Accounting and Reporting section of the CPA exam.

First, candidates' preparation should emphasize an understanding of the basic principles and objectives underlying accounting (e.g., revenue and expense recognition rules, etc.). By focusing in on the key concepts, candidates will be able to develop a solution for whatever question format is tested.

Candidates should then evaluate their competence by working 10 to 20 multiple-choice questions from each of the Modules (22-33) in this volume. This diagnostic routine will acquaint you with the specific nature of the questions tested on each topic as well as indicate the amount of study required per topic. You should work toward a 75-80% correct response rate as a minimum on each topic.

Third, work actual CPA practice problems and essay questions from recent exams under examination conditions. **This is a critical step that candidates should not overlook.** It is not enough to just work multiple-choice and other objective-type questions. CPA problems are more involved and longer than typical problems found on undergraduate accounting examinations. You must develop these skills **before** the examination by applying the "Solutions Approach" described in Chapter 3. Similarly, most CPA candidates have little experience with accounting essay questions; undergraduate accounting examinations generally consist of problems. You should write out complete solutions to essay questions. Do not wait until the examination to develop answering techniques. Selected essays or portions thereof are graded for writing skills. Candidates should also recognize the value of the keyword outline (prepared in the exam margin or on the ruled paper). Practice it while answering old examination questions, and perhaps more importantly, orient your study habits to the keyword outline approach. As you review material, think of it in "outline" or "list" form. While you should use the keyword outline to organize your answer, your answer must be written out for the grader. **Lists of keywords, even in outline form, are not acceptable to the AICPA.** Finally, get yourself in good physical and mental condition. Commit yourself to stay and to work until the end of the session. It is very easy to get up and leave an hour early.

BASIC THEORY AND FINANCIAL REPORTING

A. Basic Concepts

This module includes the basic financial statements except the Statement of Cash Flows. It also includes revenue and expense recognition rules, accounting changes, and error correction. **The relevant accounting pronouncements are indicated in the discussion, complete with cross-references to outlines of the pronouncements at the end of this chapter**. (Note these outlines appear in the following sequence: ARB, APB, SFAS, and SFAC. The page headers in the outlines identify the sources of the pronouncements outlined on those pages.) Turn to each outline as directed and study the outline while reviewing the related journal entries, computations, etc.

1. Basic Accounting Theory

The foundation of financial accounting is generally accepted accounting principles (GAAP). GAAP is the conventions, rules, and procedures necessary to define accepted practice at a particular time and includes among other items, SFAS, FASB Interpretations, APB Opinions, ARB and SEC releases. These are the pronouncements to which practitioners look when determining if financial statements fairly present financial position, results of operations, and changes in cash flows.

SAS 69 (AU 411) expanded on the above list and established the hierarchy of GAAP for business enterprises shown below. If the accountant/auditor cannot find a specified accounting treatment in category (A), s/he would proceed to the next lowest category.

- **Category (A),** officially established accounting principles, consists of Financial Accounting Standards Board (FASB) Statements of Financial Accounting Standards and Interpretations, Accounting Principles Board (APB) Opinions, and AICPA Accounting Research Bulletins.
- **Category (B)** consists of FASB Technical Bulletins and, if cleared by the FASB, AICPA Industry Audit and Accounting Guides and AICPA Statements of Position.
- **Category (C)** consists of AICPA Accounting Standards Executive Committee (AcSEC) Practice Bulletins that have been cleared by the FASB and consensus positions of the FASB Emerging Issues Task Force.
- **Category (D)** includes AICPA accounting interpretations and implementation guides ("Qs and As") published by the FASB staff, and practices that are widely recognized and prevalent either generally or in the industry.

In addition, the above four categories are supplemented by "other accounting literature."

In cases of conflict between the accounting treatment suggested by the categories, the higher category normally prevails over lower categories. For conflicts within a category the treatment most closely approximating the transaction's economic substance prevails (i.e., substance over form).

Although GAAP is the current basis for financial reporting, it does not constitute a cohesive body of accounting theory. Generally, SFAS and the other authoritative pronouncements have been the result of a problem-by-problem approach. The pronouncements have dealt with specific problems as they occur and are not predicated on an underlying body of theory.

Theory can be defined as a coherent set of hypothetical, conceptual, and pragmatic principles forming a general frame of reference for a field of inquiry; thus, accounting theory should be the basic principles of accounting rather than its practice (which GAAP describes or dictates). Accounting has a definite need for conceptual theoretical structure. Such a structure is necessary if an authoritative body such as the FASB is to promulgate consistent standards. A body of accounting theory should be the foundation of the standard-setting process and should provide guidance where no authoritative GAAP exists.

There have been efforts to develop such a frame of reference. The most recent attempt to develop accounting theory led to the establishment of the Statements of Financial Accounting Concepts (SFAC), of which seven have been issued. The purpose of this series is "to set forth fundamentals on which financial accounting and reporting standards will be based." In other words, the SFAC attempt to organize a framework that can serve as a reference point in formulating SFAS. However, it is important to note that the SFAC do not constitute authoritative GAAP. They merely serve as a theoretical framework for the development of accounting standards.

Financial Reporting. "Financial reporting includes not only financial statements but also other means of communicating information that relates, directly or indirectly, to the information provided by a business enterprise's accounting system—that is, information about an enterprise's resources, obligations, earnings, etc." (SFAC 1). It is important to note that not all informational needs are met by accounting or financial reporting. The following diagram from SFAC 5 describes the information spectrum.

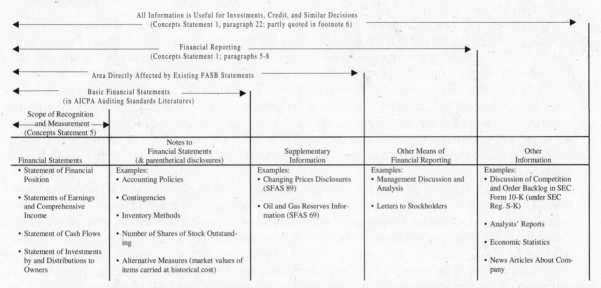

Financial Statements	Notes to Financial Statements (& parenthetical disclosures)	Supplementary Information	Other Means of Financial Reporting	Other Information
• Statement of Financial Position	Examples: • Accounting Policies	Examples: • Changing Prices Disclosures (SFAS 89)	Examples: • Management Discussion and Analysis	Examples: • Discussion of Competition and Order Backlog in SEC Form 10-K (under SEC Reg. S-K)
• Statements of Earnings and Comprehensive Income	• Contingencies	• Oil and Gas Reserves Information (SFAS 69)	• Letters to Stockholders	
• Statement of Cash Flows	• Inventory Methods			• Analysts' Reports
• Statement of Investments by and Distributions to Owners	• Number of Shares of Stock Outstanding			• Economic Statistics
	• Alternative Measures (market values of items carried at historical cost)			• News Articles About Company

Components of the Conceptual Framework. The components of the conceptual framework for financial accounting and reporting include objectives, qualitative characteristics, elements, recognition, measurement, financial statements, earnings, funds flow, and liquidity. The relationship between these components is illustrated in the following diagram, from *Financial Statements and Other Means of Financial Reporting*, a FASB Invitation to Comment.

In the diagram below, components to the left are more basic and those to the right depend on components to their left. Components are closely related to those above or below them.

Conceptual Framework
For Financial Accounting and Reporting

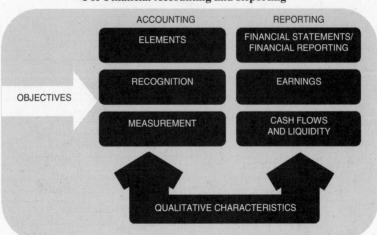

The most basic component of the conceptual framework is the objectives. The objectives underlie the other phases and are derived from the needs of those for whom financial information is intended. The objectives provide a focal point for financial reporting by identifying what types of information are relevant.

The qualitative characteristics also underlie most of the other phases. They are the criteria to be used in choosing and evaluating accounting and reporting policies.

Elements of financial statements are the components from which financial statements are created. They include assets, liabilities, equity, investments by owners, distributions to owners, comprehensive income, revenues, expenses, gains, and losses.

In order to be included in financial statements, an element must meet criteria for recognition and possess an attribute which is relevant and can be reliably measured.

Finally, reporting and display considerations are concerned with what information should be provided, who should provide it, and where it should be displayed. How the financial statements (financial position, earnings, and cash flow) are presented is the focal point of this part of the conceptual framework project.

Objectives of Financial Reporting. (See outline of SFAC 1.) Remember, objectives of financial reporting underlie the conceptual framework. They are the basis upon which a body of theory is established. The objectives described in SFAC 1 have not been verified by an empirical process, but they are an attempt by the FASB to provide a foundation for a cohesive set of interrelated concepts.

The objectives focus on users of financial information. They are derived from "the needs of external users who lack the authority to prescribe the information they want and must rely on information management communicates to them." The external users who are emphasized in the objectives are actual and potential investors and creditors. These users are particularly interested in the amounts, timing, and relative uncertainty of future cash flows, whether they be return of capital, interest, dividends, etc.

Three basic objectives are listed in SFAC 1. The objectives state that financial reporting should provide (1) information useful in investment and credit decisions, (2) information useful in assessing cash flow prospects (amount, timing, and uncertainty), and (3) information about enterprise resources, claims to those resources, and changes therein. A focal point in SFAC 1 is information about earnings and earning power. Earnings are a major cause of changes in resources. Despite the emphasis on cash flows, earnings are to be computed on the accrual basis, because accrual accounting "provides a better indication of an enterprise's present and continuing ability to generate favorable cash flows than information limited to the financial effects of cash receipts and payments."

Qualitative Characteristics. (See outline of SFAC 2.) The qualitative characteristics also underlie the conceptual framework, but in a different way. While the objectives provide an overall basis, the qualitative characteristics establish criteria for selecting and evaluating accounting alternatives which will meet the objectives. In other words, information must possess the qualitative characteristics if that information is to fulfill the objectives.

SFAC 2 views these characteristics as a hierarchy of accounting qualities, as represented in the diagram below.

A HIERARCHY OF ACCOUNTING QUALITIES

The diagram reveals many important relationships. At the top and bottom are constraints. If information falls outside these constraints, it would not be reported although it may possess some qualitative characteristics. Thus, information is not disclosed if the costs of disclosure outweigh the benefits or if the information is not material enough to influence users.

The first two qualities in the hierarchy (understandability and decision usefulness) are not qualities relating solely to information. They also depend on qualities of particular decision makers. The usefulness and understandability of information depends on the knowledge and ability of those using it. SFAC 1 states that "financial information is a tool, and like most tools, cannot be of direct help to those who are unable or unwilling to use it or who misuse it."

The primary qualities that accounting information should possess are relevance and reliability. As the chart indicates, each of these is broken down into three components. Comparability is a secondary quality which interacts with relevance and reliability to enhance usefulness of information.

Accounting information is relevant if it has the "capacity to make a difference" in a decision. To be relevant in an investment or credit decision, information must help users form predictions about future cash flows (refer to objectives). This can occur through predictive value (improving capacity to predict) or feedback value (confirmation or correction of prior predictions). Of course, to be relevant, information must be available before it loses its capacity to affect decisions (timeliness).

Information is reliable if it is reasonably free from error and bias, and faithfully represents what it claims to represent. Reliability consists of verifiability, representational faithfulness, and neutrality.

The secondary qualities of comparability and consistency become important when assessing cash flows of different enterprises or of the same enterprises over different periods. Comparability of information enables users to identify similarities in and differences between two enterprises, while consistency (unchanging policies and procedures from period to period) does the same between periods for each enterprise.

Basic Elements. (See outline of SFAC 6.) Elements of financial statements are the ten basic building blocks from which financial statements are constructed. These definitions are based upon the objectives of SFAC 1. They are intended to assure that users will receive decision-useful information about enterprise resources (assets), claims to those resources (liabilities and equity), and changes therein (the other seven elements). In order to be included in the statements, an item must qualify as an element, meet recognition criteria, and be measurable.

The meaning of financial statement elements depends on the conceptual view of earnings which is adopted. Two basic views are the asset-liability view and the revenue-expense view. Under the asset-liability view, earnings are measured by the change (other than investments or withdrawals) in the net economic resources of an enterprise during a period. Therefore, definitions of assets and liabilities are the key under this view, and definitions of revenues, expenses, gains, and losses are secondary and are based on assets and liabilities.

The revenue-expense view holds that earnings are a measure of an enterprise's effectiveness in using its inputs to obtain and sell outputs. Thus, definitions of revenues and expenses are basic to this view, and definitions of assets, liabilities, and other elements are derived from revenues and expenses.

The definitions of all ten elements are contained in the outline of SFAC 6. Let us examine one definition in more detail. "Assets are probable future economic benefits obtained or controlled by a particular entity as a result of past transactions or events." This definition is based on the objectives and qualities of SFAC 1 and 2. The overall thrust of the objectives—predicting and evaluating future cash flows—is reflected in the phrase "probable future economic benefits." "Control by a particular entity" is crucial if reporting an item as an asset is to have decision usefulness (or relevance). The quality of reliability is assured by the phrase "as a result of past transactions." Information is more verifiable, valid, and neutral (the components of reliability) if based on past transactions. A similar analysis can be applied to liabilities, equity, investments by owners, distributions to owners, comprehensive income, revenues, expenses, gains and losses.

SFAC 6 also defines some other concepts in addition to the ten elements. Especially important among these eleven additional concepts are accrual accounting, realization, recognition, and matching. Realization and recognition are addressed by the FASB in SFAC 5. The definition of accrual accounting is important because SFAC 1 stated that accrual accounting should be used since it provides a better indication of future cash flows than the cash basis. This is true because accrual accounting records transactions with cash consequences (involving future cash flows) as they occur, not when the cash actually moves. Matching is referred to in most accounting literature as a principle, or fundamental law, of accounting.

Recognition and Measurement. (See outline of SFAC 5.) Recognition principles establish criteria concerning when an element should be included in the statements, while measurement principles govern the valuation of those elements.

SFAC 5 established four fundamental recognition criteria: definitions, measurability, relevance, and reliability. If an item meets the definition of an element, can be reliably measured, is capable of making a difference in user decisions, and is verifiable, neutral, and representationally faithful, it should be included in the financial statements.

Five different attributes are used to measure assets and liabilities in present practice. These are discussed below in an excerpt from SFAC 5.

a.   ***Historical cost (historical proceeds).*** Property, plant, and equipment and most inventories are reported at their historical cost, which is the amount of cash, or its equivalent, paid to acquire an asset, commonly adjusted after acquisition for amortization or other allocations. Liabilities that involve obligations to provide goods or services to customers are generally reported at historical proceeds, which is the amount of cash, or its equivalent, received when the obligation was incurred and may be adjusted after acquisition for amortization or other allocations.

b.   ***Current cost.*** Some inventories are reported at their current (replacement) cost, which is the amount of cash, or its equivalent, that would have to be paid if the same or an equivalent asset were acquired currently.

c.   ***Current market value.*** Some investments in marketable securities are reported at their current market value, which is the amount of cash or its equivalent, that could be obtained by selling an asset in orderly liquidation. Current market value is also generally used for assets expected to be sold at prices lower than previous carrying amounts. Some liabilities that involve marketable commodities and securities, for example, the obligations of writers of options or sellers of common shares who do not own the underlying commodities or securities, are reported at current market value. Current market value is sometimes referred to as fair market value.

d.   ***Net realizable (settlement) value.*** Short-term receivables and some inventories are reported at their net realizable value, which is the nondiscounted amount of cash, or its equivalent, into which an asset is expected to be converted in due course of business less direct costs, if any, necessary to make that conversion. Liabilities that involve known or estimated amounts of money payable at unknown future dates, for example, trade payables or warranty obligations, generally are reported at their net settlement value, which is the nondiscounted amount of cash, or its equivalent, expected to be paid to liquidate an obligation in the due course of business, including direct costs, if any, necessary to make that payment.

e.   ***Present (or discounted) value of future cash flows.*** Long-term receivables are reported at their present or discounted value (discounted at the implicit or historical rate), which is the present value of future cash inflows into which an asset is expected to be converted in due course of business less present values of cash outflows necessary to obtain those inflows. Long-term payables are similarly reported at their present or discounted value (discounted at the implicit or historical rate), which is the present or discounted value of future cash outflows expected to be required to satisfy the liability in due course of business.

SFAC 5 states that each of these attributes is appropriate in different situations and that all five attributes will continue to be used in the future.

Similarly, SFAC 5 states that nominal units of money will continue to be the measurement unit. However, if inflation increases to a level where the FASB feels that financial statements become too distorted, another unit (such as units of constant purchasing power) could be adopted.

SFAC 5 is based on the concept of financial capital maintenance. Two basic concepts of capital maintenance (financial and physical) can be used to separate return **on** capital (earnings) from return **of** capital (capital recovery). Remember, any capital which is "used up" during a period must be returned before earnings can be recognized. In other words, earnings is the amount an entity can distribute to its owners and be as well-off at the end of the year as at the beginning.

One way "well-offness" can be measured is in terms of financial capital. This concept of capital maintenance holds that the capital to be maintained is measured by the amount of cash (possibly restated into constant dollars) invested by owners. Earnings may not be recognized until the dollar investment in net assets, measured in units of money or purchasing power, is returned. The financial capital maintenance concept is the traditional view which is reflected in most present financial statements.

An alternative definition of "well-offness" is expressed in terms of physical capital. This concept holds that the capital to be maintained is the physical productive capacity of the enterprise. Earnings may not be recognized until the current replacement costs of assets with the same productive capabilities of the assets used up are returned. The physical capital maintenance concept supports current cost accounting. Again, the physical productive capacity may be measured in nominal or constant dollars.

A simple example can further clarify the two capital maintenance concepts. Suppose an enterprise invests $10 in an inventory item. At year-end, the enterprise sells the item for $15. In order to replace the item at year-end, they would have to pay $12 rather than $10. To further simplify, assume the increase in replacement cost is due to specific price changes, and there is no general inflation.

The financial capital concept would maintain that the firm is as well-off once the dollar investment ($10) is returned. At that point, the financial capital is maintained and the remaining $5 is a return **on** capital, or income. The physical capital concept maintains that the firm is not as well-off until the physical capacity (a similar inventory item) is returned. Therefore, the firm must reinvest $12 to be as well-off. Then physical capital is maintained, and only the remaining $3 is a return **on** capital or income.

SFAC 5 also gives specific guidance as to recognition of revenues and gains, and expenses and losses, as indicated below.

Revenues	When realized or realizable (when related assets received or held are readily convertible to known amounts of cash or claims to cash) and earned
Gains	When realized or realizable
Expenses	When economic benefits are consumed in revenue-earning activities, or when future economic benefits are reduced or eliminated
Losses	When future economic benefits are reduced or eliminated

When economic benefits are consumed during a period, the expense may be recognized by matching (such as cost of goods sold), immediate recognition (such as selling and administrative salaries), or systematic and rational allocation (such as depreciation).

Revenues, expenses, gains, and losses are used to compute **earnings**. Earnings is the extent to which revenues and gains associated with cash-to-cash cycles substantially completed during the period exceed expenses and losses directly or indirectly associated with those cycles. Earnings adjusted for cumulative accounting adjustments and other nonowner changes in equity (such as foreign currency translation adjustments) is **comprehensive income**. Per SFAC 5, comprehensive income would reflect all changes in the equity of an entity during a period, except investments by owners and distributions to owners. SFAS 130, covered in Section D.3. of this module, only goes part way in implementing this concept.

Cash Flow Information and Present Value. (See outline of SFAC 7.) As discussed earlier, the attributes most often used to measure assets and liabilities include observable marketplace-determined amounts. These observable marketplace amounts (such as current cost) are generally more reliable and are determined more efficiently than measurements which employ estimates of future cash flows. However, when observable amounts are unavailable, accountants often turn to estimated cash flows to determine the carrying amount of an asset or liability. Since those cash flows often occur in one or more future periods, questions arise regarding whether the accounting measurement should reflect the present value or the undiscounted sum of those cash flows.

In February 2000, the FASB issued SFAC 7, *Using Cash Flow Information and Present Value in Accounting Measurements*. SFAC 7 provides a framework for using future cash flows as the basis of an accounting measurement. The framework provides general principles governing the use of present value, especially when the amount of future cash flows, their timing, or both, are uncertain. The framework provided by SFAC 7 also describes the objective of present value in accounting measurements. Note that SFAC 7 addresses measurement issues, not recognition questions. SFAC 7 does not specify when fresh-start measurements are appropriate. Fresh-start measurements are defined by the FASB as measurements in periods following initial recognition that establish a new carrying amount unrelated to previous amounts and accounting conventions. SFAC 7 applies only to measurements at initial recognition, fresh-start measurements, and amortization techniques based on future cash flows. SFAC 7 does not apply to measurements based on the amount of cash or other assets paid or received, or on observation of fair values in the marketplace. If such observations or transactions are present, the measurement would be based on them, not on future cash flows. The marketplace assessment of present value is already embodied in the transaction price.

The present value formula is a tool used to incorporate the time value of money in a measurement. Thus, it is useful in financial reporting whenever an item is measured using estimated future cash flows. The FASB defines present value as the current measure of an estimated future cash inflow or outflow, discounted at an interest rate for the number of periods between today and the date of the estimated cash flow. The objective of using present value in an accounting measurement is to capture, to the extent possible, the economic difference between sets of future cash flows.

Assets with the same cash flows are distinguished from one another by the timing and uncertainty of those cash flows. Note that an accounting measurement based on undiscounted cash flows would measure assets with the same cash flows at the same amount. For example, an asset with a contractual cash flow of $28,000 due in ten days would be equal to an asset with an *expected* cash flow of $28,000 due in ten years. Present value helps to distinguish between cash flows that might otherwise appear similar. A present value measurement that incorporates the uncertainty in estimated cash flows always provides more relevant information than a measurement based on the undiscounted sum of those cash flows, or a discounted measurement that ignores uncertainty.

To provide relevant information for financial reporting, present value must represent some observable measurement attribute of assets or liabilities. This attribute is fair value. The fair value of an asset (or liability) is defined by the FASB as the amount at which that asset (or liability) could be bought (or incurred) or sold (or settled) in a current transaction between willing parties.

The only objective of present value, when used in accounting measurements at initial recognition and fresh-start measurements, is to estimate fair value. In the absence of observed transaction prices, accounting measurements at initial recognition and fresh-start measurements should attempt to capture the elements that taken together would comprise a market price if one existed, that is, fair value.

Marketplace participants attribute prices to assets and liabilities. In doing so they distinguish the risks and rewards of one asset or liability from those of another. An observed market price encompasses the consensus view of all marketplace participants about an asset's or liability's utility, future cash flows, the uncertainties surrounding those cash flows, and the amount that marketplace participants demand for bearing those uncertainties.

While the expectations of an entity's management are often useful and informative in estimating asset and liability values, the marketplace is the final judge of asset and liability values. An entity is required to pay the market's price when it acquires an asset or settles a liability in a current transaction, regardless of the intentions or expectations of the entity's management. Therefore, for measurements at initial recognition or for fresh-start measurements, fair value provides the most complete and representationally faithful measurement of the economic characteristics of an asset or a liability.

A present value measurement that is able to capture the economic differences between various assets and liabilities would include the following elements according to SFAC 7:

a.   An estimate of the future cash flow, or in more complex cases, series of future cash flows at different times.
b.   Expectations about possible variations in the amount or timing of those cash flows.
c.   The time value of money, represented by the risk-free rate of interest.
d.   The price for bearing the uncertainty inherent in the asset or liability.
e.   Other, sometimes unidentifiable factors, including illiquidity and market imperfections.

SFAC 7 contrasts two approaches to computing present value. Either approach may be used to estimate the fair value of an asset or a liability, depending on the circumstances. In the expected cash flow approach only the time value of money, represented by the risk-free rate of interest, is included in the discount rate; the other factors cause adjustments in arriving at risk-adjusted expected cash flows. In a traditional approach to present value, adjustments for factors b. - e. are embedded in the discount rate.

While techniques used to estimate future cash flows and interest rates vary due to situational differences, certain general principles govern any application of present value techniques in measuring assets. These are discussed in the outline of SFAC 7.

Traditionally, accounting applications of present value have used a single set of estimated cash flows and a single interest rate, often described as "the rate commensurate with risk." The traditional approach assumes that a single interest rate convention can reflect all of the expectations about future cash flows and the appropriate risk premium. While the traditional approach may be adequate for some simple measurements, the FASB found that it does not provide the tools needed to address more complex problems. The expected cash flow approach was found to be a more effective measurement tool than the traditional approach in many situations. **The expected cash flow approach** uses all expectations about possible cash flows instead of the single most-likely cash flow. The expected cash flow approach focuses on direct analysis of the cash flows in question and on explicit assumptions about the range of possible estimated cash flows and their respective probabilities.

EXAMPLE: A cash flow might be $100, $200, or $300 with probabilities of 10%, 60%, and 30%, respectively. The expected cash flow is $220 ($100 x .1) + ($200 x .6) + ($300 x .3) = $220. However, the traditional approach would choose $200 as the best estimate or most-likely amount.

When the timing of cash flows is uncertain, the expected cash flow approach allows present value techniques to be utilized. The following example is from SFAC 7.

EXAMPLE: A cash flow of $1,000 may be received in one year, two years, or three years with probabilities of 10%, 60%, and 30%, respectively. Notice that the expected present value of $892.36 differs from the traditional notion of a best estimate of $902.73 (the 60% probability). The following shows the computation of expected present value:

Present value of $1,000 in one year at 5%	$952.38	
Probability	10.00%	$95.24
Present value of $1,000 in two years at 5.25%	$902.73	
Probability	60.00%	541.64
Present value of $1,000 in three years at 5.50%	$851.61	
Probability	30.00%	255.48
Expected present value		$892.36

An interest rate in a traditional present value computation is unable to reflect any uncertainties in the timing of cash flows. By incorporating a range of possible outcomes (with their respective timing differences), the expected cash flow approach accommodates the use of present value techniques when the timing of cash flows is uncertain.

An estimate of fair value should include an adjustment for risk. The risk adjustment is the price that marketplace participants are able to receive for bearing the uncertainties in cash flows. This assumes that the amount is identifiable, measurable, and significant. Present value measurements occur under conditions of uncertainty. In SFAC 7, the term **uncertainty** refers to the fact that the cash flows used in a present value measurement are estimates, rather than known amounts. Uncertainty has accounting implications because it has economic consequences. Business and individuals routinely enter into transactions based on expectations about uncertain future events. The outcome of those events will place the entity in a financial position that may be better or worse than expected, but until the uncertainties are resolved, the entity is **at risk**.

In common usage, the word **risk** refers to any exposure to uncertainty in which that exposure has potential negative consequences. Risk is a relational concept. A particular risk can only be understood in context. In most situations, marketplace participants are said to be **risk adverse**. They prefer situations with less uncertainty relative to an expected outcome. Marketplace participants seek compensation for accepting uncertainty. This is referred to as a **risk premium**. They demand more compensation (a higher premium) to assume a liability with expected cash flows that are uncertain, than to assume a liability with cash flows of the same expected amount but no uncertainty. This phenomenon can be described with the financial axiom, "the greater the risk, the greater the return." The objective of including uncertainty and risk in accounting measurements is to imitate, to the extent possible, the market's behavior toward assets and liabilities with uncertain cash flows.

If prices for an asset or liability or an essentially similar asset or liability can be observed in the marketplace, there is no need to use present value measurements. The marketplace assessment of present value is already embodied in the price. However, if observed prices are unavailable, present value measurements are often the best available technique with which to estimate what a price would be.

The measurement of liabilities sometimes involves problems different from those encountered in the measurement of assets. Thus, measurement of liabilities may require different techniques in arriving at fair value. Liabilities can be held by individuals who sell their rights differently than they would sell other assets. Liabilities are sometimes settled through assumption by a third party. To estimate the liability's fair value, accountants must estimate the price necessary to pay the third party to assume the liability.

The most relevant measure of a liability always reflects the credit standing of the entity obligated to pay. An entity's credit standing affects the interest rate at which it borrows in the marketplace. The initial proceeds of a loan, therefore, always reflect the entity's credit standing at that time. Likewise, the price at which others buy and sell the entity's loan includes their assessment of the entity's ability to repay. The failure to include changes in credit standing in the measurement of a liability ignores economic differences between liabilities.

Present value techniques are also used in periodic reporting conventions knows collectively as **interest methods of allocation**. Financial statements usually attempt to represent changes in assets and liabilities from one period to the next. In principle, the purpose of all accounting allocations is to report changes in the value, utility, or substance of assets and liabilities over time.

Accounting allocations attempt to relate the change in an asset or liability to some observable real-world phenomenon. An interest method of allocation relates changes in the reported amount with changes in the present value of a set of future cash inflows or outflows. However, allocation methods are only representations. They are not measurements of an asset or liability. The selection of a particular allocation method and the underlying assumptions always involves a degree of arbitrariness. As a result, no allocation method can be demonstrated to be superior to others in all circumstances. The FASB will continue to decide whether to require an interest method of allocation on a project-by-project basis. Refer to the outline of SFAC 7 for further information regarding the interest method of allocation.

2. **Income Determination** (See outlines of SFAC 1, 2, 5, and 6.)

The primary objective of accounting is to measure income. Income is a measure of management's efficiency in combining the factors of production into desired goods and services.

Efficient firms with prospects of increased efficiency (higher profits) have greater access to financial capital and at lower costs. Their stock usually sells at a higher price-earnings ratio than the stock of a company with less enthusiastic prospects. The credit rating of the prospectively efficient company is probably higher than the prospectively less efficient company. Thus, the "cost of capital" will be lower for the company with the brighter outlook (i.e., lower stock dividend yield rates and/or lower interest rates).

The entire process of acquiring the factors of production, processing them, and selling the resulting goods and services produces revenue. The acquisition of raw materials is part of the revenue-producing process, as is providing warranty protection.

Under the accrual basis of accounting, revenue is generally recognized at the point of sale (ARB 43, chap 1A,) or as service is performed. The point of sale is when title passes: generally when seller ships (FOB shipping point) or when buyer receives (FOB destination).

Three exceptions exist to the general revenue recognition rule: during production, at the point where production is complete, and at the point of cash collection. The table below compares the three exceptions with the general revenue recognition rule (point of sale).

Recognition basis/ source of GAAP	*Accounting method*	*Criteria for use of basis*	*Reason(s) for departing from sale basis*
• **Point of sale ARB 43 (Ch 1A)**	• Transactions approach (sales basis)	• Exchange has taken place • Earnings process is (virtually) complete	
• **During production basis ARB 45 and AICPA Contractors Guide**	• Percentage-of-completion	• Long-term construction,* property, or service contract • Dependable estimates of extent of progress and cost to complete • Reasonable assurance of collectibility of contract price	• Availability of evidence of ultimate proceeds • Better measure of periodic income • Avoidance of fluctuations in revenues, expenses, and income
• **Completion-of-production basis ARB 43 (Ch 4)**	• Net realizable value	• Immediate marketability at quoted prices • Unit interchangeability • Difficulty of determining costs	• Known or determinable revenues • Inability to determine costs and thereby defer expense recognition until sale
• **Cash collection basis APB 10**	• Installment and cost recovery methods	• Absence of a reasonable basis for estimating degree of collectibility	• Level of uncertainty with respect to collection of the receivable precludes recognition of gross profit before cash is received

Note that the "completed contract" method for construction contracts is not a departure from the sale basis.

Source: *Adapted from Henry R. Jaenicke,* **Survey of Present Practices in Recognizing Revenues, Expenses, Gains, and Losses***, FASB, 1981.*

Under accrual accounting, expenses are recognized as related revenues are recognized, that is, (product) expenses are matched with revenues. Some (period) expenses, however, cannot be associated with particular revenues. These expenses are recognized as incurred.

(1) Product costs are those which can be associated with particular sales (e.g., cost of sales). Product costs attach to a unit of product and become an expense only when the unit to which they attach is sold. This is known as associating "cause and effect."

(2) Period costs are not particularly or conveniently assignable to a product. They become expenses due to the passage of time by

(a) Immediate recognition if the future benefit cannot be measured (e.g., advertising)
(b) Systematic and rational allocation if benefits are produced in certain future periods (e.g., asset depreciation)

Thus, income is the net effect of inflows of revenue and outflows of expense during a period of time. The period in which revenues and expenses are taken to the income statement (recognized) is determined by the above criteria.

Cash basis accounting, in contrast to accrual basis accounting, recognizes income when cash is received and expenses when cash is disbursed. Cash basis accounting is subject to manipulation (i.e., cash receipts and expenses can be switched from one year to another by management). Another reason for adopting accrual basis accounting is that economic transactions have become more involved and multiperiod. An expenditure for a fixed asset may produce revenue for years and years.

3. **Accruals and Deferrals**

Accrual—accrual-basis recognition precedes (leads to) cash receipt/expenditure

Revenue—recognition of revenue earned, but not received
Expense—recognition of expense incurred, but not paid

Deferral—cash receipt/expenditure precedes (leads to) accrual-basis recognition

Revenue—postponement of recognition of revenue; cash is received,
       but revenue is not earned
Expense—postponement of recognition of expense; cash is paid,
       but expense is not incurred

A deferral postpones recognition of revenue or expense by placing the amount in liability or asset accounts. Two methods are possible for deferring revenues and expenses depending on whether real or nominal accounts are originally used to record the cash transaction.

BOOKKEEPING METHODS

Deferrals of Expense

	Expense method			*Asset method*		
When paid	Insurance expense	xx		Prepaid insurance	xx	
	Cash		xx	Cash		xx
Year-end	Prepaid insurance	xx		Insurance expense	xx	
	Insurance expense		xx	Prepaid insurance		xx
Reverse	Yes			No		

Deferrals of Revenue

	Revenue method			*Liability method*		
When received	Cash	xx		Cash	xx	
	Rent revenue		xx	Unearned rent		xx
Year-end	Rent revenue	xx		Unearned rent	xx	
	Unearned rent		xx	Rent revenue		xx
Reverse	Yes			No		

Accruals

	Expense			*Revenue*		
Adjustment	Wages expense	xx		Interest receivable	xx	
	Wages payable		xx	Interest revenue		xx
Reverse	Yes			Yes		

Entries are reversed for bookkeeping expediency. If accruals are reversed, the subsequent cash transaction is reflected in the associated nominal account. If accruals are not reversed, the subsequent cash transaction must be apportioned between a nominal and real account.

Cash		(amount received)
Revenue		(earned in current period)
Revenue receivable		(accrual at last year-end)

Accruals do not have two methods, but can be complicated by failure to reverse adjusting entries (also true for deferrals initially recorded in nominal accounts).

4. **Cash to Accrual**

Many smaller companies use the **cash basis** of accounting, where revenues are recorded when cash is received and expenses are recorded when cash is paid (except for purchases of fixed assets, which are capitalized and depreciated). Often the accountant is called upon to convert cash basis accounting records to the accrual basis. This type of problem is also found on the CPA examination.

When making journal entries to adjust from the cash basis to the accrual basis, it is important to identify two types of amounts: the **current balance** in the given account (cash basis) and the **correct balance** in the account (accrual basis). The journal entries must adjust the account balances from their current amounts to the correct amounts.

It is also important to understand relationships between balance sheet accounts and income statement accounts. When adjusting a balance sheet account from the cash basis to the accrual basis, the other half of the entry will generally be to the related income statement account. Thus, when adjusting accounts receivable, the related account is sales; for accounts payable, purchases; for prepaid rent, rent expense; and so on.

For example, assume a company adjusts to the accrual basis every 12/31; during the year, they use the cash basis. The 12/31/01 balance in accounts receivable, after adjustment, is $17,000. During 2002, whenever cash is collected, the company debits cash and credits sales. Therefore, the 12/31/02 balance in accounts receivable **before adjustment** is still $17,000. Suppose the **correct** 12/31/02 balance in accounts receivable is $28,000. The necessary entry is

Accounts receivable	11,000	
Sales		11,000

This entry not only corrects the accounts receivable account, but also increases sales since unrecorded receivables means that there are also unrecorded sales. On the other hand, suppose the **correct** 12/31/02 balance of accounts receivable is $12,500. The necessary entry is

Sales	4,500	
Accounts receivable		4,500

Sales is debited because during 2001, $4,500 more cash was collected on account than should be reported as sales. When cash is received on account the transaction is recorded as a credit to sales, not accounts receivable. This overstates the sales account.

Some problems do not require journal entries, but instead a computation of accrual amounts from cash basis amounts, as in the example below.

	12/31/01	*12/31/02*	*2002*
Rent payable	$4,000	$6,000	
Prepaid rent	8,000	4,500	
Cash paid for rent			$27,000

The rent expense can be computed using either T-accounts or a formula.

T-accounts are shown below.

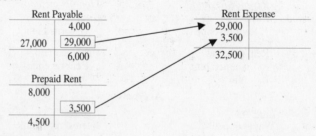

The use of a formula is illustrated next.

Payments		Beginning prepaid		Ending payable		Ending prepaid		Beginning payable		Expense
$27,000	+	8,000	+	6,000	−	4,500	−	4,000	=	$32,500

Formulas for conversion of various income statement amounts from the cash basis to the accrual basis are summarized in the following table.

Cash basis		Additions			Deductions		Accrual basis
Collections from sales	+	(Ending AR (a) AR written off (b))	−		Beginning AR (c)	=	Sales
Collections from other revenues	+	(Beginning unearned revenue (d) Ending revenue receivable (e))	−		(Ending unearned revenue (f) Beginning revenue receivable (g))	=	Other revenues
Payments for purchases	+	(Beginning inventory (h) Ending AP (i))	−		(Ending inventory (j) Beginning AP (k))	=	Cost of goods sold
Payments for expenses	+	(Beginning prepaid expenses (l) Ending accrued expenses payable (m))	−		(Ending prepaid expenses (n) Beginning accrued expenses payable (o))	=	Operating expenses*

*Provision must also be made for depreciation expense and similar write-offs and bad debt expense.

(a) Ending AR and related sales have not yet been recorded
(b) AR written off reduced AR but did not result in cash collected
(c) Beginning AR was collected and recorded as sale during the period but was sale of the prior period
(d) Beginning unearned revenue was collected and recorded as revenue in the prior period but was earned in the current period
(e) Ending revenue receivable was earned during the period but has not yet been recorded because it has not been collected
(f) Ending unearned revenue was recorded upon collection as revenue but has not yet been earned
(g) Beginning revenue receivable was recorded during the current period upon collection as revenue but was earned last period
(h) Beginning inventory was sold during the period
(i) Ending AP and related purchases have not yet been recorded
(j) Ending inventory must be excluded from cost of goods sold
(k) Beginning AP reflects purchases last period which were not paid for or recorded until the current period
(l) Beginning prepaid expenses were recorded as expenses when paid in a prior period but are expenses of the current period
(m) Ending accrued expenses payable have not yet been recorded
(n) Ending prepaid expenses were recorded as expenses when paid this period but are expenses of future periods
(o) Beginning accrued expenses payable were recorded currently as expenses when paid but are expenses of the prior period

Since the accrual-basis numbers can be derived with T-accounts, you should not have to memorize the formulas.

5. **Installment Sales**

Revenue is recognized as cash is collected. Thus, revenue recognition takes place at the point of cash collection rather than the point of sale. Installment sales accounting can only be used where "collection of the sale price is not reasonably assured" (APB 10).

Under the installment sales method, gross profit is deferred to future periods and recognized proportionately to collection of the receivables. Installment receivables and deferred gross profit accounts must be kept separate by year, because the gross profit rate usually varies from year to year.

EXAMPLE:

			Collections of	
Year	Sales	Cost of sales	Year 1	Year 3
1	300,000	225,000 *	80,000	--
2	--	--	120,000	--
3	200,000	160,000 **	100,000	100,000

*25% gross profit rate
**20% gross profit rate

	Year 1		Year 2		Year 3	
To record sale						
Install AR-1	300,000		--		--	
Install AR-3	--		--		200,000	
Install sales		300,000		--		200,000
To record cash receipt						
Cash	80,000		120,000		200,000	
Install AR-1		80,000		120,000		100,000
Install AR-3		--		--		100,000
To record CGS						
Install cost of sales	225,000		--		160,000	
Inventory (or Purchases)		225,000		--		160,000
To defer gross profit						
Install sales	300,000		--		200,000	
Install cost of sales		225,000		--		160,000
Deferred install GP-1		75,000		--		--
Deferred install GP-3		--		--		40,000
To recognize gross profit						
Deferred install GP-1	20,000 [a]		30,000 [b]		25,000 [c]	
Deferred install GP-3	--		--		20,000 [d]	
GP realized on install method		20,000		30,000		45,000

[a](25% x 80,000)   [c](25% x 100,000)
[b](25% x 120,000)   [d](20% x 100,000)

Summary of Accounts Used in Installment Sales Accounting

BALANCE SHEET

Cash		Installment AR—Year 1		Installment AR—Year 2	
(B)		Ending balance from year 1 sales	(B)	(A)	(B)

Inventory (or Purchases)		Deferred Gross Profit—Year 1		Deferred Gross Profit—Year 2	
	(C)	(E)	Ending balance from year 1 installment sales	(E)	(D)

INCOME STATEMENT

Cost of Installment Sales		Installment Sales	
(C)	(D)	(D)	(A)

Realized Gross Profit on Installment Sales		Income Summary	
(F)	(E)		(F)

Explanation of Journal Entries Made in Year Two

(A) To record installment sales
(B) To record cash collected from year one and year two installment receivables
(C) To record cost of goods sold (perpetual or periodic)
(D) To close installment sales and cost of installment sales accounts
(E) To remove gross profit realized through collections from the deferred gross profit account

    (Gross profit rate for year one x Cash collections from year one receivables)
    (Gross profit rate for year two x Cash collections from year two receivables)

(F) To close realized gross profit at year-end

6. **Cost Recovery Method**

The cost recovery method is similar to the installment sales method in that gross profit on the sale is deferred. The difference is that no profit is recognized until the cumulative receipts exceed the cost of the asset sold. For example, in the installment sales example, the entire profit from year one sales ($75,000) would be recognized in year three. Profit on year three sales will be recognized in year four to the extent that in year four cash collections on year three sales exceed the $60,000 ($160,000 cost – $100,000 cash collected) unrecovered cost on year three sales. If interest revenue was to be earned by the seller, it would likewise be deferred until the entire cost was recovered. The cost recovery method is used when the uncertainty of collection is so great that even use of the installment method is precluded.

7. **Franchise Agreements**

SFAS 45 (see outline) provides that the initial franchise fee be recognized as revenue by the franchiser **only** upon substantial performance of their initial service obligation. The amount and timing of revenue recognized depends upon whether the contract contains bargain purchase agreements, tangible property, and whether the continuing franchise fees are reasonable in relation to future service obligations. Direct franchise costs are deferred until the related revenue is recognized.

8. **Real Estate Transactions**

Accounting treatment for real estate sales is provided by SFAS 66. Due to the variety of methods of financing real estate transactions, determining when the risks and rewards of ownership have been clearly transferred and when revenue should be recognized becomes very complex.

Profit from real estate sales may be recognized in full, provided the profit is determinable and the earnings process is virtually complete. Additionally, the following four criteria must be met to recognize profit in full at the point of sale:

1. A sale is consummated.
2. The buyer's initial and continuing investments are adequate to demonstrate a commitment to pay for the property.
3. The seller's receivable is not subject to future subordination.
4. The seller has transferred to the buyer the usual risks and rewards of ownership in a transaction that is, in substance, a sale and does not have a substantial continuing involvement in the property.

Depending on which combination of criteria is met, the real estate sales will be recorded using one of the following methods:

1. Deposit
2. Cost recovery
3. Installment
4. Reduced profit
5. Percentage-of-completion
6. Full accrual

The deposit and reduced profit methods require explanation. In accordance with the deposit method, payments received are recorded as a liability until the contract is canceled or a sale is achieved. Under the reduced profit method, the seller recognizes a portion of profit at the time of sale with the remaining portion recognized in future periods. Profit recognized at the time of sale is determined by calculating the present value of the buyer's receivable and applying a formula. The reduced profit recognized at the time of sale is the gross profit less the present value of the receivable as determined above. The remaining profit is recognized in future periods. See the outline of SFAS 66.

9. **Software Revenue Recognition**

Statement of Position 97-2 provides guidance on recognizing revenue for software transactions. Software products that require significant production, modification, or customization should be accounted for using ARB 45, *Long-Term Construction-Type Contracts.* Software products that do not require significant production, modification, or customization should recognize revenue when all of the following criteria are met:

a. Persuasive evidence of an arrangement exists.
b. Delivery has occurred.
c. Vendor's fee is fixed or determinable.
d. Collectibility is probable.

The portion of the fee allocated to an element should be recognized using the same list of criteria.

a. Delivery of an element is considered not to have occurred if other elements essential to the functionality of it are undelivered.
b. No portion of the fee meets the criterion of collectibility if the portion of the fee allocable to delivered elements is subject to forfeiture, refund, or other concession if undelivered elements are not delivered.

Arrangement that includes multiple elements should allocate the fee to the elements based on vendor-specific objective evidence of fair value, regardless of stated prices in a contract.

a. Multiple elements

(1) Arrangements consisting of multiple software deliverables including

(a) Software products
(b) Upgrades/enhancements
(c) Postcontract customer service (PCS)
(d) Services
(e) Elements deliverable on a when-and-if-available basis

b. Vendor-specific objective evidence of fair value

(1) Limited to

(a) Price charged when the same element is sold separately.
(b) Price established by management if not sold separately yet. It should be probable that the price will not change before being sold separately.

(2) Amount allocated to an undelivered element should not be adjusted. If it is probable that the amount allocated will result in a loss, SFAS 5, *Accounting for Contingencies,* should be followed

c. Insufficient vendor-specific objective evidence of fair value

(1) Defer revenue until whichever one of the following occurs first

    (a) Sufficient vendor-specific objective evidence does exist

    (b) All elements have been delivered

(2) Exceptions

    (a) The PCS is the only undelivered element—recognize entire fee ratably

    (b) Only undelivered element is services that don't require significant production, modification, or customization—recognize the entire fee over the period in which the services will be performed

    (c) Arrangement is a subscription in substance—recognize entire fee ratably

    (d) Fee based on the number of copies

d. Separate accounting for service element of an arrangement is required if both of following criteria met

(1) Services not essential to functionality of any other element of the transaction.

(2) Services are described in the contract such that total price of the arrangement would be expected to vary as result of inclusion or exclusion of the services.

10. Sales Basis Criteria for Selected Transactions

Under GAAP, specific rules have been developed which are stated in the form of conditions which must be met before it is acceptable to recognize profit from "a sale in the ordinary course of business." Unfortunately, these rules represent a patchwork set of criteria for applying the sales basis of revenue recognition. This patchwork set of criteria contains many inconsistencies either in the results obtained or in the rationale justifying the criteria. The table below summarizes the criteria which have been devised for applying the sales basis to selected transactions involving the sale of assets.

Recognition issue/ source of GAAP	Factors to be considered before recognizing revenue on the sale basis	Conditions that cause recognition to be delayed beyond time of sale
• **Sale with a right of return** SFAS 48	• Whether economic substance of the transaction is a sale or a financing arrangement • Determination of sales price • Probability of collection of sales price • Seller's future obligations • Predictability of returns	• Sales price not fixed or determinable • Payment excused until product is sold • Payment excused if property stolen or damaged • Buyer without separate economic substance • Seller's obligation to bring about resale of the property • Inability to predict future returns
• **Product financing arrangement** SFAS 49	• Whether risks and rewards of ownership are transferred	• Agreement requires repurchase at specified prices or provides compensation for losses
• **Real estate sale** SFAS 66	• Probability of collection • Seller's continued involvement • Whether economic substance of the transaction is a sale of real estate or another type of transaction such as a service contract	• Inadequate buyer investment in the property • Seller's continuing obligations, such as participation in future losses, responsibility to obtain financing, construct buildings, or initiate or support operations
• **Sales-type lease** SFAS 13	• Transfer of benefits and risks of ownership • Probability of collection • Predictability of future unreimbursable costs	• Inability to meet conditions specified above for real estate sales • Inability to meet specified conditions (four criteria) indicating transfer of benefits and risks of ownership • Collectibility not predictable • Uncertainty about future unreimbursable costs
• **Sale of receivables with recourse** SFAS 125	• Isolation of transferred assets • Right to pledge or exchange transferred assets • Control of receivables	• Transferred assets can be reached by transferor or its creditors • Transferee's inability to pledge or exchange transferred assets • Control of receivables not surrendered due to repurchase or redemption agreement
• **Nonmonetary exchange** APB 29	• Completion of earning process	• Exchanges of similar inventory or productive assets
• **Sale-leaseback transaction** SFAS 13	• Substance of the transaction • Portion of property leased back • Length of leaseback period	• All sale-leaseback transactions are financing transactions and not sales transactions unless leaseback covers only a small part of the property or is for a short period of time

*Source: Adapted from Henry R. Jaenicke, **Survey of Present Practices in Recognizing Revenues, Expenses, Gains, and Losses**, FASB, 1981.*

MULTIPLE-CHOICE QUESTIONS (1-70)

1. What are the Statements of Financial Accounting Concepts intended to establish?
a. Generally accepted accounting principles in financial reporting by business enterprises.
b. The meaning of "Present fairly in accordance with generally accepted accounting principles."
c. The objectives and concepts for use in developing standards of financial accounting and reporting.
d. The hierarchy of sources of generally accepted accounting principles.

2. According to the FASB conceptual framework, the objectives of financial reporting for business enterprises are based on
a. Generally accepted accounting principles.
b. Reporting on management's stewardship.
c. The need for conservatism.
d. The needs of the users of the information.

3. According to the FASB conceptual framework, the usefulness of providing information in financial statements is subject to the constraint of
a. Consistency.
b. Cost-benefit.
c. Reliability.
d. Representational faithfulness.

4. During a period when an enterprise is under the direction of a particular management, its financial statements will directly provide information about
a. Both enterprise performance and management performance.
b. Management performance but not directly provide information about enterprise performance.
c. Enterprise performance but not directly provide information about management performance.
d. Neither enterprise performance nor management performance.

5. According to Statements of Financial Accounting Concepts, neutrality is an ingredient of

	Reliability	*Relevance*
a.	Yes	Yes
b.	Yes	No
c.	No	Yes
d.	No	No

6. According to the FASB conceptual framework, which of the following relates to both relevance and reliability?
a. Comparability.
b. Feedback value.
c. Verifiability.
d. Timeliness.

7. According to the FASB conceptual framework, the process of reporting an item in the financial statements of an entity is
a. Allocation.
b. Matching.
c. Realization.
d. Recognition.

8. Under FASB Statement of Financial Accounting Concepts 5, which of the following items would cause earnings

to differ from comprehensive income for an enterprise in an industry **not** having specialized accounting principles?
a. Unrealized loss on investments classified as available-for-sale securities.
b. Unrealized loss on investments classified as trading securities.
c. Loss on exchange of similar assets.
d. Loss on exchange of dissimilar assets.

9. Under FASB Statement of Financial Accounting Concepts 5, comprehensive income excludes changes in equity resulting from which of the following?
a. Loss from discontinued operations.
b. Prior period error correction.
c. Dividends paid to stockholders.
d. Unrealized loss on securities classified as available-for-sale.

10. According to the FASB conceptual framework, which of the following situations violates the concept of reliability?
a. Data on segments having the same expected risks and growth rates are reported to analysts estimating future profits.
b. Financial statements are issued nine months late.
c. Management reports to stockholders regularly refer to new projects undertaken, but the financial statements never report project results.
d. Financial statements include property with a carrying amount increased to management's estimate of market value.

11. According to the FASB conceptual framework, which of the following statements conforms to the realization concept?
a. Equipment depreciation was assigned to a production department and then to product unit costs.
b. Depreciated equipment was sold in exchange for a note receivable.
c. Cash was collected on accounts receivable.
d. Product unit costs were assigned to cost of goods sold when the units were sold.

12. What is the underlying concept that supports the immediate recognition of a contingent loss?
a. Substance over form.
b. Consistency.
c. Matching.
d. Conservatism.

13. What is the underlying concept governing the generally accepted accounting principles pertaining to recording gain contingencies?
a. Conservatism.
b. Relevance.
c. Consistency.
d. Reliability.

14. FASB's conceptual framework explains both financial and physical capital maintenance concepts. Which capital maintenance concept is applied to currently reported net income, and which is applied to comprehensive income?

	Currently reported net income	*Comprehensive income*
a.	Financial capital	Physical capital
b.	Physical capital	Physical capital
c.	Financial capital	Financial capital
d.	Physical capital	Financial capital

15. According to the FASB conceptual framework, an entity's revenue may result from
   a.   A decrease in an asset from primary operations.
   b.   An increase in an asset from incidental transactions.
   c.   An increase in a liability from incidental transactions.
   d.   A decrease in a liability from primary operations.

16. According to the FASB conceptual framework, which of the following is an essential characteristic of an asset?
   a.   The claims to an asset's benefits are legally enforceable.
   b.   An asset is tangible.
   c.   An asset is obtained at a cost.
   d.   An asset provides future benefits.

17. According to the FASB conceptual framework, which of the following attributes would **not** be used to measure inventory?
   a.   Historical cost.
   b.   Replacement cost.
   c.   Net realizable value.
   d.   Present value of future cash flows.

18. According to SFAC 7, *Using Cash Flow Information and Present Value in Accounting Measurements*, the most relevant measurement of an entity's liabilities at initial recognition and fresh-start measurements should always reflect
   a.   The expectations of the entity's management.
   b.   Historical cost.
   c.   The credit standing of the entity.
   d.   The single most-likely minimum or maximum possible amount.

19. Which of the following is **not** covered by SFAC 7, *Using Cash Flow Information and Present Value in Accounting Measurements*?
   a.   Measurements at initial recognition.
   b.   Interest method of amortization.
   c.   Expected cash flow approach.
   d.   Determining when fresh-start measurements are appropriate.

20. In calculating present value in a situation with a range of possible outcomes all discounted using the same interest rate, the expected present value would be
   a.   The most-likely outcome.
   b.   The maximum outcome.
   c.   The minimum outcome.
   d.   The sum of probability-weighted present values.

21. A cash flow of $200,000 may be received by Lydia Nickels, Inc. in one year, two years, or three years, with probabilities of 20%, 50%, and 30%, respectively. The rate of interest on default risk-free investments is 5%. The present value factors are

PV of 1, at 5%, for 1 year is	.95238
PV of 1, at 5%, for 2 years is	.90703
PV of 1, at 5%, for 3 years is	.86384

What is the expected present value of Lydia Nickels' cash flow (in whole dollars)?
   a. $181,406
   b. $180,628
   c. $ 90,703
   d. $ 89,925

22. Which of the following statements regarding interest methods of allocations is **not** true?
   a.   The term "interest methods of allocation" refers both to the convention for periodic reporting and to the several approaches to dealing with changes in estimated future cash flows.
   b.   Interest methods of allocation are reporting conventions that use present value techniques in the absence of a fresh-start measurement to compute changes in the carrying amount of an asset or liability from one period to the next.
   c.   Interest methods of allocation are grounded in the notion of current cost.
   d.   Holding gains and losses are generally excluded from allocation systems.

23. Which of the following is **not** an objective of using present value in accounting measurements?
   a.   To capture the value of an asset or a liability in the context of a particular entity.
   b.   To estimate fair value.
   c.   To capture the economic difference between sets of future cash flows.
   d.   To capture the elements that taken together would comprise a market price if one existed.

24. On December 31, 2002, Brooks Co. decided to end operations and dispose of its assets within three months. At December 31, 2002, the net realizable value of the equipment was below historical cost. What is the appropriate measurement basis for equipment included in Brooks' December 31, 2002 balance sheet?
   a.   Historical cost.
   b.   Current reproduction cost.
   c.   Net realizable value.
   d.   Current replacement cost.

25. In the hierarchy of generally accepted accounting principles, APB Opinions have the same authority as AICPA
   a.   Statements of Position.
   b.   Industry Audit and Accounting Guides.
   c.   Issues Papers.
   d.   Accounting Research Bulletins.

26. On October 1, 2002, Acme Fuel Co. sold 100,000 gallons of heating oil to Karn Co. at $3 per gallon. Fifty thousand gallons were delivered on December 15, 2002, and the remaining 50,000 gallons were delivered on January 15, 2003. Payment terms were: 50% due on October 1, 2002, 25% due on first delivery, and the remaining 25% due on second delivery. What amount of revenue should Acme recognize from this sale during 2002?
   a. $ 75,000
   b. $150,000
   c. $225,000
   d. $300,000

27. Amar Farms produced 300,000 pounds of cotton during the 2002 season. Amar sells all of its cotton to Brye Co., which has agreed to purchase Amar's entire production at the prevailing market price. Recent legislation assures that the market price will not fall below $.70 per pound during the next two years. Amar's costs of selling and distributing the cotton are immaterial and can be reasonably estimated. Amar reports its inventory at expected exit value. During 2002, Amar sold and delivered to Brye 200,000 pounds at the market price of $.70. Amar sold the remaining 100,000 pounds during 2003 at the market price of $.72. What amount of revenue should Amar recognize in 2002?

   a. $140,000
   b. $144,000
   c. $210,000
   d. $216,000

28. Lin Co., a distributor of machinery, bought a machine from the manufacturer in November 2002 for $10,000. On December 30, 2002, Lin sold this machine to Zee Hardware for $15,000, under the following terms: 2% discount if paid within thirty days, 1% discount if paid after thirty days but within sixty days, or payable in full within ninety days if not paid within the discount periods. However, Zee had the right to return this machine to Lin if Zee was unable to resell the machine before expiration of the ninety-day payment period, in which case Zee's obligation to Lin would be canceled. In Lin's net sales for the year ended December 31, 2002, how much should be included for the sale of this machine to Zee?

   a. $0
   b. $14,700
   c. $14,850
   d. $15,000

29. Under a royalty agreement with another company, Wand Co. will pay royalties for the assignment of a patent for three years. The royalties paid should be reported as expense

   a. In the period paid.
   b. In the period incurred.
   c. At the date the royalty agreement began.
   d. At the date the royalty agreement expired.

30. Clark Co.'s advertising expense account had a balance of $146,000 at December 31, 2002, before any necessary year-end adjustment relating to the following:

• Included in the $146,000 is the $15,000 cost of printing catalogs for a sales promotional campaign in January 2003.

• Radio advertisements broadcast during December 2002 were billed to Clark on January 2, 2003. Clark paid the $9,000 invoice on January 11, 2003.

What amount should Clark report as advertising expense in its income statement for the year ended December 31, 2002?

   a. $122,000
   b. $131,000
   c. $140,000
   d. $155,000

31. An analysis of Thrift Corp.'s unadjusted prepaid expense account at December 31, 2002, revealed the following:

• An opening balance of $1,500 for Thrift's comprehensive insurance policy. Thrift had paid an annual premium of $3,000 on July 1, 2001.

• A $3,200 annual insurance premium payment made July 1, 2002.

• A $2,000 advance rental payment for a warehouse Thrift leased for one year beginning January 1, 2003.

In its December 31, 2002 balance sheet, what amount should Thrift report as prepaid expenses?

   a. $5,200

   b. $3,600
   c. $2,000
   d. $1,600

32. Roro, Inc. paid $7,200 to renew its only insurance policy for three years on March 1, 2002, the effective date of the policy. At March 31, 2002, Roro's unadjusted trial balance showed a balance of $300 for prepaid insurance and $7,200 for insurance expense. What amounts should be reported for prepaid insurance and insurance expense in Roro's financial statements for the three months ended March 31, 2002?

	Prepaid insurance	Insurance expense
a.	$7,000	$300
b.	$7,000	$500
c.	$7,200	$300
d.	$7,300	$200

33. Aneen's Video Mart sells one- and two-year mail order subscriptions for its video-of-the-month business. Subscriptions are collected in advance and credited to sales. An analysis of the recorded sales activity revealed the following:

	2001	2002
Sales	$420,000	$500,000
Less cancellations	20,000	30,000
Net sales	$400,000	$470,000
Subscriptions expirations:		
2001	$120,000	
2002	155,000	$130,000
2003	125,000	200,000
2004		140,000
	$400,000	$470,000

In Aneen's December 31, 2002 balance sheet, the balance for unearned subscription revenue should be

   a. $495,000
   b. $470,000
   c. $465,000
   d. $340,000

34. Regal Department Store sells gift certificates, redeemable for store merchandise, that expire one year after their issuance. Regal has the following information pertaining to its gift certificates sales and redemptions:

Unredeemed at 12/31/01	$ 75,000
2002 sales	250,000
2002 redemptions of prior year sales	25,000
2002 redemptions of current year sales	175,000

Regal's experience indicates that 10% of gift certificates sold will not be redeemed. In its December 31, 2002 balance sheet, what amount should Regal report as unearned revenue?

   a. $125,000
   b. $112,500
   c. $100,000
   d. $ 50,000

35. Wren Corp.'s trademark was licensed to Mont Co. for royalties of 15% of sales of the trademarked items. Royalties are payable semiannually on March 15 for sales in July through December of the prior year, and on September 15 for sales in January through June of the same year. Wren received the following royalties from Mont:

	March 15	September 15
2001	$10,000	$15,000
2002	12,000	17,000

Mont estimated that sales of the trademarked items would total $60,000 for July through December 2001. In Wren's 2002 income statement, the royalty revenue should be

- a. $26,000
- b. $29,000
- c. $38,000
- d. $41,000

36. In 2001, Super Comics Corp. sold a comic strip to Fantasy, Inc. and will receive royalties of 20% of future revenues associated with the comic strip. At December 31, 2002, Super reported royalties receivable of $75,000 from Fantasy. During 2003, Super received royalty payments of $200,000. Fantasy reported revenues of $1,500,000 in 2003 from the comic strip. In its 2003 income statement, what amount should Super report as royalty revenue?

- a. $125,000
- b. $175,000
- c. $200,000
- d. $300,000

37. Rill Co. owns a 20% royalty interest in an oil well. Rill receives royalty payments on January 31 for the oil sold between the previous June 1 and November 30, and on July 31 for oil sold between December 1 and May 31. Production reports show the following oil sales:

June 1, 2001 - November 30, 2001	$300,000
December 1, 2001 - December 31, 2001	50,000
December 1, 2001 - May 31, 2002	400,000
June 1, 2002 - November 30, 2002	325,000
December 1, 2002 - December 31, 2002	70,000

What amount should Rill report as royalty revenue for 2002?

- a. $140,000
- b. $144,000
- c. $149,000
- d. $159,000

38. Decker Company assigns some of its patents to other enterprises under a variety of licensing agreements. In some instances advance royalties are received when the agreements are signed, and in others, royalties are remitted within sixty days after each license year-end. The following data are included in Decker's December 31 balance sheet:

	2001	2002
Royalties receivable	$90,000	$85,000
Unearned royalties	60,000	40,000

During 2002 Decker received royalty remittances of $200,000. In its income statement for the year ended December 31, 2002, Decker should report royalty income of

- a. $195,000
- b. $215,000
- c. $220,000
- d. $225,000

39. Cooke Company acquires patent rights from other enterprises and pays advance royalties in some cases, and in others, royalties are paid within ninety days after year-end. The following data are included in Cooke's December 31 balance sheets:

	2001	2002
Prepaid royalties	$55,000	$45,000
Royalties payable	80,000	75,000

During 2002 Cooke remitted royalties of $300,000. In its income statement for the year ended December 31, 2002, Cooke should report royalty expense of

- a. $295,000
- b. $305,000
- c. $310,000
- d. $330,000

40. The premium on a three-year insurance policy expiring on December 31, 2004, was paid in total on January 1, 2002. The original payment was initially debited to a prepaid asset account. The appropriate journal entry has been recorded on December 31, 2002. The balance in the prepaid asset account on December 31, 2002, should be

- a. Zero.
- b. The same as it would have been if the original payment had been debited initially to an expense account.
- c. The same as the original payment.
- d. Higher than if the original payment had been debited initially to an expense account.

41. On January 1, 2002, Sip Co. signed a five-year contract enabling it to use a patented manufacturing process beginning in 2002. A royalty is payable for each product produced, subject to a minimum annual fee. Any royalties in excess of the minimum will be paid annually. On the contract date, Sip prepaid a sum equal to two years' minimum annual fees. In 2002, only minimum fees were incurred. The royalty prepayment should be reported in Sip's December 31, 2002 financial statements as

- a. An expense only.
- b. A current asset and an expense.
- c. A current asset and noncurrent asset.
- d. A noncurrent asset.

42. A retail store received cash and issued gift certificates that are redeemable in merchandise. The gift certificates lapse one year after they are issued. How would the deferred revenue account be affected by each of the following transactions?

	Redemption of certificates	*Lapse of certificates*
a.	No effect	Decrease
b.	Decrease	Decrease
c.	Decrease	No effect
d.	No effect	No effect

43. Jersey, Inc. is a retailer of home appliances and offers a service contract on each appliance sold. Jersey sells appliances on installment contracts, but all service contracts must be paid in full at the time of sale. Collections received for service contracts should be recorded as an increase in a

- a. Deferred revenue account.
- b. Sales contracts receivable valuation account.
- c. Stockholders' valuation account.
- d. Service revenue account.

44. Ward, a consultant, keeps her accounting records on a cash basis. During 2002, Ward collected $200,000 in fees from clients. At December 31, 2001, Ward had accounts receivable of $40,000. At December 31, 2002, Ward had accounts receivable of $60,000, and unearned fees of $5,000. On an accrual basis, what was Ward's service revenue for 2002?

- a. $175,000
- b. $180,000

   c. $215,000
   d. $225,000

45. Zeta Co. reported sales revenue of $4,600,000 in its income statement for the year ended December 31, 2002. Additional information is as follows:

	12/31/01	12/31/02
Accounts receivable	$1,000,000	$1,300,000
Allowance for uncollectible accounts	(60,000)	(110,000)

Zeta wrote off uncollectible accounts totaling $20,000 during 2002. Under the cash basis of accounting, Zeta would have reported 2002 sales of
   a. $4,900,000
   b. $4,350,000
   c. $4,300,000
   d. $4,280,000

46. Marr Corp. reported rental revenue of $2,210,000 in its cash basis federal income tax return for the year ended November 30, 2002. Additional information is as follows:

Rents receivable—November 30, 2002	$1,060,000
Rents receivable—November 30, 2001	800,000
Uncollectible rents written off during the fiscal year	30,000

Under the accrual basis, Marr should report rental revenue of
   a. $1,920,000
   b. $1,980,000
   c. $2,440,000
   d. $2,500,000

47. The following information pertains to Eagle Co.'s 2002 sales:

Cash sales

Gross	$ 80,000
Returns and allowances	4,000

Credit sales

Gross	120,000
Discounts	6,000

On January 1, 2002, customers owed Eagle $40,000. On December 31, 2002, customers owed Eagle $30,000. Eagle uses the direct writeoff method for bad debts. No bad debts were recorded in 2002. Under the cash basis of accounting, what amount of net revenue should Eagle report for 2002?
   a. $ 76,000
   b. $170,000
   c. $190,000
   d. $200,000

48. The following balances were reported by Mall Co. at December 31, 2002 and 2001:

	12/31/02	12/31/01
Inventory	$260,000	$290,000
Accounts payable	75,000	50,000

Mall paid suppliers $490,000 during the year ended December 31, 2002. What amount should Mall report for cost of goods sold in 2002?
   a. $545,000
   b. $495,000
   c. $485,000
   d. $435,000

49. Class Corp. maintains its accounting records on the cash basis but restates its financial statements to the accrual method of accounting. Class had $60,000 in cash-basis pretax income for 2002. The following information pertains to Class's operations for the years ended December 31, 2002 and 2001:

	2002	2001
Accounts receivable	$40,000	$20,000
Accounts payable	15,000	30,000

Under the accrual method, what amount of income before taxes should Class report in its December 31, 2002 income statement?
   a. $25,000
   b. $55,000
   c. $65,000
   d. $95,000

50. On February 1, 2002, Tory began a service proprietorship with an initial cash investment of $2,000. The proprietorship provided $5,000 of services in February and received full payment in March. The proprietorship incurred expenses of $3,000 in February, which were paid in April. During March, Tory drew $1,000 against the capital account. In the proprietorship's financial statements for the two months ended March 31, 2002, prepared under the cash basis method of accounting, what amount should be reported as capital?
   a. $1,000
   b. $3,000
   c. $6,000
   d. $7,000

51. Compared to the accrual basis of accounting, the cash basis of accounting understates income by the net decrease during the accounting period of

	Accounts receivable	Accrued expenses
a.	Yes	Yes
b.	Yes	No
c.	No	No
d.	No	Yes

52. White Co. wants to convert its 2002 financial statements from the accrual basis of accounting to the cash basis. Both supplies inventory and office salaries payable increased between January 1, 2002, and December 31, 2002. To obtain 2002 cash basis net income, how should these increases be added to or deducted from accrual-basis net income?

	Supplies inventory	Office salaries payable
a.	Deducted	Deducted
b.	Deducted	Added
c.	Added	Deducted
d.	Added	Added

53. Before 2002, Droit Co. used the cash basis of accounting. As of December 31, 2002, Droit changed to the accrual basis. Droit cannot determine the beginning balance of supplies inventory. What is the effect of Droit's inability to determine beginning supplies inventory on its 2002 accrual-basis net income and December 31, 2002 accrual-basis owners' equity?

	2002 net income	12/31/02 owners' equity
a.	No effect	No effect
b.	No effect	Overstated
c.	Overstated	No effect
d.	Overstated	Overstated

54. Gant Co., which began operations on January 1, 2002, appropriately uses the installment method of accounting.

The following information pertains to Gant's operations for the year 2002:

Installment sales	$500,000
Regular sales	300,000
Cost of installment sales	250,000
Cost of regular sales	150,000
General and administrative expenses	50,000
Collections on installment sales	100,000

In its December 31, 2002 balance sheet, what amount should Gant report as deferred gross profit?

a. $250,000
b. $200,000
c. $160,000
d. $ 75,000

55. Since there is no reasonable basis for estimating the degree of collectibility, Astor Co. uses the installment method of revenue recognition for the following sales:

	2002	2001
Sales	$900,000	$600,000
Collections from:		
2001 sales	100,000	200,000
2002 sales	300,000	--
Accounts written off:		
2001 sales	150,000	50,000
2002 sales	50,000	--
Gross profit percentage	40%	30%

What amount should Astor report as deferred gross profit in its December 31, 2002 balance sheet for the 2001 and 2002 sales?

a. $150,000
b. $160,000
c. $225,000
d. $250,000

56. Luge Co., which began operations on January 2, 2002, appropriately uses the installment sales method of accounting. The following information is available for 2002:

Installment accounts receivable, December 31, 2002	$800,000
Deferred gross profit, December 31, 2002 (before recognition of realized gross profit for 2002)	560,000
Gross profit on sales	40%

For the year ended December 31, 2002, cash collections and realized gross profit on sales should be

	Cash collections	Realized gross profit
a.	$400,000	$320,000
b.	$400,000	$240,000
c.	$600,000	$320,000
d.	$600,000	$240,000

57. Dolce Co., which began operations on January 1, 2001, appropriately uses the installment method of accounting to record revenues. The following information is available for the years ended December 31, 2001 and 2002:

	2001	2002
Sales	$1,000,000	$2,000,000
Gross profit realized on sales made in:		
2001	150,000	90,000
2002	--	200,000
Gross profit percentages	30%	40%

What amount of installment accounts receivable should Dolce report in its December 31, 2002 balance sheet?

a. $1,225,000
b. $1,300,000
c. $1,700,000
d. $1,775,000

58. On December 31, 2001, Mill Co. sold construction equipment to Drew, Inc. for $1,800,000. The equipment had a carrying amount of $1,200,000. Drew paid $300,000 cash on December 31, 2001, and signed a $1,500,000 note bearing interest at 10%, payable in five annual installments of $300,000. Mill appropriately accounts for the sale under the installment method. On December 31, 2002, Drew paid $300,000 principal and $150,000 interest. For the year ended December 31, 2002, what total amount of revenue should Mill recognize from the construction equipment sale and financing?

a. $250,000
b. $150,000
c. $120,000
d. $100,000

59. On January 2, 2001, Blake Co. sold a used machine to Cooper, Inc. for $900,000, resulting in a gain of $270,000. On that date, Cooper paid $150,000 cash and signed a $750,000 note bearing interest at 10%. The note was payable in three annual installments of $250,000 beginning January 2, 2002. Blake appropriately accounted for the sale under the installment method. Cooper made a timely payment of the first installment on January 2, 2002, of $325,000, which included accrued interest of $75,000. What amount of deferred gross profit should Blake report at December 31, 2002?

a. $150,000
b. $172,500
c. $180,000
d. $225,000

60. For financial statement purposes, the installment method of accounting may be used if the

a. Collection period extends over more than twelve months.
b. Installments are due in different years.
c. Ultimate amount collectible is indeterminate.
d. Percentage-of-completion method is inappropriate.

61. According to the installment method of accounting, gross profit on an installment sale is recognized in income

a. On the date of sale.
b. On the date the final cash collection is received.
c. In proportion to the cash collection.
d. After cash collections equal to the cost of sales have been received.

62. Income recognized using the installment method of accounting generally equals cash collected multiplied by the

a. Net operating profit percentage.
b. Net operating profit percentage adjusted for expected uncollectible accounts.
c. Gross profit percentage.
d. Gross profit percentage adjusted for expected uncollectible accounts.

63. It is proper to recognize revenue prior to the sale of merchandise when

I. The revenue will be reported as an installment sale.
II. The revenue will be reported under the cost recovery method.

a. I only.
b. II only.
c. Both I and II.
d. Neither I nor II.

64. The following information pertains to a sale of real estate by Ryan Co. to Sud Co. on December 31, 2001:

Carrying amount		$2,000,000
Sales price:		
Cash	$ 300,000	
Purchase money mortgage	2,700,000	3,000,000

The mortgage is payable in nine annual installments of $300,000 beginning December 31, 2002, plus interest of 10%. The December 31, 2002, installment was paid as scheduled, together with interest of $270,000. Ryan uses the cost recovery method to account for the sale. What amount of income should Ryan recognize in 2002 from the real estate sale and its financing?

- a. $570,000
- b. $370,000
- c. $270,000
- d. $0

65. Wren Co. sells equipment on installment contracts. Which of the following statements best justifies Wren's use of the cost recovery method of revenue recognition to account for these installment sales?

- a. The sales contract provides that title to the equipment only passes to the purchaser when all payments have been made.
- b. No cash payments are due until one year from the date of sale.
- c. Sales are subject to a high rate of return.
- d. There is no reasonable basis for estimating collectibility.

66. According to the cost recovery method of accounting, gross profit on an installment sale is recognized in income

- a. After cash collections equal to the cost of sales have been received.
- b. In proportion to the cash collections.
- c. On the date the final cash collection is received.
- d. On the date of sale.

67. On December 31, 2002, Rice, Inc. authorized Graf to operate as a franchisee for an initial franchise fee of $150,000. Of this amount, $60,000 was received upon signing the agreement and the balance, represented by a note, is due in three annual payments of $30,000 each beginning December 31, 2003. The present value on December 31, 2002, of the three annual payments appropriately discounted is $72,000. According to the agreement, the nonrefundable down payment represents a fair measure of the services already performed by Rice; however, substantial future services are required of Rice. Collectibility of the note is reasonably certain. In Rice's December 31, 2002 balance sheet, unearned franchise fees from Graf's franchise should be reported as

- a. $132,000
- b. $100,000
- c. $ 90,000
- d. $ 72,000

68. Each of Potter Pie Co.'s twenty-one new franchisees contracted to pay an initial franchise fee of $30,000. By December 31, 2002, each franchisee had paid a nonrefundable $10,000 fee and signed a note to pay $10,000 principal plus the market rate of interest on December 31, 2003, and December 31, 2004. Experience indicates that one franchisee will default on the additional payments. Services for the initial fee will be performed in 2003. What amount of net unearned franchise fees would Potter report at December 31, 2002?

- a. $400,000
- b. $600,000
- c. $610,000
- d. $630,000

69. In which of the following examples of real estate transactions would the seller not transfer the usual risks and rewards of ownership?

 I. The buyer can compel the seller to repurchase the property.
 II. The seller guarantees the return of the buyer's investment.
 III. The seller is required to support operations of the buyer and will be reimbursed on a cost plus 5% basis.

- a. I.
- b. II.
- c. III.
- d. I and II.

70. Esker Inc. specializes in real estate transactions other than retail land sales. On January 1, 2002, Esker consummated a sale of property to Kame Ltd. The amount of profit on the sale is determinable and Esker is not obligated to perform any additional activities to earn the profit. Kame's initial and continuing investments were adequate to demonstrate a commitment to pay for the property under SFAS 66. However, Esker's receivable may be subject to future subordination. Esker should account for the sale using the

- a. Deposit method.
- b. Reduced recovery method.
- c. Cost recovery method.
- d. Full accrual method.

OTHER OBJECTIVE QUESTIONS

Problem 1 (15 to 25 minutes)

This question consists of ten items that represent descriptions or definitions of the various elements of the FASB's *Statements of Financial Accounting Concepts.*

Required:

Select the **best** answer for each item from the terms listed in A - L. A term may be used once, more than once, or not at all.

Concept statement definitions	*Terms*
1. Component of relevance.	A. Recognition
2. Increases in net assets from incidental or peripheral transactions affecting an entity.	B. Comprehensive Income
3. The process of converting noncash resources and rights into cash or claims to cash.	C. Representational Faithfulness
4. Ingredient of relevance **and** reliability.	D. Revenues
5. The process of formally recording an item in the financial statements of an entity after it has met existing criteria and been subject to cost-benefit constraints and materiality thresholds.	E. Predictive Value
6. All changes in net assets of an entity during a period except those resulting from investments by owners and distributions to owners.	F. Consistency
	G. Gains
	H. Net Income
7. Inflows or other enhancements of assets of an entity or settlements of its liabilities from delivering or producing goods, rendering services, or other activities that constitute the entity's ongoing operations.	I. Earnings
	J. Realization
8. The amount of cash, or its equivalent, that could be obtained by selling an asset in orderly liquidation.	K. Replacement Cost
	L. Current Market Value
9. The quality of information that helps users to increase the likelihood of correctly forecasting the outcome of past or present events.	
10. A performance measure concerned primarily with cash-to-cash cycles.	

PROBLEM

Problem 1   (30 to 40 minutes)

The following information pertains to Baron Flowers, a calendar-year sole proprietorship, which maintained its books on the cash basis during the year.

Baron Flowers
TRIAL BALANCE
December 31, 2002

	Dr.	Cr.
Cash	$ 25,600	
Accounts receivable, 12/31/01	16,200	
Inventory, 12/31/01	62,000	
Furniture & fixtures	118,200	
Land improvements	45,000	
Accumulated depreciation, 12/31/01		$ 32,400
Accounts payable, 12/31/01		17,000
Baron, Drawings		
Baron, Capital, 12/31/01		124,600
Sales		653,000
Purchases	305,100	
Salaries	174,000	
Payroll taxes	12,400	
Insurance	8,700	
Rent	34,200	
Utilities	12,600	
Living expenses	13,000	
	$827,000	$827,000

Baron has developed plans to expand into the wholesale flower market and is in the process of negotiating a bank loan to finance the expansion. The bank is requesting 2002 financial statements prepared on the accrual basis of accounting from Baron. During the course of a review engagement, Muir, Baron's accountant, obtained the following additional information.

1. Amounts due from customers totaled $32,000 at December 31, 2002.

2. An analysis of the above receivables revealed that an allowance for uncollectible accounts of $3,800 should be provided.

3. Unpaid invoices for flower purchases totaled $30,500 and $17,000, at December 31, 2002, and December 31, 2001, respectively.

4. The inventory totaled $72,800 based on a physical count of the goods at December 31, 2002. The inventory was priced at cost, which approximates market value.

5. On May 1, 2002, Baron paid $8,700 to renew its comprehensive insurance coverage for one year. The premium on the previous policy, which expired on April 30, 2002, was $7,800.

6. On January 2, 2002, Baron entered into a twenty-five-year operating lease for the vacant lot adjacent to Baron's retail store for use as a parking lot. As agreed in the lease, Baron paved and fenced in the lot at a cost of $45,000. The improvements were completed on April 1, 2002, and have an estimated useful life of fifteen years. No provision for depreciation or amortization has been recorded. Depreciation on furniture and fixtures was $12,000 for 2002.

7. Accrued expenses at December 31, 2001 and 2002, were as follows:

	2001	2002
Utilities	$ 900	$1,500
Payroll taxes	1,100	1,600
	$2,000	$3,100

8. Baron is being sued for $400,000. The coverage under the comprehensive insurance policy is limited to $250,000. Baron's attorney believes that an unfavorable outcome is probable and that a reasonable estimate of the settlement is $300,000.

9. The salaries account includes $4,000 per month paid to the proprietor. Baron also receives $250 per week for living expenses.

Required:

a. Using the worksheet on the following page, prepare the adjustments necessary to convert the trial balance of Baron Flowers to the accrual basis of accounting for the year ended December 31, 2002. Formal journal entries are not required to support your adjustments. However, use the numbers given with the additional information to cross-reference the postings in the adjustment columns on the worksheet.

b. Write a brief memo to Baron explaining why the bank would require financial statements prepared on the accrual basis instead of the cash basis.

Baron Flowers
WORKSHEET TO CONVERT TRIAL BALANCE TO ACCRUAL BASIS
December 31, 2002

Account title	Cash basis Dr.	Cash basis Cr.	Adjustments Dr.	Adjustments Cr.	Accrual basis* Dr. *	Accrual basis* Cr. *
Cash	25,600					
Accounts receivable	16,200					
Inventory	62,000					
Furniture & fixtures	118,200					
Land improvements	45,000					
Accumulated depreciation & amortization		32,400				
Accounts payable		17,000				
Baron, Drawings						
Baron, Capital		124,600				
Sales		653,000				
Purchases	305,100					
Salaries	174,000					
Payroll taxes	12,400					
Insurance	8,700					
Rent	34,200					
Utilities	12,600					
Living expenses	13,000					
	827,000	827,000				

Completion of these columns is not required.

Problem 2   (30 to 40 minutes)

Wyatt, CPA, is meeting with Brown, the controller of Emco, a wholesaler, to discuss the accounting issues regarding two unrelated items.

•   Emco is considering offering its customers the right to return its products for a full refund within one year of purchase. Emco expects its sales to increase as a result, but is unable to estimate the amount of future returns.

•   Brown is aware that Statement of Financial Accounting Standards (SFAS) 106, *Employers' Accounting for Postretirement Benefits other than Pensions*, is effective for years beginning after December 15, 1992. Brown is uncertain about the benefits and beneficiaries covered by this Statement. Brown believes that, regardless of SFAS 106, no estimate of postretirement obligation can be reasonable because it would be based on too many assumptions. For this reason, Brown wishes to continue to account for the postretirement benefits that Emco pays to its retirees on the pay-as-you-go (cash) basis.

Brown has asked Wyatt to write a brief memo to Brown that Brown can use to explain these issues to Emco's president.

Required:

Write a brief advisory memo from Wyatt to Brown to

a.   Explain the general principle of revenue recognition, the method of revenue recognition when right to return exists, and the impact of offering a right to return on Emco's ability to recognize revenue, if any.

b.   State the principal benefit covered by SFAS 106 and give an example of other benefits covered by SFAS 106. Explain the reasoning given in SFAS 106 for requiring accruals based on estimates. Indicate the primary recipients of postretirement benefits other than pensions.[*]

[*]   *This requirement should not be completed until you have done Module 26D, Present Value: Pensions. A cross-reference in the Module 26D problem material will direct you to return to it.*

MULTIPLE-CHOICE ANSWERS*

1. c	__ __	16. d	__ __	31. b	__ __	46. d	__ __	61. c	__ __
2. d	__ __	17. d	__ __	32. b	__ __	47. d	__ __	62. c	__ __
3. b	__ __	18. c	__ __	33. c	__ __	48. a	__ __	63. d	__ __
4. c	__ __	19. d	__ __	34. d	__ __	49. d	__ __	64. c	__ __
5. b	__ __	20. d	__ __	35. a	__ __	50. c	__ __	65. d	__ __
6. a	__ __	21. b	__ __	36. d	__ __	51. d	__ __	66. a	__ __
7. d	__ __	22. c	__ __	37. c	__ __	52. b	__ __	67. d	__ __
8. a	__ __	23. a	__ __	38. b	__ __	53. c	__ __	68. c	__ __
9. c	__ __	24. c	__ __	39. b	__ __	54. b	__ __	69. d	__ __
10. d	__ __	25. d	__ __	40. b	__ __	55. d	__ __	70. c	__ __
11. b	__ __	26. b	__ __	41. b	__ __	56. d	__ __		
12. d	__ __	27. c	__ __	42. b	__ __	57. c	__ __		
13. a	__ __	28. a	__ __	43. a	__ __	58. a	__ __		
14. c	__ __	29. b	__ __	44. c	__ __	59. a	__ __	1st: __/70 = __%	
15. d	__ __	30. c	__ __	45. d	__ __	60. c	__ __	2nd: __/70 = __%	

MULTIPLE-CHOICE ANSWER EXPLANATIONS

A.1. Basic Accounting Theory

1. (c) The Statements of Financial Accounting Concepts (SFAC) were issued to establish a framework from which financial accounting and reporting standards could be developed. The SFAC provide the theory behind accounting and reporting and provide guidance when no GAAP exists. The SFAC are not included as GAAP.

2. (d) Per SFAC 1, the objectives of financial reporting focus on providing present and potential investors with information useful in making investment decisions. Financial statement users do not have the authority to prescribe the data they desire. Therefore, they must rely on external financial reporting to satisfy their information needs, and the objectives must be based on the needs of those users.

3. (b) The FASB conceptual framework has identified two constraints to the usefulness of providing information in financial statements, cost benefit and materiality. Information is **not** disclosed if the costs of disclosure outweigh the benefits or if the information is not material enough to influence users. Consistency is a secondary quality of accounting information; reliability and relevance are the primary qualities of accounting information; and representational faithfulness is a component of reliability.

4. (c) Per SFAC 1, the primary focus of financial reporting is to provide information about an enterprise's performance. SFAC 1 states that financial reporting does not directly provide information about the performance of a particular management for the period since actions of past management may also affect the current period earnings. Financial reporting primarily focuses on the enterprise's performance and management performance would only be indirectly illustrated.

5. (b) SFAC 2 defines neutrality as the quality of information which requires freedom from bias toward a predetermined result. Since unbiased information would always be more reliable than biased information, this quality contributes to reliability. Other components of reliability include verifiability and representational faithfulness. Neutrality is not an ingredient of relevance because relevance refers to the usefulness of information, characterized by its predictive value, feedback value, and timeliness.

6. (a) Per SFAC 2, comparability is a secondary quality which relates to **both** of the primary qualities of relevance and reliability. Both feedback value and timeliness are described by SFAC 2 as ingredients only of relevance. They are not considered ingredients of reliability. Verifiability is described as an ingredient only of reliability.

7. (d) Per SFAC 5, recognition is the process of formally recording or incorporating an item into the financial statements as an asset, liability, revenue, expense, or the like. According to SFAC 6, allocation is the process of assigning or distributing an amount according to a plan or formula, matching is the simultaneous recognition of revenues with expenses that are related directly or jointly to the same transactions or events, and realization is the process of converting noncash resources and rights into money.

8. (a) Per SFAC 5, earnings and comprehensive income have the same broad components—revenues, expenses, gains, and losses—but are not the same because certain classes of gains and losses are excluded from earnings. Changes in market values of investments in marketable equity securities classified as available-for-sale securities are included in comprehensive income, but are excluded from earnings until realized. Answers (b), (c), and (d) are incorrect because they would be included in both earnings and comprehensive income. Note that unrealized gains and losses on marketable equity securities classified as trading securities are included in earnings. This treatment is in accordance with SFAS 115.

9. (c) Per SFAC 6, comprehensive income includes all changes in equity during a period except those resulting from investments by owners and distributions to owners. Dividends paid to stockholders is a change in equity resulting from a distribution to owners, so it is excluded from comprehensive income. Answers (a), (b), and (d) are all included in comprehensive income because they **are** changes in equity, but are **not** investments by, or distributions to, owners.

Under SFAS 130, prior period error corrections would also be excluded from comprehensive income. This standard

---

* *Explanation of how to use this performance record appears on page 11.*

addresses only the display of unrealized gains (losses) on foreign currency items, available-for-sale marketable securities, and the minimum pension liability adjustment. Other changes suggested in SFAC 5 and 6 will be addressed in future SFAS.

10. (d) Reliability has three subcomponents, as defined in SFAC 2: neutrality, representational faithfulness, and verifiability. **Neutrality** means that information should **not** be prepared or reported in such a way as to obtain a predetermined result, and **should** be free from bias. **Representational faithfulness** is defined as the correspondence between a measure and what it purports to represent. **Verifiability** means that two or more individuals who are independent of each other would arrive at a similar conclusion based on an examination of the same evidence. Answer (d) violates verifiability because different individuals would come up with different estimates of market value. Answer (a) is incorrect because reporting data to analysts does not violate reliability. Answers (b) and (c) are incorrect because they are examples of violations of relevance, not reliability. Answer (b) violates the relevance subcomponent of **timeliness,** while answer (c) violates the relevance subcomponent of **feedback value.**

11. (b) According to SFAC 6, realization is the process of converting noncash resources and rights into money through the sale of assets for cash or claims to cash. When equipment is sold for a note receivable, money is realized since a note qualifies as a claim to cash. Answers (a) and (d) relate to cost allocation. Answer (c) is incorrect because accounts receivable represents a claim to cash. Realization occurs at the time of sale rather than when cash is collected.

12. (d) A loss contingency is accrued by a charge to expense if it is reasonably estimable and it is **probable that a liability has been incurred** as of the balance sheet date. The **cause of the liability must have occurred on or before the date of the financial statements** if the liability is to be accrued, because the intention is to recognize the loss in the same period that the underlying cause took place. Therefore, some authorities would say that matching is the underlying concept supporting the immediate recognition of a contingent loss. A larger number, however, would mention conservatism as the more pervasive underlying concept supporting the immediate recognition of these losses.

13. (a) Conservatism means that when in doubt, accountants should choose the procedure that will be least likely to overstate assets and income. This concept underlies the GAAP pertaining to recording gain contingencies. In an effort to not overstate assets or income, gain contingencies are not recorded until they are no longer contingencies, and are disclosed only when probabilities are high that a gain contingency will become reality.

14. (c) Per SFAC 6, the major difference between financial and physical capital maintenance is related to the effects of price changes on assets held and liabilities owed during a period. The financial capital concept is applied in current GAAP. Under this concept, the effects of the price changes described above are considered "holding gains and losses," and are included in computing return on capital. Comprehensive income, which is described in SFAC 5, is "the change in equity of a business enterprise during a period from transactions and other events and circumstances from nonowner sources." It is also a measure of return on **financial** capital. The concept of physical capital maintenance seeks to measure the effects of price changes that are not currently captured under GAAP (e.g., replacement costs of nonmonetary assets). Under this concept, holding gains and losses are considered "capital maintenance adjustments" which would be included directly in equity and excluded from return on capital.

15. (d) Per SFAC 6, revenues are inflows of assets or settlements of liabilities, or both, during a period as a result of an entity's major or primary operations. Two essential characteristics of revenues are that revenues (1) arise from a company's primary earnings activities and (2) are recurring or continuing in nature. Therefore, answer (d) is correct because it meets the above criteria. Answers (b) and (c) are incorrect because they result from incidental transactions. Answer (a) is incorrect because a decrease of an asset is not a revenue.

16. (d) Per SFAC 6, the common quality shared by all assets is "service potential" or "future economic benefit." Per SFAC 6, assets commonly have other distinguishing features, such as being legally enforceable, tangible or acquired at a cost. These features, however, are not essential characteristics of assets.

17. (d) Per SFAC 5, five different attributes are used to measure assets and liabilities in present practice: historical cost, current (replacement) cost, current market value, net realizable value, and present value of future cash flows. Three of these (historical cost, replacement cost, and net realizable value) are used in measuring inventory at lower of cost or market. Present value of future cash flows is not used to measure inventory.

Cash Flow Information and Present Value (SFAC 7)

18. (c) The most relevant measure of a liability always reflects the credit standing of the entity obligated to pay, according to SFAC 7. Those who hold the entity's obligations as assets incorporate the entity's credit standing in determining the prices they are willing to pay.

19. (d) SFAC 7 provides a framework for using future cash flows as the basis for accounting measurements at initial recognition or fresh-start measurements and for the interest method of amortization. **FASB limited SFAC 7 to measurement issues** (how to measure) **and chose not to address recognition questions** (when to measure). SFAC 7 introduces the expected cash flow approach, which differs from the traditional approach by focusing on explicit assumptions about the range of possible estimated cash flows and their respective probabilities.

20. (d) The expected cash flow approach uses all expectations about possible cash flows in developing a measurement, rather than just the single most-likely cash flow. By incorporating a range of possible outcomes (with their respective timing differences), the expected cash flow approach accommodates the use of present value techniques when the timing of cash flows is uncertain. Thus, the expected cash flow is likely to provide a better estimate of fair value than the minimum, most-likely, or maximum taken alone. According to SFAC 7, expected present value refers to the sum of probability-weighted present values in a range of estimated cash flows, all discounted using the same interest rate convention.

21.   (b)   The computation of expected present value using a single interest rate is as follows:

PV of $200,000 in one year at 5%	$190,476	
Probability	20%	$38,095
PV of $200,000 in two years at 5%	$181,406	
Probability	50%	90,703
PV of $200,000 in three years at 5%	$172,768	
Probability	30%	51,830
		$180,628

According to SFAC 7, expected present value refers to the sum of probability-weighted present values in a range of estimated cash flows, all discounted using the same interest rate convention.

22.   (c)   Like depreciation and amortization conventions, interest methods are grounded in notions of historical cost, not current cost.

23.   (a)   According to SFAC 7, the objective of using present value in an accounting measurement is to capture, to the extent possible, the economic difference between sets of future cash flows. The objective of present value, when used in accounting measurements at initial recognition and fresh-start measurements, is to estimate fair value. Stated differently, present value should attempt to capture the elements that taken together would comprise a market price, if one existed, that is fair value. Value-in-use and entity-specific measurements attempt to capture the value of an asset or liability in the context of a particular entity. An entity-specific measurement substitutes the entity's assumptions for those that marketplace participants would make.

24.   (c)   SFAS 141 provides guidance on the determination of gain or loss on disposal of a component of a business. According to this guidance, such determination should be based on estimates of the net realizable value of the component. Since Brooks Co. plans to discontinue its entire operations, the appropriate measurement basis for its equipment is net realizable value. Historical cost and current reproduction and replacement costs are not appropriate measurement bases for assets once an entity has decided to discontinue its operations because these amounts do not reflect the entity's probable future benefit, which is a characteristic of assets per SFAC 6.

25.   (d)   Per AU 411, there are four primary levels of authority and an "Other" category in the hierarchy of generally accepted accounting principles. The most authoritative level includes FASB Statements and Interpretations, APB Opinions, and AICPA Accounting Research Bulletins. Statements of Position, Industry Audit and Accounting Guides, and Issues Papers are all sources of support for accounting principles but are lesser in authority.

A.2.   Income Determination

26.   (b)   Generally, sales revenue is recognized at the date of delivery, because that generally is the time at which a sale has occurred. At that point the two criteria for revenue recognition were met; the revenue is (1) realized or realizable and (2) it is earned (SFAC 6). Therefore, the amount of sales revenue recognized in 2002 is $150,000 (50,000 x $3 = $150,000).

27.   (c)   Per ARB 43, Chapter 4, income generally accrues only at the time of sale, and gains may not be anticipated by reflecting assets at their **current** sales prices. Ex-

ception to this general rule is granted, however, for agricultural products that are homogenous and have an immediate marketability at quoted prices (such as the cotton in this problem). When these inventories are stated at sales prices, they should be reduced by expenditures to be incurred in disposal. Amar Farms should, therefore, recognize revenue on the entire 300,000 pound crop in 2002 at the guaranteed (and prevailing) market price of $.70 per pound. This amounts to $210,000 (300,000 pounds x $.70 per pound = $210,000). Note that the additional $.02 per pound for the cotton sold in 2003 would be recognized in 2003, since its selling price exceeded the current (2002) market price.

28.   (a)   Per SFAS 48, revenue from the sale of a product may be recognized at the time of sale only if **all** of the following conditions are met:

1.   The seller's price is fixed or readily determinable.
2.   The buyer has paid the seller or is obligated to pay the seller, the obligation not being contingent on resale of the product.
3.   The buyer's obligation to the seller remains unchanged in the event of damage or destruction of the product.
4.   The buyer is independent from the seller.
5.   The seller does not have any significant obligations regarding resale of the product by the buyer.
6.   The amount of future returns can be reasonably estimated.

Because the buyer, Zee, has the right to return the machine to the seller, Lin, condition (2) above has not been met. Therefore, the recognition of sales revenue and cost of sales is not allowable for this transaction.

A.3.   Accruals and Deferrals

29.   (b)   Under accrual accounting, events that change an entity's financial position are recorded in the period in which the events occur. This means revenues are recognized when earned rather than when cash is received, and expenses are recognized when incurred rather than when cash is paid. Therefore, when the royalties are paid, Wand should debit an asset account (prepaid royalties) rather than an expense account. The royalties paid should be reported as expense in the period incurred (by debiting royalty expense and crediting prepaid royalties).

30.   (c)   The balance in the advertising expense account on 12/31/02 before adjustment is $146,000. Since the sales promotional campaign is to be conducted in January, any associated costs are an expense of 2003. Thus, the $15,000 cost of printing catalogs should be removed from the advertising expense account and recorded as a prepaid expense as of 12/31/02. In addition, advertising expense must be increased by the $9,000 cost of December's radio advertisements, which are an expense of 2002 even though they were not billed to Clark or paid until 2003. The $9,000 must be accrued as an expense and a liability at 12/31/02. Therefore, 2002 advertising expense should total $140,000 ($146,000 – $15,000 + $9,000).

31.   (b)   The opening balance in prepaid expenses ($1,500) results from a one-year insurance premium paid on 7/1/01. Since this policy would have expired by 6/30/02, no part of the $1,500 is included in 12/31/02 prepaid expenses. The insurance premium paid on 7/1/02 ($3,200) would be partially expired (6/12) by 12/31/02. The remainder (6/12 x

$3,200 = $1,600) would be a prepaid expense at year-end. The entire advance rental payment ($2,000) is a prepaid expense at 12/31/02 because it applies to 2003. Therefore, total 12/31/02 prepaid expenses are $3,600.

Prepaid insurance ($3,200 x 6/12)	$1,600
Prepaid rent	2,000
Total prepaid expenses	$3,600

32.   (b)   Apparently Roro records policy payments as charges to insurance expense and records prepaid insurance at the end of the quarter through an adjusting entry. The unadjusted trial balance amounts at 3/31/02 must represent the final two months of the old policy ($300 of prepaid insurance) and the cost of the new policy ($7,200 of insurance expense). An adjusting entry must be prepared to reflect the correct 3/31/02 balances. Since the new policy has been in force one month (3/1 through 3/31), thirty-five months remain unexpired. Therefore, the balance in prepaid insurance should be $7,000 ($7,200 x 35/36). Insurance expense should include the cost of the last two months of the old policy and the first month of the new policy [$300 + ($7,200 x 1/36) = $500]. Roro's adjusting entry would transfer $6,700 from insurance expense to prepaid insurance to result in the correct balances.

33.   (c)   At 12/31/02, the liability account unearned subscription revenue should have a balance which reflects all unexpired subscriptions. Of the 2001 sales, $125,000 expires during 2003 and would still be a liability at 12/31/02. Of the 2002 sales, $340,000 ($200,000 + $140,000) expires during 2003 and 2004, and therefore is a liability at 12/31/02. Therefore, the total liability is $465,000 ($125,000 + $340,000). This amount would have to be removed from the sales account and recorded as a liability in a 12/31/02 adjusting entry.

34.   (d)   Regal's unredeemed gift certificates at 12/31/01 are $75,000. During 2002, these certificates are either redeemed ($25,000) or expire by 12/31/02 ($75,000 – $25,000 = $50,000). Therefore, none of the $75,000 affects the 12/31/02 unearned revenue amount. During 2002, additional certificates totaling $250,000 were sold. Of this amount, $225,000 is expected to be redeemed in the future [$250,000 – (10% x $250,000)]. Since $175,000 of 2002 certificates were redeemed in 2002, 12/31/02 unearned revenue is $50,000 ($225,000 – $175,000).

35.   (a)   The requirement is to calculate Wren's royalty revenue for 2002. The 3/15/02 royalty receipt ($12,000) would not affect 2002 revenue because this amount pertains to revenues earned for July through December of 2001 and would have been accrued as revenue on 12/31/01. On 9/15/02, Wren received $17,000 in royalties for the first half of 2002. Royalties for the second half of 2002 will not be received until 3/15/03. However, the royalty payment to be received for the second six months (15% x $60,000 = $9,000) has been earned and should be accrued at 12/31/02. Therefore, 2002 royalty revenue is $26,000 ($17,000 + $9,000).

36.   (d)   The agreement states that Super is to receive royalties of 20% of revenues associated with the comic strip. Since Fantasy's 2003 revenues from the strip were $1,500,000, Super's royalty revenue is $300,000 ($1,500,000 x 20%). The other information in the problem about the receivable and cash payments is not needed to compute revenues. Super's 2003 summary entries would be

Cash	200,000	
Royalties rec.		75,000
Royalty revenue		125,000 ($200,000 – $75,000)
Royalties rec.	175,000	
Royalty revenue		175,000 ($300,000 – $125,000)

37.   (c)   Royalty revenues should be recognized when earned, regardless of when the cash is collected. Royalty revenue earned from 12/1/01 to 5/31/02 is $80,000 ($400,000 x 20%). Of this amount, $10,000 ($50,000 x 20%) was earned in December of 2001, so the portion earned in the first five months of 2002 is $70,000 ($80,000 – $10,000). Royalty revenue earned from 6/1/02 to 11/30/02 is $65,000 ($325,000 x 20%). The amount earned from 12/1/02 to 12/31/02, which would be accrued at 12/31, is $14,000 ($70,000 x 20%). Therefore, 2002 royalty revenue is $149,000.

1/1/02 - 5/31/02	$70,000
6/1/02 - 11/30/02	65,000
12/1/02 - 12/31/02	14,000
	$149,000

38.   (b)   The requirement is to calculate the amount of royalty income to be recognized in 2002. Cash collected for royalties totaled $200,000 in 2002. However, this amount must be adjusted for changes in the related accounts, as follows:

2002 cash received	$200,000
Royalties receivable 12/31/01	(90,000)
Royalties receivable 12/31/02	85,000
Unearned royalties 12/31/01	60,000
Unearned royalties 12/31/02	(40,000)
Royalty income	$215,000

The beginning receivable balance ($90,000) is subtracted because that portion of the cash collected was recognized as revenue last year. The ending receivable balance ($85,000) is added because that amount is 2002 revenue, even though it has not yet been collected. The beginning balance of unearned royalties ($60,000) is added because that amount is assumed to be earned during the year. Finally, the ending balance of unearned royalties ($40,000) is subtracted since this amount was collected, but not earned as revenue, by 12/31/02.

39.   (b)   The requirement is to determine the amount of royalty expense to be recognized in 2002. Cash paid for royalties totaled $300,000 in 2002. However, this amount must be adjusted for changes in the related accounts, as follows:

2002 cash paid	$300,000
Royalties payable 12/31/01	(80,000)
Royalties payable 12/31/02	75,000
Prepaid royalties 12/31/01	55,000
Prepaid royalties 12/31/02	(45,000)
	$305,000

The beginning payable balance ($80,000) is subtracted because that portion of the cash paid was recognized as expense during the previous year. The ending payable balance ($75,000) is added because that amount has been accrued as 2002 expense, even though it has not yet been paid. The beginning balance of prepaid royalties ($55,000) is added because that amount is assumed to have expired during the year. Finally, the ending balance of prepaid royalties ($45,000) is subtracted since this amount was paid, but not incurred as an expense, by 12/31/02.

40. (b) When the insurance policy was initially purchased, the entire balance was debited to a prepaid asset account (i.e., prepaid insurance). The adjusting entry at December 31, 2002, to recognize the expiration of one year of the policy would be

Insurance expense   (1/3 of original pymt.)
  Prepaid insurance   (1/3 of original pymt.)

After the adjusting entry, the prepaid asset account would contain 2/3 of the original payment. If the original payment had instead been debited to an expense account (i.e., insurance expense), then the adjusting entry at December 31, 2002 would be

Prepaid insurance   (2/3 of original pymt.)
  Insurance expense   (2/3 of original pymt.)

This alternate approach would also result in 1/3 of the original payment being expensed in 2002 and 2/3 of the original payment being carried forward as a prepaid asset. Thus, answer (b) is correct. Answer (a) is incorrect because the premium paid was for a three-year policy, 2/3 of which had not yet expired and would therefore be carried forward in the prepaid asset account. Answer (c) is incorrect because 1/3 of the original payment was already expensed. Answer (d) is incorrect because the amount would be the same as it would have been if the original payment had been debited initially to an expense account (as explained for answer (b) above).

41. (b) Per ARB 43, chap 3A, current assets are identified as resources that are reasonably expected to be realized in cash or sold or **consumed** during the normal operating cycle of the business. These resources include prepaid expenses such as royalties. Since the balance remaining in Sip Co.'s royalty prepayment (the payment relating to 2003 royalties) will be consumed within the next year, it should be reported as a current asset. Additionally, the payment relating to 2002 should be reported as an expense.

42. (b) At the time the gift certificates were issued, the following entry was made, reflecting the store's future obligation to honor the certificates:

Cash   xx
  Deferred revenue   xx

Upon redemption of the certificates, the obligation recorded in the deferred revenue account becomes satisfied and the revenue is earned. Similarly, as the certificates expire, the store is no longer under any obligation to honor the certificates and the deferred revenue should be taken into income. In both instances, the deferred revenue account must be reduced (debited) to reflect the earning of revenue. This is done through the following entry:

Deferred revenue   xx
  Revenue   xx

43. (a) The revenues from service contracts should be recognized on a pro rata basis over the term of the contract. This treatment allocates the contract revenues to the period(s) in which they are earned. Since the sale of a service contract does not culminate in the completion of the earnings process (i.e., does not represent the seller's performance of the contract), payments received for such a contract should be recorded initially in a deferred revenue account.

A.4. Cash to Accrual

44. (c) The following formula is used to adjust service revenue from the cash basis to the accrual basis:

$$\underset{\text{collected}}{\text{Cash fees}} + \underset{\text{AR}}{\text{End.}} - \underset{\text{AR}}{\text{Beg.}} + \underset{\substack{\text{unearned}\\\text{fees}}}{\text{Beg.}} - \underset{\substack{\text{unearned}\\\text{fees}}}{\text{End.}} = \underset{\substack{\text{service}\\\text{revenue}}}{\text{Accrual basis}}$$

$200,000 + $60,000 − $40,000 + 0 − $5,000 = \underline{$215,000}

As an alternative, T-accounts can be used.

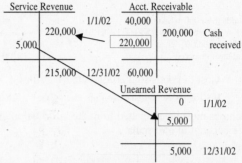

45. (d) To determine cash basis revenue, the solutions approach is to prepare a T-account for accounts receivable.

	Accounts Receivable		
12/31/01	1,000,000		
Sales	4,600,000	20,000	Write-offs
		?	Collections
12/31/02	1,300,000		

The missing amount for cash collections is $4,280,000. Another approach is to use the following formula:

Sales	+	Decrease (− increase) in AR	−	Write-offs	=	Collections
$4,600,000	−	$300,000	−	$20,000	=	$4,280,000

The increase in receivables ($300,000) means that cash collected during the period was less than sales during the period and therefore is deducted from sales revenue. The write-offs ($20,000) represent recognized sales that will never be collected in cash and therefore must also be deducted to compute collections.

46. (d) To determine rental revenue, the solutions approach is to prepare a T-account for rents receivable and rent revenues.

Rent Receivable			Rent Revenues	
800,000	800,000 a	a 800,000	2,210,000
11/30/01			
b 1,090,000	30,000 c		1,090,000 b
Bal 1,060,000	1,060,000 + 30,000		Bal 2,500,000

a. To remove 2001 revenue from the $2,210,000 of cash collected and relieve rent receivable of collections from 2001 receivables
b. To recognize unrecorded rent earned including write-offs
c. To recognize write-offs. Debit would be to the allowance account.

47. (d) Under the cash basis method of accounting, revenue is recognized as it is collected. Cash sales after returns and allowances totaled $76,000 ($80,000 − $4,000). Net credit sales for 2002 were $114,000 ($120,000 credit sales − $6,000 discounts). As made evident by the T-account below, cash collections from credit sales must equal $124,000 ($40,000 + $114,000 − $30,000), since $10,000 in excess of current credit sales was received and reduced Accounts Receivable by this amount.

	Accounts Receivable		
Bal. 1/1	40,000		
Net credit sales	114,000	?	Collections
Bal. 12/31	30,000		

A summary journal entry would be

Cash	124,000	
Sales discounts	6,000	
Accounts receivable		130,000

Total cash basis revenue for 2002 is $200,000 as shown below.

Cash sales ($80,000 – $4,000)	$ 76,000
Collections of credit sales [($40,000 + $120,000 – $30,000) – $6,000]	124,000
Total cash received	$200,000

48.   (a)   Cost of goods sold is computed as follows:

Beg. inv. + Net purchases – End. inv. = CGS

Net purchases must be computed from the information given using a T-account or a formula.

AP

		50,000	12/31/01
Payments	490,000	?	Purchases
		75,000	12/31/02

The missing amount for purchases is $515,000. Another approach is to use the following formula:

Payments	+	Ending AP	–	Beginning AP	=	Purchases
$490,000	+	$75,000	–	$50,000	=	$515,000

This amount can be used to determine cost of goods sold

Beg. inventory	$290,000
+ Net purchases	515,000
Cost of goods available	805,000
– End. inventory	260,000
Cost of goods sold	$545,000

49.   (d)   Cash-basis income of $60,000 must be adjusted for changes in accounts receivable and accounts payable to compute accrual income

Cash-basis income	$ 60,000
12/31/01 AR	(20,000)
12/31/02 AR	40,000
12/31/01 AP	30,000
12/31/02 AP	(15,000)
Accrual income	$ 95,000

The beginning AR ($20,000) is subtracted because although this amount was **collected in 2002,** it is properly accrued as **2001 revenue**. The ending AR is added because although **not collected in 2002,** it should be accrued as **2002 revenue**. The beginning AP is added because although this amount was **paid in 2002,** it is properly accrued as **2001 expense**. The ending AP is subtracted because although **not paid in 2002,** it should be accrued as **2002 expense**.

50.   (c)   The ending balance in Tory's capital account on either the accrual or cash basis is computed as follows:

$$\frac{\text{Beginning}}{\text{capital}} + \text{Investments} + \text{Income} - \text{Drawings} = \frac{\text{Ending}}{\text{capital}}$$

Tory's beginning capital is his initial cash investment of $2,000. No other investments were made. Under the cash basis method of accounting, income is the excess of cash revenues ($5,000) over cash expenses ($0, since the expenses were not paid until after March 31). Therefore, cash basis income is $5,000. Drawings are $1,000. Therefore, ending capital is $6,000 ($2,000 + $0 + $5,000 – $1,000).

51.   (d)   The requirement of this question is to determine if a decrease in accounts receivable and/or a decrease in accrued expenses would result in **cash-basis income** being **lower** than accrual-basis income.

A decrease in the accounts receivable balance would generally mean that cash was collected. In accordance with the cash basis of accounting when cash is received it is recorded as revenue (Dr. Cash, Cr. Revenue). Whereas under the accrual basis the revenue would have recorded when the receivable was recorded (Dr. AR, Cr. Revenue). Thus, a decreased accounts receivable balance would result in increased revenue/income. Therefore, the answer for this account is No.

A decrease in the accrued expenses account would generally mean cash was paid on some expenses. Under the cash basis, when the cash is paid the expense is recorded (Dr. Expense, Cr. Cash). Whereas under the accrual basis the expense would have been recorded when the accrued expense was recorded (Dr. Expense, Cr. Accrued Expense). Thus, a decreased accrued expenses account would result in increased expenses/lower income for the cash basis. Thus, the answer for this account is Yes.

52.   (b)   When a company operates on the accrual basis, supplies are inventoried and expensed as they are used. Under the cash method, however, supplies are expensed as they are paid for. Therefore if White Co. experiences an increase in supplies inventory during the year, this increase must be deducted from accrual income to get to the cash basis, because the cost of the supplies would be expensed at the time of purchase.

Office salaries payable works the opposite way. Under the accrual method, a liability would have been established resulting in additional expense over the amount of cash paid to employees. Under the cash method, no liability is accrued and the unpaid salaries are not expensed. Therefore, the increase must be added to the accrual basis net income.

53.   (c)   Prior to 2002, Droit Co. used the cash basis of accounting. Accordingly, Droit would have expensed all purchases of supplies as incurred. In contrast, under the accrual basis of accounting, the cost of unused supplies at each year-end would have been carried as an asset and, therefore, excluded from the current year's supplies expense. In 2002, the year Droit adopted the accrual basis of accounting, Droit would have inventoried unused supplies at December 31 and excluded those costs from 2002 net income. Since the cost of 2002's beginning balance of supplies was expensed during 2001, even though the supplies were not used until 2002, Droit's inability to determine the beginning supplies inventory would result in an understatement of supplies expense and overstatement of 2002 net income. However, since Droit properly inventoried supplies at December 31, 2002, its cumulative (inception-to-date) supplies expense would be properly stated. Therefore, Droit's inability to determine 2002's beginning supplies expense would have no impact on Droit's December 31, 2002 retained earnings.

A.5. Installment Sales

54.   (b)   Under the installment method, gross profit is deferred at the time of sale and is recognized by applying the gross profit rate to subsequent cash collections. At the time of sale, gross profit of $250,000 is deferred ($500,000 installment sales less $250,000 cost of installment sales). The gross profit rate is 50% ($250,000 ÷ $500,000). Since 2002 collections on installment sales were $100,000, gross profit of $50,000 (50% x $100,000) is recognized in 2002. This would decrease the deferred gross profit account to a 12/31/02 balance of $200,000 ($250,000 – $50,000). Note that regular sales, cost of regular sales, and general and administrative expenses do not affect the deferred gross profit account.

55. **(d)** Under the installment sales method, gross profit is deferred to future periods and recognized proportionately to collection of the receivables. Therefore, at each year-end, deferred gross profit can be computed by multiplying the gross profit percentage by the accounts receivable balance, as indicated below.

	2002	*2001*
Sales	$900,000	$600,000
2001 Collections		(200,000)
2002 Collections	(300,000)	(100,000)
2001 Write-offs		(50,000)
2002 Write-offs	(50,000)	(150,000)
12/31/02 AR	$550,000	$100,000
Gross profit %	x 40%	x 30%
12/31/02 Deferred GP	$220,000	$30,000

Thus, total deferred gross profit at 12/31/02 is $250,000 ($220,000 + $30,000).

56. **(d)** Under the installment sales method, gross profit is deferred to future periods and is recognized proportionately as cash is collected. To determine cash collections in this case, first compute the 2002 installment sales by dividing deferred gross profit by the gross profit percentage ($560,000 ÷ 40% = $1,400,000). Then, the 12/31/02 installment accounts receivable is subtracted to determine cash collections ($1,400,000 – $800,000 = $600,000). Realized gross profit is then computed by multiplying cash collections by the gross profit percentage ($600,000 x 40% = $240,000).

57. **(c)** When using the installment method, gross profit realized is computed as indicated below.

Cash collections   x   GP%   =   GP realized

This equation can be rearranged as follows:

GP realized   ÷   GP%   =   Cash collections

Therefore, cash collected to date on 2001 sales is $800,000 [($150,000 + $90,000) ÷ 30%], and on 2002 sales is $500,000 ($200,000 ÷ 40%). Installment accounts receivable at 12/31/02 is computed by subtracting cash collections from the original sales amount.

Installment AR - 2001 ($1,000,000 – $800,000)	$ 200,000
Installment AR - 2002 ($2,000,000 – $500,000)	1,500,000
Total 12/31/02 installment AR	$1,700,000

58. **(a)** The equipment sale is accounted for using the installment method. The gross profit percentage on the sale is 33 1/3% ($600,000 profit ÷ $1,800,000 selling price). Since $300,000 of the sales price is collected in 2002, gross profit of $100,000 is recognized (33 1/3% x $300,000). The **total** revenue recognized is $250,000 ($100,000 gross profit + $150,000 interest revenue).

59. **(a)** The machine sale is accounted for using the installment method, where gross profit is deferred and recognized in proportion to cash collected. Initially, the entire $270,000 gain is deferred. In 2001, $150,000 of the sales price was collected, and the gross profit percentage is 30% ($270,000 ÷ $900,000), so gross profit recognized was $45,000 (30% x $150,000). In 2002, $250,000 of the sales price was collected, so gross profit recognized was $75,000 (30% x $250,000). Therefore, at 12/31/02, deferred gross profit is $150,000 ($270,000 – $45,000 – $75,000). As a

shortcut, you can compute the 12/31/02 note receivable balance ($750,000 – $250,000 = $500,000), and multiply by the 30% gross profit percentage (30% x $500,000 = $150,000). Note that the **interest** collected ($75,000) does not affect the computation because it is not a collection of sales price.

60. **(c)** Per APB 10, the profit on a sale in the ordinary course of business is considered to be realized at the time of sale unless it is uncertain whether the sale price will be collected. The Board concluded that use of the installment method of accounting is not acceptable unless this uncertainty exists. Answers (a), (b), and (d) are incorrect because they do not involve the element of uncertainty regarding the collectibility of the sale price.

61. **(c)** According to the **installment method** of accounting, gross profit on an installment sale is recognized in income in proportion to the cash collection. The cash collected from a given year's sales is multiplied by that year's gross profit percentage to compute the amount of gross profit to be recognized. Answer (a) describes the **point-of-sale** recognition basis, while answer (d) describes the **cost recovery** method. Answer (b) does not describe any recognition basis currently used.

62. **(c)** Per APB 10, the installment method of accounting is used when there is a high degree of uncertainty regarding the collectibility of the sale price. Under this method, sales revenues and the related cost of goods sold are recognized in the period of the sale. However, the gross profit is deferred to the periods in which cash is collected. Income recognized in the period of collection is generally computed by multiplying the cash collected by the gross margin percentage. The installment method is based upon deferral of the gross profit, not the net operating profit. APB 10 states that the installment method is generally only applicable when the reporting company is unable to estimate the amount of uncollectible accounts.

63. **(d)** Under the installment method (case I) revenue (gross profit) is recognized **after** the sale, in proportion to cash collected. Under the cost recovery method (case II), revenue (gross profit) is again recognized **after** the sale, when cumulative receipts exceed the cost of the asset sold. Therefore, revenue is not recognized prior to the sale of merchandise in either case I or case II.

A.6. Cost Recovery Method

64. **(d)** Under the cost recovery method **no profit of any type** is recognized until the cumulative receipts (principal and interest) exceed the cost of the asset sold. This means that the entire gross profit ($3,000,000 – $2,000,000 = $1,000,000) and the 2002 interest received ($270,000) will be deferred until cash collections exceed $2,000,000. Therefore, no income is recognized in 2002.

65. **(d)** The **installment method** is used when collection of the selling price is not reasonably assured. However, when the uncertainty of collection is so great that even the use of the installment method is precluded, then the cost recovery method may be used. Having no reasonable basis for estimating collectibility would provide a great enough uncertainty to use the cost recovery method. It is important to note that anytime the installment method is used, some risk of 100% collection exists, but the risk must be extreme before the cost recovery method is employed.

66.   (a)   Per APB 10, installment methods of recognizing revenue are appropriate only when "collection of the sale price is not reasonably assured." Under the cost recovery method, gross profit is deferred and recognized only when the cumulative receipts exceed the cost of the asset sold.

A.7. Franchise Agreements

67.   (d)   Per SFAS 45, Franchise fee revenue is recognized when all material services have been substantially performed by the franchiser. Substantial performance means the franchiser has performed substantially all of required initial services and has no remaining obligation to refund any cash received. The $60,000 nonrefundable down payment applies to the initial services already performed by Rice. Therefore, the $60,000 may be recognized as revenue in 2002. The three remaining $30,000 installments relate to substantial future services to be performed by Rice. The present value of these payments ($72,000) is recorded as unearned franchise fees and recognized as revenue once substantial performance of the future services has occurred.

Cash	60,000	
Notes receivable	90,000	
Discount on notes receivable		18,000
Franchise revenue		60,000
Unearned franchise fees		72,000

68.   (c)   Initial franchise fees are not recognized as revenue until the franchisor makes substantial performance of the required services, and collection is reasonably assured. Since Potter Pie has not yet performed the required services, the initial franchise fee (21 x $30,000 = $630,000) is reported as **unearned franchise fees** at 12/31/02. The estimated uncollectible amount ($20,000) normally would be recorded as a debit to **bad debt expense** and a credit to **allowance for uncollectible accounts**. However, since no revenue has yet been recognized, it is inappropriate to record bad debt expense. Instead, **unearned franchise fees** is debited, because an unearned revenue should not be recorded when, in effect, no related asset has been received. Therefore, the **net** unearned franchise fees is $610,000 ($630,000 – $20,000).

A.8. Real Estate Transactions

69.   (d)   Items I and II do not transfer the risks and rewards of ownership to the buyer since both scenarios entitle the buyer to a return of his/her initial investment. Thus, the risks of ownership still remain with the seller. The economic substance of such arrangements is that of financing, leasing, or profit-sharing transactions. Item III transfers the risks and rewards of ownership since the seller will be reimbursed for cost plus a 5% profit on the support provided. Therefore, the seller is not required to support operations of the property at its **own** risk.

70.   (c)   The problem states that the sale has been consummated and that Kame's initial and continuing investments are adequate to demonstrate a commitment to pay for the property. However, the fact that Esker's receivable is subject to future subordination precludes recognition of the profit in full. Instead, the cost recovery method must be used to account for the sale. The deposit method is to be used

1.   Until the sale is consummated, when all activities necessary for closing have been performed.

2.   If the buyer's initial and continuing investments are not adequate to demonstrate a commitment to pay for the property and the seller is not reasonably assured of recovering the cost of the property if the buyer defaults.

The problem states that the sale has been consummated and that Kame's initial and continuing investments are adequate. Therefore, the deposit method will not be used to account for the sale. The reduced profit method is used only when the initial investment is adequate to demonstrate a commitment to pay for the property but the continuing investments are not. The continuing investments must also meet certain additional requirements for the reduced profit method to be used. Since Kame's continuing investments are adequate, the reduced profit method will not be used to account for the sale. The full accrual method may be used only if profit on the sale is determinable, the earning process is virtually complete, and all of the following:

1.   A sale is consummated.
2.   The buyer's initial and continuing investments are adequate to demonstrate a commitment to pay for the property.
3.   The seller's receivable is not subject to future subordination.
4.   The seller has transferred to the buyer the usual risks and rewards of ownership in a transaction that is, in substance, a sale and does not have a substantial continuing involvement in the property.

OTHER OBJECTIVE ANSWERS AND ANSWER EXPLANATIONS

Problem 1

1. **(E)** SFAC 5 states that "Relevance is a primary qualitative characteristic. To be relevant, information about an item must have feedback value or predictive value (or both) for users and must be timely."

2. **(G)** SFAC 6 states that "Gains are increases in equity (net assets) from peripheral or incidental transactions of an entity and from all other transactions and other events and circumstances affecting the entity except those that result from revenues or investments by owners."

3. **(J)** SFAC 5 states that "Revenues and gains are realized when products (goods or services), merchandise, or other assets are exchanged for cash or claims to cash."

4. **(F)** SFAC 2 states that "Comparability, including consistency, is a secondary quality that interacts with relevance and reliability to contribute to the usefulness of information."

5. **(A)** SFAC 5 states that "Recognition is the process of formally recording or incorporating an item into the financial statements of an entity as an asset, liability, revenue, expense, or the like." SFAC 5 continues the recognition concept by stating, "An item and information about it should meet four fundamental recognition criteria to be recognized and should be recognized when the criteria are met, subject to a cost-benefit constraint and a materiality threshold."

6. **(B)** SFAC 5 states that "Comprehensive income is a broad measure of the effects of transactions and other events on an entity, comprising all recognized changes in equity (net assets) of the entity during a period from transactions and other events and circumstances except those resulting from investments by owners and distributions to owners."

7. **(D)** SFAC 6 defines revenues as "inflows or other enhancements of assets of an entity or settlements of its liabilities (or a combination of both) from delivering or producing goods, rendering services, or other activities that constitute the entity's ongoing major or central operations."

8. **(L)** SFAC 5 defines current market value as "the amount of cash, or its equivalent, that could be obtained by selling an asset in orderly liquidation."

9. **(E)** SFAC 2 defines predictive value as "the quality of information that helps users to increase the likelihood of correctly forecasting the outcome of past or present events."

10. **(I)** SFAC 5 states that "Earnings is a measure of performance during a period that is concerned primarily with the extent to which asset inflows associated with cash-to-cash cycles substantially completed (or completed) during the period exceed (or are less than) asset outflows associated, directly or indirectly, with the same cycles."

SOLUTION GUIDE

Problem 1   Cash to Accrual Worksheet; Comparison of These Bases

a.

1.   This problem consists of two related parts. Part (a) requires the entering of adjustments to convert from cash to accrual on the worksheet provided. Part (b) requires a brief memo explaining why the bank would require accrual-basis financial statements.

2.   To complete the worksheet provided in part (a), you must refer back to the additional information given (labeled 1 through 9). The solutions approach is to treat each of the nine items as an independent problem.

2.1   Amounts due from customers total $32,000 at 12/31/02. The balance in the accounts receivable account from the last year-end is $16,200. This account must be debited for $15,800 to bring the balance up to $32,000. The corresponding credit is to Sales, since unrecorded receivables means that there are also unrecorded sales.

2.2   An allowance for doubtful accounts of $3,800 is required at 12/31/02. Since the balance in the allowance account is $0, an adjusting entry for $3,800 is required.

Doubtful accounts expense	3,800	
Allowance for doubtful accounts		3,800

2.3   Unpaid invoices for flower (the company's product) purchases total $30,500 at 12/31/02. The balance in accounts payable from last year is $17,000. This account must be credited for $13,500 to bring the balance up to $30,500. The corresponding debit is to Purchases, since these purchases were never recorded. Accrual basis Purchases for 2002 thus equals $318,600 ($305,100 + $30,500 – $17,000).

2.4   The 12/31/02 inventory is $72,800, but the books now reflect the 12/31/01 inventory of $62,000. The beginning inventory must be removed from the books, and the ending inventory must be recorded.

Income summary	62,000	
Inventory		62,000
Inventory	72,800	
Income summary		72,800

The net adjustment to inventory is $10,800. You may make either both of the above entries or a net entry on the worksheet.

     An alternative method of adjusting the inventory and purchases account using a Cost of goods sold account exists. The adjustments to the inventory account could be made to a Cost of goods sold account instead of to Income summary—inventory. In this case, the appropriate journal entries for information item (4) would be as follows:

Cost of goods sold	62,000	
Inventory (12/31/01)		62,000
Inventory (12/31/02)	72,800	
Cost of goods sold		72,800

An additional entry transferring net purchases to Cost of goods sold is then required to obtain the correct ending balance for that account. This entry should be recorded after the purchases account is adjusted to the correct accrual basis balance of $318,600 calculated in item (3).

Cost of goods sold	318,600	
Purchases		318,600

Although the AICPA Unofficial Answer did not require the balance of Cost of goods sold, accrual basis CGS equals $307,800 ($62,000 BI + $318,600 purch. – $72,800 EI).

If this method were used, the accrual basis ending balances in the debit column of the worksheet as of 12/31/02 for those accounts affected would be as follows:

Inventory	$ 72,800
Purchases	--
Cost of Goods Sold	$307,800

2.5   The insurance coverage is paid one year in advance. The $8,700 payment made on May 1 was recorded as insurance expense. Therefore, $2,900 (4/12 x 8,700) must be removed from the insurance expense account and recorded as prepaid insurance. An additional entry must be made to record some of the 4/1/01 insurance premium as 2002 expense. The last four months of that payment ($7,800 x 4/12 = $2,600) should be expensed in 2002. The credit is to Baron, capital, since the 12/31/01 balance was understated when the total premium was expensed in 2001.

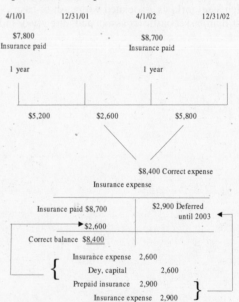

Alternatively, these entries could be netted as is done in the AICPA Unofficial Answer.

2.6   Depreciation on furniture and fixtures is $12,000. In addition, land improvements must be depreciated. The depreciation period is the useful life (fifteen years), because it is less than the lease term of twenty-five years. Depreciation on the land improvements is $2,250 ($45,000 x 1/15 x 9/12), and total depreciation is $14,250 ($12,000 + $2,250).

The entry is

| Depreciation expense | 14,250 | |
| Accumulated depreciation | | 14,250 |

2.7 Accrued expenses were unrecorded at both 12/31/01 and 12/31/02. Those unrecorded at 12/31/01 would have been recorded as an expense when paid in 2002. Therefore, those amounts must be removed from the 2002 expense accounts. The corresponding debit is to Baron, capital, since the 12/31/01 balance of that account was overstated when the accrued expenses were not recorded in 2001.

Baron, capital	2,000	
Utilities expense		900
Payroll taxes expense		1,100

The accrued expenses unrecorded at 12/31/02 must be recorded with an adjusting entry to debit the expenses and credit the related liability.

Utilities expense	1,500	
Payroll taxes expense	1,600	
Accrued expenses		3,100

Alternatively, these entries could be netted as is done in the AICPA Unofficial Answer.

2.8 The contingent lawsuit liability must be accrued because it meets the **probable** and **reasonably estimable** criteria. The estimate of the settlement is $300,000, but $250,000 of that amount is covered by insurance. Therefore the net loss and liability of $50,000 ($300,000 – $250,000) must be accrued.

| Lawsuit loss | 50,000 | |
| Lawsuit liability | | 50,000 |

2.9 Baron's "salary" (12 x $4,000 = $48,000) and living expenses ($250 x 52 = $13,000) must be reclassified from expense accounts to the drawing account.

Baron, drawing	61,000	
Salaries		48,000
Living expenses		13,000

NOTE: With regard to the treatment of Baron's salary, no authoritative pronouncement addresses this issue. However, elementary accounting textbooks treat such salaries as drawings.

b. Advantages of accrual basis instead of cash basis
- More complete information regarding earnings, assets, and claims to assets
- Cannot manipulate earnings via the timing of receipts and payments
- Events that change financial position are reported in the period of occurrence
- Revenues and expenses reflect amounts owed or receivable, which is more meaningful than cash payments/receipts

UNOFFICIAL ANSWER

Problem 1   Cash to Accrual Worksheet; Comparison of These Bases

a.

Baron Flowers
WORKSHEET TO CONVERT TRIAL BALANCE TO ACCRUAL BASIS
December 31, 2002

Account title	Cash basis Dr.	Cash basis Cr.	Adjustments Dr.	Adjustments Cr.	Accrual basis* Dr.*	Accrual basis* Cr.*
Cash	25,600				25,600	
Accounts receivable	16,200		(1) 15,800		32,000	
Inventory	62,000		(4) 10,800		72,800	
Furniture & fixtures	118,200				118,200	
Land improvements	45,000				45,000	
Accumulated depreciation & amortization		32,400		(6) 14,250		46,650
Accounts payable		17,000		(3) 13,500		30,500
Baron, Drawings			(9) 61,000		61,000	
Baron, Capital		124,600	(7) 2,000	(5) 2,600		125,200
Allowance for uncollectible accounts				(2) 3,800		3,800
Prepaid insurance			(5) 2,900		2,900	
Accrued expenses				(7) 3,100		3,100
Estimated liability from lawsuit				(8) 50,000		50,000
Sales		653,000		(1) 15,800		668,800
Purchases	305,100		(3) 13,500		318,600	
Salaries	174,000			(9) 48,000	126,000	
Payroll taxes	12,400		(7) 500		12,900	
Insurance	8,700			(5) 300	8,400	
Rent	34,200				34,200	
Utilities	12,600		(7) 600		13,200	
Living expenses	13,000			(9) 13,000		
Income summary—inventory			(4) 62,000	(4) 72,800		10,800
Uncollectible accounts			(2) 3,800		3,800	
Depreciation & amortization			(6) 14,250		14,250	
Estimated loss from lawsuit			(8) 50,000		50,000	
	827,000	827,000	237,150	237,150	938,850	938,850

Explanations of Adjustments

[1] To convert 2002 sales to accrual basis.

Accounts receivable balances:
December 31, 2002	$32,000
December 31, 2001	16,200
Increase in sales	$15,800

[2] To record provision for uncollectible accounts.

[3] To convert 2002 purchases to accrual basis.

Accounts payable balances:
December 31, 2002	$30,500
December 31, 2001	17,000
Increase in purchases	$13,500

[4] To record increase in inventory from 12/31/01 to 12/31/02.

Inventory balances:
December 31, 2002	$72,800
December 31, 2001	62,000
Increase in inventory	$10,800

[5] To adjust prepaid insurance.

Prepaid balances:
December 31, 2002 ($8,700 x 4/12)	$2,900
December 31, 2001 ($7,800 x 4/12)	2,600
Decrease in insurance expense	$ 300

[6] To record 2002 depreciation and amortization expense.

Cost of leasehold improvement	$45,000
Estimated life	15 years
Amortization ($45,000 x 1/15 x 9/12)	2,250
Depreciation expense on fixtures and equipment	12,000
	$14,250

[7] To convert expenses to accrual basis.

	Balances December 31, 2002	2001	Increase in expenses
Utilities	$1,500	$ 900	$ 600
Payroll taxes	1,600	1,100	500
	$3,100	$2,000	$1,100

[8] To record lawsuit liability at 12/31/02.

Attorney's estimate of probable loss	$300,000
Amount covered by insurance	250,000
Baron's estimated liability	$ 50,000

[9] To record Baron's drawings for 2002.

Salary ($4,000 x 12)	$48,000
Living expenses	13,000
	$61,000

---

* *Completion of these columns was not required.*

b.

To: Baron Flowers

From: Muir

Re: Accrual basis financial statements

You have asked me to explain why the bank would require financial statements prepared on the accrual basis instead of the cash basis. The bank is concerned about your ability to repay the loan. To assess that ability, it wants information about your earnings for the period, total assets, and all claims on those assets. This information about your enterprise's performance and financial position is provided more completely by accrual-basis financial statements than by cash-basis financial statements.

Under the cash basis, revenues are recognized when received and expenses when paid. Earnings can be manipulated by the timing of cash receipts and disbursements. Accrual basis accounting, while grounded in cash flows, reports transactions and other events with cash consequences at the time the transactions and events occur. Revenues and expenses are reported in the accounting period benefited and reflect receivables and payables, not just what the enterprise was able to collect or chose to pay.

ANSWER OUTLINE

Problem 2   Revenue Recognition and Postretirement Benefits other than Pensions

a.   Revenue recognition
   • Recognized when realized or realizable and earned
   • Sales with right of return
      • Revenue and cost of sales, net of returns, recognized at time of sale only if specified conditions met
      • Recognition postponed if conditions not met
   • Impact of right of return on Emco
      • Cannot reasonably estimate returns
      • Emco must defer recognition until either return privilege expires or it can reasonably estimate returns

b.   SFAS 106, *Employers' Accounting for Postretirement Benefits other than Pensions*
   • Primary recipients: retired employees, their beneficiaries, and covered dependents
   • Principal benefit is health care
   • Other benefits: tuition assistance, legal services, life insurance benefits, day care, and housing subsidies
   • Accruals based on estimates required because failure to accrue implies that no obligation exists

UNOFFICIAL ANSWER

Problem 2   Revenue Recognition and Postretirement Benefits other than Pensions

TO: Brown
FROM: Wyatt

As we discussed, here is a brief overview of revenue recognition and Statement of Financial Accounting Standards 106.

a.   Revenue recognition

The revenue recognition principle provides that revenue is recognized when it is realized or realizable and it is earned. Accordingly, revenues from the sale of products ordinarily are recognized at the time of sale. Revenue from sales transactions in which the buyer has a right to return the product are recognized at time of sale only if specified conditions are met. If all these conditions are not met, revenue recognition is postponed; if they are met, sales revenue and cost of sales should be reported in the income statement, reduced to reflect estimated returns.

One of the specified conditions is that the amount of future returns can be reasonably estimated. Since Emco cannot reasonably estimate future returns, Emco should defer recognition of sales revenue and cost of sales until the return privilege has substantially expired or it can reasonably estimate returns, which ever occurs first.

b.   Statement of Financial Accounting Standards 106, *Employers' Accounting for Postretirement Benefits other than Pensions.*

The primary recipients of postretirement benefits other than pensions are retired employees, their beneficiaries, and covered dependents. The principal benefit covered by SFAS 106 is postretirement health care benefits. Examples of other benefits include tuition assistance, legal services, life insurance benefits, day care, and housing subsidies.

The reasoning given in SFAS 106 is that accrual of the obligation based on best estimates is superior to implying, by a failure to accrue, that no obligation exists prior to the payment of benefits.

B. Error Correction

Accountants must be in a position to anticipate, locate, and correct errors in their functions of systems and procedures design, controllership, and attestation. Errors which are discovered in the same year that they are made are corrected by

1. Determining the entry that was made
2. Determining the correct entry
3. Analyzing increases or decreases needed in affected accounts
4. Making the correct entry

Errors in classification (e.g., sales expense instead of R&D expense) affect only one period. Non-systematic errors in adjusting entries (e.g., an error in ending inventory of one period) affect two periods and are known as self-correcting (counterbalancing) errors. For example, overstating ending inventory of 2002 will overstate the income of 2002 and understate the income of 2003. Other errors will affect the income of several periods, such as misrecording the cost of a long-lived asset (i.e., depreciation will be misstated for all periods).

The chart below shows four examples of counterbalancing errors.

ERRORS WHICH WILL SELF-CORRECT AFTER TWO YEARS
Omitting Accruals
Case #1

	12/31/02	12/31/03	1/1/04
Expense (wages)	Understated	Overstated	Correct
Net income	Overstated	Understated	Correct
Payable (wages)	Understated	Correct	Correct
Retained earnings	Overstated	Correct	Correct

Case #2

	12/31/02	12/31/03	1/1/04
Revenue (interest)	Understated	Overstated	Correct
Net income	Understated	Overstated	Correct
Receivable (interest)	Understated	Correct	Correct
Retained earnings	Understated	Correct	Correct

Omitting Deferrals (Prepaids)
Case #3

	12/31/02	12/31/03	1/1/04
Expense (insurance)	Overstated	Understated	Correct
Net income	Understated	Overstated	Correct
Prepaid asset	Understated	Correct	Correct
Retained earnings	Understated	Correct	Correct

Case #4

	12/31/02	12/31/03	1/1/04
Revenue (unearned)	Overstated	Understated	Correct
Net income	Overstated	Understated	Correct
Liability (un. rev.)	Understated	Correct	Correct
Retained earnings	Overstated	Correct	Correct

Notice that in all four cases the income statement errors have the opposite effect in 2002 and 2003. Also notice that by the end of 2003 the balance sheet accounts are correct. Therefore, even if the error is not discovered, the financial statements will be correct by the beginning of the third year.

When an error is discovered in a period subsequent to the period when the error occurred, an entry must be made to correct the accounts as if the error had not been made. For example, assume the entry to accrue wage expense in the amount of $10,000 is omitted on 12/31/02. The effects that would be caused by such an omission may be categorized as follows:

	2002	2003	2004
Expense	Understated	Overstated	Correct
Income	Overstated	Understated	Correct
Wages payable	Understated	Correct	Correct
Retained earnings	Overstated	Correct	Correct

If the company follows the policy of reversing adjusting entries for accruals, then correction of the error any time during 2003 will require

Adjustment to correct error	10,000	
Wage expense		10,000

The adjustment account, when closed to retained earnings, will correct for the 1/1/03 overstatement in retained earnings due to the overstatement of 2002 income. The credit to wage expense will reduce the expense account for 2003 to an amount equal to 2003 wages.

If the error was discovered in 2004, no entry would be required since the error self-corrects during 2003. The 2004 balances would be the same with or without the error.

The requirements of error analysis questions vary considerably. When asked for the effect of errors, be careful to determine the effect rather than the correction; they are opposite. The effect of revenue overstatement on income is over or plus; therefore, the correction to income is to subtract. Also distinguish between correcting/adjusting entries (which can be made in the accounts to correct the current period) and "worksheet entries" which adjust amounts reported in prior periods (i.e., journal entries are not recorded to correct nominal accounts of prior periods).

Correction of errors meets the criteria for prior period adjustments (refer to the outline of SFAS 16). They should be reported as adjustments to beginning retained earnings of single-year statements and to retained earnings of each year presented in comparative statements for the error effects prior to each of the years presented. Note that reporting of prior years' errors is required even if a journal entry is not required because the errors have self-corrected. Adjustments to the comparative years should be made to reflect retroactive application of the prior period adjustments to specific accounts affected.

The example below shows the revision of prior years' financial statements, including the format of the retained earnings statement for the $10,000 wage expense discussed above.

EXAMPLE: Assume $10,000 of wages were not recorded in Year 1; the error was not discovered until Year 3 after the books were closed for Year 2. The income tax rate was 30%.

Income Statement Effects

	Year 1	Year 2	Year 3
Wages expense	–$10,000	+$10,000	-0-
Income tax expense	+ 3,000	– 3,000	-0-
Net income	+$ 7,000	– 7,000	-0-

Comparative Income Statement
Issued in Year 3, for Year 2 and Year 3

	Year 2 Restated	Year 3
Wages expense	($ xxxx –10,000)	$ xxxx
Income tax expense	($ xxx + 3,000)	$ xxxx
Net income	($ xxx + 7,000)	$ xxxx

Balance Sheet

	Year 1	Year 2	Year 3
Wages payable	–$10,000	-0-	-0-
Taxes payable	+ 3,000	-0-	-0-
Retained earnings	+ 7,000	-0-	-0-

Comparative Retained Earnings Statement
Issued in Year 3, for Year 2 and Year 3

	Year 2 as restated	Year 3
Beginning balance	$ xxxx	$ xxxx
Prior period adjustment--Understatement of wages expense (net of tax, $3,000)	– 7,000	--
Retained earnings as adjusted	$ xxxx	$ xxxx
Net income as corrected	xxxx	xxxx
Dividends	(xxxx)	(xxxx)
Ending retained earnings	$ xxxx	$ xxxx

Inventory errors have an impact on both the balance sheet and the income statement. Inventory errors include a misstatement of the ending inventory balance, which is followed by a misstatement of the beginning balance for the next period, or an inventory error could be a misstatement of purchases for the period. The analysis of inventory errors in a periodic inventory system is facilitated by setting up a statement of cost of good sold. The statement of cost of good sold shows the relationship between the inventory and purchases accounts and the impact of incorrect amounts. The four examples shown below use the statement of cost of goods sold to analyze different inventory errors. Items that are correct are identified by an "OK," while items that are incorrect are listed as overstated (over) or understated (under).

INVENTORY ERRORS

	Case #1 (Overstated Inventory Count)		Case #2 (Understated Inventory Count)	
	2002	2003	2002	2003
Beginning inventory	OK	Over	OK	Under
+ Purchases	OK	OK	OK	OK
Goods available for sale	OK	Over	OK	Under
– Ending inventory*	Over	OK	Under	OK
Cost of goods sold	Under	Over	Over	Under
Net income	Over	Under	Under	Over
Retained earnings	Over	OK	Under	OK
Accounts payable	OK	OK	OK	OK

*   *Determined by physical count.*

	Case #3 (Overstated Purchases**)		Case #4 (Understated Purchases***)	
	2002	2003	2002	2003
Beginning inventory	OK	OK	OK	Under
+ Purchases	Over	Under	Under	Over
Goods available for sale	Over	Under	Under	OK
– Ending inventory*	OK	OK	Under	OK
Cost of goods sold	Over	Under	OK	OK
Net income	Under	Over	OK	OK
Retained earnings	Under	OK	OK	OK
Accounts payable	Over	OK	Under	OK

*   *Determined by physical count.*
**   *Vendor shipped goods FOB destination. Goods were not received by 12/31, but recorded as purchases and not included in physical inventory count.*
*** *Vendor shipped goods FOB shipping point prior to 12/31, but not recorded as purchases or included in physical inventory count.*

MULTIPLE-CHOICE QUESTIONS (1-11)

1. Loeb Corp. frequently borrows from the bank in order to maintain sufficient operating cash. The following loans were at a 12% interest rate, with interest payable at maturity. Loeb repaid each loan on its scheduled maturity date.

Date of loan	Amount	Maturity date	Term of loan
11/1/01	$ 5,000	10/31/02	1 year
2/1/02	15,000	7/31/02	6 months
5/1/02	8,000	1/31/03	9 months

Loeb records interest expense when the loans are repaid. As a result, interest expense of $1,500 was recorded in 2002. If no correction is made, by what amount would 2002 interest expense be understated?
- a. $540
- b. $620
- c. $640
- d. $720

2. During 2002, Paul Company discovered that the ending inventories reported on its financial statements were incorrect by the following amounts:

2000	$60,000 understated
2001	75,000 overstated

Paul uses the periodic inventory system to ascertain year-end quantities that are converted to dollar amounts using the FIFO cost method. Prior to any adjustments for these errors and ignoring income taxes, Paul's retained earnings at January 1, 2002 would be
- a. Correct.
- b. $ 15,000 overstated.
- c. $ 75,000 overstated.
- d. $135,000 overstated.

3. Tack, Inc. reported a retained earnings balance of $150,000 at December 31, 2001. In June 2002, Tack discovered that merchandise costing $40,000 had not been included in inventory in its 2001 financial statements. Tack has a 30% tax rate. What amount should Tack report as adjusted beginning retained earnings in its statement of retained earnings at December 31, 2002?
- a. $190,000
- b. $178,000
- c. $150,000
- d. $122,000

4. Conn Co. reported a retained earnings balance of $400,000 at December 31, 2001. In August 2002, Conn determined that insurance premiums of $60,000 for the three-year period beginning January 1, 2001, had been paid and fully expensed in 2001. Conn has a 30% income tax rate. What amount should Conn report as adjusted beginning retained earnings in its 2002 statement of retained earnings?
- a. $420,000
- b. $428,000
- c. $440,000
- d. $442,000

5. Lore Co. changed from the cash basis of accounting to the accrual basis of accounting during 2002. The cumulative effect of this change should be reported in Lore's 2002 financial statements as a
- a. Prior period adjustment resulting from the correction of an error.
- b. Prior period adjustment resulting from the change in accounting principle.
- c. Component of income before extraordinary item.
- d. Component of income after extraordinary item.

6. Bren Co.'s beginning inventory at January 1, 2002, was understated by $26,000, and its ending inventory was overstated by $52,000. As a result, Bren's cost of goods sold for 2002 was
- a. Understated by $26,000.
- b. Overstated by $26,000.
- c. Understated by $78,000.
- d. Overstated by $78,000.

7. On January 2, 2002, Air, Inc. agreed to pay its former president $300,000 under a deferred compensation arrangement. Air should have recorded this expense in 2001 but did not do so. Air's reported income tax expense would have been $70,000 lower in 2001 had it properly accrued this deferred compensation. In its December 31, 2002 financial statements, Air should adjust the beginning balance of its retained earnings by a
- a. $230,000 credit.
- b. $230,000 debit.
- c. $300,000 credit.
- d. $370,000 debit.

8. Net income is understated if, in the first year, estimated salvage value is excluded from the depreciation computation when using the

	Straight-line method	Production or use method
a.	Yes	No
b.	Yes	Yes
c.	No	No
d.	No	Yes

9. At the end of 2001, Ritzcar Co. failed to accrue sales commissions earned during 2001 but paid in 2002. The error was not repeated in 2002. What was the effect of this error on 2001 ending working capital and on the 2002 ending retained earnings balance?

	2001 ending working capital	2002 ending retained earnings
a.	Overstated	Overstated
b.	No effect	Overstated
c.	No effect	No effect
d.	Overstated	No effect

10. On December 31, 2002, special insurance costs, incurred but unpaid, were not recorded. If these insurance costs were related to work in process, what is the effect of the omission on accrued liabilities and retained earnings in the December 31, 2002 balance sheet?

	Accrued liabilities	Retained earnings
a.	No effect	No effect
b.	No effect	Overstated
c.	Understated	No effect
d.	Understated	Overstated

11. Which of the following errors could result in an overstatement of both current assets and stockholders' equity?
- a. An understatement of accrued sales expenses.
- b. Noncurrent note receivable principal is misclassified as a current asset.
- c. Annual depreciation on manufacturing machinery is understated.
- d. Holiday pay expense for administrative employees is misclassified as manufacturing overhead.

PROBLEM

Problem 1   (40 to 50 minutes)

Cord Corp., a nonpublic enterprise, requires audited financial statements for credit purposes. After making normal adjusting entries, but before closing the accounting records for the year ended December 31, 2002, Cord's controller prepared the following financial statements for 2002:

Cord Corp.
STATEMENT OF FINANCIAL POSITION
December 31, 2002

Assets	
Cash	$1,225,000
Marketable equity securities	125,000
Accounts receivable	460,000
Allowance for doubtful accounts	(55,000)
Inventories	530,000
Property and equipment	620,000
Accumulated depreciation	(280,000)
Total assets	$2,625,000
Liabilities and Stockholders' Equity	
Accounts payable and accrued liabilities	$1,685,000
Income tax payable	110,000
Common stock, $20 par	300,000
Additional paid-in capital	75,000
Retained earnings	455,000
Total liabilities and stockholders' equity	$2,625,000

Cord Corp.
STATEMENT OF INCOME
For the Year Ended December 31, 2002

Net sales	$1,700,000
Operating expenses:	
Cost of sales	570,000
Selling and administrative	448,000
Depreciation	42,000
Total operating expenses	1,060,000
Income before income tax	640,000
Income tax expense	192,000
Net income	$ 448,000

Cord's tax rate for all income items was 30% for all affected years, and it made estimated tax payments when due. Cord has been profitable in the past and expects results in the future to be similar to 2002. During the course of the audit, the following additional information (not considered when the above statements were prepared) was obtained:

1.   The investment portfolio consists of short-term investments, classified as available-for-sale, for which total market value equaled cost at December 31, 2001. On February 2, 2002, Cord sold one investment with a carrying value of $100,000 for $130,000. The total of the sale proceeds was credited to the investment account.

2.   At December 31, 2002, the market value of the remaining securities in the portfolio was $142,000.

3.   The $530,000 inventory total, which was based on a physical count at December 31, 2002, was priced at cost. Subsequently, it was determined that the inventory cost was overstated by $66,000. At December 31, 2002, the inventory's market value approximated the adjusted cost.

4.   Pollution control devices costing $48,000, which is high in relation to the cost of the original equipment, were installed on December 29, 2001, and were charged to repairs in 2001.

5.   The original equipment referred to in Item 4, which had a remaining useful life of six years on December 20, 2001, is being depreciated by the straight-line method for both financial and tax reporting.

6.   A lawsuit was filed against Cord in October 2002 claiming damages of $250,000. Cord's legal counsel believes that an unfavorable outcome is probable, and a reasonable estimate of the court's award to the plaintiff is $60,000, which will be paid in 2003 if the case is settled.

7.   Cord determined that its accumulated benefits obligation under the pension plan exceeded the fair value of plan assets by $40,000 at December 31, 2002. Cord has unrecognized prior service cost of $50,000 at December 31, 2002. Cord funds the total pension expense each year.

Required:

Prepare journal entries, without explanations, to record the effects of the foregoing data on Cord's accounting records at December 31, 2002. Do **not** prepare corrected financial statements for 2002. The journal entries should be numbered to correspond with the numbers in the additional information. Include as the last entry any necessary adjustments to the 2002 income tax expense, and support your computations for this entry.

MULTIPLE-CHOICE ANSWERS

1. a __ __	4. b __ __	7. b __ __	10. c __ __	1st: __/11 = __%	
2. c __ __	5. a __ __	8. b __ __	11. d __ __	2nd: __/11 = __%	
3. b __ __	6. c __ __	9. d __ __			

MULTIPLE-CHOICE ANSWER EXPLANATIONS

B. Error Correction

1. (a) The correct amount of 2002 interest expense is $2,040, as computed below.

11/1/01 note	
Interest from 1/1/02 to 10/31/02	
($5,000 x 12% x 10/12)	$500
2/1/02 note	
Interest from 2/1/02 to 7/31/02	
($15,000 x 12% x 6/12)	900
5/1/02 note	
Interest from 5/1/02 to 12/31/02	
($8,000 x 12% x 8/12)	640
Total 2002 interest	$2,040

Since interest expense of $1,500 was recorded, 2002 interest expense was understated by $540 ($2,040 – $1,500).

2. (c) The error in understating the 2000 ending inventory would have reversed by 1/1/02 (2000 income understated by $60,000; 2001 income overstated by $60,000). The error in overstating the 2001 ending inventory would **not** have been reversed by 1/1/02. This error overstates both 2001 income and the 1/1/02 retained earnings balance by $75,000.

3. (b) A correction of an error is treated as a prior period adjustment, recorded in the year the error is discovered, and is reported in the financial statements as an adjustment to the beginning balance of retained earnings. The adjustment is reported net of the related tax effect. In this case the net-of-tax effect is $28,000 [$40,000 – ($30% x $40,000)]. This should **increase** beginning retained earnings because the understatement of 12/31/01 inventory would have resulted in an overstatement of cost of goods sold and therefore an understatement of retained earnings. Thus, the adjustment 1/1/02 retained earnings is $178,000 ($150,000 + $28,000). Tack's journal entry to record the adjustment is

Inventory	40,000	
Retained earnings		28,000
Taxes payable		12,000

4. (b) A correction of an error is treated as a prior period adjustment and is reported in the financial statements as an adjustment to the beginning balance of retained earnings in the year the error is discovered. The adjustment is reported net of the related tax effect. In 2001, insurance expense of $60,000 was recorded. The correct 2001 insurance expense was $20,000 ($60,000 x 1/3). Therefore, before taxes, 1/1/02 retained earnings is understated by $40,000. The net of tax effect is $28,000 [$40,000 – (30% x $40,000)], so the adjusted beginning retained earnings is $428,000 ($400,000 + $28,000).

5. (a) A change in accounting principle is a change from one **generally accepted** principle to another **generally accepted** principle. A correction of an error is the correction of a mathematical mistake, a mistake in the application of an accounting principle, an oversight or misuse of existing facts, or **a change from an unacceptable prin-**ciple to a generally accepted one. Therefore, a switch from the cash basis (unacceptable) to the accrual basis (acceptable) is a correction of an error reported as a prior period adjustment.

6. (c) The requirement is to determine the effect of inventory errors on cost of goods sold. The effect of the errors on Bren's 2002 cost of goods sold (CGS) is illustrated below.

BI	– $26,000	CGS understated $26,000
+ P		
CGAS		
– EI	(+ $52,000)	CGS understated 52,000
CGS		CGS understated $78,000

Beginning inventory is the starting point for the CGS computation, so BI errors have a direct effect on CGS. The understatement of BI ($26,000) causes an **understatement** of goods available for sale (CGAS) and thus of CGS. Ending inventory is subtracted in the CGS computation, so EI errors have an inverse effect on CGS. The overstatement of EI ($52,000) means that too much was subtracted in the CGS computation, causing another **understatement** of CGS. Therefore, CGS is understated by a total of $78,000.

7. (b) The failure to record the $300,000 of deferred compensation expense in 2001 is considered an error. The profession requires that the correction of an error be treated as a prior period adjustment. Thus, the requirement is to determine the retroactive adjustment that should be made to the beginning balance of the retained earnings for 2002 (**including** any income tax effect). The net adjustment to beginning retained earnings would be a debit for $230,000 ($300,000 less the income tax benefit of $70,000).

8. (b) The depreciable base used to compute depreciation expense under both the straight-line and production methods is equal to the cost less estimated salvage value of the asset. Depreciation expense is overstated and net income is, therefore, understated when the estimated salvage value is excluded from the depreciation computation under both of these methods.

9. (d) The entry Ritzcar should have made to accrue sales commissions earned but unpaid at the end of its 2001 fiscal year is

Commission expense	xxx	
Commissions payable		xxx

Since Commissions payable is a current liability, the 2001 ending working capital is overstated due to Ritzcar's failure to record this entry. Since this error was not repeated at the end of Ritzcar's 2002 fiscal year, the income impact of the 2001 error "self-corrected" during 2002, when Ritzcar recorded both the earned but unpaid 2001 commissions plus the 2002 earned commissions. Therefore, the 2002 ending retained earnings would not be impacted by the error.

10.   (c)   A liability is accrued when an obligation to pay or perform services has been incurred. This is the case even if the liability will not be satisfied until a future date. Therefore, accrued liabilities will be understated on the December 31, 2002 balance sheet because the special insurance costs were not recorded. However, there will be no effect on the December 31, 2002, balance of retained earnings because these costs relate to work in process, and work in process does not affect net income currently. Please note that if the special insurance costs related to goods that were sold, cost of goods sold would have been understated that would have caused both net income and retained earnings to be overstated.

11.   (d)   The classification of holiday pay expense for administrative employees as manufacturing overhead would result in the capitalization of some or all of these costs as a component of ending inventory, while these costs should be expensed as incurred. This error could overstate ending inventory, a current asset. The overstatement of ending inventory also understates the cost of goods sold (Beginning inventories + Net purchases – Ending inventories = Cost of goods sold), and overstates net income and stockholders' equity. The understatement of accrued sales expenses would not affect current assets. The misclassification of the noncurrent note receivable principal as a current asset would have no impact on stockholders' equity. The understatement of depreciation on **manufacturing** machinery would understate the overhead added to inventories, a current asset.

SOLUTION GUIDE

Problem 1   Correcting Journal Entries

1.   This problem requires the preparation of correcting journal entries necessary to reflect the effects of seven items of data given in the problem. In addition, an entry to adjust 2002 income tax expense is required. The solutions approach is to simply go through the additional data, preparing the correcting entry for each item as you come to it.

1.1   On the sale of MES, Cord debited **cash** and credited **MES** for $130,000. It should have credited **MES** for the carrying value of $100,000 and also credited **gain on sale** for $30,000 ($130,000 proceeds less $100,000 carrying value). Therefore, the correcting entry must debit **MES** for $30,000 (to offset the additional $30,000 credited to that account) and credit **gain on sale** for the same amount.

1.2   In the balance sheet given, the MES are reported at $125,000. The first correcting entry included a $30,000 debit to MES. Therefore, the adjusted carrying value is $155,000 ($125,000 + $30,000). Since market value is $142,000, an **unrealized loss** of $13,000 ($155,000 – $142,000) must be recorded as a credit to an Adjustment to Market account or directly to the MES account and a debit to unrealized loss. Because these securities are carried in an available-for-sale portfolio, the unrealized loss is reported as an element of comprehensive income net of tax in the section termed other comprehensive income and part of accumulated other comprehensive income in the stockholders' equity section of the balance sheet.

1.3   Cord overstated the 12/31/02 inventory by $66,000. Therefore, **inventories** must be credited for $66,000. Since ending inventory was used to compute cost of sales (cost of goods available for sale less ending inventory equals cost of sales), the inventory error means **cost of sales** was understated by $66,000, and therefore this account must be debited.

1.4   The pollution control devices (cost of $48,000) should have been recorded as an asset instead of being expensed in 2001. Therefore, **property and equipment** must be debited for $48,000 in the correcting entry. For tax purposes, apparently the entire $48,000 was also expensed. Thus, Kern owes additional taxes for 2001 of $14,400 ($48,000 x 30%). This amount is credited to **income tax payable**. The prior period adjustment, net of the tax effect ($48,000 – $14,400 = $33,600) is credited to **retained earnings,** since a prior year's earnings (2001) was understated by that amount.

1.5   **Depreciation expense** on the pollution control devices must be recorded for 2002, with an offsetting credit to **accumulated depreciation**. 2002 depreciation is $8,000 ($48,000 x 1/6).

1.6   The **lawsuit liability** must be accrued by debiting **loss on lawsuit** and crediting the liability account because it is both **probable** that a liability has been incurred at 12/31/02 and the amount of the liability is **reasonably estimable** ($60,000).

1.7   SFAS 87 states that a minimum liability must be reported for the excess of the accumulated benefit obligation over the fair value of the plan assets. The amount to be **recorded** is the minimum liability required to be **reported** ($40,000 in this case) plus prepaid pension cost or minus accrued pension cost. There is no prepaid/accrued pension cost in this situation because Cord funds the total pension expense each year, so the amount to be recorded is $40,000. When recording the minimum liability, a **pension liability** account is credited. The debit is to the **intangible asset** account and/or the **contra equity** account. The contra equity account must be **used** if the debit ($40,000) exceeds the unrecognized prior service cost ($50,000). In this case, it does not, so the entire amount is debited to the intangible asset account.

2.   The final entry required is necessary to adjust 2002 income tax expense.

2.1   The first step is to compute the adjustment to income taxes payable and income tax expense. Income before taxes was reported at $640,000. This amount did not include the gain on sale of MES ($30,000), the increase in cost of goods sold ($66,000), or the increase in depreciation expense ($8,000). After adjusting for these items, **taxable income** is $596,000 ($640,000 + $30,000 – $66,000 – $8,000). Note that the unrealized loss on MES ($13,000) and the accrued loss on lawsuit ($60,000) does not affect **taxable** income because it is not deductible on the tax return until realized. The current portion of income tax expense and income taxes payable is therefore $178,800 (30% x $596,000).

2.2   The unrealized loss on MES ($13,000) and the lawsuit loss ($60,000) are both temporary differences that result in future deductible amounts. A **deferred tax asset** and reduction in income tax expense should be **recognized** for these future deductible amounts. Therefore, the deferred tax asset and reduction in income tax expense is measured using the tax rate of 30% (30% x $73,000 = $21,900). Corrected total income tax expense is $156,900.

2.3   The adjustment to income tax payable is $13,200 ($192,000 **originally recorded less the correct amount of $178,800**). **Note** that the balance in the income tax payable account of $110,000 at 12/31/02 is net of payments made during the year.

2.4   The adjustment to get the correct total **income tax expense** can be plugged into the entry now that the adjustments to income tax payable and deferred tax asset have been computed, or it can be computed as follows. Income tax expense was reported at $192,000. The correct 2002 income tax expense is $156,900 ($178,800 current portion of tax expense less the $21,900 reduction from the future deductible amounts). Therefore, income tax expense must be adjusted with a $35,100 credit ($192,000 – $156,900).

UNOFFICIAL ANSWER

Problem 1   Correcting Journal Entries

Cord Corp.
ADJUSTING JOURNAL ENTRIES
December 31, 2002
(Explanations not required)

	Dr.	Cr.
(1)		
Marketable equity securities	$ 30,000	
Realized gain on sale of marketable equity securities		$ 30,000 [a]
(2)		
Unrealized loss on marketable equity securities (other comprehensive income)	13,000	
Adjustment to reduce marketable equity securities to market value		13,000 [b]
(3)		
Cost of sales	66,000	
Inventories		66,000
(4)		
Property and equipment	48,000	
Income tax payable		14,400 [c]
Retained earnings		33,600 [c]
(5)		
Depreciation	8,000	
Accumulated depreciation		8,000 [d]
(6)		
Estimated loss from lawsuit	60,000	
Estimated liability from lawsuit		60,000
(7)		
Deferred pension cost	40,000	
Additional pension liability		40,000
(8)		
Deferred tax asset	21,900 [i]	
Income tax payable	13,200 [ii]	
Income tax expense		35,100 [iii]

Supporting Computations for Number 8

Corrected total income tax expense for 2002			
Income before income tax, as reported			$640,000
Add adjustment increasing income			
Realized gain on sale of securities			30,000 [1]
			670,000
Deduct adjustments decreasing income			
Increase cost of sales for inventory overstatement	$66,000		
Depreciation on pollution control devices	8,000		74,000
Adjusted taxable income before income tax			$596,000
Corrected current portion income tax expense and income taxes payable ($596,000 x 30%)			$178,800
Deferred income tax benefits—based on following temporary differences:			
Lawsuit expected to be settled in 2003	$60,000 [6]		
Unrealized loss on short-term marketable equity securities	13,000 [2]		
Total future deductible amounts	$73,000		

[i]	Deferred tax benefit of future deductible amounts ($73,000 x 30%)	21,900
	Corrected total income tax expense	$156,900
[ii]	Income tax expense as reported (all current, no deferred)	$192,000
	Corrected income tax payable and income tax expense	178,800
		$ 13,200
[iii]	Income tax expense, as reported	$192,000
	Corrected total income tax expense	156,900
		$ 35,100

Explanations of Amounts

[a]	Gain on sale of marketable equity securities	
	Selling price	$130,000
	Cost	100,000
	Gain	$ 30,000

[b] Adjustment to reduce marketable equity securities to market value

Marketable equity securities, at cost		
Balance, 2/2/02 as reported		$125,000
Adjustment for recording error		30,000
Adjusted balance, 12/31/02		155,000
Market valuation, 12/31/02		142,000
Adjustment required, 12/31/02		$ 13,000

[c] Prior year adjustment for pollution control devices

Cost of installation, 12/29/01	$ 48,000
Deduct income tax effect ($48,000 x 30%)	14,400
Credit adjustment to retained earnings, 1/1/02	$ 33,600

[d] Depreciation for 2002 on pollution control devices

Cost of the installation on 12/29/01	$ 48,000
Depreciation for 2002 ($48,000 ÷ 6 years)	$ 8,000

Keep practicing! Wiley's CPA Examination Review Software has over 2,800 questions.

Available at www.wiley.com/cpa

C. Accounting Changes

1. Changes in Accounting Principle

One type of accounting change that may occur is a change in accounting principle. A change in accounting principle occurs when there is a change from one generally accepted accounting principle to another. A change from an accounting principle that is not generally accepted to a generally accepted method is a correction of an error, not a change in principle.

Changes in accounting principles (or the method of applying them) must be justified by management unless they are made in order to comply with a FASB pronouncement. Presumption exists that, once adopted, accounting principles should not be changed for events and transactions of a similar type. Changes in accounting principle may be treated as a retroactive or as a cumulative adjustment to the financial statements. Study the outline of APB 20.

a. Retroactive-effect-type changes in accounting principle

A retroactive change in accounting principle is determined by computing the effect on beginning retained earnings of applying the new principle to affected prior years and reporting the amount net of tax in the retained earnings statement as an adjustment to the beginning balance. Additionally, financial statements from earlier periods that are presented with the current period's FS must be retroactively restated. Retroactive restatement means redoing all statements presented as if they had originally been prepared using the new accounting principle. Any part of the cumulative effect that is attributed to financial statements of prior years that are not being presented in the current period should be an adjustment of retained earnings of the earliest period being presented.

There are five special changes that require retroactive restatement of all periods presented as if the new method had been used in all prior periods. These five special changes are

(1) Change from LIFO to another inventory method
(2) Change in method of accounting for long-term contracts
(3) Change to or from the full cost method of accounting for exploration costs in the extractive industries
(4) Any change made by a company first issuing financial statements to the public for the purpose of obtaining additional equity capital or effecting a business combination or registering securities (APB 20)
(5) Change for which the retroactive approach is mandated by an authoritative pronouncement

When a retroactive restatement is made, the reasons for the change must be disclosed. The effects on net income and earnings per share should also be disclosed for each period presented.

b. Cumulative-effect-type changes in accounting principle

All other changes in principle are accounted for as current changes in accordance with the cumulative effect method. When a change in accounting principle is accounted for as a current change, the entire cumulative effect of the change is reported in the current period's financial statements. The entire cumulative effect would be recorded as an adjustment to an income statement account, and reported as a special item displayed after extraordinary items on the income statement. The cumulative effect should be reported net of tax. The following steps summarize the procedures to account for an accounting change under the cumulative effect method:

1. **Compute** the prior years' effect of the change on retained earnings at the beginning of the year in which the change is made.
2. **Use** the new principle in determining the current year's net income.
3. **Report** the effect of the new method on beginning retained earnings less tax effects as "cumulative effect on prior years of new accounting method (described), net of tax" to be displayed after extraordinary items and before net income on the income statement.
4. **Present** comparative years' data as previously reported (no restatement).

It is important to note that under the cumulative effect method there is no restatement of the prior year's financial statements. Instead, "pro forma" (as if) data concerning EPS and net income must be presented as supplementary information for all past years being reported upon. These pro forma data are presented as if the new accounting method had been used in the determination of prior years' EPS and net incomes. The retroactive methodology described above would be used to determine pro forma amounts. Thus, the face of the income statement must disclose the net income and EPS under both the retroactive and cumulative methods. The disclosure of the effects of both methods is intended to provide supplementary information to the users of the financial statements. The following illustrates the pro forma disclosure:

PRO FORMA AMOUNTS ASSUMING RETROACTIVE APPLICATION OF NEW METHOD

	20X2	*20X1*
Income from continuing operations	$xxx	$xxx
Basic earnings per share	x	x
Diluted earnings per share	x	x
Net income	$xxx	xxx
Basic earnings per share	x	x
Diluted earnings per share	x	x

There are two exceptions to be considered when using the cumulative effect method.

1. Changes in inventory method **to** LIFO, because the cumulative effect is usually not determinable. For changes to LIFO, no recognition is given to any cumulative effect associated with the change. The base year inventory for all subsequent LIFO calculations is the opening inventory under the old method in the year LIFO is adopted.
2. The application of a depreciation method to **newly** acquired assets that is different than the method that has been applied to existing assets. No cumulative effect results from this type of change.

The following example is adapted from APB 20. Assume a change in 2002 from accelerated to straight-line depreciation. It describes the

1. Depreciation effect per year (decrease in expense, increase in income)
2. Depreciation effect, net of tax (constant 40%)

Year	*Excess of accelerated depreciation over straight-line depreciation*	*Excess less tax effect*
Prior to 1998	$ 20,000	$ 12,000
1998	80,000	48,000
1999	70,000	42,000
2000	50,000	30,000
2001	30,000	18,000
Total at beginning of 2001	$250,000	$150,000

Example income statements, EPS disclosures, and pro forma retroactive disclosures are presented below for 2002 and 2001. (Assume 1,000,000 shares outstanding.)

	2002	*2001*
Income before extraordinary item and cumulative effect of a change in accounting principle	$1,200,000	$1,100,000
Extraordinary item (description)	(40,000)	100,000
Cumulative effect on prior years (to December 31, 2001) of changing to a different depreciation method (net of tax $100,000)	150,000	
Net income	$1,310,000	$1,200,000
Earnings per common share		
Income before extraordinary item and cumulative effect of a change in accounting principle	$ 1.20	$1.10
Extraordinary item	(0.04)	0.10
Cumulative effect on prior years (to December 31, 2001) of changing to a different depreciation method	0.15	
Net income	$ 1.31	$1.20

Pro forma amounts assuming the new depreciation method is applied retroactively

	2002	*2001*
Income before extraordinary item	$1,200,000	$1,118,000
Earnings per common share	$1.20	$1.12 (rounded)
Net income	$1,160,000	$1,218,000
Earnings per common share	$1.16	$1.22 (rounded)

Special points to note about the preceding example include

1. The 2002 income before extraordinary items of $1,200,000 is the same as pro forma income for that year, because the new accounting method was used in 2002.
2. The 2002 net income is different from the 2002 pro forma net income because the pro forma amount does not include the cumulative effect. The amounts that comprise the cumulative effect are reported as pro forma amounts in the years to which they pertain.
3. In 2001, both incomes in the income statement differ from those in the pro forma data by $18,000 (depreciation less tax effects).

4. If this company had a complex capital structure, all EPS amounts, actual and pro forma, would have to be reported as both basic EPS and diluted EPS.

2. **Changes in Accounting Estimates**

A change in estimate occurs when, based upon new information or experience, a better estimate may be made. Some examples that may require a change in estimate are changes in estimates of useful lives, salvage value, collectibility of receivables, etc. Changes in estimates should be treated prospectively—that is, no retroactive restatement. For example, if the useful life of an asset is increased from ten years to fifteen years during year six, the remaining depreciable cost is amortized over the years six through fifteen.

Sometimes an event may have characteristics of both a change in accounting principle and a change in estimate; in these cases the change should be treated as a change in estimate.

3. **Change in Reporting Entity**

The final type of accounting change which may occur is a change in reporting entity. A change in reporting entity occurs when a change in the structure of the organization is made which results in financial statements that represent a different or changed entity. Some examples of a change in reporting entity include presenting consolidated statements in place of individual statements, a pooling of interests, a change in subsidiaries, or a change in the use of the equity method for an investment.

A change in reporting entity should be disclosed by retroactively restating all of the prior period financial statements presented. A disclosure of the type of change and the reasons for the change should be added to the financial statements in the year of the change. The disclosure should also include the effect of the change on the net income before extraordinary items, net income, and earnings per share.

The following chart summarizes the three types of accounting changes and the related financial statement treatment and disclosure requirements:

TYPES OF ACCOUNTING CHANGES

Type of accounting change	Definition	Financial statement treatment	Financial statement disclosure
1. Change in accounting principle	Change from the use of one generally accepted accounting principle to another generally accepted accounting principle	**Cumulative:** Required for all items not requiring retroactive treatment. Record the entire effects of the change net of tax in the current period. Record after extraordinary items on the income statement. No prior period restatement occurs.	Income statement must disclose pro forma net income and EPS for all periods presented, as if the retroactive method had been used.
		Retroactive: Required for 5 special changes listed in module. Restatement of all prior period financial statements presented is required.	Disclose the effect of the change on prior net incomes and EPS presented in the year of the change.
2. Change in estimate	Change of estimated FS amount based on new information or experience	**Prospective:** Report the current period's financial statements in accordance with the new method. No restatement of prior period information is required.	Disclose the effect on income before extraordinary items, net income, and related per share amounts if the change affects several future periods.
3. Change in reporting entity	Change that results in the financial statements representing a different entity	**Retroactive:** Restate all prior periods presented.	Disclose the type of change and the reasons for the change and the related effects on net income and EPS for all prior periods presented.

MULTIPLE-CHOICE QUESTIONS (1-23)

1. On January 1, 2000, Bray Company purchased for $240,000 a machine with a useful life of ten years and no salvage value. The machine was depreciated by the double-declining balance method and the carrying amount of the machine was $153,600 on December 31, 2001. Bray changed retroactively to the straight-line method on January 1, 2002. Bray can justify the change. What should be the depreciation expense on this machine for the year ended December 31, 2002?

    a. $15,360
    b. $19,200
    c. $24,000
    d. $30,720

Items 2 and 3 are based on the following:

On January 1, 2000, Warren Co. purchased a $600,000 machine, with a five-year useful life and no salvage value. The machine was depreciated by an accelerated method for book and tax purposes. The machine's carrying amount was $240,000 on December 31, 2001. On January 1, 2002, Warren changed retroactively to the straight-line method for financial statement purposes. Warren can justify the change. Warren's income tax rate is 30%.

2. In its 2002 income statement, what amount should Warren report as the cumulative effect of this change?

    a. $120,000
    b. $ 84,000
    c. $ 36,000
    d. $0

3. On January 1, 2002, what amount should Warren report as deferred income tax liability as a result of the change?

    a. $120,000
    b. $ 72,000
    c. $ 36,000
    d. $0

4. On January 2, 2002, to better reflect the variable use of its only machine, Holly, Inc. elected to change its method of depreciation from the straight-line method to the units of production method. The original cost of the machine on January 2, 2000, was $50,000, and its estimated life was ten years. Holly estimates that the machine's total life is 50,000 machine hours.

Machine hours usage was 8,500 during 2000 and 3,500 during 2001.

Holly's income tax rate is 30%. Holly should report the accounting change in its 2002 financial statements as a(n)

    a. Cumulative effect of a change in accounting principle of $2,000 in its income statement.
    b. Adjustment to beginning retained earnings of $2,000.
    c. Cumulative effect of a change in accounting principle of $1,400 in its income statement.
    d. Adjustment to beginning retained earnings of $1,400.

5. The cumulative effect of a change in accounting principle should be recorded separately as a component of income after continuing operations, when the change is from the

    a. Cash basis of accounting for vacation pay to the accrual basis.

    b. Straight-line method of depreciation for previously recorded assets to the double declining balance method.
    c. Presentation of statements of individual companies to their inclusion in consolidated statements.
    d. Completed-contract method of accounting for long-term construction-type contracts to the percentage-of-completion method.

6. When a company changes from the straight-line method of depreciation for previously recorded assets to the double-declining balance method, which of the following should be reported?

	Cumulative effects of change in accounting principle	Pro forma effects of retroactive application
a.	No	No
b.	No	Yes
c.	Yes	Yes
d.	Yes	No

Items 7 and 8 are based on the following:

During 2002, Orca Corp. decided to change from the FIFO method of inventory valuation to the weighted-average method. Inventory balances under each method were as follows:

	FIFO	*Weighted-average*
January 1, 2002	$71,000	$77,000
December 31, 2002	79,000	83,000

Orca's income tax rate is 30%.

7. In its 2002 financial statements, what amount should Orca report as the cumulative effect of this accounting change?

    a. $2,800
    b. $4,000
    c. $4,200
    d. $6,000

8. Orca should report the cumulative effect of this accounting change as a(n)

    a. Prior period adjustment.
    b. Component of income from continuing operations.
    c. Extraordinary item.
    d. Component of income after extraordinary items.

9. On January 1, 2002, Roem Corp. changed its inventory method to FIFO from LIFO for both financial and income tax reporting purposes. The change resulted in a $500,000 increase in the January 1, 2002 inventory. Assume that the income tax rate for all years is 30%. The cumulative effect of the accounting change should be reported by Roem in its 2002

    a. Retained earnings statement as a $350,000 addition to the beginning balance.
    b. Income statement as a $350,000 cumulative effect of accounting change.
    c. Retained earnings statement as a $500,000 addition to the beginning balance.
    d. Income statement as a $500,000 cumulative effect of accounting change.

10. Is the cumulative effect of an inventory pricing change on prior years earnings reported separately between extraordinary items and net income for a change from

	LIFO to weighted-average	*FIFO to weighted-average*
a.	Yes	Yes
b.	Yes	No
c.	No	No
d.	No	Yes

11. On August 31, 2002, Harvey Co. decided to change from the FIFO periodic inventory system to the weighted-average periodic inventory system. Harvey is on a calendar year basis. The cumulative effect of the change is determined

   a. As of January 1, 2002.
   b. As of August 31, 2002.
   c. During the eight months ending August 31, 2002, by a weighted-average of the purchases.
   d. During 2002 by a weighted-average of the purchases.

12. In 2002, Brighton Co. changed from the individual item approach to the aggregate approach in applying the lower of FIFO cost or market to inventories. The cumulative effect of this change should be reported in Brighton's financial statements as a

   a. Prior period adjustment, with separate disclosure.
   b. Component of income from continuing operations, with separate disclosure.
   c. Component of income from continuing operations, without separate disclosure.
   d. Component of income after continuing operations, with separate disclosure.

13. On January 1, 2002, Poe Construction, Inc. changed to the percentage-of-completion method of income recognition for financial statement reporting but not for income tax reporting. Poe can justify this change in accounting principle. As of December 31, 2001, Poe compiled data showing that income under the completed-contract method aggregated $700,000. If the percentage-of-completion method had been used, the accumulated income through December 31, 2001, would have been $880,000. Assuming an income tax rate of 40% for all years, the cumulative effect of this accounting change should be reported by Poe in the 2002

   a. Retained earnings statement as a $180,000 credit adjustment to the beginning balance.
   b. Income statement as a $180,000 credit.
   c. Retained earnings statement as a $108,000 credit adjustment to the beginning balance.
   d. Income statement as a $108,000 credit.

14. On January 1, 1999, Taft Co. purchased a patent for $714,000. The patent is being amortized over its remaining legal life of fifteen years expiring on January 1, 2014. During 2002, Taft determined that the economic benefits of the patent would not last longer than ten years from the date of acquisition. What amount should be reported in the balance sheet for the patent, net of accumulated amortization, at December 31, 2002?

   a. $428,400
   b. $489,600
   c. $504,000
   d. $523,600

15. On January 1, 1999, Flax Co. purchased a machine for $528,000 and depreciated it by the straight-line method using an estimated useful life of eight years with no salvage value. On January 1, 2002, Flax determined that the machine had a useful life of six years from the date of acquisition and will have a salvage value of $48,000. An accounting change was made in 2002 to reflect these additional data. The accumulated depreciation for this machine should have a balance at December 31, 2002 of

   a. $292,000
   b. $308,000
   c. $320,000
   d. $352,000

16. How should the effect of a change in accounting estimate be accounted for?

   a. By restating amounts reported in financial statements of prior periods.
   b. By reporting pro forma amounts for prior periods.
   c. As a prior period adjustment to beginning retained earnings.
   d. In the period of change and future periods if the change affects both.

17. During 2002, Krey Co. increased the estimated quantity of copper recoverable from its mine. Krey uses the units of production depletion method. As a result of the change, which of the following should be reported in Krey's 2002 financial statements?

	Cumulative effect of a change in accounting principle	*Pro forma effects of retroactive application of new depletion base*
a.	Yes	Yes
b.	Yes	No
c.	No	No
d.	No	Yes

18. Oak Co. offers a three-year warranty on its products. Oak previously estimated warranty costs to be 2% of sales. Due to a technological advance in production at the beginning of 2002, Oak now believes 1% of sales to be a better estimate of warranty costs. Warranty costs of $80,000 and $96,000 were reported in 2000 and 2001, respectively. Sales for 2002 were $5,000,000. What amount should be disclosed in Oak's 2002 financial statements as warranty expense?

   a. $ 50,000
   b. $ 88,000
   c. $100,000
   d. $138,000

19. For 2001, Pac Co. estimated its two-year equipment warranty costs based on $100 per unit sold in 1998. Experience during 2002 indicated that the estimate should have been based on $110 per unit. The effect of this $10 difference from the estimate is reported

   a. In 2002 income from continuing operations.
   b. As an accounting change, net of tax, below 2002 income from continuing operations.
   c. As an accounting change requiring 2001 financial statements to be restated.
   d. As a correction of an error requiring 2001 financial statements to be restated.

20. The effect of a change in accounting principle that is inseparable from the effect of a change in accounting estimate should be reported

   a. By restating the financial statements of all prior periods presented.
   b. As a correction of an error.

   c.   As a component of income from continuing operations, in the period of change and future periods if
the change affects both.

   d.   As a separate disclosure after income from continuing operations, in the period of change and future periods if the change affects both.

21. A company has included in its consolidated financial
statements this year a subsidiary acquired several years ago
that was appropriately excluded from consolidation last year.
This results in

   a.   An accounting change that should be reported prospectively.

   b.   An accounting change that should be reported by
restating the financial statements of all prior periods presented.

   c.   A correction of an error.

   d.   Neither an accounting change nor a correction of
an error.

22. Which of the following statements is correct regarding
accounting changes that result in financial statements that
are, in effect, the statements of a different reporting entity?

   a.   Cumulative-effect adjustments should be reported
as separate items on the financial statements pertaining to the year of change.

   b.   No restatements or adjustments are required if the
changes involve consolidated methods of accounting for subsidiaries.

   c.   No restatements or adjustments are required if the
changes involve the cost or equity methods of accounting for investments.

   d.   The financial statements of all prior periods presented should be restated.

23. At December 31, 2000, Off-Line Co. changed its
method of accounting for demo costs from writing off the
costs over two years to expensing the costs immediately.
Off-Line made the change in recognition of an increasing
number of demos placed with customers that did not result
in sales. Off-Line had deferred demo costs of $500,000 at
December 31, 1999, $300,000 of which were to be written
off in 2000 and the remainder in 2001. Off-Line's income
tax rate is 30%. In its 2000 income statement, what amount
should Off-Line report as cumulative effect of change in
accounting principle?

   a. $140,000

   b. $200,000

   c. $350,000

   d. $500,000

OTHER OBJECTIVE QUESTIONS

Problem 1   (15 to 25 minutes)

On January 2, 2002, Quo, Inc. hired Reed to be its controller. During the year, Reed, working closely with Quo's president and outside accountants, made changes in accounting policies, corrected several errors dating from 2001 and before, and instituted new accounting policies.

Quo's 2002 financial statements will be presented in comparative form with its 2001 financial statements.

Required:

Items 1 through 10 represent Quo's transactions. List A represents possible classifications of these transactions as: a change in accounting principle, a change in accounting estimate, a correction of an error in previously presented financial statements, or neither an accounting change nor an accounting error.

List B represents the general accounting treatment for these transactions. These treatments are:

- Cumulative effect approach—Include the cumulative effect of the adjustment resulting from the accounting change or error correction in the 2002 financial statements, and do **not** restate the 2001 financial statements.
- Retroactive restatement approach—Restate the 2001 financial statements and adjust 2001 beginning retained earnings if the error or change affects a period prior to 2001 financial statements.
- Prospective approach—Report 2002 and future financial statements on the new basis, but do **not** restate 2001 financial statements.

For each item, select one from List A and one from List B.

List A (Select one)	*List B (Select one)*
A. Change in accounting principle.	X. Cumulative effect approach.
B. Change in accounting estimate.	Y. Retroactive restatement approach.
C. Correction of an error in previously presented financial statements.	Z. Prospective approach.
D. Neither an accounting change nor an accounting error.	

Items to be answered

1. Quo manufactures heavy equipment to customer specifications on a contract basis. On the basis that it is preferable, accounting for these long-term contracts was switched from the completed-contract method to the percentage-of-completion method.

2. As a result of a production breakthrough, Quo determined that manufacturing equipment previously depreciated over fifteen years should be depreciated over twenty years.

3. The equipment that Quo manufactures is sold with a five-year warranty. Because of a production breakthrough, Quo reduced its computation of warranty costs from 3% of sales to 1% of sales.

4. Quo changed from LIFO to FIFO to account for its finished goods inventory.

5. Quo changed from FIFO to average cost to account for its raw materials and work in process inventories.

6. Quo sells extended service contracts on its products. Because related services are performed over several years, in 2002 Quo changed from the cash method to the accrual method of recognizing income from these service contracts.

7. During 2002, Quo determined that an insurance premium paid and entirely expensed in 2001 was for the period January 1, 2001, through January 1, 2003.

8. Quo changed its method of depreciating office equipment from an accelerated method to the straight-line method to more closely reflect costs in later years.

9. Quo instituted a pension plan for all employees in 2002 and adopted Statement of Financial Accounting Standards 87, *Employers' Accounting for Pensions*. Quo had not previously had a pension plan.

10. During 2002, Quo increased its investment in Worth, Inc. from a 10% interest, purchased in 2001, to 30%, and acquired a seat on Worth's board of directors. As a result of its increased investment, Quo changed its method of accounting for investment in subsidiary from the cost adjusted for fair value method to the equity method.

Problem 2   (15 to 25 minutes)

On January 2, 2002, Falk Co. hired a new controller. During the year, the controller, working closely with Falk's president and outside accountants, made changes in existing accounting policies, instituted new accounting policies, and corrected several errors dating from prior to 2002.

Falk's financial statements for the year ended December 31, 2002, will not be presented in comparative form with its 2001 financial statements.

Required:

Items 1 through 4 represent Falk's transactions.

List A represents possible classifications of these transactions as a change in accounting principle, a change in accounting estimate, correction of an error in previously presented financial statements, or neither an accounting change nor an error correction.

List B represents the general accounting treatment required for these transactions. These treatments are

- Cumulative effect approach—Include the cumulative effect of the adjustment resulting from the accounting change or error correction in the 2002 financial statements.
- Retroactive restatement approach—Adjust 2002 beginning retained earnings if the error or change affects a period prior to 2002.
- Prospective approach—Report 2002 and future financial statements on the new basis, but do not adjust beginning retained earnings or include the cumulative effect of the change in the 2002 income statements.

List A-Type of change (Select one)	*List B-General accounting treatment (Select one)*
A. Change in accounting principle.	X. Cumulative effect approach.
B. Change in accounting estimate.	Y. Retroactive restatement approach.
C. Correction of an error in previously presented in financial statements.	X. Prospective approach.
D. Neither an accounting change nor an error correction.	

For **Items 1 and 2**, select a classification for each transaction from List A and the general accounting treatment required to report the change from List B.

1. Falk manufactures customized equipment to customer specifications on a contract basis. Falk changed its method of accounting for these long-term contracts from the completed-contract method to the percentage-of-completion method because Falk is now able to make reasonable estimates of future construction costs.

2. Based on improved collection procedures, Falk changed the percentage of credit sales used to determine the allowance for uncollectible accounts from 2% to 1%.

For **Items 3 and 4**, in addition to selecting a classification for each transaction from List A **and** the general accounting treatment required to report the change from List B, a third response is required. For these items, determine the amount, if any, of the cumulative change or prior period adjustment, ignoring income tax effects. The CPA exam would provide a list of numeric answers to choose from.

3. Effective January 1, 2002, Falk changed from average cost to FIFO to account for its inventory. Cost of goods sold under each method was as follows:

Year	*Average cost*	*FIFO*
Years prior to 2001	$71,000	$77,000
2001	79,000	82,000

4. In January 2001, Falk purchased a machine with a five-year life and no salvage value for $40,000. The machine was depreciated using the straight-line method. On December 30, 2002, Falk discovered that depreciation on the machine had been calculated using a 25% rate.

PROBLEM

Problem 1   (15 to 25 minutes)

Boulder Company appropriately changed its depreciation method for its production machinery from the double-declining balance method to the production method effective January 1, 2002.

In addition, effective January 1, 2002, Boulder appropriately changed the salvage values used in computing depreciation for its office equipment.

On December 31, 2002, Boulder appropriately changed the specific subsidiaries constituting the group of companies for which consolidated financial statements are presented.

Required:

a.   Identify any accounting changes in the three situations described above. For each accounting change identified, indicate whether Boulder should show

- The cumulative effect of a change in accounting principle in net income of the period of change.
- Pro forma effects of retroactive application for all prior periods presented currently.
- Restatement of the financial statements of all prior periods presented currently.

b.   1.   Why are accounting principles, once adopted, normally continued?
2.   What is the rationale for disclosure of a change from one generally accepted accounting principle to another generally accepted accounting principle?

Problem 2   (15 to 25 minutes)

On January 1, 2002, Windsor Corp. made the following changes in its accounting policies:

- Changed from the LIFO inventory method to the FIFO inventory method.
- Adopted the straight-line depreciation method for all future machinery acquisitions, but continued to use sum-of-the-years' digits depreciation method for all machinery purchased before 2002.
- Changed from the cash to the accrual basis of accounting for accumulated vacation pay.

Windsor prepares two-year comparative financial statements.

Required:

a.   What type of accounting change is the change from the LIFO to the FIFO inventory costing method? How should Windsor report this change in its 2002 comparative financial statements?

b.   What type of accounting change is Windsor's change from the sum-of-the-years' digits to the straight-line depreciation method for all machinery purchased after 2001? How should Windsor report this change?

c.   What type of change occurs when recognition of vacation pay expense is changed from the cash basis to the accrual basis? How should Windsor report this change?

MULTIPLE-CHOICE ANSWERS

1. c	__ __	6. c	__ __	11. a	__ __	16. d	__ __	21. b	__ __
2. b	__ __	7. c	__ __	12. d	__ __	17. c	__ __	22. d	__ __
3. c	__ __	8. d	__ __	13. c	__ __	18. a	__ __	23. c	__ __
4. c	__ __	9. a	__ __	14. b	__ __	19. a	__ __	1st: __/23 = __%
5. b	__ __	10. d	__ __	15. a	__ __	20. c	__ __	2nd: __/23 = __%

MULTIPLE-CHOICE ANSWER EXPLANATIONS

C.1. Changes in Accounting Principles

1. **(c)** Per APB 20, when a change in principle is made, generally the current or catch-up approach is used. The cumulative effect of the adjustment of prior years is reported in the current income statement, and the new method is used in the current year. Do not be misled by the statement in the question that says Bray changed retroactively. The term retroactive is being used in this question to refer to the way in which the catch-up or cumulative amount is computed, not the manner of reporting it. In comparative financial statements, no changes are made to the previously published financial statements for catch-up adjustments as an accounted for catch-up or cumulative type change. In this case the cumulative effect is $38,400 ($86,400 double-declining balance accumulated depreciation – $48,000 straight-line accumulated depreciation). The journal entry to reflect this cumulative effect would be

Accumulated depreciation	38,400	
Cumulative effect		38,400

In 2002, depreciation expense would be computed using straight-line depreciation, computed as follows:

Depreciation exp. is $24,000 ($240,000 ÷ 10).

Depreciation expense	24,000	
Accumulated depreciation		24,000

2. **(b)** Per APB 20, a change in principle is generally recorded using the current approach. The cumulative effect of the adjustment on prior years is reported in the current income statement net of the related tax effect. In this case, the accumulated depreciation account must be decreased by $120,000 [$360,000 – ($600,000 x 2/5)], the excess of accelerated depreciation over straight-line. The tax effect is $36,000 (30% x $120,000), so the cumulative effect reported is $84,000 ($120,000 – $36,000). The journal entry is

Accumulative depreciation	120,000	
Cumulative effect		84,000
Deferred tax liability		36,000

3. **(c)** Per APB 20, a change in principle is generally recorded using the current approach. The cumulative effect of the adjustment on prior years is reported in the current income statement net of the related tax effect. The cause of the tax effect is that while **before the change**, the tax basis and accounting book value of the asset were both $240,000, and **after the change**, the tax basis remains at $240,000 but the accounting book value is now $360,000 [$600,000 – (2/5 x $600,000)]. When the book value of an asset is greater than its tax basis due to a temporary difference, the result is future taxable amounts for which a deferred tax liability must be recorded. The deferred tax liability is the future tax rate times the future taxable amounts [$30% x ($360,000 – $240,000) = $36,000]

4. **(c)** Per APB 20, when a change in principle is made, generally, the **current** approach is used. The cumulative effect of the change on prior years, net of tax, is reported in the current income statement, and the new method is used in the current year. Depreciation recorded in the prior years (2000-01) using the straight-line method totaled $10,000 [($50,000 x 1/10) x 2]. If the units of production method had been used, depreciation would have been $12,000 [($50,000/50,000) x (8,500 + 3,500)]. Therefore, the cumulative effect on prior years before taxes is $2,000 ($12,000 – $10,000), and the net-of-tax effect is $1,400 [$2,000 – (30% x $2,000)]. Using the current approach, this amount is recorded as a cumulative effect in the income statement rather than as an adjustment to the beginning balance of retained earnings.

5. **(b)** The requirement is to determine which accounting change should be reported as the cumulative effect of a change in accounting principle. Per APB 20, a change from straight-line depreciation to the double-declining balance method should be reported as a cumulative effect of a change in accounting principle after income from continuing operations. A change from the cash basis to the accrual basis of accounting is a change from non-GAAP to GAAP accounted for as the correction of an error. A change in reporting entity requires restatement of the financial statements of all prior periods presented in order to show financial information for the new reporting entity for all periods (APB 20). A change in the method of accounting for long-term contracts qualifies as a "special" change under APB 20, requiring restatement of prior periods as if the new method had been used.

6. **(c)** The requirement is to determine whether a change in depreciation method from straight-line to double-declining balance should be reported as a cumulative effect of a change in accounting principle and if the pro forma effects of retroactive application should also be reported. APB 20 requires the presentation of the cumulative effect of the change and the pro forma effects of retroactive application (for a change in accounting principle). Additionally, the pro forma effects of retroactive application are to be shown on the face of the income statement in a separate section, below earnings per share.

7. **(c)** The cumulative effect of a change in accounting principle is the cumulative effect on prior years' income as if the new method had been used in those prior years. For the years prior to 2002, beginning inventory would be the same for both methods ($0 inventory at the formation of the firm), and ending inventory would be $71,000 (FIFO) or $77,000 (WA). Therefore, the cumulative effect on prior years' income, before taxes, would be $6,000 ($77,000 – $71,000). Since APB 20 requires that a cumulative effect be recorded net of the related tax effect, Orca should report a cumulative effect of $4,200 [$6,000 – (30% x $6,000)].

8.   (d)   Per APB 20, a change in accounting principle generally should be recognized by including in the net income of the period of change the cumulative effect, based on retroactive computation, of changing to the new accounting principle. The cumulative effect is to be reported as a special item after extraordinary items. Only retroactive-type accounting changes (not cumulative effect-type) and error corrections are reported as prior period adjustments. The cumulative effect is reported separately after income from continuing operations. Extraordinary items are a separate category distinct from cumulative effect of change in accounting principle, and are defined as unusual and infrequent nonrecurring events that have material effects.

9.   (a)   APB 20 states that a change in inventory methods from LIFO is one of the exceptions requiring the use of the **retroactive** approach rather than the **current** approach. The cumulative effect at the beginning of the period of change is entered directly to retained earnings as a prior period adjustment, and the prior year statements are retroactively restated. The cumulative effect is recorded net of the related tax effect. In this case, the cumulative effect is $350,000 [$500,000 – (30% x $500,000)]. The journal entry is

Inventory	500,000	
Retained earnings		350,000
Deferred tax liability		150,000

10.   (d)   Per APB 20, certain "special" changes in accounting principle are reported by retroactively applying the new method in restatements of prior periods including reporting the cumulative effect of the change as an adjustment to the beginning balance of retained earnings. A change from the LIFO method of inventory pricing to another method is designated as such a change. In contrast, a change from FIFO to weighted-average should be accounted for by presenting the cumulative effect of the change in the income statement between the captions "extraordinary items" and "net income."

11.   (a)   Per APB 20, the amount shown in the income statement for the cumulative effect of changing to a new accounting principle is the difference between (a) the amount of retained earnings **at the beginning of the period** of a change and (b) the amount of retained earnings that would have been reported at that date if the new accounting principle had been applied retroactively for all prior periods which would have been affected and by recognizing only the direct effects of the change and related income tax effect.

12.   (d)   Per APB 20, a change in accounting principle includes both accounting principles and practices and the methods of applying them. Such a change should be recognized by including the cumulative effect, based on retroactive computation, of changing to the new accounting principle in the net income of the period of the change. The effect of adopting the new accounting principle on income before extraordinary items (if any) and net income of the period of the change should be disclosed. The cumulative effect of the change is **excluded** from income from continuing operations due to the unique nature of this component of net income. Corrections of errors, not accounting changes, are treated as prior period adjustments.

13.   (c)   The requirement is to indicate how a change in accounting principle from the completed-contract method to the percentage-of-completion method should be reported. Per APB 20, a change in the method of accounting for long-term contracts is one of the exceptions requiring the use of the **retroactive**, rather than the **current**, approach. The cumulative effect at the beginning of the period of change is entered directly to retained earnings as a prior period adjustment, and prior year statements are retroactively restated. The cumulative effect is recorded net of the related tax effect. In this case, the cumulative effect is $108,000 [($880,000 – $700,000) x (1 – .40)]. The journal entry is as follows:

Construction-in-progress	180,000	
Deferred taxes		72,000
Retained earnings		108,000

C.2. Change in Accounting Estimates

14.   (b)   This situation is a change in accounting estimate and should be accounted for currently and prospectively. From 1/1/99 to 12/31/01, patent amortization was recorded using a fifteen-year life. Yearly amortization was $47,600 ($714,000 ÷ 15), accumulated amortization at 12/31/01 was $142,800 ($47,600 x 3), and the book value of the patent at 12/31/01 was $571,200 ($714,000 – $142,800). Beginning in 2002, this book value must be amortized over its remaining useful life of 7 years (10 years – 3 years). Therefore, 2002 amortization is $81,600 ($571,200 ÷ 7) and the 12/31/02 book value is $489,600 ($571,200 – $81,600).

15.   (a)   From 1/1/99 to 12/31/01, depreciation was recorded using an eight-year life. Yearly depreciation was $66,000 ($528,000 ÷ 8), and accumulated depreciation at 12/31/01 was $198,000 (3 x $66,000). In 2002, the estimated useful life was changed to six years total with a salvage value of $48,000. Therefore, the 12/31/01 book value ($528,000 – $198,000 = $330,000) is depreciated down to the $48,000 salvage value over a remaining useful life of three years (six years total – three years already recorded). Depreciation expense for 2002 is $94,000 [($330,000 – $48,000) ÷ 3], increasing accumulated depreciation to $292,000 ($198,000 + $94,000).

16.   (d)   APB 20 states that changes in accounting estimate are to be accounted for in the period of change and in future periods if the change affects both (i.e., **prospectively**). Pro forma amounts are presented for changes in accounting principle accounted for using the **current** (cumulative effect) approach. Answers (a) and (c) are incorrect because they apply to **retroactive**-type changes in principle and error correction, respectively.

17.   (c)   APB 20 provides examples of items for which estimates are required to prepare financial statements. Recoverable mineral reserves is one of the provided examples. APB 20 states that the effect of a change in accounting estimate should be accounted for in (a) the period of change if the change affects that period only, or (b) the period of change and future periods if the change affects both. APB 20 further states that a change in an estimate should not be accounted for by restating amounts reported in financial statements of prior periods or by reporting pro forma amounts for prior periods.

18.   (a)   A change in estimated warranty costs due to technological advances in production qualifies as a change in accounting estimate. Changes in estimate are treated prospectively; there is no retroactive restatement, and the new estimate is used in current and future years. Therefore, in 2002, Oak should use the new estimate of 1% and report warranty expense of $50,000 ($5,000,000 x 1%).

19.   (a)   A change in equipment warranty costs based on additional information obtained through experience qualifies as a change in accounting estimate. Changes in estimate should be accounted for in the period of change as a component of income from continuing operations and in future periods if necessary. Accounting changes reported net of tax below income from continuing operations are cumulative effects of changes in accounting principle. No restatement is required for a change in estimate.

20.   (c)   Per APB 20, the effect of a change in accounting principle which is inseparable from the effect of a change in accounting estimate should be accounted for as a change in accounting estimate. Changes in estimate should be accounted for in the period of change and also in any affected future periods as a component of income from continuing operations (APB 20). Financial statements are only restated for "special" changes in accounting principle, changes in entity, and changes due to an error. Errors include mathematical mistakes, mistakes in applying accounting principles, oversights or misuse of available facts, and changes from unacceptable accounting principles to GAAP (APB 20). The situation described in this question does not meet the description of an error.

C.3. Change in Reporting Entity

21.   (b)   The requirement is the determination of the consequences of including a subsidiary in the current year's statements when it was appropriately excluded in last year's. Per APB 20, when (1) consolidated or combined statements are presented in place of individual statements; (2) there is a change in the group of subsidiaries for which consolidated statements are prepared [answer (b)]; (3) there is a change in companies included in combined statements; or (4) there is a business combination accounted for as a pooling of interests, then a change in the reporting entity has occurred. Such changes should be reported by restating the financial statements of all prior periods presented to show financial information for the new reporting entity for all periods (APB 20). Answer (a) is incorrect because retroactive restatement is required. Answer (c) is incorrect since errors consist of correcting mathematical mistakes, mistakes in applying principles, oversights or misuse of avoidable facts, and changes from unacceptable to acceptable GAAP. Answer (d) is incorrect since a change in reporting entity is an accounting change.

22.   (d)   An accounting change that results in financial statements that are, in effect, the statements of a different reporting entity is treated as a change in reporting entity. Per APB 20, when a change in reporting entity occurs, it should be reported by restating the financial statements of all prior periods presented to show financial information for the new reporting entity for all periods. Cumulative effect adjustments are not reported when the retroactive approach is used. A change in entity **does** require restatement.

23.   (c)   The cumulative effect is the net-of-tax difference in retained earnings between the new principle and the old principle as of the beginning of the fiscal year of the change.

The cumulative effect will be computed as of January 1, 2000, for the change in accounting principle made during the 2000 fiscal year, regardless of when during the year the change in accounting principle is actually made. As of January 1, 2000, the amount of deferred demo costs were $500,000. Therefore, the net-of-tax cumulative effect in the 2000 income statement will be $350,000 ($500,000 x .70 net of tax.)

OTHER OBJECTIVE ANSWERS AND ANSWER EXPLANATIONS

Problem 1

1. (A,Y)   This situation represents a change in the method of accounting for long-term construction-type contracts and requires retroactive restatement of past financial statements.

2. (B,Z)   This situation is not a change in accounting principle but is a change in an estimate and should be handled prospectively.

3. (B,Z)   This situation is a change in an estimate. The change in the percentage of warranty costs is not a change in accounting principle. Changes in estimate are handled prospectively.

4. (A,Y)   This situation is a change from one acceptable accounting principle to another and requires retroactive restatement.

5. (A,X)   This situation is a change from one acceptable accounting method to another and requires the cumulative effect approach.

6. (C,Y)   The use of the cash method is considered an error since that method is generally **not** acceptable. The switch to an acceptable method (accrual) is considered the correction of an error and requires the retroactive restatement approach.

7. (C,Y)   The write-off of the insurance premium was an error. Since comparative financial statements are prepared, past years must be corrected using the retroactive restatement approach even though this error is self-correcting after two years.

8. (A,X)   This situation is a change in method which is considered a change in principle and requires the cumulative effect approach.

9. (D,Z)   Since the company did not previously account for pensions this situation is simply the adoption of an appropriate accounting principle for pensions. No change in principle occurs.

10. (D,Y)   Quo's increase in ownership interest (10% to 30%) and its acquisition of a seat on Worth's board of directors has given Quo the ability to exercise significant influence in the operating decisions of Worth. Therefore, according to APB 18, Quo should adopt the equity method to account for its investment in Worth. The cost adjusted for fair value method is no longer applicable due to the change in Quo's investment in Worth. However, the change from the cost adjusted for fair value method to the equity method is not a change in accounting principle. A change in accounting principle occurs when an accounting principle different from the one used previously for reporting purposes is adopted. For a change to occur, a choice between two or more accounting principles must exist (APB 20). In this case, the change in Quo's situation dictates that the equity method be used to account for the investment. Quo's current economic situation is clearly different and this necessitates the adoption of a different accounting principle (APB 20). Consequently, this is not an accounting change. However, APB 18 requires that the investment account be retroactively restated to reflect balances as if the equity method had always been used.

Problem 2

1. (A,Y)   Changing from using the completed-contract method to the percentage-of-completion method is a change in accounting principle per APB 20. The three situations below are examples of changes in accounting principle that require retroactive restatement of all periods presented as if the new method had been used in all prior periods. Per APB 20, a change in the method of accounting for long-term contracts requires a retroactive restatement.

  1.   Change from LIFO to another inventory method
  2.   Change in method of accounting for long-term contracts
  3.   Change to or from the full cost method of accounting for exploration costs in the extractive industries

2. (B,Z)   The percentage of net credit sales used in determining the amount to be added to the allowance for uncollectible accounts is an estimate made by management. Changing the percentage is a change in accounting estimate, which is treated prospectively.

3. (A,X, $9,000)   Changing from average cost to FIFO is a change in accounting principle. Most changes in accounting principle are treated as a cumulative effect approach. However, the five special situations above require retroactive restatement. This situation does not fit any of the five scenarios in number 1. above, so the change in accounting principle should be treated using the cumulative effect approach. To determine the amount, the prior years' effect of the change on the beginning retained earnings needs to be computed and displayed net of tax after extraordinary items and before net income. Because the change is effective in 2002, all prior years, including 2001, need to be included. The cost of goods sold would have been $6,000 higher in years prior to 2001 and $3,000 higher in 2001 under the FIFO method. The total cumulative effect ignoring income taxes is $6,000 + $3,000 = $9,000. The entry to record the cumulative effect is as follows:

Cumulative effect of a change in accounting principle	9,000	
Inventory		9,000

Note that this situation represents a situation where prices have been decreasing causing FIFO inventory (latest prices) to be less than average cost inventory and cost of goods sold to be greater under FIFO.

4. (C,Y, $2,000)   An error has occurred because using the straight-line method for a five-year-life asset should compute depreciation using a 20% rate (100%/5 years). A correction of an error in previously presented financial statements is treated as a prior period adjustment with retroactive restatement and should be reported as adjustments to beginning retained earnings of each year presented. The amount of the adjustment is the difference in the amount of depreciation taken and what should have been taken in 2001 only. Because the error was found in 2002, depreciation expense for 2002 could be corrected. Depreciation in 2001 was $10,000 ($40,000 x 25%). It should have been $8,000 ($40,000 x 20%) or [($40,000 – 0) /5]. The difference of $2,000 is the adjustment necessary.

Accumulated depreciation	2,000	
Retained earnings		2,000

ANSWER OUTLINE

Problem 1   Types of Accounting Changes

a.   Changes in depreciation method is change in accounting principle
    Show cumulative effect of change in accounting principle in net income of period of change
    Show pro forma effects of retroactive application for all prior periods presented currently
    Do not restate FS of all prior periods presented currently
    Change in salvage values is change in accounting estimate
        Do not report cumulative effect
        Do not report pro forma effects
        Do not restate prior period FS
    Change in subsidiaries constituting group of companies for consolidated FS is change in reporting entity
        Do not report cumulative effect
        Do not report pro forma effects
        Restate FS of prior periods presented currently

b.   **1.**   Accounting principles normally continued
        Consistency enhances comparability of accounting information across accounting periods
        Consistency increases usefulness of FS
    2.   Disclosure of change in accounting principle
        Avoids misleading FS users
        Presumption exists that once adopted, accounting principle should not be changed
            For events and transactions of similar type

UNOFFICIAL ANSWER

Problem 1   Types of Accounting Changes

a.   Boulder's change in depreciation method is a change in accounting principle. This change in accounting principle should show the cumulative effect of a change in accounting principle in net income of the period of change, and the pro forma effects of retroactive application for all prior periods presented currently. Financial statements of prior periods should not be restated.

Boulder's change in salvage values is a change in accounting estimate. Boulder would not report a cumulative effect, nor pro forma effects, nor would prior period financial statements be restated.

Boulder's change in the specific subsidiaries constituting the group of companies for which consolidated financial statements are presented is a change in reporting entity. Neither the cumulative effect nor the pro forma effects of the change should be reported. However, financial statements of prior periods presented currently should be restated.

b.   **1.**   Consistent use of accounting principles from one accounting period to another enhances the comparability of accounting information across accounting periods, and thus increases the usefulness of financial statements.
2.   If a change in accounting principle occurs, the nature and effect of a change in accounting principle should be disclosed to avoid misleading financial statement users. Disclosure is required because there is a presumption that an accounting principle once adopted should not be changed in accounting for events and transactions of a similar type.

ANSWER OUTLINE

Problem 2   Types of Accounting Changes

a.   Change from LIFO to FIFO
    Change in accounting principle
    Restate 2001 FS
        Adjust for effect on 1/1/01 RE
    Disclosures
        For 2002
            Nature and justification for change
        For all periods presented
            Effects on IS components

b.   Adoption of straight-line method
    Adoption for newly acquired assets
    2001 FS unaffected
    No cumulative effect in 2002
        Because change not being applied to existing assets
    Disclosures for 2002
        Nature and justification for change
            Effect on 2002 income components

c.   Change from cash basis to accrual basis
    Error correction
        Change from non-GAAP to GAAP
    Restate 2001 FS
        Adjust for effect on 1/1/01 RE
    Disclosures for 2002
        Nature and details of corrections

UNOFFICIAL ANSWER

Problem 2   Types of Accounting Changes

a.   A change from the LIFO inventory method to the FIFO inventory method is a change in accounting principle. Windsor should restate the 2001 financial statements, including adjustment for the effect on January 1, 2001, retained earnings, as if the FIFO method had been adopted at the beginning of 2001. The nature and justification for the change in inventory method should be disclosed in the notes to the 2002 financial statements. The effects of the change on income statement components should be disclosed for all periods presented.

b.   Windsor's change to the straight-line depreciation method for all future machinery acquisitions is not a change in accounting principle because the previously recorded assets will continue to be depreciated using the sum-of-the-years' digits method. The nature and justification for the change in depreciation methods should be disclosed in the notes to the 2002 comparative financial statements. The 2001 financial statements are unaffected by the change, but the effects of the change on 2002 income components should be disclosed.

c.   A change from the cash basis of vacation pay expense recognition to the accrual basis is a change from an accounting principle that is not generally accepted to one that is generally accepted. Such a change is considered an error correction. Windsor should restate the 2001 financial statements, including adjustment for the effect on January 1, 2001 retained earnings, to correct prior errors. Windsor should disclose the nature and details of the corrections in notes to the 2002 financial statements.

D. Financial Statements

648   658   693   705-707

1. Income and Retained Earnings Statement Formats

Review the outlines of APB 9, APB 30, SFAS 130, and SFAS 144 before proceeding. Income statements may be prepared using a multiple-step or single-step form. The income (earnings) and comprehensive income statement illustrated below for Totman Company includes separate categories for continuing operations, discontinued operations, extraordinary items, and changes in accounting principles. The other comprehensive income is required per SFAS 130. The purpose of these separate categories is to enable users to assess future cash flows. The Totman Co. statement is a combined statement of income and comprehensive income.

Totman Company
STATEMENT OF EARNINGS AND COMPREHENSIVE INCOME
For the Year Ended December 31, 2002

	Sales		$2,677
	Cost of goods sold		1,489
See	Gross margin on sales		1,188
Note	Operating expenses		
#5	Selling expenses	$ 220	
below	Administrative expenses	255	475
	Operating income		713
	Other revenues and gains		
	Interest revenue	$ 5	
	Equity in Huskie Co. earnings	15	
	Gain on sale of available-for-sale securities	45	65
	Other expenses and losses		
	Interest expense	(60)	
	Loss from permanent impairment of value of manufacturing facilities	(120)	(180)
	Income from continuing operations before provision for income taxes		598
	Provision for income taxes		
	Current	$ 189	
	Deferred	50	239
	Income from continuing operations		359(a)
	Discontinued operations:		
	Loss from operations of discontinued Division Z, including loss on disposal of $230	(1,265)	
	Income tax benefit	(466)	(799)(b)
	Income (loss) before extraordinary item and cumulative effect of an accounting change		(440)
	Extraordinary item: Loss due to earthquake (less applicable income taxes of $30)		(45)(b)
	Cumulative effect on prior years of retroactive application of new depreciation method (less		
	applicable income taxes of $80)		(120)(b)
	Net earnings (loss)		(605)(a)
	Other comprehensive income:		
	Foreign currency translation adjustments (less applicable income taxes of $6)		26
	Unrealized gains on securities:		
	Unrealized holding gains arising during period (less applicable income taxes of $43)	179	
	Less: reclassification adjustment (less applicable income taxes of $10) for gain included		
	in net income	(35)	144
	Minimum pension liability (less applicable income taxes of $12) taxes		(53)
	Other comprehensive income		117
	Comprehensive income		$(488)

Note:
1. Assumes a tax rate of 40% on applicable items
2. (a) indicates where earnings per share (EPS) amounts would be necessary on the face of the IS. (b) EPS may be shown on the face of the income statement or in the notes. On the CPA exam, rather than memorizing these, simply calculate an EPS number for all numbers starting with income from continuing operations through net earnings.
3. Footnote explanations would also be required for many of the above events and transactions.
4. In the multiple-step format above, the Securities and Exchange Commission (SEC) requires that public companies place impairment losses in operating income instead of under "Other expenses and losses."
5. This is the format for a multiple-step income statement. A single-step income statement would differ only for the portion of the statement shown below. Otherwise, the single-step statement format is the same.

Revenues		
Sales	$2,677	
Interest	5	
Gain on sale of available-for-sale securities	45	
Equity in Huskie Co. earnings	15	
Total revenues		$2,742
Expenses		
Cost of goods sold	1,489	
Selling expenses	220	
Administrative expenses	255	
Interest expense	60	
Loss from permanent impairment of value of manufacturing facilities	120	
Total expenses		2,144
Income from continuing operations before provision for income taxes		598

The following chart summarizes the various category definitions and their placement on the income statement and retained earnings statement. These categories are all discussed in various parts of this module.

INCOME STATEMENT AND RETAINED EARNINGS STATEMENT CATEGORIES

Description	*Definition*	*Placement on income statement or retained earnings statement*
1. **Unusual or Infrequent Items**	An unusual or infrequent event considered to be material that does not qualify as extraordinary	Placed as part of income from continuing operations after normal recurring revenues and expenses
2. **Discontinued Operations***	Results from disposal of a business segment or a line of business	Placed as a separate category after income from continuing operations
3. **Extraordinary Items***	An unusual and infrequent nonrecurring event which has material effects	Placed as a separate category after discontinued operations
4. **Change in Accounting Principle:***		
Cumulative effect:	Change from one generally accepted accounting principle to another	Placed as a separate category after extraordinary items
Restatement:	Change which requires restatement of all prior periods presented	Placed as a separate category in retained earnings
5. **Correction of an Error***	A correction of a material error from a prior period	Placed as a separate category in retained earnings

* These items are all presented net of applicable income tax effects.

2. Unusual or Infrequent Items

Items that are unusual or infrequent but not both should not be presented as extraordinary items. However, they are often presented in a separate section in the income statement above income before extraordinary items. A common example of such items is a "restructuring charge."

A restructuring is a program that is planned and controlled by management and materially changes either (1) the scope of the **business** undertaken by the company, or (2) the manner in which that business is conducted. Examples include

  a. Sale or termination of a line of business
  b. Closure of business activities in a particular location
  c. Relocation of business activities from one location to another
  d. Changes in management structure, or
  e. Fundamental reorganizations that affect the nature and focus of operations

SFAS 146 deals with accounting for the costs of exit and disposal activities (which include, among other items, restructurings) and provides that a liability for a cost associated with an exit or disposal activity should be recognized and measured initially at fair value in the period in which the liability is incurred. The fair value is usually determined by determining the present value of the estimate future payments discounted at the credit-adjusted risk-free rate of interest. In the unusual circumstance when fair value cannot be reasonably estimated, the liability shall be initially recognized in the period in which fair value can be reasonably estimated. Examples of such liabilities include

  a. Onetime termination benefits provided to current employees that are involuntarily terminated
  b. Costs to terminate a contract that is not a capital lease
  c. Costs to consolidate facilities or relocate employees

The recognition of the liability and expense for onetime termination benefits depends on whether the employees are required to provide services beyond the minimum retention period. If so, the expense is recognized over the period that the services are provided. If they are not required to provide future services, the liability is recognized when the plan is communicated to the employees.

In periods subsequent to initial measurement, changes to the liability shall be measured using the credit-adjusted risk-free rate that was used to measure the liability initially.

Costs associated with an exit or disposal activity that does not involve discontinued operations shall be included in income from continuing operations before income taxes. The footnotes to the financial statements shall provide extensive disclosure of the activities (See outline of SFAS 146).

3. **Discontinued Operations**

As shown on the Totman Co. income statement, "Discontinued operations" is broken out separately. The "Loss from discontinued operations includes the loss or income of the component for the period, and the gain or loss on its disposal. Income taxes or tax benefit are deducted from or added to that amount to determine the gain or loss after taxes. To qualify for treatment as discontinued operations the assets must comprise a component of the entity with operations and cash flows that are clearly distinguished, operationally and for financial reporting purposes, from the rest of the entity. A component may be a reportable or operating segment (see the outline of SFAS 131), a reporting unit (see the outline of SFAS 142), a subsidiary, or an asset group.

Many of the assets disposed of as discontinued operations are long-lived assets. Such assets are subject to the requirements of SFAS 144. Accordingly, the component is classified as discontinued operations in the first period that it meets the criteria as being "held for sale":

   a.   Management commits to a plan of disposal
   b.   The assets are available for sale
   c.   An active program to locate a buyer have been initiated
   d.   The sale is probable
   e.   The asset is being actively marketed for sale at a fair price
   f.   It is unlikely that the disposal plan will significantly change

To be reported as discontinued operations, SFAS 144 also requires (1) the operations and cash flows of the component have been (or will be) eliminated from the ongoing operations of the entity as a result of the disposal, and (2) the entity will not have any significant involvement in the operations of the component after disposal.

Long-lived assets classified as "held for sale" are reported at the lower of their carrying amounts or fair values less costs to sell. Therefore, the gain or loss on disposal of discontinued operations is the actual gain or loss if disposal occurs in the same period that the component meets the criteria to be classified as "held for sale" (see the outline of SFAS 144). If the criteria to classify the component as "held for sale" is met in a period before it is disposed of, the amount of the loss (if applicable) on disposal is an estimated loss resulting from the write-down of the group of assets to their estimated fair values. Estimated gains cannot be initially recognized. However, if the component is held for sale over several reporting periods estimated gains can be recognized based on new information but are limited to the amount of losses previously recognized. Thus, the assets can be written up but not above their carrying amounts when they met the criteria as being held for sale.

When "discontinued operations" are disclosed in a comparative income statement, the income statement presented for each previous year must be adjusted retroactively to enhance comparability with the current year's income statement. Accordingly, the revenues, cost of goods sold, and operating expenses (including income taxes) for the discontinued component are removed from the revenues, cost of goods sold, and operating expenses of continuing operations and are netted into one figure, that is, "Income (loss) from operations." The following excerpt from a comparative income statement shows the proper disclosure (2001 figures assumed).

	2002	*2001*
Discontinued operations:		
Loss from operations of discontinued Division Z, including loss on disposal in 2002 of $230	$699	$990
Income tax benefit	$466	$300

4. **Comprehensive Income**

Reporting. Comprehensive income is the sum of net earnings (loss) and other comprehensive income. Refer to the outline of SFAS 130. This standard goes part way in implementing the concept of comprehensive income per SFAC 5 and 6. These two concept statements would require reporting all transactions other than those with owners in comprehensive income. However, SFAS 130 leaves prior period adjustments in retained earnings. It requires disclosure of **changes during a period** of the following components of other comprehensive income: unrealized gains and losses on available-for-sale investments and foreign currency items, including any reclassification adjustments and the minimum pension liability adjustment.

This standard allows the management of an enterprise three choices for presenting **other comprehensive income**. These are as follows:

1. At the bottom of IS, continue from net income to arrive at a comprehensive income figure (illustrated on page 788), or
2. In a separate statement that starts with net income, (illustrated below), or
3. In the statement of changes in stockholders' equity illustrated on page 723.

The first two alternatives are preferred by the FASB. If either the second or third one is used, it is necessary to begin with net earnings so that net earnings would be reconciled to comprehensive income as it is in the single statement. The new standard continues the required disclosure of the **accumulated** amounts of these components in the stockholders' equity section of the balance sheet, in a statement of changes in stockholders' equity, or in the notes to financial statements. (See the balance sheet on the following page and the statement of changes in stockholders' equity at the beginning of Module 28.)

Recycling or reclassification adjustments. As unrealized gains (losses) recorded and reported in other comprehensive income for the current or prior periods are later realized, they are recognized and reported in net income. To avoid double counting it is necessary to reverse the unrealized amounts that have been recognized. Assume that an available-for-sale security was sold April 1, 2002, for a $45 gain. There was $30 of unrealized gain that arose in years prior to 2002 and is in **accumulated other** comprehensive income. The other $15 unrealized gain was reported in the first quarter statements and is part of the $179 reported below under other comprehensive income for 2002.

Totman Company
STATEMENT OF EARNINGS AND COMPREHENSIVE INCOME
For the Year Ended December 31, 2002

Sales		$2,677
Operating income		713
Other revenues and gains		
Interest revenue	$ 5	
Equity in Huskie Co. earnings	15	
Gain on sale of available-for-sale securities	45	65
Other expenses and losses		
Interest expense	(60)	
Loss from permanent impairment of value of manufacturing facilities	(120)	(180)
Income from continuing operations before provision for income taxes		598
Provision for income taxes		
Current	$ 189	
Deferred	50	239
Income from continuing operations		359
Net earnings (loss)		(605)
Other comprehensive income:		
Foreign currency translation adjustments (less applicable income taxes of $6)		26
Unrealized gains on securities:		
Unrealized holding gains arising during period (less applicable income taxes of $43)	179	
Less: reclassification adjustment (less applicable income taxes of $10) for gain included in net income	(35)	144
Minimum pension liability (less applicable income taxes of $12) taxes		(53)
Other comprehensive income		117
Comprehensive income		$(488)

The reclassification adjustment to avoid double counting is $45 less a tax effect of $10 or $35 net. Since the $45 was realized in the current period, a realized gain of $45 was reported in the income from continuing operations under other revenues and gains above before provisions for income taxes of $598. The $10 of income tax on the $45 is reported as part of provision for income taxes in the current portion of income tax expense of $189. Recall that all items reported above the provision for income taxes are reported "gross," not the net of tax treatment as in the case of items such as discontinued operations. Also, note the tax effects reported under other comprehensive income are **deferred** since the unrealized components are not recognized for tax purposes until realized.

Totman Company
BALANCE SHEET
December 31, 2002

Assets			Liabilities and Stockholders' Equity		
Current assets:			*Current liabilities:*		
Cash and bank deposits:			Commercial paper and other short-term	$xxx	
Restricted to current bond maturity	$xxx		notes		
Unrestricted	xxx	$xxx	Accounts payable	xxx	
Short-term investments:			Salaries, wages, and commissions	xxx	
Marketable securities (Trading)		xxx	Taxes withheld from employees	xxx	
Refundable income taxes		xxx	Income taxes payable	xxx	
Receivables from affiliates		xxx	Dividends payable	xxx	
Accounts receivable	xxx		Rent revenue collected in advance	xxx	
Less allowance for doubtful accounts	(xxx)	xxx	Other advances from customers	xxx	
Notes receivable due in 2003		xxx	Current portion of long-term debt	xxx	
Installment notes due in 2003		xxx	Current obligations under capital leases	xxx	
Interest receivable		xxx	Deferred tax liability	xxx	
Creditors' accounts with debit balances		xxx	Short-term portion of accrued warranty	xxx	
Advances to employees		xxx	Other accrued liabilities	xxx	
Inventories (carried at lower of cost or			Total current liabilities		$xxx
market by FIFO)			*Noncurrent liabilities:*		
Finished goods	xxx		Notes payable due after 2002	xxx	
Work in process	xxx		Plus unamortized note premium	xxx	$xxx
Raw materials	xxx	xxx	Long-term bonds:		
Prepaid expenses:			10% debentures due 2013	xxx	
Prepaid rent	xxx		9-1/2% collateralized obligations ma-		
Prepaid insurance	xxx	xxx	turing serially to 2005	xxx	
Total current assets		$xxx	8% convertible subordinated debentures		
Long-term investments:			due 2018	xxx	
Investments in marketable securities			Less unamortized discounts net of	(xxx)	xxx
(available-for-sale)		xxx	premiums		
Investments in bonds (held-to-maturity)		xxx	Accrued pension cost		xxx
Investments in unused land		xxx	Obligations under capital leases		xxx
Cash surrender value of officers' life in-			Deferred tax liability		xxx
surance policies		xxx	Long-term portion of accrued warranty		xxx
Sinking fund for bond retirement		xxx	Total noncurrent liabilities		$xxx
Plant expansion fund		xxx	Total liabilities		$xxx
Total long-term investments		$xxx	*Capital stock:*		
Property, plant, and equipment:			$12.50 convertible preferred stock, $100		
Land		xxx	stated value, 200,000 shares authorized,		
Buildings		xxx	175,000 outstanding	xxx	
Machinery and equipment		xxx	12% cumulative preferred stock, $100		
Furniture and fixtures		xxx	stated value, callable at $115, 100,000		
Leasehold improvements		xxx	shares authorized and outstanding	xxx	
Leased assets		xxx	Common stock, $10 stated value, 500,000		
Less accumulated depreciation and am-	(xxx)		shares authorized, 450,000 issued, 15,000		
ortization			held in treasury	xxx	
Total property, plant, and equipment		$xxx	Common stock subscribed 10,000 shares	xxx	
Intangible assets net of amortization:			Less: Subscriptions receivable	(xxx)	xxx
Excess of cost over net assets of acquired			*Additional paid-in capital:*		
businesses	xxx		From 12% cumulative preferred	xxx	
Patents	xxx		From common stock	xxx	
Trademarks	xxx		From treasury stock transactions	xxx	
Total intangible assets, net		$xxx	From stock dividends	xxx	
Other assets:			From expiration of stock options	xxx	
Installment notes due after 2002	xxx		Warrants outstanding	xxx	xxx
Unamortized bond issue costs	xxx		*Retained earnings:*		
Equipment to be disposed of	xxx		Appropriated for bond indebtedness	xxx	
Total other noncurrent assets		$xxx	Free and unappropriated	xxx	xxx
Total assets		$xxx	*Accumulated other comprehensive income:*		xxx*
			Total stockholders' equity		$xxx
			Less: Treasury stock at cost		(xxx)
			Total liabilities and stockholders' equity		$xxx

*Assumes components thereof are disclosed either in a statement of changes in stockholders' equity or in the notes to FS.

Balance sheet. Accumulated other comprehensive income is reported in the stockholders' equity section of the balance sheet. When an entity has components of other comprehensive income, the total of these is closed to the balance sheet account entitled **accumulated other comprehensive income,** not retained earnings. In the case above, the other comprehensive income of $117 for the period would need to be closed to accumulated other comprehensive income, not retained earnings as would the ($605) net loss.

5. **Balance Sheets (Statements of Financial Position)**

Balance sheets or statements of financial position present assets, liabilities, and stockholders' equity. The balance sheet reports the effect of transactions at a point in time, whereas the statement of earnings (income) and comprehensive income, statement of retained earnings, and statement of cash flows report the effect of transactions over a period of time.

An example of balance sheet classification and presentation is illustrated by the comprehensive balance sheet on the previous page.

Distinction between current and noncurrent assets and liabilities is almost universal.

Current assets—"cash and other assets or resources commonly identified as those which are reasonably expected to be realized in cash or sold or consumed during the normal operating cycle of the business."   (ARB 43, chap 3A)

Current liabilities—"obligations whose liquidation is reasonably expected to require the use of existing resources properly classifiable as current assets or the creation of other current liabilities" (during the normal operating cycle of the business).   (ARB 43, chap 3A)

Note current assets include those expected to be

    a.   Realized in cash
    b.   Sold
    c.   Consumed

Current liabilities are those expected to

    a.   Use current assets
    b.   Create other current liabilities

The operating cycle is the average time between acquisition of materials and final cash realization. Review the outline of ARB 43, chap 3A.

6. **Other Financial Statement Concepts**

    a.   **Disclosures.** Related-party disclosures are covered by SFAS 57 (refer to that outline). Additional disclosures required for specific situations are specified at the end of most pronouncements (e.g., APB and SFAS). Study these disclosure requirements by assuming you are a financial analyst analyzing the statements: "What would you want disclosed? Note any required disclosures that are not 'common sense.'" It is not necessary to memorize them for the exam.

    b.   **Accounting policies** must be set forth as the initial footnote to the statements. Disclosures are required of

        (1)   Accounting principles used when alternatives exist
        (2)   Principles peculiar to a particular industry
        (3)   Unusual or innovative applications of accounting principles

        Turn to the outline of APB 22.

    c.   **Development stage enterprise accounting** should be per generally accepted accounting principles. The only additional disclosure required is that cumulative amounts from inception of losses, revenues, expenses, and cash flows should be shown in the income statement and statement of cash flows. Furthermore, the stockholders' equity section of the balance sheet should include cumulative net losses termed "deficit accumulated during development stage." These statements should be identified as those of a development stage enterprise. (More detailed coverage appears in Module 24.)

    d.   **Constant dollar accounting.** SFAS 89 encourages, but does not require, a business enterprise that prepares its financial statements in US dollars and in accordance with US generally accepted accounting principles to disclose supplementary information on the effects of changing prices. This statement presents requirements to be followed by enterprises that voluntarily elect to disclose this information.

Constant dollar accounting is a method of reporting financial statement elements in dollars which have the same purchasing power. This method is often described as accounting in units of current purchasing power.

Purchasing power indicates the ability of a dollar to command goods and services. If the inflation rate during a given year for a group of items is 10%, then 110 end-of-year dollars are needed to purchase the same group of items which cost $100 at the beginning of the year. Similarly, a machine purchased at the beginning of that year for $1,000 would be presented in a year-end constant dollar balance sheet at a restated cost of $1,100. This represents the basic thrust of constant dollar accounting: the adjustment of historical data (nominal dollars) for changes in the general price level.

The adjustment of nominal dollar data is facilitated by the use of the Consumer Price Index, which reflects the average change in the retail prices of a wide variety of consumer goods. The adjustment is made by multiplying historical cost by the TO/FROM ratio.

$$\text{Historical cost (nominal dollars)} \quad x \quad \frac{\text{Price level adjusting to}}{\text{Price level adjusting from}} \quad = \quad \text{Restated historical cost (constant dollar)}$$

For example, an asset was purchased on 12/31/00 for $20,000 and the Consumer Price Index was 100 on 12/31/00, 110 on 12/31/01, and 120 on 12/31/02. Restatement for end-of-year balance sheets would be

$$12/31/00 \quad \$20,000 \quad x \quad \frac{100}{100} \quad = \quad \$20,000$$

$$12/31/01 \quad \$20,000 \quad x \quad \frac{110}{100} \quad = \quad \$22,000$$

$$12/31/02 \quad \$20,000 \quad x \quad \frac{120}{100} \quad = \quad \$24,000$$

or

$$\$22,000 \quad x \quad \frac{120}{110} \quad = \quad \$24,000$$

The preparation of constant dollar financial statements requires the classification of balance sheet items as either monetary or nonmonetary. Items are monetary if their amounts are fixed by statute or contract in terms of numbers of dollars. Examples include cash, accounts and notes receivable, accounts and notes payable, and bonds payable. By contract or statute, these items are already stated in current dollars and require no restatement. Nonmonetary items, on the other hand, do require restatement to current dollars. Inventory, property, plant, and equipment, and unearned service revenue are examples of nonmonetary items. Under some increasingly popular loan arrangements, when the repayment of loan principal is adjusted by an index, the receivable/payable is classified as a nonmonetary item.

The holding of a nonmonetary asset such as land during a period of inflation need not result in a loss of purchasing power because the value of that land can "flow" with the price level (hence, the need for restatement). However, if a monetary asset such as cash is held during a period of inflation with no interest, purchasing power is lost because the cash will be able to purchase less goods and services at year-end than at the beginning of the year. This type of loss is simply called a "purchasing power loss." Holding a monetary liability has the opposite effect. Therefore, if a firm's balance sheet included more monetary liabilities than monetary assets throughout a given year, a purchasing power **gain** would result, since the firm could pay its liabilities using cash which is "worth less" than the cash it borrowed.

A simple example can illustrate both the restatement process and the effect of holding monetary assets. Assume that the Static Company has the following balance sheet at the beginning of period 1:

Static Co.
Beginning of Period 1
Consumer Price Index = 100

Cash	$1,000	Common Stock	$2,000
Land	1,000		
	$2,000		$2,000

Further assume

- Index increases to 110 by the end of year 1
- No transactions have taken place, land and common stock would be restated to end-of-year dollars.
- Cash is still stated at $1,000.

- To have the same level of purchasing power that was present at the beginning of the year, Static Co. should also have cash of $1,100 at year-end. The fact that the company held $1,000 cash throughout the year has resulted in a $100 purchasing power loss. The balance sheet at the end of period 1 would therefore be

Static Co.
End of Period 1
Consumer Price Index = 110

Cash	$1,000	Common Stock	$2,200[b]
Land	1,100[a]	Retained Earnings	(100)[c]
	$2,100		$2,100

$$^a \$1,000 \ \times \frac{110}{100} \qquad ^b \$2,000 \ \times \frac{110}{100} \qquad ^c \text{Purchasing power loss } \$1,000 - (\$1,000 \ \times \frac{110}{100})$$

What if the entity had acquired equipment costing $1,000 at the beginning of the year by issuing a $1,000 note payable? At the end of the year, under constant dollar accounting, the equipment would be carried at $1,100 and the note payable would be still reported at $1,000. What would the net purchasing power gain (loss) be? The answer is zero because the ($100) is offset by a $100 gain from holding the note payable.

e. **Current cost accounting** is a method of valuing and reporting assets, liabilities, revenues, and expenses at their current cost at the balance sheet date or at the date of their use or sale.

It is important to distinguish between constant dollar and current cost accounting. Constant dollar accounting is concerned only with changes in the unit of measure—from nominal dollars to units of general purchasing power. Current cost accounting discards historical cost as a reporting model.

Preparation of a current cost income statement requires an understanding of certain basic current cost concepts. **Current cost income from continuing operations** is sales revenue less expenses on a current cost basis. **Realized holding gains** (the difference between current cost and historical cost of assets consumed) are then added to arrive at **realized income,** which will always be equal to historical cost net income. Finally, **unrealized holding gains** (increases in the current cost of assets held throughout the year) are included to result in **current cost net income**.

An example should help clarify these terms. Bell Co. went into business on 1/1/02. 2002 sales revenue was $200,000 and purchases totaled $150,000. Inventory with a historical cost of $100,000 was sold when its current cost was $160,000. Ending inventory (historical cost, $50,000) had a year-end current cost of $80,000. No other revenue was realized or expenses incurred during 2002. Historical and current cost income statements for 2002 are presented below.

Bell Company
INCOME STATEMENTS

Historical cost		*Current cost*	
Sales	$200,000	Sales	$200,000
Less CGS	(100,000)	Less CGS	(160,000)
		Cur. cost income from cont. oper.	40,000
		Realized holding gains (160,000 – 100,000)	60,000
Net income	$100,000	Realized income	100,000
		Unrealized holding gains (80,000 – 50,000)	30,000
		Current cost net income	$130,000

2002 journal entries for Bell Company in current cost system would be as follows:

a)	Inventory	150,000			d)	Cost of goods sold	160,000	
	Cash		150,000			Inventory		160,000
b)	Inventory	90,000			e)	Realizable holding gain	90,000	
	Realizable					Realized holding gain		60,000
	holding gain		90,000			Unrealized holding gain		30,000
c)	Cash	200,000						
	Sales revenue		200,000					

In general, sales and some expense amounts (salaries, rent, etc.) will be the same under historical and current cost systems. However, whenever an expense represents the use or consumption of an asset whose current cost has changed since its acquisition (as with the inventory in the Bell Co. example), that expense must be expressed at the current cost of the asset when used. Realized holding gains are computed by comparing the current cost of assets when used or consumed with their historical cost. Unrealized holding gains for the period are determined by identifying changes in the current cost of assets held throughout the year (not used or consumed). Notice that the holding gains do not reflect changes in the general purchasing power. In other words, the holding gains are not reported net of general inflation when the reporting model is current cost/nominal dollar.

      Current cost/constant dollars. The relationship measured is current cost, but the measuring unit is restated dollars. Changes in both the general and specific price levels are separately recorded.

f.   **Risks and Uncertainties.** AICPA Statement of Position 94-6, *Disclosure of Certain Significant Risks and Uncertainties,* requires disclosure in financial statements about the risks and uncertainties existing as of the date of those statements. The four areas of disclosure are

  (1) Nature of operations

      (a) Major products/services and principal markets served
      (b) Industries operating within and relative importance of each industry, including basis of determination (assets, revenue or earnings).

        NOTE: Quantification not required and words such as predominantly, equally, major, or other may be used.

  (2) Use of estimates in preparation of financial statements

      (a) This fact must be disclosed by an explanation that management must use estimates
      (b) Purpose is to alert users clearly to pervasiveness of estimates

  (3) Certain significant estimates

      (a) Potential impact of estimates to value assets, liabilities, gains or losses when

         1] Reasonably possible the estimate will change in the near term
         2] Effect of change would be material to financial statements

           NOTE: Near term is defined as not to exceed one year from date of financial statements.

      (b) This is not a change in SFAS 5, *Accounting for Contingencies*
      (c) Disclosure of factors causing the estimate to be sensitive to change is encouraged, but not required
      (d) Materiality is measured by the effect that using a different estimate would have on the financial statements

  (4) Current vulnerability due to concentrations

      (a) Before issuance of financial statements, management knows that concentrations

         1] Exist at balance sheet date
         2] Make entity vulnerable to risk of near-term severe impact
         3] Reasonably possible events could cause severe impact in near future

           NOTE: Severe impact is defined as higher than materiality and would have a significant financially disruptive effect on the normal functioning of the entity.

      (b) Examples are concentrations in

         1] Volume of business transacted with a particular customer, supplier, lender, grantor, or contributor
         2] Revenue from particular products, services, or fund-raising events
         3] Available sources of supply of materials, labor, or services, or of licenses or other rights used in the entity's operations
         4] Market or geographical area in which an entity conducts its operations

      (c) Disclose the percentage of labor covered by a collective bargaining agreement and the percentage covered whose agreement expires within one year
      (d) Describe for operations outside of home country, the carrying value of net assets and location

7. **Comparative Financial Statements**

The Totman Company balance sheet and income statement illustrated in this module are presented for a single year. Most companies present comparative financial statements. Comparative financial statements present not only the current year's information, but prior periods also. The purpose of comparative financial statements is to enable users to evaluate trends which may reveal information about the company's future performance. The SEC requires that a two-year comparative balance sheet and a three-year comparative income statement and statement of cash flows be presented.

8. **Other Comprehensive Bases of Accounting**

Financial statements may be prepared in conformity with a comprehensive basis of accounting other than generally accepted accounting principles. Other comprehensive bases are illustrated in the chart below.

Accounting method	*Characteristics*
1. Cash basis (pure)	Fixed assets would be expensed in the period paid for
2. Income tax bases	
• Modified cash basis—hybrid method of IRS	Reflects use of accrual basis for inventories, cost of goods sold, sales, and depreciation if these are significant
• Accrual basis—IRS	Use accruals and deferrals with several exceptions (e.g., prepaid income, warranty expense)
3. Prescribed basis by regulatory agency	Determined by regulatory agency

Guidance for preparing these statements is found in the AICPA publication entitled *Preparing and Reporting on Cash- and Tax-Basis Financial Statements*. When financial statements are prepared on an income tax basis, the financial statements should not simply repeat items and amounts reported in the tax return. Thus, items such as nontaxable municipal interest and the nondeductible portion of travel and entertainment expense should be **fully** reflected in the income statement on the basis used for tax purposes (cash or accrual) with footnote disclosure of the differences between the amounts reported in the income statement and tax return.

9. **Prospective Financial Information**

• Definitions:

  • Prospective financial information—any financial information about the future
  • Responsible party—person(s), usually management, who are responsible for assumptions underlying the information
  • Users of prospective financial information:

    • General—use of FS by parties with whom responsible party is not negotiating directly
    • Limited use—use of prospective financial information by the responsible party only or by responsible party and third parties with whom responsible party is negotiating directly

  • Financial forecast—prospective FS that present the knowledge and belief of responsible party in terms of expected financial position, results of operations, and cash flows

    • May be prepared for **general or limited** use
    • Monetary amounts are expressed as a single-point estimate of results or range

  • Financial projection—prospective FS that present the knowledge and belief of responsible party, based on one or more **hypothetical** assumptions, the enterprise's financial position, results of operations, and cash flows

    • Assumptions **not necessarily** expected to occur
    • May contain a single-point estimate of results or a range of dollars
    • May be prepared only for **limited** use

• Reasons for preparation:

  • Needed to obtain external financing
  • Consider change in accounting or operations
  • Prepare budget

• Process for preparing forecasts and projections may consist of any of the following:

  • Formal system
  • Carrying out a work program that outlines steps followed in preparation
  • Documented procedures, methods, and practices used in preparation

- Financial forecasts and projections should reflect **a reasonably objective basis** as a result of preparing them:
  - In good faith
  - With due care by qualified personnel
  - In accordance with GAAP
  - With the highest quality information that is reasonably available
  - Using information that is in accordance with plans of the entity
  - Identifying key factors as basis for assumptions
    - Key factors are important matters for which outcomes are expected to depend
  - Using appropriate assumptions
    - Quality of these is crucial
    - **Hypothetical** assumptions used in projections do **not** need to meet a strict reasonableness test; they must, however, be appropriate in light of the purpose of the projection's purpose
  - Providing ways to determine relative effect of variations in main assumptions (i.e., sensitivity analysis)
  - Documenting forecast/projection and process used
  - Providing for comparison of forecast/projection with attained results
  - Providing adequate review of the responsible party at appropriate levels of authority in the organization
- Prospective financial statement disclosures include:
  - Summary of significant accounting policies
  - Summary of significant assumptions.

MULTIPLE-CHOICE QUESTIONS (1-81)

1. In Baer Food Co.'s 2002 single-step income statement, the section titled "Revenues" consisted of the following:

Net sales revenue		$187,000
Results from discontinued operations:		
Loss from discontinued component Z in-		
cluding loss on disposal of $1,200	$ 16,400	
Less tax benefit	4,000	(12,400)
Interest revenue		10,200
Gain on sale of equipment		4,700
Cumulative change in 2000 and 2001 income		
due to change in depreciation method (net of		
$750 tax effect)		1,500
Total revenues		$191,000

In the revenues section of the 2002 income statement, Baer Food should have reported total revenues of

- a. $216,300
- b. $215,400
- c. $203,700
- d. $201,900

Items 2 and 3 are based on the following:

Vane Co.'s trial balance of income statement accounts for the year ended December 31, 2003, included the following:

	Debit	Credit
Sales		$575,000
Cost of sales	$240,000	
Administrative expenses	70,000	
Loss on sale of equipment	10,000	
Sales commissions	50,000	
Interest revenue		25,000
Freight out	15,000	
Loss on early retirement of long-term debt		
	20,000	
Uncollectible accounts expense	15,000	
Totals	$420,000	$600,000

Other information

Finished goods inventory:	
January 1, 2003	$400,000
December 31, 2003	360,000

Vane's income tax rate is 30%. In Vane's 2003 multiple-step income statement,

2. What amount should Vane report as the cost of goods manufactured?

- a. $200,000
- b. $215,000
- c. $280,000
- d. $295,000

3. What amount should Vane report as income after income taxes from continuing operations?

- a. $126,000
- b. $129,500
- c. $140,000
- d. $147,000

4. Brock Corp. reports operating expenses in two categories: (1) selling, and (2) general and administrative. The adjusted trial balance at December 31, 2002, included the following expense and loss accounts:

Accounting and legal fees	$120,000
Advertising	150,000
Freight-out	80,000
Interest	70,000
Loss on sale of long-term investment	30,000
Officers' salaries	225,000
Rent for office space	220,000
Sales salaries and commissions	140,000

One-half of the rented premises is occupied by the sales department.

Brock's total selling expenses for 2002 are

- a. $480,000
- b. $400,000
- c. $370,000
- d. $360,000

5. The following costs were incurred by Griff Co., a manufacturer, during 2002:

Accounting and legal fees	$ 25,000
Freight-in	175,000
Freight-out	160,000
Officers salaries	150,000
Insurance	85,000
Sales representatives salaries	215,000

What amount of these costs should be reported as general and administrative expenses for 2002?

- a. $260,000
- b. $550,000
- c. $635,000
- d. $810,000

6. Which of the following should be included in general and administrative expenses?

	Interest	Advertising
a.	Yes	Yes
b.	Yes	No
c.	No	Yes
d.	No	No

7. In Yew Co.'s 2002 annual report, Yew described its social awareness expenditures during the year as follows:

The Company contributed $250,000 in cash to youth and educational programs. The Company also gave $140,000 to health and human service organizations, of which $80,000 was contributed by employees through payroll deductions. In addition, consistent with the Company's commitment to the environment, the Company spent $100,000 to redesign product packaging.

What amount of the above should be included in Yew's income statement as charitable contributions expense?

- a. $310,000
- b. $390,000
- c. $410,000
- d. $490,000

8. During 2002 both Raim Co. and Cane Co. suffered losses due to the flooding of the Mississippi River. Raim is located two miles from the river and sustains flood losses every two to three years. Cane, which has been located fifty miles from the river for the past twenty years, has never before had flood losses. How should the flood losses be reported in each company's 2002 income statement?

	Raim	Cane
a.	As a component of income from continuing operations	As an extraordinary item
b.	As a component of income from continuing operations	As a component of income from continuing operations
c.	As an extraordinary item	As a component of income from continuing operations
d.	As an extraordinary item	As an extraordinary item

9. Witt Co. incurred the following infrequent losses during 2002:

- $175,000 from a major strike by employees.
- $150,000 from an early extinguishment of debt.
- $125,000 from the abandonment of equipment used in the business.

In Witt's 2002 income statement, the total amount of infrequent losses **not** considered extraordinary should be
- a. $275,000
- b. $300,000
- c. $325,000
- d. $450,000

10. Kent Co. incurred the following infrequent losses during 2001:

- A $300,000 loss was incurred on disposal of one of four dissimilar factories.
- A major currency devaluation caused a $120,000 exchange loss on an amount remitted by a foreign customer.
- Inventory valued at $190,000 was made worthless by a competitor's unexpected product innovation.

In its 2002 income statement, what amount should Kent report as losses that are **not** considered extraordinary?
- a. $610,000
- b. $490,000
- c. $420,000
- d. $310,000

11. Midway Co. had the following transactions during 2002:

- $1,200,000 pretax loss on foreign currency exchange due to a major unexpected devaluation by the foreign government.
- $500,000 pretax loss from discontinued operations of a division.
- $800,000 pretax loss on equipment damaged by a hurricane. This was the first hurricane ever to strike in Midway's area. Midway also received $1,000,000 from its insurance company to replace a building, with a carrying value of $300,000, that had been destroyed by the hurricane.

What amount should Midway report in its 2002 income statement as extraordinary loss before income taxes?
- a. $ 100,000
- b. $1,300,000
- c. $1,800,000
- d. $2,500,000

12. Ocean Corp.'s comprehensive insurance policy allows its assets to be replaced at current value. The policy has a $50,000 deductible clause. One of Ocean's waterfront warehouses was destroyed in a winter storm. Such storms occur approximately every four years. Ocean incurred $20,000 of costs in dismantling the warehouse and plans to replace it. The following data relate to the warehouse:

| Current carrying amount | $ 300,000 |
| Replacement cost | 1,100,000 |

What amount of gain should Ocean report as a separate component of income before extraordinary items?
- a. $1,030,000
- b. $ 780,000
- c. $ 730,000
- d. $0

13. Purl Corporation's income statement for the year ended December 31, 2002, shows the following:

Income before income tax and extraordinary item	$900,000
Gain on life insurance coverage—included in the above $900,000 income amount	100,000
Extraordinary item—loss due to earthquake damage	300,000

Purl's tax rate for 2002 is 40%. How much should be reported as the provision for income tax in Purl's 2002 income statement?
- a. $200,000
- b. $240,000
- c. $320,000
- d. $360,000

14. Thorpe Co.'s income statement for the year ended December 31, 2003, reported net income of $74,100. The auditor raised questions about the following amounts that had been included in net income:

Unrealized loss on decline in market value of noncurrent investments in stock classified as available-for-sale (net of tax)	$(5,400)
Gain on early retirement of bonds payable (net of $11,000 tax effect)	22,000
Adjustment to profits of prior years for errors in depreciation (net of $3,750 tax effect)	(7,500)
Loss from fire (net of $7,000 tax effect)	(14,000)

The loss from the fire was an infrequent but not unusual occurrence in Thorpe's line of business. Thorpe's December 31, 2002 income statement should report net income of
- a. $65,000
- b. $66,100
- c. $81,600
- d. $87,000

15. On January 1, 2002, Brecon Co. installed cabinets to display its merchandise in customers' stores. Brecon expects to use these cabinets for five years. Brecon's 2002 multi-step income statement should include
- a. One-fifth of the cabinet costs in cost of goods sold.
- b. One-fifth of the cabinet costs in selling, general, and administrative expenses.
- c. All of the cabinet costs in cost of good sold.
- d. All of the cabinet costs in selling, general, and administrative expenses.

16. A material loss should be presented separately as a component of income from continuing operations when it is
- a. An extraordinary item.
- b. A cumulative-effect-type change in accounting principle.
- c. Unusual in nature and infrequent in occurrence.
- d. Not unusual in nature but infrequent in occurrence.

17. During 2002, Peg Construction Co. recognized substantial gains from

- An increase in value of a foreign customer's remittance caused by a major foreign currency revaluation.
- A court-ordered increase in a completed long-term construction contract's price due to design changes.

Should these gains be included in continuing operations or reported as an extraordinary item in Peg's 2002 income statement?

	Gain from major currency revaluation	*Gain from increase in contract's price*
a.	Continuing operations	Continuing operations
b.	Extraordinary item	Continuing operations
c.	Extraordinary item	Extraordinary item
d.	Continuing operations	Extraordinary item

18. An extraordinary item should be reported separately on the income statement as a component of income

	Net of income taxes	Before discontinued operations of a component of a business
a.	Yes	Yes
b.	Yes	No
c.	No	No
d.	No	Yes

19. In 2002, hail damaged several of Toncan Co.'s vans. Hailstorms had frequently inflicted similar damage to Toncan's vans. Over the years, Toncan had saved money by not buying hail insurance and either paying for repairs, or selling damaged vans and then replacing them. In 2002, the damaged vans were sold for less than their carrying amount. How should the hail damage cost be reported in Toncan's 2002 financial statements?

    a.   The actual 2002 hail damage loss as an extraordinary loss, net of income taxes.

    b.   The actual 2002 hail damage loss in continuing operations, with **no** separate disclosure.

    c.   The expected average hail damage loss in continuing operations, with **no** separate disclosure.

    d.   The expected average hail damage loss in continuing operations, with separate disclosure.

20. A transaction that is unusual in nature and infrequent in occurrence should be reported separately as a component of income

    a.   After cumulative effect of accounting changes and before discontinued operations.

    b.   After cumulative effect of accounting changes and after discontinued operations.

    c.   Before cumulative effect of accounting changes and before discontinued operations.

    d.   Before cumulative effect of accounting changes and after discontinued operations.

21. In 2002, Teller Co. incurred losses arising from its guilty plea in its first antitrust action, and from a substantial increase in production costs caused when a major supplier's workers went on strike. Which of these losses should be reported as an extraordinary item?

	Antitrust action	Production costs
a.	No	No
b.	No	Yes
c.	Yes	No
d.	Yes	Yes

22. In open market transactions, Gold Corp. simultaneously sold its long-term investment in Iron Corp. bonds and purchased its own outstanding bonds. The broker remitted the net cash from the two transactions. Gold's gain on the purchase of its own bonds exceeded its loss on the sale of the Iron bonds. Gold should report the

    a.   Net effect of the two transactions as an extraordinary gain.

    b.   Net effect of the two transactions in income before extraordinary items.

    c.   Effect of its own bond transaction gain in income before extraordinary items, and report the Iron bond transaction as a loss in income before extraordinary items.

    d.   Effect of its own bond transaction as an extraordinary gain, and report the Iron bond transaction loss in income before extraordinary items.

23. Under SFAS 130, *Reporting Comprehensive Income,* corrections of errors are reported in

    a.   Other comprehensive income.

    b.   Other income/(expense).

    c.   Retained earnings.

    d.   Stockholders' equity

24. Service Corp. incurred costs associated with relocating employees in a restructuring of its operations. How should the company account for these costs?

    a.   Measured at fair value and recognized over the next two years.

    b.   Measured at fair value and recognized when the liability is incurred.

    c.   Recognized when the costs are paid.

    d.   Measured at fair value and treated as a prior period adjustment.

25. On January 1, 2002, Deer Corp. met the criteria for discontinuance of a business component. For the period January 1 through October 15, 2002, the component had revenues of $500,000 and expenses of $800,000. The assets of the component were sold on October 15, 2002, at a loss for which no tax benefit is available. In its income statement for the year ended December 31, 2002, how should Deer report the component's operations from January 1 to October 15, 2002?

    a. $500,000 and $800,000 should be included with revenues and expenses, respectively, as part of continuing operations.

    b. $300,000 should be reported as part of the loss on operations and disposal of a component.

    c. $300,000 should be reported as an extraordinary loss.

    d. $500,000 should be reported as revenues from operations of a discontinued component.

26. Which of the following criteria is not required for a component's results to be classified as discontinued operations?

    a.   Management must have entered into a sales agreement.

    b.   The component is available for immediate sale.

    c.   The operations and cash flows of the component will be eliminated from the operations of the entity as a result of the disposal.

    d.   The entity will not have any significant continuing involvement in the operations of the component after disposal.

27. On November 1, 2002, management of Herron Corporation committed to a plan to dispose of Timms Company, a major subsidiary. The disposal meets the requirements for classification as discontinued operations. The carrying value of Timms Company was $8,000,000 and management estimated the fair value less costs to sell to be $6,500,000. For 2002, Timms Company had a loss of $2,000,000. How much should Herron Corporation present as loss from discontinued operations before the effect of taxes in its income statement for 2002?

    a. $0

    b. $1,500,000

    c. $2,000,000

    d. $3,500,000

28. On December 1, 2002, Greer Co. committed to a plan to dispose of its Hart business component's assets. The disposal meets the requirements to be classified as discontinued operations. On that date, Greer estimated that the loss from the disposition of the assets would be $700,000 and Hart's 2002 operating losses were $200,000. Disregarding income taxes, what net gain (loss) should be reported for discontinued operations in Greer's 2002 income statement?

    a. $0
    b. $(200,000)
    c. $(700,000
    d. $(900,000)

29. A component of Ace, Inc. was discontinued during 2003. Ace's loss on disposal should

    a.   Exclude the associated employee relocation costs.
    b.   Exclude operating losses for the period.
    c.   Include associated employee termination costs.
    d.   Exclude associated lease cancellation costs.

30. When a component of a business has been discontinued during the year, this component's operating losses of the current period should be included in the

    a.   Income statement as part of revenues and expenses.
    b.   Income statement as part of the loss on disposal of the discontinued component.
    c.   Income statement as part of the income (loss) from continuing operations.
    d.   Retained earnings statement as a direct decrease in retained earnings.

31. When a component of a business has been discontinued during the year, the loss on disposal should

    a.   Include operating losses of the current period.
    b.   Exclude operating losses during the period.
    c.   Be an extraordinary item.
    d.   Be an operating item.

32. On January 1, 2003, Shine Co. agreed to sell a business component on March 1, 2003. The gain on the disposal should be

    a.   Presented as an extraordinary gain.
    b.   Presented as an adjustment to retained earnings.
    c.   Netted with the loss from operations of the component as a part of discontinued operations.
    d.   None of the above.

33. What is the purpose of reporting comprehensive income?

    a.   To report changes in equity due to transactions with owners.
    b.   To report a measure of overall enterprise performance.
    c.   To replace net income with a better measure.
    d.   To combine income from continuing operations with income from discontinued operations and extraordinary items.

34. During 2002, the "other revenues and gains" section of Totman Company's Statement of Earnings and Comprehensive Income contains $5,000 in interest revenue, $15,000 equity in Harpo Co. earnings, and $25,000 gain on sale of available-for-sale securities. Assuming the sale of the securities increased the current portion of income tax expense by

$10,000, determine the amount of Totman's reclassification adjustment to other comprehensive income.

    a. $ 5,000
    b. $ 2,500
    c. $35,000
    d. $15,000

35. Which of the following is **not** an acceptable option of reporting other comprehensive income and its components?

    a.   In a separate statement of comprehensive income.
    b.   In a statement of earnings and comprehensive income.
    c.   In the footnotes.
    d.   In a statement of changes in stockholders' equity.

36. Accumulated other comprehensive income should be reported on the balance sheet as a component of

	Retained earnings	*Additional paid-in capital*
a.	No	Yes
b.	Yes	Yes
c.	Yes	No
d.	No	No

37. Which of the following changes during a period is not a component of other comprehensive income?

    a.   Unrealized gains or losses as a result of a debt security being transferred from held-to-maturity to available-for-sale.
    b.   Stock dividends issued to shareholders.
    c.   Foreign currency translation adjustments.
    d.   Minimum pension liability adjustments.

Items 38 and 39 are based on the following:

A company buys ten shares of securities at $2,000 each on December 31, 2000. The securities are classified as available for sale. The fair value of the securities increases to $2,500 on December 31, 2001, and to $2,750 on December 31, 2002. On December 31, 2002, the company sells the securities. Assume no dividends are paid and that the company has a tax rate of 30%.

38. In 2002, what is the amount of the reclassification adjustment for other comprehensive income?

    a. $ 7,500
    b. $ (7,500)
    c. $ 5,250
    d. $ (5,250)

39. What is the amount of the holding gain arising during the period that is classified in other comprehensive income for the period ending December 31, 2002?

    a.   0
    b. $7,500
    c. $2,500
    d. $1,750

40. What amount of comprehensive income should Searles Corporation report on its statement of income and comprehensive income given the following net of tax figures that represent changes during a period?

Minimum pension liability	$ (3,000)
Unrealized gain on available-for-sale securities	15,000
Reclassification adjustment, for securities gain included in net income	(2,500)
Stock warrants outstanding	4,000
Net income	77,000

a. $86,500
b. $89,000
c. $89,500
d. $90,500

41. If ($2,450) net of tax is the reclassification adjustment included in other comprehensive income in the year the securities are sold, what is the gain (loss) that is included in income from continuing operations before income taxes? Assume a 30% tax rate.
    a. $(2,450)
    b. $(3,500)
    c. $ 2,450
    d. $ 3,500

42. Which of the following changes during a period is **not** a component of other comprehensive income?
    a.   Minimum pension liability.
    b.   Treasury stock, at cost.
    c.   Foreign currency translation adjustment.
    d.   Reclassification adjustment, for securities gain included in net income.

43. Which of the following is true?
    a.   Separate EPS amounts must be presented for both other comprehensive income and comprehensive income.
    b.   Separate EPS amounts must be presented for other comprehensive income but not for comprehensive income.
    c.   Separate EPS amounts must be presented for comprehensive income but not for other comprehensive income.
    d.   Separate EPS amounts are not required to be presented for either other comprehensive income or comprehensive income.

44. Which of the following options for displaying comprehensive income is(are) preferred by FASB?
   I.   A continuation from net income at the bottom of the income statement.
   II.   A separate statement that begins with net income.
   III.   In the statement of changes in stockholders' equity.

    a.   I.
    b.   II.
    c.   II and III.
    d.   I and II.

45. Which of the following is not classified as other comprehensive income?
    a.   A net loss of an additional pension liability not yet recognized as net periodic pension cost.
    b.   Subsequent decreases of the fair value of available-for-sale securities that have been previously written down as impaired.
    c.   Decreases in the fair value of held-to-maturity securities.
    d.   None of the above.

46. When a full set of general-purpose financial statements are presented, comprehensive income and its components should
    a.   Appear as a part of discontinued operations, extraordinary items, and cumulative effect of a change in accounting principle.

    b.   Be reported net of related income tax effect, in total and individually.
    c.   Appear in a supplemental schedule in the notes to the financial statements.
    d.   Be displayed in a financial statement that has the same prominence as other financial statements.

Items 47 through 49 are based on the following:

The following trial balance of Mint Corp. at December 31, 2002, has been adjusted except for income tax expense.

	Dr.	Cr.
Cash	$ 600,000	
Accounts receivable, net	3,500,000	
Cost in excess of billings on long-term contracts	1,600,000	
Billings in excess of costs on long-term contracts		$ 700,000
Prepaid taxes	450,000	
Property, plant, and equipment, net	1,480,000	
Note payable—noncurrent		1,620,000
Common stock		750,000
Additional paid-in capital		2,000,000
Retained earnings—unappropriated		900,000
Retained earnings—restricted for note payable		160,000
Earnings from long-term contracts		6,680,000
Costs and expenses	5,180,000	
	$12,810,000	$12,810,000

Other financial data for the year ended December 31, 2002, are

    •   Mint uses the percentage-of-completion method to account for long-term construction contracts for financial statement and income tax purposes. All receivables on these contracts are considered to be collectible within twelve months.
    •   During 2002, estimated tax payments of $450,000 were charged to prepaid taxes. Mint has not recorded income tax expense. There were no temporary or permanent differences, and Mint's tax rate is 30%.

In Mint's December 31, 2002 balance sheet, what amount should be reported as

47. Total retained earnings?
    a. $1,950,000
    b. $2,110,000
    c. $2,400,000
    d. $2,560,000

48. Total noncurrent liabilities?
    a. $1,620,000
    b. $1,780,000
    c. $2,320,000
    d. $2,480,000

49. Total current assets?
    a. $5,000,000
    b. $5,450,000
    c. $5,700,000
    d. $6,150,000

50. Mirr, Inc. was incorporated on January 1, 2002, with proceeds from the issuance of $750,000 in stock and borrowed funds of $110,000. During the first year of operations, revenues from sales and consulting amounted to $82,000, and operating costs and expenses totaled $64,000. On December 15, Mirr declared a $3,000 cash dividend, payable to stockholders on January 15, 2003. No additional activities affected owners' equity in 2002. Mirr's liabilities increased to $120,000 by December 31, 2002. On Mirr's December 31, 2002 balance sheet, total assets should be reported at

a. $885,000
b. $882,000
c. $878,000
d. $875,000

51. The following changes in Vel Corp.'s account balances occurred during 2002:

	Increase
Assets	$89,000
Liabilities	27,000
Capital stock	60,000
Additional paid-in capital	6,000

Except for a $13,000 dividend payment and the year's earnings, there were no changes in retained earnings for 2002. What was Vel's net income for 2002?

a. $ 4,000
b. $ 9,000
c. $13,000
d. $17,000

52. When preparing a draft of its 2002 balance sheet, Mont, Inc. reported net assets totaling $875,000. Included in the asset section of the balance sheet were the following:

Treasury stock of Mont, Inc. at cost, which approximates market value on December 31	$24,000
Idle machinery	11,200
Cash surrender value of life insurance on corporate executives	13,700
Allowance for decline in market value of noncurrent equity investments	8,400

At what amount should Mont's net assets be reported in the December 31, 2002 balance sheet?

a. $851,000
b. $850,100
c. $842,600
d. $834,500

53. In analyzing a company's financial statements, which financial statement would a potential investor primarily use to assess the company's liquidity and financial flexibility?

a. Balance sheet.
b. Income statement.
c. Statement of retained earnings.
d. Statement of cash flows.

54. During 2002, Jones Company engaged in the following transactions:

Salary expense to key employees who are also principal owners	$100,000
Sales to affiliated enterprises	250,000

Which of the two transactions would be disclosed as related-party transactions in Jones' 2002 financial statements?

a. Neither transaction.
b. The $100,000 transaction only.
c. The $250,000 transaction only.
d. Both transactions.

55. Dean Co. acquired 100% of Morey Corp. prior to 2002. During 2002, the individual companies included in their financial statements the following:

	Dean	*Morey*
Officers' salaries	$ 75,000	$50,000
Officers' expenses	20,000	10,000
Loans to officers	125,000	50,000
Intercompany sales	150,000	--

What amount should be reported as related-party disclosures in the notes to Dean's 2002 consolidated financial statements?

a. $150,000
b. $155,000
c. $175,000
d. $330,000

56. For which type of material related-party transactions does Statement of Financial Accounting Standard 57, *Related-Party Disclosures*, require disclosure?

a. Only those not reported in the body of the financial statements.
b. Only those that receive accounting recognition.
c. Those that contain possible illegal acts.
d. All those other than compensation arrangements, expense allowances, and other similar items in the ordinary course of business.

57. Financial statements shall include disclosures of material transactions between related parties except

a. Nonmonetary exchanges by affiliates.
b. Sales of inventory by a subsidiary to its parent.
c. Expense allowance for executives which exceed normal business practice.
d. A company's agreement to act as surety for a loan to its chief executive officer.

58. Dex Co. has entered into a joint venture with an affiliate to secure access to additional inventory. Under the joint venture agreement, Dex will purchase the output of the venture at prices negotiated on an arm's-length basis. Which of the following is(are) required to be disclosed about the related-party transaction?

I. The amount due to the affiliate at the balance sheet date.
II. The dollar amount of the purchases during the year.

a. I only.
b. II only.
c. Both I and II.
d. Neither I nor II.

59. What is the purpose of information presented in notes to the financial statements?

a. To provide disclosures required by generally accepted accounting principles.
b. To correct improper presentation in the financial statements.
c. To provide recognition of amounts **not** included in the totals of the financial statements.
d. To present management's responses to auditor comments.

60. Which of the following information should be included in Melay, Inc.'s 2002 summary of significant accounting policies?

a. Property, plant, and equipment is recorded at cost with depreciation computed principally by the straight-line method.
b. During 2002, the Delay component was sold.

c. Business component 2002 sales are Alay $1M, Belay $2M, and Celay $3M.

d. Future common share dividends are expected to approximate 60% of earnings.

61. Which of the following information should be disclosed in the summary of significant accounting policies?

a. Refinancing of debt subsequent to the balance sheet date.

b. Guarantees of indebtedness of others.

c. Criteria for determining which investments are treated as cash equivalents.

d. Adequacy of pension plan assets relative to vested benefits.

62. A company that wishes to disclose information about the effect of changing prices in accordance with SFAS 89, *Financial Accounting and Changing Prices*, should report this information in

a. The body of the financial statements.

b. The notes to the financial statements.

c. Supplementary information to the financial statements.

d. Management's report to shareholders.

63. Lewis Company was formed on January 1, 2001. Selected balances from the historical cost balance sheet at December 31, 2002, were as follows:

Land (purchased in 2001)	$120,000
Investment in nonconvertible bonds (purchased in 2001, and expected to be held to maturity)	60,000
Long-term debt	80,000

The average Consumer Price Index was 100 for 2001, and 110 for 2002. In a supplementary constant dollar balance sheet (adjusted for changing prices) at December 31, 2002, these selected account balances should be shown at

	Land	Investment	Long-term debt
a.	$120,000	$60,000	$88,000
b.	$120,000	$66,000	$88,000
c.	$132,000	$60,000	$80,000
d.	$132,000	$66,000	$80,000

64. The following items were among those that appeared on Rubi Co.'s books at the end of 2002:

Merchandise inventory	$600,000
Loans to employees	20,000

What amount should Rubi classify as monetary assets in preparing constant dollar financial statements?

a. $0

b. $ 20,000

c. $600,000

d. $620,000

65. In its financial statements, Hila Co. discloses supplemental information on the effects of changing prices in accordance with Statement of Financial Accounting Standards 89, *Financial Reporting and Changing Prices*. Hila computed the increase in current cost of inventory as follows:

Increase in current cost (nominal dollars)	$15,000
Increase in current cost (constant dollars)	$12,000

What amount should Hila disclose as the inflation component of the increase in current cost of inventories?

a. $ 3,000

b. $12,000

c. $15,000

d. $27,000

66. When computing purchasing power gain or loss on net monetary items, which of the following accounts is classified as nonmonetary?

a. Advances to unconsolidated subsidiaries.

b. Allowance for uncollectible accounts.

c. Unamortized premium on bonds payable.

d. Accumulated depreciation of equipment.

67. During a period of inflation in which a liability account balance remains constant, which of the following occurs?

a. A purchasing power gain, if the item is a nonmonetary liability.

b. A purchasing power gain, if the item is a monetary liability.

c. A purchasing power loss, if the item is a nonmonetary liability.

d. A purchasing power loss, if the item is a monetary liability.

68. The following information pertains to each unit of merchandise purchased for resale by Vend Co.:

March 1, 2002	
Purchase price	$ 8
Selling price	$12
Price level index	110

December 31, 2002	
Replacement cost	$10
Selling price	$15
Price level index	121

Under current cost accounting, what is the amount of Vend's holding gain on each unit of this merchandise?

a. $0

b. $0.80

c. $1.20

d. $2.00

69. Kerr Company purchased a machine for $115,000 on January 1, 2002, the company's first day of operations. At the end of the year, the current cost of the machine was $125,000. The machine has no salvage value, a five-year life, and is depreciated by the straight-line method. For the year ended December 31, 2002, the amount of the current cost depreciation expense which would appear in supplementary current cost financial statements is

a. $14,000

b. $23,000

c. $24,000

d. $25,000

70. At December 31, 2002, Jannis Corp. owned two assets as follows:

	Equipment	Inventory
Current cost	$100,000	$80,000
Recoverable amount	$ 95,000	$90,000

Jannis voluntarily disclosed supplementary information about current cost at December 31, 2002. In such a disclosure, at what amount would Jannis report total assets?

a. $175,000

b. $180,000

c. $185,000

d. $190,000

71. Could current cost financial statements report holding gains for goods sold during the period and holding gains on inventory at the end of the period?

	Goods sold	Inventory
a.	Yes	Yes
b.	Yes	No
c.	No	Yes
d.	No	No

72. Manhof Co. prepares supplementary reports on income from continuing operations on a current cost basis in accordance with SFAS 89, *Financial Reporting and Changing Prices*. How should Manhof compute cost of goods sold on a current cost basis?

    a.   Number of units sold times average current cost of units during the year.

    b.   Number of units sold times current cost of units at year-end.

    c.   Number of units sold times current cost of units at the beginning of the year.

    d.   Beginning inventory at current cost plus cost of goods purchased less ending inventory at current cost.

73. Which of the following are examples of concentrations that create vulnerabilities and therefore would require disclosure of risks and uncertainties?

  I.   Market in which an entity conducts its operations.

  II. Available sources of supply of materials used in operations of an entity.

 III. Volume of business transacted with a certain contributor.

    a.   I and II.

    b.   II and III.

    c.   I and III.

    d.   I, II, and III.

74. Which of the following is required to be disclosed regarding the risks and uncertainties that exist?

    a.   Factors causing an estimate to be sensitive.

    b.   The potential impact of estimates about values of assets and liabilities when it is reasonably possible that the estimate will change in the near future.

    c.   The potential impact of estimates about values of assets and liabilities when it is remotely possible that the estimate will change in the near future.

    d.   A description of the operations both within and outside of the home country.

75. Which of the following accounting bases may be used to prepare financial statements in conformity with a comprehensive basis of accounting other than generally accepted accounting principles?

  I.   Basis of accounting used by an entity to file its income tax return.

  II. Cash receipts and disbursements basis of accounting.

    a.   I only.

    b.   II only.

    c.   Both I and II.

    d.   Neither I nor II.

76. Income tax basis financial statements differ from those prepared under GAAP in that income tax basis financial statements

    a.   Do **not** include nontaxable revenues and nondeductible expenses in determining income.

    b.   Include detailed information about current and deferred income tax liabilities.

    c.   Contain **no** disclosures about capital and operating lease transactions.

    d.   Recognize certain revenues and expenses in different reporting periods.

77. In financial statements prepared on the income tax basis, how should the nondeductible portion of expenses such as meals and entertainment be reported?

    a.   Included in the expense category in the determination of income.

    b.   Included in a separate category in the determination of income.

    c.   Excluded from the determination of income but included in the determination of retained earnings.

    d.   Excluded from the financial statements.

78. Which of the following is false?

    a.   Prospective financial information may be prepared for general or limited users.

    b.   The responsible party is the only limited user.

    c.   The financial projection may contain assumptions not necessarily expected to occur.

    d.   The financial projection may be expressed as a range of dollars.

79. Prospective financial information is defined as

    a.   Any financial information about the past, present, or future.

    b.   Any financial information about the present or future.

    c.   Any financial information about the future related to the day-to-day operations.

    d.   Any financial information about the future.

80. To achieve a reasonably objective basis, financial forecasts and projections should be prepared

  I.   In accordance with GAAP

  II. Using information that is in accordance with the plans of the entity.

 III. With due professional care.

    a.   I and III.

    b.   II and III.

    c.   I, II, and III.

    d.   I and II.

81. Which of the following disclosures should prospective financial statements include?

	Summary of significant accounting policies	Summary of significant assumptions
a.	Yes	Yes
b.	Yes	No
c.	No	Yes
d.	No	No

OTHER OBJECTIVE QUESTIONS

Problem 1   (15 to 25 minutes)

The illustrations below represent accounting transactions that affect the recognition of income for an accounting period. Their classification is the subject of this objective format matching question.

Required:

For each of the ten illustrations below, select the best classification from those listed A-I below. A classification may be used once, more than once, or not at all.

Illustration	*Classification*
1. Newly acquired assets are depreciated using the sum-of-the-years' digits method; previously recorded assets are depreciated using the straight-line method.	A. Change in reporting entity.
2. Accounting for a pooling of interests.	B. Correction of an error.
3. Reported as a prior period adjustment on the Retained Earnings Statement.	C. Change in accounting principle.
4. Write-down of inventory due to obsolescence.	D. Change in estimate.
5. Gains or losses on the disposal of the net assets of a component are included in this calculation.	E. Extraordinary item.
6. Changing from the gross profit method for determining year-end inventory balances to dollar value LIFO.	F. Discontinued Operations—Gain or loss from operations.
7. Accounting for existing construction contracts is changed from completed contract to percentage-of-completion.	G. Not an accounting change.
8. The effects of a change in estimate and a change in principle are inseparable for the same event.	H. Part of net income before extraordinary items.
9. The excess of cash paid over the carrying value to extinguish bonds.	I. Discontinued Operations—Gain or loss on disposal.
10. Income or loss of the component for the period of disposal included in this calculation.	

Problem 2   (10 to 15 minutes)

Pucket Corp. is in the process of preparing its financial statements for the year ended December 31, 2002. Items 1 through 8 represent various transactions or situations that occurred during 2002.

Required:

Select from the list of financial statement categories below the category in which the item should be presented. A financial statement category may be selected once, more than once, or not at all.

Financial Statement Categories
A. Income from continuing operations, with **no** separate disclosure.
B. Income from continuing operations, with separate disclosure (either on the face of statement or in the notes).
C. Other comprehensive income for the period.
D. Extraordinary items.
E. Separate component of stockholders' equity.
F. None of the above categories include this item.

Items to be answered

1. An increase in the unrealized excess of cost over market value of marketable equity securities classified as trading type securities.
2. The accumulated amount of the unrealized excess of cost over market value of available-for-sale marketable equity securities.
3. Income from operations of a discontinued component in the component's disposal year.
4. A gain on remeasuring a foreign subsidiary's financial statements from the local currency into the functional currency.
5. A loss on translating a foreign subsidiary's financial statements from the functional local currency into the reporting currency during this period.
6. A loss caused by a major earthquake in an area previously considered to be subject to only minor tremors.
7. The probable receipt of $1,000,000 from a pending lawsuit.
8. The purchase of research and development services. There were **no** other research and development activities.

Problem 3   (15 to 20 minutes)

You have been asked to assist the chief accountant of the Baker Corporation in the preparation of a balance sheet. The outline presented below represents the various classifications suggested by the chief accountant for the balance sheet.

Assets	*Liabilities and capital*
A. Current	G. Current
B. Investments	H. Long-term
C. Plant and equipment	I. Other liabilities
D. Intangibles	J. Preferred stock
E. Deferred charges	K. Common stock
F. Other assets	L. Paid-in capital excess of par
	M. Retained earnings
	N. Items excluded from the balance sheet.
	X. Contra valuation account

Required:

Items 1 through 18 represent accounts of the Baker Corporation. Determine how each account would be classified from the list above. If the account is a contra or valuation account, mark "X" before the letter. For example: "Allowance for Doubtful Accounts" would be "X-A." An answer may be selected once, more than once, or not at all.

Items to be answered

1. Dividend payable (on Baker's preferred stock).

2. Plant construction in progress by the company.

3. Factory building (retired from use and held for sale).

4. Land (held for possible future building site).

5. Merchandise inventory (held by Baker corporation on consignment).

6. Stock dividend distributable (in common stock to common stockholders and to be issued at par).

7. Office supplies inventory.

8. Sinking fund cash (First National Bank, Trustee).

9. Installment sales accounts receivable (average collection period eighteen months). All sales are installment sales.

10. Temporary decline in inventory value.

11. Advances to officers (indefinite repayment date).

12. Estimated warranty costs. The warranty costs are for a one-year warranty on parts and labor.

13. Inventory of small tools used in the business.

14. Treasury stock under par value method.

15. Common stock subscribed (Baker Corporation's stock).

16. Convertible bonds.

17. Securities held as collateral.

18. Bank overdraft (only account with bank).

PROBLEMS[1]

Problem 1　　　　(15 to 25 minutes)

Hillside Company had a loss during the year ended December 31, 2002, that is properly reported as an extraordinary item.

On July 1, 2002, Hillside committed itself to a formal plan for sale of a business component that meets the requirements for treatment as discontinued operations. A loss is expected from the proposed sale. Component operating losses were incurred continuously throughout 2002, and were expected to continue until final disposition in 2003. Costs were incurred in 2002 to relocate component employees.

Required:

a.　How should Hillside report the extraordinary item in its income statement? Why?

b.　How should Hillside report the effect of the discontinued operations in its 2002 income statement?

c.　How should Hillside report the costs that were incurred to relocate employees of the discontinued component? Why?

Do not discuss earnings per share requirements.

Problem 2　　　　(40 to 50 minutes)

The following condensed trial balance of Powell Corp., a publicly owned company, has been adjusted except for income tax expense:

Powell Corp.
CONDENSED TRIAL BALANCE
June 30, 2002

	Debit	Credit
Total assets	$25,080,000	
Total liabilities		$9,900,000
5% cumulative preferred stock		2,000,000
Common stock		10,000,000
Retained earnings		2,900,000
Machine sales		750,000
Service revenues		250,000
Interest revenue		10,000
Gain on sale of factory		250,000
Cost of sales—machines	425,000	
Cost of services	100,000	
Administrative expenses	300,000	
Research and development expenses	110,000	
Interest expense	5,000	
Loss from asset disposal	40,000	
	$26,060,000	$26,060,000

Other information and financial data for the year ended June 30, 2002, follows:

•　The weighted-average number of common shares outstanding during 2002 was 200,000. The potential dilution from the exercise of stock options held by Powell's officers and directors was not material.

•　There were no dividends-in-arrears on Powell's preferred stock at July 1, 2001. On May 1, 2002, Powell's directors declared a 5% preferred stock dividend to be paid in August 2002.

•　During 2002, one of Powell's foreign factories was expropriated by the foreign government, and Powell received a $900,000 payment from the foreign government in settlement. The carrying value of the plant was $650,000. Powell has never disposed of a factory.

•　Administrative expenses includes a $5,000 premium payment for a $1,000,000 life insurance policy on Powell's president, of which the corporation is the beneficiary.

•　Powell depreciates its assets using the straight-line method for financial reporting purposes and an accelerated method for tax purposes. The differences between book and tax depreciation are as follows:

	Financial statements over
June 30	*(under) tax depreciation*
2002	$(15,000)
2003	10,000
2004	5,000

There were no other temporary differences.

•　Powell's enacted tax rate for the current and future years is 30%.

Required:

a.　Using the single-step format, prepare Powell's income statement for the year ended June 30, 2002.

b.　Prepare a schedule reconciling Powell's financial statement net income to taxable income for the year ended June 30, 2002.

Problem 3　　　　(40 to 50 minutes)

Presented below is the unaudited balance sheet as of December 31, 2002, prepared by the bookkeeper of Zues Manufacturing Corp.

Zues Manufacturing Corp.
BALANCE SHEET
For the Year Ended December 31, 2002

Assets	
Cash	$ 225,000
Accounts receivable (net)	345,700
Inventories	560,000
Prepaid income taxes	40,000
Investments	57,700
Land	450,000
Building	1,750,000
Machinery and equipment	1,964,000
Goodwill	37,000
Total assets	$5,429,400

Liabilities & Stockholders' Equity	
Accounts payable	$ 133,800
Mortgage payable	900,000
Notes payable	500,000
Lawsuit liability	80,000
Income taxes payable	61,200
Deferred tax liability	28,000
Accumulated depreciation	420,000
Total liabilities	$2,123,000
Common stock, $50 par; 40,000 shares issued	2,231,000
Retained earnings	1,075,400
Total stockholders' equity	$3,306,400
Total liabilities and stockholders' equity	$5,429,400

---

[1]　*The Financial Accounting and Reporting Exam format (FARE) will consist of 20% - 30% essays/problems; thus, it is important that candidates work as many problems as possible so as to be prepared for them. Additionally, the experience of doing them will give candidates a better comprehension of the concepts in preparation for the multiple-choice and other objective type questions. At this point you may want to peruse the FARE Sample Exam in the Appendix of this volume, noting the format of the exam.*

Your firm has been engaged to perform an audit, during which the following data are found:

• Checks totaling $14,000 in payment of accounts payable were mailed on December 30, 2002, but were not recorded until 2003. Late in December 2002, the bank returned a customer's $2,000 check, marked "NSF," but no entry was made. Cash includes $100,000 restricted for building purposes.

• Included in accounts receivable is a $30,000 note due on December 31, 2005, from Zues' president.

• During 2002, Zues purchased 500 shares of common stock of a major corporation that supplies Zues with raw materials. Total cost of this stock was $51,300, and market value on December 31, 2002, was $47,000. The decline in market value is considered temporary. Zues plans to hold these shares indefinitely.

• Treasury stock was recorded at cost when Zues purchased 200 of its own shares for $32 per share in May 2002. This amount is included in investments.

• On December 30, 2002, Zues borrowed $500,000 from a bank in exchange for a 10% note payable, maturing December 30, 2007. Equal principal payments are due December 30 of each year, beginning in 2003. This note is collateralized by a $250,000 tract of land acquired as a potential future building site, which is included in land.

• The mortgage payable requires $50,000 principal payments, plus interest, at the end of each month. Payments were made on January 31 and February 28, 2003. The balance of this mortgage was due June 30, 2004. On March 1, 2003, prior to issuance of the audited financial statements, Zues consummated a noncancelable agreement with the lender to refinance this mortgage. The new terms require $100,000 annual principal payments, plus interest, on February 28 of each year, beginning in 2004. The final payment is due February 28, 2011.

• The lawsuit liability will be paid in 2003.

• The following is an analysis of the deferred tax liability at December 31, 2002:

Deferred taxes related to depreciation	$48,000
Deferred taxes related to a lawsuit liability	(20,000)
Net deferred tax liability	$28,000

• The current income tax expense reported in Zues' 2002 income statement was $61,200.

• The company was authorized to issue 100,000 shares of $50 par value common stock.

Required:

Prepare a corrected classified balance sheet as of December 31, 2002. This financial statement should include a proper heading, format, and necessary descriptions.

Problem 4 (15 to 25 minutes)

SFAS 130 requires enterprises to disclose comprehensive income.

Required:

a. Define comprehensive income, **other** comprehensive income, and **accumulated** other comprehensive income. You **do not** need to list specific items of other comprehensive income.

b. How shall comprehensive income be reported in the financial statements?

c. Explain the purpose of recycling adjustments in measuring comprehensive income. How should they be reported?

d. What earnings per share disclosures are required for other comprehensive income items and comprehensive income for public companies?

Problem 5

This problem is covered in Chapter 3 under "Problem Solutions Approach Example."

MULTIPLE-CHOICE ANSWERS

1. d __ __	18. b __ __	35. c __ __	52. a __ __	69. c __ __
2. a __ __	19. b __ __	36. d __ __	53. a __ __	70. a __ __
3. a __ __	20. d __ __	37. b __ __	54. c __ __	71. a __ __
4. a __ __	21. c __ __	38. d __ __	55. c __ __	72. a __ __
5. a __ __	22. c __ __	39. d __ __	56. d __ __	73. d __ __
6. d __ __	23. c __ __	40. a __ __	57. b __ __	74. b __ __
7. a __ __	24. b __ __	41. d __ __	58. c __ __	75. c __ __
8. a __ __	25. b __ __	42. b __ __	59. a __ __	76. d __ __
9. b __ __	26. a __ __	43. d __ __	60. a __ __	77. a __ __
10. a __ __	27. d __ __	44. d __ __	61. c __ __	78. b __ __
11. a __ __	28. d __ __	45. c __ __	62. c __ __	79. d __ __
12. c __ __	29. c __ __	46. d __ __	63. c __ __	80. c __ __
13. c __ __	30. b __ __	47. b __ __	64. b __ __	81. a __ __
14. d __ __	31. a __ __	48. a __ __	65. a __ __	
15. b __ __	32. c __ __	49. c __ __	66. d __ __	
16. d __ __	33. b __ __	50. a __ __	67. b __ __	1st: __/81 = __%
17. a __ __	34. d __ __	51. b __ __	68. d __ __	2nd: __/81 = __%

MULTIPLE-CHOICE ANSWER EXPLANATIONS

D.1. Income and Retained Earnings Statements

1. (d)   Baer Food's 2002 revenues should include net sales revenue ($187,000), interest revenue ($10,200), and gain on sale of equipment ($4,700), for a total of $201,900. Discontinued operations (loss of $12,400) and the change in accounting principle ($1,500) are both special items that should be reported as separate components of income, after **income from continuing operations**. Therefore, these items should **not** be included in the revenues section of the income statement (which is placed **before** income from continuing operations).

2. (a)   To directly compute cost of goods manufactured (CGM), the formula is

>   Beginning work in process
> + Direct materials used
> + Direct labor
> + Factory overhead
> – Ending work in process
>   Cost of goods manufactured

However, none of these elements are given in this problem, so CGM must be computed indirectly, using the cost of sales formula

Beginning finished goods	$400,000
+ Cost of goods manufactured	+ CGM
– Ending finished goods	–360,000
Cost of sales	$240,000

Solving for the missing amount, CGM is $200,000.

3. (a)   All of the revenues, gains, expenses, and losses given in this problem are components of income from continuing operations. Income before income taxes is $180,000, as computed below.

Revenues ($575,000 + $25,000)	$600,000
Expenses and losses ($240,000 + $70,000 + $10,000 + $50,000 + $15,000 + $15,000 + $20,000)	420,000
Income before income taxes	$180,000

To compute income from continuing operations (after taxes), income taxes ($180,000 x 30% = $54,000) must also be deducted ($180,000 – $54,000 = $126,000).

4. (a)   The requirement is to compute the amount of expenses to be included in selling expenses for 2002. Advertising ($150,000) and sales salaries and commissions

($140,000) are clearly selling expenses, as is the rent for the office space occupied by the sales department ($220,000 x 1/2 = $110,000). Additionally, freight-out ($80,000) is a selling expense because shipping the goods **from** the point of sale to the customer is the final effort in the selling process. The total selling expense is, therefore, $480,000 ($150,000 + $140,000 + $110,000 + $80,000). The remaining expenses given are general and administrative expenses, except for interest and the loss on sale of long-term investment, which are nonoperating items (other expenses and losses).

5. (a)   Operating expenses are usually divided into two categories, **selling expenses** and **general and administrative (G&A) expenses**. Selling expenses are related to the sale of a company's products, while G&A expenses are related to the company's general operations. Therefore, Griff should include the following costs in G&A expense:

Accounting and legal fees	$ 25,000
Officers' salaries	150,000
Insurance	85,000
G&A expense	$260,000

Freight-in ($175,000) is an inventoriable cost which should be reflected in cost of goods sold and ending inventory. Freight-out, the cost of delivering goods to customers ($160,000), is included in selling expenses. Sales representatives salaries ($215,000) is also a selling expense.

6. (d)   Interest expense is generally considered to be a nonoperating item and is therefore included in **other expenses and losses**. Operating expenses are usually divided into two categories, **selling expenses** and **general and administrative expenses**. Since advertising expense is directly related to the sale of the company's products, it is included in selling expenses. Therefore, neither of the expenses given are general and administrative expenses.

7. (a)   Charitable contributions expense should include all expenses incurred in 2002 by Yew Co. which involve charitable contributions to other entities. The total charitable contributions expense is $310,000, consisting of the $250,000 donated to youth and educational programs and the $60,000 ($140,000 – $80,000) donated to health and human service organizations. The other $80,000 was given to these organizations **by the employees,** with the company merely acting as an agent collecting that amount through payroll deductions and forwarding it on to the organizations. The expenditure for redesigning product packaging ($100,000) would be properly classified as research and development expense.

8. (a) Per APB 30, extraordinary items are material gains or losses which are both **unusual** in nature and **infrequent** in occurrence. For Raim Co., which sustains flood losses every two to three years, the 2002 flood loss is not infrequent, and should be recognized as a component of income from continuing operations. For Cane Co., the 2002 flood loss is both unusual and infrequent, so it should be recognized as an extraordinary item.

9. (b) Per APB 30, extraordinary items are material items which are **both unusual** in nature and **infrequent** in occurrence. APB 30 specifically states that the effect of a strike ($175,000) and a gain or loss from sale or abandonment of equipment ($125,000) are **not** considered extraordinary. However, SFAS 4 states that gains and losses from extinguishment of debt are to be classified as extraordinary even if they do not meet the **unusual** and **infrequent** criteria. Therefore the $150,000 loss is extraordinary, and the total amount of infrequent losses **not** considered extraordinary is $300,000 ($175,000 + $125,000).

10. (a) Per APB 30, extraordinary items are material items which are **both unusual** in nature and **infrequent** in occurrence. Disposals of plant assets, foreign currency losses, and inventory losses are not considered to be unusual in nature, and thus are not extraordinary. Items that may qualify as extraordinary items include some casualties, expropriations, and prohibitions under a new law. In Kent Co.'s 2002 income statement, losses not considered extraordinary amount to $610,000. The factory disposal ($300,000) is classified as discontinued operations because the operations carried on there are dissimilar from operations carried on at the other factories. The $120,000 foreign currency loss and $190,000 inventory loss are not extraordinary because they are not unusual in nature.

11. (a) Per APB 30, extraordinary items are material gains or losses which are both **unusual** in nature and **infrequent** in occurrence. Foreign currency losses ($1,200,000) and losses due to discontinued operations ($500,000) are not considered to be unusual in nature and thus are not extraordinary. Items that may qualify as extraordinary include some casualties, expropriations, prohibitions under a new law, and extinguishment of debt. Midway's casualty loss appears to be extraordinary because the hurricane was the first ever to strike in Midway's area. The net pretax loss was $100,000 [$800,000 equipment loss – $700,000 building gain ($1,000,000 – $300,000)].

12. (c) A gain (loss) must be recognized when a nonmonetary asset is involuntarily converted into monetary assets even if the company reinvests the monetary assets in replacement nonmonetary assets. The gain or loss is the difference between the insurance proceeds ($1,100,000 replacement cost – $50,000 deductible = $1,050,000) and the carrying amount of the assets destroyed or used up as a result of the casualty loss. The warehouse (carrying amount of $300,000) was destroyed, and cash of $20,000 was used to cover removal costs. Therefore, the gain is $730,000 [$1,050,000 – ($300,000 + $20,000)]. It is **not** an extraordinary item because storms similar to the one that destroyed the warehouse occur frequently (every four years).

13. (c) In this situation, the provision for income tax (income tax expense) will be the amount of the tax liability to the government determined without including the extraordinary loss. This amount is determined by applying the 40% tax rate to pretax accounting income before extraordinary items adjusted for any permanent differences. Accounting income before taxes is $900,000, but that amount includes a gain on life insurance coverage ($100,000). A gain on life insurance coverage is a **permanent** difference because it is included in accounting income but will **never** be included in taxable income. Therefore, the amount of accounting income which will be subject to taxes is $800,000 ($900,000 – $100,000), and the provision for income taxes is $320,000 ($800,000 x 40%). The tax savings from the extraordinary loss ($300,000 x 40% = $120,000) will not affect the provision for income taxes because the extraordinary item must be reported together with its tax effect (extraordinary loss of $180,000; net of tax).

14. (d) Net income as reported ($74,100) properly included the gain on early retirement of bonds payable ($22,000) and the loss from fire ($14,000). The fact that the gain and loss were reported net of taxes in the income statement was incorrect, but does not cause the net income amount to be in error. However, the other two items should **not** be reported in the income statement at all. An unrealized loss on **noncurrent** investments in stock ($5,400) is reported in other comprehensive income, not in net income. A correction of an error ($7,500) is treated as a prior period adjustment. It is reported in the financial statements as an adjustment to the beginning balance of retained earnings, rather than in the income statement. Since both of these items were subtracted in the computation of reported net income, they must be added back to compute the correct net income of $87,000 ($74,100 + $5,400 + $7,500).

15. (b) In 2002, Brecon Co. would report one fifth of the cabinet costs as depreciation expense in selling, general, and administrative expenses. Four fifths of the cabinet cost would remain capitalized as fixed assets at the end of 2001. The cabinets are considered fixed assets and not a part of cost of goods sold.

16. (d) APB 30 states that a material gain or loss that is unusual in nature or infrequent in occurrence, but not both, should be presented as a separate component of income or loss from continuing operations. Both extraordinary items and cumulative effect type changes in accounting principle are reported separately **after** income from continuing operations.

17. (a) Per APB 30, for an item to qualify as an extraordinary item it must be **both** unusual in nature and infrequent in occurrence. The above criteria must take into account the environment in which the entity operates. An entity with sales in different countries will experience foreign currency revaluations on a regular basis, so a currency revaluation would not be infrequent in occurrence and it is not an extraordinary item. Gains from increases in contract prices are neither infrequent nor unusual, so they cannot qualify as extraordinary items.

18. **(b)** Per APB 30, extraordinary items are reported **net of income taxes** as a separate component of income **after** discontinued operations but before cumulative effect of a change in accounting principle.

19. **(b)** Per APB 30, extraordinary items are events and transactions that are distinguished by both their unusual nature and the infrequency of their occurrence. Losses of this type are both common and frequent for Toncan. Per SFAS 5, estimates of the losses would not be presented in the financial statements. No amount is recorded until a loss actually occurs.

20. **(d)** Per APB 30, a transaction that is unusual in nature and infrequent in occurrence is considered an extraordinary item. An extraordinary item is reported **after** discontinued operations but **before** cumulative effect of accounting changes.

21. **(c)** Per APB 30, extraordinary items are events and transactions that are distinguished by both their unusual nature and the infrequency of their occurrence. Teller Co.'s loss arising from its **first** antitrust action meets both of these criteria (particularly since they pleaded guilty) and should therefore be reported as an extraordinary item. The strike against Teller's major supplier, however, should not be reported as an extraordinary item because it is usual in nature but may be expected to recur as a consequence of customary and continuing business activities.

22. **(c)** Per APB 30, extraordinary items are material items which are **both unusual** in nature and **infrequent** in occurrence. Therefore, the loss on sale of a bond investment is not extraordinary. In addition, SFAS 145 rescinded SFAS 4 which required gains or losses on extinguishment of debt to be reported as an extraordinary item. Thus, neither item is treated as extraordinary.

23. **(c)** SFAS 130 does not completely operationalize the concept of comprehensive income per SFAC 5 and 6 which state all transactions and events other than those with owners should be reported in comprehensive income. Under SFAS 130, corrections of errors shall continue to be reported net of tax in retained earnings as an adjustment of the beginning balance.

24. **(b)** SFAS 146 provides that costs of exit activities (including restructuring charges) should be measured and recognized at fair value when they are incurred.

D.2. Discontinued Operations

25. **(b)** The operating loss of $300,000 ($500,000 revenues less $800,000 expenses) relates to a discontinued component, so it is part of discontinued operations, **not** continuing operations. It is combined with the loss from disposal on the income statement. **Discontinued operations** is a category distinct from **extraordinary items**.

26. **(a)** SFAS 44 includes a number of requirements for disposal of a component to be presented as discontinued operations. However, management is not required to have entered into a sales agreement. It is sufficient if management is committed to a disposal plan that is reasonable. The other items are all required for presentation as discontinued operations.

27. **(d)** In discontinued operations, SFAS 144 requires the presentation of the income or loss from operations of the component and the gain or loss on disposal. Since the company met the requirements for "held for sale" status in 2002, the subsidiary should be written down to its fair value less cost to sell. This would result in a loss of $1,500,000 ($8,000,000 carrying amount – $6,500,000 fair value). Therefore, the loss from discontinued operations would be $3,500,000 ($2,000,000 loss from operations + $1,500,000 loss on planned disposal).

28. **(d)** According to SFAS 144, the loss from discontinued operations would equal the loss from operations plus the estimated loss from disposal of the component.

29. **(c)** SFAS 146 states that costs of termination benefits, lease termination, and consolidating facilities or relocating employees related to a disposal activity that involves discontinued operations should be included in the results of discontinued operations.

30. **(b)** The requirement is to determine how a discontinued component's operating losses for the current period should be classified in the financial statements. According to SFAS 144, the "income (loss) from operations" is combined with the loss on disposal.

31. **(a)** Per SFAS 144, gains or losses from the operation of a discontinued business component realized for the period are combined with the loss of disposal to determine the loss from discontinued operations.

32. **(c)** Per SFAS 144, discontinued operations should include the gain or loss on disposal plus the results of operations during the period.

D.3. Comprehensive Income

33. **(b)** Per SFAS 130, the purpose of reporting comprehensive income is to report a measure of overall enterprise performance by displaying all changes in equity of an enterprise that result from recognized transactions and other economic events of the period other than transactions with owners in their capacity as owners. An enterprise should continue to display an amount for net income with equal prominence to the comprehensive income amount displayed.

34. **(d)** Once unrealized items recorded and reported in the current or prior period are recognized as realized and reported in net income, it is necessary to reverse them out of other comprehensive income. The reclassification adjustment is to avoid double counting. The reclassification adjustment in this situation is $15,000 ($25,000 gain on AFS securities, net of $10,000 tax).

35. **(c)** SFAS 130 allows flexibility in the presentation of comprehensive income in the financial statements. However, the statement should be presented as a primary financial statement. The FASB allows three presentation formats [answer choices (a), (b), and (d)] with a preference for the first two alternatives.

36. **(d)** The accumulated balance of other comprehensive income should be reported as a component of equity, separate from retained earnings and additional paid-in capital.

37. (b) Comprehensive income is defined as the change in equity of a business during a period from transactions of nonowner sources. Stockholders are owners of the corporation or entity, therefore, transactions between the entity and shareholder are not a component of comprehensive income.

38. (d) The calculation of holding gains recognized in other comprehensive income is as follows:

	Before tax	Income tax	Net of tax
Year ended 12/31/01	$5,000	$1,500	$3,500
Year ended 12/31/02	2,500	750	1,750
Total gain	$7,500	$2,250	$5,250

The reclassification adjustment should be shown net of tax, so ($5,250) is the adjustment amount. $5,250 had been previously added to other comprehensive income when the gains occurred. The $5,250 needs to be taken out in order to avoid counting the gains twice. The securities have been sold so the gains are now realized and will be part of net income.

39. (d) The gain for the period is 10 shares times the increase in fair value, which is $250. This gain of $2,500 must be shown net of tax, so the holding gain is $1,750.

40. (a) Per SFAS 130, comprehensive income is computed as follows:

Net income		77,000
Other comprehensive income net of tax:		
Unrealized gain on securities	15,000	
Less: reclassification adjustment	(2,500)	12,500
Minimum pension liability adjustment		(3,000)
Other comprehensive income		9,500
Comprehensive income		86,500

Notice that stock warrants outstanding are not included as part of comprehensive income.

41. (d) If $2,450 (net of tax) is being deducted from other comprehensive income as a reclassification adjustment, $2,450 must be the amount of unrealized gains (net of tax) that have been recognized in other comprehensive income. The realized gains will then be recognized in income from continuing operations before tax. The gains before tax effects are $3,500 ($2,450 ÷ 70%).

42. (b) SFAS 130 requires disclosure of changes during a period of the following components of other comprehensive income: unrealized gains and losses on available-for-sale investments and foreign currency items, including any reclassification adjustments, and the minimum pension liability adjustment. Treasury stock is deducted from stockholders' equity and **not** a component of other comprehensive income.

43. (d) Separate EPS calculations are not required for other comprehensive income or comprehensive income according to SFAS 130.

44. (d) The FASB prefers that comprehensive income be shown at the bottom of the income statement as a continuation of net income or in a separate statement beginning with net income. Presenting comprehensive income in the statement of changes in stockholders' equity is not a method that is preferred by the FASB.

45. (c) Held-to-maturity securities are reported at amortized cost. Any decreases or increases in fair value are reported neither in net income nor as part of other comprehen-

sive income. Answer (a) and (b) are incorrect because per SFAS 132, a net loss of an additional pension liability not yet recognized as net periodic pension cost and subsequent decreases of the fair value of available-for-sale securities that have been previously written down as impaired are included in other comprehensive income. Answer (d) is incorrect because decreases in the fair value of held-to-maturity securities are no part of other comprehensive income.

46. (d) According to SFAS 130, *Reporting Comprehensive Income*, comprehensive income (net income plus other comprehensive income) should be displayed in a financial statement that has the same prominence as other financial statements. Answer (a) is incorrect because the FASB prefers that comprehensive income be displayed either at the bottom of the income statement, continuing from net income to arrive at a comprehensive income figure (equals net income plus other comprehensive income), or in a separate statement of comprehensive income. Answer (b) is incorrect because components of other comprehensive income may be displayed net of related tax effects or before related tax effects with one amount shown for the aggregate income tax effect. Answer (c) is incorrect because comprehensive income can be displayed in the two methods preferred by the FASB (mentioned above) or in the statement of changes in stockholders' equity.

D.4. Balance Sheets

47. (b) Total retained earnings includes both unappropriated retained earnings and restricted retained earnings. Therefore, before closing entries, total retained earnings is $1,060,000 ($900,000 + $160,000). Before computing 2002 net income, tax expense must be recorded. Earnings ($6,680,000) less costs and expenses ($5,180,000) result in pretax income of $1,500,000. Since the tax rate is 30%, tax expense is $450,000 (30% x $1,500,000). Therefore, an adjustment is necessary to debit **income tax expense** and credit **prepaid taxes** for $450,000. After the adjustment, net income is $1,050,000 ($6,680,000 – $5,180,000 – $450,000). After closing entries, total retained earnings is $2,110,000 ($1,060,000 + $1,050,000).

48. (a) The only liabilities included in the trial balance are billings in excess of costs on long-term contracts ($700,000) and note payable-noncurrent ($1,620,000). Only the note is noncurrent. Billings in excess of costs on long-term contracts is similar to unearned revenue and is always reported as a current liability.

49. (c) Current assets listed in the trial balance are cash ($600,000), accounts receivable ($3,500,000), cost in excess of billings on long-term contracts ($1,600,000) and prepaid taxes ($450,000). However, income tax expense has not yet been recorded. Earnings ($6,680,000) less costs and expenses ($5,180,000) result in pretax income of $1,500,000. Since the tax rate is 30%, tax expense is $450,000 (30% x $1,500,000). Therefore, an adjustment is necessary to debit **income tax expense** and credit **prepaid taxes** for $450,000. Total current assets, after this adjustment, are $5,700,000.

Cash	$ 600,000
Accounts receivable	3,500,000
Cost in excess of billings	1,600,000
	$5,700,000

50. (a) Mirr began operations on 1/1/02 with the following balance sheet elements:

Assets   =   Liabilities   +   Owners' equity
$860,000   = $110,000   + $750,000

During 2002, liabilities increased to $120,000, and owners' equity increased to $765,000 [$750,000 beginning balance + $18,000 net income ($82,000 revenues – $64,000 expenses) – $3,000 dividends declared]. Therefore, 12/31/02 assets must be $885,000.

Assets   =   Liabilities   +   Owners' equity
Assets   = $120,000   + $765,000
Assets   = $885,000

51. (b) The requirement is to determine the net income for 2002 by analyzing changes in the balance sheet. Recall the accounting equation: Assets – Liabilities = Stockholders' equity. By inserting the changes given into this formula, we find an increase of $62,000 exists in the entire stockholders' equity section ($89,000 – $27,000 = $62,000). Stockholders' equity is composed of capital stock, additional paid-in capital and retained earnings. Because increases in the other two balances are given that total $66,000 ($60,000 + $6,000), the retained earnings balance must have decreased by $4,000 ($66,000 – $62,000). When dividends are paid, this reduces retained earnings, while Vel Corp. net income increases the balance of retained earnings. For the equation to balance, the changes in retained earnings account must reduce total stockholders' equity by $4,000. Therefore, if $13,000 in dividends are paid, which reduce retained earnings, and total retained earnings are to be reduced by $4,000, then net income, which increases retained earnings, must be $9,000. This creates the $4,000 difference needed to make the equation balance ($89,000 – $27,000 = $66,000 – $4,000). The following shows the analysis of the retained earnings account:

Retained earnings (beg.)	$ xxx
Net income (plug)	**9,000**
Dividends	(13,000)
Retained earnings (decrease)	($ 4,000)

52. (a) Idle machinery ($11,200) and cash surrender value of life insurance ($13,700) are both assets. The allowance for decline in market value of noncurrent marketable equity securities ($8,400) is a contra asset that is properly included in the asset section of the balance sheet (as a deduction). The only item listed which should **not** be included in the asset section of the balance sheet is the treasury stock ($24,000). Although the treasury stock account has a debit balance, it is not an asset; instead, it is reported as a contra equity account. Therefore, the $24,000 must be excluded from the asset section, reducing the net asset amount to $851,000 ($875,000 – $24,000).

53. (a) Although the statement of cash flows provides information about liquidity, solvency, and financial flexibility, a potential investor would **primarily** use the balance sheet to assess liquidity and financial flexibility. The balance sheet helps users analyze the company's ability to use current assets to pay current liabilities (liquidity) and the company's ability to alter the amounts and timing of future cash flows to adapt to unexpected needs or to take advantage of opportunities (flexibility).

D.5.a. Disclosures

54. (c) SFAS 57 requires that financial statements include disclosures of material transactions between related parties. Compensation arrangements in the ordinary course of business, however, are specifically excluded from this disclosure requirement. Therefore, only the $250,000 sale to affiliated enterprises must be disclosed.

55. (c) SFAS 57 requires disclosure of material transactions between related parties except: (1) compensation agreements, expense allowances, and other similar items in the ordinary course of business, and (2) transactions which are eliminated in the preparation of consolidated or combined financial statements. The officers' salaries and officers' expenses fall into category (1), while the intercompany sales fall into category (2). Therefore, only the loans to officers ($125,000 + $50,000 = $175,000) are reported as related-party disclosures.

56. (d) SFAS 57 requires disclosure of material transactions between related parties except: (1) compensation agreements, expense allowances, and other similar items in the ordinary course of business and (2) transactions eliminated in the preparation of consolidated or combined financial statements.

57. (b) SFAS 57 requires disclosure of any material related-party transactions except

1. Compensation agreements, expense allowances, and similar items in the ordinary course of business.
2. Transactions that are eliminated in the preparation of consolidated or combined financial statements.

Since sales of inventory between subsidiary and parent are eliminated in preparing consolidated financial statements, such sales need not be disclosed as a related-party transaction. Nonmonetary exchanges by affiliates are not specifically exempted from disclosure by SFAS 57, and therefore must be disclosed as related-party transactions. SFAS 57 states that compensation arrangements, expense allowances, and similar items in the ordinary course of business need not be disclosed as related-party transactions. However, in this case the allowances are in excess of normal business practice and therefore must be disclosed. Surety and guaranty agreements between related parties are not specifically exempted from disclosure by SFAS 57 and therefore must be disclosed as related-party transactions.

58. (c) According to SFAS 57, *Related-Party Disclosures*, disclosures of material transactions shall include (1) nature of relationship(s), (2) description of transaction(s), including those assigned zero or nominal amounts, (3) dollar amounts of transactions for each income statement period and effect of any change in method of establishing terms, and (4) amounts due to/from related parties, including terms and manner of settlement.

59. (a) The users of the information are the focus of financial reporting. GAAP requires disclosures in the notes to facilitate the users' understanding of the financial statements. Answer (b) is incorrect because the financial statements should be properly presented in accordance with GAAP; thus no improper presentation should exist. Answer (c) is incorrect because the totals of the financial statements should include all items; thus, no items would be excluded. Answer (d) is incorrect because management's responses to the auditor's comments would be contained in the management letter, which is a separate report typically presented to the audit committee or the board of directors.

D.5.b. Accounting Policies

60. **(a)** The requirement is to determine which information should be included in the summary of significant accounting policies. Per APB 22, disclosure of accounting policies should identify and describe the accounting principles followed by the reporting entity and methods of applying those principles. Answer (a) is correct because the method of recording and depreciating assets is an example of such a required disclosure. Answers (b) and (c) are incorrect because both represent detail presented elsewhere in the financial statements. Answer (d) is incorrect because it is an estimate of earnings rather than an accounting policy.

61. **(c)** Per APB 22, disclosure of accounting policies should identify and describe the accounting principles followed by the reporting entity and methods of applying those principles. The criteria for determining which investments are treated as cash equivalents is an example of how the entity applies accounting principles. APB 22 states that these disclosures should not duplicate details presented elsewhere as part of the financial statements. Answers (a), (b), and (d) are not disclosures of accounting **policies,** and also would be presented elsewhere in the financial statements.

D.5.d. Constant Dollar Accounting

62. **(c)** SFAS 89 encourages, but does not require, business enterprises to disclose **supplementary information** on the effects of changing prices. The statement presents requirements to be followed by enterprises that voluntarily elect to disclose this information. Answers (a) and (b) are incorrect because the information is not reported in the body of the financial statements or in the notes to the financial statements. Answer (d) is incorrect because management's report to shareholders identifies management's responsibilities, including responsibilities for the internal control system, and would not include information about changing prices.

63. **(c)** The requirement is to determine the amounts to be reported for three balance sheet accounts in a supplementary **constant dollar** balance sheet. In a constant dollar balance sheet, **nonmonetary** items are restated to the current price level, while monetary items are **not** restated because they are already stated in current dollars. The investment in bonds and the long-term debt are monetary items since their amounts are fixed by contract in terms of number of dollars. Therefore, these items are not restated and are reported at $60,000 and $80,000, respectively. The land, however, is a nonmonetary item and its cost ($120,000) must be restated to current dollars by using the TO/FROM ratio (110/100), resulting in an adjusted amount of $132,000 ($120,000 x 110/100). Reference to SFAS 89 will provide guidance on monetary/nonmonetary classifications.

64. **(b)** According to SFAS 89, "loans to employees" is a monetary asset account since its payment amount is fixed at some point in the future. Conversely, merchandise inventory is considered a nonmonetary asset account since its value will change based on relative price levels in the future. The total value of monetary assets is the balance of the loans to employees account, or $20,000.

65. **(a)** The increase in current cost (nominal dollars) of $15,000 is the **total** increase in current cost, including any increase caused by inflation. The effect of changes in the general price level is **not** separated from the effect of changes in specific value. The increase in current cost (constant dollars) of $12,000 is the increase in current cost after eliminating any increase caused by inflation. Therefore, the inflation component of the increase in current cost of inventories is $3,000 ($15,000 – $12,000).

66. **(d)** The requirement is to determine which item is classified as nonmonetary when computing the purchasing power gain or loss on net monetary items. SFAS 89 defines a monetary item as one that is fixed or determinable without reference to future prices. Accumulated depreciation is not a monetary item. Advances to unconsolidated subsidiaries, allowance for doubtful accounts, and unamortized premium on bonds payable are all monetary items.

67. **(b)** Per SFAS 89, a purchasing power gain or loss is the net gain or loss determined by restating in units of constant purchasing power the opening and closing balances of, and transactions in, **monetary** assets and liabilities. During a period of rising prices, monetary liabilities give rise to purchasing power gains because they will be settled with cash which can be used to purchase relatively fewer goods or services at a future time.

D.5.e. Current Cost Accounting

68. **(d)** Current cost accounting is a method of valuing and reporting assets, liabilities, revenues, and expenses at their current cost at the balance sheet date or at the date of their use or sale. A holding gain is recorded as an increase in an item's value. At December 31, 2002, Vend Co. is holding merchandise which is currently valued at $10 per unit (replacement cost), while the original recorded value of the merchandise was $8 per unit (purchase price). Therefore, the holding gain is $2 per unit.

69. **(c)** The requirement is to calculate the amount of current cost depreciation expense which would appear in supplementary current cost financial statements. Per SFAS 89, depreciation is to be measured based on the **average** current cost of the asset during the period of use. The average current cost of this machine during 2002 is $120,000 [($115,000 + $125,000) ÷ 2]. Therefore, 2002 depreciation expense is $24,000 ($120,000 ÷ 5-year useful life).

70. **(a)** SFAS 89 requires that current cost for inventories and equipment be measured at the lower of current cost or recoverable amount. For equipment, recoverable amount ($95,000) is lower than current cost; for inventory, current cost ($80,000) is lower than recoverable amount. Therefore, the total amount to be reported for these assets is $175,000 ($95,000 + $80,000).

71. **(a)** Per SFAS 89, increases or decreases in the current cost of inventory result from the difference between the measures of assets at their entry dates (beginning of year or purchase date) and measures of assets at their exit dates (end of year or date of use/sale). Based on this definition, holding gains would be reported both when inventory is sold during the year (realized gains), and when inventory is held at the end of the year (unrealized gains).

72. **(a)** SFAS 89 illustrates the computation of cost of goods sold under the current cost method. The current cost of goods sold is computed by multiplying the average cost of units produced or purchased during the year times the number of units sold.

73.   (d)   The market in which an entity conducts its operations, the available sources of supply of materials used in operations of an entity, and the volume of business transacted with a certain contributor are all examples of concentrations that create vulnerabilities that are required to be disclosed per SOP 94-6, *Disclosures of Certain Significant Risks and Uncertainties.*

74.   (b)   The potential impact of estimates about values of assets and liabilities when it is reasonably possible that the estimate will change in the near future is a required disclosure regarding significant risks and uncertainties. Factors causing an estimate to be sensitive is not a required disclosure, only recommended. The potential impact of estimates about values of assets and liabilities when it is remotely possible that the estimate will change in the near future is not a required disclosure. It is only a required disclosure if it is reasonably possible that the estimates will change in the near future. Only a description of operations outside the home country is a required disclosure.

D.7.   Other Comprehensive Bases of Accounting

75.   (c)   Other than generally accepted accounting principles, the only other bases which may be used to prepare financial statements in conformity with a comprehensive basis of accounting are the **cash basis** and a **basis of accounting used to file an income tax return**.

76.   (d)   When financial statements are prepared using an income tax basis, two accounting methods can be used: (1) modified cash basis—hybrid method of IRS and (2) accrual basis—IRS. The modified cash basis reflects the use of accrual basis for inventories, cost of goods sold, sales, and depreciation, if these are significant. The accrual basis uses accruals and deferrals with several exceptions (e.g., prepaid income, warranty expense). When financial statements are prepared on an income tax basis, the financial statements should not simply repeat items and amounts reported in the tax return. Thus, items such as nontaxable municipal interest and the nondeductible portion of travel and entertainment expense should be fully reflected in the income statement on the basis used for tax purposes, with footnote disclosure of the differences between the amounts reported in the income statements and tax return.

77.   (a)   In financial statements prepared on the income tax basis, the nondeductible portion of meals and entertainment expense should be included with the deductible portion as a total amount of travel and entertainment expense. Additionally, the nondeductible portion should be footnoted. Answer (a) is the best answer among the alternatives given, although it does not indicate that a footnote is required. The answer to this question is found in an AICPA practice publication entitled *Preparing and Reporting on Cash- and Tax-basis Financial Statements* that gives guidance to practitioners on preparing financial statements on other comprehensive bases of accounting.

D.8.   Prospective Financial Information

78.   (b)   The responsible party is not the only limited user. Third parties with whom the responsible party is ne-

gotiating directly are also limited users. Answer (a) is incorrect because prospective financial information may be prepared for general or limited use. Answer (c) is incorrect because it is true that assumptions not necessarily expected to occur may be included in the financial projection. Answer (d) is incorrect because the financial projection may be expressed as a range of dollars.

79.   (d)   Prospective financial information is defined as any financial information about the future.

80.   (c)   Financial forecasts and projections must be prepared in accordance with GAAP, with the plans of the entity, and with due professional care in order to achieve a reasonably objective basis.

81.   (a)   According to the AICPA *Accounting and Auditing Guide*, prospective financial statements include information on the purpose of the statements, assumptions, and significant accounting policies.

OTHER OBJECTIVE ANSWERS AND ANSWER EXPLANATIONS

Problem 1

1. **(G)** The acquisition of assets does not necessitate that the same method of depreciation be used for the newly acquired assets as for the existing assets. Therefore, no change in accounting principle has occurred because the previously recorded assets will continue to be depreciated using the straight-line method.

2. **(A)** Accounting for a pooling of interests is properly accounted for as a change in reporting entity.

3. **(B)** According to SFAS 16, all corrections of errors should be treated as prior period adjustments. This requires prompt recording of the error in the year in which the error was discovered, and reporting the effects of the error in the financial statements as an adjustment to the beginning balance of retained earnings.

4. **(H)** According to APB 30, for an item to qualify as an extraordinary item it must be both unusual in nature and infrequent in occurrence. Clearly, the write-down of inventory due to obsolescence does not qualify for extraordinary treatment; therefore, it should be disclosed separately in the income statement before extraordinary items.

5. **(I)** Gains or losses on the disposal of net assets is included in the calculation of gain or loss on disposal of discontinued operations. Therefore, the total gain or loss on disposal should consist of the following two calculations: the net asset gain or loss mentioned above and the income or loss from operations from the measurement date to the disposal date (the phase-out period).

6. **(B)** The use of the gross profit method to determine year-end inventory balances is not proper GAAP. Therefore, if a situation such as this existed, it should be treated as a correction of an error.

7. **(C)** The change from one generally accepted accounting principle to another is considered a change in accounting principle. Since both the completed contract method and the percentage-of-completion methods are recognized GAAP, the change from one to the other is properly accounted for as a change in accounting principle.

8. **(D)** According to APB 20, when it is impossible to determine whether a change in accounting principle or a change in estimate has occurred, the change should be considered as a change in estimate.

9. **(H)** Gains or losses on extinguishment of debt are no longer treated as extraordinary items.

10. **(I)** Income or loss from operations during the phase-out period (from the measurement date to the disposal date) is properly included in the calculation of the gain or loss on the disposal of discontinued operations. Therefore, this calculation includes both the income or loss from operations during the phase-out period and the gain or loss on the disposal of net assets.

Problem 2

1. **(B)** Per SFAS 115, changes in the market value of (trading type) marketable securities shall be included in the determination of income from continuing operations of the period in which the change in market value occurs.

2. **(E)** Per SFAS 130, the accumulated changes in the valuation (unrealized excess of cost over market value) of **available-for-sale** marketable equity securities shall be reported as accumulated other comprehensive income.

3. **(F)** Per SFAS 144, results of operations of a component that has been or will be discontinued should be reported **separately** as a component of income, after income from continuing operations but before extraordinary items and the cumulative effect of accounting changes.

4. **(B)** Per SFAS 52, a foreign subsidiary must **remeasure** its financial statements when its functional currency (the currency of the primary economic environment in which the entity operates) is different from its local currency (the currency currently used by the entity). The effect of the remeasurement process (gain or loss) should be recognized currently in income. Aggregate gain or loss for the period should also be disclosed either in the financial statements or in the notes.

5. **(C)** Per SFAS 52, when translating a foreign subsidiary's financial statements from functional currency to reporting currency, a translation adjustment will result. The translation adjustment is not included in net income but is reported as a component of comprehensive income and called other comprehensive income.

6. **(D)** Per APB 30, extraordinary items are events and transactions that are **both** unusual and infrequent. The earthquake in this problem occurred in an area previously considered subject to only minor tremors. Therefore, the earthquake would be considered an extraordinary event. Per APB 30, extraordinary items should be shown separately on the income statement, after income from continuing operations.

7. **(F)** The question indicates that it is probable that Pucket Corp. will **receive** $1,000,000 from a pending lawsuit. Thus, the $1,000,000 is a **gain** contingency. Per SFAS 5, contingencies that may result in **gains** are not reflected in the accounts, as doing so might result in the recognition of revenue before its realization. Adequate disclosure of the gain contingency should be made, but care should be taken to avoid misleading implications as to the likelihood of realization.

8. **(B)** Per SFAS 2, the cost of research and development services performed by others on behalf of the enterprise are included in R&D costs. R&D costs are charged to expense when incurred and thus are included in income from continuing operations of that period. In addition, separate disclosure of the total R&D costs for the period should be made either in the financial statements or in the notes.

Problem 3

1. (**G**) When a corporation declares a cash or property dividend, the amount to be paid becomes a liability of the corporation. The dividends payable amount would be classified as a current liability on the balance sheet. It is important to note that dividends payable represent the amount distributed to stockholders as a return on their investment. Dividends are not expenses.

2. (**C**) When an item of property, plant, or equipment is being constructed by the company that intends to use it, all of the relevant costs related to the construction should be included in the asset. The asset would be classified as plant and equipment.

3. (**F**) A factory building that has been retired from use and held for sale should be classified as an **other asset** rather than as property, plant and equipment. The property, plant and equipment account should include only those tangible assets that are being used in operations.

4. (**B**) Land that is held for speculative or investment purposes should be classified as an investment rather than as property, plant, and equipment. The property, plant, and equipment account should represent only those assets being used in current operations.

5. (**N**) Consigned inventory is excluded from the balance sheet because it is not owned by Baker. Consigned inventory represents an arrangement whereby the owner of the goods transfers physical possession to an agent (Baker). The agent (consignee) will attempt to sell the goods on the owner's behalf. The inventory remains an asset of its owner.

6. (**K**) A stock dividend distributable represents a dividend to be distributed to shareholders in the form of additional shares of the corporation's stock. Each shareholder will receive a proportional share of additional stock. The declaration of a stock dividend does not result in a liability, as it does not result in any of the corporation's assets being paid. Thus, a stock dividend distributable would be classified as an addition in the stockholders' equity section in the common stock account.

7. (**A**) Current assets represent cash or other assets that are expected to be used within the operating cycle. Office supplies inventory represents an asset that could be expected to be used within the operating cycle.

8. (**B**) Generally, a fund is a group of assets set aside for a future nonoperating purpose. A sinking fund contains assets to be used in the future to retire bonds. These assets are generally invested while waiting to be used and are noncurrent.

9. (**A**) An installment sales accounts receivable results when the corporation makes a sale to a customer and does not receive payment in full on the date of sale. Since this company normally sells on the installment basis, its operating cycle becomes eighteen months. Its receivables are current assets because their average life falls within the operating cycle.

10. (**N**) Temporary decline in inventory value is a loss and appears on the income statement.

11. (**F**) Advances to officers are considered nontrade receivables. These types of receivables should be reported separately on the balance sheet as other assets.

12. (**G**) A warranty is a guarantee made by the seller to the purchaser against defects in the product's quality. Estimated warranty expense for a given period can be estimated as a percentage of sales. The percentage is based on past warranty experience. The estimated warranty cost represents the warranty expenditures in the future for past sales and is a current liability.

13. (**C**) Property, plant, and equipment consists of items used in the normal operations of a business. The inventory of small tools represents tools **used** in the business and are not for sale.

14. (**X-K**) Treasury stock is a corporation's own stock which has been issued and reacquired by the corporation. Treasury stock may be accounted for under the cost or par value method. When the par value method is used, treasury stock would be recorded on the balance sheet as a reduction or contra to the common stock account.

15. (**K**) Common stock subscribed represents stock subscriptions that have not been fully paid. The stock is not considered to be issued until the full price is paid. This account should be classified as an increase in the common stock and it is offset in stockholders' equity by a contra account for the balance of the subscription due.

16. (**H**) A convertible bond is a bond which may be converted to another form of the corporation's securities during a specified time frame. A bond is typically classified as a long-term liability on the balance sheet.

17. (**N**) Corporations do not own securities they hold as collateral. The corporation will retain the securities only in the event of a default on the receivable the securities are collateralizing. Thus, the securities are excluded from the balance sheet of Baker and they appear on the balance sheets of their owners.

18. (**G**) A bank overdraft occurs when a check is written for a greater amount than the balance in the bank account. A bank overdraft should be classified as a current liability. It should not be offset against other cash account balances unless the cash account is in the same bank.

ANSWER OUTLINE

Problem 1   Discontinued Operations and Extraordinary
Items

a.   Report extraordinary item after continuing operations
and discontinued operations
    Net of tax
    Presentation required to enable users to assess future
    cash flows

b.   Report discontinued operations in separate section
after continuing operations
    Present as two components
        Loss from operations of discontinued compo-
        nent, including any loss or gain on disposal
        Income tax benefit

c.   Report relocation costs as part of "loss on disposal"
component
    Reason for treating as part of "loss on disposal" com-
    ponent is that they directly relate to decision to dis-
    pose

UNOFFICIAL ANSWER

Problem 1   Discontinued Operations and X/O Items

a.   Hillside should report the extraordinary item separately,
net of applicable income taxes, below the continuing operations section in the income statement. Exclusion of extraordinary items from the results of continuing operations is
intended to produce a measure of income from continuing
operations that is useful in projecting future operating cash
flows.

b.   Hillside should report the discontinued operations separately in the 2002 income statement immediately below income from continuing operations. Discontinued operations
should be comprised of

• Loss from operations of the discontinued component and the loss on disposal.
• Income tax benefit.

c.   Hillside should include the costs incurred to relocate
employees in the loss on disposal of the discontinued component in its 2002 income statement. These costs are a direct result of the commitment to dispose of its component.

SOLUTION GUIDE

Problem 2   Prepare Single-Step IS; Reconcile Net Income
to Taxable Income

1.   This problem consists of two related parts requiring a
single-step income statement and a schedule reconciling net income to taxable income.

2.   Part a. requires preparation of a single-step income
statement. In a single-step income statement, total
expenses and losses are subtracted from total revenues and gains to compute income. There are no
"steps" resulting in subtotals such as gross profit, income from operations, etc. For any format income
statement, however, nonrecurring items such as extraordinary items, discontinued operations, and cumulative effect of change in accounting principle are
reported separately.

2.1   Revenues and gains listed in the trial balance include
machine sales, service revenues, interest revenue, and
gain on sale of factory. The gain is not listed in the
revenues and gains section because it is an extraordinary item. The gain is extraordinary because it is unusual, infrequent and results from an expropriation.
APB 30 specifies expropriations as an example of an
extraordinary item.

2.2   Expenses and losses listed in the trial balance include
cost of sales, cost of services, administrative expenses, research and development expenses, interest
expense, and loss from asset disposal.

2.3   One expense **not** listed in the trial balance is income
tax expense, which has not yet been recorded. To
compute the current portion of income tax expense
on ordinary income, first the expenses and losses
listed in 2.1 are subtracted from the revenues (excluding the extraordinary item) listed in 2.2. The difference of $30,000 is income before income tax and
extraordinary item. The amount must be adjusted for
permanent and temporary differences to compute
taxable income (excluding extraordinary item). The
$5,000 life insurance premium payment must be
added back because it was deducted to compute accounting income, but is not deductible for tax purposes, (permanent difference). The $15,000 excess
tax depreciation (temporary difference) must be subtracted. Therefore, taxable income, excluding the
extraordinary item, is $20,000 ($30,000 + $5,000 –
$15,000). Since the tax rate is 30%, the current por-
tion of income tax expense is $6,000 ($20,000 x
30%).

2.4   The deferred portion of income tax expense is computed by multiplying the future taxable amounts
($10,000 + $5,000 = $15,000) by the future enacted
tax rate of 30% (30% x $15,000 = $4,500).

2.5   After computing tax expense, other revenues
($1,010,000) less total expenses ($990,500) equals
income before extraordinary item ($19,500). Note
that the two components of income taxes could have
been disclosed after "income before income taxes
and extraordinary item," which would be $30,000
(see 2.3).

2.6   As discussed in 2.1, the gain from the expropriation
of the factory ($250,000) is an extraordinary item.
Per APB 30, extraordinary items must be reported
separately, and net of their tax effect. Since the
$250,000 gain is taxable, the gain must be reported at
$175,000 ($250,000 less tax effect of 30% x
$250,000). Therefore, net income is $194,500
($19,500 + $175,000).

2.7   Earnings per share (EPS) must be reported on income
before extraordinary items and on net income, in accordance with SFAS 128. EPS on the extraordinary
gain may be shown either on the face of the IS or in
the notes to the FS. The 2001 cumulative preferred
dividends ($2,000,000 x 5% = $100,000) must be
subtracted from the income amounts to determine the
amount available to common stockholders. This result is then divided by the weighted-average number

of common shares outstanding. Earnings per share on income before extraordinary gain is

$$\frac{\$19,500 \text{ income} - \$100,000 \text{ pref. dividends}}{200,000 \text{ weighted-average shares}} = (\underline{\$0.40})$$

Next, the extraordinary gain per share is $0.87 $\left(\frac{\$175,000}{200,000}\right)$.

Finally, net income per share is $.47 ($0.40 + $0.87).

3.   Part b. requires the preparation of a schedule reconciling net income to taxable income.

3.1   Net income from part a. is $194,500. This must be adjusted for any items that affect net income but not taxable income, or vice versa.

3.2   Income taxes (current, deferred, and on the extraordinary item) decrease net income, but do not affect taxable income. Therefore, these amounts ($6,000; $4,500; $75,000) must be added back to net income.

3.3   The officer's life insurance expense ($5,000) also reduces net income, but is not deductible for tax purposes. Therefore, it, too, must be added back to net income.

3.4   The excess tax depreciation ($15,000) is deductible on the tax return but is not an expense on the income statement. This item must be deducted to reconcile to taxable income.

3.5   The resulting taxable income ($270,000) can be computed directly to check its correctness as follows:

Revenues and gains		
Machine sales		$750,000
Service revenues		250,000
Interest revenue		10,000
Gain on sale of factory		250,000
		1,260,000
Expenses and losses		
Cost of sales ($425,000 + $15,000)*	$440,000	
Cost of services	100,000	
Administrative expenses ($300,000 – $5,000)	295,000	
Research and development expense	110,000	
Interest expense	5,000	
Loss from asset disposal	40,000	990,000
Taxable income		$ 270,000

*Assumes depreciation is included in cost of sales

Note that taxable income times the tax rate results in taxes currently payable of $81,000 ($270,000 x 30%), which corresponds to **income tax expense—current** ($6,000) plus the tax expense applicable to the extraordinary item ($75,000).

UNOFFICIAL ANSWER

Problem 2   Prepare Single-Step IS; Reconcile Net Income to Taxable Income

a.

Powell Corp.
INCOME STATEMENT
For the Year Ended June 30, 2002

Revenues:		
Machine sales	$750,000	
Service revenues	250,000	
Interest revenue	10,000	
Total revenues		$1,010,000

Expenses:		
Cost of sales—machines	425,000	
Cost of services	100,000	
Administrative expenses	300,000	
Research and development expenses	110,000	
Interest expense	5,000	
Loss from asset disposal	40,000	
Current income tax expense	6,000	
Deferred income tax expense	4,500	
Total expenses and losses		990,500
Income before extraordinary gain		19,500
Extraordinary gain, net of income taxes of $75,000		175,000
Net income		$ 194,500
Earnings (loss) per share:		
Income before extraordinary gain		($0.40)
Extraordinary gain		.87
Net income		$0.47

b.

Net income	$ 194,500
Add:	
Taxes on extraordinary gain	75,000
Provision for income taxes	10,500
Financial statement income before income taxes	280,000
Permanent difference—officer's life insurance	5,000
Temporary difference—excess of tax over financial statement depreciation	(15,000)
Taxable income	$ 270,000

SOLUTION GUIDE

Problem 3   Prepare Balance Sheet

1.   In this problem, a corrected, classified 12/31/02 balance sheet with proper format and necessary descriptions must be prepared. The solutions approach is to first write the correct statement heading on paper. Second, skim the incorrect balance sheet provided, then go through the additional data to determine the necessary adjustments and disclosures. As you do this, label each item CA, CL, investment, etc.

2.   The unrecorded payment on accounts payable should be recorded at 12/30/02, resulting in a $14,000 decrease in cash and accounts payable.

2.1   No entry was made for the customer's NSF check ($2,000), which should be recorded as a decrease in cash and an increase in accounts receivable (since the customer still owes Zues $2,000).

2.2   Cash restricted for building purposes ($100,000) must be reported separately from unrestricted cash. Restricted cash is classified either as current or long-term depending on the expected date of disbursement. In this case, since the cash is restricted for future **building purposes,** it is classified as long-term.

2.3   The $30,000 note receivable from Zues' president should be reported separately from accounts receivable, reducing AR by the same amount. The note should be classified as long-term since it is not due until 12/31/05.

2.4   Current assets should include cash ($225,000 – $14,000 – $2,000 – $100,000 = $109,000), accounts receivable, net ($345,700 + $2,000 – $30,000 = $317,700) and inventories ($560,000). The restricted cash ($100,000) and notes receivable ($30,000) are reported as other assets.

3. The next two items of additional data concern the investments account, which is reported in the bookkeeper's balance sheet at $57,700 [$51,300 cost of investment plus $6,400 cost of treasury stock (200 x $32)].

3.1 The cost of treasury stock ($6,400) should be removed from the investments account and reported as a separate reduction of stockholders' equity. This brings the investment account down to a balance of $51,300 ($57,700 – $6,400), which is the cost of the investment.

3.2 The remaining investment consists of shares of stock of a **major** corporation, which indicates that these are **marketable** equity securities (MES), which should be reported at market. Since cost is $51,300 and market value is $47,000, an unrealized loss should be recorded at $4,300 ($51,300 – $47,000). The unrealized loss is reported as a separate component of stockholders' equity entitled "accumulated other comprehensive income" because these MES should be classified as "available-for-sale." Additionally, the investment account should be reduced by $4,300. Note that the shares acquired were those of a supplier. Since the percentage of outstanding shares represented by the 500 shares is unknown, "available for sale" appears to be the proper treatment.

3.3 The land held as a potential future building site ($250,000) is shown under "other assets" in the AICPA answer. It would also be acceptable to classify the land as an investment.

4. None of the additional data gives any information on the amounts reported as land, building, machinery, and equipment, or accumulated depreciation, except for the information about the land held as a potential future plant site (see 3.3 above).

4.1 Property, plant, and equipment consists of land ($450,000 – $250,000 = $200,000), building ($1,750,000), and machinery and equipment ($1,964,000). Accumulated depreciation ($420,000) is subtracted from the building, machinery, and equipment.

4.2 Goodwill ($37,000) is reported as an intangible asset.

5. The next few items of additional information involve liabilities. The main concern is determining classification as current or long-term.

5.1 The notes payable ($500,000) are classified as $100,000 current (for the installment due 12/30/02) and $400,000 long-term (for the remaining four installments).

5.2 The mortgage payable would generally be reported as $600,000 current (12 x $50,000) and the remaining $300,000 long-term ($900,000 – $600,000). However, after two $50,000 installments were paid, the remaining $800,000 was refinanced on a long-term

basis. Per SFAS 6, a short-term obligation can be reclassified as long-term if the enterprise intends to refinance the obligation on a long-term basis **and** the intent is supported by the ability to refinance. Zues demonstrated its intent and ability to refinance $800,000 of the mortgage when it actually refinanced that amount on 3/1/03, before the 12/31/02 financial statements were issued. Therefore, in the 12/31/02 balance sheet, $100,000 of the mortgage should be classified as current and $800,000 as long-term.

5.3 The lawsuit liability ($80,000) is classified as current since it will be paid in 2002.

5.4 Income taxes payable ($61,200) is the amount recorded as the current portion of income tax expense in the 2002 income statement. Zues also has recorded $40,000 of prepaid income taxes, which apparently represents estimated tax payments made during 2002. Therefore, the net income taxes payable to be reported as a current liability at 12/31/02 is $21,200 ($61,200 – $40,000).

5.5 The classification of deferred tax liabilities and assets is a two-step process. First, all deferred tax liabilities and assets are classified as current or long-term. Once classified, all current items are netted to determine either a current asset or liability, and all long-term items are similarly netted. In this case, a noncurrent DT liability of $48,000 exists due to the depreciation difference and a current DT asset of $20,000 exists due to the lawsuit liability difference. These should not be netted. A $20,000 current deferred tax asset is reported. In addition, there is a long-term deferred tax liability of $48,000 caused by the depreciation difference.

5.6 Accounts payable is reported as a current liability at $119,800 ($133,800 less the $14,000 adjustment discussed in item 2 above).

6. In the stockholders' equity section common stock is reported at the par value of the shares issued ($40,000 x $50 = $2,000,000). Additional disclosures for the common stock are the number of shares authorized, issued, and outstanding, and the par value per share.

6.1 Paid-in capital in excess of par is the excess of the issue price of the stock (the $2,231,000 balance reported in the bookkeeper's balance sheet) over the par value of $2,000,000 ($2,231,000 – $2,000,000 = $231,000).

6.2 The other stockholders' equity items are retained earnings (given at $1,075,400) and the two items discussed earlier: treasury stock (see 3.1 above) and the unrealized loss (see 3.2 above).

6.3 Once you have identified where each element should go in the BS, prepare the statement.

UNOFFICIAL ANSWER

Problem 3   Prepare Balance Sheet

Zues Manufacturing Corp.
BALANCE SHEET
December 31, 2002

Assets

	Current Assets			
[1]*	Cash		$ 109,000	
[2]	Accounts receivable (net)		317,700	
	Inventories		560,000	
	Deferred tax asset		$ 20,000	
	Total current assets			$1,006,700
[3]	Long-term investment, at cost			47,000
	Property, plant, and equipment, at cost			
[4]	Land		200,000	
	Building	$1,750,000		
	Machinery and equipment	1,964,000		
	Total	3,714,000		
	Less accumulated depreciation	420,000	3,294,000	
	Total property, plant, and equipment			3,494,000
	Intangible asset			
	Goodwill			37,000
	Other assets			
[1]	Cash restricted for building purposes		100,000	
[2]	Officer's note receivable		30,000	
[4]	Land held for future building site		250,000	380,000
	Total assets			$4,964,700

Liabilities and Stockholders' Equity

	Current Liabilities			
[5]	Accounts payable		$ 119,800	
[6&7]	Current installments of long-term debt		200,000	
	Lawsuit liability		80,000	
[8]	Income taxes payable		21,200	
	Total current liabilities			$ 421,000
[6]	Long-term debt			
	Mortgage payable		800,000	
[7]	Note payable		400,000	
	Deferred tax liability		48,000	
	Total long-term debt			1,248,000
	Stockholders' equity			
[9]	Common stock, authorized 100,000 shares of $50 par value; issued 40,000 shares; outstanding 39,800 shares		2,000,000	
[9]	Additional paid-in capital		231,000	
	Total paid-in capital		2,231,000	
	Retained earnings		1,075,400	
	Accumulated other comprehensive income:			
	Unrealized loss on long-term investment		(4,300)	
	Total		3,302,100	
[3]	Less: Cost of treasury stock		($6,400)	
	Total stockholders' equity			3,295,700
	Total liabilities and stockholders' equity			$4,964,700

*Numbers in brackets are keyed to explanations of amounts

Explanations of Amounts

[1]	Cash, per unaudited balance sheet	$ 225,000
	Less: Unrecorded checks in payment of accounts payable	(14,000)
	NSF check not recorded	(2,000)
	Cash restricted for rebuilding purposes (reported in other assets)	(100,000)
	Corrected balance	$109,000
[2]	Accounts receivable (net), per unaudited balance sheet	$345,700
	Add charge-back for NSF check (see [1])	2,000
	Less officer's note receivable (reported in other assets)	(30,000)
	Corrected balance	$317,700
[3]	Investments, per unaudited balance sheet	$ 57,700
	Less: Long-term investment (reported separately)	(47,000)
	Write-down of investment to market	(4,300)

	Treasury stock (reported in stockholders' equity)	(6,400)
	Corrected balance	$ 0
[4]	Land, per unaudited balance sheet	$ 450,000
	Less land acquired for future building site (reported in other assets)	(250,000)
	Correct balance	(250,000)
[5]	Accounts payable, per unaudited balance sheet	$ 133,800
	Less unrecorded payments (see [1])	(14,000)
	Corrected balance	$ 119,800
[6]	Mortgage payable, per unaudited balance sheet	$ 900,000
	Less current portion ($50,000 x 2)	(100,000)
	Refinanced as long-term mortgage payable	$ 800,000
[7]	Note payable, per unaudited balance sheet	$ 500,000
	Less current portion	(100,000)
	Long-term note payable	$ 400,000

[8]	Income taxes payable, per unaudited		
	balance sheet	$ 61,200	
	Less prepaid income taxes	(40,000)	
	Corrected balance	$21,200	

[9]	Common stock, per unaudited balance		
	sheet	$2,231,000	
	Less additional paid-in capital in excess		
	of par value	(231,000)	
	Corrected balance	$2,000,000	

ANSWER OUTLINE

Problem 4   Comprehensive Income

a. Comprehensive income (CI) = Net income + Other comprehensive income (OCI)

> OCI = Rev., gains, exp., loss not included in NI under GAAP
>
> AOCI = Cumulative BS amounts vs. single period OCI items

b. Alternatives for reporting comprehensive income

- Continuation of IS, or
- Separate FS starting with NI, or
- Statement of changes in SE

Reported net of tax or total tax effect for all items with detail in notes.

c. Recycling (reclassification) adjustments

> Avoid double counting for items realized in net income of current period
>
>> Shown as increases or decreases to related items in OCI except for min. pen. liability

Reported net of tax in other comprehensive income or total tax effect for all items with detail in notes.

d. EPS not required for CI or OCI components

UNOFFICIAL ANSWER

Problem 4   Comprehensive Income

a. Comprehensive income as used in SFAS 130 includes the total of all items of comprehensive income of which net income is a part. Additional items are called other comprehensive income and include revenues, gains, expenses, and losses that are not included in net income under generally accepted accounting principles. Accumulated other comprehensive income represents cumulative amounts on the stockholders' equity section of the balance sheet, whereas other comprehensive income components are single period amounts.

b. Comprehensive income may be reported in the financial statements under one of three alternatives.

- At the bottom of the income statement, continue from net income to arrive at a **comprehensive income** figure, or

- In a separate comprehensive income statement that starts with net income, or

- In the statement of changes in stockholders' equity; the first two are preferred by the FASB.

All components shall be shown net of tax or a total tax expense may be shown with the detail for each component disclosed in the notes.

c. Recycling adjustments are necessary to avoid double counting of items recognized as realized in net income of the current period that were recognized as unrealized in other comprehensive income in the current or prior period. The adjustments are shown as additions or subtractions (net of tax) from each item adjusted, except for those relating to the minimum pension liability that shall be shown net of adjustment for the period.

d. Disclosure of earnings per share is not required for other comprehensive income items or for comprehensive income.

Keep practicing! Wiley's CPA Examination Review Software has over 2,800 questions.

Available at www.wiley.com/cpa

INVENTORY

Inventory is defined in ARB 43 (see outline) as tangible personal property (1) held for sale in the ordinary course of business, (2) in the process of production for such sale, or (3) to be used currently in the production of items for sale.

Inventory is tested on the Financial Accounting and Reporting section of the exam. The primary topics covered by questions on the exam are

1. **Ownership of goods:** the determination of which items are to be included in inventory.
2. **Cost:** the determination of which costs are to be assigned to inventory.
3. **Cost flow assumptions:** the determination of costs assigned to cost of goods sold and inventory under the various cost flow methods.
4. **Valuation:** the determination of how and when inventories should reflect their market values.

ARB 43, chap 4 is the primary authoritative pronouncement regarding the accounting for inventories. You should review the outline before continuing your study of this module.

A. Determining Inventory and Cost of Goods Sold

The primary basis of accounting for inventories is cost, which includes the cash or other fair value of consideration given in exchange for it. Inventory cost is a function of two variables

1. The number of units included in inventory, and
2. The costs attached to those units

The units to be included in inventory are those which the firm owns; ownership is usually determined by legal title.

The costs to be included in inventory include all costs necessary to prepare the goods for sale. For a manufacturing entity, this would include direct materials, direct labor, and both direct and indirect factory overhead. These costs are then allocated to the work in process and finished goods inventory accounts. Per SFAS 34, interest on inventories routinely produced, or repetitively produced in large quantities, is not capitalized as part of inventory cost.

For a merchandising concern, the costs to be included in inventory include the purchase price of the goods, freight-in, insurance, warehousing, and any other costs incurred in the preparation of these goods for sale. The amount used as a purchase price for the goods will vary depending upon whether the gross or net method is used in the recording of purchases. If the gross method is used to record the purchases, then any subsequent discount taken is shown as purchase discount which is netted against the purchases account in determining cost of goods sold. If the net method is used to record purchases, then any purchase discounts offered are assumed taken and the purchase account reflects the net price. If subsequent to the recording of the purchases the discount is not taken (i.e., payment is tendered after the discount period has elapsed), a purchase discounts lost account is debited. The balance in the purchase discounts lost account does **not** enter into the determination of cost of goods sold; this amount is treated as a period expense. Note that regardless of the method used, purchases are always recorded net of any allowable trade discounts. These are discounts that are allowed to the entity because of its being a wholesaler, a good customer, or merely the fact that the item is on sale at a reduced price. Also note that interest paid to vendors is not included in the cost of inventory.

The determination of cost of goods sold and inventory under each of the cost flow assumptions depends upon the method used to record the inventory: periodic or perpetual.

Periodic system. Inventory is counted periodically and then priced. The ending inventory is usually recorded in the cost of goods sold (CGS) entry.

Ending inventory (EI)	xx	
CGS	(plug)	
Beginning inventory (BI)		xx
Purchases		xx

CGS = Purchases – (the change in inventory). For example, if ending inventory decreases, all of the purchases and some of the beginning inventory have been sold. If ending inventory increases, not all of the purchases have been sold.

Perpetual system. A running total is kept of the units on hand (and possibly their value) by recording all increases and decreases as they occur. When inventory is purchased, the inventory account, rather than purchases, is debited. As inventory is sold, the following entry is recorded.

CGS   (cost)
   Inventory   (cost)

B. Inventory Valuation and Cost-Flow Methods

1. Specific identification	8. Last-in, first-out (LIFO)
2. Weighted-average	9. Dollar-value LIFO
3. Simple average	10. Gross profit
4. Moving average	11. Standard costs
5. Lower of cost or market	12. Direct costing
6. Losses on purchase commitments	13. Market
7. First-in, first-out (FIFO)	14. Cost apportionment by relative sales value

1. **Specific Identification**

The seller determines which item is sold. For example, a seller has for sale four identical machines costing $260, $230, $180, and $110. Since the machines are identical, a purchaser will have no preference as to which machine s/he receives when purchased. Note that the seller is able to manipulate income as s/he can sell any machine (and charge the appropriate amount to CGS). Significant dollar value items are frequently accounted for by specific identification. The use of the specific identification method is appropriate when there is a relatively small number of significant dollar value items in inventory.

2. **Weighted-Average**

The seller averages the cost of all items on hand and purchased during the period. The units in ending inventory and units sold (CGS) are costed at this average cost. For example

	Cost	Units	
Beginning inventory	$200	100	($2.00 unit)
Purchase 1	315	150	($2.10 unit)
Purchase 2	85	50	($1.70 unit)
	$600	300	

Weighted-average cost $600/300 = $2.00 unit

3. **Simple Average**

The seller does not weight the average for units purchased or in beginning inventory (e.g., the above $2.00, $2.10, and $1.70 unit costs would be averaged to $1.93). The method is fairly accurate if all purchases, production runs, and beginning inventory quantities are equal.

4. **Moving Average**

The average cost of goods on hand must be recalculated any time additional inventory is purchased at a unit cost different from the previously calculated average cost of goods on hand. For example

	Dollar cost of units on hand	Units on hand	Inventory unit cost
Beginning inventory	$200	100	$2.00
Sale of 50 units @ $2.00 = $100	100	50	2.00
Purchase of 150 units for $320	420	200	2.10
Sale of 50 units @ $2.10 = $105	315	150	2.10
Purchase of 50 units for $109	424	200	2.12

Note that sales do not change the unit price because they are taken out of inventory at the average price. Moving average may only be used with perpetual systems which account for changes in value with each change in inventory (and not with perpetual systems only accounting for changes in the number of units).

5. **Lower of Cost or Market**

"A departure from the cost basis of pricing the inventory is required when the utility of the goods is no longer as great as its cost." (ARB 43, chap 4)

The following steps should be used to apply the lower of cost or market rule given in chapter 4 of ARB 43.

a. Determine market

Market is replacement cost limited to

(1) **Ceiling**—which is net realizable value (selling price less selling costs and costs to complete).

(2) **Floor**—which is net realizable value less normal profit.

Note that if replacement cost is greater than net realizable value, market equals net realizable value. Likewise, market equals net realizable value minus normal profit if replacement cost is less than net realizable value minus normal profit.

b. Determine cost
    Note that the floor and ceiling have nothing to do with cost
c. Select the lower of cost or market either for each individual item or for inventory as a whole (compute total market and total cost, and select lower)

LOWER OF COST OR MARKET EXAMPLE

Item	Cost	Replacement cost	Selling price	Selling cost	Normal profit
A	$10.50	$10.25	$15.00	$2.50	$2.50
B	5.75	5.25	8.00	1.50	1.00
C	4.25	4.75	5.50	1.00	1.50

Item	Replacement cost	NRV (ceiling)	NRV-Profit (floor)	Designated market value	Cost	LCM
A	$10.25	$12.50	$10.00	$10.25	$10.50	$10.25
B	5.25	6.50	5.50	5.50	5.75	5.50
C	4.75	4.50	3.00	4.50	4.25	4.25

Item A—Market is replacement cost, $10.25, because it is between the floor ($10.00) and the ceiling ($12.50). Lower of cost or market is $10.25.
Item B—Market is limited to the floor, $5.50 ($8.00 – $1.50 – $1.00) because the $5.25 replacement cost is beneath the floor. Lower of cost or market is $5.50.
Item C—Market is limited to the ceiling, $4.50 ($5.50 – $1.00) because the $4.75 replacement cost is above the ceiling. Lower of cost or market is $4.25.

Observations about the ARB 43 rule

(1) The floor limitation on market prevents recognition of more than normal profit in future periods (if market is less than cost).
(2) The ceiling limitation on market prevents recognition of a loss in future periods (if market is less than cost).
(3) Cost or market applied to individual items will always be as low as, and usually lower than, cost or market applied to the inventory as a whole. They will be the same when all items at market or all items at cost are lower.
(4) Once inventory has been written down there can be no recovery from the write-down until the units are sold. Recall that this differs from marketable securities where recoveries of prior write-downs are required to be taken into the income stream.

Methods of recording the write-down
If market is less than cost at the end of any period, there are two methods available to record the market decline. The entry to establish the ending inventory can be made using the market figure. The difficulty with this procedure is that it forces the loss to be included in the cost of goods sold, thus overstating the cost of goods sold by the amount of the loss. Note that under this method the loss is not separately disclosed.

An alternative treatment is to debit the inventory account for the actual cost (not market) of goods on hand, and then to make the following entry to give separate recognition to the market decline.

Loss due to market decline   xx
    Inventory   xx

6. **Losses on Purchase Commitments**

    Purchase commitments (PC) result from legally enforceable contracts to purchase specific quantities of goods at fixed prices in the future. When there is a decline in market value below the contract price at the balance sheet date and the contracts are noncancellable, an unrealized loss has occurred and, if material, should be recorded in the period of decline.

Estimated loss on PC   (excess of PC over mkt.)
    Accrued loss on PC   (excess of PC over mkt.)

If further declines in market value are estimated to occur before delivery is made, the amount of the loss to be accrued should be increased to include this additional decline in market value per SFAS 5. The loss is taken to the income statement; the accrued loss on PC is a liability account and shown on the balance sheet.

When the goods are subsequently received

Purchases	xx	
Accrued loss on PC	xx	
Cash		xx

If a partial or full recovery occurs before the inventory is received, the accrued loss account would be reduced by the amount of the recovery. Likewise, an income statement account, "Recovery on Loss of PC," would be credited.

7. **First-In, First-Out (FIFO)**

The goods from beginning inventory and the earliest purchases are assumed to be the goods sold first. In a period of rising prices, cost of goods sold is made up of the earlier, lower-priced goods resulting in a larger profit (relative to LIFO). The ending inventory is made up of more recent purchases and thus represents a more current value (relative to LIFO) on the balance sheet. It should be noted that this cost-flow assumption may be used even when it does not match the physical flow of goods. Whenever the FIFO method is used, the results of inventory and cost of goods sold are the same at the end of the period under either a perpetual or a periodic system.

8. **Last-In, First-Out (LIFO)**

Under this cost-flow method, the most recent purchases are assumed to be the first goods sold; thus, ending inventory is assumed to be composed of the oldest goods. Therefore, the cost of goods sold contains relatively current costs (resulting in the matching of current costs with sales). Again, this cost-flow assumption usually does not parallel the physical flow of goods.

LIFO is widely adopted because it is acceptable for tax purposes and because in periods of rising prices it reduces tax liability due to the lower reported income (resulting from the higher cost of goods sold). LIFO smoothes out fluctuations in the income stream relative to FIFO because it matches current costs with current revenues. A primary disadvantage of LIFO is that it results in large profits if inventory decreases because earlier, lower valued layers are included in the cost of goods sold. This is generally known as a LIFO liquidation. Another disadvantage is the cost involved in maintaining separate LIFO records for each item in inventory. If LIFO is used for tax purposes, it must be used for financial reporting purposes. This is known as the LIFO conformity rule. Under current tax law, inventory layers may be added using the (1) earliest acquisition costs, (2) weighted-average unit cost for the period, or (3) latest acquisition costs. In solving questions on the CPA Exam, use the earliest acquisition costs unless you are instructed to use one of the other alternatives.

When a company uses LIFO for external reporting purposes and another inventory method for internal purposes, a **LIFO Reserve** account is used to reduce inventory from the internal valuation to the LIFO valuation. LIFO Reserve is a contra account to inventory, and is adjusted up or down at year-end with a corresponding increase or decrease to **Cost of Goods Sold**.

9. **Dollar-Value LIFO**

Dollar-value LIFO is LIFO applied to **pools** of inventory items rather than to **individual** items. Thus, the cost of keeping inventory records is less under dollar-value LIFO than under unit LIFO. Because the LIFO conformity rule (if LIFO is used for tax, it must also be used for external financial statements) also applies to dollar-value LIFO, companies using dollar-value LIFO define their LIFO pools so as to conform with IRS regulations. Under these regulations, a LIFO pool can contain all of the inventory items for a natural business unit, or a multiple pool approach can be elected whereby a business can group similarly used inventory items into several groups or pools.

The advantage of using inventory pools is that an involuntary liquidation of LIFO layers is less likely to occur because of the increased number of items in the pool (if the level of one item decreases it can be offset by increases in the levels of other items), and because the pools can be adjusted for changes in product composition or product mix.

Like unit LIFO, dollar-value LIFO is a layering method. Unlike unit LIFO, dollar-value LIFO determines increases or decreases in ending inventory in terms of dollars of the same purchasing power rather than in terms of units. Dollar-value LIFO seeks to determine the real dollar change in inventory. Therefore, ending inventory is deflated to base-year cost by dividing ending inventory by the current year's conversion price index and comparing the resulting amount with the beginning inventory, which has also been stated in base-year dollars.

The difference represents the layer which, after conversion, must be added or subtracted to arrive at the appropriate value of ending inventory. Always remember that the individual layers in a dollar-value LIFO inventory are valued as follows:

$$\text{\$ value LIFO} = \text{Inventory at base-year prices} \quad \text{x} \quad \text{Conversion price index}$$

In applying dollar-value LIFO, manufacturers develop their own indexes while retailers and wholesalers use published figures. In computing the conversion price index, the **double-extension technique** is used, named so because each year the ending inventory is extended at both base-year prices and current-year prices. The index, computed as follows, measures the change in the inventory prices since the base year.

$$\frac{\text{EI at end-of-year prices}}{\text{EI at base-year prices}} = \text{Conversion price index}$$

To illustrate the computation of the index, assume that the base-year price of products A and B is $3 and $5, respectively, and at the end of the year, the price of product A is $3.20 and B, $5.75, with 2,000 and 800 units on hand, respectively. The index for the year is 110%, computed as follows:

	EI at end-of-year prices	÷	EI at base-year prices	=	Conversion price index
Product A	2,000 @ $3.20 = $ 6,400		2,000 @ $3 = $ 6,000		
Product B	800 @ $5.75 = $ 4,600		800 @ $5 = $ 4,000		
	$11,000		$10,000		1.10 (or 110%)

Steps in dollar-value LIFO

Manufacturers	*Retailers and wholesalers*
1. Compute the conversion price index	1. Determine index from appropriate published source
2. Compare BI at base-year prices to EI at base-year prices to determine the	2. Divide EI by conversion price index to restate to base-year prices
a. New inventory layer added, or b. Old inventory layer removed (LIFO liquidation)	3. Same as "2." opposite
3. If there is an increase at base-year prices, value this new layer by multiplying the layer (stated in base-year dollars) by the conversion price index. If there is a decrease at base-year prices, the remaining layers are valued at the index in effect when the layer was first added.	4. Same as "3." opposite

For example, assume the following:

	EI at end-of-year prices	÷	Conversion price index	=	EI at base-year prices		Change as measured in base-year dollars
Year 1 (base)	$100,000		1.00		$100,000		
Year 2	121,000		1.10		110,000	>	$10,000
Year 3	150,000		1.20		125,000	>	15,000
Year 4	135,000		1.25		108,000	>	(17,000)

In both year 2 and year 3, ending inventory in terms of base-year dollars increased 10,000 and 15,000 base-year dollars, respectively. Since layers are added every year that ending inventory at base-year prices is greater than the previous year's ending inventory at base-year prices, the ending inventory for year 3 would be computed as follows:

Ending inventory, Year 3

	Base-year prices	x	Index	=	EI at dollar-value LIFO cost
Year 1 (base)	$100,000		1.00		$100,000
Year 2 layer	10,000		1.10		11,000
Year 3 layer	15,000		1.20		18,000
Ending inventory	$125,000				$129,000

Note that each layer added is multiplied by the conversion price index in effect when the layer was added. Thus, the year 2 layer is multiplied by the year 2 index of 1.10 and the year 3 layer is multiplied by the year 3 index of 1.20.

In year 4, ending inventory decreased by 17,000 base-year dollars. Therefore, a LIFO liquidation has occurred whereby 17,000 base-year dollars will have to be removed from the previous year's ending inventory. Because LIFO is being used, the liquidation affects the most recently added layer first and then, if necessary, the next most recently added layer(s). Ending inventory in year 4 is composed of

	Base-year prices	x	*Index*	=	*EI at dollar-value LIFO cost*
Year 1 (base)	$100,000		1.00		$100,000
Year 2 layer	8,000		1.10		8,800
Ending inventory	$108,000				$108,800

Note that the liquidation of 17,000 base-year dollars in year 4 caused the entire year 3 layer of 15,000 base-year dollars to be liquidated as well as 2,000 base-year dollars from year 2. Also note that the remaining 8,000 base-year dollars in the year 2 layer is still multiplied by the year 2 index of 1.10.

Link-chain technique. The computations for application of the double-extension technique can become very arduous even if only a few items exist in the inventory. Also, consider the problems that arise when there is a constant change in the inventory mix or in situations in which the breadth of the inventory is large.

The link-chain method was originally developed for (and limited to) those companies that wanted to use LIFO but, because of a substantial change in product lines over time, were unable to recreate or keep the historical records necessary to make accurate use of the double-extension method.

The link-chain method is the process of developing a single cumulative index. Technological change is allowed for by the method used to calculate each current year index. The index is derived by double extending a representative sample (generally thought to be between 50% and 75% of the dollar value of the pool) at both beginning-of-year prices and end-of-year prices. This annual index is then applied (multiplied) to the previous period's cumulative index to arrive at the new current year cumulative index.

The brief example below illustrates how the links and cumulative index are computed.

End of period	*Ratio of end of period prices to beginning prices**	*Cumulative index number***
0	--	1.000
1	1.10	1.100
2	1.05	1.155
3	1.07	1.236

* $\dfrac{\text{End of period prices}}{\text{Beginning of period prices}}$ = *Index number for* **this period only**

** *Multiply the cumulative index number at the beginning of the period by the ratio computed with the formula shown above.*

The ending inventory is divided by the cumulative index number to derive the ending inventory at base period prices. An increase (layer) in base period dollars for the period is priced using the newly derived index number.

10. **Gross Profit**

Ending inventory is estimated by using the gross profit (GP) percentage to convert sales to cost of goods presumed sold. Since ending inventory is only estimated, the gross method is not acceptable for either tax or annual financial reporting purposes. Its major uses are to estimate ending inventory for internal use, for use in interim financial statements, and for establishing the amount of loss due to the destruction of inventory by fire, flood, or other catastrophes.

As an example, suppose the inventory of the Luckless Company has been destroyed by fire and the following information is available from duplicate records stored at a separate facility: beginning inventory of $30,000, purchases for the period of $40,000, sales of $60,000, and an average GP percentage of 25%. The cost of the inventory destroyed is computed as follows:

Beginning inventory	$30,000
+ Purchases	40,000
Goods available	70,000
− Cost of goods sold	45,000*
Inventory destroyed	$25,000

*Cost of goods sold is computed as (1) sales of $60,000 – ($60,000 x 25%) or (2) sales of $60,000 x 75%.

If you need to convert a GP rate on cost to a markup (MU) rate on the selling price, divide the GP rate on cost by 1 **plus** the GP rate on cost, that is, if the GP rate on cost is 50%, then $.50/(1 + .50) = 33$ 1/3% is the MU rate on the selling price. If you need to convert a MU rate on the selling price to a GP rate on cost, divide the MU rate on the selling price by 1 **minus** the MU rate on the selling price, that is, if the MU rate on the selling price is 20%, then $.20/(1 − .20) = 25\%$ GP rate on cost. Always be cautious about gross profit rates (on cost or the selling price).

11. **Standard Costs**

Standard costs are predetermined costs in a cost accounting system, generally used for control purposes. Inventory may be costed at standard only if variances are reasonable (i.e., not large). Large debit (unfavorable) variances would indicate inventory (and cost of sales) were undervalued, whereas large credit (favorable) variances would indicate inventory is overvalued.

12. **Direct (Variable) Costing**

Direct costing is not an acceptable method for valuing inventory (ARB 43, chap 4). Direct costing considers only variable costs as product costs and fixed production costs as period costs. In contrast, absorption costing considers both variable and fixed manufacturing costs as product costs.

13. **Market**

Inventory is usually valued at market value when market is lower than cost. However, occasionally, inventory will be valued at market even if it is above cost. This usually occurs with

a. Precious metals with a fixed market value
b. Industries such as meatpacking where costs cannot be allocated and

(1) Quoted market prices exist
(2) Goods are interchangeable (e.g., agricultural commodities)

14. **Cost Apportionment By Relative Sales Value**

Basket purchases and similar situations require cost allocation based on relative value. For example, a developer may spend $400,000 to acquire land, survey, curb and gutter, pave streets, etc. for a subdivision. Due to location and size, the lots may vary in selling price. If the total of all selling prices were $600,000, the developer could cost each lot at 2/3 (400/600; COST/RETAIL ratio) of its selling price.

C. Items to Include in Inventory

Goods shipped FOB shipping point which are in transit should be included in the inventory of the buyer since title passes to the buyer when the carrier receives the goods. Goods shipped FOB destination should be included in the inventory of the seller until the goods are received by the buyer since title passes to the buyer when the goods are received at their final destination. The more complicated UCC rules concerning transfer of title should be used for the law portion, not the financial accounting and reporting portion, of the exam.

D. Consignments

Consignors consign their goods to consignees who are sales agents of the consignors. Consigned goods remain the property of the consignor until sold. Therefore, any unsold goods (including a proportionate share of freight costs incurred in shipping the goods to the consignee) must be included in the consignor's inventory.

Consignment sales revenue should be recognized by the consignor when the consignee sells the consigned goods to the ultimate customer. Therefore, no revenue is recognized at the time the consignor ships the goods to the consignee. Note that sales commission made by the consignee would be reported as a selling expense by the consignor and would **not** be netted against the sales revenue recognized by the consignor. The UCC rules concerning consignments should be used for the law portion, not the financial accounting and reporting portion, of the exam.

E. Ratios

The two ratios below relate to inventory.

1. **Inventory turnover**—Measures the number of times inventory was sold and reflects inventory order and investment policies

$$\frac{\text{Cost of goods sold}}{\text{Average inventory}}$$

2. **Number of days' supply in average inventory**—Number of days inventory is held before sale; reflects on efficiency of inventory policies

$$\frac{365}{\text{Inventory turnover}}$$

F. Long-Term Construction Contracts

The outline of ARB 45 should be reviewed before continuing to study long-term construction contracts. This section also reflects the treatment of these contracts in the AICPA's *Construction Contractors Audit and Accounting Guide.*

Long-term contracts are accounted for by two methods: completed-contract method and percentage-of-completion method.

1. Completed-contract method—Recognition of contract revenue and profit at contract completion. All related costs are deferred until completion and then matched to revenues.
2. Percentage-of-completion—Recognition of contract revenue and profit during construction based on expected total profit and estimated progress towards completion in the current period. All related costs are recognized in the period in which they occur.

The use of the percentage-of-completion method depends on the ability to make reasonably dependable estimates of contract revenues, contract costs, and the extent of progress toward completion. For entities which customarily operate under contractual arrangements and for whom contracting represents a significant part of their operations, the **presumption** is that they have the ability to make estimates that are sufficiently dependable to justify the use of the percentage-of-completion method of accounting.

In Statement of Position 81-1, the Accounting Standards Division states that the percentage-of-completion method is **preferable** in circumstances in which reasonably dependable estimates can be made and in which all of the following conditions exist:

- Contracts executed by the parties normally include provisions that clearly specify the enforceable rights regarding goods or services to be provided and received by the parties, the consideration to be exchanged, and the manner and terms of settlement.
- The buyer can be expected to satisfy obligations under the contract.
- The contractor can be expected to perform contractual obligation.

The completed-contract method is **preferable** in circumstances in which estimates cannot meet the criteria for reasonable dependability or one of the above conditions does not exist.

The advantage of percentage-of-completion is periodic recognition of income, and the disadvantage is dependence on estimates. The advantage of the completed-contract method is that it is based on results, not estimates, and the disadvantage is that current performance is not reflected and income recognition may be irregular.

In practice, various procedures are used to measure the extent of progress toward completion under the percentage-of-completion method, but the most widely used one is **cost-to-cost** which is based on the assumed relationship between a unit of input and productivity. Under cost-to-cost, either revenue and/or profit to be recognized in the current period can be determined by the following formula.

$$\text{Revenue (profit)} = \left(\frac{\text{Cost to date}}{\substack{\text{Total expected} \\ \text{cost based on} \\ \text{latest estimate}}} \times \substack{\text{Contract price} \\ \text{(Expected profit)}} \right) - \substack{\text{Revenue (profit)} \\ \text{recognized in} \\ \text{previous periods}}$$

It is important to note that revenue and profit are two different terms. Profit is calculated by subtracting construction expenses from revenue. Revenue is the contract price. Therefore, pay particular attention to what item the CPA exam asks you to calculate.

The ledger account titles used in the following discussion are unique to long-term construction contracts. In practice, there are numerous account titles for the same item (e.g., "billings on LT contracts" vs. "partial billings on construction in progress") and various methodologies for journalizing the same transactions (e.g., separate revenue and expense control accounts in lieu of an "income on LT contracts" account). The following example has been simplified to highlight the main concepts.

EXAMPLE: *Assume a 3-year contract at a contract price of $500,000 as well as the following data:*

	Year 1	Year 2	Year 3
Cost incurred this year	$135,000	$225,000	$ 45,000
Prior years' costs	-0-	135,000	360,000
Estimated costs to complete	$315,000	40,000	-0-
Total costs	$450,000	400,000	$405,000
Progress billings made during the year	$200,000	$200,000	$100,000
Collection of billings each year	$175,000	$200,000	$125,000

From the above information, the following may be determined.

Percent of completion *(costs to date/total costs)*

Year 1: $135,000/$450,000 = 30%
Year 2: $360,000/$400,000 = 90%
Year 3: $405,000/$405,000 = 100%

	Year 1	Year 2	Year 3
Total revenue	$500,000	$500,000	$500,000
x Percent of completion	x 30%	x 90%	x 100%
Total revenue to be recognized by end of year	$150,000	$450,000	$500,000
– Revenue recognized in prior periods	--	(150,000)	(450,000)
Current year's revenue (to be recognized)	$150,000	$300,000	$ 50,000
Contract price	$500,000	$500,000	$500,000
– Total estimated costs	(450,000)	(400,000)	(405,000)
Estimated profit	$ 50,000	$100,000	$ 95,000
x Percent of completion	x 30%	x 90%	x 100%
Total profit to be recognized by end of year	$ 15,000	$ 90,000	$ 95,000
– Profit recognized in prior periods	--	(15,000)	(90,000)
Current year's profit (to be recognized)	$ 15,000	$ 75,000	$ 5,000

		Percentage-of-completion		Completed-contract	
Year 1 Costs	Construction in progress	135,000		135,000	
	Cash		135,000		135,000
Year 1 Progress billings	Accounts receivable	200,000		200,000	
	Billings on LT contracts		200,000		200,000
Year 1 Cash collected	Cash	175,000		175,000	
	Accounts receivable		175,000		175,000
Year 1 Profit recognition	Construction expenses	135,000		none	
	Construction in progress	15,000			
	Construction revenue		150,000		
Year 2 Costs	Construction in progress	225,000		225,000	
	Cash		225,000		225,000
Year 2 Progress billings	Accounts receivable	200,000		200,000	
	Billings on LT contracts		200,000		200,000
Year 2 Cash collected	Cash	200,000		200,000	
	Accounts receivable		200,000		200,000
Year 2 Profit recognition	Construction expenses	225,000		none	
	Construction in progress	75,000			
	Construction revenue		300,000		
Year 3 Costs	Construction in progress	45,000		45,000	
	Cash		45,000		45,000
Year 3 Progress billings	Accounts receivable	100,000		100,000	
	Billings on LT contracts		100,000		100,000
Year 3 Cash collected	Cash	125,000		125,000	
	Accounts receivable		125,000		125,000
Year 3 Profit recognition and closing of special accounts	Construction expenses	45,000			
	Construction in progress	5,000			
	Construction revenue		50,000		
	Billings on LT contracts	500,000			
	Const. in progress		500,000		
	Construction expenses			405,000	
	Const. in progress				405,000
	Billings on LT contracts			500,000	
	Construction revenue				500,000

The "construction in progress" (CIP) account is a cost accumulation account similar to "work in process" for job-order costing, except that the percentage-of-completion method includes interim profits in the account. The "billings on LT contracts" account is similar to an unearned revenue account. At each financial statement date, the "construction in progress" account should be netted against the "billings on LT contracts" account on a project-by-project basis, resulting in a net current asset and/or a net current liability. Under the percentage-of-completion method in the above example, a net current asset of $50,000 [($135,000 + $15,000 + $225,000 + $75,000) − ($200,000 + $200,000)] would be reported at the end of year 2. A net current liability of $40,000 would result under the completed-contract method [($200,000 + $200,000) − ($135,000 + $225,000)] for the same year.

SUMMARY OF ACCOUNTS USED IN CONSTRUCTION ACCOUNTING
(NO LOSS EXPECTED OR INCURRED)

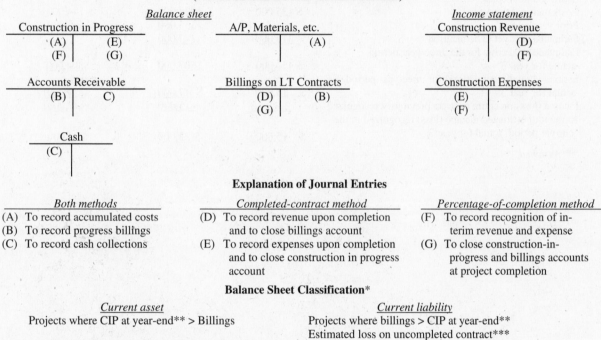

Balance sheet

Construction in Progress
(A)	(E)
(F)	(G)

A/P, Materials, etc.
	(A)

Income statement

Construction Revenue
	(D)
	(F)

Accounts Receivable
(B)	(C)

Billings on LT Contracts
(D)	(B)
(G)	

Construction Expenses
(E)	
(F)	

Cash
(C)	

Explanation of Journal Entries

Both methods	*Completed-contract method*	*Percentage-of-completion method*
(A) To record accumulated costs	(D) To record revenue upon completion and to close billings account	(F) To record recognition of interim revenue and expense
(B) To record progress billings		
(C) To record cash collections	(E) To record expenses upon completion and to close construction in progress account	(G) To close construction-in-progress and billings accounts at project completion

Balance Sheet Classification*

Current asset	*Current liability*
Projects where CIP at year-end** > Billings	Projects where billings > CIP at year-end**
	Estimated loss on uncompleted contract***

*   *Evaluate and classify on a project-by-project basis.*
** *Construction in progress including income (when percentage-of-completion method is used) or loss recognized.*
*** *When recognizing and reporting losses, it is necessary to use a current liability account instead of reducing CIP in those cases in which a contract's billings exceed its accumulated costs.*

Contract Losses. In any year when a **percentage-of-completion** contract has an expected loss on the entire contract, the amount of the loss reported in that year is the total expected loss on the entire contract **plus** all profit previously recognized. For example, if the expected costs yet to be incurred at the end of year two were $147,000, the total expected loss is $7,000 [$500,000 − ($135,000 + $225,000 + $147,000)] and the total loss reported in year two would be $22,000 ($7,000 + $15,000). Similarly, under the **completed-contract** method, total expected losses on the entire contract are recognized as soon as they are estimated. The loss recognized is similar to that for percentage-of-completion except the amount is for the expected loss on the entire contract. In the aforementioned example, the loss to be recognized is only $7,000 (the entire loss on the contract expected in year two) because interim profits have not been recorded. Journal entries and a schedule for profit or loss recognized on the contract under the percentage-of-completion method follow:

Journal entry at end of year 2	*Percentage-of-completion*		*Completed-contract*	
Construction expenses	227,000*			
Construction in progress (loss)		22,000		
Construction revenue		205,000**		
Loss on uncompleted LT contracts			7,000	
Construction in progress (loss)				7,000

Journal entry at end of year 2	Percentage-of-completion	Completed-contract
Supporting Calculations:		
* Year 2 costs		$225,000
Loss attributable to year 3:		
Year 3 revenue ($500,000 – $150,000 – $205,000)	$145,000	
Year 3 costs (expected)	147,000	2,000
Total		$227,000

** ($360,000/$507,000) (Costs to date/Total estimated costs) = 71% (rounded); (71% x $500,000) – $150,000 = $205,000

PERCENTAGE-OF-COMPLETION METHOD

	Year 1	Year 2	Year 3
Contract price:	$ 500,000	$500,000	$500,000
Estimated total costs:			
Costs incurred this year	$ 135,000	$225,000	$ 144,000***
Prior year's costs	--	135,000	360,000
Estimated cost yet to be incurred	315,000	147,000	--
Estimated total costs for the three-year period, actual for year 3	$ 450,000	$507,000	$504,000
Estimated total income (loss) for three-year period, actual for year 3	$ 15,000	$ (7,000)	$ (4,000)
Income (loss) on entire contract previously recognized	--	15,000	(7,000)
Amount of estimated income (loss) recognized in the current period, actual for year 3	$ 15,000	$(22,000)	$ 3,000

***Assumed

MULTIPLE-CHOICE QUESTIONS (1-57)

1. The following information applied to Fenn, Inc. for 2002:

Merchandise purchased for resale	$400,000
Freight-in	10,000
Freight-out	5,000
Purchase returns	2,000

Fenn's 2002 inventoriable cost was
a. $400,000
b. $403,000
c. $408,000
d. $413,000

2. On December 28, 2002, Kerr Manufacturing Co. purchased goods costing $50,000. The terms were FOB destination. Some of the costs incurred in connection with the sale and delivery of the goods were as follows:

Packaging for shipment	$1,000
Shipping	1,500
Special handling charges	2,000

These goods were received on December 31, 2002. In Kerr's December 31, 2002 balance sheet, what amount of cost for these goods should be included in inventory?
a. $54,500
b. $53,500
c. $52,000
d. $50,000

3. On June 1, 2002, Pitt Corp. sold merchandise with a list price of $5,000 to Burr on account. Pitt allowed trade discounts of 30% and 20%. Credit terms were 2/15, n/40 and the sale was made FOB shipping point. Pitt prepaid $200 of delivery costs for Burr as an accommodation. On June 12, 2002, Pitt received from Burr a remittance in full payment amounting to
a. $2,744
b. $2,940
c. $2,944
d. $3,140

4. The following information was taken from Cody Co.'s accounting records for the year ended December 31, 2002:

Decrease in raw materials inventory	$ 15,000
Increase in finished goods inventory	35,000
Raw material purchased	430,000
Direct labor payroll	200,000
Factory overhead	300,000
Freight-out	45,000

There was no work in process inventory at the beginning or end of the year. Cody's 2002 cost of goods sold is
a. $895,000
b. $910,000
c. $950,000
d. $955,000

5. The following information pertains to Deal Corp.'s 2002 cost of goods sold:

Inventory, 12/31/01	$ 90,000
2002 purchases	124,000
2002 write-off of obsolete inventory	34,000
Inventory, 12/31/02	30,000

The inventory written off became obsolete due to an unexpected and unusual technological advance by a competitor. In its 2002 income statement, what amount should Deal report as cost of goods sold?

a. $218,000
b. $184,000
c. $150,000
d. $124,000

6. How should the following costs affect a retailer's inventory?

	Freight-in	*Interest on inventory loan*
a.	Increase	No effect
b.	Increase	Increase
c.	No effect	Increase
d.	No effect	No effect

7. According to the net method, which of the following items should be included in the cost of inventory?

	Freight costs	*Purchase discounts not taken*
a.	Yes	No
b.	Yes	Yes
c.	No	Yes
d.	No	No

8. The following information pertained to Azur Co. for the year:

Purchases	$102,800
Purchase discounts	10,280
Freight in	15,420
Freight out	5,140
Beginning inventory	30,840
Ending inventory	20,560

What amount should Azur report as cost of goods sold for the year?
a. $102,800
b. $118,220
c. $123,360
d. $128,500

9. Bach Co. adopted the dollar-value LIFO inventory method as of January 1, 2000. A single inventory pool and an internally computed price index are used to compute Bach's LIFO inventory layers. Information about Bach's dollar value inventory follows:

	Inventory	
	at base	*at current*
Date	*year cost*	*year cost*
1/1/00	$90,000	$90,000
2000 layer	20,000	30,000
2001 layer	40,000	80,000

What was the price index used to compute Bach's 2001 dollar value LIFO inventory layer?
a. 1.09
b. 1.25
c. 1.33
d. 2.00

10. Nest Co. recorded the following inventory information during the month of January:

	Units	*Unit cost*	*Total cost*	*Units on hand*
Balance on 1/1	2,000	$1	$2,000	2,000
Purchased on 1/8	1,200	3	3,600	3,200
Sold on 1/23	1,800			1,400
Purchased on 1/28	800	5	4,000	2,200

Nest uses the LIFO method to cost inventory. What amount should Nest report as inventory on January 31 under each of the following methods of recording inventory?

	Perpetual	Periodic
a.	$2,600	$5,400
b.	$5,400	$2,600
c.	$2,600	$2,600
d.	$5,400	$5,400

11. The weighted-average for the year inventory cost flow method is applicable to which of the following inventory systems?

	Periodic	Perpetual
a.	Yes	Yes
b.	Yes	No
c.	No	Yes
d.	No	No

12. During January 2002, Metro Co., which maintains a perpetual inventory system, recorded the following information pertaining to its inventory:

	Units	Unit cost	Total cost	Units on hand
Balance on 1/1/02	1,000	$1	$1,000	1,000
Purchased on 1/7/02	600	3	1,800	1,600
Sold on 1/20/02	900			700
Purchased on 1/25/02	400	5	2,000	1,100

Under the moving-average method, what amount should Metro report as inventory at January 31, 2002?
- a. $2,640
- b. $3,225
- c. $3,300
- d. $3,900

13. Moss Co. has determined its December 31, 2002 inventory on a FIFO basis to be $400,000. Information pertaining to that inventory follows:

Estimated selling price	$408,000
Estimated cost of disposal	20,000
Normal profit margin	60,000
Current replacement cost	360,000

Moss records losses that result from applying the lower of cost or market rule. At December 31, 2002, what should be the net carrying value of Moss' inventory?
- a. $400,000
- b. $388,000
- c. $360,000
- d. $328,000

14. Based on a physical inventory taken on December 31, 2002, Chewy Co. determined its chocolate inventory on a FIFO basis at $26,000 with a replacement cost of $20,000. Chewy estimated that, after further processing costs of $12,000, the chocolate could be sold as finished candy bars for $40,000. Chewy's normal profit margin is 10% of sales. Under the lower of cost or market rule, what amount should Chewy report as chocolate inventory in its December 31, 2002 balance sheet?
- a. $28,000
- b. $26,000
- c. $24,000
- d. $20,000

15. Reporting inventory at the lower of cost or market is a departure from the accounting principle of
- a. Historical cost.
- b. Consistency.
- c. Conservatism.
- d. Full disclosure.

16. The original cost of an inventory item is below both replacement cost and net realizable value. The net realizable value less normal profit margin is below the original cost. Under the lower of cost or market method, the inventory item should be valued at
- a. Replacement cost.
- b. Net realizable value.
- c. Net realizable value less normal profit margin.
- d. Original cost.

17. Which of the following statements are correct when a company applying the lower of cost or market method reports its inventory at replacement cost?

  I. The original cost is less than replacement cost.
  II. The net realizable value is greater than replacement cost.

- a. I only.
- b. II only.
- c. Both I and II.
- d. Neither I nor II.

18. The original cost of an inventory item is above the replacement cost and the net realizable value. The replacement cost is below the net realizable value less the normal profit margin. As a result, under the lower of cost or market method, the inventory item should be reported at the
- a. Net realizable value.
- b. Net realizable value less the normal profit margin.
- c. Replacement cost.
- d. Original cost.

19. On January 1, 2002, Card Corp. signed a three-year noncancelable purchase contract, which allows Card to purchase up to 500,000 units of a computer part annually from Hart Supply Co. at $.10 per unit and guarantees a minimum annual purchase of 100,000 units. During 2002, the part unexpectedly became obsolete. Card had 250,000 units of this inventory at December 31, 2002, and believes these parts can be sold as scrap for $.02 per unit. What amount of probable loss from the purchase commitment should Card report in its 2002 income statement?
- a. $24,000
- b. $20,000
- c. $16,000
- d. $ 8,000

20. Thread Co. is selecting its inventory system in preparation for its first year of operations. Thread intends to use either the periodic weighted-average method or the perpetual moving-average method, and to apply the lower of cost or market rule either to individual items or to the total inventory. Inventory prices are expected to generally increase throughout 2002, although a few individual prices will decrease. What inventory system should Thread select if it wants to maximize the inventory carrying amount at December 31, 2002?

	Inventory method	Cost or market application
a.	Perpetual	Total inventory
b.	Perpetual	Individual item
c.	Periodic	Total inventory
d.	Periodic	Individual item

21. Marsh Company had 150 units of product A on hand at January 1, 2002, costing $21 each. Purchases of product A during the month of January were as follows:

	Units	Unit cost
Jan. 10	200	$22
18	250	23
28	100	24

A physical count on January 31, 2002, shows 250 units of product A on hand. The cost of the inventory at January 31, 2002, under the LIFO method is

a. $5,850
b. $5,550
c. $5,350
d. $5,250

22. During January 2002, Metro Co., which maintains a perpetual inventory system, recorded the following information pertaining to its inventory:

	Units	Unit cost	Total cost	Units on hand
Balance on 1/1/02	1,000	$1	$1,000	1,000
Purchased on 1/7/02	600	3	1,800	1,600
Sold on 1/20/02	900			700
Purchased on 1/25/02	400	5	2,000	1,100

Under the LIFO method, what amount should Metro report as inventory at January 31, 2002?

a. $1,300
b. $2,700
c. $3,900
d. $4,100

23. Drew Co. uses the average cost inventory method for internal reporting purposes and LIFO for financial statement and income tax reporting. At December 31, 2002, the inventory was $375,000 using average cost and $320,000 using LIFO. The unadjusted credit balance in the LIFO Reserve account on December 31, 2002, was $35,000. What adjusting entry should Drew record to adjust from average cost to LIFO at December 31, 2002?

		Debit	Credit
a.	Cost of goods sold	$55,000	
	Inventory		$55,000
b.	Cost of goods sold	$55,000	
	LIFO reserve		$55,000
c.	Cost of goods sold	$20,000	
	Inventory		$20,000
d.	Cost of goods sold	$20,000	
	LIFO reserve		$20,000

24. A company decided to change its inventory valuation method from FIFO to LIFO in a period of rising prices. What was the result of the change on ending inventory and net income in the year of the change?

	Ending inventory	Net income
a.	Increase	Increase
b.	Increase	Decrease
c.	Decrease	Decrease
d.	Decrease	Increase

25. Generally, which inventory costing method approximates most closely the current cost for each of the following?

	Cost of goods sold	Ending inventory
a.	LIFO	FIFO
b.	LIFO	LIFO
c.	FIFO	FIFO
d.	FIFO	LIFO

26. During periods of rising prices, a perpetual inventory system would result in the same dollar amount of ending inventory as a periodic inventory system under which of the following inventory cost flow methods?

	FIFO	LIFO
a.	Yes	No
b.	Yes	Yes
c.	No	Yes
d.	No	No

27. On January 1, 2001, Poe Company adopted the dollar-value LIFO inventory method. Poe's entire inventory constitutes a single pool. Inventory data for 2001 and 2002 are as follows:

Date	Inventory at current year cost	Inventory at base year cost	Relevant price index
1/1/01	$150,000	$150,000	1.00
12/31/01	220,000	200,000	1.10
12/31/02	276,000	230,000	1.20

Poe's LIFO inventory value at December 31, 2002, is

a. $230,000
b. $236,000
c. $241,000
d. $246,000

28. Brock Co. adopted the dollar-value LIFO inventory method as of January 1, 2001. A single inventory pool and an internally computed price index are used to compute Brock's LIFO inventory layers. Information about Brock's dollar-value inventory follows:

	Inventory		
Date	At base year cost	At current year cost	At dollar value LIFO
1/1/01	$40,000	$40,000	$40,000
2001 layer	5,000	14,000	6,000
12/31/01	45,000	54,000	46,000
2002 layer	15,000	26,000	?
12/31/02	$60,000	$80,000	?

What was Brock's dollar-value LIFO inventory at December 31, 2002?

a. $80,000
b. $74,000
c. $66,000
d. $60,000

29. Estimates of price-level changes for specific inventories are required for which of the following inventory methods?

a. Conventional retail.
b. Dollar-value LIFO.
c. Weighted-average cost.
d. Average cost retail.

30. When the double-extension approach to the dollar-value LIFO inventory method is used, the inventory layer added in the current year is multiplied by an index number. Which of the following correctly states how components are used in the calculation of this index number?

a. In the numerator, the average of the ending inventory at base year cost and at current year cost.
b. In the numerator, the ending inventory at current year cost, and, in the denominator, the ending inventory at base year cost.
c. In the numerator, the ending inventory at base year cost, and, the denominator, the ending inventory at current year cost.

d.   In the denominator, the average of the ending inventory at base year cost and at current year cost.

31. Jones Wholesalers stocks a changing variety of products. Which inventory costing method will be most likely to give Jones the lowest ending inventory when its product lines are subject to specific price increases?
a.   Specific identification.
b.   Weighted-average.
c.   Dollar-value LIFO.
d.   FIFO periodic.

32. Dart Company's accounting records indicated the following information:

Inventory, 1/1/02	$ 500,000
Purchases during 2002	2,500,000
Sales during 2002	3,200,000

A physical inventory taken on December 31, 2002, resulted in an ending inventory of $575,000. Dart's gross profit on sales has remained constant at 25% in recent years. Dart suspects some inventory may have been taken by a new employee. At December 31, 2002, what is the estimated cost of missing inventory?
a. $ 25,000
b. $100,000
c. $175,000
d. $225,000

33. On July 1, 2002, Casa Development Co. purchased a tract of land for $1,200,000. Casa incurred additional cost of $300,000 during the remainder of 2002 in preparing the land for sale. The tract was subdivided into residential lots as follows:

Lot class	Number of lots	Sales price per lot
A	100	$24,000
B	100	16,000
C	200	10,000

Using the relative sales value method, what amount of costs should be allocated to the Class A lots?
a. $300,000
b. $375,000
c. $600,000
d. $720,000

34. Herc Co.'s inventory at December 31, 2002, was $1,500,000 based on a physical count priced at cost, and before any necessary adjustment for the following:

•   Merchandise costing $90,000, shipped FOB shipping point from a vendor on December 30, 2002, was received and recorded on January 5, 2003.
•   Goods in the shipping area were excluded from inventory although shipment was not made until January 4, 2003. The goods, billed to the customer FOB shipping point on December 30, 2002, had a cost of $120,000.

What amount should Herc report as inventory in its December 31, 2002 balance sheet?
a. $1,500,000
b. $1,590,000
c. $1,620,000
d. $1,710,000

35. Kew Co.'s accounts payable balance at December 31, 2002, was $2,200,000 before considering the following data:

•   Goods shipped to Kew FOB shipping point on December 22, 2002, were lost in transit. The invoice cost of $40,000 was not recorded by Kew. On January 7, 2003, Kew filed a $40,000 claim against the common carrier.
•   On December 27, 2002, a vendor authorized Kew to return, for full credit, goods shipped and billed at $70,000 on December 3, 2002. The returned goods were shipped by Kew on December 28, 2002. A $70,000 credit memo was received and recorded by Kew on January 5, 2003.
•   Goods shipped to Kew FOB destination on December 20, 2002, were received on January 6, 2003. The invoice cost was $50,000.

What amount should Kew report as accounts payable in its December 31, 2002 balance sheet?
a. $2,170,000
b. $2,180,000
c. $2,230,000
d. $2,280,000

36. Lewis Company's usual sales terms are net sixty days, FOB shipping point. Sales, net of returns and allowances, totaled $2,300,000 for the year ended December 31, 2002, before year-end adjustments. Additional data are as follows:

•   On December 27, 2002, Lewis authorized a customer to return, for full credit, goods shipped and billed at $50,000 on December 15, 2002. The returned goods were received by Lewis on January 4, 2003, and a $50,000 credit memo was issued and recorded on the same date.
•   Goods with an invoice amount of $80,000 were billed and recorded on January 3, 2003. The goods were shipped on December 30, 2002.
•   Goods with an invoice amount of $100,000 were billed and recorded on December 30, 2002. The goods were shipped on January 3, 2003.

Lewis' adjusted net sales for 2002 should be
a. $2,330,000
b. $2,280,000
c. $2,250,000
d. $2,230,000

37. On January 1, 2002, Dell, Inc. contracted with the city of Little to provide custom built desks for the city schools. The contract made Dell the city's sole supplier and required Dell to supply no less than 4,000 desks and no more than 5,500 desks per year for two years. In turn, Little agreed to pay a fixed price of $110 per desk. During 2002, Dell produced 5,000 desks for Little. At December 31, 2002, 500 of these desks were segregated from the regular inventory and were accepted and awaiting pickup by Little. Little paid Dell $450,000 during 2002. What amount should Dell recognize as contract revenue in 2002?
a. $450,000
b. $495,000
c. $550,000
d. $605,000

38. On October 20, 2002, Grimm Co. consigned forty freezers to Holden Co. for sale at $1,000 each and paid $800 in transportation costs. On December 30, 2002, Holden reported the sale of ten freezers and remitted $8,500. The remittance was net of the agreed 15% commission. What amount should Grimm recognize as consignment sales revenue for 2002?
a. $ 7,700

b. $ 8,500
c. $ 9,800
d. $10,000

39. The following items were included in Opal Co.'s inventory account at December 31, 2002:

Merchandise out on consignment, at sales price, including 40% markup on selling price $40,000
Goods purchased, in transit, shipped FOB shipping point   36,000
Goods held on consignment by Opal   27,000

By what amount should Opal's inventory account at December 31, 2002, be reduced?
a. $103,000
b. $ 67,000
c. $ 51,000
d. $ 43,000

40. On December 1, 2002, Alt Department Store received 505 sweaters on consignment from Todd. Todd's cost for the sweaters was $80 each, and they were priced to sell at $100. Alt's commission on consigned goods is 10%. At December 31, 2002, five sweaters remained. In its December 31, 2002 balance sheet, what amount should Alt report as payable for consigned goods?
a. $49,000
b. $45,400
c. $45,000
d. $40,400

41. Southgate Co. paid the in-transit insurance premium for consignment goods shipped to Hendon Co., the consignee. In addition, Southgate advanced part of the commissions that will be due when Hendon sells the goods. Should Southgate include the in-transit insurance premium and the advanced commissions in inventory costs?

	Insurance premium	*Advanced commissions*
a.	Yes	Yes
b.	No	No
c.	Yes	No
d.	No	Yes

42. Jel Co., a consignee, paid the freight costs for goods shipped from Dale Co., a consignor. These freight costs are to be deducted from Jel's payment to Dale when the consignment goods are sold. Until Jel sells the goods, the freight costs should be included in Jel's
a. Cost of goods sold.
b. Freight-out costs.
c. Selling expenses.
d. Accounts receivable.

43. Heath Co.'s current ratio is 4:1. Which of the following transactions would normally increase its current ratio?
a. Purchasing inventory on account.
b. Selling inventory on account.
c. Collecting an account receivable.
d. Purchasing machinery for cash.

44. During 2002, Rand Co. purchased $960,000 of inventory. The cost of goods sold for 2002 was $900,000, and the ending inventory at December 31, 2002, was $180,000. What was the inventory turnover for 2002?
a. 6.4
b. 6.0
c. 5.3
d. 5.0

45. In a comparison of 2002 to 2001, Neir Co.'s inventory turnover ratio increased substantially although sales and inventory amounts were essentially unchanged. Which of the following statements explains the increased inventory turnover ratio?
a. Cost of goods sold decreased.
b. Accounts receivable turnover increased.
c. Total asset turnover increased.
d. Gross profit percentage decreased.

46. Selected data pertaining to Lore Co. for the calendar year 2002 is as follows:

Net cash sales $ 3,000
Cost of goods sold   18,000
Inventory at beginning of year   6,000
Purchases   24,000
Accounts receivable at beginning of year   20,000
Accounts receivable at end of year   22,000

Lore would use which of the following to determine the average days' sales in inventory?

	Numerator	*Denominator*
a.	365	Average inventory
b.	365	Inventory turnover
c.	Average inventory	Sales divided by 365
d.	Sales divided by 365	Inventory turnover

47. Cord Builders, Inc. has consistently used the percentage-of-completion method of accounting for construction-type contracts. During 2001 Cord started work on a $9,000,000 fixed-price construction contract that was completed in 2003. Cord's accounting records disclosed the following:

	December 31	
	2001	2002
Cumulative contract costs incurred	$3,900,000	$6,300,000
Estimated total cost at completion	7,800,000	8,100,000

How much income would Cord have recognized on this contract for the year ended December 31, 2002?
a. $100,000
b. $300,000
c. $600,000
d. $700,000

48. State Co. recognizes construction revenue and expenses using the percentage-of-completion method. During 2001, a single long-term project was begun, which continued through 2002. Information on the project follows:

	2001	2002
Accounts receivable from construction contract	$100,000	$300,000
Construction expenses	105,000	192,000
Construction in progress	122,000	364,000
Partial billings on contract	100,000	420,000

Profit recognized from the long-term construction contract in 2002 should be
a. $ 50,000
b. $108,000
c. $128,000
d. $228,000

49. Lake Construction Company has consistently used the percentage-of-completion method of recognizing income. During 2001, Lake entered into a fixed-price contract to construct an office building for $10,000,000. Information relating to the contract is as follows:

	At December 31,	
	2001	2002
Percentage of completion	20%	60%
Estimated total cost at completion	$7,500,000	$8,000,000
Income recognized (cumulative)	500,000	1,200,000

Contract costs incurred during 2002 were
   a. $3,200,000
   b. $3,300,000
   c. $3,500,000
   d. $4,800,000

50. Hansen Construction, Inc. has consistently used the percentage-of-completion method of recognizing income. During 2002, Hansen started work on a $3,000,000 fixed-price construction contract. The accounting records disclosed the following data for the year ended December 31, 2002:

Costs incurred	$ 930,000
Estimated cost to complete	2,170,000
Progress billings	1,100,000
Collections	700,000

How much loss should Hansen have recognized in 2002?
   a. $230,000
   b. $100,000
   c. $ 30,000
   d. $0

Items 51 and 52 are based on the following data pertaining to Pell Co.'s construction jobs, which commenced during 2002:

	Project 1	Project 2
Contract price	$420,000	$300,000
Costs incurred during 2002	240,000	280,000
Estimated costs to complete	120,000	40,000
Billed to customers during 2002	150,000	270,000
Received from customers during 2002	90,000	250,000

51. If Pell used the completed contract method, what amount of gross profit (loss) would Pell report in its 2002 income statement?
   a. $ (20,000)
   b. $ 0
   c. $ 340,000
   d. $ 420,000

52. If Pell used the percentage-of-completion method, what amount of gross profit (loss) would Pell report in its 2002 income statement?
   a. $(20,000)
   b. $ 20,000
   c. $ 22,500
   d. $ 40,000

53. Which of the following is used in calculating the income recognized in the fourth and final year of a contract accounted for by the percentage-of-completion method?

	Actual total costs	Income previously recognized
a.	Yes	Yes
b.	Yes	No
c.	No	Yes
d.	No	No

54. A company used the percentage-of-completion method of accounting for a five-year construction contract. Which of the following items will the company use to calculate the income recognized in the third year?

	Progress billings to date	Income previously recognized
a.	Yes	No
b.	No	Yes
c.	No	No
d.	Yes	Yes

55. The calculation of the income recognized in the third year of a five-year construction contract accounted for using the percentage-of-completion method includes the ratio of
   a.   Total costs incurred to date to total estimated costs.
   b.   Total costs incurred to date to total billings to date.
   c.   Cost incurred in year three to total estimated costs.
   d.   Costs incurred in year three to total billings to date.

56. When should an anticipated loss on a long-term contract be recognized under the percentage-of-completion method and the completed-contract method, respectively?

	Percentage-of-completion	Completed-contract
a.	Over life of project	Contract complete
b.	Immediately	Contract complete
c.	Over life of project	Immediately
d.	Immediately	Immediately

57. In accounting for a long-term construction contract using the percentage-of-completion method, the progress billings on contracts account is a
   a.   Contra current asset account.
   b.   Contra noncurrent asset account.
   c.   Noncurrent liability account.
   d.   Revenue account.

OTHER OBJECTIVE QUESTIONS

Problem 1   (15 to 25 minutes)

Items 1 through 13 represent True or False statements concerning inventory accounting methods.

Required:

Respond to each statement as either True or False.

Items to be answered

1. The gross margin method uses historical sales margins to estimate the cost of inventory.

2. The dollar-value LIFO method preserves old inventory costs by charging current costs to cost of goods sold.

3. Inventory should be reported at the lower of cost or market and it may be based on the values of individual items, categories, or the total inventory.

4. A loss on a purchase commitment should be recorded when the contract price is greater than the market and it is anticipated that a loss will occur when the contract is completed.

5. Under the dollar-value LIFO method, increases and decreases in a layer would be measured based upon the change in the total dollar value of the layer.

6. The link-chain method uses a cumulative index to value the base cost of ending inventory.

7. The price index for dollar-value LIFO is a measure of changes in price levels between the current year and the base year.

8. Under the LIFO method, an inventory liquidation will result in higher profits in a period of rising prices.

9. A holding gain results from holding an item while the market value experiences a decline.

10. During a period of rising prices, the LIFO cost flow assumption results in a higher net income as compared to FIFO.

11. In a period of rising prices, when a company changes from FIFO to LIFO the net income will tend to decline as will working capital.

12. The use of LIFO for book and tax purposes will result in a lower tax payment in a period of rising prices.

13. Under the LIFO method, the cost of goods sold balance would be the same whether a perpetual or periodic inventory system is used.

PROBLEMS

Problem 1   (15 to 25 minutes)

Happlia Co. imports expensive household appliances. Each model has many variations and each unit has an identification number. Happlia pays all costs for getting the goods from the port to its central warehouse in Des Moines. After repackaging, the goods are consigned to retailers. A retailer makes a sale, simultaneously buys the appliance from Happlia, and pays the balance due within one week.

To alleviate the overstocking of refrigerators at a Minneapolis retailer, some were reshipped to a Kansas City retailer where they were still held in inventory at December 31, 2002. Happlia paid the costs of this reshipment.

Happlia uses the specific identification inventory costing method.

Required:

a. In regard to the specific identification inventory costing method
  1. Describe its key elements.
  2. Discuss why it is appropriate for Happlia to use this method.

b. 1. What general criteria should Happlia use to determine inventory carrying amounts at December 31, 2002? Ignore lower of cost or market considerations.
  2. Give four examples of costs included in these inventory carrying amounts.

c. What costs should be reported in Happlia's 2002 income statement? Ignore lower of cost or market considerations.

Problem 2   (15 to 25 minutes)

Blaedon Co. makes ongoing design refinements to lawnmowers that are produced for it by contractors. Blaedon stores the lawnmowers in its own warehouse and sells them at list price, directly to retailers. Blaedon uses the FIFO inventory method. Approximately two-thirds of new lawnmower sales involve trade-ins. For each used lawnmower traded in and returned to Blaedon, retailers receive a $40 allowance regardless of whether the trade-in was associated with a sale of a 2002 or 2003 model. Blaedon's net realizable value on a used lawnmower averages $25.

At December 31, 2002, Blaedon's inventory of new lawnmowers includes both 2002 and 2003 models. When the 2003 model was introduced in September 2002, the list price of the remaining 2002 model lawnmowers was reduced below cost. Blaedon is experiencing rising costs.

Required:

a. At December 31, 2002, how should Blaedon determine the carrying amounts assigned to its lawnmower inventory of
  1. 2003 models?
  2. 2002 models?

b. Considering only the 2003 model lawnmower, explain the impact of the FIFO cost flow assumptions on Blaedon's 2002
  1. Income statement amounts.
  2. Balance sheet amounts.

Problem 3   (30 to 40 minutes)

York Co. sells one product, which it purchases from various suppliers. York's trial balance at December 31, 2002, included the following accounts:

Sales (33,000 units @ $16)	$528,000
Sales discounts	7,500
Purchases	368,900
Purchase discounts	18,000
Freight-in	5,000
Freight-out	11,000

York Co.'s inventory purchases during 2002 were as follows:

	Units	Cost per unit	Total cost
Beginning inventory, January 1	8,000	$8.20	$ 65,600
Purchases, quarter ended March 31	12,000	8.25	99,000
Purchases, quarter ended June 30	15,000	7.90	118,500
Purchases, quarter ended September 30	13,000	7.50	97,500
Purchases, quarter ended December 31	7,000	7.70	53,900
	55,000		$434,500

Additional information

York's accounting policy is to report inventory in its financial statements at the lower of cost or market, applied to total inventory. Cost is determined under the last-in, first-out (LIFO) method.

York has determined that, at December 31, 2002, the replacement cost of its inventory was $8 per unit and the net realizable value was $8.80 per unit. York's normal profit margin is $1.05 per unit.

Required:

a. Prepare York's schedule of cost of goods sold, with a supporting schedule of ending inventory. York uses the direct method of reporting losses from market decline of inventory.

b. Explain the rule of lower of cost or market and its application in this situation.

Problem 4   (20 to 25 minutes)

On January 1, 2000, Silver Industries, Inc. adopted the dollar-value LIFO method of determining inventory costs for financial and income tax reporting. The following information relates to this change:

• Silver has continued to use the FIFO method, which approximates current costs, for internal reporting purposes. Silver's FIFO inventories at December 31, 2000, 2001, and 2002 were $100,000, $137,500, and $195,000, respectively.

• The FIFO inventory amounts are converted to dollar-value LIFO amounts using a single inventory pool and cost indices developed using the link-chain method. Silver estimated that the current year cost change indices, which measure year-to-year cost changes, were 1.25 for 2001 and 1.20 for 2002.

Required:

Prepare a schedule showing the computation of Silver's dollar-value LIFO inventory at December 31, 2001 and 2002. Show all calculations.

Problem 5 (15 to 25 minutes)

On July 1, 2001, Bow Construction Co. commenced operations and began constructing a building for Crecy under a fixed price contract. Anticipated completion date was June 15, 2003. Bow projects a large profit because it purchased most of the contract materials at exceptionally low prices in August 2001.

At the end of each month, Crecy is billed for completed work, for which it pays within thirty days. On December 31, 2002, all costs incurred exceed billings on the contract.

For the Crecy contract, Bow uses the percentage-of-completion (cost-to-cost) method for financial statement purposes. For income tax purposes, Bow qualifies for and uses the completed-contract method. Bow has no other contracts and no other differences between financial statement and income tax reporting.

Required:

a. How should Bow determine that the percentage-of-completion method is appropriate for the Crecy contract?

b. How should Bow calculate its 2002 income to be recognized on the Crecy contract? Explain any special treatment of unused material costs and why it is required.

c. Ignoring income tax effects, specify how the accounts related to the Crecy contract should be reported on Bow's December 31, 2002 balance sheet.

d. What are the income tax effects of the Crecy contract on Bow's 2002 balance sheet and income statement?*

---

* *This requirement should not be completed until you have done Module 27, Deferred Taxes. A cross-reference in the Module 27 problem material will direct you to return to it.*

Problem 6 (40 to 50 minutes)

London, Inc. began operation of its construction division on October 1, 2001, and entered into contracts for two separate projects. The Beta project contract price was $600,000 and provided for penalties of $10,000 per week for late completion. Although during 2002 the Beta project had been on schedule for timely completion, it was completed four weeks late in August 2003. The Gamma project's original contract price was $800,000. Change orders during 2003 added $40,000 to the original contract price.

The following data pertains to the separate long-term construction projects in progress:

	Beta	Gamma
As of September 30, 2002:		
Costs incurred to date	$360,000	$410,000
Estimated costs to complete	40,000	410,000
Billings	315,000	440,000
Cash collections	275,000	365,000
As of September 30, 2003:		
Costs incurred to date	450,000	720,000
Estimated costs to complete	--	180,000
Billings	560,000	710,000
Cash collections	560,000	625,000

Additional information

• London accounts for its long-term construction contracts using the percentage-of-completion method for financial reporting purposes and the completed-contract method for income tax purposes.

• Enacted income tax rates are 25% for 2002 and 30% for future years.

• London's income before income taxes from all divisions, before considering revenues from long-term construction projects, was $300,000 for the year ended September 30, 2002. There were no other temporary or permanent differences.

Required:

a. Prepare a schedule showing London's gross profit (loss) recognized for the years ended September 30, 2002, and 2003, under the percentage-of-completion method.

b. Prepare a schedule showing London's balances in the following accounts at September 30, 2002, under the percentage-of-completion method:

- Accounts receivable
- Costs and estimated earnings in excess of billings
- Billings in excess of costs and estimated earnings

c. Prepare a schedule reconciling London's financial statement income and taxable income for the year ended September 30, 2002, and showing all components of taxes payable and current and deferred income tax expense for the year then ended. Do not consider estimated tax requirements.*

---

* *This requirement should not be completed until you have done Module 27, Deferred Taxes. A cross-reference in the Module 27 problem material will direct you to return to it.*

MULTIPLE-CHOICE ANSWERS

1. c __ __	13. c __ __	25. a __ __	37. c __ __	49. b __ __
2. d __ __	14. c __ __	26. a __ __	38. d __ __	50. b __ __
3. c __ __	15. a __ __	27. c __ __	39. d __ __	51. a __ __
4. b __ __	16. d __ __	28. c __ __	40. c __ __	52. b __ __
5. c __ __	17. b __ __	29. b __ __	41. c __ __	53. a __ __
6. a __ __	18. b __ __	30. b __ __	42. a __ __	54. b __ __
7. a __ __	19. c __ __	31. c __ __	43. b __ __	55. __ __
8. b __ __	20. a __ __	32. a __ __	44. b __ __	56. d __ __
9. d __ __	21. c __ __	33. c __ __	45. d __ __	57. a __ __
10. b __ __	22. b __ __	34. d __ __	46. b __ __	
11. b __ __	23. d __ __	35. a __ __	47. a __ __	1st: __/57 = __%
12. b __ __	24. c __ __	36. d __ __	48. a __ __	2nd: __/57 = __%

MULTIPLE-CHOICE ANSWER EXPLANATIONS

A.   Determining Inventory and Cost of Goods Sold

1.   (c)   Inventoriable costs include all costs necessary to prepare goods for sale. For a merchandising concern these costs include the purchase price of the goods, freight-in, insurance, warehousing, and any costs necessary to get the goods to the point of sale (except interest on any loans obtained to purchase the goods). In this problem, inventoriable costs total $408,000.

Purchase price less returns ($400,000 – $2,000)	$398,000
Freight-in	10,000
	$408,000

Note that freight-out is a **selling expense**, not an inventoriable cost, as the diagram below indicates.

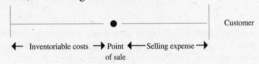

2.   (d)   When the shipping terms are FOB destination, the seller bears **all** costs of transporting the goods to the buyer. Therefore, the seller is responsible for the payment of packaging costs ($1,000), shipping costs ($1,500), and the special handling charges ($2,000). The only amount to be included as the buyer's cost of the inventory purchased is the purchase price ($50,000).

3.   (c)   Purchases are always recorded net of trade discounts. When more than one trade discount is applied to a list price, it is called a chain discount. Chain discounts are applied in steps; each discount applies to the previously discounted price. The cost, net of trade discounts, is $2,800 [$5,000 – (30% x $5,000) = $3,500; and $3,500 – (20% x $3,500) = $2,800]. Payment was made within the discount period, so the net purchase price is $2,744 [$2,800 – (2% x $2,800)]. The remittance from Burr would also include reimbursement of the $200 of delivery costs. Since the terms were FOB shipping point, Burr is responsible for paying this amount, and must reimburse Pitt, who prepaid the freight. Thus, the total remittance is $2,944 ($2,744 + $200).

4.   (b)   Three computations must be performed: raw materials used, cost of goods manufactured, and cost of goods sold.

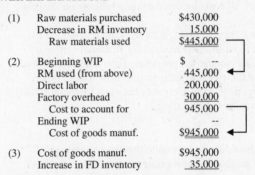

The decrease in RM inventory is added when computing RM used because RM were used in excess of those purchased. The increase in FG inventory is deducted when computing cost of goods sold because it represents the portion of goods manufactured which were not sold. The freight-out is irrelevant for this question because freight-out is a selling expense and therefore does not affect cost of goods sold.

5.   (c)   To compute cost of goods sold, the solutions approach is to set up a T-account for inventory

	Inventory		
12/31/01	90,000		
Purchases	124,000	34,000	Write-off
		?	Cost of goods sold
12/31/02	30,000		

Purchases increase inventory, while the write-off and cost of goods sold decrease inventory. Cost of goods sold can be computed as $150,000 using the T-account. An alternate solutions approach is to use the CGS computation

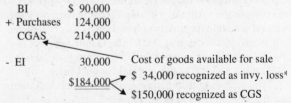

* *Theoretically correct treatment.*

6.   (a)   Per ARB 43, the cost of inventory should include all expenditures (direct and indirect) incurred to bring an item to its existing condition and location. Freight-in charges are thus appropriately included in inventory costs. Per SFAS 34, interest cost shall not be capitalized for assets that are in use or ready for their intended use in the earnings activities of the enterprise. Thus, interest on an inventory loan should not be included in inventory (it should be expensed as incurred).

7. **(a)** Per ARB 43, the cost of inventory should include all expenditures (direct and indirect) incurred to bring an item to its existing condition and location. Freight charges are thus appropriately included in inventory costs. Under the net purchase method, purchase discounts not taken are recorded in a Purchase Discounts Lost account. When this method is used, purchase discounts lost are considered a financial (i.e., "other") expense, and are thus excluded from the cost of inventory.

8. **(b)** Azur should report cost of goods sold calculated as

Cost of goods sold (CGS) = Beg. Inventory + Net purchases* + Freight in – Ending Inventory

CGS = $ 30,840 + $92,520** + $15,420 – $20,560

CGS = $118,220

Freight out is a selling expense and does not enter the calculation of cost of goods sold.

 * *Net purchase = Purchases – Purchase returns and allowances – Purchase discounts*

 ** *($102,800 – $10,280)*

B. Inventory Valuation and Cost-Flow Methods

9. **(d)** The index is calculated as 2.00 = ($80,000 current cost / $40,000 base year cost). The index for a particular period is calculated by dividing the base year cost of the inventory layer into the current cost of the layer.

10. **(b)** The inventory valuations are calculated as follows:

Valuations of ending inventory under LIFO perpetual

1,400 units at $1.00	=	$1,400
800 units at $5.00	=	4,000
Total		$5,400

Value of ending inventory under LIFO periodic

2,000 units at $1.00	=	$2,000
200 units at $3.00	=	600
Total		$2,600

B.2. Weighted-Average

11. **(b)** The requirement is to determine whether the weighted-average inventory method is applicable to a periodic and/or a perpetual inventory system. The weighted-average method computes a weighted-average unit cost of inventory for the entire period and is used with periodic records. The moving-average method requires that a new unit of cost be computed each time new goods are purchased and is used with perpetual records.

B.4. Moving-Average

12. **(b)** The moving-average method requires that a new unit cost be computed each time goods are purchased. The new unit cost is used to cost all sales of inventory until the next purchase. After the 1/7/02 purchase, Metro owns 1,600 units (1,000 + 600) at a total cost of $2,800 ($1,000 + $1,800). Therefore, the moving-average unit cost at that time is $1.75 ($2,800 ÷ 1,600 units). After the 1/20/02 sale of 900 units (at a unit of cost of $1.75), Metro owns 700 units at a unit cost of $1.75 (700 x $1.75 = $1,225). The 1/25/02 purchase of 400 units at a total cost of $2,000 increases inventory to its 1/31/02 balance of $3,225 ($1,225 +

$2,000). The new unit cost (not required) is $2.93 ($3,225 ÷ 1,100).

B.5. Lower of Cost or Market

13. **(c)** ARB 43 requires the use of lower of cost or market (LCM) for financial reporting of inventories. The market value of inventory is defined as the replacement cost (RC), as long as it is less than the ceiling (net realizable value, or NRV) and more than the floor (NRV less a normal profit, or NRV – NP). In this case, the amounts are

Ceiling: NRV = $408,000 est. sell. price – $20,000 dep. cost =	$388,000
Replacement cost	$360,000
Floor: NRV – NP = $388,000 – $60,000 =	$328,000

The designated market value is the replacement cost of $360,000 because it falls between the floor and the ceiling. Once market value is designated, LCM can be determined by simply picking the lower of cost ($400,000) or market ($360,000). Thus, the inventory should be reported at market.

14. **(c)** ARB 43 requires the use of lower of cost or market (LCM) for financial reporting of inventories. The market value of inventory is defined as the replacement cost (RC), as long as it is less than the ceiling (net realizable value, or NRV) and more than the floor (NRV less a normal profit, or NRV – NP). In this case, the amounts are

Ceiling: NRV = $40,000 est. sell. price – $12,000 disp. cost =	$28,000
Floor: NRV – NP = $28,000 – (10% x $40,000)	$24,000
RC:	$20,000

Since RC falls below the floor, the floor (NRV – NP) is the designated market value. Once market value is designated, LCM can be determined by simply determining the lower of cost ($26,000) or market ($24,000). Therefore, inventory is reported at $24,000.

15. **(a)** SFAC 5 establishes five different attributes on which assets can be measured. The attribute used should be determined by the nature of the item and the relevance and reliability of the attribute measured. The five attributes are historical cost, current cost, current market value, net realizable value, and present value. Historical cost is defined as the amount of cash, or its equivalent, paid to acquire an asset. Reporting inventory at lower of cost or market is a departure from the historical cost principle as the inventory could potentially be carried at the market value if lower. Although, reporting inventory at lower of cost or market does not create a departure from conservatism as this method carries at inventory the lowest or most conservative value. The use of LCM does not violate the principle of consistency either, as it would be reported on this basis continually. Finally the use of LCM would not violate the principle of full disclosure as its use would be discussed in the footnotes.

16. **(d)** According to ARB 43, inventory is to be valued at the lower of cost or market. Under this method, market is replacement cost provided that replacement cost is lower than net realizable value (ceiling) and higher than net realizable value less the normal profit margin (floor). The question does not specify whether replacement cost is above or below net realizable value, but since the original cost is below **both** of these values, that information is irrelevant.

Either NRV or RC will be designated as the market value of the inventory, and since the original cost is below **both** of these values, the inventory will be valued at its original cost. Answer (c) is incorrect because NRV-NP represents the market floor. Answers (a) and (b) are incorrect because they are both **above** the original cost.

17. (b) ARB 43 requires the use of lower of cost or market (LCM) for financial reporting of inventories. The market value of inventory is defined as the replacement cost (RC) as long as it is less than the ceiling (net realizable value, or NRV) and more than the floor (NRV less a normal profit, or NRV – NP). Therefore, if inventory is reported at RC, RC must be less than original cost (meaning statement I is **not** correct), and RC must be less than NRV (meaning statement II **is** correct) and greater than NRV – NP.

18. (b) ARB 43 requires the pricing of inventory at market when market value is less than cost. Market value is defined as current replacement cost, subject to a ceiling of net realizable value (NRV) and a floor of net realizable value minus a normal profit margin.

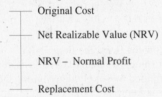

In this situation, replacement cost lies outside of (below) the floor and ceiling limitations. Therefore, NRV less a normal profit margin (the floor), will be used as the market to determine LCM. Since original cost is greater than market, market will be used to price the inventory for the period.

19. (c) The requirement is to determine the amount of probable loss from the purchase commitment that Card should report in its 2002 income statement. When there is a decline in market value below the contract price at the balance sheet date and the contract is noncancelable, an unrealized loss should be recorded in the period of decline and reported in the income statement. In this case, Card has a contract to purchase a minimum of 100,000 units both in 2003 and 2004 at $.10 per unit. The $20,000 loss (200,000 x $.10) on these obsolete units should be reduced by the amount Card believes is unrealizable from the sale of these units. Therefore, the loss on **purchase commitment** is $16,000 [$20,000 – (200,000 x .02)]. Additionally, Card Corp. would need to record a loss of $20,000 ($.08 x 250,000) from **inventory obsolescence**.

20. (a) To maximize its inventory carrying amount at December 31, 2002, Thread should use the perpetual moving-average method with the lower of cost or market rule applied to the total inventory. First, when using the perpetual moving-average method, the cost of sales throughout the year are determined using the average cost of purchases up to the time of the sale. On the other hand, under the periodic weighted-average method, the cost of each item

is the weighted-average of **all** units purchased during the year. During a period of rising prices, the perpetual moving-average method results in a lower cost of goods sold and a higher ending inventory because the cost of items sold throughout the year is the average of the earlier, lower prices. Second, the application of the lower of cost or market rule to the total inventory will result in a higher ending inventory because market values lower than cost are offset against market values higher than cost.

B.7. & B.8. First-In, First-Out (FIFO), and Last-In, First-Out (LIFO)

21. (c) The requirement is to determine the cost of the 1/31/02 inventory, using the LIFO method. LIFO stands for last-in, first-out; this means that the cost of the units purchased most recently are included in cost of goods sold. Therefore, the 1/31/02 inventory consists of the 250 units that were purchased at the earliest date(s). Thus, the 1/31/02 inventory would consist of the 150 units on hand at 1/1/02 (150 x $21 = $3,150) plus an additional 100 units purchased at the earliest purchase date in January (January 10; 100 x $22 = $2,200). The total value of the inventory at 1/31/02 would be $5,350 ($3,150 + $2,200).

22. (b) LIFO stands for last-in, first-out; this means that it is assumed that any units sold are the units most recently purchased. In a perpetual system, LIFO is applied at the time of each sale rather than once a year as in a periodic system. Using LIFO, the 900 units sold on 1/20/02 would consist of the 600 units purchased on 1/7/02 and 300 of the 1,000 units in the 1/1/02 balance. This would leave in inventory 700 units from the 1/1/02 balance. After the 1/25/02 purchase, inventory included those 700 units plus the 400 units purchased on 1/25/02. Therefore, ending inventory is $2,700 [(700 x $1) + (400 x $5)].

23. (d) When a company uses LIFO for external reporting purposes and another inventory method for internal purposes, a **LIFO Reserve** account is used to reduce inventory from the internal valuation to the LIFO valuation. LIFO Reserve is a contra account to inventory, and is adjusted up or down at year-end with a corresponding increase or decrease to **Cost of Goods Sold**. In this case, the LIFO Reserve account must be adjusted from a balance of $35,000 to a balance of $55,000 ($375,000 – $320,000). Therefore, LIFO Reserve is credited for $20,000 ($55,000 – $35,000) with a corresponding debit to Cost of Goods Sold.

24. (c) In a change **to** LIFO, no recognition is given to any cumulative effect associated with the change because it is usually not determinable. Thus, the effect on ending inventory and net income is the result solely of current year effects. In a period of rising prices, LIFO will result in a **lower ending inventory** amount than FIFO because the earlier lower costs are assumed to remain in ending inventory. LIFO will also result in a **lower net income** because the more recent higher costs are assigned to cost of goods sold.

25. (a) The inventory costing method which most closely approximates the current cost for cost of goods sold is LIFO, while the method which more accurately reflects ending inventory is FIFO. Under LIFO, the most recent purchases are assumed to be the first goods sold; thus, cost of goods sold contains relatively current costs. On the other hand, since FIFO assumes that the goods from beginning inventory and the earliest purchases are sold first, the ending inventory is made up of more recent purchases and thus represents a more current value.

26. **(a)**   Under the FIFO method, the first goods purchased are considered to be the first goods used or sold. Ending inventory is thus made up of the latest (most recent) purchases. Whenever the FIFO method is used, the ending inventory is the same whether a perpetual or periodic system is used. This is true even during periods of rising or falling prices because the inventory flow is always in chronological order. Under the LIFO method, the latest (most recent) purchases are considered to be the first goods used or sold. Ending inventory is thus made up of the first (oldest) purchases. When a periodic method is used, the first/last purchase determination is made only at the end of the year, based upon the actual chronological order of all purchases. When a perpetual method is used, however, the first/last purchase determination is made continuously throughout the year. When inventory levels get low under the perpetual method, early purchase costs will often be assigned to goods sold, a situation that is much less likely to occur in a periodic system. Therefore, in times of either rising or falling prices, LIFO ending inventory is usually different under a periodic system than under a perpetual system.

B.9.   Dollar-Value LIFO

27. **(c)**   When using dollar-value LIFO, the ending inventory at current year cost must first be converted to base year cost. This amount is given at 12/31/02 ($230,000), but it could be computed as follows: $276,000 \div 1.20 =$ $230,000. The next step is to determine the incremental LIFO layers at base year cost. The 1/1/01 (base year) layer is $150,000, the 2001 layer is $50,000 ($200,000 – $150,000), and the 2002 layer is $30,000 ($230,000 – $200,000). Finally, the LIFO layers are restated using the price index in effect at the time each layer was added.

	Base coat		*Ending inventory at DV LIFO cost*
1/1/01 layer	150,000	x 1.00 =	$150,000
2001 layer	50,000	x 1.10 =	55,000
2002 layer	30,000	x 1.20 =	36,000
	$230,000		$241,000

28. **(c)**   When using dollar-value LIFO, the ending inventory at current year cost must first be converted to base year cost. The 12/31/02 inventory at base year cost is given as $60,000. Since the 12/31/01 inventory at base year cost was $45,000 ($40,000 base layer and $5,000 2001 layer), a new layer of $15,000 was added in 2002 ($60,000 – $45,000). This layer must be restated using the 2002 price index. The 2002 price index is computed using the double-extension technique, as illustrated below.

$$\frac{\text{EI at year-end prices}}{\text{EI at base year prices}} = \frac{\$80,000}{\$60,000} = \underline{1.33}$$

Therefore, the 12/31/02 inventory using dollar-value LIFO is $66,000 as computed below.

	Base cost		*DV LIFO*
Base layer	$40,000		$40,000
2001 layer	5,000		6,000
2002 layer	15,000	x 1.33	20,000
			$66,000

29. **(b)**   The requirement is to determine which inventory method requires estimates of price level changes for specific inventories. In accordance with the dollar-value LIFO method, the ending inventory is first converted to the base year cost so that the incremental layers can be determined. The incremental layers are then restated using the price index which was in effect at the time each of the layers were added to the inventory. Thus, the specific layers of the ending inventory are adjusted to the current price level. Therefore, answer (b) is correct. Answers (a), (c), and (d) are incorrect because these methods do not specifically adjust for price level changes.

30. **(b)**   The requirement is to determine the appropriate use of ending inventory at current year cost and ending inventory at base year cost in calculating the dollar-value LIFO index. According to ARB 43, chap 4, the index number used to convert the current year's inventory layer is calculated as follows:

$$\text{Index} = \frac{\text{Ending inventory at current year cost}}{\text{Ending inventory at base year cost}}$$

This index indicates the relationship between current and base year prices as a percentage, and when multiplied by the new layer (which is the increase in inventory in base year dollars), it will convert the layer to current dollars.

31. **(c)**   During periods of rising prices, the inventory costing methods which will give Jones the lowest ending inventory balance are LIFO methods, because inventory items that were purchased at the earliest date (when prices were lower) will remain in inventory and the most recently purchased and more expensive items will be expensed through cost of goods sold. Any FIFO method will produce a higher ending inventory balance during inflation since the items purchased earliest (at lower prices) will be expensed through COGS, while the more expensive items remain in inventory. Answers (a) and (b) are incorrect because neither will give Jones a lower ending inventory balance than dollar-value LIFO, particularly as Jones' inventory changes (because dollar-value LIFO allows the LIFO "layers" to be made up of similar, not necessarily identical, items).

B.10.   Gross Profit

32. **(a)**   The gross profit method can be used to estimate the cost of missing inventory. The first step is to compute the cost of goods available for sale.

Beginning inventory	$ 500,000
Purchases	2,500,000
Cost of goods available for sale	$3,000,000

The second step is to estimate cost of goods sold based on the gross profit percentage.

Sales	$3,200,000
Estimated gross profit ($3,200,000 x 25%)	(800,000)
Cost of goods sold ($3,200,000 x 75%)	$2,400,000

Note that a shortcut is to realize that if gross profit is 25% of sales, cost of goods sold must be 75% of sales. The third step is to compute estimated ending inventory.

Cost of goods available for sale	$ 3,000,000
Estimated cost of goods sold	(2,400,000)
Estimated ending inventory	$ 600,000

Since the actual count of ending inventory at December 31 was only $575,000, the estimated shortage in inventory is $25,000 ($600,000 – $575,000).

B.14.   Cost Apportionment by Relative Sales Value

33.   (c)   The total cost of acquiring the land and preparing it for sale ($1,200,000 + $300,000 = $1,500,000) should be allocated to the residential lots based on their relative sales value, as computed below.

Lot class	# of lots		Sales price		Total sales value
A	100	x	$24,000	=	$2,400,000
B	100	x	16,000	=	1,600,000
C	200	x	10,000	=	2,000,000
					$6,000,000

Total cost		Fraction allocated to Class A		Allocated cost
$1,500,000	x	($2,400/$6,000)	=	$600,000

C. Items to Include in Inventory

34.   (d)   Before adjustment, the inventory based on a physical count was $1,500,000. The $90,000 of merchandise shipped FOB shipping point by a vendor on 12/30/02 should also be included in Herc's 12/31/02 inventory because Herc, the buyer, owns the goods while in transit under these terms. The goods in the shipping area (cost, $120,000) are also owned by Herc because they were not shipped until 2003 and Herc still retains the risks of ownership until that point. Therefore, 12/31/02 inventory is $1,710,000 ($1,500,000 + $90,000 + $120,000).

35.   (a)   Before adjustment, the balance in the Accounts Payable account is $2,200,000. The $40,000 of goods lost in transit from a vendor were shipped FOB **shipping point**. This means the buyer owns the goods while they were in transit; therefore, Kew should record the purchase and accounts payable in 2002. Kew, not the vendor, is ultimately responsible for the lost goods (note that Kew, not the vendor, is suing the common carrier). The $70,000 return that was recorded on 1/5/03 should have been recorded in 2002 when the return was authorized (December 27, 2002). Therefore, Kew should reduce 12/31/02 Accounts Payable by $70,000. The $50,000 of goods received on 1/6/03 were properly recorded in 2003, since the terms were FOB destination (the buyer does not own the goods until they are physically received). Therefore, no adjustment is necessary for this amount. Kew should report 12/31/02 Accounts Payable at $2,170,000 ($2,200,000 + $40,000 − $70,000).

36.   (d)   Net sales is $2,300,000, subject to three possible adjustments. The goods returned ($50,000) should be recorded as a return in 2002, when Lewis authorized the return. Since this return was not recorded until 2003, 2002 sales must be adjusted downward. The goods shipped on 12/30/02 ($80,000) were recorded as a sale in 2003. Since the terms were FOB shipping point, the sale must be recorded in 2002 when the goods were shipped; therefore, 2002 sales must be adjusted upward. The goods shipped on 1/3/03 ($100,000) should not be recorded as a sale until 2003. Since the sale was recorded in 2002, 2002 sales must be adjusted downward. Therefore, adjusted net sales for 2002 should be $2,230,000 ($2,300,000 − $50,000 + $80,000 − $100,000).

37.   (c)   Generally, goods are considered sold when legal title to the goods passes to the buyer. In certain situations, however, the transfer of title criteria does not reflect the underlying economics of the situation. In this situation,
although transfer of legal title may not have occurred for the 500 segregated desks, the economic substance of the transaction is that the seller no longer retains the risks of ownership. Therefore, all 5,000 desks (including the 500 segregated and accepted desks) are considered sold in 2002, and revenue of $550,000 is recognized (5,000 x $110). Note that the amount of cash collected ($450,000) does not affect the amount of revenue recognized in this case.

D. Consignments

38.   (d)   A consignor recognizes sales revenue from consignments when the consignee sells the consigned goods to the ultimate customer. Sales commissions earned by the consignee ($10,000 x 15% = $1,500) are reported as a selling expense by the consignor and are **not** netted against sales revenue. Therefore, sales revenue is reported at the total selling price of $10,000 (10 x $1,000). Note that the transportation costs ($800) do not affect sales either; one-fourth (10/40) is reflected in cost of goods sold and three-fourths (30/40) is included in ending inventory.

39.   (d)   No adjustment is necessary for the goods in transit ($36,000). The goods were shipped **FOB shipping point**, which means the buyer (Opal) owns the goods while in transit. Therefore, Opal properly included these goods in 12/31/02 inventory. The merchandise **out** on consignment is owned by the consignor (Opal) and should be included in Opal's inventory **at cost** [$40,000 − (40% x $40,000) = $24,000]. Therefore, inventory must be reduced by $16,000 for this item ($40,000 − $24,000). The goods **held** on consignment ($27,000) are owned by the consignor, not Opal; therefore, inventory must be reduced $27,000 for this item. The total reduction in inventory is $43,000 ($16,000 + $27,000).

40.   (c)   Alt sold 500 of the consigned sweaters (505 − 5) at $100 each, resulting in total sales of $50,000 (500 x $100). Alt must report a payable to Todd for this amount, less Alt's commission [$50,000 − (10% x $50,000) = $45,000]. Alt does not owe Todd anything for the unsold sweaters until they are sold.

41.   (c)   Inventoriable costs include all costs necessary to prepare goods for sale. These costs include the purchase price or manufacturing cost of the goods, freight, and any other costs necessary to get the goods to the point of sale. The in-transit insurance premium would therefore be included in inventory costs. Commissions paid to the consignee are selling expenses in the period the consigned goods are sold that are not required to ready the goods for sale. These costs, therefore, are not included in inventory.

42.   (d)   In a consignment, the manufacturer or wholesaler is referred to as the consignor and the dealer or retailer is referred to as the consignee. In such an arrangement, title to the goods remains with the consignor until they are sold to a third party. Jel's payment of reimbursable freight costs results in an account receivable from Dale, which Jel will subtract from the sale proceeds it remits to Dale. Answers (a), (b), and (c) are incorrect because the consignee, Jel, generally does not bear any costs associated with the sale of consigned goods.

E. Ratios

43. (b) The formula to compute the current ratio is

$$\text{Current ratio} = \frac{\text{Current assets}}{\text{Current liabilities}}$$

The following entries would be recorded when inventory is sold on account:

| Accounts receivable | } Sales price |
| Sales | of merchandise |

| Cost of goods sold | } Cost of |
| Inventory | merchandise |

Since the selling price (increase to AR) is normally higher than the cost of the merchandise sold (decrease to merchandise inventory) the sale would normally cause a net increase in current assets, and therefore, a net increase in the current ratio. When the existing current ratio is greater than one, increases of equal amounts to the numerator (inventory, a component of current assets) and denominator (accounts payable, a component of current liabilities) will reduce the ratio. When an account receivable is collected, cash (a current asset) is increased by the same amount that accounts receivable (another current asset) is decreased. Thus, the transaction has no impact on the current ratio. When machinery (a noncurrent asset) is purchased for cash (a current asset), there is a **decrease** in the current ratio.

44. (b) The formula for inventory turnover is

$$\frac{\text{Cost of goods sold}}{\text{Average inventory}}$$

Average inventory is equal to beginning inventory plus ending inventory, divided by two. Since beginning inventory is not given, it must be computed using the cost of goods sold relationship

	Cost of goods sold	$ 900,000
+	Ending inventory	180,000
	Cost of goods available for sale	$1,080,000
−	Purchases	− 960,000
	Beginning inventory	$ 120,000

Therefore, average inventory is $150,000 [($120,000 + $180,000) ÷ 2], and inventory turnover is 6.0 times ($900,000 ÷ 150,000).

45. (d) The solutions approach is to create a numerical example that conforms to the facts given in the question. The inventory turnover ratio is calculated as follows:

$$\frac{\text{Cost of goods sold}}{\text{Average inventory}}$$

If we assume that cost of goods sold has increased from 100 to 150 and average inventory has remained unchanged at 50 then the following ratios result:

$$\frac{\text{Cost of goods sold}}{\text{Average inventory}} \qquad \frac{100}{50} = 2 \qquad \frac{150}{50} = 3$$

Thus, if cost of goods sold increases while inventory remains unchanged, then the inventory turnover ratio will increase.

In addition, we must examine the effects of the increase in cost of goods sold on the gross profit percentage when sales remain constant. Assuming the same facts as above, and sales of $200, we get the following results:

	Sales	200	200
−	Cost of goods sales	− 100	− 150
	Gross profit	100	50

Thus, as cost of goods sold increases, the gross profit and the gross profit percentage will decrease.

Answer (a) is incorrect because a decrease in cost of goods sold will cause the inventory ratio to increase. Answers (b) and (c) are incorrect because they are not related to inventory turnover.

46. (b) Average days' sales in inventory measures the number of days inventory is held before sale; it reflects on efficiency of inventory policies. It is computed using the following formula:

$$\frac{365}{\text{Inventory turnover}}$$

F. Long-Term Construction Contracts

47. (a) The total expected income on the contract at 12/31/02 is $900,000 ($9,000,000 – $8,100,000). The formula for recognizing profit under the percentage-of-completion method is

$$\frac{\text{Costs to date}}{\text{Total expected costs}} \times \overset{\text{Expected}}{\text{profit}} = \overset{\text{Profit recog-}}{\text{nized to date}}$$

$$\frac{\$6,300,000}{\$8,100,000} \times \$900,000 = \$700,000$$

This result is the **total** profit on the contract in 2001 and 2002. The 2001 profit recognized must be subtracted from $700,000 to determine the 2002 profit. At 12/31/01, the total expected income on the contract was $1,200,000 ($9,000,000 – $7,800,000). The income recognized in 2001 was $600,000, as computed below.

$$\frac{\$3,900,000}{\$7,800,000} \times \$1,200,000 = \$600,000$$

Therefore, 2002 income is $700,000 less $600,000, or $100,000.

48. (a) Profit to be recognized using the percentage-of-completion method is generally computed as follows:

$$\left(\frac{\text{Cost to date}}{\text{Total expected cost}} \times \overset{\text{Expected}}{\text{profit}} \right) - \overset{\text{Profit recognized}}{\text{in previous periods}}$$

Not enough information is given in this problem to perform this computation, so 2002 profit must be computed indirectly. Since only construction expenses and profit are debited to the construction-in-progress (CIP account), 2001 profit must have been $17,000 ($122,000 CIP less $105,000 const. exp.). Cumulative profit recognized by the end of 2002 must be $67,000 [$364,000 CIP less $297,000 cumulative const. exp. ($105,000 + $192,000)]. Therefore, 2002 profit was $50,000 ($67,000 – $17,000).

	CIP	
2001 Exp.	105,000	
2001 Profit	?	2001 Profit = $17,000
2001 End. bal	122,000	
2002 Exp.	192,000	
2002 Profit	?	2002 Profit = $50,000
2002 End. bal.	364,000	

49. (b) Based on the information given, it must be assumed that costs incurred are used to measure the extent of progress toward project completion. At 12/31/01, the project was 20% complete and total estimated costs were $7,500,000. Therefore, costs incurred as of 12/31/01 were 20% of $7,500,000, or $1,500,000. At 12/31/02, the project was 60% complete and total estimated costs were $8,000,000. Therefore, costs incurred as of 12/31/02 are

60% of $8,000,000 or $4,800,000. The costs incurred during 2002 were $4,800,000 less $1,500,000, or $3,300,000.

50. (b) The requirement is to determine the amount of loss to recognize in 2002 on a long-term, fixed-price construction contract. Under both the percentage-of-completion method and the completed-contract method, an expected **loss** on a contract must be recognized in **full** in the period in which the expected loss is discovered. Therefore, Hanson must recognize a loss of $100,000 in 2002.

Expected contract revenue	$3,000,000
Expected contract costs ($930,000 + $2,170,000)	3,100,000
Expected loss	$ (100,000)

51. (a) The expected income on project 1 [$420,000 – ($240,000 + $120,000) = $60,000] is **not** recognized until the project is completed under the completed contract method. However, under the completed contract method, an expected **loss** on a contract must be recognized in full in the period in which it is discovered. Project two has an expected loss of ($20,000) [$300,000 – ($280,000 + $40,000)] which must be recognized immediately in 2002.

52. (b) Construction companies that use the percentage-of-completion method in accounting for long-term construction contracts usually recognize gross profit according to the cost-to-cost method.

$$\frac{\text{Costs to date}}{\text{Total estimated costs}} \times \text{Estimated profit} = \text{Gross profit to date}$$

Pell would recognize gross profit of $40,000 on project 1

$$\frac{\$240,000}{\$240,000 + \$120,000} \times [\$420,000 - (\$240,000 + \$120,000)] = \$40,000$$

Note that prior years' gross profit need not be subtracted from $40,000 because the project commenced during 2002. Under both the percentage-of-completion method and the completed-contract method, an expected **loss** must be recognized in full in the period in which the expected loss is discovered. Project two has an expected loss of ($20,000) [$300,000 – ($280,000 + $40,000)] which must be recognized in full in 2002. The net gross profit recognized on the two projects is $20,000 ($40,000 profit less ($20,000) loss).

53. (a) In the **final year** of a contract accounted for by the percentage-of-completion method, the percentage of completion is 100%, since costs to date equal total costs. Therefore, the formula to calculate income to be recognized in the final year is simply

$$\underbrace{(\text{Contract price} - \text{Actual total costs}) - \binom{\text{Income previously}}{\text{recognized}}}_{\text{Actual income}}$$

Therefore both **actual total costs** and **income previously recognized** are used in calculating income.

54. (b) Under the percentage-of-completion method of accounting for long-term contracts, the cost-to-cost formula is used to compute the amount of income to be recognized in a particular year. The formula to calculate current income is as follows:

$$\left(\frac{\text{Cost to date}}{\text{Total expected cost}} \times \begin{array}{c}\text{Expected} \\ \text{profit}\end{array}\right) - \begin{array}{c}\text{Profit recognized} \\ \text{in previous periods}\end{array}$$

Progress billings do not impact the amount of income recognized.

55. (a) The requirement is to determine the ratio to be used to calculate income in the third year using the percentage-of-completion method. ARB 45 suggests that income be recognized on a cost-to-cost basis when the percentage-of-completion method is used.

$$\left(\frac{\text{Cost to date}}{\text{Total expected cost}} \times \begin{array}{c}\text{Expected} \\ \text{profit}\end{array}\right) - \begin{array}{c}\text{Profit recognized} \\ \text{in previous periods}\end{array}$$

Answers (b) and (d) are incorrect because billings to date are not used as a basis for recognizing revenues. Answer (c) is incorrect as the cost-to-cost calculation requires a cumulative calculation so changes in expected costs and expected income can be adjusted for; thus, costs incurred in year three would be an incorrect basis for recognition of income.

56. (d) Per ARB 45, an anticipated loss on a long-term contract should be recognized immediately under **both** the percentage-of-completion and the completed-contract methods.

57. (a) The requirement is to determine the proper classification for the progress billings on contracts account under the percentage-of-completion method. In the construction industry, operating cycles for construction contracts generally exceed one year. Therefore, the predominant practice is to classify all contract-related assets and liabilities as current. On the balance sheet, the Construction in Progress (CIP) account is netted with the contra account, progress billings. If CIP exceeds billings, the excess is reported as a current asset [answer (a)]. If billings exceed CIP, the excess is reported as a current liability. Answers (b) and (c) are incorrect because the accounts related to construction contracts are classified as current. Answer (d) is incorrect because progress billings is not used as a basis for recognizing revenues.

OTHER OBJECTIVE ANSWERS AND ANSWER EXPLANATIONS

Problem 1

1. **(T)** The gross margin method uses historical margins on sales to estimate the cost of inventory. This method is typically used for interim reporting only because it may not be precise enough for the year-end financial statements.

2. **(T)** The dollar-value LIFO method groups inventory into layers and charges the most recent items to cost of goods sold before using older layers which have older inventory costs.

3. **(T)** Inventory should be carried at the lower of cost or market. In determining the lower of cost or market it may be based on the values of individual items, item categories, or even total inventory.

4. **(T)** When the market price of a contract to purchase goods falls below the contract price and it is foreseeable that the contract will result in a loss, then a loss on the purchase commitment should be recorded.

5. **(T)** The dollar-value LIFO method measures changes in inventory layers based upon the total dollar value change in the layer.

6. **(T)** The link-chain method uses a cumulative index to compute the base cost of inventory. The cumulative index is equal to the current year's prices divided by the prior year's prices, multiplied by the prior year's cumulative index. The link-chain method is only used in limited circumstances.

7. **(T)** A price index provides a measure of the changes in price between base year and the current year. The price index is generally used to compute changes in inventory levels.

8. **(T)** In a period of rising prices, a liquidation of older inventory, which carries lower costs, will result in a decline in the cost of goods sold and higher profits.

9. **(F)** A holding gain results from holding an item while the market value **increases**. Thus, the holding gain would be equal to the current market value less the value on the books.

10. **(F)** During a period of rising prices, the LIFO method will result in higher priced items being charged to cost of goods sold, thus lowering net income. It is the FIFO method which would produce a higher net income because the cost of goods sold would reflect the older or lower cost goods.

11. **(T)** A change from FIFO to LIFO will tend to result in a decrease in net income and working capital. This is because the LIFO method will put the more recent/higher priced items on the income statement (last in) and the older/less expensive goods will be carried in inventory. Thus, net income will be lower due to higher cost of goods sold, and working capital will be lower due to the lower inventory asset balance.

12. **(T)** The LIFO method results in the most recently purchased inventory items being expensed first. In a period of rising prices this would result in a lower net income and thus a lower taxes payable. The IRS allows the use of LIFO for tax only if it is also used for external reporting purposes as well.

13. **(F)** The cost of goods sold would be different because a periodic system will compute the cost of goods sold based on the total goods sold and total purchases for a period, whereas a perpetual one will match each good sold with the most recent purchase on an ongoing basis.

ANSWER OUTLINE

Problem 1   Specific Identification Method, LCM, and
                 Inventoriable Costs

a. 1. Specific identification method (SIM)
        Each unit distinguished from similar units
        Cost flows identical to physical flows
        Recording of costs to each unit is not burdensome
        If similar units have different costs, CGS in-
          fluenced by units sold
    2. SIM appropriate because
        Units are costly,
        Identifiable by # and description, and
        Good records exist
        Inventory at retailers not subject to CGS manipu-
          lation by Happlia

b. 1. General criteria for cost inclusion
        Include all necessary and reasonable costs to get
          units in place for sale
            Allocate common or joint costs
    2. Costs included in inventory
        Invoice costs
        Des Moines Freight
        Insurance costs
        Repackaging costs

c. 2002 IS
        Report as CGS all costs attached to units sold in 2002
        Deduct reshipment costs in finding operating income

UNOFFICIAL ANSWER

Problem 1   Specific Identific. Method, LCM, and Inven-
                 toriable Costs

a. 1. The specific identification method requires **each
unit to be clearly distinguished** from similar units either by
description, identification number, location, or other characteristic. Costs are accumulated for specific units and expensed as the units are sold. Thus, the specific identification
method results in recognized **cost flows being identical to
actual physical flows**. Ideally, each unit is relatively expensive and the number of such units relatively few so that
recording of costs is not burdensome. Under the specific
identification method, if similar items have different costs,
cost of goods sold is influenced by the specific units sold.

2. It is appropriate for Happlia to use the specific
identification method because each appliance is expensive,
and easily identified by number and description. The specific identification method is feasible because Happlia already maintains records of its units held by individual retailers. Management's ability to manipulate cost of goods sold
is minimized because once the inventory is in retailers'
hands Happlia's management cannot influence the units
selected for sale.

b. 1. Happlia should include in inventory carrying
amounts all necessary and reasonable costs to get an appliance into a useful condition and place for sale. Common (or
joint) costs should be allocated to individual units. Such
costs exclude the excess costs incurred in transporting refrigerators to Minneapolis and their reshipment to Kansas
City. These units' costs should only include normal freight
costs from Des Moines to Kansas City. In addition, costs
incurred to provide time utility to the goods (i.e., ensuring
that they are available when required) will also be included
in inventory carrying amounts.

2. Examples of inventoriable costs include the unit invoice price, plus an allocated proportion of the port handling
fees, import duties, freight costs to Des Moines and to retailers, insurance costs, repackaging, and warehousing costs.

c. The 2002 income statement should report in cost of
goods sold all inventory costs related to units sold in 2002,
regardless of when cash is received from retailers. Excess
freight costs incurred for shipping the refrigerators from
Minneapolis to Kansas City should be included in determining operating income.

ANSWER OUTLINE

Problem 2   Inventory Costs, LCM, and FIFO FS Effects

a. 1. Costs included in 2003 inventory
        All necessary and reasonable costs
        Design costs
        Purchase price from contractors
        Freight-in
        Warehousing costs

    2. Carrying amount for 2002 inventory
        Reported at net realizable value (NRV)
        Net realizable value below original cost
        NRV = Current list price – disposition costs – [2/3
          ($40 allowance – carrying amount of trade-ins)]
        Trade-ins' carrying amount = $25 average NRV –
          profit margin (if any)

b. 1. Effect of FIFO on income statement when costs are
          rising
        Earliest costs assigned to CGS (CGS lower)
        Low costs matched against current revenues
        Net income higher than under other inventory
          methods

    2. Effect of FIFO on balance sheet when costs are ris-
          ing
        Latest costs assigned to EI (EI higher)
        EI approximates replacement cost
        RE higher than under other inventory methods

UNOFFICIAL ANSWER

Problem 2   Inventory Costs, LCM, and FIFO FS Effects

a. 1. For its 2003 models, Blaedon should include in
inventory carrying amounts all necessary and reasonable
costs. These costs may include design costs, purchase price
from contractors, freight-in, and warehousing costs.

2. Blaedon's 2002 model inventory should be assigned a carrying amount equal to its net realizable value,
which is its current list price reduced by both its disposition
costs and two-thirds of the difference between the $40 al-
lowance given and the carrying amount assigned to trade-
ins. The trade-ins' carrying amount should equal the $25
average net realizable value less the profit margin, if any,
assigned.

b. 1. Using FIFO, Blaedon would assign the earliest
lawnmower costs to cost of goods sold. With rising costs,
this would result in matching old, relatively low inventory
costs against current revenues. Net income would be higher
than that reported using certain other inventory methods.

2. Blaedon would assign the latest costs to ending inventory. Normally, the carrying amount of Blaedon's FIFO
ending inventory would approximate replacement cost at

December 31, 2002. Retained earnings would be higher than that reported using certain other inventory methods.

SOLUTION GUIDE

Problem 3   LIFO and LCM

a.

1.   This problem requires preparation of a cost of goods sold (CGS) schedule with a supporting schedule of ending inventory at lower of cost or market (LCM). York uses the direct method for LCM, which means the LCM amount is used directly in the CGS computation with no separate disclosure of any LCM loss.

2.   The cost of goods sold schedule can be prepared first, leaving the last two lines (ending inventory and CGS) blank for now. The computation starts with **beginning inventory** plus **cost of goods purchased** equals **cost of goods available for sale** (cost of goods purchased is **purchases** less **purchase discounts** plus **freight-in**). **Freight-out** is a selling expense which does not affect CGS.

3.   When determining LCM, the market value of inventory is defined as the **replacement cost**, as long as it is less than the ceiling [**net realizable value** (NRV)] and more than the floor (**NRV less a normal profit**).

3.1   There are 22,000 units in ending inventory (55,000 units available less 33,000 units sold). Using LIFO, the earliest units in are assumed to remain in ending inventory. Therefore, ending inventory consists of the 8,000 units from beginning inventory, plus the 12,000 units purchased in the first quarter, plus 2,000 more units from second quarter purchases to get up to the 22,000 unit total. The cost of ending inventory is $180,400 [(8,000 x $8.20) + (12,000 x $8.25) + (2,000 x $7.90)].

3.2   The replacement cost of the inventory is $176,000 (22,000 x $8).

3.3   The ceiling (NRV) is $193,600 (22,000 x $8.80).

3.4   The floor (NRV less a normal profit) is $170,500 [22,000 x ($8.80 – $1.05)].

3.5   Because replacement cost ($176,000) falls between the floor ($170,500) and the ceiling ($193,600), the replacement cost of $176,000 is the designated market value.

3.6   Since the designated market value of $176,000 is less than cost ($180,400), the LCM valuation of ending inventory is $176,000. This amount can be put into the cost of goods sold schedule, resulting in CGS of $245,500.

b.   Value inventory at LCM
Market is replacement with limits
  Market must ≤ NRV and
  Market must ≥ NRV – normal profit
Market is replacement cost in this situation
  Replacement cost ($176,000) falls between above limits
Inventory reported at market because < cost

UNOFFICIAL ANSWER

Problem 3   LIFO and LCM

a.

York Co.
SCHEDULE OF COST OF GOODS SOLD
For the Year Ended December 31, 2002

Beginning inventory	$ 65,600
Add: Purchases	368,900
Less: Purchase discounts	(18,000)
Add: Freight-in	5,000
Goods available for sale	421,500
Less: Ending inventory	(176,000) [1]
Cost of Goods Sold	$245,500

York Co.
SUPPORTING SCHEDULE OF ENDING INVENTORY
December 31, 2002

Inventory at cost (LIFO):

	Units	Cost per unit	Total cost
Beginning inventory, January 1	8,000	$8.20	$ 65,600
Purchases, quarter ended March 31	12,000	8.25	99,000
Purchases, quarter ended June 30	2,000	7.90	15,800
	22,000		$180,400

Inventory at market:
22,000 units @ $8 = $176,000 [1]

b.   Inventory should be valued at the lower of cost or market. Market means current replacement cost, except that

(1)   Market should not exceed the net realizable value; and

(2)   Market should not be less than net realizable value reduced by an allowance for an approximately normal profit margin.

In this situation, because replacement cost ($8 per unit) is less than net realizable value, but greater than net realizable value reduced by a normal profit margin, replacement cost is used as market. Because inventory valued at market ($176,000) is lower than inventory valued at cost ($180,400), inventory should be reported in the financial statements at market.

SOLUTION GUIDE

Problem 4   Dollar-Value LIFO Using Link-Chain Method

1.   This problem requires the preparation of a schedule showing the computation of Silver's dollar-value LIFO inventory at December 31, 2001 and 2002.

2.   The solutions approach is to first make the calculations for each year, and then to organize the information into a schedule.

2.1   Under the link-chain method, an index number is computed for **each period**

$$\frac{\text{End of current period prices}}{\text{Beginning of current period prices}} = \frac{\text{Current year}}{\text{index number}}$$

2.2   The link-chain (cumulative) index number is

$$\frac{\text{Cumulative index number}}{\text{at beginning of period}} \times \frac{\text{Current year}}{\text{index number}}$$

This link-chain (cumulative) index number is divided into the ending inventory amount to reach ending inventory at base year prices.

2.3   The new layer added is

$$\left(\frac{\text{Ending inventory}}{\text{at base prices}} - \frac{\text{Beginning inventory}}{\text{at base prices}}\right) \times \frac{\text{Link-chain}}{\text{(cumulative)}}\text{ index number}$$

2.4　Ending dollar-value LIFO inventory is the base layer plus all layers added.

3.　Silver's inventory of $100,000 at 12/31/00 constitutes the base layer. The index number for this layer is 1.00. The current year index number for 2001 is 1.25, so the cumulative index number at 12/31/02 is 1.25 x 1.00 = 1.25

3.1　Ending inventory at 12/31/01 prices was $137,500. This is converted to base prices as $137,500 ÷ 1.25 = $110,000.

3.2　The new 2001 layer is ($110,000 – $100,000) x 1.25 = $12,500.

3.3　Ending dollar-value LIFO inventory at 12/31/01 is

2000 Base layer	$100,000
2001 Layer added	12,500
	$112,500

4.　The cumulative index number at 12/31/01 is 1.25. The current year index number for 2002 is 1.20, so the cumulative index number at 12/31/02 is 1.20 x 1.25 = 1.50.

4.1　Ending inventory at 12/31/02 prices was $195,000, which is converted to base prices as $195,000 ÷ 1.50 = $130,000.

4.2　The new 2002 layer is calculated by subtracting the beginning inventory at base prices ($110,000 from 3.1 above) from $130,000. ($130,000 – $110,000) x 1.50 = $30,000.

4.3　Ending dollar-value LIFO inventory at 12/31/02 is the two layers shown in 3.3 plus the $30,000 layer added in 2002.

UNOFFICIAL ANSWER

Problem 4　Dollar-Value LIFO Using Link-Chain Method

Silver, Inc.
COMPUTATION OF DOLLAR-VALUE INVENTORY
December 31, 2001 and 2002

Year	FIFO inventory	Current year cost change index	Link-chain cost index	Inventory at base-year costs
2000	$100,000	1.00	1.00	$100,000
2001	137,500	1.25	1.25	110,000
2002	195,000	1.20	1.50	130,000

Year	LIFO inventory layers at base-year costs	Link-chain cost index	2001 dollar-value LIFO inventory	2002 dollar-value LIFO inventory
2000	$100,000	1.00	$100,000	$100,000
2001	10,000	1.25	12,500	12,500
2002	20,000	1.50		30,000
	$130,000		$112,500	$142,500

ANSWER OUTLINE

Problem 5　LT Contracts

a.　Percentage-of-completion
　　Use if two conditions met
　　　Reasonable estimates of profitability at completion
　　　Reliable measures of progress toward completion

b.　Income recognized in 2002

$$\text{2002 Income} = \left(\frac{\text{Costs incured to date - Cost of unused materials}}{\text{Total estimatd costs to complete}} \times \text{Total profit} \right) - \text{Income recognized in 2001}$$

Exclude costs of unused materials
　　May cause overstatement of income compared with efforts of period

c.　BS reporting
　　AR on contract—current asset
　　Excess of costs + Gross profit > billings—current asset

d.　Income tax effects
　　BS

$$\frac{\text{Current deferred tax liability}}{} = \frac{\text{Total net income reported in 2001 and 2002}}{} \times \frac{\text{Enacted 2003 average tax rate}}{}$$

　　IS

$$\frac{\text{Deferred income tax expense}}{} = \frac{\text{Increase in deferred tax liability during 2002}}{}$$

- Reasonable estimates of profitability at completion.
- Reliable measures of progress toward completion.

b.　At December 31, 2002, Bow should calculate the percentage of completion by comparing the costs incurred to date, less costs of unused materials, to the estimated total cost to complete Crecy. Income to date equals the percentage of completion multiplied by the estimated total profit to be earned on the contract. The 2002 income equals the income to be recognized to December 31, 2002, less the income reported under the contract in 2001.

　　When contract materials are purchased but not used, costs of the unused materials are excluded from income recognition calculations. Otherwise, the early period income reported may be overstated compared with the income earning efforts of that period.

c.　Bow should report a current asset for the Crecy account receivable, and another for the excess of costs incurred plus total profit recognized over contract billings.

d.　Bow should report a current deferred tax liability equal to its total net income reported in 2001 and 2002 multiplied by its enacted 2003 average tax rate. A deferred income tax expense should be recognized for the increase during 2002 in the deferred tax liability balance.

UNOFFICIAL ANSWER

Problem 5　LT Contracts

a.　Bow must have a system that is capable of meeting both of the following conditions for the Crecy contract:

SOLUTION GUIDE

Problem 6 LT Construction Contracts and Deferred Taxes

1. This problem consists of three related requirements concerning long-term construction contracts. The candidates must compute gross profit recognized for two years using the percentage-of-completion method, compute balances in various accounts, and reconcile financial statement income and taxable income.

2. Using the percentage-of-completion method, gross profit is recognized periodically based on progress toward completion of the project using the following formula.

$$\frac{\text{Costs to date}}{\text{Total estimated costs}} \times \begin{array}{c}\text{Estimated}\\\text{profit}\end{array} = \begin{array}{c}\text{Gross profit}\\\text{to date}\end{array}$$

For the Beta project, London would recognize gross profit of $180,000 the first year.

$$\frac{\$360,000}{(\$360,000 + \$40,000)} \times [\$600,000 - (\$360,000 + \$40,000)] = \$180,000$$

The estimates available at 9/30/02 are used above.

2.1 By the end of the second year, the Beta project is complete and has resulted in actual gross profit of $110,000 ($560,000 revenues less $450,000 costs). Since gross profit of $180,000 was recognized the first year, a loss of $70,000 must be recognized the second year [$110,000 − $180,000 = $(70,000)]. The loss of $70,000 is in effect an adjustment of the excessive gross profit recognized the first year. Instead of restating the prior period, the prior period misstatement is absorbed in the current period, as is appropriate for a change in estimate.

2.2 Under both the percentage-of-completion method and the completed contract method, for financial accounting purposes, an expected **loss** on a contract must be recognized in full in the period in which the expected loss is discovered. At the end of the first year, London has an expected loss on the Gamma contract [$800,000 − ($410,000 + $410,000) = $(20,000)] that must be recognized immediately.

2.3 By the end of the second year, the expected loss on the Gamma contract has increased to $60,000 [$840,000 − ($720,000 + $180,000)]. Since a loss of $20,000 was recognized the first year, an additional loss of $40,000 must be recognized in the second year to bring the cumulative loss recognized up to the new estimate of $60,000.

3. Part (b) requires the computation of the 9/30/02 balances of accounts receivable, costs and estimated earnings in excess of billings, and billings in excess of costs and estimated earnings. At 10/1/01, the balances in all three accounts were $0 since the construction division began operations on that date.

3.1 **Accounts receivable** is increased by billings

Accounts receivable
    Billings on LT contracts

It is decreased by cash collections

Cash
    Accounts receivable

Therefore, 9/30/02 AR is computed by adding the billings on the two projects ($315,000 + $440,000 = $755,000) and subtracting the collections on the two projects ($275,000 + $365,000 = $640,000). The 9/30/02 balance is $115,000 ($755,000 − $640,000).

3.2 **Construction-in-progress** is debited for costs incurred and profit recognized. **Billings on LT contracts** is credited for billings made. In the balance sheet, the two accounts are netted on a project-by-project basis, resulting in a net current asset and/or a net current liability. At 9/30/01, the costs incurred on the Beta project ($360,000) and the estimated earnings ($180,000 from item two of this solution guide) exceed billings ($315,000) by $225,000.

3.3 On the Gamma project billings ($440,000) exceed costs ($410,000) by $30,000. There is no estimated earnings on this project because it is expected, at 9/30/02, to result in a $20,000 loss (see item 2.2 above). This estimated loss does not affect the excess of billings over costs and estimated earnings because it is reported separately as a current liability.

4. Financial statement income consists of income before taxes before considering construction projects ($300,000) plus gross profit from construction contracts [$160,000 from part (a) of the solution], less income tax expense. The **pretax** financial income, therefore, is $460,000 ($300,000 + $160,000). The income not from construction projects will be taxed this year, so current income tax expense is $75,000 ($300,000 x 25%). Because the completed contract method is used for tax purposes, the $160,000 gross profit from construction contracts will not be taxed until future years (note that for **tax** purposes no gross profit or gross **loss** is recognized until completion under the completed contract method). Therefore, deferred tax expense is $48,000 (future enacted rate of 30% times $160,000). Financial statement income is $337,000 [$460,000 − ($75,000 + $48,000)].

4.1 Since the $160,000 gross profit will not be recognized for tax purposes until later years, taxable income is $300,000. To reconcile financial statement income ($337,000 from above) to taxable income, the current and deferred income tax must be added back to compute pretax financial income ($337,000 + $75,000 + $48,000 = $460,000). Then the gross profit not recognized for tax purposes is subtracted to reconcile to taxable income ($460,000 − $160,000 = $300,000).

UNOFFICIAL ANSWER

Problem 6   LT Construction Contracts and Deferred Taxes

a.
London Inc.
SCHEDULE OF GROSS PROFIT (LOSS)

	Beta	*Gamma*
For the Year Ended September 30, 2002:		
Estimated gross profit (loss):		
Contract price	$600,000	$800,000
Less total costs	400,000	820,000
Estimated gross profit (loss)	$200,000	$ (20,000)
Percent complete:		
Costs incurred to date	$360,000	$410,000
Total costs	400,000	820,000
Percent complete	90%	50%
Gross profit (loss) recognized	$180,000	$ (20,000)
For the Year Ended September 30, 2003:		
Estimated gross profit (loss):		
Contract price	$560,000	$840,000
Less total costs	450,000	900,000
Estimated gross profit (loss)	$110,000	$ (60,000)
Percent complete:		
Costs incurred to date	$450,000	$720,000
Total costs	450,000	900,000
Percent complete	100%	80%
Gross profit (loss) recognized	110,000	(60,000)
Less gross profit (loss) recognized in prior year	180,000	(20,000)
Gross profit (loss) recognized	$ (70,000)	$ (40,000)

b.
London Inc.
SCHEDULE OF SELECTED BALANCE SHEET ACCOUNTS
September 30, 2002

Accounts receivable		$115,000
Costs and estimated earnings in excess of billings:		
Construction in progress	$540,000	
Less: Billings	315,000	
Costs and estimated earnings in excess of billings		225,000
Billings in excess of costs and estimated earnings		30,000
Estimated loss on contract		20,000

c.
London Inc.
SCHEDULE OF INCOME TAXES PAYABLE AND INCOME TAX EXPENSE
September 30, 2002

Financial statement income:		
From other divisions		$300,000
From Beta project		180,000
From Gamma project		(20,000)
Total financial statement income		$460,000
Less temporary differences:		
Beta project income		(180,000)
Gamma project loss		20,000
Total taxable income		$300,000
Taxes payable ($300,000 x 25%)		$ 75,000
Deferred tax liability ($160,000 x 30%)		48,000
Tax expense:		
Current	$ 75,000	
Deferred	48,000	123,000

FIXED ASSETS

A. Acquisition Cost

Fixed assets represent the capitalized amount of expenditures made to acquire tangible property which will be used for a period of more than one year. Their cost, therefore, is deferred to future periods in compliance with the matching principle. Tangible property includes land, buildings, equipment, or any other property that physically exists. All of the costs necessary to get the asset to the work site and to prepare it for use are capitalized, including the cost of negotiations, sales taxes, finders' fees, razing an old building, shipment, installation, preliminary testing, and so forth. When capitalizing such costs it is necessary to associate them with the asset which is being prepared for use. Thus, the cost of razing an old building is added to the cost of acquiring the land on which the building stood. Charges for self-constructed fixed assets include direct materials, direct construction labor, variable overhead, and a fair share of fixed overhead. Assets received through donation should be recorded at FMV with a corresponding credit to revenue; if FMV is not determinable, book value should be used (see outline of SFAS 116). If the entity incurs a liability associated with future retirement of the asset, the fair value (present value) of that obligation should be added to the carrying value of the asset (see outline of SFAS 143).

B. Capitalization of Interest

SFAS 34 (see outline) requires the capitalization of interest as part of the cost of certain assets. Only assets which require a period of time to be prepared for use qualify for interest capitalization. These include assets constructed for sale produced as discrete projects (e.g., ships) and assets constructed for a firm's own use, whether by the entity itself or by an outsider. For example, a building purchased by an entity **would not** qualify, but one constructed over a period of time **would**. Other assets that do **not** qualify include those in use or ready for use and ones not being used in the earnings activities of a firm (e.g., idle land).

The amount of interest to be capitalized is the amount which could have been avoided if the project had not been undertaken. This amount includes amortization of any discount, premium, or issue costs; but, it shall not exceed the actual interest incurred during the period. The amount of "avoidable" interest is computed as

$$\frac{\text{Average accumulated expenditures}}{\text{during construction}} \quad \text{x} \quad \text{Interest rate} \quad \text{x} \quad \frac{\text{Construction}}{\text{period}}$$

The interest rate used is the rate on specific borrowings for the asset, or a weighted-average of other borrowings when a specific rate is not available. Capitalized interest should be compounded. This is usually accomplished by including the interest capitalized in a previous period in the calculation of average accumulated expenditures of subsequent periods. Furthermore, noninterest-bearing payables (e.g., trade payables and accruals) are excluded in determining these expenditures. In practice, both the weighted-average interest rate and the average accumulated expenditures have been computed on the following bases: monthly, quarterly, semiannual, and annual. The interest capitalization period begins when, and continues as long as, all three of the following conditions are met:

1. Expenditures for the asset have been made
2. Activities necessary to get the asset ready for its intended use are in progress
3. Interest cost is being incurred

The period ends when the asset is substantially complete. Brief interruptions and delays do not suspend interest capitalization, while suspension of the activities will. In no case should the amount capitalized exceed the interest actually incurred.

EXAMPLE: Interest Capitalization

Assume the company is constructing an asset which qualifies for interest capitalization. By the beginning of July $3,000,000 had been spent on the asset, and an additional $800,000 was spent during July. The following debt was outstanding for the entire month.

1. A loan of $2,000,000, interest of 1% per month, specifically related to the asset.
2. A note payable of $1,500,000, interest of 1.5% per month.
3. Bonds payable of $1,000,000, interest of 1% per month.

The amount of interest to be capitalized is computed below.

Average accumulated expenditures *(for the month of July)*
($3,000,000 + $3,800,000) ÷ 2 = $3,400,000

Avoidable interest			Actual interest		
$2,000,000 x 1%	=	$20,000	$2,000,000 x 1%	=	$20,000
1,400,000 x 1.3%*	=	18,200	1,500,000 x 1.5%	=	22,500
			1,000,000 x 1%	=	10,000
$3,400,000		$38,200	$4,500,000		$52,500

$38,200 \le $52,500

∴ $38,200 is capitalized

Amount of interest to be capitalized is $38,200

Asset	38,200	
Interest expense		38,200

The average rate on other borrowings is ($22,500 + $10,000) ÷ ($1,500,000 + $1,000,000) = 1.3%. Notice that a specific rate is used to the extent possible and the average rate is used only on any excess. Alternatively, the rate on all debt may be used.

Interest on expenditures made to acquire land on which a building is to be constructed qualifies for interest capitalization. The capitalization period begins when activities necessary to construct the building commence and ends when the building is substantially complete. Interest so capitalized becomes part of the cost of the building. Thus, it is charged to expense as the building is depreciated.

Frequently, the funds borrowed to finance the construction project are temporarily invested until needed. Per SFAS 62, the interest earned on these funds must be recognized as revenue and may not be offset against the interest expense to be capitalized.

The diagram below outlines the requirements pertaining to capitalization of interest.

***Rationale* for interest capitalization**

1. To reflect asset's acquisition cost
2. To match asset's cost with revenue of periods that benefit from its use

C. Nonmonetary Exchanges

Study the outline of APB 29 and FASB Interpretation 30. The exchange of nonmonetary assets (such as inventory, property, and equipment) for other nonmonetary assets requires special consideration of two amounts.

1. Gain or loss, if any
2. Fair market value of the nonmonetary assets received

Gain or loss on a nonmonetary exchange is computed as follows:

Fair value of the asset given – Book value of the asset given = Gain (loss)

If the fair value (FV) of the asset given up cannot be determined, assume it is equal to the fair value of the asset received. If neither fair values are determinable, gain or loss cannot be computed.

The asset received is generally recorded at the fair value of the asset surrendered (or the FV of the asset received if "more clearly evident"). Some exceptions do exist. Remember, however, that the asset given up will always be removed from the books at book value.

The following rules apply in recording nonmonetary exchanges:

- Losses are always recognized (conservatism).
- Gains are recognized when **dissimilar assets** are exchanged (i.e., a machine for a truck).
- Gains are **not** recognized when **similar assets** are exchanged (i.e., a machine for a machine) because the earnings process is **not** considered complete.
- The asset received is recorded at the **fair value** of the asset given up (or the FV of the asset received if "more clearly evident") whenever gains and losses are recognized.
- The asset received is recorded at the **book value** of the asset given up when gains and losses are **not** recognized. Gains and losses are not recognized when (1) the earnings process is not considered complete, and (2) gain or loss cannot be computed.

SUMMARY OF ACCOUNTING FOR INTEREST CAPITALIZATION

Capitalization of Interest During Construction

Qualifying Assets:

Capitalize means to include an expenditure in an asset's cost.

Interest costs, when material, incurred in acquiring the following types of assets, shall be capitalized

    1. Assets constructed or produced for a firm's own use

        a. Including construction by outside contractors requiring progress payments

    2. Assets intended for lease or sale that are produced as discrete projects

        a. For example, ships and real estate developments

    3. But **not** on

        a. Routinely produced inventories (e.g., widgets)
        b. Assets ready for their intended use when acquired
        c. Assets not being used nor being readied for use (e.g., idle equipment)
        d. Land, unless it is being developed (e.g., as a plant site, real estate development, etc.). Then capitalized interest resulting from land expenditure (cash outlay) is added to building.

When to Capitalize Interest (All three must be met):
    1. Expenditures for asset have been made
    2. Activities intended to get asset ready are in progress
    3. Interest cost is being incurred

Applicable Interest (Net of discounts, premiums, and issue costs):
    1. Interest obligations having explicit rates
    2. Imputed interest on certain payables/receivables
    3. Interest related to capital leases

How Much Interest Cost Is Capitalized?

$$\left(\begin{array}{l}\text{Accumulated expenditures beg. of period (C - I - P bal.) +}\\ \text{Accumulated expenditures end of period (C - I - P bal.)}\end{array}\right) \div 2 \times \text{Portion of year} = \text{Weighted-average accumulated expenditures}$$

$$\text{Weighted-average accumulated expenditures} \times \left(\begin{array}{c}\text{Interest*}\\ \text{rate}\end{array}\right) = \text{Amount capitalized (cannot exceed total interest incurred)}$$

* *AICPA questions have given the specific borrowing rate on debt incurred to finance a project and indicated that expenditures were incurred evenly throughout the year. SFAS 34 requires that the firm's weighted-average borrowing rate be used after the amount of a specific borrowing is exhausted. Alternatively, only the firm's weighted-average borrowing rate may be used on all expenditures.*

Qualifications:
    1. Amount of interest to be capitalized cannot exceed total interest costs incurred during the entire reporting period
    2. Interest earned on temporarily invested borrowings may not be offset against interest to be capitalized

Exceptions to these rules occur when boot (cash) is involved in the exchange.

The chart on the next page summarizes the process involved in accounting for nonmonetary exchanges. Refer to this chart as you work through the following examples.

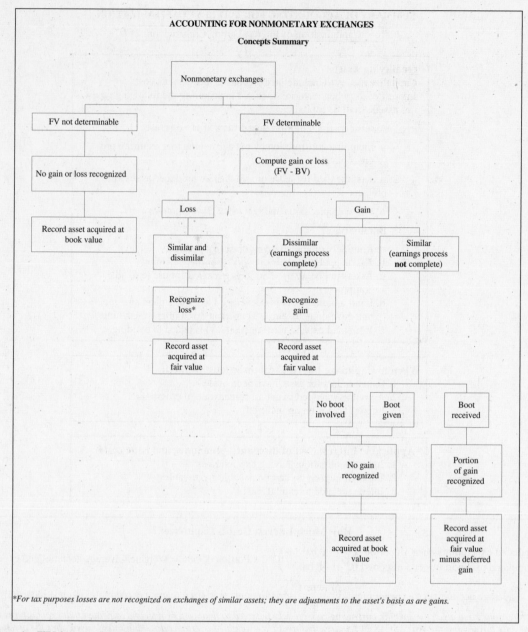

ACCOUNTING FOR NONMONETARY EXCHANGES

Concepts Summary

For tax purposes losses are not recognized on exchanges of similar assets; they are adjustments to the asset's basis as are gains.

Situation 1. FV is not determinable.

EXAMPLE: A company trades a machine (cost, $10,000; accumulated depreciation, $3,000) for land. Neither the FV of the machine or the land is determinable.

Land	7,000	*(BV given)*
Accumulated depreciation	3,000	
Machine		10,000

Since FV is unknown, no gain can be computed, and the asset received is recorded at the BV of the asset given up ($10,000 – $3,000).

Situation 2. Loss, no boot involved.

EXAMPLE: A company trades a machine with a FV of $5,000 (cost, $10,000; accumulated depreciation, $3,000) for land.

	FV	BV	Gain (loss)
Machine given	$5,000	$7,000	$(2,000)
Land received			

The loss (FV – BV) is recognized immediately and the land is recorded at the FV of the machine given up.

Land	5,000	(FV given)
Accumulated depreciation	3,000	
Loss	2,000	
Machine		10,000

(Note that this transaction would be treated the same way if similar assets had been exchanged.)

EXAMPLE: *A company trades a machine (cost, $10,000; accumulated depreciation, $3,000) for another machine with a FV of $6,000.*

	FV	BV	Gain (loss)
Machine given		$7,000	$(1,000)
Machine received	$6,000		

In this case, the FV of the asset given is unknown. You can substitute the FV of the asset received for FV given when computing gain/loss. The fair value of the asset given is implied in this case.

$6,000		$7,000		$(1,000)
FV given	–	BV given	=	Loss
(assumed or implied)				

Machine	6,000	(FV received)
Accumulated depreciation	3,000	
Loss	1,000	
Machine		10,000

Situation 3. Loss, boot given.

EXAMPLE: *A company trades a machine with a FV of $6,000 (cost, $10,000; accumulated depreciation, $3,000) and $500 cash for land.*

	Boot	FV	BV	Gain (loss)
Machine given	$500	$6,000	$7,000	$(1,000)
Land received				

Gain (loss) still equals FV less BV. Boot given is added to the value of the asset given.

Land	6,500	(FV given + Boot given)
Accumulated depreciation	3,000	
Loss	1,000	
Machine		10,000
Cash		500

Assume the FV of the machine was unknown, but the FV of the land received was known to be $6,000.

	Boot	FV	BV	Gain (loss)
Machine given	$500		$7,000	$(1,500)
Land received		$6,000		

To compute gain (loss), you can assume FV given is equal to FV received less boot given ($6,000 – $500).

$5,500		$7,000		$(1,500)
FV given	–	BV given	=	Loss
(assumed)				

Land	6,000	(FV received)
Accumulated depreciation	3,000	
Loss	1,500	
Machine		10,000
Cash		500

Situation 4. Loss, boot received.

EXAMPLE: *A company trades a machine with a FV of $6,000 (cost, $10,000; accumulated depreciation, $3,000) for land and $500 cash.*

	Boot	FV	BV	Gain (loss)
Machine given		$6,000	$7,000	$(1,000)
Land received	$500			

Boot received is deducted from the value of the asset given.

Land	5,500	(FV given – Boot received)
Accumulated depreciation	3,000	
Cash	500	
Loss	1,000	
Machine		10,000

Now assume the FV of the machine is unknown but the FV of the land received is known to be $6,000.

	Boot	FV	BV	Gain (loss)
Machine given			$7,000	$(500)
Land received	$500	$6,000		

In this case, you can assume FV given is equal to FV received **plus** the boot received ($6,000 + $500).

$6,500		$7,000		$(500)
FV given	–	BV given	=	Loss
(assumed)				

Land	6,000		(FV received)
Accumulated depreciation	3,000		
Cash	500		
Loss	500		
Machine		10,000	

Situation 5. Gain, dissimilar assets.

EXAMPLE: A company trades a computer with a FV of $12,000 (cost, $11,000; accumulated depreciation, $4,000) for a building.

	FV	BV	Gain (loss)
Computer given	$12,000	$7,000	$5,000
Building received			

Since the assets traded are dissimilar, the earnings process is considered complete and the entire gain is recognized.

Building	12,000		(FV received)
Accumulated depreciation	4,000		
Computer		11,000	
Gain		5,000	

If boot had been involved, the accounting would be the same as that illustrated in the loss situation.

Situation 6. Gain, similar assets, no boot involved.

EXAMPLE: A company trades equipment with a FV of $12,000 (cost, $11,000; accumulated depreciation, $4,000) for similar equipment.

	FV	BV	Gain (loss)
Equipment given	$12,000	$7,000	$5,000
Equipment received			

Since similar assets have been traded, the earnings process is **not** considered complete and no gain is recognized. The asset received is debited at the book value (**not** fair value) of the asset given.

Equipment	7,000		(BV given)
Accumulated depreciation	4,000		
Equipment		11,000	

The unrecognized gain of $5,000 will be deferred; it will be recognized as the equipment received is depreciated (lower depreciation results than if FV had been used) and/or sold or disposed of in a subsequent transaction.

Situation 7. Gain, similar assets, boot given.

EXAMPLE: A company trades a machine (cost, $10,000; accumulated depreciation, $2,000) and $4,000 in cash for a similar machine with a FV of $16,000.

	Boot	FV	BV	Gain (loss)
Machine given	$4,000		$8,000	$4,000
Machine received		$16,000		

As in the loss situation, the FV of the asset given can be assumed equal to the FV received less the boot given ($16,000 – $4,000).

$12,000		$8,000		$4,000
FV given	–	BV given	=	Gain
(assumed)				

Boot given is added to the value of the asset received (in this case, book value). Gain is still unrecognized.

Machine	12,000		(BV given + Boot given)
Accumulated depreciation	2,000		
Machine		10,000	
Cash		4,000	

Below are alternative ways to calculate the asset received.

FV received	$16,000	BV given	$ 8,000
Gain deferred	(4,000)	Cash paid	4,000
	12,000		12,000

Situation 8. Gain, similar assets, boot received.

An exception to nonrecognition of gain on exchange of similar assets arises when boot is received in the exchange. This type of exchange is treated as a hybrid transaction—part sale and part exchange. The earnings process is assumed complete for the portion related to the boot received (i.e., "sale" portion), but is **not** assumed complete for the portion related to the asset received (i.e., "exchange" portion). Therefore, a gain is recognized only for that portion related to the boot. Gain recognized is computed as follows:

$$\left(\frac{\text{Boot received}}{\text{Boot received + FV of asset received}} \right) \times \text{Total gain} = \text{Gain recognized}$$

If the FV of the asset received is not given, it may be determined by subtracting the boot received from the FV of the asset given up.

EXAMPLE: A company trades a machine with a FV of $12,000 (cost, $9,000; accumulated depreciation, $2,000) for a similar machine and $2,000 cash.

	Boot received	Machine FV	Machine BV	Gain (loss)
Given		$12,000	$7,000	$5,000
Received	$2,000	?	?	

Since boot was received, the portion of the gain relating to the boot must be recognized.

$$\left(\frac{\$2,000}{\$2,000 + \$10,000 \text{ *}} \right) \times (\$5,000) = \$833$$

*The FV of the asset received ($10,000) was derived by deducting boot received from the FV of the machine given.

$12,000		$2,000		$10,000
FV given	–	Boot received	=	FV received
				(assumed)

Thus, only $833 of the gain will be recognized. The machine received would be recorded at its FV less the gain deferred [$10,000 – ($5,000 gain – $833 gain recognized)]. Alternatively, the asset received will be debited at BV given less boot received, plus gain recognized ($7,000 – $2,000 + $833 = $5,833).

Cash	2,000			
Machine (received)	5,833			
Accumulated depreciation	2,000	$\left(\begin{array}{c} \text{FV received} - \\ \text{Gain deferred} \end{array} \right)$	or	$\left(\begin{array}{c} \text{BV given} - \text{Boot received} \\ + \text{Gain recognized} \end{array} \right)$
Machine (given)		9,000		
Gain		833		

D. Purchase of Groups of Fixed Assets (Basket purchase)

Cost should be allocated based on relative market value.

$$\text{Cost of all assets acquired} \times \frac{\text{Market value of A}}{\text{Market value of all assets acquired}}$$

EXAMPLE: Purchase of Asset 1 with a FMV of $60,000, Asset 2 with a FMV of $120,000, and Asset 3 with a FMV of $20,000 all for $150,000 cash.

	FMV	Relative FMV	x	Total cost	=	Allocated cost
Asset 1	$ 60,000	60/200		$150,000		$45,000
Asset 2	120,000	120/200		150,000		90,000
Asset 3	20,000	20/200		150,000		15,000
Total FMV	$200,000					

Journalized:

Asset 1	$45,000	
Asset 2	90,000	
Asset 3	15,000	
Cash		$150,000

E. Capital vs. Revenue Expenditures

Capital expenditures and revenue expenditures are charges that are incurred after the acquisition cost has been determined and the related fixed asset is in operation.

Capital expenditures are not normal, recurring expenses; they benefit the operations of more than one period. The cost of major rearrangements of assets to increase efficiency is an example of a capital expenditure.

Revenue expenditures are normal recurring expenditures. However, some expenditures that meet the test for capital expenditures are expensed because they are immaterial (e.g., less than $50).

Expenditures to improve the efficiency or extend the asset life should be capitalized and charged to future periods. A subtle distinction is sometimes made between an improvement in efficiency and an extension of the asset life. Some accountants feel improvements in efficiency should be charged to the asset account, and improvements extending the asset life should be charged to the accumulated depreciation account. The rationale is that improvements extending the asset life will need to be depreciated over an extended period of time, requiring revision of depreciation schedules.

The chart on the following page summarizes the appropriate treatment of expenditures related to fixed assets.

F. Depreciation

Depreciation is the annual charge to income for asset use during the period. Since depreciation is a noncash expense, it does not provide resources for the replacement of assets. It is simply a means of spreading asset costs to periods in which the assets produce revenue. Essentially, the "depreciation base" is allocated over the asset's useful life in a rational and systematic manner. The meaning of the key terms is as follows:

> **Systematic**—*Formula or plan*
> **Rational**—*Representational faithfulness (fits with reality)*
> **Allocation**—*Not a process of valuation*

The objective is to match asset cost with revenue produced. The depreciation base is cost less salvage value (except for the declining balance method which ignores salvage value). The cost of an asset will include any reasonable cost incurred in bringing an asset to an enterprise and getting it ready for its intended use. The useful life can be limited by

1. Technological change
2. Normal deterioration
3. Physical usage

The first two indicate depreciation is a function of time whereas the third indicates depreciation is a function of the level of activity. Other depreciation methods include inventory, retirement, replacement, group, composite, etc. Depreciation methods based on time are

1. Straight-line (SL)
2. Accelerated

    a. Declining balance (DB)

        (1) Most common is double-declining balance (DDB)

    b. Sum-of-the-years' digits (SYD)

Straight-line and **accelerated** depreciation are illustrated by the following example: $10,000 asset, four-year life, $2,000 salvage value.

Year	Straight line	DDB	SYD
1	$2,000	$5,000	$3,200
2	$2,000	$2,500	$2,400
3	$2,000	$ 500*	$1,600
4	$2,000	--	$ 800

Straight-line $\dfrac{\$10,000-\$2,000}{4}$

DDB   Twice the straight-line rate (2 x 25%) times the net book value at beginning of each year, but not below salvage value (salvage value is not deducted for depreciation base).

* $10,000 – ($5,000 + 2,500) = $2,500 Book value at beginning of year three. $2,500 – 2,000 salvage value = \underline{$500}.

SYD   4/10**, 3/10, 2/10, 1/10 of ($10,000 – $2,000).

** $\dfrac{n(n+1)}{2} = \dfrac{4 \times 5}{2} = 10$

Physical usage depreciation is based on activity (e.g., machine hours) or output (e.g., finished widgets).

COSTS SUBSEQUENT TO ACQUISITION OF PROPERTY, PLANT, AND EQUIPMENT

Type of expenditure / Characteristics	Expense when incurred	Capitalize — Debit (credit) to asset	Capitalize — Debit (credit) to accum. deprec.	Other
1. Additions				
• Extensions, enlargements, or expansions made to an existing asset		x		
2. Repairs and maintenance				
a. Ordinary				
• Recurring, relatively small expenditures				
1. Maintain normal operating condition	x			
2. **Do not** add materially to use value	x			
3. **Do not** extend useful life	x			
b. Extraordinary (major)				
• Not recurring, relatively large expenditures				
1. Primarily increase the quality and/or output of services		x		
2. Primarily extend the useful life			x	
3. Replacements and improvements				
• Major component of asset is removed and replaced with the same type of component with comparable performance capabilities (replacement) or a different type of component having superior performance capabilities (betterment)				
a. Book value of old component is known				
• Old component amounts		(x)	x	• Recognize any proceeds and loss (or gain) on old asset
• New component outlay		x		
b. Book value of old component is not known				
• Primarily increases the use value		x		
• Primarily extends the useful life			x	
4. Reinstallations and rearrangements				
• Provide greater efficiency in production or reduce production costs				
1. Material costs, benefits extend into future accounting periods		x		
2. No measurable future benefit	x			

$$\frac{\text{Annual}}{\text{depreciation}} = \frac{\text{Current activity or output}}{\text{Total expected activity or output}} \times \text{Depreciation base}$$

EXAMPLE: A machine costs $60,000. The machine's total output is expected to be 500,000 units. If 100,000 units are produced in the first year, $12,000 of depreciation would be incurred (100/500 x $60,000).

Note that physical usage depreciation results in a varying charge (i.e., not constant). Also physical usage depreciation is based on asset activity rather than expiration of time.

Straight-line and accelerated depreciation methods are illustrated by the following graphs:

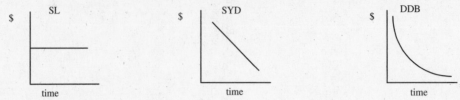

Accelerated depreciation is justified by

1. Increased productivity when asset is new
2. Increasing maintenance charges with age
3. Risk of obsolescence

Accelerated depreciation methods result in a better matching of costs and revenues when one or more of these factors are present.

Inventory depreciation is a method typically used in situations where there are many low-cost tangible assets, such as hand tools for a manufacturer or utensils for a restaurant. Using this method, an inventory of the assets is taken at the beginning and the end of the year. Valuation of these assets is based on appraisal value. Depreciation is calculated as follows:

$$\frac{\text{Annual}}{\text{depreciation}} = \frac{\text{Beginning}}{\text{inventory}} + \frac{\text{Cost of}}{\text{acquisitions}} - \frac{\text{Ending}}{\text{inventory}}$$

The inventory method is advantageous in situations involving such small assets because it is not practical to maintain separate depreciation schedules for them. On the other hand, this method is often criticized because it is not systematic and rational.

Composite (group) depreciation averages the service life of a number of property units and depreciates the group as if it were a single unit. The term "group" is used when the assets are similar; "composite" when they are dissimilar. The depreciation rate is the following ratio:

$$\frac{\text{Sum of annual SL depreciation of individual assets}}{\text{Total asset cost}}$$

Thus, composite depreciation is a weighted-average of a group of assets—usually of a similar nature, expected life, etc.

EXAMPLE: Three types of assets (A, B, and C) are depreciated under the composite method.

Asset type	Asset cost	Salvage value	Depreciation base	Useful life (yrs.)	SL annual depreciation
A	$ 45,000	$ 15,000	$ 30,000	5	$ 6,000
B	90,000	50,000	40,000	4	10,000
C	145,000	25,000	120,000	3	40,000
	$280,000	$ 90,000	$190,000		$56,000

Depreciation or composite rate $= \dfrac{\$56,000}{\$280,000} = 20\%$

Composite life $= 3.39$ *years ($190,000 ÷ $56,000)*

Note that the composite life is the depreciation base divided by the annual depreciation. Depreciation is recorded until the book value of the composite group is depreciated to the salvage value of the then remaining assets. As assets are retired the composite group salvage value is reduced. Also note that gains and losses are not recognized on disposal (i.e., gains and losses are netted into accumulated depreciation). This latter practice also affects the length of time required to reduce the book value (cost less accumulated depreciation) to the group salvage value. The entry to record a retirement is

Cash, other consideration	(amount received)	
Accumulated depreciation	(plug)	
Asset		(original cost)

Changes in depreciation. The exam tests changes in depreciation due to changes in expected useful life and salvage value. Make the change prospectively from the beginning of the year in which the change in estimate is made. The procedure for straight-line depreciation is

1. Divide the periods remaining (from the beginning of the year of change) into
2. The remaining depreciation base (i.e., undepreciated cost to date less revised salvage value)

Fractional year depreciation. Many conventions exist for accounting for depreciation for midyear asset acquisitions. They include

1. A whole year's depreciation in year of acquisition and none in year of disposal
2. One-half year's depreciation in year of acquisition and year of disposal
3. Depreciation to nearest whole month in both year of acquisition and year of disposal

CPA exam questions generally specify the convention to be followed. If not and the question is an essay/problem, select a convention reasonable in the circumstances and provide an explanation to the grader.

G. **Disposals and Impairment of Value** (see the outline of SFAS 121)

The entry to record the disposal (sale) of an asset is

Cash	(amount received)	
Accumulated depreciation	(old asset)	
Old asset		(cost)
Gain or loss	(loss)	(gain)

Do not forget to record depreciation for disposed assets up to the point of disposal.

EXAMPLE: Jimco, a manufacturer of sports equipment, purchased a machine for $6,000 on 1/1/96. The machine had an eight-year life, a $600 salvage value, and was depreciated using the straight-line method. Thus, depreciation was charged at a rate of $56.25 per month [($6,000 cost – $600 salvage) ÷ (8 yrs x 12 mos/yr)]. If Jimco sells the asset on 9/1/01 for $3,000, the following entries must be made to record 2000 depreciation and to record the sale:

Depreciation expense	450	
Accumulated depreciation		450
($56.25 x 8 mos)		
Cash	3,000	
Accumulated depreciation	3,825	
($56.25 x 68 mos)		
Equipment		6,000
Gain on sale of equip.		825
[$3,000 cash – ($6,000 – $3,825)CV]		

In some cases, assets are intended to be **disposed of** in a future reporting period rather than held for use. Per SFAS 144, if management has adopted such a plan for disposal, a loss is recognized if the fair value minus selling costs (NRV) is less than the recorded carrying value.

Assume that the asset in the above example has not been sold yet. However, management intends to dispose of it in the next year at NRV of $1,500. The entry to record management's intents would be as follows:

*Loss on planned disposition	675	
Equipment to be disposed of	1,500	
Accumulated depreciation	3,825	
Equipment		6,000

*[($1,500 – ($6,000 – 3,825) CV]

Fixed assets intended for disposal are not subsequently depreciated. The equipment to be disposed of would be classified as other assets on the balance sheet.

Losses on fixed assets to be disposed of can be recovered due to changes in the fair value or selling costs associated with the asset. This write-up, however, **cannot** exceed the carrying amount prior to recognition of impairment. If the NRV for this asset increases in the next period, the maximum recovery (gain) that could be recognized is $675.

In some cases, the carrying (book) value of fixed assets **intended to be held and used for productive purposes** may have to be reduced due to an **impairment** of value. This means that not all of the asset's cost will be recovered. If one or more factors (see the outline of SFAS 144) indicate that an asset or group of assets might be impaired, it is necessary to do the **recovery** test, which is to compare the undiscounted expected net future cash flows generated by a fixed asset to its carrying amount on the balance sheet. If the cash flows are equal to or greater than the asset's carrying value, the asset's cost will be recovered and no accounting recognition is required. However, if the cash flows are less than the carrying value a loss must be recognized. The subsequent loss is measured by the difference between the carrying value and the **fair value not the undiscounted net cash flows,** at the impairment date. The asset's carrying value is adjusted to reflect its fair value.

Assume that the asset in the above example is not sold. A test for impairment indicates that the net undiscounted cash flows from the machine are less than its carrying value. Thus, the asset is impaired as of 9/1/01. The machine's actual fair value at this date is $1,400, with **no** salvage value. Therefore, its carrying value is reduced,

Loss on impairment	775	
[($6,000 – $3,825)CV – $1,400 FV]		
Accumulated depreciation		775

and it will continue to be depreciated at $50.00 per month for its remaining useful life ($1,400 ÷ 28 mos = $50.00). At 12/31/03, when the asset is fully depreciated, Jimco retires it and writes the machine off with the following entry:

Accumulated depreciation	6,000	
Equipment		6,000

Note that the entire cost has been depreciated because upon impairment of the asset it was determined that the equipment did not have a salvage value.

When management has alternative courses of action to recover the carrying amount of the assets or a particular course has multiple outcomes in terms of cash flow, SFAS 144 indicates that probability-weighted cash flow approach should be considered. Subsequent to the impairment loss, the asset is depreciated based on its new carrying value. **Recoveries of previously recognized impairment losses may not be recognized in subsequent periods.**

H. Depletion

Depletion is "depreciation" of natural resources. The depletion base is the total cost of the property providing the natural resources. This includes all development costs such as exploring, drilling, excavating, and other preparatory costs.

The depletion base is usually allocated by the ratio of extracted units over the total expected recoverable units.

$$\frac{\text{Units extracted}}{\text{Total expected recoverable units}} \text{ x } \text{Depletion base}$$

The unit depletion rate is frequently revised due to the uncertainties surrounding the recovery of natural resources. The revised unit rate in any year takes the following form:

$$\frac{\text{Orig. cost + Addl. cost incurred – Resid. value – Depletion taken in prev. yrs.}}{\text{Units withdrawn currently + Estimated units recoverable at year - end}}$$

Note that the adjustment is being made prospectively (i.e., the remaining undepleted cost is being expensed over the remaining recoverable units).

Depletion on resources extracted during an accounting period is allocated between inventory and cost of goods sold.

I. Insurance

Loss account for fixed assets. When an insured loss occurs, an insurance loss account should be set up and charged for all losses. These losses include decreases in asset value, earned insurance premiums, etc. The account should be credited for any payments from the insurance company. The remainder is closed to revenue and expense summary.

Coinsurance. This area is tested on the Business Law and Professional Responsibilities section of the exam.

J. Goodwill and Other Intangible Assets (See the outline of SFAS 142)

Intangible assets are nonphysical assets. Intangible assets normally include only noncurrent intangibles (e.g., accounts receivable are not considered intangibles). Examples of intangible assets include copyrights, leaseholds, organizational costs, trademarks, franchises, patents, and goodwill. These intangibles may be categorized according to the following characteristics:

1. Identifiability. Separately identifiable or lacking specific identification.

2. Manner of acquisition. Acquired singly, in groups, or in business combinations; or developed internally.
3. Expected period of benefit. Limited by law or contract, related to human or economic factors, or indefinite or indeterminate duration.
4. Separability from enterprise. Rights transferable without title, salable, or inseparable from the entire enterprise.

Acquisition of intangibles. Purchased intangibles should be recorded at cost, which represents the fair value of the intangible at time of acquisition. Internally developed intangibles are written off as research and development expense; an exception is the cost to register a patent.

Acquisition of goodwill and allocation to reporting units. Goodwill is recorded only when an entire business is purchased. Purchase of goodwill as part of acquiring a business is discussed in the Investment and Business Combinations and Consolidations modules.

In a business acquisition, the recognized goodwill should be assigned to one or more reporting units. In essence, the goodwill assigned to a reporting unit is the difference between the fair value of the unit and the value of its individual assets and liabilities. A reporting unit can be an operating segment (see SFAS 131) or one level below.

EXAMPLE: Allocation of Goodwill to a Reporting Unit

Dunn Corporation acquired all of the assets of Yeager Corporation for $12,000,000 cash. The assets were seen as relating to three different reporting units (operating segments)—Communications, Technology, and Consulting. The fair value of the Communications reporting unit at the date of acquisition was $4,700,000. Goodwill associated with the unit would be assigned based on a comparison of its total fair value to the value of its assets and liabilities as shown below.

Communications Reporting Unit
(In 000s)

	Fair value
Cash	$ 200
Accounts receivable	900
Net Equipment	2,700
Patents	1,000
Customer contracts	700
Current liabilities	(1,200)
Fair value of net assets	$4,400

The amount of goodwill assigned to the reporting unit would be $300,000 ($4,700,000 – $4,400,000), the excess of the fair value of the reporting unit over the value of its net assets. Goodwill would be assigned to the other two reporting units in a similar manner.

Amortization of intangibles. Intangible assets that have a definite useful life are amortized by crediting the intangible account directly (ordinarily, contra accounts are not used).

Amortization expense	xx	
Intangible asset		xx

The method of amortization of intangibles should mirror the pattern that the asset is consumed. If the pattern cannot be reliably determined, the straight-line basis should be used. Factors to consider in determining economic life are listed in the outline of SFAS 142.

EXAMPLE: Determination of Useful Life of an Intangible Asset

Yeager Communications owns several radio stations and has $5,000,000 recorded as the carrying value of broadcast rights. The rights have a legal life of 7 more years but may be extended upon appropriate application for an indefinite period. Since the company has the right and intent to extend the rights indefinitely, the useful life of the asset should be considered indefinite and the rights should not be amortized.

Impairment of intangible assets. An intangible asset that is amortized should be tested for impairment in accordance with SFAS 121.

An intangible asset that is determined to have an indefinite useful life should not be amortized. However, it should be reevaluated every reporting period to determine if facts and circumstances have changed creating a limited life and requiring it to be amortized. Also, such intangible assets should be tested for impairment annually or more frequently if facts and circumstances indicate that impairment may have occurred—see the outline of SFAS 121 for such facts and circumstances. If the fair value of the intangible asset exceeds its carrying amount, an impairment loss should be recorded in the amount of the difference.

EXAMPLE: Impairment of an Intangible Asset with an Indefinite Life

    Wilson Company acquired a trademark for a major consumer product several years ago for $50,000. At the time it was expected that the asset had an indefinite life. During its annual impairment test of this asset, the company determined that unexpected competition has entered the market that will significantly reduce the future sales of the product. Based on an analysis of cash flows, the trademark is determined to have a fair market value of $30,000 and is expected to continue to have an indefinite useful life. The $20,000 ($50,000 – $30,000) impairment loss should be recognized as shown below.

Impairment loss	20,000	
Trademark		20,000

Impairment of goodwill. The goodwill assigned to a reporting unit should be tested for impairment on an annual basis and between annual tests in certain circumstances. These circumstances are listed in the outline of SFAS 142. The annual test may be performed any time during the company's fiscal year as long as it is done at the same time every year. Different reporting units may be tested at different times during the year. The test of impairment is a two-step process as described below.

1. Compare the fair value of the reporting unit with its carrying amount. If the carrying amount of the unit exceeds its fair value, the second step is performed. In estimating the fair value of a reporting unit, a valuation technique based on multiples of earnings or revenue, or other performance measure should be used.

2. Compare the implied fair value of the reporting unit goodwill with the carrying amount of that goodwill. The implied fair value of goodwill is determined in the same manner as the amount of goodwill recognized in a business combination—see outline of SFAS 141. That is, all assets in the segment are valued in accordance with SFAS 141, and the excess of the fair value of the reporting unit as a whole over the amounts assigned to its assets and liabilities is the implied goodwill. If the implied value of goodwill is less than its carrying amount, goodwill is written down to its implied value and an impairment loss is recognized.

EXAMPLE: Test of Impairment of Goodwill

    Dunn Corporation is performing the test of impairment of the Communication reporting unit at 9/30/01. In performing the first step in the test of impairment, the Communication reporting unit is valued through a multiple of earnings approach at $4,450,000. The carrying amount of the unit at 9/30/01 is $4,650,000, requiring the second step to be performed. The fair value of the assets and liabilities are valued as shown below.

Communications Reporting Unit
Estimated Fair Values
9/30/01
(In 000s)

	Fair value
Cash	$ 150
Accounts receivable	1,000
Net Equipment	2,600
Patents	950
Customer contracts	800
Current liabilities	(1,100)
Fair value of net assets	$4,400

The implied value of goodwill is $250,000 ($4,650,000 - $,400,000) and this exceeds the carrying amount of $300,000. Therefore, an impairment of goodwill should be recognized as shown below.

Impairment loss	50,000	
Goodwill-Communications		50,000

    In performing step one of the test, a detailed determination of fair value of a reporting unit may be carried forward from one year to the next if (1) there are no significant changes in the assets and liabilities that make up the reporting unit, (2) the most recent determined fair value exceeded the unit's carrying amount by a significant margin, and (3) based on an analysis of events or circumstances since the last valuation, the likelihood that the carrying amount exceeds fair value is remote.

K. Reporting on the Costs of Start-up Activities

    SOP 98-5 provides guidance on financial reporting of start-up costs, including organization costs. It requires such costs to be expensed as incurred. Start-up costs are defined as one-time activities related to opening a new facility or new class of customer, initiating a new process in an existing facility, or some new operation. In practice, these are referred to as preopening costs, preoperating costs, and organization costs. Routine ongoing efforts to improve existing quality of products, services, or facilities, are not start-up costs.

L. Research and Development Costs (SFAS 2)

SFAS 2 (see outline) require R&D costs to be expensed as incurred except for intangibles or fixed assets purchased from others having alternative future uses. These should be capitalized and amortized over their useful life. Thus, the cost of patents and R&D equipment purchased from third parties may be deferred and amortized over the asset's useful life. Internally developed R&D may not be deferred.

Finally, R&D done under contract for others is not required to be expensed per SFAS 2. The costs incurred would be matched with revenue using the completed-contract or percentage-of-completion method.

M. Computer Software Costs

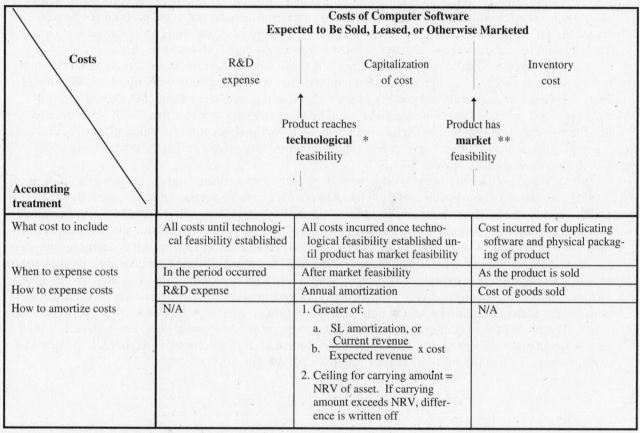

Costs	Costs of Computer Software Expected to Be Sold, Leased, or Otherwise Marketed		
	R&D expense	Capitalization of cost	Inventory cost
		Product reaches **technological** * feasibility	Product has **market** ** feasibility
Accounting treatment			
What cost to include	All costs until technological feasibility established	All costs incurred once technological feasibility established until product has market feasibility	Cost incurred for duplicating software and physical packaging of product
When to expense costs	In the period occurred	After market feasibility	As the product is sold
How to expense costs	R&D expense	Annual amortization	Cost of goods sold
How to amortize costs	N/A	1. Greater of: a. SL amortization, or b. $\dfrac{\text{Current revenue}}{\text{Expected revenue}} \times \text{cost}$ 2. Ceiling for carrying amount = NRV of asset. If carrying amount exceeds NRV, difference is written off	N/A

* *Software creation process includes a detail program design.*
** *Product ready for release to customers.*

Software developed for sale or lease. SFAS 86 (see outline) establishes the standards for recording internally developed or purchased computer software costs which are to be either sold, leased, or marketed as an individual product or as part of a process. The costs which are incurred internally to create the software should be expensed as research and development until technological feasibility is established. Thereafter, all costs should be capitalized and reported at the lower of unamortized cost or net realizable value. Capitalization should cease when the software is available for general release to customers.

The annual amortization of capitalized computer software costs will be the greater of the ratio of current revenues to anticipated total revenues or the straight-line amortization which is based on the estimated economic life.

Once the software is available for general release to customers, the inventory costs should include costs for duplicating software and for physically packaging the product. The cost of maintenance and customer support should be charged to expense in the period incurred.

Software developed for internal use. SOP 98-1 was developed to provide guidance for internally developed software. Software must meet two criteria to be accounted for as internally developed software. First, the software's specifications must be designed or modified to meet the reporting entity's internal needs, including costs to customize purchased software. Second, during the period in which the software is being developed, there can be no plan or intent to market the software externally, although development of the software can be jointly funded by several entities that each plan to use the software internally.

In order to justify capitalization of related costs, it is necessary for management to conclude that it is probable that the project will be completed and that the software will be used as intended. Absent that level of expectation, costs must be expensed currently as research and development costs are required to be. Entities which historically were engaged in both research and development of software for internal use and for sale to others would have to carefully identify costs with one or the other activity, since the former would (if all conditions are met) be subject to capitalization, while the latter might be expensed as research and development costs until technological feasibility had been demonstrated, per SFAS 86.

Under terms of the standard, cost capitalization commences when an entity has completed the conceptual formulation, design, and testing of possible project alternatives, including the process of vendor selection for purchased software, if any. These early-phase costs (referred to as "preliminary project stage" in SOP 98-1) are analogous to research and development costs and must be expensed as incurred. These cannot be later restored to an asset account if the development proves to be successful.

Costs incurred subsequent to the preliminary stage, and which meet the criteria under GAAP as long-lived assets, can be capitalized and amortized over the asset's expected economic life. Capitalization of costs will begin when both of two conditions are met. First, management having the relevant authority authorizes and commits to funding the project and believes that it is probable that it will be completed and that the resulting software will be used as intended. Second, the conceptual formulation, design, and testing of possible software project alternatives (i.e., the preliminary project stage) have been completed.

N. Development Stage Enterprises (SFAS 7)

SFAS 7 (see outline) defines a development stage enterprise as one devoting substantially all of its efforts to establishing a new business and (1) planned principal operations have not commenced, or (2) planned principal operations have commenced, but there has been no significant revenue. It is important to note that generally accepted accounting principles are to be followed in preparing the financial statements of a development stage enterprise. Therefore, no special treatment is allowed concerning capitalization or deferral of costs; only costs that may be deferred for an established enterprise may be capitalized by a development stage enterprise. Additionally, the balance sheet should show cumulative losses since inception under stockholders' equity. The income statement and statement of cash flows should include both current period and cumulative amounts, since inception, of revenues, expenses, losses, and cash flows. The financial statements must be identified as those of a development stage enterprise. It should also be noted that the first fiscal year after the development stage, a disclosure is required in the financial statements stating that the entity was previously in the development stage.

MULTIPLE-CHOICE QUESTIONS (1-77)

1. Merry Co. purchased a machine costing $125,000 for its manufacturing operations and paid shipping costs of $20,000. Merry spent an additional $10,000 testing and preparing the machine for use. What amount should Merry record as the cost of the machine?

- a. $155,000
- b. $145,000
- c. $135,000
- d. $125,000

2. On December 1, 2002, Boyd Co. purchased a $400,000 tract of land for a factory site. Boyd razed an old building on the property and sold the materials it salvaged from the demolition. Boyd incurred additional costs and realized salvage proceeds during December 2002 as follows:

Demolition of old building	$50,000
Legal fees for purchase contract and recording ownership	10,000
Title guarantee insurance	12,000
Proceeds from sale of salvaged materials	8,000

In its December 31, 2002 balance sheet, Boyd should report a balance in the land account of

- a. $464,000
- b. $460,000
- c. $442,000
- d. $422,000

3. Cole Co. began constructing a building for its own use in January 2002. During 2002, Cole incurred interest of $50,000 on specific construction debt, and $20,000 on other borrowings. Interest computed on the weighted-average amount of accumulated expenditures for the building during 2002 was $40,000. What amount of interest cost should Cole capitalize?

- a. $20,000
- b. $40,000
- c. $50,000
- d. $70,000

4. Clay Company started construction of a new office building on January 1, 2002, and moved into the finished building on July 1, 2003. Of the building's $2,500,000 total cost, $2,000,000 was incurred in 2002 evenly throughout the year. Clay's incremental borrowing rate was 12% throughout 2002, and the total amount of interest incurred by Clay during 2002 was $102,000. What amount should Clay report as capitalized interest at December 31, 2002?

- a. $102,000
- b. $120,000
- c. $150,000
- d. $240,000

5. During 2002, Bay Co. constructed machinery for its own use and for sale to customers. Bank loans financed these assets both during construction and after construction was complete. How much of the interest incurred should be reported as interest expense in the 2002 income statement?

	Interest incurred for machinery for own use	Interest incurred for machinery held for sale
a.	All interest incurred	All interest incurred
b.	All interest incurred	Interest incurred after completion
c.	Interest incurred after completion	Interest incurred after completion
d.	Interest incurred after completion	All interest incurred

6. On July 1, 2002, Balt Co. exchanged a truck for twenty-five shares of Ace Corp.'s common stock. On that date, the truck's carrying amount was $2,500, and its fair value was $3,000. Also, the book value of Ace's stock was $60 per share. On December 31, 2002, Ace had 250 shares of common stock outstanding and its book value per share was $50. What amount should Balt report in its December 31, 2002 balance sheet as investment in Ace?

- a. $3,000
- b. $2,500
- c. $1,500
- d. $1,250

7. On March 31, 2002, Winn Company traded in an old machine having a carrying amount of $16,800, and paid a cash difference of $6,000 for a new machine having a total cash price of $20,500. On March 31, 2002, what amount of loss should Winn recognize on this exchange?

- a. $0
- b. $2,300
- c. $3,700
- d. $6,000

8. Amble, Inc. exchanged a truck with a carrying amount of $12,000 and a fair value of $20,000 for a truck and $5,000 cash. The fair value of the truck received was $15,000. At what amount should Amble record the truck received in the exchange?

- a. $ 7,000
- b. $ 9,000
- c. $12,000
- d. $15,000

9. In an exchange of similar assets, Transit Co. received equipment with a fair value equal to the carrying amount of equipment given up. Transit also contributed cash. As a result of the exchange, Transit recognized

- a. A loss equal to the cash given up.
- b. A loss determined by the proportion of cash paid to the total transaction value.
- c. A gain determined by the proportion of cash paid to the total transaction value.
- d. Neither gain **nor** loss.

10. May Co. and Sty Co. exchanged nonmonetary assets. The exchange did not culminate an earning process for either May or Sty. May paid cash to Sty in connection with the exchange. To the extent that the amount of cash exceeds a proportionate share of the carrying amount of the asset surrendered, a realized gain on the exchange should be recognized by

	May	Sty
a.	Yes	Yes
b.	Yes	No
c.	No	Yes
d.	No	No

11. Vik Auto and King Clothier exchanged goods, held for resale, with equal fair values. Each will use the other's goods to promote their own products. The retail price of the car that Vik gave up is less than the retail price of the clothes received. What profit should Vik recognize for the nonmonetary exchange?

a. A profit is **not** recognized.
b. A profit equal to the difference between the retail prices of the clothes received and the car.
c. A profit equal to the difference between the retail price and the cost of the car.
d. A profit equal to the difference between the fair value and the cost of the car.

12. Yola Co. and Zaro Co. are fuel oil distributors. To facilitate the delivery of oil to their customers, Yola and Zaro exchanged ownership of 1,200 barrels of oil without physically moving the oil. Yola paid Zaro $30,000 to compensate for a difference in the grade of oil. On the date of the exchange, cost and market values of the oil were as follows:

	Yola Co.	Zaro Co.
Cost	$100,000	$126,000
Market values	120,000	150,000

In Zaro's income statement, what amount of gain should be reported from the exchange of the oil?
a. $0
b. $ 4,800
c. $24,000
d. $30,000

13. An entity disposes of a nonmonetary asset in a nonreciprocal transfer. A gain or loss should be recognized on the disposition of the asset when the fair value of the asset transferred is determinable and the nonreciprocal transfer is to

	Another entity	A stockholder of the entity
a.	No	Yes
b.	No	No
c.	Yes	No
d.	Yes	Yes

14. On July 1, 2002, one of Rudd Co.'s delivery vans was destroyed in an accident. On that date, the van's carrying value was $2,500. On July 15, 2002, Rudd received and recorded a $700 invoice for a new engine installed in the van in May 2002, and another $500 invoice for various repairs. In August, Rudd received $3,500 under its insurance policy on the van, which it plans to use to replace the van. What amount should Rudd report as gain (loss) on disposal of the van in its 2002 income statement?
a. $1,000
b. $ 300
c. $0
d. $ (200)

15. Lano Corp.'s forest land was condemned for use as a national park. Compensation for the condemnation exceeded the forest land's carrying amount. Lano purchased similar, but larger, replacement forest land for an amount greater than the condemnation award. As a result of the condemnation and replacement, what is the net effect on the carrying amount of forest land reported in Lano's balance sheet?
a. The amount is increased by the excess of the replacement forest land's cost over the condemned forest land's carrying amount.
b. The amount is increased by the excess of the replacement forest land's cost over the condemnation award.
c. The amount is increased by the excess of the condemnation award over the condemned forest land's carrying amount.
d. No effect, because the condemned forest land's carrying amount is used as the replacement forest land's carrying amount.

16. On July 1, 2002, Town Company purchased for $540,000 a warehouse building and the land on which it is located. The following data were available concerning the property:

	Current appraised value	Seller's original cost
Land	$200,000	$140,000
Warehouse building	300,000	280,000
	$500,000	$420,000

Town should record the land at
a. $140,000
b. $180,000
c. $200,000
d. $216,000

17. During 2002, King Company made the following expenditures relating to its plant building:

Continuing and frequent repairs	$40,000
Repainted the plant building	10,000
Major improvements to the electrical wiring system	32,000
Partial replacement of roof tiles	14,000

How much should be charged to repair and maintenance expense in 2002?
a. $96,000
b. $82,000
c. $64,000
d. $54,000

18. On June 18, 2002, Dell Printing Co. incurred the following costs for one of its printing presses:

Purchase of collating and stapling attachment	$84,000
Installation of attachment	36,000
Replacement parts for overhaul of press	26,000
Labor and overhead in connection with overhaul	14,000

The overhaul resulted in a significant increase in production. Neither the attachment nor the overhaul increased the estimated useful life of the press. What amount of the above costs should be capitalized?
a. $0
b. $84,000
c. $120,000
d. $160,000

19. A building suffered uninsured fire damage. The damaged portion of the building was refurbished with higher quality materials. The cost and related accumulated depreciation of the damaged portion are identifiable. To account for these events, the owner should
a. Reduce accumulated depreciation equal to the cost of refurbishing.
b. Record a loss in the current period equal to the sum of the cost of refurbishing and the carrying amount of the damaged portion of the building.
c. Capitalize the cost of refurbishing and record a loss in the current period equal to the carrying amount of the damaged portion of the building.
d. Capitalize the cost of refurbishing by adding the cost to the carrying amount of the building.

20. Derby Co. incurred costs to modify its building and to rearrange its production line. As a result, an overall reduction in production costs is expected. However, the modifications did not increase the building's market value, and the rearrangement did not extend the production line's life. Should the building modification costs and the production line rearrangement costs be capitalized?

	Building modification costs	*Production line rearrangement costs*
a.	Yes	No
b.	Yes	Yes
c.	No	No
d.	No	Yes

21. On January 2, 2002, Lem Corp. bought machinery under a contract that required a down payment of $10,000, plus twenty-four monthly payments of $5,000 each, for total cash payments of $130,000. The cash equivalent price of the machinery was $110,000. The machinery has an estimated useful life of ten years and estimated salvage value of $5,000. Lem uses straight-line depreciation. In its 2002 income statement, what amount should Lem report as depreciation for this machinery?

    a. $10,500
    b. $11,000
    c. $12,500
    d. $13,000

22. Turtle Co. purchased equipment on January 2, 2000, for $50,000. The equipment had an estimated five-year service life. Turtle's policy for five-year assets is to use the 200% double-declining depreciation method for the first two years of the asset's life, and then switch to the straight-line depreciation method. In its December 31, 2002 balance sheet, what amount should Turtle report as accumulated depreciation for equipment?

    a. $30,000
    b. $38,000
    c. $39,200
    d. $42,000

23. Rago Company takes a full year's depreciation expense in the year of an asset's acquisition, and no depreciation expense in the year of disposition. Data relating to one of Rago's depreciable assets at December 31, 2002, are as follows:

Acquisition year	2000
Cost	$110,000
Residual value	20,000
Accumulated depreciation	72,000
Estimated useful life	5 years

Using the same depreciation method as used in 2000, 2001, and 2002, how much depreciation expense should Rago record in 2003 for this asset?

    a. $12,000
    b. $18,000
    c. $22,000
    d. $24,000

24. On January 2, 1999, Union Co. purchased a machine for $264,000 and depreciated it by the straight-line method using an estimated useful life of eight years with no salvage value. On January 2, 2002, Union determined that the machine had a useful life of six years from the date of acquisition and will have a salvage value of $24,000. An accounting change was made in 2002 to reflect the additional data.

The accumulated depreciation for this machine should have a balance at December 31, 2002, of

    a. $176,000
    b. $160,000
    c. $154,000
    d. $146,000

25. Weir Co. uses straight-line depreciation for its property, plant, and equipment, which, stated at cost, consisted of the following:

	12/31/02	*12/31/01*
Land	$ 25,000	$ 25,000
Buildings	195,000	195,000
Machinery and equipment	695,000	650,000
	915,000	870,000
Less accumulated depreciation	400,000	370,000
	$515,000	$500,000

Weir's depreciation expense for 2002 and 2001 was $55,000 and $50,000, respectively. What amount was debited to accumulated depreciation during 2002 because of property, plant, and equipment retirements?

    a. $40,000
    b. $25,000
    c. $20,000
    d. $10,000

26. On January 1, 1998, Crater, Inc. purchased equipment having an estimated salvage value equal to 20% of its original cost at the end of a ten-year life. The equipment was sold December 31, 2002, for 50% of its original cost. If the equipment's disposition resulted in a reported loss, which of the following depreciation methods did Crater use?

    a. Double-declining balance.
    b. Sum-of-the-years' digits.
    c. Straight-line.
    d. Composite.

27. A depreciable asset has an estimated 15% salvage value. At the end of its estimated useful life, the accumulated depreciation would equal the original cost of the asset under which of the following depreciation methods?

	Straight-line	*Productive output*
a.	Yes	No
b.	Yes	Yes
c.	No	Yes
d.	No	No

28. In which of the following situations is the units-of-production method of depreciation most appropriate?

    a. An asset's service potential declines with use.
    b. An asset's service potential declines with the passage of time.
    c. An asset is subject to rapid obsolescence.
    d. An asset incurs increasing repairs and maintenance with use.

29. A machine with a five-year estimated useful life and an estimated 10% salvage value was acquired on January 1, 1999. On December 31, 2002, accumulated depreciation, using the sum-of-the-years' digits method, would be

    a. (Original cost less salvage value) multiplied by 1/15.
    b. (Original cost less salvage value) multiplied by 14/15.
    c. Original cost multiplied by 14/15.
    d. Original cost multiplied by 1/15.

30. Spiro Corp. uses the sum-of-the-years' digits method to depreciate equipment purchased in January 2000 for $20,000. The estimated salvage value of the equipment is $2,000 and the estimated useful life is four years. What should Spiro report as the asset's carrying amount as of December 31, 2002?

    a. $1,800
    b. $2,000
    c. $3,800
    d. $4,500

31. The graph below depicts three depreciation expense patterns over time.

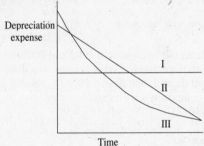

Which depreciation expense pattern corresponds to the sum-of-the-years' digits method and which corresponds to the double-declining balance method?

	Sum-of-the-years' digits	Double-declining balance
a.	III	II
b.	II	I
c.	I	III
d.	II	III

32. Which of the following uses the straight-line depreciation method?

	Group depreciation	Composite depreciation
a.	No	No
b.	Yes	No
c.	Yes	Yes
d.	No	Yes

33. A company using the composite depreciation method for its fleet of trucks, cars, and campers retired one of its trucks and received cash from a salvage company. The net carrying amount of these composite asset accounts would be decreased by the

    a.   Cash proceeds received and original cost of the truck.
    b.   Cash proceeds received.
    c.   Original cost of the truck less the cash proceeds.
    d.   Original cost of the truck.

34. During 2002, the management of West Inc. decided to dispose of some of its older equipment and machinery. By year-end, December 31, 2002, these assets had not been sold, although the company was negotiating their sale to another company. On the December 31, 2002 balance sheet of West Inc., this equipment and machinery should be reported at

    a.   Fair value.
    b.   Carrying amount.
    c.   The lower of carrying amount or fair value.
    d.   The lower of carrying amount or fair value less cost to sell.

35. At December 31, 2002, Matson Inc. was holding long-lived assets that it intended to sell. The assets do not constitute a separate component of the company. The company appropriately recognized a loss in 2002 related to these assets. On Matson's income statement for the year ended December 31, 2002, this loss should be reported as a(n)

    a.   Extraordinary item.
    b.   Component of income from continuing operations before income taxes.
    c.   Separate component of selling or general and administrative expenses, disclosed net of tax benefit.
    d.   Component of the gain (loss) from sale of discontinued operations, disclosed net of income taxes.

36. Taft Inc. recognized a loss in 2001 related to long-lived assets that it intended to sell. These assets were not sold during 2002, and the company estimated, at December 31, 2002, that the loss recognized in 2001 had been more than recovered. On the December 31, 2002 balance sheet, Taft should report these long-lived assets at their

    a.   Fair value on December 31, 2001.
    b.   Fair value less cost to sell on December 31, 2001.
    c.   Fair value on December 31, 2002.
    d.   Carrying amount on December 31, 2001.

37. Cranston Inc. reported an impairment loss of $150,000 on its income statement for the year ended December 31, 2001. This loss was related to long-lived assets which Cranston intended to use in its operations. On the company's December 31, 2001 balance sheet, Cranston reported these long-lived assets at $920,000 and, as of December 31, 2001, Cranston estimated that these long-lived assets would be used for another five years. On December 31, 2002, Cranston determined that the fair values of its impaired long-lived assets had increased by $25,000 over their fair values at December 31, 2001. On the company's December 31, 2002 balance sheet, what amount should be reported as the carrying amount for these long-lived assets? Assume straight-line depreciation and no salvage value for the impaired assets.

    a. $761,000.
    b. $736,000.
    c. $945,000.
    d. $756,000.

38. Assets intended to be held and used for productive purposes may suffer from impairment in each of the following circumstances **except**

    a.   A change in the way the assets are used or physical change in the assets.
    b.   Asset costs incurred exceed the original amounts planned.
    c.   Discounted expected future cash flows and interest charges are less than the carrying amount of the assets.
    d.   A significant adverse change in legal factors that might affect the assets' fair value.

39. Synthia, Inc., a clothing manufacturer, purchased a sewing machine for $10,000 on July 1, 2000. The machine had a ten-year life, a $500 salvage value, and was depreciated using the straight-line method. On December 31, 2002, a test for impairment indicates that the undiscounted cash flows from the sewing machine are less than its carrying value. The machine's actual fair value on December 31,

2002 is $3,000. What is Synthia's loss on impairment on December 31, 2002?

- a. $6,500
- b. $4,750
- c. $4,625
- d. $4,150

40. With regard to impaired assets, an FASB standard provides for

	Recognition of loss upon impairment	Restoration of previously recognized impairment losses
a.	Yes	Yes
b.	Yes	No
c.	No	Yes
d.	No	No

41. Scarbrough Company had purchased equipment for $280,000 on January 1, 1999. The equipment had an eight-year useful life and a salvage value of $40,000. Scarbrough depreciated the equipment using the straight-line method. In August 2002, Scarbrough questioned the recoverability of the carrying amount of this equipment. At August 31, 2002, the expected net future cash inflows (undiscounted) related to the continued use and eventual disposal of the equipment total $175,000. The equipment's fair value on August 31, 2002, is $150,000. After any loss on impairment has been recognized, what is the carrying value of Scarbrough's equipment as of August 31, 2002?

- a. $175,000
- b. $170,000
- c. $150,000
- d. $130,000

42. Under the reporting requirements of SFAS 144, impairment losses for assets to be held and used shall be reported

- a. As an extraordinary item.
- b. As a component of discontinued operations.
- c. As a component of income from continuing operations.
- d. As a change in accounting estimate.

43. During December 2002, Bubba Inc. determined that there had been a significant decrease in the market value of its equipment used in its manufacturing process. At December 31, 2002, Bubba compiled the information below.

Original cost of the equipment	$500,000
Accumulated depreciation	300,000
Expected net future cash inflows (undiscounted) related to the continued use and eventual disposal of the equipment	175,000
Fair value of the equipment	125,000

What is the amount of impairment loss that should be reported on Bubba's income statement prepared for the year ended December 31, 2002?

- a. $ 75,000
- b. $ 25,000
- c. $325,000
- d. $375,000

44. Marjorie, Inc., acquired a machine for $320,000 on August 31, 1999. The machine has a five-year life, a $50,000 salvage value, and was depreciated using the straight-line method. On May 31, 2002, a test for recoverability reveals that the expected net future undiscounted cash inflows related to the continued use and eventual disposal of the machine total $150,000. The machine's actual fair value on May 31, 2002, is $135,000, with no salvage value. As-

suming a loss on impairment is recognized May 31, 2002, what is Marjorie's depreciation expense for June 2002?

- a. $6,352
- b. $5,000
- c. $4,500
- d. $3,148

45. Which of the following statements is(are) correct about the carrying amount of a long-lived asset after an impairment loss has been recognized? Assume the long-lived asset is being held for use in the business and that the asset is depreciable.

- I. The reduced carrying amount of the asset may be increased in subsequent years if the impairment loss has been recovered.
- II. The reduced carrying amount of the asset represents the amount that should be depreciated over the asset's remaining useful life.

- a. I only.
- b. II only.
- c. Both I and II.
- d. Neither I nor II.

46. According to SFAS 144, if a long-lived asset is determined to be impaired, how is the loss calculated?

- a. Future discounted cash flows less asset's carrying (book) value.
- b. Future undiscounted cash flows less asset's carrying (book) value.
- c. Fair value less asset's carrying (book) value.
- d. Cash outflows needed to obtain cash inflows.

47. In accordance with SFAS 144, long-lived assets are required to be reviewed for impairment

- a. At the balance sheet date, every three years.
- b. When the asset is fully depreciated.
- c. When circumstances indicate that the carrying amount of an asset might not be recoverable.
- d. At the balance sheet date, every year.

48. During December 2002, Toni Corp. determined that there had been a significant decrease in the market value of its equipment used in its roofing business. At December 31, 2002, Toni compiled the information below.

Original cost of equipment	$800,000
Accumulated depreciation	450,000
Expected net future cash inflows (undiscounted) related to the continued use and eventual disposal of the equipment	300,000
Fair value of the equipment	250,000

What is the amount of the impairment loss that should be reported on Toni's income statement prepared for the year ended December 31, 2002?

- a. $ 50,000
- b. $100,000
- c. $150,000
- d. $200,000

49. Miller Company acquired a machine for $420,000 on June 30, 2000. The machine has a seven-year life, no salvage value, and was depreciated using the straight-line method. On August 31, 2002, a test for recoverability reveals that the expected net future undiscounted cash inflows related to the continued use and eventual disposal of the machine total $275,000. The machine's actual fair value on

August 31, 2002, is $261,000. Assuming a loss on impairment is recognized August 31, 2002, what is Miller's depreciation expense for September 2002?

     a. $4,000
     b. $4,350
     c. $4,500
     d. $5,000

50. In January 2002, Vorst Co. purchased a mineral mine for $2,640,000 with removable ore estimated at 1,200,000 tons. After it has extracted all the ore, Vorst will be required by law to restore the land to its original condition at an estimated cost of $220,000. The present value of the estimated restoration costs is $180,000. Vorst believes it will be able to sell the property afterwards for $300,000. During 2002, Vorst incurred $360,000 of development costs preparing the mine for production and removed and sold 60,000 tons of ore. In its 2002 income statement, what amount should Vorst report as depletion?

     a. $135,000
     b. $144,000
     c. $150,000
     d. $159,000

51. On December 31, 2000, Byte Co. had capitalized software costs of $600,000 with an economic life of four years. Sales for 2001 were 10% of expected total sales of the software. At December 31, 2001, the software had a net realizable value of $480,000. In its December 31, 2001 balance sheet, what amount should Byte report as net capitalized cost of computer software?

     a. $432,000
     b. $450,000
     c. $480,000
     d. $540,000

52. On January 2, 2002, Judd Co. bought a trademark from Krug Co. for $500,000. Judd retained an independent consultant, who estimated the trademark's remaining life to be fifty years. Its unamortized cost on Krug's accounting records was $380,000. In Judd's December 31, 2002 balance sheet, what amount should be reported as accumulated amortization?

     a. $ 7,600
     b. $ 9,500
     c. $10,000
     d. $12,500

53. On January 2, 2002, Paye Co. purchased Shef Co. at a cost that resulted in recognition of goodwill of $200,000. During the first quarter of 2002, Paye spent an additional $80,000 on expenditures designed to maintain goodwill. In its December 31, 2002 balance sheet, what amount should Paye report as goodwill?

     a. $180,000
     b. $200,000
     c. $252,000
     d. $280,000

54. Northern Airline purchased airline gate rights at Newark International Airport for $2,000,000 with a legal life of five years. However, Northern has the ability and right to extend the rights every ten years for an indefinite period of time. Over what period of time should Northern amortize the gate rights?

     a.   5 years.
     b.   15 years
     c.   40 years.
     d.   The rights should not be amortized.

55. On January 2, 1999, Lava, Inc. purchased a patent for a new consumer product for $90,000. At the time of purchase, the patent was valid for fifteen years; however, the patent's useful life was estimated to be only ten years due to the competitive nature of the product. On December 31, 2002, the product was permanently withdrawn from sale under governmental order because of a potential health hazard in the product. What amount should Lava charge against income during 2002, assuming amortization is recorded at the end of each year?

     a. $ 9,000
     b. $54,000
     c. $63,000
     d. $72,000

56. What does SFAS 142 require with respect to accounting for goodwill?

     a.   Goodwill should be amortized over a five-year period.
     b.   Goodwill should be amortized over its expected useful life.
     c.   Goodwill should be recorded and never adjusted.
     d.   Goodwill should be recorded and periodically evaluated for impairment.

57. Which of the following statements concerning patents is correct?

     a.   Legal costs incurred to successfully defend an internally developed patent should be capitalized and amortized over the patent's remaining economic life.
     b.   Legal fees and other direct costs incurred in registering a patent should be capitalized and amortized on a straight-line basis over a five-year period.
     c.   Research and development contract services purchased from others and used to develop a patented manufacturing process should be capitalized and amortized over the patent's economic life.
     d.   Research and development costs incurred to develop a patented item should be capitalized and amortized on a straight-line basis over seventeen years.

58. Under SFAS 142, goodwill should be tested periodically for impairment

     a.   For the entity as a whole.
     b.   At the subsidiary level.
     c.   At the industry segment level.
     d.   At the operating segment level or one level below.

59. On July 12, 2002, Carver, Inc. acquired Jones Company in a business combination. As a result of the combination, the following amounts of goodwill were recorded for each of the three reporting units of the acquired company.

Retailing	$30,000
Service	$20,000
Financing	$40,000

Near the end of 2002 a new major competitor entered the company's market and Carver was concerned that this might cause a significant decline in the value of goodwill. Accordingly, Carver computed the implied value of the goodwill for the three major reporting units at December 31, 2002 as follows:

Retailing	$25,000
Service	$10,000
Financing	$60,000

Determine the amount of impairment of goodwill that should be recorded by Carver at December 31, 2002.

   a. $0
   b. $10,000
   c. $15,000
   d. $25,000

60. Sloan Corporation is performing its annual test of the impairment of goodwill for its Financing reporting unit. It has determined that the fair value of the unit exceeds it carrying value. Which of the following is correct concerning this test of impairment?

   a. Impairment is not indicated and no additional analysis is necessary.
   b. Goodwill should be written down as impaired.
   c. The assets and liabilities should be valued to determine if there has been an impairment of goodwill.
   d. Goodwill should be retested at the entity level.

61. Wilson Corporation is performing the test of impairment of its Technology reporting unit at 9/30/02. In the first step of the process, Wilson has valued the unit using a multiple of earnings approach at $2,000,000. The carrying value of the net assets of the Technology unit is $2,100,000. What should Wilson do with this information?

   a. Record an impairment loss of $100,000.
   b. Record no impairment loss.
   c. Value goodwill individually.
   d. Perform step two of the test of impairment.

62. Brunson Corp., a major US winery, begins construction of a new facility in Italy. Following are some of the costs incurred in conjunction with the start-up activities of the new facility:

Production equipment	$815,000
Travel costs of salaried employees	40,000
License fees	14,000
Training of local employees for production and maintenance operations	120,000
Advertising costs	85,200

What portion of the organizational costs will be expensed?

   a. $975,000
   b. $160,000
   c. $0
   d. $139,200

63. On January 1, 2002, Kew Corp. incurred organization costs of $24,000. What portion of the organization costs will Kew defer to years subsequent to 2002?

   a. $23,400
   b. $19,200
   c. $ 4,800
   d. $0

64. Which of the following statements is(are) correct regarding the treatment of start-up activities related to the opening of a new facility?

  I. Costs of raising capital should be expensed as incurred.
  II. Costs of acquiring or constructing long-lived assets and getting them ready for their intended use should be expensed as incurred.

  III. Cost of research and development should be expensed as incurred.

   a. I only.
   b. III only.
   c. Both I and III.
   d. I, II, and III.

65. Cody Corp. incurred the following costs during 2002:

Design of tools, jigs, molds, and dies involving new technology	$125,000
Modification of the formulation of a process	160,000
Troubleshooting in connection with breakdowns during commercial production	100,000
Adaptation of an existing capability to a particular customer's need as part of a continuing commercial activity	110,000

In its 2002 income statement, Cody should report research and development expense of

   a. $125,000
   b. $160,000
   c. $235,000
   d. $285,000

66. In 2002, Ball Labs incurred the following costs:

Direct costs of doing contract research and development work for the government to be reimbursed by governmental unit	$400,000

Research and development costs not included above were

Depreciation	$300,000
Salaries	700,000
Indirect costs appropriately allocated	200,000
Materials	180,000

What was Ball's total research and development expense in 2002?

   a. $1,080,000
   b. $1,380,000
   c. $1,580,000
   d. $1,780,000

67. West, Inc. made the following expenditures relating to Product Y:

  • Legal costs to file a patent on Product Y—$10,000. Production of the finished product would not have been undertaken without the patent.
  • Special equipment to be used solely for development of Product Y—$60,000. The equipment has no other use and has an estimated useful life of four years.
  • Labor and material costs incurred in producing a prototype model—$200,000.
  • Cost of testing the prototype—$80,000.

What is the total amount of costs that will be expensed when incurred?

   a. $280,000
   b. $295,000
   c. $340,000
   d. $350,000

68. Brill Co. made the following expenditures during 2002:

Costs to develop computer software for internal use in Brill's general management information system	$100,000
Costs of market research activities	75,000

What amount of these expenditures should Brill report in its 2002 income statement as research and development expenses?

a. $175,000
b. $100,000
c. $ 75,000
d. $0

69. On January 1, 2002, Jambon purchased equipment for use in developing a new product. Jambon uses the straight-line depreciation method. The equipment could provide benefits over a ten-year period. However, the new product development is expected to take five years, and the equipment can be used only for this project. Jambon's 2002 expense equals

a. The total cost of the equipment.
b. One-fifth of the cost of the equipment.
c. One-tenth of the cost of the equipment.
d. Zero.

Items 70 and 71 are based on the following:

During 2002, Pitt Corp. incurred costs to develop and produce a routine, low-risk computer software product, as follows:

Completion of detailed program design	$13,000
Costs incurred for coding and testing to establish technological feasibility	10,000
Other coding costs after establishment of technological feasibility	24,000
Other testing costs after establishment of technological feasibility	20,000
Costs of producing product masters for training materials	15,000
Duplication of computer software and training materials from product masters (1,000 units)	25,000
Packaging product (500 units)	9,000

70. In Pitt's December 31, 2002 balance sheet, what amount should be reported in inventory?

a. $25,000
b. $34,000
c. $40,000
d. $49,000

71. In Pitt's December 31, 2002 balance sheet, what amount should be capitalized as software cost, subject to amortization?

a. $54,000
b. $57,000
c. $59,000
d. $69,000

72. On December 31, 2001, Bit Co. had capitalized costs for a new computer software product with an economic life of five years. Sales for 2002 were 30% of expected total sales of the software. At December 31, 2002, the software had a net realizable value equal to 90% of the capitalized cost. What percentage of the original capitalized cost should be reported as the net amount on Bit's December 31, 2002 balance sheet?

a. 70%
b. 72%
c. 80%
d. 90%

73. Which of the following statements is incorrect regarding internal-use software?

a. The application and development costs of internal-use software should be amortized on a straight-line

basis unless another systematic and rational basis is more representative of its costs.
b. Internal-use software is considered to be software that is marketed as a separate product or as part of a product or process.
c. The costs of testing and installing computer hardware should be capitalized as incurred.
d. The costs of training and application maintenance should be expensed as incurred.

74. Which of the following statements is(are) correct regarding the proper accounting treatment for internal-use software costs?

I. Preliminary costs should be capitalized as incurred.
II. Application and development costs should be capitalized as incurred.

a. I only.
b. II only.
c. Both I and II.
d. Neither I nor II.

75. What is the proper accounting treatment for the following stages of internal-use software costs?

	Preliminary stage costs	*Post-implementation costs*
a.	Capitalized as incurred	Capitalized as incurred
b.	Expensed as incurred	Capitalized as incurred
c.	Capitalized as incurred	Expensed as incurred
d.	Expensed as incurred	Expensed as incurred

76. Financial reporting by a development stage enterprise differs from financial reporting for an established operating enterprise in regard to footnote disclosures

a. Only.
b. And expense recognition principles only.
c. And revenue recognition principles only.
d. And revenue and expense recognition principles.

77. A development stage enterprise

a. Issues an income statement that shows only cumulative amounts from the enterprise's inception.
b. Issues an income statement that is the same as an established operating enterprise, but does **not** show cumulative amounts from the enterprise's inception as additional information.
c. Issues an income statement that is the same as an established operating enterprise, and shows cumulative amounts from the enterprise's inception as additional information.
d. Does **not** issue an income statement.

OTHER OBJECTIVE QUESTION

Problem 1   (15 to 25 minutes)

Items 1 through 6 represent expenditures for goods held for resale and equipment.

Required:

For **items 1 through 6,** determine for each item whether the expenditure should be capitalized(C) or expensed as a period cost (E) .

1. Freight charges paid for goods held for resale.

2. In-transit insurance on goods held for resale purchased FOB shipping point.

3. Interest on note payable for goods held for resale.

4. Installation of equipment.

5. Testing of newly purchased equipment.

6. Cost of current year service contract on equipment.

Items 7 through 10 are based on the following 2002 transactions:[1]

• Link Co. purchased an office building and the land on which it is located by paying $800,000 cash and assuming an existing mortgage of $200,000. The property is assessed at $960,000 for realty tax purposes, of which 60% is allocated to the building.

• Link leased construction equipment under a seven-year capital lease requiring annual year-end payments of $100,000. Link's incremental borrowing rate is 9%, while the lessor's implicit rate, which is not known to Link, is 8%. Present value factors for an ordinary annuity for seven periods are 5.21 at 8% and 5.03 at 9%. Fair value of the equipment is $515,000.

• Link paid $50,000 and gave a plot of undeveloped land with a carrying amount of $320,000 and a fair value of $450,000 to Club Co. in exchange for a plot of undeveloped land with a fair value of $500,000. The land was carried on Club's books at $350,000.

Required:

For **items 7 through 10,** calculate the amount to be recorded for each item.[1]

7.   Building.

8.   Leased equipment.

9.   Land received from Club on Link's books.

10. Land received from Link on Club's books.

Items 11 through 14 are based on the following information:[1]

On January 2, 2001, Half, Inc. purchased a manufacturing machine for $864,000. The machine has an eight-year estimated life and a $144,000 estimated salvage value. Half expects to manufacture 1,800,000 units over the life of the machine. During 2002, Half manufactured 300,000 units.

Required:

Items 11 through 14 represent various depreciation methods. For each item, calculate depreciation expense for 2002 (the second year of ownership) for the machine described above under the method listed.[1]

11. Straight-line.

12. Double-declining balance.

13. Sum-of-the-years' digits.

14. Units of production.

---

[1] *On the CPA exam, a list of numeric answer choices would be presented for the candidate to select from.*

PROBLEMS

Problem 1   (15 to 25 minutes)

Winter Sports Co. rents winter sports equipment to the public. Snowmobiles are depreciated by the double-declining balance method. Before the season began, the estimated lives of several snowmobiles were extended because engines were replaced. Winter was given thirty days to pay for the engines. Winter gave the old engines to a local mechanic who agreed to provide repairs and maintenance service in the next year equal to the fair value of the engines. Rental skis, poles, and boots are capitalized and depreciated according to the inventory (appraisal) method.

Required:

a. How would Winter account for the purchase of the new engines and the transfer of the old engines to the local mechanic if the old engines' costs are

  1. Known?
  2. Unknown?

b. 1. What are two assumptions underlying use of an accelerated depreciation method?
   2. How should Winter calculate the snowmobiles' depreciation?

c. How should Winter calculate and report the costs of the skis, poles, and boots in its balance sheets and income statements?

Problem 2   (15 to 25 minutes)

Portland Co. uses the straight-line depreciation method for depreciable assets. All assets are depreciated individually except manufacturing machinery, which is depreciated by the composite method.

During the year, Portland exchanged a delivery truck with Maine Co. for a larger delivery truck. It paid cash equal to 10% of the larger truck's value.

Required:

a. What factors should have influenced Portland's selection of the straight-line depreciation method?

b. How should Portland account for and report the truck exchange transaction?

c. 1. What benefits should Portland derive from using the composite method rather than the individual basis for manufacturing machinery?
   2. How should Portland have calculated the manufacturing machinery's annual depreciation expense in its first year of operation?

Problem 3   (15 to 25 minutes)

Jones Corporation has significant amounts of property, plant, and equipment.

Required:

a. Define what is meant by impairment of an operational asset (e.g., equipment).

b. How is the definition of impairment applied in practice? Include in the answer signs or indicators of impairment, loss determination, and measurement of losses.

c. Describe the accounting and reporting for an impairment loss in current and future periods.

d. How are losses on operational assets that management expects to dispose of measured, accounted for, and reported on the financial statements?

Problem 4   (30 to 40 minutes)

During 2002, Broca Co. had the following transactions:

• On January 2, Broca purchased the net assets of Amp Co. for $360,000. The fair value of Amp's identifiable net assets was $172,000. Broca believes that, due to the popularity of Amp's consumer products, the life of the resulting goodwill is unlimited.

• On February 1, Broca purchased a franchise to operate a ferry service from the state government for $60,000 and an annual fee of 1% of ferry revenues. The franchise expires after five years.

• On April 5, Broca was granted a patent that had been applied for by Amp. During 2002, Broca incurred legal costs of $51,000 to register the patent and an additional $85,000 to successfully prosecute a patent infringement suit against a competitor. Broca estimates the patent's economic life to be ten years.

Broca has determined that it is appropriate to amortize these intangibles on the straight-line basis over the maximum period permitted by generally accepted accounting principles, taking a full year's amortization in the year of acquisition.

Required:

a. 1. Describe the characteristics of intangible assets. Discuss the accounting for the purchase or internal development of intangible assets with an indeterminable life, such as goodwill.
   2. Over what period should intangible assets be amortized? How should this period be determined?

   3. Describe the financial statement disclosure requirements relating to Broca's intangible assets and expenses. Do not write the related footnotes.

b. Prepare a schedule showing the intangibles section of Broca's balance sheet at December 31, 2002, and a schedule showing the related expenses that would appear on Broca's 2002 income statement. Show supporting computations. (Assume none of the intangibles have been determined to be impaired.)

Problem 5   (15 to 20 minutes)

Carson Corporation is performing its annual test of the impairment of the goodwill related to its Technology reporting unit. The carrying value of goodwill allocated to the unit is $500,000. Using a multiple of revenue, Carson has determined the fair value of the Technology reporting unit to be $1,700,000 at 12/31/02, and the fair value and carrying value of the assets and liabilities were determined as follows:

	(In 000s)	
	Carrying value	*Fair value*
Cash	$ 200	$ 200
Accounts receivable	250	250
Inventory	350	400
Net Equipment	700	700
Patents	400	450
Goodwill	500	?
Accounts payable	(200)	(200)
Long-term debt	(300)	(300)
	1,900	

Required:

a. Contrast the accounting for goodwill acquired through a business combination with goodwill that is internally generated.

b. The first step in determining whether goodwill of a reporting unit is impaired is to compare the fair value of the unit to its carrying value. Make this comparison for the Technology reporting unit of Carson Company and describe the course of action that should be taken based on the results.

c. Calculate the amount of impairment of goodwill (if any) that should be recorded for the Technology reporting unit of Carson Corporation at 12/31/02, and prepare related journal entry.

Problem 6   (15 to 25 minutes)

Mono Tech Co. began operations in 1999 and confined its activities to one project. It purchased equipment to be used exclusively for research and development on the project, and other equipment that is to be used initially for research and development and subsequently for production. In 2000, Mono constructed and paid for a pilot plant that was used until December 2001 to determine the best manufacturing process for the project's product. In December 2001, Mono obtained a patent and received cash from the sale of the pilot plant. In 2002, a factory was constructed and commercial manufacture of the product began.

Required:

a.   **1.** According to the FASB conceptual framework, what are the three essential characteristics of an asset?

     2. How do Mono's project expenditures through 2001 meet the FASB conceptual framework's three essential characteristics of an asset? Do **not** discuss why the expenditures may **not** meet the characteristics of an asset.

     3. Why is it difficult to justify the classification of research and development expenditures as assets?

b. How should Mono report

     1. The effects of equipment expenditures in its income statements and balance sheets from 1999 through 2002?

     2. Pilot plant construction costs and sale proceeds in its 2000 and 2001 statements of cash flows using the direct method?

MULTIPLE-CHOICE ANSWERS

1. a	__ __	17. c	__ __	33. b	__ __	49. c	__ __	65. d	__ __
2. a	__ __	18. d	__ __	34. d	__ __	50. b	__ __	66. b	__ __
3. b	__ __	19. c	__ __	35. b	__ __	51. b	__ __	67. c	__ __
4. a	__ __	20. b	__ __	36. d	__ __	52. c	__ __	68. d	__ __
5. d	__ __	21. a	__ __	37. b	__ __	53. b	__ __	69. a	__ __
6. a	__ __	22. b	__ __	38. c	__ __	54. d	__ __	70. b	__ __
7. b	__ __	23. a	__ __	39. c	__ __	55. c	__ __	71. c	__ __
8. b	__ __	24. d	__ __	40. b	__ __	56. d	__ __	72. a	__ __
9. a	__ __	25. b	__ __	41. b	__ __	57. a	__ __	73. b	__ __
10. c	__ __	26. c	__ __	42. c	__ __	58. d	__ __	74. b	__ __
11. d	__ __	27. d	__ __	43. a	__ __	59. c	__ __	75. d	__ __
12. b	__ __	28. a	__ __	44. a	__ __	60. a	__ __	76. a	__ __
13. d	__ __	29. b	__ __	45. b	__ __	61. d	__ __	77. c	__ __
14. b	__ __	30. c	__ __	46. c	__ __	62. b	__ __		
15. a	__ __	31. d	__ __	47. c	__ __	63. d	__ __	1st: __/77 = __%	
16. d	__ __	32. c	__ __	48. b	__ __	64. b	__ __	2nd: __/77 = __%	

MULTIPLE-CHOICE ANSWER EXPLANATIONS

A. Acquisition Cost

1. **(a)** The cost of machinery includes all expenditures incurred in acquiring the asset and preparing it for use. Cost includes the purchase price, freight and handling charges, insurance on the machine while in transit, cost of special foundations, and costs of assembling, installation, and testing. All of the costs given in this problem are properly recorded as the cost of the machine. Therefore the cost to be recorded is $155,000 ($125,000 + $20,000 + $10,000).

2. **(a)** Any cost involved in preparing land for its ultimate use (such as a factory site) is considered part of the cost of the land. Before the land can be used as a building site, it must be purchased (involving costs such as purchase price, legal fees, and title insurance) and the old building must be razed (cost of demolition less proceeds from sale of scrap). The total balance in the land account should be $464,000.

Purchase price	$400,000
Legal fees	10,000
Title insurance	12,000
Net cost of demolition ($50,000 – $8,000)	42,000
	$464,000

B. Capitalization of Interest

3. **(b)** The amount of interest cost which should be capitalized during building construction is the **lower** of **avoidable interest** or **actual interest**. Avoidable interest equals the interest computed on the weighted-average amount of accumulated expenditures on the building ($40,000). Since actual interest is $70,000 ($50,000 + $20,000), the amount capitalized should be $40,000.

4. **(a)** The requirement is to calculate the amount of capitalized interest at 12/31/02. The requirements of SFAS 34 for capitalization of interest are met: (1) expenditures for the asset have been made, (2) activities that are necessary to get the asset ready for its intended use are in progress, and (3) interest cost is being incurred. The amount to be capitalized is the lower of avoidable interest or actual interest. Avoidable interest is the average accumulated expenditures multiplied by the appropriate interest rate or rates. Since $2,000,000 was spent on the building evenly throughout the year, the average accumulated expenditures were $1,000,000

($2,000,000 ÷ 2) and the avoidable interest was $120,000 ($1,000,000 x 12%). Since actual interest ($102,000) is less than avoidable interest, the actual interest cost is capitalized.

5. **(d)** SFAS 34 defines certain assets for which interest costs incurred in their production should be capitalized rather than expensed. Assets which "qualify" for interest capitalization are those constructed or otherwise produced for an enterprise's own use and those intended for sale or lease that are constructed or otherwise produced as **discrete projects**. SFAS 34 further stipulates that the capitalization period shall end when the asset is substantially complete and ready for its intended use. Based upon these criteria, the interest costs associated with the machinery for Bay's own use should be capitalized during the construction period and expensed after completion. Additionally, all costs associated with the machinery held for sale should be expensed because the machinery does not meet the "discrete project" criterion.

C. Nonmonetary Exchanges

6. **(a)** When the investment was acquired, it was recorded at cost—the fair market value of the asset surrendered to acquire it. The July 1 entry was

Inv. in Ace stock	3,000	
Truck		2,500
Gain on disposal		500 ($3,000 – $2,500)

The investment would be reported in the 12/31/02 balance sheet at $3,000. The book value of Ace's stock does not affect the amount recorded on Balt's books.

7. **(b)** The cash price of the new machine represents its fair market value (FMV). The FMV of the old machine can be determined by subtracting the cash portion of the purchase price ($6,000) from the total cost of the new machine: $20,500 – $6,000 = $14,500. Since the book value of the machine ($16,800) exceeds its FMV on the date of the trade-in ($14,500), the difference of $2,300 must be recognized as a loss. Note, however, that if the FMV of the old machine had **exceeded** its book value, the gain would not be recognized. In accordance with APB 29, gains on nonmonetary transactions involving similar productive assets are not recognized when boot is given.

8. **(b)** When similar assets are exchanged, boot is received, and a gain results, the exchange is treated as part sale and part exchange. The earnings process is assumed to be complete for the portion relating to the boot received. The gain recognized is computed as follows:

$$\frac{\text{Boot received}}{\text{Boot received} + \text{FMV of assets received}} \times \text{Total Gain} = \text{Gain Recognized}$$

Total Gain = (15,000 + 5,000) – 12,000 = 8,000

Assets received   Book Value of asset
  by Amble   given up by Beam

The gain recognized would be calculated as follows:

$$\frac{5,000}{15,000 + 5,000} \times 8,000 = \$2,000 \text{ gain recognized}$$

The asset acquired is recorded at its FMV less the gain not recognized ($15,000 – $6,000 = $9,000). This amount can also be computed as the **book** value of the asset surrendered plus the gain recognized less boot received ($12,000 + $2,000 – $5,000 = $9,000). The journal entry is

Truck (new)	9,000	
Cash	5,000	
Truck (old)		12,000
Gain on sale		2,000

9. **(a)** Per APB 29 if a loss is indicated by the terms of the transaction, the entire loss on the exchange should be recognized. In this case, a loss results because Transit received a similar asset whose book value equaled the fair market value of the asset received and paid cash. Therefore, Transit gave up more than they received, the difference being the loss.

10. **(c)** Per APB 29 when the exchange of nonmonetary assets includes an amount of monetary consideration, the Board believes that the receiver of monetary consideration has realized a partial gain on the exchange. To determine the partial gain to be recognized, first compute the total gain which is the difference between the fair market value of the nonmonetary asset given up and its book value. Then multiply the ratio of the **monetary** consideration received to the **total** consideration received (i.e., monetary consideration plus the estimated fair market value of the asset received) times the total gain. The result is the realized gain to be recognized. The Board further believes that the entity paying the monetary consideration should **not** recognize any gain until the earnings process is culminated. Note, however, that **all losses** on sales or exchanges are recognized immediately.

11. **(d)** Per APB 29, nonmonetary exchanges of dissimilar assets are accounted for on the basis of fair values, and both gains and losses recognized. The gain (or loss) for Vik is calculated as the difference between the fair value and cost of the car. Note that the retail/list price of an asset is not always representative of the FMV of the asset. An asset can often be purchased for less than the retail/list price.

12. **(b)** When similar assets are exchanged, in this case inventory, boot is received, and a gain results, the exchange is treated as part sale and part exchange. The earnings process is assumed to be complete for the portion relating to the boot received. The gain recognized is computed as follows:

$$\frac{\text{Boot received}}{\text{Boot received} + \text{FMV of assets received}} \times \text{Total gain} = \text{Gain Recognized}$$

Total Gain = (120,000 + 30,000) – 126,000 = 24,000

Assets received by Zaro   Book value of
                            asset given up by Zaro

In this case, it would be calculated as follows:

$$\frac{30,000}{(30,000 + 120,000)} \times 24,000 = \$4,800$$

13. **(d)** Per APB 29, a transfer of a nonmonetary asset in a nonreciprocal transfer should be recorded at the fair value of the asset transferred, with a gain or loss recognized on the disposition, whether the transfer is made to a stockholder or to another entity.

14. **(b)** A gain (loss) must be recognized when a nonmonetary asset is involuntarily converted into monetary assets even if the company reinvests the monetary assets in replacement nonmonetary assets. The gain or loss is the difference between the insurance proceeds received ($3,500) and the carrying value of the asset destroyed. The unadjusted carrying value ($2,500) must be adjusted for the capital expenditure ($700) which has not yet been recorded. When a major component of an asset like an engine is replaced, the preferred treatment is to take the old component off the books (with a loss recognized) and record the new component. When the book value of the component is unknown (as in this case), the cost of the new component ($700) is simply debited to the accumulated depreciation account. This increases the van's carrying value to $3,200 ($2,500 + $700), which means the gain is $300 ($3,500 – $3,200). Note that the $500 invoice should be recorded as repairs expense, and therefore does not affect the van's carrying value.

15. **(a)** Per FASB Interpretation 30, involuntary conversions of nonmonetary assets to monetary assets are monetary transactions for which gain or loss shall be recognized even though an enterprise reinvests or is obligated to reinvest the monetary assets in replacement nonmonetary assets. Accordingly, Lano would record the condemnation and replacement of the forest land as two separate transactions. Lano should recognize a gain on the condemnation and subsequently record the replacement land at the total purchase price. The net effect of these events is to increase the amount of forest land on Lano's balance sheet by the excess of the replacement land's cost over the condemned land's carrying amount, as shown below.

```
               ┌──── Purchase price of replacement land
               │
───────────────┼──── Condemnation award
               │
               │┌─── Gain recognized
               ├┤
               │└─── Condemned land's book value
```

D. Purchase of Groups of Fixed Assets

16. **(d)** The requirement is to determine the amount at which land acquired in a group purchase of fixed assets should be recorded. The total cost ($540,000) of the land and building should be allocated based on their relative fair market value (FMV). Current appraised value is a better indicator of FMV than the seller's original cost. Therefore, the land should be recorded at $216,000.

$$\frac{\text{FMV land}}{\text{Total FMV of asets purchased}} \quad x \quad \begin{array}{c}\text{Purchase price}\\\text{of group assets}\end{array}$$

$$\frac{200,000}{500,000} \quad x \quad 540,000 \quad = \quad \$216,000$$

There is no problem in recording the land at more than its appraised value since value is only an estimate of FMV.

E. Capital Versus Revenue Expenditures

17. (c) The requirement is to calculate the amount to be charged to repair and maintenance expense in 2002. Generally, a cost should be capitalized if it improves the asset and expensed if it merely maintains the asset at its current level. Continuing and frequent repairs ($40,000) should be expensed. Similarly, the cost of repainting the plant building ($10,000) and the cost of partially replacing the roof tiles ($14,000) should be expensed. These are ordinary, regularly occurring expenditures which maintain, rather than improve, the plant building. The work on the electrical wiring system ($32,000) is capitalized instead of expensed since it is a major improvement. Therefore, the total amount expensed is $64,000 ($40,000 + $10,000 + $14,000).

18. (d) The cost of the attachment ($84,000) should be capitalized because it is an **addition**. The cost of installing the attachment ($36,000) is also capitalized because this expenditure was required to get the attachment ready for its intended use. The overhaul costs ($26,000 + $14,000 = $40,000) are also capitalized. Even though the overhaul did not increase useful life, it is a capital expenditure because it increased productivity. The total amount capitalized is $160,000 ($84,000 + $36,000 + $40,000).

19. (c) When an entity suffers a casualty loss to an asset, the accounting loss is recorded at the net carrying value of the damaged asset, if known. In this case, the cost and related accumulated depreciation are identifiable. The entity should therefore recognize a loss in the current period equal to the carrying amount of the damaged portion of the building. The refurbishing of the building, which is an economic event separate from the fire damage, should be treated similarly to the purchase of other assets or betterments. The cost of refurbishing the building should therefore be capitalized and depreciated over the shorter of the refurbishment's useful lives or the useful life of the building.

Loss	xxx	(Plug)
Acc. Depr.	xxx	
Building		xxx
Building	xxx	
Cash		xxx

Answer (a) is incorrect because in order to reduce the accumulated depreciation account, the useful life of the asset must be extended. In this case, there is no mention of this fact. Answer (d) is incorrect because it fails to recognize the casualty loss and properly remove the cost and accumulated depreciation on the damaged portion of the building from the accounting records.

NOTE: If the components of the damaged portion are not identifiable, the following entry would be made:

Loss	xxx	
Cash		xxx

20. (b) Generally, a cost should be capitalized if it improves the efficiency of the asset or extends its useful life and expensed if it merely maintains the asset at its current

level. Since an overall reduction in production costs is expected, efficiency must have been improved by the steps taken by Derby. In this problem, it appears that both the building modification and the production line rearrangement contributed to the improved efficiency in the production process. Therefore, both costs should be capitalized.

F. Depreciation

21. (a) Machinery is recorded at its historical cost, which is measured by the cash or **cash equivalent price** of obtaining the machine and preparing it for use. The journal entry to record this acquisition would be

Machinery	110,000		(cash equiv.)
Discount on N.P.	20,000		($130,000 – $110,000)
Notes payable		120,000	(24 x $5,000)
Cash		10,000	

The $20,000 discount represents future interest expense (the cost associated with paying for the asset over two years instead of immediately) rather than part of the cost of the machine. Straight-line depreciation for 2002 is computed as follows:

(Cost – Salvage value)	x	1/useful life	=	Depr. expense
($110,000 – $5,000)	x	1/10	=	$10,500

22. (b) The formula for 200% double-declining balance (DDB) depreciation is

$$\left(\begin{array}{c}\text{Beginning-of-year}\\\text{book value}\end{array}\right) x \left(\begin{array}{c}\text{DDB}\\\text{rate}\end{array}\right) = \text{Depreciation expense}$$

The DDB rate is two times the straight-line rate (in this case, 1/5 x 2 = 2/5 or 40%). Therefore, depreciation for the first two years is

2000: $50,000 x 40%	=	$20,000
2001: ($50,000 – $20,000) x 40%	=	12,000
		$32,000

In 2002, Turtle switches to the straight-line method. The book value ($50,000 – $32,000 = $18,000) would be depreciated over the remaining three years (five years less two gone by). Therefore, 2002 depreciation is $6,000 ($18,000 x 1/3) and 12/31/02 accumulated depreciation is $38,000 ($32,000 + $6,000).

23. (a) The requirement is to calculate the amount of depreciation expense to be recorded in 2002. After three years (2000-2002), accumulated depreciation is $72,000. Therefore, the method that was used was the sum-of-the-years' digits (SYD) method. Using this method, after three years the balance in accumulated depreciation would be 12/15 of the depreciable base (5/15 + 4/15 + 3/15). The depreciable base is the cost ($110,000) less the residual value ($20,000), or $90,000. Thus, using the SYD method, accumulated depreciation at 12/31/01 would be $72,000 ($90,000 x 12/15), which matches the amount given in the problem. 2002 depreciation expense, using the SYD method is $12,000 ($90,000 x 2/15).

24. (d) From 1/2/99 to 12/31/01, depreciation was recorded using an eight-year life. Yearly depreciation was $33,000 ($264,000 ÷ 8), and accumulated depreciation at 12/31/01 was $99,000 (3 x $33,000). In 2002, the estimated useful life was changed to six years total with a salvage value of $24,000. Therefore, the 12/31/01 book value ($264,000 – $99,000 = $165,000) is depreciated down to the $24,000 salvage value over a remaining useful life of three years (6 years total – 3 years already recorded). The 2002 depreciation expense is $47,000 [($165,000 – $24,000) ÷ 3], increasing accumulated depreciation to $146,000 ($99,000 + $47,000).

25. **(b)** The solutions approach is to set up a T-account for **accumulated depreciation** and solve for the unknown.

	Accumulated Depreciation		
		370,000	12/31/01
2002 retirements	?	55,000	2002 depr. expense
		400,000	12/31/02

The 12/31/01 and 12/31/02 balances were given in the schedule. The 2002 depreciation expense would be recorded by debiting the expense account and crediting accumulated depreciation. The accumulated depreciation would be debited for the property, plant, and equipment retirements. To balance the T-account, the debit must be $25,000. Alternatively, an equation can be used as shown below.

$$\$370,000 + \$55,000 - X = \$400,000$$
$$425,000 - X = 400,000$$
$$X = 25,000$$

$$370,000 = 12/31/01 \text{ balance}$$
$$55,000 = 2002 \text{ depreciation expense}$$
$$400,000 = 12/31/02 \text{ balance}$$
$$X = \text{retirements}$$

26. **(c)** After reviewing the different methods, you might realize that the method with the highest carrying amount would result in a loss or

Gain/loss = Proceeds – Carrying amount
$$= 50\% \, C - [C - 50\% \, (C - S)]$$
$$= 50\% \, C - [C - 50\% \, (C - 20\%C)]$$
$$= .5C - [1.00C - .5(1.00C - .2C)]$$
$$= .5C - [.6C]$$

Carrying amount > Proceeds
$$\therefore \text{Loss}$$

27. **(d)** The formula to compute straight-line depreciation is

$$\frac{\text{Original cost less salvage value}}{\text{Estimated useful life}}$$

The formula to determine depreciation using the productive output method is

$$\frac{\text{Current activity (output)}}{\text{Total expected activity}} \times \frac{\text{Original cost less}}{\text{salvage value}}$$

Note that both of these methods use cost minus salvage value as the depreciable base of the asset. This means that after all depreciation has been recorded using either method, the net asset will be recorded at salvage value, and accumulated depreciation will equal the original cost minus salvage value.

28. **(a)** Depreciation is a method of allocating the cost of an asset in a systematic and rational manner. Since the units-of-production method of depreciation is most appropriate when depreciation is a function of activity, answer (a) is correct. Answer (b) is incorrect because this situation warrants the use of a depreciation method based on the passage of time. Answers (c) and (d) are incorrect because both support the use of an accelerated method of depreciation.

29. **(b)** Under the sum-of-the-years' digits (SYD) method, depreciation expense is computed by applying declining fractions to the depreciable cost of the asset. The denominator is the sum of the years in the life of the asset (1 + 2 + 3 + 4 + 5 = 15 in this case). Annual depreciation would be computed as follows:

1999	Original cost less salvage value	x	5/15
2000	Original cost less salvage value	x	4/15
2001	Original cost less salvage value	x	3/15
2002	Original cost less salvage value	x	2/15
Total	Original cost less salvage value	x	14/15

Accumulated depreciation at December 31, 2002, would be (original cost less salvage value) multiplied by 14/15.

30. **(c)** Sum-of-the-years' digits (SYD) depreciation = (Cost less Salvage value) x Applicable fraction.

Where applicable fraction = $\dfrac{\text{Number of years of estimated life remaining as of the beginning of the year}}{\text{SYD}}$

and SYD = $\dfrac{n(n+1)}{2}$ where n = estimated useful life

Calculated as

Year 1 (2000) = $18,000* $\times \dfrac{4}{10}$ = $7,200

Year 2 (2001) = $18,000 $\times \dfrac{3}{10}$ = $5,400

Year 3 (2002) = $18,000 $\times \dfrac{2}{10}$ = $3,600

* ($20,000 – $2,000)

On December 31, 2002, the carrying amount of Spiro's asset equals $3,800 (the asset's cost of $20,000 minus accumulated depreciation of $16,200**).

** ($7,200 + $5,400 + $3,500)

31. **(d)** Line I represents depreciation expense that stays constant over time (i.e., straight-line). Both sum-of-the-years' digits and double-declining balance are accelerated depreciation methods, and hence the depreciation expense for these two methods does not stay constant over time. Line II represents depreciation expense that decreases at a constant rate (i.e., a linear function) and thus would be the pattern of depreciation for sum-of-the-years' digits. Line III represents depreciation expense that decreases at a decreasing rate (i.e., a nonlinear function) and thus would be the pattern of depreciation for the double-declining balance method.

32. **(c)** Composite (group) depreciation averages the service life of a number of property units and depreciates the group as if it were a single unit. The term "group" is used when the assets are similar; the term "composite" is used when they are dissimilar. The mechanical application of both of these methods is identical. The depreciation rate is the following ratio:

$$\frac{\text{Sum of annual SL depreciation of individual assets}}{\text{Total asset cost}}$$

Thus, both group and composite depreciation utilize the straight-line depreciation method.

33. **(b)** The solutions approach is to prepare the journal entry that would be made when an asset is retired under the composite depreciation method.

Cash	(cash proceeds)	
Accumulated depreciation	(plug)	
Truck		(original cost)

The net decrease in the carrying amount of the assets is the credit to the asset account less the plug to accumulated depreciation. This amount would be equal to the **cash proceeds received**.

G. Disposals and Impairment of Value

34. **(d)**   SFAS 144 requires that when management plans to dispose of long-lived assets and limited-lived intangibles, the assets shall be reported at the lower of carrying amount or fair value less cost to sell.

35. **(b)**   Per SFAS 144, losses associated with long-lived assets which are to be disposed of are to be reported as a component of income from continuing operations before income taxes for entities preparing income statements. Losses on long-lived assets to be disposed of are neither unusual nor infrequent occurrences. These losses are not part of selling or general and administrative expenses and they are not disclosed net of tax. Discontinued operations result from disposal of a separate business component.

36. **(d)**   In 2001, Taft recognized a loss on the long-lived assets that were to be sold and changed the carrying amount of these assets to fair value less cost to sell. In 2002, the assets have still not been sold. The loss recognized has been more than recovered. Per SFAS 144, subsequent revisions in estimates of fair value less cost to sell shall be reported as adjustments of the carrying amount of an asset to be disposed of. However, the carrying amount may not be increased above the carrying amount prior to impairment. The same amount recognized as a loss in 2001 would be recognized as a recovery (gain) in the 2002 income statement.

37. **(b)**   According to SFAS 144, the reduced carrying amount of Cranston's assets ($920,000) should be accounted for as their new cost, and this amount should be depreciated over the remaining useful life of five years. Restoration of previously recognized impairment losses is prohibited. Therefore, Cranston should report .80 x $920,000 or $736,000 as the carrying amount of its impaired long-lived assets on its December 31, 2002 balance sheet.

38. **(c)**   The requirement is to determine when an asset is impaired. An asset is impaired when the sum of the expected future cash flows is less than the carrying amount of the asset. Per SFAS 144, the expected future cash flows are **not** discounted and do not consider interest charges. Answer (c) refers to one way to measure a loss once it has been determined that an asset has been impaired.

39. **(c)**   The loss on impairment is calculated by subtracting the machine's actual fair value from its carrying value at the date of impairment.

$10,000	initial cost of machine		$10,000	Cost on 7/1/00
−$ 500	salvage value		− 2,375	accumulated depreciation
$ 9,500	depreciable base		$ 7,625	carrying value on 12/31/02
÷ 10	year life		− $ 3,000	actual fair value on 12/31/02
$950	depreciation per year		$ 4,625	loss on impairment
x 2.5	years (7/1/00 - 12/31/02)			
$ 2,375	accumulated depreciation			

40. **(b)**   Under SFAS 144, when an asset has been determined to be impaired, it is written down to fair value and loss on impairment is recognized. SFAS 144 specifically states that restoration of previously recognized impairment losses is prohibited.

41. **(b)**   According to SFAS 144, a long-lived asset is considered impaired if the future cash flows expected to result from the use of the asset and its eventual disposition are less than the carrying amount of the asset. If deemed impaired, the asset's carrying value is reduced to fair value and a loss on impairment is recognized for the difference (Carrying value – Fair value). In this case, the asset is **not** impaired, as the net cash inflows of $175,000 are greater than the 8/31/02 carrying amount (book value) of $170,000. Therefore, the carrying amount of the asset ($170,000) remains unchanged.

42. **(c)**   SFAS 144, states, "an impairment loss for assets to be held and used shall be reported as a component of income from continuing operations before income taxes for entities presenting an income statement and in the statement of activities of a not-for-profit organization. Although there is no requirement to report a subtotal such as "income from operations," entities that present such a subtotal must include the impairment loss in that subtotal.

43. **(a)**   The undiscounted expected future cash flows ($175,000) are less than the carrying amount of the equipment ($200,000). Therefore, the equipment is deemed impaired. The impairment loss is calculated in the following way:

Carrying amount of the equipment on December 31, 2002	$200,000
Fair value of the equipment on December 31, 2002	125,000
Impairment loss reported on 2002 income statement	$ 75,000

44. **(b)**   According to SFAS 144, "after an impairment loss is recognized, the reduced carrying amount of the asset shall be accounted for as its new cost." This new cost (the fair value of the asset at the date of impairment, or $135,000) shall be depreciated over the asset's remaining useful life (twenty-seven months). Therefore, the depreciation expense for June is $5,000 ($135,000 ÷ 27 months x 1 month).

45. **(b)**   Per SFAS 144, recoveries of impairment losses shall not be recognized.

46. **(c)**   According to SFAS 144, the loss due to impairment of long-lived assets is measured by deducting the asset's fair value from the carrying (book) value.

47. **(c)**   SFAS 144 requires long-lived assets and limited lived intangibles to be reviewed for impairment whenever circumstances and situations change such that there is an indication that the carrying amount might not be recoverable. A specific time frame for review of asset impairment, every year or every three years, is not required.

48. **(b)**   The undiscounted expected future cash flows ($300,000) are less than the carrying amount of the equipment ($350,000). Thus, the equipment is determined to be impaired. The impairment loss is calculated as follows:

Carrying value - 12/31/02	$350,000
Fair value - 12/31/02	250,000
Impairment loss reported on 2002 income statement	$100,000

49. **(c)**   According to SFAS 144, after an impairment loss is recognized, the reduced carrying amount of the asset shall be accounted for as its new cost. This new cost (the fair value of the asset at the date of impairment, or $261,000) shall be depreciated over the asset's remaining useful life (58 months). Therefore, the depreciation expense for September is $4,500 ($261,000 ÷ 58 months x 1 month).

H. Depletion

50. (b) The depletion charge per unit is the **depletion base** (net cost of the resource) divided by the **estimated units of the resource**. Vorst's depletion base is $2,880,000, as computed below.

Cost of mine	$2,640,000
Development cost	360,000
Restoration cost	180,000
Residual value	(300,000)
	$2,880,000

Note that the present value of the restoration costs are recorded as required by SFAS 143. The depletion charge is $2.40 per ton ($2,880,000 ÷ 1,200,000 tons). Since 60,000 tons were removed and sold, depletion of $144,000 (60,000 x $2.40) is included in Vorst's 2002 income statement. Note that the amount of depletion included in the income statement depends on the tons **sold**. If more tons were removed than sold, part of the depletion would be included in the cost of ending inventory rather than in the income statement.

J. Intangible Assets (APB 17)

51. (b) The software should be valued at the lower of its unamortized cost or its net realizable value. The software's unamortized cost is $450,000, which is equal to $600,000 – $150,000 ($600,000/4). Answer (c) is incorrect because the software's unamortized cost is less than its net realizable value.

52. (c) Judd Company would record the trademark at its cost of $500,000. The unamortized cost on the seller's books ($380,000) is irrelevant to the buyer. The trademark has a remaining useful life of fifty years. Therefore, the 2002 amortization expense and 12/31/02 accumulated amortization is $10,000 ($500,000 ÷ 50 years).

53. (b) SFAS 142 states that a company should record as an asset the cost of intangible assets such as goodwill **acquired from other entities**. SFAS 142 also states that **costs of developing** intangible assets such as goodwill "which are not specifically identifiable, have indeterminate lives, or are inherent in a continuing business and related to an entity as a whole" should be expensed when incurred. Therefore, only the $200,000 (and not the additional $80,000) should be capitalized as goodwill. In accordance with SFAS 142 goodwill should not be amortized.

54. (d) In determining the useful life of an intangible, SFAS 142 indicates that consideration should be given to the legal, regulatory or contractual life, including rights to extension. Since Northern has the ability and intent to renew the rights indefinitely, the intangible should not be amortized.

55. (c) Before 2001, Lava would record total amortization of $27,000 [($90,000 x 1/10) x 3 years], resulting in a 12/31/01 carrying amount of $63,000 ($90,000 – $27,000). Since the patent became worthless at 12/31/02 due to government prohibition of the product, the entire carrying amount ($63,000) should be charged against income in 2002 as an impairment loss.

56. (d) SFAS 142 states that goodwill should not be amortized. Instead, goodwill remains at the amount established at the time of the business combination unless it is determined to be impaired. SFAS 142 requires the testing of goodwill for impairment annually, or more often if events and circumstances indicate that goodwill may be impaired.

57. (a) Costs incurred in connection with securing a patent, as well as attorney's fees and other unrecovered costs of a successful legal suit to protect the patent, can be capitalized as part of patent costs. Therefore, answer (a) is correct because legal fees and other costs incurred to successfully defend a patent should be amortized along with the acquisition cost over the remaining economic life of the patent. Answer (b) is incorrect because legal fees and other direct costs incurred in registering a patent should be capitalized and amortized on a straight-line basis over its economic life, not five years. Answers (c) and (d) are incorrect because research and development costs related to the development of the product, process or idea that is subsequently patented must be expensed as incurred, not capitalized and amortized.

58. (d) SFAS 142 requires goodwill to be allocated to reporting units which are operating segments of the business or one level below. Goodwill is also tested for impairment at the level of the reporting unit.

59. (c) Goodwill impairment is determined at the level of the individual reporting unit. It is the difference between the carrying amount of goodwill and its implied value. The carrying amounts of goodwill of the Retailing and Service reporting units are greater than their implied values. Therefore, an impairment loss should be recognized in the amount of $15,000 ($30,000 + $20,000) – ($25,000 + $10,000).

60. (a) There are two steps in the test of impairment of goodwill. The first is to compare the carrying value of the reporting unit to its fair value. If the fair value exceeds the carrying value there is no need to perform the second step of valuing the unit's assets and liabilities. Goodwill is never tested at the entity level.

61. (d) Since the fair value of the reporting unit is less than its carrying amount, the second step in the test should be performed. The assets and liabilities of the unit should be valued and compared to value of the total unit. The implied value of goodwill is the difference. The impairment is equal to the difference between the implied value and the carrying amount of the goodwill.

K. Reporting on the Costs of Start-Up Activities

62. (b) Start-up activities are defined broadly as those onetime activities related to opening a new facility as well as introducing a new product or service and conducting business in a new territory (SOP 98-5). Certain costs that may be incurred in conjunction with start-up activities are not subject to these provisions. These costs include the costs of acquiring long-lived assets such as production equipment, costs of advertising, and license fees, and are not subject to the provisions of SOP 98-5. Answer (b) which includes the costs of training local employees ($120,000) and travel costs of salaried employees ($40,000) is the correct answer.

63. (d) Organization costs are those incurred in the formation of a corporation. Per SOP 98-5, these costs should be expensed as incurred. The rationale is that uncertainty exists concerning the future benefit of these costs in future years. Thus, they are properly recorded as an expense in 2002.

64. **(b)** According to SOP 98-5, the costs of raising capital and the costs of acquiring or constructing long-lived assets and getting them ready for their intended use are not expensed as incurred. Such costs should be accounted for in accordance with other existing authoritative accounting literature. Research and development (R&D) costs are expensed as incurred per SFAS 2.

L.   Research and Development Costs (SFAS 2)

65. **(d)** Research and development (R&D) costs are defined in SFAS 2. SFAS 2 provides detailed lists of examples of activities that would be included in R&D costs and expenses, and that would be excluded from R&D costs and possibly capitalized. Among those items listed as being part of R&D costs are design of tools, jigs, molds, and dies involving new technology ($125,000) and modification of the formulation of a process ($160,000), for a total R&D expense of $285,000. Included in the items listed in SFAS 2 as **not** being part of R&D costs are troubleshooting breakdowns during production ($100,000), and adaptation of existing capability for a specific customer ($110,000).

66. **(b)** Per SFAS 2, all R&D costs must be expensed when incurred. However, R&D costs incurred when performing R&D work under contract for other entities are specifically excluded from the requirements of SFAS 2. Generally such costs are deferred and matched with revenue under the completed-contract or percentage-of-completion method. The other costs listed would all be expensed in 2002. Therefore, Ball's 2002 research and development expense is $1,380,000 ($300,000 + $700,000 + $200,000 + $180,000).

67. **(c)** Per SFAS 2, all R&D costs are to be charged to expense when incurred. SFAS 2 specifically includes as R&D costs the cost of designing, constructing, and testing preproduction prototypes, and the cost of R&D equipment (unless it has alternative future uses). Therefore, $340,000 ($60,000 + $200,000 + $80,000) is classified as R&D costs and expensed. The legal costs incurred to obtain a patent ($10,000) are capitalized in the patents account.

68. **(d)** In SFAS 2, the FASB excludes from its definitions of research and development expense the acquisition, development, or improvement of a product or process for use in its **selling or administrative activities**. Both costs given in this problem relate to selling or administrative activities, so the expenditures of $175,000 would not be reported as research and development expense.

69. **(a)** SFAS 2 requires research and development costs to be expensed as incurred except for fixed assets, intangible assets, or materials purchased that have alternative future uses. Tambon purchased equipment to be used for research and development, but the equipment can only be used for that project. Therefore, the cost of the equipment must be expensed in 2002 as it has no alternative future uses.

M.   Computer Software Costs (SFAS 86)

70. **(b)** Costs incurred in creating a computer software product should be charged to research and development

expense when incurred until **technological feasibility** has been established for the product. Technological feasibility is established upon completion of a detailed program design or working model. In this case, $23,000 would be recorded as expense ($13,000 for completion of detailed program design and $10,000 for coding and testing to establish technological feasibility). Costs incurred from the point of technological feasibility until the time when product costs are incurred are capitalized as software costs. In this situation, $59,000 is capitalized as software cost ($24,000 + $20,000 + $15,000). Product costs that can be easily associated with the inventory items are reported as inventory (in this case, $25,000 for duplication of computer software and training materials and $9,000 of packaging costs, for a total of $34,000).

71. **(c)** Costs incurred in creating a computer software product should be charged to research and development expense when incurred until **technological feasibility** has been established. Technological feasibility is established upon completion of a detailed program design or working model. In this case, $23,000 would be recorded as expense ($13,000 for completion of detailed program design and $10,000 for coding and testing to establish technological feasibility). Costs incurred from the point of technological feasibility until the time when product costs are incurred are capitalized as software costs. In this situation, $59,000 is capitalized as software cost ($24,000 + $20,000 + $15,000). Product costs that can be easily associated with the inventory items are reported as inventory (in this case, $25,000 for duplication of computer software and training materials and $9,000 of packaging costs, for a total of $34,000).

72. **(a)** Per SFAS 86, the annual amortization of capitalized software costs shall be the greater of

1.   The ratio of the software's current sales to its expected total sales, or
2.   The straight-line method over the economic life of the product.

In this case, the ratio of current to expected total sales is 30% (given). The annual straight-line rate is 20% per year (1 ÷ economic life of five years). The 30% amortization should be recorded in 2002, since it is the higher of the two. The unamortized cost on the 12/31/02 balance sheet should, therefore, be 70% (100% – 30% amortization). Note that SFAS 86 requires that the unamortized cost of capitalized software products must be compared to the net realizable value of those assets at each balance sheet date. Any excess of the amortized cost over the net realizable value must be written off. In this case, the net realizable value (90%) was **above** the unamortized cost (70%), so no additional write-off was required.

73. **(b)** According to SOP 98-1, *Accounting for the Costs of Computer Software Developed or Obtained for Internal Use*, internal-use software is software having the following characteristics: (1) The software is acquired, internally developed, or modified solely to meet the entity's internal needs, and (2) during the software's development or modification, no substantive plan exists to market the software externally.

74. **(b)** Application and development costs create probable future benefit. Therefore, they should be capitalized as incurred. However, preliminary costs are similar to research and development costs and are expensed as incurred, not capitalized.

75.   (d)   Preliminary costs are similar to research and development costs; therefore, they are expensed as incurred. Postimplementation costs such as training are not considered software development costs at all and are expensed as incurred.

N.   Development Stage Enterprises (SFAS 7)

76.   (a)   Per SFAS 7, a development stage enterprise shall follow the same revenue and expense recognition principles and issue the same basic financial statements as an established operating enterprise, but shall disclose certain additional information. Per SFAS 7, a development stage company shall use the same generally accepted accounting principles that apply to established operating enterprises to govern the recognition of revenue and to determine whether a cost is to be capitalized or expensed as incurred.

77.   (c)   Per SFAS 7, a development stage enterprise shall issue the same basic financial statements as an established operating enterprise, but shall disclose certain additional information. An income statement, in addition to showing amounts of revenues and expenses for each period covered by the income statement, shall include the cumulative amounts from the enterprise's inception.

OTHER OBJECTIVE ANSWERS AND ANSWER EXPLANATIONS

Problem 1

Items 1 through 6 represent questions concerning expenditures for goods held for resale and equipment and whether these expenditures should be capitalized or expensed as a period cost. The general concept that determines whether expenditures should be product costs and, therefore, capitalized or expensed as period costs is whether or not these expenditures "attach" themselves to the assets of inventory or equipment. Costs that "attach" themselves to assets are those that are directly connected with bringing the goods or equipment to the place of business of the buyer and converting such goods to a salable (inventory) or unusable (equipment) condition.

1. **(C)** Freight charges are directly connected with bringing the goods to the place of business of the buyer.

2. **(C)** Insurance charges are directly connected with bringing the goods to the place of business of the buyer.

3. **(E)** Only interest costs related to continued assets constructed for internal use or assets produced as discrete products for sale or lease should be capitalized. The informational benefit of capitalization does not justify the cost of the accounting for the interest as a product cost.

4. **(C)** Direct cost of bringing the equipment to the buyer.

5. **(C)** Direct cost of converting the equipment to a usable condition.

6. **(E)** Does not relate to bringing the equipment to the buyer or putting it into a usable condition.

7. **($600,000)** Since the land and building were purchased together, the cost of each must be allocated based on the relative market value. The land and building were purchased together for a total cost of $1,000,000 ($800,000 cash + $200,000 mortgage assumption). For property tax purposes, the building is deemed to be 60% of the value of the land and building. Therefore, the cost of the building should be recorded at $600,000 ($1,000,000 x 60%).

8. **($503,000)** As the lease is classified as a capital lease, Link must record an asset and liability based on the present value of the minimum lease payments. However, the leased assets cannot be recorded at an amount greater than the fair value. To determine the minimum value of the lease payments, Link should discount the future payments using the **lesser** of the lessee's (Link's) incremental borrowing rate (9%) or the lessor's implicit rate if **known** by the lessee. Therefore, since Link does not know the lessor's implicit rate, Link's rate of 9% should be used. The recorded value would be $100,000 x 5.03 = $503,000, which is less than the fair value.

9. **($370,000)** In recording a nonmonetary exchange, the asset received is recorded at the book value of the asset given up plus any boot given when gains and losses are not recognized. Gains and losses are not recognized when the earnings process is not considered complete (when **similar** assets are exchanged), and when the gain or loss cannot be computed. In Link's case, the earnings process is not complete as similar assets are being exchanged. The following fact pattern exists for Link:

	Boot	*FV*	*BV*	*Gain (Loss)*
Land given	50,000	450,000	320,000	130,000
Land received		500,000		

Link will record the land received from Club at the book value of the land given up plus the boot given ($320,000 + 50,000 = $370,000).

An alternative method to calculate the value to record the land at is to subtract the deferred gain from the fair value of the land received ($500,000 – 130,000 = $370,000).

10. **($315,000)** On Club's books the following situation exists:

	Boot	*FV*	*BV*	*Gain (Loss)*
Land given		500,000	350,000	150,000
Land received	50,000	450,000		

An exception to the nonrecognition of gain on similar assets exists when boot is received. The earnings process is considered complete for the portion related to the boot received, but not complete for the portion related to the asset received. A gain is recognized only for the portion related to the boot. The gain is computed as follows:

$$\frac{\text{Boot received}}{\text{Boot received} + \text{FV of asset received}} \times \text{Total gain} = \text{Gain recognized}$$

$$\frac{50,000}{50,000 + 450,000} \times 150,000 = \$15,000$$

The land received will be recorded at its fair value less the gain deferred.

$$\$450,000 - (150,000 - 15,000) = \$315,000.$$

An alternative method is to record the land received at the book value of the land given less the boot received plus the gain recognized, as follows:

$$\$350,000 - 50,000 + 15,000 = \$315,000.$$

11. **($90,000)** Under the straight-line method of depreciation, the depreciation expense would be calculated as follows:

$$\frac{\text{Cost salvage value}}{\text{Estimated life}} = \frac{\$864,000 - 144,000}{8} = \$90,000$$

Depreciation expense would be $90,000 for all eight years, 2001-2009.

12.   (**$162,000**)   The double-declining balance method is calculated by taking two times the straight-line rate times the net book value at the beginning of each year, but not below the salvage value. Furthermore the salvage value is not deducted to arrive at the depreciable base. The calculation would be as follows:

	NBV		*Depreciation expense*
2001	$864,000 x (1/8 x 2)	=	$216,000
2002	($864,000 – 216,000) x (1/8 x 2)	=	$162,000

13.   (**$140,000**)   Under the sum-of-the-years' digits method, the depreciation expense is calculated as follows:

$$2001 \qquad 8 \div \frac{8(8+1)}{2} \qquad x \qquad (\$864,000 - \$144,000) \qquad = \qquad \$160,000$$

$$2002 \qquad (7 \div 36) \qquad x \qquad (\$864,000 - \$144,000) \qquad = \qquad \$140,000$$

14.   (**$120,000**)   The units of production method is a type of physical usage depreciation that is based on activity. The formula is as follows:

$$\frac{\text{Current activity/output}}{\text{Total expected activity/output}} \qquad x \qquad \text{Depreciable base} \qquad = \qquad \text{Annual depreciation}$$

Depreciation expense for 2002 is calculated as follows:

$$\frac{300,000 \text{ units}}{1,800,000 \text{ units}} \qquad x \qquad (\$864,000 - \$144,000) \qquad = \qquad \$120,000$$

ANSWER OUTLINE

Problem 1   Replacement of Components; Accelerated
                Depreciation; Inventory Method of Depre-
                ciation

a.   1.   Old engines' costs **known**

    •   Remove old engines' costs and accumulated
depreciation from account balances
    •   Record current asset (prepaid repairs and
maintenance) at FMV of old engines
    •   Operating gain/loss = difference between old
engines' carrying value and fair value
    •   Record new engines and related liability at new
engines' cost

2.   Old engines' costs **unknown**

    •   Record current asset (prepaid repairs and
maintenance) at FMV of old engines
    •   Increase snowmobiles account by difference be-
tween new engines' costs and old engines' fair value or
    •   Decrease accumulated depreciation by same
amount
    •   Record liability at new engines' cost

b.   1.   Assumptions underlying use of accelerated de-
             preciation

    •   Asset productivity greater in earlier years
    •   Provides a more constant cost over the years
    •   Avoids risk of obsolescence

2.   Depreciation expense = double the straight-line
         rate times book value

c.   Balance Sheet

    •   Report as noncurrent asset
    •   Record amount equal to physical quantities of
items times an appraised amount

    Income Statement

    •   Report depreciation expense
    •   Depreciation exp. = BI + Purchases – EI

UNOFFICIAL ANSWER

Problem 1   Replacement of Components; Accelerated
                Depreciation; Inventory Method of Depre-
                ciation

a.   1.   When the old engines' costs are known, the snowmobiles account is decreased by the old engines' costs, and
accumulated depreciation is decreased by the accumulated
depreciation on the old engines. A current asset would be
recorded for the fair value of the future repair and maintenance services. The net difference between the old engines'
carrying amounts and their fair values is recorded as an operating gain or loss. To record the new engines' acquisition,
both the snowmobiles account and accounts payable are
increased by the new engines' costs.

2.   If the old engines' costs are unknown, then either
the snowmobiles account would be increased or accumulated depreciation would be decreased by the difference
between the new engines' costs and the old engines' fair
values.

b.   1.   Assumptions underlying use of an accelerated depreciation method include

    •   An asset is more productive in the earlier years
of its estimated useful life. Therefore, greater depreciation charges in the earlier years would be matched
against the greater revenues generated in the earlier
years.
    •   Repair and maintenance costs are often higher
in later periods and an accelerated depreciation method
results in a more nearly annual constant total cost over
the years of use.
    •   An asset may become obsolete before the end
of its originally estimated useful life. The risk associated with estimated long-term cash flows is greater than
the risk associated with near-term cash flows. Accelerated depreciation recognizes this condition.

2.   Winter should calculate snowmobile depreciation
by applying twice the straight-line rate to their carrying
amounts.

c.   Under the inventory (appraisal) method, Winter calculates the ending undepreciated cost on the skis, poles, and
boots by multiplying the physical quantities of these items
on hand by an appraised amount. This ending undepreciated
cost is classified as a noncurrent asset. Depreciation included in continuing operations equals the sum of the beginning balance and purchases for the year less the ending undepreciated cost.

ANSWER OUTLINE

Problem 2   Selection of Deprec. Method, Nonmonetary
                Exchange, and Composite Deprec. Method

a.   Factors influencing selection of SL method
        Equal amounts of asset's service potential used each pe-
        riod
        If reasons for decline in service potential are unclear,
        other reasons are
            Ease of recordkeeping
            Use of SL for similar assets
            Use by others in industry

b.   Accounting for the truck exchange
        First, record AD to date of exchange
        Then, if original truck's carrying value > FMV

Truck (new)	xxx		(Recorded at FMV)
Loss	xxx		(Part of income from
			continuing operations)
AD	xxx		
Truck (old)		xxx	} (Original truck's carrying value)
Cash		xxx	

        If original truck's carrying value is < FMV

Truck (new)	xxx		(FMV – unrecognized gain)
AD	xxx		
Truck (old)		xxx	} (Original truck's carrying value)
Cash		xxx	

        Gain not recognized, but decreases carrying value of
        new truck

c.   1.   Benefits derived from using composite method
             Bookkeeping greatly simplified
             Avoids income fluctuations as result of recognizing
                gains (losses) on dispositions
                 Unrecognized losses on early dispositions offset
                    by continuing depreciation on machines used
                    beyond average life
2.   Calculation of manufacturing machinery's annual
         depreciation expense

(a) $$\frac{\text{Depreciable cost (CRV) for a single machine}}{\text{Estimated life for that machine}}$$

= Annual S-L depreciation for each machine

(b) $$\frac{S \text{ Annual depreciation for each machine}}{S \text{ Individual capitalized cost}}$$

= Annual composite depreciation rate (%)

UNOFFICIAL ANSWER

Problem 2 Selection of Deprec. Method, Nonmonetary Exchange, and Composite Deprec. Method

a. Portland should have selected the straight-line depreciation method when approximately the same amount of an asset's service potential is used up each period. If the reasons for the decline in service potential are unclear, then the selection of the straight-line method could be influenced by the ease of recordkeeping, its use for similar assets, and its use by others in the industry.

b. Portland should record depreciation expense to the date of the exchange. If the original truck's carrying amount is greater than its fair value, a loss results. The truck's capitalized cost and accumulated depreciation are eliminated, and the loss on trade-in is reported as part of income from continuing operations. The newly acquired truck is recorded at fair value. If the original truck's carrying amount is less than its fair value at trade-in, then there is an unrecognized gain. The newly acquired truck is recorded at fair value less the unrecognized gain. Cash is decreased by the amount paid.

c. 1. By associating depreciation with a group of machines instead of each individual machine, Portland's bookkeeping process is greatly simplified. Also, since actual machine lives vary from the average depreciable life, unrecognized net losses on early dispositions are expected to be offset by continuing depreciation on machines usable beyond the average depreciable life. Periodic income does not fluctuate as a result of recognizing gains and losses on manufacturing machine dispositions.

2. Portland should divide the depreciable cost (capitalized cost less residual value) of each machine by its estimated life to obtain its annual depreciation. The sum of the individual annual depreciation amounts should then be divided by the sum of the individual capitalized costs to obtain the annual composite depreciation rate.

ANSWER OUTLINE

Problem 3 Impairment of Fixed Assets

a. Asset impaired if carry. amt. not recoverable

b. One or more factors indicate possible impairment

- FMV decline
- Δ in asset use or physical Δ.
- Legal factors, Δ business climate, or regular action
- Asset cost > planned
- Operating (xxx) or cash flow (xxx)

If possible impairment indicated, do recoverability test
   $\sum$ fut. cash flows < or > carry. amt.
   If cash flows
      < carry amt., assets impaired
      > carry amt., assets not impaired

If impairment confirmed by recoverability test, measure loss
   Fair value – Carry. amt.

c. Current period
   Impairment loss   xx
      A/D   xx
Future periods
   Recognize additional losses
   Recoveries prohibited
Losses reported in income from cont. oper.

d. Compare NRV to carry. amt.
   Report lower amt.
   Loss = Carry. amt. – NRV
   Asset no longer depreciated
   Recoveries in future periods recognized limited to previous losses
   Report losses in continuing operations income
   Report assets under other assets

UNOFFICIAL ANSWER

Problem 3 Impairment of Fixed Assets

a. An operational asset is impaired if some or all of the carrying amount of that asset will not be recovered.

b. An asset could be impaired if one or more of the following conditions exists:

- Significant decrease in market value
- Change in way asset used or physical change in asset
- Legal factors or change in business climate that might affect asset's fair value or adverse action or assessment by regulator
- Asset cost incurred greater than planned
- Operating or cash flow losses from the asset

If a least one of these conditions exist, a recoverability test shall be performed. Under this test, a loss on operational assets shall be recognized if the expected total net future cash flows are less than the carrying amounts of the assets. Assets should be grouped at lowest level for which there are identifiable cash flows independent of other groupings. Expected net future cash flows are future cash inflows to be generated by the assets less the future cash outflows expected to be necessary to obtain those inflows. Expected future cash flows are not discounted. If the ability to recover the asset is not demonstrated (sum of future cash flows < carrying amount) a loss shall be measured and recorded. The loss is measured as the difference between the fair value of the asset(s) and the carrying amount.

c. A loss is recognized in the current period by a debit to an impairment loss account and a credit to accumulated depreciation. In future periods, if additional impairment is confirmed, an additional loss shall be recognized. However, recoveries of losses recognized in prior periods are not permitted. Impairment losses are reported in income from continuing operations.

d. In situations in which management has made a decision to dispose of an asset, such asset should be recorded at the lower of the asset's carrying amount or net realizable value (NRV). These assets shall no longer be depreciated. In future periods, recoveries are permitted, but are limited to losses previously recognized on these assets. Losses recognized are reported as part of income from continuing operations. The assets to be disposed of shall be reported under other assets on the company's balance sheet.

ANSWER OUTLINE

Problem 4   Intangible Assets

a.   1.   Characteristics of intangible assets

- Lack physical existence
- Value difficult to estimate
- High degree of uncertainty concerning future benefits

Purchased intangibles

- Record at cost

Internally generated intangibles

- Expense currently

2.   Amortized over useful lives
Factors affecting useful life

- Legal life
- Contractual provisions
- Effects of obsolescence, demand, etc.
- Expected actions of competitors
- Other economic factors

Useful life may be indefinite

- Do not amortize
- Periodically test for impairment

3.   Disclose the following:

- The amounts assigned to the intangibles acquired, in total and by class of asset
- The gross carrying amounts by class of asset
- The aggregate amount of amortization expense and the estimated amount for the five succeeding periods.
- The weighted-average amortization period, in total and by major class of asset
- The aggregate amount of goodwill impairment loss recognized during the period

b.   1.   Part (b) consists of two requirements: a schedule showing the intangibles section of Broca's 12/31/02 balance sheet, and a schedule showing the related expenses that would appear on Broca's 2002 income statement. The solutions approach for problems in which the requirements are interrelated is to make all the computations for each item at one time. After making the computations, label each computation according to the requirement (BS = balance sheet, IS = income statement) to which it relates.

2.   In a purchase, the net assets acquired are recorded at their FMV. The excess of the cost of the investment ($360,000) over the FMV of the net assets acquired ($172,000) is allocated to goodwill ($360,000 – $172,000 = $188,000). Intangible assets with an indeterminate or unlimited life, such as this goodwill, are not amortized. The goodwill is reported in the 12/31/02 balance at its cost.

3.   The franchise acquired on 2/1/02 is recorded at its cost of $60,000. Since Broca amortizes these intangibles on a straight-line basis, and takes a full year's amortization in the year of acquisition, 2002 amortization is $12,000 ($60,000 x 1/5), and the franchise is reported at cost less accumulated amortization at 12/31/02 ($60,000 – $12,000 = $48,000). In addition to the amortization expense, there is also an annual fee that must be expensed, equal to 1% of ferry revenues. For 2002, this fee is $200 ($20,000 x 1%).

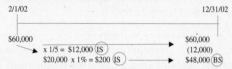

4.   Patents are initially recorded at cost of acquisition, which is purchase price for a purchased patent, or legal and other costs of registration ($51,000) for an internally generated patent. Legal fees incurred in **successfully** defending the patent ($85,000) are also capitalized because such fees help establish the legal right of the holder to any future benefits that will be derived from the patent. Therefore, this patent is capitalized at a total amount of $136,000 ($51,000 + $85,000). Since Broca amortizes these intangibles on a straight-line basis and takes a full-year's amortization in the year of acquisition, amortization is $13,600 ($136,000 x1/10). The patent is reported at cost less accumulated amortization at 12/31/02 ($136,000 – $13,600 = $122,400).

UNOFFICIAL ANSWER

Problem 4   Intangible Assets

a.   1.   The main characteristics of intangible assets are their lack of physical substance, the difficulty of estimating their value, and the high degree of uncertainty regarding their future life. Accounting for intangible assets depends on whether they have been purchased or developed internally.

Intangible assets purchased from others should be recorded at cost. The costs of developing intangible assets with indeterminable lives, such as goodwill, are ordinarily not distinguishable from the current costs of operations and thus are not assignable to specific assets but are expensed immediately. Intangible assets with as indeterminate life are not amortized. Instead they are periodically tested for impairment.

2.   Intangible assets should be amortized over their estimated useful life. Estimated useful life should be determined by consideration of such factors as legal life; provisions for renewal or extensions of contracts; the effects of

obsolescence, demand, and competition; and other economic factors.

   3.   The financial statements should disclose the amounts assigned to the intangible assets and their gross carrying amounts; the aggregated amount of amortization expense and the estimated amounts for the five succeeding periods; and the weighted-average amortization period, in total and by major class of asset.

b.

Broca Co.
INTANGIBLES SECTION OF BALANCE SHEET
December 31, 2002

Goodwill	$188,000 [1]
Franchise, net of accumulated amortization of $12,000	48,000 [2]
Patent, net of accumulated amortization of $13,600	122,400 [3]

[1]	Cash paid	$360,000
	Value of net assets	(172,000)
	Goodwill	188,000
[2]	Franchise	$60,000
	Amortization over 5 years	(12,000)
	Balance	$48,000
[3]	Legal costs ($51,000 + $85,000)	$136,000
	Amortization over 10 years	(13,600)
	Balance	$122,400

EXPENSES RESULTING FROM INTANGIBLES
For the Year Ended December 31, 2002

Amortization:		
Franchise	12,000	
Patent	13,600	
	$25,600	
Franchise fee	200	
	$25,800	

ANSWER OUTLINE

Problem 5   Impairment of Goodwill

a. • Only goodwill acquired through a business combination is recorded as an asset

• Recorded goodwill is not amortized but it is tested for impairment periodically

• The cost of internally developing or maintaining goodwill is expensed as incurred

b. • The first step in the test of goodwill impairment is a comparison of the fair value of the reporting unit to its carrying value

• If the carrying value is greater than the fair value the second step in the test of impairment must be performed

c. • The second step in the test of impairment involves determining the fair values of the net assets of the reporting unit

• The implied value of goodwill is the difference between the fair value of the unit and the fair value of its net assets

• Impairment is recorded by debiting Impairment Loss and crediting Goodwill

UNOFFICIAL ANSWER

Problem 5   Impairment of Goodwill

a.   Goodwill acquired through a business combination is the only type of goodwill that is recognized. Such goodwill is not amortized but is tested periodically for impairment. Internally generated goodwill is not recorded. Expenditures to develop, maintain, or enhance goodwill are expensed as incurred.

b.   Since the carrying value of the reporting unit ($1,900,000) exceeds the fair value of the unit ($1,700,000), the second step in the test of impairment should be performed.

c.   The implied value of goodwill is the difference between the fair value of the unit ($1,700,00) and the fair value of its assets and liabilities ($1,500,00). Therefore, the implied value of goodwill is $200,000. Since the carrying value of goodwill is $500,000, there is a $300,000 impairment that must be recognized as shown below.

Impairment loss	$300,000	
Goodwill		$300,000

To recognize impairment of goodwill for the Technology reporting unit at 12/31/02.

ANSWER OUTLINE

Problem 6   R&D Costs

a. **1.**   Asset characteristics
Probable future benefit in form of net cash inflows
Obtain benefit and control access to it
Transaction or event that gives entity right to or control of benefit has already occurred

   2.   Intent to produce the product, presuming future net cash inflows
Patent enables control of benefits
Consequences of past events (R&D)

   3.   Future benefits are uncertain and difficult to measure as R&D expenditures incurred

b. **1.**   Equipment exclusively for R&D
Expensed on IS as R&D in period incurred
Equipment used for R&R and production
Capitalize as fixed assets less accumulation depr. on BS for 1999 through 2002
Depreciate asset from 1999 to 2002 as R&D expense in IS
Depreciation for 2002 should be added to cost of inventory, via overhead, and expensed as CGS in the IS

   2.   Cash payments for pilot plant as cash outflow in operating activities in 2000 SCF
Cash received from sale as cash inflow from operating activities in 2001 SCF

UNOFFICIAL ANSWER

Problem 6   R&D Costs

a. **1.**   According to the FASB conceptual framework, the three essential characteristics of an asset are

• It embodies a probable future benefit that involves a capacity to contribute to future net cash inflows.

• A particular entity can obtain the benefit and control others' access to it.

• The transaction or other event giving rise to the entity's right to or control of the benefit has already occurred.

2. Mono's project expenditures through 2001 meet the FASB conceptual framework's three essential characteristics of an asset as follows:

- Since Mono intends to produce the product, it presumably anticipates future net cash inflows.
- Mono has obtained a patent that will enable it to control the benefits arising from the product.
- The control is a consequence of past events.

3. It is difficult to justify the classification of research and development expenditures as assets because at the time expenditures are made the future benefits are uncertain, and difficult to measure.

b. 1. Expenditures for equipment to be used exclusively for research and development should be reported as research and development expense in the period incurred. Expenditures for equipment to be used both for research and development and for production should be capitalized and reported as fixed assets, less accumulated depreciation, on Mono's balance sheets from 1999 through 2002. An appropriate depreciation method should be used, with depreciation from 1999 through 2002 reported as research and development expense. Depreciation for 2002 should be added to cost of inventory, via factory overhead, and expensed as cost of goods sold.

2. Cash payments for the pilot plant construction should be reported as cash outflows from operating activities on Mono's 2000 statement of cash flows. Cash received from the sale of the pilot plant should be reported as a cash inflow from operating activities on Mono's 2001 statement of cash flows.

Keep practicing! Wiley's CPA Examination Review Software has over 2,800 questions.

Available at www.wiley.com/cpa

MONETARY CURRENT ASSETS AND CURRENT LIABILITIES

Chapter 3A of ARB 43 defines current assets and current liabilities. This study module reviews the accounting for current assets (except inventory which is presented in Module 23 and short-term investments which are presented in Module 29). This module also reviews current liabilities.

A. Cash

Per SFAS 95 (see outline), the definition of cash includes both cash (cash on hand and demand deposits) and cash equivalents (short-term, highly liquid investments). Cash equivalents have to be readily convertible into cash and so near maturity that they carry little risk of changing in value due to interest rate changes. Generally this will include only those investments with original maturities of three months or less from the **date of purchase** by the enterprise. Common examples of cash equivalents include Treasury bills, commercial paper, and money market funds. Unrestricted cash and cash equivalents available for general use are presented as the first current asset.

Cash set aside for special uses is usually disclosed separately. The entry to set up a special fund is

Special cash fund	xx	
Cash		xx

Cash restricted as to use (e.g., not transferable out of a foreign country) should be disclosed separately, but not as a current asset if it cannot be used in the next year (this is true of special funds also).

Imprest (petty) cash funds are generally included in the total cash figure, but unreimbursed expense vouchers are excluded.

1. Bank Reconciliations

Bank reconciliations are prepared by bank depositors when they receive their monthly bank statements. The reconciliation is made to determine any required adjustments to the cash balance. Two types of reconciling items are possible.

a.   Reconciling items not requiring adjustment on the books (type A)
b.   Reconciling items requiring adjustment on the books (type B)

There are three type A reconciling items. They do not require adjusting journal entries.

(1) Outstanding checks
(2) Deposits in transit
(3) Bank errors

All other reconciling items (type B) require adjusting journal entries. Examples of type B reconciling items include

(1) Unrecorded returned nonsufficient funds (NSF) checks
(2) Unrecorded bank charges
(3) Errors in the cash account
(4) Unrecorded bank collections of notes receivable

Two types of formats are used in bank reconciliations.

Format 1	*Format 2*
Balance per bank	Balance per bank
+(–) A adjustments	+(–) A adjustments
Correct cash balance	+(–) B adjustments
	Balance per books
Balance per books	+(–) B adjustments
+(–) B adjustments	Correct cash balance
Correct cash balance	

Type A and B adjustments can be either added or subtracted depending upon the type of format and the nature of the item.

Reconciling items must be analyzed to determine whether they are included in (1) the balance per bank, and/or (2) the balance per books. If they are included in one, but not the other, an adjustment is required. For instance, the $1,800 deposit in transit in the following example is included in the balance per books but not in the balance per bank. Thus, it must be added to the balance per bank to reconcile to the correct cash balance. Deposits in transit do not require an adjusting journal entry. Analyze all reconciling items in this manner, but remember, only journalize type B reconciling items.

SAMPLE BANK RECONCILIATION (FORMAT 1)

Per bank statement	$ 4,702
Deposits in transit	1,800
Outstanding checks	(1,200)
Bank error	50
Correct cash balance	$ 5,352
Per books	$ 5,332
Service charges	(5)
Note collected by bank	150
Customer's NSF check	(170)
Deposit of July 10 recorded as $749 instead of $794	45
Correct cash balance	$ 5,352

Note that the balance per bank and balance per books each are reconciled directly to the corrected balance.

a. **Adjusting journal entries**

All of the items in the per books section of a bank reconciliation (type B) require adjusting entries. The entries for the above example appear below.

Miscellaneous expense	5		AR	170	
Cash		5	Cash		170
Cash	150		Cash	45	
Notes receivable		150	AR (or sales)		45

b. **Four-column cash reconciliation**

Unlike the bank reconciliation above, which is as of a specific date, a four-column cash reconciliation, also known as a "proof of cash," reconciles bank and book cash balances over a specified time period. A proof of cash consists of four columns: beginning of the period bank reconciliation, receipts, disbursements, and end-of-the-period bank reconciliation. Thus, the proof of cash cross-foots as well as foots.

SAMPLE PROOF OF CASH (FORMAT 2)

	Bank reconciliation June 30, 2002	Receipts	Disbursements	Bank reconciliation July 31, 2002
Balance per bank statement	$3,402	$25,200	$23,900	$ 4,702
Deposits in transit				
June 30, 2002	1,610	(1,610)		
July 31, 2002		1,800		1,800
Outstanding checks				
June 30, 2002	(450)		(450)	
July 31, 2002			1,200	(1,200)
Service charges			(5)	5
Note collected by bank		(150)		(150)
Customer's NSF check			(170)	170
Deposit of July 10 recorded as $749 instead of $794		(45)		(45)
Bank error			(50)	50
Balance per books	$4,562	$25,195	$24,425	$ 5,332

Note that there are no type B reconciling items in the beginning reconciliation column. This is because the $4,562 has been adjusted when the June bank statement was reconciled. Notice that figures appearing in the center columns have unlike signs if they are adjacent and like signs if they are not adjacent to amounts in the side columns.

The purpose of the proof of cash is to disclose any cash misstatements, such as unrecorded disbursements and receipts within a month, which would not be detected by a bank reconciliation. For example, if the center two columns each required a negative $1,000 to make the top line reconcile with the bottom line, there may be unrecorded receipts and deposits of $1,000.

B. Receivables

Accounts receivable should be disclosed in the balance sheet at net realizable value (gross amount less estimated uncollectibles) by source (e.g., trade, officer, etc.). Officer, employee, and affiliate company receivables should be separately disclosed (ARB 43, chap 1A). Unearned interest and finance charges should be deducted from gross receivables (APB 6).

1. **Anticipation of Sales Discounts**

    Cash discounts are generally recognized as expense when cash payment is received within the discount period. As long as cash discounts to be taken on year-end receivables remain constant from year to year, there is no problem. If, however, discounts on year-end receivables fluctuate, a year-end allowance can be set up or sales can be recorded net of the discounts. The entries to record sales at net are shown below in comparison to the sales recorded at gross.

		Sales at net		*Sales at gross*	
a.	Sale	AR	(net)	AR	(gross)
		Sales	(net)	Sales	(gross)
b.	Cash receipt within discount period	Cash	(net)	Sales disc.	(disc.)
		AR	(net)	Cash	(net)
				AR	(gross)
c.	Cash receipt after discount period	Cash	(gross)	Cash	(gross)
		AR	(net)	AR	(gross)
		Disc. not			
		taken	(disc.)		

    The rationale for the net method is that sales are recorded at the cash equivalent amount and receivables nearer realizable value. Note that under both the net and gross methods, sales and accounts receivable are recorded net of trade discounts for the same reason. If a sales discount allowance method is used, the entry below is made with the gross method entries. The entry should be reversed.

Sales discounts	(expected disc. on year-end AR)
Allowance for sales disc.	(expected disc. on year-end AR)

Similarly, when using the "net method," an entry should be made to pick up discounts not expected to be taken on year-end receivables. Generally, however, these latter adjustments are not made, because they are assumed to be about the same each period.

2. **Bad Debts Expense**

    There are two approaches to bad debts.

    - Direct write-off method
    - Allowance method

    a. Under the direct write-off method, bad debts are considered expenses in the period in which they are written off. **Note that this method is not considered acceptable under GAAP**, unless the amounts are immaterial.

Bad debts expense	(uncollectible AR)
AR	(uncollectible AR)

    b. The allowance method seeks to estimate the amount of uncollectible receivables, and establishes a contra valuation account (allowance for bad debts) for the amount estimated to be uncollectible. The adjusting entry to set up the allowance is

Bad debts expense	(estimated)
Allowance for bad debts	(estimated)

    The entry to write off bad debts is

Allowance for bad debts	(uncollectible AR)
AR	(uncollectible AR)

    There are two methods to determine the annual charge to bad debts expense.

    (1) Annual sales
    (2) Year-end AR

For example, charging bad debts expense for 1% of annual sales is based on the theory that bad debts are a function of sales; this method emphasizes the income statement.

    Charging bad debts on year-end AR is based on the theory that bad debts are a function of AR collections during the period; this method emphasizes the balance sheet. A bad debts percentage can be applied to total AR or subsets of AR. Often an aging schedule is prepared for this purpose. An AR aging schedule classifies AR by their age (e.g., 30, 60, 90, 120, etc., days overdue).

    When bad debts expense is estimated as a function of sales, any balance in the allowance account is ignored in making the adjusting entry. Bad debts expense under this method is simply the total amount computed (i.e., Sales x Percentage). However, when bad debts expense is estimated using outstanding receivables, the expense is the amount needed to adjust the allowance account to the amount computed (i.e., AR x Percentage[s]). Thus, bad debts expense under this method is the amount computed less any credit balance currently in the allowance account (or plus any debit balance).

Net accounts receivable is the balance in accounts receivable less the allowance for bad debts. Also remember that net receivables **do not change** when a specific account is written off since both accounts receivable and the allowance account are reduced by the same amount.

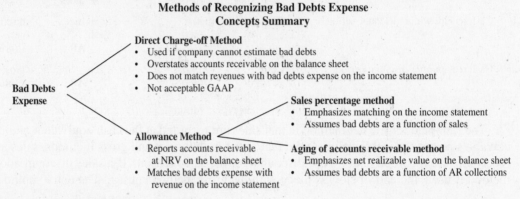

Methods of Recognizing Bad Debts Expense
Concepts Summary

Bad Debts Expense

Direct Charge-off Method
• Used if company cannot estimate bad debts
• Overstates accounts receivable on the balance sheet
• Does not match revenues with bad debts expense on the income statement
• Not acceptable GAAP

Allowance Method
• Reports accounts receivable at NRV on the balance sheet
• Matches bad debts expense with revenue on the income statement

Sales percentage method
• Emphasizes matching on the income statement
• Assumes bad debts are a function of sales

Aging of accounts receivable method
• Emphasizes net realizable value on the balance sheet
• Assumes bad debts are a function of AR collections

3. **Pledging and Selling (Factoring) AR**[1]

Sometimes businesses cannot wait for the cash flow from the normal collection of AR.

Pledging of receivables. Pledging is an agreement where accounts receivable are used as collateral for loans. Generally, the lender has limited rights to inspect the borrower's records to achieve assurance that the receivables do exist. The customers whose accounts have been pledged are not aware of this event, and their payments are still remitted to the original obligee. The pledged accounts merely serve as security to the lender, giving comfort that sufficient assets exist which will generate cash flows adequate in amount and timing to repay the debt. However, the debt is paid by the borrower whether or not the pledged receivables are collected and whether or not the pattern of such collections matches the payments due on the debt.

The only accounting issue relating to pledging is that of adequate disclosure. The accounts receivable, which remain assets of the borrowing entity, continue to be shown as current assets in its financial statements but must be identified as having been pledged. This identification can be accomplished either parenthetically or by footnote disclosures. Similarly, the related debt should be identified as having been secured by the receivables.

EXAMPLE: *Proper disclosure for pledged receivables shown parenthetically on the balance sheet*

Current assets:
  Accounts receivable, net of allowance for doubtful accounts of $600,000
    ($3,500,000 of which has been pledged as collateral for bank loans)   8,450,000

Current liabilities:
  Bank loans payable (secured by pledged accounts receivable)   2,700,000

Factoring of receivables. This category of financing is the most significant in terms of accounting implications. Factoring traditionally has involved the outright sale of receivables to a financing institution known as a factor. These arrangements involved (1) notification to the customer to forward future payments to the factor and (2) the transfer of receivables **without recourse** which means that the factor assumes the risk of loss from noncollection. Thus, once a factoring arrangement is completed, the entity has no further involvement with the accounts, except for a return of merchandise. In its simplistic form, the receivables are sold and the difference between the cash received and the carrying value is recognized as a gain or loss.

The classical variety of factoring (i.e., without recourse) provides two financial services to the business: it permits the entity to obtain cash earlier and the risk of bad debts is transferred to the factor. The factor is compensated for each of the services. Interest is charged based on the anticipated

[1] *Taken from Delaney, et. al.,* **GAAP: Interpretation and Application**, *2002 Edition, John Wiley & Sons, Inc., New York, NY, pp. 126-154.*

length of time between the date the factoring is consummated and the expected collection date of the receivables sold. A fee is charged based upon the factor's anticipated bad debt losses.

> *EXAMPLE: Thirsty Corp., on July 1, 2002, enters into an agreement with Rich Company to sell a group of its receivables **without recourse**. A total face value of $200,000 of accounts receivable are involved. The factor will charge 20% interest computed on the weighted-average time to maturity of the receivables of thirty-six days plus a 3% fee.*
>
> *The entries required are as follows:*

Cash	190,055	
Interest expense (or prepaid) (200,000 x .20 x 36/365)	3,945	
Factoring fee (200,000 x .03)	6,000	
Accounts receivable		200,000

> *The interest expense and factor's fee can be combined into a $9,945 loss on the sale of receivables.*

Merchandise returns will normally be the responsibility of the original vendor, who must then make the appropriate settlement with the factor. To protect against the possibility of merchandise returns which diminish the total of receivables to be collected, very often a factoring arrangement will **not** advance the full amount of the factored receivables (less any interest and factoring fee deductions). Rather, the factor will retain a certain fraction of the total proceeds relating to the portion of sales which are anticipated to be returned by customers. This sum is known as the factor's holdback (due from factor). When merchandise is returned to the borrower, an entry is made reducing the receivable from the factor. At the end of the return privilege period, any remaining holdback will become due and payable to the borrower.

> *EXAMPLE: Accounting for the transfer of receivables without recourse*
>
> 1. *Thirsty Corp., on July 1, 2002, enters into an agreement with Rich Company to sell a group of its receivables **without recourse**. A total face value of $200,000 accounts receivable are involved. The factor will charge 20% interest computed on the weighted-average time to maturity of the receivables of thirty-six days plus a 3% fee. A 5% holdback will also be retained.*
> 2. *Thirsty's customers return for credit $4,800 of merchandise.*
> 3. *The customer return privilege period expires and the remaining holdback is paid to the transferor.*
>
> *The entries required are as follows:*

1.	Cash	180,055	
	Loss on sale of receivables	9,945*	
	Factor's holdback receivable (200,000 x .05)	10,000	
	Accounts receivable		200,000
	*($3,945 interest expense + $6,000 factoring fee)		
2.	Sales returns and allowances	4,800	
	Factor's holdback receivable		4,800
3.	Cash	5,200	
	Factor's holdback receivable		5,200

Factoring does transfer title. Thus, if there is a **without recourse** provision, the removal of these receivables from the borrower's balance sheet is clearly warranted.

Another variation is known as factoring **with recourse**. Some entities had such a poor history of uncollectible accounts that factors were only willing to purchase their accounts if a substantial fee were collected to compensate for the risk. When the company believed that the receivables were of a better quality, a way to avoid excessive factoring fees was to sell these receivables with recourse. This variation of factoring was really an assignment of receivables with notification to the customers.

In computing the gain or loss to be recognized at the date of the transfer of the receivables, the borrower (transferor) must take into account the anticipated chargebacks from the transferee for bad debts to be incurred. This action requires an estimate by the transferor, based on past experience. Adjustments should also be made at the time of sale for the estimated effects of any prepayments by customers (where the receivables are interest-bearing or where cash discounts are available), and for the effects of any defects in the eligibility of the transferred receivables.

> *EXAMPLE: Accounting for the transfer of receivables with recourse*
>
> 1. *Thirsty Corp., on July 1, 2002, enters into an agreement with Rich Company to sell a group of its receivables with a face value of $200,000. Rich Company (the factor) will charge 20% interest computed on the weighted-average time to maturity of the receivables of thirty-six days and a 3% fee. A 5% holdback will also be retained.*
> 2. *Generally, 40% of Thirsty's customers take advantage of a 2% cash discount.*

3.   *Assume Thirsty Corp. surrenders control of the receivables, per SFAS 140, Thirsty's future obligation is reasonably estimable, and Rich Co. does not have a unilateral ability to require Thirsty to repurchase the receivables.*

4.   *The factor accepts the receivables **subject to recourse** for nonpayment. This means that the transferor has **continuing involvement**. The recourse obligation has a fair value of $10,000.*

   According to the requirements of SFAS 140, this situation qualifies as a sale. Under this standard, Thirsty must record a liability for the recourse liability due to its continuing involvement with the receivables transferred. It has accepted the obligation for all credit losses and has, in effect, guaranteed the receivables.
   The entries required to record the sale are

Cash	180,055	
Interest expense	3,945	
Factoring fee	6,000	
Factor's holdback receivable (200,000 x .05)	10,000	
Loss on sale of receivables	11,600	
Due to factor (200,000 x .40 x .02)		1,600
Accounts receivable		200,000
Recourse obligation		10,000

Simplified, the entry is

Cash	180,055	
Factor's holdback receivable [(200,000 x .05) – 1,600]	8,400	
Loss on sale of receivables (3,945 + 6,000 + 11,600)	21,545	
Accounts receivable		200,000
Recourse obligation		10,000

The accounts receivable are removed from the transferor's books because they have been sold. The loss on sale of receivables is the sum of the interest charged by the factor ($3,945), the factor's fee ($6,000), the expected chargeback for cash discounts to be taken ($1,600), and the fair value of the recourse obligation ($10,000).

Because the transaction resulted in a "sale" rather than a borrowing, the "interest" and "fee" elements relate directly to the sale transaction. Note that in a sale, these components are in essence part of a negotiated price for the receivables. All you need to remember is that in sales transactions, amounts that would ordinarily be income statement amounts are netted together to get the total loss.

If, subsequent to the sale of the receivables, the actual experience relative to the recourse terms differs from the provision made at the time of the sale, a change in an accounting estimate results. It is reflected as an additional gain or loss in the subsequent period. These changes are not corrections of errors or retroactive adjustments.

Secured borrowings. If the facts in the example above apply, but the transfer does **not** qualify as a sale, because the transferor does not surrender control of the receivables, the borrower's entry will be

Cash	190,055	
Interest expense (or prepaid)	3,945	
Factoring fee	6,000	
Factor borrowing payable		200,000

The accounts receivable remain on the borrower's books. Both the accounts receivable and the factor borrowing payable should be cross-referenced in the balance sheet.

Transfers of financial assets under SFAS 140. The FASB uses a financial-components approach for SFAS 140. In doing so, the previous approach that viewed a financial asset as an indivisible unit has become obsolete. **Under the financial component approach, financial assets are now to be viewed as a variety of components with a focus on who controls the components and on whether control has changed with a given transaction.**

The basic accounting problem in this area involves instances of possible continuing involvement through recourse, repurchase agreements, options generated, servicing, and collateral. The issue is whether the transfer has resulted in a sale or a secured borrowing. A sale results, to the extent that consideration other than beneficial interests has been received, when the transferor gives up control.

Under SFAS 140, transfers of financial assets are disaggregated into separate assets and liabilities. Each entity involved in the transaction then

1.   Recognizes only the assets controlled and liabilities incurred, and
2.   Derecognizes assets where control has been given up or lost and liabilities where extinguishment has occurred.

The chart below summarizes the accounting for the transfer of receivables.

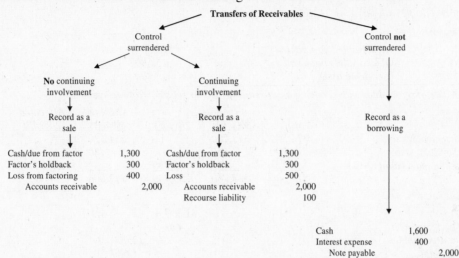

The "factor's holdback" provides a margin of protection against sales discounts, sales returns and allowances, and disputed accounts. It may be referred to as "Due from factor" or "Receivable from factor." Additionally, when a recourse obligation exists, an amount is included as protection for the transferee against uncollectible accounts.

Control is deemed to have been surrendered by the transferor only if **all** of the following conditions are met:

1. The **assets** transferred are **beyond the reach of the transferor** and its affiliates, its creditors, bankruptcy trustees or other receivers, except for an affiliate that is a qualifying special-purpose entity.

2. The **transferee can pledge or exchange freely** the assets transferred without unreasonable constraints or conditions imposed on its contractual right **or** the holders of beneficial interests in a qualifying special-purpose entity can pledge or exchange those interests freely without unreasonable constraints or conditions imposed on their right.

3. The **transferor has not kept effective control** of the financial assets transferred through a repurchase or redemption agreement that entitles and obligates repurchase or redemption before maturity at a determinable price **or** the ability to unilaterally cause the holder to return specific assets (except for a cleanup call). To meet this condition, the transferor must have received cash or other collateral sufficient at all time to substantially fund repurchase or redemption.

Retained interests. In most cases, the outright transfer of assets and/or liabilities result(s) in changes in control that are obvious from the nature of the transaction. Problems generally occur when there is some sort of continuing involvement by the transferor. Retained interests include undivided interests for which control has not been given up by the transferor, servicing (mortgages, credit card receivables, etc.) assets and liabilities and beneficial interests in transferred assets to a qualifying special-purpose entity (SPE) in a securitization. In general, the more that the transferor of assets retains an interest, the less likely the transaction will be classified as a sale and the more likely the transaction will be classified as a secured borrowing. The primary reason for this result is that in a sale, the transferor should give up control. If a determination cannot be made between classification as proceeds of a sale or as retained interests, the asset should be classified as proceeds and should be measured at fair value. Interests in transferred assets that are not a part of the proceeds are considered retained interests that are still under the control of the transferor.

Retained interests are to be measured at their previous carrying value before the transfer through an allocation at the date of sale based on relative fair values of the assets sold and the assets retained. This allocation must be applied to all transfers that have retained interests, regardless of whether or not they qualify as sales. It should be noted that this fair value allocation may result in a relative change in basis unless the fair values are proportionate to their carrying values. Thus, the gain or loss from any sale component could also be affected.

EXAMPLE: Retained interests

Sale of receivable with servicing

Facts given:

Receivable's fair value	$16,500
Receivable's book value	15,000
Servicing asset	700

Partial sale of receivables with servicing asset retained. Seller sells 80% of receivables.

	FV	80% FV	20% FV	Allocated 80% BV	Allocated 20% BV
Receivables sold	$16,500	$13,200		$11,520	
Servicing asset	700	560		480	
Retained amount (20%)			$3,440		$3,000
	$17,200	$13,760	$3,440	$12,000	$3,000

Journal entry

Cash	13,200	
Servicing asset	480	
Receivables		12,000
Gain		1,680

Seller reports retained amount at $3,000.

The retained interests continue to be the transferor's assets since control of these assets has not been transferred. They are carried at the allocated book value without recognition of any gain or loss. Thus, the retained interest is considered continuing control over a previous asset (although the form may have changed) and it should not be remeasured at fair value.

Servicing of financial assets. This includes

1. Collecting payments
2. Paying taxes and insurance
3. Monitoring delinquencies
4. Foreclosing
5. Investing
6. Remitting fees
7. Accounting

Although inherent in transfers of most financial assets, servicing is a distinct asset or liability only when separated contractually from the underlying financial asset. The servicing asset usually results either from separate purchase or assumption of rights or from securitization with retained servicing. The servicer's obligations are specified in the contract.

Typically, the servicing contract results in an asset since the benefits are more than adequate compensation for the servicing. The benefits include

1. Fees
2. Late charges
3. Float
4. Other income

If the above benefits do not provide fair compensation, the contract results in a liability. With regard to the sale of assets, a servicing liability would reduce the net proceeds and would affect the gain or loss calculation.

The fair value of a servicing contract is based on its value in the market and is not based on the internal cost structure of the servicer. Thus, the concept of adequate compensation is judged by requirements that would be imposed by a new or outside servicer. In cases where there are few servicing contracts that are purchased or sold, present value methods may be used for valuation.

In summary, the servicer should classify the components into one of the following categories:

1. More than adequate—resulting in a recorded asset
2. Adequate compensation (no asset or liability)
3. Less than adequate—resulting in a recorded liability

If, under a servicing contract, the transferor transfers assets to a qualifying special purpose entity in a guaranteed mortgage securitization, retains the securities, and classifies them as held-to-maturity debt securities under SFAS 115, the asset or liability can be reported together with the asset being serviced. However, if the entity sells or securitizes with service retained or if the entity purchases or assumes servicing, a servicing asset or liability results. If servicing is retained, resulting assets are measured at book value based on relative fair value at the date of sale, if practical. Servicing liabilities undertaken, servicing assets purchased, and servicing liabilities assumed are measured at fair value.

Specifically, servicing assets or servicing liabilities are to be accounted for separately as follows:

1. Assets are to be reported separately from liabilities. They are not netted.
2. Initially measure retained servicing assets at allocated book value based on relative fair values at date of sale or securitization.
3. Initially measure at fair value all purchased assets, assumed liabilities, and liabilities undertaken in a sale or securitization.
4. Account separately for interest-only strips (future interest income from serviced assets that exceeds servicing fees).
5. Amortize assets in proportion to and over the period of net servicing income.
6. Evaluate and measure impairment as follows:

    a. Stratify recognized assets based on predominant risk (asset size, type, interest rate, terms, location, date of organization, etc.).
    b. Individual stratum should have impairment recognized through a valuation allowance in the amount of the excess of book value over fair value.
    c. Adjust the valuation allowances to reflect needed changes. Excess fair value for a stratum should not be recognized.

7. Amortize liabilities in proportion to and over the period of net servicing loss. In cases where changes have increased the fair value above the book value, an increased liability and a loss should be recognized.

Securitizations. Securitization is the transformation of financial assets into securities (asset-backed securities). Various assets including mortgages, credit cards, trade receivables, loans, and leases are grouped and securitized. These groupings of relatively homogeneous assets are then pooled and divided into securities with cash-flows that can be quite different from those of the original assets. With an established market, most of these securities cost less than the alternative use of the assets as collateral for borrowing. Thus, the benefits of most securitizations include lower financing costs, increased liquidity, and lower credit risk.

The transferor (also called issuer or sponsor) forms a securitization mechanism (separate corporation or qualifying special-purpose entity [QSPE]) to buy the assets and to issue the securities. Sometimes, another transfer is made to a trust and the trust issues the securities. These different structures are generally referred to as one-tier or two-tier. The securitization mechanism then generates beneficial interests in the assets or resulting cash flows which are sold. The form of the securities chosen depends on such things as the nature of the assets, income tax considerations, and returns to be received.

Payments by the securitization mechanism are usually classified as **pay-through, pass-through,** or **revolving-period**. In a **pay-through,** cash flows from the assets pay off the debt securities. The assets are essentially collateral. In a **pass-through,** undivided interests are issued and the investors share in the net cash flows. In a **revolving-period,** undivided interests are issued, but until liquidation, the net cash flows are split between buying additional assets and paying off investors.

Various financial components arise from securitizations. Examples include servicing contracts, interest-only strips, retained interests, recourse obligations, options, swaps, and forward contracts. All controlled assets and liabilities must be recognized under SFAS 140.

EXAMPLE: Sale of loans

Facts given:

Loan's fair value	*$16,500*
Loan's book value	*15,000*
Fair value of recourse obligation	*(900)*
Fair value of call option	*800*
Fair value of interest rate swap	*700*

   1.   Sale with recourse obligation, call and swap (seller provides floating interest rate return although the basic sale is at fixed interest rate terms).

Journal entry

Cash	16,500	
Call option	800	
Interest rate swap	700	
Loans		15,000
Recourse obligation		900
Gain		2,100

2. *Partial sale with recourse obligation, call and swap. Seller sells 80% of loans.*

	FV	80% FV	20% FV	Allocated 80% BV	Allocated 20% BV
Cash	$16,500	$13,200		$12,000	
Call option	800	640			
Interest rate swap	700	560			
Resource obligation	(900)	(720)			
Retained amount (20%)			$3,420		$3,000
	$17,100	$13,680	$3,420	$12,000	$3,000

Journal entry

Cash	13,200	
Call option	640	
Interest rate swap	560	
Loans		12,000
Recourse obligation		720
Gain		1,680

Seller reports retained amount at $3,000.

The transferor generally desires for the assets to be taken off the balance sheet. This result can be accomplished if the transaction results in a sale. The key criterion in this case is to be sure that the assets are beyond control of the transferor even in bankruptcy.

Accounting for collateral. The treatment depends both on control of the assets and on the liabilities incurred under the collateral agreement. Ordinarily, the transferor should carry the collateral as an asset and the transferee should not record the pledged asset.

If the transferee, however, has control, the secured party should record the asset at fair value and also the liability to return it. The transferor-debtor should reclassify the asset (probably as a receivable) and report it separately in the balance sheet. If the debtor's rights to the collateral are impaired by the transferee's sale or repledge of the collateral, the secured party should recognize the proceeds and also the liability to return the collateral to the extent it hasn't done so.

If the transferor defaults and is not entitled to the return of the collateral, it should be derecognized. If not already recognized, the transferee should record its asset at fair value.

C. Current Liabilities

"Obligations whose liquidation is reasonably expected to require the use of existing resources properly classifiable as current assets, or the creation of other current liabilities" (ARB 43, chap 3).

1. **Examples of current liabilities** (as they fall within the above definition)

a. Trade accounts and notes payable

b. Loan obligations—Including current portions of long-term debt. This is not true if the current portion of long-term debt will not require the use of current assets (e.g., be paid from a sinking fund which is not classified as current).

c. Short-term obligations expected to be refinanced cannot be reclassified as noncurrent liabilities unless there is both an intent and an ability to refinance. See the outline of SFAS 6.

d. Dividends payable—Cash dividends are a liability when declared. They cannot be rescinded.

e. Accrued liabilities—Adjusting entries to reflect the use of goods or services before paying for them. Will pay in future periods even though the expense is incurred in this period (e.g., interest, payroll, rent expenses).

Expense account	xx	
Liability (usually current) account		xx

f. Payroll—There are two entries to record payroll. The first records the employee's payment and deductions on behalf of the employee. The second is to record the employer's taxes.

Payroll expense	xx (gross pay)	
Payroll payable, cash		xx (net pay)
Income taxes payable		xx
FICA taxes payable		xx
Union dues payable		xx
Medical insurance payable		xx
Payroll tax expense	xx	
FICA taxes payable		xx
Federal unemployment tax payable		xx
State unemployment tax payable		xx

g. Property taxes. See the outline of ARB 43, chap 10A. Generally, there is a monthly accrual for property taxes over the fiscal period of the taxing authority. If taxes are payable at the end of the tax authority's fiscal period, the monthly accrual would be

Property tax expense	xx
Property tax payable	xx

If the taxes were paid at the beginning of the period, the entry to record the prepayment would be followed by monthly entries to expense the prepayment.

Prepaid property taxes	xx	Property tax expense	xx
Cash	xx	Prepaid property taxes	xx

If taxes are due, but not paid at the beginning of the year, the liability should be recorded and the deferred charge expensed over the fiscal year of the taxing body.

Deferred property taxes	xx	Property tax expense	xx
Property tax payable	xx	Deferred property taxes	xx

h. Bonus arrangements

Bonus expense	xx
Bonus payable	xx

Set up equations to describe the terms of the bonus agreement. The general forms of the equations follow:

$$\begin{aligned}
B &= P(NI - B - T) \\
T &= R(NI - B) \\
B &= \text{Bonus} \\
P &= \text{Bonus or profit sharing rate (10\%)} \\
NI &= \text{Net income (\$150,000)} \\
T &= \text{Taxes} \\
R &= \text{Tax rate (40\%)}
\end{aligned}$$

EXAMPLE: Work through the above equations using the data in parentheses.

$$\begin{aligned}
T &= .40(150,000 - B) \\
T &= 60,000 - .4B \\
B &= .10(150,000 - B - T) \\
B &= .10(150,000 - B - 60,000 + .4B) \\
B &= 15,000 - .1B - 6,000 + .04B \\
1.06B &= 9,000 \\
B &= \$8,491
\end{aligned}$$

i. Advances from customers—Record as deferred revenue and recognize as revenue when earned

Cash	xx	Deferred revenue	xx
Deferred revenue	xx	Revenue	xx

2. **Contingencies**

a. **Definitions**—An obligation may be either determinable (fixed) or contingent in accordance with the following definitions.

(1) **Determinable liabilities**—The amount of cash and time of payment are known and reasonably precise. Such liabilities are usually evidenced by written contracts but may also arise from implied agreements or imposed legal statutes. Examples include notes payable and liabilities for various taxes as shown above.

(2) **Contingent liabilities**—Such obligations **may** exist but are dependent on uncertain future events. According to SFAS 5 a contingency is defined as an existing condition, situation, or

set of circumstances involving uncertainty as to possible gain or loss to an enterprise that will ultimately be resolved when one or more future events occur or fail to occur.

b. **Recording and disclosing contingencies**—The accounting problems related to contingencies involve the following issues.

(1) When is it appropriate to record and report the effects of a contingency in the financial statements? Should the financial impact of the contingency be reported in the period when the contingency is still unresolved or in the period in which the contingency is resolved?

(2) For contingencies not recorded and reported on the financial statements before they are resolved, what disclosures, if any, are needed in the footnotes to the financial statements?

According to SFAS 5 (see outline), a loss contingency should be accrued if it is **probable** that an asset has been impaired or a liability has been incurred at the balance sheet date **and** the amount of the loss is **reasonably estimable**. When loss contingencies are accrued, a debit should be made to an expense or to a loss account and a credit should be made to either a liability or to a contra asset account. Note that to accrue a loss contingency means that the financial effects are reported in the financial statements **before** the contingency is resolved.

When making the decision concerning the accrual of a loss contingency, the term **probable** relates to the likelihood of a future event taking place or failing to take place which would resolve the uncertainty. However, the likelihood of a future event taking place or failing to take place may not always be judged to be probable. The likelihood of the future event taking place or failing to take place may instead be judged to be **reasonably possible** or **remote**. In these last two situations, it is **not** appropriate to accrue the loss contingency as of the balance sheet date, although footnote disclosure may be necessary. Footnote disclosure will be discussed later in this section.

In addition to being probable, the accrual of a loss contingency also requires that the amount of the loss be **reasonably estimable**. In most situations, a single amount can be estimated, and this represents the loss that is accrued. In other situations, the loss may be estimated in terms of a range, for example, the range of loss may be $100,000 to $500,000. In these situations, the amount of loss to accrue is the best estimate within the range. For example, if the best estimate within the range is $200,000, the loss should be accrued in the amount of $200,000. However, if no number in the range is a better estimate of the loss than any other number in the range, the lower number in the range is accrued as the loss. Thus, $100,000 would be accrued if no other number in the range from $100,000 to $500,000 were a better estimate of the loss than any other number in the range.

c. **Examples of loss contingencies**—The accounting problems related to contingencies involve the following issues:

- Collectibility of receivables (Bad debts expense/Allowance for uncollectible accounts),
- Obligations related to product warranties and product defects (Warranty expense/ Warranty liability), and
- Premiums offered to customers (Premium expense/Premium liability)

These contingencies are usually accrued because it is **probable** that some receivables will not be collected, that some of the products sold will be defective and may need warranty work, and that some customers will take advantage of premiums offered by the company. In addition, the **amounts** in each case can usually be **estimated** because of past experience with each of these situations.

To illustrate the accrual of a loss contingency, let's focus on a **product warranty** situation. Here are the facts related to the illustration for ABC Company.

Year	Sales	*Actual warranty expenditures*	*Estimated warranty costs related to dollar sales*
2002	$500,000	$15,000	Year of sale 4%
2003	$700,000	$47,000	Year after sale 6%

In 2002, ABC should accrue a loss contingency related to product warranties for $50,000 [$500,000 x (4% + 6%)]. The entry would appear as follows:

Warranty expense	50,000	
Liability for product warranty		50,000

The **actual** warranty expenditures in 2002 would be recorded in the following manner. (Note that the actual expenditures reduce the liability and have no effect on the expense account.)

Liability for product warranty	15,000	
Cash, parts inventory, etc.		15,000

ABC's income statement for 2002 would report an expense for $50,000 related to its product warranty, and its December 31, 2002 balance sheet would report a current liability for product warranty of $35,000 ($50,000 – $15,000). In 2003, ABC should accrue a loss contingency related to product warranties for $70,000 [$700,000 x (4% + 6%)]. The entry would appear as follows:

Warranty expense	70,000	
Liability for product warranty		70,000

The actual warranty expenditures for 2003 would be recorded in the following manner. (Again, note that the actual expenditures only affect the liability account.)

Liability for product warranty	47,000	
Cash, parts inventory, etc.		47,000

ABC's income statement for 2003 should report an expense related to product warranties of $70,000, and its December 31, 2003 balance sheet should report a current liability for product warranty of $58,000 (the 1/1/03 balance of $35,000 + the 2003 expense of $70,000 less the actual warranty expenditures of $47,000 in 2003).

Another example of accrual of a contingent liability involves companies offering **premiums** (e.g., towels, knives, and other prizes) to promote their products. Such companies often have premium liability for outstanding coupons when it is probable that some of the coupons will be redeemed and the amount can be estimated. The expense should be accrued in the period of sale based on the estimated redemption rate.

Premium plan expense	xx	
Premium plan liability		xx

As coupons are actually redeemed by customers, the liability is reduced.

Premium plan liability	xx	
Premiums		xx

Loss contingencies that may be accrued (depending upon whether or not the two conditions of probable and reasonably estimable are satisfied) include the following events.

- Threat of expropriation of assets
- Pending or threatened litigation
- Actual or possible claims and assessments
- Guarantees of indebtedness of others
- Obligations of commercial banks under "Standby letters of credit," and
- Agreements to repurchase receivables (or the related property) that have been sold

Litigation—The one event listed above that appears frequently on the exam involves pending litigation. If the loss from litigation is reasonably estimable, and it is probable as of the balance sheet date that the lawsuit will be lost, the loss should be accrued.

To illustrate this point, assume that XYZ Company is presently involved in litigation involving patent infringement that allegedly occurred during 2002. The financial statements for 2002 are being prepared, and XYZ's legal counsel believes it is probable that XYZ will lose the lawsuit and that the damages will be in the range from $500,000 to $800,000 with the most likely amount being $700,000. Based upon XYZ's legal counsel, it should accrue the loss contingency in the following manner at December 31, 2002.

Loss from litigation	700,000	
Liability from litigation		700,000

The $700,000 loss from litigation should be reported on XYZ's 2002 income statement, and the liability should be reported on the December 31, 2002 balance sheet.

If XYZ settles the litigation in 2003 by paying damages of $600,000, the following journal entry should be made.

Liability from litigation	700,000	
Cash		600,000
Recovery of loss from litigation		100,000

The above entry results in a loss recovery for 2003 because the damages were settled for less than their estimated amount. This situation is not unusual because the loss contingency related to the litigation was based upon an estimate. Note that the loss recovery cannot exceed the estimated loss, which in this case was $700,000. It would be incorrect to revise the 2002 financial statements so that the loss contingency reflected the actual damages of $600,000. When the financial statements for 2002 were issued, the best estimate of loss was $700,000. This estimate is not revised subsequent to the issuance of the 2002 financial statements.

Since loss contingencies involving litigation are only accrued if the conditions of probable and reasonably estimable are present, you should be aware of what is reported if either or both of these conditions are not present. For XYZ's case, suppose that its legal counsel believed it was only **reasonably possible** (not probable) as of the balance sheet date, December 31, 2002, that XYZ would lose its lawsuit. In this situation, it would **not** be appropriate for XYZ to accrue a loss at December 31, 2002. However, because XYZ's legal counsel believes it is reasonably possible to lose the lawsuit, XYZ should disclose this litigation in its footnotes for its 2002 financial statements. The range of loss, noted before as being from $500,000 to $800,000, would also be disclosed in the footnote. In 2003, when the actual damages of $600,000 are known, XYZ would record a loss of this amount and report it on its 2003 income statement.

If XYZ's legal counsel believed that it was **remote** as of December 31, 2002, that the lawsuit would be lost, no accrual or disclosure of the litigation would be necessary.

Loss contingencies that are not accrued or even disclosed in the footnotes include the following events.

- Risk of loss or damage of enterprise property by fire, explosion, or other hazards
- General or unspecified business risks
- Risk of loss from catastrophes assumed by property and casualty insurance companies including reinsurance companies

Losses that result from the above events are recorded and reported in the period when the event occurs that causes the loss. For example, if XYZ's factory is destroyed by fire in 2002, the loss from this event should be recorded and reported in 2002. If the damages from the fire amount to $1,000,000, and XYZ's insurance company reimburses XYZ $800,000, XYZ's loss is $200,000. If XYZ does not insure for fire with an insurance company, XYZ's loss for 2002 would be $1,000,000.

Compensated absences—Knowledge of the conditions that must be present in order to accrue a loss contingency is helpful in the accounting for **compensated absences** (vacation, sick leave pay, etc.). According to SFAS 43 (see outline), an employer shall accrue a liability for employees' compensation for future absences if all of the following conditions are met.

- The employer's obligation relating to employees' rights to receive compensation for future absences is attributable to employees' **services already rendered**
- The obligation relates to rights that **vest or accumulate**
- Payment of the compensation is **probable**
- The amount can be reasonably **estimated**

Note that the last two criteria are the general criteria for recognizing a loss contingency per SFAS 5.

To illustrate the accounting for compensated absences, assume MNO Company employees earn two weeks of paid vacation for each year of employment. Unused vacation time can be accumulated and carried forward to succeeding years, and will be paid at the salary level in effect when the vacation is taken. As of December 31, 2002, when John Baker's salary was $600 per week, John Baker had earned eighteen weeks vacation time and had used twelve weeks of accumulated vacation time. At December 31, 2002, MNO should report a liability for John Baker's accumulated vacation time of $3,600 (six weeks of accumulated vacation time times $600 per week). The journal entry at December 31, 2002, would appear as follows (assume previous year's entry was reversed).

| Salary and wages expense | 3,600 | |
| Accrued liability for compensated absences | | 3,600 |

Gain contingencies—The discussion relating to contingencies has focused on the accounting for loss contingencies. On the other hand, contingencies exist that may also result in possible **gains**. According to SFAS 5, contingencies that might result in gains usually are not reflected in the accounts since to do so might be to recognize revenue prior to its realization. This means that any gains that result from gain contingencies should be recorded and reported in the period during which the contingency is resolved. For example, the plaintiff in a lawsuit should not record or report the expected damages to be received until the lawsuit has been decided.

D. Ratios

1. **Solvency**—Measure short-term viability

    a. **Acid-test (quick) ratio**—Measures ability to pay current liabilities from cash and near-cash items

    $$\frac{\text{Cash, Net receivables, Marketable securities}}{\text{Current liabilities}}$$

    b. **Current ratio**—Measures ability to pay current liabilities from cash, near-cash, and cash flow items

    $$\frac{\text{Current assets}}{\text{Current liabilities}}$$

2. **Operational efficiency**—Measures utilization of assets

    a. **Receivable turnover**—Measures how rapidly cash is collected from credit sales

    $$\frac{\text{Net credit sales}}{\text{Average net receivables}}$$

    b. **Number of days' sales in average receivables**—Average length of time receivables are outstanding, which reflects credit and collection policies

    $$\frac{365}{\text{Receivable turnover}}$$

    c. **Inventory turnover**—Indicates how rapidly inventory is sold

    $$\frac{\text{Cost of goods sold}}{\text{Average inventory}}$$

    d. **Number of days' supply in average inventory**—Measures the number of days inventory is held before sale and therefore reflects the effeciency of the entity's inventory policies

    $$\frac{365}{\text{Inventory turnover}}$$

    e. **Length of operating cycle**—Measures length of time from purchase of inventory to collection of cash

    $$\begin{array}{c}\text{Number of days'} \\ \text{supply in average} \\ \text{inventory}\end{array} + \begin{array}{c}\text{Number of days'} \\ \text{sales in average} \\ \text{receivables}\end{array}$$

MULTIPLE-CHOICE QUESTIONS (1-108)

1. Burr Company had the following account balances at December 31, 2002:

Cash in banks	$2,250,000
Cash on hand	125,000
Cash legally restricted for additions to plant (expected to be disbursed in 2003)	1,600,000

Cash in banks includes $600,000 of compensating balances against short-term borrowing arrangements. The compensating balances are not legally restricted as to withdrawal by Burr. In the current assets section of Burr's December 31, 2002 balance sheet, total cash should be reported at

    a. $1,775,000
    b. $2,250,000
    c. $2,375,000
    d. $3,975,000

2. Ral Corp.'s checkbook balance on December 31, 2002, was $5,000. In addition, Ral held the following items in its safe on that date:

Check payable to Ral Corp., dated January 2, 2003, in
payment of a sale made in December 2002, not included in December 31 checkbook balance $2,000
Check payable to Ral Corp., deposited December 15 and
included in December 31 checkbook balance, but returned by bank on December 30 stamped "NSF." The
check was redeposited on January 2, 2003, and cleared
on January 9   500
Check drawn on Ral Corp.'s account, payable to a vendor, dated and recorded in Ral's books on Decem-
ber 31 but not mailed until January 10, 2003   300

The proper amount to be shown as Cash on Ral's balance sheet at December 31, 2002 is

    a. $4,800
    b. $5,300
    c. $6,500
    d. $6,800

3. Trans Co. had the following balances at December 31, 2002:

Cash in checking account	$ 35,000
Cash in money market account	75,000
US Treasury bill, purchased 11/1/2002, maturing 1/31/2003	350,000
US Treasury bill, purchased 12/1/2002, maturing 3/31/2003	400,000

Trans's policy is to treat as cash equivalents all highly liquid investments with a maturity of three months or less when purchased. What amount should Trans report as cash and cash equivalents in its December 31, 2002 balance sheet?

    a. $110,000
    b. $385,000
    c. $460,000
    d. $860,000

4. On October 31, 2002, Dingo, Inc. had cash accounts at three different banks. One account balance is segregated solely for a November 15, 2002 payment into a bond sinking fund. A second account, used for branch operations, is overdrawn. The third account, used for regular corporate operations, has a positive balance. How should these accounts be reported in Dingo's October 31, 2002 classified balance sheet?

    a.   The segregated account should be reported as a
         noncurrent asset, the regular account should be re-

ported as a current asset, and the overdraft should
be reported as a current liability.
    b.   The segregated and regular accounts should be re-
         ported as current assets, and the overdraft should
         be reported as a current liability.
    c.   The segregated account should be reported as a
         noncurrent asset, and the regular account should be
         reported as a current asset net of the overdraft.
    d.   The segregated and regular accounts should be re-
         ported as current assets net of the overdraft.

5. In preparing its August 31, 2002 bank reconciliation, Apex Corp. has available the following information:

Balance per bank statement, 8/31/02	$18,050
Deposit in transit, 8/31/02	3,250
Return of customer's check for insufficient funds, 8/31/02	600
Outstanding checks, 8/31/02	2,750
Bank service charges for August	100

At August 31, 2002, Apex's correct cash balance is

    a. $18,550
    b. $17,950
    c. $17,850
    d. $17,550

6. Poe, Inc. had the following bank reconciliation at March 31, 2002:

Balance per bank statement, 3/31/02	$46,500
Add deposit in transit	10,300
	56,800
Less outstanding checks	12,600
Balance per books, 3/31/02	$44,200

Data per bank for the month of April 2002 follow:

Deposits	$58,400
Disbursements	49,700

All reconciling items at March 31, 2002, cleared the bank in April. Outstanding checks at April 30, 2002, totaled $7,000. There were no deposits in transit at April 30, 2002. What is the cash balance per books at April 30, 2002?

    a. $48,200
    b. $52,900
    c. $55,200
    d. $58,500

7. On the December 31, 2002 balance sheet of Mann Co., the current receivables consisted of the following:

Trade accounts receivable	$ 93,000
Allowance for uncollectible accounts	(2,000)
Claim against shipper for goods lost in transit (November 2002)	3,000
Selling price of unsold goods sent by Mann on consignment at 130% of cost (**not** included in Mann's ending inventory)	26,000
Security deposit on lease of warehouse used for storing some inventories	30,000
Total	$150,000

At December 31, 2002, the correct total of Mann's current net receivables was

    a. $ 94,000
    b. $120,000
    c. $124,000
    d. $150,000

8. The following information relates to Jay Co.'s accounts receivable for 2002:

Accounts receivable, 1/1/02	$ 650,000
Credit sales for 2002	2,700,000
Sales returns for 2002	75,000
Accounts written off during 2002	40,000
Collections from customers during 2002	2,150,000
Estimated future sales returns at 12/31/02	50,000
Estimated uncollectible accounts at 12/31/02	110,000

What amount should Jay report for accounts receivable, before allowances for sales returns and uncollectible accounts, at December 31, 2002?

- a. $1,200,000
- b. $1,125,000
- c. $1,085,000
- d. $ 925,000

9. Frame Co. has an 8% note receivable dated June 30, 2000, in the original amount of $150,000. Payments of $50,000 in principal plus accrued interest are due annually on July 1, 2001, 2002, and 2003. In its June 30, 2002 balance sheet, what amount should Frame report as a current asset for interest on the note receivable?

- a. $0
- b. $ 4,000
- c. $ 8,000
- d. $12,000

10. On December 1, 2002, Tigg Mortgage Co. gave Pod Corp. a $200,000, 12% loan. Pod received proceeds of $194,000 after the deduction of a $6,000 nonrefundable loan origination fee. Principal and interest are due in sixty monthly installments of $4,450, beginning January 1, 2003. The repayments yield an effective interest rate of 12% at a present value of $200,000 and 13.4% at a present value of $194,000. What amount of accrued interest receivable should Tigg include in its December 31, 2002 balance sheet?

- a. $4,450
- b. $2,166
- c. $2,000
- d. $0

11. On Merf's April 30, 2002 balance sheet a note receivable was reported as a noncurrent asset and its accrued interest for eight months was reported as a current asset. Which of the following terms would fit Merf's note receivable?

- a. Both principal and interest amounts are payable on August 31, 2002, and August 31, 2003.
- b. Principal and interest are due December 31, 2002.
- c. Both principal and interest amounts are payable on December 31, 2002, and December 31, 2003.
- d. Principal is due August 31, 2003, and interest is due August 31, 2002, and August 31, 2003.

12. On August 15, 2002, Benet Co. sold goods for which it received a note bearing the market rate of interest on that date. The four-month note was dated July 15, 2002. Note principal, together with all interest, is due November 15, 2002. When the note was recorded on August 15, which of the following accounts increased?

- a. Unearned discount.
- b. Interest receivable.
- c. Prepaid interest.
- d. Interest revenue.

13. Delta, Inc. sells to wholesalers on terms of 2/15, net 30. Delta has no cash sales but 50% of Delta's customers take

advantage of the discount. Delta uses the gross method of recording sales and trade receivables. An analysis of Delta's trade receivables balances at December 31, 2002, revealed the following:

Age		Amount	Collectible
0 - 15	days	$100,000	100%
16 - 30	days	60,000	95%
31 - 60	days	5,000	90%
Over 60 days		2,500	$500
		$167,500	

In its December 31, 2002 balance sheet, what amount should Delta report for allowance for discounts?

- a. $1,000
- b. $1,620
- c. $1,675
- d. $2,000

14. Fenn Stores, Inc. had sales of $1,000,000 during December, 2002. Experience has shown that merchandise equaling 7% of sales will be returned within thirty days and an additional 3% will be returned within ninety days. Returned merchandise is readily resalable. In addition, merchandise equaling 15% of sales will be exchanged for merchandise of equal or greater value. What amount should Fenn report for net sales in its income statement for the month of December 2002?

- a. $900,000
- b. $850,000
- c. $780,000
- d. $750,000

15. At January 1, 2002, Jamin Co. had a credit balance of $260,000 in its allowance for uncollectible accounts. Based on past experience, 2% of Jamin's credit sales have been uncollectible. During 2002, Jamin wrote off $325,000 of uncollectible accounts. Credit sales for 2002 were $9,000,000. In its December 31, 2002 balance sheet, what amount should Jamin report as allowance for uncollectible accounts?

- a. $115,000
- b. $180,000
- c. $245,000
- d. $440,000

16. The following accounts were abstracted from Roxy Co.'s unadjusted trial balance at December 31, 2002:

	Debit	Credit
Accounts receivable	$1,000,000	
Allowance for uncollectible accounts	8,000	
Net credit sales		$3,000,000

Roxy estimates that 3% of the gross accounts receivable will become uncollectible. After adjustment at December 31, 2002, the allowance for uncollectible accounts should have a credit balance of

- a. $90,000
- b. $82,000
- c. $38,000
- d. $30,000

17. In its December 31 balance sheet, Butler Co. reported trade accounts receivable of $250,000 and related allowance for uncollectible accounts of $20,000. What is the total amount of risk of accounting loss related to Butler's trade accounts receivable, and what amount of that risk is off-balance-sheet risk?

	Risk of accounting loss	Off-balance-sheet risk
a.	$0	$0
b.	$230,000	$0
c.	$230,000	$20,000
d.	$250,000	$20,000

18. Inge Co. determined that the net value of its accounts receivable at December 31, 2002, based on an aging of the receivables, was $325,000. Additional information is as follows:

Allowance for uncollectible accounts—1/1/02	$ 30,000
Uncollectible accounts written off during 2002	18,000
Uncollectible accounts recovered during 2002	2,000
Accounts receivable at 12/31/02	350,000

For 2002, what would be Inge's uncollectible accounts expense?

   a. $ 5,000
   b. $11,000
   c. $15,000
   d. $21,000

19. The following information pertains to Tara Co.'s accounts receivable at December 31, 2002:

Days outstanding	Amount	Estimated % uncollectible
0 – 60	$120,000	1%
61 – 120	90,000	2%
Over 120	100,000	6%
	$310,000	

During 2002, Tara wrote off $7,000 in receivables and recovered $4,000 that had been written off in prior years. Tara's December 31, 2001 allowance for uncollectible accounts was $22,000. Under the aging method, what amount of allowance for uncollectible accounts should Tara report at December 31, 2002?

   a. $ 9,000
   b. $10,000
   c. $13,000
   d. $19,000

20. A method of estimating uncollectible accounts that emphasizes asset valuation rather than income measurement is the allowance method based on

   a. Aging the receivables.
   b. Direct write-off.
   c. Gross sales.
   d. Credit sales less returns and allowances.

21. Which method of recording uncollectible accounts expense is consistent with accrual accounting?

	Allowance	Direct write-off
a.	Yes	Yes
b.	Yes	No
c.	No	Yes
d.	No	No

22. When the allowance method of recognizing uncollectible accounts is used, the entry to record the write-off of a specific account

   a. Decreases both accounts receivable and the allowance for uncollectible accounts.
   b. Decreases accounts receivable and increases the allowance for uncollectible accounts.
   c. Increases the allowance for uncollectible accounts and decreases net income.
   d. Decreases both receivable and net income.

23. A company uses the allowance method to recognize uncollectible accounts expense. What is the effect at the time of the collection of an account previously written off on each of the following accounts?

	Allowance for uncollectible accounts	Uncollectible accounts expense
a.	No effect	Decrease
b.	Increase	Decrease
c.	Increase	No effect
d.	No effect	No effect

24. Which of the following is a method to generate cash from accounts receivables?

	Assignment	Factoring
a.	Yes	No
b.	Yes	Yes
c.	No	Yes
d.	No	No

25. Gar Co. factored its receivables. Control was surrendered in the transaction which was on a without recourse basis with Ross Bank. Gar received cash as a result of this transaction, which is best described as a

   a. Loan from Ross collateralized by Gar's accounts receivable.
   b. Loan from Ross to be repaid by the proceeds from Gar's accounts receivable.
   c. Sale of Gar's accounts receivable to Ross, with the risk of uncollectible accounts retained by Gar.
   d. Sale of Gar's accounts receivable to Ross, with the risk of uncollectible accounts transferred to Ross.

Items 26 through 28 are based on the following:

Taylored Corp. factored $400,000 of accounts receivable to Rich Corp. on July 1, 2002. Control was surrendered by Taylored. Rich accepted the receivables subject to recourse for nonpayment. Rich assessed a fee of 2% and retains a holdback equal to 5% of the accounts receivable. In addition, Rich charged 15% interest computed on a weighted-average time to maturity of the receivables of forty-one days. The fair value of the recourse obligation is $8,000.

26. Taylored will receive and record cash of

   a. $385,260
   b. $357,260
   c. $365,260
   d. $377,260

27. Which of the following statements is correct?

   a. Rich should record an asset of $8,000 for the recourse obligation.
   b. Taylored should record a liability and corresponding loss of $8,000 related to the recourse obligation.
   c. Taylored should record a liability of $8,000, but no loss, related to the recourse obligation.
   d. No entry for the recourse obligation should be made by Taylored or Rich until the debtor fails to pay.

28. Assuming all receivables are collected, Taylored's cost of factoring the receivables would be

   a. $ 8,000
   b. $34,740
   c. $42,740
   d. $14,740

29. Which of the following is used to account for probable sales discounts, sales returns, and sales allowances?

	Due from factor	*Recourse liability*
a.	Yes	No
b.	Yes	Yes
c.	No	Yes
d.	No	No

30. Scarbrough Corp. factored $600,000 of accounts receivable to Duff Corp. on October 1, 2001. Control was surrendered by Scarbrough. Duff accepted the receivables subject to recourse for nonpayment. Duff assessed a fee of 3% and retains a holdback equal to 5% of the accounts receivable. In addition, Duff charged 15% interest computed on a weighted-average time to maturity of the receivables of fifty-four days. The fair value of the recourse obligation is $9,000. Scarbrough will receive and record cash of
- a. $529,685
- b. $538,685
- c. $547,685
- d. $556,685

31. Synthia Corp. factored $750,000 of accounts receivable to Thomas Company on December 3, 2002. Control was surrendered by Synthia. Thomas accepted the receivables subject to recourse for nonpayment. Thomas assessed a fee of 2% and retains a holdback equal to 4% of the accounts receivable. In addition, Thomas charged 12% interest computed on a weighted-average time to maturity of the receivables of fifty-one days. The fair value of the recourse obligation is $15,000. Assuming all receivables are collected, Synthia's cost of factoring the receivables would be
- a. $12,575
- b. $15,000
- c. $27,575
- d. $42,575

32. Bannon Corp. transferred financial assets to Chapman, Inc. The transfer meets the conditions to be accounted for as a sale. As the transferor, Bannon should do each of the following, **except**
- a. Remove all assets sold from the balance sheet.
- b. Record all assets received and liabilities incurred as proceeds from the sale.
- c. Measure the assets received and liabilities incurred at cost.
- d. Recognize any gain or loss on the sale.

33. If financial assets are exchanged for cash or other consideration, but the transfer does not meet the criteria for a sale, the transferor and the transferee should account for the transaction as a

	Secured borrowing	*Pledge of collateral*
a.	No	Yes
b.	Yes	Yes
c.	Yes	No
d.	No	No

34. All but one of the following are required before a transfer of receivables can be recorded as a sale.
- a. The transferred receivables are beyond the reach of the transferor and its creditors.
- b. The transferor has not kept effective control over the transferred receivables through a repurchase agreement.
- c. The transferor maintains continuing involvement.
- d. The transferee can pledge or sell the transferred receivables.

35. Which of the following is not an objective for each entity accounting for transfers of financial assets?
- a. To derecognize assets when control is gained.
- b. To derecognize liabilities when extinguished.
- c. To recognize liabilities when incurred.
- d. To derecognize assets when control is given up.

36. Which of the following is false?
- a. A servicing asset shall be assessed for impairment based on its fair value.
- b. A servicing liability shall be assessed for increased obligation based on its fair value.
- c. An obligation to service financial assets may result in the recognition of a servicing asset or servicing liability.
- d. A servicing asset or liability should be amortized for a period of five years.

37. Which of the following is true?
- a. A debtor may not grant a security interest in certain assets to a lender to serve as collateral with recourse.
- b. A debtor may not grant a security interest in certain assets to a lender to serve as collateral without recourse.
- c. The arrangement of having collateral transferred to a secured party is known as a pledge.
- d. Secured parties are never permitted to sell collateral held under a pledge.

Items 38 through 40 are based on the following:

Company ABC sells loans with a $2,200 fair value and a carrying amount of $2,000. ABC Company obtains an option to purchase similar loans and assumes a recourse obligation to repurchase loans. ABC Company also agrees to provide a floating rate of interest to the transferee company. The fair values are listed.

Fair values	
Cash proceeds	$2,100
Interest rate swap	140
Call option	80
Recourse obligation	(120)

38. What is the gain (loss) on the sale?
- a. $ 320
- b. $ 200
- c. $(100)
- d. $ 120

39. The journal entry to record the transfer for ABC Company includes
- a. A debit to call option.
- b. A credit to interest rate swap.
- c. A debit to loans.
- d. A credit to cash.

40. Assume for this problem that ABC Company agreed to service the loans without explicitly stating the compensation. The fair value of the service is $50. What are the net proceeds received and the gain (loss) on the sale?

	Net proceeds received	Gain (loss)
a.	$2,200	$ 200
b.	$2,250	$ 250
c.	$2,150	$ 150
d.	$2,200	$(250)

41. In accordance with SFAS 140, *Accounting for Transfers and Servicing of Financial Assets and Extinguishments of Liabilities,* financial assets subject to prepayment should be measured
    a.   Like investments in debt securities classified as held-to-maturity.
    b.   At cost.
    c.   Like investments in debt securities classified as available-for-sale or trading.
    d.   At fair value.

42. In accordance with SFAS 140, *Accounting for Transfers and Servicing of Financial Assets and Extinguishments of Liabilities,* all of the following would be disclosed except
    a.   Policy for requiring collateral or other security due to repurchase agreements or securities lending transactions.
    b.   Cash flows between the securitization special-purpose entity (SPE) and the transferor.
    c.   Accounting policies for measuring retained interest.
    d.   Description of assets or liabilities with estimimable fair values.

43. Taft Inc. borrowed $1,000,000 from Wilson Company on July 2, 2000. As part of the loan agreement, Taft granted Wilson a security interest in land that originally cost $750,000 when it was acquired by Taft in 1994. The land had a fair value of $900,000 on July 2, 2000. In June 2002, Taft defaulted on its loan to Wilson, and the land was transferred to Wilson in full settlement of the debt on June 30. The land had a fair value of $950,000 on June 30, 2002. In accordance with SFAS 140, *Accounting for Transfers and Servicing of Financial Assets and Extinguishments of Liabilities,* what amount should Wilson record for land on June 30, 2002?
    a. $0.
    b. $750,000.
    c. $900,000.
    d. $950,000.

44. Lyle, Inc. is preparing its financial statements for the year ended December 31, 2002. Accounts payable amounted to $360,000 before any necessary year-end adjustment related to the following:

    •   At December 31, 2002, Lyle has a $50,000 debit balance in its accounts payable to Ross, a supplier, resulting from a $50,000 advance payment for goods to be manufactured to Lyle's specifications.
    •   Checks in the amount of $100,000 were written to vendors and recorded on December 29, 2002. The checks were mailed on January 5, 2003.

What amount should Lyle report as accounts payable in its December 31, 2002 balance sheet?
    a. $510,000
    b. $410,000
    c. $310,000
    d. $210,000

45. Rabb Co. records its purchases at gross amounts but wishes to change to recording purchases net of purchase discounts. Discounts available on purchases recorded from October 1, 2001, to September 30, 2002, totaled $2,000. Of this amount, $200 is still available in the accounts payable balance. The balances in Rabb's accounts as of and for the year ended September 30, 2002, before conversion are

Purchases	$100,000
Purchase discounts taken	800
Accounts payable	30,000

What is Rabb's accounts payable balance as of September 30, 2002, after the conversion?
    a. $29,800
    b. $29,200
    c. $28,800
    d. $28,200

46. On March 1, 2001, Fine Co. borrowed $10,000 and signed a two-year note bearing interest at 12% per annum compounded annually. Interest is payable in full at maturity on February 28, 2003. What amount should Fine report as a liability for accrued interest at December 31, 2002?
    a. $0
    b. $1,000
    c. $1,200
    d. $2,320

47. On September 1, 2001, Brak Co. borrowed on a $1,350,000 note payable from Federal Bank. The note bears interest at 12% and is payable in three equal annual principal payments of $450,000. On this date, the bank's prime rate was 11%. The first annual payment for interest and principal was made on September 1, 2002. At December 31, 2002, what amount should Brak report as accrued interest payable?
    a. $54,000
    b. $49,500
    c. $36,000
    d. $33,000

48. In its 2002 financial statements, Cris Co. reported interest expense of $85,000 in its income statement and cash paid for interest of $68,000 in its cash flow statement. There was no prepaid interest or interest capitalization either at the beginning or end of 2002. Accrued interest at December 31, 2001, was $15,000. What amount should Cris report as accrued interest payable in its December 31, 2002 balance sheet?
    a. $ 2,000
    b. $15,000
    c. $17,000
    d. $32,000

49. Ames, Inc. has $500,000 of notes payable due June 15, 2003. Ames signed an agreement on December 1, 2002, to borrow up to $500,000 to refinance the notes payable on a long-term basis with no payments due until 2003. The financing agreement stipulated that borrowings may not exceed 80% of the value of the collateral Ames was providing. At the date of issuance of the December 31, 2002 financial statements, the value of the collateral was $600,000 and is not expected to fall below this amount during 2003. In Ames' December 31, 2002 balance sheet, the obligation for these notes payable should be classified as

	Short-term	Long-term
a.	$500,000	$0
b.	$100,000	$400,000
c.	$ 20,000	$480,000
d.	$0	$500,000

50. A company issued a short-term note payable with a stated 12% rate of interest to a bank. The bank charged a .5% loan origination fee and remitted the balance to the company. The effective interest rate paid by the company in this transaction would be

   a. Equal to 12.5%.
   b. More than 12.5%.
   c. Less than 12.5%.
   d. Independent of 12.5%.

51. Cali, Inc. had a $4,000,000 note payable due on March 15, 2002. On January 28, 2002, before the issuance of its 2001 financial statements, Cali issued long-term bonds in the amount of $4,500,000. Proceeds from the bonds were used to repay the note when it came due. How should Cali classify the note in its December 31, 2001 financial statements?

   a. As a current liability, with separate disclosure of the note refinancing.
   b. As a current liability, with no separate disclosure required.
   c. As a noncurrent liability, with separate disclosure of the note refinancing.
   d. As a noncurrent liability, with no separate disclosure required.

52. On December 31, 2002, Largo, Inc. had a $750,000 note payable outstanding, due July 31, 2003. Largo borrowed the money to finance construction of a new plant. Largo planned to refinance the note by issuing long-term bonds. Because Largo temporarily had excess cash, it prepaid $250,000 of the note on January 12, 2003. In February 2003, Largo completed a $1,500,000 bond offering. Largo will use the bond offering proceeds to repay the note payable at its maturity and to pay construction costs during 2003. On March 3, 2003, Largo issued its 2002 financial statements. What amount of the note payable should Largo include in the current liabilities section of its December 31, 2003 balance sheet?

   a. $750,000
   b. $500,000
   c. $250,000
   d. $0

53. Rice Co. salaried employees are paid biweekly. Advances made to employees are paid back by payroll deductions. Information relating to salaries follows:

	12/31/01	12/31/02
Employee advances	$24,000	$ 36,000
Accrued salaries payable	40,000	?
Salaries expense during the year		420,000
Salaries paid during the year (gross)		390,000

In Rice's December 31, 2002 balance sheet, accrued salaries payable was

   a. $94,000
   b. $82,000
   c. $70,000
   d. $30,000

54. Fay Corp. pays its outside salespersons fixed monthly salaries and commissions on net sales. Sales commissions are computed and paid on a monthly basis (in the month following the month of sale), and the fixed salaries are treated as advances against commissions. However, if the fixed salaries for salespersons exceed their sales commissions earned for a month, such excess is not charged back to them. Pertinent data for the month of March 2002 for the three salespersons are as follows:

Salesperson	Fixed salary	Net sales	Commission rate
A	$10,000	$ 200,000	4%
B	14,000	400,000	6%
C	18,000	600,000	6%
Totals	$42,000	$1,200,000	

What amount should Fay accrue for sales commissions payable at March 31, 2002?

   a. $70,000
   b. $68,000
   c. $28,000
   d. $26,000

55. Lime Co.'s payroll for the month ended January 31, 2002, is summarized as follows:

Total wages	$10,000
Federal income tax withheld	1,200

All wages paid were subject to FICA. FICA tax rates were 7% each for employee and employer. Lime remits payroll taxes on the 15th of the following month. In its financial statements for the month ended January 31, 2002, what amounts should Lime report as total payroll tax liability and as payroll tax expense?

	Liability	Expense
a.	$1,200	$1,400
b.	$1,900	$1,400
c.	$1,900	$ 700
d.	$2,600	$ 700

56. Under state law, Acme may pay 3% of eligible gross wages or it may reimburse the state directly for actual unemployment claims. Acme believes that actual unemployment claims will be 2% of eligible gross wages and has chosen to reimburse the state. Eligible gross wages are defined as the first $10,000 of gross wages paid to each employee. Acme had five employees, each of whom earned $20,000 during 2002. In its December 31, 2002 balance sheet, what amount should Acme report as accrued liability for unemployment claims?

   a. $1,000
   b. $1,500
   c. $2,000
   d. $3,000

57. Pine Corp. is required to contribute, to an employee stock ownership plan (ESOP), 10% of its income after deduction for this contribution but before income tax. Pine's income before charges for the contribution and income tax was $75,000. The income tax rate is 30%. What amount should be accrued as a contribution to the ESOP?

   a. $7,500
   b. $6,818
   c. $5,250
   d. $4,773

58. Able Co. provides an incentive compensation plan under which its president receives a bonus equal to 10% of the corporation's income before income tax but after deduction of the bonus. If the tax rate is 40% and net income after bonus and income tax was $360,000, what was the amount of the bonus?

a. $36,000
b. $60,000
c. $66,000
d. $90,000

59. Ivy Co. operates a retail store. All items are sold subject to a 6% state sales tax, which Ivy collects and records as sales revenue. Ivy files quarterly sales tax returns when due, by the twentieth day following the end of the sales quarter. However, in accordance with state requirements, Ivy remits sales tax collected by the twentieth day of the month following any month such collections exceed $500. Ivy takes these payments as credits on the quarterly sales tax return. The sales taxes paid by Ivy are charged against sales revenue.

Following is a monthly summary appearing in Ivy's first quarter 2002 sales revenue account:

	Debit	Credit
January	$ --	$10,600
February	600	7,420
March	--	8,480
	$600	$26,500

In its March 31, 2002 balance sheet, what amount should Ivy report as sales taxes payable?
a. $ 600
b. $ 900
c. $1,500
d. $1,590

60. Hudson Hotel collects 15% in city sales taxes on room rentals, in addition to a $2 per room, per night, occupancy tax. Sales taxes for each month are due at the end of the following month, and occupancy taxes are due fifteen days after the end of each calendar quarter. On January 3, 2003, Hudson paid its November 2002 sales taxes and its fourth quarter 2002 occupancy taxes. Additional information pertaining to Hudson's operations is

2002	Room rentals	Room nights
October	$100,000	1,100
November	110,000	1,200
December	150,000	1,800

What amounts should Hudson report as sales taxes payable and occupancy taxes payable in its December 31, 2002 balance sheet?

	Sales taxes	Occupancy taxes
a.	$39,000	$6,000
b.	$39,000	$8,200
c.	$54,000	$6,000
d.	$54,000	$8,200

61. On July 1, 2002, Ran County issued realty tax assessments for its fiscal year ended June 30, 2003. On September 1, 2002, Day Co. purchased a warehouse in Ran County. The purchase price was reduced by a credit for accrued realty taxes. Day did not record the entire year's real estate tax obligation, but instead records tax expenses at the end of each month by adjusting prepaid real estate taxes or real estate taxes payable, as appropriate. On November 1, 2002, Day paid the first of two equal installments of $12,000 for realty taxes. What amount of this payment should Day record as a debit to real estate taxes payable?
a. $ 4,000
b. $ 8,000
c. $10,000
d. $12,000

62. Kemp Co. must determine the December 31, 2002 year-end accruals for advertising and rent expenses. A $500 advertising bill was received January 7, 2003, comprising costs of $375 for advertisements in December 2002 issues, and $125 for advertisements in January 2003 issues of the newspaper.

A store lease, effective December 16, 2001, calls for fixed rent of $1,200 per month, payable one month from the effective date and monthly thereafter. In addition, rent equal to 5% of net sales over $300,000 per calendar year is payable on January 31 of the following year. Net sales for 2002 were $550,000.

In its December 31, 2002 balance sheet, Kemp should report accrued liabilities of
a. $12,875
b. $13,000
c. $13,100
d. $13,475

63. On May 1, 2002, Marno County issued property tax assessments for the fiscal year ended June 30, 2003. The first of two equal installments was due on November 1, 2002. On September 1, 2002, Dyur Co. purchased a four-year-old factory in Marno subject to an allowance for accrued taxes. Dyur did not record the entire year's property tax obligation, but instead records tax expenses at the end of each month by adjusting prepaid property taxes or property taxes payable, as appropriate. The recording of the November 1, 2002 payment by Dyur should have been allocated between an increase in prepaid property taxes and a decrease in property taxes payable in which of the following percentages?

	Percentage allocated to	
	Increase in prepaid property taxes	Decrease in paid property taxes
a.	66 2/3%	33 1/3%
b.	0%	100%
c.	50%	50%
d.	33 1/3%	66 2/3%

64. Black Co. requires advance payments with special orders for machinery constructed to customer specifications. These advances are nonrefundable. Information for 2002 is as follows:

Customer advances—balance 12/31/01	$118,000
Advances received with orders in 2002	184,000
Advances applied to orders shipped in 2002	164,000
Advances applicable to orders cancelled in 2002	50,000

In Black's December 31, 2002 balance sheet, what amount should be reported as a current liability for advances from customer?
a. $0
b. $ 88,000
c. $138,000
d. $148,000

65. Marr Co. sells its products in reusable containers. The customer is charged a deposit for each container delivered and receives a refund for each container returned within two years after the year of delivery. Marr accounts for the containers not returned within the time limit as being retired by sale at the deposit amount. Information for 2002 is as follows:

Container deposits at December 31, 2001, from deliveries in

2000	$150,000	
2001	430,000	$580,000

Deposits for containers delivered in 2002   780,000

Deposits for containers returned in 2002 from deliveries in

2000	$ 90,000
2001	250,000
2002	286,000 626,000

In Marr's December 31, 2002 balance sheet, the liability for deposits on returnable containers should be
- a. $494,000
- b. $584,000
- c. $674,000
- d. $734,000

66. Kent Co., a division of National Realty, Inc., maintains escrow accounts and pays real estate taxes for National's mortgage customers. Escrow funds are kept in interest-bearing accounts. Interest, less a 10% service fee, is credited to the mortgagee's account and used to reduce future escrow payments. Additional information follows:

Escrow accounts liability, 1/1/02	$ 700,000
Escrow payments received during 2002	1,580,000
Real estate taxes paid during 2002	1,720,000
Interest on escrow funds during 2002	50,000

What amount should Kent report as escrow accounts liability in its December 31, 2002 balance sheet?
- a. $510,000
- b. $515,000
- c. $605,000
- d. $610,000

67. Cobb Company sells appliance service contracts agreeing to repair appliances for a two-year period. Cobb's past experience is that, of the total dollars spent for repairs on service contracts, 40% is incurred evenly during the first contract year and 60% evenly during the second contract year. Receipts from service contract sales for the two years ended December 31, 2002, are as follows:

2001	$500,000
2002	600,000

Receipts from contracts are credited to unearned service contract revenue. Assume that all contract sales are made evenly during the year. What amount should Cobb report as unearned service contract revenue at December 31, 2002?
- a. $360,000
- b. $470,000
- c. $480,000
- d. $630,000

68. Toddler Care Co. offers three payment plans on its twelve-month contracts. Information on the three plans and the number of children enrolled in each plan for the September 1, 2002 through August 31, 2003 contract year follows:

Plan	Initial payment per child	Monthly fees per child	Number of children
#1	$500	$ --	15
#2	200	30	12
#3	--	50	9
			36

Toddler received $9,900 of initial payments on September 1, 2002, and $3,240 of monthly fees during the period September 1 through December 31, 2002. In its December 31, 2002 balance sheet, what amount should Toddler report as deferred revenues?
- a. $3,300
- b. $4,380
- c. $6,600
- d. $9,900

69. For $50 a month, Rawl Co. visits its customers' premises and performs insect control services. If customers experience problems between regularly scheduled visits, Rawl makes service calls at no additional charge. Instead of paying monthly, customers may pay an annual fee of $540 in advance. For a customer who pays the annual fee in advance, Rawl should recognize the related revenue
- a. When the cash is collected.
- b. At the end of the fiscal year.
- c. At the end of the contract year after all of the services have been performed.
- d. Evenly over the contract year as the services are performed.

70. A retail store received cash and issued gift certificates that are redeemable in merchandise. The gift certificates lapse one year after they are issued. How would the deferred revenue account be affected by each of the following transactions?

	Redemption of certificates	Lapse of certificates
a.	Decrease	No effect
b.	Decrease	Decrease
c.	No effect	No effect
d.	No effect	Decrease

71. On March 31, 2002, Dallas Co. received an advance payment of 60% of the sales price for special-order goods to be manufactured and delivered within five months. At the same time, Dallas subcontracted for production of the special-order goods at a price equal to 40% of the main contract price. What liabilities should be reported in Dallas' March 31, 2002 balance sheet?

	Deferred revenues	*Payables to subcontractor*
a.	None	None
b.	60% of main contract price	40% of main contract price
c.	60% of main contract price	None
d.	None	40% of main contract price

72. In June 2002, Northan Retailers sold refundable merchandise coupons. Northan received $10 for each coupon redeemable from July 1 to December 31, 2002, for merchandise with a retail price of $11. At June 30, 2002, how should Northan report these coupon transactions?
- a. Unearned revenues at the merchandise's retail price.
- b. Unearned revenues at the cash received amount.
- c. Revenues at the merchandise's retail price.
- d. Revenues at the cash received amount.

73. Delect Co. provides repair services for the AZ195 TV set. Customers prepay the fee on the standard one-year service contract. The 2001 and 2002 contracts were identical, and the number of contracts outstanding was substantially the same at the end of each year. However, Delect's December 31, 2002 deferred revenues' balance on unperformed service contracts was significantly less than the balance at December 31, 2001. Which of the following situations might account for this reduction in the deferred revenue balance?
- a. Most 2002 contracts were signed later in the calendar year than were the 2001 contracts.
- b. Most 2002 contracts were signed earlier in the calendar year than were the 2001 contracts.

   c.   The 2002 contract contribution margin was greater than the 2001 contract contribution margin.

   d.   The 2002 contribution margin was less than the 2001 contract contribution margin.

74. Brad Corp. has unconditional purchase obligations associated with product financing arrangements. These obligations are reported as liabilities on Brad's balance sheet, with the related assets also recognized. In the notes to Brad's financial statements, the aggregate amount of payments for these obligations should be disclosed for each of how many years following the date of the latest balance sheet?

   a.   0
   b.   1
   c.   5
   d.   10

75. On January 17, 2002, an explosion occurred at a Sims Co. plant causing extensive property damage to area buildings. Although no claims had yet been asserted against Sims by March 10, 2002, Sims' management and counsel concluded that it is likely that claims will be asserted and that it is reasonably possible Sims will be responsible for damages. Sims' management believed that $1,250,000 would be a reasonable estimate of its liability. Sims' $5,000,000 comprehensive public liability policy has a $250,000 deductible clause. In Sims' December 31, 2001 financial statements, which were issued on March 25, 2002, how should this item be reported?

   a.   As an accrued liability of $250,000.

   b.   As a footnote disclosure indicating the possible loss of $250,000.

   c.   As a footnote disclosure indicating the possible loss of $1,250,000.

   d.   No footnote disclosure or accrual is necessary.

76. Brite Corp. had the following liabilities at December 31, 2002:

Accounts payable	$55,000
Unsecured notes, 8%, due 7/1/03	400,000
Accrued expenses	35,000
Contingent liability	450,000
Deferred income tax liability	25,000
Senior bonds, 7%, due 3/31/03	1,000,000

The contingent liability is an accrual for possible losses on a $1,000,000 lawsuit filed against Brite. Brite's legal counsel expects the suit to be settled in 2004, and has estimated that Brite will be liable for damages in the range of $450,000 to $750,000.

   The deferred income tax liability is not related to an asset for financial reporting and is expected to reverse in 2004.

   What amount should Brite report in its December 31, 2002 balance sheet for current liabilities?

   a. $ 515,000
   b. $ 940,000
   c. $1,490,000
   d. $1,515,000

77. On February 5, 2003, an employee filed a $2,000,000 lawsuit against Steel Co. for damages suffered when one of Steel's plants exploded on December 29, 2002. Steel's legal counsel expects the company will lose the lawsuit and estimates the loss to be between $500,000 and $1,000,000. The employee has offered to settle the lawsuit out of court for $900,000, but Steel will not agree to the settlement. In its December 31, 2002 balance sheet, what amount should Steel report as liability from lawsuit?

   a. $2,000,000
   b. $1,000,000
   c. $ 900,000
   d. $ 500,000

78. On November 5, 2002, a Dunn Corp. truck was in an accident with an auto driven by Bell. Dunn received notice on January 12, 2003, of a lawsuit for $700,000 damages for personal injuries suffered by Bell. Dunn Corp.'s counsel believes it is probable that Bell will be awarded an estimated amount in the range between $200,000 and $450,000, and that $300,000 is a better estimate of potential liability than any other amount. Dunn's accounting year ends on December 31, and the 2002 financial statements were issued on March 2, 2003. What amount of loss should Dunn accrue at December 31, 2002?

   a. $0
   b. $200,000
   c. $300,000
   d. $450,000

79. During 2002, Haft Co. became involved in a tax dispute with the IRS. At December 31, 2002, Haft's tax advisor believed that an unfavorable outcome was probable. A reasonable estimate of additional taxes was $200,000 but could be as much as $300,000. After the 2002 financial statements were issued, Haft received and accepted an IRS settlement offer of $275,000. What amount of accrued liability should Haft have reported in its December 31, 2002 balance sheet?

   a. $200,000
   b. $250,000
   c. $275,000
   d. $300,000

80. Management can estimate the amount of loss that will occur if a foreign government expropriates some company assets. If expropriation is reasonably possible, a loss contingency should be

   a.   Disclosed but not accrued as a liability.
   b.   Disclosed and accrued as a liability.
   c.   Accrued as a liability but not disclosed.
   d.   Neither accrued as a liability nor disclosed.

81. Invern, Inc. has a self-insurance plan. Each year, retained earnings is appropriated for contingencies in an amount equal to insurance premiums saved less recognized losses from lawsuits and other claims. As a result of a 2002 accident, Invern is a defendant in a lawsuit in which it will probably have to pay damages of $190,000. What are the effects of this lawsuit's probable outcome on Invern's 2002 financial statements?

   a.   An increase in expenses and no effect on liabilities.
   b.   An increase in both expenses and liabilities.
   c.   No effect on expenses and an increase in liabilities.
   d.   No effect on either expenses or liabilities.

82. In 2001, a personal injury lawsuit was brought against Halsey Co. Based on counsel's estimate, Halsey reported a $50,000 liability in its December 31, 2001 balance sheet. In November 2002, Halsey received a favorable judgment, requiring the plaintiff to reimburse Halsey for expenses of $30,000. The plaintiff has appealed the decision, and Halsey's counsel is unable to predict the outcome of the appeal. In its December 31, 2002 balance sheet, Halsey should report what amounts of asset and liability related to these legal actions?

	Asset	Liability
a.	$30,000	$50,000
b.	$30,000	$0
c.	$0	$20,000
d.	$0	$0

83. During January 2002, Haze Corp. won a litigation award for $15,000 that was tripled to $45,000 to include punitive damages. The defendant, who is financially stable, has appealed only the $30,000 punitive damages. Haze was awarded $50,000 in an unrelated suit it filed, which is being appealed by the defendant. Counsel is unable to estimate the outcome of these appeals. In its 2002 financial statements, Haze should report what amount of pretax gain?

- a. $15,000
- b. $45,000
- c. $50,000
- d. $95,000

84. In May 1999 Caso Co. filed suit against Wayne, Inc. seeking $1,900,000 damages for patent infringement. A court verdict in November 2002 awarded Caso $1,500,000 in damages, but Wayne's appeal is not expected to be decided before 2004. Caso's counsel believes it is probable that Caso will be successful against Wayne for an estimated amount in the range between $800,000 and $1,100,000, with $1,000,000 considered the most likely amount. What amount should Caso record as income from the lawsuit in the year ended December 31, 2002?

- a. $0
- b. $ 800,000
- c. $1,000,000
- d. $1,500,000

85. During 2001, Smith Co. filed suit against West, Inc. seeking damages for patent infringement. At December 31, 2001, Smith's legal counsel believed that it was probable that Smith would be successful against West for an estimated amount in the range of $75,000 to $150,000, with all amounts in the range considered equally likely. In March 2002, Smith was awarded $100,000 and received full payment thereof. In its 2001 financial statements, issued in February 2002 how should this award be reported?

- a. As a receivable and revenue of $100,000.
- b. As a receivable and deferred revenue of $100,000.
- c. As a disclosure of a contingent gain of $100,000.
- d. As a disclosure of a contingent gain of an undetermined amount in the range of $75,000 to $150,000.

86. In 2002, a contract dispute between Dollis Co. and Brooks Co. was submitted to binding arbitration. In 2002, each party's attorney indicated privately that the probable award in Dollis' favor could be reasonably estimated. In 2003, the arbitrator decided in favor of Dollis. When should Dollis and Brooks recognize their respective gain and loss?

	Dollis' gain	Brooks' loss
a.	2002	2002
b.	2002	2003
c.	2003	2002
d.	2003	2003

87. Eagle Co. has cosigned the mortgage note on the home of its president, guaranteeing the indebtedness in the event that the president should default. Eagle considers the likelihood of default to be remote. How should the guarantee be treated in Eagle's financial statements?

- a. Disclosed only.
- b. Accrued only.
- c. Accrued and disclosed.
- d. Neither accrued nor disclosed.

88. North Corp. has an employee benefit plan for compensated absences that gives employees 10 paid vacation days and 10 paid sick days. Both vacation and sick days can be carried over indefinitely. Employees can elect to receive payment in lieu of vacation days; however, no payment is given for sick days not taken. At December 31, 2002, North's unadjusted balance of liability for compensated absences was $21,000. North estimated that there were 150 vacation days and 75 sick days available at December 31, 2002. North's employees earn an average of $100 per day. In its December 31, 2002 balance sheet, what amount of liability for compensated absences is North required to report?

- a. $36,000
- b. $22,500
- c. $21,000
- d. $15,000

89. Ross Co. pays all salaried employees on a Monday for the five-day workweek ended the previous Friday. The last payroll recorded for the year ended December 31, 2002, was for the week ended December 25, 2002. The payroll for the week ended January 1, 2003, included regular weekly salaries of $80,000 and vacation pay of $25,000 for vacation time earned in 2002 not taken by December 31, 2002. Ross had accrued a liability of $20,000 for vacation pay at December 31, 2001. In its December 31, 2002 balance sheet, what amount should Ross report as accrued salary and vacation pay?

- a. $64,000
- b. $68,000
- c. $69,000
- d. $89,000

90. Gavin Co. grants all employees two weeks of paid vacation for each full year of employment. Unused vacation time can be accumulated and carried forward to succeeding years and will be paid at the salaries in effect when vacations are taken or when employment is terminated. There was no employee turnover in 2002. Additional information relating to the year ended December 31, 2002, is as follows:

Liability for accumulated vacations at 12/31/01	$35,000
Pre-2001 accrued vacations taken from 1/1/02 to 9/30/02 (the authorized period for vacations)	20,000
Vacations earned for work in 2002 (adjusted to current rates)	30,000

Gavin granted a 10% salary increase to all employees on October 1, 2002, its annual salary increase date. For the year ended December 31, 2002, Gavin should report vacation pay expense of

- a. $45,000
- b. $33,500
- c. $31,500
- d. $30,000

91. At December 31, 2002, Taos Co. estimates that its employees have earned vacation pay of $100,000. Employees will receive their vacation pay in 2003. Should Taos accrue a liability at December 31, 2002, if the rights to this compensation accumulated over time or if the rights are vested?

	Accumulated	Vested
a.	Yes	No
b.	No	No
c.	Yes	Yes
d.	No	Yes

92. If the payment of employees' compensation for future absences is probable, the amount can be reasonably estimated, and the obligation relates to rights that accumulate, the compensation should be

- a. Accrued if attributable to employees' services not already rendered.
- b. Accrued if attributable to employees' services already rendered.
- c. Accrued if attributable to employees' services whether already rendered or not.
- d. Recognized when paid.

93. During 2002, Gum Co. introduced a new product carrying a two-year warranty against defects. The estimated warranty costs related to dollar sales are 2% within twelve months following the sale and 4% in the second twelve months following the sale. Sales and actual warranty expenditures for the years ended December 31, 2002 and 2003, are as follows:

	Sales	Actual warranty expenditures
2002	$150,000	$2,250
2003	250,000	7,500
	$400,000	$9,750

What amount should Gum report as estimated warranty liability in its December 31, 2003 balance sheet?

- a. $ 2,500
- b. $ 4,250
- c. $11,250
- d. $14,250

94. Vadis Co. sells appliances that include a three-year warranty. Service calls under the warranty are performed by an independent mechanic under a contract with Vadis. Based on experience, warranty costs are estimated at $30 for each machine sold. When should Vadis recognize these warranty costs?

- a. Evenly over the life of the warranty.
- b. When the service calls are performed.
- c. When payments are made to the mechanic.
- d. When the machines are sold.

95. Case Cereal Co. frequently distributes coupons to promote new products. On October 1, 2002, Case mailed 1,000,000 coupons for $.45 off each box of cereal purchased. Case expects 120,000 of these coupons to be redeemed before the December 31, 2002, expiration date. It takes thirty days from the redemption date for Case to receive the coupons from the retailers. Case reimburses the retailers an additional $.05 for each coupon redeemed. As of December 31, 2002, Case had paid retailers $25,000 related to these coupons and had 50,000 coupons on hand that had not been processed for payment. What amount should Case report as a liability for coupons in its December 31, 2002 balance sheet?

- a. $35,000
- b. $29,000
- c. $25,000
- d. $22,500

96. Dunn Trading Stamp Co. records stamp service revenue and provides for the cost of redemptions in the year stamps are sold to licensees. Dunn's past experience indicates that only 80% of the stamps sold to licensees will be redeemed. Dunn's liability for stamp redemptions was $6,000,000 at December 31, 2001. Additional information for 2002 is as follows:

Stamp service revenue from stamps sold to licensees	$4,000,000
Cost of redemptions (stamps sold prior to 1/1/02)	2,750,000

If all the stamps sold in 2002 were presented for redemption in 2003, the redemption cost would be $2,250,000. What amount should Dunn report as a liability for stamp redemptions at December 31, 2002?

- a. $7,250,000
- b. $5,500,000
- c. $5,050,000
- d. $3,250,000

Items 97 and 98 are based on the following:

The following trial balance of Trey Co. at December 31, 2002, has been adjusted except for income tax expense.

	Dr.	Cr.
Cash	$ 550,000	
Accounts receivable, net	1,650,000	
Prepaid taxes	300,000	
Accounts payable		$ 120,000
Common stock		500,000
Additional paid-in capital		680,000
Retained earnings		630,000
Foreign currency translation adjustment	430,000	
Revenues		3,600,000
Expenses	2,600,000	
	$5,530,000	$5,530,000

Additional information

- During 2002, estimated tax payments of $300,000 were charged to prepaid taxes. Trey has not yet recorded income tax expense. There were no differences between financial statement and income tax income, and Trey's tax rate is 30%.
- Included in accounts receivable is $500,000 due from a customer. Special terms granted to this customer require payment in equal semiannual installments of $125,000 every April 1 and October 1.

97. In Trey's December 31, 2002 balance sheet, what amount should be reported as total current assets?

- a. $1,950,000
- b. $2,200,000
- c. $2,250,000
- d. $2,500,000

98. In Trey's December 31, 2002 balance sheet, what amount should be reported as total retained earnings?

- a. $1,029,000
- b. $1,200,000
- c. $1,330,000
- d. $1,630,000

99. The following is Gold Corp.'s June 30, 2002 trial balance:

Cash overdraft		$ 10,000
Accounts receivable, net	$ 35,000	
Inventory	58,000	
Prepaid expenses	12,000	
Land held for resale	100,000	
Property, plant, and equipment, net	95,000	

Accounts payable and accrued expenses	32,000
Common stock	25,000
Additional paid-in capital	150,000
Retained earnings	83,000
	$300,000 $300,000

Additional information

• Checks amounting to $30,000 were written to vendors and recorded on June 29, 2002, resulting in a cash overdraft of $10,000. The checks were mailed on July 9, 2002.

• Land held for resale was sold for cash on July 15, 2002.

• Gold issued its financial statements on July 31, 2002.

In its June 30, 2002 balance sheet, what amount should Gold report as current assets?

- a. $225,000
- b. $205,000
- c. $195,000
- d. $125,000

100. Mill Co.'s trial balance included the following account balances at December 31, 2002:

Accounts payable	$15,000
Bonds payable, due 2003	25,000
Discount on bonds payable, due 2003	3,000
Dividends payable 1/31/03	8,000
Notes payable, due 2004	20,000

What amount should be included in the current liability section of Mill's December 31, 2002 balance sheet?

- a. $45,000
- b. $51,000
- c. $65,000
- d. $78,000

Items 101 and 102 are based on the following:

Rey, Inc.
SELECTED FINANCIAL DATA
December 31,

	2002	2001
Cash	$ 170,000	$ 90,000
Accounts receivable (net)	450,000	400,000
Merchandise inventory	540,000	420,000
Short-term marketable securities	80,000	40,000
Land and building (net)	1,000,000	1,000,000
Mortgage payable—current portion	60,000	50,000
Accounts payable and accrued liabilities	240,000	220,000
Short-term notes payable	100,000	140,000

Net credit sales totaled $3,000,000 and $2,000,000 for the years ended December 31, 2002 and 2001, respectively.

101. At December 31, 2002, Rey's quick (acid-test) ratio was

- a. 1.50 to 1.
- b. 1.75 to 1.
- c. 2.06 to 1.
- d. 3.10 to 1.

102. For 2002, Rey's accounts receivable turnover was

- a. 1.13
- b. 1.50
- c. 6.67
- d. 7.06

103. Which of the following ratios is(are) useful in assessing a company's ability to meet currently maturing or short-term obligations?

	Acid-test ratio	Debt to equity ratio
a.	No	No
b.	No	Yes
c.	Yes	Yes
d.	Yes	No

104. North Bank is analyzing Belle Corp.'s financial statements for a possible extension of credit. Belle's quick ratio is significantly better than the industry average. Which of the following factors should North consider as a possible limitation of using this ratio when evaluating Belle's creditworthiness?

- a. Fluctuating market prices of short-term investments may adversely affect the ratio.
- b. Increasing market prices for Belle's inventory may adversely affect the ratio.
- c. Belle may need to sell its available-for-sale investments to meet its current obligations.
- d. Belle may need to liquidate its inventory to meet its long-term obligations.

105. On December 30, 2002, Vida Co. had cash of $200,000, a current ratio of 1.5:1 and a quick ratio of .5:1. On December 31, 2002, all cash was used to reduce accounts payable. How did these cash payments affect the ratios?

	Current ratio	Quick ratio
a.	Increased	Decreased
b.	Increased	No effect
c.	Decreased	Increased
d.	Decreased	No effect

106. Tod Corp. wrote off $100,000 of obsolete inventory at December 31, 2002. The effect of this write-off was to decrease

- a. Both the current and acid-test ratios.
- b. Only the current ratio.
- c. Only the acid-test ratio.
- d. Neither the current nor the acid-test ratios.

107. The following computations were made from Clay Co.'s 2002 books:

Number of days' sales in inventory	61
Number of days' sales in accounts receivable	33

What was the number of days in Clay's 2002 operating cycle?

- a. 33
- b. 47
- c. 61
- d. 94

108. On December 31, 2002, Northpark Co. collected a receivable due from a major customer. Which of the following ratios would be increased by this transaction?

- a. Inventory turnover ratio.
- b. Receivable turnover ratio.
- c. Current ratio.
- d. Quick ratio.

OTHER OBJECTIVE QUESTIONS

Problem 1   (15 to 25 minutes)

The following items relate to the transfer of accounts and notes receivable.

Required:

a.   Items 1 through 6. For each item, match the transaction with the appropriate journal entry. Entries may be used once, more than once, or not at all.

Transaction	*Journal entry*

1. A company transfers receivables by surrendering control. Collection is to be made by the purchaser (factor), who assumes risk of loss.	A. Cash xxx
	   Interest expense xxx
	      Liability on discounted NR xxx
	      Interest revenue xxx

2. A company specifically assigns a portion of its receivables as collateral for a loan. Collections from the assigned receivables will be used to repay the loan and interest.	B. Cash xxx
	   Factor's holdback xxx
	   Interest expense (Discount) xxx
	      Liability on transferred AR xxx

3. A company pledges its receivables as collateral to secure a loan and the debtor collects the proceeds.	C. Cash xxx
	   Finance charge xxx
	   AR assigned xxx
	      Note payable xxx
	      AR xxx

4. A company sells accounts receivable to a factor in a transaction considered a borrowing.	

5. A company transfers a note receivable by surrendering control over it. The transfer was on a without recourse basis.	D. Cash xxx
	   Factor's holdback xxx
	   Loss on sale of AR xxx
	      AR xxx

6. A company pledges its accounts receivable as security for a loan.	E. Parenthetical or note disclosure only.

	F. Cash xxx
	   Loss on sale of NR xxx
	      NR xxx
	      Interest revenue xxx

b.   Items 7 through 11. Determine whether each statement is true or false.

7. The balance in "factor's holdback" (due from factor) is reported as an expense of the period.

8. In a specific assignment of receivables, collections on the assigned accounts are generally remitted to the assignor.

9. Factors are banks or finance companies that purchase receivables for a fee and then collect the remittances directly from the selling company.

10. A transfer of receivables with recourse may be accounted for as a sale, provided the transferee can require the transferor to repurchase the receivables.

11. In a transfer of receivables with recourse accounted for as a borrowing, the difference between the receivables and the total of the factor's holdback plus the proceeds is a financing cost that should be amortized to interest expense over the term of the receivables.

Problem 2   (10 to 15 minutes)

Items 1 through 6 are based on the following:

Town, Inc. is preparing its financial statements for the year ended December 31, 2002.

Required:

Items 1 through 6 represent various commitments and contingencies of Town at December 31, 2002, and events subsequent to December 31, 2002, but prior to the issuance of the 2002 financial statements. For each item, select from the following list the reporting requirement. A reporting requirement may be selected once, more than once, or not at all.

Reporting requirement
D.   Disclosure only.
A.   Accrual only.
B.   Both accrual and disclosure.
N.   Neither accrual nor disclosure.

1. On December 1, 2002, Town was awarded damages of $75,000 in a patent infringement suit it brought against a competitor. The defendant did not appeal the verdict, and payment was received in January 2003.

2. A former employee of Town has brought a wrongful-dismissal suit against Town. Town's lawyers believe the suit to be without merit.

3. At December 31, 2002, Town had outstanding purchase orders in the ordinary course of business for purchase of a raw material to be used in its manufacturing process. The market price is currently higher than the purchase price and is not anticipated to change within the next year.

4. A government contract completed during 2002 is subject to renegotiation. Although Town estimates that it is reasonably possible that a refund of approximately $200,000 – $300,000 may be required by the government, it does not wish to publicize this possibility.

5. Town has been notified by a governmental agency that it will be held responsible for the cleanup of toxic materials at a site where Town formerly conducted operations. Town estimates that it is probable that its share of remedial action will be approximately $500,000.

6. On January 5, 2003, Town redeemed its outstanding bonds and issued new bonds with a lower rate of interest. The reacquisition price was in excess of the carrying amount of the bonds.

Problem 3

See the solutions approach example in Chapter 3, Solutions Approach, Problem 2.

PROBLEMS

Problem 1   (15 to 25 minutes)

Magrath Company has an operating cycle of less than one year and provides credit terms for all of its customers. On April 1, 2002, the company transferred some of its accounts receivable. Control over the receivables was surrendered by Magrath.

On July 1, 2002, Magrath sold special order merchandise and received a noninterest-bearing note due June 30, 2003. The market rate of interest for this note is determinable.

Magrath uses the allowance method to account for uncollectible accounts. During 2002, some accounts were written off as uncollectible and other accounts previously written off as uncollectible were collected.

Required:

a. How should Magrath account for and report the accounts receivable factored on April 1, 2002? Why is this accounting treatment appropriate?

b. How should Magrath report the effects of the noninterest-bearing note on its income statement for the year ended December 31, 2002, and its December 31, 2002 balance sheet?

c. How should Magrath account for the collection of the accounts previously written off as uncollectible?

d. What are the two basic approaches to estimating uncollectible accounts under the allowance method? What is the rationale for each approach?

Problem 2   (20 to 25 minutes)

Sigma Co. began operations on January 1, 2001. On December 31, 2001, Sigma provided for uncollectible accounts based on 1% of annual credit sales. On January 1, 2002, Sigma changed its method of determining its allowance for uncollectible accounts by applying certain percentages to the accounts receivable aging as follows:

Days past invoice date	Percent deemed to be uncollectible
0 - 30	1
31 - 90	5
91 - 180	20
Over 180	80

In addition, Sigma wrote off all accounts receivable that were over one year old. The following additional information relates to the years ended December 31, 2002, and 2001:

	2002	2001
Credit sales	$3,000,000	$2,800,000
Collections	2,915,000	2,400,000
Accounts written off	27,000	None
Recovery of accounts previously written off	7,000	None
Days past invoice date at 12/31		
0 - 30	300,000	250,000
31 - 90	80,000	90,000
91 - 180	60,000	45,000
Over 180	25,000	15,000

Required:

a. Prepare a schedule showing the calculation of the allowance for uncollectible accounts at December 31, 2002.

b. Prepare a schedule showing the computation of the provision for uncollectible accounts for the year ended December 31, 2002.

Problem 3   (15 to 25 minutes)

Gregor Wholesalers Co. sells industrial equipment for a standard three-year note receivable. Revenue is recognized at time of sale. Each note is secured by a lien on the equipment and has a face amount equal to the equipment's list price. Each note's stated interest rate is below the customer's market rate at date of sale. All notes are to be collected in three equal annual installments beginning one year after sale. Some of the notes are subsequently discounted at a bank with recourse that qualify as sales, some are subsequently discounted without recourse, and some are retained by Gregor. At year-end, Gregor evaluates all outstanding notes receivable and provides for estimated losses arising from defaults.

Required:

a. What is the appropriate valuation basis for Gregor's notes receivable at the date it sells equipment?

b. How should Gregor account for the discounting, without recourse, of a February 1, 2002 note receivable discounted on May 1, 2002? Why is it appropriate to account for it in this way?

c. At December 31, 2002, how should Gregor measure and account for the impact of estimated losses resulting from notes receivable that it

1. Retained and did **not** discount?
2. Discounted at a bank with recourse?

Problem 4   (15 to 25 minutes)

Smith, Inc. is planning to obtain cash by transferring some of its accounts receivable to a factor.

a. With regard to transfers of financial assets, what is the meaning of the financial components approach?

b. Describe the criteria for determining when control has been surrendered in a transfer of receivables.

c. How are transfers of receivables accounted for if one or more of the criteria for determining whether control has been surrendered are not met?

d. Describe the accounting for transfers of receivables in which control is surrendered, but the agreement contains a recourse provision that allows the transferee to recover losses from the transferor and provides for a factor's holdback.

Problem 5   (15 to 25 minutes)

Chester Company has the following contingencies:

• A threat of expropriation exists for one of its manufacturing plants located in a foreign country. Expropriation is deemed to be reasonably possible. Any compensation from the foreign government would be less than the carrying amount of the plant.

• Potential costs exist due to the discovery of a safety hazard related to one of its products. These costs are probable and can be reasonably estimated.

• One of its warehouses located at the base of a mountain could no longer be insured against rock slide losses. No rock slide losses have occurred.

Required:

a. How should Chester report the threat of expropriation of assets? Why?

b. How should Chester report the potential costs due to the safety hazard? Why?

c. How should Chester report the noninsurable rock slide risk? Why?

Problem 6   (15 to 25 minutes)

Supey Chemical Co. encountered the following two situations in 2002:

• Supey must pay an indeterminate amount for toxic waste cleanup on its land. An adjoining land owner, Gap Toothpaste, sold its property because of possible toxic contamination by Supey of the water supply and resulting potential adverse public reaction towards its product. Gap sued Supey for damages. There is a reasonable possibility that Gap will prevail in the suit.

• At December 31, 2002, Supey had a noncancellable purchase contract for 10,000 pounds of Chemical XZ, for delivery in June 2003. Supey does not hedge its contracts. Supey uses this chemical to make Product 2-Y. In December 2002, the US Food and Drug Administration banned the sale of Product 2-Y in concentrated form. Supey will be allowed to sell Product 2-Y in a diluted form; however, it will take at least five years to use the 10,000 pounds of Chemical XZ. Supey believes the sales price of the diluted product will not be sufficient to recover the contract price of Chemical XZ.

Required:

a. **1.** In its 2002 financial statements, how should Supey report the toxic waste cleanup? Why is this reporting appropriate?

2. In its 2002 financial statements, how should Supey report Gap's claim against it? Why is this reporting appropriate?

b. In its 2002 financial statements, how should Supey report the effects of the contract to purchase Chemical XZ? Why is this reporting appropriate?

MULTIPLE-CHOICE ANSWERS

1. c __ __	20. a __ __	39. a __ __	58. b __ __	77. d __ __	96. c __ __
2. a __ __	21. b __ __	40. c __ __	59. b __ __	78. c __ __	97. a __ __
3. c __ __	22. a __ __	41. c __ __	60. b __ __	79. a __ __	98. c __ __
4. a __ __	23. c __ __	42. d __ __	61. b __ __	80. a __ __	99. a __ __
5. a __ __	24. b __ __	43. d __ __	62. d __ __	81. b __ __	100. a __ __
6. a __ __	25. d __ __	44. a __ __	63. d __ __	82. d __ __	101. b __ __
7. a __ __	26. c __ __	45. a __ __	64. b __ __	83. a __ __	102. d __ __
8. c __ __	27. b __ __	46. d __ __	65. c __ __	84. a __ __	103. d __ __
9. c __ __	28. d __ __	47. c __ __	66. c __ __	85. a __ __	104. a __ __
10. c __ __	29. a __ __	48. d __ __	67. d __ __	86. c __ __	105. a __ __
11. d __ __	30. b __ __	49. c __ __	68. c __ __	87. a __ __	106. b __ __
11. b __ __	31. c __ __	50. b __ __	69. d __ __	88. d __ __	107. d __ __
13. a __ __	32. c __ __	51. c __ __	70. b __ __	89. d __ __	108. b __ __
14. a __ __	33. b __ __	52. c __ __	71. c __ __	90. c __ __	
15. a __ __	34. c __ __	53. c __ __	72. b __ __	91. c __ __	
16. d __ __	35. a __ __	54. c __ __	73. b __ __	92. b __ __	
17. b __ __	36. d __ __	55. d __ __	74. c __ __	93. d __ __	
18. b __ __	37. c __ __	56. a __ __	75. b __ __	94. d __ __	1st: __/108 = __%
19. a __ __	38. b __ __	57. b __ __	76. c __ __	95. a __ __	2nd: __/108 = __%

MULTIPLE-CHOICE ANSWER EXPLANATIONS

A. Cash

1.   (c)   Cash on hand ($125,000) and cash in banks ($2,250,000) are both reported as cash in the current asset section of the balance sheet because they are both unrestricted and readily available for use. Cash legally restricted for additions to plant ($1,600,000) is not available to meet current operating needs, and therefore should be excluded from current assets. Instead, it should be shown in the long-term asset section of the balance sheet as an investment.

2.   (a)   To be classified as cash, the item must be readily available for current needs with no legal restrictions limiting its use. A postdated check is not acceptable for deposit and therefore is not considered cash. Thus, the $2,000 check was correctly excluded from the 12/31 checkbook balance and no adjustment is necessary. An NSF check should not be included in cash until it has been redeposited and has cleared the bank. At 12/31, the NSF check ($500) had not yet been redeposited, so it was incorrectly included in the 12/31 checkbook balance, and an adjustment must be made. The check which was not mailed until 1/10/03 ($300) should not be subtracted from cash until the company gives up physical control of that amount. Therefore, $300 must be added back to the checkbook balance. As a result of these adjustments, the correct cash balance is $4,800 ($5,000 – $500 + $300).

3.   (c)   Per SFAS 95, *Statement of Cash Flows*, the definition of cash includes both cash (cash on hand and demand deposits) and cash equivalents (short-term, highly liquid investments). Cash equivalents have to be readily convertible into cash and so near maturity that they carry little risk of changing in value due to interest rate changes. This will include only those investments with original maturities of three months or less from the date of purchase by the enterprise. Common examples of cash equivalents include treasury bills, commercial paper, and money market funds. Trans should report a total of $460,000 ($35,000 + $75,000 + $350,000) on its December 31, 2002 balance sheet. The US treasury bill purchased on 12/1/02 is not included in the

calculation because its original maturity is not within three months or less from the date of purchase.

4.   (a)   Cash which is segregated and deposited into a bond sinking fund is presented in a classified balance sheet as a noncurrent asset because its use us restricted. Bank overdrafts are presented as current liabilities, unless other accounts at the **same bank** contain sufficient cash to offset the overdraft. The operating account that has a positive balance, should be presented as a current asset.

A.1. Bank Reconciliations

5.   (a)   To determine the correct 8/31/02 cash balance, a partial bank reconciliation should be prepared. The balance per bank statement ($18,050) must be adjusted for any items which the bank has not yet recorded and also for any bank errors (none in this problem).

Balance per bank statement	$18,050
Deposits in transit	3,250
Outstanding checks	(2,750)
Correct balance	$18,550

The deposits in transit and outstanding checks represent transactions that the company has recorded, but the bank has not yet recorded. The insufficient funds check ($600) and bank service charge ($100) are both items which the bank has recorded but the company has not. They would be adjustments to the **book balance**, not the **bank balance**.

6.   (a)   The balance per books at 3/31/02 is $44,200. The amount would be increased by cash receipts per books and decreased by cash disbursements per books. Cash receipts per the bank in April were $58,400, but this amount includes the $10,300 in transit at 3/31. Therefore, cash receipts per books in April are $48,100 ($58,400 – $10,300). Cash disbursements per the bank in April were $49,700. This amount includes the 3/31 outstanding checks ($12,600) but does **not** include the 4/30 outstanding checks ($7,000). Therefore, April cash disbursements per books is $44,100 ($49,700 – $12,600 + $7,000). The cash balance per books at 4/30/99 is $48,200 ($44,200 at 3/31/02, plus $48,100 receipts, less $44,100 disbursements). An alternative solutions approach is to first compute the 4/30/02 bank balance ($46,500 + $58,400 – $49,700 = $55,200), and then adjust for outstanding checks ($55,200 – $7,000 = $48,200).

B. Receivables

7. **(a)** The 12/31/02 current net receivables would include the trade receivables, net of the allowance account ($93,000 – $2,000 = $91,000). The claim against a shipper for goods lost in transit ($3,000) is also a valid receivable at year-end. Therefore, the total current net receivables are $94,000 ($91,000 + $3,000). The **unsold** goods on consignment do not represent a receivable until sold. Therefore, the $26,000 should be removed from receivables and sales and the cost ($26,000 ÷ 130% = $20,000) should be removed from cost of goods sold and reported as ending inventory. The security deposit ($30,000) should be reported as a **long-term** receivable.

8. **(c)** The solutions approach is to set up a T-account for accounts receivable.

AR			
1/1/02	650,000		
Credit sales	2,700,000	75,000	Sales returns
		40,000	Write-offs
		2,150,000	Collections
12/31/02	1,085,000		

Credit sales are debited to **AR** and credited to **sales**. Sales returns are debited to **sales returns** and credited to **AR**; write-offs are debited to the **allowance for doubtful accounts** and credited to **AR**; and cash collections are debited to **cash** and credited to **AR**. The estimated future sales returns ($50,000) and estimated uncollectible accounts ($110,000) do not affect the accounts receivable account but are instead recorded in separate allowance accounts. Since the requirement is to determine accounts receivable **before** these allowances, the balance of accounts receivable should include only sales returns and write-offs for 2002.

9. **(c)** Accrued interest receivable at 6/30/02 is interest revenue which has been earned by 6/30/02, but has not yet been received by that date. Interest was last received on 7/1/01; the accrued interest receivable includes interest revenue earned from 7/1/01 through 6/30/02 (a full year). The original balance of the note receivable was $150,000 but the 7/1/01 principal payment of $50,000 reduced this balance to $100,000. Therefore, the 6/30/02 interest receivable is $8,000 ($100,000 x 8%).

10. **(c)** Per SFAS 91, loan origination fees are recognized over the life of the related loan as an adjustment of yield. These fees are recorded as a discount on the note receivable. Therefore, Tigg's 12/1/02 entry is

Notes receivable	200,000	
Discount on NR		6,000
Cash		194,000

Using the effective interest method, Tigg's 12/31/02 adjusting entry is

Int. receivable	2,000	
Discount on NR	166	
Int. revenue		2,166

The interest receivable is

Face value	x	Stated rate	x	Time		
$200,000	x	12%	x	1/12	=	$2,000

The interest revenue is

Carrying amount	x	Effective rate	x	Time		
$194,000	x	13.4%	x	1/12	=	$2,166

11. **(d)** A current asset is an asset that can be reasonably expected to be converted into cash, sold or consumed in operations, within a single operating cycle or within a year if more than one cycle is completed each year. A noncurrent asset is an asset that can not be expected to be converted to cash, sold or consumed within a single operating cycle or within one year, whichever is longer. Because accrued interest was reported as a current asset on the 2002 balance sheet, it can be assumed interest will be received on August 31, 2002, since current assets are received within one year. Also, because the note receivable was reported as a noncurrent asset it can be assumed that the principal will not be collected within the next twelve months. Principal that is not due until August 31, 2003, coincides with reporting the note as a noncurrent asset.

12. **(b)** Upon receipt of the interest-bearing note for the sale of goods, Benet would record the following entry:

Notes receivable	(face value)	
Interest receivable	(interest from 7/15 to 8/15)	
Sales		(face + interest)

Note that the interest that accrued on the note from July 15 to August 15 represents part of the sales price of the merchandise (rather than interest income) because Benet did not hold the note during this period. On November 15, Benet will record the following entry:

Cash	(Plug)	
Note receivable		(face value)
Interest revenue		(interest from 8/15 to 11/15)
Interest receivable		(interest from 7/15 to 8/15)

B.1. Anticipation of Sales Discounts

13. **(a)** If material, an allowance for discounts must be reported at year-end in order to match the discounts with the related sales and to report receivables at their collectible amount. At 12/31/02, $100,000 of the accounts receivable have the potential to be discounted by 2% because they are less than fifteen days old (terms 2/15, net 30). Since 50% of the customers are expected to take advantage of the 2% discount, the allowance for discounts should be $1,000 [($100,000 x 50%) x 2%]. None of the other categories require a discount allowance because they are older than the maximum age of fifteen days to receive the 2% discount.

14. **(a)** SFAS 48 requires that when revenue is recognized from sales where a right of return exists, sales revenue must be reduced to reflect estimated returns. In this case, sales of $1,000,000 must be reduced by estimated returns of $100,000 [(7% + 3%) x $1,000,000], resulting in net sales of $900,000. The estimated exchanges (15%) will not result in a future reduction of sales.

B.2. Bad Debts Expense

15. **(a)** To compute the 12/31/02 allowance for uncollectible accounts, the solutions approach is to set up a T-account for the allowance.

Allowance for U.A.			
		260,000	1/1/02
		180,000	Expense (2% x 9,000,000)
Write-offs	325,000		
		115,000	12/31/02

The 1/1/02 balance is increased by bad debts expense recorded (2% x credit sales of $9,000,000) and decreased by write-offs of specific uncollectible accounts.

16. (d) The balance in the allowance for doubtful accounts should reflect the amount of accounts receivable that are estimated to be uncollectible. Since it is estimated that 3% of the gross accounts receivable will become uncollectible, the allowance account should have a 12/31/02 balance of $30,000 (3% x $1,000,000). Note that **bad debt expense** of $38,000 would be recorded for 2002, as indicated below.

	Allowance		
Bal. before adj.	8,000		
		?	Bad debt expense ($38,000)
		30,000	12/31/02 (3% x $1,000,000)

17. (b) The total amount of risk of accounting loss related to Butler's trade accounts receivable is $230,000 ($250,000 trade accounts receivable – $20,000 uncollectible amount). The accounting loss cannot exceed the amount of the account receivable recognized as an asset in the balance sheet ($230,000). Off-balance-sheet risk refers to a potential loss that may exceed the amount recognized as an asset. There is no off-balance-sheet risk in this example.

18. (b) The solutions approach is to set up a T-account for the allowance for doubtful accounts.

	Allowance		
		30,000	1/1/02
2002 Write-offs	18,000	2,000	2002 Recoveries
		14,000	12/31/02 Before adj.
		?	Unc. accts. expense
		25,000	12/31/02

In 2002, $18,000 of accounts were written off as uncollectible (debit allowance, credit AR). Also, $2,000 of AR were recovered (debit AR, credit allowance; then, debit cash, credit AR), leaving a balance in the allowance account of $14,000 ($30,000 – $18,000 + $2,000). The desired 12/31/02 balance is $25,000 ($350,000 AR less $325,000 net value per aging schedule). Therefore, to increase the allowance from $14,000 to $25,000, uncollectible accounts expense of $11,000 must be recorded.

19. (a) When an aging schedule is used to estimate uncollectibles, the total uncollectibles computed is the amount used for the ending balance in the allowance account. As computed below, the 12/31/02 allowance for uncollectible accounts should be $9,000.

$$
\begin{array}{rcl}
\$120,000 \times 1\% & = & \$1,200 \\
90,000 \times 2\% & = & 1,800 \\
100,000 \times 6\% & = & \underline{6,000} \\
& & \$9,000
\end{array}
$$

The other information given (12/31/01 allowance, write-offs, and recoveries) would be used to determine the bad debt expense adjustment, not the allowance balance. In this case, apparently due to a change in estimate, the bad debt expense adjustment would actually be a credit (to offset the necessary debit to the allowance account).

	Allowance for U.A.		
		22,000	12/31/01
Write-offs	7,000	4,000	Recoveries
		19,000	
Adjustment	10,000		
		9,000	12/31/02

20. (a) The aging of receivables method of estimating uncollectible accounts is based on the theory that bad debts are a function of accounts receivable collections during the period. The aging of receivables method emphasizes reporting accounts receivable at their net realizable value. It is a "balance-sheet" approach, which stresses the collectibility (valuation) of the receivable balance. Once the balance of the allowance account required to reduce net accounts receivable to their realizable value has been computed, bad debts expense is merely the amount needed to adjust the allowance account to the computed balance. Answer (b) is incorrect because under the direct write-off method, bad debts are considered expenses in the period in which they are written off; no consideration is given to the valuation of accounts receivable. Answers (c) and (d) are incorrect because both of these methods are based on the theory that bad debts are a function of sales. Thus, these methods emphasize reporting the bad debts expense amount accurately on the income statement.

21. (b) A primary objective of accrual accounting is to record the cash consequences of events that change an entity's financial position in the period in which the events occur. This means recognizing revenues when earned rather than when cash is received, and recognizing expenses when incurred rather than when cash is paid. Expenses are incurred when they help the firm earn revenue. Under the allowance method, uncollectible accounts expense is recognized in the same period as the related revenue. The same credit decisions that enabled the entity to earn revenue caused it to incur uncollectible accounts expense. Therefore, under accrual accounting that expense should be recognized in the same period. On the other hand, when the direct write-off method is used, the uncollectible accounts expense is generally recognized after the period in which the revenue is recognized; after the event (credit decision) which changed financial position. Therefore, the direct write-off method is **not** consistent with accrual accounting.

22. (a) When the allowance method for recognizing uncollectible accounts is used, the entry to write off a specific account is

Allowance for unc. accts.	xxx	
Accts. receivable		xxx

Answer (a) is correct because this entry decreases both accounts.

23. (c) When an account receivable that was previously written off is collected, two entries must be made. The first entry reverses the write-off and reestablishes the receivable.

Accounts receivable	xxx	
Allowance for uncollectible accounts		xxx

The second entry records the cash receipt.

Cash	xxx	
Accounts receivable		xxx

The credit to the allowance account in the first entry increases its balance. Uncollectible accounts expense, however, is not affected by this transaction.

B.3. Pledging and Selling AR

24. (b) An **assignment** of accounts receivable is a financing arrangement whereby the owner of the receivables (assignor) obtains a loan from the lender (assignee) by pledging the accounts receivable as collateral. A **factoring**

of accounts receivable is basically a sale of, or borrowing on, the receivables. "Factors" are intermediaries that buy receivables from companies (for a fee) and then collect payments directly from the customers. Thus, both of these are methods of generating cash from accounts receivable.

25.   (d)   When receivables are factored and control is surrendered the transaction is treated as a **sale**. Under SFAS 125, a transfer in which control is surrendered will not be treated as a borrowing. The risk of uncollectible accounts is **not** retained by the seller in a sale without recourse.

26.   (c)   Taylored will receive the value of the receivables ($400,000), reduced by $20,000 for the amount of the holdback ($400,000 x .05), $8,000 withheld as fee income ($400,000 x .02), and $6,740 withheld as interest expense ($400,000 x .15 x 41/365). Answer (c) is therefore correct ($400,000 – $8,000 – $6,740 – $20,000).

27.   (b)   Under SFAS 140, a sale of receivables with recourse is recorded using a financial components approach because the seller has a continuing involvement. Under this approach the seller would reduce receivables, recognize assets obtained and liabilities incurred, and record gain or loss. The entry would be

Cash	$365,260	
Factor's holdback	20,000	
Loss	22,740*	
Accounts receivable		$400,000
Liability under recourse provision		8,000

* ($6,740 + $8,000 + $8,000)

28.   (d)   If all receivables are collected, Taylored would eliminate its recourse liability and the corresponding loss. The costs incurred by Taylored would include a fee of $8,000 ($400,000 x .02) and interest expense of $6,740 ($400,000 x .15 x 41/365) for a total of $14,740.

29.   (a)   The seller uses a Due from Factor or Factor's Holdback account to account for probable sales discounts, sales returns, and sales allowances. The Recourse liability account is recorded to indicate probable uncollectible accounts.

30.   (b)   Scarbrough will receive the value of the receivables ($600,000), reduced by $30,000 for the amount of the holdback ($600,000 x .05), $18,000 withheld as fee income ($600,000 x .03), and $13,315 withheld as interest expense ($600,000 x .15 x 54/365). Answer (b) is therefore correct ($600,000 – $30,000 – $18,000 – $13,315).

31.   (c)   If all receivables are collected, Synthia would eliminate its recourse liability and the corresponding loss. The costs incurred by Synthia would include a fee of $15,000 ($750,000 x .02) and interest expense of $12,575 ($750,000 x .12 x 51/365) for a total of $27,575.

32.   (c)   According to SFAS 140, the transferor, Bannon, should measure the assets received and liabilities incurred at fair value, not at cost. The transferee, Chapman, should record any assets obtained and liabilities incurred at fair value.

33.   (b)   According to SFAS 140, if financial assets are exchanged for cash or other consideration, but the transfer does not meet the criteria to be accounted for as a sale, both

the transferor and the transferee should account for the transfer as a secured borrowing and a pledge of collateral.

34.   (c)   Under SFAS 140, a sale occurs if the seller surrenders control of the receivables transferred. Control is deemed to have been surrendered by the seller only if all three conditions listed in (a), (b), and (d) are met. Answer (c) is used to determine whether a recourse liability is recorded as part of the sale, not whether a transaction can be recorded as a sale.

35.   (a)   To derecognize assets when control is gained is not an objective in accounting for transfers of financial assets. When control is gained, the assets should be recognized. Answer (b) is incorrect because an objective is to derecognize liabilities when extinguished. A liability no longer exists, and it should be removed from the balance sheet. Answer (c) is incorrect because recognizing liabilities when incurred is an objective. Answer (d) is incorrect because derecognizing assets when control is given up is an objective in accounting for transfers of financial assets.

36.   (d)   A servicing asset or liability should be amortized in proportion to and over the period of estimated net servicing income or net servicing loss as stated in SFAS 140. Answer (a) is incorrect because a servicing asset shall be assessed for impairment based on its fair value. Answer (b) is incorrect because a servicing liability shall be assessed for increased obligation based on its fair value. Answer (c) is incorrect because an obligation to service financial assets may result in the recognition of a servicing asset or a servicing liability.

37.   (c)   The arrangement of having collateral transferred to a secured party is known as a pledge. Answer (a) is incorrect because a debtor may grant a security interest in certain assets to a lender to serve as collateral with recourse. Answer (b) is incorrect because a debtor may grant a security interest in certain assets to a lender to serve as collateral without recourse. Answer (d) is incorrect because secured parties are sometimes permitted to sell collateral held under a pledge.

38.   (b)   Net proceeds from the sale are equal to $2,200.

Net proceeds	
Cash received	$2,100
Plus: Interest rate swap	140
Call option	80
Less: Recourse obligation	(120)
Net proceeds	$2,200

The gain is computed as follows:

Net proceeds	$2,200
Carrying amount of loans sold	2,000
Gain on sale	$ 200

39.   (a)   The journal entry to record the transfer for ABC Company is as follows:

Cash	2,100	
Interest rate swap	140	
Call option	80	
Loans		2,000
Recourse obligation		120
Gain on sale		200

Answer (b) is incorrect because is should be a debit to interest rate swap, not a credit. Answer (c) is incorrect because loans should be credited. It was on ABC Company's books as an asset and must be taken off. Answer (d) is incorrect because cash is being received, so it must be debited.

40.   (c)   ABC Company must report a servicing obligation of $50. The calculation of net proceeds is

Cash received	$2,100
Plus: Interest rate swap	140
Call option	80
Less: Recourse obligation	(120)
Servicing obligation	(50)
Net proceeds	$2,150

The gain is

Net proceeds	$2,150
Carrying amount of loans sold	2,000
Gain on sale	$ 150

41.   (c)   Under SFAS 140, financial assets subject to prepayment should be measured like investments in debt securities classified as available-for-sale or trading.

42.   (d)   SFAS 140 requires disclosure of (a), (b), and (c). Answer (d) is the correct answer as disclosure is only required of assets and liabilities with nonestimatable fair values.

43.   (d)   According to SFAS 140, if the debtor defaults under the terms of the secured contract and is no longer entitled to redeem the pledged asset, it (Taft) shall derecognize the pledged asset, and the secured party (Wilson) shall recognize the collateral as its asset initially measured at fair value.

C.1. Examples of Current Liabilities

44.   (a)   Before adjustment, the balance in the Accounts Payable account is $360,000. This amount is net of a $50,000 debit balance in Lyle's account payable to Ross resulting from a $50,000 advance payment for goods to be manufactured to Lyle's specifications. The $50,000 should be reclassified as a current asset, **Advance to Suppliers**. The checks recorded on 12/29/02 incorrectly reduced the accounts payable balance by $100,000. The $100,000 reduction should not have been recorded until the checks were mailed on 1/5/03. The 12/31/02 accounts payable must be increased by $100,000. Therefore, the corrected 12/31/02 accounts payable is $510,000.

Unadjusted AP	$360,000
Reclassification of advance	50,000
Error correction	100,000
	$510,000

45.   (a)   When purchases are recorded using the net method, purchases and accounts payable are recorded at an amount net of the cash discounts, and the failure to take advantage of a discount is recorded in a Purchase Discounts Lost account. Therefore, when Rabb changes to the net method, gross accounts payable ($30,000) must be adjusted down to the net amount. Since $200 of discounts are still available in the accounts payable balance, the net accounts payable at 9/30/02 is $29,800 ($30,000 – $200). The journal entry is

Purchase discounts lost	1,000	
Purchase discounts	800	
Accts. payable	200	
Purchases		2,000

46.   (d)   Accrued interest payable at 12/31/02 is interest expense which has been incurred by 12/31/02, but has not

yet been paid by that date. The note was issued on 3/1/01 and interest is payable in full at maturity on 2/28/03. Therefore, there is one year and ten months of unpaid interest at 12/31/02 (3/1/01 to 12/31/02). Interest for the first year is $1,200 ($10,000 x 12%). Since interest is compounded annually, the new principal amount for the second year includes the original principal ($10,000) plus the first year's interest ($1,200). Therefore, accrued interest for the ten months ended 12/31/02 is $1,120 ($11,200 x 12% x 10/12), and total accrued interest at 12/31/02 is $2,320 ($1,200 + $1,120).

47.   (c)   Accrued interest payable at 12/31/02 is interest expense which has been incurred by 12/31/02, but has not yet been paid by that date. Interest was last paid on 9/1/02; the accrued interest payable includes interest expense incurred from 9/1/02 through 12/31/02 (four months). The original balance of the note payable was $1,350,000 but the 9/1/02 principal payment of $450,000 reduced this balance to $900,000. Therefore, the interest payable at 12/31/02 is $36,000 ($900,000 x 12% x 4/12). The prime rate (11%) does not affect the computation because it is not the stated rate on this note.

48.   (d)   The solutions approach is to analyze the interest payable T-account for 2002, assuming all interest payments flow through interest payable.

Interest Payable		
	15,000	12/31/01
2002 Int. paid 68,000	85,000	2002 Expense
	?	12/31/02

The beginning interest payable balance ($15,000) is increased by interest expense (debit interest expense, credit interest payable for $85,000) and decreased by interest paid (debit interest payable, credit cash for $68,000), resulting in a 12/31/02 balance of $32,000 ($15,000 + $85,000 – $68,000).

49.   (c)   All of the notes are due 6/15/03, and normally the entire amount would be classified as current. However, SFAS 6 states that a short-term obligation can be reclassified as long-term if the enterprise intends to refinance the obligation on a long-term basis **and** the intent is supported by the ability to refinance. Ames demonstrated its ability by entering into a financing agreement before the statements are issued. SFAS 6 further states that the amount to be excluded from current liabilities cannot exceed the amount available for refinancing under the agreement. Ames expects to be able to refinance at least $480,000 (80% x $600,000) of the notes. Therefore, that amount can be classified as long-term, while the remaining $20,000 must be classified as short-term.

50.   (b)   The effective rate of interest paid on a note is computed as follows:

$$\frac{\text{Effective}}{\text{interest rate}} = \frac{\text{Interest paid}}{\text{Cash received}}$$

In this case, let's assume the short-term note payable was in the amount of $100,000. The effective interest rate would be 12.56%.

$$\frac{(\$100,000 \times .12) + (\$100,000 \times .005)}{\$100,000} = 12.56$$

This is because the loan origination fee increases the interest paid on the note and reduces the net cash received from the note.

51. **(c)** The $4,000,000 note payable is due March 15, 2002, and normally would be classified as a current liability in the December 31, 2001 financial statements. However, SFAS 6 states that a short-term obligation can be reclassified as long-term if the enterprise intends to refinance the obligation on a long-term basis and the intent is supported by the ability to refinance. Cali demonstrated its ability to refinance by actually issuing bonds and refinancing the note prior to the issuance of the December 31, 2001 financial statements. Since the proceeds from the bonds exceeded the amount needed to retire the note, the entire $4,000,000 notes payable would be classified as a noncurrent liability, with separate disclosure of the note refinancing required by SFAS 6.

52. **(c)** The notes payable ($750,000) are due 7/31/03, and would normally be included in 12/31/02 current liabilities. However, SFAS 6 states that a short-term obligation can be reclassified as long-term if the enterprise intends to refinance the obligation on a long-term basis and the intent is supported by the ability to refinance. Largo demonstrated its ability to refinance by actually issuing $1,500,000 of bonds in February 2003 before the 12/31/02 financial statements were issued on 3/3/03. The bond proceeds will be used to retire the note at maturity. SFAS 6 also states that the amount excluded from current liabilities cannot exceed the amount actually refinanced. Since Largo prepaid $250,000 of the note on 1/12/03 with excess cash, that amount must be included in 12/31/02 current liabilities. Only the remaining $500,000 can be excluded from current liabilities.

53. **(c)** A key to solving this problem is understanding that the employee advances do **not** affect the accrued salaries payable. When advances are made to employees, they are a cash payment separate from the payroll function. The advances made, therefore, are not reflected in salaries expense ($420,000) or **gross** salaries paid ($390,000). Therefore, the solutions approach is to analyze the salaries payable T-account for 2002 (disregarding the employee advances).

	Salaries Payable		
		40,000	12/31/01
2002 sal. paid	390,000	420,000	2002 sal. expense
		?	12/31/02

The beginning salaries payable balance ($40,000) is increased by salaries expense ($420,000) and decreased by salaries paid ($390,000), resulting in a 12/31/02 balance of $70,000.

54. **(c)** No sales commission is due to salesperson A because his commissions earned ($200,000 x 4% = $8,000) are less than his fixed salary ($10,000). Note that the excess of the fixed salary over commissions earned is not charged back against A. Commissions totaling $28,000 are due to salespersons B and C as computed below.

	Commissions earned		Fixed salary paid	Commissions payable
B	(6% x $400,000)	–	$14,000	$10,000
C	(6% x $600,000)	–	$18,000	18,000
				$28,000

55. **(d)** Lime's payroll tax liability includes amounts withheld from payroll checks [$1,200 of federal income taxes withheld and $700 of the **employees'** share of FICA ($10,000 x 7%)] plus the **employer's** share of FICA (an additional $700). Therefore, the total payroll tax liability is $2,600 ($1,200 + $700 + $700). The amount recorded as payroll tax expense consists only of the employer's share of FICA ($700), since no unemployment taxes are mentioned in the problem.

56. **(a)** The contingent unemployment claims liability is both probable and reasonably estimable, so it must be accrued at 12/31/02. Acme's reasonable estimate of its probable liability is 2% of eligible gross wages. Eligible gross wages are the first $10,000 of gross wages paid to each of the five employees (5 x $10,000 = $50,000), so the accrued liability should be $1,000 (2% x $50,000). Note that the 3% rate is not used because Acme has chosen the option to reimburse the state directly, and its best estimate of this liability is based on 2%, not 3%.

57. **(b)** To compute the amount of the contribution, the requirements described in the problem must be translated into an equation. The contribution must equal 10% of income **after** deduction of the contribution, but **before** income tax. Therefore, the tax rate (30%) does not enter into the computation. The equation is solved below.

$$
\begin{aligned}
C &= .10 \text{ x } (\$75,000 - C) \\
C &= \$7,500 - .10C \\
1.1C &= \$7,500 \\
C &= \$7,500 \div 1.1 \\
C &= \$6,818
\end{aligned}
$$

The amount to be accrued as an expense and liability is $6,818.

58. **(b)** If net income **after** bonus and income tax is $360,000, income before taxes can be computed by dividing **$360,000** by **1 minus the tax rate**.

$$
\text{Income before taxes} = \frac{\$360,000}{1 - .40} = \underline{\$600,000}
$$

The bonus is equal to 10% of income **before** income tax but **after** the bonus. The $600,000 computed above **is** income before tax but after all other expenses including the bonus. Therefore, the bonus must be $60,000 (10% x $600,000). Note that this problem is different from other bonus problems because usually the income before taxes and bonus ($660,000 in this case) is given as the starting point, rather than net income.

59. **(b)** To determine the correct amount for sales revenue, Ivy must divide the total of sales and sales taxes by 100% plus the sales tax percentage (6%) as indicated below.

Month	Total		Percentage		Sales revenue
Jan.	$10,600	÷	106%	=	$10,000
Feb.	$7,420	÷	106%	=	7,000
March	$8,480	÷	106%	=	8,000
Total					$25,000

Sales taxes payable would include all sales taxes collected, less any sales taxes already remitted.

January sales taxes ($10,600 – $10,000)	$600
*February sales taxes ($7,420 – $7,000)	420
March sales taxes ($8,480 – $8,000)	480
Total	$1,500
Less taxes remitted	600
Sales taxes payable	$ 900

Note February sales taxes were not remitted since they did not exceed $500.

60. (b) As of 12/31/02 the October sales taxes should have been paid, so there would be no 12/31/02 current liability for those taxes. However, at 12/31/02 sales taxes payable must be reported for the November room rentals as they were not paid until 1/3/03 and the December room rentals [15% x ($110,000 + $150,000) = $39,000]. The fourth quarter occupancy taxes were not paid until 1/3/03, so they would also represent a current liability at 12/31/02 [(1,100 + 1,200 + 1,800) x $2 = $8,200].

61. (b) When the warehouse was purchased on 9/1/02, it would be recorded at its total cost before any credit for accrued realty taxes. The offsetting credits would be to **cash** for the net amount paid, and to **real estate taxes payable** for two months' taxes ($12,000 x 2/6 = $4,000). At the end of September and of October, Day would record property tax expense each month as follows:

Real estate tax expense	2,000	
Real estate taxes payable		2,000

Therefore, at October 31, Day has a balance of $8,000 in the payable account ($4,000 + $2,000 + $2,000). On 11/1/02, Day would record the semiannual payment as follows:

Real estate taxes payable	8,000	
Prepaid real estate taxes	4,000	
Cash		12,000

The prepaid real estate taxes would then be expensed $2,000 per month at the end of November and December.

62. (d) An accrued liability is an expense which has been incurred, but has not been paid. Of the $500 advertising bill, $375 had been incurred as an expense as of 12/31/02 and should be reported as an accrued liability at that time. For the store lease, the fixed portion ($1,200 per month) is payable on the 16th of each month for the preceding month. Therefore, on 12/16/02, rent was paid for the period 11/16/02 to 12/15/02. An additional one-half month's rent expense (1/2 x $1200 = $600) has been incurred but not paid as of 12/31/02. The variable portion of the rent [5% x ($550,000 – $300,000), or $12,500] was incurred during 2002, but will not be paid until 1/31/03. It, too, is an accrued liability at 12/31/02. Total 12/31/02 accrued liabilities are $13,475.

Advertising	$ 375
Fixed rent (1/2 x $1,200)	600
Variable rent [5% x ($550,000 – $300,000)]	12,500
Total	$13,475

63. (d) The solutions approach to this problem is to construct a time line documenting the events in the question.

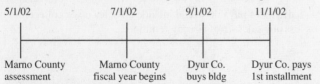

5/1/02	7/1/02	9/1/02	11/1/02
Marno County assessment	Marno County fiscal year begins	Dyur Co. buys bldg	Dyur Co. pays 1st installment

Note that on May 1, 2002, the County has merely determined the amount of property tax owed by each property

owner, and no entries would be made by companies subject to property taxes on that date. The fiscal year 2003 taxes are for the period from July 1, 2002, to June 30, 2003. On September 1, 2002, the date on which Dyur purchased the building, two months of the fiscal year had passed, and the property tax expense related to those months was borne by the seller. At October 31, 2002, Dyur would have a liability for four months of property taxes (even though only the months of September and October would have been expensed by Dyur). On November 1, 2002, four months of the fiscal year had passed, and Dyur paid taxes for the first six months of the fiscal year. The entry recorded upon the payment would be

Property taxes payable	(four months)
Prepaid property taxes	(two months)
Cash	(six months)

The payment would therefore be allocated as two-sixths (33 1/3%) to an increase in prepaid property taxes and four-sixths (66 2/3%) to a decrease in property taxes payable.

64. (b) To determine the 12/31/02 balance of the liability for customer advances, the solutions approach is to set up a T-account for the liability.

Customer Advances			
		118,000	12/31/01
		184,000	2002 adv. received
2002 adv. applied	164,000		
2002 cancellations	50,000		
		88,000	12/31/02

When advances are received ($184,000), cash is debited and the liability account is credited. When advances are applied to orders shipped ($164,000), the liability account is debited and sales is credited. When an order is cancelled ($50,000), the liability account is debited and a revenue account is credited, since the advance payments are nonrefundable. Thus, the customer advances balance on 12/31/02 is $88,000.

65. (c) The solutions approach is to set up a T-account for the liability.

Liability for Deposits			
		580,000	12/31/01 balance
		780,000	2002 deliveries
2002 returns	626,000		
2002 sales	60,000		
		674,000	12/31/02 balance

When customers pay the deposit for a container, cash is debited and the liability is credited. Therefore, at 12/31/01 the liability consists of deposits for containers still held by customers from the last two years ($580,000). During 2002, the liability was increased for deposits on containers delivered ($780,000). When containers are returned, the deposits are returned to the customers; in 2002, the liability was debited and cash credited for $626,000. Also, at 12/31/02, some customers still held containers from 2000 ($150,000 – $90,000 = $60,000). The two-year time limit has expired on these, so the company is no longer obligated to return the deposit. The containers are considered sold to the customers, so the liability account is debited and sales credited for $60,000. This results in a 12/31/02 balance of $674,000.

66. (c) To compute the escrow liability, the solutions approach is to use a T-account.

	Escrow Liability		
		700,000	1/1/02
Taxes paid	1,720,000	1,580,000	Receipts
		45,000	Net interest
		605,000	12/31/02

Escrow payments received ($1,580,000) would increase the liability because these amounts are payable to taxing authorities. Taxes paid ($1,720,000) decrease the liability. The net interest credited to the escrow accounts [$50,000 – (10% x $50,000) = $45,000] would increase the liability, resulting in a 12/31/02 balance of $605,000.

67. (d) All contract sales are made **evenly** during the year. Therefore, the 2001 contracts range from one year expired (if sold on 12/31/01) to two years expired (if sold on 1/1/01), for an average of one and one-half years expired [(2+1)/2]. Similarly, the 2002 contracts range from zero years expired to one year expired, for an average of one-half year expired [(0+1)/2]. The average **unearned** portion of the 2001 contracts is one-half year (two years – one and one-half years), the last half of the second contract year. The amount of unearned revenue related to 2001 contracts is computed as follows:

$$\$500,000 \times 60\% \times 1/2 = \underline{\$150,000}$$

The average **unearned** portion of the 2002 contracts is one and one-half years (two years – one-half year), the last half of the first contract year and all of the second contract year. The amount of unearned revenue related to the 2002 contracts is computed as follows:

2002:	$600,000 x 40% x ½	=	$120,000
	$600,000 x 60%	=	360,000
			$480,000

Therefore, the total unearned revenue is $630,000 ($150,000 + $480,000).

68. (c) Revenue is earned by Toddler Care Co. as time goes by and care is provided. Therefore, revenue should be recognized on a straight-line basis regardless of the timing of cash receipts. The monthly fees can simply be recognized on a monthly basis, but the initial payment must be deferred and recognized as revenue on a straight-line basis over the twelve-month period. The 12/31/02 deferred revenues are $6,600, as computed below.

Plan	Initial fees	2002 revenue (4/12)	12/31/02 def. rev. (8/12)
1	15 x $500 = $7,500	$2,500	$5,000
2	12 x $200 = $2,400	800	1,600
3	$ 0	0	0
	$9,900	$3,300	$6,600

Since the total initial payments received are given ($9,900), a shortcut is to multiply that amount by 8/12 ($9,900 x 8/12 = $6,600).

69. (d) Revenue is generally recognized when **realized or realizable** and **earned**. Revenues are considered earned when the entity has substantially accomplished what it must do to be entitled to the benefits represented by the revenues. Therefore, service revenue generally is earned as the work is performed, and it should be recognized evenly over the contract year as the monthly services are performed. Answer (a) is incorrect because accrual basis accounting is preferable; SFAC 6 explains that cash method provides little information about the results of operations. Answer (b) is incorrect because revenue should be recognized when earned. Answer (c) is incorrect because the completed-contract method should only be used when reasonable esti-

mates of contract costs, revenues, and the extent of progress toward completion cannot be reasonably estimated.

70. (b) When a company issues gift certificates for cash, the following journal entry is made:

Cash	(amount of certificate)	
Deferred revenue		(amount of certificate)

When the gift certificates are subsequently redeemed, the following journal entry is made:

Deferred revenue	(amount of certificate)	
Revenue		(amount of certificate)

However, if the gift certificates are not redeemed and lapse, the following journal entry is made:

Deferred revenue	(amount of certificate)	
Gain on lapse of certificates		(amount of certificate)

Please note that although different accounts are credited depending on whether the certificates are redeemed or lapse, the Deferred Revenue account is decreased in both cases.

71. (c) Per SFAC 5, revenues are generally recognized when they are both **realized** or **realizable** and **earned**. Therefore, Dallas Co. should report a liability for deferred revenues equal to the advance payment of 60% of the main contract price. Per SFAC 6, one of three essential characteristics of a liability is that the transaction or other event obligating the entity has already happened. Since the subcontractor had not produced the special-order goods as of March 31, Dallas should not record a liability at that time. Therefore, no payable to the subcontractor would be reported for this activity as of March 31.

72. (b) At June 30, 2002, Northan Retailers should report the coupon transactions as unearned revenues because the sale of the coupons is not the culmination of the earnings process (i.e., Northan must allow customers to exchange the coupons for merchandise or refund the cost of the coupons at some later date). The unearned revenues should be recorded at the amount of the cash received by debiting cash and crediting an unearned revenue account. The retail price of the merchandise for which coupons may be redeemed does not impact the monetary amount of Northan's liability to its customers, and each coupon redeemed will ultimately result in the recognition of sales of $10, the amount of cash previously received.

73. (b) The requirement is to determine the situation that might account for the reduction in the deferred revenue balance. When a service contract is purchased by a customer and the fee prepaid, deferred revenue is recognized at the date of payment. Revenue cannot be recorded because revenue has not yet been earned. Revenue is only recorded when services are performed under the contract. The deferred revenue balance is reduced by the **actual** amount of revenue earned when services are performed under the services contract. If more contracts were signed earlier in one year than another year, there is a greater period of time in which to perform actual services. As previously stated, when actual services are performed, the deferred revenue balance is decreased. Therefore, the more actual services that are performed, the greater the reduction in the deferred revenue balance. If more 2002 contracts were signed later in 2002 than 2001, the deferred revenue balance in 2002 would be larger than 2001. There would be less time to perform actual services, therefore less actual revenue would be recognized, creating a larger deferred revenue balance at year-end. There is no contribution margin recognized on service contracts.

74.   (c)   Per SFAS 47, the aggregate amount of payments for unconditional purchase obligations that have been recognized on the purchaser's balance sheet shall be disclosed for each of the **five** years following the date of the latest balance sheet presented.

C.2.   Current Liabilities—Contingencies

75.   (b)   Per SFAS 5, a loss contingency should be accrued if it is **probable** that a liability has been incurred at the balance sheet date and the amount of the loss is reasonably estimable. With respect to unfiled claims, the enterprise must consider both the probability that a claim will be filed and the probability of an unfavorable outcome. Although it is probable that claims will be asserted against Sims, it is only **reasonably possible** that the claims will be successful. Therefore, this contingent liability should not be accrued, but should be disclosed. The potential loss to be disclosed is $250,000, since the additional amount above the deductible would be covered by the insurance policy, and therefore is not a loss or liability for Sims.

76.   (c)   ARB 43 states that current liabilities are obligations whose liquidation is reasonably expected to require the use of current assets or the creation of other current liabilities. This means that generally, current liabilities are the liabilities that are due within one year of the balance sheet date. Clearly, accounts payable ($55,000) and accrued expenses ($35,000) are current liabilities. Notes payable ($400,000) and bonds payable ($1,000,000) are usually considered to be long-term, but the maturity dates given (7/1/03 and 3/1/03 respectively) indicate they are current liabilities at 12/31/02. The contingent liability ($450,000) and deferred tax liability ($25,000) will not be settled until 2004 and therefore should be classified as long-term at 12/31/02. Thus, the 12/31/02 current liabilities total is $1,490,000 as follows:

Accounts payable	$ 55,000
Accrued expenses	35,000
Unsecured notes 8%—due 7/1/03	400,000
Senior bonds 7%—due 3/1/03	1,000,000
Total current liabilities	$1,490,000

77.   (d)   The lawsuit damages must be accrued as a loss contingency in accordance with SFAS 5 because an unfavorable outcome is **probable** and the amount of the loss is **reasonably estimable**. Per FASB Interpretation 14, when a range of possible loss exists, the best estimate within the range is accrued. When no amount within the range is a better estimate than any other amount, the dollar amount at the low end of the range is **accrued** (in this case, $500,000) and the dollar amount of the high end of the range is **disclosed**.

78.   (c)   Per SFAS 5, a loss contingency should be accrued if it is **probable** that a liability has been incurred at the balance sheet date and the amount of the loss is **reasonably estimable**. This loss must be accrued because it meets both criteria. Notice that even though the lawsuit was not initiated until 1/12/03, the liability was incurred on 11/5/02 when the accident occurred. FASB Interpretation 14 requires that when some amount within an estimated range is a better estimate than any other amount in the range, that amount is accrued. Therefore, a loss of $300,000 should be accrued. If no amount within the range is a better estimate than any other amount, the amount at the low end of the range is accrued and the amount at the high end is disclosed.

79.   (a)   The additional tax liability must be accrued as a loss contingency in accordance with SFAS 5 because an unfavorable outcome is **probable** and the amount of the loss is **reasonably estimable**. Since $200,000 is the reasonable estimate, that amount should be accrued by debiting Income Tax Expense and crediting Income Tax Payable. The possibility of the liability being as high as $300,000 would be disclosed in the notes. The settlement offer of $275,000 is not accrued at 12/31/02 because prior to financial statement issuance, Haft was unaware of the offer, and $200,000 was the best estimate. In 2003, when the settlement offer was accepted, Haft would record an additional $75,000 of expense and liability.

80.   (a)   Per SFAS 5, a loss contingency is accrued if it is **probable** that a liability has been incurred at the balance sheet date and the amount of the loss is reasonably estimable. If no accrual is made for a loss contingency because one or both of the conditions above are not met, disclosure of the contingency shall be made when it is at least **reasonably possible** that a loss was incurred. Therefore, this loss should be disclosed, but not accrued as a liability.

81.   (b)   Invern's appropriation of retained earnings for contingencies is merely a reclassification of retained earnings on the balance sheet which tells the readers of the financial statements that such amounts are generally not available to pay dividends. This appropriation has no effect on the income statement. When a loss contingency is probable (as in this instance) **and** reasonably estimable ($190,000 in this instance), SFAS 5 requires accrual of the loss. Therefore, Invern must accrue both a liability and an expense of $190,000. Note that Invern will also reclassify $190,000 of appropriated retained earnings into the "general" retained earnings.

82.   (d)   At 12/31/02, Halsey's contingent liability of $50,000 is no longer probable due to the favorable judgment and the inability to predict the outcome of the appeal. Therefore, no liability should be reported in the balance sheet. SFAS 5 states that **gain** contingencies are not reflected in the accounts until realized, so the $30,000 asset is not reported in the 12/31/02 balance sheet, either.

83.   (a)   SFAS 5 states that gain contingencies are not recognized in the income statement until realized. As only $15,000 of the litigation awards has been resolved as of December 31, 2002, Haze should report only $15,000 as a gain in its 2002 financial statements.

84.   (a)   SFAS 5 states that **gain** contingencies are not reflected in the accounts until realized. Since the case is unresolved at 12/31/02, none of this contingent gain should be recorded as income in 2002. Adequate disclosure should be made of the gain contingency, but care should be taken to avoid misleading implications as to the likelihood of realization.

85.   (d)   SFAS 5 states that **gain** contingencies are not reflected in the accounts until realized. Since the case was unresolved at 12/31/01, none of this contingent gain can be recorded as a receivable and/or revenue in 2001. Since the contingency is probable, it should be disclosed along with the 12/31/01 estimate of a range of $75,000 to $150,000. A gain contingency would not be accrued as a receivable. The amount disclosed should be the range because all amounts within the range are considered equally likely.

86.   (c)   Per SFAS 5, an estimated loss from a loss contingency shall be accrued by a charge to income if **both** of the following conditions are met:

1. Information available indicates that it is **probable** that an asset has been impaired or a liability has been incurred.
2. The amount of the loss can be **reasonably estimated**.

However, per SFAS 5, gain contingencies are only recognized when a specific event actually occurs, not prior to the event, because to do so would recognize the gain prior to its realization. Therefore, Brooks should recognize the loss in 2002 due to the fact that the event is probable and can be reasonably estimated. Dollis, on the other hand, cannot recognize the gain until 2003, the year they receive the actual award.

87.   (a)   Eagle Co. has a contingent liability where the possibility of loss is **remote**. Loss contingencies are accrued when they are **probable** and **reasonably estimable**. All others are disclosed unless remote. However, per SFAS 5, some contingencies, such as guarantees of others' debts, standby letters of credit by banks, and agreements to repurchase receivables, are disclosed even if remote. Eagle's contingent liability is **not** accrued, because it is not probable. It **is** disclosed for two reasons: it is a guarantee of other's debt, and it is a related-party transaction.

88.   (d)   SFAS 43 states that accrual of a liability for future vacation pay is required if all the conditions below are met.

1. Obligation arises from employee services already performed.
2. Obligation arises from rights that vest or accumulate.
3. Payment is probable.
4. Amount can be reasonably estimated.

The criteria are met for the vacation pay (150 x $100 = $15,000), so North is required to report a $15,000 liability. The same criteria apply to accrual of a liability for future sick pay, **except** that if sick pay benefits accumulate but do not vest, accrual is **permitted** but not **required** because its payment is contingent upon future employee sickness. Therefore, no liability is **required** for these sick pay benefits (75 x $100 = $7500). Note that the unadjusted balance of the liability account ($21,000) does not affect the computation of the required 12/31/02 liability.

89.   (d)   The week ended 1/1/03 included four days in 2002 and one day in 2003. The pay due for this week won't be paid until the following Monday (1/4/03). Therefore, Ross has a liability for four days' accrued salaries at 12/31/02 (4/5 x $80,000 = $64,000). The entire $25,000 of vacation pay is an accrued liability at 12/31/02 because it represents vacation time earned by employees in 2002 but not taken by 12/31/02. Therefore, the total accrued salary and vacation pay is $89,000 ($64,000 + $25,000).

90.   (c)   Per SFAS 43, an employer is required to accrue a liability for employees' rights to receive compensation for future absences, such as vacations, when certain conditions are met. The Statement does **not**, however, specify how such liabilities are to be measured. Since vacation time is paid by Gavin Co. at the salaries in effect when vacations are taken or when employment is terminated, Gavin adjusts its vacation liability and expense to current salary levels. Gavin's 2002 vacation pay expense consists of vacations earned for work in 2002 (adjusted to current rates) of $30,000 plus the amount necessary to adjust its pre-2002 vacation liability for the 10% salary increase. The amount of this adjustment is equal to 10% of the preexisting liability balance at December 31, 2002 [($35,000 − $20,000) x 10% = $1,500]. Therefore, total vacation pay expense for the period is equal to $31,500 ($30,000 + $1,500).

91.   (c)   Per SFAS 43, an employer shall accrue a liability for employees' future absences if **all** of the following conditions are met: (1) the employer's obligation relates to employees' service already rendered, (2) the employees' rights vest **or** accumulate, (3) payment of the compensation is probable, and (4) the amount can be reasonably estimated. All of these conditions are met whether Taos Co.'s employees' rights either accumulate or vest.

92.   (b)   SFAS 43 states that accrual of a liability for employees' compensation for future absences is required if all of the conditions below are met.

1. Obligation arises from employee services already performed.
2. Obligation arises from rights that vest or accumulate.
3. Payment is probable.
4. Amount can be reasonably estimated.

93.   (d)   The solutions approach is to set up a T-account for warranty liability.

Warranty Liability			
2002 payments	2,250	9,000	2002 exp. (6% x $150,000)
2003 payments	7,500	15,000	2003 exp. (6% x $250,000)
		14,250	12/31/03 liability

Each year warranty expense is estimated at 6% of sales and recorded by debiting the expense account and crediting the liability. As warranty expenditures are made, the liability is debited and cash is credited. Note that the total estimated warranty cost for **both** years (2% + 4% = 6%) is recorded in the year of sale in compliance with the matching principle.

94.   (d)   The warranty expense of $30 for each machine sold, although it will be incurred over the three-year warranty period, is directly related to the sales revenue as an integral and inseparable part of the sale and recognized at the time of the sale. The warranty costs make their contribution to revenue in the year of sale by making the product more attractive to the customer. Therefore, in accordance with the matching principle, the warranty costs should be expensed when the machines are sold with a corresponding credit to accrued liability. Answers (a) and (b) are incorrect; this is a sales warranty approach in which the warranty is sold separately from the product. The revenue is recognized on the straight-line basis and they are expensed as incurred.

Answer (c) is incorrect because this describes a cash basis method.

95.   (a)   Case expects 120,000 coupons to be redeemed at a total cost of $.50 per coupon ($.45 + $.05). Therefore, total expected redemptions are $60,000 (120,000 x $.50). By 12/31/02, $25,000 has been paid on coupon redemptions, so a liability of $35,000 must be established ($60,000 – $25,000). Note that this liability would include both payments due for the 50,000 coupons on hand, and payments due on coupons to be received within the first thirty days after the expiration date.

96.   (c)   Dunn records stamp service revenue and provides for the cost of redemptions in the year stamps are sold. Therefore, Dunn's entries are

To record sales of stamps		
Cash	4,000,000	
Stamp service revenue		4,000,000
To record cost of redemptions		
Liability for stamp reds.	2,750,000	
Inventory		2,750,000
To provide for cost of future redemptions		
Cost of redemptions	1,800,000	
Liability for stamp reds.		1,800,000
(80% x $2,250,000)		

The 12/31/02 liability balance is $5,050,000 as shown below.

Liability for Stamp Redemptions

		6,000,000	12/31/01
Redemptions	2,750,000	1,800,000	Provision for reds.
		5,050,000	12/31/02

Miscellaneous

97.   (a)   Current assets listed in the trial balance are cash ($550,000), accounts receivable ($1,650,000), and prepaid taxes ($300,000). However, part of the AR must be reclassified, and income tax expense has not yet been recorded. Included in AR is $500,000 due from a customer, for which $250,000 is collectible in 2003 (2 x $125,000) and $250,000 is collectible in 2004. The portion collectible in 2003 should be reclassified as a noncurrent asset. Revenues ($3,600,000) less expenses ($2,600,000) result in pretax income of $1,000,000. Since the tax rate is 30%, tax expense is $300,000 (30% x $1,000,000). Therefore, an adjustment is necessary to debit **income tax expense** and credit **prepaid taxes** for $300,000. Total current assets, after reclassification and adjustment, are $1,950,000 [answer (a)] as calculated below.

Cash	$ 550,000
AR ($1,650,000 – $250,000)	1,400,000
Prepaid taxes ($300,000 – $300,000)	--
	$1,950,000

98.   (c)   Before closing entries, retained earnings is $630,000. 2002 net income is revenues ($3,600,000) less expenses ($2,600,000) and income tax expense [30% x ($3,600,000 – $2,600,000) = $300,000]. After adjusting for income tax expense, net income is $700,000 [$3,600,000 – ($2,600,000 + $300,000)]. After closing entries, 12/31/02 retained earnings is $1,330,000 ($630,000 + $700,000). The foreign currency translation adjustment ($430,000) does not affect retained earnings; it is reported as a separate component of stockholders' equity.

99.   (a)   Current assets are cash and other assets that are expected to be converted into cash, sold, or consumed either in one year, or in the operating cycle, whichever is longer. Generally included in this category are cash, temporary investments, short-term receivables, inventories, and prepaid expenses. In this situation, there are two special items. Cash must be adjusted because checks that were not mailed until July 9 were recorded June 29. To compute the correct June 30 cash balance, this $30,000 of checks must be added back to the cash balance, turning the $10,000 overdraft into a $20,000 positive balance [(– $10,000) + $30,000 = $20,000]. Also, land held for resale ($100,000) must be included in current assets because, like inventory, at June 30 it is expected to be sold for cash within the next year. Therefore, June 30 current assets total $225,000.

Cash	$20,000
AR, net	35,000
Inventory	58,000
Prepaid expenses	12,000
Land held for resale	100,000
	$225,000

100.   (a)   ARB 43 states that current liabilities are obligations whose liquidation is reasonably expected to require the use of current assets or the creation of other current liabilities. This means that generally, current liabilities are liabilities due within one year of the balance sheet date. Clearly, accounts payable ($15,000) and dividends payable ($8,000) are current liabilities. Generally, bonds payable are a long-term liability; however, since these bonds are due in 2003, they must be reported as a current liability at 12/31/02 ($25,000 fair value less $3,000 discount, or $22,000). Therefore, total current liabilities are $45,000 ($15,000 + $8,000 + $22,000). The notes payable ($20,000) are classified as long-term because they are not due until 2004.

D.   Ratios

101.   (b)   The quick (acid-test) ratio is quick assets (cash, temporary investments in marketable equity securities, and net receivables) divided by current liabilities. The quick ratio measures the ability to pay current liabilities from cash and near-cash items. In this case, quick assets total $700,000 ($170,000 + $450,000 + $80,000) and current liabilities total $400,000 ($60,000 + $240,000 + $100,000), resulting in a quick ratio of 1.75 to 1 ($700,000 ÷ $400,000).

102.   (d)   The formula to compute accounts receivable turnover is

$$\frac{\text{Net credit sales}}{\text{Average accounts receivable}}$$

The average receivable is the sum of the beginning and ending net accounts receivable divided by 2. The 2002 beginning accounts receivable equals the 2001 ending balance in accounts receivable. Average accounts receivable is $425,000 [($450,000 + $400,000) ÷ 2]. Applying the formula, the 2002 accounts receivable turnover is 7.06 times ($3,000,000 ÷ $425,000).

103.   (d)   Ratios that are useful in assessing a company's ability to meet currently maturing or short-term obligations are referred to as solvency ratios. The acid-test ratio is classified as a solvency ratio, and it measures the ability to pay current liabilities from cash and near-cash items. The acid-test ratio is

$$\frac{\text{Cash + Net receivables + Marketable securities}}{\text{Current liabilities}}$$

The debt to equity ratio is a leverage ratio that measures the relative amount of leverage or debt a company has. The debt to equity ratio is

$$\frac{\text{Total liabilities}}{\text{Common stockholders equity}}$$

Therefore, answer (d) is correct because the acid-test ratio is useful in assessing a company's ability to meet currently maturing or short-term obligations while the debt to equity ratio is not.

104. (a)   The quick (acid-test) ratio measures the ability to pay current liabilities from cash and near-cash items.

$$\text{Quick ratio} = \frac{\text{Cash, Net receivables, Marketable securities}}{\text{Current liabilities}}$$

Fluctuating market prices of short-term investments may adversely affect Belle's quick ratio and creditworthiness. Inventory and available-for-sale investment items do not affect the quick ratio.

105. (a)   The solutions approach is to create a numerical example that conforms to the facts given in the question. Assume the following:

$$\text{Current ratio} = \frac{\$900,000}{\$600,000} = 1.5 \text{ to } 1$$

$$\text{Quick ratio} = \frac{\$300,000}{\$600,000} = .5 \text{ to } 1$$

Payments of accounts payable decrease both cash (a current and quick asset) and accounts payable (a current liability). After payment the following ratios result:

$$\text{Current ratio} = \frac{900 - 200}{600 - 200} = \frac{700}{400} = 1.75 \text{ to } 1$$

$$\text{Quick ratio} = \frac{300 - 200}{600 - 200} = \frac{100}{400} = .25 \text{ to } 1$$

Subtracting equal amounts from the numerator and the denominator of a ratio **greater than one** will **increase** the ratio. Subtracting equal amounts from the numerator and the denominator of a ratio **less than one** will **decrease** the ratio. Therefore, the current ratio will increase while the quick ratio decreases.

106. (b)   The formula to compute the current ratio is

$$\text{Current ratio} = \frac{\text{Current assets}}{\text{Current liabilities}}$$

The write-off of inventory would decrease current assets and the current ratio. The formula to compute the acid-test (quick) ratio is

$$\text{Acid-test ratio} = \frac{\text{Cash + Net receivables + Marketable securities}}{\text{Current liabilities}}$$

The write-off of inventory has no effect on the acid-test ratio.

107. (d)   The number of days in the operating cycle measures the length of time from purchase of inventory to collection of cash. The formula is

$$\begin{pmatrix} \text{Number of days'} \\ \text{sales in} \\ \text{inventories} \end{pmatrix} + \begin{pmatrix} \text{Number of days'} \\ \text{sales in} \\ \text{accts. receivable} \end{pmatrix} = \begin{pmatrix} \text{Number of days} \\ \text{in} \\ \text{operating cycle} \end{pmatrix}$$

$$61 \text{ days} \quad + \quad 33 \text{ days} \quad = \quad \underline{94 \text{ days}}$$

Note that the number of days' sales in inventories measures the number of days from the purchase of inventory to the sale of inventory, while the number of days' sales in accounts receivable measures the number of days from the sale of inventory to the collection of cash.

108. (b)   Collection of a receivable results in an increase in cash and a decrease in the accounts receivable balance. The accounts receivable turnover ratio is computed by dividing net credit sales by the average net accounts receivable balance. Collection of a receivable reduces the average net accounts receivable balance. Thus the receivable turnover ratio increases. Since this transaction does not affect cost of goods sold or inventory, the inventory turnover ratio is unaffected. Neither the current ratio nor the quick ratio is affected by the collection; neither current assets nor quick assets would change as a result of the collection.

OTHER OBJECTIVE ANSWERS AND ANSWER EXPLANATIONS

Problem 1

Part a.

1.   **(D)** In this transaction, receivables are factored by surrendering control and without recourse. This constitutes an outright sale of the receivables in that title, risk of loss, and rights to future benefits are all transferred. Therefore, a loss on the transaction is recognized.

2.   **(C)** In a specific assignment of receivables, AR assigned are identified by placing them in an AR assigned account. A finance charge is assessed on assignment transactions that are borrowings.

3.   **(E)** When AR are pledged, the receivables serve as collateral for a loan but the proceeds are not remitted to the lender. In this case, the amount of AR pledged is reported at the balance sheet date either parenthetically or in the notes.

4.   **(B)** In this transaction, considered a borrowing, receivables are considered to be factored with recourse. Thus, the transaction is viewed as a loan collateralized by AR and the amount of the proceeds plus the factor's holdback and interest charged should be reported as a liability.

5.   **(F)** A note discounted on which control is surrendered and the terms include without recourse is considered a sales transaction upon which a loss should be recognized. Notes receivable should be credited.

6.   **(E)** A general assignment of receivables is another term for pledging AR, and thus should be disclosed parenthetically or in the notes to the financial statements (no journal entry).

Part b.

7.   **(F)** "Factor's holdback" accounts for the proceeds retained by the factor to cover estimated sales discounts, sales returns, and sales allowances. When all amounts have been collected by the factor, the balance in factor's margin is returned to the seller. Therefore, this account is a receivable reported as a current asset on the balance sheet.

8.   **(T)** A specific assignment of receivables bestows more formal rights upon the assignee (lender) in that the AR do not simply collateralize the loan, but collections on the assigned accounts are actually remitted to the assignor who remits them to the assignee (lender).

9.   **(F)** Once a company sells receivables to a factor it normally has no further involvement with the receivables. The factor usually collects the remittances directly from the **customer**.

10.   **(F)** Per SFAS 125, transfers of receivables in which the transferee can require the transferor to repurchase the receivables may not be considered a sale.

11.   **(T)** The difference between the amount of receivables sold to a factor in a borrowing transaction and the total of the factor's holdback plus the proceeds is recorded in a "Discount on Transferred AR" or interest expense account (see journal entry (B) in part a.). This account represents interest cost and should be recognized over the term of the receivables. If interest expense is debited, an adjusting entry to defer some of the interest as "Discount" would be required if some of the discount pertains to a later period.

Problem 2

1.   **(B)** SFAS 5 states "contingencies that might result in gains usually are not reflected in the accounts since to do so might be to recognize revenue prior to its realization." Since this gain contingency was resolved before the issuance of the financial statements, it is handled similar to an ordinary transaction that occurred prior to the year-end and is accrued in the year of its occurrence.

     SFAS 5 states "adequate disclosure shall be made of contingencies that might result in gains...."

2.   **(N)** To accrue an estimated loss from a loss contingency it is necessary that it is probable that an asset has been impaired or a liability has been incurred and that the amount of loss can be reasonably estimated. Since Town's lawyers believe the suit to be without merit, neither condition has been met.

     SFAS 5 states "disclosure is also required of some loss contingencies that do not meet 'the accrual requirements mentioned above if' there is a **reasonable possibility** that a loss may be incurred." Again, this condition has not been met.

3.   **(N)** The conditions described in this question would be considered general or unspecified business risks that do not meet the conditions for accrual or disclosure.

4.   **(D)** The words "reasonably possible" require the disclosure of this item. No accrual need be made since the question does not state it is **probable** that an asset has been impaired or a liability incurred and that the amount of loss can be reasonably estimated.

5.   **(B)** The word "probable" and the inclusion of the estimated amount of $500,000 mean that this situation meets the criteria of (1) a probable incurrence of a liability and (2) a reasonable estimate of an amount.

6.   **(D)** SFAS 5 quotes ARB 50 which "required disclosure of a number of situations including...commitments such as those for an obligation to reduce debts." SFAS 5 states "situations of the type described...shall continue to be disclosed in financial statements." Since the entire transaction took place in the next accounting period it does not meet the conditions for an accrual in the current period even though it would be disclosed in a footnote.

ANSWER OUTLINE

Problem 1   AR Factored, Noninterest NR, Bad Debts

a.   Accounting for AR factored
     Cash (amount received)
     Loss (cash received – AR factored)
       AR (amount factored)

    Loss reported on IS
    Transfers with control surrendered equivalent to sale

b.   Carrying value at 7/1/02 is maturity value discounted
    for two years at market interest rate
    Income Statement effects
      Interest revenue for 2002 = Carrying value at 7/1/02
      x Market rate of interest at 7/1/02 x 1/2 year
    Balance Sheet effects
      Noninterest-bearing NR should be reported as non-
      current asset at face value less unamortized discount
        Because it is due more than one year from BS date

c.   Reinstatement of AR previously WO
    AR   xx
      Allowance for DA   xx

    Collection of AR previously WO
    Cash   xx
      AR   xx

d.   **Credit Sales Basis**
    Emphasizes IS
    Attempts to match uncollectible accounts with reve-
    nue earned in same period
    Receivable Account Basis
    Emphasizes BS
    Reports receivables at estimated future collectible
    amounts (net realizable value)

UNOFFICIAL ANSWER

Problem 1   AR Factored, Noninterest NR, Bad Debts

a.   To account for the accounts receivable factored on
April 1, 2002, Magrath should decrease accounts receivable
by the amount of accounts receivable factored, increase cash
by the amount received from the factor, and record a loss
equal to the difference. The loss should be reported in the
income statement. Transfers of accounts receivable with
control over the receivables surrendered is equivalent to a
sale.

b.   The carrying amount of the note at July 1, 2002, is the
maturity amount discounted for two years at the market interest rate. For the noninterest-bearing note receivable, the
interest revenue for 2002 should be determined by multiplying the carrying amount of the note at July 1, 2002, times
the market rate of interest at the date of the note times one-
half.

    The noninterest-bearing note receivable should be re-
ported in the December 31, 2002 balance sheet, as a noncurrent asset at its face amount less the unamortized discount.

c.   Magrath should account for the collection of the accounts previously written off as uncollectible as follows:

    •   Increase both accounts receivable and the allow-
ance for uncollectible accounts.
    •   Increase cash and decrease accounts receivable.

d.   One approach estimates uncollectible accounts based on
credit sales. This approach focuses on income determination
by attempting to match uncollectible accounts expense with
the revenues generated.

    The other allowance approach estimates uncollectible
accounts based on the balance in or aging of receivables.
The approach focuses on asset valuation by attempting to
report receivables at realizable value.

ANSWER OUTLINE

Problem 2   Schedule to Calculate Provision and Allow-
               ance for Bad Debts

1.   This problem consists of two related parts: part a.
requires a calculation of the allowance for uncollectible accounts at 12/31/02 using an aging approach,
and part b. requires a computation of the 2002 provision for uncollectible accounts (uncollectible accounts expense). The solutions approach is to
quickly review the basics of accounting for uncollectible accounts, visualize the solution format, and
begin. Some candidates may benefit from preparation of T-accounts (see item 4 below).

2.   When using the aging approach, the **total** uncollectible accounts (in other words, the required ending
balance in the allowance account) is estimated by applying a different percentage to the various age categories. The percentage increases as the age of the receivables increases because the older a receivable is,
the less likely is its ultimate collection.

2.1   In this case, Sigma estimates that 1% of its receivables in the zero-thirty days age category will prove
to be uncollectible. Therefore, of that $300,000 of
accounts receivable, it is estimated that $3,000 (1% x
$300,000) will be uncollectible. Similar computa-
tions are performed for the other age categories, resulting in an estimate that $<u>39,000</u> of the $465,000
accounts receivable will prove to be uncollectible.
This is the required 12/31/02 balance in the allowance account.

3.   When using the aging approach, the first step is to
compute the required ending balance in the allowance account (as discussed in items 2 and 2.1 above).
The second step is to compute the uncollectible accounts expense necessary to bring the **unadjusted**
allowance balance up to the **required** allowance balance.

3.1   The only item affecting the allowance account in
2001 was the recording of uncollectible accounts expense of $28,000 (1% x $2,800,000 credit sales).
Therefore, the 1/1/02 balance in this account is
$28,000. No adjustment is necessary for the change
in the method of estimating this expense (from percent of sales to aging schedule) because any such
change is handled prospectively.

    *NOTE: Using the aging percents given also results in a
$28,000 balance at 1/1/02. Even if the result was differ-
ent, though, no adjustment is necessary.*

3.2   During 2002, this $28,000 credit balance was de-
creased by write-offs of $27,000 (debit allowance,
credit AR) and increased by $7,000 of recoveries
(debit AR, credit allowance; and debit cash, credit
AR). Therefore, the 12/31/02 balance in the allowance account, **before adjustment,** is $8,000 ($28,000
– $27,000 + $7,000).

3.3   To increase the allowance account from $8,000 (see 3.2 above) to $39,000 (see 2.1 above), a provision for uncollectible accounts (uncollectible accounts expense) of $31,000 must be recorded for 2002.

4.   Some candidates may benefit from the preparation of T-accounts for the allowance account and accounts receivable. These T-accounts are provided below.

T-accounts for 2001

```
                         AR
       Sales  2,800,000  | 2,400,000  Collections
     12/31/01   400,000  |

                      Allowance
                           |  28,000   Provision
                           |  28,000   12/31/01
```

T-accounts for 2002

```
                         AR
      1/1/02    400,000  |
      Sales   3,000,000  |
                         |  2,908,000*  Collections
    Recoveries    7,000  |     27,000   Write-offs
                         |      7,000   Recoveries
     12/31/02   465,000  |

                      Allowance
                           |  28,000   1/1/02
    Write-offs  27,000     |
                           |   7,000   Recoveries
                           |   8,000   12/31/02 before adj.
                           |  31,000   Provision
                           |  39,000   12/31/02
```

The collections given ($2,915,000) apparently includes the recoveries of $7,000. In the T-accounts above these are shown separately, but total collections are $2,915,000. Note that the ending balance of AR ($465,000) corresponds to the information given in the problem ($300,000 + $80,000 + $60,000 + $25,000 = $465,000)

UNOFFICIAL ANSWER

Problem 2   Schedule to Calculate Provision and Allowance for Bad Debts

a.

Sigma Co.
SCHEDULE OF CALCULATION OF
ALLOWANCE FOR UNCOLLECTIBLE ACCOUNTS
December 31, 2002

0 to 30 days	$300,000	x	1%	$ 3,000
31 to 90 days	80,000	x	5%	4,000
91 to 180 days	60,000	x	20%	12,000
Over 180 days	25,000	x	80%	20,000
Accounts receivable	$465,000			
Allowance for uncollectible accounts				$39,000

b. Computation of 2002 provision

Balance December 31, 2001	$28,000
Write-offs during 2002	(27,000)
Recoveries during 2002	7,000
Balance before 2002 provision	8,000
Required allowance at December 31, 2002	39,000
2002 provision	$31,000

ANSWER OUTLINE

Problem 3   Notes Receivable: Valuation, Discounting, and Estimating Losses

a.   Note's valuation basis
     Discounted present value of the future principal and interest receivable at customer's market rate of % on sale date

b.   Discounting of note
     Increase CV of note by effective interest revenue earned to 5/1/02
     Discounting shall be treated as sale
     Recognize a gain (loss)
     Since note discounted without recourse, treat as sale

c.   1.   NR not discounted
     Uncollectible notes expense equals adjustment necessary to make balance needed in allowance for uncollectible notes equal estimated uncollectible less FMV of recoverable equipment
   2.   Recognize recourse liability at time of transfer
     Review and adjust this liability at year-end

       Adjustment of prior year amounts are Δs in estimate

UNOFFICIAL ANSWER

Problem 3   Notes Receivable: Valuation, Discounting, and Estimating Losses

a.   The appropriate valuation basis of a note receivable at the date of sale is its discounted present value of the future amounts receivable for principal and interest using the customer's market rate of interest, if known or determinable, at the date of the equipment's sale.

b.   Gregor should increase the carrying amount of the note receivable by the effective interest revenue earned for the period February 1 to May 1, 2002. Gregor should account for the discounting of the note receivable without recourse by increasing cash for the proceeds received, eliminating the carrying amount of the note receivable, and recognizing a loss (gain) for the resulting difference.

This reporting is appropriate since the note's carrying amount is correctly recorded at the date it was discounted and the discounting of a note receivable without recourse is equivalent to a sale of that note. Thus the difference between the cash received and the carrying amount of the note at the date it is discounted is reported as a loss (gain).

c. 1.   For notes receivable not discounted, Gregor should recognize an uncollectible notes expense. The expense equals the adjustment required to bring the balance of the allowance for uncollectible notes receivable equal to the estimated uncollectible amounts less the fair values of recoverable equipment.

2.   When a transfer with recourse qualifies as a sale, a components approach is used. The notes receivable are removed from the books but a liability for recourse provisions is recognized. At year-end, the recourse liability must be reviewed and adjusted upward or downward with a corresponding gain (loss) recognized. Any changes relating to prior years is a change of accounting estimate.

ANSWER OUTLINE

Problem 4   Receivable Transfers

a.   Financial components approach
   Accounts for transactions as part asset and part liability using surrender of control criteria

b.   Transferred assets isolated
   Transferee may pledge/exchange assets
   Transferor has no effective control
      No obligatory repurchase agreement
      No entitlement to repurchase based on availability

c.

Cash	xx	
Finance expense	xx	
Liability for loan		xx

d.

Cash	xx	
Factor's holdback	xx	
Loss from transfer	xx	
Receivables		xx
Recourse obligation		xx

UNOFFICIAL ANSWER

Problem 4   Receivable Transfers

a.   The financial components approach as applied to transfers of financial assets provides that the transaction can be separated into the elements comprising it using criteria to ascertain whether control is surrendered. This means that the event can be accounted for by recognizing assets and liabilities in a transfer rather than only as an exchange of assets or an incurrence of a liability.

b.   The criteria for determining when control has been surrendered are

- Transferred assets have been isolated from the transferor or its creditors,
- Transferee has the unconstrained right to pledge or exchange the transferred assets, and
- Transferor does not maintain effective control over the transferred assets through

  - An agreement that obligates the transferor to repurchase or redeem them before their maturity, or
  - An agreement that entitles transferor to repurchase transferred assets that are not obtainable elsewhere

c.   If one or more criteria for determining whether control has been surrendered are not met, the transfer should be recorded as a borrowing by debiting cash and finance expense and crediting a loan liability account.

d.   If control is surrendered in a transfer of receivables, the transaction shall be accounted for by derecognizing the receivables with an entry that debits cash, an asset account entitled "Factor's Holdback," and a loss account. Additionally, the entry would include credits to receivables and a liability account entitled "Recourse Obligation."

ANSWER OUTLINE

Problem 5   Contingencies

a.   Disclose threat of expropriation in notes to FS
   Include estimate of possible loss or range thereof
   Accrual inappropriate because threat only reasonably possible, not probable

b.   Accrue loss and liability from safety hazard and report in FS
   Because both recognition conditions met
      Probable that liability incurred
      Amount of loss can be reasonably estimated
   Additionally, disclose nature of hazard in notes to FS

c.   Do not recognize loss and liability
   Because no asset impaired/liability incurred at BS date
   Disclosure of uninsured risk permitted, but not required

UNOFFICIAL ANSWER

Problem 5   Contingencies

a.   Chester should disclose the threat of expropriation of assets in the notes to the financial statements. Disclosure would include an estimate of the possible loss or an estimate of the range of loss. Accrual of a loss is inappropriate because the threat of expropriation is only reasonably possible.

b.   Chester should report the potential costs due to the safety hazard by accruing a loss in the income statement and a liability in the balance sheet. Accrual is required because both of the following conditions are met:

- It is considered probable that a liability has been incurred.
- The amount of the loss can be reasonably estimated.

In addition, Chester should separately disclose in the notes to the financial statements the nature of the safety hazard.

c.   Chester should not accrue a loss because an asset has not been impaired nor has a liability been incurred. Disclosure of the uninsured rockslide risk, while permitted, is not required.

ANSWER OUTLINE

Problem 6   Contingencies

a. 1.   Reporting toxic waste cleanup in 2002 FS
   Footnote disclosure of loss
      Nature of loss
      Indication that an estimate cannot be made

No accrual
Loss not reasonably estimable
Uncertain amount would impair integrity of FS

2. Reporting Gap's claim in 2002 FS
Footnote disclosure
Nature of claim
Include estimate of potential loss
No accrual
Only reasonably possible that Supey will lose the suit

b. Reporting effects of contract to purchase Chemical XZ in 2002 FS
Report estimated loss equal to unrecoverable amount of contract price
Part of income from continuing operations
CL

Reporting appropriate because
Net loss on purchase commitment should be measured and recognized in period it occurs
Reporting loss recognizes commitment's impact on future cash flows

UNOFFICIAL ANSWER

Problem 6   Contingencies

a.   1.   Notes to Supey's 2002 financial statements should disclose the nature of the loss on cleanup and indicate that an estimate of the loss, or range of the loss, cannot be made. No accrual should be made because the loss cannot be reasonably estimated and accrual of an uncertain amount would impair the integrity of the financial statements.

2.   Supey should disclose the nature of Gap's claim in the notes to the 2002 financial statements. Disclosure should include an estimate of the potential loss. Supey should not accrue the loss because it is only reasonably possible that it will have to pay for Gap's losses.

b.   An estimated loss on the purchase commitment, equal to the unrecoverable amount of the contract price, should be reported as part of 2002 income from continuing operations and as a current liability at December 31, 2002. The net loss on the purchase commitment should be measured and recognized in the period in which it occurs. Since Supey did not hedge this contract, reporting this loss recognizes the commitment's impact on future cash flows.

Keep practicing! Wiley's CPA Examination Review Software has over 2,800 questions.

Available at www.wiley.com/cpa

PRESENT VALUE

This module begins by reviewing the basic concepts related to time value of money. The module then covers four major topics in which time value of money applications are used extensively: (1) bonds payable and bond investments, (2) debt restructure, (3) pensions, and (4) leases.

A. Fundamentals

The concepts of time value of money are essential for successful completion of the CPA exam. Time value of money concepts are central to capital budgeting, leases, pensions, bonds, and other topics. You must understand the mechanics as well as the concepts. After studying the next few pages, work the multiple-choice questions entitled "Fundamentals." Note that the following abbreviations are used in the text that follows.

> i = interest rate
> n = number of periods or rents

On the CPA exam, you do not have to know the complex formulas that are used to compute time value of money factors (TVMF). The factors will be given to you or enough information will be given to you so that you can easily compute them (see A.8. TVMF Applications). Your main focus of attention should be centered on understanding which TVMF should be used in a given situation.

1. **Future Value (FV) of an Amount** (future value of $1)

The future value of an amount is the amount that will be available at some point in the future if an amount is deposited today and earns compound interest for "n" periods. The most common application is savings deposits. For example, if you deposited $100 today at 10%, you would have $110 [$100 + ($100 x 10%)] at the end of the first year, $121[$100 + ($110 x 10%)] at the end of the second year, etc. The compounding feature allows you to earn interest on interest. In the second year of the example you earn $11 interest: $10 on the original $100 and $1 on the first year's interest of $10.

2. **Present Value (PV) of a Future Amount** (present value of $1)

The present value of a future amount is the amount you would pay now for an amount to be received "n" periods in the future given an interest rate of "i." A common application would be the money you would lend today for a noninterest-bearing note receivable in the future. For example, if you were lending money at 10%, you would lend $100 for a $110 note due in one year or for a $121 note due in two years.

The present value of $1 is the inverse of the future value of $1. Thus, given a future value of $1 table, you have a present value of $1 by dividing each value into 1.00. Look at the present value of $1 and future value of $1 tables on the next page. The future value of $1 at 10% in five years is 1.611. Thus, the present value of $1 in five years would be 1.00 ÷ 1.611 which is .621 (check the table). Conversely, the future value of $1 is found by dividing the present value of $1 into 1.00, that is, 1.00 ÷ .621 = 1.611.

3. **Compounding**

When interest is compounded more than once a year, two extra steps are needed. First, **multiply** "n" by the number of times interest is compounded annually. This will give you the total number of interest periods. Second, **divide** "i" by the number of times interest is compounded annually. This will give you the appropriate interest rate for each interest period. For example, if the 10% was compounded semiannually, the amount of $100 at the end of one year would be $110.25 [$(1.05)^2$] instead of $110.00. The extra $.25 is 5% of the $5.00 interest earned in the first half of the year.

4. **Future Value of an Ordinary Annuity**

The future value of an ordinary annuity is the amount available "n" periods in the future as a result of the deposit of an amount (A) at the end of every period 1 through "n." Compound interest is earned at the rate of "i" on the deposits. A common application is a bond sinking fund. A deposit is made at the end of the first period and earns compound interest for n-1 periods (not during the first period, because the deposit is made at the end of the first period). The next to the last payment earns one period's interest, that is, n – (n-1) = 1. The last payment earns no interest, because it is deposited at the end of the last (nth) period. Remember that in the FUTURE AMOUNT OF AN ORDINARY ANNUITY TABLE, all of the factors for any "n" row are based on one less interest period than the number of payments.

TIME VALUE OF MONEY FACTOR (TVMF) TABLES

Future Value (Amount) of $1

n	6%	8%	10%	12%	15%
1	1.060	1.080	1.100	1.120	1.150
2	1.124	1.166	1.210	1.254	1.323
3	1.191	1.260	1.331	1.405	1.521
4	1.262	1.360	1.464	1.574	1.749
5	1.338	1.469	1.611	1.762	2.011

Present Value of $1

n	6%	8%	10%	12%	15%
1	.943	.926	.909	.893	.870
2	.890	.857	.826	.797	.756
3	.840	.794	.751	.712	.658
4	.792	.735	.683	.636	.572
5	.747	.681	.621	.567	.497

Future Value (Amount) of an Ordinary Annuity of $1

n	6%	8%	10%	12%	15%
1	1.000	1.000	1.000	1.000	1.000
2	2.060	2.080	2.100	2.120	2.150
3	3.184	3.246	3.310	3.374	3.473
4	4.375	4.506	4.506	4.641	4.993
5	5.637	5.867	6.105	6.353	6.742

Present Value of an Ordinary Annuity of $1

n	6%	8%	10%	12%	15%
1	.943	.926	.909	.893	.870
2	1.833	1.783	1.736	1.690	1.626
3	2.673	2.577	2.487	2.402	2.283
4	3.465	3.312	3.170	3.037	2.855
5	4.212	3.993	3.791	3.605	3.352

5. Present Value of an Ordinary Annuity

The present value of an ordinary annuity is the value today, given a discount rate, of a series of future payments. A common application is the capitalization of lease payments by either lessors or lessees. Payments "1" through "n" are assumed to be made at the end of years "1" through "n," and are discounted back to the present.

> EXAMPLE: *Assume a five-year lease of equipment requiring payments of $1,000 at the end of each of the five years, which is to be capitalized. If the discount rate is 10%, the present value is $3,791 ($1,000 x 3.791).*

The behavior of the present value of the lease payment stream over the five-year period is shown below. Note that the liability (principal amount) grows by interest in the amount of 10% during each period and decreases by $1,000 at the end of each period.

0	1	2	3	4	5

$3,791 + 380 Int. = $4,171
                   − 1,000 Pay
                   $3,171 + 320 Int. = $3,491
                                    − 1,000 Pay
                                    $2,491 + 250 Int. = $2,741
                                                      − 1,000
                                                      $1,741 + 170 Int. = $1,911
                                                                        − 1,000
                                                                        $ 911 + 91 Int. = $1,002
                                                                                        − 1,000
                                                                                             2*

* *Due to rounding*

6. Distinguishing a Future Value of an Annuity from a Present Value of an Annuity

Sometimes confusion arises in distinguishing between the future value (amount) of an annuity and the present value of an annuity. These two may be distinguished by determining whether the total dollar amount in the problem comes at the beginning (e.g., cost of equipment acquired for leasing) or at the end (e.g., the amount needed to retire bonds) of the series of payments as illustrated below.

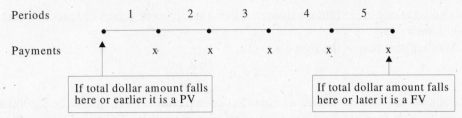

Remember: if the total amount comes at the end of the series of payments, it is a **future value** of annuity situation. If the total amount comes at the beginning of the series of payments, it is a **present value** of annuity situation. The total dollar amount may be given in the problem or you may have to compute it; either way, it makes no difference in determining whether a problem involves a present value or future value situation.

Some students feel the need to "convert" all time value of money problems into either present value or future value problems, depending on which they're most comfortable with. This process involves more work and more chance for errors, because an additional TVMF equation must be solved in the conversion. This is inefficient, and unnecessary if you are able to correctly identify between the two initially. Become proficient at determining present value and future value situations, so that you may efficiently select the correct TVMF from the corresponding table.

7. **Annuities Due**

In some cases, the payments or annuities may not conform to the assumptions inherent in the annuity tables. For example, the payments might be made at the beginning of each of the five years instead of at the end of each year. This is an annuity due (annuity in advance) in contrast to an ordinary annuity (annuity in arrears). Both annuity due and ordinary annuity payments are represented by the "x's" in the illustration below.

Periods		1		2		3		4		5	
Annuity			x		x		x		x		x
Annuity Due	x		x		x		x		x	

If the payments in the 5-period lease example above were made at the beginning of the period, the present value of the first payment which is made today is $1,000 (i.e., the TVMF is 1.00). The remaining 4 payments comprise an ordinary annuity for 4 periods as you can see on the above diagram. Always use time diagrams to analyze application of annuities.

To convert either a future value of an ordinary annuity or the present value of an ordinary annuity factor to an annuity due factor, multiply the ordinary annuity factor times (1 + i). For the above lease example, you would find the present value of an ordinary annuity factor for n = 5 which is 3.993. Then multiply 3.993 by 1.08 to arrive at the annuity due factor, 4.312. The present value of the payments would be $4,312 (4.312 x $1,000). Notice that the present value of the annuity due in the above example is $319 greater than the present value of the ordinary annuity because the payments are moved closer to the present.

8. **TVMF Applications**

The basic formula to use is

$$FV \text{ or } PV = TVMF \times Amount$$

If an annuity is involved, the amount is the periodic payment or deposit; if not, it is a single sum. Note that FV or PV is determined by three variables: time, interest rate, and payment. TVMF represents two variables: time and interest rate. The tables usually have the interest rate on the horizontal axis and time on the vertical axis. The above formula may also be stated as

$$Amount = \frac{FV \text{ or } PV}{TVMF}$$

For example, if we need to accumulate $12,210 in five years to repay a loan, we could determine the required annual deposit with the above formula. If the savings rate were 10%, we would divide the FV ($12,210) by the TVMF of the future value of annuity, n=5, i=.10 (6.105) and get $2,000. Thus, $2,000 deposited at the end of each of five years earning 10% will result in $12,210. This formula may also be used to find future values of an amount, present values of amounts, and annuities in the same manner.

Another variation of the formula is

$$TVMF = \frac{FV \text{ or } PV}{Amount}$$

For example, we may be offered a choice between paying $3,312 in cash or $1,000 a year at the end of each of the next four years. We determine the interest rate by dividing the annual payment into the present value of the annuity to obtain the TVMF (3.312) for n=4. We then find the interest rate which has the same or similar TVMF (in this case 8%).

Alternatively, using the above formula, we may know the interest rate but not know the number of payments. Given the TVMF, we can determine "n" by looking in the TVMF table under the known interest rate. Remember the TVMF reflects two variables: time and interest rate.

9. **Notes Receivable and Payable**

     Notes should be recorded at their present values (see outline of APB 21). Upon receipt or issuance of a note, record the net value of the note receivable or payable (i.e., note plus or minus premium or discount) at

     1.   Cash received or paid

         a.   Assumes no other rights or privileges

     2.   Established exchange price (fair market value) or property or services received or provided

         a.   If not determinable, determine present value with imputed interest rate

Record interest revenue (on notes receivable) or interest expense (on notes payable) as the effective rate of interest times the net receivable or payable during the period.

     a.   **Note exchanged for cash only**—When a note is exchanged for cash and no other rights or privileges are exchanged, the present value of the note is equivalent to the cash exchanged. The cash exchanged, however, may not be equal to the face amount of the note (the amount paid at maturity). When the face amount of a note does not equal its present value, the difference is either a discount or a premium. A discount results when the face of the note exceeds its present value, and a premium results when the present value of the note exceeds its face (see Section B.1. in this module for a more detailed discussion of discounts and premiums).

     b.   **Note exchanged for cash and unstated rights and privileges**—In the preceding discussion, notes were issued solely for cash, and no other rights or privileges were exchanged. The accounting treatment differs, however, when a note is issued for cash and unstated rights and/or privileges are also exchanged. The cash exchanged for such a note consists of two elements: (1) the present value of the note, and (2) the present value of the unstated right or privilege. Proper accounting for this situation requires that one of the two present values above be determined. Once this is done, the remaining present value is simply the difference between the face amount of the note and the present value that was determined.

         For example, on January 1, 2002, Zilch Company borrowed $200,000 from its major customer, Martha Corporation. The borrowing is evidenced by a note payable due in three years. The note is noninterest-bearing. In consideration for the borrowing, Zilch Company agrees to supply Martha Corporation's inventory needs for the loan period at favorable prices. This last feature of the transaction is the unstated right or privilege; that is, the ability of Martha to purchase inventory at less than regular prices.

         The present value of the note (assuming it is easier to determine) should be based upon the interest rate Zilch would have to pay in a normal borrowing of $200,000 (i.e., in a transaction that did not include unstated rights or privileges). Assume that Zilch would have to pay interest at 12% in a normal borrowing. The present value of $200,000 discounted for three years at 12% is $142,400 ($200,000 x .712). The difference between the face amount of the note, $200,000, and its present value of $142,400 represents the present value of the unstated right or privilege. The amount of this present value is $57,600.

         The entries below show how both Zilch and Martha should account for this transaction during 2002.

	Zilch			*Martha*	
1/1/02			*1/1/02*		
Cash	142,400		Note receivable	200,000	
Discount on note payable	57,600		Discount on note receivable		57,600
Note payable		200,000	Cash		142,400
Cash	57,600		Advance payments on inventory	57,600	
Deferred revenue		57,600	Cash		57,600
12/31/02			*12/31/02*		
Interest expense	17,088*		Discount on note receivable	17,088	
Discount on note payable		17,088	Interest income		17,088
* $142,400 x .12 = $17,088					
Deferred revenue	xx		Inventory (purchases)	xx	
Sales		xx	Advance payments on in-		
			ventory		xx

The amounts represented by "xx" in the entries above depend upon the amount of goods acquired by Martha during 2002.

On the December 31, 2002 balance sheets of both Zilch and Martha, the above notes should be disclosed in the noncurrent liability (Zilch) and asset (Martha) sections net of the unamortized discount applicable to each note.

c. **Note exchanged in a noncash transaction**—In addition to notes issued for cash, a note may also be received or issued in a noncash transaction; that is, for goods, property, or services. The problem created in this situation is how to determine the note's present value in the absence of cash. One way to solve this problem is to assume that the stated rate or contractual rate stated on the note represents a fair rate of return to the supplier for the use of the related funds. If the interest rate is presumed to be fair, then the face amount of the note is presumed to equal its present value. Interest revenue (expense) is computed by multiplying the interest rate stated on the face of the note by the face of the note. There is no discount or premium to consider because the face of the note is assumed to be equal to its present value.

The assumption that the interest rate on the face of the note is fair is not always valid. According to APB 21, the assumption is not valid if

1. The interest rate is not stated (usually, this means the note is noninterest-bearing), or
2. The stated rate is unreasonable (this refers to both unreasonably low and high rates), or
3. The stated face amount of the note is materially different from the current cash sales price for the same or similar items, or from the market value of the note at the date of the transaction.

When the interest rate is not fair, the face amount of the note does not equal its present value. In the absence of cash, the present value of a note is determined according to the following priorities:

1. First, determine if the goods, property, or services exchanged have a reliable fair market value. If they do, the fair market value is presumed to be the present value of the note.
2. If a reliable fair market value does not exist for the goods, property, or services exchanged, then determine if the note has a market value. If it does, the note's market value is equal to the present value of the note.
3. Finally, if market values do not exist for either the goods, property, or services or for the note, then an interest rate must be **imputed**. This imputed interest rate is then used to determine the present value of the note. The imputed interest rate represents the **debtor's** incremental borrowing rate.

To illustrate the situation where the interest rate on a note is not fair, yet the fair market value of the property exchanged is known, assume the following facts: Doink Co. sold a building on January 1, 2002, which originally cost $7,000,000 and which had a book value of $4,000,000 for a $14,000,000 (face amount) noninterest-bearing note due in three years. Since zero interest is not considered to be a fair rate of return, the face amount of Doink's note does not equal its present value. In Doink's case, the face of its note is $14,000,000. The present value of the note is the unknown and must be calculated.

To determine the present value of Doink's $14,000,000 noninterest-bearing note, you should first see if the building sold had a reliable fair market value at the date it was sold. Assume that Doink's building could have sold on January 1, 2002, for $10,000,000 in a straight cash transaction. Given the information about the building, its fair market value of $10,000,000 on January 1, 2002 represents the note's present value. Since the face of the note is $14,000,000 and its present value is $10,000,000, the $4,000,000 difference represents the discount. Doink should record this transaction in the following manner:

Note receivable	14,000,000	
Accumulated depreciation	3,000,000	
Building		7,000,000
Gain on sale of building		6,000,000
Discount on note receivable		4,000,000

It is important that you note how the gain is calculated in the entry above. The gain is the difference between the present value of the note ($10,000,000) and the book value of the property sold ($4,000,000). The difference between the face amount of the note ($14,000,000) and its present value ($10,000,000) represents the discount of $4,000,000. This discount should be amortized to interest income using the effective interest method. However, before this discount can be amortized, the interest rate must be determined. In situations like this, the interest rate can be determined by reference to present value tables. In Doink's situation, the present value of the note, $10,000,000, divided by its face amount, $14,000,000, results in the number .714. This number represents a factor from the present value of $1 table. Since Doink's note is for 3 periods, the factor .712 in the present value of $1 table is under the 12% interest rate. Thus, Doink's interest rate is approximately 12%.

If the building sold by Doink did not have a reliable fair market value on January 1, 2002, the next step would be to determine if the note had a market value on that date.

Finally, if the building sold by Doink did not possess a reliable fair market value on January 1, 2002, and the note did not have a market value on that date, the present value of Doink's note would have to be determined by **imputation**. This means that Doink would determine the present value of its note by reference to the incremental borrowing rate of the company which acquired its building.

The following diagram represents the forementioned relationships and procedures for determining the present value of a note receivable or payable (monetary assets and liabilities) and the amount of a discount/premium.

**ACCOUNTING FOR MONETARY ASSETS AND LIABILITIES WHICH HAVE
MATURITIES GREATER THAN ONE YEAR FROM THE BALANCE SHEET DATE**

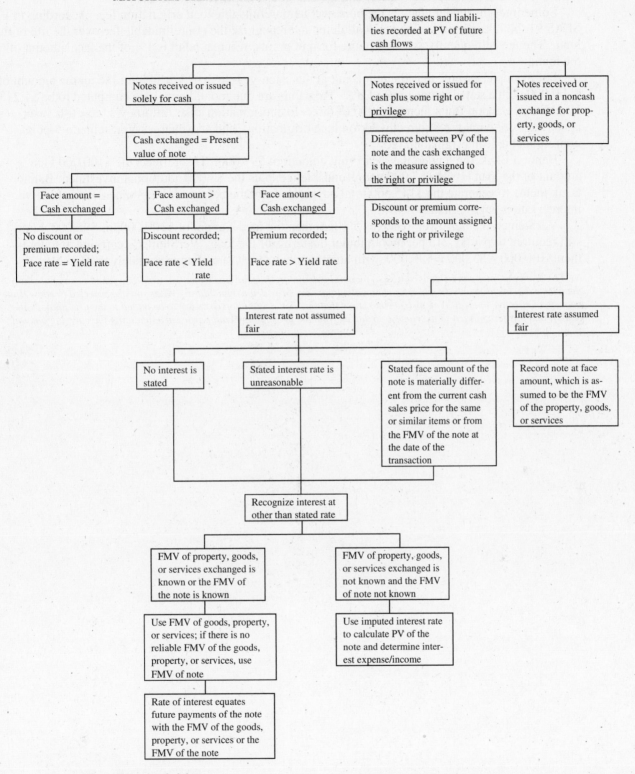

10.   **Lending Activities**

The basic loan situation involves a borrower receiving the face amount of a loan from a lender, with no related discount or premium. The liability is the face amount, and the effective interest rate is the stated interest rate.

Sometimes the lender incurs various loan origination costs when originating or acquiring a loan. According to SFAS 91, the lender shall defer and recognize these costs over the life of the loan only when the costs relate directly to the loan, and would not have been incurred but for the loan. Otherwise, the costs are considered indirect and are charged to expense as incurred.

Sometimes the lender charges the borrower a nonrefundable loan origination fee. According to SFAS 91, both lender and borrower shall defer and recognize the nonrefundable fee over the life of the loan. The fee is frequently assessed in the form of points, where a point is 1% of the face amount of the loan.

For example, assume that Bannon Bank grants a ten-year loan to VerSteiner, Inc. in the amount of $100,000 with a stated interest rate of 8%. Payments are due monthly, and are computed to be $1,213. In addition, Bannon Bank incurs $3,000 of direct loan origination costs (attorney's fees, title insurance, wages of employees' direct work on loan origination), and also charges VerSteiner a 5-point nonrefundable loan origination fee.

Bannon Bank, the lender, has a carrying amount of $98,000. This reflects the $100,000 face amount of the loan less the $5,000 nonrefundable fee, plus the $3,000 additional investment Bannon Bank incurs to generate the $145,560 total payments from the borrower, VerSteiner. The effective interest rate is approximately 8.5%.

VerSteiner, the borrower, receives 5% less than the face amount of $100,000, or $95,000, but is still required to pay $1,213 per month under the terms of the loan. VerSteiner's carrying amount is then $100,000 – $5,000 = $95,000, with an effective interest rate of approximately 9.2%.

NOTE: Both the rates can be derived with a financial calculator. It is not likely that you would be asked to compute these on the CPA exam because only simple 4-function calculators are provided to candidates. What you are expected to know is the concept of effective interest. You also need to know that the loan origination costs are to be added to the principal, by the lender, and any fee charged to the client is deducted from the principal by both parties in calculating the carrying amount.

MULTIPLE-CHOICE QUESTIONS (1-22)

1. On March 15, 2002, Ashe Corp. adopted a plan to accumulate $1,000,000 by September 1, 2006. Ashe plans to make four equal annual deposits to a fund that will earn interest at 10% compounded annually. Ashe made the first deposit on September 1, 2002. Future value and future amount factors are as follows:

Future value of $1 at 10% for 4 periods	1.46
Future amount of ordinary annuity of $1 at 10% for four periods	4.64
Future amount of annuity in advance of $1 at 10% for four periods	5.11

Ashe should make four annual deposits (rounded) of
- a. $250,000
- b. $215,500
- c. $195,700
- d. $146,000

2. On July 1, 2002, James Rago signed an agreement to operate as a franchisee of Fast Foods, Inc. for an initial franchise fee of $60,000. Of this amount, $20,000 was paid when the agreement was signed and the balance is payable in four equal annual payments of $10,000 beginning July 1, 2003. The agreement provides that the down payment is not refundable and no future services are required of the franchisor. Rago's credit rating indicates that he can borrow money at 14% for a loan of this type. Information on present and future value factors is as follows:

Present value of $1 at 14% for four periods	0.59
Future amount of $1 at 14% for four periods	1.69
Present value of an ordinary annuity of $1 at 14% for four periods	2.91

Rago should record the acquisition cost of the franchise on July 1, 2002 at
- a. $43,600
- b. $49,100
- c. $60,000
- d. $67,600

3. On November 1, 2002, a company purchased a new machine that it does not have to pay for until November 1, 2004. The total payment on November 1, 2004, will include both principal and interest. Assuming interest at a 10% rate, the cost of the machine would be the total payment multiplied by what time value of money concept?
- a. Present value of annuity of $1.
- b. Present value of $1.
- c. Future amount of annuity of $1.
- d. Future amount of $1.

4. For which of the following transactions would the use of the present value of an annuity due concept be appropriate in calculating the present value of the asset obtained or liability owed at the date of incurrence?
- a. A capital lease is entered into with the initial lease payment due one month subsequent to the signing of the lease agreement.
- b. A capital lease is entered into with the initial lease payment due upon the signing of the lease agreement.
- c. A ten-year 8% bond is issued on January 2 with interest payable semiannually on July 1 and January 1 yielding 7%.
- d. A ten-year 8% bond is issued on January 2 with interest payable semiannually on July 1 and January 1 yielding 9%.

5. Jole Co. lent $10,000 to a major supplier in exchange for a noninterest-bearing note due in three years and a contract to purchase a fixed amount of merchandise from the supplier at a 10% discount from prevailing market prices over the next three years. The market rate for a note of this type is 10%. On issuing the note, Jole should record

	Discount on note receivable	*Deferred charge*
a.	Yes	Yes
b.	Yes	No
c.	No	Yes
d.	No	No

6. On December 30, 2002, Chang Co. sold a machine to Door Co. in exchange for a noninterest-bearing note requiring ten annual payments of $10,000. Door made the first payment on December 30, 2002. The market interest rate for similar notes at date of issuance was 8%. Information on present value factors is as follows:

Period	*Present value of $1 at 8%*	*Present value of ordinary annuity of $1 at 8%*
9	0.50	6.25
10	0.46	6.71

In its December 31, 2002 balance sheet, what amount should Chang report as note receivable?
- a. $45,000
- b. $46,000
- c. $62,500
- d. $67,100

Items 7 and 8 are based on the following:

On January 2, 2002, Emme Co. sold equipment with a carrying amount of $480,000 in exchange for a $600,000 noninterest-bearing note due January 2, 2005. There was no established exchange price for the equipment. The prevailing rate of interest for a note of this type at January 2, 2002, was 10%. The present value of $1 at 10% for three periods is 0.75.

7. In Emme's 2002 income statement, what amount should be reported as interest income?
- a. $ 9,000
- b. $45,000
- c. $50,000
- d. $60,000

8. In Emme's 2002 income statement, what amount should be reported as gain (loss) on sale of machinery?
- a. $(30,000) loss.
- b. $ 30,000 gain.
- c. $120,000 gain.
- d. $270,000 gain.

9. On December 31, 2002, Jet Co. received two $10,000 notes receivable from customers in exchange for services rendered. On both notes, interest is calculated on the outstanding principal balance at the annual rate of 3% and payable at maturity. The note from Hart Corp., made under customary trade terms, is due in nine months and the note from Maxx, Inc. is due in five years. The market interest rate for similar notes on December 31, 2002, was 8%. The compound interest factors to convert future values into present values at 8% follow:

Present value of $1 due in nine months	.944
Present value of $1 due in five years	.680

At what amounts should these two notes receivable be reported in Jet's December 31, 2002 balance sheet?

	Hart	*Maxx*
a.	$ 9,440	$6,800
b.	$ 9,652	$7,820
c.	$10,000	$6,800
d.	$10,000	$7,820

10. Leaf Co. purchased from Oak Co. a $20,000, 8%, five-year note that required five equal annual year-end payments of $5,009. The note was discounted to yield a 9% rate to Leaf. At the date of purchase, Leaf recorded the note at its present value of $19,485. What should be the total interest revenue earned by Leaf over the life of this note?
- a. $5,045
- b. $5,560
- c. $8,000
- d. $9,000

Items 11 and 12 are based on the following:

House Publishers offered a contest in which the winner would receive $1,000,000, payable over twenty years. On December 31, 2002, House announced the winner of the contest and signed a note payable to the winner for $1,000,000, payable in $50,000 installments every January 2. Also on December 31, 2002, House purchased an annuity for $418,250 to provide the $950,000 prize monies remaining after the first $50,000 installment, which was paid on January 2, 2003.

11. In its December 31, 2002 balance sheet, what amount should House report as note payable—contest winner, net of current portion?
- a. $368,250
- b. $418,250
- c. $900,000
- d. $950,000

12. In its 2002 income statement, what should House report as contest prize expense?
- a. $0
- b. $ 418,250
- c. $ 468,250
- d. $1,000,000

13. On December 31, 2002, Roth Co. issued a $10,000 face value note payable to Wake Co. in exchange for services rendered to Roth. The note, made at usual trade terms, is due in nine months and bears interest, payable at maturity, at the annual rate of 3%. The market interest rate is 8%. The compound interest factor of $1 due in nine months at 8% is .944. At what amount should the note payable be reported in Roth's December 31, 2002 balance sheet?
- a. $10,300
- b. $10,000
- c. $ 9,652
- d. $ 9,440

14. On January 1, 2002, Parke Company borrowed $360,000 from a major customer evidenced by a noninterest-

bearing note due in three years. Parke agreed to supply the customer's inventory needs for the loan period at lower than market price. At the 12% imputed interest rate for this type of loan, the present value of the note is $255,000 at January 1, 2002. What amount of interest expense should be included in Parke's 2002 income statement?
- a. $43,200
- b. $35,000
- c. $30,600
- d. $0

15. Pie Co. uses the installment sales method to recognize revenue. Customers pay the installment notes in twenty-four equal monthly amounts, which include 12% interest. What is an installment note's receivable balance six months after the sale?
- a. 75% of the original sales price.
- b. Less than 75% of the original sales price.
- c. The present value of the remaining monthly payments discounted at 12%.
- d. Less than the present value of the remaining monthly payments discounted at 12%.

16. On July 1, 2002, a company obtained a two-year 8% note receivable for services rendered. At that time the market rate of interest was 10%. The face amount of the note and the entire amount of the interest are due on June 30, 2004. Interest receivable at December 31, 2002 was
- a. 5% of the face value of the note.
- b. 4% of the face value of the note.
- c. 5% of the July 1, 2002, present value of the amount due June 30, 2004.
- d. 4% of the July 1, 2002, present value of the amount due June 30, 2004.

17. Which of the following is reported as interest expense?
- a. Pension cost interest.
- b. Postretirement health care benefits interest.
- c. Imputed interest on noninterest-bearing note.
- d. Interest incurred to finance construction of machinery for own use.

18. The discount resulting from the determination of a note payable's present value should be reported on the balance sheet as a(n)
- a. Addition to the face amount of the note.
- b. Deferred charge separate from the note.
- c. Deferred credit separate from the note.
- d. Direct reduction from the face amount of the note.

19. In calculating the carrying amount of a loan, the lender adds to the principal

	Direct loan origination costs incurred by the lender	*Loan origination fees charged to the borrower*
a.	Yes	Yes
b.	Yes	No
c.	No	Yes
d.	No	No

20. Duff, Inc. borrowed from Martin Bank under a ten-year loan in the amount of $150,000 with a stated interest rate of 6%. Payments are due monthly, and are computed to be $1,665. Martin Bank incurs $4,000 of direct loan origination costs and $2,000 of indirect loan origination costs. In addition, Martin Bank charges Duff, Inc. a four-point nonrefundable loan origination fee.

Martin Bank, the lender, has a carrying amount of
a. $144,000
b. $148,000
c. $150,000
d. $152,000

21. Martin Bank grants a ten-year loan to Duff, Inc. in the amount of $150,000 with a stated interest rate of 6%. Payments are due monthly, and are computed to be $1,665. Martin Bank incurs $4,000 of direct loan origination costs and $2,000 of indirect loan origination costs. In addition, Martin Bank charges Duff, Inc. a four-point nonrefundable loan origination fee.

Duff, the borrower, has a carrying amount of
a. $144,000
b. $148,000
c. $150,000
d. $152,000

22. On December 1, 2002, Money Co. gave Home Co. a $200,000, 11% loan. Money paid proceeds of $194,000 after the deduction of a $6,000 nonrefundable loan origination fee. Principal and interest are due in sixty monthly installments of $4,310, beginning January 1, 2003. The repayments yield an effective interest rate of 11% at a present value of $200,000 and 12.4% at a present value of $194,000. What amount of income from this loan should Money report in its 2002 income statement?
a. $0
b. $1,833
c. $2,005
d. $7,833

OTHER OBJECTIVE QUESTIONS

Problem 1   (15 to 25 minutes)

Presented below is selected information regarding the sale of a building by Catrina Corporation.

On January 1, 2002, Catrina Corporation sold a building that originally cost $300,000 with accumulated depreciation of $75,000 for a noninterest-bearing note with a face value of $300,000 due January 1, 2006. The FMV of the building is readily determinable and the market rate for a note of this type is 6%.

Required:

a. Items 1 through 5 represent statements regarding the proper treatment of items in the sale of the building. Determine if the statement is true or false.

Items to be answered

1. The gain or loss on the sale of the building would be equal to the face value of the note less the book value of the building.

2. The difference between the face value of the note and the present value of the note represents the discount or premium on the note.

3. If the fair market value of the building was not determinable, then 6% would be considered the imputed interest rate.

4. Even though the note is a noninterest-bearing note, the interest revenue for Catrina Corp. can be computed using the effective interest method.

5. The amount recorded as the present value of the note should be equal to the fair market value of the building.

b. Items 6 through 14 require the candidate to select the best answer from the Responses to be selected.

Items to be answered	*Responses to be selected*
6. Annuity due	**A.** Effective interest rate x Net receivable or payable balance at the beginning of the period
7. Imputed interest rate	**B.** Periodic interest is computed on principal balance and interest earned to date
8. Market value of note	**C.** Represents the debtor's incremental borrowing rate
9. Note issued at a discount	**D.** Series of payments/receipts which occur at beginning of the period
10. Premium on a note	**E.** The difference between the present value of the note and the cash exchanged when the market rate of interest < rate on note
11. Simple interest method	**F.** Periodic interest is computed based on the principal balance only
12. Interest revenue/expense	**G.** Maturity value of note and interest payments discounted to the present value
13. Future value of annuity	**H.** This will result when face rate of the note < yield rate
14. Face of note equals present value of the note	**I.** The amount which will be available in the future as a result of consecutive payments/receipts at the end of each period—compounded at a specified interest rate
	J. Series of payments/receipts which are made at the end of the period
	K. No premium or discount exists

PROBLEM

Problem 1   (45 to 55 minutes)

Kern, Inc. had the following long-term receivable account balances at December 31, 2001:

Note receivable from the sale of an idle building	$750,000
Note receivable from an officer	200,000

Transactions during 2002 and other information relating to Kern's long-term receivables follow:

• The $750,000 note receivable is dated May 1, 2001, bears interest at 9%, and represents the balance of the consideration Kern received from the sale of its idle building to Able Co. Principal payments of $250,000 plus interest are due annually beginning May 1, 2002. Able made its first principal and interest payment on May 1, 2002. Collection of the remaining note installments is reasonably assured.

• The $200,000 note receivable is dated December 31, 1999, bears interest at 8%, and is due on December 31, 2004. The note is due from Frank Black, president of Kern, Inc., and is collateralized by 5,000 shares of Kern's common stock. Interest is payable annually on December 31, and all interest payments were made through December 31, 2002. The quoted market price of Kern's common stock was $45 per share on December 31, 2002.

• On April 1, 2001, Kern sold a patent to Frey Corp. in exchange for a $100,000 noninterest-bearing note due on April 1, 2004. There was no established exchange price for the patent, and the note had no ready market. The prevailing interest rate for this type of note was 10% at April 1, 2002. The present value of $1 for two periods at 10% is 0.826. The patent had a carrying amount of $40,000 at January 1, 2002, and the amortization for the year ended December 31, 2002, would have been $8,000. Kern is reasonably assured of collecting the note receivable from Frey.

• On July 1, 2002, Kern sold a parcel of land to Barr Co. for $400,000 under an installment sale contract. Barr made a $120,000 cash down payment on July 1, 2001, and signed a four-year 10% note for the $280,000 balance. The equal annual payments of principal and interest on the note will be $88,332, payable on July 1 of each year from 2003 through 2006. The fair value of the land at the date of sale was $400,000. The cost of the land to Kern was $300,000. Collection of the remaining note installments is reasonably assured.

Required:

Prepare the following and show supporting computations:

a. Long-term receivables section of Kern's December 31, 2002 balance sheet.

b. Schedule showing current portion of long-term receivables and accrued interest receivable to be reported in Kern's December 31, 2002 balance sheet.

c. Schedule showing interest revenue from long-term receivables and gains recognized on sale of assets to be reported in Kern's 2002 income statement.

MULTIPLE-CHOICE ANSWERS

1. c __ __	6. c __ __	11. b __ __	16. b __ __	21. a __ __
2. b __ __	7. b __ __	12. c __ __	17. c __ __	22. c __ __
3. b __ __	8. a __ __	13. b __ __	18. d __ __	
4. b __ __	9. d __ __	14. c __ __	19. b __ __	1st: __/22 = __%
5. a __ __	10. b __ __	15. c __ __	20. b __ __	2nd: __/22 = __%

MULTIPLE-CHOICE ANSWER EXPLANATIONS

A. Fundamentals

1.   (c)   The desired fund balance on September 1, 2006, ($1,000,000) is a **future amount**. The series of four equal annual deposits is an **annuity in advance,** as illustrated in the diagram below.

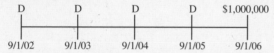

This is an annuity in advance, rather than an ordinary annuity, because the last deposit (9/1/05) is made one year prior to the date the future amount is needed. Therefore, these are beginning-of-year payments. The deposit amount is computed by dividing the future amount by the factor for the future amount of an annuity in advance.

$$\$1,000,000 \div 5.11 = \$195,700$$

2.   (b)   The requirement is to determine the acquisition cost of a franchise. The cost of this franchise is the down payment of $20,000 plus the present value of the four equal annual payments of $10,000. The annual payments represent an annuity, so the $10,000 annual payment is multiplied by the present value factor of 2.91. Therefore, the franchise cost is $49,100 ($20,000 + $29,100). The journal entry is

Franchise	49,100	
Discount on notes payable	10,900	
Notes payable		40,000
Cash		20,000

3.   (b)   The requirement is to determine what time value of money concept would be used to determine the cost of a machine when a payment (principal plus interest) is to be made in two years. Answer (b) is correct because the cost of the machine is to be recorded immediately; therefore, the cost of the present value of a lump-sum payment would be used. Answer (c) is incorrect because a future amount would be used in computing the payment and not the cost of the machine. Also, a lump-sum payment is involved and not an annuity. Answer (d) is incorrect because a future amount would be used in computing the payment and not the cost. Answer (a) is incorrect because a lump-sum payment is involved, not an annuity.

4.   (b)   The requirement is the situation which illustrates an annuity due. An annuity due (annuity in advance) is a series of payments where the first payment is made at the beginning of the first period, in contrast to an ordinary annuity (annuity in arrears), in which the first payment is made at the end of the first period. Answer (b) is correct because the initial lease payment is due immediately (at the beginning of the first period). Answers (a), (c), and (d) all illustrate situations in which the first lease or interest payment occurs at the end of the first period. Note that in answers (c) and (d), the stated rate and yield rate of the bonds differ; while this would affect the present value of the bonds, it has

no effect on the classification as an annuity due or an ordinary annuity.

5.   (a)   In recording the transaction recognition should be given to both the imputed interest rate and the deferred charge related to the merchandise discount. Answer (b) is incorrect because the deferred charge should also be recognized. Answer (c) is incorrect because a discount on the noninterest-bearing note should also be recognized. Answer (d) is incorrect because both the discount and the deferred charge should be recognized.

A.9. Notes Receivable and Payable

6.   (c)   If the FMV of the machine and the FMV of the note are not known, the transaction should be recorded at the PV of the note by imputing interest at the prevailing rate (8%) for similar notes. This series of ten payments is an **annuity in advance,** because the first payment is due immediately on 12/30/02. However, the problem requires the amount to be reported for the note receivable on **12/31/02,** after the first payment is received. The remaining nine payments are an ordinary annuity, as illustrated in the diagram below.

PV = ?

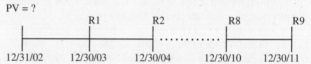

In a PV computation, one must look at the first rent to see if it is an ordinary annuity or annuity in advance. If the first rent occurs one period after the computation date, it is an ordinary annuity. Therefore, the PV to be reported for the note receivable at 12/31/02 is $62,500 (10,000 x 6.25).

7.   (b)   The $600,000 noninterest-bearing note should be recorded at its present value of $450,000 ($600,000 x .75). The journal entry is

Loss on sale of equip.	30,000	
Note receivable	600,000	
Discount on NR		150,000 } 450,000
Equipment (net)		480,000

At 12/31/02, interest income would be recognized using the effective interest method. Using this method, interest is computing by multiplying the book value of the note ($600,000 – $150,000 = $450,000) by the effective interest rate ($450,000 x 10% = $45,000).

8.   (a)   The $600,000 noninterest-bearing note should be recorded at its present value of $450,000 ($600,000 x .75). The journal entry is

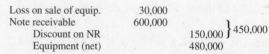

The loss is recognized because the fair value of the note received ($450,000) is $30,000 less than the carrying amount of the equipment sold ($480,000).

9. **(d)** APB 21 states that receivables bearing an unreasonably low stated interest rate should be recorded at their present value. However, APB 21 does **not** apply to receivables arising through the normal course of business that mature in less than one year. Therefore, the Hart receivable would be recorded at face value ($10,000), since it matures in nine months. The Maxx receivable would be recorded at its present value, since it matures in five years. The Maxx receivable will result in a lump-sum collection of $11,500 [$10,000 + (10,000 x 3% x 5)], so its present value is $7,820 ($11,500 x .680).

10. **(b)** The total interest revenue earned over the life of the note equals the excess of the cash received over the cash paid to acquire the note. The cash received over the five years is $25,045 (5 receipts of $5,009 each). The cash paid to acquire the $20,000 note was $19,485. Therefore, the total interest revenue is $5,560 ($25,045 – $19,485).

11. **(b)** The $1,000,000 note is payable $50,000 in 2001 (current portion) and $950,000 after 2002 (long-term portion). Per APB 21, this noninterest-bearing long-term note should be recorded at its present value, which can be measured as the amount required to purchase an annuity sufficient to provide the funds to satisfy the obligation. Therefore, the note payable, net of current portion, should be reported at $418,250.

12. **(c)** The contest prize expense must be recognized at the present value of the obligation incurred as a result of the contest. The obligation consists of $50,000 payable in two days, and $950,000 payable over the next nineteen years. The $950,000 long-term portion has a present value of $418,250, as evidenced by the cost of an annuity contract sufficient to satisfy it. Therefore, the total PV of the obligation is $468,250 ($50,000 + $418,250). The journal entry to record the expense is

Contest prize expense	$468,250	
Discount on NP	$531,750	
Notes payable		$1,000,000

13. **(b)** APB 21 states that all receivables and payables are subject to present value measurement techniques and interest imputation, if necessary, with certain exceptions. One exception is normal course of business receivables and payables maturing in less than one year. Therefore this note payable, due in nine months at usual trade terms, would be reported at face value ($10,000) rather than at present value ($10,225 x .944 = $9,652).

14. **(c)** The requirement is to determine the amount of interest expense to be recognized in 2002 from a noninterest-bearing note. Parke Company is able to borrow on a noninterest basis because they agree to sell their product at less than the market price. In this type of situation, the note payable is recorded at present value, and the difference between the present value and the cash received is recorded as **unearned sales revenue** (to be recognized when the product is sold at less than market value). The initial journal entry is

Cash	360,000	
Discount on NP	105,000	
Note payable		360,000 ⎤ 255,000
Unearned sales revenue		105,000 ⎦

When interest expense is recognized at the end of 2002, the effective interest method must be used. Using this method, interest expense is computed by multiplying the book value of the liability ($360,000 – $105,000 = $255,000) by the effective interest rate (12%), resulting in interest expense of $30,600.

15. **(c)** The entry made to record an installment sale (ignoring the cost of sale and inventory) is as follows:

Note receivable	(Sale price)
Installment sales	(PV of note @ 12%)
Discount on notes receivable	(Plug)

Although the customer would have paid 25% (six out of twenty-four months) of the total payments due under the terms of the installment sale, the **net** carrying value of the note (equal to the principal balance of the note less the unamortized discount) is equal to the present value of the remaining monthly payments discounted at 12%. Under the effective interest method, the carrying value of the note will at all times be equal to the present value of the remaining installment payments, regardless of whether the note is recorded gross or net in Pie Co.'s accounts.

16. **(b)** When a note is issued with a stated rate (8% in this case) below the market rate (10% in this case), the note will be issued at a discount. The entry for the recipient of the note on July 1 would be as follows:

Notes receivable	xxx	
Disc. on notes rec.		xxx
Service revenue		xxx

On December 31, the company must accrue interest on the note. The following entry would be made:

Interest receivable	(6 months at stated rate)
Disc. on notes rec.	(6 months amortization)
Interest revenue	(6 months interest at market rate)

Note that interest receivable is debited for an amount based upon the **stated** (face) rate of the note. This is because the stated rate will determine the amount of cash interest that will be received upon maturity of the note. Since the bond was held for six months (7/1/02 to 12/31/02) as of 12/31/02, the amount of the receivable would be determined as follows:

$$\begin{array}{l} \text{Interest} \\ \text{receivable} \end{array} = \begin{array}{c} \text{Face value} \\ \text{of note} \end{array} \times \begin{array}{c} \text{Stated} \\ \text{rate} \end{array} \times \begin{array}{c} \text{Period} \\ \text{held} \end{array}$$
$$= \text{Face value} \times 8\% \times (6/12 \text{ months})$$
$$= 4\% \times \text{Face value}$$

17. **(c)** When a noninterest-bearing note is issued, APB 21 states that interest must be imputed on the note and amortized to interest expense over the life of the note using the effective interest rate. Answers (a) and (b) are incorrect because interest on pension cost and postretirement healthcare benefits is included as a component of future benefit obligation. Answer (d) is incorrect because interest incurred to finance construction of machinery for a company's own use may be capitalized and amortized.

18. **(d)** **Discount on notes payable** is a liability valuation account. It should be reported as a direct reduction from the face amount of the note (contra account). A **premium on notes payable** would be reported as an addition to the face amount of the note. A discount is not recorded as a separate asset because it does not provide any future economic benefit. It is not a deferred credit separate from the note because it is a debit, not a credit, and because it is inseparable from the note. Thus, a discount on notes payable should be reported on the balance sheet as a direct reduction from the face amount of the note.

A.10. Lending Activities

19.   (b)   In calculating the carrying amount of a loan, loan origination costs are added to the principal by the lender. Any fee charged to the borrower is **deducted** from the principal by both parties (the lender and the borrower) in calculating the carrying amount.

20.   (b)   The lender's carrying amount of the loan is calculated by adding the direct loan origination costs to the principal and deducting the loan origination fee charged to the borrower. Indirect loan origination costs are charged to expense as incurred, and are not considered when calculating the carrying amount of the loan. Therefore, Martin Bank has a carrying amount of $148,000 [$150,000 principal plus $4,000 direct loan origination costs minus $6,000 ($150,000 x 0.04) nonrefundable loan origination fee]. The $2,000 indirect loan origination costs are expensed in the period incurred.

21.   (a)   Duff, Inc., the borrower, receives 4% less than the face amount of $150,000. Duff's carrying amount is, therefore, $150,000 – $6,000, or $144,000. Loan origination fees charged to the borrower are deducted from the principal in calculating the carrying amount.

NOTE: Loan origination fees are frequently assessed in the form of points, where a point is 1% of the face amount of the loan.

22.   (c)   Money Co. made a cash outflow of $194,000 for the $200,000 loan Money gave to Home Co. The book value of the loan is $194,000 on Money's books. Money will receive an effective interest rate of 12.4% on its cash outflow. Income from the loan would be calculated by multiplying the book value, times the effective interest rate, and the number of months of the year (in this case just one— December). $194,000 x .124 x 1/12 = $2,004.67. The stated rate is 11% and is not used in the calculation. Money Co. will receive equal monthly installments over the sixty-month life of the loan. Money Co. will effectively earn 12.4% on its initial cash outflow of $194,000, because Home Co. will repay principal for the total loan amount of $200,000.

OTHER OBJECTIVE ANSWERS AND ANSWER EXPLANATIONS

Problem 1

   1.   **(F)** The gain or loss on the sale of the building is calculated by taking the difference between the present value of the note and the book value of the building. When the fair market value (FMV) of the building is readily determinable then the FMV will represent the present value of the note. If the FMV of building was not readily determinable then the PV would be calculated using the market rate. Therefore, this statement is false because the gain or loss would be equal to the **present value of the note** less the book value of the building.

   2.   **(T)** The difference between the face value of the note and its present value will be equal to the discount or premium. If the face of the note > present value, then a discount exists and if the face of the note < present value, then a premium exists. Therefore, the statement is true.

   3.   **(T)** Then the stated interest rate is not fair, and the FMV of the goods being exchanged does not exist, an interest rate must be imputed. The imputed rate would be used to determine the present value of the note. The imputed interest rate represents the rate at which a debtor could obtain financing of a similar nature from a different source, which is known as the incremental borrowing rate. The problem states that the market rate of interest for a note of this type is 6%, thus the debtor's incremental borrowing rate is 6%. Therefore, the statement is true.

   4.   **(T)** The difference between the face value of the note and the present value will equal the discount or premium. The discount or premium should be amortized using the effective interest method. The effective interest rate is assumed to be equal to the imputed interest rate. Therefore, the statement is true.

   5.   **(T)** The present value of the note will be equal to the fair market value of the building if it is determinable. Therefore, this statement is true because the problem states that the FMV is readily determinable.

   6.   **(D)** An annuity due (annuity in advance) represents a series of payments made or received at the beginning of the period.

   7.   **(C)** An imputed interest rate is used when the rate on a note is not fair and the market value of the items being exchanged is not readily determinable. An imputed interest rate represents the rate at which the debtor could obtain financing from a different source, this is known as the debtor's incremental borrowing rate.

   8.   **(G)** The market value of a note is equal to the maturity value and the interest payments discounted to the present value. The present value represents the amount you would pay now for an amount to be received in the future. Thus, answer G is the correct response, as the present value equals the current market value of the principal and interest amounts.

   9.   **(H)** When a note is exchanged for cash and no other rights or privileges exist, the present value of the note will equal the cash received if the stated rate on the note equals the market yield rate. However, if the stated rate is less than the market rate, then the note will be issued at a discount to compensate.

  10.   **(E)** A premium on a note occurs when the interest rate on a note is greater than the market yield rate. The market bids up the price of the bond above par until the effective interest rate on the note equals the market yield rate.

  11.   **(F)** The simple interest method computes interest based upon the amount of principal only. Interest is computed as Principal x Interest x Time. The compound interest method computes interest on principal and any interest earned and not withdrawn.

  12.   **(A)** The interest revenue or expense on a note is computed by taking the effective interest rate times the net receivable or payable balance.

  13.   **(I)** An annuity is a periodic payment or receipt made in consecutive intervals over time compounded at a stated interest rate. The future value of an annuity represents the total of the periodic payments and accumulated interest at some point in the future.

  14.   **(K)** When a note is exchanged for cash and no other rights or privileges exist, the present value of the note will be equal to the cash exchanged if the stated rate of interest equals the market yield rate. No premium or discount exists if the stated rate on the note equals the market yield rate.

SOLUTION GUIDE

Problem 1   Notes Receivable

1.   This problem consists of three related requirements. The candidate is required to prepare a long-term receivables section, prepare a schedule showing the current portion of the receivables and accrued interest receivable, and prepare a schedule showing the interest income and gains recognized on the sale of assets. Information pertaining to four notes is given.

1.1   The solutions approach for problems of this type where the requirements are interrelated is to prepare time lines for each note, make all computations for each note at one time, and label each computation according to the requirement to which it relates. For example, if a number or computation relates to requirement **a.**, it can be labeled "a." Using this approach, the candidate will be solving a part of two to three requirements as each note is covered, but not necessarily in the same order as given on the exam. After working through all the information given, the formal required schedules can be prepared.

1.2   The requirement in part **a.** is to prepare the long-term receivables section of the balance sheet dated 12/31/02. The solutions approach is to determine the amount of each note that is due after 12/31/03. In preparing the receivables section, all relevant information must be disclosed, [interest rates, due dates, less current installment (if applicable), etc.].

1.3   Part **b.** is essentially two subrequirements requiring the preparation of a schedule showing the current portion of the long-term receivables (label as b1.) and accrued interest receivable (label as b2.) that would appear in the balance sheet at 12/31/02.

1.4   Part **c.** is also essentially two subrequirements requiring the preparation of a schedule showing interest income from long-term receivables (c1.) and gains recognized on the sale of assets (c2.) that would appear on the income statement for the year ending 12/31/02.

2.   For the note arising from the sale of the building, $250,000 of the $750,000 principal was received on 5/1/02, leaving $500,000 to be received. Of this amount, $250,000 is due on 5/1/03 and represents the current portion. The remaining principal amount of $250,000 is due after 12/31/03 and is classified as long-term (see time line after 2.2).

2.1   Interest has accrued on this note since the last interest payment date (5/1/02) in the amount of $30,000 ($500,000 x 9% x 8/12). See time line after 2.2.

2.2   The interest income on this note is $52,500. This is equal to 9% of the note's balance outstanding from 1/1/02 to the first principal payment on 5/1/02 ($750,000 x 9% x 4/12 = $22,500) plus the interest earned on the remaining balance from the payment date to 12/31/02 ($500,000 x 9% x 8/12 = $30,000).

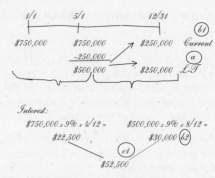

3.   The $200,000 note receivable from the officer is due 12/31/04; therefore, the entire amount is classified as long-term (see time line after 3.3).

3.1   Since the interest is payable annually on 12/31 and all the schedule interest payments have been made, there is no accrued interest from this note at 12/31/02.

3.2   A full year's interest was earned on the officer's note ($200,000 x 8% = $16,000). See the time line after 3.3.

3.3   No gain or loss is recorded on the stock acting as collateral. However, data relating to the collateral should be disclosed.

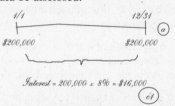

4.   The carrying value of the patent is its 1/1/02 book value of $40,000, less the 1/1/02 to 4/1/02 amortization of $2,000 ($8,000 x 3/12), or $38,000. Subtracting the 4/1/02 carrying value from the present value of the note received for the patent ($82,600) equals the gain on the sale of the patent, $44,600 (see time line after 4.2).

4.1   The $100,000 note arising from the sale of the patent is due 4/1/04 and is therefore considered long-term. Per APB 21, a noninterest-bearing note should be recorded at its present value using the prevailing rate of interest on similar notes with any difference recorded as a discount or premium. Therefore, at the time this note was received, a discount was recorded for the difference between the face value ($100,000) and present value ($100,000 x .826 = $82,600) of the note, or $17,400, which will be amortized as interest revenue over the life of the note. The effective interest method should be used. The straight-line method is used for intraperiod allocation. Interest was earned for nine months (4/1 - 12/31) on the carrying value of the note; therefore, the 2001 interest revenue and discount amortization is $6,195 ($82,600 x 10% x 9/12). After this amortization is recorded, the unamortized discount on 12/31/02 is $11,205 ($17,400 – $6,195). The note is presented net of the discount (see time line after 4.2).

4.2   No accrued interest will be recorded in the receivable account pertaining to this note. Even though interest revenue is recorded, the interest is a direct result of amortizing the related discount on the note and is not recorded as a receivable.

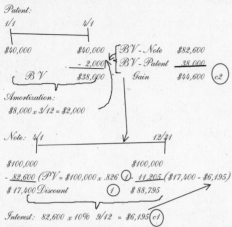

5. The gain on the land sale is the selling price, $400,000 less its cost, $300,000, or $100,000 (see time line after 5.2).

5.1 Since the principal (and interest) on this note will be paid in four equal annual installments, the note must be divided between its current and long-term por-

tions. Subtracting the first year's interest, ($280,000 x 10% = $28,000) from the installment to be received on 7/1/02 equals the current portion ($88,332 – $28,000 = $60,332). The remainder of the note ($280,000 – $60,332 = $219,668) is the long-term receivable (see time line after 5.2).

5.2 Six months' interest was earned and accrued in 2002 on this note ($280,000 x 10% x 6/12 = $14,000).

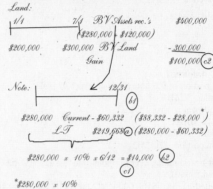

UNOFFICIAL ANSWER

Problem 1   Notes Receivable

a.

Kern, Inc.
LONG-TERM RECEIVABLES SECTION
OF BALANCE SHEET
December 31, 2002

9% note receivable from sale of idle building, due in annual installments of $250,000 to May 1, 2004, less current installment	$250,000	[1]
8% note receivable from officer, due December 31, 2004, collateralized by 5,000 shares of Kern, Inc. common stock with a fair value of $225,000	200,000	
Noninterest-bearing note from sale of patent, net of 10% imputed interest, due April 1, 2004	88,795	[2]
Installment contract receivable, due in annual installments of $88,332 to July 1, 2006, less current installment	219,668	[3]
Total long-term receivables	$758,463	

b.

Kern, Inc.
SELECTED BALANCE SHEET ACCOUNTS
December 31, 2002

Current portion of long-term receivables:		
Note receivable from sale of idle building	$250,000	[1]
Installment contract receivable	60,332	[3]
Total	$310,332	
Accrued interest receivable:		
Note receivable from sale of idle building	$30,000	[4]
Installment contract receivable	14,000	[5]
Total	$44,000	

c.

Kern, Inc.
INTEREST REVENUE FROM LONG-TERM RECEIVABLES
AND GAINS RECOGNIZED ON SALE OF ASSETS
For the Year Ended December 31, 2002

Interest revenue:

Note receivable from sale of idle building	$52,500	[6]
Note receivable from sale of patent	6,195	[2]
Note receivable from officer	16,000	[7]
Installment contract receivable from sale of land	14,000	[5]
Total interest revenue	$88,695	

Gains recognized on sale of assets:

Patent	$ 44,600	[8]
Land	100,000	[9]
Total gains recognized	$144,600	

Explanation of Amounts

[1] Long-term portion of 9% note receivable at 12/31/02

Face amount, 5/1/01	$750,000
Less installment received 5/1/02	250,000
Balance, 12/31/02	500,000
Less installment due 5/1/03	250,000
Long-term portion, 12/31/02	$250,000

[2] Noninterest-bearing note, net of imputed interest at 12/31/02

Face amount, 4/1/02	$100,000
Less imputed interest [$100,000 – $82,600 ($100,000 x 0.826)]	17,400
Balance, 4/1/02	82,600
Add interest earned to 12/31/02 [$82,600 x 10% x 9/12]	6,195
Balance, 12/31/02	$ 88,795

[3] Long-term portion of installment contract receivable at 12/31/02

Contract selling price, 7/1/02	$400,000
Less cash down payment	120,000
Balance, 12/31/02	280,000
Less installment due 7/1/03 [$88,332 – $28,000 ($280,000 x 10%)]	60,332
Long-term portion, 12/31/02	$219,668

[4] Accrued interest—note receivable, sale of idle building at 12/31/02

Interest accrued from 5/1 to 12/31/02 [$500,000 x 9% x 8/12]	$ 30,000

[5] Accrued interest—installment contract at 12/31/02

Interest accrued from 7/1 to 12/31/02 [$280,000 x 10% x 1/2]	$ 14,000

[6] Interest revenue—note receivable, sale of idle building, for 2002

Interest earned from 1/1/ to 5/1/02 [$750,000 x 9% x 4/12]	$ 22,500
Interest earned from 5/1 to 12/31/02 [$500,000 x 9% x 8/12]	30,000
Interest revenue	$ 52,500

[7] Interest revenue—note receivable, officer, for 2002

Interest earned 1/1 to 12/31/02 [$200,000 x 8%]	$ 16,000

[8] Gain recognized on sale of patent

Stated selling price		$100,000
Less imputed interest		17,400 [2]
Actual selling price		82,600
Less cost of patent (net)		
Carrying value 1/1/02	$40,000	38,000
Less amortization 1/1 to 4/1/02 [$8,000 x 1/4]	2,000	2,000
Gain recognized		$ 44,600

[9] Gain recognized on sale of land

Selling price	$400,000
Less cost	300,000
Gain recognized	$100,000

B. Bonds

1. **Bonds Payable and Bond Investments**

Investment in bonds and bonds payable are discussed together to contrast their treatment.[1] Bonds generally provide for periodic fixed interest payments at a contract rate of interest. At issuance, or thereafter, the market rate of interest for the particular type of bond may be above, the same, or below the contract rate. If the market rate exceeds the contract rate, the book value will be less than the maturity value. The difference (discount) will make up for the contract rate being below the market rate.

Conversely, when the contract rate exceeds the market rate, the bond will sell for more than maturity value to bring the effective rate to the market rate. This difference (premium) will make up for the contract rate being above the market rate. When the contract rate equals the market rate, the bond will sell for the maturity value.

The market value of a bond is equal to the maturity value and interest payments discounted to the present. You may have to refer to the discussion of time value of money concepts in the previous section before working with the subsequent material. Finally, when solving bond problems, candidates must be careful when determining the number of months to use in the calculation of interest and discount/premium amortization. For example, candidates frequently look at a bond issue with an interest date of September 1 and count three months to December 31. This error is easy to make because candidates focus only on the fact that September is the ninth month instead of also noting whether the date is at the beginning or end of the month. Candidates should also be aware that bond issues that mature on a single date are called term bonds, and bond issues that mature in installments are called serial bonds.

2. **Bond Valuation Example**

$10,000 in bonds, semiannual interest at 6% contract rate, maturing in six years, and market rate of 5%.

a. Find present value of maturity value. Use present value of $1 factor. Discount $10,000 back 12 periods at 2 1/2% interest (Factor = .7436). (Semiannual compounding is going to be required to discount the semiannual payments so it is also assumed here.)

$$\$10,000 \qquad x \qquad .7436 \qquad = \qquad \$7,436$$

b. Find the present value of the annuity of twelve $300 interest payments. Use present value of an ordinary annuity of $1 factor for twelve periods at 2 1/2% interest (Factor = 10.26).

$$\$300 \qquad x \qquad 10.26 \qquad = \qquad \$3,078$$

c. Today's value is $10,514 (7,436 + 3,078)

The $514 premium is to be recognized over the life of the bond issue. It is a reduction of interest expense on the books of the issuer and a reduction of interest revenue on the books of the investor. Amortization is to be the interest, or present value basis. (See outline of APB 21.)

The following summarizes when bonds are issued/acquired at a premium or discount:

ISSUE/ACQUISITION PRICE OF BONDS—PRESENT VALUE OF INTEREST ANNUITY PLUS THE PRESENT VALUE OF THE MATURITY AMOUNT USING THE YIELD OR MARKET RATE

Face amount	*Premium*	*Discount*
Yield rate = Face rate	Yield rate < Face rate	Yield rate > Face rate

3. **Journal Entries**

The issuer's books will be illustrated at gross (including a premium or discount account) and the investor's books will be illustrated at net (no discount or premium account). The investor may record the bonds either net or gross, but the issuer records at gross. In the past, CPA examination problems and solutions have followed the net method on the books of the investor.

---

[1] *Coverage in this module focuses on a bond's book or carrying value. Issues concerning FMV, holding gains and losses, and financial statement presentation of bond investments are covered with other marketable debt securities in Module 29, Investments.*

		Issuer			Investor		
a.	Issue and	Cash	10,514		Bond invest.	10,514	
	Acquisition	Bonds pay.		10,000	Cash		10,514
		Bonds prem.		514			
b.	First int.	Interest exp.	300		Cash	300	
	payment	Cash		300	Interest rev.		300
c.	Premium—	Bond prem.	37.15*		Interest rev.	37.15	
	Amortization	Interest exp.	37.15		Bond invest.		37.15*

* *Interest receipt (payment) minus effective interest = 300 – 262.85 = 37.15*
Effective interest = net book value times effective rate = 10,514 x .025 = 262.85

Entry a. assumes that the bonds are issued on the interest payment date. If bonds are purchased between interest payment dates, the purchaser will also include accrued interest through the purchase date in the total cash paid for the bonds. The payment of this accrued interest on the purchase date will serve to reduce the subsequent receipt of interest income (which covers a time period longer than the time the purchaser held the bond).

Subsequent interest payments are recorded the same as entry b. shown above. The amount of subsequent amortization (entry c. above) changes. Interest to be recorded under the interest method is always computed by

Effective interest rate x Net book value

This formula is true of all applications of the interest method. The effective rate of interest times net book value is the actual interest revenue or expense for the period. The difference between the actual interest and the amount received or paid is the amortization. The amortization table below shows the effective interest amounts and premium amortizations for the first 4 periods.

Period	3% cash interest	2 1/2% effective interest	Decrease in book value	Book value of bonds
0				$10,514.00
1	$300[a]	$262.85[b]	$37.15[c]	10,476.85[d]
2	300	261.92	38.08	10,438.77
3	300	260.97	39.03	10,399.74
4	300	259.99	40.01	10,359.73

(a) 3% x $10,000   (c) $300 – $262.85
(b) 2 1/2% x $10,514.00   (d) $10,514.00 – $37.15

Since the interest is paid semiannually, interest (including premium amortization) is recorded every six months. The journal entries for periods 2, 3, and 4 are

	Issuer			Investor		
Period 2	Interest expense	261.92		Cash	300.00	
	Bond premium	38.08		Interest rev.		261.92
	Cash		300.00	Bond invest.		38.08
Period 3	Interest expense	260.97		Cash	300.00	
	Bond premium	39.03		Interest rev		260.97
	Cash		300.00	Bond invest.		39.03
Period 4	Interest expense	259.99		Cash	300.00	
	Bond premium	40.01		Interest rev.		259.99
	Cash		300.00	Bond invest		40.01

Notice that the interest (revenue and expense) decreases over time. This is because the net book value (which is also the present value) is decreasing from the maturity value plus premium to the maturity value. Thus, the effective rate is being multiplied by a smaller amount each six months.

Also, note that the change in interest each period is the prior period's premium amortization times the effective rate. For example, the interest in period 3 is $.95 less than in period 2, and $38.08 of premium was amortized in period 2. The effective rate of 2.5% (every six months) times $38.08 is $.95. Thus, if the interest changes due to the changing level of net book value, the change in interest will be equal to the change in the net book value times the effective rate of interest.

Another complication may arise if the year-end does not coincide with the interest dates. In such a case, an adjusting entry must be made. The proportional share of interest payable or receivable should be recognized along with the amortization of discount or premium. The amortization of discount or premium should be straight-line within the amortization period.

EXAMPLE: Assume that in the above example, both issuer and investor have reporting periods ending three months after the issuance of the bonds.

	Issuer		Investor	
Entries on the	Interest expense	150	Interest receivable	150
closing date	Interest payable	150	Interest revenue	150
	Bond premium	18.57	Interest revenue	18.57
	Interest expense	18.57	Bond investment	18.57

Reverse at beginning of new period and make regular entry at next interest payment date.

If bonds are sold (bought) between interest dates, premium/discount amortization must be computed for the period between sale (purchase) date and last (next) interest date. This is accomplished by straight-lining the six-month amount which was calculated using the effective interest method.

EXAMPLE: The investor sold $5,000 of bonds in the above example, two months after issuance, for $5,250 plus interest.

1. The bond premium which must be amortized to the point of sale ($5,000 for two months) is 1/2 x 1/3 x $37.15 or $6.19.

Interest revenue	6.19	
Investment		6.19

2. The sale is recorded. The investment account was $5,257 before amortization of $6.19. The cash received would be $5,250 plus $50 interest (1/2 x 1/3 x $300). The loss is a forced figure.

Cash	5,300.00	
Loss	.81	
Interest revenue		50.00
Investment		5,250.81 [($10,514.00/2) – $6.19]

3. Check the interest revenue recorded ($50.00 – $6.19) to the interest earned: $5,257 x 2 1/2% x 1/3 (which equals $43.81).

Costs incurred in connection with the issuance of bonds (e.g., printing and engraving, accounting and legal fees, and commissions), according to SFAC 6, may be treated two ways. **However**, APB 21 currently allows the treatment of bond issue costs only in one of these ways.

SFAC 6 (see outline) states that the bond issue costs can be treated as either an expense or a reduction of the related bond liability. Bond issue costs are not considered as assets because they provide no future economic benefit. The argument for treating them as a reduction of the related bond liability is that they reduce bond proceeds, thereby increasing the effective interest rate. Thus, they should be accounted for the same as unamortized discounts.

In practice, however, the only acceptable GAAP for bond issue costs is to treat them as deferred charges and amortize them on a straight-line basis over the life of the bond.

4. **Comparison of Effective Interest and Straight-Line Amortization Methods**

Method of Amortization	Interest Revenue/Expense	Interest Rate**
Effective interest method	Changes each period*	Constant each period
Straight-line method	Constant each period	Changes each period

* Carrying amount of the bond investment or bonds payable at the beginning of the interest period multiplied times the yield rate
** Interest revenue/expense for a period divided by the carrying amount of the bond investment or bond liability at the beginning of the interest period

The following table summarizes the various behavior patterns related to the use of the effective interest method:

Description	Amortization of	
	Discount	Premium
Interest revenue/expense	↑Increases each period	↓Decreases each period
Amount of amortization	↑Increases each period	↑Increases each period
Carrying amount of bonds payable/investment in bonds	↑Increases each period	↓Decreases each period

5. **Convertible Bonds** (See outlines of APB 14 and SFAS 84)

Bonds are frequently issued with the right to convert the bonds into common stock. When issued, no value is apportioned to the conversion feature. Two approaches are possible to account for bond conversions: valuing the transaction at cost (book value of the bonds), or valuing at market (of the stocks or bonds), whichever is more reliable. At market, assuming market value exceeds book value, the entries would be

Issuer			*Investor*	
Loss on redemption	(plug)		Stock invest	(mkt)
Bonds payable	(book value)		Invest in bonds	(carrying value)
Bond premium	(book value)		Gain on conversion	(plug)
Common stock		(par)		
Paid-in excess of par		(mkt-par)		

On the issuer's books, the debit (credit) to the loss (gain) account (ordinary) would be for the difference between the market value of the stock (bonds) and the book value of the bonds. The conversion is treated as the culmination of an earnings process; thus the loss (gain) should be recognized. The bonds and the related accounts must be written off, and paid-in excess of par is credited for the excess of the market value of the stock (bonds) over the stock's par value. On the investor's books, the gain (loss) would also be the difference between the market value the stock (bonds) and the book value of the bonds. Remember in both cases that the accrued interest and discount or premium amortization must be recorded prior to the conversion.

Conversion under the cost method would result in debits to bonds payable and bond premium (or a credit to bond discount) equal to the book value of the bonds, and credits to common stock and paid-in excess of par equal to the book value. In practice, conversions are usually recorded at book value. Note that under this method no gain (loss) is recorded, as no gain (loss) should result from an equity transaction.

To induce conversion, firms sometimes change the original conversion privilege or give additional considerations to the bondholders. Per SFAS 84 (see outline), the fair market value of these "sweeteners" should be recognized as an expense (ordinary in nature) upon conversion, determined as the excess of the FMV of all securities and consideration transferred over the FMV of the securities issuable per the original conversion terms.

6. **Debt Issued with Detachable Purchase Warrants**

APB 14 (see outline) requires the proceeds of debt issued with detachable stock purchase warrants to be allocated between the debt and stock warrants based on relative market values. Example: units of one bond and one warrant (to buy 10 shares of stock at $50/share) are issued for $1,030. Thereafter, warrants trade at $40 and the bonds at $960. The relative market value of the warrants is 4% (40/1,000) and the relative market value of the bonds is 96% (960/1,000). Thus, $41.20 (.04 x $1,030) of the issue price is assigned to the warrants.

Cash	1,030.00	
Bond discount	11.20	
Bonds payable		1,000.00
Paid-in capital—stock warrants		41.20

If one warrant was subsequently exercised

Cash	500.00	
Paid-in capital—stock warrants	41.20	
Common stock		(par of 10 shs)
Paid-in excess		(plug)

Alternatively, the example above could have indicated the market value of the stock (e.g., $54) rather than the market values of the bonds and warrants. In such a case, one would value the warrants based on the difference between option price and market price, for example, [$54 (market) – $50 (option)] x 10 shares = $40 value for the warrants.

Notice the effect of requiring allocation of the cash received to the stock warrants. The final effect is to increase interest costs on the bond issue by reducing the premium or increasing the discount.

Note that the allocation to equity shown above is only applicable where the purchase warrants are **detachable**. In contrast, no allocation is made to equity if the bonds are issued with **nondetachable** stock purchase warrants. Detachable warrants are often traded separately from the debt and therefore have a readily determinable market value of their own. The inseparability of nondetachable warrants prevents the determination of a separate market value; therefore, no allocation to equity is permitted by APB 14.

7. **Extinguishment of Debt** (See outline of APB 26)

Debt is considered extinguished whenever the debtor pays the creditor and is relieved of all obligations relating to the debt. Typical examples of this are the calling of a bond by the debtor, requiring the bondholder to sell the bond to the issuing corporation at a certain date and stated price, and the open market repurchase of a debt issue. Refunding of debt (replacement of debt with other debt) is also considered an extinguishment. However, troubled debt restructures (situations where creditors agree to grant relief to debtors) and debt conversions initiated by the debt holders are not. Additionally, when the debtor is legally released from being the primary obligor of the debt either judicially or by the creditor, and it is probable the debtor will make no further payments on it, the debt is considered extinguished.

All gains (losses) resulting from the extinguishment of debt should be recognized in the period of extinguishment. The gain (loss) is the difference between the bond's reacquisition price and its net book value [face value plus (minus) any unamortized premium (discount) and issue costs]. The rule is not affected by the reissuance of debt before or after the refunding. Furthermore, this rule applies to convertible bonds when reacquired with cash. The gain or loss is **extraordinary** (see SFAS 4 and 64).

Loss or gain	xx	xx
Bonds payable	xx	
Bond premium	xx	
Unamortized issue costs		xx
Bond discount		xx
Cash		xx

MULTIPLE-CHOICE QUESTIONS (1-42)

1. Hancock Co.'s December 31, 2002 balance sheet contained the following items in the long-term liabilities section:

Unsecured

9.375% registered bonds ($25,000 maturing annually beginning in 2006)	$275,000
11.5% convertible bonds, callable beginning in 2010, due 2022	125,000

Secured

9.875% guaranty security bonds, due 2022	$275,000
10.0% commodity backed bonds ($50,000 maturing annually beginning in 2007)	200,000

What are the total amounts of serial bonds and debenture bonds?

	Serial bonds	*Debenture bonds*
a.	$475,000	$400,000
b.	$475,000	$125,000
c.	$450,000	$400,000
d.	$200,000	$650,000

2. Blue Corp.'s December 31, 2002 balance sheet contained the following items in the long-term liabilities section:

9 3/4% registered debentures, callable in 2013, due in 2018	$700,000
9 1/2% collateral trust bonds, convertible into common stock beginning in 2011, due in 2021	600,000
10% subordinated debentures ($30,000 maturing annually beginning in 2008)	300,000

What is the total amount of Blue's term bonds?
- a. $ 600,000
- b. $ 700,000
- c. $1,000,000
- d. $1,300,000

3. Bonds payable issued with scheduled maturities at various dates are called

	Serial bonds	*Term bonds*
a.	No	Yes
b.	No	No
c.	Yes	No
d.	Yes	Yes

4. The following information pertains to Camp Corp.'s issuance of bonds on July 1, 2002:

Face amount	$800,000
Term	Ten years
Stated interest rate	6%
Interest payment dates	Annually on July 1
Yield	9%

	At 6%	*At 9%*
Present value of one for ten periods	0.558	0.422
Future value of one for ten periods	1.791	2.367
Present value of ordinary annuity of one for ten periods	7.360	6.418

What should be the issue price for each $1,000 bond?
- a. $1,000
- b. $ 864
- c. $ 807
- d. $ 700

5. Perk, Inc. issued $500,000, 10% bonds to yield 8%. Bond issuance costs were $10,000. How should Perk calculate the net proceeds to be received from the issuance?
- a. Discount the bonds at the stated rate of interest.

- b. Discount the bonds at the market rate of interest.
- c. Discount the bonds at the stated rate of interest and deduct bond issuance costs.
- d. Discount the bonds at the market rate of interest and deduct bond issuance costs.

6. The market price of a bond issued at a discount is the present value of its principal amount at the market (effective) rate of interest
- a. Less the present value of all future interest payments at the market (effective) rate of interest.
- b. Less the present value of all future interest payments at the rate of interest stated on the bond.
- c. Plus the present value of all future interest payments at the market (effective) rate of interest.
- d. Plus the present value of all future interest payments at the rate of interest stated on the bond.

7. On July 1, 2002, Eagle Corp. issued 600 of its 10%, $1,000 bonds at 99 plus accrued interest. The bonds are dated April 1, 2002 and mature on April 1, 2012. Interest is payable semiannually on April 1 and October 1. What amount did Eagle receive from the bond issuance?
- a. $579,000
- b. $594,000
- c. $600,000
- d. $609,000

8. During 2002, Lake Co. issued 3,000 of its 9%, $1,000 face value bonds at 101 1/2. In connection with the sale of these bonds, Lake paid the following expenses:

Promotion costs	$ 20,000
Engraving and printing	25,000
Underwriters' commissions	200,000

What amount should Lake record as bond issue costs to be amortized over the term of the bonds?
- a. $0
- b. $220,000
- c. $225,000
- d. $245,000

9. Dixon Co. incurred costs of $3,300 when it issued, on August 31, 2002, five-year debenture bonds dated April 1, 2002. What amount of bond issue expense should Dixon report in its income statement for the year ended December 31, 2002?
- a. $ 220
- b. $ 240
- c. $ 495
- d. $3,300

10. On November 1, 2002, Mason Corp. issued $800,000 of its ten-year, 8% term bonds dated October 1, 2002. The bonds were sold to yield 10%, with total proceeds of $700,000 plus accrued interest. Interest is paid every April 1 and October 1. What amount should Mason report for interest payable in its December 31, 2002 balance sheet?
- a. $17,500
- b. $16,000
- c. $11,667
- d. $10,667

11. On July 1, 2002, Day Co. received $103,288 for $100,000 face amount, 12% bonds, a price that yields 10%. Interest expense for the six months ended December 31, 2002, should be
- a. $6,197

b. $6,000
c. $5,164
d. $5,000

12. On January 2, 2002, West Co. issued 9% bonds in the amount of $500,000, which mature on January 2, 2012. The bonds were issued for $469,500 to yield 10%. Interest is payable annually on December 31. West uses the interest method of amortizing bond discount. In its June 30, 2002 balance sheet, what amount should West report as bonds payable?
   a. $469,500
   b. $470,475
   c. $471,025
   d. $500,000

13. Webb Co. has outstanding a 7%, ten-year $100,000 face-value bond. The bond was originally sold to yield 6% annual interest. Webb uses the effective interest rate method to amortize bond premium. On June 30, 2002, the carrying amount of the outstanding bond was $105,000. What amount of unamortized premium on bond should Webb report in its June 30, 2003 balance sheet?
   a. $1,050
   b. $3,950
   c. $4,300
   d. $4,500

14. A bond issued on June 1, 2002, has interest payment dates of April 1 and October 1. Bond interest expense for the year ended December 31, 2002, is for a period of
   a. Three months.
   b. Four months.
   c. Six months.
   d. Seven months.

15. For the issuer of a ten-year term bond, the amount of amortization using the interest method would increase each year if the bond was sold at a

	Discount	Premium
a.	No	No
b.	Yes	Yes
c.	No	Yes
d.	Yes	No

16. On January 2, 2002, Nast Co. issued 8% bonds with a face amount of $1,000,000 that mature on January 2, 2008. The bonds were issued to yield 12%, resulting in a discount of $150,000. Nast incorrectly used the straight-line method instead of the effective interest method to amortize the discount. How is the carrying amount of the bonds affected by the error?

	At December 31, 2002	At January 2, 2008
a.	Overstated	Understated
b.	Overstated	No effect
c.	Understated	Overstated
d.	Understated	No effect

17. The following information relates to noncurrent investments that Fall Corp. placed in trust as required by the underwriter of its bonds:

Bond sinking fund balance, 12/31/02	$ 450,000
2003 additional investment	90,000
Dividends on investments	15,000
Interest revenue	30,000
Administration costs	5,000
Carrying amount of bonds payable	1,025,000

What amount should Fall report in its December 31, 2003 balance sheet related to its noncurrent investment for bond sinking fund requirements?
   a. $585,000
   b. $580,000
   c. $575,000
   d. $540,000

18. Witt Corp. has outstanding at December 31, 2003, two long-term borrowings with annual sinking fund requirements and maturities as follows:

	Sinking fund requirements	Maturities
2002	$1,000,000	$ --
2003	1,500,000	2,000,000
2004	1,500,000	2,000,000
2005	2,000,000	2,500,000
2006	2,000,000	3,000,000
	$8,000,000	$9,500,000

In the notes to its December 31, 2003 balance sheet, how should Witt report the above data?
   a. No disclosure is required.
   b. Only sinking fund payments totaling $8,000,000 for the next five years detailed by year need be disclosed.
   c. Only maturities totaling $9,500,000 for the next five years detailed by year need to be disclosed.
   d. The combined aggregate of $17,500,000 of maturities and sinking fund requirements detailed by year should be disclosed.

19. On March 1, 1998, a company established a sinking fund in connection with an issue of bonds due in 2010. At December 31, 2002, the independent trustee held cash in the sinking fund account representing the annual deposits to the fund and the interest earned on those deposits. How should the sinking fund be reported in the company's balance sheet at December 31, 2002?
   a. The cash in the sinking fund should appear as a current asset.
   b. Only the accumulated deposits should appear as a noncurrent asset.
   c. The entire balance in the sinking fund account should appear as a current asset.
   d. The entire balance in the sinking fund account should appear as a noncurrent asset.

20. An issuer of bonds uses a sinking fund for the retirement of the bonds. Cash was transferred to the sinking fund and subsequently used to purchase investments. The sinking fund
  I. Increases by revenue earned on the investments.
  II. Is **not** affected by revenue earned on the investments.
  III. Decreases when the investments are purchased.

   a. I only.
   b. I and III.
   c. II and III.
   d. III only.

21. On July 2, 2002, Wynn, Inc., purchased as a short-term investment a $1,000,000 face value Kean Co. 8% bond for $910,000 plus accrued interest to yield 10%. The bonds mature on January 1, 2009, pay interest annually on January 1, and are classified as trading securities. On December 31, 2002, the bonds had a market value of $945,000. On February 13, 2003, Wynn sold the bonds for $920,000. In its December 31, 2002 balance sheet, what amount should Wynn

report for short-term investments in trading debt securities? (Answer should be in accordance with SFAS 115.)
- a. $910,000
- b. $920,000
- c. $945,000
- d. $950,000

22. On July 1, 2002, East Co. purchased as a long-term investment $500,000 face amount, 8% bonds of Rand Corp. for $461,500 to yield 10% per year. The bonds pay interest semiannually on January 1 and July 1. In its December 31, 2002 balance sheet, East should report interest receivable of
- a. $18,460
- b. $20,000
- c. $23,075
- d. $25,000

23. On October 1, 2001, Park Co. purchased 200 of the $1,000 face value, 10% bonds of Ott, Inc., for $220,000, including accrued interest of $5,000. The bonds, which mature on January 1, 2008, pay interest semiannually on January 1 and July 1. Park used the straight-line method of amortization and appropriately classified the bonds as held-to-maturity. On Park's December 31, 2002 balance sheet, the bonds should be reported at
- a. $215,000
- b. $214,400
- c. $214,200
- d. $212,000

24. On July 1, 2002, York Co. purchased as a held-to-maturity investment $1,000,000 of Park, Inc.'s 8% bonds for $946,000, including accrued interest of $40,000. The bonds were purchased to yield 10% interest. The bonds mature on January 1, 2009, and pay interest annually on January 1. York uses the effective interest method of amortization. In its December 31, 2002 balance sheet, what amount should York report as investment in bonds?
- a. $911,300
- b. $916,600
- c. $953,300
- d. $960,600

25. In 2001, Lee Co. acquired, at a premium, Enfield, Inc. ten-year bonds as a long-term investment. At December 31, 2002, Enfield's bonds were quoted at a small discount. Which of the following situations is the most likely cause of the decline in the bonds' market value?
- a. Enfield issued a stock dividend.
- b. Enfield is expected to call the bonds at a premium, which is less than Lee's carrying amount.
- c. Interest rates have declined since Lee purchased the bonds.
- d. Interest rates have increased since Lee purchased the bonds.

26. An investor purchased a bond as a held-to-maturity investment on January 2. The investor's carrying value at the end of the first year would be highest if the bond was purchased at a
- a. Discount and amortized by the straight-line method.
- b. Discount and amortized by the effective interest method.
- c. Premium and amortized by the straight-line method.
- d. Premium and amortized by the effective interest method.

27. An investor purchased a bond as a long-term investment on January 1. Annual interest was received on December 31. The investor's interest income for the year would be highest if the bond was purchased at
- a. Par.
- b. Face value.
- c. A discount.
- d. A premium.

28. On March 1, 2002, Clark Co. issued bonds at a discount. Clark incorrectly used the straight-line method instead of the effective interest method to amortize the discount. How were the following amounts, as of December 31, 2002, affected by the error?

	Bond carrying amount	Retained earnings
a.	Overstated	Overstated
b.	Understated	Understated
c.	Overstated	Understated
d.	Understated	Overstated

29. Jent Corp. purchased bonds at a discount of $10,000. Subsequently, Jent sold these bonds at a premium of $14,000. During the period that Jent held this investment, amortization of the discount amounted to $2,000. What amount should Jent report as gain on the sale of bonds?
- a. $12,000
- b. $22,000
- c. $24,000
- d. $26,000

30. On July 1, 2002, after recording interest and amortization, York Co. converted $1,000,000 of its 12% convertible bonds into 50,000 shares of $1 par value common stock. On the conversion date the carrying amount of the bonds was $1,300,000, the market value of the bonds was $1,400,000, and York's common stock was publicly trading at $30 per share. Using the book value method, what amount of additional paid-in capital should York record as a result of the conversion?
- a. $ 950,000
- b. $1,250,000
- c. $1,350,000
- d. $1,500,000

31. On March 31, 2002, Ashley, Inc.'s bondholders exchanged their convertible bonds for common stock. The carrying amount of these bonds on Ashley's books was less than the market value but greater than the par value of the common stock issued. If Ashley used the book value method of accounting for the conversion, which of the following statements correctly states an effect of this conversion?
- a. Stockholders' equity is increased.
- b. Additional paid-in capital is decreased.
- c. Retained earnings is increased.
- d. An extraordinary loss is recognized.

Items 32 and 33 are based on the following:

On January 2, 1999, Chard Co. issued ten-year convertible bonds at 105. During 2002, these bonds were converted into common stock having an aggregate par value equal to the total face amount of the bonds. At conversion, the market price of Chard's common stock was 50% above its par value.

32. On January 2, 1999, cash proceeds from the issuance of the convertible bonds should be reported as
  a. Contributed capital for the entire proceeds.
  b. Contributed capital for the portion of the proceeds attributable to the conversion feature and as a liability for the balance.
  c. A liability for the face amount of the bonds and contributed capital for the premium over the face amount.
  d. A liability for the entire proceeds.

33. Depending on whether the book value method or the market value method was used, Chard would recognize gains or losses on conversion when using the

	Book value method	Market value method
a.	Either gain or loss	Gain
b.	Either gain or loss	Loss
c.	Neither gain **nor** loss	Loss
d.	Neither gain **nor** loss	Gain

34. On December 30, 2002, Fort, Inc. issued 1,000 of its 8%, ten-year, $1,000 face value bonds with detachable stock warrants at par. Each bond carried a detachable warrant for one share of Fort's common stock at a specified option price of $25 per share. Immediately after issuance, the market value of the bonds without the warrants was $1,080,000 and the market value of the warrants was $120,000. In its December 31, 2002 balance sheet, what amount should Fort report as bonds payable?
  a. $1,000,000
  b. $ 975,000
  c. $ 900,000
  d. $ 880,000

35. On December 31, 2002, Moss Co. issued $1,000,000 of 11% bonds at 109. Each $1,000 bond was issued with fifty detachable stock warrants, each of which entitled the bondholder to purchase one share of $5 par common stock for $25. Immediately after issuance, the market value of each warrant was $4. On December 31, 2002, what amount should Moss record as discount or premium on issuance of bonds?
  a. $ 40,000 premium.
  b. $ 90,000 premium.
  c. $110,000 discount.
  d. $200,000 discount.

36. On March 1, 2002, Evan Corp. issued $500,000 of 10% nonconvertible bonds at 103, due on February 28, 2012. Each $1,000 bond was issued with thirty detachable stock warrants, each of which entitled the holder to purchase, for $50, one share of Evan's $25 par common stock. On March 1, 2002, the market price of each warrant was $4. By what amount should the bond issue proceeds increase stockholders' equity?
  a. $0
  b. $15,000
  c. $45,000
  d. $60,000

37. Main Co. issued bonds with detachable common stock warrants. Only the warrants had a known market value. The sum of the fair value of the warrants and the face amount of the bonds exceeds the cash proceeds. This excess is reported as
  a. Discount on bonds payable.

  b. Premium on bonds payable.
  c. Common stock subscribed.
  d. Contributed capital in excess of par—stock warrants.

38. When bonds are issued with stock purchase warrants, a portion of the proceeds should be allocated to paid-in capital for bonds issued with

	Detachable stock purchase warrants	Nondetachable stock purchase warrants
a.	No	Yes
b.	No	No
c.	Yes	No
d.	Yes	Yes

39. On June 30, 2002, King Co. had outstanding 9%, $5,000,000 face value bonds maturing on June 30, 2007. Interest was payable semiannually every June 30 and December 31. On June 30, 2002, after amortization was recorded for the period, the unamortized bond premium and bond issue costs were $30,000 and $50,000, respectively. On that date, King acquired all its outstanding bonds on the open market at 98 and retired them. At June 30, 2002, what amount should King recognize as gain before income taxes on redemption of bonds?
  a. $ 20,000
  b. $ 80,000
  c. $120,000
  d. $180,000

40. On January 1, 1997, Fox Corp. issued 1,000 of its 10%, $1,000 bonds for $1,040,000. These bonds were to mature on January 1, 2007 but were callable at 101 any time after December 31, 2000. Interest was payable semiannually on July 1 and January 1. On July 1, 2002, Fox called all of the bonds and retired them. Bond premium was amortized on a straight-line basis. Before income taxes, Fox's gain or loss in 2002 on this early extinguishment of debt was
  a. $30,000 gain.
  b. $12,000 gain.
  c. $10,000 loss.
  d. $ 8,000 gain.

41. On January 1, 2002, Hart, Inc. redeemed its fifteen-year bonds of $500,000 par value for 102. They were originally issued on January 1, 1990 at 98 with a maturity date of January 1, 2005. The bond issue costs relating to this transaction were $20,000. Hart amortizes discounts, premiums, and bond issue costs using the straight-line method. What amount of extraordinary loss should Hart recognize on the redemption of these bonds?
  a. $16,000
  b. $12,000
  c. $10,000
  d. $0

42. Weald Co. took advantage of market conditions to refund debt. This was the fifth refunding operation carried out by Weald within the last four years. The excess of the carrying amount of the old debt over the amount paid to extinguish it should be reported as a(n)
  a. Deferred credit to be amortized over life of new debt.
  b. Part of continuing operations.
  c. Extraordinary gain, net of income taxes.
  d. Extraordinary loss, net of income taxes.

OTHER OBJECTIVE QUESTIONS

Problem 1   (15 to 25 minutes)

Items 1 through 7 are based on the following:

On January 2, 2002, North Co. issued bonds payable with a face value of $480,000 at a discount. The bonds are due in ten years and interest is payable semiannually every June 30 and December 31. On June 30, 2002, and on December 31, 2002, North made the semiannual interest payments when due, and recorded interest expense and amortization of bond discount.

Required:

Items 1 through 7, contained in the partially completed amortization table below, represent information needed to complete the table. For each item, select from the following lists the correct numerical response. A response may be selected once, more than once, or not at all.

	Cash	Interest expense	Amortization	Discount	Carrying amount
1/2/02					(3)
6/30/02	(2)	18,000	3,600	(1)	363,600
12/31/02	$14,400	(6)	(7)		

Annual Interest Rates: Stated   (4)
                          Effective (5)

Rates			Amounts		
A.	3.0%		G.	$ 3,420	P.	$ 21,600
B.	4.5%		H.	$ 3,600	Q.	$116,400
C.	5.0%		I.	$ 3,780	R.	$120,000
D.	6.0%		J.	$ 3,960	S.	$123,600
E.	9.0%		K.	$14,400	T.	$360,000
F.	10.0%		L.	$17,820	U.	$363,600
			M.	$18,000	V.	$367,200
			N.	$18,180	W.	$467,400
			O.	$18,360	X.	$480,000

Problem 2   (5 to 15 minutes)

Items 1 through 5 are based on the following:

Hamnoff, Inc.'s $50 par value common stock has always traded above par. During 2001, Hamnoff had several transactions that affected the following balance sheet accounts:

    I.   Bond discount
   II.   Bond premium
  III.   Bonds payable
  IV.   Common stock
   V.   Additional paid-in capital
  VI.   Retained earnings

Required:

For **items 1 through 5,** determine whether the transaction increased (I), decreased (D), or had no effect (N) on each of the balances in the above accounts.

1.   Hamnoff issued bonds payable with a nominal rate of interest that was less than the market rate of interest.

2.   Hamnoff issued convertible bonds, which are common stock equivalents, for an amount in excess of the bonds' face amount.

3.   Hamnoff issued common stock when the convertible bonds described in item 2 were submitted for conversion. Each $1,000 bond was converted into twenty common shares. The book value method was used for the early conversion.

4.   Hamnoff issued bonds, with detachable stock warrants, for an amount equal to the face amount of the bonds. The stock warrants have a determinable value.

5.   Hamnoff declared and issued a 2% stock dividend.

PROBLEMS

Problem 1   (15 to 25 minutes)

On January 2, 2000, Drew Company issued 9% term bonds dated January 2, 2000 at an effective annual interest rate (yield) of 10%. Drew uses the effective interest method of amortization. On July 1, 2002, the bonds were extinguished early when Drew acquired them in the open market for a price greater than their face amount.

On September 1, 2002, Drew issued for cash 7% nonconvertible bonds dated September 1, 2002, with detachable stock purchase warrants. Immediately after issuance, both the bonds and the warrants had separately determined market values.

Required:

a.   1.   Were the 9% term bonds issued at face amount, at a discount, or at a premium? Why?

2.   Would the amount of interest expense for the 9% term bonds using the effective interest method of amortization be higher in the first or second year of the life of the bond issue? Why?

b.   1.   How should gain or loss on early extinguishment of debt be determined? Does the early extinguishment of the 9% term bonds result in a gain or loss? Why?

2.   How should Drew report the early extinguishment of the 9% term bonds on the 2002 income statement?

c.   How should Drew account for the issuance of the 7% nonconvertible bonds with detachable stock purchase warrants?

Problem 2   (15 to 25 minutes)

On June 30, 1999, Corval Co. issued fifteen-year 12% bonds at a premium (effective yield 10%). On November 30, 2002, Corval transferred both cash and property to the bondholders to extinguish the entire debt. The fair value of the transferred property equaled its carrying amount. The fair value of the cash and property transferred exceeded the bonds carrying amount. [Ignore income taxes.]

Required:

a.   Explain the purpose of the effective interest method and the effect of applying the method in 1999 on Corval's bond premium.

b.   What would have been the effect on 1999 interest expense, net income, and the carrying amount of the bonds if Corval had incorrectly adopted the straight-line interest method instead of the effective interest method?

c.   How should Corval calculate and report the effects of the November 30, 2002 transaction in its 2002 income statement? Why is this presentation appropriate?

d.   How should Corval report the effects of the November 30, 2002 transaction in its statement of cash flows using the indirect method?

Problem 3   (10 to 15 minutes)

Columbine Co.'s ten-year convertible bonds, were issued and dated October 1, 2000. Each $1,000 bond is convertible, at the holder's option, into twenty shares of Columbine's $25 par value common stock. The bonds were issued at a premium when the common stock traded at $45 per share. After payment of interest on October 1, 2002, 30% of the bonds were tendered for conversion when the common stock was trading at $57 per share. Columbine used the book value method to account for the conversion.

Required:

a.   1.   How would the issue price of Columbine's convertible bonds be determined?

2.   How should Columbine account for the issuance of the convertible bonds? Give the rationale for this accounting practice.

3.   How should Columbine account for the conversion of the bonds into common stock?

Problem 4

This problem can be found in Module 27. It is Problem 2 and requires preparation of the long-term liabilities section of the balance sheet and a schedule of interest expense.

MULTIPLE-CHOICE ANSWERS

1. a __ __	10. b __ __	19. d __ __	28. c __ __	37. a __ __
2. d __ __	11. c __ __	20. a __ __	29. b __ __	38. c __ __
3. c __ __	12. b __ __	21. c __ __	30. b __ __	39. b __ __
4. c __ __	13. c __ __	22. b __ __	31. a __ __	40. d __ __
5. d __ __	14. d __ __	23. d __ __	32. d __ __	41. a __ __
6. c __ __	15. b __ __	24. a __ __	33. c __ __	42. c __ __
7. d __ __	16. b __ __	25. d __ __	34. c __ __	
8. d __ __	17. b __ __	26. d __ __	35. c __ __	1st: __/42 = __%
9. b __ __	18. d __ __	27. c __ __	36. d __ __	2nd: __/42 = __%

MULTIPLE-CHOICE ANSWER EXPLANATIONS

B.1.-4. Bonds

1. **(a)** **Serial** bonds are bond issues that mature in installments (usually on the same date each year over a period of years). In this case, serial bonds total $475,000 ($275,000 + $200,000). **Debenture** bonds are bonds that are **not** secured by specifically designated collateral, but rather by the general assets of the corporation. The unsecured bonds total $400,000 ($275,000 + $125,000).

2. **(d)** **Term bonds** are bond issues that mature on a single date, as opposed to **serial bonds**, which mature in installments. In this case, the 9 3/4% bonds and the 9 1/2% bonds are term bonds ($700,000 + $600,000 = $1,300,000), while the 10% bonds are serial bonds ($300,000).

3. **(c)** Serial bonds are bond issues that mature in installments (i.e., on the same date each year over a period of years). Term bonds, on the other hand, are bond issues that mature on a single date.

4. **(c)** The issue price of each bond is equal to the present value (PV) of the maturity value plus the PV of the interest annuity. The PV must be computed using the yield rate (9%). The computation is

Amount		PV factor		PV
$1,000	x	.422	=	$422
60	x	6.418	=	385
				$807

The annuity interest amount above ($60) is the principal ($1,000) times the stated cash rate (6%).

5. **(d)** The question asks for net proceeds to be received from the issuance. The market value of a bond is equal to the maturity value and the interest payments discounted at the market rate of interest. The net proceeds will be the market value of the bond less the bond issuance costs.

6. **(c)** The market price of a bond issued at any amount (par, premium, or discount) is equal to the present value of all of its future cash flows, discounted at the current market (effective) interest rate. The market price of a bond issued at a discount is equal to the present value of both its principal and periodic future cash interest payments at the stated (cash) rate of interest, discounted at the current market (effective) rate.

7. **(d)** To determine the net cash received from the bond issuance, the solutions approach is to prepare the journal entry for the issuance

Cash	?	
Discount on BP	6,000	
Bonds payable		600,000
Interest expense		15,000

The bonds were issued at 99 ($600,000 x 99% = $594,000), so the discount is $6,000 ($600,000 – $594,000). The accrued interest covers the three months from 4/1 to 7/1 ($600,000 x 10% x 3/12 = $15,000). The cash received includes the $594,000 for the bonds and the $15,000 for the accrued interest, for a total of $609,000.

8. **(d)** SFAS 91 states that engraving and printing costs, legal and accounting fees, commissions, promotion costs, and other similar costs should be recorded as bond issue costs and amortized over the term of the bonds. All the costs given are bond issue costs, so the amount reported as bond issue costs is $245,000 ($20,000 + $25,000 + $200,000).

9. **(b)** Bond issue costs are treated as deferred charges and amortized on a straight-line basis over the life of the bond. These five-year bonds were issued five months late (4/1/02 to 8/31/02), so they will be outstanding only fifty-five months (60 – 5). During 2002, the bonds were outstanding for four months (8/31/02 to 12/31/02). Therefore, the bond issue costs must be amortized for four months out of fifty-five months total, resulting in bond issue expense of $240 ($3,300 x 4/55).

10. **(b)** Interest payable reported in the 12/31/02 balance sheet would consist of interest due from the bond date (10/1/02) to the year-end (12/31/02); in other words, three months' interest. The formula for interest payable is

$$\begin{pmatrix}\text{Face}\\\text{value}\end{pmatrix} \times \begin{pmatrix}\text{Stated}\\\text{rate}\end{pmatrix} \times \begin{pmatrix}\text{Time}\\\text{period}\end{pmatrix} = \begin{pmatrix}\text{Interest}\\\text{payable}\end{pmatrix}$$

$$\$800,000 \quad \times \quad 8\% \quad \times \quad 3/12 \quad = \quad \$16,000$$

This amount would result from two entries.

Issuance

Cash	705,333	
Discount on BP	100,000	
Bonds payable		800,000
Int. payable		5,333 (800,000 x 8% x 1/12)

Adjusting entry

Interest expense	11,667	(700,000 x 10% x 2/12)
Int. payable		10,667 (800,000 x 8% x 2/12)
Discount on BP		1,000

11. **(c)** A bond premium must be amortized using the interest method or the straight-line method if the results are not materially different. To use the straight-line method, the amount of time the bonds will be outstanding must be known. Since this time period is not given, the interest method must be used. Under the interest method, interest expense is computed as follows:

$$\begin{pmatrix}\text{BV of}\\\text{bonds}\end{pmatrix} \times \begin{pmatrix}\text{Yield}\\\text{rate}\end{pmatrix} \times \begin{pmatrix}\text{Time}\\\text{period}\end{pmatrix} = \begin{pmatrix}\text{Interest}\\\text{expense}\end{pmatrix}$$

$$\$103,288 \quad \times \quad 10\% \quad \times \quad 6/12 \quad = \quad \$5,164$$

The interest payable at 12/31/02 is $6,000 ($100,000 x 12% x 6/12), so the 12/31/02 journal entry is

Interest expense	5,164	
Premium on BP	836	
Interest payable		6,000

12. (b)   Under the effective interest method, interest expense is computed as follows:

$$\begin{pmatrix} BV\ of \\ bonds \end{pmatrix} \times \begin{pmatrix} Yield \\ rate \end{pmatrix} \times \begin{pmatrix} Time \\ period \end{pmatrix} = \begin{pmatrix} Interest \\ expense \end{pmatrix}$$

$$\$469,500 \quad \times \quad 10\% \quad \times \quad 6/12 \quad = \quad \$23,475$$

The cash interest payable is computed below.

$$\begin{pmatrix} FV\ of \\ bonds \end{pmatrix} \times \begin{pmatrix} Stated \\ rate \end{pmatrix} \times \begin{pmatrix} Time \\ period \end{pmatrix} = \begin{pmatrix} Interest \\ payable \end{pmatrix}$$

$$\$500,000 \quad \times \quad 9\% \quad \times \quad 6/12 \quad = \quad \$22,500$$

The bond discount amortization is the difference between these two amounts computed above ($23,475 – $22,500 = $975). This amortization would increase the carrying amount of the bonds to $470,475 ($469,500 original carrying amount + $975 amortization).

13. (c)   Under the effective interest method, interest expense is computed as follows:

$$\begin{pmatrix} CA\ of \\ bonds \end{pmatrix} \times \begin{pmatrix} Yield \\ rate \end{pmatrix} \times \begin{pmatrix} Time \\ period \end{pmatrix} = \begin{pmatrix} Interest \\ expense \end{pmatrix}$$

$$\$105,000 \quad \times \quad 6\% \quad \times \quad 12/12 \quad = \quad \$6,300$$

The cash interest payable is computed as follows:

$$\begin{pmatrix} FV\ of \\ bonds \end{pmatrix} \times \begin{pmatrix} Stated \\ rate \end{pmatrix} \times \begin{pmatrix} Time \\ period \end{pmatrix} = \begin{pmatrix} Cash \\ interest \end{pmatrix}$$

$$\$100,000 \quad \times \quad 7\% \quad \times \quad 12/12 \quad = \quad \$7,000$$

The bond premium amortization is the difference between these two amounts ($7,000 – $6,300 = $700). Therefore, the unamortized premium at 6/30/03 is $4,300 ($5,000 – $700).

14. (d)   Under the accrual basis of accounting, expenses should be recognized when incurred, regardless of when cash is paid. Therefore, expense from the bond issue date (6/1/01) through year-end (12/31/02) should be recognized in 2002.

The seven months (6/1/02 - 12/31/02) of interest expense would be the net effect of entries prepared on the issuance date, the October 1 interest date, and December 31 (adjusting entry).

15. (b)   The requirement is to determine whether the amount of amortization increases each year using the interest method when a bond is sold either at a discount or premium or both. Using the interest method, interest expense for the period is based on the carrying value of the bond multiplied by the effective rate of interest. Cash interest paid for the period equals the face value of the bond multiplied by the stated rate of interest. The difference between these two resulting figures is the amortization of the discount or premium each period. The solutions approach is to prepare a table for a bond issued at a discount and at a premium and examine the direction of the successive amortization amounts. Consider $100,000 of 8% bonds issued on January 1, 2002, due on January 1, 2009, with interest payable each July 1 and January 1. Investors wish to obtain a yield of 10% on the issue. The amortization for the first two periods is as follows:

Dates	Credit cash	Debit interest expense	Credit bond discount	Carrying value of bonds
1/1/02				$92,278
7/1/02	$4,000	$4,614	$614	92,892
1/1/03	4,000	4,645	645	93,537

Assume the same facts, except the investors wish to obtain a yield of only 6% on the issue.

Dates	Credit cash	Debit interest expense	Credit bond discount	Carrying value of bonds
1/1/02				$108,530
7/1/02	$4,000	$3,256	$744	107,786
1/1/03	4,000	3,234	766	107,020

The above tables show that when bonds are sold at either a discount or a premium, the amount of amortization using the interest method will increase each year.

16. (b)   Using the effective interest method, interest expense is computed as the **carrying amount** of the bonds multiplied by the **effective rate** of interest. Cash interest paid equals the **face value** of the bonds multiplied by the **stated rate** of interest. The difference between interest expense and cash interest paid is discount amortization. When bonds are issued at a discount, the carrying amount increases each year, so interest expense increases each year, which causes a larger difference between interest expense and interest paid. Therefore, under the effective interest method, the discount amortization amount increases yearly. Under the straight-line method, discount amortization is constant each period. After one year, the incorrect use of the straight-line method would overstate the carrying amount of the bonds since more discount would have been amortized than under the effective interest method. By the time the bonds mature at 1/2/08, the entire discount would have been amortized under both methods, so the carrying amount would be the same for both methods.

17. (b)   The 12/31/02 bond sinking fund balance ($450,000) was increased by the additional investment ($90,000), dividends ($15,000), and interest ($30,000). It was decreased by administration costs ($5,000), resulting in a 12/31/03 balance of $580,000 ($450,000 + $90,000 + $15,000 + $30,000 – $5,000).

18. (d)   SFAS 47 requires disclosure at the balance sheet date of future payments for sinking fund requirements and maturity amounts of long-term debt during each of the next five years. Therefore, the combined aggregate of $17,500,000 of maturities and sinking fund requirements detailed by year should be disclosed.

19. (d)   Companies sometimes place assets in segregated funds for special needs. These funds may become unavailable for normal operations due to debt covenants or other contractual requirements. Funds segregated for long-term needs, such as the bond sinking fund established in this problem, are reported as investments in the noncurrent section of the balance sheet. When interest is earned on investments held in a bond sinking fund, the following journal entry would be made:

| Bond sinking fund cash | (revenue earned) | |
| Bond sinking fund revenue | | (revenue earned) |

The debit to the bond sinking fund increases the balance of the fund. The amount credited to bond sinking fund revenue is reported in the "Other Income (Expense)" section of the income statement.

20. (a)   Businesses occasionally accumulate a fund of cash and/or investments for a specific purpose, such as the retirement of bonds in this problem. These funds are referred to as "sinking funds." The sinking fund is increased when periodic additions are made to the fund and when revenue is earned on the investments held in the fund. When cash is used to purchase investments, the components of the fund change (i.e., cash is invested and replaced by bonds or other securities), but the total fund balance is not affected.

21. (c)   Debt and equity securities that are classified as **trading securities** are reported at fair market value, with unrealized gains and losses included in earnings. Therefore, at 12/31/02 Wynn would recognize an unrealized holding gain of $35,000 ($945,000 – $910,000) on the income statement, and report the securities at their fair market value of $945,000. In accordance with SFAS 115, securities classified as trading securities are reported at fair market value on the balance sheet.

22. (b)   Interest **receivable** on an investment in bonds is computed using the basic interest formula

$$\begin{pmatrix} \text{Face} \\ \text{value} \end{pmatrix} \times \begin{pmatrix} \text{Stated} \\ \text{rate} \end{pmatrix} \times \begin{pmatrix} \text{Time} \\ \text{period} \end{pmatrix} = \begin{pmatrix} \text{Interest} \\ \text{receivable} \end{pmatrix}$$

$$\$500{,}000 \times 8\% \times 6/12 = \$20{,}000$$

Note that interest **revenue** is $23,075 ($461,500 x 10% x 6/12) using the interest method.

23. (d)   The bonds should be recorded at an original cost of $215,000 ($220,000 less accrued interest of $5,000). The premium of $15,000 is amortized using the straight-line method over the period from the 10/1/01 date of purchase to the 1/1/08 maturity date (seventy-five months). By 12/31/02, amortization has been recorded for fifteen months (10/1/01 to 12/31/02), so total amortization is $3,000 ($15,000 x 15/75). Therefore, the bonds should be reported on the 12/31/02 balance sheet at $212,000 ($215,000 – $3,000).

24. (a)   When using the interest method of amortization, interest revenue is computed as follows:

$$\begin{pmatrix} \text{BV of} \\ \text{bonds} \end{pmatrix} \times \begin{pmatrix} \text{Yield} \\ \text{rate} \end{pmatrix} \times \begin{pmatrix} \text{Time} \\ \text{period} \end{pmatrix} = \begin{pmatrix} \text{Interest} \\ \text{expense} \end{pmatrix}$$

$$\$906{,}000 \times 10\% \times 6/12 = \$45{,}300$$

The initial BV is the total amount paid less the accrued interest ($946,000 – $40,000 = $906,000). The amount of interest receivable for the six months is computed below.

$$\begin{pmatrix} \text{FV of} \\ \text{bonds} \end{pmatrix} \times \begin{pmatrix} \text{Stated} \\ \text{rate} \end{pmatrix} \times \begin{pmatrix} \text{Time} \\ \text{period} \end{pmatrix} = \begin{pmatrix} \text{Interest} \\ \text{receivable} \end{pmatrix}$$

$$\$1{,}000{,}000 \times 8\% \times 6/12 = \$40{,}000$$

The discount amortized at 12/31/02 is the difference in these two amounts ($45,300 – $40,000 = $5,300). This increases the book value of the investment to $911,300 ($906,000 + $5,300).

25. (d)   The requirement is to determine the most likely cause of the decline in the bonds' market value. When the bonds were acquired at a premium, they sold above their face value. This meant that the stated rate of the bonds was greater than the market rate of interest on an alternative investment of equal risk. Thus, the investors paid more than the face value to acquire the bonds. However, when bonds are quoted at a discount, the stated rate of the bonds is less than the market rate. Therefore, the market rate of interest has increased since Lee purchased the bonds.

26. (d)   At any point in time, an investor's carrying value of a bond held as a long-term investment is equal to the par value of the bond, plus the amount of the unamortized premium, or less the amount of the unamortized discount. A bond purchased at a premium, thus, has a higher carrying value at any point in time than if it had been purchased at a discount. This is logical since its initial cost is also higher when purchased at a premium.

Having determined that the bond purchased at a premium will result in the highest carrying value, we must now determine which amortization method will result in the higher carrying value at the end of the first year. Under the straight-line method, the periodic amortization is constant; it is computed by dividing the total premium by the number of periods involved. Under the effective interest method, the periodic amortization changes over the term of the bond. A review of amortization tables for bonds issued at a premium will demonstrate that the periodic amortization of the premium is lowest in the first period, but increases over subsequent periods. Therefore, the straight-line method would result in higher amortization of the premium at the end of the first year than under the effective interest method. The higher amortization would result in a smaller unamortized premium and lower, overall carrying value at the end of the first year under the straight-line method than under the effective interest method.

27. (c)   The requirement is to determine the purchase price of a bond which will yield the highest interest income for the investor. If the bond's market rate of interest on the date of acquisition is different than the stated rate, the bonds will sell at a premium or discount. If the market rate of interest is higher than the bond's stated rate, the purchase price will be lower than the face value (i.e., discounted). The discount will be recognized over the life of the investment as an addition to interest income. Annual interest income will equal the cash interest received plus the discount amortization for the year. If the bonds are purchased at par (face value), the interest income will equal the cash interest received. The interest income for a bond purchased at a premium would equal the cash interest received less the premium amortization for the year.

28. (c)   When a company uses the effective interest method to amortize a discount on bonds payable, interest expense (which is based on the carrying value of the bonds) is lower in earlier years when compared to interest expense under the straight-line method. Therefore, the straight-line method results in higher interest expense, lower net income, and **understated** retained earnings. Since more interest expense is recorded under the straight-line method, amortization of the discount on bonds payable will be greater under the straight-line method when compared to the effective-interest method. Therefore, the carrying amount of the bonds under the straight-line method is **overstated**.

29. (b)   The gain on sale of the bond investment is the excess of the selling price over the carrying amount. The selling price was $14,000 **above** face value. The bonds were purchased at a discount of $10,000, but after amortization of $2,000 the carrying amount at the time of sale was $8,000 **below** face value. Therefore, the selling price exceeded the carrying amount by $22,000 ($14,000 premium + $8,000 remaining discount).

B.5. Convertible Bonds

30. (b) Using the book value method, the common stock is recorded at the carrying amount of the converted bonds, less any conversion expenses. Since there are no conversion expenses in this case, the common stock is recorded at the $1,300,000 carrying amount of the converted bonds. The par value of the stock issued is $50,000 (50,000 x $1), so additional paid-in capital (APIC) of $1,250,000 ($1,300,000 – $50,000) is recorded. The entry is

Bonds payable	1,000,000	
Premium on B.P.	300,000	
Common stock		50,000
APIC		1,250,000

Note that when the book value method is used, FMV are not considered, and no gain or loss is recognized.

31. (a) Under the book value method, the common stock will be recorded at the book value of the bonds at the date of conversion. Thus, no gain or loss is recognized on the conversion. The conversion entry credits common stock and APIC, which increases stockholders' equity. The amount of additional paid-in capital is the difference between the book value of the bonds and the par value of the stock. The effect of the conversion would be to increase the APIC. The conversion has no effect on retained earnings. No gain or loss is recognized.

32. (d) Per APB 14, convertible debt securities which may be converted into common stock at the option of the holder, and whose issue price is not significantly greater than face value, should be reported as debt upon issuance for the entire proceeds of the bonds. This reasoning is based on the inseparability of the debt and the conversion option, and the mutually exclusive options of the holder (i.e., holding either bonds or stock). Contributed capital would be recorded only upon conversion of the bonds to common stock.

33. (c) When the **book value method** of accounting for the conversion of bonds into common stock is used, the common stock will be recorded at the book value of the bonds at the date of conversion. Thus, no gain or loss is recognized on the conversion. When the **market value method** of accounting for the conversion is used, the following journal entry would be made on the books of the issuer (assuming market value > book value):

Loss on redemption	(plug)	
Bonds payable	(book value)	
Common stock		(par)
APIC-common stock		(mkt.-par)

The debit to the loss account would be for the difference between the market value of the stock and the book value of the bonds. The market value method assumes a culmination of the earnings process, and a gain or loss on the conversion may be recognized. In this case, the market value of the stock exceeds the book value of the bonds, and a loss is recognized.

B.6. Debt Issued with Detachable Purchase Warrants

34. (c) APB 14 states that the proceeds of bonds issued with **detachable** warrants are allocated between the bonds and the warrants based upon their relative FMV at the time of issuance. In this case, the portion allocated to the bonds is $900,000, calculated as follows:

$$\frac{\$1,080,000}{\$1,080,000 + \$120,000} = 90\%; \ 90\% \ x \ \$1,000,000 = \$900,000$$

Therefore, the bonds payable are reported at $900,000 (face value $1,000,000 less discount $100,000).

35. (c) APB 14 states that the proceeds from the issuance of debt with **detachable** stock warrants should be allocated between the debt and equity elements. 1,000 bonds ($1,000,000 ÷ $1,000) were issued with fifty detachable stock warrants each, for a total of 50,000 warrants. Paid-in capital from stock warrants is $200,000 (50,000 x $4). Since the bonds and warrants were issued for $1,090,000 ($1,000,000 x 109%), the portion of the proceeds allocated to the bonds is $890,000 ($1,090,000 – $200,000) and the discount is $110,000 ($1,000,000 – $890,000). Note that if a FMV is given for the **bonds without warrants,** APB 14 states that the proceeds should be allocated between the bonds and warrants based on their relative FMV at the time of issuance.

36. (d) APB 14 states that the proceeds from the issuance of debt with **detachable** stock warrants should be allocated between the debt and equity elements. 500 bonds ($500,000 ÷ $1,000) were issued with thirty detachable stock warrants each, for a total of 15,000 warrants. Paid-in capital from stock warrants is $60,000 (15,000 x $4). Note that if a FMV was given for the **bonds without warrants,** APB 14 states that the proceeds should be allocated between the bonds and warrants based on their relative FMV at the time of issuance.

37. (a) The solutions approach is to set up the original journal entry on the books of the issuer. The entry would be made as follows:

Cash	(proceeds)	
Discount on bonds payable	(plug)	
Bonds payable		(face)
APIC—Stock warrants		(fair value)

Since the APIC—Stock warrants account is already stated at market value, any remaining difference must be allocated to the **bonds**. Bonds payable would be credited only at their face (par) value. Therefore, Discount on bonds payable is debited for the excess of the fair value of the warrants and the face amount of the bonds over cash proceeds.

38. (c) Bonds issued with stock purchase warrants are, in substance, composed of two elements: a debt element, and a stockholders' equity element. Per APB 14, proceeds from bonds issued with **detachable** stock purchase warrants should be allocated between the bonds and the warrants on the basis of their relative fair market values. Detachable warrants trade separately from the debt; thus, a market value is available. The amount allocated to the warrants should be accounted for as paid-in capital. Bonds issued with **nondetachable** stock purchase warrants must be surrendered in order to exercise the warrants. Since this inseparability prevents the determination of individual market values, no allocation is permitted under APB 14.

B.7. Extinguishment of Debt

39. (b) A gain or loss on redemption of bonds is the difference between the **cash paid** ($5,000,000 x 98% = $4,900,000) and the **net book value of the bonds**. To compute the net book value, premium or discount and bond issue costs must be considered. Book value is $4,980,000 ($5,000,000 face value, less $50,000 bond issue costs, plus $30,000 premium). Therefore the gain or redemption is $80,000 ($4,980,000 book value less $4,900,000 cash paid).

40.   (d)   The gain on early extinguishment of debt is the excess of the book value of the bonds at the time of retirement over the cash paid ($1,000,000 x 101% = $1,010,000). On 1/1/97, the original balance in the premium account was $40,000 ($1,040,000 − $1,000,000). At 7/1/02, the premium had been amortized for five and one-half years, or eleven six-month periods (1/1/97 to 7/1/02). Since the bond term was ten years, or twenty six-month periods, the total premium amortized was $22,000 ($40,000 x 11/20). Therefore, the unamortized premium was $18,000 ($40,000 − $22,000) and the book value of the bonds was $1,018,000 ($1,000,000 + $18,000). A shortcut approach is to take the 1/1/97 book value ($1,040,000) and subtract the amortization ($22,000) to determine the 7/1/02 book value of $1,018,000. The gain is $8,000 ($1,018,000 book value less $1,010,000 cash paid).

41.   (a)   The total bond discount and bond issue costs were $30,000 at the time of issuance [(.02 x $500,000) + $20,000]. By 1/1/02, twelve years have passed since the bonds were issued on 1/1/90. Since the bonds have a fifteen-year life, 12/15 of the discount and issue costs have been amortized, leaving 3/15 unamortized (3/15 x $30,000 = $6,000). When bonds are retired, the bonds and unamortized premium or discount, and/or issue costs must be removed from the books. In this situation, the difference between the net book value of the bonds ($500,000 − $6,000 = $494,000) and the cash paid ($500,000 x 1.02 = $510,000) is recognized as an extraordinary loss ($510,000 − $494,000 = $16,000).

42.   (c)   APB 30 provides general guidance on the reporting of extraordinary items. This guidance requires events and transactions that are both unusual in nature and infrequent in occurrence to be reported as extraordinary items. SFAS 4, however, amends APB 30 to the extent that classification of gains or losses from extinguishment of debt are always reported as an extraordinary item, without regard to the criteria in APB 30. When the carrying value of the old debt exceeds the amount paid to extinguish the debt, the following entry would be recorded:

Debt	(carrying value)	
Cash		(amount paid)
Extraordinary gain		(difference)

OTHER OBJECTIVE ANSWER EXPLANATIONS

Problem 1

1. **(Q; $116,400)** The "discount" column in the problem is the **unamortized** discount. The unamortized discount at any point in time is equal to the difference between the face value of the bonds ($480,000) and the carrying amount of the bonds ($363,600) at that point in time.

2. **(K; $14,400)** The cash interest is the product of the stated interest rate x the face value of the bonds. The cash interest is a constant as long as neither the stated interest rate nor the face value of the bonds changes. Since neither one has changed in the problem, the **given** amount of cash interest on 12/31/02 is the same as the missing amount of cash interest on 6/30/02.

3. **(T; $360,000)** The carrying amount is equal to the face value minus the unamortized discount. The amortization of the unamortized discount increases the carrying amount. The carrying amount was increased by the amortization of $3,600 at 6/30/02. To obtain the carrying amount at 1/2/02 one reverses the increase of $3,600 that occurred at 6/30/02. Thus

Carrying amount 6/30/02	$363,600
Reverse increase in carrying amount at 6/30/02 due to amortization of discount	(3,600)
Carrying amount 1/2/02	$360,000

4. **(D; 6.0%)** The stated interest rate is equal to cash interest $14,400 ÷ face value $480,000. $14,000 ÷ $480,000 = .03. Since the table is set up on a semiannual basis and the answer required is on an annual basis, the .03 is doubled to equal 6.0%

5. **(F; 10.0%)** Effective interest is equal to interest expense. Interest expense is the product of the effective interest rate x the carrying value at the beginning of the interest period. In this case, interest expense is $18,000; carrying amount at the beginning of the period is $360,000 (from question 3). Thus: $18,000 ÷ $360,000 = .05 for six months; .05 x 2 =.10 on an annual basis.

6. **(N; $18,180)** As stated in question 5, interest expense is the product of the effective interest rate (.05) x the carrying value at the beginning of the period $363,600. Thus: $363,600 x .05 = $18,180.

7. **(I; $3,780)** Amortization is the difference between interest expense $18,180 and cash interest $14,400. Thus: $18,180 – $14,400 = $3,780.

Problem 2

		1	2	3	4	5
I.	Bond discount	I	N	N	I	N
II.	Bond premium	N	I	D	N	N
III.	Bonds payable	I	I	D	I	N
IV.	Common stock	N	N	I	N	I
V.	Additional paid-in capital	N	N	I	I	I
VI.	Retained earnings	N	N	N	N	D

1. Since the nominal rate of interest was less than the market rate of interest, the bonds sold at a discount. In other words, the investors paid less than the face value to acquire the bonds. The journal entry to record the transaction is

Cash	xx	
Discount on bonds payable	xx	
Bonds payable		xx

Therefore, the issuance of the bonds would increase both bonds payable and discount on bonds payable.

2. Per APB 14, convertible debt securities which may be converted into common stock at the option of the holder, and whose issue price is not significantly greater than face value, should be reported as debt upon issuance for the entire proceeds of the bonds. This reasoning is based on the inseparability of the debt and the conversion option, and the mutually exclusive options of the holder (i.e., holding either bonds or stock). The journal entry to record the transaction is

Cash	xx	
Premium on bonds payable		xx
Bonds payable		xx

Therefore, the issuance of the convertible bonds would increase both bonds payable and premium on bonds payable.

3. When the book value method of accounting for the conversion of bonds into common stock is used, the common stock will be recorded at the book value of the bonds at the date of conversion. Thus, no gain or loss is recognized on the conversion. The journal entry to record the transaction is

Bonds payable	xx	
Premium on bonds payable	xx	
Common stock		xx
Additional paid-in capital		xx

Therefore, the conversion of the bonds would decrease bonds payable and premium on bonds payable while increasing common stock and additional paid-in capital.

4. APB 14 states that the proceeds of bonds issued with detachable warrants are allocated between the bonds and the warrants based upon their relative fair market values at the time of issuance. In this case, the bonds, with detachable stock warrants, were issued for an amount equal to the face amount of the bonds. Since part of the proceeds are allocated to the stock warrants, the bonds were issued at a discount. The journal entry to record the transaction is

Cash	xx	
Discount on bonds payable	xx	
Bonds payable		xx
Additional paid-in capital - Stock warrants		xx

Therefore, the issuance of the bonds, with detachable stock warrants, would increase bonds payable, discount on bonds payable, and additional paid-in capital.

5. The issuance of a "small" stock dividend (less than 20-25%) requires that the market value of the stock be transferred from retained earnings. The journal entry to record the transaction is

Retained earnings	xx	
Common stock		xx
Additional paid-in capital		xx

Therefore, a 2% stock dividend would decrease retained earnings while increasing both common stock and additional paid-in capital.

ANSWER OUTLINE

Problem 1   Issuance of Bonds

a.   1.   9% bonds issued at discount
   Stated rate (9%) < market rate (10%)
   Bonds must sell at discount to yield 10%
   (Issue price = PV) < face amount

   2.   Interest expense higher in second year than in first year
   10% effective rate applied to increasing bond carrying value each year
   Results in higher interest expense each successive year

b.   1.   Gain (loss) on early extinguishment is difference between net carrying value of bonds and acquisition price
   Net carrying value > acquisition price — gain results
   Net carrying value < acquisition price — loss results
   Early extinguishment of 9% bonds results in loss
   Bonds issued at discount
   Carrying value at date of extinguishment must be less than face value
   Acquisition price exceeds net carrying value

   2.   Report loss on early extinguishment in 2001 IS
   Extraordinary item, net of tax

c.   Proceeds from issuance increases cash
   Allocate proceeds between bonds and warrants on basis of relative FMV
   Portion allocated to bonds accounted for as LT debt
   Portion allocated to warrants accounted for as APIC

UNOFFICIAL ANSWER

Problem 1   Issuance of Bonds

a.   1.   The 9% bonds were issued at a discount (less than face amount). Although the bonds provide for payment of interest of 9% of face amount, this rate was less than the prevailing or market rate for bonds of similar quality at the time the bonds were issued. Thus, the issue price of the bonds, which is the present value of the principal and interest payments discounted at 10%, is less than the face amount.

   2.   The amount of interest expense would be higher in the second year of the life of the bond issue than in the first year of the life of the bond issue. According to the effective interest method of amortization, the 10% effective interest rate is applied to the bond carrying amount. In a discount situation, the bond carrying amount increases each year, and this results in a greater interest in each successive year.

b.   1.   Gain or loss on early extinguishment of debt should be determined by comparing the carrying amount of the bonds at the date of extinguishment with the acquisition price. If the carrying amount exceeds the acquisition price, a gain results. If the carrying amount is less than the acquisition price, a loss results.

   In this case, a loss results. The term bonds were issued at a discount. Therefore, the carrying amount of the bonds at the date of extinguishment must be less than the face amount, which is less than the acquisition price.

2.   Drew should report the loss from early extinguishment of debt in its 2002 income statement as an extraordinary item, net of income taxes.

c.   The proceeds from the issuance of the 7% nonconvertible bonds with detachable stock purchase warrants should be recorded as an increase in cash. These proceeds should be allocated between the bonds and the warrants on the basis of their relative market values. The portion of the proceeds allocable to the bonds should be accounted for as long-term debt, while the portion allocable to the warrants should be accounted for as paid-in capital.

ANSWER OUTLINE

Problem 2   Effective Interest Method; Effect of Using SL versus Effective Interest Method; Extinguishment of Debt in IS and SCF

a.   Effective interest method
   Periodic interest expense = constant percentage of BV of bonds
   In 1999, premium decrease less than if straight-line method used

b.   For 1999,
   Interest expense   —   understated
   Net income   —   overstated
   BV of bonds   —   understated

c.   Report as XO loss after income from continuing operations
   Loss = excess of FMV of cash and property transferred over BV of bonds
   Early extinguishment of debt is XO item

d.   Operating activities
   Add gross extraordinary loss to NI
   Financing activities
   Show extinguishment as cash outflow

   Significant noncash transactions
   Show noncash elements of transaction at bottom of SCF/notes to FS

UNOFFICIAL ANSWER

Problem 2   Effective Interest Method; Effect of Using SL versus Effective Interest Method; Extinguishment of Debt in IS and SCF

a.   The purpose of the effective interest method is to provide periodic interest expense based on a constant rate over the life of the bonds. The impact of applying the effective interest method on Corval's bond premium is to decrease the premium by a lesser amount in 1999 compared to using the straight-line method of amortization.

b.   Under the straight-line interest method, the premium is amortized at a constant periodic amount, and in 1999 the premium amortization would have been greater than amortization under the effective interest method. Consequently, for 1999, interest expense would have been understated, net income would have been overstated, and the carrying amount of the bonds would have been understated.

c.   The November 30, 2002 transaction is reported as an extraordinary loss after income from continuing operations. This loss equals the excess of the fair value of the cash and property transferred over the bonds' carrying amount on

November 30, 2002. This presentation is appropriate because this is an early extinguishment of debt.

d.   The gross amount of the extraordinary loss is added to
net income under cash flows from operating activities. The
cash payment is reported as a cash outflow from financing
activities.

Corval should disclose details of the noncash elements
of the transaction either on the same page as the statement of
cash flows or in the notes to the financial statements.

ANSWER OUTLINE

Problem 3   Convertible Debt and EPS

a.   1.   Issue price = Expected future cash flows discounted at market rate + Value of conversion option

2.   Accounting for issuance

Cash	(issue price)	
Bonds payable		(face amount)
Premium		(plug)

Convertible debt accounted for as debt
Conversion option not recognized

3.   Accounting for conversion

Bonds payable	(30% of balance)	
Premium	(30% of balance)	
Common stock		($25/share issued)
Additional PIC		(plug)

UNOFFICIAL ANSWER

Problem 3   Convertible Debt and EPS (592,T3)

a.   1.   The bond issue price would be determined by the
expected future cash flows of principal and interest, discounted at the market rate of interest, plus the value of the
conversion option at the date of issuance.

2.   Columbine should account for the issuance of the
convertible bonds by increasing cash for the issue price,
increasing bonds payable by the face amount, and increasing
premium on bonds payable for the balance. The convertible
debt is accounted for solely as debt. The conversion option
is not recognized primarily because it is inseparable from the
debt, and secondarily because of the practical difficulty of
assigning it a value.

3.   Columbine should account for the conversion of
the bonds into common stock by decreasing both bonds payable and unamortized bond premium by 30%, increasing
common stock by $25 for each share issued, and increasing
additional paid-in capital by the difference between the three
previous amounts.

C. Debt Restructure

SFAS 15 (see outline) prescribes accounting for debtors in situations where creditors are compelled to grant relief (i.e., restructure debt) to debtors. Two types of restructure are described. The first is a settlement of the debt at less than the carrying amount and the second is a continuation of the debt with a modification of terms.

SFAS 114 (see outline), as amended by SFAS 118, addresses the accounting by creditors for impairment of certain loans. Impaired loans include all loans that are restructured in a troubled debt restructuring involving a modification of terms.

1. **Settlement of Debt**

a. **Debtors**—If the debt is settled by the exchange of assets, an extraordinary gain is recognized for the difference between the carrying amount of the debt and the consideration given to extinguish the debt. If a noncash asset is given, a separate, ordinary gain or loss is recorded to revalue the noncash asset to FMV as the basis of the noncash asset given. Thus, a two-step process is used: (1) revalue the noncash asset to FMV and (2) determine the restructuring gain. If stock is issued to settle the liability, record the stock at FMV.

b. **Creditors**

(1) Assets received in full settlement are recorded at FMV

(a) Excess of receivable over asset FMV is an ordinary loss

(b) Subsequently account for the assets as if purchased for cash

EXAMPLE 1: SETTLEMENT OF DEBT—Debtor company transfers land in full settlement of its loan payable.

Loan payable (5 years remaining)	*$90,000*
Accrued interest payable on loan	*10,000*
Land:	
Book value	*70,000*
Fair value	*80,000*

Debtor			*Creditor*		
1. Land	*10,000*		*1. Land*	*80,000*	
Gain on transfer of			*Loss on settlement*	*20,000*	
assets		*10,000*	*Loan receivable*		*90,000*
2. Loan payable	*90,000*		*Interest receivable*		*10,000**
Interest payable	*10,000*				
Land		*80,000*			
Extraordinary gain					
on settlement of debt		*20,000*			

* *If the creditor was a bank or other finance company, this amount would be included as part of Loan receivable.*

2. **Impairment**

If the creditor determines that, based on current information and events, it is probable that they will be unable to collect all amounts due on an outstanding note receivable, then the note is considered to be impaired. The criteria for determining uncollectibility of a note should be based on the creditor's normal review procedures. When a note receivable is considered to be impaired, a loss should be recorded at the time the impairment is discovered. The loss will be based upon the difference between the current carrying value of the note and the present value of the expected future cash flows from the impaired note, discounted at the loan's contractual rate.

EXAMPLE:

On January 1, 2002, Spot Corporation issued a $100,000, three-year noninterest-bearing note to yield 10%, to Grover Corporation. On December 31, 2002, Spot Co. management determines that it is probable that Grover Co. will be unable to repay the entire note. It appears as though only $75,000 will be repaid. Using the effective interest method the impairment is calculated as follows:

Date	*10% interest*	*Carrying value*	
1/1/02	*--*	*$ 75,132*	*(present value of 100,000 at 10% for 3 periods, 100,000 x .75132)*
12/31/02	*7,513*	*82,645*	*(75,132 + 7,513)*
12/31/03	*8,265*	*90,910*	*(82,645 + 8,265)*
12/31/04	*9,090*	*100,000*	*(90,910 + 9,090)*

Carrying value at 12/31/02	*$82,645*
Present value of future receipts	
($75,000, 10%, 2 periods = $75,000 x .82645)	*61,984*
Impairment at 12/31/02	*$20,661*

The loss due to the impairment of the Grover Co. note will be recorded on the creditor's books as follows:

Bad debt expense	20,661	
Allowance for doubtful accounts		20,661

The debtor, Grover Co., should not record anything, as it still has a legal obligation to repay the entire $100,000. The future interest revenue recorded by Spot Co. will be based upon the new carrying value of $61,984. If there is a significant change in the expected future cash flows, then the impairment should be recalculated and the allowance adjusted accordingly.

3. **Modification of Terms**

   a. **Debtors**

   If the debt is continued with a modification of terms, it is necessary to compare the total future cash flows of the restructured debt (both principal and stated interest) with the prerestructured carrying value. If the total amount of future cash flows is greater than the carrying value, no adjustment is made to the carrying value of the debt; however, a new effective interest rate must be computed. This rate makes the present value of the total future cash flows equal to the present carrying value of debt (principal and accrued interest). If the total future cash flows of the restructured debt are less than the present carrying value, the current debt should be reduced to the amount of the future cash flows and an extraordinary gain should be recognized. No interest expense would be recognized in subsequent periods because the loan was written down below its carrying value. All payments including those designated as interest would be applied to the principal amount.

   If the restructuring consists of part settlement and part modification of payments, first account for the part settlement per the above, and then account for the modification of payments per the above.

   b. **Creditors**

   Under SFAS 114 a creditor measures impairment based on the present value of expected future cash flows discounted at the loan's effective interest rate. The effective interest rate for a loan restructured in a troubled debt restructuring is based on the original contractual rate, not the rate specified in the restructuring agreement. As a practical expedient, a creditor may measure impairment based on a loan's observable market price, or the fair value of the collateral if the loan is collateral dependent. A loan is collateral dependent if the repayment of the loan is expected to be provided solely by the underlying collateral.

   If the measure of the impaired loan is less than the recorded investment in the loan (including accrued interest, net deferred loan fees or costs, and unamortized premium or discount), a creditor shall recognize an impairment by creating a valuation allowance with a corresponding charge to bad debt expense or by adjusting an existing valuation allowance for the impaired loan with a corresponding charge or credit to bad debt expense.

   The present value of an impaired loan's expected future cash flows will change from one reporting period to the next because of the passage of time and also may change because of revised estimates in the amount or timing of those cash flows. No guidance is provided on how the creditor should recognize the change in the present value.

   The following example of the treatment of modification of terms for creditors demonstrates the accounting for the **debtor** under SFAS 15 and for the **creditor** under SFAS 114.

   EXAMPLE 2: MODIFICATION OF TERMS—GAIN/LOSS RECOGNIZED—Assume the interest rate on above loan is 5% and the following modification of terms is made:

   1. *Interest rate is reduced to 4%.*
   2. *The accrued interest is forgiven.*
   3. *The principal at date of restructure is reduced to $80,000.*

   Debtor

Future cash flows (after restructuring):	
Principal	$80,000
Interest (5 years x $80,000 x 4%; $3,200 per year)	+ 16,000
Total cash to be received	$96,000
Amount prior to restructure	
($90,000 principal + $10,000 accrued interest)	– 100,000
Extraordinary gain to be recognized	$ 4,000

Analysis of Debtor's Loan Payable Account

Gain	4,000			
	3,200*		90,000	Loan payable before modification
4% modified interest	3,200			of terms
payments in years 1-5	3,200			
	3,200		10,000	Additional amount payable from
	3,200			accrued interest
				Bal. before principal pay 80,000

* Note that the $3,200 is recorded as a reduction of principal, not as an interest expense.

Creditor

Present value of future cash flows (after restructuring) discounted at the original effective interest rate of 5% for the 5
years remaining:

Principal ($80,000 x .78353)**	$ 62,682
Interest ($80,000 x 4% x 4.32948)***	13,854
Present value of future cash flows	$ 76,536
Recorded investment in loan by creditor	$100,000
Present value of future cash flows after restructuring	76,536
Impairment loan loss to be recognized by creditor	$ 23,464

** PV of 1 for 5 periods at 5%.
*** PV of ordinary annuity for 5 periods at 5%.

Debtor (SFAS 15)			Creditor (SFAS 114)		
Beginning of Year 1			**Beginning of Year 1**		
Interest payable	10,000		Bad debt expense	23,464	
Loan payable	4,000		Loan receivable		10,000
Loan payable		10,000	Accrued interest receivable		10,000
Extraordinary gain on			Valuation allowance for impaired		
restructure of debt		4,000	loans		3,464
End of Year 1			**End of Year 1**		
Loan payable	3,200		Cash	3,200	
Cash		3,200	Valuation allowance for impaired loans	627	
			Interest revenue/bad debts expense		3,827*
			* [($80,000 – $3,464)] x 5% = $3,827		
End of Year 2			**End of Year 2**		
Loan payable	3,200		Cash	3,200	
Cash		3,200	Valuation allowance for impaired loans	658	
			Interest revenue/bad debts expense		3,858*
			* [$80,000 – ($3,464 – $627)] x 5% = $3,858		
End of Year 3			**End of Year 3**		
Loan payable	3,200		Cash	3,200	
Cash		3,200	Valuation allowance for impaired loans	691	
			Interest revenue/bad debts expense		3,891*
			* [$80,000 – ($3,464 – $627 – $658)] x 5% = $3,891		
End of Year 4			**End of Year 4**		
Loan payable	3,200		Cash	3,200	
Cash		3,200	Valuation allowance for impaired loans	726	
			Interest revenue/bad debts expense		3,926*
			* [$80,000 – ($3,464 – $627 – $658 – $691)] x 5% = $3,926		
End of Year 5			**End of Year 5**		
Loan payable	3,200		Cash	3,200	
Cash		3,200	Valuation allowance for impaired loans	762	
			Interest revenue/bad debts expense		3,962*
			* [$80,000 – ($3,464 – $627 – $658 – $691 – $726)] x 5% = $3,962		
Loan payable	80,000		Cash	80,000	
Cash		80,000	Loan receivable		80,000

NOTE: This example does not include any future changes in the amount and timing of future cash flows, due to the
complexity of the accounting.

EXAMPLE 3: MODIFICATION OF TERMS—NO GAIN RECOGNIZED BY DEBTOR—Assume the $90,000 principal is reduced to $85,000. The interest rate of 5% is reduced to 4%.

Future cash flows (after restructuring):	
Principal	$ 85,000
Interest (5 years x $85,000 x 4%)	17,000
Total cash to be received	$102,000
Amount prior to restructure:	
($90,000 principal + $10,000 accrued interest)	– 100,000
Interest expense/revenue to be recognized over 5 years	$ 2,000

In Example 3, a new effective interest rate must be computed so that the PV of future payments = $100,000. A trial and error approach would be used. For the exam, you need to be prepared to describe this process and the related entries, but you will not have to make such a computation.

End of Year 1-5

		Debtor	
Loan payable		xxxx	
Interest expense		xxx	
Cash			3,400

End of Year 5

Loan payable		85,000	
Cash			85,000

NOTE: x's equal different amounts each year based on effective interest rate computed.

By Creditor—The creditor would account for the modification in the same way as in the previous example that shows the SFAS 114 approach. That is, the original effective rate would be used to measure the loss.

To summarize the two basic situations

1. **Settlement of debt:** The debtor transfers assets or grants an equity interest to the creditor in full satisfaction of the claim. Both debtor and creditor account for the fair values of assets transferred and equity interest granted. A gain or loss is recognized on the asset transferred. The debtor recognizes a gain and the creditor recognizes a loss for the difference between the recorded value of the debt and the fair values accounted for.

2. **Restructuring of the debt:** Under SFAS 15, the terms of the debt are modified in order to reduce or defer cash payments that the debtor is obligated to make to the creditor, but the debt itself is continued. The debtor accounts for the modification of terms as a reduction in interest expense from the date of restructuring until maturity. Gains and losses will generally not be recognized unless the total future cash payments specified by the new terms are less than the recorded amount of the debt. Then the debtor would recognize a gain for the difference. The debtor's gain is considered extraordinary. Under SFAS 114, the creditor accounts for a restructuring using the original effective rate to measure losses.

Refer to the outlines of SFAS 15 and SFAS 114 for the disclosure requirements.

MULTIPLE-CHOICE QUESTIONS (1-8)

1. For a troubled debt restructuring involving only a modification of terms, which of the following items specified by the new terms would be compared to the carrying amount of the debt to determine if the debtor should report a gain on restructuring?

a. The total future cash payments.
b. The present value of the debt at the original interest rate.
c. The present value of the debt at the modified interest rate.
d. The amount of future cash payments designated as principal repayments.

Items 2 and 3 are based on the following:

The following information pertains to the transfer of real estate pursuant to a troubled debt restructuring by Knob Co. to Mene Corp. in full liquidation of Knob's liability to Mene:

Carrying amount of liability liquidated	$150,000
Carrying amount of real estate transferred	100,000
Fair value of real estate transferred	90,000

2. What amount should Knob report as a pretax extraordinary gain (loss) on restructuring of payables?

a. $(10,000)
b. $0
c. $50,000
d. $60,000

3. What amount should Knob report as ordinary gain (loss) on transfer of real estate?

a. $(10,000)
b. $0
c. $50,000
d. $60,000

4. On October 15, 2002, Kam Corp. informed Finn Co. that Kam would be unable to repay its $100,000 note due on October 31 to Finn. Finn agreed to accept title to Kam's computer equipment in full settlement of the note. The equipment's carrying value was $80,000 and its fair value was $75,000. Kam's tax rate is 30%. What amounts should Kam report as ordinary gain (loss) and extraordinary gain for the year ended September 30, 2003?

	Ordinary gain (loss)	Extraordinary gain
a.	$(5,000)	$17,500
b.	$0	$20,000
c.	$0	$14,000
d.	$20,000	$0

5. Colt, Inc. is indebted to Kent under an $800,000, 10%, four-year note dated December 31, 1999. Annual interest of $80,000 was paid on December 31, 2000 and 2001. During 2002, Colt experienced financial difficulties and is likely to default unless concessions are made. On December 31, 2002, Kent agreed to restructure the debt as follows:

• Interest of $80,000 for 2002, due December 31, 2002, was made payable December 31, 2003.
• Interest for 2003 was waived.
• The principal amount was reduced to $700,000.

Assuming an income tax rate of 40%, how much should Colt report as extraordinary gain in its income statement for the year ended December 31, 2002?

a. $0
b. $ 60,000
c. $100,000
d. $108,000

6. Grey Company holds an overdue note receivable of $800,000 plus recorded accrued interest of $64,000. The effective interest rate is 8%. As the result of a court-imposed settlement on December 31, 2002, Grey agreed to the following restructuring arrangement:

• Reduced the principal obligation to $600,000.
• Forgave the $64,000 accrued interest.
• Extended the maturity date to December 31, 2004.
• Annual interest of $40,000 is to be paid to Grey on December 31, 2003 and 2004.

The present value of the interest and principal payments to be received by Grey Company discounted for two years at 8% is $585,734. On December 31, 2002, Grey would recognize a valuation allowance for impaired loans of

a. $ 14,266
b. $184,000
c. $278,266
d. $0

7. On December 31, 2000, Marsh Company entered into a debt restructuring agreement with Saxe Company, which was experiencing financial difficulties. Marsh restructured a $100,000 note receivable as follows:

• Reduced the principal obligation to $70,000.
• Forgave $12,000 of accrued interest.
• Extended the maturity date from December 31, 2000 to December 31, 2002.
• Reduced the interest rate from 12% to 8%. Interest was payable annually on December 31, 2001 and 2002.

Present value factors:

Single sum, two years @ 8%	.85734
Single sum, two years @ 12%	.79719
Ordinary annuity, two years @ 8%	1.78326
Ordinary annuity, two years @ 12%	1.69005

In accordance with the agreement, Saxe made payments to Marsh on December 31, 2001 and 2002. How much interest income should Marsh report for the year ended December 31, 2002?

a. $0
b. $ 5,600
c. $ 8,100
d. $11,200

8. Casey Corp. entered into a troubled debt restructuring agreement with First State Bank. First State agreed to accept land with a carrying amount of $85,000 and a fair value of $120,000 in exchange for a note with a carrying amount of $185,000. Disregarding income taxes, what amount should Casey report as extraordinary gain in its income statement?

a. $0
b. $ 35,000
c. $ 65,000
d. $100,000

MULTIPLE-CHOICE ANSWERS

| 1. a __ __ | 3. a __ __ | 5. b __ __ | 7. c __ __ | 1st: __/8 = __% |
| 2. d __ __ | 4. a __ __ | 6. a __ __ | 8. c __ __ | 2nd: __/8 = __% |

MULTIPLE-CHOICE ANSWER EXPLANATIONS

C. Debt Restructure

1. **(a)** In a restructuring involving only a change in terms, the total future cash payments should be compared to the carrying amount to determine if a gain should be recognized. Answers (b) and (c) are incorrect because the undiscounted future cash flows are compared to the carrying amount. Answer (d) is incorrect because the total amount of future cash flows are compared to the carrying amount.

2. **(d)** In this restructure, the debt is retired by the transfer of real estate to the creditor. Per SFAS 15, an ordinary operating gain or loss is recognized on the transfer of real estate, and an extraordinary gain or loss is recognized on the restructuring. The ordinary loss is the excess of the real estate's carrying amount over its FMV ($100,000 – $90,000 = $10,000). The extraordinary gain is the excess of the carrying amount of the liability over the FMV of the real estate transferred, net of the related tax effect. The pretax extraordinary gain is $60,000 ($150,000 – $90,000). The journal entry is

Liability	150,000	
Loss on transfer	10,000	
Real estate		100,000
X/O gain		60,000

3. **(a)** In this restructure, the debt is retired by the transfer of real estate to the creditor. Per SFAS 15, an ordinary operating gain or loss is recognized on the transfer of real estate, and an extraordinary gain or loss is recognized on the restructuring. The ordinary loss is the excess of the real estate's carrying amount over its FMV ($100,000 – $90,000 = $10,000). The extraordinary gain is the excess of the carrying amount of the liability over the FMV of the real estate transferred, net of the related tax effect. The pretax extraordinary gain is $60,000 ($150,000 – $90,000). The journal entry is

Liability	150,000	
Loss on transfer	10,000	
Real estate		100,000
X/O gain		60,000

4. **(a)** In this restructure, the debt is retired by the transfer of equipment to the creditor. Per SFAS 15, an ordinary operating gain or loss is recognized on the transfer of the equipment, and an extraordinary gain or loss is recognized on the retirement of the debt. The ordinary loss is the excess of the equipment's carrying amount over its fair value ($80,000 – $75,000 = $5,000). The extraordinary gain is the excess of the carrying amount of the debt over the fair value of the equipment transferred, net of the related tax effect [$100,000 – $75,000 = $25,000; $25,000 – (30% x $25,000) = $17,500].

5. **(b)** The requirement is to determine the amount of extraordinary gain to be recognized from a troubled debt restructure. According to SFAS 15, if the debt is continued with a modification of terms, an extraordinary gain is recognized by the debtor if the future cash payments on the debt are less than the carrying value of the debt. For troubled debt restructures, carrying value is defined as the principal amount ($800,000) plus accrued interest ($80,000), or $880,000. The future payments total $780,000 ($700,000 reduced principal and $80,000 interest). The $100,000 difference ($880,000 – $780,000) is recognized as an extraordinary gain, net of the related tax effect [$100,000 – (40% x $100,000) = $60,000]. The following entry would be made:

Notes payable	800,000	
Interest payable	80,000	
Notes payable (restructured amt)		780,000
Extraordinary gain		100,000

6. **(a)** Under SFAS 114, if the present value of future cash flows is less than the carrying amount of the loan (Principal + Accrued interest) then bad debt expense should be recorded for the total impairment, the accrued interest account should be written off, and the principal balance in the loan receivable account should be reduced to reflect any amounts forgiven. Any remaining balance should be recorded in an allowance account, as follows:

Present value of interest and principal payments to be received by Grey Company (as stated in the problem)	585,734
Recorded investment by Grey Company ($800,000 principal + $64,000 interest)	864,000
Less present value of future cash flows	(585,734)
	278,266

Bad debt expense	278,266	
Loan receivable		200,000
Accrued interest receivable		64,000
Valuation allowance for impaired loans		14,266

Thus, under SFAS 114, the valuation allowance Grey must recognize is $14,266.

7. **(c)** The requirement is to determine the amount of interest revenue to be recorded by Marsh, after a modification of terms type of troubled debt restructure on December 31, 2000.

Under SFAS 114, when a modification of terms results in the present value of future cash flows being less than the carrying amount, then the interest revenue is calculated by using the effective interest method. In this problem the expected future cash flows is determined by discounting the principal and interest at the original effective rate of 12%.

70,000	x	.79719	=	55,803
5,600	x	1.69005	=	9,464
Present value of future cash flows				65,267

The interest revenue to be recognized can then be determined using the effective interest method.

PV at 12/31/00		$65,267
Interest income at 12/31/01 ($65,267 x 12%)	$7,832	
Interest receivable at 12/31/01 (70,000 x 8%)	5,600	
Increase in carrying value of loan		2,232
PV at 12/31/00		67,499
Interest revenue at 12/31/02 (67,499 x 12%)	$8,100	

8. **(c)** If a debt is settled by the exchange of assets, an extraordinary gain is recognized for the difference between the carrying amount of the debt and the fair value of the consideration given to extinguish the debt. If a noncash asset is given, a separate ordinary gain or loss is recorded to

revalue the nonasset to fair market value as the basis of the
noncash asset given. Therefore, an ordinary gain of $35,000
($120,000 – $85,000) will be recorded to revalue the land to
fair market value, and an extraordinary gain of $65,000
($185,000 – $120,000) will be recorded for the extinguishment of the debt in Casey's income statement.

Keep practicing! Wiley's CPA Examination Review Software has over 2,800 questions.

Available at www.wiley.com/cpa

D. Pensions

Accounting for pensions involves the use of special terminology. Mastery of this terminology is essential both to an understanding of problem requirements and to the ability to respond correctly to theory questions. Review the definitions at the beginning of the outline of SFAS 87 before proceeding with this section of the module. When you are finished with this section, review the remaining portion of the outline of SFAS 87. Additionally, you should look over the contents of SFAS 88 and SFAS 132; SFAS 88 has been tested lightly. SFAS 132 deals solely with employer disclosures about pensions and other postretirement benefits. It amends Statements 87, 88, and 106. SFAS 106, which deals with postemployment benefits other than pensions, is modeled very closely after SFAS 87. Therefore, your knowledge of pensions from SFAS 87 and SFAS 132 should enable you to answer questions on SFAS 106.

In this section the key points covered are as follows:

1. The differences between a defined contribution pension plan and a defined benefit pension plan and the resulting accounting and reporting differences between these two types of plans.
2. The bookkeeping entries made to record an employer's pension expense and the funding of pension cost.
3. The difference between the accumulated benefits actuarial approach and the benefits-years-of-service approach.
4. The calculation and reporting of the additional minimum liability for employers who sponsor defined benefit pension plans.
5. The five elements which, if they all exist, an employer sponsoring a defined benefit pension plan must evaluate for inclusion in its pension expense each year. These factors are: (1) service cost, (2) interest cost, (3) actual return on plan assets, (4) amortization of unrecognized prior service cost, and (5) gain or loss.
6. The required disclosures in the financial statements of employers who sponsor pension plans.

1. **Employer Sponsor's vs. Plan's Accounting and Reporting**

In order to understand the accounting and reporting requirements for pension plans, you must keep in mind that there are two accounting entities involved: (1) the employer sponsor of the plan, and (2) the pension plan which is usually under the control of a pension trustee.

The employer sponsor reports Pension Expense in its income statement. In its balance sheet it usually reports a pension liability labeled Accrued/Prepaid Pension Cost (the sum of two accounts, Accrued/Prepaid Pension Cost and Additional Pension Liability, if required) and an Intangible Asset—Deferred Pension Cost (if required). As discussed later, a third balance sheet account, Net Loss Not Recognized As Pension Expense, is possible. In order to fund the plan, the employer sponsor contributes money to the plan.

A separate accounting entity, the pension plan, maintains the following accounts: Projected Benefit Obligation, Accumulated Benefit Obligation (for reporting purposes only), Vested Benefits (for reporting purposes only), and Plan Assets. The pension plan pays benefits to the retired employees.

The diagram below shows the relationship of the entities involved in a pension plan, the accounts usually used by each, and the flow of cash.

In addition to the accounts shown in the diagram below, the employer sponsor must also maintain, on a memo basis, accounts for Unrecognized Past Service Cost and Unrecognized Gains and Losses.

You should note as you read the sections below that the projected benefit obligations of the pension plan, the interest on these obligations, the pension plan assets available to meet these obligations, and returns (income) on these plan assets are all economic variables which impact the employer sponsor's yearly calculations of pension expense and its year-end pension liability (or prepaid pension cost).

In the following presentation, key concepts are **boldfaced** to call attention to those terms and phrases that must be clearly understood.

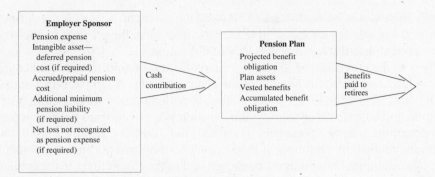

2.   An Overview of Employer's Accounting for Pension Plans

Under a **defined contribution plan** the employer agrees to make a defined contribution to a pension plan as determined by the provisions of the plan. Consequently, plan participants will receive at retirement whatever benefits (i.e., payments) the contributions can provide. Accounting for a defined contribution plan is relatively straightforward. Each year the employer records an expense and a related liability for the agreed-upon contribution. Payments are charged against the liability with an offsetting reduction in cash. Additional disclosure requirements include a description of the plan including: employee groups covered, the basis for determining contributions, and the nature and effects of events affecting comparability.

Under a **defined benefit plan** the employer agrees to provide a benefit at retirement that is defined or fixed by a formula. Because the benefits are defined, the employer accepts the risk associated with changes in the variables that determine the amounts needed to meet the obligation to plan participants. These amounts require the use of estimates that may become very complex. However, these estimates are made by actuaries hired by the management of the employer sponsor. They are not made by the sponsoring company's accountants. The remainder of our pension coverage is devoted to a discussion of the issues that arise under this type of plan.

The **accrual accounting objective** for pension costs recognizes the compensation cost of an employee's pension benefits including prior service costs over that employee's service period. Under accrual accounting, pension expense should not be determined on the basis of the employer's cash payout (funding) practices. The **funding of the pension obligation** refers to the amount that the employer contributes to an independent trustee for the pension plan (plans where the fund is under the control of the employer are considered unfunded). Many factors including tax considerations, working capital management, and contractual agreements influence funding decisions. Thus, the amount selected for funding should not govern the determination of the amount to be reported as pension expense under accrual accounting; these events should be distinguished. Although both events can be recorded with one entry, we use two entries to better illustrate this distinction.

Pension expense	xxxx	
Accrued/prepaid pension cost		xxxx

This adjusting entry is to record the accrued expense. The optional use of the Accrued/Prepaid Pension Cost account simplifies the accounting. If the account has a net debit balance, it is a prepaid asset account. If the account has a net credit balance, it is a liability.

Accrued/prepaid pension cost	xxxx	
Cash		xxxx

This entry is to record the funding of the pension obligation at the time cash is transferred to the plan's trustee.

The determination of the amounts to be used in the above entries requires the professional expertise of actuaries who assess the benefits to be provided under the pension formula and the characteristics of the employees covered under the plan (e.g., average age). With these factors as given, the actuaries must estimate the values of the variables that will influence the actual amounts to be paid at retirement by making **actuarial assumptions** about factors such as longevity, early retirements, turnover rate, and the rates of return to be earned on invested funds.

The actuarial present value of the obligation determined under the benefits-years-of-service method is referred to as the **projected benefit obligation**. If the defined benefit formula is not dependent on the amount of a future salary (say a retiree receives a fixed amount for each month worked), there would be no difference between the two approaches. If the defined benefit formula is pay-related and salaries are assumed to increase over time, the projected benefit obligation will be a greater amount than the accumulated benefit obligation.

Many of the provisions of SFAS 87 employ the use of amortization procedures that will significantly reduce, over time, the amount of the unrecognized pension liability associated with defined benefit plans. While the FASB conceptually supported immediate recognition of the projected benefit obligation as a balance sheet liability, this position was not adopted because it represented too significant a departure from past practices. The FASB did, however, require a minimum pension liability. This minimum liability requirement is independent of other reporting requirements for defined benefit plans. The minimum liability must be recognized to the extent that the accumulated benefit obligation at year-end exceeds the fair value of the plan assets at year-end. However, it should be noted that an asset may not be recorded by the employer when the fair value of plan assets exceeds the amount of the accumulated benefit obligation.

The accounting for the **minimum liability (ML)** is complex because the ML is a combination of two accounts: the Additional Pension Liability and the Accrued/Prepaid Pension Cost. Assume that the excess of the ABO over the fair value of the plan assets (i.e., ML) is $5,000. That amount is the **final** liability balance that must appear in the balance sheet. If a credit balance (assume $1,000) already exists in the Accrued/Prepaid Pension Cost Account, only an additional $4,000 credit is required to make the combination of the two credit accounts equal to $5,000. The adjusting journal entry is

Intangible asset—deferred pension cost	4,000	
Additional pension liability		4,000

Assume that instead of a credit of $1,000 in the Accrued/Prepaid account there is a debit of $1,000 in the account. Since the **final** liability must be a $5,000 credit, and that liability is a combination of a debit of $1,000 in the Accrued/Prepaid account, and a credit amount in the Additional Liability account which must equal a credit balance of $5,000, the adjusting entry will be

Intangible asset—deferred pension cost	6,000	
Additional pension liability		6,000

The $6,000 Additional Pension Liability credit will be combined with the $1,000 Accrued/Prepaid Pension Cost debit to result in a final liability credit in the balance sheet which will be labeled Accrued Pension Liability $5,000. **The account title Minimum Liability is not used in the balance sheet.**

The Intangible Asset—Deferred Pension Cost Account that results from the adjusting entry for the minimum liability cannot exceed the unrecognized prior service cost. If any excess does exist, the debits in the adjusting entry will be: (1) a debit to the intangible asset equal to the unrecognized prior service cost and (2) a second debit for the excess to an "other comprehensive income" account that is closed to "accumulated other comprehensive income." In the example immediately above where the ML is $5,000 assume that the unrecognized prior service cost is $2,000. The adjusting entry would be

Intangible asset—deferred pension cost	2,000 (equal to unrecognized service cost)	
Minimum pension liability adjustment		
(Other comprehensive income)	4,000	
Additional pension liability		6,000

The minimum pension liability adjustment is closed along with other comprehensive income accounts to "accumulated other comprehensive income account" which is a component of stockholders' equity. It is important to note that the debit balance accounts in the above entry are not amortized. Instead, at each statement date the amount of the Additional Liability account and the offsetting debit account (or accounts) are adjusted upward or downward to reflect the relationship between the excess of the accumulated benefit obligation over the fair value of plan assets at that date.

This completes the overview of the accounting required by employers for pension plans. In the next section, the determination of Pension Cost is thoroughly reviewed. The general term "**Pension Cost**" is preferred over pension expense because pension cost is included in overhead in the determination of product costs and therefore may be part of inventory in the balance sheet. When permissible the term "Pension Expense" is used instead because it is simpler and clearer. The disclosure of the elements included in pension expense is one of the most significant disclosures required by SFAS 132 and should be carefully studied. A comprehensive illustration is presented in Section 5 below. This illustration integrates the concepts and calculations that have been introduced in the preceding discussions. Section 4 below is concerned with the additional disclosure requirements that apply.

3. **Determination of Pension Expense**

Pension Expense is a net amount calculated by adding together five factors. These factors are: (1) service cost, (2) interest on the projected benefit obligation, (3) expected return on plan assets, (4) amortization of unrecognized prior service cost, and (5) the effect of gains and losses. Each of these components is discussed below.

a. **Service cost—Increases pension expense**

Service cost is defined as the actuarial present value of benefits attributed by the pension benefit formula to employee service during the current period. SFAS 87 requires that future salary levels be taken into consideration in this calculation (i.e., the benefits-years-of-service approach).

b. **Interest on projected benefit obligation—Increases expense**

The **interest on the projected benefit obligation** is defined as the increase in the amount of the projected benefit obligation due to the passage of time. Since the pension plan's obligation at the beginning of the year is stated in terms of present value, a provision for interest is required. By the end of the period, the plan's obligation will increase by the amount of interest that would accrue based on the discount (settlement) rate selected. The discount rate selected should be determined by reference to market conditions using such rates as the return on high quality investments or the implicit rate of return in retirement annuities as a basis for comparison. Also, the rate selected must be **explicit** and an unreasonable rate cannot be justified by an argument that the unreasonable rate is **implicitly** valid because of other offsetting actuarial assumptions. The selected discount rate is referred to as the **settlement rate** because it is the rate at which the plan's obligation could be settled.

> EXAMPLE: Compute the "interest" component of net pension expense for 2001, if the projected benefit obligation was $4,800,000 on January 1, 2001, and the settlement rate is 9%. Answer: Net pension expense for 2001 is increased by $432,000 (9% x $4,800,000) to provide for interest on the projected benefit obligation.

c. **Actual return on plan assets—Decreases or possibly increases pension expense**

The **actual return on plan assets** is defined as the difference in the fair value of plan assets at the beginning and the end of the period adjusted for contributions made to the plan and benefit payments made by the plan during the period. The formula for determining the actual return is as follows:

Actual return = (End. Bal. of plan assets at fair value – Beg. bal. of plan assets at fair value) + Benefits – Contributions

The **fair value or market value** of plan assets is defined as the price expected in a sales transaction between a willing buyer and seller. **Plan assets** typically include marketable securities and other investments such as real estate that are held in trust for the plan participants. Assets that are under the control of the employer are not considered to be plan assets. In calculating the return on plan assets, considerable leeway has been allowed in measuring the fair value of plan assets.

> EXAMPLE: Compute the "actual return on plan assets" component of net pension expense, if the fair value of plan assets was $3,100,000 at the beginning of the year and $3,820,000 at year-end. The employer sponsor contributed $450,000 to the plan and the plan paid benefits of $200,000 during the year. Answer: Net pension expense is decreased by $470,000 [($3,820,000 – $3,100,000)] due to the actual return earned on the fair value of plan assets.

Although the **actual** return on plan assets is measured and disclosed as one of the components of net pension expense, net pension expense will include only an amount equal to the **expected** return on plan assets. This methodology is followed because the difference between the actual return on plan assets and the expected return on plan assets is a canceling adjustment that is included in the gain or loss calculation to be discussed below.

d. **Prior service cost—Increases or possibly decreases pension expense**

Prior service costs are retroactive adjustments that are granted to recognize services rendered in previous periods. These costs are caused by either an amendment to an existing plan or the initiation of a new plan where a **retroactive allowance** is made for past services rendered. If, as a result of an amendment to an existing plan, the benefits are increased, then the amount of the plan's projected benefit obligation will increase. The amount of the prior service costs is measured by the increase in the projected benefit obligation caused by the amendment or the initiation of the plan.

While the prior service costs are related to the past, it is assumed that the initiation or amendment of the plan was made with the intent of benefiting the employer's future operations rather than its past operations. Because of this assumption, prior service costs should be amortized over the present and future periods affected. Two methods approved for use in determining the assignment of prior service costs are (1) the expected future years of service method, and (2) the straight-line basis over the average remaining service period of active employees method.

Under the **expected future years of service** method, the total number of employee service years is calculated by grouping employees according to the time remaining to their retirement, based on actuarial assumptions, and multiplying the number in each group by the number of periods remaining to retirement. For example, eight employees expected to work ten years until retirement would contribute eighty expected future years of service to the total. To calculate the amortization of prior service costs for a given year, the number of employee service years applicable to that period is used as the numerator of the fraction and the denominator is the total employee service years based on all the identified groups. This method produces a declining pattern similar to the amortization applicable to premiums or discounts on serial bonds and the sum-of-the-years' digits method of depreciation.

The **straight-line basis over the average remaining service period** of active employees is a simpler method. The projected average remaining service period for the affected participants is estimated by the use of a weighted-average method. For example, ten employees with ten years remaining to retirement, and fifteen employees with twenty years remaining to retirement would have a weighted-average service life of sixteen years computed as follows: $(10 \times 10 + 15 \times 20)/25$. In this example, the prior service costs would be amortized and included in pension expense over sixteen years. Note by including these prior service costs in pension expense, these costs will also be included in the employer's Accrued/Prepaid Pension Cost account over the sixteen years. Thus, the employer will gradually record on its balance sheet the unrecognized liability associated with these prior service costs.

> *EXAMPLE: Compute the "amortization of prior service cost" component of net pension expense for the first three years after an amendment, based on the following facts. The prior service cost associated with the amendment is determined by the actuaries to be $650,000 (the difference between the projected benefit obligation before and after the amendment). The employer has 200 employees at the time of the amendment. It is expected that workers will retire or terminate at the rate of 4% per year, and the employer will use the "expected future years of service" method of amortization. Answer: Since the workers will leave at the rate of 8 per year, the denominator of the amortization fraction is computed by summing $200 + 192 + 184 + ... + 8$. This series can be written as $8(25 + 24 + 23 + ... + 1)$ or $8n(n+1)/2 = 8(25)(26)/2 = 2,600$. The calculations for the first three years and the unamortized balance at year-end are presented in the table below.*

Year	Amortization fraction	Annual amortization	Unamortized balances
0			$650,000
1	200/2,600	$50,000	600,000
2	192/2,600	48,000	552,000
3	184/2,600	46,000	506,000

e. **Gain or loss—Increases or decreases pension expense**

Net gain or loss is defined as the change in the amount of the projected benefit obligation as well as the change in the value of plan assets (realized and unrealized), resulting from experience being different from that assumed, or from a change in an actuarial assumption. For this calculation, plan assets are valued at the market-related value, discussed under c. above.

The gain or loss component included in net pension expense consists of two items: (1) the current period difference between the actual and expected return [(Expected rate of return on plan assets) x (Market-related value of plan assets a the beginning of the period)] on plan assets, and (2) amortization of the unrecognized net gain or loss from **previous** periods. The current period difference is reported as a component of the current period net pension expense and the unrecognized net gain or loss is subject to amortization. In the unusual case when a gain or loss arises from an event such as the discontinuation of a business component, the gain or loss should be recognized immediately and associated with the event that was the cause (e.g., discontinued operations) rather than the pension plan.

When the amortization of the cumulative unrecognized net gain or loss from previous periods is required, the procedure is comparable to the amortization of prior service cost and, in general, it requires the use of a systematic method applied on a consistent basis that is dependent on the average remaining service period for active employees. Unlike past service cost, however, the amount to be amortized is not necessarily the calculated amount of the cumulative unrecognized net gain or loss. Instead, the minimum amount subject to amortization is determined by the use of a method sometimes referred to as the "corridor" approach. The minimum amount of the cumulative unrecognized gain or loss required to be amortized is determined by computing, at the beginning of the fiscal year, the excess of the cumulative unrecognized gain or loss over 10% of the greater of the projected benefit obligation or the market-related asset value. If the cumulative unrecognized gain or loss is equal to or less than the 10% calculated value, no amount need be amortized.

> EXAMPLE: *Compute the "gain or loss" component of net pension expense and the other elements of pension expense based on the following facts:*
>
> *At the beginning of the year the cumulative unrecognized net loss was $500,000, the fair value and market-related value of plan assets was $3,100,000, and the projected benefit obligation was $4,800,000. The expected return on assets for the year was 9% and the settlement rate was 11%. The fair value of plan assets at the end of the year was $3,400,000. There were no contributions to the plan during the year. The plan made no benefit payments during the year. Service costs for the year were $400,000. At the beginning of the year the average remaining service period of active employees was ten years. There are no other factors to be considered in computing pension expense for the year.*
>
> Answer: *The elements of net pension expense are calculated as follows:*
>
> | | | |
> |---|---:|---|
> | Service cost | $400,000 | |
> | Interest (.11 x $4,800,000) | 528,000 | |
> | Actual return on plan assets | (300,000) | (1) |
> | Amortization of unrecognized net loss | 2,000 | (2) |
> | Asset gain deferred | <u>21,000</u> | (3) |
> | Net pension expense | <u>$651,000</u> | |

NOTE: *The above components of pension expense are required to be disclosed in the employer sponsor's financial statements. This would be done in the footnotes to those statements.*

> (1) *$3,400,000 less $3,100,000 less contributions to the plan of $0 plus benefit payments of the plan of $0.*
> (2) *Amortization of unrecognized net loss is calculated as follows:*
>
> | | |
> |---|---:|
> | *"Corridor" 10% x $4,800,000* | *$480,000* |
> | *Cumulative unrecognized net loss at the beginning of the year* | <u>*500,000*</u> |
> | *Excess to be amortized* | <u>*$ 20,000*</u> |
> | *Amortization of unrecognized loss is: $20,000/10 years = $2,000.* | |
>
> (3) *The asset gain deferred of $21,000 is calculated as follows: Actual return on plan assets of $300,000 less expected return on plan assets of $279,000. The expected return on plan assets is determined by multiplying the expected return on plan assets of 9% times the market-related value of plan assets at the beginning of the year of $3,100,000. Note that in the above computation of pension expense actual return on assets of $300,000 is included as required by SFAS 87. However, the expected return on plan assets of $279,000 ($300,000 – $21,000) is the amount that is actually included in pension expense for the year.*

4. **Disclosures**

Under SFAS 87 and SFAS 132, disclosure in the statement of financial position follows the practice of **offsetting** the financial effects of plan assets and obligations where the plan's assets can be used directly to satisfy its obligations. This practice and the practice of **netting** the components of pension expense in the income statement, and the complexities inherent in pension accounting, put added emphasis on the use of notes to the financial statements to provide disclosure. The required disclosures are as follows:

a. A reconciliation schedule of the benefit obligation showing the components separately
b. A reconciliation schedule of the fair value of plan assets with the components shown separately
c. The funded status of the plan(s) and the amounts recognized and not recognized in the statement of financial position (balance sheet)
d. The net periodic benefit cost recognized with the components shown separately
e. The amount of change in the additional minimum pension liability recognized within other comprehensive income
f. The rates and assumptions used for the assumed discount rate, rate of compensation increase, and expected long-term rate of return on plan assets

g.   The assumed health care cost trend rate, a description of the pattern of change, and what effect a 1-percentage-point increase or decrease would have on the aggregated service and interest cost components

h.   An explanation of any significant changes in the plan assets or the benefit obligation

If an employer sponsors more than one pension plan, the plans may be shown aggregated or disaggregated.

5.   **Comprehensive Illustration**

Schaefer Company has sponsored a noncontributory (i.e., employees make no contributions) defined benefit plan for its 100 employees for several years. Within this group of 100 employees, it is expected that workers will retire or terminate at the rate of 5 per year for the next twenty years starting January 1, 2001. Prior to 2000, cumulative pension expense recognized in compliance with SFAS 87 exceeded cumulative contributions by $150,000, resulting in a $150,000 balance sheet liability. As of January 1, 2001, the company has agreed to an amendment to its plan that includes a retroactive provision to recognize prior service. To illustrate how the provisions of SFAS 87 should be applied, assumptions about the facts relevant to the pension plan for the years 2000 and 2001 are presented in the tables that follow:

	1/1/2000	1/1/2001	12/31/2001
Plan assets (at fair value = market-related value)	$400,000	$ 455,000	$ 760,500
Accumulated benefit obligation (ABO; 60% vested)	460,000	640,000*	710,000*
Projected benefit obligation	550,000	821,500*	1,033,650*
Unrecognized cumulative gain (loss)—due to unexpected decrease in asset value	--	(106,000)	?
Prior service cost amendment	--	105,000	?
Accrued pension cost (liability)	(150,000)	?	?

* *Includes effects of amendment*

	12/31/2000	12/31/2001
Service cost	$117,000	$130,000
Employer's funding contribution	125,000	260,000
Plan assets (at fair value = market-related value)	455,000	760,500
Accumulated benefit obligation (60% vested)	620,000	710,000
Benefits paid by the plan	--	--
Unrecognized cumulative gain (loss)—due to unexpected decrease in asset value	(106,000)	(103,729)
Rate of return on assets	9%	10%
Settlement rate	9%	10%

Schedule of Changes in Plan Assets

	2000	2001
Plan assets at 12/31	$455,000	$760,500
Plan assets at 1/1	400,000	455,000
Increase in plan assets	55,000	305,500
Add: Benefits paid	--	--
Less: Funding contributions for the year	(125,000)	(260,000)
Actual return or (loss) on plan assets	(70,000)	45,500
Expected return on plan assets		
2000: 9% x $400,000	36,000	
2001: 10% x $455,000		45,500
Unrecognized gain (loss)	$(106,000)	$ --

Required:

A.   Prepare a supporting schedule to determine the amounts to be reported as pension expense for 2000 and 2001. The company has decided to use the "expected future years of service" method to amortize the effects of the amendment made in 2001.

B.   Prepare the journal entries required for 2000 and 2001 with respect to the pension plan including any entry necessary to comply with the **minimum liability** requirement.

C.   Prepare pension worksheets for 2000 and 2001. Note these worksheets summarize Schaefer's general journal entries and changes in its pension-related accounts. These worksheets also summarize the changes in the pension plan's accounts, unrecognized prior service cost, and unrecognized gain or loss. Study these worksheets as they are an excellent tool for pulling together the elements of this comprehensive illustration.[1]

---

[1]   *From Paul B. W. Miller, "The New Pension Accounting (Part 2)," **Journal of Accountancy** (February 1987), pp. 86-94.*

D. Indicate the pension-related amounts that should appear in the company's financial statements prepared at the end of 2000 and 2001.

E. Prepare disclosures of the funded status of the plan to the liability shown in the company's balance sheet at 1/1/00, 12/31/00, and 12/31/01.

Solution
Part A

REQUIRED FOOTNOTE DISCLOSURE
Pension Expense

	12/31/00	*12/31/01*
Components of net periodic benefit cost		
1. Service cost	$117,000	$130,000
2. Interest cost on projected benefit obligation	49,500	82,150
3. Actual loss or (actual return) on plan assets	70,000	(45,500)
4. Amortization of prior service cost	--	10,000
5. Deferral of "gain" or (loss)	(106,000)	--
6. Loss amortization	--	2,271
7. Recognized actuarial loss	--	--
Net periodic benefit cost	$130,500	$178,921

NOTE: This is one of the required disclosures by SFAS 87 and 132 as discussed above.

Calculations

1. **Service cost** is given.

2. **Interest:** 9% x $550,000 (2000), and 10% x $821,500 (2001).

3. **Actual return:** ($70,000) for 2000 and $45,500 (same as expected) for 2001. Note that in 2000, the $70,000 actual loss on plan assets less the $106,000 unrecognized loss equals the expected return ($36,000).

4. **Prior service:** Compute the denominator of the fraction for amortization by calculating the sum of the estimated remaining service years by adding 100 + 95 + 90 + ... + 10 + 5. This series can be written as 5(20 + 19 + 18 + ... + 2 + 1) or 5n(n+1)/2 = 5(20)(21)/2 = 1,050. For 2001 the amount is (100/1,050) x $105,000 = $10,000.

5. **Loss:** The $106,000 unrecognized loss that arose in 2000 is not amortized until 2001, because no unrecognized net gain or loss existed at the **beginning** of the year. The amortization of the unrecognized net gain or loss should be included as a component of pension expense only if the unrecognized net gain or loss existed as of the **beginning** of the year and the unrecognized gain or loss exceeded the corridor. At 1/1/2001 10% of the greater of the projected benefit obligation ($821,500) or the market-related asset value ($455,000) is equal to $82,150. The **minimum loss** to be amortized is $106,000 – $82,150 or $23,850. The average employee service remaining as of 1/1/2000 assuming a constant work force of 100 and an attrition rate of 5 workers per year is (100 + 95 + 90 + ... + 10 + 5)/100 or 1,050/100 = 10.5 years. The amount of the loss recognized in 2001 is $23,850/10.5 = $2,271. Since actual and expected returns are equal in 2001, no further adjustment is required.

Part B

Journal Entries

	2000		2001	
Pension expense	130,500		178,921	
Accrued/prepaid pension cost		130,500		178,921
To record pension expense				
Accrued/prepaid pension cost	125,000		260,000	
Cash		125,000		260,000
To record funding				

The amount of the **minimum liability** is the excess, if any, at the balance sheet date of the accumulated benefit obligation over the fair value of plan assets. An adjustment is required to the extent that the liability has not already been reflected. (Note that this adjustment does not impact the determination of pension expense.)

	2000	2001
Intangible asset—deferred pension cost	9,500	
Additional minimum liability	9,500	

To adjust as of 12/31/2000 for the minimum liability by increasing the liability from $155,500 (credit balance in the "Accrued/Prepaid Pension Cost" account below) to $165,000 ($620,000 ABO – $455,000 FMV of plan assets)

	2000	2001
Additional minimum liability	9,500	
Intangible asset—deferred pension cost		9,500

To adjust as of 12/31/2001 the balance in additional liability account; no balance is required because the FMV of plan assets ($760,500) exceeds the ABO ($710,000)

Pension Expense	
2000	130,500
2001	178,921

Accrued/Prepaid Pension Cost			
2000 Funding	125,000	150,000	1/1/2000 balance
		130,500	2000 accrual
2001 Funding	260,000	155,500	12/31/2000 balance
		178,921	2001 accrual
		74,421	12/31/2001 balance

Intangible Asset—Def. Pension Cost			
2000	9,500	9,500	2001

Additional Minimum Liability			
2001	9,500	9,500	2000

Part C

SCHAEFER COMPANY
Pension Work Sheet—2000

	Debit (credit)					Debit (credit)			
	General journal entries					Memo entries			
Items	Pension expense	Cash	Prepaid/ accrued cost	Add'l liability	Intangible asset	Projected benefit obligation	Plan assets	Unrecognized prior service cost	Unrecognized net gain or loss
Bal. 1/1/2000			(150,000)			(550,000)	400,000		
Service cost	117,000					(117,000)			
Interest cost	49,500					(49,500)			
Actual loss	70,000						(70,000)		
Deferred gain	(106,000)								106,000
Contribution		(125,000)					125,000		
Min. lia. adj.				(9,500)	9,500				
Journal entry for 2000	130,500	(125,000)	(5,500)						
Bal. 12/31/2000			(155,500)	(9,500)	9,500	(716,500)	455,000		106,000

SCHAEFER COMPANY
Pension Work Sheet—2001

	Debit (credit)					Debit (credit)			
	General journal entries					Memos entries			
Items	Pension expense	Cash	Prepaid/ accrued cost	Add'l liability	Intangible asset	Projected benefit obligation	Plan assets	Unrecognized prior service cost	Unrecognized net gain or loss
Bal. 1/1/2001			(155,500)	(9,500)	9,500	(716,500)	455,000		106,000
Prior service cost amendment						(105,000)		105,000	
Service cost	130,000					(130,000)			
Interest cost	82,150					(82,150)			
Actual return	(45,500)						45,500		
Prior service cost amort.	10,000							(10,000)	
Gain amort.	2,271								(2,271)
Contribution		(260,000)					260,000		
Min. lia. adj.				9,500	(9,500)				
Journal entry for 2001	178,921	(260,000)	81,079						
Bal. 12/31/2001			(74,421)	--	--	(1,033,650)	760,500	95,000	103,729

Part D

Financial Statements

	12/31/2000	12/31/2001
Assets		
Intangible asset—deferred pension cost	$ 9,500	$ --
Liabilities		
Accrued pension cost**	165,000*	74,421
Income statement		
Pension expense	130,500	178,921

* *Accrued liability ($155,500) plus adjustment for minimum liability ($9,500)*

** *Although not specifically addressed by SFAS 87, we believe these amounts **should be** classified as noncurrent, unless evidence indicates otherwise, in accordance with ARB 43, Chapter 3A (current assets and liabilities).*

Part E

Required Footnote Disclosure

	12/31/2000	12/31/2001
Change in benefit obligation		
Benefit obligation at beginning of year*	$550,000	$ 716,500*
Service cost	117,000	130,000
Interest cost	49,500	82,150
Amendment (prior service cost)	--	105,000
Actuarial loss (gain)	--	--
Benefits paid	--	--
Benefit obligation at end of year	$716,500	$1,033,650

* *Before effect of plan amendment.*

	12/31/2000	12/31/2001
Change in plan assets		
Fair value of plan assets at beginning of year	$400,000	$ 55,000
Actual return (loss) on plan assets	(70,000)	45,500
Employer contribution	125,000	260,000
Benefits paid	--	--
Fair value of plan assets at end of year	$ 455,000	$ 760,500
Funded status	$(261,500)	$ (273,150)
Unrecognized loss on assets	106,000	103,729
Unrecognized prior service cost	--	95,000
Net amount recognized	$(155,500)	$ (74,421)

	12/31/2000	12/31/2001
Amounts recognized in the statement of financial position (balance sheet) consist of		
Accrued benefit liability	$(165,000)*	$ (74,421)
Intangible asset	9,500	--
Accumulated other comprehensive income	--	--
Net amount recognized	$(155,500)	$ (74,421)

* *Accrued pension cost plus adjustment for minimum liability ($9,500).*

6. Postretirement Benefits other than Pensions (OPEB)

SFAS 106 (refer to outline) establishes the standard for employers' accounting for other (than pension) postretirement benefits (OPEB). This standard requires a single method for measuring and recognizing an employer's accumulated postretirement benefit obligation (APBO). It applies to all forms of postretirement benefits, although the most material benefit is usually postretirement health care. It uses the fundamental framework established by SFAS 87 and SFAS 88. To the extent that the promised benefits are similar, the accounting provisions are similar. Only when there is a compelling reason is the accounting different. SFAS 132 states the required disclosures for employers with postretirement benefits and pensions.

There are, however, some fundamental differences between defined benefit pension plans and postretirement benefits other than pensions. The following list presents these differences.

Differences between Pensions and Postretirement Health Care Benefits*

Item	Pensions	Health care benefits
Funding	Generally funded.	Generally *NOT* funded.
Benefit	Well-defined and level dollar amount.	Generally uncapped and great variability.
Beneficiary	Retiree (maybe some benefit to surviving spouse).	Retiree, spouse, and other dependents.
Benefit payable	Monthly	As needed and used.
Predictability	Variables are reasonably predictable.	Utilization difficult to predict. Level of cost varies geographically and fluctuates over time.

* *D. Gerald Searfoss and Naomi Erickson, "The Big Unfunded Liability: Postretirement Health Care Benefits," **Journal of Accountancy**, November 1988, pp. 28-39.*

SFAS 106 requires accrual accounting and adopts the three primary characteristics of pension accounting: (1) delayed recognition (changes are not recognized immediately, but are subsequently recognized in a gradual and systematic way), (2) reporting net cost (aggregates of various items are reported as one net amount), and (3) offsetting assets and liabilities (assets and liabilities are sometimes shown net).

SFAS 106 distinguishes between the **substantive** plan and **written** plan. Although generally the same, the substantive plan (the one understood as evidenced by past practice or by communication of intended changes) is the basis for the accounting if it differs from the written plan.

OPEBs are considered to be deferred compensation earned in an exchange transaction during the time periods that the employee provides services. The expected cost generally should be attributed in equal amounts (unless the plan attributes a disproportionate share of benefits to early years) over the periods from the employee's hiring date (unless credit for the service is only granted from a later date) to the date that the employee attains full eligibility for all benefits expected to be received. This accrual should be followed even if the employee provides service beyond the date of full eligibility.

The transition obligation, under SFAS 106, is the unrecognized and unfunded APBO (accumulated postretirement benefit obligation) for all of the participants in the plan. This obligation can either (1) be recognized immediately as the effect of an accounting change, subject to certain limitations, or (2) be recognized on a delayed basis over future service periods with disclosure of the unrecognized amount. The delayed recognition has to result in, at least, as rapid a recognition as would have been recognized on a pay-as-you-go basis.

EXAMPLE: A sample illustration of the basic accounting for OPEB as established by SFAS 106 follows: Firstime Accrual Co. plans to adopt accrual accounting for OPEB as of January 1, 2001. All employees were hired at age 30 and are fully eligible for benefits at age 60. There are no plan assets. This first calculation determines the unrecognized transition obligation (UTO).

Firstime Accrual
December 31, 2000

Employee	Age	Years of service	Total years when fully eligible	Expected retirement age	Remaining service to retirement	EPBO	APBO
A	35	5	30	60	25	$ 14,000	$ 2,333
B	40	10	30	60	20	22,000	7,333
C	45	15	30	60	15	30,000	15,000
D	50	20	30	60	10	38,000	25,333
E	55	25	30	65	10	46,000	38,333
F	60	30	30	65	5	54,000	54,000
G	65	RET	--		--	46,000	46,000
H	70	RET	--		--	38,000	38,000
					85	$288,000	$226,332

Calculations

1. *EPBO (expected postretirement benefit obligation) is usually determined by an actuary, although it can be calculated if complete data is available.*
2. *APBO is calculated using the EPBO. Specifically, it is EPBO x (Years of service/total years when fully eligible)*
3. *The unrecognized transition obligation (UTO) is the APBO at 12/31/00 since there are no plan assets to be deducted. The $226,332 can be amortized over the average remaining service to retirement of 14.17 (85/6) years or an optional period of twenty years, if longer. Firstime Accrual selected the twenty-year period of amortization.*
4. *Note that Employee F has attained full eligibility for benefits and yet plans to continue working.*
5. *Note that the above 2000 table is used in the calculation of the 2001 components of OPEB cost that follows.*

After the establishment of UTO, the next step is to determine the benefit cost for the year ended December 31, 2001. This calculation follows the framework established by SFAS 87. The discount rate is assumed to be 10%.

Firstime Accrual
OPEB COST
December 31, 2001

1.	Service Cost	$ 5,000
2.	Interest Cost	22,633
3.	Actual Return on Plan Assets	--
4.	Gain or Loss	--
5.	Amortization of Unrecognized Prior Service Cost	--
6.	Amortization of UTO	11,317
	Total OPEB Cost	$38,950

Calculations

1. *Service cost calculation uses only employees not yet fully eligible for benefits.*

Employee	1/1/01 EPBO	Total years when fully eligible	Service cost
A	$14,000	30	$ 467
B	22,000	30	733
C	30,000	30	1,000
D	38,000	30	1,267
E	46,000	30	1,533
Total service cost			$5,000

2.   *Interest cost is the 1/1/01 APBO of $226,332 x 10% = $22,633.*
3.   *There are no plan assets so there is no return.*
4.   *There is no gain (loss) since there are no changes yet.*
5.   *There is no unrecognized prior service cost initially.*
6.   *Amortization of UTO is the 1/1/01 UTO of $226,332/20 year optional election = $11,317.*

     Assume that Firstime Accrual makes a year-end cash benefit payment of $20,000. Firstime Accrual's year-end entry to record other postretirement benefit cost for 2001 would be as follows:

Postretirement benefit cost	38,950	
Cash		20,000
Accrued postretirement benefit cost		18,950

Required disclosures for a postretirement benefit plan are stated in SFAS 106 and SFAS 132. The requirements are the same as the requirements for pensions, which have already been covered in this module.

7.   **Postemployment Benefits** (See the outline of SFAS 112)

Benefits made available to former/inactive employees after employment but before retirement. Examples include continuation of health care and life insurance coverage, severance pay, and disability-related benefits. Criteria for accrual of these benefits are the same as for compensated absences.

   a.   Obligation relates to **services already provided** by the employee,
   b.   Rights to compensation **vest or accumulate,**
   c.   Payment of obligation is **probable,** and
   d.   Amount to be paid is **reasonably estimable**.

Note that the last two are the general criteria for recognizing a loss contingency per SFAS 5. If is not possible to reliably estimate benefits, disclosure of that fact is required in FS.

8.   **Deferred Compensation**

Deferred compensation is the payment at a future date for work done in an earlier period(s). Account for these contracts individually on an accrual basis that reflects the terms of the agreement. Accrue amounts to be paid in future over the employment period from date agreement is signed to full eligibility date. The rationale for this treatment is matching.

MULTIPLE-CHOICE QUESTIONS (1-38)

1. The following information pertains to Lee Corp.'s defined benefit pension plan for 2002:

Service cost	$160,000
Actual and expected gain on plan assets	35,000
Unexpected loss on plan assets related to a 2001 disposal of a subsidiary	40,000
Amortization of unrecognized prior service cost	5,000
Annual interest on pension obligation	50,000

What amount should Lee report as pension expense in its 2002 income statement?

   a. $250,000
   b. $220,000
   c. $210,000
   d. $180,000

2. Jordon Corporation obtains the following information from its actuary. All amounts given are **as of** 1/1/02 (beginning of the year).

	1/1/02
Projected benefit obligation	$1,530,000
Market-related asset value	1,650,000
Unrecognized net loss	235,000
Average remaining service period	5.5 years

What amount of unrecognized net loss should be recognized as part of pension expense in 2002?

   a. $70,000
   b. $42,727
   c. $14,909
   d. $12,727

3. Which of the following disclosures is not required of companies with a defined benefit pension plan?

   a.   A description of the plan.
   b.   The amount of pension expense by component.
   c.   The weighted-average discount rate.
   d.   The estimates of future contributions.

4. Bulls Corporation amends its pension plan on 1/1/02. The following information is available:

	1/1/02 amendment	*1/1/02 after amendment*
Accumulated benefit obligation	$ 950,000	$1,425,000
Projected benefit obligation	1,300,000	1,900,000

The total amount of unrecognized prior service cost to be amortized over future periods as a result of this amendment is

   a. $950,000
   b. $600,000
   c. $475,000
   d. $125,000

5. On January 2, 2002, Loch Co. established a noncontributory defined benefit plan covering all employees and contributed $1,000,000 to the plan. At December 31, 2002, Loch determined that the 2002 service and interest costs on the plan were $620,000. The expected and the actual rate of return on plan assets for 2002 was 10%. There are no other components of Loch's pension expense. What amount should Loch report in its December 31, 2002 balance sheet as prepaid pension cost?

   a. $280,000
   b. $380,000
   c. $480,000
   d. $620,000

6. Webb Co. implemented a defined benefit pension plan for its employees on January 1, 1999. During 1999 and 2000, Webb's contributions fully funded the plan. The following data are provided for 2002 and 2001:

	2002 *Estimated*	2001 *Actual*
Projected benefit obligation, December 31	$750,000	$700,000
Accumulated benefit obligation, December 31	520,000	500,000
Plan assets at fair value, December 31	675,000	600,000
Projected benefit obligation in excess of plan assets	75,000	100,000
Pension expense	90,000	75,000
Employer's contribution	?	50,000

What amount should Webb contribute in order to report an accrued pension liability of $15,000 in its December 31, 2002 balance sheet?

   a. $ 50,000
   b. $ 60,000
   c. $ 75,000
   d. $100,000

7. Visor Co. maintains a defined benefit pension plan for its employees. The service cost component of Visor's net periodic pension cost is measured using the

   a.   Unfunded accumulated benefit obligation.
   b.   Unfunded vested benefit obligation.
   c.   Projected benefit obligation.
   d.   Expected return on plan assets.

8. Which of the following components should be included in the calculation of net pension cost recognized for a period by an employer sponsoring a defined benefit pension plan?

	Actual return on plan assets, if any	*Amortization of unrecognized prior service cost, if any*
a.	No	Yes
b.	No	No
c.	Yes	No
d.	Yes	Yes

9. Interest cost included in the net pension cost recognized by an employer sponsoring a defined benefit pension plan represents the

   a.   Amortization of the discount on unrecognized prior service costs.
   b.   Increase in the fair value of plan assets due to the passage of time.
   c.   Increase in the projected benefit obligation due to the passage of time.
   d.   Shortage between the expected and actual returns on plan assets.

10. On July 31, 2002, Tern Co. amended its single employee defined benefit pension plan by granting increased benefits for services provided prior to 2002. This prior service cost will be reflected in the financial statement(s) for

   a.   Years before 2002 only.
   b.   Year 2002 only.
   c.   Year 2002, and years before and following 2002.
   d.   Year 2002, and following years only.

11. Effective January 1, 2002, Flood Co. established a defined benefit pension plan with no retroactive benefits. The first of the required equal annual contributions was paid on December 31, 2002. A 10% discount rate was used to calculate service cost and a 10% rate of return was assumed for plan assets. All information on covered employees for 2002 and 2003 is the same. How should the service cost for 2003 compare with 2002, and should the 2002 balance sheet report an accrued or a prepaid pension cost?

	Service cost for 2003 compared to 2002	Pension cost reported on the 2002 balance sheet
a.	Equal to	Accrued
b.	Equal to	Prepaid
c.	Greater than	Accrued
d.	Greater than	Prepaid

12. A company that maintains a defined benefit pension plan for its employees reports an unfunded accrued pension cost. This cost represents the amount that the

a. Cumulative net pension cost accrued exceeds contributions to the plan.
b. Cumulative net pension cost accrued exceeds the vested benefit obligation.
c. Vested benefit obligation exceeds plan assets.
d. Vested benefit obligation exceeds contributions to the plan.

13. The following information pertains to Seda Co.'s pension plan:

Actuarial estimate of projected benefit obligation at 1/1/02	$72,000
Assumed discount rate	10%
Service costs for 2002	18,000
Pension benefits paid during 2002	15,000

If **no** change in actuarial estimates occurred during 2002, Seda's projected benefit obligation at December 31, 2002 was

a. $64,200
b. $75,000
c. $79,200
d. $82,200

14. Which of the following terms includes assumptions concerning projected changes in future compensation when the pension benefit formula is based on future compensation levels (e.g., pay-related and final pay plans)?

	Service cost component	Projected benefit obligation	Accumulated benefit obligation
a.	Yes	Yes	Yes
b.	Yes	Yes	No
c.	No	Yes	No
d.	Yes	No	Yes

15. For a defined benefit pension plan, the discount rate used to calculate the projected benefit obligation is determined by the

	Expected return on plan assets	Actual return on plan assets
a.	Yes	Yes
b.	No	No
c.	Yes	No
d.	No	Yes

16. At December 31, 2002, the following information was provided by the Kerr Corp. pension plan administrator:

Fair value of plan assets	$3,450,000
Accumulated benefit obligation	4,300,000
Projected benefit obligation	5,700,000

What is the amount of the pension liability that should be shown on Kerr's December 31, 2002 balance sheet?

a. $5,700,000

b. $2,250,000
c. $1,400,000
d. $ 850,000

17. Nome Co. sponsors a defined benefit plan covering all employees. Benefits are based on years of service and compensation levels at the time of retirement. Nome determined that, as of September 30, 2002, its accumulated benefit obligation was $380,000, and its plan assets had a $290,000 fair value. Nome's September 30, 2002 trial balance showed prepaid pension cost of $20,000. In its September 30, 2002 balance sheet, what amount should Nome report as additional pension liability?

a. $110,000
b. $360,000
c. $380,000
d. $400,000

18. Payne, Inc. implemented a defined benefit pension plan for its employees on January 2, 2002. The following data are provided for 2002, as of December 31, 2002:

Accumulated benefit obligation	$103,000
Plan assets at fair value	78,000
Net periodic pension cost	90,000
Employer's contribution	70,000

What amount should Payne record as additional minimum pension liability at December 31, 2002?

a. $0
b. $ 5,000
c. $20,000
d. $45,000

Items 19 and 20 are based on the following:

The following data pertains to Hall Co.'s defined-benefit pension plan at December 31, 2002:

Unfunded accumulated benefit obligation	$25,000
Unrecognized prior service cost	12,000
Net periodic pension cost	8,000

Hall made no contributions to the pension plan during 2002.

19. At December 31, 2002, what amount should Hall record as additional pension liability?

a. $ 5,000
b. $13,000
c. $17,000
d. $25,000

20. In its December 31, 2002 statement of stockholders' equity, what amount should Hall report as excess of additional pension liability over unrecognized prior service cost?

a. $ 5,000
b. $13,000
c. $17,000
d. $25,000

21. An employer sponsoring a defined benefit pension plan is subject to the minimum pension liability recognition requirement. An additional liability must be recorded equal to the unfunded

a. Accumulated benefit obligation plus the previously recognized accrued pension cost.
b. Accumulated benefit obligation less the previously recognized accrued pension cost.
c. Projected benefit obligation plus the previously recognized accrued pension cost.

    d.   Projected benefit obligation less the previously recognized accrued pension cost.

22. In which of the following pension instances would the account adjustment for minimum pension liability be reported on the balance sheet for a particular year?

    a.   When the additional pension liability required to be recognized exceeds the unrecognized prior service cost.

    b.   When the unrecognized prior service cost exceeds the additional pension liability required to be recognized.

    c.   Only when an employer sponsors two or more separate defined benefit pension plans.

    d.   Only when there is an amendment to a defined benefit pension plan.

23. On September 1, 2002, Howe Corp. offered special termination benefits to employees who had reached the early retirement age specified in the company's pension plan. The termination benefits consisted of lump-sum and periodic future payments. Additionally, the employees accepting the company offer receive the usual early retirement pension benefits. The offer expired on November 30, 2002. Actual or reasonably estimated amounts at December 31, 2002, relating to the employees accepting the offer are as follows:

• Lump-sum payments totaling $475,000 were made on January 1, 2003.

• Periodic payments of $60,000 annually for three years will begin January 1, 2004. The present value at December 31, 2002 of these payments was $155,000.

• Reduction of accrued pension costs at December 31, 2002 for the terminating employees was $45,000.

In its December 31, 2002 balance sheet, Howe should report a total liability for special termination benefits of

    a. $475,000
    b. $585,000
    c. $630,000
    d. $655,000

24. SFAS 132, *Employers' Disclosures about Pensions and Other Postretirement Benefits*, requires a reconciliation of the beginning and ending balances of the benefit obligation for both defined benefit pension plans and defined postretirement plans. Which of the following items would appear in the schedule related to defined benefit pension plans?

	Service cost	Benefits paid
a.	Yes	No
b.	Yes	Yes
c.	No	Yes
d.	No	No

25. A company with a defined benefit pension plan must disclose in the notes to its financial statements a reconciliation of

    a.   The vested and nonvested benefit obligation of its pension plan with the accumulated benefit obligation.

    b.   The accrued or prepaid pension cost reported in its balance sheet with the pension expense reported in its income statement.

    c.   The accumulated benefit obligation of its pension plan with its projected benefit obligation.

    d.   The funded status of its pension plan with the accrued or prepaid pension cost reported in its balance sheet.

26. SFAS 132, *Employers' Disclosures about Pensions and Other Postretirement Benefits*, requires a reconciliation of the beginning and ending balances of the plan assets for both defined pension plans and defined postretirement plans. Which of the following items would appear in the reconciliation schedule related to defined pension plans?

	Benefit payments	Actual return on plan assets
a.	No	Yes
b.	No	No
c.	Yes	No
d.	Yes	Yes

27. Which of the following defined benefit pension plan disclosures should be made in a company's financial statements?

  I. The amount of net periodic pension cost for the period.
  II. The fair value of plan assets.

    a.   Both I and II.
    b.   I only.
    c.   II only.
    d.   Neither I nor II.

28. Which of the following is not a required disclosure for defined benefit pension plans?

    a.   An explanation of a significant change in plan assets if not apparent from other disclosures.

    b.   The amount of any unamortized prior service cost not recognized in the statement of financial position (balance sheet).

    c.   The effect of a two-percentage-point increase in the assumed health care cost trend rate(s).

    d.   Reconciliation of beginning and ending balance of the benefit obligation.

29. Which of the following rates must be disclosed for defined benefit pension plans?

  I. Assumed discount rate
  II. Expected long-term rate of return on all of the employer's assets
  III. Rate of compensation increase

    a.   I and III.
    b.   II and III.
    c.   I, II, and III.
    d.   III only.

30. Jan Corp. amended its defined benefit pension plan, granting a total credit of $100,000 to four employees for services rendered prior to the plan's adoption. The employees, A, B, C, and D, are expected to retire from the company as follows:

A will retire after three years.
B and C will retire after five years.
D will retire after seven years.

What is the amount of prior service cost amortization in the first year?

    a. $0
    b. $ 5,000
    c. $20,000
    d. $25,000

31. The effects of a one-percentage-point increase or decrease in the trend rates for health care costs must be disclosed for which of the following relating to defined benefit postretirement plans?

I. The aggregate of the service and interest cost components.
II. The accumulated postretirement benefit obligation.

    a.   Both I and II.
    b.   I only.
    c.   II only.
    d.   Neither I nor II.

32. A company with a defined benefit pension plan must disclose in the notes to its financial statements all of the following **except**

    a.   A reconciliation of the funded status of its pension plan with the accrued or prepaid cost reported in its balance sheet.
    b.   Rates for assumed discount rate, rate of compensation increase, and expected long-term rate of return on plan assets.
    c.   A reconciliation of the accrued or prepaid pension cost reported in its balance sheet with the pension expense reported in its income statement.
    d.   The recognized amount of the net periodic benefit cost with the components shown separately.

33. The following information pertains to Foster Co.'s defined benefit postretirement plan for the year 2002.

Service cost	$120,000
Benefit payment	55,000
Interest on the accumulated postretirement benefit obligation	20,000
Unrecognized transition obligation (to be amortized over twenty years)	200,000

Foster Co.'s 2002 net periodic postretirement benefit cost was

    a. $205,000
    b. $150,000
    c. $ 95,000
    d. $285,000

34. Kemp Company provides a defined benefit postretirement plan for its employees. Kemp adopted the plan on January 1, 2002, in accordance with the provisions of SFAS 106, *Employer's Accounting for Postretirement Benefits other than Pensions*. Data relating to the pension plan for 2002 are as follows:

Service cost for 2002	28,000
Interest on the accumulated postretirement benefit obligation	5,000
Amortization of the unrecognized transition obligation	8,000

At the end of 2002, Kemp makes a benefit payment of $10,000 to employees. In its December 31, 2002 balance sheet, Kemp should record accrued postretirement benefit cost of

    a. $35,000
    b. $31,000
    c. $51,000
    d. $15,000

35. Bounty Co. provides postretirement health care benefits to employees who have completed at least ten years service and are aged fifty-five years or older when retiring. Employees retiring from Bounty have a median age of sixty-

two, and no one has worked beyond age sixty-five. Fletcher is hired at forty-eight years old. The attribution period for accruing Bounty's expected postretirement health care benefit obligation to Fletcher is during the period when Fletcher is aged

    a.   48 to 65.
    b.   48 to 58.
    c.   55 to 65.
    d.   55 to 62.

36. An employer's obligation for postretirement health benefits that are expected to be provided to or for an employee must be fully accrued by the date the

    a.   Employee is fully eligible for benefits.
    b.   Employee retires.
    c.   Benefits are utilized.
    d.   Benefits are paid.

37. Which of the following are correct regarding a transition obligation resulting from the adoption of a defined benefit postretirement plan?

I. A transition obligation may be recognized immediately.
II. The transition obligation represents the difference between the accumulated postretirement benefit obligation and the fair value of plan assets at the beginning of the year the plan is adopted.
III. A transition obligation may be amortized on a straight-line basis over a maximum period of twenty years.

    a.   I and II.
    b.   II only.
    c.   I, II, and III.
    d.   II and III.

38. Which of the following information should be disclosed by a company providing health care benefits to its retirees?

I. The assumed health care cost trend rate used to measure the expected cost of benefits covered by the plan.
II. The accumulated postretirement benefit obligation.

    a.   Both I and II.
    b.   I only.
    c.   II only.
    d.   Neither I nor II.

OTHER OBJECTIVE QUESTION

Problem 1   (15 to 25 minutes)

The following information pertains to Sparta Co.'s defined benefit pension plan.

Discount rate	8%
Expected rate of return	10%
Average service life	12 years

At January 1, 2002:

Projected benefit obligation	$600,000
Fair value of pension plan assets	720,000
Unrecognized prior service cost	240,000
Unamortized prior pension gain	96,000

At December 31, 2002:

Projected benefit obligation	910,000
Fair value of pension plan assets	825,000

Service cost for 2002 was $90,000. There were no contributions made or benefits paid during the year. Sparta's unfunded accrued pension liability was $8,000 at January 1, 2002. Sparta uses the straight-line method of amortization over the maximum period permitted.

Required:

a.   For items 1 through 5, calculate the amounts to be recognized as components of Sparta's unfunded accrued pension liability at December 31, 2002. On the CPA exam, a list of numeric answers would be presented for the candidate to choose from.

Amounts to be calculated

1. Interest cost.

2. Expected return on plan assets.

3. Actual return on plan assets.

4. Amortization of prior service costs.

5. Minimum amortization of unrecognized pension gain.

b.   For items 6 through 10, determine whether the component increases or decreases Sparta's unfunded accrued pension liability.

Items to be answered

6. Service cost.

7. Deferral of gain on plan assets.

8. Actual return on plan assets.

9. Amortization of prior service costs.

10. Amortization of unrecognized pension gain.

PROBLEMS

Problem 1   (15 to 25 minutes)

Essex Company has a single-employer defined benefit pension plan, and a compensation plan for future vacations for its employees.

Required:

a.   Define the interest cost component of net pension cost for a period. How should Essex determine its interest cost component of net pension cost for a period?

b.   Define prior service cost. How should Essex account for prior service cost? Why?

c.   What conditions must be met for Essex to accrue compensation for future vacations? What is the theoretical rationale for accruing compensation for future vacations?

NOTE: Part C of this question is covered in Module 25.

Problem 2   (15 to 25 minutes)

At December 31, 2002, as a result of its single employer defined benefit pension plan, Bighorn Co. had an unrecognized net loss and an unfunded accrued pension cost. Bighorn's pension plan and its actuarial assumptions have not changed since it began operations in 1998. Bighorn has made annual contributions to the plan.

Required:

a.   Identify the components of net pension cost that should be recognized in Bighorn's 2002 financial statements.

b.   What circumstances caused Bighorn's
1.   Unrecognized net loss?
2.   Unfunded accrued pension cost?

c.   How should Bighorn compute its minimum pension liability and any additional pension liability?

Problem 3   (30 to 40 minutes)

Deck Co. has just hired a new president, Palmer, and is reviewing its employee benefit plans with the new employee. For current employees, Deck offers a compensation plan for future vacations. Deck also provides postemployment benefits to former or inactive employees.

On the date of Palmer's hire, Palmer entered into a deferred compensation contract with Deck. Palmer is expected to retire in ten years. The contract calls for a payment of $150,000 upon termination of employment following a minimum three-year service period. The contract also provides that interest of 10%, compounded annually, be credited on the amount due each year after the third year.

Required:

a.   Give an example of postemployment benefits. State the conditions under which Deck is required to accrue liabilities for compensated absences and postemployment benefits. State Deck's disclosure requirements if these conditions, in full or in part, are not met.

b.   Describe the general accrual period for amounts to be paid under a deferred compensation contract. State the theoretical rationale for requiring accrual of these liabilities and related expenses.

c.   Prepare a schedule of the expense and accrued liability related to Palmer's deferred compensation agreement to be reported in Deck's financial statements for the first four years of the contract.

Problem 4

Return to Module 22A and complete Problem 2, requirement b. that covers postretirement benefits other than pensions.

1. d	__ __	9. c	__ __	17. a	__ __	25. d	__ __	33. b	__ __
2. d	__ __	10. d	__ __	18. b	__ __	26. d	__ __	34. b	__ __
3. d	__ __	11. d	__ __	19. c	__ __	27. a	__ __	35. b	__ __
4. b	__ __	12. a	__ __	20. a	__ __	28. c	__ __	36. a	__ __
5. c	__ __	13. d	__ __	21. b	__ __	29. a	__ __	37. c	__ __
6. d	__ __	14. b	__ __	22. a	__ __	30. c	__ __	38. a	__ __
7. c	__ __	15. b	__ __	23. c	__ __	31. a	__ __	1st: __/38 = __%
8. d	__ __	16. d	__ __	24. b	__ __	32. c	__ __	2nd: __/38 = __%

MULTIPLE-CHOICE ANSWER EXPLANATIONS

D.1.-5. Pensions

1. (d) Per SFAS 87, the six elements which an employer sponsoring a defined benefit pension plan must include in its net pension cost are service cost, interest cost, actual return on plan assets, amortization of unrecognized prior service cost, deferral of unexpected gain or loss, and amortization of the unrecognized net obligation or unrecognized net asset existing at the date of initial application of SFAS 87. Lee Corp's pension expense is calculated as follows:

Service cost	$160,000
Gain (actual and expected) on plan assets	(35,000)
Amortization	5,000
Interest	50,000
	180,000

Note that per SFAS 87, gains and losses that arise from a single occurrence which is not directly related to the operation of the plan should be reported as part of that occurrence and not as part of the plan's activity. Therefore, the $40,000 unexpected loss on plan assets related to a 2002 disposal of a subsidiary should be reported as part of the "loss on disposal" and not as part of the 2002 pension cost.

2. (d) The requirement is to determine the amount of unrecognized net loss to be recognized as a part of pension expense in 2002. Per SFAS 87, the **corridor approach** is to be used to determine gain or loss amortization. Under this approach, only the unrecognized net gain or loss in excess of 10% of the **greater** of the projected benefit obligation (PBO) or the market-related asset value (M-RAV) is amortized. In this case, the M-RAV ($1,650,000) is larger than the PBO ($1,530,000). The corridor is $165,000 (10% x $1,650,000). The unrecognized net loss ($235,000) exceeds the corridor by $70,000 ($235,000 – $165,000). This excess is amortized over the average remaining service period of active employees expected to participate in the plan ($70,000 ÷ 5.5 = $12,727).

3. (d) Estimates of future contributions to a defined benefit pension plan are not required to be disclosed. Answer (a) is incorrect because a description of the plan is a required disclosure. Answer (b) is incorrect because the amount of pension expense by component is a required disclosure. Answer (c) is incorrect because the weighted-average discount rate is a required disclosure.

4. (b) The requirement is to calculate the total amount of unrecognized prior service cost to be amortized over future periods as a result of a pension plan amendment. Prior service cost is the present value of retroactive benefits given to employees for years of service provided before the date of an amendment to the plan. Per SFAS 87, the cost of these retroactive benefits is measured by the increase in the projected benefit obligation at the date of amendment ($1,900,000 – $1,300,000 = $600,000). This amount will be recognized as expense (amortized) during the service periods of those employees who are expected to receive benefits under the plan.

5. (c) Prepaid pension cost is the cumulative excess of the amount funded over the amount recorded as pension expense. In 2002, pension expense is $520,000.

Service cost and interest on PBO	$620,000
Actual return on plan assets ($1,000,000 x 10%)	(100,000)
Pension expense	$520,000

Since 2002 funding was $1,000,000, 12/31/02 prepaid pension cost is $480,000 ($1,000,000 – $520,000).

6. (d) The solutions approach is to set up a T-account for prepaid/accrued pension cost

Prepaid/Accrued Pension Cost

		0	1/1/01 bal.
2001 cont.	50,000	75,000	2001 expense
2002 cont.	?	90,000	2002 expense
		15,000	Desired 12/31/02 bal.

The 1/1/01 balance is $0 because prior to 2001, Webb's contributions fully funded the plan. The missing amount can be solved as $100,000. Note that minimum liability considerations do not affect the accrued pension liability because in both years the fair value of plan assets exceeds the accumulated benefit obligation.

7. (c) The requirement is to determine how the service cost component of the net periodic pension cost is measured in a defined benefit pension plan. Per SFAS 87 the service cost component recognized shall be determined as "the actuarial present value of benefits attributed by the pension benefit formula to employee service during the period" that is known as the **projected benefit obligation**.

8. (d) Per SFAS 87, among the components which should be included in the net pension cost recognized for a period by an employer sponsoring a defined benefit pension plan are **both** actual return on plan assets, if any, and amortization of unrecognized prior service cost, if any.

9. (c) Net pension cost (expense) is comprised of six elements. One of these elements is interest on the projected benefit obligation, which is defined as the increase in the amount of the projected benefit obligation due to the passage of time. Candidates must be careful so as not to confuse "interest cost" with the "actual return" component of net pension cost which is the earnings on the plan assets. If the latter component is positive, it reduces the net pension cost for the period.

10.   (d)   Per SFAS 87, "because plan amendments are granted with the expectation that the employer will realize economic benefits in future periods, this Statement ... provides for recognition during the future periods of those employees." Therefore, the prior service cost will be reflected in the financial statements for 2002 and future years only.

11.   (d)   This question addresses the behavior of the components of pension expense over a period of time. SFAS 87 defines service cost as the actuarial present value of benefits attributed by the pension benefit formula to services rendered by employees during that period. This problem states that "all information on covered employees for 2002 and 2003 is the same," which indicates that there has been no change in Flood's work force during this two-year period. The only difference in the service cost for these two years would, therefore, be attributable to differences in the discounting of the benefits. Each year a group of employees works, the group becomes one year closer to retirement age and to collecting their retirement benefits. The present value of the benefits earned by employees each year grows as their retirement date grows nearer, because the benefits are discounted over a shorter period of time. If, for instance, the "average" retirement date for Flood's employees is January 1, 2013, the present value of the benefits for 2003's service will be greater than the present value of 2002 service, because it is discounted eleven years for 2002 versus ten years for 2003. (This is because every additional year of discounting reduces the present value of the benefits.) Therefore, the service cost for 2003 will be greater than for 2002. The problem also states that Flood intends to fund the plan in equal annual installments, and that the discount rate which was used to calculate the service cost is equal to the assumed rate of return on plan assets. Under these circumstances, to fully fund the pension obligation in equal payments, Flood will contribute an amount which exceeds the pension cost in the first years of the plan and which is less than the pension cost in later years. The glossary of SFAS 87 defines prepaid pension cost as the cumulative employer contributions in excess of accrued pension cost. Since 2002's funding would exceed its pension cost, Flood would report a prepaid pension cost on its 2002 balance sheet. The journal entry to record the funding would be

Pension expense	xxx	
Prepaid pension cost	xxx	
Cash		xxx

12.   (a)   The requirement is to determine what the "unfunded accrued pension cost" represents. Per SFAS 87, the unfunded accrued pension cost is a liability recognized when the net periodic pension cost exceeds the amount the employer has contributed to the plan.

13.   (d)   The projected benefit obligation is the actuarial present value of the pension obligation at the end of the period. Since there were no changes in actuarial estimates during the year, the end of period projected benefit obligation is computed as follows:

Projected benefit obligation, 1/1/02	$72,000
Service cost	18,000
Interest on projected benefit obligation (10% x $72,000)	7,200
Benefit payments	(15,000)
Pension benefit obligation, 12/31/02	$82,200

Service cost and interest on the projected benefit obligation increase the projected benefit obligation; benefit payments decrease the projected benefit obligation.

14.   (b)   The requirement is to determine which of the listed pension terms includes assumptions concerning projected changes in future compensation levels if the pension benefit formula is based on future compensation levels. Per SFAS 87, the service cost component and the projected benefit obligation reflect projected future compensation levels while the accumulated benefit obligation is measured based on employees' history of service and compensation without an estimate of projected future compensation levels.

15.   (b)   Per SFAS 87, the assumed discount rate should reflect the rates at which pension benefits could be effectively settled. This rate is sometimes referred to as the "settlement rate." To determine the settlement rate, it is appropriate to look at rates implicit in current prices of annuity contracts that could be used to settle the obligation under the defined benefit plan. The expected return on plan assets is **not** used to calculate the projected benefit obligation. The actual return on plan assets is also **not** used to calculate the projected benefit obligation.

16.   (d)   SFAS 87 requires that a minimum pension liability be reported for the excess of the accumulated benefit obligation over the fair value of the plan assets ($4,300,000 – $3,450,000 = **$850,000**). Note that this is the amount to be **reported in the balance sheet**. The amount of **additional liability to be recorded** would be this amount plus prepaid pension cost or less accrued pension cost.

17.   (a)   SFAS 87 requires the recognition of a **minimum liability** if the accumulated benefit obligation (ABO) exceeds the FV of the plan assets. In this case, the excess of the ABO over the FV of plan assets is $90,000 ($380,000 – $290,000). The **additional liability** to be recorded is the minimum liability **less accrued pension cost,** or plus **prepaid pension cost**. Therefore, the additional liability is $110,000 ($90,000 + $20,000).

18.   (b)   SFAS 87 requires the reporting of a **minimum liability** if the accumulated benefit obligation (ABO) exceeds the FV of the plan assets. In this case, the excess of the ABO over the FV of plan assets is $25,000 ($103,000 – $78,000). The **additional liability** to be recorded is equal to the minimum liability **less accrued pension cost,** or **plus prepaid pension cost**. At the end of the first year, accrued pension cost is $20,000 ($90,000 pension expense less $70,000 cash contribution). Therefore, the additional liability is $5,000 ($25,000 – $20,000).

19.   (c)   SFAS 87 requires that a **minimum pension liability** be reported for the excess of the accumulated benefit obligation (ABO) over the fair value of the plan assets. This excess is also called the unfunded ABO ($25,000). The **additional liability** to be recorded is the minimum liability less **accrued pension cost** or plus **prepaid pension cost**. Since Hall made no contributions to the pension plan during 2002, accrued pension cost equals net periodic pension cost of $8,000. Therefore, the additional pension liability to be recorded is $17,000 ($25,000 – $8,000).

20.   (a)   SFAS 87 requires that a **minimum pension liability** be reported for the excess of the accumulated benefit obligation (ABO) over the fair value of the plan assets. This excess is also called the unfunded ABO ($25,000). The **additional liability** to be recorded is the minimum liability less **accrued pension cost** or plus **prepaid pension cost**.

Since Hall made no contributions to the pension plan during 2002, accrued pension cost equals net periodic pension cost of $8,000. Therefore, the additional liability to be recorded is $17,000 ($25,000 – $8,000). Generally, the credit to **additional liability** is offset by a debit to an **intangible asset** account. However, when the additional liability exceeds the unrecognized prior service cost, the excess is reported as a component of **other comprehensive income** entitled "adjustment for minimum pension liability" and as accumulated other comprehensive income which is reported in one of three places, including the statement of changes in stockholder's equity, rather than as an intangible asset. For Hall, the excess reported in the equity account is $5,000 ($17,000 additional liability less $12,000 unrecognized prior service cost).

21.   (b)   Per SFAS 87, the recognition of an additional minimum liability is required if an unfunded accumulated benefit obligation (excess of accumulated benefit obligation over fair value of plan assets) exists and (1) an asset has been recognized as prepaid pension cost, (2) the liability already recognized as unfunded accrued pension cost is less than the unfunded accumulated benefit obligation, or (3) no accrued or prepaid pension cost has been recognized. The additional liability that must be recorded is the amount necessary to make the **total** liability equal to the unfunded accumulated benefit obligation (i.e., the accumulated benefit obligation **less** the fair market value of plan assets). The **projected** benefit obligation is not involved in the calculation of the minimum liability.

22.   (a)   The requirement is to determine when the **accumulated other comprehensive income** account, adjustment for minimum pension liability, should be reported on the balance sheet for a particular year. Per SFAS 87, when the additional liability required to be recognized exceeds the unrecognized prior service cost, the excess should be reported as a separate component (that is, a reduction) of **other comprehensive income and accumulated other comprehensive income,** net of any tax benefits. An employer that sponsors only one defined benefit pension plan may be required to report the equity account as well as an employer with two or more defined benefit pension plans. An amendment to an existing plan does not always cause the difference between the fair value of the plan assets and the accumulated benefit obligation.

23.   (c)   Per SFAS 88, when special termination benefits are offered to employees, a loss and liability must be recognized when the employee accepts the offer and the amount can be reasonably estimated. The amount to be recognized shall include any lump-sum payments ($475,000) and the present value of any expected future payments ($155,000). Therefore, the total liability for special termination benefits is $630,000 ($475,000 + $155,000). Note that the reduction of accrued pension costs ($45,000) would reduce the amount of the loss, but would **not** affect the liability. Instead it would be recorded as a reduction of accrued pension costs. The journal entry would be

Loss from termination benefits	585,000	
Accrued pension costs	45,000	
Liability from termination benefits		630,000

24.   (b)   The reconciliation schedule for the benefit obligation related to defined benefit pension plans would disclose both the amounts for service cost and benefits paid. Other items that would be disclosed in this reconciliation schedule include (1) interest cost, (2) contributions by plan participants, (3) actuarial gains and losses, (4) plan amendments, (5) divestitures, curtailments, and settlements, and (6) special termination benefits.

25.   (d)   SFAS 132 requires disclosure of a schedule reconciling the funded status of the pension plan (PBO less FV of plan assets) with the accrued or prepaid pension cost reported in the balance sheet.

26.   (d)   The reconciliation schedule for the plan assets related to defined benefit pension plans would disclose both the benefit payments and the actual return on plan assets. Other items that would be disclosed in this reconciliation schedule include (1) contributions by the employer, (2) contributions by plan participants, and (3) settlements and divestitures.

27.   (a)   Per SFAS 132, an employer sponsoring a defined benefit pension plan must disclose a great deal of information related to the plan. These disclosures include the amount of net periodic pension cost for the period and the fair value of plan assets.

28.   (c)   The effect of a one-percentage-point increase in the assumed health care cost trend rate(s) is required, not a two-percentage-point increase. An explanation of a significant change in plan assets, if not apparent from other disclosures, is required according to SFAS 132. The amount of any unamortized prior service cost not recognized in the statement of financial position (balance sheet) is a required disclosure. Another required disclosure per SFAS 132 is a reconciliation of beginning and ending balances of the benefit obligation.

29.   (a)   According to SFAS 132, the assumed discount rate and the rate of compensation increase are both required disclosures. The expected long-term rate of return on all of the employer's assets is not required. The expected long-term rate of return on plan assets is required, however.

30.   (c)   There are two methods approved for use in determining the assignment of prior service cost: the expected years of service method, and the straight-line basis over the average remaining service period of active employees method. Under the expected future years of service method, the total number of employee service years is calculated by grouping employees according to the time remaining to their retirement and multiplying the number in each group by the number of periods remaining to retirement. [(1 person x 3) + (2 people x 5) + (1 person x 7) = 20]. To calculate the amortization of prior service costs for a given year, the number of employee service years applicable to that period is used as the numerator of the fraction, and the denominator is the total employee service years based on all the identified groups. (4/20 x $100,000 = $20,000) For the straight-line basis over the average remaining service period method, the total number of service years (calculated above) is divided by the number of employees to find the weighted-average service life of each employee. (20/4 = 5 yrs.) The $100,000 of prior service cost will be amortized over the five years, or at $20,000 ($100,000 ÷ 5 = $20,000) a year.

31.   (a)   SFAS 132 requires the disclosure of the effects of a one-percentage-point increase or decrease of the trend rates for health care costs on: the aggregate of the service and interest cost components and the accumulated postretirement obligation.

32.   (c)   A reconciliation of the accrued or prepaid pension cost reported in its balance sheet with the pension expense reported in its income statement is not required. Answer (a) is incorrect because a reconciliation of the funded status of its pension plan with the accrued or prepaid cost reported in its balance sheet is required according to SFAS 132. Answer (b) is also incorrect because rates for assumed discount rate, rate of compensation increase, and expected long-term rate of return on plan assets are also required. Another required disclosure of SFAS 132 is the recognized amount of the net periodic benefit cost with the components shown separately.

D.6.   Postretirement Benefits other than Pensions (OPEB)

33.   (b)   Net periodic postretirement benefit cost is a net amount calculated by adding or subtracting six components. Three components present in this problem are combined as follows:

Service cost	$120,000
Interest on the accumulated postretirement benefit obligation	20,000
Amortization of transition obligation ($200,000 ÷ 20 years)	10,000
Postretirement benefit cost	$150,000

Service cost and interest on the accumulated postretirement benefit obligation always increase postretirement benefit cost. Foster Co. has elected to amortize the unrecognized transition obligation over a twenty-year period. Amortization of the $200,000 obligation on the straight-line basis increases postretirement benefit cost by $10,000 per year. The benefit payment represents a cash payment made for benefits by the employer; however, this is not a component of net periodic postretirement benefit cost.

34.   (b)   To determine the accrued postretirement benefit cost, the net periodic postretirement benefit cost must first be calculated as follows:

Service cost	$28,000
Interest on the accumulated postretirement benefit obligation	5,000
Amortization of the unrecognized transition obligation	8,000
Net periodic postretirement benefit cost	$41,000

An adjusting entry is required at year-end to record net periodic postretirement benefit cost and the cash benefit payments made to employees. An accrued postretirement benefit cost will be recorded if the net postretirement benefit cost exceeds the cash payments to employees. The journal entry would be

Postretirement benefit cost	41,000	
Cash		10,000
Accrued postretirement benefit cost		31,000

The balance in the accrued postretirement benefit cost account would be $31,000.

35.   (b)   The requirement is to determine the attribution period for accruing the expected postretirement health care benefit obligation. In accordance with SFAS 106, the beginning of the attribution period is generally the date of hire, and the end shall be the date of full eligibility. Fletcher's

age at the date of hire is forty-eight and the period of eligibility is ten years. Thus, the attribution period is forty-eight to fifty-eight.

36.   (a)   SFAS 106 requires an employer's obligation for postretirement benefits expected to be provided to an employee be fully accrued by the full eligibility date of the employee, even if the employee is to render additional service beyond that date.

37.   (c)   Per SFAS 106, a transition obligation is measured as the difference between the accumulated postretirement benefit obligation and the fair value of plan assets at the beginning of the fiscal year for which SFAS 106 is adopted. A transition obligation may be recognized immediately in net income of the period of the change, or recognized on a delayed basis as a component of net periodic postretirement benefit cost. If delayed recognition is elected, SFAS 106, states that in general the transition obligation should be amortized on a straight-line basis over the average remaining service period of plan participants. If the average remaining service period is less than twenty years, the employer may elect to use a twenty-year amortization period.

38.   (a)   SFAS 106 requires that the employer disclose the amount of the accumulated postretirement benefit obligation. The employer must also disclose the assumed health care cost trend rate used to measure the expected cost of benefits covered by the plan.

OTHER OBJECTIVE ANSWER EXPLANATIONS

Problem 1

1.   **($48,000)** The solutions approach is to set up the formula for calculating interest cost

Beginning balance of projected benefit obligation (1/1/02)	x	Discount rate	=	Interest cost
$600,000	x	.08	=	$48,000

2.   **($72,000)** The solutions approach is to set up the formula for calculating the expected return on plan assets

Beginning balance of fair value of the plan assets (1/1/02)	x	Expected rate of return on plan assets	=	Expected return on plan assets
$720,000	x	10%	=	$72,000

3.   **($105,000)** The solutions approach is to set up a T-account for the fair value of pension plan assets

	Fair Value of Pension Plan Assets		(Pension plan account, but not on Sparta's books)
1/1/02	720,000		
Contributions during the year	0	0	Pension benefits paid during 2002
Actual return on plan assets	?		
12/31/02	825,000		

Actual return on plan assets = $825,000 – $720,000 + $0 – $0 = $105,000

The problem states that there were no contributions made or benefits paid, thus the actual return on plan assets is the only change not accounted for.

4.   **($20,000)** The solutions approach is to set up the formula for amortization of prior service cost

Unrecognized prior service cost (1/1/02)	÷	Average service life of employees	=	Amortization of prior service costs

$$\frac{\$240,000}{12} = \$20,000$$

5.   **($2,000)** The solutions approach is to set up the steps needed to calculate the minimum amortization of unrecognized pension gain

(1)   Determine the greater of the

  Projected benefit obligation ($600,000), or
  Fair value of the plan assets ($720,000)

(2)   Multiply the larger amount in #1 by 10%

  $720,000 x 10% = $72,000

(3)   Calculate the difference between the value in #2 and the unamortized prior pension gain

  $96,000 – $72,000 = $24,000

(4)   Amortize the value in #3 by dividing it by the average service life of employees

$$\frac{\$24,000}{12} = \$2,000$$

  Minimum amortization   = $2,000

When the amortization of the cumulative unrecognized net gain or loss from previous periods is required, the procedure is comparable to the amortization of prior service cost and, in general, it requires the use of the average remaining service period for active employees. Unlike prior service cost, however, the amount to be amortized is not necessarily the calculated amount of the cumulative unrecognized net gain or loss. Instead, the minimum amount subject to amortization, is determined by the use of a method sometimes referred to as the "corridor" approach. The minimum amount of the cumulative unrecognized gain or loss required to be amortized is determined by computing, at the beginning of the fiscal year, the excess of the cumulative unrecognized gain or loss over 10% of the greater of the projected benefit obligation or the market-related asset value. If the cumulative unrecognized gain or loss is equal to or less than the 10% calculated value, no amount need be amortized.

6.   **(I)** Service cost increases the unfunded accrued pension liability. Service cost is defined as the actuarial present value of benefits attributed by the pension benefit formula to employee services performed during the current period. In other words, this represents the obligation a company is responsible to pay, for work employees perform during the current year, which increases a company's pension liability.

7.   **(I)** The deferral of a gain on pension plan assets will increase the unfunded pension liability. A gain consists of two components: (1) the current period difference between the expected return on plan assets and the actual return on plan assets **and** (2) the unrecognized net gain from **previous periods**. When the expected return is less than the actual return, a gain arises. However, the pension cost for the year will report the expected return on plan assets, not the actual return on plan assets. This is done to record a more consistent, smooth yearly return, rather than one which is erratic, based on actual results. Therefore, if the expected return is less than the actual return, the actual return which originally decreased pension cost, will be offset by an increase in pension cost for the difference between the actual and expected return. A numerical example will help to clarify this point.

Actual return	=	$60,000
Expected return	=	25,000
Difference		$35,000 gain

The $35,000 gain cannot be recognized, because only the expected return is recorded as a decrease in pension cost. Therefore, because $60,000 was recorded, and only $25,000 should be used to decrease pension cost, the $35,000 gain will be subtracted from pension cost, **increasing** pension liability by $35,000.

8. **(D)** The actual return on plan assets will decrease the unfunded accrued pension liability. The actual return represents the return on the assets that are invested, to generate income, for paying pension benefits. This return will then decrease the amount of funds a company must contribute, to accumulate funds to pay pension benefits to their employees, thereby decreasing pension liability. Recall, from the discussion in (7), there will be an adjustment in the calculation of pension cost for the difference between the actual return and the expected return on plan assets.

9. **(I)** The amortization of prior service costs will increase the unfunded accrued pension liability. Prior service costs represent additional benefits, which are granted to employees, for services performed in previous periods. These benefits are then amortized over the average service life of the employees, from the time period the benefits were granted. The benefits increase the pension liability on Sparta's books as they are amortized because they represent the additional benefits that must be paid to employees.

10. **(D)** The amortization of unrecognized pension gain decreases the unfunded accrued pension liability. Please refer to question (7) for an explanation of how a pension gain arises. Also, refer to question (5) for an explanation of how gain amortization is calculated. The amortization decreases the pension liability because it is a deduction in the pension cost calculation. Therefore, the pension liability decreases.

ANSWER OUTLINE

Problem 1   Pension Terms and Accrual of Vacation Pay

a.   Interest cost component = Increase in PBO caused by
          passage of time
          Calculation
             Assumed discount rate x Beginning PBO

b.   PSC = Increased benefits based on services rendered in
          prior periods
          Granted at adoption or amendment date
          Accounting
             Include amortization of PSC in net pension cost dur-
                ing future service periods of employees active at
                date of adoption/amendment
             Because PSC incurred in anticipation of future eco-
                nomic benefits to employer

c.   Conditions necessary for accrual of future vacation
          compensation
             Obligation stems from services already performed
             Obligation relates to vested/accumulated rights
             Payment is probable
             Amount can reasonably be estimated
          Rationale for accrual
             Matches costs and revenues
             Recognizes measurable liability

UNOFFICIAL ANSWER

Problem 1   Pension Terms and Accrual of Vacation Pay

a.   The interest cost component of the net pension cost for
a period is the increase in the projected benefit obligation
due to the passage of time. Essex would determine its interest cost component by applying an assumed discount rate to
the beginning projected benefit obligation.

b.   Prior service cost is the cost of retroactive benefits (increased benefits based on services rendered in prior periods)
granted at the date of adoption or amendment of a pension
plan. Prior service cost should be included in net pension
cost during the future service periods of those employees
active at the date of the pension plan adoption or amendment, as appropriate, who are expected to receive benefits
under the pension plan. Prior service cost is incurred with
the expectation that the employer will realize economic
benefits in future periods.

c.   Essex must accrue compensation for future vacations if
all of the following conditions are met:

   •   Essex's obligation relating to employees' rights to
receive compensation for future vacations is attributable to
employees' services already rendered.
   •   The obligation relates to rights that vest or accumulate.
   •   Payment of the vacation benefits is probable.
   •   The amount can be reasonably estimated.

   The theoretical rationale is that accruing compensation
matches the cost of vacation benefits to the period in which
services are rendered, and results in recognition of a measurable liability.

ANSWER OUTLINE

Problem 2   Pension Cost Components; Causes of Unrec-
          ognized Net Loss and Accrual Pension Cost;
          Minimum Liability (592,T5)

a.   Components of net pension cost

   •   Service cost
   •   Interest cost
   •   Actual return on plan assets
   •   Gain or loss
          (Actual – Expected return) + Amortization of un-
             recognized gain/loss

b.   **1.**   Unrecognized net loss
             Actuarial assumptions ≠ Experience for PBO
                and returns on plan assets
      2.   Unfunded accrued pension cost
             Cumulative net pension expense > Cash contrib-
                uted to fund

c.   Minimum pension liability = ABO – FV of plan assets
          Additional pension liability = Minimum liability –
             Unfunded accrued pension cost

UNOFFICIAL ANSWER

Problem 2   Pension Cost Components; Causes of Un-
          recognized Net Loss and Accrual Pension
          Cost; Minimum Liability

a.   The components of Bighorn's 2002 net pension cost
calculation are

   •   Service cost.
   •   Interest cost.
   •   Actual return on plan assets.
   •   Gain or loss consisting of

      •   The difference between the actual and expected re-
turn on plan assets.
      •   Any amortization of the unrecognized gain or loss
from previous periods.

b.   **1.**   Bighorn's unrecognized net loss results from differences between actuarial assumptions and experiences for
both its projected benefit obligation and returns on plan assets.
      2.   Bighorn's unfunded accrued pension cost occurs
because cumulative net pension expense exceeds cash contributed to the pension fund.

c.   Bighorn's minimum pension liability equals the excess
of the accumulated benefit obligation over the fair value of
plan assets. Bighorn's additional pension liability would
equal any excess of this minimum pension liability over the
unfunded accrued pension cost.

ANSWER OUTLINE

Problem 3 Postemployment Benefits; Deferred Compensation Contracts

a. Example of postemployment benefits:
    Health care benefits
    Conditions that require accrued liabilities:
        Obligation is attributable to employees' services already rendered,
        Employee's rights accumulate or vest,
        Payment is probable, and
        Amount of benefits can be reasonably estimated
    Disclosure requirements
        Mention that obligation amount is **not** reasonably estimable

b. General accrual period
        Active employment period through full eligibility date
            Beginning with contract date
    Theoretical rationale
        Matching
            Cost of benefits matched to period services rendered
        Recognize measurable liability

c. Record deferred compensation expense and increase accrued liability first three years (2002-2004)
    Record interest in year four (2005)

UNOFFICIAL ANSWER

Problem 3 Postemployment Benefits; Deferred Compensation Contracts

a. An example of postemployment benefits offered by employers is continuation of health care benefits. Deck is required to accrue liabilities for compensated absences and postemployment benefits if all of the following conditions are met:

- The obligation is attributable to employees' services already rendered,
- The employees' rights accumulate or vest,
- Payment is probable, and
- The amount of the benefits can be reasonably estimated

If an obligation cannot be accrued solely because the amount cannot be reasonably estimated, the financial statements should disclose that fact.

b. Estimated amounts to be paid under a deferred compensation contract should be accrued over the period of an employee's active employment from the time the contract is signed to the employee's full eligibility date. The theoretical rationale for accrual of these obligations to be paid in the future is that accrual matches the cost of the benefits to the period in which services are rendered, and results in recognition of a measurable liability.

c.   *Deck Co.*
SCHEDULE OF DEFERRED COMPENSATION AMOUNTS
For the Years 2002 through 2005

For the year ended	Accrued liability	Deferred compensation expense
12/31/02	$ 50,000	$50,000 [a]
12/31/03	$100,000	$50,000
12/31/04	$150,000	$50,000
12/31/05	$165,000	$15,000 [b]

[a] $150,000 ÷ 3 (straight-line method)
[b] $150,000 x 10%

E. Leases

A lease is a contract between two parties—a lessor and a lessee. A lease contract gives a lessee rights to use the lessor's property for a specified period of time in return for periodic cash payments (rent) to the lessor.

A major goal in accounting for leases is to recognize the economic substance of the lease agreement over its mere legal form. For example, many lease agreements are similar to the purchase of an asset financed by the issuance of debt. The economic substance of a lease agreement generally takes one of two forms:

1. Periodic payments of rent by the lessee for the **use** of the lessor's property
2. Periodic payments similar to an installment purchase by the lessee for the rights to **acquire** the lessor's property in the future (i.e., acquisition of property by financing)

In (1), the risks and rewards of owning the asset remain with the lessor. Accordingly, the asset is **not** treated as sold by the lessor to the lessee, and remains on the lessor's books. This form of leasing arrangement is called an **operating lease**. By contrast, in (2), a lease agreement may transfer many of the risks and rewards of ownership to the lessee. This form of lease is treated as a sale by the lessor and as a purchase by the lessee. This concept is clearly stated in SFAS 13 as follows:

> A lease that transfers substantially all of the benefits and risks incident to ownership of property should be accounted for as the acquisition of an asset and the incurrence of an obligation by the lessee and as a sale or financing by the lessor.

When the risks and rewards of ownership are deemed to have been passed from the lessor to the lessee, the lessor will account for the lease as either a **direct financing** or as a **sales-type lease,** and the lessee will account for the lease as a **capital lease**.

To determine whether the risks and rewards of ownership have been transferred to the lessee, **at least one** of the following four criteria must be met:

1. The lease **transfers title** to the lessee
2. The lease contains a **bargain purchase** option
3. The lease **term is 75% or more** of useful life and the lease is not first executed within the last 25% of the original useful life
4. The **present value** of minimum lease payments **is 90% or more** of the net of the **fair market value** of the asset reduced by the investment tax credit (when in effect) retained by the lessor and the lease is not executed in the last 25% of the original useful life

These four criteria apply to both the lessor and to the lessee. The lessor, however, must meet two additional criteria:

1. **Collectibility** of minimum lease payments is predictable, and
2. There are **no important uncertainties** concerning costs yet to be incurred by the lessor under the lease.

Both of the above must be satisfied by the lessor in order for the lessor to treat the lease in substance as an installment sale.

The classification of leases can be summarized as follows:

	Lessor	*Lessee*
Risks and rewards remain with lessor (no sale and purchase of asset)	Operating	Operating
Risks and rewards transfer to lessee (sale and purchase of asset)	Direct financing .... Sales-type	Capital

1. Study Program for Leases

a. Begin by reviewing the terms peculiar to leases that appear at the beginning of the outline of SFAS 13 in the pronouncement outlines that begin after Module 33.

b.   Review the material in this module so that you will be familiar with the major concepts and applications in the leasing area.
c.   After you have developed a solid base of understanding, you should review the outline of SFAS 13.
d.   The discussion of accounting for leases is structured to follow the lease classification matrix listed above.

(1) Operating Lease—Lessor/Lessee

An operating lease is any lease not meeting the criteria for a direct financing or sales-type lease in the case of a lessor, or for a capital lease in the case of a lessee. Under an operating lease, leased assets continue to be carried on the lessor's balance sheet and are depreciated in the normal manner. These assets, however, are not shown on the lessee's balance sheet since the lessee cannot expect to derive any future economic benefit from the assets beyond the lease term. Several issues are frequently encountered when dealing with operating leases. These issues are discussed in the remainder of this section.

(a)   Free rent/uneven payments

Some lease agreements might call for uneven payments or scheduled rent increases over the lease term. Other agreements might include, as an incentive to the lessee, several months of "free rent" during which the lessee may use the asset without owing rent to the lessor. In these cases, rental revenue (expense) is still recognized by the lessor (lessee) on a straight-line basis and is prorated over the full term of the lease during which the lessee has possession of the asset. This is due to the matching principle; if physical usage is relatively the same over the lease term, then an equal amount of benefit is being obtained by both parties to the lease.

NOTE: Another method to allocate rental revenue (expense) may be used if it better represents the actual physical use of the leased asset.

When the pattern of actual cash received (paid) as rent is other than straight-line, it will be necessary for both parties to record accruals, or deferrals, depending upon the payment schedule.

		Accruals	(or)	*Deferrals*
Lessor	--	Rent receivable		Unearned rent
Lessee	--	Rent payable		Prepaid rent

Numerical Example 1:

Lease Information

1)   A ten-year lease is initiated on 1/1/01
2)   Payments are $100,000 per year payable January 1 (except for the first year)
3)   Payment for the first year is $50,000, due on 7/1/01

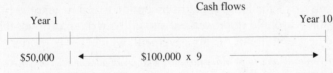

Cash flows

Recognition of revenue/expense:

Actual cash received/paid = (9 years   x $100,000) + $50,000 = $950,000 total

Revenue and expense per year = $950,000   ÷   10 years   = $95,000 per year

Journal entries for the lessor			*Journal entries for the lessee*		
Year 1			*Year 1*		
Cash	50,000		Rent expense	50,000	
Rent revenue		50,000	Cash		50,000
Rent receivable	45,000		Rent expense	45,000	
Rent revenue		45,000	Rent payable		45,000

Years 2-10

Cash	100,000	
Rent revenue		95,000
Rent receivable		5,000 (a)

Years 2-10

Rent expense	95,000	
Rent payable	5,000 (b)	
Cash		100,000

	Rent Receivable		(a)		(b)	Rent Payable		
yr. 1	45,000	5,000	yr. 2		yr. 2	5,000	45,000	yr. 1
		•				•		
		•				•		
		•	yr. 10		yr. 10	•		

(b)   Initial direct costs

The lessor may incur costs in setting up the lease agreement. Such costs might include finder's fees, appraisal fees, document processing fees, negotiation fees, and any costs in closing the transaction. These costs, called initial direct costs, are carried as an asset on the lessor's balance sheet. Initial direct costs are amortized on a straight-line basis to expense over the lease term by the lessor, and are shown net of accumulated amortization on the lessor's balance sheet.

(c)   Lease bonus (fee)

At the inception of the lease, the lessee may pay a nonrefundable lease bonus (fee) to the lessor in order to obtain more favorable leasing terms (e.g., a lease term of three years instead of five years). The lease bonus (fee) would be treated as unearned rent by the lessor and would be amortized to rental revenue on a straight-line basis over the lease term. The lessee would treat the lease bonus (fee) as prepaid rent and would recognize it as rental expense over the lease term on a straight-line basis.

(d)   Security deposits

Some lease agreements may require that the lessee pay the lessor a security deposit at the inception of the lease. Security deposits may be either refundable or nonrefundable. A **refundable** security deposit is treated as a liability by the lessor and as a receivable by the lessee until the deposit is returned to the lessee. A **nonrefundable** security deposit is recorded as unearned revenue by the lessor and as prepaid rent by the lessee until the deposit is considered earned by the lessor (usually at the end of the lease term).

(e)   Leasehold improvements

Frequently, the lessee will make improvements to leased property by constructing new buildings or improving existing structures. The lessee has the right to use these leasehold improvements over the term of the lease; however, these improvements will revert to the lessor at the expiration of the lease. Leasehold improvements are capitalized to "Leasehold Improvements" (a property, plant and equipment account) by the lessee and are amortized over the **shorter** of (1) the remaining lease term, **or** (2) the useful life of the improvement. Improvements made in lieu of rent should be expensed in the period incurred. If the lease contains an option to renew and the likelihood of renewal is uncertain, the leasehold improvement should be written off over the life of the initial lease term or useful life of the improvement, whichever is shorter.

*NOTE: Moveable equipment or office furniture that is not attached to the leased property is **not** considered a leasehold improvement.*

The summary below lists the elements commonly encountered in operating leases:

Operating Lease FS Elements

	Lessor	*Lessee*
Balance sheet:	• Leased asset (net of accumulated depreciation)	• Prepaid rent (including lease bonus/fee and nonrefundable security deposit)
	• Rent receivable	• Leasehold improvements (net of accumulated amortization)
	• Initial direct costs (net of accumulated amortization)	• Deposit receivable
	• Unearned rent (including lease bonus/fee and nonrefundable security deposit)	
	• Deposit liability	

Income statement:	• Rent revenue (including amortization of lease bonus/fee and nonrefundable security deposit)	• Rent expense (including amortization of lease bonus/fee and nonrefundable security deposit)
	• Depreciation expense	• Amortization of leasehold improvements
	• Amortization of initial direct costs	
	• Other maintenance expenses	

Knowledge of these elements is helpful in answering questions that require a determination of lessor's net income or lessee's total expense in connection with an operating lease.

(f) **Termination costs**

Occasionally, a lessee will decide to terminate an operating lease and incur costs to do so. SFAS 146 indicates that such costs should be measured and recognized at fair value at the date the agreement is terminated or the entity no longer receives rights to the assets (See outline of SFAS 146).

(2) **Direct Financing Lease—Lessor**

Although most discussions, including SFAS 13, begin with the lessee's accounting for a capital lease, we have chosen to present the lessor's accounting first because the lessor is the party that determines the fixed cash schedule of lease payments that are to be made by the lessee.

A direct financing lease arises when a consumer needs equipment but does not want to purchase the equipment outright, and/or is unable to obtain conventional financing. In this situation, the consumer will turn to a leasing company (e.g., a bank) which will purchase the desired asset from a manufacturer (or dealer) and lease it to the consumer. Direct financing leases apply to leasing companies, as opposed to manufacturers or dealers, because leasing companies purchase the assets solely for leasing, not for resale. Leasing companies are usually involved in financing activities (e.g., banking and insurance), not in the sale of property of the type being leased. The following situation shows when a direct financing lease would arise:

> ABC Company needs new equipment to expand its manufacturing operations but does not have enough capital to purchase the equipment at present. ABC Company employs Universal Leasing Company to purchase the equipment. ABC will lease the asset from Universal. Universal records a direct financing lease.

The relationships in a direct financing lease arrangement are illustrated below.

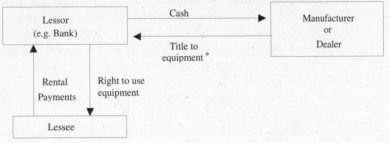

* *Title would stay with the lessor unless criterion (1) or (2) above is met in which case title would pass to the lessee.*

As mentioned, a lease is considered to be a direct financing lease by the **lessor** if at least one of the four criteria applicable to both lessors and lessees is met, and **both** of the additional criteria applicable to lessors is met.

Direct financing leases result in only interest revenue for the lessor. In essence, no product has been sold by the lessor, so no gain/loss, sales, or cost of sales is recognized from the lease transaction. Thus the FMV (selling price) of the leased asset equals its cost to the lessor.

The lessor's entry to record the acquisition of title to the asset to be leased is as follows:

Asset to be leased	(cost of asset = FMV)
Cash	(cash paid)

At the inception of the lease, the lessor makes the following entry:

Lease receivable	xx	
Asset to be leased		xx
Unearned interest revenue		xx

In effect, the asset is removed from the lessor's books; it will be transferred to the lessee's books if one of the four criteria applicable to lessees is met. It is possible that the lessee's analysis might result in an operating lease.

In order to calculate the amounts in the entry above, you must first become familiar with several important terms.

(a) **Minimum lease payments (MLP)**

MLP are the payments that the lessor/lessee is or can be required to make in connection with the leased property.

1. Rent payments (excluding executory costs and contingent rentals)
2. Bargain purchase option (if any)
3. Guaranteed residual value (if any)
4. Penalty for failure to renew (if any)

Executory costs (e.g., property taxes, insurance, etc.) and contingent rentals are treated as revenues in the period earned.

(b) **Bargain purchase option (BPO)**

This option allows the lessee to purchase leased property for an amount substantially lower than the expected FMV at the exercise date of the option.

(c) **Residual value**

Residual value can be unguaranteed or guaranteed. Some lease contracts require lessees to guarantee residual value to lessors. The lessee can either buy the leased asset at the end of the lease term for the guaranteed residual value or allow the lessor to sell the leased asset (with the lessee paying any deficiency or receiving any excess over the guaranteed residual value).

Guaranteed residual value (GRV) is considered part of the "minimum lease payment" and is reflected in the lessor's lease receivable account and the lessee's lease payable account. At the end of the lease term, the receivable and payable on the respective lessor's and lessee's books should be equal to the guaranteed residual value. Both lessor and lessee consider the guaranteed residual value a final lease payment. The lessee should amortize (depreciate) the asset down to the guaranteed residual value.

Unguaranteed residual value is the estimated residual value of the leased asset at the end of the lease (if a guaranteed residual value exists, the unguaranteed residual value is the excess of estimated value over the guaranteed residual value). The present value of the unguaranteed residual value should be included in the lessor's net investment in the lease unless the lease transfers title to the leased asset or there is a bargain purchase option.

At the end of the lease, the lessor's receivable account should be equal to the unguaranteed residual value. The lessor must review the estimated residual value annually and recognize any decreases as a loss. No upward adjustments of the residual value are permitted.

Now you are ready to calculate the amounts for the lessor's entry using the following formulas:

Lease receivable* (= gross investment)	=	Total MLP**	+	URV (if any)
Asset to be leased (= net investment) (= FMV or cost of asset)	=	PV of gross investment		
Unearned interest revenue	=	Gross investment	–	FMV (or cost) of asset

* The title **Gross investment** is used when there is an unguaranteed residual value because the lower probability of collection of the residual value makes the use of the term **Receivable** undesirable.

** Include guaranteed residual value.

Alternative methods of recording the lease transaction are shown below.

Lease receivable (gross)	xx			Lease receivable (net)	xx	
Asset to be leased		xx	-or-	Asset to be leased		xx
Unearned interest revenue		xx				

We will follow the gross method in our examples for the lessor because it is consistent with SFAS 13 and the questions on the CPA exam.

SFAS 13 specifies additional guidelines when accounting for the lessor.

- The lease receivable should be separated into current and noncurrent components on the lessor's balance sheet.
- Unearned interest revenue must be amortized to produce a constant periodic rate of return on the net investment using the interest method.
- No residual value is assumed to accrue to the value of the lessor if the lease transfers ownership or contains a BPO.
- At the termination of the lease, the balance in the receivable should equal the guaranteed or unguaranteed residual value, assuming title is not transferred and there is no bargain purchase option.

Numerical Example 2:

Lease Information

1) A three-year lease is initiated on 1/1/02 for equipment costing $131,858 with an expected useful life of five years. The FMV of the equipment on 1/1/02 is $131,858.
2) Three annual payments are due to the lessor beginning 12/31/02. The property reverts back to the lessor upon termination of the lease.
3) The guaranteed residual value at the end of year 3 is $10,000.
4) The lessor is to receive a 10% return (implicit rate).
5) Collectivity of minimum lease payments is predictable, and there are no important uncertainties concerning costs yet to be incurred by the lessor under the lease.
6) The cost (FMV) of the asset incurred by the lessor to acquire the asset for leasing is to be recovered through two components: annual rent payments and guaranteed residual value using a discount (implicit) rate of 10%.
7) The annual rent payment to the lessor is computed as follows:

   a) Find PV of guaranteed residual value

   $$\$10,000 \quad \times \quad .7513 \quad = \quad \$7,513$$
   GRV

   b) Find PV of annual rent payments

   $$\$131,858 \quad - \quad \$7,513 \quad = \quad \$124,345$$
   FMV of asset

   c) Find annual rent payment

   $$\$124,345 \quad \div \quad PVA_{n=3; i=10\%}$$
   $$\$124,345 \quad \div \quad 2.4869 \quad = \quad \$50,000$$

Lease Classification

This lease is a direct financing lease because criterion 4 (the 90% test) is satisfied.

$$\$124,345 + \$7,513 \geq (.9)(\$131,858)$$

(Since the residual value is guaranteed, the PV of the MLP is 100% of the FMV.) The two additional criteria for the lessor are satisfied, and FMV equals cost. If the residual value had been unguaranteed, the 90% test would still have been met because $124,345 \geq (.9)($131,858)$.

Accounting for Lease

1) The lease should be recorded at the beginning of year 1 by the lessor.
2) The lease receivable is calculated as follows:

(Annual rent payment	x	Lease term)	+	GRV	
$50,000		3 yrs.		$10,000	= $160,000

3) Unearned interest revenue is calculated as follows:

Lease receivable	–	FMV of asset		
$160,000		$131,858		= $ 28,142

4) Unearned interest is amortized during the lease term using the following amortization schedule:

AMORTIZATION SCHEDULE

Carrying value at beg. of yr. 1 (= PV of gross investment)		$131,858
Interest revenue (10%)	$ 13,186	
Rent payment	(50,000)	(36,814)
Carrying value at beg. of yr. 2		95,044
Interest revenue	9,504	
Rent payment	(50,000)	(40,496)
Carrying value at beg. of yr. 3		54,548
Interest revenue	5,452	
Rent payment	(50,000)	(44,548)
Carrying value at end of yr. 3 (= residual value)		10,000

Lease receivable on balance sheet:

End of Year 1	–	current portion	=	$40,496	principal reduction in year 2
		noncurrent portion	=	$54,548	principal reductions after year 2
End of Year 2	–	current portion	=	$54,548	principal reduction in the following year (includes residual value)

NOTE: As the lease expires, interest revenue decreases and the reduction of principal increases.

5) The journal entries for the lessor are shown below.

JOURNAL ENTRIES FOR THE LESSOR

Initial entries (Beg. of Yr. 1)

Equipment for leasing	131,858	
Cash		131,858
Lease receivable	160,000	
Equipment for leasing		131,858
Unearned interest		28,142

End of Year 1

Cash	50,000	
Lease receivable		50,000
Unearned interest	13,186	
Interest revenue		13,186

End of Year 2

Cash	50,000	
Lease receivable		50,000
Unearned interest	9,504	
Interest revenue		9,504

End of Year 3

Cash	50,000	
Lease receivable		50,000
Unearned interest	5,452	
Interest revenue		5,452

6) Assume that when the asset is returned at the end of year 3 the asset has a FMV of only $4,000. The lessee will need to make a payment of $6,000 ($10,000 – $4,000) because the residual value was guaranteed. The lessor would make the following entry:

Cash	6,000	
Residual value of equipment	4,000	
Lease receivable		10,000

(3) Sales-Type Lease—Lessor

A sales-type lease arises when a manufacturer or dealer leases an asset which otherwise might be sold outright for a profit. These manufacturers (dealers) use leasing as a way to market their own products (e.g., a car dealership). The leasing, or financing arrangement, is a means for the manufacturer to sell its products and realize a profit from sales. (By contrast, direct financing leases serve purely as financing arrangements.) The following situation shows when a sales-type lease would arise:

ABC Company needs equipment to expand its manufacturing operations. ABC Company enters into a lease agreement with XYZ Manufacturing, Inc. for the equipment. XYZ Manufacturing Inc. records a sales-type lease.

The relationships in a sales-type lease arrangement are illustrated below.

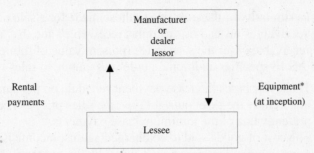

* *Title stays with lessor and property will be returned to lessor at the end of the lease term unless criterion (1) or (2) above is met.*

Sales-type leases, unlike direct financing leases, result in **both** (1) gross profit (loss) in the period of sales, **and** (2) interest revenue to be earned over the lease term using the effective interest method. The diagram below compares and contrasts direct financing leases with sales-type leases.

Direct Financing Lease (Lessor)

Gross investment
= Total amount lessor receives
= MLPs + URV
= Lease Receivable

FMV
= Cost of asset
= PV of gross investment
= Asset

0

Unearned interest revenue
• *Recognize as revenue using the (effective) interest method*

Sales-Type Lease (Lessor)

Gross investment
= Total amount lessor receives
= MLPs + URV
= Lease Receivable

FMV
= Sales price
= PV of MLPs
= Sales

Cost
= Cost of Goods Sold

0

Unearned interest revenue
• *Recognize as revenue using the (effective) interest method*

Gross (dealer's) profit
• *Recognize immediately*
• *Sales less CGS on income statement*

A lease is considered to be a sales-type lease from the viewpoint of the lessor if the criteria mentioned earlier for direct financing leases are satisfied. However, in the case of a sales-type lease, the FMV of the asset, which is the sales price in the ordinary course of the lessor's business is **greater than** the cost or carrying value of the leased asset. Because of this difference, a sales-type lease is more complex than a direct financing lease. The journal entries to record a sales-type are

Lease receivable (Gross)	xx	
Sales		xx
Unearned interest		xx
CGS	xx	
Inventory		xx

Note the similarity of these entries to those made for a sale on account. The differences are "lease receivable" instead of "accounts receivable" and the "unearned interest" for the excess of the receivables over the sales price (present value of future payments).

SFAS 13 specifies additional guidelines unique to sales-type leases:

- The lessor bases the lease payment schedule on the amount the lessee would have paid to purchase the asset outright (i.e., the sales price). Therefore, sales are equal to the present value of the minimum lease payments.
- The cost of goods sold to be charged against income is equal to the historic cost or carrying value of the leased asset (most likely inventory) **less** the present value of any unguaranteed residual value.
- The difference between the selling price and cost of goods sold is the gross profit (loss) recognized by the lessor at the inception of the lease.
- When accounting for sales-type leases, guaranteed residual value is considered part of sales revenue because the lessor knows the entire asset has been sold. Unguaranteed residual value, however, is excluded from both sales and cost of sales at its present value because there is less certainty that unguaranteed residual value will be realized.

Numerical Example 3:

Lease Information

Assume same information as in previous example except

1) The cost of the equipment is $100,000 (either manufactured cost or purchase price paid by dealer).
2) The normal selling price of the equipment is $131,858 which is greater than the $100,000 cost.
3) The residual value is **unguaranteed**.
4) The lease payments are $50,000, the same as computed in the previous example, because the lessor treats an **un**guaranteed residual value in the same way as a guaranteed residual value. However, as mentioned below, the present value of the unguaranteed residual value is not included in the 90% test.

Lease Classification

This is a sales-type lease since the 90% test is satisfied; 90% of the $131,858 FMV = $118,672, which is less than $124,345, the present value of the minimum lease payments (see Numerical Example 2); the present value of the residual value is excluded because it is unguaranteed. Additionally, the cost of the asset is less than its fair market value (also the present value of the minimum lease payments plus the unguaranteed residual value). Assume the two additional criteria for the lessor have been satisfied.

Accounting for Lease

1) The gross investment is: $160,000 [3 payments of $50,000 (same as Numerical Example 2) plus a $10,000 unguaranteed residual value]
   The PV of gross investment is: $131,858 [($50,000 x 2.4869) + ($10,000 x .7513)]
   The unearned interest revenue is: $28,142 ($160,000 – $131,858)
   Sales are: $124,345 [$131,858 – ($10,000 x .7513)*]
   CGS is: $92,487 [$100,000 – ($10,000 x .7513)*]

   * *Note that there is no effect on gross profit of not including the present value of the unguaranteed residual value in either sales or cost of goods sold. In both cases, the gross profit is $31,858. If the residual value were guaranteed, this adjustment would not be made.*

2) The entry to record the lease is

Lease receivable**	160,000	
Cost of goods sold	92,487	
Sales		124,345
Inventory***		100,000
Unearned interest		28,142

   ** *On the balance sheet this amount is termed gross investment since it includes an unguaranteed residual value.*
   *** *Either acquisition cost to dealer or manufacturer's cost of production.*

Interest revenue will be recognized at 10% of the outstanding net investment (lease receivable less unearned interest) each period (i.e., interest revenue in year 1 is $131,858 x 10% = $13,186).

At the end of year 1, the following entry(ies) would be made:

Cash	50,000	
Lease receivable		50,000
Unearned interest revenue	13,186	
Interest revenue		13,186

At termination, the lease receivable will have a balance of $10,000 which is the unguaranteed residual value. Note that the same amortization schedule that appears in Numerical Example 2 above is applicable to this one. The fact that the residual value is unguaranteed in this example does not affect the amortization schedule because the lessor is projecting that it will get back an asset worth $10,000. If the asset is returned to the lessor and its fair market value is only $4,000, the following entry is made on the lessor's books:

Loss	6,000	
Residual value of equipment	4,000	
Lease receivable		10,000

Now that we have completed our discussion of lessor's direct financing and sales-type leases, it should be helpful to review the financial statement elements for the lessor, and to preview elements that appear on the lessee's financial statements. These balance sheet elements are shown below.

Lessor

	Direct financing lease	Sales-type lease
Balance sheet:	Lease receivable (current and noncurrent)	Lease receivable (current and noncurrent)
	Initial direct costs (added to net investment causing a new implicit rate of interest)	
Income statement:	Unearned interest revenue	Unearned interest revenue
	Interest revenue	Interest revenue
	Amortization of initial direct costs	Initial direct costs (expensed immediately)
		Dealer's profit

Lessee

	Capital lease
Balance sheet:	Leased asset (net of accumulated depreciation)
	Lease obligation (current and noncurrent)
Income statement:	Depreciation expense
	Interest expense
	Other maintenance expense

(4) **Capital Leases—Lessee**

When a lessor records a direct financing or sales-type lease, the lessee, in turn, must record a capital lease. Capital leases reflect the transfer of risks and benefits associated with the asset to the lessee. A lease is considered to be a capital lease to the lessee if **any one** of the four criteria of SFAS 13 is satisfied.

1. Transfer of title
2. Bargain purchase
3. 75% of useful life
4. 90% of net FMV

Lease agreements not meeting at least one of the criteria for capital leases are treated as operating leases on the lessee's books. If the lease is classified as a capital lease, the lessee must record an asset and a liability based on the present value of the minimum lease payments as follows:

Leased asset	(PV of MLP)	
Lease obligation		(PV of MLP)

Note that the above entry reflects recording the transaction "net" (i.e., at present value). If the lease was recorded gross, the lease obligation would be credited for the total amount of the MLP and there would be a debit to "Discount on lease obligation."

Leased asset	(PV of MLP)	
Discount on lease obligation	(plug)	
Lease obligation		(gross MLP)

The gross method is similar to the accounting for deferred payment contracts.

To determine the present value of the MLP, the lessee discounts the future payments using the **lesser** of

1. The lessee's incremental borrowing rate, **or**
2. The lessor's implicit rate if known by the lessee

NOTE: Using a lower interest rate increases the present value.

Leased assets, however, should **not** be recorded at an amount greater than the FMV of the asset. If the FMV is less than the PV of the MLP, the lease should be recorded at the FMV and a new implicit interest rate calculated to reflect a constant periodic rate applied to the remaining balance of the obligation.

During the term of the lease, the lessee must use the (effective) interest method to allocate cash paid between interest expense and reduction of the lease obligation. This method is the same as the one used by the lessor as previously described.

Lessees must amortize leased assets recorded on the books under a capital lease. The amortization (depreciation) method used should be consistent with the lessee's normal depreciation policy. The term over which the asset is amortized may differ depending upon which criteria qualified the lease as a capital lease.

1. If the lease transfers ownership or contains a BPO (criteria 1 or 2), the asset will be amortized over its estimated useful life (since the asset actually becomes the property of the lessee at the end of the lease term and will be used for the remainder of its useful life).
2. If the 75% of useful life or the 90% test (criteria 3 or 4) is met, the leased asset is amortized over the lease term only (since the property will revert to the lessor at the end of the lease term and will be used for the remainder of its useful life).

The lease term does not extend beyond the date of a bargain purchase option. Lease terms, however, may include the following:

1. Bargain renewal periods
2. Periods when the lessor has the option to renew or extend
3. Periods during which the lessee guarantees the debt of the lessor
4. Periods in which a material penalty exists for failure to renew

When the lease terminates, the balance in the obligation account should equal the bargain purchase option price or the expected residual value (guaranteed residual value, or salvage value if lower).

Leased assets and obligations should be disclosed as such in the balance sheet. The lease obligation should be separated into both current and noncurrent components.

Numerical Example 4:

Lease Information

1) A three-year lease is initiated on 1/1/02 for equipment with an expected useful life of five years. The equipment reverts back to the lessor upon expiration of the lease agreement.
2) Three payments are due to the lessor in the amount of $50,000 per year **beginning 12/31/02.** An additional sum of $1,000 is to be paid annually by the lessee for insurance.
3) Lessee guarantees a $10,000 residual value on 12/31/04 to the lessor.
4) The leased asset is expected to have only a $7,000 salvage value on 12/31/04 despite the $10,000 residual value guarantee; therefore, the asset should be depreciated down to the $7,000 expected residual value.
5) The lessee's incremental borrowing rate is 10% (same as lessor's implicit rate).
6) The present value of the lease obligation is

PV of guaranteed residual value	=	$10,000	x	.7513	=	$ 7,513
PV of annual payments	=	$50,000	x	2.4869	=	124,345
						$131,858

Note that since the lessee's incremental borrowing rate is 10% and the residual value is guaranteed, the present value of $131,858 is the same amount used by the lessor in the direct financing lease example (Numerical Example 2) to determine the payments to be made by the lessee. If an incremental borrowing rate different than the lessor's is used and/or the lease contains an unguaranteed residual value, the present value computed by the lessee will differ from the lessor's present value (FMV). These differences account for the fact that many leases are not capitalized by lessees because they don't meet the 90% test.

Lease Classification
The 90% test is met because the present value of the minimum lease payments ($131,858) is 100% of the FMV of the leased asset.

Accounting for Lease
1) Note that executory costs (e.g., insurance, property taxes, etc.) are not included in the present value calculations
2) The entry to recognize the lease is

1/1/02	Leased equipment	131,858	
	Lease obligation		131,858

3) The entries to record the payments and depreciation are

	12/31/02		12/31/03		12/31/04	
Insurance expense	1,000		1,000		1,000	
Lease obligation*	36,814		40,496		44,548	
Interest expense*	13,186		9,504		5,452	
Cash		51,000		51,000		51,000
Depreciation expense**	41,619		41,619		41,620	
Accumulated depreciation		41,619		41,619		41,620***

  * Refer to the amortization table in the direct financing lease discussion (Numeric Example 2). Note that classification of the lease obligation into current and noncurrent on the lessee's books would parallel classification of the lease receivable on the lessor's books.

  ** [($131,858 − 7,000) ÷ 3 years]

  *** Rounding error of $1

4) The 12/31/04 entry to record the guaranteed residual value payment (assuming salvage value = estimated residual value = $7,000) and to clear the lease related accounts from the lessee's books is

Lease obligation	10,000	
Accumulated depreciation	124,858	
Cash		3,000
Leased equipment		131,858

If the actual residual value were only $5,000, the credit to "cash" would be $5,000 and a $2,000 loss would be recognized by the lessee.

Remember that leased assets are amortized over the lease term unless title transfers or a bargain purchase option exists—then over the useful life of the leased asset. At the end of the lease, the balance of the lease obligation should equal the guaranteed residual value or the bargain purchase option price. To illustrate, consider the example below.

Numerical Example 5:

Lease Information
1) A three-year lease is initiated on 1/1/02 for equipment with an expected useful life of five years.
2) Three annual $50,000 payments are due the lessor **beginning 1/1/02.**
3) The lessee can exercise a bargain purchase option on 12/31/04 for $10,000. The expected residual value at 12/31/06 is $1,000.
4) The lessee's incremental borrowing rate is 10% (lessor's implicit rate is unknown).

Lease Classification
Although the lease term is for only 60% of the asset's useful life, the lessee would account for this as a capital lease because it contains a bargain purchase option. Also, the PV of the minimum lease payments is greater than 90% of the FMV of the leased asset.

Accounting for Lease

1) The present value of the lease obligation is

PV of bargain purchase option	=	$10,000	x	.7513	=	$ 7,513
PV of annual payments	=	$50,000	x	2.7355	=	136,775
						$144,288

2) The following amortization table summarizes the liability amortization:

AMORTIZATION TABLE

Carrying value at beg. of yr. 1		$144,288
Lease payment	$(50,000)	(50,000)
Carrying value at beg. of yr. 1 after first payment		94,288
Interest expense	9,429	
Lease payment	(50,000)	(40,571)
Carrying value at beg. of year 2 after second payment		53,717
Interest expense	5,372	
Lease payment	(50,000)	(44,628)
Carrying value at beg. of yr. 3 after third payment		9,089
Interest expense	911*	911
Bargain purchase option		10,000
Option payment	(10,000)	(10,000)
		--

* *Rounding error of $2*

NOTE: *This table reflects the fact that the lease is an annuity due with cash payments on 1/1 and interest expense accruals on 12/31; thus, the first payment does not include any interest expense.*

3) The entry to record the lease is

1/1/00	Leased equipment	144,288	
	Lease obligation		144,288

4) The entries to record the payments, interest expense, depreciation (amortization) expense, and the exercise of the bargain purchase are

		2002		2003		2004	
1/1	Lease obligation	50,000		40,571		44,628	
	Accrued interest payable or interest expense*			9,429		5,372	
	Cash		50,000		50,000		50,000
12/31	Interest expense	9,429		5,372		911	
	Accrued int. payable		9,429		5,372		
	Lease obligation						911
12/31	Depreciation expense**	28,658		28,658		28,658	
	Accumulated depreciation		28,658		28,658		28,658
12/31	Lease obligation					10,000	
	Cash						10,000

*　*If 12/31 accruals are reversed*
**　*(143,288 ÷ 5 years)*

2.　Other Considerations

To supplement the review of lease accounting presented above, the following topics have been selected for further discussion:

a.　Initial direct costs
b.　Sale-leaseback
c.　Disclosure requirements

a.　Initial direct costs

Initial direct costs are the lessor's costs directly associated with negotiation and consummation of leases. These costs include commissions, legal fees, credit investigations, document preparation, etc. In operating leases, initial direct costs are capitalized and subsequently amortized to expense in proportion to the recognition of rental revenue (which is usually straight-line).

Initial direct costs of direct financing and sales-type leases are accounted for differently: (1) In sales-type leases, charge initial direct costs to operations in the year the sale is recorded; (2) In direct financing leases add the initial direct costs to the net investment in the lease. Compute a new effective interest rate that equates the minimum lease payments and any unguaranteed residual value with the combined outlay for the leased asset and initial direct costs. Finally, the unearned lease (interest) revenue and the initial direct costs are to be amortized to income over the lease term so that a constant periodic rate is earned on the net investment.

b. **Sale-leaseback**

Sale-leaseback describes a transaction where the owner of property (seller-lessee) sells the property, and then immediately leases all or part of it back from the new owner (buyer-lessor). The important consideration in this type of transaction is the recognition of two separate and distinct economic transactions. It is important, however, to note that there is not a physical transfer of property. First, there is a sale of property, and second, there is a lease agreement for the same property in which the seller is the lessee and the buyer is the lessor. This is illustrated below.

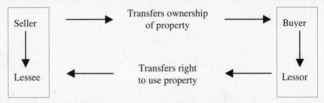

Note that sale-leaseback transactions only affect accounting for the seller-lessee. Buyer-lessor accounting is unaffected.

The accounting treatment from the seller-lessee's point of view will depend upon the degree of rights to use the property retained by the seller-lessee. The degree of rights may be categorized in one of three ways:

1. Substantially all
2. Minor
3. More than minor but less than substantially all

A seller-lessee retains **substantially all** the rights to use the property if the PV of the rental payments is 90% or more of the fair value of the asset sold. This test is based on the criteria used earlier to classify leases. Since the seller-lessee retains use of the asset, this type of sale-leaseback is considered, in substance, a form of financing to the seller-lessee rather than a sale. In this case, any gain on the sale is deferred by the seller-lessee.

Cash	(selling price)		
Asset		(carrying value)	
Deferred gain		(excess)	

The asset would be reported on the seller-lessee's balance sheet as follows:

Leased asset	xx
Less: Deferred gain	(xx)
	xx

The net value of the leased asset is the same amount the asset would be if it had not been sold.

If the lease is classified as a capital lease, the deferred gain is amortized over the life of the asset at the same rate as the asset is being depreciated. As deferred gain is amortized, it is charged to depreciation expense.

Deferred gain	xx
Depreciation expense	xx

Alternatively, the gain may be recognized as income over the term of the lease.

Although most leases in the "substantially all" category are capital leases, a sale-leaseback occurring in the last 25% of an asset's economic life would be classified as an operating lease.

If the lease is classified as an operating lease, any deferred gain is amortized over the lease term in proportion to the related gross rental charges to expense over the lease term. Amortization in this case is charged to rent expense by the seller-lessee.

```
Deferred gain              xx
    Rent expense                      xx
```

The seller-lessee retains only a **minor** portion of rights to use the property when the PV of the rental payments is 10% or less of the fair value of the asset sold. Since the seller-lessee has given up the right to use the asset, the leaseback is considered in substance a sale. Any gain on the sale is recognized in full since the earnings process is considered complete.

```
Cash                   (selling price)
    Asset                                  (carrying value)
    Gain                                   (excess)
```

When only a minor portion of use is retained, the seller-lessee accounts for the lease as an operating lease.

The seller-lessee retains **more than a minor portion but less than substantially all** the rights to use the property when the PV of the rental payments is more than 10% but less than 90% of the fair value of the asset sold. In this situation, gain is recognized only to the extent that it exceeds the PV of the rental payments.

```
Cash                   (selling price)
    Asset                                  (carrying value)
    Deferred gain                          (PV of rental payments)
    Gain                                   (excess)
```

Recognized gain for capital and operating leases is derived as follows:

1. If the leaseback is classified as an operating lease, recognized gain is the portion of gain that exceeds the PV of the MLP over the lease term. The seller-lessee should use its incremental borrowing rate to compute the PV of the MLP. If the implicit rate of interest in the lease is known and lower, it should be used instead.
2. If the leaseback is classified as a capital lease, recognized gain is the amount of gain that exceeds the recorded amount of the leased asset.

In all cases, the seller-lessee should immediately recognize a loss when the fair value of the property at the time of the leaseback is less than its undepreciated cost (book value). In the example below, the sales price is less than the book value of the property. However, there is no economic loss because the FMV which equals the PV is greater than the book value.

The artificial loss must be deferred and amortized as an addition to depreciation.

In the chart below, when the leased asset is land only, any amortization should be on a straight-line basis over the lease term, regardless of whether the lease is classified as a capital or operating lease.

The buyer-lessor should account for the transaction as a purchase and a direct financing lease if the agreement meets the criteria of **either** a direct financing lease **or** a sales-type lease. Otherwise, the agreement should be accounted for as a purchase and an operating lease.

To illustrate a sale-leaseback transaction, consider the example below.

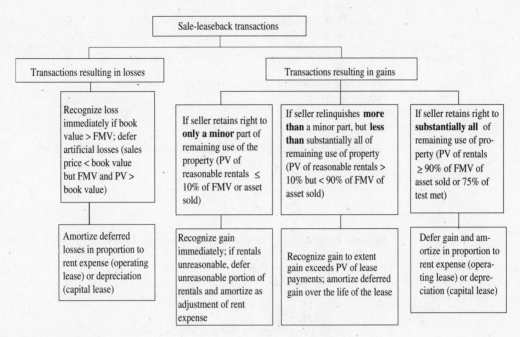

Numerical Example 6:

Lease Information

1) Lessee Corporation sells equipment that has a book value of $80,000 and a fair value of $100,000 to Lessor Corporation, and then immediately leases it back.

2) The sale date is January 1, 2000, and the equipment has a fair value of $100,000 on that date and an estimated useful life of fifteen years.

3) The lease term is fifteen years, noncancelable, and requires equal rental payments of $13,109 at the beginning of each year.

4) Lessee Corp. has the option to renew the lease annually at the same rental payments upon expiration of the original lease.

5) Lessee Corp. has the obligation to pay all executory costs.

6) The annual rental payments provide the lessor with a 12% return on investment.

7) The incremental borrowing rate of Lessee Corp. is 12%.

8) Lessee Corp. depreciates similar equipment on a straight-line basis.

Lease Classification

Lessee Corp. should classify the agreement as a capital lease since the lease term exceeds 75% of the estimated economic life of the equipment, and because the present value of the lease payments is greater than 90% of the fair value of the equipment. Assuming that collectibility of the lease payments is reasonably predictable and that no important uncertainties exist concerning the amount of unreimbursable costs yet to be incurred by the lessor, Lessor Corp. should classify the transaction as a direct financing lease because the present value of the minimum lease payments is equal to the fair market value of $100,000.

Accounting for Lease

Lessee Corp. and Lessor Corp. would normally make the following journal entries during the first year:

Upon Sale of Equipment on January 1, 2000

Lessee Corp.			Lessor Corp.		
Cash	100,000		Equipment	100,000	
Equipment		80,000	Cash		100,000
Unearned profit on			Lease receivable	196,635*	
sale-leaseback		20,000	Equipment		100,000
Leased equipment	100,000		Unearned interest		96,635
Lease obligations		100,000			

* ($13,109 x 15)

To Record First Payment on January 1, 2000

Lessee Corp.			Lessor Corp.		
Lease obligations	13,109		Cash	13,109	
Cash		13,109	Lease receivable		13,109

To Record Incurrence and Payment of Executory Costs

Lessee Corp.		Lessor Corp.
Insurance, taxes, etc.	xxx	(No entry)
Cash (accounts payable)	xxx	

To Record Depreciation Expense on the Equipment, December 31, 2000

Lessee Corp.		Lessor Corp.
Depreciation expense	6,667	(No entry)
Accum. depr.—		
capital leases		
($100,000 ÷ 15)	6,667	

To Amortize Profit on Sale-Leaseback by Lessee Corp., December 31, 2000

Lessee Corp.		Lessor Corp.
Unearned profit on		(No entry)
sale-leaseback	1,333	
Depr. expense		
($20,000 ÷ 15)	1,333	

To Record Interest for 1999, December 31, 2000

Lessee Corp.			Lessor Corp		
Interest expense	10,427		Unearned interest income	10,427	
Accrued interest payable		10,427	Interest income		10,427

(Carrying value $86,891 x .12 = $10,427)

c. **Disclosure requirements**

The disclosures required of the lessor and lessee are very comprehensive and detailed. In essence, all terms of the leasing arrangement are required (i.e., contingent rentals, subleases, residual values, unearned interest revenue, etc.). For the details see the outline of SFAS 13 (D.5.). There are, however, a couple of generic disclosure requirements. First, a **general description** of the leasing arrangement is required. Second, the minimum future payments to be received (paid) by the lessor (lessee) for each of the **five succeeding fiscal years** should also be disclosed.

SUMMARY OF KEY PROBLEM SOLUTION POINTS

(1) *Lessor—direct financing and sales-type leases*

(a) Periodic lease payments (PLP) $=\dfrac{\text{FMV of leased property} - \text{PV of RV*/BPO}}{\left[\begin{array}{c}\text{PV of an annuity factor** using}\\ \text{the lessor's implicit rate}\end{array}\right]}$

    * *Guaranteed/unguaranteed*
  ** *Annuity due or ordinary*

(b) Lease payments receivable/ = $\left[\begin{array}{c}\text{Periodic lease}\\ \text{payments}\end{array} \text{ x }\begin{array}{c}\text{Number}\\ \text{of rents}\end{array}\right]$ + Residual value/
    Gross investments   Bar. Pur. Opt.

(c) Unearned interest revenue = Gross investment – PV of PLP,
     PV of G/U RV,
     PV of BPO

(d) Net investment = Gross investment – Unearned interest revenue

(e) Gross profit (only for sales-type leases) = Selling price* – Cost of leased asset sold

    * *(FMV/PV of PLP + G/URV + BPO)*

(f) Interest revenue = $\left[\begin{array}{c}\text{Carrying value}\\ \text{of lease}\\ \text{receivable*}\end{array}\right]$ x Implicit % x Time

    * *(Gross investment – Unearned interest)*

Periodic Journal Entries

Unearned interest revenue	xxx	
Interest revenue		xxx
Cash	xxx	
Lease payments receivable		xxx

(2) *Lessee—capital lease*

(a) Determine capital lease liability

$$\text{Determine capital lease liability} = \begin{pmatrix} \text{Periodic} \\ \text{lease} \\ \text{payment (PLP)} \end{pmatrix} \times \begin{pmatrix} \text{Present} \\ \text{value} \\ \text{factor*} \end{pmatrix} + \begin{bmatrix} \text{G/URV} & \text{PV} \\ \text{OR} & \text{of} \\ \text{BPO} & \times & 1.00 \\ & & \text{factor} \end{bmatrix}$$

* Annuity due or ordinary annuity

- Use lessee's incremental borrowing %, unless lessor's implicit % is lower and lessee knows it
- PLP is exclusive of executory costs

(b) Leased asset = Capital lease liability at inception of lease as computed above—PV x MLP [Exception: where FMV of leased asset < PV of MLP (PLP + GRV or BPO), then leased asset and capital lease liability are recorded at the FMV of leased asset.]

(c) Depreciation (amortization) of leased asset

- Over useful life, regardless of lease term, if either criterion (1) or (2) is met: title transfer or bargain purchase option.

- Over lease term if criterion (3) or (4) is met: $\geq 75\%$ test or $\geq 90\%$ test

(d) Lease liability =

(1) Carrying value at inception of lease	$xxx
(2) Less first payment (usually the first payment is all principal because the lease liability is the PV of an annuity due)	(xx)
(3) Carrying value (CV)	$xxx

(e) CV x % = Interest expense

(4) Less principal part of 2**nd** payment [PLP – (CV x interest %)]	(xxx)
(5) Carrying value	$xxx
	etc.

MULTIPLE-CHOICE QUESTIONS (1-53)

1. Rapp Co. leased a new machine to Lake Co. on January 1, 2002. The lease expires on January 1, 2007. The annual rental is $90,000. Additionally, on January 1, 2002, Lake paid $50,000 to Rapp as a lease bonus and $25,000 as a security deposit to be refunded upon expiration of the lease. In Rapp's 2002 income statement, the amount of rental revenue should be

    a. $140,000
    b. $125,000
    c. $100,000
    d. $ 90,000

2. Wall Co. leased office premises to Fox, Inc. for a five-year term beginning January 2, 2002. Under the terms of the operating lease, rent for the first year is $8,000 and rent for years two through five is $12,500 per annum. However, as an inducement to enter the lease, Wall granted Fox the first six months of the lease rent-free. In its December 31, 2002 income statement, what amount should Wall report as rental income?

    a. $12,000
    b. $11,600
    c. $10,800
    d. $ 8,000

3. On January 1, 2002, Wren Co. leased a building to Brill under an operating lease for ten years at $50,000 per year, payable the first day of each lease year. Wren paid $15,000 to a real estate broker as a finder's fee. The building is depreciated $12,000 per year. For 2002, Wren incurred insurance and property tax expense totaling $9,000. Wren's net rental income for 2002 should be

    a. $27,500
    b. $29,000
    c. $35,000
    d. $36,500

4. On July 1, 2000, Gee, Inc. leased a delivery truck from Marr Corp. under a three-year operating lease. Total rent for the term of the lease will be $36,000, payable as follows:

    12 months at $ 500 = $ 6,000
    12 months at $ 750 =   9,000
    12 months at $1,750 = 21,000

All payments were made when due. In Marr's June 30, 2002 balance sheet, the accrued rent receivable should be reported as

    a. $0
    b. $ 9,000
    c. $12,000
    d. $21,000

5. On January 1, 2002, Glen Co. leased a building to Dix Corp. for a ten-year term at an annual rental of $50,000. At inception of the lease, Glen received $200,000 covering the first two years' rent of $100,000 and a security deposit of $100,000. This deposit will not be returned to Dix upon expiration of the lease but will be applied to payment of rent for the last two years of the lease. What portion of the $200,000 should be shown as a current and long-term liability, respectively, in Glen's December 31, 2002 balance sheet?

	Current liability	*Long-term liability*
a.	$0	$200,000
b.	$ 50,000	$100,000
c.	$100,000	$100,000
d.	$100,000	$ 50,000

6. As an inducement to enter a lease, Graf Co., a lessor, granted Zep, Inc., a lessee, twelve months of free rent under a five-year operating lease. The lease was effective on January 1, 2002, and provides for monthly rental payments to begin January 1, 2003. Zep made the first rental payment on December 30, 2002. In its 2002 income statement, Graf should report rental revenue in an amount equal to

    a.   Zero.
    b.   Cash received during 2002.
    c.   One-fourth of the total cash to be received over the life of the lease.
    d.   One-fifth of the total cash to be received over the life of the lease.

7. Quo Co. rented a building to Hava Fast Food. Each month Quo receives a fixed rental amount plus a variable rental amount based on Hava's sales for that month. As sales increase so does the variable rental amount, but at a reduced rate. Which of the following curves reflects the monthly rentals under the agreement?

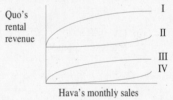

    a.   I
    b.   II
    c.   III
    d.   IV

8. As an inducement to enter a lease, Arts, Inc., a lessor, grants Hompson Corp., a lessee, nine months of free rent under a five-year operating lease. The lease is effective on July 1, 2002 and provides for monthly rental of $1,000 to begin April 1, 2003. In Hompson's income statement for the year ended June 30, 2002, rent expense should be reported as

    a. $10,200
    b. $ 9,000
    c. $ 3,000
    d. $ 2,550

9. On January 1, 2002, Park Co. signed a ten-year operating lease for office space at $96,000 per year. The lease included a provision for additional rent of 5% of annual company sales in excess of $500,000. Park's sales for the year ended December 31, 2002, were $600,000. Upon execution of the lease, Park paid $24,000 as a bonus for the lease. Park's rent expense for the year ended December 31, 2002, is

    a. $ 98,400
    b. $101,000
    c. $103,400
    d. $125,000

10. On July 1, 2002, South Co. entered into a ten-year operating lease for a warehouse facility. The annual minimum lease payments are $100,000. In addition to the base rent,

South pays a monthly allocation of the building's operating expenses, which amounted to $20,000 for the year ended June 30, 2003. In the notes to South's June 30, 2003 financial statements, what amounts of subsequent years' lease payments should be disclosed?

a. $100,000 per annum for each of the next five years and $500,000 in the aggregate.
b. $120,000 per annum for each of the next five years and $600,000 in the aggregate.
c. $100,000 per annum for each of the next five years and $900,000 in the aggregate.
d. $120,000 per annum for each of the next five years and $1,080,000 in the aggregate.

11. On January 1, 2002, Mollat Co. signed a seven-year lease for equipment having a ten-year economic life. The present value of the monthly lease payments equaled 80% of the equipment's fair value. The lease agreement provides for neither a transfer of title to Mollat nor a bargain purchase option. In its 2002 income statement Mollat should report

a. Rent expense equal to the 2002 lease payments.
b. Rent expense equal to the 2002 lease payments less interest expense.
c. Lease amortization equal to one-tenth of the equipment's fair value.
d. Lease amortization equal to one-seventh of 80% of the equipment's fair value.

12. A twenty-year property lease, classified as an operating lease, provides for a 10% increase in annual payments every five years. In the sixth year compared to the fifth year, the lease will cause the following expenses to increase

	Rent	Interest
a.	No	Yes
b.	Yes	No
c.	Yes	Yes
d.	No	No

13. On December 1, 2002, Clark Co. leased office space for five years at a monthly rental of $60,000. On the same date, Clark paid the lessor the following amounts:

First month's rent	$ 60,000
Last month's rent	60,000
Security deposit (refundable at lease expiration)	80,000
Installation of new walls and offices	360,000

What should be Clark's 2002 expense relating to utilization of the office space?

a. $ 60,000
b. $ 66,000
c. $120,000
d. $140,000

14. Star Co. leases a building for its product showroom. The ten-year nonrenewable lease will expire on December 31, 2007. In January 2002, Star redecorated its showroom and made leasehold improvements of $48,000. The estimated useful life of the improvements is eight years. Star uses the straight-line method of amortization. What amount of leasehold improvements, net of amortization, should Star report in its June 30, 2002 balance sheet?

a. $45,600
b. $45,000
c. $44,000
d. $43,200

15. On January 2, 2002, Ral Co. leased land and building from an unrelated lessor for a ten-year term. The lease has a renewal option for an additional ten years, but Ral has not reached a decision with regard to the renewal option. In early January of 2002, Ral completed the following improvements to the property:

Description	Estimated life	Cost
Sales office	10 years	$47,000
Warehouse	25 years	75,000
Parking lot	15 years	18,000

Amortization of leasehold improvements for 2002 should be

a. $ 7,000
b. $ 8,900
c. $12,200
d. $14,000

16. On January 1, 2000, Nobb Corp. signed a twelve-year lease for warehouse space. Nobb has an option to renew the lease for an additional eight-year period on or before January 1, 2004. During January 2002, Nobb made substantial improvements to the warehouse. The cost of these improvements was $540,000, with an estimated useful life of fifteen years. At December 31, 2002, Nobb intended to exercise the renewal option. Nobb has taken a full year's amortization on this leasehold. In Nobb's December 31, 2002 balance sheet, the carrying amount of this leasehold improvement should be

a. $486,000
b. $504,000
c. $510,000
d. $513,000

17. During January 2002, Vail Co. made long-term improvements to a recently leased building. The lease agreement provides for neither a transfer of title to Vail nor a bargain purchase option. The present value of the minimum lease payments equals 85% of the building's market value, and the lease term equals 70% of the building's economic life. Should assets be recognized for the building and the leasehold improvements?

	Building	Leasehold improvements
a.	Yes	Yes
b.	No	Yes
c.	Yes	No
d.	No	No

18. A lessee incurred costs to construct office space in a leased warehouse. The estimated useful life of the office is ten years. The remaining term of the nonrenewable lease is fifteen years. The costs should be

a. Capitalized as leasehold improvements and depreciated over fifteen years.
b. Capitalized as leasehold improvements and depreciated over ten years.
c. Capitalized as leasehold improvements and expensed in the year in which the lease expires.
d. Expensed as incurred.

19. Glade Co. leases computer equipment to customers under direct-financing leases. The equipment has no residual value at the end of the lease and the leases do not contain bargain purchase options. Glade wishes to earn 8% interest on a five-year lease of equipment with a fair value of $323,400. The present value of an annuity due of $1 at 8%

for five years is 4.312. What is the total amount of interest revenue that Glade will earn over the life of the lease?
   a. $ 51,600
   b. $ 75,000
   c. $129,360
   d. $139,450

20. On January 1, 2000, JCK Co. signed a contract for an eight-year lease of its equipment with a ten-year life. The present value of the sixteen equal semiannual payments in advance equaled 85% of the equipment's fair value. The contract had no provision for JCK, the lessor, to give up legal ownership of the equipment. Should JCK recognize rent or interest revenue in 2002, and should the revenue recognized in 2002 be the same or smaller than the revenue recognized in 2001?

	2002 revenues recognized	2002 amount recognized compared to 2001
a.	Rent	The same
b.	Rent	Smaller
c.	Interest	The same
d.	Interest	Smaller

21. Peg Co. leased equipment from Howe Corp. on July 1, 2001 for an eight-year period expiring June 30, 2010. Equal payments under the lease are $600,000 and are due on July 1 of each year. The first payment was made on July 1, 2002. The rate of interest contemplated by Peg and Howe is 10%. The cash selling price of the equipment is $3,520,000, and the cost of the equipment on Howe's accounting records is $2,800,000. The lease is appropriately recorded as a sales-type lease. What is the amount of profit on the sale and interest revenue that Howe should record for the year ended December 31, 2002?

	Profit on sale	Interest revenue
a.	$720,000	$176,000
b.	$720,000	$146,000
c.	$ 45,000	$176,000
d.	$ 45,000	$146,000

22. Howe Co. leased equipment to Kew Corp. on January 2, 2002, for an eight-year period expiring December 31, 2009. Equal payments under the lease are $600,000 and are due on January 2 of each year. The first payment was made on January 2, 2002. The list selling price of the equipment is $3,520,000 and its carrying cost on Howe's books is $2,800,000. The lease is appropriately accounted for as a sales-type lease. The present value of the lease payments is $3,300,000. What amount of profit on the sale should Howe report for the year ended December 31, 2002?
   a. $720,000
   b. $500,000
   c. $ 90,000
   d. $0

23. The excess of the fair value of leased property at the inception of the lease over its cost or carrying amount should be classified by the lessor as
   a.   Unearned income from a sales-type lease.
   b.   Unearned income from a direct-financing lease.
   c.   Manufacturer's or dealer's profit from a sales-type lease.
   d.   Manufacturer's or dealer's profit from a direct-financing lease.

24. In a lease that is recorded as a sales-type lease by the lessor, interest revenue
   a.   Should be recognized in full as revenue at the lease's inception.
   b.   Should be recognized over the period of the lease using the straight-line method.
   c.   Should be recognized over the period of the lease using the interest method.
   d.   Does **not** arise.

25. Lease M does not contain a bargain purchase option, but the lease term is equal to 90% of the estimated economic life of the leased property. Lease P does not transfer ownership of the property to the lessee at the end of the lease term, but the lease term is equal to 75% of the estimated economic life of the leased property. How should the lessee classify these leases?

	Lease M	Lease P
a.	Capital lease	Operating lease
b.	Capital lease	Capital lease
c.	Operating lease	Capital lease
d.	Operating lease	Operating lease

26. On December 31, 2002, Day Co. leased a new machine from Parr with the following pertinent information:

Lease term	6 years
Annual rental payable at beginning of each year	$50,000
Useful life of machine	8 years
Day's incremental borrowing rate	15%
Implicit interest rate in lease (known by Day)	12%
Present value of annuity of 1 in advance for 6 periods at	
12%	4.61
15%	4.35

The lease is not renewable, and the machine reverts to Parr at the termination of the lease. The cost of the machine on Parr's accounting records is $375,500. At the beginning of the lease term, Day should record a lease liability of
   a. $375,500
   b. $230,500
   c. $217,500
   d. $0

27. On January 1, 2002, Day Corp. entered into a ten-year lease agreement with Ward, Inc. for industrial equipment. Annual lease payments of $10,000 are payable at the end of each year. Day knows that the lessor expects a 10% return on the lease. Day has a 12% incremental borrowing rate. The equipment is expected to have an estimated useful life of ten years. In addition, a third party has guaranteed to pay Ward a residual value of $5,000 at the end of the lease.

The present value of an ordinary annuity of $1 at
   12% for ten years is 5.6502
   10% for ten years is 6.1446

The present value of $1 at
   12% for ten years is .3220
   10% for ten years is .3855

In Day's October 31, 2002 balance sheet, the principal amount of the lease obligation was
   a. $63,374
   b. $61,446
   c. $58,112
   d. $56,502

28. Robbins, Inc. leased a machine from Ready Leasing Co. The lease qualifies as a capital lease and requires ten annual payments of $10,000 beginning immediately. The lease specifies an interest rate of 12% and a purchase option of $10,000 at the end of the tenth year, even though the machine's estimated value on that date is $20,000. Robbins' incremental borrowing rate is 14%.

> The present value of an annuity due of one at
> 12% for ten years is 6.328
> 14% for ten years is 5.946
>
> The present value of one at
> 12% for ten years is .322
> 14% for ten years is .270

What amount should Robbins record as lease liability at the beginning of the lease term?

    a. $62,160
    b. $64,860
    c. $66,500
    d. $69,720

29. Neal Corp. entered into a nine-year capital lease on a warehouse on December 31, 2002. Lease payments of $52,000, which includes real estate taxes of $2,000, are due annually, beginning on December 31, 2003, and every December 31 thereafter. Neal does not know the interest rate implicit in the lease; Neal's incremental borrowing rate is 9%. The rounded present value of an ordinary annuity for nine years at 9% is 5.6. What amount should Neal report as capitalized lease liability at December 31, 2001?

    a. $280,000
    b. $291,200
    c. $450,000
    d. $468,000

30. East Company leased a new machine from North Company on May 1, 2002, under a lease with the following information:

Lease term	10 years
Annual rental payable at beginning of each lease year	$40,000
Useful life of machine	12 years
Implicit interest rate	14%
Present value of an annuity of one in advance for ten periods at 14%	5.95
Present value of one for ten periods at 14%	0.27

East has the option to purchase the machine on May 1, 2012 by paying $50,000, which approximates the expected fair value of the machine on the option exercise date. On May 1, 2002, East should record a capitalized lease asset of

    a. $251,500
    b. $238,000
    c. $224,500
    d. $198,000

31. On January 1, 2002, Babson, Inc. leased two automobiles for executive use. The lease requires Babson to make five annual payments of $13,000 beginning January 1, 2002. At the end of the lease term, December 31, 2006, Babson guarantees the residual value of the automobiles will total $10,000. The lease qualifies as a capital lease. The interest rate implicit in the lease is 9%. Present value factors for the 9% rate implicit in the lease are as follows:

For an annuity due with five payments	4.240
For an ordinary annuity with five payments	3.890
Present value of $1 for five periods	0.650

Babson's recorded capital lease liability immediately after the first required payment should be

    a. $48,620
    b. $44,070
    c. $35,620
    d. $31,070

32. On December 30, 2002, Rafferty Corp. leased equipment under a capital lease. Annual lease payments of $20,000 are due December 31 for ten years. The equipment's useful life is ten years, and the interest rate implicit in the lease is 10%. The capital lease obligation was recorded on December 30, 2002, at $135,000, and the first lease payment was made on that date. What amount should Rafferty include in current liabilities for this capital lease in its December 31, 2002 balance sheet?

    a. $ 6,500
    b. $ 8,500
    c. $11,500
    d. $20,000

33. Oak Co. leased equipment for its entire nine-year useful life, agreeing to pay $50,000 at the start of the lease term on December 31, 2001, and $50,000 annually on each December 31 for the next eight years. The present value on December 31, 2001, of the nine lease payments over the lease term, using the rate implicit in the lease which Oak knows to be 10%, was $316,500. The December 31, 2001 present value of the lease payments using Oak's incremental borrowing rate of 12% was $298,500. Oak made a timely second lease payment. What amount should Oak report as capital lease liability in its December 31, 2002 balance sheet?

    a. $350,000
    b. $243,150
    c. $228,320
    d. $0

34. On December 31, 2001, Roe Co. leased a machine from Colt for a five-year period. Equal annual payments under the lease are $105,000 (including $5,000 annual executory costs) and are due on December 31 of each year. The first payment was made on December 31, 2001, and the second payment was made on December 31, 2002. The five lease payments are discounted at 10% over the lease term. The present value of minimum lease payments at the inception of the lease and before the first annual payment was $417,000. The lease is appropriately accounted for as a capital lease by Roe. In its December 31, 2002 balance sheet, Roe should report a lease liability of

    a. $317,000
    b. $315,000
    c. $285,300
    d. $248,700

35. In the long-term liabilities section of its balance sheet at December 31, 2001, Mene Co. reported a capital lease obligation of $75,000, net of current portion of $1,364. Payments of $9,000 were made on both January 2, 2002, and January 2, 2003. Mene's incremental borrowing rate on the date of the lease was 11% and the lessor's implicit rate, which was known to Mene, was 10%. In its December 31, 2002 balance sheet, what amount should Mene report as capital lease obligation, net of current portion?

    a. $66,000
    b. $73,500
    c. $73,636
    d. $74,250

36. For a capital lease, the amount recorded initially by the lessee as a liability should normally
     a.   Exceed the total of the minimum lease payments.
     b.   Exceed the present value of the minimum lease payments at the beginning of the lease.
     c.   Equal the total of the minimum lease payments.
     d.   Equal the present value of the minimum lease payments at the beginning of the lease.

37. At the inception of a capital lease, the guaranteed residual value should be
     a.   Included as part of minimum lease payments at present value.
     b.   Included as part of minimum lease payments at future value.
     c.   Included as part of minimum lease payments only to the extent that guaranteed residual value is expected to exceed estimated residual value.
     d.   Excluded from minimum lease payments.

38. A six-year capital lease entered into on December 31, 2002, specified equal minimum annual lease payments due on December 31 of each year. The first minimum annual lease payment, paid on December 31, 2002, consists of which of the following?

	Interest expense	*Lease liability*
a.	Yes	Yes
b.	Yes	No
c.	No	Yes
d.	No	No

39. A six-year capital lease expiring on December 31 specifies equal minimum annual lease payments. Part of this payment represents interest and part represents a reduction in the net lease liability. The portion of the minimum lease payment in the fifth year applicable to the reduction of the net lease liability should be
     a.   Less than in the fourth year.
     b.   More than in the fourth year.
     c.   The same as in the sixth year.
     d.   More than in the sixth year.

40. A lessee had a ten-year capital lease requiring equal annual payments. The reduction of the lease liability in year two should equal
     a.   The current liability shown for the lease at the end of year one.
     b.   The current liability shown for the lease at the end of year two.
     c.   The reduction of the lease obligation in year one.
     d.   One-tenth of the original lease liability.

41. On January 2, 2002, Cole Co. signed an eight-year noncancelable lease for a new machine, requiring $15,000 annual payments at the beginning of each year. The machine has a useful life of twelve years, with no salvage value. Title passes to Cole at the lease expiration date. Cole uses straight-line depreciation for all of its plant assets. Aggregate lease payments have a present value on January 2, 2002, of $108,000 based on an appropriate rate of interest. For 2002, Cole should record depreciation (amortization) expense for the leased machine at
     a. $0
     b. $ 9,000
     c. $13,500
     d. $15,000

42. On January 2, 2002, Nori Mining Co. (lessee) entered into a five-year lease for drilling equipment. Nori accounted for the acquisition as a capital lease for $240,000, which includes a $10,000 bargain purchase option. At the end of the lease, Nori expects to exercise the bargain purchase option. Nori estimates that the equipment's fair value will be $20,000 at the end of its eight-year life. Nori regularly uses straight-line depreciation on similar equipment. For the year ended December 31, 2002, what amount should Nori recognize as depreciation expense on the leased asset?
     a. $48,000
     b. $46,000
     c. $30,000
     d. $27,500

43. The lessee should amortize the capitalizable cost of the leased asset in a manner consistent with the lessee's normal depreciation policy for owned assets for leases that

	Contain a bargain purchase option	*Transfer ownership of the property to the lessee by the end of the lease term*
a.	No	No
b.	No	Yes
c.	Yes	Yes
d.	Yes	No

44. On January 1, 2002, Harrow Co. as lessee signed a five-year noncancelable equipment lease with annual payments of $100,000 beginning December 31, 2002. Harrow treated this transaction as a capital lease. The five lease payments have a present value of $379,000 at January 1, 2002, based on interest of 10%. What amount should Harrow report as interest expense for the year ended December 31, 2002?
     a. $37,900
     b. $27,900
     c. $24,200
     d. $0

45. On January 1, 2001, West Co. entered into a ten-year lease for a manufacturing plant. The annual minimum lease payments are $100,000. In the notes to the December 31, 2002 financial statements, what amounts of subsequent years' lease payments should be disclosed?

	Amount for appropriate required period	*Aggregate amount for the period thereafter*
a.	$100,000	$0
b.	$300,000	$500,000
c.	$500,000	$300,000
d.	$500,000	$0

46. Cott, Inc. prepared an interest amortization table for a five-year lease payable with a bargain purchase option of $2,000, exercisable at the end of the lease. At the end of the five years, the balance in the leases payable column of the spreadsheet was zero. Cott has asked Grant, CPA, to review the spreadsheet to determine the error. Only one error was made on the spreadsheet. Which of the following statements represents the best explanation for this error?
     a.   The beginning present value of the lease did **not** include the present value of the bargain purchase option.
     b.   Cott subtracted the annual interest amount from the lease payable balance instead of adding it.

c. The present value of the bargain purchase option was subtracted from the present value of the annual payments.

d. Cott discounted the annual payments as an ordinary annuity, when the payments actually occurred at the beginning of each period.

47. On December 31, 2002, Lane, Inc. sold equipment to Noll, and simultaneously leased it back for twelve years. Pertinent information at this date is as follows:

Sales price	$480,000
Carrying amount	360,000
Estimated remaining economic life	15 years

At December 31, 2002, how much should Lane report as deferred gain from the sale of the equipment?

a. $0
b. $110,000
c. $112,000
d. $120,000

48. The following information pertains to a sale and leaseback of equipment by Mega Co. on December 31, 2002:

Sales price	$400,000
Carrying amount	$300,000
Monthly lease payment	$3,250
Present value of lease payments	$36,900
Estimated remaining life	25 years
Lease term	1 year
Implicit rate	12%

What amount of deferred gain on the sale should Mega report at December 31, 2002?

a. $0
b. $ 36,900
c. $ 63,100
d. $100,000

49. On December 31, 2002, Parke Corp. sold Edlow Corp. an airplane with an estimated remaining useful life of ten years. At the same time, Parke leased back the airplane for three years. Additional information is as follows:

Sales price	$600,000
Carrying amount of airplane at date of sale	$100,000
Monthly rental under lease	$ 6,330
Interest rate implicit in the lease as computed by Edlow and known by Parke (this rate is lower than the lessee's incremental borrowing rate)	12%
Present value of operating lease rentals ($6,330 for 36 months @ 12%)	$190,581

The leaseback is considered an operating lease. In Parke's December 31, 2002 balance sheet, what amount should be included as deferred revenue on this transaction?

a. $0
b. $190,581
c. $309,419
d. $500,000

50. On June 30, 2002, Lang Co. sold equipment with an estimated useful life of eleven years and immediately leased it back for ten years. The equipment's carrying amount was $450,000; the sale price was $430,000; and the present value of the lease payments, which is equal to the fair value of the equipment, was $465,000. In its June 30, 2002 balance sheet, what amount should Lang report as deferred loss?

a. $35,000
b. $20,000
c. $15,000
d. $0

51. On January 1, 2002, Hooks Oil Co. sold equipment with a carrying amount of $100,000, and a remaining useful life of ten years, to Maco Drilling for $150,000. Hooks immediately leased the equipment back under a ten-year capital lease with a present value of $150,000 and will depreciate the equipment using the straight-line method. Hooks made the first annual lease payment of $24,412 in December 2002. In Hooks' December 31, 2002 balance sheet, the unearned gain on equipment sale should be

a. $50,000
b. $45,000
c. $25,588
d. $0

52. In a sale-leaseback transaction, the seller-lessee has retained the property. The gain on the sale should be recognized at the time of the sale-leaseback when the lease is classified as a(n)

	Capital lease	*Operating lease*
a.	Yes	Yes
b.	No	No
c.	No	Yes
d.	Yes	No

53. Able sold its headquarters building at a gain, and simultaneously leased back the building. The lease was reported as a capital lease. At the time of sale, the gain should be reported as

a. Operating income.
b. An extraordinary item, net of income tax.
c. A separate component of stockholders' equity.
d. An asset valuation allowance.

PROBLEMS

Problem 1　(15 to 20 minutes)

On January 2, 2002, Elsee Co. leased equipment from Grant, Inc. Lease payments are $100,000, payable annually every December 31 for twenty years. Title to the equipment passes to Elsee at the end of the lease term. The lease is noncancelable.

Additional facts
- The equipment has a $750,000 carrying amount on Grant's books. Its estimated economic life was twenty-five years on January 2, 2002.
- The rate implicit in the lease, which is known to Elsee, is 10%. Elsee's incremental borrowing rate is 12%.
- Elsee uses the straight-line method of depreciation.

The rounded present value factors of an ordinary annuity for twenty years are as follows:

12%	7.5
10%	8.5

Required:

Prepare the necessary journal entries, without explanations, to be recorded by Elsee for

1. Entering into the lease on January 2, 2002.
2. Making the lease payment on December 31, 2002.
3. Expenses related to the lease for the year ended December 31, 2002.

Show supporting calculations for all entries.

Problem 2　(15 to 25 minutes)

On December 31, 2002, Jen, Inc. sold a building for its fair value and leased it back. The building was sold for more than its carrying amount and a gain was recorded. Lease payments are due at the end of each month. Jen accounted for the transaction as a capital lease. The lease's interest rate was equal to Jen's incremental borrowing rate.

Required:

a. How should Jen account for the sale portion of the sale-leaseback transaction at December 31, 2002? Why is this an appropriate method of accounting for this portion of the contract?

b. How should Jen report the leaseback portion of the sale-leaseback transaction on its December 31, 2003 balance sheet? How are these reported amounts determined?

Problem 3　(30 to 50 minutes)

The following information relates to the obligations of Villa Watch Co. as of December 31, 2002:

- Accounts payable for goods and services purchased on open account amounted to $35,000 at December 31, 2002.
- On December 15, 2002, Villa declared a cash dividend of $.05 per common share, payable on January 12, 2003, to shareholders of record as of December 31, 2002. Villa had 1,000,000 shares of common stock issued and outstanding throughout 2002.
- On December 31, 2002, Villa entered into a six-year capital lease on a warehouse and made the first an-

nual lease payment of $100,000. Villa's incremental borrowing rate was 12%, and the interest rate implicit in the lease, which was known to Villa, was 10%. The rounded present value factors for an annuity due for six years are 4.6 at 12% and 4.8 at 10%.
- On July 1, 2002, Villa issued $500,000, 8% bonds for $440,000 to yield 10%. The bonds mature on June 30, 2008, and pay interest annually every June 30. At December 31, 2002, the bonds were trading on the open market at 86 to yield 12%. Villa uses the effective interest method.
- Villa's 2002 pretax financial income was $850,000 and its taxable income was $600,000. The difference is due to $100,000 of permanent differences and $150,000 of temporary differences related to noncurrent assets. At December 31, 2002, Villa had cumulative taxable differences of $300,000 related to noncurrent assets. Villa's effective tax rate is 30%. Villa made no estimated tax payments during the year.
- Contingency information
  - Villa has been named a liable party for toxic waste cleanup on its land, and must pay an as-yet-undetermined amount for environmental remediation activities.
  - An adjoining landowner, Clear Toothpaste Co., sold its property because of possible toxic contamination of the water supply and resulting potential adverse public reaction toward its product. Clear sued Villa for damages. There is a reasonable possibility that Clear will prevail and be awarded between $250,000 and $600,000.
  - As a result of comprehensive risk assessment, Villa has discontinued rockslide insurance for its warehouse, which is located at the base of a mountain. The warehouse has never sustained rockslide damage, and the probability of sustaining future damage is only slight.

Required:

Begin the answer to each requirement (i.e., a., b., and c.) on the top of a new page.*

a. Prepare the liabilities section of Villa's December 31, 2002 balance sheet.

b. Discuss the information Villa is required to disclose, either in the body of the financial statements or the notes thereto, related to bonds payable and capital leases included in the liabilities presented above.

c. Explain how Villa should account for each contingency in its 2002 financial statements. Discuss the theoretical justification for each accounting treatment.

* The AICPA has just recently started including this statement.

MULTIPLE-CHOICE ANSWERS

1. c __ __	13. b __ __	25. b __ __	37. a __ __	49. b __ __
2. c __ __	14. c __ __	26. b __ __	38. c __ __	50. b __ __
3. a __ __	15. d __ __	27. b __ __	39. b __ __	51. b __ __
4. b __ __	16. b __ __	28. c __ __	40. a __ __	52. b __ __
5. b __ __	17. b __ __	29. a __ __	41. b __ __	53. d __ __
6. d __ __	18. b __ __	30. b __ __	42. d __ __	
7. a __ __	19. a __ __	31. a __ __	43. c __ __	
8. a __ __	20. d __ __	32. b __ __	44. a __ __	
9. c __ __	21. b __ __	33. b __ __	45. c __ __	
10. c __ __	22. b __ __	34. d __ __	46. a __ __	
11. a __ __	23. c __ __	35. b __ __	47. d __ __	1st: __/53 = __%
12. d __ __	24. c __ __	36. d __ __	48. a __ __	2nd: __/53 = __%

MULTIPLE-CHOICE ANSWER EXPLANATIONS

E.1.d.(1) Operating Leases: Lessor/Lessee

1. **(c)** SFAS 13 specifies that, in an operating lease, the lessor should recognize rental revenue on a straight-line basis. This means that the lease bonus ($50,000) should be recorded as unearned revenue on 1/1/02, and recognized as rental revenue over the five-year lease term. Therefore, 2002 rental revenue should be $100,000 [$90,000 + ($50,000 ÷ 5)]. The security deposit ($25,000) does not affect rental revenue. Since it is to be refunded to the lessee upon expiration of the lease, it is recorded as a deposit, a long-term liability when received.

2. **(c)** SFAS 13 states that rental revenue on operating leases should be recognized on a straight-line basis unless another method more reasonably reflects the pattern of use given by the lessor. When the pattern of cash flows under the lease agreement is other than straight-line, this will result in the recording of rent receivable or unearned rent. Wall's total rent revenue [(1/2 x $8,000) + (4 x $12,500) = $54,000] should be recognized on a straight-line basis over the five-year lease term ($54,000 x 1/5 = $10,800). Since cash collected in 2002 is only $4,000 (one-half of $8,000, since the first six months are rent-free), Wall would accrue rent receivable and rental revenue of $6,800 ($10,800 – $4,000) at year-end to bring the rental revenue up to $10,800.

3. **(a)** Net rental income on an operating lease is equal to rental revenue less related expenses, as computed below.

Rental revenue	$50,000
Depreciation expense	(12,000)
Executory costs	(9,000)
Finder's fee ($15,000 ÷ 10)	(1,500)
Net rental income	$27,500

The finder's fee ($15,000) is capitalized as a deferred charge at the inception of the lease and amortized over ten years to match the expense to the revenues it enabled the lessor to earn.

4. **(b)** SFAS 13 states that for an operating lease, rental revenue should be recognized on a straight-line basis unless another method more reasonably reflects the pattern of use given by the lessor. When the pattern of cash flows under the lease agreement is other than straight-line, this will result in the recording of rent receivable or unearned rent. Gee's total rent revenue ($36,000) should be recognized on a straight-line basis over the thirty-six-month lease, resulting in monthly entries debiting **rent receivable** and crediting **rent revenue** for $1,000. Cash collections will result in

entries debiting **cash** and crediting **rent receivable** for $500 per month for the first twelve months and $750 per month for the second twelve months. Therefore, rent receivable at 6/30/02 is $9,000, as indicated by the T-account below.

	Rent Receivable		
Accruals (24 x $1,000)	24,000	6,000	Collections (12 x $500)
		9,000	Collections (12 x $750)
6/30/02 Balance	9,000		

5. **(b)** At 1/1/02, Glen would record as a current liability unearned rent of $50,000, and as a long-term liability unearned rent of $150,000. During 2002, the current portion of unearned rent was earned and would be recognized as revenue. At 12/31/02, the portion of the long-term liability representing the second year's rent ($50,000) would be reclassified as current, leaving as a long-term liability the $100,000 representing the last two years' rent.

6. **(d)** SFAS 13 states that rental revenue on operating leases should be recognized on a straight-line basis unless another method more reasonably reflects the pattern of use given by the lessor. When the pattern of cash flows under the lease agreement is other than straight-line, this will result in the recording of rent receivable or unearned rent. Therefore, even though Graf received only one monthly payment in 2002 (1/48 of the total rent to received over the life of the lease), they would accrue as rent receivable and rent revenue an amount sufficient to increase the rent revenue account to a balance equal to one-fifth of the total cash to be received over the five-year life of the lease.

7. **(a)** The graph presented in the problem can be interpreted as follows:

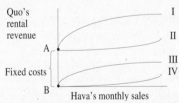

Line AB is considered to be fixed rental costs per month. Therefore, answers (c) and (d) are incorrect because lines III and IV do not include the fixed portion of the rental payment, in its graphical representation. The problem states that as the variable rental amount increases, it does so at a decreasing rate. Answer (b) is incorrect because line II is increasing, but at an increasing rate, not a decreasing rate, as line I represents. Therefore, answer (a) is the correct answer because line I is increasing, at a decreasing rate.

8. **(a)** SFAS 13 states that rent on operating leases should be expensed on a straight-line basis unless another method is better suited to the particular benefits and costs associated with the lease. In this lease, the lessee must pay rent of $1,000 monthly for five years excluding the first nine months, or fifty-one months (60 – 9). Therefore, total rent expense for the five years is $51,000 (51 x $1,000). Recognizing rent expense on a straight-line basis, rent expense for the first year is $10,200 ($51,000 ÷ 5 years).

9. **(c)** SFAS 13 specifies that, in an operating lease, the lessee should recognize rent expense on a straight-line basis unless another method is better suited to the particular lease. Therefore, the lease bonus should be recognized as rent expense on a straight-line basis over the ten-year lease term ($24,000 ÷ 10 = $2,400). However, the contingent rentals, which are based on company sales, shall be expensed in the period to which they relate. Therefore, in 2002, contingent rentals of $5,000 [5% x ($600,000 – $500,000)] should be included in rent expense. Total rent expense is $103,400, as computed below.

Base rental	$ 96,000
Lease bonus ($24,000 ÷ 10)	2,400
Cont. rental [5% x ($600,000 – $500,000)]	5,000
	$103,400

10. **(c)** For operating leases having noncancellable remaining lease terms of more than one year, the lessee must disclose future minimum lease payments in the aggregate and for each of the five succeeding fiscal years. Since the annual **minimum** lease payments are $100,000, South must disclose subsequent years' lease payments of $100,000 per annum for each of the next five years and $900,000 (nine remaining payments x $100,000) in the aggregate.

11. **(a)** To qualify for treatment as a capital lease, a lease must meet one or more of the following criteria:

1. Transfers ownership to lessee.
2. Contains bargain purchase option.
3. Lease term is ≥ 75% of the economic life of the leased asset.
4. Present value of minimum lease payments is ≥ 90% of the FMV of the leased asset.

Since the lease signed by Mollat Company does not meet any of these criteria, it must be classified as an operating lease. For operating leases, the lessee's lease payments are recorded as debits to rent expense. Mollat would report rent expense equal to the 2002 lease payments in its 2002 income statement.

12. **(d)** When a leasing agreement is accounted for as an operating lease, the lessor and the lessee recognize rental revenue and rental expense respectively on a straight-line basis unless another systematic and rational basis more clearly reflects the time pattern in which use benefit is given (received) by the respective parties. Per FASB Technical Bulletin 85-3, the straight-lining of uneven lease payments includes scheduled rent increases. Even though the amount of the annual lease payment increases in year six, rental expense would not change. Interest is not an element of revenue (expense) in operating leases.

E.1.d.(1)(e)   Leasehold Improvements

13. **(b)** The first month's rent ($60,000) should be expensed in 2002. The prepayment of the last month's rent

(also $60,000) should be deferred and recognized as an expense in November 2007. The security deposit ($80,000) should be recorded as a long-term receivable, since Clark can expect to receive the deposit back at lease end. The installation of new walls and offices ($360,000) is recorded as a leasehold improvement at 12/1/02. At 12/31/02, amortization must be recorded for one month ($360,000 x 1/60 = $6,000). Therefore, 2002 expense is $66,000 ($60,000 + $6,000). The journal entries are

Rent expense	60,000	
Prepaid rent	60,000	
Sec. deposit receivable	80,000	
Leasehold improvements	360,000	
Cash		560,000
Amortization expense	6,000	
Leasehold improvements		6,000

14. **(c)** Leasehold improvements are capitalized and amortized over the shorter of the remaining life of the lease (six years from 1/1/02 to 12/31/07) or the useful life of the improvements (eight years). Therefore, the $48,000 cost is amortized over six years, resulting in annual amortization of $8,000 ($48,000 ÷ 6). For the period 1/1/02 to 6/30/02, amortization is $4,000 ($8,000 x 6/12), so the 6/30/02 net amount for leasehold improvements is $44,000 ($48,000 – $4,000).

15. **(d)** Leasehold improvements are properly capitalized and amortized over the shorter of the remaining life of the lease or the useful life of the improvement. If the lease contains an option to renew and the likelihood of renewal is uncertain (as it is in this case), then the remaining life of the lease is based on the initial lease term. In this case, the remaining life of the lease is therefore ten years. Since the estimated lives of all improvements in this case are greater than or equal to ten years, the appropriate amortization period is ten years. The 2002 amortization is thus computed as the total cost of $140,000 ($47,000 + $75,000 + $18,000 = $140,000), divided by ten years, or $14,000. There is no salvage value for leasehold improvements, because the assets revert to the lessor at the end of the lease term. Note that if the renewal of the lease for an additional ten years were considered a certainty, the amortization periods would be as follows: ten years for the sales office (estimated life); twenty years for the warehouse (lease term); and fifteen years for the parking lot (estimated life).

16. **(b)** The cost of the leasehold improvements ($540,000) should be amortized over the remaining life of the lease, or over the useful life of the improvements, whichever is **shorter**. The remaining life of the lease should include periods covered by a renewal option **if** it is probable that the option will be exercised. In this case, the remaining life of the lease is eighteen years (12 years of original lease + 8 years in option period – 2 years gone by), and the useful life of the improvements is fifteen years. Therefore, amortization is based on a fifteen-year life ($540,000 ÷ 15 = $36,000). The 12/31/02 carrying amount is $504,000 ($540,000 – $36,000).

17. **(b)** Per SFAS 13, a lease should be classified as a capital lease by the lessee if the lease terms meet any one of the following four criteria: (1) the lease transfers ownership of the property to the lessee by the end of the lease term, (2) the lease contains a bargain purchase option, (3) the lease term is greater than or equal to 75% of the economic life of the leased property, or (4) the present value of the minimum lease payments is greater than or equal to 90% of the fair market value of the leased property. In this question, the terms of Vail's lease do not meet any of the four criteria for treatment as a capital lease, so the lease should be accounted for as an operating lease. Vail should therefore **not** recognize the building as an asset. In an operating lease, the lessee should capitalize the cost of the leasehold improvements, recognizing them as assets, and amortize their cost over the shorter of their useful lives or the term of the lease.

18. **(b)**   Leasehold improvements are properly capitalized and amortized over the remaining life of the lease, or the useful life of the improvements, whichever is shorter. Since the useful life of the office is only ten years and the remaining term of the lease is fifteen years, the cost should be depreciated over the ten-year period.

E.1.d.(2) Direct Financing Leases: Lessor

19. **(a)**   The annual lease payment is $75,000 ($323,400 ÷ 4.312). After five years, total lease payments will be $375,000 (5 x $75,000). The total interest revenue over the life of the lease is the excess of total lease payments over the fair value of the leased asset ($375,000 – $323,400 = $51,600).

20. **(d)**   This lease qualifies as a direct financing lease; therefore interest revenue will be recognized rather than rent revenue. Had the lease qualified as an operating lease, rent revenue would have been recognized. The lessor's criteria for direct financing classification is as follows:

(1) The lease transfers ownership to the lessee, at the end of the lease
(2) The lease contains a bargain purchase option
(3) The lease term is ≥ 75% of an asset's economic life
(4) The present value of the minimum lease payments is ≥ 90% of the fair market value of the leased asset.

Note that the question is silent concerning the two additional criteria that apply to lessors: (1) collectibility of minimum lease payments is predictable, and (2) no important uncertainties exist concerning costs yet to be incurred by the lessee. Recall that if one of the four criteria are met, the lease is treated as a capital lease. In this case, since the lease term is for 80% of the asset's economic life, test (3) is met, and the lease is properly treated as a capital lease. In addition, the amount of interest revenue will be smaller in 2002 than the revenue in 2001. This result occurs because the present value of the minimum lease payments or carrying value of the obligation decreases each year as lease payments are received. As this occurs, the amount of interest revenue on the outstanding amount of the investment will decrease as well. Over the course of time, the investment reduction portion of each level payment increases and the amount of interest declines.

E.1.d.(3) Sales-Type Leases: Lessor

21. **(b)**   This is a sales-type lease, so at the inception of the lease, the lessor would recognize sales of $3,520,000 and cost of goods sold of $2,800,000, resulting in a **profit on sale of $720,000**. In addition, interest revenue is recognized for the period July 1, 2002, to December 31, 2002. The initial net lease payments receivable on 7/1/02 is

$3,520,000. The first rental payment received on 7/1/02 consists entirely of principal, reducing the net receivable to $2,920,000 ($3,520,000 – $600,000). Therefore, 2002 **interest revenue for the six months from 7/1/02 to 12/31/02 is $146,000** ($2,920,000 x 10% x 6/12).

22. **(b)**   This is a sales-type lease, so at the inception of the lease, the lessor would recognize sales of $3,300,000 (the PV of the lease payments), and cost of goods sold of $2,800,000, resulting in profit on the sale of $500,000 ($3,300,000 – $2,800,000). Note that the list selling price of an asset ($3,520,000 in this case) is not always representative of its FMV. An asset can often be purchased for less than its list price.

23. **(c)**   Per SFAS 13, the excess of the fair value of leased property at the inception of the lease over the lessor's cost is defined as the manufacturer's or dealer's profit. Answer (a) is incorrect because the unearned income from a sales-type lease is defined as the difference between the gross investment in the lease and the sum of the present values of the components of the gross investment. Answer (b) is incorrect because the unearned income from a direct-financing lease is defined as the excess of the gross investment over the cost (also the PV of lease payments) of the leased property. Answer (d) is incorrect because a sales-type lease involves a manufacturer's or dealer's profit while a direct financing lease does not.

24. **(c)**   Per SFAS 13, revenue is to be recognized for a sales-type lease over the lease term so as to produce a **constant rate** of return on the net investment in the lease. This requires the use of the **interest method**. Per SFAS 13, interest revenue **does** arise in a sales-type lease. Answer (a) is incorrect because the interest is to be earned over the life of the lease, not in full at the lease's inception.

E.1.d.(4) Capital Leases: Lessee

25. **(b)**   SFAS 13 provides criteria for classifying leases as either "capital" or "operating." If **any** of the criteria for classification as a capital lease are met, the lease is classified as such. One of the capital lease criterion is that the lease term is equal to 75% or more of the estimated economic life of the leased property. Thus, both leases M and P should be classified as capital leases.

26. **(b)**   This is a capital lease for the lessee because the lease term is 75% of the useful life of the machine [6 years = (75% x 8 years)]. For a capital lease, the lessee records as a **leased asset** and a **lease obligation** the lower of the PV of the minimum lease payments or the FV of the leased asset (not given in this problem). The PV of the minimum lease payments is computed using the lower of the lessee's incremental borrowing rate (15%) or the implicit rate used by the lessor if known by the lessee (12%). Since the implicit rate is lower, and known by the lessee, it is used to compute the PV ($50,000 x 4.61 = $230,500). The cost of the asset on the lessor's books ($375,500) is irrelevant.

27. **(b)**   This is a capital lease since the lease term (ten years) is the same as the useful life of the leased asset. In a capital lease, the lessee records an asset and a liability based on the PV of the minimum lease payments. The minimum lease payments includes rentals and a guaranteed residual value, **if guaranteed by the lessee**. In this case the minimum lease payments include only the rentals, since the residual value is guaranteed by a third party. The minimum lease payments are discounted using the **lower** of the lessee's incremental borrowing rate or the implicit rate used by the lessor, if known. In this case, the lessee knows the implicit rate is 10%, which is lower than the incremental borrowing rate of 12%. Thus, the present value or principal amount of the lease obligation is $61,446 ($10,000 x 6.1446) through the first year. Although accrued interest would be recognized at 10/31/02, the principal amount does not change until 1/1/03.

28.   (c)   The lessee records a capital lease at the present value of the minimum lease payments. The minimum lease payments includes rental payments and bargain purchase options (among other items). The $10,000 purchase option is a **bargain** purchase option because it allows the lessor to purchase the leased asset at an amount **less** than its expected fair value. In accordance with SFAS 13, the lessee computes the present value using its incremental borrowing rate (14%), unless the lessor's implicit rate (12%) is lower and is known by the lessee. This question indicates that the implicit rate is stated in the lease; therefore it would be known to the lessee. At the beginning of the lease term, Robbins should record a leased asset and lease liability at $66,500.

PV of rentals	($10,000 x 6.328)	=	$63,280
PV of BPO	($10,000 x .322)	=	3,220
PV at 12%			$66,500

29.   (a)   The annual executory costs (real estate taxes of $2,000) are **not** an expense or liability until incurred; therefore they are excluded from the minimum lease payments and are **not** reflected in the initial lease liability. The 12/31/02 capital lease liability is recorded at the PV of the minimum lease payments [5.6 x ($52,000 – $2,000) = $280,000].

30.   (b)   The requirement is to determine the amount to be recorded as a capitalized leased asset. This is a capital lease for the lessee because the lease term exceeds 75% of the economic life of the leased asset (10/12 > 75%). In a capital lease, the lessee records as an asset and liability the present value (PV) of the minimum lease payments (unless the PV exceeds the asset's FMV, in which case the FMV is recorded). The minimum lease payments include rentals, and a lessee-guaranteed residual value or a bargain purchase option. Only rentals apply in this case. Note that the $50,000 purchase option is not a **bargain** purchase option that the lessee would be compelled to exercise. A bargain purchase option is an option to purchase the leased asset at an amount **less** than its expected fair value. Therefore, the present value of the minimum lease payments is $238,000 ($40,000 x 5.95).

31.   (a)   The initial lease liability at 1/1/02, before the 1/1/02 payment, is the present value of the five rental payments (an **annuity due** since the first payment is made on 1/1/02) plus the present value of the guaranteed residual value. The computation is below.

PV of rentals ($13,000 x 4.240)	$55,120
PV of residual ($10,000 x 0.650)	6,500
Initial liability	$61,620

The 1/1/02 payment consists entirely of principal, bringing the 1/1/02 liability down to $48,620 ($61,620 – $13,000).

32.   (b)   The initial lease obligation at 12/30/02 was $135,000. The first lease payment was made the same day,

and therefore consisted entirely of principal reduction. After the payment, the lease obligation was $115,000 ($135,000 – $20,000). This balance will be reported as current (for the portion to be paid in 2003) and long-term (for the portion to be paid beyond 2003). The next lease payment of $20,000 will be paid 12/31/03, and will consist of both interest ($115,000 x 10% = $11,500) and principal reduction ($20,000 – $11,500 = $8,500). Thus, the portion of the $115,000 lease obligation to be paid in the next year (and therefore reported as a current liability) is $8,500. Note that the interest to be paid next year ($11,500) is not a liability at 12/31/02 because it has not yet been incurred.

33.   (b)   This is a capital lease for the lessee because the lease term (nine years) exceeds 75% of the useful life of the machine (also nine years). For a capital lease, the lessee records as a **leased asset** and a **lease obligation** at the lower of the PV of the minimum lease payments or the FV of the leased asset (not given in this problem). The PV of the minimum lease payments is computed using the lower of the lessee's incremental borrowing rate (12%) or the implicit rate used by the lessor if known by the lessee (10%). Since the implicit rate is lower, and known by the lessee, it is used to compute the PV ($316,500). The initial lease payment ($50,000) is entirely principal because it was made at the inception of the lease. Therefore, after the 12/31/01 payment, the lease liability is $266,500 ($316,500 – $50,000). The 12/31/02 payment consists of interest incurred during 2002 ($266,500 x 10% = $26,650) and principal reduction ($50,000 – $26,650 = $23,350). Therefore, the 12/31/02 capital lease liability is $243,150 ($266,500 – $23,350).

34.   (d)   The initial lease liability at 12/31/01 is $417,000 (the PV of the minimum lease payments). The annual executory costs ($5,000) are **not** an expense or liability until incurred; therefore, they are excluded from the minimum lease payments and are **not** reflected in the initial lease liability. The 12/31/01 payment of $105,000 includes $5,000 of executory costs; the remainder ($100,000) is entirely principal since the payment was made at the inception of the lease. Therefore, after the 12/31/01 payment, the lease liability is $317,000 ($417,000 – $100,000). The 12/31/02 payment consists of executory costs ($5,000), interest incurred during 2002 ($317,000 x 10% = $31,700), and reduction of principal ($105,000 – $5,000 – $31,700 = $68,300). Therefore, the 12/31/02 balance sheet should include a lease liability of $248,700 ($317,000 – $68,300).

35.   (b)   On 1/2/02, Mene made a lease payment of $9,000, which included payment of the current portion of the lease obligation ($1,364) and interest ($9,000 – $1,364 = $7,636). After this payment, the total lease obligation was $75,000. The 1/2/03 payment would include interest of $7,500 ($75,000 x 10%), and principal of $1,500 ($9,000 – $7,500). This $1,500 amount would represent the current portion of the lease obligation at 12/31/02, so the long-term lease obligation net of the current portion at 12/31/02 is $73,500 ($75,000 – $1,500).

36.   (d)   SFAS 13 specifies that if a lease is classified as a capital lease, the lessee must record an asset and a liability, each for an amount equal to the present value of the minimum lease payments at the beginning of the lease.

37.   (a)   At the inception of a capital lease, the lessee must record an asset and a liability based on the PV of the minimum lease payments. The minimum lease payments are the payments that lessee is required to make in connection with the leased property, including rent payments, bargain purchase option, and guaranteed residual value. Minimum lease payments (MLP) are recorded at present value. The whole guaranteed residual value is included in MLP.

38. **(c)** In a capital lease where the first annual lease payment is made immediately upon signing the lease (annuity due), the first payment consists solely of lease liability reduction, since no time has transpired during which interest expense could be incurred. Subsequent payments include both interest expense and reduction of the liability.

39. **(b)** Per SFAS 13, each minimum lease payment shall be allocated between a reduction of the obligation and interest expense so as to produce a constant periodic rate of interest on the remaining balance of the obligation. Since the interest will be computed based upon a **declining** obligation balance, the interest component of each payment will also be declining. The result will be a relatively larger portion of the minimum lease payment allocated to the reduction of the lease obligation in the latter portion of the lease term.

40. **(a)** When a leasing agreement is accounted for as capital lease, the lessee recognizes a liability on its books equal to the present value of the minimum lease payments. The liability should be divided between current and noncurrent based upon when each lease payment is due. At the end of year one, the current lease liability should equal the principal portion of the lease payment due in year two. Therefore, when the lease payment is made in year two, the reduction of the lease liability will equal the current liability shown at the end of year one.

41. **(b)** This is a capital lease since title passes to Cole, the lessee, at the end of the lease. At the inception of the lease on 1/2/02, the lessee records the PV of the lease payments ($108,000) as an asset and a liability. The asset is depreciated on a straight-line basis over its useful life of twelve years, resulting in a yearly depreciation charge of $9,000 ($108,000 ÷ 12). The asset is depreciated over its useful life rather than over the lease term (eight years) because title transfers to the lessee, allowing the lessee to use the asset for twelve years.

42. **(d)** A leased asset acquired in a capital lease should be depreciated over the period of time the lessee expects to use the asset (either the lease term or the useful life, depending on the situation). In this case, Nori expects to use the leased asset for its entire eight-year useful life, due to the expected exercise of the bargain purchase option at the end of the five-year lease term. Therefore, Nori's 2002 depreciation expense is $27,500

$$\frac{(\$240,000 \text{ cost}) - (\$20,000 \text{ salvage})}{8 \text{ years}} = \$27,500$$

43. **(c)** The requirement is to determine whether a lessee should amortize the capitalizable cost of a leased asset in a manner consistent with the lessee's normal depreciation policy for owned assets for leases that contained a bargain purchase option and/or transferred ownership at the end of the lease term. Transfer of ownership of the property to the lessee by the end of the lease term and a lease that contains a bargain purchase option are properly classified as capital

leases (SFAS 13). Per SFAS 13, if the lease meets either of the above criteria, the asset shall be amortized in a manner consistent with the lessee's normal depreciation policy for owned assets.

44. **(a)** At the inception of the lease on 1/1/02, the capitalized liability is $379,000 (the present value of the lease payments). Since the first payment is not due until the **end** of the first year, 2002 interest expense is based on the full initial liability ($379,000 x 10% = $37,900).

45. **(c)** SFAS 13, as amended and interpreted, requires the disclosure of future minimum lease payments (MLP) for each of the next five years and the aggregate amount of MLP due after five years. At 12/31/02, eight annual payments of $100,000 each have not yet been paid. Therefore, future MLP are $800,000 (8 x $100,000). The amount for the appropriate required period (five years) is $500,000, while the aggregate amount for the period thereafter is $300,000 ($800,000 – $500,000).

46. **(a)** At the end of the lease, the balance in the lease payable column should equal the bargain purchase option price. Failure to include the present value of the bargain purchase option price in the beginning present value of the lease would result in an ending balance in the lease payable column of zero. Both answers (b) and (c) would have resulted in an ending balance of less than zero, while answer (d) would have resulted in an ending balance greater than zero.

E.2.b. Sale-Leaseback

47. **(d)** According to SFAS 13, sale-leaseback arrangements are treated as though two transactions were a single financing transaction, if the lease qualifies as a capital lease. Any gain or loss on the sale is deferred and amortized over the lease term (if possession reverts to the lessor) or the economic life (if ownership transfers to the lessee). In this case, the lease qualifies as a capital lease because the lease term (twelve years) is 80% of the remaining economic life of the leased property (fifteen years). Therefore, at 12/31/02, all of gain ($480,000 – $360,000 = $120,000) would be deferred and amortized over twelve years. Since the sale took place on 12/31/02, there is no amortization for 2002.

48. **(a)** SFAS 13 generally treats a sale-leaseback as a single financing transaction in which any profit on the sale is deferred and amortized by the seller. However, SFAS 28 amends this general rule when either **only a minor part** of the remaining use of the leased asset is retained (case one) or when **more than a minor part but less than substantially all** of the remaining use of the leased asset is retained (case two). Case one occurs when the PV of the lease payments is 10% or less of the FMV of the sale-leaseback property. Case two occurs when the leaseback is more than minor but does **not** meet the criteria of a capital lease. This problem is an example of case one, because the PV of the lease payments ($36,900) is less than 10% of the FMV of the asset (10% x $400,000 = $40,000). SFAS 28 specifies that under these circumstances, the full gain ($400,000 – $300,000 = $100,000) is recognized, and **none is deferred**.

49. **(b)** SFAS 13 generally treats a sale-leaseback as a single financing transaction in which any profit on the sale is deferred and amortized by the seller. However, SFAS 28 amends this general rule when either **only a minor part** of the remaining use of the leased asset is retained (case one or when **more than a minor part but less than substantially all** of the remaining use of the leased asset is retained (case two). Case one occurs when the PV of the lease payments is 10% or less of the FMV of the sale-leaseback property. Case two occurs when the leaseback is more than minor but does **not** meet the criteria of a capital lease. This is an example of case two because while the PV of the lease payments ($190,581) is more than 10% of the FMV of the asset ($600,000), the lease falls into the operating lease category. SFAS 28 specifies that under these circumstances the gain on sale ($600,000 – $100,000 = $500,000) is recognized to the extent that it exceeds the PV of the lease payments ($190,581). The gain reported would be $309,419 ($500,000 – $190,581). The portion of the gain represented by the $190,581 PV of the lease payments is deferred and amortized on a straight-line basis over the life of the lease.

50. (b)   On a sale-leaseback, generally **losses** are recognized immediately. However, there can be two types of losses in sale-leasebacks. The type that is **recognized immediately** is a **real economic loss,** where the carrying amount of the asset is higher than its FMV. The type that is **deferred** is an **artificial loss** where the sale price ($430,000) is below the carrying amount ($450,000), but the FMV ($465,000) is above the carrying amount ($450,000). The loss in this problem ($450,000 – $430,000 = $20,000) is an artificial loss that must be deferred.

51. (b)   According to SFAS 13, sale-leaseback transactions are treated as though two transactions were a single financing transaction, if the lease qualifies as a capital lease. Any gain on the sale is deferred and amortized over the lease term (if possession reverts to the lessor) or the economic life (if ownership transfers to the lessee); both are ten years in this case. Since this is a capital lease, the entire gain ($150,000 – $100,000 = $50,000) is deferred at 1/1/02. At 12/31/02, an adjusting entry must be prepared to amortize 1/10 of the unearned gain (1/10 x $50,000 = $5,000), because the lease covers ten years. Therefore, the unearned gain at 12/31/02 is $45,000 ($50,000 – $5,000).

52. (b)   Per SFAS 28, any profit related to a sale-leaseback transaction in which the seller-lessee retains the property leased (i.e., the seller-lessee retains substantially all of the benefits and risks of the ownership of the property sold), shall be deferred and amortized in proportion to the amortization of the leased asset, if a capital lease. If it is an operating lease, the profit will be deferred in proportion to the related gross rental charged to expense over the lease term. It is important to note that **losses,** however, are recognized immediately for either a capital or operating lease. Since the gain on the sale should be deferred in either case, no gain is recognized at the time of the sale.

NOTE: An example of an operating lease in which substantially all of the remaining use of the leased asset is retained by the lessee occurs when the lease term begins within the last 25% of the asset's original useful life.

53. (d)   In a sale-leaseback transaction, if the leaseback is recorded as a capital lease and the lessee has retained **substantially all** of the rights to use the property, then any gain on the sale must be deferred and amortized over the life of the property in proportion to the amortization of the leased asset. This deferred gain acts as an asset valuation allowance resulting in the net amount shown for the leased asset being equal to the same carrying value as if the sale and leaseback transaction had not occurred.

SOLUTION GUIDE

Problem 1   Capital Lease Entries

1.   This problem requires preparation of the lessee's journal entries for the first year of a lease. The lease is a capital lease because title passes to the lessee at the end of the lease and the lease term (twenty years) is greater than 75% of the useful life (twenty-five years).

2.   In a capital lease, the lessee records a **leased asset** and a **lease obligation** at the present value of the minimum lease payments. The lessee's incremental borrowing rate (12%) should be used to determine the present value unless the lessor's implicit rate is lower and is known by the lessee. The lessor's 10% rate is lower and is known by the lessee, so it is used to compute the PV of $850,000 ($100,000 x 8.5).

3.   The first lease payment on 12/31/02 consists of interest expense incurred during 2001 ($850,000 x 10% = $85,000) and reduction of lease obligation ($100,000 payment – $85,000 interest = $15,000). The $100,000 credit to cash is offset by debits to interest expense ($85,000) and lease obligation ($15,000)

4.   The only other expense related to this lease is depreciation of the leased asset. Leased assets are depreciated over the lease term (twenty years) unless the lease transfers ownership (as this one does) or contains a bargain purchase option. If either of these is present, then the asset is depreciated over the estimated useful life of the asset (twenty-five years). Depreciation expense is cost ($850,000) divided by useful life ($850,000 ÷ 25 years = $34,000). If a salvage value had been given, it would be subtracted from cost before dividing by useful life.

UNOFFICIAL ANSWER

Problem 1   Capital Lease Entries

	Debits	Credits
1. January 2, 2002—to record lease:		
Equipment	850,000	
Capital lease liability		850,000
2. December 31, 2002—to record payment:		
Capital lease liability	100,000	
Cash		100,000
3. December 31, 2002—to record depreciation:		
Depreciation expense	34,000	
Accumulated depreciation		34,000
Interest expense	85,000	
Capital lease liability		85,000

ANSWER OUTLINE

Problem 2   Sale-Leaseback Accounting and Reporting

a.   Accounting for sale-leaseback, 12/31/02

Cash	xx	
PP&E		xx
Deferred gain		xx

Appropriate because Jen retains substantial ownership rights and obligations
   Earning process not complete
   Financing transaction, not a sale
   Gain should be deferred

b.   BS reporting 12/31/03
   Leased property at discounted PV 12/31/02 less acc. depr. and unamortized deferred gain on sale
      Discounted PV at 12/31/02 represents future lease payments, discounted at Jen's interest rate
   Lease obligation equals the 12/31/02 PV less principal repaid in 2003
      2004 principal reduction reported as CL
      Balance due reported as NCL

UNOFFICIAL ANSWER

Problem 2   Sale-Leaseback Accounting and Reporting

a.   Jen should account for the sale portion of the sale-leaseback transaction by increasing cash for the sale price, decreasing property, plant, and equipment for the building's carrying amount, and recording a deferred gain for the excess of the sale price over the building's carrying amount.

   This accounting is appropriate because Jen still retains substantial ownership rights and obligations pertaining to the building. Since no earning process occurred, this sale-leaseback is not in substance a sale but a financing transaction. Therefore, the gain should be deferred.

b.   The leased building is included on Jen's December 31, 2003 balance sheet as leased property at its discounted present value on December 31, 2002, less accumulated depreciation, and less unamortized deferred gain on the sale. Its discounted present value at December 31, 2002, represents the future lease payments, discounted at Jen's interest rate.

   The lease obligation on Jen's December 31, 2003 balance sheet equals the building's December 31, 2002 present value less principal repaid in 2003. An amount equal to the principal to be repaid in 2004 should be reported as a current liability. The balance of the obligation should be reported as a noncurrent liability.

SOLUTION GUIDE AND ANSWER OUTLINE

Problem 3   Liabilities Section of BS; Bond and Lease Disclosures; Contingencies

1.   The accounts payable are current because these amounts are typically due in less than one year.

2.   The cash dividends payable are current because they will be paid in the following January. The cash dividends payable is computed as follows:

Dividend per share		# outstanding shares		Dividends Payable
$.05	x	1,000,000	=	$50,000

3.   The lease obligation must be separated into a current and noncurrent portion. The current portion is the amount by which the lease obligation's principal will be reduced in the next year. The carrying value of the lease obligation at 12/31/02 is $380,000 and is computed as follows:

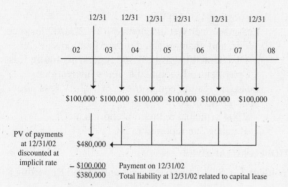

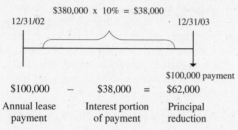

$380,000 - $100,000 = $380,000 Total liability at 12/31/02 related to capital lease

The amount of principal reduction (current liability) for 2003 is $62,000 and is computed as follows:

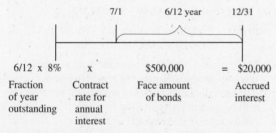

$380,000 x 10% = $38,000

$100,000	–	$38,000	=	$62,000
Annual lease payment		Interest portion of payment		Principal reduction

The noncurrent liability is $318,000 as computed below.

$380,000	–	$62,000	=	$318,000
Capital lease liability		Current portion of liability		Noncurrent liability

Note that because the lessor's implicit rate of 10% is lower than Villa's incremental borrowing rate and Villa is aware of the lessor's implicit rate, it shall be used per SFAS 13.

4. Accrued interest on the bonds is a current liability. The amount is $20,000 for the six months they are outstanding in 2002 and is computed as follows:

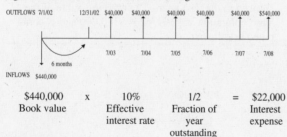

6/12 x 8%	x	$500,000	=	$20,000
Fraction of year outstanding		Contract rate for annual interest	Face amount of bonds	Accrued interest

5. The bonds payable are all noncurrent because they do not mature until 2006. The carrying amount of the bonds payable is the issue amount of the bonds plus the amortization of the bond discount for six months, or $442,000 and is computed below.

Diagram of cash inflows and outflows relating to the bonds

OUTFLOWS 7/1/02   12/31/02 $40,000 $40,000 $40,000 $40,000 $40,000 $540,000

6 months
INFLOWS $440,000

$440,000	x	10%	1/2	=	$22,000
Book value		Effective interest rate	Fraction of year outstanding		Interest expense

$22,000	–	$20,000	=	$2,000
Effective interest		Cash interest		Increase in book value (Amortization of bond discount)

$440,000	+	$2,000	=	$442,000
Book value 7/1/04		Increase in book value		Book value 12/31/04

Note that the information about the current market price and yield rate is not relevant because under the historical cost model per GAAP, the bonds market price and yield rate at the issue date are used throughout the life of the bond issue.

6. Income taxes payable is a current liability of $180,000 as computed below.

$600,000	x	30%	=	$180,000
Taxable income		Effective tax rate		Income taxes payable

7. Deferred income tax liability is a long-term liability because it relates to noncurrent assets. Only temporary differences have future taxable or deductible amounts that result in deferred tax liabilities or deferred tax assets. Current pretax financial income was reduced by the $150,000 temporary difference, a current deductible amount that will result in future taxable amount(s). The cumulative temporary differences including the $150,000 that arose this period are $300,000. Therefore, the deferred tax liability is $90,000 and is computed as follows:

$300,000	x	30%	=	$90,000
Cumulative taxable differences related to noncurrent assets		Effective tax rate		Deferred tax liability

b. Capital lease disclosures on face of BS or in notes
   • Gross amount of assets
     • Major classes
   • Future minimum lease payments
   • General description of arrangement
     • Existence and terms or renewal
     • Escalation clauses
     • Restrictions
Bonds payable disclosures on face of
   • BS or in notes
   • Face amount
   • Nature and terms
     • Credit and market risk
     • Cash requirements
     • Related accounting policies

c. Toxic waste
   • Loss incurred
   • Disclose nature and cannot be estimated
Clear's claim
   • Not probable, so do not accrue
   • Disclose existence, nature, and estimate
Rockslide insurance
   • No impairment
   • No liability incurred
   • Do not accrue
   • Remote, disclosure not needed

UNOFFICIAL ANSWER

Problem 3 Liabilities Section of BS; Bond and Lease
Disclosures; Contingencies

a.

Villa Co.
BALANCE SHEET—LIABILITIES SECTION
December 31, 2002

Accounts payable	$ 35,000	
Accrued interest payable	20,000	[2]
Income taxes payable	180,000	[3]
Dividends payable	50,000	
Current portion, long-term debt	62,000	[1]
Total current liabilities	347,000	
Capital lease payable, less $62,000 current		
portion	318,000	[1]
Bonds payable	442,000	[2]
Deferred tax liability	90,000	[3]
Total liabilities	$1,197,000	

[1]	$100,000 x 4.8	=	$480,000	
	$480,000 – $100,000	=	$380,000	
	$380,000 x 10%	=	$ 38,000	
	$100,000 – $38,000	=	$ 62,000	
	$380,000 – $62,000	=	$318,000	
[2]	500K x 8% x 1/2	=	20K	
	440K x 10% x 1/2	=	22K	
	440 K + (22K – 20K)	=	442K	
[3]	600K x 30%	=	180K	
	300K x 30%	=	90K	

b.   Villa should disclose the following information about
the capital leases, either in the body of the financial statements or in the notes thereto:

- The gross amount of assets recorded under the capital
  leases, presented by major classes. This information
  may be combined with owned assets.
- Future minimum lease payments as of the balance
  sheet date, in the aggregate and for each of the five
  succeeding years.

- A general description of the leasing arrangement, including the existence and terms of renewal, escala-
  tion clauses, and restrictions imposed by the lease
  agreements.

Villa should disclose the following information about the
bonds payable, either in the body of the financial statements
or in the notes thereto:

- The face amount.
- The nature and terms of the bonds and a discussion of
  their credit and market risk, cash requirements, and
  related accounting policies.
- The fair value of the bonds and the method used to
  estimate their fair value. The price at which the
  bonds are trading is the most reasonable estimate of
  their fair value at December 31, 2002.

c.   Villa should account for each contingency in a slightly
different way because the likelihood of Villa's incurring a
loss differs in each situation.

For the toxic waste cleanup, a loss has been incurred.
In the notes to its financial statements, Villa should disclose
the nature of the loss on cleanup and indicate that an estimate of the loss, or range of the loss, cannot be made. No
accrual should be made because the loss cannot be reasonably estimated and accrual of an uncertain amount would
impair the integrity of the financial statements.

With regard to Clear's claim it is only reasonably possible, and not probable, that Villa will have to pay. Accordingly, Villa should not accrue the loss. Villa should
disclose the existence and nature of Clear's claim in the
notes to its financial statements. Disclosure should include
an estimate of the potential range of loss.

Regarding the lack of rockslide insurance, no asset has
been impaired, and no liability has been incurred. Accordingly, Villa should not accrue a loss. Since the likelihood of
a rockslide is remote, disclosure of the uninsured risk, while
permitted, is not required.

DEFERRED TAXES

SFAS 109, *Accounting for Income Taxes*, requires an asset and liability (balance sheet) approach to recognizing and measuring deferred taxes. To understand the basic concepts of deferred taxes, study this module and the outlines of SFAS 109 and APB 23.

A. Overview of Deferred Tax Theory

There are numerous differences between the recognition and measurement of pretax financial (book) income and asset/liability valuation under GAAP and the recognition and measurement of taxable income and asset/liability valuation under the Internal Revenue Code. Because of these differences between the two bodies of promulgated rules, pretax financial (book) income usually differs from taxable income. The amount of Income Tax Expense and the amount of Income Taxes Payable are, therefore, often different amounts.

According to SFAS 109, financial income tax expense (the **current and deferred** tax consequences of **all** events that have been recognized in the financial statements) is charged to Income Tax Expense. Income Tax Expense equals the taxes actually owed (a current tax liability) for the current period plus or minus the change during the current period in amounts payable in the future and in future tax benefits. By using this procedure, any possible income statement or balance sheet distortion that may result from differences in the timing of revenue recognition or expense deductibility and asset or liability valuation between GAAP and the Internal Revenue Code is avoided. The Income Tax Expense reported in the entity's income statement reflects the amount of taxes related to transactions recognized in the financial statements prepared under GAAP for the specific period. The deferred tax asset or liability (the difference between Income Tax Expense and Income Tax Payable) reported in the entity's balance sheet clearly reflects the amount of taxes that the entity has prepaid (an asset) or will have to pay in the future (a liability) because of temporary differences that result from differences in timing of revenue recognition or expense deductibility between GAAP and the Internal Revenue Code.

B. Permanent and Temporary Differences Defined

Differences between pretax financial (book) income and taxable income can be divided into two types: temporary differences or permanent differences. SFAS 109 does **not** use the term permanent differences. However, to ease our explanation and your comprehension, the term "permanent difference" will be used in this module, as it is in several intermediate accounting textbooks.

1. Temporary Differences

SFAS 109 defines a temporary difference as "a difference between the tax basis of an asset or liability and its reported amount in the financial statements that will result in taxable or deductible amounts in future years when the reported amount of the asset or liability is recovered or settled, respectively." This definition of a temporary difference is based on the assumption that assets and liabilities reported on an entity's balance sheet will eventually be recovered or settled at their net reported (book) value. This recovery or settling process will create income statement items (revenues/gains or expenses/losses) as the life of the asset or liability progresses. If the reported financial (book) value of the balance sheet item differs from its tax basis, the correct period for recognition of the related income statement item will differ between the entity's financial statements and the entity's tax return. Thus, from an income statement perspective, a temporary difference occurs when a revenue or expense item: (1) is included in both financial accounting income and taxable income, **and**, (2) is recognized in one period for financial accounting purposes and in another period for income tax purposes because of differences between the promulgated rules of GAAP and the Internal Revenue Code. If such a temporary difference exists, an amount will be recorded and reported as either a deferred tax liability or a deferred tax asset depending upon the relationship between the reported net financial (book) value and the tax basis of the related asset or liability. When the temporary difference reverses, the recorded deferred tax amount is removed from the balance sheet; the amount removed results in an increase or decrease in income tax expense. Some examples of temporary differences are presented below.

a. **Estimated warranty liability:** Expense recognized in the financial statements when the liability is incurred. Deduction recognized for tax purposes when the work is actually performed.

b. **Unearned rent (royalty) revenue:** Recognized in the financial statements as a liability when the rent (royalty) is received and as revenue when earned. Recognized as revenue for tax purposes when the cash is received. (Note that the Internal Revenue Code refers to revenue received in advance as "prepaid income," not "unearned revenue.")

c. **Plant assets and accumulated depreciation:** Changes in these assets and the related contra asset are recognized in the financial statements according to depreciation methods acceptable to GAAP. Changes in these assets and the related contra asset are usually recognized for tax purposes according to accelerated methods acceptable to the IRS such as ACRS and MACRS. Note that recovery of these assets occurs as the asset is used in the entity's operations to generate revenue. In essence, a portion of the investment in the asset is being recovered as the product or service is sold.

d. **Donated asset:** According to GAAP, initial valuation in the financial statements of a donated asset is based upon fair market value, and revenue is recognized for the same amount. Depreciation on the asset is computed according to the entity's normal policies. Upon sale of the asset, a gain is recognized for the difference between cash received and net book value. According to the Internal Revenue Code, a donated asset has the same basis for the donee as it did in the donor's hands. Thus, no tax deductions for depreciation are allowed for the asset if the tax basis is zero. When the asset is sold, the entire amount received is a taxable gain.

e. **Involuntary conversion of assets:** According to GAAP (FASB Interpretation 30), a gain (loss) must be recognized when a nonmonetary asset is involuntarily converted into a monetary asset, even though the entity reinvests the monetary assets in replacement nonmonetary assets. The replacement asset is valued at its cost or fair market value on date of acquisition. According to the Internal Revenue Code, no gain is recognized on an involuntary conversion if the amount reinvested in replacement property equals or exceeds the amount realized from the converted property. The tax basis of the replacement asset is valued at its cost less the deferred gain.

f. **Goodwill:** Under GAAP, goodwill is not amortized. The Internal Revenue Code however, mandates an amortization period of fifteen years.

2. **Permanent Differences**

A permanent difference occurs when a revenue or expense item is only included in pretax financial (book) income or in taxable income but will never be included in both. For example, interest income on municipal bonds is included in pretax financial (book) income but is never included in taxable income because it is tax exempt by law. No deferred taxes need to be recognized because no future tax consequences are created. The tax exempt income (or deduction not allowed for taxes) is simply subtracted from (or added to) book income in the book to tax reconciliation. Thus, a permanent difference affects only the current reconciliation of book income to taxable income, and has no effect on the computation of deferred taxes. Some common permanent differences are

a. **State and municipal bond interest income:** included in book income but not included in taxable income.

b. **Life insurance premium expense when the corporation is the beneficiary:** deducted for book income but not for taxable income; proceeds received on such policies result in a book gain but are not taxable.

c. **Federal income tax expense:** deducted for book income but not for taxable income.

d. **Payment of penalty or fine:** deducted for book income but not for taxable income.

e. **Dividend received deduction (DRD):** deducted for taxable income but not for book income.

The example below shows how permanent and temporary differences are used in calculating taxable income, given a corporation's pretax financial (book) income.

EXAMPLE 1: A corporation has pretax financial accounting (book) income of $146,000 in 2001. Additional information is as follows:

1. *Municipal bond interest income is $35,000.*
2. *Life insurance premium expense, where the corporation is the beneficiary, per books is $4,000.*
3. *Accelerated depreciation is used for tax purposes, while straight-line is used for books. Tax depreciation is $10,000; book depreciation is $5,000.*
4. *Estimated warranty expense of $500 is accrued for book purposes.*

Taxable income can be determined as follows:

Financial (book) income before income taxes	*$146,000*
Permanent differences	
Life insurance premium	*4,000*
Municipal bond interest	*(35,000)*
Temporary differences	
Amount added to tax accum. depr. and deducted on the tax return >	
Amount added to book accum. deprec. and deprec. exp.	*(5,000)*
Amount recognized for book estimated warranty	
liability and warranty exp. not recognized on the tax return	*500*
Taxable income	*$110,500*

The above schedule is known as the reconciliation of book income to taxable income. It is similar to the Schedule M-1 of the US Corporate Income Tax Return (Form 1120) except it starts with pretax financial accounting income instead of net income as Schedule M-1 does. Note that the permanent differences only impact the current year (2000 in this case) whereas the temporary differences will have future tax consequences.

C. Deferred Tax Assets and Liabilities

SFAS 109 defines a deferred tax asset as the deferred tax consequences attributable to deductible temporary differences and carryforwards. SFAS 109 requires that the deferred tax asset be reduced by a valuation allowance if a portion or all of the deferred tax asset will not be realized in the future. A deferred tax liability is defined as an amount that is recognized for the deferred tax consequence of temporary differences that will result in taxable amounts in future years. SFAS 109, like its predecessor pronouncements, does **not** permit discounting of these deferred tax assets and liabilities.

1. Identification and Measurement of Deferred Tax Items

The candidate's ability to work an income tax accounting problem depends upon his/her ability to correctly identify permanent and temporary differences. In order to recognize the tax consequences of a temporary difference, it must be the result of event(s) that have already been recognized in the entity's financial statements for the current or previous years. With regard to a fixed asset, this means that the fixed asset has been acquired before the end of the year for which income taxes are being determined. Thus, planned asset acquisitions for future years cannot result in temporary differences and thereby affect the determination of deferred income taxes.

A **temporary difference** between pretax financial (book) income and taxable income occurs when the tax basis of an asset (or liability) differs from its reported financial statement amount. As shown in *Example 1,* a temporary difference resulting from timing of GAAP recognition vs. timing of recognition for tax purposes can create the need for additions to or subtractions from book income in order to arrive at taxable income. These **additions (taxable amounts)** or **subtractions (deductible amounts)** can occur in the year an asset is acquired or a liability is incurred as well as in future years as the asset is recovered or the liability is settled. The table below presents the various possible relationships between financial statement (book) and tax recognition of revenue and expense and assets and liabilities as well as the nature of the resulting future tax consequences.

Acctg. income *>or<* *taxable income**	*B/S relationships*	*Temp. differ.*** *Cur.*	*Fut.*	*Type of BS tax deferral*	*Current deferred tax expense effect*	*Future deferred tax expense effect*
	Assets					
>	*(1) on books > tax return*	*D*	*T*	*Liability*	*(+)*	*(–)*
<	*(2) on books < tax return*	*T*	*D*	*Asset*	*(–)*	*(+)*
	Liabilities					
<	*(3) on books > tax return*	*T*	*D*	*Asset*	*(–)*	*(+)*
	(4) on books < tax return	*D*	*T*	*Liability*	*(+)*	*(–)*

* Relationship in the year the temporary difference originates.
** Deductible (D) /Taxable (T)

For example, a type 1 temporary difference (such as the difference between the financial statement amount and the **zero** tax basis of an asset obtained by a donation) creates a deferred tax liability. If the donated asset is sold for more than its tax basis, recognition of the difference between the asset's financial statement amount and its tax return basis results in a gain for taxable income and either a smaller gain or a loss for book income depending on the amount of book depreciation taken on the asset since it was received by the enterprise. The amount of cash that will be needed to pay the taxes due will be increased because the entire amount of cash received for the donated asset will be reported as gain (taxable amount) on the tax return. A liability is defined in SFAC 6 as "probable future sacrifices of economic benefits arising from present obligations of a particular entity to transfer assets...as a result of past transactions or events." The increase in cash paid out for taxes (a sacrifice of economic benefits) will result when the donated asset (from a past transaction or event) is disposed of; therefore, the future tax impact of the current period difference between financial statement value and tax basis represents a deferred liability. When the liability is recognized, deferred income tax expense is also recognized.

In contrast, a contingent liability recognized in the current period financial statements represents a type 3 temporary difference because a contingent liability has a zero basis for tax accounting. The amount of expense stemming from this contingent liability must be added back to financial (book) income to arrive at taxable income. Therefore, a deferred tax asset is created. When the probable and measurable future event does actually occur, the contingent liability will then represent a loss (deductible amount) on the tax return. Because the tax loss recognized will reduce taxable income and income taxes payable, the amount of cash that will be needed to pay the taxes due will be decreased. Remember, an asset is defined in SFAC 6 as a "probable future economic benefit obtained or controlled by a particular entity as a result of past transactions or events." The reduction of current tax expense and the resulting future decrease in cash paid out for taxes (an economic benefit) will result from the contingent liability (a past transaction or event). Therefore, the future tax impact of the current period difference between the financial statement value and tax basis represents a deferred tax asset in the year the contingency is recognized. Note that the deferred tax expense recorded in this situation is a credit because it represents a current period benefit.

2. **Scheduling and Recording Deferred Tax Amounts**

An entity's total income statement provision for income taxes is the sum of that entity's current and deferred tax amounts. The current tax expense or benefit is defined by SFAS 109 as "the amount of income taxes paid or payable (or refundable) for a year as determined by applying the provisions of the tax law to the taxable income or excess of deductions over revenues for that year." The deferred tax expense or benefit is defined as "the change during the year in an enterprise's deferred tax liabilities or assets." Thus, SFAS 109 requires that current and deferred tax amounts be computed independently.

The deferred tax amount (the future tax consequences of temporary differences) should be recorded in the current financial statements at the amounts that will be paid or recovered based upon tax laws and rates that are already in place and due to be in effect at the date of payment or recovery. These are known as **enacted** tax laws and **enacted** tax rates. In order to comply with SFAS 109, an entity must, therefore, determine when the identified and measured temporary differences will become taxable or deductible. Future **taxable amounts** cause taxable income to be greater than financial (book) income in future periods. They are a result of existing temporary differences and are reported as deferred tax liabilities in the current year. Future **deductible amounts** cause taxable income to be less than financial (book) income in future periods. They are a result of existing temporary differences and are reported as a deferred tax asset in the current year. For illustrative purposes, the following examples show the scheduling of future temporary differences. However, in practice and on the CPA exam, extensive scheduling is generally not necessary unless (1) there is a change in future enacted tax rates or (2) the problem requires the use of a valuation allowance account.

According to SFAS 109, deferred tax liabilities and assets are determined separately for each taxpaying component (an individual entity or group of entities that is consolidated for tax purposes) in each tax jurisdiction. That determination includes the following procedures:

1. Identify the types and amounts of existing temporary differences
2. Identify the nature and amount of each type of operating loss and tax credit carryforward and the remaining length of the carryforward period
3. Measure the total deferred tax liability for taxable temporary differences using the applicable tax rate
4. Measure the total deferred tax asset for deductible temporary differences and operating loss carryforwards using the applicable tax rate
5. Measure deferred tax assets for each type of tax credit carryforward
6. Reduce deferred tax assets by a valuation allowance if, based on the weight of available evidence, it is *more likely than not* (a likelihood of more than 50%) that some portion or all of the deferred tax assets will not be realized. The valuation allowance should be sufficient to reduce the deferred tax asset to the amount that is more likely than not to be realized.
7. Deferred tax assets and liabilities are **not** discounted to reflect their present value.

EXAMPLE 2: *This example shows the* **deferred tax accounting in 2001, 2002, and 2003** *for the temporary differences included in EXAMPLE 1 earlier in this module. Additional details are*

a.   *On 1/1/99 the enterprise acquired a depreciable asset for $30,000 that had an estimated life of six years and is depreciated on a straight-line basis for book purposes. For tax purposes, the asset is depreciated using the straight-line election under MACRS and qualifies as a three-year asset.*

b.   *The enterprise deducted warranty expense of $500 for book purposes in 2001 that is expected to be deductible for tax purposes in 2002.*

c.   *Taxable income was $110,500 in 2001, $112,000 in 2002, and $113,500 in 2003.*

d.   *The applicable tax rate is 40% for all years affected.*

The deferred component of income tax expense for 2001 is computed as follows. First, a schedule of the **temporary depreciation differences** *for all affected years is prepared:*

	1999	2000	2001	2002	2003	2004
Book depreciation	$ 5,000	$ 5,000	$ 5,000	$5,000	$5,000	$5,000
Tax depreciation	5,000*	10,000	10,000	5,000*	-	-
Temporary difference:						
No difference	$ 0			$ 0		
Book deprec. < Tax deprec.		$ (5,000)	$ (5,000)			
Book deprec. > Tax deprec.					$5,000	$5,000

* *Due to MACRS half-year convention*

Then, a schedule of **future taxable (deductible) amounts** *is prepared.*

	2002 Taxable (deductible)	2003 Taxable (deductible)	2004 Taxable (deductible)	Tax rate	Deferred tax liability (asset)
Scheduled taxable (deductible) amounts:					
Depreciation differences:					
taxable amounts		$5,000	$5000	40%	$4,000 Noncurrent
Warranty differences:					
deductible amounts	$(500)			40%	$(200) Current

The above schedule shows that the future tax benefit (deductible amount) in 2002 of the $500 temporary difference resulting from the Warranty Expense Liability must be recognized automatically as a deferred tax asset in 2001. The deferred tax asset of $200 ($500 x 40%) should be reported as a current asset at 12/31/01 because the classification of the temporary difference is based on the related asset or liability, in this case a warranty liability that is expected to be satisfied in the next year. The amount of future taxes payable (deferred tax liability) associated with the total temporary difference of $10,000 resulting from excess depreciation [$5,000 (2002) + $5,000 (2003)] is $4,000 [($5,000 + 5,000) x 40%]. The $4,000 amount is reported as a noncurrent deferred tax liability at 12/31/01, because classification as current or noncurrent is based on the classification of the related asset or liability, in this case a depreciable asset that is noncurrent.

Once the deferred tax asset and deferred tax liability have been measured at year-end, a journal entry is necessary to adjust the deferred tax account balances to the current year-end amount. As stated earlier, income tax expense for the year will consist of the taxes currently payable (based on taxable income) plus or minus any change in the deferred tax accounts.

EQUATION FOR DETERMINING INCOME TAX EXPENSE

$$\text{Income tax expense for financial reporting} = \text{Income tax payable from the tax return} \pm \text{Change in deferred taxes (net)*}$$

* *Ending balance of deferred tax liability/asset (net) less beginning balance of deferred tax liability/asset (net)*

NOTES:

1.   *Income Tax Expense is the sum of the two numbers on the right side of the equation. Each of these two numbers is determined directly using independent calculations. It is not possible to derive Income Tax Expense from pretax financial accounting income adjusted for permanent differences, unless the tax rate is constant for all years affected.*

2.   *The $\pm$ refers to whether the change is a credit or additional liability (+) or a debit or additional asset (−).*

3.   *Income Tax Payable is the amount of taxes calculated on the corporate tax return. It is the amount legally owed the government (after credits).*

4.   *One deferred tax (net) balance sheet account may be used in practice. If separate asset and liability accounts are used, the changes in each account would all be netted to determine the deferred tax component of income tax expense.*

To illustrate, we will use the deferred tax liability computed in Example 2 above and the taxable income derived in Example 1. Note that prior to adjustment, the deferred tax asset account had a zero balance and the deferred tax liability account had a balance of $2,000 ($5,000 x 40%) that was recognized as a result of the accumulated depreciation temporary difference that originated in 1996. (Refer to the schedule following the additional information given in Example 2 showing depreciation and the pattern of temporary differences and to the T-account under (c) below.) To focus on the two components of income tax expense, two entries rather than the typical combined entry will be used.

Income tax expense—current	44,200	
Income tax payable (a)		44,200

(a) $110,500 taxable income (from Example 1) x 40% = $44,200

Income tax expense—deferred (d)	1,800	
Deferred tax asset—current (b)	200	
Deferred tax liability—noncurrent (c)		2,000

(b) $500 x 40% = $200 needed Ending balance; $200 Ending balance – $0 Beginning balance = $200 increase needed in the account

Deferred Tax Asset

Beg. bal.	0	
Increase (b)	200	
End. bal.	<u>200</u>	

(c) $10,000 x 40% = $4,000 needed Ending balance; $4,000 Ending balance – $2,000 Beginning balance = $2,000 increase needed in the account

Deferred Tax Liability

	2,000	Beg. bal.
	2,000	Increase (c)
	<u>4,000</u>	End. bal.

(d) $2,000 increase in noncurrent deferred tax liability account – $200 increase in current deferred tax asset account = $1,800

The bottom of the income statement for 2001 would appear as follows:

Income before income tax		$146,000
Income tax expense		
Current	$44,200	
Deferred	<u>1,800</u>	<u>46,000</u>
Net income		<u>$100,000</u>

To determine the deferred component of income tax expense for **2002**, a schedule of future taxable (deductible) amounts is prepared.

	2002 Taxable (deductible)	2003 Taxable (deductible)	2004 Taxable (deductible)	Tax rate	Deferred tax liability (asset)
Scheduled taxable (deductible) amounts:					
Depreciation differences:					
taxable amounts	-0-	$5,000	$5,000	40%	$4,000 Noncurrent

The temporary depreciation difference of $10,000 results in future taxes payable (a deferred tax liability) of $4,000 [($5,000 + 5,000) x 40%]. Note that the amount of the deferred tax liability in this example does not change from 2000 to 2001. The $4,000 amount would be reported as a noncurrent deferred tax liability at 12/31/02, based upon the noncurrent classification of the related depreciable asset. The $500 warranty expense deducted in 2001 for book purposes is deducted in 2002 for tax purposes. Therefore, the deferred tax asset related to warranty expense is realized in 2002 and the temporary difference related to warranty expense no longer exists.

Once the deferred tax amounts have been measured at year-end, a journal entry is required to adjust the deferred tax account balances to the current year-end amount. Income tax expense for the year consists of the taxes currently payable plus or minus any change in the deferred tax accounts. The following journal entries are needed to record income tax expense for 2002:

Income tax expense—current	44,800	
Income tax payable (a)		44,800

(a) $112,000 taxable income x 40% = $44,800

Income tax expense deferred (c)	200	
Deferred tax asset current (b)		200

(b)   The credit to the deferred tax asset is the adjustment necessary to reduce the existing balance to the desired ending balance.

Deferred Tax Asset

Beg. bal.	200		
		200	Decrease (b)
End. bal.	0		

(c)   Income tax expense—deferred results from the decrease in the deferred tax asset. There is no adjustment to the deferred tax liability account.

Deferred Tax Liability

	4,000	Beg. bal.
	0	
	4,000	End. bal.

To determine the deferred component of income tax expense for **2003** the following journal entries are required:

| Income tax expense—current | 45,400 | |
| Income tax payable (a) | | 45,400 |

(a) $113,500 taxable income x 40% = $45,400

| Deferred tax liability—noncurrent (b) | 2,000 | |
| Income tax expense—deferred (c) | | 2,000 |

(b)   The debit to the deferred tax liability is the adjustment necessary to reduce the existing balance to the desired ending balance.

Deferred Tax Liability

	4,000	Beg. bal.
2,000		Decrease (b)
	2,000	End. bal.

(c)   Income tax expense—deferred results from the decrease in the deferred tax liability. The deferred tax asset account was closed in 2002 because all temporary differences have reversed.

The income tax liability per the tax return in 2003 is higher than total tax expense reported on the income statement since depreciation is not deducted for tax purposes anymore. In effect, the income tax liability in 2003 includes a portion of the tax deferred from 2001-2002 that was recorded as a liability; therefore, the deferred tax liability is reduced in 2003. There is a corresponding decrease in income tax expense—deferred that will reconcile the income tax liability per the tax return to income tax expense on the books.

Income tax expense—current	45,400
Income tax expense—deferred	(2,000)
Income tax expense per income statement	43,400

Changing tax rates. The previous examples assumed a constant enacted tax rate of 40%. Under the liability method upon which SFAS 109 is predicated, future taxable or deductible amounts must be measured using enacted tax rates expected to be in effect in the periods such amounts will impact taxable income. Similarly, a deferred tax asset is measured using the applicable enacted tax rate and provisions of the enacted tax law. However, when tax rates change, adjustments to reflect such changes are automatically included in the journal entry amount to increase or decrease the deferred tax accounts to the balances needed to properly reflect balance sheet amounts and to recognize the deferred component of income tax expense. The rate change effect would be included because the amount of the journal entry is determined by comparing the needed balance in deferred taxes at the end of the period which would be based on the newly enacted rates with the balance at the beginning of the period and taking the difference.

EXAMPLE 3: Assume that in June 2003 a new income tax law is passed which lowers the corporate tax rate to 35% effective January 1, 2004. The entry debiting income tax expense—current and crediting income tax payable for 2003 is identical to that above.

However, the debit to the deferred tax liability account is the adjustment necessary to reduce the existing balance to the desired ending balance **under the new tax rate**.

| Deferred tax liability—noncurrent | 2,250 | |
| Income tax expense—deferred | | 2,250 |

Deferred Tax Liability

	4,000	Beg. bal.
2,250		Decrease
	1,750	End. bal.

The $1,750 is the necessary balance for the 2004 reversal of the remaining $5,000 at 35%.

EXAMPLE 4: Dart Corporation has the following temporary differences from its first year of operations:

		Treatment in the book to tax reconciliation
1. **Long-term contracts:**		
Year 1 (Current year):	Book contract income > tax contract income	$300 subtraction
Year 2:	Book contract income < tax contract income	$300 addition
2. **Accumulated depreciation:**		
Year 1 (Current year):	Book deprec. < tax deprec.	$1,000 subtraction
Year 2:	Book deprec. < tax deprec.	$500 subtraction
Year 3:	Book deprec. > tax deprec.	$600 addition
Year 4:	Book deprec. > tax deprec.	$400 addition
Year 7:		$500 addition
3. **Estimated expense liability:**		
Year 1 (Current year):	Book est. exp./loss > tax deduction	$200 addition
Year 7:	Book exp./loss < tax deduction	$200 subtraction
4. **Rent revenue:**		
Year 1 (Current year):	Book rev. < tax rev.	$500 addition
Year 4:	Book rev. > tax rev.	$200 subtraction
Year 7:	Book rev. > tax rev.	$300 subtraction

5. **Tax rates:**

Current year:	40%
Years 2-4:	35%
Years 5-7:	30%

The schedule below combines (1) the pretax accounting income to taxable income reconciliation and (2) the future taxable (deductible) amounts schedule. Remember that **taxable amounts** are added to financial (book) income in the book to tax reconciliation schedule in the future years in which they increase taxable income. **Deductible amounts** are subtracted from financial (book) income in the book to tax reconciliation schedule in the future years in which they decrease taxable income. Taxable income and deferred tax liability (asset) balances for year 1 (the current year) would be determined as follows:

	Current year	Future years				
	Year 1	Year 2 taxable (deductible)	Year 3 taxable (deductible)	Year 4 taxable (deductible)	Year 7 taxable (deductible)	Deferred tax liability (asset)
Tax rate	40%	35%	35%	35%	30%	
Pretax accounting income	$1,600					
Temporary differences:						
LT contracts	(300)	300				$105 Current
Accumulated deprec.	(1,000)	(500)*	600	400	500	$325 Noncurrent
Estimated expense liability	200				(200)	$ (60) Noncurrent
Rent revenue	500			(200)	(300)	$(160) Noncurrent
Taxable income	$1,000					
Income tax payable ($1,000 x 40%)	$ 400					

* Note that in year 2 there is excess tax depreciation as there was in year 1.

Income tax expense would be computed as follows:

$$\text{Income tax expense} = \text{Income taxes payable} \pm \text{Change in deferred taxes (net)}$$

Under SFAS 109, deferred tax assets and liabilities are classified as current or long-term based on the related asset or liability, rather than on the expected timing of the future deductible or taxable amounts. However, if a deferred tax asset or liability is not related to an asset or liability for financial reporting purposes, it is classified based upon its expected reversal date. Presented below is a solution for Example 4.

Temporary difference	Deferred tax asset or liability	Related account	Classification*
LT contracts	$300 x 35% = $105 liability	Const-in-Progress	Current
Depreciation	[(500) + 600 + 400] x 35% + $500 x 30% = $325 liability	Accumulated depr.	Noncurrent
Est. expense	$200 x 30% = $60 asset	Estimated liability	Noncurrent
Rent revenue	$200 x 35% + $300 x 30% = $160 asset	Unearned rent	Noncurrent

* Balance sheet disclosure is explained for this example in Section F.3.

The journal entries required are as follows:

Income tax expense current	400	
Income tax payable		400 (a)

(a) $1,000 taxable income x 40% = $400

Income tax expense deferred (e)	210	
Deferred tax asset noncurrent (b)	220	
Deferred tax liability current (c)		105
Deferred tax liability noncurrent (d)		325

(b) $200 x 30% + $200 x 35% + $300 x 30% = $220 needed Ending balance; $220 Ending balance – $0 Beginning balance = $220 increase needed in the account.

Deferred Tax Asset—Noncurrent	
Beg. bal.	-0-
Increase (b)	220
End. bal.	220

(c) $300 x 35% = $105 Ending balance; $105 Ending balance – $0 Beginning balance = $105 increase needed in the account

Deferred Tax Liability—Current	
-0-	Beg. bal.
105	Increase (c)
105	End. bal.

(d) $1,000 x 35% + ($500) x 35% + $500 x 30% = $325 Ending balance; $325 Ending balance –$0 Beginning balance = $325 increase needed in the account.

Deferred Tax Liability—Noncurrent	
-0-	Beg. bal.
325	Increase (d)
325	End. bal.

(e) $105 increase in current deferred tax liability amount + $325 increase in noncurrent deferred tax liability account – $220 increase in noncurrent deferred tax asset account = $210.

Note that since this is the firm's first year of operations, there are no beginning balances in the deferred tax accounts. If there were any permanent differences, such differences would affect only the current year as they did in Example 1. In addition, the need for a valuation allowance to reduce the deferred tax asset to its net realizable value would need to be considered.

Deferred tax asset valuation allowance. SFAS 109 does require that a deferred tax asset be reduced by a valuation allowance if, based on the weight of available evidence, it is more likely than not (a likelihood of more than 50%) that some portion or all of the deferred tax asset will not be realized. All available evidence, both positive and negative, should be considered to determine whether a valuation allowance is needed. The need for a valuation allowance ultimately depends on the existence of sufficient taxable income (necessary to receive the benefit of a future deductible amount) within the carryback/carryforward period, as described in Section E of this module. SFAS 109 provides the following list of possible sources of taxable income; if any one of these sources is sufficient to support a conclusion that a valuation allowance is not necessary, other sources need not be considered.

1. Possible Sources of Taxable Income

   a. Future reversals of existing taxable temporary differences
   b. Future taxable income exclusive of reversing temporary differences and carryforwards
   c. Taxable income in prior carryback year(s) if carryback is permitted under the tax law
   d. **Tax-planning strategies** that would, if necessary, be implemented to

      (1) Accelerate taxable amounts to utilize expiring carryforwards
      (2) Change the character of taxable or deductible amounts from ordinary income or loss to capital gain or loss
      (3) Switch from tax-exempt to taxable investments.

SFAS 109 also provides some examples of evidence to be considered when evaluating the need for a valuation allowance. These are summarized in the table below.

1. Negative Evidence—Indicates Need for a Valuation Allowance

   a. Cumulative losses in recent years
   b. A history of operating loss or tax credit carryforwards expiring unused
   c. Losses expected in early future years (by a presently profitable entity)
   d. Unsettled circumstances that, if unfavorably resolved, would adversely affect future operations and profit levels on a continuing basis in future years
   e. A carryback/carryforward period that is so brief that it would limit realization of tax benefits if (1) a significant deductible temporary difference is expected to reverse in a single year or (2) the enterprise operates in a traditionally cyclical business.

2. Positive Evidence—Can Offset the Impact of Negative Evidence

   a. Existing contracts or firm sales backlog that will produce more than enough taxable income to realize the deferred tax asset based on existing sales prices and cost structures
   b. An excess of appreciated asset value over the tax basis of the entity's net assets in an amount sufficient to realize the deferred tax asset
   c. A strong earnings history exclusive of the loss that created the future deductible amount (tax loss carryforward or deductible temporary difference) coupled with evidence indicating that the loss (for example, an unusual, infrequent, or extraordinary item) is an aberration rather than a continuing condition.

For an example of the recording of a valuation allowance, assume Jeremiah Corporation has determined it has a noncurrent deferred tax asset of $800,000. Note that in the current and prior periods when this asset was recognized, income tax expense was reduced. Based on the weight of available evidence, Jeremiah feels it is more likely than not that $300,000 of this deferred tax asset will not be realized. Jeremiah would prepare the following journal entry:

Income tax expense	300,000	
Allowance to reduce deferred tax asset to		
expected realizable value		300,000

The balance sheet presentation is

Other Assets (Noncurrent)	
Deferred tax asset	$800,000
Less Allowance to reduce deferred tax asset to expected realizable value	(300,000)
	$ 500,000

At each year-end, the balance on the allowance account is adjusted upward or downward based on the evidence available at that time, resulting in an increase or decrease of income tax expense. For example, if $600,000 was deemed to be the net realizable value at the end of the next year, the following entry would be made:

Allowance to reduce deferred tax asset to expected realizable value	100,000	
Deferred income tax expense		100,000

D. Deferred Tax Related to Business Investments

One additional issue concerns temporary differences from income on long-term investments that are accounted for using the equity method. For these investments a corporation may assume that the temporary difference (the undistributed income since date of acquisition) will ultimately become taxable in the form of a dividend or in the form of a capital gain. Obviously, the tax expense and deferred tax liability recorded when the difference originates will be a function of whichever of these assumptions is made.

To illustrate the application of the requirements of SFAS 109 and APB 23 assume Parent Company owns 70% of the outstanding common stock of Subsidiary Company and 30% of the outstanding common stock of Investee Company. Additional data for Subsidiary and Investee Companies for the year 2000 are as follows:

	Investee Co	Subsidiary Co
Net income	$50,000	$100,000
Dividends paid	20,000	60,000

1. Income Tax Effects from Investee Co.

The pretax accounting income of Parent Company will include equity in Investee income equal to $15,000 ($50,000 x 30%). Parent's taxable income, however, will include dividend income of $6,000 ($20,000 x 30%), and a dividends received deduction of 80% of the $6,000, or $4,800, will also be allowed for the dividends received. This 80% dividends received deduction is a permanent difference between pretax accounting and taxable income and is allowed for dividends received from domestic corporations in which the ownership percentage is less than 80% and equal to or greater than 20%. The originating temporary difference results from Parent's equity ($9,000) in Investee's undistributed income of $30,000 ($50,000 – $20,000). The amount by which the deferred tax liability account would increase in 2000 depends upon the expectations of Parent Co. as to the manner in which the $9,000 of undistributed income will be received. If the expectation of receipt is via dividends, then the temporary difference is 20% of $9,000 because 80% of the expected dividend will be excluded from taxable income when received. This temporary difference in 2000 of $1,800, multiplied by the tax rate, will give the amount of the increase in the deferred tax liability. If the expectation of receipt, however, is through future sale of the investment, then the temporary difference is $9,000, and the change in the deferred tax liability is the capital gains rate (currently the same as ordinary rate) times the $9,000.

The entries below illustrate these alternatives. A tax rate of 34% is used for both ordinary income and capital gains. Note that the amounts in the entries below relate only to Investee Company's incremental impact upon Parent Company's tax accounts.

	Expectations for undistributed income	
	Dividends	*Capital gains*
Income tax expense	1,020	3,468
Deferred taxes (net)	612[b]	3,060[c]
Income taxes payable	408[a]	408[a]

[a]*Computation of income taxes payable*

Dividend income—30% ($20,000)	*$6,000*
Less: 80% dividends received deduction	*(4,800)*
Amount included in Parent's taxable income	*$1,200*
Tax liability—34% ($1,200)	*$ 408*

[b]*Computation of deferred tax liability (dividend assumption)*
   Temporary difference—Parent's share of undistributed income—
      30% ($30,000) ... $ 9,000
   Less: 80% dividends received deduction ... *(7,200)*
   Originating temporary difference ... *$1,800*
   Deferred tax liability—34% ($1,800) ... *$ 612*
[c]*Computation of deferred tax liability (capital gain assumption)*
   Temporary difference—Parent's share of undistributed income—
      30% ($30,000) ... *$9,000*
   Deferred tax liability—34% ($9,000) ... *$3,060*

2. Income Tax Effects from Subsidiary Co.

The pretax accounting income of Parent will also include equity in Subsidiary income of $70,000 (70% of $100,000). Note also that this $70,000 will be included in pretax consolidated income if Parent and Subsidiary consolidate. For tax purposes, Parent and Subsidiary cannot file a consolidated tax return because the minimum level of control (80%) is not present. Consequently, the taxable income of Parent will include dividend income of $42,000 (70% of $60,000) and there will be an 80% dividends received deduction of $33,600. The temporary difference results from Parent's equity ($28,000) in Subsidiary's undistributed earnings of $40,000 ($100,000 – $60,000). Remember that the undistributed income of Subsidiary has been recognized for book purposes, but only distributed income (dividends) has been included in taxable income. The amount of the deferred tax liability in 2000 depends upon the expectations of Parent Company as to the manner in which this $28,000 of undistributed income will be received in the future. The same expectations can exist as previously discussed for Parent's equity in Investee's undistributed earnings (i.e., through future dividend distributions or capital gains). Determination of the amounts and the accounts affected for these two assumptions would be similar. The diagram below illustrates the accounting and income tax treatment of the undistributed investee/subsidiary earnings by corporate investors under different levels of ownership.

SUMMARY OF TEMPORARY DIFFERENCES OF INVESTEES AND SUBSIDIARIES

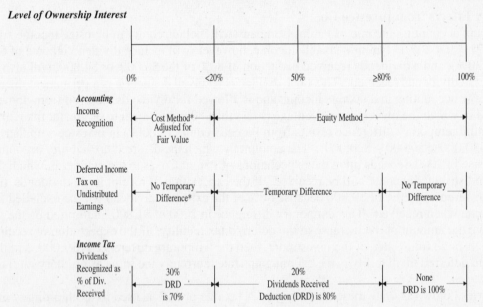

Recognition of Temporary Differences

*   *Both pretax financial accounting and taxable income would include only dividends declared by the investee. If evidence indicates that significant influence exists at an ownership level less than 20%, a temporary difference would be recognized.*

E. Loss Carryforwards and Carrybacks

Operating losses of a particular period can be carried back to the two immediate past periods' income resulting in a refund. Losses still remaining after carrybacks may also be carried forward for twenty years to offset income if income arises in any of those twenty years. Companies may at the time of the loss elect to use only the carryforward provision.

Loss carrybacks occur when losses in the current period are carried back to periods in which there was income. Loss carrybacks result in tax refunds in the loss period and thus should be recognized in the year of the loss. The entry to record the benefit is

| Tax refund receivable | (based on tax credit due to loss) | |
| Tax loss benefit (income tax expense) | | (same) |

The tax loss benefit account would be closed to revenue and expense summary in the year of the loss.

Tax loss carryforwards are recognized in the year the loss occurs. Under SFAS 109, the benefit of a loss carryforward is **always** recognized as a deferred tax asset which may be reduced by a valuation allowance if necessary. For example, assume Caleb Corporation has a loss carryforward of $300,000 which could result in future tax savings of $120,000 (40% x $300,000). Caleb feels that based on the weight of available evidence it is more likely than not that $50,000 of these savings will not be realized. Caleb's entries to record the benefit and the valuation allowance are

Deferred tax asset	120,000	
Tax loss benefit (income tax expense)		120,000
Tax loss benefit (income tax expense)	50,000	
Allowance to reduce deferred tax asset to expected realizable value		50,000

Income statement presentation

The income statement for the year in which both a loss carryback and carryforward are realized would appear as follows:

Loss before income taxes		$ (xx)
Less:		
Benefit from operating loss carryback	xx	
Benefit from operating loss carryforward	xx	xx
Net loss		$ (xx)

F. Financial Statement Presentation of Income Tax

1. Income Statement

    Continuing operations. For each year presented, the significant components of income tax expense arising from continuing operations shall be disclosed on the face of the income statement or in the notes. These components would include

    a. Current tax expense or benefit
    b. Deferred tax expense or benefit (exclusive of the effects of other components listed below)
    c. The benefits of operating loss carryforwards
    d. Adjustments of a deferred tax liability or asset for enacted changes in tax laws or rates or a change in the tax status of the enterprise
    e. Adjustments of the beginning-of-the-year balance of a valuation allowance because of a change in circumstances that causes a change in judgment about the realizability of the related deferred tax asset in future years.

    Other components of net income. Income tax expense must be allocated within an accounting period between continuing operations and other components of net income (i.e., discontinued operations, extraordinary items, etc.). The amount of income tax expense allocated to continuing operations is equal to the tax on pretax income or loss from continuing operations. However, if net income includes "special items" such as discontinued operations, extraordinary items, and accounting changes, the amount of income tax expense allocated to continuing operations must consider these items. The amount allocated to an item other than continuing operations (e.g., discontinued operations, extraordinary items, and accounting changes) is equal to the incremental effect on income taxes resulting from that item.

    EXAMPLE: Alco Co. has income from continuing operations of $2,000,000, an extraordinary gain of $450,000, and no permanent or temporary differences. The current tax rate is 34%. Total income tax expense is $833,000 ($2,450,000 x 34%). This amount will first be allocated to income from continuing operations, and the remainder (incremental tax consequences attributable to the remaining components of net income) will be allocated to the extraordinary gain.

Total income tax expense	*$ 833,000*
Tax consequences associated with income from continuing operations ($2,000,000 x 34%)	*680,000*
Remainder to extraordinary gain	*$ 153,000*

The bottom of the income statement would appear as follows:

Income from continuing operations	$2,000,000
Income tax expense	680,000
Income before extraordinary item	$1,320,000
Extraordinary gain (net of $153,000 tax)	297,000
Net income	$1,617,000

EXAMPLE: *Benjamin Corporation's ordinary loss from continuing operations is $1,000. Benjamin also has an extraordinary gain of $1,800 that is a capital gain for tax purposes. The tax rate is 40% on ordinary income and 30% on capital gains. Income taxes currently payable are $240 [($1,800 – $1,000) x 30%]. Since the effect of the $1,000 loss was to offset a capital gain, the benefit allocated to continuing operations is $300 (30% x $1,000) rather than $400 (40% x $1,000). The incremental tax expense allocated to the extraordinary gain is $540 (difference between the $300 tax benefit and the $240 total tax expense).*

Other comprehensive income. Components of other comprehensive income may be displayed net of related deferred tax effects or before related deferred tax effects with one amount shown for the aggregate income tax effect (with detail shown in notes). Refer to Module 22D for more information regarding comprehensive income.

2. Retained Earnings

Any income tax effects associated with adjustments of the opening balance of retained earnings for a **special type** change in accounting principle or correction of an error are to be charged or credited directly to retained earnings. The income tax effects of other stockholders' equity items (e.g., cumulative translation adjustment) are charged or credited to stockholders' equity.

3. Balance Sheet

The classification of deferred tax liabilities and assets is a two-stage process. First, all deferred tax liabilities and assets are classified as current or noncurrent. Deferred tax liabilities and assets are classified as current or long-term based on the related asset or liability. A deferred tax liability or asset is related to an asset or liability if reduction of the asset or liability will cause the temporary difference to reverse. If the deferred tax liability or asset is **not** related to any asset or liability for financial reporting purposes (such as a deferred tax asset caused by a loss carryforward), it is classified based on the timing of its expected reversal or utilization date. Once classification has been determined, all current amounts are netted to get a net current asset or liability and the noncurrent amounts are likewise netted to obtain a net noncurrent amount.

This process is illustrated in Example 4 that appeared earlier in this module. In Example 4, the only current deferred tax asset/liability is the $105 current liability. Thus the net current amount is a $105 liability. The other amounts are netted to find the net noncurrent amount. In this case the net noncurrent amount is a $105 liability ($325 – $220).

If an allowance account has been recognized for a deferred tax asset, it would be deducted from the related deferred tax asset before the netting process described above is done. If the allowance account balance relates to a deferred tax asset that is classified partially as current and partially as noncurrent, the allowance balance should be allocated between them in the ratio of each asset balance to the total asset balance.

Note that if a tax refund receivable results from a loss carryback in the current period, this element would not be included in the netting process; only deferred tax assets and liabilities are netted.

G. Treatment of Selected Temporary Differences

On the following page we have summarized the treatment of selected temporary differences from the period of origination to the period of reversal.

TREATMENT OF SELECTED TEMPORARY DIFFERENCES

	Book value		Tax basis		Previous and current reconciliations of book income to tax income	Future years(s) reconciliation of book income to tax income	Deferred consequence*
a. Estimated liability under warranties	56,000	Less	--	=	56,000 addition(s)	56,000 subtraction(s)	Asset (3)
b. Unearned rent (royalty) revenue received (liability)	40,000	Less	--	=	40,000 addition(s)	40,000 subtraction(s)	Asset (3)
c. Long-term contracts:							
Construction in process (asset)	1,125,000	Less	1,000,000	=	125,000 subtraction	125,000 addition	Liability (1)
d. Plant assets and accumulated depreciation:							
Equipment (asset)	50,000	Less	50,000				
Accumulated depreciation (contra asset)	10,000	Less	18,500				
End of period basis	40,000	Less	31,500	=	8,500 subtraction(s)	8,500 addition(s)	Liability (1)
e. Donated assets:							
Year of acquisition:							
Machinery (asset)	90,000	Less	--	=	Not included because donat. recorded in S/E	See deprec. below	Liability (1)
Depreciation:							
Machinery (asset)	90,000	Less	--				
Accumulated depreciation (contra asset)	18,000	Less	--				
End of period basis	72,000	Less	--	=	18,000 addition(s)	18,000 addition(s)	Reduction of liability
Sale of asset:							
Cash received	80,000	Less	80,000				
Basis of asset	72,000	Less	80,000				
Gain (revenue)	8,000	Less	80,000	=		72,000 addition	Reduction of liability
f. Replacement asset for involuntarily converted asset:							
Year of acquisition:							
Building (asset)	280,000	Less	280,000				
Deferred gain from involuntary conversion	--**	Less	(110,000)				
Initial basis of asset	280,000	Less	170,000	=	110,000 subtraction		Liability (1)
Depreciation:							
Building (asset)	280,000	Less	170,000				
Accumulated depreciation (contra asset)	(14,000)	Less	(28,900)				
End of period basis	266,000	Less	141,100	=	14,900 subtraction		Liability (1)
Sale of replacement asset:							
Cash received	270,000	Less	270,000				
Basis of asset	(266,000)	Less	(141,100)				
Gain (revenue)	4,000	Less	128,900	=		124,900 addition	Reduction of liability

* The numbers in parenthesis refer to the relationships presented on p. 394.
** The $10,000 gain was recognized in the financial statements in the period the involuntary conversion occurred.

MULTIPLE-CHOICE QUESTIONS (1-41)

1.   Justification for the method of determining periodic deferred tax expense is based on the concept of
   a.   Matching of periodic expense to periodic revenue.
   b.   Objectivity in the calculation of periodic expense.
   c.   Recognition of assets and liabilities.
   d.   Consistency of tax expense measurements with actual tax planning strategies.

2.   Among the items reported on Cord, Inc.'s income statement for the year ended December 31, 2002, were the following:

Payment of penalty	$ 5,000
Insurance premium on life of an officer with Cord as owner and beneficiary	10,000

Temporary differences amount to
   a. $0
   b. $ 5,000
   c. $10,000
   d. $15,000

3.   Caleb Corporation has three financial statement elements for which the December 31, 2002, book value is different than the December 31, 2002, tax basis

	Book value	Tax basis	Difference
Equipment	$200,000	$120,000	$80,000
Prepaid officers insurance policy	75,000	0	75,000
Warranty liability	50,000	0	50,000

As a result of these differences, future taxable amounts are
   a. $ 50,000
   b. $ 80,000
   c. $155,000
   d. $205,000

4.   Temporary differences arise when revenues are taxable

	After they are recognized in financial income	Before they are recognized in financial income
a.	Yes	Yes
b.	Yes	No
c.	No	No
d.	No	Yes

5.   Which of the following differences would result in future taxable amounts?
   a.   Expenses or losses that are deductible after they are recognized in financial income.
   b.   Revenues or gains that are taxable before they are recognized in financial income.
   c.   Expenses or losses that are deductible before they are recognized in financial income.
   d.   Revenues or gains that are recognized in financial income but are never included in taxable income.

6.   Dunn Co.'s 2002 income statement reported $90,000 income before provision for income taxes. To compute the provision for federal income taxes, the following 2002 data are provided:

Rent received in advance	$16,000
Income from exempt municipal bonds	20,000
Depreciation deducted for income tax purposes in excess of depreciation reported for financial statements purposes	10,000
Enacted corporate income tax rate	30%

If the alternative minimum tax provisions are ignored, what amount of current federal income tax liability should be reported in Dunn's December 31, 2002 balance sheet?
   a. $18,000
   b. $22,800
   c. $25,800
   d. $28,800

7.   Pine Corp.'s books showed pretax income of $800,000 for the year ended December 31, 2002. In the computation of federal income taxes, the following data were considered:

Gain on an involuntary conversion	$350,000
(Pine has elected to replace the property within the statutory period using total proceeds.) Depreciation deducted for tax purposes in excess of depreciation deducted for book purposes	50,000
Federal estimated tax payments, 2002	70,000
Enacted federal tax rates, 2002	30%

What amount should Pine report as its current federal income tax liability on its December 31, 2002 balance sheet?
   a. $ 50,000
   b. $ 65,000
   c. $120,000
   d. $135,000

8.   For the year ended December 31, 2002, Tyre Co. reported pretax financial statement income of $750,000. Its taxable income was $650,000. The difference is due to accelerated depreciation for income tax purposes. Tyre's effective income tax rate is 30%, and Tyre made estimated tax payments during 2002 of $90,000. What amount should Tyre report as current income tax expense for 2002?
   a. $105,000
   b. $135,000
   c. $195,000
   d. $225,000

9.   Tower Corp. began operations on January 1, 2001. For financial reporting, Tower recognizes revenues from all sales under the accrual method. However, in its income tax returns, Tower reports qualifying sales under the installment method. Tower's gross profit on these installment sales under each method was as follows:

Year	Accrual method	Installment method
2001	$1,600,000	$ 600,000
2002	2,600,000	1,400,000

The income tax rate is 30% for 2001 and future years. There are no other temporary or permanent differences. In its December 31, 2002 balance sheet, what amount should Tower report as a liability for deferred income taxes?
   a. $840,000
   b. $660,000
   c. $600,000
   d. $360,000

10.   On June 30, 2002, Ank Corp. prepaid a $19,000 premium on an annual insurance policy. The premium payment was a tax deductible expense in Ank's 2002 cash basis tax return. The accrual basis income statement will report a $9,500 insurance expense in 2002 and 2003.

Ank's income tax rate is 30% in 2002 and 25% thereafter. In Ank's December 31, 2002 balance sheet, what amount related to the insurance should be reported as a deferred income tax liability?
   a. $5,700
   b. $4,750

c. $2,850
d. $2,375

11. Mill, which began operations on January 1, 2000, recognizes income from long-term construction contracts under the percentage-of-completion method in its financial statements and under the completed-contract method for income tax reporting. Income under each method follows:

Year	Completed-contract	Percentage-of-completion
2000	$ --	$300,000
2001	400,000	600,000
2002	700,000	850,000

The income tax rate was 30% for 2000 through 2002. For years after 2002, the enacted tax rate is 25%. There are no other temporary differences. Mill should report in its December 31, 2002 balance sheet a deferred income tax liability of

a. $ 87,500
b. $105,000
c. $162,500
d. $195,000

Items 12 and 13 are based on the following:

Zeff Co. prepared the following reconciliation of its pretax financial statement income to taxable income for the year ended December 31, 2002, its first year of operations:

Pretax financial income	$160,000
Nontaxable interest received on municipal securities	(5,000)
Long-term loss accrual in excess of deductible amount	10,000
Depreciation in excess of financial statement amount	(25,000)
Taxable income	$140,000

Zeff's tax rate for 2002 is 40%.

12. In its 2002 income statement, what amount should Zeff report as income tax expense—current portion?

a. $52,000
b. $56,000
c. $62,000
d. $64,000

13. In its December 31, 2002 balance sheet, what should Zeff report as deferred income tax liability?

a. $2,000
b. $4,000
c. $6,000
d. $8,000

14. West Corp. leased a building and received the $36,000 annual rental payment on June 15, 2002. The beginning of the lease was July 1, 2002. Rental income is taxable when received. West's tax rates are 30% for 2002 and 40% thereafter. West had no other permanent or temporary differences. West determined that no valuation allowance was needed. What amount of deferred tax asset should West report in its December 31, 2002 balance sheet?

a. $ 5,400
b. $ 7,200
c. $10,800
d. $14,400

15. Black Co., organized on January 2, 2002, had pretax accounting income of $500,000 and taxable income of $800,000 for the year ended December 31, 2002. The only temporary difference is accrued product warranty costs that are expected to be paid as follows:

2003	$100,000
2004	50,000
2005	50,000
2006	100,000

Black has never had any net operating losses (book or tax) and does not expect any in the future. There were no temporary differences in prior years. The enacted income tax rates are 35% for 2002, 30% for 2003 through 2005, and 25% for 2006. In Black's December 31, 2002 balance sheet, the deferred income tax asset should be

a. $ 60,000
b. $ 70,000
c. $ 85,000
d. $105,000

16. A temporary difference that would result in a deferred tax liability is

a. Interest revenue on municipal bonds.
b. Accrual of warranty expense.
c. Excess of tax depreciation over financial accounting depreciation.
d. Subscriptions received in advance.

17. Orleans Co., a cash basis taxpayer, prepares accrual basis financial statements. In its 2003 balance sheet, Orleans' deferred income tax liabilities increased compared to 2002. Which of the following changes would cause this increase in deferred income tax liabilities?

I. An increase in prepaid insurance.
II. An increase in rent receivable.
III. An increase in warranty obligations.

a. I only.
b. I and II.
c. II and III.
d. III only.

18. At the end of year one, Cody Co. reported a profit on a partially completed construction contract by applying the percentage-of-completion method. By the end of year two, the total estimated profit on the contract at completion in year three had been drastically reduced from the amount estimated at the end of year one. Consequently, in year two, a loss equal to one-half of the year one profit was recognized. Cody used the completed-contract method for income tax purposes and had no other contracts. The year two balance sheet should include a deferred tax

	Asset	Liability
a.	Yes	Yes
b.	No	Yes
c.	Yes	No
d.	No	No

19. A deferred tax liability is computed using

a. The current tax laws, regardless of expected or enacted future tax laws.
b. Expected future tax laws, regardless of whether those expected laws have been enacted.
c. Current tax laws, unless enacted future tax laws are different.
d. Either current or expected future tax laws, regardless of whether those expected laws have been enacted.

20. For the year ended December 31, 2002, Grim Co.'s pretax financial statement income was $200,000 and its taxable income was $150,000. The difference is due to the following:

Interest on municipal bonds	$70,000
Premium expense on keyman life insurance	(20,000)
Total	$50,000

Grim's enacted income tax rate is 30%. In its 2002 income statement, what amount should Grim report as current provision for income tax expense?

- a. $45,000
- b. $51,000
- c. $60,000
- d. $66,000

Items 21 and 22 are based on the following:

Venus Corp.'s worksheet for calculating current and deferred income taxes for 2002 follows:

	2002	2003	2004
Pretax income	$1,400		
Temporary differences:			
Depreciation	(800)	$(1,200)	$2,000
Warranty costs	400	(100)	(300)
Taxable income	$1,000		
Enacted rate	30%	30%	25%

Deferred tax accounts	Asset	Liability
Current	$ (30)[a]	
Noncurrent (before netting)	$ (75)[b]	$ 140[c]

[a] *[($100) x 30%]*
[b] *[($300) x 25%]*
[c] *[($1,200) x 30%] + [$2,000 x 25%]*

Venus had no prior deferred tax balances. In its 2002 income statement, what amount should Venus report as

21. Current income tax expense?
- a. $420
- b. $350
- c. $300
- d. $0

22. Deferred income tax expense?
- a. $350
- b. $300
- c. $120
- d. $ 35

23. Shear, Inc. began operations in 2002. Included in Shear's 2002 financial statements were bad debt expenses of $1,400 and profit from an installment sale of $2,600. For tax purposes, the bad debts will be deducted and the profit from the installment sale will be recognized in 2003. The enacted tax rates are 30% in 2002 and 25% in 2003. In its 2002 income statement, what amount should Shear report as deferred income tax expense?
- a. $300
- b. $360
- c. $650
- d. $780

24. Quinn Co. reported a net deferred tax asset of $9,000 in its December 31, 2001 balance sheet. For 2002, Quinn reported pretax financial statement income of $300,000. Temporary differences of $100,000 resulted in taxable income of $200,000 for 2002. At December 31, 2002, Quinn had cumulative taxable differences of $70,000. Quinn's effective income tax rate is 30%. In its December 31, 2002,

income statement, what should Quinn report as deferred income tax expense?
- a. $12,000
- b. $21,000
- c. $30,000
- d. $60,000

25. Rein Inc. reported deferred tax assets and deferred tax liabilities at the end of 2001 and at the end of 2002. For the year ended 2002, Rein should report deferred income tax expense or benefit equal to the
- a. Decrease in the deferred tax assets.
- b. Increase in the deferred tax liabilities.
- c. Amount of the current tax liability plus the sum of the net changes in deferred tax assets and deferred tax liabilities.
- d. Sum of the net changes in deferred tax assets and deferred tax liabilities.

26. On its December 31, 2002 balance sheet, Shin Co. had income taxes payable of $13,000 and a current deferred tax asset of $20,000 before determining the need for a valuation account. Shin had reported a current deferred tax asset of $15,000 at December 31, 2001. No estimated tax payments were made during 2002. At December 31, 2002, Shin determined that it was more likely than not that 10% of the deferred tax asset would not be realized. In its 2002 income statement, what amount should Shin report as total income tax expense?
- a. $ 8,000
- b. $ 8,500
- c. $10,000
- d. $13,000

27. Under current generally accepted accounting principles, which approach is used to determine income tax expense?
- a. Asset and liability approach.
- b. A "with and without" approach.
- c. Net of tax approach.
- d. Periodic expense approach.

28. Bart, Inc., a newly organized corporation, uses the equity method of accounting for its 30% investment in Rex Co.'s common stock. During 2002, Rex paid dividends of $300,000 and reported earnings of $900,000. In addition

- The dividends received from Rex are eligible for the 80% dividends received deductions.
- All the undistributed earnings of Rex will be distributed in future years.
- There are no other temporary differences.
- Bart's 2002 income tax rate is 30%.
- The enacted income tax rate after 2002 is 25%.

In Bart's December 31, 2002 balance sheet, the deferred income tax liability should be
- a. $10,800
- b. $ 9,000
- c. $ 5,400
- d. $ 4,500

29. Leer Corp.'s pretax income in 2002 was $100,000. The temporary differences between amounts reported in the financial statements and the tax return are as follows:

- Depreciation in the financial statements was $8,000 more than tax depreciation.

• The equity method of accounting resulted in financial statement income of $35,000. A $25,000 dividend was received during the year, which is eligible for the 80% dividends received deduction.

Leer's effective income tax rate was 30% in 2002. In its 2002 income statement, Leer should report a current provision for income taxes of

   a. $26,400
   b. $23,400
   c. $21,900
   d. $18,600

30. Dix, Inc., a calendar-year corporation, reported the following operating income (loss) before income tax for its first three years of operations:

   2000 $100,000
   2001   (200,000)
   2002   400,000

There are no permanent or temporary differences between operating income (loss) for financial and income tax reporting purposes. When filing its 2001 tax return, Dix did not elect to forego the carryback of its loss for 2001. Assume a 40% tax rate for all years. What amount should Dix report as its income tax liability at December 31, 2002?

   a. $160,000
   b. $120,000
   c. $ 80,000
   d. $ 60,000

31. Town, a calendar-year corporation incorporated in January 2000, experienced a $600,000 net operating loss (NOL) in 2002 due to a prolonged strike. Town never had a strike in the past that significantly affected its income and does not expect such a strike in the future. Additionally, there is no other negative evidence concerning future operating income. For the years 2000-2001, Town reported a taxable income in each year, and a total of $450,000 for the two years. Assume that: (1) there is no difference between pretax accounting income and taxable income for all years, (2) the income tax rate is 40% for all years, (3) the NOL will be carried back to the profit years 2000-2001 to the extent of $450,000, and $150,000 will be carried forward to future periods. In its 2002 income statement, what amount should Town report as the reduction of loss due to NOL carryback and carryforward?

   a. $240,000
   b. $180,000
   c. $270,000
   d. $360,000

32. Bishop Corporation began operations in 2000 and had operating losses of $200,000 in 2000 and $150,000 in 2001. For the year ended December 31, 2002, Bishop had pretax book income of $300,000. For the three-year period 2000 to 2002, assume an income tax rate of 40% and no permanent or temporary differences between book and taxable income. Because Bishop began operations in 2000, the entire amount of deferred tax assets recognized in 2000 and 2001 were offset with amounts added to the allowance account. In Bishop's 2002 income statement, how much should be reported as current income tax expense?

   a. $0
   b. $ 40,000
   c. $ 60,000
   d. $120,000

33. Mobe Co. reported the following operating income (loss) for its first three years of operations:

   2000 $ 300,000
   2001   (700,000)
   2002   1,200,000

For each year, there were no deferred income taxes, and Mobe's effective income tax rate was 30%. In its 2001 income tax return, Mobe elected to carry back the maximum amount of loss possible. Additionally, there was more negative evidence than positive evidence concerning profitability for Mobe in 2002. In its 2002 income statement, what amount should Mobe report as total income tax expense?

   a. $120,000
   b. $150,000
   c. $240,000
   d. $360,000

34. In 1999, Rand, Inc. reported for financial statement purposes the following items, which were not included in taxable income:

Installment gain to be collected equally in 2003 through 2005	$1,500,000
Estimated future warranty costs to be paid equally in 2003 through 2005	2,100,000

There were no temporary differences in prior years. Rand's enacted tax rates are 30% for 2002 and 25% for 2003 through 2005.

In Rand's December 31, 2002 balance sheet, what amounts of the deferred tax asset should be classified as current and noncurrent?

	Current	Noncurrent
a.	$60,000	$100,000
b.	$60,000	$120,000
c.	$50,000	$100,000
d.	$50,000	$120,000

35. Thorn Co. applies Statement of Financial Accounting Standards 109, *Accounting for Income Taxes*. At the end of 2002, the tax effects of temporary differences were as follows:

	Deferred tax assets (liabilities)	Related asset classification
Accelerated tax depreciation	$(75,000)	Noncurrent asset
Additional costs in inventory for tax purposes	25,000	Current asset
	$(50,000)	

A valuation allowance was not considered necessary. Thorn anticipates that $10,000 of the deferred tax liability will reverse in 2003. In Thorn's December 31, 2002 balance sheet, what amount should Thorn report as noncurrent deferred tax liability?

   a. $40,000
   b. $50,000
   c. $65,000
   d. $75,000

36. Because Jab Co. uses different methods to depreciate equipment for financial statement and income tax purposes, Jab has temporary differences that will reverse during the next year and add to taxable income. Deferred income taxes that are based on these temporary differences should be classified in Jab's balance sheet as a

   a. Contra account to current assets.
   b. Contra account to noncurrent assets.

   c.   Current liability.

   d.   Noncurrent liability.

37. At the most recent year-end, a company had a deferred income tax liability arising from accelerated depreciation that exceeded a deferred income tax asset relating to rent received in advance which is expected to reverse in the next year. Which of the following should be reported in the company's most recent year-end balance sheet?

   a.   The excess of the deferred income tax liability over the deferred income tax asset as a noncurrent liability.

   b.   The excess of the deferred income tax liability over the deferred income tax asset as a current liability.

   c.   The deferred income tax liability as a noncurrent liability.

   d.   The deferred income tax liability as a current liability.

38. On December 31, 2002, Oak Co. recognized a receivable for taxes paid in prior years and refundable through the carryback of all of its 2002 operating loss. Also, Oak had a 2002 deferred tax liability derived from the temporary difference between tax and financial statement depreciation, which reverses over the period 2003-2007. The amount of this tax liability is less than the amount of the tax asset. Which of the following 2002 balance sheet sections should report tax-related items?

   I.   Current assets.

  II.   Current liabilities.

 III.   Noncurrent liabilities.

   a.   I only.

   b.   I and III.

   c.   I, II, and III.

   d.   II and III.

39. The amount of income tax applicable to transactions that are not reported in the continuing operations section of the income statement is computed

   a.   By multiplying the item by the effective income tax rate.

   b.   As the difference between the tax computed based on taxable income without including the item and the tax computed based on taxable income including the item.

   c.   As the difference between the tax computed on the item based on the amount used for financial reporting and the amount used in computing taxable income.

   d.   By multiplying the item by the difference between the effective income tax rate and the statutory income tax rate.

40. No net deferred tax asset (i.e., deferred tax asset net of related valuation allowance) was recognized in the 2001 financial statements by the Chaise Company when a loss from discontinued operations was carried forward for tax purposes because it was more likely than not that none of this deferred tax asset would be realized. Chaise had no temporary differences. The tax benefit of the loss carried forward reduced current taxes payable on 2002 continuing operations. The 2002 income statement would include the tax benefit from the loss brought forward in

   a.   Income from continuing operations.

   b.   Gain or loss from discontinued operations.

   c.   Extraordinary gains.

   d.   Cumulative effect of accounting changes.

41. Which of the following statements is correct regarding the provision for income taxes in the financial statements of a sole proprietorship?

   a.   The provision for income taxes should be based on business income using individual tax rates.

   b.   The provision for income taxes should be based on business income using corporate tax rates.

   c.   The provision for income taxes should be based on the proprietor's total taxable income, allocated to the proprietorship at the percentage that business income bears to the proprietor's total income.

   d.   No provision for income taxes is required.

OTHER OBJECTIVE QUESTIONS

Problem 1   (15 to 25 minutes)

Required:

a.   Items 1 through 4, describe circumstances resulting in differences between financial statement income and taxable income. For each numbered item, determine whether the difference is

List

    A. A temporary difference resulting in a deferred tax asset.
    B. A temporary difference resulting in a deferred tax liability.
    C. A permanent difference.

An answer may be selected once, more than once, or not at all.

1.   For plant assets, the depreciation expense deducted for tax purposes is in excess of the depreciation expense used for financial reporting purposes.

2.   A landlord collects some rents in advance. Rents received are taxable in the period in which they are received.

3.   Interest is received on an investment in tax-exempt municipal obligations.

4.   Costs of guarantees and warranties are estimated and accrued for financial reporting purposes.

b.   The following partially completed worksheet contain Lane Co.'s reconciliation between financial statement income and taxable income for the three years ended April 30, 2001, and additional information.

Lane Co.
INCOME TAX WORKSHEET
For the Three Years Ended April 30, 2002

	April 30, 2000	*April 30, 2001*	*April 30, 2002*
Pretax financial income	$900,000	$1,000,000	$1,200,000
Permanent differences	100,000	100,000	100,000
Temporary differences	200,000	100,000	150,000
Taxable income	$600,000	$ 800,000	$ 950,000
Cumulative temporary differences (future taxable amounts)	$200,000	$ (6)	$ 450,000
Tax rate	20%	25%	30%
Deferred tax liability	$ 40,000	$ 75,000	$ (8)
Deferred tax expense	$ --	$ (7)	$ --
Current tax expense	$ (5)	$ --	$ --

The tax rate changes were enacted at the beginning of each tax year and were not known to Lane at the end of the prior year.

Required:

Items 5 through 8 represent amounts omitted from the worksheet. For each item, determine the amount omitted from the worksheet. Select the amount from the following list. An answer may be used once, more than once, or not at all.

5.   Current tax expense for the year ended April 30, 2000.

6.   Cumulative temporary differences at April 30, 2001.

7.   Deferred tax expense for the year ended April 30, 2001.

8.   Deferred tax liability at April 30, 2002.

Amount			
A.	$ 25,000	H.	$135,000
B.	$ 35,000	I.	$140,000
C.	$ 45,000	J.	$160,000
D.	$ 75,000	K.	$180,000
E.	$100,000	L.	$200,000
F.	$112,500	M.	$300,000
G.	$120,000	N.	$400,000

PROBLEMS

Problem 1   (15 to 25 minutes)

Chris Green, CPA, is auditing Rayne Co.'s 2002 financial statements. The controller, Dunn, has provided Green with the following information relating to income taxes:

• Dunn has prepared a schedule of all differences between financial statement and income tax return income. Dunn believes that as a result of pending legislation, the enacted tax rate at December 31, 2002, will be increased for 2003. Dunn is uncertain which differences to include and which rates to apply in computing deferred taxes under SFAS 109. Dunn has requested an overview of SFAS 109 from Green.

Required:

Part a. of this problem required a schedule of interest expense; we did not add it to this volume because it was similar to many other questions and problems.

b.   Prepare a brief memo to Dunn from Green

• Identifying the objectives of accounting for income taxes,
• Defining temporary differences,
• Explaining how to measure deferred tax assets and liabilities, and
• Explaining how to measure deferred income tax expense or benefit.

Problem 2   (30 to 40 minutes)

The only difference between Tempo's taxable income and pretax accounting income is depreciation on a machine acquired on January 1, 2001, for $250,000. The machine's estimated useful life is five years, with no salvage value. Depreciation is computed using the straight-line method for financial reporting purposes and the MACRS method for tax purposes. Depreciation expense for tax and financial reporting purposes for 2002 through 2005 is as follows:

Year	Tax depreciation	Financial depreciation	Tax depreciation (over) under financial depreciation
2002	$80,000	$50,000	$(30,000)
2003	40,000	50,000	10,000
2004	35,000	50,000	15,000
2005	30,000	50,000	20,000

The enacted federal income tax rates are 30% for 2001 and 2002. A 35% tax rate for 2003 through 2005 was enacted during 1998.

For the year ended December 31, 2002, Tempo's income before income taxes was $430,000.
The balance in the deferred tax liability account was $4,500 at December 31, 2001.

Required:

a.   Prepare a schedule showing Tempo's income before income taxes, current income tax expense, deferred income tax expense, and net income. Show supporting calculations for current and deferred income tax amounts.

Problem 3   (45 to 55 minutes)

[See Problem 2 in Module 22 D. (Requirement b.)]

Problem 4   (45 to 55 minutes)

[See Problem 3 in Module 22 D.]

Problem 5   (40 to 50 minutes)

[See Problem 4 in Module 22 D.]

Problem 6   (15 to 25 minutes)

[See Problem 5 in Module 23 (Requirement d.)]

Problem 7   (40 to 50 minutes)

[See Problem 6 in Module 23 (Requirement c.)]

MULTIPLE-CHOICE ANSWERS

1.	c	__ __	10.	d	__ __	19.	c	__ __	28.	b	__ __	37.	c	__ __
2.	a	__ __	11.	c	__ __	20.	a	__ __	29.	b	__ __	38.	b	__ __
3.	b	__ ·	12.	b	__ __	21.	c	__ __	30.	b	__ __	39.	b	__ __
4.	a	__ __	13.	c	__ __	22.	d	__ __	31.	a	__ __	40.	a	__ __
5.	c	__ __	14.	b	__ __	23.	a	__ __	32.	a	__ __	41.	d	
6.	b	__ __	15.	c	__ __	24.	c	__ __	33.	c	__ __			
7.	a	__ __	16.	c	__ __	25.	d	__ __	34.	c	__ __			
8.	c	__ __	17.	b	__ __	26.	c	__ __	35.	d	__ __	1st:	__/41 = __%	
9.	b	__ __	18.	b	__ __	27.	a	__ __	36.	d	__ __	2nd:	__/41 = __%	

MULTIPLE-CHOICE ANSWER EXPLANATIONS

A. Overview of Deferred Tax Theory

1. **(c)** SFAS 109 states that the objective of accounting for income taxes is to recognize the amount of current and deferred taxes payable or refundable at the date of the financial statements. The standard further states that this objective is implemented through recognition of deferred tax liabilities or assets. Deferred tax expense results from changes in deferred tax assets and liabilities.

B. Permanent and Temporary Differences Defined

2. **(a)** **Temporary** differences are differences between taxable income and accounting income which originate in one period and reverse in one or more subsequent periods. The payment of a penalty ($5,000) and insurance premiums where the corporation is the beneficiary ($10,000) are **not** temporary differences because they never reverse. These are examples of **permanent** differences, which are items that either enter into accounting income but never into taxable income (such as these two items), or enter into taxable income but never into accounting income.

3. **(b)** The officer insurance policy difference ($75,000) is a permanent difference which does not result in future taxable or deductible amounts. The warranty difference ($50,000) is a temporary difference, but it results in future **deductible** amounts in future years when tax warranty expense exceeds book warranty expense. However, the equipment difference ($80,000) is a temporary difference that results in future taxable amounts in future years when tax depreciation is less than book depreciation.

4. **(a)** SFAS 109 cites examples of temporary differences. Among these examples are revenues which are taxable both before and after they are recognized in financial income. Note that emphasis is placed on the difference between book and tax, not the chronological order of the reporting.

5. **(c)** Expenses or losses that are deductible before they are recognized in financial income would result in future taxable amounts. For example, the cost of an asset may have been deducted for tax purposes faster than it was depreciated for financial reporting. In future years, tax depreciation will be less than financial accounting depreciation, meaning future taxable income will exceed future financial accounting income. Answers (a) and (b) are temporary differences that would result in future deductible amounts. Answer (d) is a permanent difference that does not result in either future taxable or future deductible amounts.

C. Deferred Tax Assets and Liabilities

6. **(b)** To determine the current federal tax liability, **book** income ($90,000) must be adjusted for any temporary or permanent differences to determine **taxable** income.

Book income	$90,000
Rent received in advance	16,000
Municipal interest	(20,000)
Excess tax depreciation	(10,000)
Taxable income	$76,000

Rent received in advance (temporary difference) is added to book income because rent is taxable when received, but is not recognized as book revenue until earned. Municipal interest (permanent difference) is subtracted from book income because it is excluded from taxable income. The excess tax depreciation (temporary difference) is subtracted because this excess amount is an additional tax deduction beyond accounting depreciation. The current tax liability is computed by multiplying taxable income by the tax rate ($76,000 x 30% = $22,800).

7. **(a)** The **current** federal income tax liability is based on **taxable** income, which is computed in the "book to tax reconciliation" below.

Accounting income	$ 800,000
Nontaxable gain	(350,000)
Excess tax depreciation	(50,000)
Taxable income	$ 400,000

The gain on involuntary conversion was included in accounting income but is deferred for tax purposes. Depreciation deducted for tax purposes in excess of book depreciation also causes taxable income to be less than accounting income. Taxes payable before considering estimated tax payments is $120,000 ($400,000 x 30%). Since tax payments of $70,000 have already been made, the 12/31/02 current federal income tax liability is $50,000 ($120,000 – $70,000).

8. **(c)** SFAS 109 states that income tax expense must be reported in two components: the amount currently payable (current portion) and the tax effects of temporary differences (deferred portion). The current portion is computed by multiplying taxable income by the current enacted tax rate ($650,000 x 30% = $195,000). The deferred portion is $30,000 ($100,000 temporary difference x 30%). The estimated tax payments ($90,000) do not affect the amount of tax expense, although the payments would decrease taxes payable.

9. **(b)** Over the two years, accounting income on the accrual basis is $4,200,000 ($1,600,000 + $2,600,000) and taxable income using the installment method is $2,000,000

($600,000 + $1,400,000). This results in future taxable amounts at 12/31/02 of $2,200,000 ($4,200,000 – $2,000,000). Therefore, at 12/31/02, Tower should report a deferred tax liability of $660,000 ($2,200,000 x 30%).

10. **(d)** For accounting purposes, prepaid insurance is $9,500 at 12/31/02. For tax purposes, there was no prepaid insurance at 12/31/02, since the entire amount was expensed on the 2002 tax return. Therefore, the temporary difference is $9,500. This temporary difference will result in a future taxable amount in 2003, when the tax rate is 25%. Therefore, at 12/31/02, a deferred tax liability of $2,375 (25% x $9,500) must be reported.

11. **(c)** Mill's total accounting income using percentage-of-completion ($300,000 + $600,000 + $850,000 = $1,750,000) will eventually be subject to federal income taxes. However, by 12/31/02, only $1,100,000 of income ($400,000 + $700,000) has been reported as taxable income using the completed-contract method. The amount of accounting income which has not yet been taxed ($1,750,000 – $1,100,000 = $650,000 temporary difference) will be taxed eventually when the related contracts are completed. The resulting future taxable amounts will all be taxed after 2002 when the enacted tax rate is 25%. Therefore, the 12/31/02 deferred tax liability is $162,500 ($650,000 x 25%). To record the liability, the following entry would be made:

Income tax expense—deferred	162,500	
Deferred tax liability		162,500

12. **(b)** SFAS 109 states that income tax expense must be reported in two components: the amount currently payable (current portion) and the tax effects of temporary differences (deferred portion). The amount currently payable, or current income tax expense, is computed by multiplying taxable income by the current enacted tax rate ($140,000 x 40% = $56,000).

13. **(c)** The deferred tax liability reported at 12/31/02 results from future taxable (and possibly deductible) amounts which exist as a result of past transactions, multiplied by the appropriate tax rate. The nontaxable interest received on municipal securities ($5,000) is a **permanent** difference that does **not** result in future taxable or deductible amounts. SFAS 109 requires the netting of current deferred tax assets and liabilities, and noncurrent deferred tax assets and liabilities. The future deductible amount ($10,000) resulting from a loss accrual results in a **long-term** deferred tax asset of $4,000 ($10,000 x 40%) because it is related to a **long-term** loss accrual. The future taxable amount ($25,000) caused by depreciation results in a **long-term** deferred tax liability of $10,000 ($25,000 x 40%) because it is related to a **long-term** asset (property, plant, and equipment). Since these are both long-term, they are netted and a long-term deferred tax liability of $6,000 is reported in the balance sheet ($10,000 liability less $4,000 asset).

14. **(b)** At 12/31/02, unearned rent for financial accounting purposes is $18,000 ($36,000 x 6/12). The tax basis of unearned rent at 12/31/02 is $0 because rental income is taxable when received. This temporary difference ($18,000 – $0 = $18,000) results in future deductible amounts because 2002 taxable rental income ($0) will be less than 2002 financial rental income ($18,000). The deferred tax asset to be recorded is measured using the future

enacted tax rate of 40% in accordance with SFAS 109. The deferred tax asset is $7,200 ($18,000 x 40%).

15. **(c)** Under SFAS 109, a deferred tax asset is recognized for all deductible temporary differences. The computation of the deferred tax asset for Black Co. arising from the accrued product warranty costs of $300,000 is shown below.

	2003	2004	2005	2006	Total
Future deductible amounts	$100,000	$50,000	$50,000	$100,000	$300,000
Tax rate	30%	30%	30%	25%	
Deferred tax asset	$30,000	$15,000	$15,000	$25,000	$85,000

Thus, the total deferred tax asset at the end of 2002 is $85,000.

16. **(c)** An excess of tax depreciation over financial accounting depreciation results in future taxable amounts and, therefore, a deferred tax liability. Answer (a) is an example of a permanent difference that does not result in future taxable or deductible amounts. Answers (b) and (d) are examples of temporary differences that result in future deductible amounts and a possible deferred tax asset.

17. **(b)** The increase in prepaid insurance in 2003 creates a deductible amount for income tax reporting purposes for the insurance paid; however, for financial reporting purposes the expense is not recognized until years subsequent to 2003. As a result, net taxable income for future years is increased, thus, the deferred income tax liability increases. The increase in rent receivable in 2003 also increases the deferred tax liability. For income tax purposes, rents are not included in income until received (i.e., years subsequent to 2003). However, the amount of the receivable is earned and recognized in the income statement in 2003. The increase in warranty obligations results in warranty expense for 2003 and will provide future deductible amounts, because under the IRC, a deduction for warranty cost is not permitted until such cost is incurred. Future deductible amounts lead to deferred tax assets.

18. **(b)** Per SFAS 109, a deferred tax liability is recognized for temporary differences that will result in **net** taxable amounts (taxable income exceeds book income) in future years. Although Cody Co. has recognized a loss (per books) in year two of the construction contract, the contract is still profitable over the three years. Therefore, in year three when the contract is completed, Cody will recognize the total profit on its tax return, and only a portion of the profit will be recorded in its income statement. Thus, the contract will result in a taxable amount in year three and a deferred tax liability exists. Note that this liability was recorded at the end of year 1 and reduced by one-half at the end of year two due to the change in estimated profit. Answers (a) and (c) are incorrect because no deferred tax asset is created. Answer (d) is incorrect because Cody will include a deferred tax liability on its balance sheet.

19. **(c)** Per SFAS 109, a deferred tax liability is recognized for the amount of taxes payable in **future** years as a result of the deferred tax consequences (as measured by the provisions of **enacted** tax laws) of events recognized in the financial statements in the current or preceding years.

20. **(a)** SFAS 109 states that income tax provision (expense) must be reported in two components: the amount currently payable (current portion) and the tax effects of temporary differences (deferred portion). The current portion is computed by multiplying taxable income by the current enacted tax rate ($150,000 x 30% = $45,000). Note that in this case, the deferred portion is $0, because both differences are permanent differences, which do not result in a deferred tax liability. Therefore, the current provision for income taxes should be reported at $45,000. It is important to note that if temporary differences did exist the tax effects would have been included in the tax expense for the current period.

21. **(c)** SFAS 109 states that income tax expense must be reported in two components: the amount currently payable (current portion) and the tax effects of temporary differences (deferred portion). The amount currently payable, or current income tax expense, is computed by multiplying taxable income by the current enacted tax rate ($1,000 x 30% = $300).

22. **(d)** SFAS 109 states that income tax expense must be reported on the IS in two components: the amount currently payable (current portion) and the tax effects of temporary differences (deferred portion). Note that scheduling is required in this question because the tax rates are not the same in all future years. The worksheet indicates two temporary differences: depreciation and warranty costs. The scheduling contained in the worksheet shows that these two temporary differences will result in a deferred tax asset of $105 ($30 + $75) and deferred tax liability of $140. The liability has the effect of increasing 2002 tax expense while the asset has the effect of decreasing 2002 tax expense. The net effect is deferred income tax expense of $35 for 2002 [$140 – ($30 + $75)].

Not required:

The balance sheet presentation would show a current deferred tax asset of $30 and a noncurrent deferred tax liability of $65 ($140 – $75).

23. **(a)** The deferred portion of income tax expense can be computed by determining the tax effect of the two temporary differences. The installment sale profit results in a future taxable amount in 2003 of $2,600, and the bad debt expense results in a future deductible amount of $1,400. The deferred tax consequences of these temporary differences will be measured by Shear in 2002 using the enacted tax rate expected to apply to taxable income in the year the deferred amounts are expected to be settled. The following journal entry is necessary to record the deferred tax liability related to the installment sale:

Deferred tax expense	650	
Deferred tax liability		650
[$2,600 x .25]		

To record the deferred tax asset related to the bad debt expense, the following journal entry is required:

Deferred tax asset	350	
Deferred tax expense		350
[$1,400 x .25]		

The amount of deferred tax expense to be reported by Shear in its 2002 income statement is $300 ($650 – $350). Note that one journal entry could have been used. Using two entries more clearly shows the opposite effect of an asset versus a liability on deferred tax expense.

24. **(c)** SFAS 109 states that income tax expense must be reported in two components: the amount currently payable (current portion) and the tax effects of temporary differences (deferred portion). The current portion is computed by multiplying taxable income by the current enacted tax rate ($200,000 x 30% = $60,000). The deferred portion is $30,000 ($100,000 temporary difference x 30%). An alternative computation for the deferred portion is shown below.

DT asset at 12/31/02	$ 0	
DT asset at 12/31/01	9,000	
Decrease in DT asset		$9,000
DT liability at 12/31/02 ($70,000 x 30%)	$21,000	
DT liability at 12/31/01	0	
Increase in DT liability		21,000
Deferred portion of tax expense		$30,000

25. **(d)** SFAS 109 defines the deferred income tax expense or benefit as the net change during the year in an enterprise's deferred tax liabilities or assets. The deferred income tax expense or benefit must consider the net effect of changes (both increases and decreases) in both deferred tax assets and deferred tax liabilities. The decrease in deferred tax assets alone or the increase in deferred tax liabilities alone will not be equal to the deferred income tax expense. The amount of income tax liability (current portion which comes off the tax return) plus the sum of the net changes in deferred tax assets and deferred tax liabilities is the total amount of income tax expense or benefit for the year. The question asks only for the deferred portion.

26. **(c)** From 12/31/01 to 12/31/02, the deferred tax asset increased by $5,000 (from $15,000 to $20,000). Income taxes payable at 12/31/02 are $13,000. Based on this information, the following journal entries can be recreated.

Income tax expense—current	13,000	
Income tax payable		13,000
Deferred tax asset	5,000	
Income tax expense—deferred		5,000

An additional entry would be prepared by Shin to record an allowance to reduce the deferred tax asset to its realizable value (10% x $20,000 = $2,000).

Income tax expense—deferred	2,000	
Allowance to reduce deferred		
tax asset to realizable value		2,000

Based on these three entries, total 2002 income tax expense is $10,000 ($13,000 – $5,000 + $2,000).

27. **(a)** SFAS 109, *Accounting for Income Taxes,* specifies that income tax expense is the sum of income taxes currently payable or refundable and the deferred tax expense or benefit which is the change during the year in an enterprise's deferred tax liabilities and assets. This method is more commonly called the asset and liability approach.

D. Deferred Tax Related to Business Investments

28. **(b)** The deferred income tax liability is the result of the undistributed earnings of an equity investee, which are expected to be distributed as dividends in future periods. For accounting purposes, investment revenue is $270,000 ($900,000 x 30%). For tax purposes, dividend revenue is $90,000 ($300,000 x 30%), which will be partially offset by the 80% dividends received deduction. Because of this 80% deduction, the difference ($270,000 – $90,000 = $180,000) is partially a permanent difference (80% x $180,000 = $144,000 which will never be subject to taxes) and partially a temporary difference (20% x $180,000 = $36,000 which will be taxable in future years). This future taxable amount of $36,000 will become taxable after 2002, when the expected tax rate is 25%. Therefore, the deferred tax liability is $9,000 (25% x $36,000). The entry to record the liability is as follows:

Income tax expense—deferred	9,000	
Deferred tax liability		9,000

29. (b) The **current** provision for income taxes is computed by multiplying taxable income on the Form 1120 by the current tax rate. Since taxable income is not given, pretax book income must be adjusted to compute taxable income.

Pretax book income	$100,000
Excess book depreciation	8,000
Excess book investment revenue	(30,000)
[$35,000 – (20% x $25,000)]	
Taxable income	$78,000

Excess book depreciation is added because it causes book income to be lower than taxable income. For book purposes, investment revenue of $35,000 was recognized using the equity method; for tax purposes, net dividend revenue of $5,000 was recognized [$25,000 – (80% x $25,000)]. The excess book revenue ($35,000 – $5,000 = $30,000) is deducted to compute taxable income. Therefore, the **current** provision for income taxes is $23,400 ($78,000 x 30%).

E. Loss Carryforwards and Carrybacks

30. (b) Dix did **not** elect to forego the loss carryback, so $100,000 of the $200,000 loss will be carried back to offset 2000 income, resulting in a tax refund of $40,000 (40% x $100,000). The remaining $100,000 of the 2001 loss will be carried forward to offset part of 2002 income. Thus, the income tax **liability** at 12/31/02 will be $120,000 [40% x ($400,000 – $100,000)].

31. (a) The requirement is to determine the amount to be reported in 2002 as the reduction of loss due to NOL carryback and carryforward (i.e., benefit [negative tax expense] on the face of the IS). Per SFAS 109, a deferred tax liability or asset is recognized for all temporary differences, operating losses, and tax credit carryforwards.

Income Tax Return Analysis

	2000-2001	2002
Inc (loss)	450,000	$(600,000)
Carryback	(450,000)	450,000
Unused NOL		$150,000

Town can thus recognize tax benefits from both the NOL carryback and carryforward. Town may carryback $450,000 of the NOL which will provide a tax benefit of $180,000 ($450,000 x .40). The journal entry to recognize the loss carryback would be as follows:

Tax refund receivable	180,000	
Benefit due to loss carryback		180,000

The additional $150,000 NOL can be carried forward to future periods to provide a benefit of $60,000 ($150,000 x .40). The following journal entry reflects the loss carryforward:

Deferred tax asset	60,000	
Benefit due to loss carryforward		60,000

Therefore, the reduction of the loss due to NOL carryback and carryforward is $240,000. Note that an allowance for

nonrealization of the deferred tax asset is not necessary because the information given about the strike indicates that it is not more likely than not that part of the deferred tax asset may not be recognized.

The carryback and carryforward would be shown in the income statement as follows:

Loss before income taxes		$(600,000)
Less:		
Benefit from operating loss carryback	$180,000	
Benefit from operating loss carryforward	60,000	240,000
Net loss		$(360,000)

32. (a) The requirement is to determine the amount of 2002 current income tax expense (or income taxes payable from tax return) to be reported in the income statement. For tax purposes, loss carryforwards should not be recognized until they are actually realized.

Income Tax Return Analysis

	2000	2001	2002
Income or loss	$(200,000)	$(150,000)	$300,000
Carryforward	200,000	100,000	(300,000)
Unused Carry-forward	-0-	$ 50,000	-0-

Bishop would recognize, in the income statement, income tax expense of $0 as the loss carryforward fully offsets the 2002 income.

Not required:

The deferred tax component for 2002 would be as follows:

Balance in the deferred tax asset and allowance accounts at 1/1/02

	Deferred Tax Asset		Allow for Reduction, etc.	
12/31/00	80,000		80,000	12/31/00
12/31/01	60,000		60,000	12/31/01
12/31/01 balance	140,000		140,000	12/31/01 balance

The deferred tax entry for 2002 would be

Allow for reduction, etc.	140,000	
Deferred tax asset		120,000
Income tax expense—deferred		20,000

The bottom of the income statement would be

Income before taxes		$300,000
Income tax expense or benefit		
Current	0	
Deferred **benefit**	20,000	
Net income		$320,000

33. (c) Per SFAS 109, a deferred tax liability or asset is recognized for all temporary differences and operating loss carryforwards. In 2001, Mobe would prepare the following entries:

Tax refund receivable ($300,000 x 30%)	90,000	
Deferred tax asset ($400,000 x 30%)	120,000	
Tax loss benefit (income tax expense)		210,000
Tax loss benefit (income tax expense)	120,000	
Allowance to reduce deferred tax asset to realizable value		120,000

The tax refund receivable results from carrying $300,000 of the 2001 loss **back** to offset 2000 taxable income. The deferred tax asset results from the potential **carryforward** of the remaining $400,000 loss ($700,000 – $300,000). However, the inconsistent performance of the company (profitable operations in the first year, loss in the second year) coupled with the lack of positive evidence concerning future operations indicate that at the end of 2001 it is more likely than not that none of the deferred tax asset will be realized. Therefore, Mobe must establish a valuation allowance to reduce this asset to its expected realizable value. In 2002, the entries are

Income tax expense ($1,200,000 x 30%)	360,000	
Deferred tax asset		120,000
Income taxes payable [($1,200,000 – $400,000) x 30%]		240,000
Allowance to reduce deferred tax asset to realizable value	120,000	
Benefit due to loss carryforward (income tax expense)		120,000

Income taxes payable is 2002 income of $1,200,000 less the $400,000 loss carryforward, times 30%. Total income tax expense for 2002 is $240,000 ($360,000 – $120,000). Note that if the facts had indicated positive evidence following 2001 for 2002 operations, the allowance account would not have been recognized and 2002 expense would have been $360,000.

F. Financial Statement Presentation of Income Tax

34. (c) The warranty temporary difference results in future deductible amounts of $700,000 per year in 2003 through 2005 ($2,100,000 ÷ 3). The installment temporary difference results in future taxable amounts of $500,000 per year in 2003 through 2005 ($1,500,000 ÷ 3). The portions of the resulting deferred tax asset and deferred tax liability that will be netted to find the amount of the current asset/current liability to be presented on the BS are shown below.

Deferred tax asset:	
$(700,000) x 25% =	$(175,000)
Deferred tax liability:	
$500,000 x 25% =	125,000
Current deferred tax asset (CDTA) shown on BS	$ (50,000)

The noncurrent deferred tax asset is $100,000 [25% x ($2,100,000 – $1,500,000)] – $50,000 CDTA.

35. (d) Per SFAS 109, deferred tax liabilities and assets are classified as current or noncurrent based on the classification of the related asset or liability for financial reporting. The deferred tax liability resulting from accelerated tax depreciation should be considered noncurrent because the related asset is classified as noncurrent. The deferred tax asset resulting from additional costs in inventory for tax purposes is classified as current because the related asset is classified as current. Therefore, Thorn would report a **noncurrent deferred tax liability** of **$75,000**.

36. (d) Deferred tax liabilities and assets are classified as current or noncurrent based on the related asset or liability. A deferred tax liability or asset is considered to be related to an asset or liability if reduction of the asset or liability will cause the temporary difference to reverse. If the deferred tax liability or asset is **not** related to any asset or liability, then it is classified based on the timing of its expected reversal or utilization date. This deferred tax liability is related to equipment, which is noncurrent, so the deferred tax liability should also be classified as a noncurrent liability. Deferred taxes are always classified as assets or liabilities, rather than as contra accounts.

37. (c) Deferred tax assets and liabilities are classified as current or noncurrent based on the classification of the related asset or liability for financial reporting. Therefore, a deferred tax liability relating to depreciation of a fixed asset would be noncurrent in nature. The deferred tax asset relating to rent received in advance that is expected to reverse in the following year would be classified as current. No netting of net current amounts and net noncurrent amounts can occur.

38. (b) Per SFAS 109, a **deferred** tax liability or asset should be classified in two categories (the current amount and the noncurrent amount) on the balance sheet based on the classification of the related asset or liability for financial reporting. The receivable for taxes paid in prior years and refundable through the carryback of the 2002 operating loss is **not** considered a **deferred** tax asset. A current asset should be reported on the balance sheet for the amount of the refund due to Oak Co. Note that if there was a current deferred tax liability it would not be netted with the refund receivable. However, a current deferred tax asset would be so netted. A noncurrent deferred tax liability should be reported on the balance sheet for temporary differences related to depreciation of fixed assets.

39. (b) Per SFAS 109, income tax expense must be associated with (i.e., allocated among) income from continuing operations, discontinued operations, extraordinary items, cumulative effect of an accounting change, and prior period adjustments. The tax effect to be associated with any of the special items (other than income from continuing operations) is computed by determining the income tax on overall taxable income and comparing it with the income tax on continuing operations. If more than one special item exists, the difference between tax on ordinary operations and tax on overall taxable income must be allocated proportionately among the special items.

40. (a) Per SFAS 109, the tax benefit of an operating loss carryforward or carryback shall be reported in the same manner as the **source of income (loss) in the current year**. Thus, in 2002, the tax benefit shall be reported under income from continuing operations.

41. (d) Sole proprietorships do not pay any income taxes as the tax items related to a sole proprietorship flow through to the owner's tax return. Because the sole proprietorship is not a taxable entity, no provision for income taxes would be included in the financial statements of the sole proprietorship. Although answer (a) illustrates the correct formula for calculating the taxes payable related to a sole proprietorship's operations, it is an incorrect response because the tax provision would not be shown on the sole proprietorship's financial statements since it flows through to the owner and is a liability of the owner. The income tax expense would be calculated using the owner's tax rates, as it is the owner's personal liability, not the entity's. The proprietorship would have **no** provision for income taxes on its books. The entire income tax liability is the personal responsibility of the owner.

OTHER OBJECTIVE ANSWERS AND ANSWER EXPLANATIONS

Problem 1

1. **(B)** In cases in which tax depreciation is greater than accounting (book) depreciation, taxable income will be less than accounting income and a deferred tax liability results. The reason is that in future years tax depreciation will be less than book depreciation and taxable income will be greater than book income. This will result in future cash flows for the income tax liability shown on the Form 1120 exceeding those that would occur based on pretax accounting income. Thus a deferred tax liability will result. The entry is

Deferred income tax expense	xx	
Deferred tax liability		xx

In the reversal year, the entry would be

Deferred tax liability	xx	
Deferred tax expense		xx

2. **(A)** Taxable income will exceed pretax accounting (book) income in the year in which the rents are received. In effect, income taxes on the portion of the rent that is unearned for financial reporting under GAAP must be prepaid under the Internal Revenue Code. Thus, a deferred tax asset would result because in future years when the rent received in advance is earned, no taxes will be payable on the amount earned, because the taxes were paid in the year rent was received. The entry is

Deferred tax asset	xx	
Deferred tax expense		xx

3. **(C)** Interest earned on a tax-exempt municipal obligation is a permanent difference. The interest is deducted in the year received from pretax accounting income to arrive at taxable income. However, it will never be reported as income on the firm's Form 1120. Therefore, such a difference does not result in deferred income taxes.

4. **(A)** Costs of guarantees and warranties are not deductible under the Internal Revenue Code until incurred. Under SFAS 5, however, they are estimated and recorded as an expense (loss) and a liability in the period of sale. In effect, income taxes are prepaid because in later years a benefit is received when these costs are incurred and deducted on the tax return. The entry in the origination year is

Deferred tax asset	xx	
Deferred tax expense		xx

The entry when the warranty costs are deducted is

Deferred tax expense	xx	
Deferred tax asset		xx

5. **(G)** Current tax expense for FY 2000 is equal to taxable income (Form 1120) of $600,000 times 20% or $120,000.

6. **(M)** The $100,000 temporary difference for FY 2001 is deducted from pretax financial income to arrive at taxable income. Therefore, cumulative temporary differences or future taxable amounts are increased. Thus, $300,000 ($200,000 + $100,000) will be added to pretax financial income in future reversal years.

7. **(B)** Deferred tax expense is equal to the increased rate on future taxable amounts outstanding at the beginning of FY 2001 plus the amount related to the $100,000 of temporary differences that originated in FY 2001. Thus, deferred tax expense is equal to $35,000 [$200,000 x (.25 – .20) + $100,000 x .25]. The entry is

Deferred tax expense	35,000	
Deferred tax liability		35,000

8. **(H)** In FY 2001 cumulative temporary differences (future taxable amounts) increased by $150,000. The deferred tax liability account for three years is shown below.

Deferred Tax Liability	
	2000
40,000	(200,000 x .20)
	2001
10,000	[200,000 x (.25 – .20)]
25,000	(100,000 x .25)
	2002
15,000	[300,000 x (.30 – .25)]
45,000	(150,000 x .30)
	Bal. 135,000

The $135,000 is equal to the cumulative temporary differences of $450,000 x .30.

ANSWER OUTLINE

Problem 1   Deferred Tax Memo

Memorandum Format (To:, From:, Subject:)
Objective of accounting for income taxes is to recognize:
   taxes payable/refundable
   deferred tax assets/liabilities
Temporary Differences
   Differences between tax basis and GAAP basis
   Result in future taxable/deductible amounts
Measurement of deferred tax asset/liability
   Based on enacted tax laws
   Allowance for unrealizable assets
Deferred income tax expense
   Equal to Δ during year in deferred tax liabilities and assets

UNOFFICIAL ANSWER

Problem 1   Deferred Tax Memo

To: Dunn
From: Green
Re: Accounting for income taxes

Below is a brief overview of accounting for income taxes in accordance with SFAS 109.

    The objectives of accounting for income taxes are to recognize (a) the amount of taxes payable or refundable for the current year, and (b) deferred tax liabilities and assets for the estimated future tax consequences of temporary differences and carryforwards. Temporary differences are differences between the tax basis of assets or liabilities and their reported amounts in the financial statements that will result in taxable or deductible amounts in future years.

    Deferred tax assets and liabilities are measured based on the provisions of enacted tax law; the effects of future changes in the tax laws or rates are not anticipated. The measurement of deferred tax assets is reduced, if necessary, by a valuation allowance to reflect the net asset amount that is more likely than not to be realized. Deferred income tax expense or benefit is measured as the change during the year in an enterprise's deferred tax liabilities and assets.

SOLUTION GUIDE

Problem 2   Schedule for Income Taxes; Schedule of Interest Expense Calculations; LT Liabilities Section of BS

1. This problem originally consisted of three related requirements concerning income taxes (part a), interest expense (part b), and long-term liabilities (part c). To avoid redundancy with modules covered previously we eliminated requirements b. and c.

2. The **current** portion of **2002** income tax expense is computed as follows:

Income before taxes	–	Excess tax depreciation	=	Taxable income
\$430,000[a]	–	\$30,000	=	\$400,000

Taxable income	x	Current tax rate	=	Current tax expense
\$400,000	x	30%	=	\$120,000[a]

The journal entry for the current portion of income taxes would be

Income tax expense—current	120,000	
Income taxes payable		120,000

2.1 The only temporary difference is the depreciation difference. It caused the \$4,500 long-term deferred tax liability that appears on the 12/31/01 balance sheet. The excess tax depreciation in 2001 was \$15,000 [\$250,000 cost – (\$80,000 + 40,000 + 35,000 + 30,000) tax depreciation – \$50,000 financial (book) depreciation]. The deferred tax liability is equal to \$4,500 (\$15,000 x 30%).

    The schedule below shows the deductible and taxable amounts for 2001 and 2002.

Schedule of (Deductible) and Taxable Amounts

	Originating Years		Future Years		
Years Ended	2001	2002	2003	2004	2005
2001	\$(15,000)*		\$10,000	\$ 5,000	
2002		\$(30,000)*		10,000	20,000
Total fut. tax. amts.			\$10,000	\$15,000	\$20,000

* *Deductions in reconciling book income to taxable income.*

The **deferred** portion of 2002 income tax expense is based on the **change** in the deferred tax liability. At 12/31/02, the deferred tax liability is \$15,750 [(\$10,000 + 15,000 + 20,000) x 35%]. At 12/31/01, the deferred liability tax was \$4,500. Therefore, the deferred portion of income tax expense is \$11,250[a] (\$15,750 – \$4,500). Total income tax expense is \$131,250 (\$120,000 + \$11,250).

Income Tax Expense—Deferred		Deferred Tax Liability	
2002			4,500 12/31/01
Adjust. 11,250			11,250 Adjust
			15,750 Bal 12/31/02

Income tax expense—deferred	11,250	
Deferred tax liability		11,250

Note that the 2002 deferred tax expense consists of two components as follows:

Rate increase on beginning balance	(35% – 30%) x \$15,000 = \$ 750
2002 originating difference	35% x 30,000 = 10,500
	\$11,250

2.2 2002 net income is \$298,750[a] (\$430,000 income before income taxes – \$131,250 income tax expense).

UNOFFICIAL ANSWER

Problem 2   Schedule for Income Taxes; Schedule of Interest Expense Calculations; LT Liabilities Section of BS

a.

Tempo Co.
INCOME TAX EXPENSE AND NET INCOME
For the Year Ended December 31, 2002

Income before income taxes		$430,000
Income tax expense:		
Current [30% x (430,000 – 30,000)]	$120,000	
Deferred [see computation below]	11,250	131,250
Net income		$298,750

Computation

Deferred income tax expense		
Temporary difference—depreciation		
2003	$10,000	
2004	15,000	
2005	20,000	$45,000
Effective tax rate for years 2003 through 2005		35%
Deferred tax liability, 12/31/02		15,750
Less:		
12/31/01 deferred tax liability		4,500
2002 deferred income tax expense		$11,250

Keep practicing! Wiley's CPA Examination Review Software has over 2,800 questions.

Available at www.wiley.com/cpa

STOCKHOLDERS' EQUITY

Stockholders' equity is the residual of assets minus liabilities (i.e., net assets). Due to the number of fraudulent manipulations involving stocks, many states have legislated accounting for stockholders' equity transactions, and they are controlled to some degree (e.g., conditions under which dividends may be paid).

Common stockholders' equity consists of two major categories: contributed capital and retained earnings. Retained earnings are either appropriated or unappropriated. Paid-in consists of paid-in excess and legal capital. Legal capital is the par or stated value of stock. An outline of stockholders' equity follows:

- Contributed capital
  - Paid-in (e.g., common and preferred stock)
    - Legal—par, stated, no par
    - Paid-in capital in excess of par or stated value
    - Paid-in capital from other transactions
      - Treasury stock
      - Retirement of stock
      - Stock dividends recorded at market
      - Stock warrants detachable from bonds
      - Lapse of stock purchase warrants
      - Conversion of convertible bonds
      - Any other gain on the company's own stock transactions
- Retained earnings
  - Appropriated
  - Unappropriated
- Accumulated other comprehensive income
- Contra stockholders' equity item (deducted after contributed capital, retained earnings, and accumulated other comprehensive income above are totaled)
  - Treasury stock (cost method)

When significant changes occur in stockholders' equity accounts, enterprises are required to disclose them. Most companies satisfy this requirement by issuing a statement of changes in stockholders' equity (illustrated below). These statements show changes in the number of shares (not included due to space limits) as well as dollars between balance sheet dates. The statement of changes in stockholders' equity may also be used to report comprehensive income per SFAS 130 (see the second column in the following statement). This is the FASB's least preferable means of disclosing it. See Module 22D, page 127.

Disclosure requirements concerning information about an entity's capital structure is covered in SFAS 129 (see outline).

Northern Corporation
Statement of Changes in Stockholders' Equity
For the Year Ended December 31, 2002

	Common stock	Comprehensive income	Retained earnings	Accumulated other comprehensive income	Total
Balances, January 1, 2002	$1,500,000		$213,675	$ (3,450)	$1,710,225
Comprehensive income					
Net income		$63,250	63,250		
Other comprehensive income:					
Foreign currency translation adjustments, net of tax		8,000			
Unrealized gains on securities:					
Unrealized holding gains arising during period, net of tax		13,000			
Less: reclassification adjustment, net of tax, for gain included in net income		(1,500)			
Minimum pension liability adjustment, net of tax		(2,500)			
Other comprehensive income		7,000		17,000	
Comprehensive income		80,250			80,250
Proceeds from issuance of shares	200,000				200,000
Dividends paid	--		(24,825)		(24,825)
Balances, December 31, 2002	$1,700,000		$252,100	$13,550	$1,965,650

A. Common Stock

The entry to record the issuance of common stock is

Cash	(amount received)
Common stock	(par or stated value)
Paid-in capital in excess of par	(forced)

If stock is sold for less than par, a discount account is debited.

Very little stock is issued at a discount because of the resulting potential liability to the original purchaser for the difference between the issue price (when less than par) and par which in many states is legal capital. This liability has been avoided by the use of stated value and no par stock, but is mainly avoided by establishing par values below market.

Control accounts are occasionally used to control unissued stock. At authorization

Unissued common stock	(total par or stated value)
Common stock authorized	(same)

At issuance

Cash	(cash received)
Unissued common stock	(par or stated value)
Paid-in capital in excess of par	(forced)

The credit balance in the authorized account is the total available for issuance. The debit balance in the unissued account is the amount not issued. Thus, authorized (cr) – unissued (dr) = issued (cr). The unissued account is an offset account to the authorized account.

No-par stock is occasionally issued (i.e., no par or stated value exists). All of the proceeds from issuance of no-par stock are credited to "common stock."

Legal expenses	(FMV)
Assets	(FMV)
Common stock	(par)
Paid-in capital in excess of par	(forced)

Costs of registering and issuing common stock are generally netted against the proceeds (i.e., reduce "paid-in capital in excess of par"). An alternative method is to consider stock issue costs an organizational cost.

B. Preferred Stock

As implied, preferred stock has preferential rights: most commonly the right to receive dividends prior to common stockholders. Generally the dividend payout is specified (e.g., 7% of par). Additional possible features are

1. Participating—share with common stockholders in dividend distributions after both preferred and common stockholders receive a specified level of dividend payment

    a. Participation with common stockholders in dividends is usually specified in terms of a percentage of legal capital. For example, 7% preferred receive 7% of their par value in dividends before common stockholders receive dividends. Fully participating preferred would receive the same percentage dividend as common stockholders if the common stockholders received over a 7% (of par value) dividend.

2. Cumulative—dividends not paid in any year (dividends in arrears) must be made up before distributions can be made to common stockholders

    a. However, dividends in arrears are not a liability until declared. They should be disclosed parenthetically or in the footnotes.

3. Convertible—preferred stockholders have an option of exchanging their stock for common stock at a specified ratio

    a. Conversion is usually accounted for at book value

Preferred stock	(par converted)
Preferred paid in accounts	(related balances)
Common stock	(par)
Paid-in capital in excess of par	(forced)

b. If market value is used, common stock and paid-in excess are credited for the market value, usually resulting in a large debit to retained earnings. (Plug figure in the journal entry.)

4. Callable—the corporation has the option to repurchase the preferred stock at a specified price

a. If called, no gain or loss is recognized. Gains are taken to a paid-in capital account; losses are charged to retained earnings

Preferred stock	(par)
Preferred paid in accounts	(related balances)
Retained earnings	(if dr. needed)
Cash	(amount paid)
Paid-in capital from preferred retirement	(if cr. needed)

Any of the above features present in a preferred stock issuance should be disclosed parenthetically in the balance sheet next to the account title.

C. Stock Subscriptions

Stock (common/preferred) can be subscribed by investors. A receivable is established and "stock subscribed" credited. When the total subscription price is received, the stock (common/preferred) is issued.

At subscription

Cash	(any cash received)
Subscription receivable	(balance)
Common stock subscribed	(par)
Paid-in capital in excess of par	(subscription price > par)

Cash receipt and issuance

Cash	(balance)
Subscriptions receivable	(balance)
Common stock subscribed	(par)
Common stock*	(par)

* *Unissued common stock, if unissued and authorized accounts are being used.*

Upon default of subscription agreements, depending on the agreement, the amount paid to date may be

1. Returned to subscriber
2. Kept by company
3. Held to cover any losses on resale and balance returned

If returned

Common stock subscribed	(par)
Paid-in capital in excess of par	(subscription price > par)
Cash	(any cash received)
Subscriptions receivable	(balance)

If kept by the company, no cash would be paid and "paid-in from subscription default" credited instead of cash.

If held to cover any losses on resale, a "refundable subscription deposit" liability would be credited instead of cash. If the stock were resold at less than the original subscription price, the difference would be debited to "refundable subscription deposit."

Cash	(payment)
Refundable subscription deposit	(forced)
Stock	(par)
Paid-in capital in excess of par	(amount from original sale)

The balance in the refundable subscription account would be paid (possibly in an equivalent number of shares) to the original subscriber.

D. Treasury Stock Transactions

A firm's own stock repurchased on the open market is known as treasury stock. Treasury stock is **not** an asset, as a firm may not own shares of itself. Instead it is treated as a reduction of stockholders' equity. There are two methods of accounting for treasury stock: cost and par value.

1. Cost Method

Under the **cost method**, treasury stock is debited for the cost of treasury stock. Any gain (loss) is recognized at the point of resale. However, such gains (losses) are not included in the determination of periodic income. Gains are credited to "paid-in capital from treasury stock transactions." Losses should be charged first to "paid-in capital from treasury stock (TS) transactions" or "paid-in capital from stock retirement" to the extent that either of these exists for that class of stock. The remainder of any loss is to be charged to retained earnings. In essence a one-transaction viewpoint is used, as the firm is treated as a middle "person" for the transfer of stock between two shareholders.

2. **Par Value Method**

Under the **par value** method, all capital balances associated with the treasury shares are removed upon acquisition. Any excess of treasury stock cost over par value is accounted for by charging "paid-in capital from common stock" for the amount in excess of par received when the shares were originally issued. Any excess of the cost of acquiring the treasury stock over the original issue cost is charged to retained earnings. If treasury stock is acquired at a cost equal to or less than the original issue cost, "paid-in capital from common stock" is charged (debited) for the original amount in excess of par and "paid-in capital from treasury stock" is credited for the difference between the original issue price and the cost to acquire the treasury stock. When the treasury stock is resold, it is treated as a typical issuance, with the excess of selling price over par credited to "paid-in capital from common stock." Note that the par value method takes on a two-transaction viewpoint. The purchase is treated as a "retirement" of the shares, while the subsequent sale of the shares is treated as a "new" issue.

EXAMPLE: 100 shares ($50 par) are originally sold at $60, reacquired at $70, and subsequently resold at $75.

<u>Cost method</u>			<u>Par value method</u>		
Treasury stock	7,000		Treasury stock	5,000	
Cash		7,000	Paid-in capital—common stock	1,000	
			Retained earnings	1,000	
			Cash		7,000
Cash	7,500		Cash	7,500	
Treasury stock		7,000	Treasury stock		5,000
Paid-in capital—			Paid-in capital—common		2,500
treasury stock		500	stock		

If the shares had been resold at $65:

<u>Cost method</u>			<u>Par value method</u>		
Cash	6,500		Cash	6,500	
Retained earnings*	500		Treasury stock		5,000
Treasury stock		7,000	Paid-in capital—common stock		1,500

* *"Paid-in capital—treasury stock" or "paid-in capital—retired stock" of that issue would be debited first to the extent it exists.*

Note that total stockholders' equity is not affected by the method selected; only the allocation among the equity accounts is different.

E. Retirement of Stock

Formal retirement or constructive retirement (purchase with no intent of reissue) of stock is handled very similarly to treasury stock. When formally retired

Common stock	xx	
Paid-in capital in excess of par*	xx	
Retained earnings*	xx	
Treasury stock*		xx

* *Assuming a loss on the retirement of treasury stock*

1. "Paid-in capital from treasury stock transactions" may be debited to the extent it exists
2. A pro rata portion of all paid-in capital existing for that issue (e.g., if 2% of an issue is retired, up to 2% of all existing paid-in capital for that issue may be debited)

Alternatively, the entire or any portion of the loss may be debited to retained earnings. Any gains are credited to a "paid-in capital from retirement" account.

F. Dividends

1. At the date of declaration, an entry is made to record the dividend liability.

Retained earnings (dividends)	xx	
Dividends payable		xx

2. No entry is made at the date of record. Those owning stock at the date of record will be paid the previously declared dividends.

    a. The stockholder records consist of

        (1) General ledger account

        (2) Subsidiary ledger

            (a) Contains names and addresses of stockholders

        (3) Stock certificate book

    b. Outside services: usually banks

        (1) Transfer agent issues new certificates, canceling old, and maintains stockholder ledger

        (2) Registrar validates new certificates and controls against overissuance

        (3) Functions are now becoming combined

3. At the payment date, the liability is paid.

Dividends payable	xx	
Cash		xx

4. Property dividends are accounted for as cash dividends. They are recorded at FMV of the asset transferred with a gain (loss) recognized on the difference between the asset's BV and FMV at disposition (see APB 29).

5. Liquidation dividends (dividends based on other than earnings) are a return of capital to stockholders and should be so disclosed. Paid-in capital is usually debited rather than retained earnings. Common stock cannot be debited because it is the legal capital which can only be eliminated upon corporate dissolution.

6. Scrip dividends are issuance of promises to pay dividends in the future (and may bear interest) instead of cash.

Retained earnings	xx	
Scrip dividends payable		xx

Scrip dividends are a liability which is extinguished by payment.

Scrip dividends payable	xx	
Interest expense (maybe)	xx	
Cash		xx

7. Unlike cash and property dividends, stock dividends are not a liability when declared. They can be rescinded, as nothing is actually being distributed to stockholders except more stock certificates. Current assets are not used to "pay" the dividend.

    a. After stock dividends, shareholders continue to own the same proportion of the corporation.

    b. At declaration

Retained earnings	(FMV of shares)	
Stock dividend distributable		(par)
Paid-in capital in excess of par		(plug)

    c. At issuance

Stock dividend distributable	xx	
Common stock		xx

    d. Charge retained earnings for FMV of stock dividend if less than 20%-25% increase in stock outstanding; charge RE for **par value** of stock dividend if greater than 20-25% increase in stock outstanding.

        (1) Not required if closely held company

G. Stock Splits

    Stock splits change the number of shares outstanding and the par value per share. Par value is reduced in proportion to the increase in the number of shares. The total par value outstanding does not change and no charge is made to retained earnings. If legal requirements preclude changing the par or stated value, charge retained earnings only for the par or stated value issued.

STOCK DIVIDENDS AND SPLITS: SUMMARY OF EFFECTS

	Total S.E.	Par value per share	Total par outstanding	RE	Legal capital	Additional paid-in capital	No. of shares outstanding
Stock dividend < 20-25% of shares outstanding	N/C	N/C	+	Decrease by market value of shares issued	+	+	+
Stock split effected in form of dividend > 20 – 25% of shares outstanding	N/C	N/C	+	Decrease by par value of shares issued	+	N/C	+
Stock split	N/C	Decrease proportion-ately	N/C	N/C	N/C	N/C	+

N/C = No Change
 + = Increase
Prepared by Professor John R. Simon, Northern Illinois University

H. Appropriations of Retained Earnings (Reserves)

An entry to appropriate retained earnings restricts the amount of retained earnings that is available for dividends.

RE (or Unappropriated RE)	xx	
Reserve for RE (or Appropriated RE)		xx

It is important to note, however, that the restriction of retained earnings does not necessarily provide cash for any intended purpose. The purpose is to show that **assets** in the amount of the appropriation are not available for dividends. SFAS 5 requires that when a reserve is no longer needed it must be returned directly to unappropriated retained earnings by reversing the entry that created it.

I. Compensation Cost

1. Stock Options

Study ARB 43, chap 13B, and APB 25 before studying this section. SFAS 123 is introduced at the end of this section. The outline of this standard should be studied at that point.

Compensation is generally measured by the dollar value difference between the option price and the market price if the option price is below the market price.

For financial reporting purposes, compensation is measured on the measurement date—that date on which both the number of shares the individual employee is entitled to and the option or purchase price are known. The measurement date is usually, though not always, the grant date.

Many options are granted at a price equal to or greater than the market price when the option is granted for a fixed number of shares. Thus, there is no compensation expense, and no journal entry involving compensation expense is recorded. Disclosure, however, as to the options outstanding, is required. When the employee acquires stock under these circumstances, the corporation debits cash for the option price, and credits common stock for par and paid-in capital for the excess.

If the measurement date is the grant date and deferred compensation is recorded, it is amortized over the periods in which the employee provides the services for which the option contract is the reward. For example, an option is granted to a corporate officer to purchase 100 shares of $1 par common at $52 when the market price is $58. The entry to record the granting of the option is

Deferred compensation expense	600	(a contra paid in capital account)
Stock options outstanding	600	(a paid-in capital account)

Deferred compensation is subtracted from stock options outstanding in the paid-in capital section of owners' equity to indicate the net contributed services on any date—that is, on the grant date nothing has yet been contributed by the option holder, and this would be measured by ($600 – $600 = 0). As the employee provides services to earn the option, an entry is made assigning compensation expense to periods (assume a five-year period).

Compensation expense	120	
Deferred compensation expense	120	

When the option is exercised, cash is received and stock is issued as reflected in the following entry (assume exercise after the five-year period):

Cash	5,200		(option price)
Stock options outstanding	600		
Common stock		100	(par)
Additional paid-in capital		5,700	(plug)

If the options are forfeited due to the employee(s) failing to fulfill an obligation (e.g., staying with the company) compensation expense is credited in the year of forfeiture. The amount credited reflects the total compensation expense previously charged to the income statement for the employee(s) who forfeited the options. In the example, assume the officer leaves the company in year 3, two years before the options can be exercised. The following entry is made in year 3:

Stock options outstanding	600	
Deferred compensation expense		360
Compensation expense		240

In the example above, the grant date and the measurement date coincide. If the measurement date follows the grant date, it is necessary to assume compensation expense based on the market values of the common stock that exist at the end of each period until the measurement date is reached. For example, assume that on 1/1/00, a company grants an option to purchase 100 shares of common stock at 90% of the market price at 12/31/02 and that the compensation period is four years. Note that at 1/1/00, the number of shares is determinable, but the option price is unknown. The market values and option prices of the common shares are as follows:

12/31/00	$10 x 90% = $ 9.00
12/31/01	13 x 90% = 11.70
12/31/02	15 x 90% = 13.50

The following entries for compensation expense are recorded:

	2000	*2001*	*2002*	*2003*
Compensation expense	25	40*	47.50*	37.50
Stock options outstanding	25	40	47.50	37.50

2000: [($10 – 9.00) x 100 shares x 1/4)] = $25
2001: [($13 – 11.70) x 100 shares x 2/4)] – expense recognized to date = $40
2002: [($15 – 13.50) x 100 shares x 3/4)] – expense recognized to date = $47.50
2003: [($15 – 13.50) x 100 shares x 4/4)] – expense recognized to date = $37.50

* *Results from change in accounting estimate.*

Note that the market value of the stock at the end of 2000 and 2001 is used as an estimate of the market price of the stock at 12/31/02. Also, in accordance with FASB Interpretation 28, changes in the market value of the stock between the date of grant and the measurement date are adjustments to compensation expense **in the period the market value of the stock changes**. The effects of such changes are not spread over future periods.

A time line depicting the actual and estimated compensation expense would appear as follows:

2000	2001	2002	2003
$25	$40	$47.50	$37.50
estimated	estimated	actual	actual

Market price is known for both years

2. **Stock Appreciation Rights**

Study the summary of FASB Interpretation 28, which follows the outline of APB 25, in conjunction with the study of this section.

Stock appreciation rights (SAR) allow employees to receive stock or cash equal in amount to the difference between the market value and some predetermined amount per share for a certain number of shares. SAR allow employees to receive share appreciation without having to make a cash outlay as is common in stock option plans.

For financial reporting purposes, compensation expense is the excess of market value over a predetermined amount. Compensation expense is recorded in each period prior to exercise based on the excess of market value at the end of each period over a predetermined amount. Compensation expense is adjusted up or down as the market value of the stock changes before the measurement date (which is the exercise date). Therefore, compensation expense could be credited if the stock's market value drops from one period to the next.

EXAMPLE: Assume a company grants 100 SAR, payable in cash, to an employee on 1/1/00. The predetermined amount for the SAR plan is $50 per right, and the market value of the stock is $55 on 12/31/00, $53 on 12/31/01, and $61 on 12/31/02. Compensation expense recorded in each year would be

Total expense – Exp. previously accrued = Current expense

2000	100 ($55 – $50)	=	$ 500 – $ 0	=	$ 500
2001	100 ($53 – $50)	=	$ 300 – $500	=	$ (200)
2002	100 ($61 – $50)	=	$1,100 – $300	=	$ 800

The total expense recognized over the three-year period is $1,100 [100($61 – $50)]. Journal entries would be

2000 and 2002			2001	
Compensation expense	$500/$800		Liability under SAR plan	$200
Liability under SAR plan		$500/$800	Compensation expense	$200

If the SAR were to be redeemed in common stock, Stock Rights Outstanding (a paid-in capital account) would replace the liability account in the above entries.

The above example assumes no service or vesting period, which is the period of time until the SAR become exercisable. If the above plan had a two-year service period, 50% of the total expense would be recognized at the end of the first year, and 100% at the end of the second year and thereafter until exercised. The compensation would be accrued as follows:

2000	$ (500)	(50%)	=	$ 250 – $ 0	=	$250
2001	$ (300)	(100%)	=	$ 300 – $250	=	$ 50
2002	$(1,100)	(100%)	=	$1,100 – $300	=	$800

J.   Stock Compensation under SFAS 123

Under this standard, the FASB encourages that compensation cost be measured at the grant date at **fair value** for stock purchase plans, stock options, restricted stock, and SAR issued to employees. Those plans requiring cash settlement shall measure the appropriate expense at the date of each reporting period.

The fair value of the compensation shall be calculated utilizing an options pricing model (such as the Black-Scholes model) which considers the following variables:

1.   Current price of the underlying stock
2.   Exercise price of the option
3.   Expected life of the option
4.   Expected volatility of the underlying stock
5.   Expected dividends on the stock
6.   Risk-free interest rate during the expected option term

The resulting fair value shall be applied to the number of options expected to vest (based on the grant date estimate) or the total number of options issued; nonpublic companies may use a simplified approach known as the minimum value method. This method considers all of the above variables except volatility. Previously recognized compensation expense shall only be revised for actual forfeitures before vesting or if certain performance conditions are not met.

SFAS 123 is also required for companies issuing stock options or other equity instruments to nonemployees in exchange for goods or services. Such transactions are recorded at the fair value of the goods or services received or the equity instrument issued, whichever is more reliably determinable.

Comparison of SFAS 123 and APB 25.

	SFAS 123 (Fair value)	APB 25 (Intrinsic value)
When to measure compensation expense	Date of grant for both fixed and variable stock-based plans; each reporting period for plans requiring cash settlement	Date at which number of shares and exercise price are known, generally grant; each reporting period for plans requiring cash settlement
How to measure compensation expense	Measure the fair value of options using option-pricing model (e.g., Black-Scholes or Binomial model); nonpublic entities may use the minimum value method	Measure the intrinsic value of options difference between market price and exercise price at measurement date
How to allocate compensation expense	Recognize on a straight-line basis over the vesting period	Recognize on a straight-line basis over the vesting period

To illustrate the recognition and measurement of stock compensation expense, suppose ABC Corporation (a nonpublic company) establishes an employee stock option plan on January 1, 2000. The plan allows its employees to acquire 10,000 shares of its $1 par value common stock at $52 per share, when the market price is also $52. The options may not be exercised until five years from the grant date. The risk-free interest rate is 8%, and the stock is expected to pay dividends of $2 annually. The schedule below shows the calculation of deferred compensation expense under SFAS 123 and APB 25.

Accounting for Stock Based Compensation under the Minimum Value Method under SFAS 123		*Accounting for Stock Based Compensation under the Method Allowed under APB 25*	
Current market value per share	$52.00	Current market value per share	$52.00
Less: Present value exercise price		Less: Exercise price per share	$52.00
($52 x .681)	$35.39	Equals	$ 0.00
Present value expected div.		Times # of options	10,000
($2 x 3.993)	$ 7.99	Deferred comp. expense	$ 0
Equals	$ 8.62		
Times # of options	10,000		
Deferred comp. expense	$86,200		

Journal Entry in Year 1:			*Journal Entries:*
Deferred comp. expense	86,200		No journal entries required because under the provisions
Stock options outstanding		86,200	of APB 25, no deferred compensation expense is rec-
Over each of the next five years:			ognized when the exercise price equals the market
Compensation expense	17,240		price.
Deferred comp. expense		17,240	

Accounting treatment per APB 25 is still acceptable for those organizations opting not to adopt the recommendations of SFAS 123. Such companies, however, are required to include pro forma net income and earnings per share under the new method. All organizations with stock-based compensation plans are required to make detailed disclosures about plan terms, exercise prices, and the assumptions made in measuring the fair value of stock-based grants (read the outline of SFAS 123).

K. Basic Earnings Per Share

CPA candidates must be able to compute both basic and diluted earnings per share (EPS). In addition to the computations, candidates should also understand the presentation and disclosure requirements. Only public entities (those who trade their stock on the major stock exchanges and over the counter) are required to present earnings per share. Nonpublic companies often choose to present such information, but they are not required to do so. Before continuing, it is recommended that candidates read the outline of SFAS 128, *Earnings Per Share,* in the back of the FARE section.

The objective of EPS is to measure the performance of an entity over the reporting period. Required presentation calls for a **basic** EPS in all situations and a **diluted** EPS in those situations where an entity's capital structure includes potential dilutive securities. Basic and dilutive (when applicable) earnings per share amounts must be presented on the face of the income statement for two elements.

1. Income from continuing operations **and**
2. Net income

In those situations where an entity also reports discontinued operations, extraordinary items, and/or cumulative effects of an accounting change in principle, the entity **may report** EPS on the face of the income statement or disclose such information in the footnotes to the financial statements. Note that the only required EPS presentations are for income from continuing operations and net income. All other presentations of EPS are optional.

Public corporations begin by computing **basic** earnings per share. In this calculation, only those shares of common stock **outstanding** are included. Any **potential** issuance of securities is **ignored**. The computational formula is as follows:

$$\text{Basic EPS} = \frac{\text{Net income available to common stockholders}}{\text{Weighted-average number of common shares \textbf{outstanding}}}$$

The **numerator** (net income available to common stockholders) for EPS on **net income** is computed by taking the **net income** and **subtracting**

1. The dividends **declared** in the period on the **noncumulative preferred stock** (whether paid or not) **and**
2. The dividends **accumulated** for the period on the **cumulative preferred stock** (whether or not declared).

The **numerator** (net income available to common stockholders) for EPS on **net income from continuing operations** is computed by taking the **net income** and subtracting any net income or adding any net loss from the following:

- Discontinued operations
- Extraordinary items
- Cumulative effect of a change in accounting principle.

The net income from continuing operations is then adjusted by subtracting the preferred stock dividends as described in points number 1. and 2. above.

The following example will illustrate the application of this formula:

Numerator information		*Denominator information*	
a. Net income	$100,000	a. Common shares outstanding	
b. Extraordinary loss		1/1/01	100,000
(net of tax)	30,000	b. Shares issued for cash 4/1	20,000
c. 6% preferred stock,		c. Shares issued in 10% stock	
$100 par, 1,000 shares		dividend declared in July	12,000
issued and outstanding		d. Shares of treasury stock	
($100,000 x .06)	6,000	purchased 10/1	10,000

Earnings per common share:

$$\text{On income from continuing operations} = \frac{\$130,000 - 6,000}{\text{Common shares outstanding}}$$

$$\text{On net income} = \frac{\$100,000 - 6,000}{\text{Common shares outstanding}}$$

When calculating the amount of the numerator, the claims of senior securities (i.e., preferred stock) should be deducted to arrive at the earnings attributable to common shareholders. In the example, the preferred stock is cumulative. Thus, regardless of whether or not the board of directors declares a preferred dividend, holders of the preferred stock have a claim of $6,000 (1,000 shares x $6 per share) against 2001 earnings. Therefore, $6,000 is deducted from the numerator to arrive at the net income attributable to common shareholders. Note that this $6,000 would have been **deducted for noncumulative preferred only if a dividend of this amount had been declared.** Cumulative preferred stock dividends are always deducted whether or not declared.

The numerator of the EPS calculation covers a particular time period such as a month, a quarter, or a year. It is, therefore, consistent to calculate the average number of common shares which were outstanding during this same time period. The calculation below in Table I illustrates the determination of weighted-average common shares outstanding. Note that for stock dividends the number of shares is adjusted retroactively for the shares which were outstanding prior to the stock dividend. Since the stock dividend was issued **after** the issuance of additional shares for cash on 4/1, the shareholders of those additional shares and the shareholders of the shares outstanding at the beginning of the year will receive the stock dividend. However, if the stock dividend had been issued **before** the issuance of additional shares of stock for cash on 4/1, only the shareholders who own the shares outstanding at the beginning of the period would have received the stock dividend. Stock splits are handled in an identical fashion.

TABLE 1

Dates	*Number common shares outstanding*	*Months outstanding*	*Fraction of year*	*Shares x Fraction of year*
1/1 to 4/1	100,000 + 10% (100,000) = 110,000	3	¼	27,500
4/1 to 10/1	110,000 + 20,000 + 10% (20,000) = 132,000	6	½	66,000
10/1 to 12/31	132,000 – 10,000 = 122,000	3	¼	30,500
	Weighted-average of common shares outstanding			124,000

In the weighted-average computation, an additional problem is created if common shares are issued in a business combination during the year. If the combination is accounted for as a purchase, the common shares are weighted from the date of issuance. If the pooling method is used, the shares are considered to be outstanding for the entire year, regardless of the date the pooling was consummated. Other complications in the weighted-average calculation are posed by actual conversions of debt and preferred stock to common during the year and by exercise of warrants and options. These situations are introduced in the example presented with diluted earnings per share in the next section.

To complete the basic EPS example, the weighted-average number of common shares determined in Table I is divided into the income elements previously computed to arrive at the following:

Earnings per common share:

On income from continuing operations $\dfrac{\$130,000 - 6,000}{124,000 \text{ common shares}} = \$1.00$

On net income $\dfrac{\$100,000 - 6,000}{124,000 \text{ common shares}} = \$ .76$

The above EPS numbers should be presented on the face of the income statement. Reporting a $.24 loss per share due to the extraordinary item is optional.

L. Diluted Earnings Per Share

Diluted EPS measures the performance of the entity over the reporting period (same as basic EPS) while also taking into account the effect of all dilutive potential common shares that were outstanding during the period. The only difference in the computation of diluted and basic EPS is that the denominator of the diluted EPS computation is increased to include the number of additional common shares that would have been outstanding if the dilutive potential common shares had been issued. In addition, the numerator is adjusted to add back any convertible preferred dividends, the after-tax amount of interest recognized in the period associated with any convertible debt, and any other changes in income (loss) that would result from the assumed conversion of the potential common shares. Diluted EPS should be based on the security holder's most advantageous conversion rate or exercise price. Similar to basic EPS, all antidilutive securities are disregarded.

The following two independent examples will illustrate the procedures necessary to calculate basic and diluted EPS. For both examples, assume net income is $50,000, and the weighted-average of common shares outstanding is 10,000.

In the first example, assume the following additional information with respect to the capital structure:

1. 4% nonconvertible, cumulative preferred stock, par $100, 1,000 shares issued and outstanding the entire year

2. Options and warrants to purchase 1,000 shares of common stock at $8 per share. The average market price of common stock during the year was $10 and the closing market price was $12 per share. The options and warrants were outstanding all year.

Diluted EPS must be computed because of the presence of the options and warrants. The preferred stock is not convertible; therefore, it is not a potentially dilutive security.

The first step in the solution of this problem is the determination of the basic EPS. This calculation appears as follows:

$$\frac{\text{Net income} - \text{Preferred dividends}}{\text{Weighted-average of common shares}} = \frac{\$50,000 - 4,000}{10,000 \text{ shares}} = \$4.60$$

Note that preferred dividends are deducted to arrive at net income applicable to common stock. When preferred stock is cumulative, this deduction is made whether or not dividends have been declared.

The calculation of diluted EPS is based upon outstanding common stock and all dilutive common shares that were outstanding during the period. In the example, the options and warrants are the only potentially dilutive security. Options and warrants are considered to be common stock equivalents at all times. Consequently, the only question that must be resolved is whether or not the options and warrants are dilutive. This question is resolved by comparing the average market price per common share of $10 with the exercise price of $8. If the average market price is > the exercise price, the effect of assuming the exercise of options and warrants is dilutive. However, if the average market price is ≤ the exercise price, the effect of assuming the exercise of options and warrants would be antidilutive (i.e., EPS would stay the same or increase). In the example, the options and warrants are dilutive ($10 > $8).

The method used to determine the dilutive effects of options and warrants is called the **treasury stock method**.

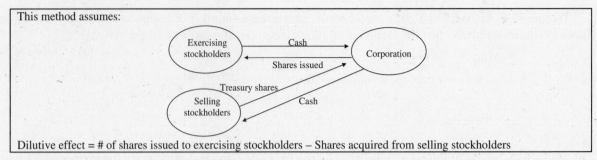

This method assumes:

Dilutive effect = # of shares issued to exercising stockholders – Shares acquired from selling stockholders

In the example above, all of the options and warrants are assumed to be exercised at the beginning of the year (the options and warrants were outstanding the entire year) and the cash received is used to reacquire shares (treasury stock) at the average market price. The computation below illustrates the "treasury stock" method.

Proceeds from assumed exercise of options and warrants	
(1,000 shares x $8)	$8,000
Number of shares issued	1,000
Number of shares reacquired ($8,000 ÷ $10)	800
Number of shares assumed issued and not reacquired	200*

* *An alternative approach that can be used to calculate this number for diluted EPS is demonstrated below.*

$$\frac{Ave.\ mar.\ price - Exer.\ price}{Average\ market\ price} \quad x \quad \frac{Number\ of\ shares}{under\ options/warrants} \quad = \quad Shares\ not\ reacquired$$

$$\frac{\$10-8}{\$10} \quad x \quad 1,000\ shares \quad = \quad 200\ shares$$

Diluted EPS can now be calculated, as follows, including the effects of applying the "treasury stock" method.

$$\frac{Net\ income - Preferred\ dividends}{Weighted\text{-}average\ of\ common\ shares\ outstanding + Number\ of\ shares\ not\ acquired\ with\ proceeds\ from\ options\ and\ warrants} = \frac{\$50,000-4,000}{10,000+200\ shares} = \$4.51$$

Note the incremental effects of the treasury stock method; there was no effect on the numerator of the EPS calculation while there were 200 shares added to the denominator. Note also that the options and warrants are dilutive. EPS is reduced from $4.60 to $4.51.

Table II summarizes the calculations made for the first example involving diluted EPS.

TABLE II

Items	Basic EPS Numerator	Denominator	Diluted EPS Numerator	Denominator
Net income	$50,000		$50,000	
Preferred div.	(4,000)		(4,000)	
Common shares outstanding		10,000 shs.		10,000 shs.
Options and warrants				200
Totals	$46,000 ÷	10,000 shs.	$46,000 ÷	10,200 shs.
EPS	$4.60		$4.51	

For the second example, assume the following additional information about the capital structure (net income of $50,000 and common shares of 10,000 as in previous example).

1. 8% convertible debt, 200 bonds each convertible into 40 common shares. The bonds were outstanding the entire year. The average AA corporate bond yield was 10% at the date the bonds were issued. The income tax rate is 40%. The bonds were issued at par ($1,000 per bond). No bonds were converted during the year.
2. 4% convertible, cumulative preferred stock, par $100, 1,000 shares issued and outstanding. Each preferred share is convertible into 2 common shares. The preferred stock was outstanding the entire year, and the average AA corporate bond yield at the date the preferred stock was issued was 10%. The preferred stock was issued at par. No preferred stock was converted during the year.

The capital structure is complex in this example because of the presence of the two convertible securities. The first step in the solution of this example is the calculation of basic EPS based upon weighted-average of common shares outstanding. This EPS is the same as it was for the first example (i.e., $4.60). The next step is the computation of diluted EPS. The diluted EPS computation will include the convertible preferred stock if it is dilutive.

To determine the dilutive effect of the preferred stock, an assumption (called the **if converted method**) is made that all of the preferred stock is converted at the earliest date that it could have occurred during the year. In this example, the date would be January 1. The effects of this assumption are twofold. One, if the preferred stock is converted, there will be no preferred dividend of $4,000 for the year; and, two, there will be an additional 2,000 shares of common stock outstanding during the year (the conversion rate is 2 common for 1 preferred). EPS is computed, as follows, reflecting these two assumptions.

$$\frac{\text{Net income}}{\substack{\text{Weighted–average of common shares} \\ \text{outstanding + Shares issued upon} \\ \text{conversion of preferred stock}}} = \frac{\$50,000}{10,000 + 2,000 \text{ shares}} = \$4.17$$

The convertible preferred stock is dilutive because it reduced EPS from $4.60 to $4.17.

In the example, the convertible bonds are assumed to have been converted at the beginning of the year. The effects of this assumption are twofold. One, if the bonds are converted, there will be no interest expense of $16,000 (8% x $200,000 face value); and, two, there will be an additional 8,000 shares (200 bonds x 40 shares) of common stock outstanding during the year. One note of caution, however, must be mentioned; namely, the effect of not having $16,000 of interest expense will increase income, but it will also increase tax expense. Consequently, the net effect of not having interest expense is $9,600 [$16,000 – (40% x $16,000)]. Diluted EPS is computed, as follows, reflecting the dilutive preferred stock and the effects noted above for the convertible bonds.

$$\frac{\text{Net income + Interest expense (net of tax)}}{\substack{\text{Weighted–average of common shares} \\ \text{outstanding + Shares issued upon} \\ \text{conversion of preferred and} \\ \text{conversion of bonds}}} = \frac{\$50,000 + 9,600}{10,000 + 2,000 + 8,000 \text{ shares}} = \$2.98$$

The convertible debt is dilutive. Both the convertible bonds and preferred stock reduced EPS from $4.60 to $2.98. Table III summarizes the computations made for the second example.

The income statement disclosures for EPS, as a result of the second example, would be as follows:

Earnings per common share (see Note X)	$4.60
Earnings per common share assuming dilution	2.98

Note X would state the assumptions made in determining both basic and diluted EPS numbers.

TABLE III

Items	Basic EPS Numerator	Basic EPS Denominator	Diluted EPS Numerator	Diluted EPS Denominator
Net income	$50,000		$50,000	
Preferred div.	(4,000)			
Common shares outstanding		10,000 shs.		10,000 shs.
Conversion of preferred				2,000
Conversion of bonds			9,600	8,000
Totals	$46,000 ÷	10,000 shs.	$59,600 ÷	20,000 shs.
EPS	$4.60		$2.98	

In the two examples, all of the potentially dilutive securities were outstanding the entire year and no conversions or exercises were made during the year. If a potentially dilutive security was not outstanding the entire year, then the numerator and denominator effects would have to be "time-weighted." For instance, suppose the convertible bonds in the second example were issued during the current year on July 1. If all other facts remain unchanged, diluted EPS would be computed as follows:

$$\frac{\text{Net income + Interest expense (net of tax)}}{\substack{\text{Weighted–average of common shares} \\ \text{outstanding + Shares issued upon} \\ \text{conversion of preferred and} \\ \text{conversion of bonds}}} = \frac{\$50,000 + 1/2(9,600)}{\substack{10,000 + 2,000 + \\ 1/2 \,(8,000)}} = \$3.43$$

The convertible debt is dilutive whether or not it is outstanding the entire year or for part of a year.

If actual conversions or exercises take place during a period, the common shares issued will be outstanding from their date of issuance and, therefore, will be in the weighted-average of common shares outstanding. These shares are then weighted from their respective times of issuance. For example, assume that all the bonds in the second example are converted on July 1 into 8,000 common shares. Several important effects should be noted, as follows:

1. The weighted-average of common shares outstanding will be increased by (8,000)(.5) or 4,000. Income will increase $4,800 net of tax, because the bonds are no longer outstanding.
2. The "if converted" method is applied to the period January 1 to July 1 because it was during this period that the bonds were potentially dilutive. The interest expense, net of tax, of $4,800 is added to the income, and 4,000 shares (.5 of 8,000) are added to the denominator.
3. Interestingly, the net effect of items 1 and 2 is the same for the period whether these dilutive bonds were outstanding the entire period or converted during the period.

It should also be noted that when convertible debt is issued for a premium or discount, the interest expense net of taxes must be computed after giving effect to premium/discount amortization.

The benchmark used to determine if including individual securities decreases income is income from continuing operations unless an enterprise has no discontinued operations. In that case income before extraordinary items or cumulative effect would be the benchmark number.

Contingent issuances of common stock. Also mentioned are **contingent issuances** of common stock (e.g., stock subscriptions). If shares are to be issued in the future with no restrictions on issuance other than the passage of time, they are to be considered issued and treated as outstanding in the computation of dilutive EPS (SFAS 128). Other issuances that are dependent upon certain conditions being met are to be evaluated in a different respect. SFAS 128 uses as examples the maintenance of current earnings levels and the attainment of specified earnings increases. If the contingency is to merely maintain the earnings levels currently being attained, then the shares are considered outstanding for the entire period and considered in the computation of dilutive EPS if the effect is dilutive. If the requirement is to increase earnings over a period of time, the diluted EPS computation shall include those shares that would be issued based on the assumption that current amount of earnings will remain unchanged, if the effect is dilutive.

EPS on comprehensive income and other comprehensive income components. EPS numbers below net income are not required per SFAS 130 for comprehensive income components.

M. Corporate Bankruptcy

The going concern assumption is one of the basic principles underlying the primary financial statements (balance sheet, income statement and statement of cash flows). However, this assumption of continued existence is threatened in corporations that are in severe financial trouble. A range of alternative actions is available to a company before it enters bankruptcy, such as seeking extensions on due dates of debt, restructuring its debt, or allowing a court-appointed trustee to manage the corporation. These pre-bankruptcy options are presented in the following modules:

Creditor's agreements—Module 11, Bankruptcy
Troubled debt restructurings—Module 26, Present Value, Section C

Bankruptcy is the final legal act for a company. In bankruptcy, the accounting and financial reporting must present the information necessary for the liquidation of the business. The **Statement of Affairs** is prepared to present the current market values of the assets and the status of the various categories of the equity interests of the corporation.

The accountant must provide a prioritization of the creditors' claims against the net assets of the corporation. The legal rights of each creditor are determined by the terms of the credit agreement it has with the company and by the National Bankruptcy Act.

The **Statement of Affairs** classifies assets in the following order of priority (highest to lowest):

1. Assets pledged with fully secured creditors—assets having a fair valuation equal to or greater than the debts for which they serve as collateral
2. Assets pledged with partially secured creditors—assets having a fair valuation less than their associated debts
3. Free assets—uncommitted assets available for remaining equity interests

The equity interests are classified in the following order (highest to lowest):

1. Preferred claims—these claims have priority as specified in the Bankruptcy Act
2. Fully secured creditors—these are claims which should be fully covered with the realizations from the assets pledged to the claims
3. Partially secured creditors—these are claims which may not be fully covered by the realizations of the pledged assets for these claims; the amount of the uncovered claims goes to the unsecured creditors category
4. Unsecured creditors—these are claims that have no priority and do not have any collateral claims to any specific assets
5. Stockholders' equity—this represents any residual claim

The historical cost valuation principles used in a balance sheet assume a going concern assumption. As a business enters bankruptcy, the liquidation values of the assets become the most relevant measures. In addition, anticipated costs of liquidation should be recognized. The Statement of Affairs begins with the present book values of the company's assets in order to articulate with the balance sheet. After relating the projected proceeds from the liquidation of the assets to the various equity interests, the statement concludes with the estimated dollar amount of unsecured claims that cannot be paid (estimated deficiency).

EXAMPLE: The Vann Corporation's balance sheet for December 31, 2002, is shown below. The corporation is entering bankruptcy and expects to incur $8,000 of costs for the liquidation process. The estimated current values of the assets are determined and the various equity claims are prioritized. The Statement of Affairs for Vann Corporation is presented on the following page.

The Vann Corporation
BALANCE SHEET
December 31, 2002

Assets	
Cash	$ 1,500
Marketable securities	10,000
Accounts receivable (net)	18,000
Merchandise inventory	41,000
Prepaid expenses	2,000
Land	6,000
Building (net of depreciation)	65,000
Machinery (net of depreciation)	21,000
Goodwill	10,000
	$174,500
Equities	
Accounts payable	$ 30,000
Notes payable	37,000
Accrued wages	6,500
Mortgages payable	45,000
Capital stock ($10 par)	100,000
Retained earnings (deficit)	(44,000)
	$174,500

N.   Reorganizations

Chapter 11 of the Bankruptcy Reform Act of 1978 allows legal protection from creditors to provide time for a bankrupt corporation to return its operations to a profitable level. SOP 90-7 provides guidance for financial reporting during Chapter 11 reorganizations. The SOP requires the balance sheet, income statement, and statement of cash flows to distinguish events and transactions related with the reorganization from those related to ongoing operations. Liabilities should be reported at expected amounts per the plan on the balance sheet. Liabilities should be classified as unsecured or secured liabilities before reorganization and liabilities incurred after the filing date for Chapter 11. Transactions directly related to the reorganization should be reported separately on the income statement in the period incurred, and disclosure should be made of any anticipated changes in common stock or common stock equivalents. Cash flows related to the reorganization should be reported separately from those related to regular operations. At confirmation of the plan of reorganization, an entity may be considered a new entity for reporting purposes if the reorganization value of assets before confirmation is less than liabilities incurred after petition for Chapter 11 and voting shareholders before confirmation receive less than 50% of the voting shares of the emerging entity. If the entity does not qualify as a new entity, the reorganization should be accounted for as troubled debt restructuring which is discussed in Module 26C.

The Vann Corporation
STATEMENT OF AFFAIRS
December 31, 2002

ASSETS

Book values		Estimated current values	Amount available to unsecured claims
	(1) Assets Pledged with Fully Secured Creditors:		
$ 6,000	Land	$12,000	
65,000	Building	41,000	
		$53,000	
	Less Mortgages Payable	45,000	$ 8,000
	(2) Assets Pledged with Partially Secured Creditors:		
10,000	Marketable Securities	$12,000	
	Notes Payable	37,000	
	(3) Free Assets		
1,500	Cash	1,500	
18,000	Accounts Receivable (net)	14,000	
41,000	Merchandise Inventory	22,500	
2,000	Prepaid Expenses	0	
21,000	Machinery	13,200	
10,000	Goodwill	0	51,200
	Estimated amount available		59,200
	Less: creditors with priority		(14,500)
	Net Estimated amount available to unsecured creditors		44,700
	(81 cents on the dollar)		
	Estimated deficiency to unsecured creditors		10,300
			$55,000
$174,500			

EQUITIES

Book values			Amount unsecured
	(1) Creditors with Priority		
	Estimated Liquidation Expenses (accounting, legal and other costs of liquidation process)	$ 8,000	
6,500	Accrued Wages	6,500	
		$14,500	
	(2) Fully Secured Creditors		
45,000	Mortgages Payable	45,000	
	(3) Partially Secured Creditors		
37,000	Notes Payable	37,000	
	Less Marketable Securities	12,000	25,000
	(4) Unsecured Creditors		
30,000	Accounts Payable		30,000
	(5) Stockholders' Equity		
100,000	Capital Stock		
(44,000)	Retained Earnings (deficit)		
$174,500			$55,000

O. Quasi Reorganization (ARB 43, Chapter 7A)

The purpose of a quasi reorganization is to allow companies to avoid formal bankruptcy proceedings through an informal proceeding. The procedure is applicable for a situation where a going concern exists except for overvalued assets and a possible deficit. The overvalued assets result in high depreciation charges and losses or lower net income. The deficit precludes payment of dividends.

The procedure is applicable during a period of declining price levels (normally associated with decreased economic activity), such as the 1930s.

The procedures involve

1. Proper authorization including that from stockholders and creditors where required
2. Revaluation of assets to current values
3. Elimination of any deficit by charging paid-in capital

    a. First, capital surplus
    b. Second, capital stock

To write down assets: here the adjustments are taken directly to retained earnings. An alternative is to use an intermediary account such as "adjustment account" which would later be closed to retained earnings.

Retained earnings	(write-down)
Assets	(write-down)

To eliminate the deficit

Paid-in capital	(deficit)
Retained earnings	(deficit)

In many cases, paid-in capital in excess of par value will be insufficient, and the par or stated value of the capital stock must be reduced to eliminate the deficit.

Existing paid-in capital	(amount on the books)
Capital stock	(total reduction in par)
Retained earnings	(deficit)
Paid-in capital from	
quasi reorganization	(forced figure)

The paid-in capital arises from reducing the par or stated value from, for example, $100 to $50 rather than to $59.415. The $59.415 would come from dividing the shares outstanding into the retained earnings deficit.

ARB 46 requires retained earnings to be dated for ten years (less than ten years justified under exceptional circumstances) after a quasi reorganization takes place. Disclosure similar to "since quasi reorganization of June 30, 1989," would be appropriate.

P. Stock Rights

Generally, before additional stock is offered to the public, stock rights are issued to existing shareholders to prevent involuntary dilution of their voting rights (e.g., the preemptive privilege). The stock rights, evidenced by warrants, indicate the number and price at which the shares may be purchased. At issuance, the issuer makes only a memorandum entry. Upon exercise, the following entry is made:

Cash	(proceeds)
Common stock	(par)
Paid-in capital	(plug)

Information relating to stock rights outstanding must be disclosed. Detachable stock rights issued with preferred stock are treated like those on bonds (see Module 26, Section B.6.). Treatment of stock rights by recipients is discussed in Module 29, Section F.

Q. Employee Stock Ownership Plan (ESOP)

An employee stock ownership plan (ESOP) is a qualified stock bonus plan designed to invest primarily in qualifying employer securities, including stock and other marketable obligations. In some instances, the ESOP will borrow funds from a bank or other lender in order to acquire shares of the employer's stock. If such an obligation of the ESOP is guaranteed by the employer (assumption by the employer of the ESOP's debt), it should be recorded as a liability in the employer's financial statements. The offsetting debit to the liability should be accounted for as a reduction of shareholders' equity. Shareholders' equity will increase symmetrically with the reduction of the liability as the ESOP makes payments on the debt. Assets held by an ESOP should not be included in the employer's financial statements, because such assets are owned by the employees, not the employer. Additionally, the employer should charge to compensation expense the amount the employer contributed or committed to be contributed to an ESOP with respect to a given year. This is done regardless of whether or not the ESOP has borrowed funds.

R. Ratios

The following ratios use stockholders' equity components in their calculations:

1. **Dividend payout**—measures percentage of earnings distributed as dividends

$$\frac{\text{Dividends per share}}{\text{Earnings per share}}$$

2. **Book value of common stock** (at a point in time)—not a meaningful measure because assets are carried at historical costs

$$\frac{\text{Common stockholders' equity}}{\text{Shares outstanding}}$$

3. **Rate of return on common stockholders' equity**—measures the return earned on the stockholders' investment in the firm

$$\frac{\text{Net income available to common stockholders}}{\text{Common stockholders' equity}}$$

4. **Debt to equity**—shows creditors the corporation's ability to sustain losses

$$\frac{\text{Total debt (all liabilities)}}{\text{Stockholders' equity}}$$

MULTIPLE-CHOICE QUESTIONS (1-91)

1. East Co. issued 1,000 shares of its $5 par common stock to Howe as compensation for 1,000 hours of legal services performed. Howe usually bills $160 per hour for legal services. On the date of issuance, the stock was trading on a public exchange at $140 per share. By what amount should the additional paid-in capital account increase as a result of this transaction?

 a. $135,000
 b. $140,000
 c. $155,000
 d. $160,000

2. On July 1, 2002, Cove Corp., a closely held corporation, issued 6% bonds with a maturity value of $60,000, together with 1,000 shares of its $5 par value common stock, for a combined cash amount of $110,000. The market value of Cove's stock cannot be ascertained. If the bonds were issued separately, they would have sold for $40,000 on an 8% yield to maturity basis. What amount should Cove report for additional paid-in capital on the issuance of the stock?

 a. $75,000
 b. $65,000
 c. $55,000
 d. $45,000

3. Beck Corp. issued 200,000 shares of common stock when it began operations in 2000 and issued an additional 100,000 shares in 2001. Beck also issued preferred stock convertible to 100,000 shares of common stock. In 2002, Beck purchased 75,000 shares of its common stock and held it in Treasury. At December 31, 2002, how many shares of Beck's common stock were outstanding?

 a. 400,000
 b. 325,000
 c. 300,000
 d. 225,000

4. A corporation was organized in January 2002 with authorized capital of $10 par value common stock. On February 1, 2002, shares were issued at par for cash. On March 1, 2002, the corporation's attorney accepted 5,000 shares of the common stock in settlement for legal services with a fair value of $60,000. Additional paid-in capital would increase on

	February 1, 2002	*March 1, 2002*
a.	Yes	No
b.	Yes	Yes
c.	No	No
d.	No	Yes

5. On April 1, 2002, Hyde Corp., a newly formed company, had the following stock issued and outstanding:

• Common stock, no par, $1 stated value, 20,000 shares originally issued for $30 per share.

• Preferred stock, $10 par value, 6,000 shares originally issued for $50 per share.

Hyde's April 1, 2002 statement of stockholders' equity should report

	Common stock	*Preferred stock*	*Additional paid-in capital*
a.	$ 20,000	$ 60,000	$820,000
b.	$ 20,000	$300,000	$580,000
c.	$600,000	$300,000	$0
d.	$600,000	$ 60,000	$240,000

6. On March 1, 2002, Rya Corp. issued 1,000 shares of its $20 par value common stock and 2,000 shares of its $20 par value convertible preferred stock for a total of $80,000. At this date, Rya's common stock was selling for $36 per share, and the convertible preferred stock was selling for $27 per share. What amount of the proceeds should be allocated to Rya's convertible preferred stock?

 a. $60,000
 b. $54,000
 c. $48,000
 d. $44,000

7. During 2000, Brad Co. issued 5,000 shares of $100 par convertible preferred stock for $110 per share. One share of preferred stock can be converted into three shares of Brad's $25 par common stock at the option of the preferred shareholder. On December 31, 2002, when the market value of the common stock was $40 per share, all of the preferred stock was converted. What amount should Brad credit to Common Stock and to Additional Paid-in Capital— Common Stock as a result of the conversion?

	Common stock	*Additional paid-in capital*
a.	$375,000	$175,000
b.	$375,000	$225,000
c.	$500,000	$ 50,000
d.	$600,000	$0

8. Quoit, Inc. issued preferred stock with detachable common stock warrants. The issue price exceeded the sum of the warrants' fair value and the preferred stock's par value. The preferred stock's fair value was not determinable. What amount should be assigned to the warrants outstanding?

 a. Total proceeds.
 b. Excess of proceeds over the par value of the preferred stock.
 c. The proportion of the proceeds that the warrants' fair value bears to the preferred stock's par value.
 d. The fair value of the warrants.

9. Blue Co. issued preferred stock with detachable common stock warrants at a price that exceeded both the par value and the market value of the preferred stock. At the time the warrants are exercised, Blue's total stockholders' equity is increased by the

	Cash received upon exercise of the warrants	*Carrying amount of warrants*
a.	Yes	No
b.	Yes	Yes
c.	No	No
d.	No	Yes

10. When collectibility is reasonably assured, the excess of the subscription price over the stated value of the no par common stock subscribed should be recorded as

 a. No par common stock.
 b. Additional paid-in capital when the subscription is recorded.
 c. Additional paid-in capital when the subscription is collected.

    d.   Additional paid-in capital when the common stock is issued.

11. On December 1, 2002, shares of authorized common stock were issued on a subscription basis at a price in excess of par value. A total of 20% of the subscription price of each share was collected as a down payment on December 1, 2002, with the remaining 80% of the subscription price of each share due in 2003. Collectibility was reasonably assured. At December 31, 2002, the stockholders' equity section of the balance sheet would report additional paid-in capital for the excess of the subscription price over the par value of the shares of common stock subscribed and

    a.   Common stock issued for 20% of the par value of the shares of common stock subscribed.

    b.   Common stock issued for the par value of the shares of common stock subscribed.

    c.   Common stock subscribed for 80% of the par value of the shares of common stock subscribed.

    d.   Common stock subscribed for the par value of the shares of common stock subscribed.

12. In 2001, Seda Corp. acquired 6,000 shares of its $1 par value common stock at $36 per share. During 2002, Seda issued 3,000 of these shares at $50 per share. Seda uses the cost method to account for its treasury stock transactions. What accounts and amounts should Seda credit in 2002 to record the issuance of the 3,000 shares?

	Treasury stock	Additional paid-in capital	Retained earnings	Common stock
a.		$102,000	$42,000	$6,000
b.		$144,000		$6,000
c.	$108,000	$ 42,000		
d.	$108,000		$42,000	

13. At December 31, 2001, Rama Corp. had 20,000 shares of $1 par value treasury stock that had been acquired in 2001 at $12 per share. In May 2002, Rama issued 15,000 of these treasury shares at $10 per share. The cost method is used to record treasury stock transactions. Rama is located in a state where laws relating to acquisition of treasury stock restrict the availability of retained earnings for declaration of dividends. At December 31, 2002, what amount should Rama show in notes to financial statements as a restriction of retained earnings as a result of its treasury stock transactions?

    a. $ 5,000
    b. $10,000
    c. $60,000
    d. $90,000

14. United, Inc.'s unadjusted current assets section and stockholders' equity section of its December 31, 2002 balance sheet are as follows:

Current assets

Cash	$ 60,000
Investments in marketable equity securities (including $300,000 of United, Inc. common stock)	400,000
Trade accounts receivable	340,000
Inventories	148,000
Total	$ 948,000

Stockholders' equity

Common stock	$2,224,000
Retained earnings (deficit)	(224,000)
Total	$2,000,000

The investments and inventories are reported at their costs, which approximate market values.

In its 2002 statement of stockholders' equity, United's total amount of equity at December 31, 2002, is

    a. $2,224,000
    b. $2,000,000
    c. $1,924,000
    d. $1,700,000

15. Cyan Corp. issued 20,000 shares of $5 par common stock at $10 per share. On December 31, 2001, Cyan's retained earnings were $300,000. In March 2002, Cyan reacquired 5,000 shares of its common stock at $20 per share. In June 2002, Cyan sold 1,000 of these shares to its corporate officers for $25 per share. Cyan uses the cost method to record treasury stock. Net income for the year ended December 31, 2002, was $60,000. At December 31, 2002, what amount should Cyan report as retained earnings?

    a. $360,000
    b. $365,000
    c. $375,000
    d. $380,000

16. Victor Corporation was organized on January 2, 2002, with 100,000 authorized shares of $10 par value common stock. During 2002 Victor had the following capital transactions:

January 5—issued 75,000 shares at $14 per share.
December 27—purchased 5,000 shares at $11 per share.

Victor used the par value method to record the purchase of the treasury shares. What would be the balance in the paid-in capital from treasury stock account at December 31, 2002?

    a. $0
    b. $ 5,000
    c. $15,000
    d. $20,000

17. On incorporation, Dee Inc. issued common stock at a price in excess of its par value. No other stock transactions occurred except treasury stock was acquired for an amount exceeding this issue price. If Dee uses the par value method of accounting for treasury stock appropriate for retired stock, what is the effect of the acquisition on the following?

	Net common stock	Additional paid-in capital	Retained earnings
a.	No effect	Decrease	No effect
b.	Decrease	Decrease	Decrease
c.	Decrease	No effect	Decrease
d.	No effect	Decrease	Decrease

18. Posy Corp. acquired treasury shares at an amount greater than their par value, but less than their original issue price. Compared to the cost method of accounting for treasury stock, does the par value method report a greater amount for additional paid-in capital and a greater amount for retained earnings?

	Additional paid-in capital	Retained earnings
a.	Yes	Yes
b.	Yes	No
c.	No	No
d.	No	Yes

19. In 1999, Rona Corp. issued 5,000 shares of $10 par value common stock for $100 per share. In 2002, Rona reacquired 2,000 of its shares at $150 per share from the estate of one of its deceased officers and immediately canceled these 2,000 shares. Rona uses the cost method in accounting for its treasury stock transactions. In connection with the retirement of these 2,000 shares, Rona should debit

	Additional paid-in capital	*Retained earnings*
a.	$ 20,000	$280,000
b.	$100,000	$180,000
c.	$180,000	$100,000
d.	$280,000	$0

20. The following accounts were among those reported on Luna Corp.'s balance sheet at December 31, 2001:

Marketable securities (market value $140,000)	$ 80,000
Preferred stock, $20 par value, 20,000 shares issued and outstanding	400,000
Additional paid-in capital on preferred stock	30,000
Retained earnings	900,000

On January 20, 2002, Luna exchanged all of the marketable securities for 5,000 shares of Luna's preferred stock. Market values at the date of the exchange were $150,000 for the marketable securities and $30 per share for the preferred stock. The 5,000 shares of preferred stock were retired immediately after the exchange. Which of the following journal entries should Luna record in connection with this transaction?

		Debit	*Credit*
a.	Preferred stock	100,000	
	Additional paid-in capital on preferred stock	7,500	
	Retained earnings	42,500	
	Marketable securities		80,000
	Gain on exchange of securities		70,000
b.	Preferred stock	100,000	
	Additional paid-in capital on preferred stock	30,000	
	Marketable securities		80,000
	Additional paid-in capital from retirement of preferred stock		50,000
c.	Preferred stock	150,000	
	Marketable securities		80,000
	Additional paid-in capital on preferred stock		70,000
d.	Preferred stock	150,000	
	Marketable securities		80,000
	Gain on exchange of securities		70,000

21. On December 31, 2002, Pack Corp.'s board of directors canceled 50,000 shares of $2.50 par value common stock held in treasury at an average cost of $13 per share. Before recording the cancellation of the treasury stock, Pack had the following balances in its stockholders' equity accounts:

Common stock	$540,000
Additional paid-in capital	750,000
Retained earnings	900,000
Treasury stock, at cost	650,000

In its balance sheet at December 31, 2002, Pack should report common stock outstanding of

  a. $0
  b. $250,000

  c. $415,000
  d. $540,000

22. In 2000, Fogg, Inc. issued $10 par value common stock for $25 per share. No other common stock transactions occurred until March 31, 2002, when Fogg acquired some of the issued shares for $20 per share and retired them. Which of the following statements correctly states an effect of this acquisition and retirement?

  a. 2002 net income is decreased.
  b. 2002 net income is increased.
  c. Additional paid-in capital is decreased.
  d. Retained earnings is increased.

23. Plack Co. purchased 10,000 shares (2% ownership) of Ty Corp. on February 14, 2001. Plack received a stock dividend of 2,000 shares on April 30, 2001, when the market value per share was $35. Ty paid a cash dividend of $2 per share on December 15, 2001. In its 2001 income statement, what amount should Plack report as dividend income?

  a. $20,000
  b. $24,000
  c. $90,000
  d. $94,000

24. Arp Corp.'s outstanding capital stock at December 15, 2002, consisted of the following:

- 30,000 shares of 5% cumulative preferred stock, par value $10 per share, fully participating as to dividends. No dividends were in arrears.
- 200,000 shares of common stock, par value $1 per share.

On December 15, 2002, Arp declared dividends of $100,000. What was the amount of dividends payable to Arp's common stockholders?

  a. $10,000
  b. $34,000
  c. $40,000
  d. $47,500

25. At December 31, 2001 and 2002, Apex Co. had 3,000 shares of $100 par, 5% cumulative preferred stock outstanding. No dividends were in arrears as of December 31, 2000. Apex did not declare a dividend during 2001. During 2002, Apex paid a cash dividend of $10,000 on its preferred stock. Apex should report dividends in arrears in its 2002 financial statements as a(n)

  a. Accrued liability of $15,000.
  b. Disclosure of $15,000.
  c. Accrued liability of $20,000.
  d. Disclosure of $20,000.

26. East Corp., a calendar-year company, had sufficient retained earnings in 2002 as a basis for dividends, but was temporarily short of cash. East declared a dividend of $100,000 on April 1, 2002, and issued promissory notes to its stockholders in lieu of cash. The notes, which were dated April 1, 2002, had a maturity date of March 31, 2003, and a 10% interest rate. How should East account for the scrip dividend and related interest?

  a. Debit retained earnings for $110,000 on April 1, 2002.
  b. Debit retained earnings for $110,000 on March 31, 2003.

   c. Debit retained earnings for $100,000 on April 1, 2002, and debit interest expense for $10,000 on March 31, 2003.

   d. Debit retained earnings for $100,000 on April 1, 2002, and debit interest expense for $7,500 on December 31, 2002.

27. On January 2, 2002, Lake Mining Co.'s board of directors declared a cash dividend of $400,000 to stockholders of record on January 18, 2002, payable on February 10, 2002. The dividend is permissible under law in Lake's state of incorporation. Selected data from Lake's December 31, 2001 balance sheet are as follows:

Accumulated depletion	$100,000
Capital stock	500,000
Additional paid-in capital	150,000
Retained earnings	300,000

The $400,000 dividend includes a liquidating dividend of

   a. $0
   b. $100,000
   c. $150,000
   d. $300,000

28. On June 27, 2002, Brite Co. distributed to its common stockholders 100,000 outstanding common shares of its investment in Quik, Inc., an unrelated party. The carrying amount on Brite's books of Quik's $1 par common stock was $2 per share. Immediately after the distribution, the market price of Quik's stock was $2.50 per share. In its income statement for the year ended June 30, 2002, what amount should Brite report as gain before income taxes on disposal of the stock?

   a. $250,000
   b. $200,000
   c. $ 50,000
   d. $0

29. On December 1, 2002, Nilo Corp. declared a property dividend of marketable securities to be distributed on December 31, 2002, to stockholders of record on December 15, 2002. On December 1, 2002, the marketable securities had a carrying amount of $60,000 and a fair value of $78,000. What is the effect of this property dividend on Nilo's 2002 retained earnings, after all nominal accounts are closed?

   a. $0.
   b. $18,000 increase.
   c. $60,000 decrease.
   d. $78,000 decrease.

30. Long Co. had 100,000 shares of common stock issued and outstanding at January 1, 2002. During 2002, Long took the following actions:

March 15	— Declared a 2-for-1 stock split, when the fair value of the stock was $80 per share.
December 15	— Declared a $.50 per share cash dividend.

In Long's statement of stockholders' equity for 2002, what amount should Long report as dividends?

   a. $ 50,000
   b. $100,000
   c. $850,000
   d. $950,000

31. A company declared a cash dividend on its common stock on December 15, 2002, payable on January 12, 2003.

How would this dividend affect stockholders' equity on the following dates?

	December 15, 2002	December 31, 2002	January 12, 2003
a.	Decrease	No effect	Decrease
b.	Decrease	No effect	No effect
c.	No effect	Decrease	No effect
d.	No effect	No effect	Decrease

32. Ole Corp. declared and paid a liquidating dividend of $100,000. This distribution resulted in a decrease in Ole's

	Paid-in capital	Retained earnings
a.	No	No
b.	Yes	Yes
c.	No	Yes
d.	Yes	No

33. Instead of the usual cash dividend, Evie Corp. declared and distributed a property dividend from its overstocked merchandise. The excess of the merchandise's carrying amount over its market value should be

   a. Ignored.
   b. Reported as a separately disclosed reduction of retained earnings.
   c. Reported as an extraordinary loss, net of income taxes.
   d. Reported as a reduction in income before extraordinary items.

34. The following stock dividends were declared and distributed by Sol Corp.:

Percentage of common share outstanding at declaration date	Fair value	Par value
10	$15,000	$10,000
28	40,000	30,800

What aggregate amount should be debited to retained earnings for these stock dividends?

   a. $40,800
   b. $45,800
   c. $50,000
   d. $55,000

35. Ray Corp. declared a 5% stock dividend on its 10,000 issued and outstanding shares of $2 par value common stock, which had a fair value of $5 per share before the stock dividend was declared. This stock dividend was distributed sixty days after the declaration date. By what amount did Ray's current liabilities increase as a result of the stock dividend declaration?

   a. $0
   b. $ 500
   c. $1,000
   d. $2,500

36. How would total stockholders' equity be affected by the declaration of each of the following?

	Stock dividend	Stock split
a.	No effect	Increase
b.	Decrease	Decrease
c.	Decrease	No effect
d.	No effect	No effect

37. On July 1, 2002, Bart Corporation has 200,000 shares of $10 par common stock outstanding and the market price of the stock is $12 per share. On the same date, Bart declared a 1-for-2 reverse stock split. The par of the stock was increased from $10 to $20 and one new $20 par share was issued for each two $10 par shares outstanding. Immediately before the 1-for-2 reverse stock split, Bart's additional paid-in capital was $450,000. What should be the balance in Bart's additional paid-in capital account immediately after the reverse stock split is effected?

    a. $0
    b. $450,000
    c. $650,000
    d. $850,000

38. How would a stock split in which the par value per share decreases in proportion to the number of additional shares issued affect each of the following?

	Additional paid-in capital	Retained earnings
a.	Increase	No effect
b.	No effect	No effect
c.	No effect	Decrease
d.	Increase	Decrease

39. At December 31, 2001, Eagle Corp. reported $1,750,000 of appropriated retained earnings for the construction of a new office building, which was completed in 2002 at a total cost of $1,500,000. In 2002, Eagle appropriated $1,200,000 of retained earnings for the construction of a new plant. Also, $2,000,000 of cash was restricted for the retirement of bonds due in 2003. In its 2002 balance sheet, Eagle should report what amount of appropriated retained earnings?

    a. $1,200,000
    b. $1,450,000
    c. $2,950,000
    d. $3,200,000

40. The following information pertains to Meg Corp.:

• Dividends on its 1,000 shares of 6%, $10 par value cumulative preferred stock have not been declared or paid for three years.

• Treasury stock that cost $15,000 was reissued for $8,000.

What amount of retained earnings should be appropriated as a result of these items?

    a. $0
    b. $1,800
    c. $7,000
    d. $8,800

41. A retained earnings appropriation can be used to

    a. Absorb a fire loss when a company is self-insured.
    b. Provide for a contingent loss that is probable and reasonably estimable.
    c. Smooth periodic income.
    d. Restrict earnings available for dividends.

42. On January 1, 2001, Doro Corp. granted an employee an option to purchase 3,000 shares of Doro's $5 par value common stock at $20 per share. The option became exercisable on December 31, 2002, after the employee completed two years of service. The option was exercised on January 10, 2003. The market prices of Doro's stock were as follows:

January 1, 2001	$30
December 31, 2002	50
January 10, 2003	45

For 2002, Doro should recognize compensation expense under APB 25 of

    a. $45,000
    b. $37,500
    c. $15,000
    d. $0

43. In connection with a stock option plan for the benefit of key employees, Ward Corp. intends to distribute treasury shares when the options are exercised. These shares were bought in 2001 at $42 per share. On January 1, 2002, Ward granted stock options for 10,000 shares at $38 per share as additional compensation for services to be rendered over the next three years. The options are exercisable during a four-year period beginning January 1, 2004, by grantees still employed by Ward. Market price of Ward's stock was $47 per share at the grant date. No stock options were terminated during 2002. In Ward's December 31, 2002 income statement, what amount should be reported as compensation expense pertaining to the options under APB 25?

    a. $90,000
    b. $40,000
    c. $30,000
    d. $0

44. On January 2, 2002, Kine Co. granted Morgan, its president, compensatory stock options to buy 1,000 shares of Kine's $10 par common stock. The options call for a price of $20 per share and are exercisable for three years following the grant date. Morgan exercised the options on December 31, 2002. The market price of the stock was $50 on January 2, 2002, and $70 on December 31, 2002. By what net amount should stockholders' equity increase as a result of the grant and exercise of the options under APB 25?

    a. $20,000
    b. $30,000
    c. $50,000
    d. $70,000

45. On January 2, 2002, Morey Corp. granted Dean, its president, 20,000 stock appreciation rights for past services. Those rights are exercisable immediately and expire on January 1, 2005. On exercise, Dean is entitled to receive cash for the excess of the stock's market price on the exercise date over the market price on the grant date. Dean did not exercise any of the rights during 2002. The market price of Morey's stock was $30 on January 2, 2002 and $45 on December 31, 2002. As a result of the stock appreciation rights, Morey should recognize compensation expense for 2002 of

    a. $0
    b. $100,000
    c. $300,000
    d. $600,000

46. Wall Corp.'s employee stock purchase plan specifies the following:

• For every $1 withheld from employees' wages for the purchase of Wall's common stock, Wall contributes $2.

• The stock is purchased from Wall's treasury stock at market price on the date of purchase.

The following information pertains to the plan's 2002 transactions:

Employee withholdings for the year	$ 350,000
Market value of 150,000 shares issued	1,050,000
Carrying amount of treasury stock issued (cost)	900,000

Before payroll taxes, what amount should Wall recognize as expense in 2002 under either APB 25 or SFAS 123 for the stock purchase plan?

- a. $1,050,000
- b. $ 900,000
- c. $ 700,000
- d. $ 550,000

47. In accounting for stock based compensation under SFAS 123, what interest rate is used to discount both the exercise price of the option and the future dividend stream?

- a. The firm's known incremental borrowing rate.
- b. The current market rate that firms in that particular industry use to discount cash flows.
- c. The risk-free interest rate.
- d. Any rate that firms can justify as being reasonable.

48. In accounting for employee stock-based compensation, if the market price is equal to the option price at the date of grant, would any deferred stock compensation expense be measured?

	Under APB 25	Under SFAS 123
a.	Yes	No
b.	No	No
c.	No	Yes
d.	Yes	Yes

49. In what circumstances is compensation expense immediately recognized, under SFAS 123?

- a. In all circumstances.
- b. In circumstances when the options are exercisable within two years for services rendered over the next two years.
- c. In circumstances when options are granted for prior service, and the options are immediately exercisable.
- d. In no circumstances is compensation expense immediately recognized.

50. What is required of companies that continue to use APB 25 for accounting for stock-based compensation rather than adopting SFAS 123?

- a. Letters of explanation to shareholders.
- b. Footnote disclosures of the effects of adoption.
- c. Approval of stock-compensated employees.
- d. A hearing before the FASB.

51. Which of the following disclosures required by SFAS 123 must be made by companies that continue to employ APB 25?

- I. The weighted-average grant date fair value of options granted during the year.
- II. A description of the method and significant assumptions used to estimate fair values.
- III. The vesting requirements of the plan.

- a. III only.
- b. I and III only.
- c. I, II, and III.
- d. None of these.

52. Shafer Corporation (a nonpublic company) establishes an employee stock option plan on January 1, 2002. The plan allows its employees to acquire 20,000 shares of its $5 par

value common stock at $75 per share, when the market price is also $75. The options may not be exercised until five years from the grant date. The risk-free interest rate is 6%, and the stock is expected to pay dividends of $3 annually. What is the amount of deferred compensation expense that should be recorded in year one under SFAS 123?

Present value of 1 at 6% for 5 years	.747
Future value of 1 at 6% for 5 years	1.338
Present value of annuity at 6% for 5 years	4.212
Future value of annuity at 6% for 5 years	5.637

- a. $ 52,080
- b. $126,780
- c. $379,500
- d. $633,780

53. Normally, dividends are not paid on shares that have not been issued. However, an entity can choose to pay dividend equivalents on options. Under the provisions of SFAS 123, how are these dividend equivalents accounted for on options that vest, and how are they accounted for on options that do not vest?

	Vest	Not Vest
a.	Compensation expense	Compensation expense
b.	Compensation expense	Charge against retained earnings
c.	Charge against retained earnings	Compensation expense
d.	Charge against retained earnings	Charge against retained earnings

54. In accounting for employee stock-based compensation, should compensation expense be recognized on a straight-line basis over the vesting period?

	Under APB 25	Under SFAS 123
a.	No	No
b.	No	Yes
c.	Yes	No
d.	Yes	Yes

55. At December 31, 2002 and 2001, Gow Corp. had 100,000 shares of common stock and 10,000 shares of 5%, $100 par value cumulative preferred stock outstanding. No dividends were declared on either the preferred or common stock in 2002 or 2001. Net income for 2002 was $1,000,000. For 2002, basic earnings per share amounted to

- a. $10.00
- b. $ 9.50
- c. $ 9.00
- d. $ 5.00

56. Ute Co. had the following capital structure during 2001 and 2002:

Preferred stock, $10 par, 4% cumulative, 25,000 shares issued and outstanding	$ 250,000
Common stock, $5 par, 200,000 shares issued and outstanding	1,000,000

Ute reported net income of $500,000 for the year ended December 31, 2002. Ute paid no preferred dividends during 2001 and paid $16,000 in preferred dividends during 2002. In its December 31, 2002 income statement, what amount should Ute report as basic earnings per share?

- a. $2.42
- b. $2.45
- c. $2.48
- d. $2.50

57. The following information pertains to Jet Corp.'s outstanding stock for 2002:

Common stock, $5 par value

Shares outstanding, 1/1/02	20,000
2-for-1 stock split, 4/1/02	20,000
Shares issued, 7/1/02	10,000

Preferred stock, $10 par value, 5% cumulative

Shares outstanding, 1/1/02	4,000

What are the number of shares Jet should use to calculate 2002 basic earnings per share?

- a. 40,000
- b. 45,000
- c. 50,000
- d. 54,000

58. Timp, Inc. had the following common stock balances and transactions during 2002:

1/1/02	Common stock outstanding	30,000
2/1/02	Issued a 10% common stock dividend	3,000
3/1/02	Issued common stock in a pooling of interests	9,000
7/1/02	Issued common stock for cash	8,000
12/31/02	Common stock outstanding	50,000

What were Timp's 2002 weighted-average shares outstanding?

- a. 40,000
- b. 44,250
- c. 44,500
- d. 46,000

59. Strauch Co. has one class of common stock outstanding and no other securities that are potentially convertible into common stock. During 2001, 100,000 shares of common stock were outstanding. In 2002, two distributions of additional common shares occurred: On April 1, 20,000 shares of treasury stock were sold, and on July 1, a 2-for-1 stock split was issued. Net income was $410,000 in 2002 and $350,000 in 2001. What amounts should Strauch report as basic earnings per share in its 2002 and 2001 comparative income statements?

	2002	2001
a.	$1.78	$3.50
b.	$1.78	$1.75
c.	$2.34	$1.75
d.	$2.34	$3.50

60. Earnings per share data must be reported on the income statement for

	Cumulative effect of a change in accounting principle	Extraordinary items
a.	Yes	No
b.	No	No
c.	No	Yes
d.	Yes	Yes

61. On January 31, 2002, Pack, Inc. split its common stock 2 for 1, and Young, Inc. issued a 5% stock dividend. Both companies issued their December 31, 2001 financial statements on March 1, 2002. Should Pack's 2001, basic earnings per share (BEPS) take into consideration the stock split, and should Young's 2001 BEPS take into consideration the stock dividend?

	Pack's 2001 BEPS	Young's 2001 BEPS
a.	Yes	No
b.	No	No
c.	Yes	Yes
d.	No	Yes

62. Mann, Inc. had 300,000 shares of common stock issued and outstanding at December 31, 2001. On July 1, 2002, an additional 50,000 shares of common stock were issued for cash. Mann also had unexercised stock options to purchase 40,000 shares of common stock at $15 per share outstanding at the beginning and end of 2002. The average market price of Mann's common stock was $20 during 2002. What is the number of shares that should be used in computing diluted earnings per share for the year ended December 31, 2002?

- a. 325,000
- b. 335,000
- c. 360,000
- d. 365,000

63. Peters Corp.'s capital structure was as follows:

	December 31	
	2001	2002
Outstanding shares of stock:		
Common	110,000	110,000
Convertible preferred	10,000	10,000

During 2002, Peters paid dividends of $3.00 per share on its preferred stock. The preferred shares are convertible into 20,000 shares of common stock and are considered common stock equivalents. Net income for 2002 was $850,000. Assume that the income tax rate is 30%. The diluted earnings per share for 2002 is

- a. $6.31
- b. $6.54
- c. $7.08
- d. $7.45

64. Cox Corporation had 1,200,000 shares of common stock outstanding on January 1 and December 31, 2002. In connection with the acquisition of a subsidiary company in June 2001, Cox is required to issue 50,000 additional shares of its common stock on July 1, 2003, to the former owners of the subsidiary. Cox paid $200,000 in preferred stock dividends in 2002, and reported net income of $3,400,000 for the year. Cox's diluted earnings per share for 2002 should be

- a. $2.83
- b. $2.72
- c. $2.67
- d. $2.56

65. On June 30, 2001, Lomond, Inc. issued twenty $10,000, 7% bonds at par. Each bond was convertible into 200 shares of common stock. On January 1, 2002, 10,000 shares of common stock were outstanding. The bondholders converted all the bonds on July 1, 2002. The following amounts were reported in Lomond's income statement for the year ended December 31, 2002:

Revenues	$977,000
Operating expenses	920,000
Interest on bonds	7,000
Income before income tax	50,000
Income tax at 30%	15,000
Net income	$ 35,000

What is Lomond's 2002 diluted earnings per share?

- a. $2.50

   b. $2.85
   c. $2.92
   d. $3.50

66. West Co. had earnings per share of $15.00 for 2002 before considering the effects of any convertible securities. No conversion or exercise of convertible securities occurred during 2002. However, possible conversion of convertible bonds, not considered common stock equivalents, would have reduced earnings per share by $0.75. The effect of possible exercise of common stock options would have increased earnings per share by $0.10. What amount should West report as diluted earnings per share for 2002?

   a. $14.25
   b. $14.35
   c. $15.00
   d. $15.10

67. In determining diluted earnings per share, dividends on nonconvertible cumulative preferred stock should be

   a.   Disregarded.
   b.   Added back to net income whether declared or not.
   c.   Deducted from net income only if declared.
   d.   Deducted from net income whether declared or not.

68. The if-converted method of computing earnings per share data assumes conversion of convertible securities as of the

   a.   Beginning of the earliest period reported (or at time of issuance, if later).
   b.   Beginning of the earliest period reported (regardless of time of issuance).
   c.   Middle of the earliest period reported (regardless of time of issuance).
   d.   Ending of the earliest period reported (regardless of time of issuance).

69. In determining earnings per share, interest expense, net of applicable income taxes, on convertible debt that is dilutive should be

   a.   Added back to weighted-average common shares outstanding for diluted earnings per share.
   b.   Added back to net income for diluted earnings per share.
   c.   Deducted from net income for diluted earnings per share.
   d.   Deducted from weighted-average common shares outstanding for diluted earnings per share.

70. For contingent issue agreements requiring passage of time or earnings threshold that is met, before issuing stock, these should be

	Included in basic earnings per share	Included in computing diluted earnings per share
a.	No	No
b.	No	Yes
c.	Yes	No
d.	Yes	Yes

71. Kent Co. filed a voluntary bankruptcy petition on August 15, 2002, and the statement of affairs reflects the following amounts:

	Book value	Estimated current value
Assets		
Assets pledged with fully secured creditors	$ 300,000	$370,000
Assets pledged with partially secured creditors	180,000	120,000
Free assets	420,000	320,000
	$ 900,000	$810,000
Liabilities		
Liabilities with priority	$ 70,000	
Fully secured creditors	260,000	
Partially secured creditors	200,000	
Unsecured creditors	540,000	
	$1,070,000	

Assume that the assets are converted to cash at the estimated current values and the business is liquidated. What amount of cash will be available to pay unsecured nonpriority claims?

   a. $240,000
   b. $280,000
   c. $320,000
   d. $360,000

72. Seco Corp. was forced into bankruptcy and is in the process of liquidating assets and paying claims. Unsecured claims will be paid at the rate of 40 cents on the dollar. Hale holds a $30,000 noninterest-bearing note receivable from Seco collateralized by an asset with a book value of $35,000 and a liquidation value of $5,000. The amount to be realized by Hale on this note is

   a. $ 5,000
   b. $12,000
   c. $15,000
   d. $17,000

73. Kamy Corp. is in liquidation under Chapter 7 of the Federal Bankruptcy Code. The bankruptcy trustee has established a new set of books for the bankruptcy estate. After assuming custody of the estate, the trustee discovered an unrecorded invoice of $1,000 for machinery repairs performed before the bankruptcy filing. In addition, a truck with a carrying amount of $20,000 was sold for $12,000 cash. This truck was bought and paid for in the year before the bankruptcy. What amount should be debited to estate equity as a result of these transactions?

   a. $0
   b. $1,000
   c. $8,000
   d. $9,000

74. On December 30, 2002, Hale Corp. paid $400,000 cash and issued 80,000 shares of its $1 par value common stock to its unsecured creditors on a pro rata basis pursuant to a reorganization plan under Chapter 11 of the bankruptcy statutes. Hale owed these unsecured creditors a total of $1,200,000. Hale's common stock was trading at $1.25 per share on December 30, 2002. As a result of this transaction, Hale's total stockholders' equity had a net increase of

   a. $1,200,000
   b. $ 800,000
   c. $ 100,000
   d. $ 80,000

75. The primary purpose of a quasi reorganization is to give a corporation the opportunity to

   a.   Obtain relief from its creditors.

b. Revalue understated assets to their fair values.
c. Eliminate a deficit in retained earnings.
d. Distribute the stock of a newly created subsidiary to its stockholders in exchange for part of their stock in the corporation.

76. When a company goes through a quasi reorganization, its balance sheet carrying amounts are stated at
a. Original cost.
b. Original book value.
c. Replacement value.
d. Fair value.

77. The stockholders' equity section of Brown Co.'s December 31, 2002 balance sheet consisted of the following:

Common stock, $30 par, 10,000 shares authorized and outstanding	$300,000
Additional paid-in capital	150,000
Retained earnings (deficit)	(210,000)

On January 2, 2003, Brown put into effect a stockholder-approved quasi reorganization by reducing the par value of the stock to $5 and eliminating the deficit against additional paid-in capital. Immediately after the quasi reorganization, what amount should Brown report as additional paid-in capital?
a. $ (60,000)
b. $150,000
c. $190,000
d. $400,000

78. On July 1, 2002, Vail Corp. issued rights to stockholders to subscribe to additional shares of its common stock. One right was issued for each share owned. A stockholder could purchase one additional share for 10 rights plus $15 cash. The rights expired on September 30, 2002. On July 1, 2002, the market price of a share with the right attached was $40, while the market price of one right alone was $2. Vail's stockholders' equity on June 30, 2002, comprised the following:

Common stock, $25 par value, 4,000 shares issued and outstanding	$100,000
Additional paid-in capital	60,000
Retained earnings	80,000

By what amount should Vail's retained earnings decrease as a result of issuance of the stock rights on July 1, 2002?
a. $0
b. $ 5,000
c. $ 8,000
d. $10,000

79. In September 1999, West Corp. made a dividend distribution of one right for each of its 120,000 shares of outstanding common stock. Each right was exercisable for the purchase of 1/100 of a share of West's $50 variable rate preferred stock at an exercise price of $80 per share. On March 20, 2002, none of the rights had been exercised, and West redeemed them by paying each stockholder $0.10 per right. As a result of this redemption, West's stockholders' equity was reduced by
a. $ 120
b. $ 2,400
c. $12,000
d. $36,000

80. On November 2, 2001, Finsbury, Inc. issued warrants to its stockholders giving them the right to purchase additional $20 par value common shares at a price of $30. The stockholders exercised all warrants on March 1, 2002. The shares had market prices of $33, $35, and $40 on November 2, 2001; December 31, 2001; and March 1, 2002, respectively. What were the effects of the warrants on Finsbury's additional paid-in capital and net income?

	Additional paid-in capital	Net income
a.	Increased in 2002	No effect
b.	Increased in 2001	No effect
c.	Increased in 2002	Decreased in 2001 and 2002
d.	Increased in 2001	Decreased in 2001 and 2002

81. A company issued rights to its existing shareholders to purchase, for $30 per share, unissued shares of $15 par value common stock. Additional paid-in capital will be credited when the

	Rights are issued	Rights lapse
a.	Yes	No
b.	No	No
c.	No	Yes
d.	Yes	Yes

Items 82 and 83 are based on the following:

On January 1, 2002, Fay Corporation established an employee stock ownership plan (ESOP). Selected transactions relating to the ESOP during 2002 were as follows:

• On April 1, 2002, Fay contributed $30,000 cash and 3,000 shares of its $10 par common stock to the ESOP. On this date the market price of the stock was $18 a share.
• On October 1, 2002, the ESOP borrowed $100,000 from Union National Bank and acquired 5,000 shares of Fay's common stock in the open market at $17 a share. The note is for one year, bears interest at 10%, and is guaranteed by Fay.
• On December 15, 2002, the ESOP distributed 6,000 shares of Fay common stock to employees of Fay in accordance with the plan formula.

82. In its 2002 income statement, how much should Fay report as compensation expense relating to the ESOP?
a. $184,000
b. $120,000
c. $ 84,000
d. $ 60,000

83. In Fay's December 31, 2002 balance sheet, how much should be reported as a reduction of shareholders' equity and as an endorsed note payable in respect of the ESOP?

	Reduction of shareholders' equity	Endorsed note payable
a.	$0	$0
b.	$0	$100,000
c.	$100,000	$0
d.	$100,000	$100,000

84. Zinc Co.'s adjusted trial balance at December 31, 2002, includes the following account balances:

Common stock, $3 par	$600,000
Additional paid-in capital	800,000
Treasury stock, at cost	50,000
Net unrealized loss on available-for-sale MES	20,000
Retained earnings: appropriated for uninsured earthquake losses	150,000
Retained earnings: unappropriated	200,000

What amount should Zinc report as total stockholders' equity in its December 31, 2002 balance sheet?

- a. $1,680,000
- b. $1,720,000
- c. $1,780,000
- d. $1,820,000

85. Rudd Corp. had 700,000 shares of common stock authorized and 300,000 shares outstanding at December 31, 2001. The following events occurred during 2002:

January 31	Declared 10% stock dividend
June 30	Purchased 100,000 shares
August 1	Reissued 50,000 shares
November 30	Declared 2-for-1 stock split

At December 31, 2002, how many shares of common stock did Rudd have outstanding?

- a. 560,000
- b. 600,000
- c. 630,000
- d. 660,000

86. Nest Co. issued 100,000 shares of common stock. Of these, 5,000 were held as treasury stock at December 31, 2001. During 2002, transactions involving Nest's common stock were as follows:

May 3	1,000 shares of treasury stock were sold.
August 6	10,000 shares of previously unissued stock were sold.
November 18	A 2-for-1 stock split took effect.

Laws in Nest's state of incorporation protect treasury stock from dilution. At December 31, 2002, how many shares of Nest's common stock were issued and outstanding?

	Shares	
	Issued	*Outstanding*
a.	220,000	212,000
b.	220,000	216,000
c.	222,000	214,000
d.	222,000	218,000

87. The following information pertains to Ali Corp. as of and for the year ended December 31, 2002:

Liabilities	$ 60,000
Stockholders' equity	$500,000
Shares of common stock issued and outstanding	10,000
Net income	$ 30,000

During 2002, Ali's officers exercised stock options for 1,000 shares of stock at an option price of $8 per share. What was the effect of exercising the stock options?

- a. Debt to equity ratio decreased to 12%.
- b. Earnings per share increased by $0.33.
- c. Asset turnover increased to 5.4%.
- d. No ratios were affected.

88. Selected information for Irvington Company is as follows:

	December 31	
	2001	*2002*
Preferred stock, 8%, par $100, non-convertible, noncumulative	$125,000	$125,000
Common stock	300,000	400,000
Retained earnings	75,000	185,000
Dividends paid on preferred stock for year ended	10,000	10,000
Net income for year ended	60,000	120,000

Irvington's return on common stockholders' equity, rounded to the nearest percentage point, for 2002 is

- a. 17%
- b. 19%
- c. 23%
- d. 25%

89. Hoyt Corp.'s current balance sheet reports the following stockholders' equity:

5% cumulative preferred stock, par value $100 per share; 2,500 shares issued and outstanding	$250,000
Common stock, par value $3.50 per share; 100,000 shares issued and outstanding	350,000
Additional paid-in capital in excess of par value of common stock	125,000
Retained earnings	300,000

Dividends in arrears on the preferred stock amount to $25,000. If Hoyt were to be liquidated, the preferred stockholders would receive par value plus a premium of $50,000. The book value per share of common stock is

- a. $7.75
- b. $7.50
- c. $7.25
- d. $7.00

90. Grid Corp. acquired some of its own common shares at a price greater than both their par value and original issue price but less than their book value. Grid uses the cost method of accounting for treasury stock. What is the impact of this acquisition on total stockholders' equity and the book value per common share?

	Total stockholders' equity	*Book value per share*
a.	Increase	Increase
b.	Increase	Decrease
c.	Decrease	Increase
d.	Decrease	Decrease

91. How are dividends per share for common stock used in the calculation of the following?

	Dividend per share payout ratio	*Earnings per share*
a.	Numerator	Numerator
b.	Numerator	Not used
c.	Denominator	Not used
d.	Denominator	Denominator

OTHER OBJECTIVE QUESTIONS

Problem 1   (10 to 15 minutes)

Required:

Items 1 through 10 require the candidate to select the best response from the responses to be selected.

Items to be answered	*Responses to be selected*
1. Par value method	A. Contains no potentially dilutive securities
2. Appropriations of retained earnings	B. A form of compensation which allows employees to receive stock or cash for the difference between the stated value and the market value
3. Stock split	C. Legal or contractual restrictions on the number of shares an employee may own
4. Simple capital structure	D. Issuance of additional shares in order to reduce the market value
5. If-converted method	E. Purchase by the corporation of its own stock
6. Scrip dividend	F. The value of treasury shares are recorded at cost of acquisition
7. Stock appreciation rights	G. A dividend paid which is considered a return of the shareholders' investment
8. Stock option	H. Actions by the board of directors to disclose amounts not available for dividends
9. Liquidating dividend	I. The balance of the treasury stock account reflects the par value
10. Treasury stock	J. A form of compensation which allows employees to purchase shares at a specified price
	K. A dividend issued in the form of a note payable
	L. A stock transaction resulting in a reduced number of shares outstanding and a higher market value
	M. Assumes convertible securities were converted at the beginning of the period

---

Problem 2   (15 to 25 minutes)

Min Co. is a publicly held company whose shares are traded in the over-the-counter market. The stockholders' equity accounts at December 31, 2001, had the following balances:

Preferred stock, $100 par value, 6% cumulative; 5,000 shares authorized; 2,000 issued and outstanding	$200,000
Common stock, $1 par value, 150,000 shares authorized; 100,000 issued and outstanding	100,000
Additional paid-in capital	800,000
Retained earnings	1,586,000
Total stockholders' equity	$2,686,000

Transactions during 2002 and other information relating to the stockholders' equity accounts were as follows:

- February 1, 2002—Issued 13,000 shares of common stock to Ram Co. in exchange for land. On the date issued, the stock had a market price of $11 per share. The land had a carrying value on Ram's books of $135,000, and an assessed value for property taxes of $90,000.

- March 1, 2002—Purchased 5,000 shares of its own common stock to be held as treasury stock for $14 per share. Min uses the cost method to account for treasury stock. Transactions in treasury stock are legal in Min's state of incorporation.

- May 10, 2002—Declared a property dividend of marketable securities held by Min to common shareholders. The securities had a carrying value of $600,000; fair value on relevant dates were

Date of declaration (May 10, 2002)	$720,000
Date of record (May 25, 2002)	758,000
Date of distribution (June 1, 2002)	736,000

- October 1, 2002—Reissued 2,000 shares of treasury stock for $16 per share.

- November 4, 2002—Declared a cash dividend of $1.50 per share to all common shareholders of record November 15, 2002. The dividend was paid on November 25, 2002.

- December 20, 2002—Declared the required annual cash dividend on preferred stock for 2002. The dividend was paid on January 5, 2003.

- January 16, 2003—Before closing the accounting records for 2002, Min became aware that no amortization had been recorded for 2001 for a patent purchased on July 1, 2001. The patent was properly capitalized at $320,000 and had an estimated useful life of eight years when purchased. Min's income tax rate is 30%. The appropriate correcting entry was recorded on the same day.

- Adjusted net income for 2002 was $838,000.

Required:

Items 1 through 8 represent amounts to be reported in Min's financial statements. **Items 9 and 10** represent other financial information. For all items, calculate the amounts requested. On the CPA exam, a list of numeric answers would be provided for the candidate to select from.

Items 1 through 4 represent amounts to be reported on Min's 2002 statement of retained earnings.

1. Prior period adjustment.

2. Preferred dividends.

3. Common dividends—cash.

4. Common dividends—property.

Items 5 through 8 represent amounts to be reported on Min's statement of stockholders' equity at December 31, 2002.

5. Number of common shares issued at December 31, 2002.

6. Amount of common stock issued.

7. Additional paid-in capital, including treasury stock transactions.

8. Treasury stock.

Items 9 and 10 represent other financial information for 2001 and 2002.

9. Book value per share at December 31, 2001, before prior period adjustment.

10. Numerator used in calculation of 2002 earnings per share for the year.

PROBLEMS

Problem 1   (15 to 25 minutes)

Field Co.'s stockholders' equity account balances at December 31, 2001, were as follows:

Common stock	$ 800,000
Additional paid-in capital	1,600,000
Retained earnings	1,845,000

The following 2002 transactions and other information relate to the stockholders' equity accounts:

- Field had 400,000 authorized shares of $5 par common stock, of which 160,000 shares were issued and outstanding.
- On March 5, 2002, Field acquired 5,000 shares of its common stock for $10 per share to hold as treasury stock. The shares were originally issued at $15 per share. Field uses the cost method to account for treasury stock. Treasury stock is permitted in Field's state of incorporation.
- On July 15, 2002, Field declared and distributed a property dividend of inventory. The inventory had a $75,000 carrying value and a $60,000 fair market value.
- On January 2, 2000, Field granted stock options to employees to purchase 20,000 shares of Field's common stock at $18 per share, which was the market price on that date. The options may be exercised within a three-year period beginning January 2, 2002. The measurement date is the same as the grant date. On October 1, 2002, employees exercised all 20,000 options when the market value of the stock was $25 per share. Field issued new shares to settle the transaction.
- Field's net income for 2002 was $240,000.
- Field intends to issue new stock options to key employees in 2003. Field's management is aware that SFAS 123, *Accounting for Stock-Based Compensation*, which was issued in 1995, discusses both the "intrinsic value" method and the "fair value" method of accounting for stock options. Field's management is unsure of the difference between the two methods.

Required:

a.   Prepare the stockholders' equity section of Field's December 31, 2002 balance sheet. Support all computations.

b.   In a brief memo to Field's management, explain how compensation cost is measured under both the "fair value" method and the "intrinsic value" method of accounting for stock options, and when the measured cost is recognized.

Problem 2   (15 to 25 minutes)

Columbine Co.'s ten-year convertible bonds were issued and dated October 1, 2002. Each $1,000 bond is convertible, at the holder's option, into 20 shares of Columbine's common stock. Columbine, a public company, had a net loss for the year. There was no change in the number of shares outstanding during the year.

Required:

a.   Describe and distinguish between basic and diluted earnings per share. Include in your discussion the meaning of dilutive securities.

b.   Determine whether to include the convertible bonds in computing 2002 diluted earnings per share.

MULTIPLE-CHOICE ANSWERS

1. a	__ __	20. a	__ __	39. a	__ __	58. d	__ __	77. c	__ __
2. b	__ __	21. c	__ __	40. a	__ __	59. b	__ __	78. a	__ __
3. d	__ __	22. c	__ __	41. d	__ __	60. b	__ __	79. c	__ __
4. d	__ __	23. b	__ __	42. c	__ __	61. c	__ __	80. a	__ __
5. a	__ __	24. c	__ __	43. c	__ __	62. b	__ __	81. b	__ __
6. c	__ __	25. d	__ __	44. a	__ __	63. b	__ __	82. c	__ __
7. a	__ __	26. d	__ __	45. c	__ __	64. d	__ __	83. d	__ __
8. d	__ __	27. b	__ __	46. c	__ __	65. b	__ __	84. a	__ __
9. a	__ __	28. c	__ __	47. c	__ __	66. a	__ __	85. a	__ __
10. b	__ __	29. c	__ __	48. c	__ __	67. d	__ __	86. a	__ __
11. d	__ __	30. b	__ __	49. c	__ __	68. a	__ __	87. a	__ __
12. c	__ __	31. b	__ __	50. b	__ __	69. b	__ __	88. c	__ __
13. c	__ __	32. d	__ __	51. c	__ __	70. b	__ __	89. d	__ __
14. d	__ __	33. d	__ __	52. b	__ __	71. d	__ __	90. c	__ __
15. a	__ __	34. b	__ __	53. c	__ __	72. c	__ __	91. b	__ __
16. c	__ __	35. a	__ __	54. d	__ __	73. d	__ __		
17. b	__ __	36. d	__ __	55. b	__ __	74. b	__ __		
18. c	__ __	37. b	__ __	56. b	__ __	75. c	__ __	1st: __/91 = __%
19. c	__ __	38. b	__ __	57. b	__ __	76. d	__ __	2nd: __/91 = __%

MULTIPLE-CHOICE ANSWER EXPLANATIONS

A. Common Stock

1. **(a)** When stock is issued for services, the transaction should be recorded at either the FMV of the stock issued or the FMV of the services received, whichever is more clearly determinable. The FMV of stock traded on a public exchange is a more objective, reliable measure than a normal billing rate for legal services, which is likely to be negotiable. If the transaction is valued at $140 per share, legal expense would be debited for $140,000 (1,000 x $140), common stock would be credited for the par value of $5,000 (1,000 x $5), and additional paid-in capital would be credited for the difference ($140,000 − $5,000 = $135,000).

2. **(b)** When stock is issued in combination with other securities (lump sum sales), the proceeds can be allocated by the **proportional method** or by the **incremental method**. If the FMV of each class of securities is determinable, the proceeds should be allocated to each class of securities based on their relative FMV. In the instances where the FMV of all classes of securities is not determinable, the incremental method should be used. The market value of the securities is used as a basis for those classes that are known, and the remainder of the lump sum is allocated to the class for which the market value is not known. In this problem, the FMV of the stock is unknown. As such, the incremental method must be used as follows:

Lump sum receipt	$110,000
FMV of bonds	40,000
Balance allocated to common stock	$ 70,000

As the par value of the common stock is $5,000 (1,000 shares x $5), $65,000 ($70,000 − $5,000) should be reported as additional paid-in capital on the issuance of the stock.

3. **(d)** The number of common shares outstanding is equal to the issued shares less treasury shares. Beck Corp. had 300,000 shares outstanding at 1/1/02. The purchase of treasury shares in 2002 reduced the number of shares outstanding to 225,000 (300,000 − 75,000). The preferred stock convertible into 100,000 shares of common stock is

recorded as preferred stock until it is **converted** by the stockholder.

4. **(d)** On February 1, 2002, when shares were issued at par for cash, the following journal entry would have been made:

Cash	(cash received)	
Common stock		(par)

On March 1, 2002, however, the issuance of 5,000 shares in settlement for legal services rendered would have been recorded as follows:

Legal fees	60,000	
Common stock ($10 x 5,000 shares)		50,000
Addl. paid-in capital		10,000

Per APB 29, stock issued for services (i.e., in a nonmonetary transaction) should be recorded at the fair market value of those services (in this case $60,000).

B. Preferred Stock

5. **(a)** When the common stock was issued, it was recorded at stated value with the excess recorded as additional paid-in capital.

Cash	600,000	
Common stock		20,000
Addl. paid-in capital		580,000

The preferred stock was recorded at par value with the excess credited to additional paid-in capital.

Cash	300,000	
Preferred stock		60,000
Addl. paid-in capital		240,000

Therefore, at 4/1/02, the balances are common stock ($20,000), preferred stock ($60,000), and additional paid-in capital ($580,000 + $240,000 = $820,000).

6. **(c)** In a lump-sum issuance of common and preferred stock, the proceeds ($80,000) are generally allocated based on the relative fair market values of the securities issued. The FMV of the convertible preferred stock is $54,000 ($27 x 2,000) and the FMV of the common stock is

$36,000 ($36 x 1,000). The proceeds are allocated as follows:

Convertible preferred	$\dfrac{\$54,000}{\$90,000}$	x	$80,000	=	$48,000
Common	$\dfrac{\$36,000}{\$90,000}$	x	$80,000	=	$32,000

7. (a) All 5,000 shares of convertible preferred stock were converted to common stock at a rate of 3 shares of common for every share of preferred. Therefore, 15,000 shares of common stock were issued (5,000 x 3). The common stock account is credited for the par value of these shares (15,000 x $25 = $375,000). APIC – CS ($550,000 – $375,000 = $175,000) is credited for the difference between the carrying amount of the preferred stock (5,000 x $110 = $550,000) and the par value of the common stock. The journal entry is

Preferred stock	500,000	
APIC-PS	50,000	
Common stock		375,000
APIC-CS		175,000

Note that the $40 market value of the common stock is ignored. The book value method must be used for conversion of preferred stock, so no gains or losses can be recognized.

8. (d) Per APB 14, when an issuance of debt, or in this case preferred stock, contains detachable common stock warrants the total proceeds from the sale should be allocated to both the preferred stock and the detachable stock warrants. This treatment arises due to the separability of the stock and the detachable warrants. The allocation of the proceeds is based on the relative fair values of both the stock and the warrants at the time of the issuance. However, in instances where only one of the fair values is known, the known fair value will be used to allocate proceeds to the security in which the fair value is determinable. The remainder is then allocated to the security for which the fair value is unknown. Therefore, because only the fair value of the warrants is known, answer (d) is correct. Answers (a) and (b) are incorrect because fair market value is used to allocate proceeds to the warrants, not the total proceeds or excess proceeds over par value. Answer (c) is incorrect because proceeds are allocated in proportion to both fair values, if determinable, not the fair market value and par value.

9. (a) When the preferred stock and detachable warrants are issued, the following journal entry is made:

Cash	(cash received)
Preferred stock	(par value)
APIC—preferred stock	(FMV of preferred stock – par value)
APIC—stock warrants	(plug)

When the stock warrants are exercised, the following journal entry is made:

Cash	(cash received)
APIC—stock warrants	(original amount credited)
Common stock	(par value)
APIC—common stock	(plug)

Therefore, stockholders' equity is increased by the cash received upon the exercise of the common stock warrants. The carrying amount of the warrants increased total stockholders' equity when the preferred stock was issued, not when the warrants were issued.

C. Stock Subscriptions

10. (b) When no par common stock is sold on a subscription basis at a price above the stock's stated value, the stock is not issued until the full subscription price is received. The journal entry on the subscription contract date would be

Cash	(amount received—if any)
Subscription receivable	(balance due)
Common stock subscribed	(stated value)
Additional paid-in capital	(plug)

The journal entry on the date the balance of the subscription is collected and the common stock issued would be

Cash	(balance due)
Common stock subscribed	(stated value)
Common stock	(stated value)
Subscription receivable	(balance due)

Additional paid-in capital increases on the date that the stock is subscribed, not paid for or issued.

11. (d) When stock is sold on a subscription basis, the full price of the stock is not received initially, and the stock is not issued until the full subscription price is received. On the subscription contract date of December 1, 2001, the journal entry would be

Cash	(amount received)
Subscriptions receivable	(balance due)
Common stock subscribed	(par)
Additional paid-in capital	(plug)

D. Treasury Stock Transactions

12. (c) Under the cost method, the treasury stock account is debited for the cost of the shares acquired. If the treasury shares are reissued at a price in excess of the acquisition cost, the excess is credited to an account titled Paid-in Capital from Treasury Stock. This question refers to it as Additional Paid-in Capital because typically companies do not segregate the two accounts on the balance sheet for reporting purposes. If the treasury shares are reissued at less than the acquisition cost, the deficiency is treated first as a reduction to any paid-in capital related to previous reissuances or retirements of treasury stock of the same class. If the balance in Paid-in Capital from Treasury Stock is not sufficient to absorb the deficiency, the remainder is recorded as a reduction of retained earnings. As the shares in this question were reissued at a price in excess of the acquisition price, the following journal entry would be made at the time of reissue:

Cash (3,000 x $50)	150,000	
Treasury stock (3,000 x $36)		108,000
Additional paid-in capital		
($150,000 – $108,000)		42,000

13. (c) The entry that Rama made on acquisition of treasury stock was as follows using the **cost method:**

Treasury stock		
(20,000 x $12)	240,000	
Cash		240,000

When some of the shares are later reissued, the entry is

Cash (15,000 x $10)	150,000	
Retained earnings	30,000	
Treasury stock		
(15,000 x $12)		180,000

It is assumed there was no balance in APIC—Treasury stock prior to this entry. If the problem had stated there was a credit balance, APIC—Treasury stock would be debited before retained earnings to the extent a credit balance existed in APIC—Treasury stock. SFAS 5 requires disclosure when retained earnings are legally restricted. In this case, the net treasury stock account balance is $60,000 ($240,000 – $180,000), and this is the amount of retained earnings that must be disclosed as legally restricted.

14. **(d)**   The unadjusted stockholders' equity section shows a total of $2,000,000. However, analysis of the current asset section reveals that United has incorrectly classified $300,000 of treasury stock as a current asset. Although this account has a debit balance, it is **not an asset**. Treasury stock should be reported as a reduction of stockholders' equity. Therefore, total equity at 12/31/02 should be $1,700,000 ($2,000,000 – $300,000).

15. **(a)**   Under the cost method, when treasury stock is acquired, **treasury stock** is debited and **cash** is credited for the cost.

Treasury stock	100,000	
Cash		100,000

When the treasury stock is resold at an amount above cost, **cash** is debited for the proceeds, **treasury stock** is credited at cost, and the difference is credited to **additional paid-in capital—treasury stock**.

Cash	25,000	
Treasury stock		20,000
APIC—TS		5,000

Neither of these two transactions affect **retained earnings**. Therefore, 12/31/02 retained earnings consists of the 12/31/01 balance ($300,000) plus 2002 net income ($60,000), or $360,000.

16. **(c)**   The requirement is to determine the balance in the paid-in capital from treasury stock account at 12/31/02. Using the par value method, treasury stock is debited for par value (5,000 x $10, or $50,000) when purchased. Any excess over par from the original issuance (5,000 x $4, or $20,000) is removed from the appropriate paid-in capital account. In effect, the total original issuance price (5,000 x $14, or $70,000) is charged to the two accounts. Any difference between the original issue price ($70,000) and the cost of the treasury stock (5,000 x $11, or $55,000) is credited to paid-in capital from treasury stock, as illustrated below.

Treasury stock	50,000		(5,000 x $10)
APIC	20,000		(5,000 x $ 4)
Cash		55,000	(5,000 x $11)
PIC—Treasury stock		15,000	($70,000 – $55,000)

17. **(b)**   When Dee Inc. issued common stock at a price in excess of its par value, the following journal entry was made:

Cash	(Cash received)
Common stock	(Par)
Additional paid-in capital	(Excess of cash capital received over par)

When Dee Inc. acquires treasury stock using the par method for an amount exceeding the issue price the following journal entry is made:

Treasury stock	(Par)
Additional paid-in capital	(Excess of original issue price over par)
Retained earnings	(Excess of acquisition price over issue price)
Cash	(Cash paid)

Net common stock decreases by the par value of treasury stock acquired. Additional paid-in capital decreases by the excess of the original issue price over the par value. Retained earnings decreases by the excess of the acquisition price over the original issue price.

18. **(c)**   In this case, the par value method does not report a greater amount for additional paid-in capital or retained earnings than the cost method. The entries for an acquisition of treasury shares at greater than par but less than the original issue price are as follows:

Cost method		*Par value method*	
Treasury stock	xxx	Treasury stock	xxx
Cash	xxx	PIC in excess of par	xxx
		Cash	xxx
		PIC from treasury stock	xxx

Since under the par value method the original paid-in capital in excess of par must be removed from the accounts upon reacquisition, the par value method actually reports a decrease in additional paid-in capital. On the other hand, under the cost method no change in additional paid-in capital is recorded. There is no change in retained earnings under either method.

E. Retirement of Stock

19. **(c)**   When accounting for the retirement of stock, common stock and additional paid-in capital are removed from the books based on the original issuance of the stock. Cash is credited for the cost of the shares. Any difference is debited to **retained earnings** or credited to **paid-in capital from retirement**. The entry in this case is

Common stock	20,000 (2,000 x $10)	
APIC	180,000 (2,000 x $90)	
Retained earnings	100,000 (2,000 x $50)	
Cash		300,000

Therefore, APIC should be debited for $180,000 and retained earnings should be debited for $100,000.

20. **(a)**   In this problem, Luna Corp. is exchanging its marketable equity securities (MES) for its preferred stock (i.e., they are retiring some of their preferred stock by exchanging MES). Upon disposition of the MES, a gain of $70,000, which is the difference between the carrying amount ($80,000) and the FMV ($150,000), must be recognized. Upon retirement of the stock, the preferred stock is debited for the $100,000 par amount (5,000 shares x $20 par). The additional paid-in capital (APIC) is debited for $7,500, which is 1/4 of the original APIC (i.e., 5,000 of the 20,000 shares were retired). The remainder of the FMV of the preferred stock ($42,500 = $150,000 – $100,000 – $7,500) is debited to retained earnings.

21. **(c)**   When accounting for the retirement of treasury stock that was initially recorded using the cost method, common stock and additional paid-in capital are removed from the books based on the original issuance of the stock. Treasury stock is credited for the cost of the shares acquired. Any difference is debited to retained earnings or credited to paid-in capital from retirement. In this problem, common stock should be debited for $125,000 (50,000 shares x $2.50), and the common stock outstanding at December 31, 2001, is $415,000 ($540,000 – $125,000).

22. **(c)**   The requirement is to determine which of the statements correctly identifies an effect of the acquisition and retirement of common stock. The entry to record the retirement of common stock appears as follows:

Common stock (par)		
Additional paid-in capital	xxx	
Retained earnings	xxx	
Cash		xxx

Additional paid-in capital is debited to the extent it exists. In this case, based on the original issuance, the additional paid-in capital (APIC) balance was $15 per share on the shares retired. When stock is repurchased, if the APIC balance is depleted to zero, retained earnings must also be debited. In this case, retained earnings would not be needed, however. Common stock would be debited for $10 per share and additional paid-in capital would be debited for $10 a share. Excess APIC remains, so retained earnings are not needed to retire the stock. When common stock is repurchased and retired, additional paid-in capital decreases. When common stock is retired, net income is never affected; only stockholders' equity balances are affected. If retained earnings are needed to retire stock, the account decreases, not increases.

F. Dividends

23. (b) Since this is an investment accounted for on the cost basis, the dividend income should be the amount of cash dividends received. Since Plack Co. had 12,000 shares at the time the cash dividend was paid, the total amount of cash dividends received is $24,000 (12,000 x $2.00).

24. (c) When preferred stock is participating, there may be different agreements as to how the participation feature is to be executed. However, in the absence of any specific agreement, the following procedure should be used:

After the preferred stock is allocated its current year dividend, the common stock will receive a "like" percentage of par value outstanding. If there are remaining declared dividends, this amount should be shared by both the preferred and common stock in proportion to the par value dollars outstanding of each stock as follows:

Current year's dividend:		
Preferred, 5% of $300,000		
(30,000 shares x $10 Par)	$15,000	
Common, 5% of $200,000		
(200,000 shares x $1 Par)	10,000	$25,000
Amount available for participation		
($100,000 – $25,000)		$ 75,000
Par value of stock that is to participate		
($300,000 + $200,000)		$500,000
Proportional share of participating dividend:		

Preferred	$\dfrac{\$300,000}{\$500,000}$	x	75,000	=	$ 45,000
Common	$\dfrac{\$200,000}{\$500,000}$	x	75,000	=	$ 30,000

Thus, the dividends payable to common shareholders is $40,000 ($10,000 + $30,000).

25. (d) For **cumulative** preferred stock, dividends not paid in **any** year will accumulate and must be paid in a later year before any dividends can be paid to common stockholders. The unpaid prior year dividends are called "dividends in arrears." The balance of dividends in arrears should be disclosed in the financial statements rather than accrued, as they are not considered a liability until they are declared. Dividends in arrears at 12/31/02 total $20,000, as computed below.

2001	$300,000 x 5%	=	$15,000
2002	$300,000 x 5%	=	15,000
Total cumulative preferred dividends			$30,000
Less 2002 dividend payment			(10,000)
Balance of dividends in arrears			$20,000

Answer (c) is incorrect because dividends in arrears are not considered to be a liability until they are declared. They should be disclosed parenthetically or in the notes to the financial statements. Answer (b) is incorrect because the total dividends amount needs to reflect both the 2001 and 2002 unpaid dividends since it is cumulative preferred stock. Answer (a) is incorrect because the dividends in arrears would not be considered a liability until they are declared and the $15,000 amount is the incorrect balance as discussed above.

26. (d) The interest is not an expense or liability until incurred, thus, none of it is recorded on April 1. The April 1 entry would be

Retained earnings	100,000	
Scrip dividends payable		100,000

By December 31 (the year-end for this calendar-year company), nine months' interest had been incurred, which would not be paid until the maturity date of 3/31/03. The $7,500 of interest expense ($100,000 x 10% x 9/12) must be accrued at 12/31/02 with the following entry:

Interest expense	7,500	
Interest payable		7,500

27. (b) Dividends that are based on funds other than retained earnings are considered to be liquidating dividends. The cash dividend declared of $400,000 is first assumed to be a return **on** capital for the distribution of the retained earnings balance of $300,000. The excess $400,000 dividend – $300,000 RE = $100,000 is considered to be a return **of** capital or a liquidating dividend rather than a return **on** capital. Note that the amount of liquidating dividend also equals the balance in accumulated depletion. Companies in the extractive industries may pay dividends equal to the accumulated income **and** depletion.

28. (c) Per APB 29, a transfer of a nonmonetary asset to a stockholder or to another entity in a nonreciprocal transfer should be recorded at the fair value of the asset transferred, and a gain or loss should be recognized on the disposition of the asset. The fair value of the nonmonetary asset distributed is measured by the amount that would be realized in an outright sale at or near the time of distribution. In this case, a gain should be recognized for the difference between the fair value of $2.50 per share and the carrying amount of $2 per share, or a total gain of $50,000 [100,000 x ($2.50 – $2.00)].

29. (c) Per APB 29, a transfer of a nonmonetary asset to a stockholder or to another entity in a nonreciprocal transfer should be recorded at the fair market value of the asset transferred, and a gain or loss should be recognized on the disposition of the asset. At the date of declaration, Nilo records

Marketable securities	18,000	
Gain on disposition of securities		18,000
Retained earnings (dividends)	78,000	
Property dividends payable		78,000

At the date of distribution, Nilo records

Property dividends payable	78,000	
Marketable securities		78,000

After all nominal accounts are closed, the effect on retained earnings from the above entries would be $60,000 ($78,000 debit to retained earnings less $18,000 credit to retained earnings when the "gain on disposition" account is closed out).

30. (b) A stock split is **not** a dividend. Stock splits change the number of shares outstanding and the par value per share. Par value per share is reduced in proportion to the increase in the number of shares. Therefore, the total par value outstanding does not change, and no journal entry is required. The only dividend to be reported in Long's 2002 statement of stockholders' equity is the 12/15 cash dividend. The stock split increased the number of shares outstanding to 200,000 (100,000 x 2), so the amount of the cash dividend is $100,000 (200,000 x $.50).

31. (b) The requirement is to determine the effect of a cash dividend on stockholders' equity at the three dates listed. On the date of declaration, December 15, 2002, the following entry should be made:

Retained earnings	xxx	
Dividends payable		xxx

Thus, at December 15, 2002, stockholders' equity is reduced due to the debit to retained earnings. On December 31, 2002, there is no effect on stockholders' equity because an entry would not be recorded. On January 12, 2003, the following entry would be made:

Dividends payable	xxx	
Cash		xxx

The net effect of this entry is to decrease assets and liabilities by an equal amount. Thus, stockholders' equity (or net assets) would be unaffected.

32. (d) Any dividend not based on earnings must be a reduction of corporate paid-in capital and, to that extent, it is a liquidating dividend. The following journal entries would be made for this situation:

At date of declaration:

Additional paid-in capital	100,000	
Dividends payable		100,000

At date of payment:

Dividends payable	100,000	
Cash		100,000

Thus, a liquidating dividend would decrease Ole's paid-in capital, not its retained earnings.

33. (d) A property dividend is a nonreciprocal transfer of nonmonetary assets between an enterprise and its owners. APB 29 requires that "nonreciprocal transfers of nonmonetary assets to a stockholder or another entity shall be recorded at the fair value of the asset transferred. Additionally, a gain or loss shall be recognized on the disposition of the asset." Accordingly, Evie Corp. should record the following journal entries to reflect the property dividend:

At the date of declaration:

Loss on decline in inventory value		
(Carrying amount – Market value)	xxx	
Merchandise inventory		xxx

Retained earnings (market value)	xxx	
Property dividends payable		xxx

At the date of distribution:

Property dividends payable	xxx	
Merchandise inventory		xxx

The loss recorded in the above journal entry does not qualify as unusual and infrequent, thus it is not an extraordinary item. The loss should be reported as a reduction in income before extraordinary items.

34. (b) The requirement is to determine the amount to be debited to retained earnings for these stock dividends. Per ARB 43, chap 7B, the issuance of a stock dividend less than **20-25%** (a "small" stock dividend) requires that the **market value** of the stock be transferred from retained earnings, and a dividend greater than **20-25%** (a "large" stock dividend) requires the **par value** of the stock to be transferred from retained earnings. Thus, a 10% stock dividend is considered to be "small" and should be transferred from retained earnings at the FMV of $15,000. A 28% stock dividend is considered to be "large" and should be transferred at the par value of $30,800. The aggregate amount to be transferred from retained earnings is $45,800.

35. (a) When the stock dividend is less than 20-25% of the common shares outstanding at the time of the declaration, generally accepted accounting principles require that the FMV of the stock issued be transferred from retained earnings. At the date of declaration, the following entry would be made:

Retained earnings (Stock dividends declared)		
(.05 x 10,000 shares x $5)	2,500	
Common stock dividend distributable		
(.05 x 10,000 x $2)		1,000
Additional paid-in capital (plug)		1,500

Note from the entry above that no asset or liability has been affected. The entry merely reflects a reclassification within the equity accounts. When a balance sheet is prepared between the dates of declaration and distribution, the common stock dividend distributable should be shown in the stockholders' equity section as an addition to capital stock.

G. Stock Splits

36. (d) ARB 43, chap 7, defines a stock dividend as an issuance by a corporation of its own common shares to its common shareholders without consideration...to give the recipient shareholders evidence of a part of their respective interests in accumulated corporate earnings without distribution of cash or other property. A stock split is defined as an issuance by a corporation of common shares to its common shareholders without consideration...prompted mainly by a desire to increase the number of outstanding shares for the purpose of effecting a reduction in their unit market price and, thereby, of obtaining wider distribution and improved marketability of the shares. Thus, neither of these transactions results in a transfer of assets among the shareholders and the corporation. While the allocation of stockholders' equity among the various accounts (retained earnings, common stock, and additional paid-in capital) will change, the **total** stockholders' equity is **not** affected.

37. (b) The requirement is to determine the balance of additional paid-in capital immediately after a reverse stock split. Stock splits change the number of shares outstanding and the par value per share, but the total par value outstanding does not change. Stock splits do not affect any account balances, including additional paid-in capital. Therefore, the balance of additional paid-in capital remains at $450,000.

38. (b) A stock split does not affect either the balance of the additional paid-in capital or the retained earnings accounts. The number of shares outstanding and the par value per share merely change in proportion to each other. When this occurs, only a memorandum entry is made.

H. Appropriations of Retained Earnings (Reserves)

39. (a) The requirement is to determine the amount of appropriated retained earnings Eagle should report in its 2002 balance sheet. The entry to record the appropriation of retained earnings in 2002 for the construction of a new plant is as follows:

RE (or Unappropriated RE)	$1,200,000	
RE Appropriated for plant expansion		$1,200,000

The cash restricted for the retirement of bonds due in 2003 should **not** be reported as an appropriation of retained earnings because the facts in the question do not indicate that appropriation was made by management. SFAS 5 requires that when an appropriation is no longer needed, it must be returned directly to unappropriated retained earnings by reversing the entry that created it. Therefore, when the office building was completed in 2002, the following entry was made:

RE Appropriated for plant expansion	$1,750,000	
RE (or Unappropriated RE)		$1,750,000

The total cost to complete the building has no effect on appropriated retained earnings.

40. (a) Retained earnings are typically appropriated due to legal requirements, contractual requirements, or through the discretion of the board of directors. Dividends in arrears are not considered a liability to the company, and retained earnings would not be appropriated for this amount. In many cases, retained earnings must be appropriated for an amount equal to the cost of treasury stock acquired. However, this appropriation would be removed upon reissuance of the treasury stock.

41. (d) SFAS 5, states that appropriations of retained earnings are not prohibited provided that the appropriation is clearly identified as such in the stockholders' equity section of the balance sheet. Costs or losses cannot be charged to an appropriation of retained earnings. A contingent loss that is probable and reasonably estimable should be accrued as a loss and liability under the guidance of SFAS 5.

I.1. Stock Options

42. (c) Under APB 25, employee compensation expense as the result of a stock option plan is calculated as the difference between the option price and the market price **at the date of grant** times the number of option shares.

$$\text{Option shares} \times \left(\text{Market price} - \text{Option price}\right) = \text{Total compensation expense}$$
$$3,000 \times (\$30 - \$20) = \$30,000$$

The total compensation expense must be recognized over the period for which the option plan represents compensation. If not otherwise specified, the required service period (two

years) is assumed to be the period benefited. Therefore, 2002 compensation expense is $15,000 ($30,000 ÷ 2). Note that compensation expense is not affected by changes in the market value of the stock after the measurement date.

43. (c) Under APB 25, total compensation expense as a result of a stock option plan is calculated as the difference between the option price and the market price at the date of grant times the number of option shares.

$$\text{Option shares} \times \left(\text{Market price} - \text{Option price}\right) = \text{Total compensation expense}$$
$$10,000 \times (\$47 - \$38) = \$90,000$$

The total compensation expense must be recognized over the period for which the option plan represents compensation. Therefore, 2001 compensation expense is $30,000 ($90,000 ÷ 3 years). Note that APB 25 states that the cost of treasury stock distributed in an option plan does not determine compensation expense.

44. (a) The net increase in stockholders' equity (SE) as a result of the grant and exercise of the options is equal to the increase in cash (1,000 shares x $20 option price = $20,000). The journal entry to record the options has no effect on SE because a SE account will be credited while a contra SE account will be debited as follows:

Deferred compensation	30,000	
Paid-in capital stock options		30,000

[1000 shares x ($50 market price – $20 option price)]

The entry to recognize compensation expense has no effect on SE because the debit decreases SE while the credit increases SE by reducing the contra account as follows:

Compensation expense	30,000	
Deferred compensation		30,000

The only entry which does affect SE is the entry for the exercise of the options, which decreases SE by $30,000 while increasing it by $50,000 (a net increase of $20,000).

Cash (1,000 x $20)	20,000	
Paid-in capital stock options (1,000 x $30)	30,000	
Common stock (1,000 x $10)		10,000
Paid-in capital in X of PV (plug)		40,000

Thus, the net increase in stockholders' equity is $20,000.

NOTE: The concept tested in this question would apply in the same way under SFAS 123. Therefore, although compensation expense would differ under the new standard, the answer would be the same.

I.2. Stock Appreciation Rights

45. (c) The 20,000 stock appreciation rights (SAR) each entitle the holder to receive cash equal to the excess of the market price of the stock on the exercise date over the market price on the grant date ($30). Since these SAR are payment for past services and are exercisable immediately, there is no required service period. Therefore, the expense computed at 12/31/02 does **not** have to be allocated to more than one period. At 12/31/02, compensation expense is measured based on the excess of the 12/31/02 market price ($45) over the predetermined price ($30), resulting in compensation expense of $300,000 [20,000 ($45 – $30)]. Note that **if** Dean was **required** to work three years **before** the SAR could be exercised, the expense would be allocated over the three years of required service ($300,000 x 1/3 = $100,000).

J. Stock Compensation under SFAS 123

46. (c) Per APB 25 or SFAS 123, when accounting for stock compensation plans, total compensation expense is computed as the excess of the market price of the stock over the amount contributed by employees. In this case, the market value of the 150,000 shares issued in 2002 is $1,050,000, and the employees' contributions for these shares is $350,000. Therefore, Wall should recognize $700,000 ($1,050,000 – $350,000) as expense in 2002 for the stock compensation plan.

47. (c) According to SFAS 123, *Accounting for Stock Option Employee Compensation Plans*, the rate of interest used to discount both the exercise price and dividends is the risk-free interest rate.

48. (c) Using the Black-Scholes method, it is more than likely that deferred compensation expense would be measured even if the market value and the option price are equal. Deferred compensation is not measured under APB 25 if the market price is equal to the option price.

49. (c) If the stock options are for past services, as indicated when the options are immediately exercisable by the holders, compensation cost must be fully expensed at the grant date. Answer (a) is incorrect because usually deferred compensation expense is recognized. Answer (b) is incorrect because deferred compensation expense is recognized when service has not yet been provided. Answer (d) is incorrect because when options are provided for prior service compensation expense must immediately be recognized.

50. (b) SFAS 123 requires that footnote disclosures be presented in the financial statements of entities that do not adopt SFAS 123, which effectively will show what the effect of adoption would have been. This includes pro forma net income and earnings per share reflecting the difference in compensation cost and the related tax effect of using SFAS 123 as opposed to APB 25.

51. (c) SFAS 123 significantly expanded the disclosures which are required by entities having stock compensation arrangements, and this expansion applies as well, for the most part, to those companies that continue to employ APB 25 for financial statement purposes. Thus, all three items listed are required to be disclosed.

52. (b) Accounting for stock-based compensation under the minimum value method under SFAS 123 is as follows:

Current market value per share	$75.00
Less: Present value of exercise price ($75 x .747)	56.025
Present value of expected dividends ($3 x 4.212)	12.636
Equals	6.339
Times # of options	x 20,000
Deferred compensation expense	$126,780

53. (c) Under the provisions of SFAS 123, dividends or dividend equivalents on options which vest are to be accounted for as other dividends—that is, charged against retained earnings—but those paid on options which do not vest are deemed to be compensation expense. The reporting entity can either estimate what fraction of options will vest and allocate such dividend equivalents between retained earnings and compensation expense accordingly, or it can charge the entire amount to retained earnings and account

for forfeitures as they occur, by reversing the charge from retained earnings to compensation cost.

54. (d) Under both APB 25 and SFAS 123, compensation expense should be recognized on a straight-line basis over the vesting period.

K. Basic Earnings Per Share

55. (b) The formula for basic earnings per share (BEPS) is

$$\frac{\underset{\text{net income}}{\$1,000,000} - \underset{\text{preferred dividends}}{\$50,000}}{100,000 \text{ common shares outstanding}} = \$9.50$$

In calculating the numerator, the claims of preferred shareholders against 2002 earnings should be deducted to arrive at the 2002 earnings attributable to common shareholders. This amount is 50,000 (5% x $100 x 10,000 shares). The $50,000 preferred dividends in arrears is not deducted to compute the numerator in determining 2002 BEPS. This is because the $50,000 dividends in arrears is a claim of preferred shareholders against 2001 earnings and would reduce 2001 BEPS.

56. (b) The formula for basic earnings per share (BEPS) is

$$\frac{\underset{\text{net income}}{\$500,000} - \underset{\text{preferred dividends}}{10,000}}{200,000 \text{ common shares outstanding}} = \$2.45$$

In calculating the numerator, the claims of preferred shareholders against 2002 earnings should be deducted to arrive at the 2002 earnings attributable to common shareholders. This amount is $10,000 ($250,000 x 4%). During 2001, the BEPS numerator would have been reduced by $10,000 even though no preferred dividends were declared, because the cumulative feature means that $10,000 of 2001 earnings are reserved for, and will ultimately be paid to, preferred stockholders. In 2002, the 2001 dividends in arrears are paid, as well as $6,000 of the $10,000 2002 preferred dividend. Even though only $6,000 is paid, the entire $10,000 is subtracted for reasons explained above.

57. (b) SFAS 128 states that for EPS purposes, shares of stock issued as a result of stock dividends or splits should be considered outstanding for the entire period in which they were issued. Therefore, both the original 20,000 shares and the additional 20,000 issued in the 4/1 stock split are treated as outstanding for the entire year (20,000 x 2 = 40,000). The 7/1 issuance of 10,000 shares results in a weighted-average of 5,000 shares (10,000 x 6/12) because the shares were outstanding for only six months during the year. Therefore, Jet should use 45,000 shares (40,000 + 5,000) to calculate EPS.

58. (d) The computation of weighted-average shares outstanding is

Date	# of shares		Fraction		WA
1/1	30,000	x	12/12	=	30,000
2/1	3,000	x	12/12	=	3,000
3/1	9,000	x	12/12	=	9,000
7/1	8,000	x	6/12	=	4,000
					46,000

The 3,000 shares issued as a result of a stock dividend are weighted at 12/12 instead of 11/12 because for EPS purposes stock dividends are treated as if they occurred at the beginning of the year. Similarly, the shares issued in a pooling of interests are treated as if outstanding the entire year for BEPS purposes (weighted at 12/12 instead of 10/12).

59. (b) The formula for computing BEPS for a simple capital structure is

$$\frac{\text{Net income} - \text{Applicable pref. stock dividends}}{\text{Weighted-average \# of common shares outstanding}}$$

Net income is $410,000 and $350,000 in 2002 and 2001, respectively, and there are no preferred dividends. The weighted-average number of common shares outstanding must be computed for 2002. Stock dividends and stock splits are handled retroactively for comparability. The 2002 computation is

Dates	Number of shares		Fraction	WA
1/1 to 3/31	100,000 x 2 =	200,000	3/12	50,000
4/1 to 6/30	(100,000 + 20,000) x 2 =	240,000	3/12	60,000
7/1 to 12/31	120,000 x 2 =	240,000	6/12	120,000
				230,000

The 2001 weighted-average of 100,000 is retroactively restated to 200,000 for comparability. Therefore, the BEPS amounts are

2002	*2001*
$\frac{\$410,000}{230,000} = \$1.78$	$\frac{\$350,000}{200,000} = \$1.75$

60. (b) Per SFAS 128, earnings per share must be shown on the face of the income statement for income from continuing operations and net income. Discontinued operations, extraordinary items, and cumulative effect of change in accounting principle may be shown on the income statement or in the notes.

61. (c) Per SFAS 128, if the number of common shares outstanding increases as a result of a stock dividend or stock split or decreases as a result of a reverse split, the computations of EPS should give retroactive recognition for all periods presented. If these events take place after the close of the period but before completion of the financial report, the per share computations should be based on the new number of shares. Note that when per share computations reflect such changes in the number of shares after the close of the period, this fact should be disclosed.

L. Diluted Earnings Per Share

62. (b) The requirement is to determine the number of shares that should be used in computing 2002 diluted earnings per share. The first step is to compute the weighted-average number of common shares outstanding. 300,000 shares were outstanding the entire year, and 50,000 more shares were outstanding for six months, resulting in a weighted-average of 325,000 [300,000 + (50,000 x 6/12)]. Second, the stock options increase the number of shares used in the computation **only** if they are dilutive. The stock options are dilutive because the exercise price is less than the market value. Thus, the denominator effect of the options must be computed. This is done using the **treasury stock method,** as illustrated below.

Assumed proceeds (40,000 x $15)	$600,000
Shares issued	40,000
Shares reacquired ($600,000 ÷ $20)	(30,000)
Shares issued, not reacquired	10,000

Therefore, the number of shares used for computing diluted earnings per share is 335,000 (325,000 + 10,000).

63. (b) Diluted earnings per share is based on common stock and all dilutive potential common shares. To determine if a security is dilutive, EPS, including the effect of the dilutive security, must be compared to the basic EPS. In this case, basic EPS is $7.45.

$$\frac{850,000\,(\text{NI}) - 30,000\,(\text{pref.div.})}{110,000\,\text{shares}} = \$7.45$$

The effect of the convertible preferred stock is to increase the numerator by $30,000 ($3.00 dividend per share x 10,000 shares) for the amount of the preferred dividends that would not be paid (assuming conversion) and increase the denominator by 20,000 shares. This security is dilutive because it decreases the EPS from $7.45 to $6.54.

$$\frac{850,000 - 30,000 + 30,000}{110,000 + 20,000} = \$6.54$$

If the EPS increases due to the inclusion of a security, that security is antidilutive and should not be included.

64. (d) The requirement is to compute the diluted earnings per share for 2002. Therefore, **all** potential common shares that **reduce** current EPS must be included in the computation. The formula for diluted EPS is

$$\frac{\text{Net income available to common shareholders}}{\text{Weighted-average common shares outstanding}}$$

The net income available to common shareholders is $3,200,000. This is the net income of $3,400,000 less the preferred stock dividend of $200,000. The weighted-average common shares outstanding is 1,250,000. This is computed as the actual common shares outstanding for the full year of 1,200,000 plus the contingent common shares of 50,000 that were outstanding for the full year because the contingency was incurred in 2001. Thus,

$$\text{Diluted EPS} = \frac{\$3,200,000}{1,250,000} = \$2.56$$

65. (b) The effect of convertible bonds is included in diluted EPS under the if converted method, if they are dilutive. The bonds are dilutive as shown below.

$$\text{Basic EPS} = \frac{\$35,000}{(1/2)10,000 + (1/2)14,000} = \$2.92$$

$$\frac{\text{Incremental}}{\text{per share effect}} = \frac{(7\% \times \$10,000) - 30\%\ (7\% \times \$10,000)}{200\ \text{shares per bond}} = \frac{\$490}{200} = \$2.45$$

Since $2.45 < $2.92, the bonds are dilutive. Under the if converted method, the assumption is made that the bonds were converted at the beginning of the current year (1/1) or later in the current year if the bonds were issued during the current year. In this case, conversion is assumed for the first six months of 2002 only because the bonds were actually converted on July 1. Under their assumed conversion, the numerator would increase because bond interest expense would not have been incurred for the first six months of the year [1/2 ($14,000 – 30% x $14,000) = $4,900]. The denominator would increase because the 4,000 shares (20 x 200) would have been outstanding for the first six months of the year (4,000 x 6/12 = 2,000). Therefore, diluted EPS is $2.85.

$$\frac{\$35,000 + \$4,900}{12,000 + 2,000} = \frac{\$39,900}{14,000} = \$2.85$$

66. **(a)** Diluted EPS takes into account the effect of all dilutive potential common shares that were outstanding during the period. Thus, the possible conversion of convertible bonds would be included because they are dilutive (i.e., EPS would be reduced), but the possible exercise of common stock options would not be included because they are antidilutive (i.e., EPS would be increased). Diluted EPS = $15.00 – $.75 = $14.25.

67. **(d)** The requirement is to determine the treatment of nonconvertible cumulative preferred dividends in determining diluted EPS. Per SFAS 128, dividends on nonconvertible cumulative preferred shares should be deducted from net income whether an actual liability exists or not. This is because cumulative preferred stock owners must receive any dividends in arrears before future dividend distributions can be made to common stockholders.

68. **(a)** Per SFAS 128, the if converted method of computing earnings per share assumes that convertible securities are converted at the beginning of the earliest period reported or, if later, at the time of issuance.

69. **(b)** Per SFAS 128, if convertible securities are deemed to be dilutive, then interest expense should be added back to net income when computing diluted earnings per share.

70. **(b)** Per SFAS 128, the effect of contingent issue agreements are not included in basic earnings per share. They are included in diluted earnings per share if the contingency is met.

M. Corporate Bankruptcy

71. **(d)** The total cash available to pay **all** unsecured claims, including priority claims, is the cash obtained from free assets ($320,000) and any excess cash available from assets pledged with fully secured creditors after they are used to satisfy those claims ($370,000 – $260,000 = $110,000). Therefore, total cash available is $430,000 ($320,000 + $110,000). After paying priority claims, $360,000 will remain to pay all unsecured nonpriority claims ($430,000 – $70,000).

72. **(c)** Bankruptcy law requires that the claims of secured creditors be satisfied before any unsecured claims are paid. Hale is a secured creditor in the amount of $5,000 (the liquidation value of the collateral). The remainder of Hale's claim ($30,000 – $5,000 = $25,000) is an unsecured claim, because it is not secured by any collateral. Therefore, Hale will receive a total of $15,000 on this note: $5,000 received in full as a secured creditor, and $10,000 received as an unsecured creditor ($25,000 x $.40).

73. **(d)** A bankruptcy trustee may establish a new set of accounting records to maintain accountability for the bankruptcy estate. Once the trustee assumes custody of the estate, the trustee will enter any unrecorded assets or liabilities in the estate equity account. Any gains or losses and liquidation expenses incurred will also be recorded. In the Kamy Corp. bankruptcy, both the $8,000 loss on sale of the truck ($20,000 carrying value – $12,000 cash selling price) and the $1,000 unrecorded liability would be debited to the estate equity account as follows:

Estate equity	1,000	
Accounts payable		1,000

Cash	12,000	
Estate equity	8,000	
Truck		20,000

N. Reorganizations

74. **(b)** The requirement is to determine the net increase in total stockholders' equity as a result of the payments to unsecured creditors pursuant to a reorganization plan under Chapter 11. The net increase in stockholders' equity can be determined as follows:

Fair value of liabilities owed to unsecured creditors	$1,200,000
Cash paid	(400,000)
Common stock issued (80,000 x $1.25)	(100,000)
Gain on settlement of debt	$ 700,000

The gain on the settlement of debt would be included in the income statement and closed to retained earnings. The net increase in stockholders' equity would equal $800,000 ($700,000 gain + $100,000 FMV of stock issued).

O. Quasi Reorganization

75. **(c)** Although assets are often revalued to fair value during a quasi reorganization, the **primary** purpose of a quasi reorganization is to eliminate a deficit in retained earnings so that dividends may be paid without waiting years to eliminate the deficit through future earnings. A quasi reorganization does not directly allow a corporation to obtain relief from creditors or result in a distribution of stock.

76. **(d)** Per ARB 43, chap 7A, in certain instances an entity may elect to restate its assets, capital stock, and surplus through a readjustment (or "quasi reorganization") and thus avail itself of permission to relieve its future income account or earned surplus account of charges which would otherwise be made there against. In such instances, the entity should present a **fair (value)** balance sheet as of the date of the reorganization.

77. **(c)** A quasi reorganization generally involves (1) revaluing assets, (2) reducing par, and (3) writing the deficit off against additional paid-in capital. In this case, no mention is made of the first step, revaluing assets. The second step, reducing par, results in a decrease to **common stock** and an increase to **additional paid-in capital** of $250,000 [10,000 x ($30 – $5)]. The third step, writing off the deficit, increases **retained earnings** by $210,000 (creating a $0 balance) and decrease **additional paid-in capital** by the same amount. Immediately after the quasi reorganization, Brown should report additional paid-in capital of $190,000 ($150,000 + $250,000 – $210,000).

P. Stock Rights

78. **(a)** When a corporation issues rights to its stockholders, it only makes a memorandum entry. If rights are later exercised, the corporation would make the following entry:

Cash	xxx	
Common stock		xxx
Additional paid-in capital		xxx

79. **(c)** The only time a journal entry is recorded for the issuance and exercise of stock rights is on the date of exercise. At the date of issuance, only a memorandum entry is recorded. The redemption of the rights issued to the shareholders should be treated like a dividend. Accordingly, retained earnings will be decreased by the amount paid to the shareholders (120,000 x $0.10 = $12,000).

80. **(a)** The requirement is to determine the effects of the stock warrants on the additional paid-in capital account and on net income. When a corporation issues stock warrants to its stockholders it only makes a memorandum entry. Then, when the warrants are exercised, the following entry is made:

Cash	xxx	
Common stock		xxx
Additional paid-in capital		xxx

Net income is not affected by the exercise of stock warrants because the transaction represents a process of raising capital and is not related to the earnings process. Additional paid-in capital is not affected until the exercise date in 2002.

81. **(b)** Note that the only time an entry related to the issuance and exercise of stock rights, which affects the equity accounts of a corporation, is recorded is on the date of exercise. At the date of issuance, only a memorandum entry is recorded, and on the date of the rights lapsing, no entry is recorded which would affect the company's equity accounts. Thus, the correct answer is (b): the additional paid-in capital account would not be credited at the time the rights are issued or at the date on which the rights lapse.

Q. Employee Stock Ownership Plan (ESOP)

82. **(c)** Per SOP 76-3, the amount contributed or committed to be contributed to an employee stock ownership plan (ESOP) in a given year should be the measure of the amount to be charged to expense by the employer. Therefore, Fay should record 2002 compensation expense of $84,000 [contribution of $30,000 cash and common stock with a FMV of $54,000 (3,000 x $18)].

83. **(d)** Per SOP 76-3, an obligation of an Employee Stock Ownership Plan (ESOP) should be recorded as a liability in the financial statements of the employer when the obligation is covered by either a guarantee of the employer or a commitment by the employer to make future contributions to the ESOP sufficient to meet the debt service requirements. Therefore, the note payable of $100,000 (which is guaranteed by Fay) should be reported in Fay's 12/31/02 balance sheet. The SOP also states that the offsetting debit to the employer's liability should be reported as a reduction of stockholders' equity. Therefore, Fay should also report $100,000 as a reduction of stockholders' equity.

Stockholders' Equity: Comprehensive

84. **(a)** All of the accounts given are stockholders' equity accounts. Total stockholders' equity is computed below.

Paid-in capital		
Common stock		$600,000
Addl. paid-in capital		800,000
		1,400,000
Retained earnings		
Appropriated	$150,000	
Unappropriated	200,000	350,000
		1,750,000
Accumulated other comprehensive income		
Unrealized loss on available-for-sale MES		(20,000)
Less: Treasury stock		(50,000)
		$1,680,000

Both **treasury stock** and **net unrealized loss on available-for-sale marketable equity securities** are contra stockholders' equity accounts.

85. **(a)** The number of shares outstanding is equal to the issued shares less treasury shares. The table below shows the effects of each of the stock transactions on the common shares outstanding.

	Outstanding shares
1/1/02	300,000
1/31/02 declaration of 10% stock dividend	30,000
6/30/02 purchase of TS	(100,000)
8/1/02 sale of TS	50,000
Subtotal	280,000
11/30/02 stock split	x 2
12/31/02	560,000

86. **(a)** Shares issued and outstanding are computed below.

	Issued	*Outstanding*
12/31/01	100,000	95,000
5/3/02		1,000
8/6/02	10,000	10,000
Subtotal	110,000	106,000
11/18/02	110,000	106,000
12/31/02	220,000	212,000

At 12/31/01, shares issued were 100,000 and outstanding 95,000 (100,000 issued less 5,000 treasury). The reissuance of treasury stock does not increase shares issued, but does increase shares outstanding by 1,000 to 96,000 (100,000 issued less 4,000 treasury). The issuance of previously unissued stock on 8/6/02 increases both issued and outstanding shares by 10,000, bringing the totals to 110,000 issued and 106,000 outstanding prior to the stock split. Since treasury stock is protected from dilution, shares issued, treasury shares, and outstanding shares are all doubled by the stock split.

R. Ratios

87. **(a)** The requirement is to determine the effect on Ali Corp. of exercising the stock options. First, the debt to equity ratio is calculated as follows:

$$\text{Debt to equity} = \frac{\text{Total liabilities}}{\text{Common stockholders' equity}}$$

The figures given in the problem reflect the account balances **after** the exercise of the stock options. Thus, Ali's debt to equity ratio after the exercise is

$$\frac{\$60,000}{\$500,000} = 12\%$$

When the options were exercised, total stockholders' equity would have increased by the amount of the option price as follows:

Common stock	↑	by par value x 1,000 shares
Paid-in capital	↑	by (option price-par) x 1,000 shares

Note that the information given is incomplete as to whether compensation was recorded under the stock option plan. However, even if compensation were recorded, the entries are made only to accounts that impact stockholders' equity, and the net effect is no change. Thus, the only change is an increase resulting from the exercise of the options. Since common stockholders' equity increased, the denominator of the debt to equity ratio also increased. As the denominator becomes larger and the numerator remains constant, the quotient becomes smaller. Therefore, the debt to equity ratio must have **decreased** to its current level of 12%. Answer (b) is incorrect because earnings per share decreased by $.15. Answer (c) is incorrect because not enough information is given to calculate the asset turnover. Answer (d) is incorrect because the debt to equity ratio, rate of return on common stock, earnings per share, price earnings ratio, and book value per share were all affected by exercising the stock options.

88. (c)   The requirement is to determine Irvington's return on common stockholders' equity for 2002, which is computed by dividing net income available to common stockholders (net income less preferred dividends) by average common stockholders' equity

$$\frac{\$120,000 - \$10,000}{(\$375,000 + \$585,000)/2} = 23\%$$

89. (d)   The requirement is to determine the book value per common share. The book value per common share is the amount each share would receive if the company were liquidated. The book value per common share is calculated as follows:

	Preferred	Common
Preferred stock, 5%	$250,000	
Common stock		$350,000
APIC in excess of par value of common stock		125,000
Retained earnings:		
Dividends in arrears	25,000	
Liquidation premium	50,000	
Remainder to common (Plug)		225,000
Totals	$325,000	$700,000
Shares outstanding		100,000
Book value per share		$ 7.00

Note that when calculating the remainder to common, total stockholders' equity before the liquidation must be equal to the amount after the assumed liquidation.

90. (c)   Under the cost method, treasury stock is debited for the cost of the treasury stock, thus decreasing total stockholders' equity. However, the book value per share will increase due to the acquisition of the treasury stock. Book value per share is calculated by dividing common stockholders' equity by the shares outstanding. An example will help illustrate.

Stockholders' equity	
Common stock (30,000 shares)	
$5 par	$150,000
Additional paid-in capital	550,000
Retained earnings	250,000
	$950,000

$$\text{Book value per share} = \frac{\$950,000}{30,000} = \$31.67$$

Per the facts in the question, treasury stock was acquired at more than par and original issue price, but less than book value per share. Therefore, the acquisition price must be greater than $23.33 per share (700,000 ÷ 30,000) and less than $31.67 per share.

Let's say 1,000 shares of treasury stock were acquired at $27.00 per share.

$$\text{Book value per share} = \frac{\$950,000 - (1,000 \times \$27)}{30,000 - 1,000}$$

$$= \frac{923,000}{29,000}$$

$$= \$31.83$$

The book value per share increased after the acquisition of the treasury stock.

91. (b)   Dividends per share is used in the numerator of the dividend payout ratio as shown below.

$$\frac{\text{Dividend}}{\text{payout ratio}} = \frac{\text{Dividends per share}}{\text{Earnings per share}}$$

However, dividends per share are not used in the calculation of earnings per share.

$$\frac{\text{Earnings}}{\text{per share}} = \frac{\text{Net income} - \text{Preferred dividends}}{\text{Weighted-average number of shares outstanding}}$$

OTHER OBJECTIVE ANSWERS AND ANSWER EXPLANATIONS

Problem 1

1. **(I)** In accordance with the par value method, treasury shares are recorded at par value by debiting treasury stock when acquired. Any additional paid-in capital from the original issue of the acquired shares is also debited, cash is credited, and either additional paid-in capital—treasury stock is credited or retained earnings are debited for the difference between cash and the other two debits previously mentioned.

2. **(H)** Appropriations of retained earnings are actions by the board of directors to disclose amounts not available for dividends.

3. **(D)** A stock split changes the number of shares outstanding and the par value per share. The purpose of a stock split is to reduce the market price per share.

4. **(A)** A simple capital structure for a corporation exists if there are no potentially dilutive securities.

5. **(M)** The if converted method for convertible securities assumes that the securities were converted at the later of the beginning of the period or the date of issue. The method thus increases the weighted-average number of shares in the denominator of the EPS equation. Since the method assumes conversion at the beginning of the period, no preferred dividends or interest would be considered to have been paid.

6. **(K)** A scrip dividend is a dividend issued by the corporation in the form of a note payable.

7. **(B)** A stock appreciation right allows an employee to receive the excess of the market value of the stock over a preestablished value in the form of cash, shares of stock, or both on the exercise date.

8. **(J)** A stock option is a form of compensation given to employees which allows them to purchase shares of stock at a specified price.

9. **(G)** A dividend paid to shareholders in excess of the retained earnings balance which is considered to be a return of capital and a liquidating dividend.

10. **(E)** When a corporation purchases its own stock in the market, the stock is termed treasury stock. Treasury stock is not an asset as a corporation cannot invest in itself. Treasury stock is recorded in a contra equity account.

Problem 2

This problem is a collection of miscellaneous stockholders' equity problems. The candidate should start the problem by scanning the required information to determine the amounts to be calculated. While scanning, the candidate should recognize that some of the required items are related, such as 2 (preferred dividends) and 10 (numerator used in calculating EPS) and 5 (number of common shares issued) and 6 (amount of common stock issued); 7 (additional paid-in capital) and 8 (treasury stock). These relationships require that the candidate label each answer, so that it will be possible to quickly find that answer when it is used in a subsequent problem.

Unlike many previous exam problems, the order of the information concerning the transactions does not coincide with the order of the required answers. This arrangement makes it necessary to read the required amount and then hunt for the transaction information needed to calculate that required amount.

1. **($14,000)** Prior period adjustment is the term generally applied to corrections of errors of prior periods. In this problem no amortization had been recorded in a prior year—an error. Since this is not a self-correcting error, it still existed in 2003. The calculation is cost ($320,000) ÷ useful life (eight years) for 1/2 year (purchased July 1). Prior period adjustments are disclosed net of tax (30%). $320,000/8 x 1/2 x (1 – .3) = $14,000.

2. **($12,000)** Preferred dividends are 6% and cumulative. They were declared during 2002 and paid in 2003. The declaration is sufficient to record and recognize the dividends legally; they do not have to be paid in the current year to be recognized during that time period. These dividends will be used in the numerator in question 10 when calculating the 2002 EPS. Since these dividends are cumulative, they would be used in the calculation of EPS even if they had not been declared. The amount of preferred dividends is derived by multiplying the par value of the stock by its rate. 6% x $200,000 par = $12,000 dividends.

3. **($165,000)** Common dividends—cash is calculated by the formula: Common shares outstanding x Dividend per share. In this problem the number of shares outstanding is affected by the beginning shares (100,000), shares issued (13,000), and treasury shares purchased and sold (5,000 purchased, 2,000 sold) prior to the dividend date of November 4. 100,000 + 13,000 – 5,000 + 2,000 = 110,000 shares outstanding x dividend rate $1.50 = $165,000.

4. **($720,000)** Common dividends—property differ from cash dividends because the property may be carried in the accounts at an amount which does not equal its fair value (cash is always at its fair value). Management intends to distribute the property at its fair value, therefore it is necessary to bring the property to fair value on the date management is legally forced to distribute it (the declaration date). Value fluctuations beyond that date are irrelevant.

5. **(113,000)** The number of shares issued differs from the number of shares outstanding which was used in question 3. Shares issued include those outstanding as well as those held in the treasury. Shares outstanding from question 3, 110,000 plus 3,000 treasury shares = 113,000 shares.

6.   **($113,000)** Amount of common stock issued—This question takes the answer from question 5 (113,000 shares) and multiplies that figure by the par value of each share, $1.

7.   **($934,000)** The additional paid-in capital, including treasury stock transactions, is derived by adding the beginning balance ($800,000) to the excess ($10) of issue price ($11) over par value ($1) for the shares issued (13,000) to acquire land on February 1, 2002. In addition, the sale of the treasury stock (2,000 shares) at an amount ($16) greater than cost ($14) gives rise to a nonoperating gain that cannot be included in net income since it was both not related to operations and is a transaction in the company's own stock. $800,000 + (13,000 x $10) + (2,000 x 16-14) = $934,000.

8.   **($42,000)** Treasury stock—Since the Min Co. follows the cost method of accounting for treasury stock, this answer is derived by multiplying the shares of treasury stock (3,000) by their cost ($14). 3,000 x $14 = $42,000.

9.   **($24.86)** Book value per share is a concept that relates common stockholders' equity to shares of common stock. The "per share" referred to is always the **common** shares unless the problem states some other type of shares. In this case it is to be calculated before the prior period adjustment. It is necessary to subtract preferred stock's total liquidating value ($100 x 2,000 sh = $200,000) from total stockholders' equity ($2,686,000) to obtain common stockholders' equity. In this problem no liquidating value is given, so par value is used. The resulting amount ($2,686,000 – $200,000 = $2,486,000) is divided by the common shares outstanding (100,000) to obtain book value per share ($24.86). ($2,686,000 – $200,000) ÷ 100,000 = $24.86.

10.   **($826,000)** The formula for calculating earnings per share is (NI – Preferred dividends) ÷ Wtd.-avg. shares outstanding. The numerator is income available to common stockholders. The problem states that adjusted net income for 2002 was $838,000. The word "adjusted" tells the candidate that net income includes all information concerning transactions in the problem and need not be changed in any way. Preferred dividends ($12,000) were calculated in question 2. $838,000 – $12,000 = $826,000.

SOLUTION GUIDE AND ANSWER OUTLINE

Problem 1 Stockholders' Equity Section and Stock Compensation

a. To prepare the stockholders' equity section of Field's December 31, 2002 balance sheet, certain computations need to be made first.

1. The common stock authorized does not change throughout the problem; it is 400,000 shares. The number of shares outstanding increases by the 20,000 shares issued when the stock options were exercised. The balance in the common stock account is the number of shares issued times the par value of the common stock (180,000 x $5 = $900,000).

2. The treasury stock is accounted for by the cost method, which means the treasury stock is recorded at cost (5,000 shares x $10 = $50,000). The journal entry for the treasury stock is

Treasury stock	50,000	
Cash		50,000

3. The information given indicates that the intrinsic value method of APB 25 is used because no fair value is given for these options which would be needed to use the fair value method of SFAS 123. Compensation cost is zero and no entry is made until the options are recognized. Additional paid-in capital is the amount of money received for stock above the par value. The exercise or option price of the stock options exercised was $18 per share. The $13 per share paid above the par value of the stock needs to be added to the additional paid-in capital account, so $260,000 ($13 x 20,000 shares) should be added to the beginning balance of $1,600,000 for a total of $1,860,000 in the additional paid-in capital account.

4. The formula for retained earnings is

    Beginning balance
    Add: Net income
    Less: Dividends
    Ending balance

    The amount of the dividends is the fair market value of the property distributed, which is $60,000 in this case. A $15,000 loss is recognized from the property dividend for the difference between the $75,000 carrying value and market value of the inventory. However, this loss would already be included in 2002 net income. Retained earnings is

Beginning balance	$1,845,000
Add: Net income	240,000
Less: Dividend	(60,000)
Ending balance	$2,025,000

b. Fair value method

- Cost measured at grant date at value of award
- Value based on option-pricing model

Intrinsic value method

- Measured at grant date (or other measurement date)
- Difference between market price at grant date over employee exercise price

Recognize expense methods over service period for both

UNOFFICIAL ANSWER

Problem 1 Stockholders' Equity Section and Stock Compensation

a.

Field Co.
STOCKHOLDERS' EQUITY SECTION OF BALANCE SHEET
December 31, 2002

Common stock, $5 par value, 400,000 shares authorized, 180,000 shares issued, 175,000 shares outstanding		$ 900,000	[1]
Additional paid-in capital		1,860,000	[2]
Retained earnings:			
Beginning balance	$1,845,000		
Add: Net income	240,000		
Less: Property dividend distributed	(60,000)	2,025,000	
		4,785,000	
Less common stock in treasury, 5,000 shares at cost		(50,000)	
Total stockholders' equity		$4,735,000	

[1] Shares issued: 160,000 + 20,000 = 180,000 x $5 = $900,000
[2] Additional paid-in capital $1,600,000 + [20,000 x ($18 – 5)] = $1,860,000 (1,600,000 + 260,000)

b. To: Management, Field Co.
Re: Accounting for Stock-Based Compensation

As you are aware, SFAS 123 discusses both the "intrinsic value" method and the "fair value" method of accounting for stock options. The purpose of this memo is to inform you of the difference between the two methods and of when the company should record compensation cost associated with 2002 stock option issuances.

Under the "fair value" method of accounting for stock options, compensation cost is measured at the grant date based on the value of the award. This value is computed using an option-pricing model. Under the "intrinsic value" method, compensation cost is the excess, if any, of the quoted market price of the stock at the grant date (or other measurement date) over the amount an employee must pay to acquire the stock.

Under both methods, compensation cost, if any, is recognized over the service period, which is usually the vesting period.

ANSWER OUTLINE

Problem 2 EPS

a. $\text{Basic EPS} = \dfrac{\text{NI} - \text{Pfd. div.}}{\text{WA out. shs.}}$

Preferred dividend deducted if declared or if stock is cumulative

$\text{Diluted EPS} = \dfrac{\text{NI} - \text{Pfd. div.} + \text{Dilutive security adjust.}}{\text{WA out. shs.} + \text{Dilutive security shs.}}$

Dilutive securities include options & warrants and convertible bonds & preferred stock
Dilutive securities decrease EPS
Antidilutive securities increase EPS

b. Effect of assuming bond conversion is antidilutive
Addition of interest, net of tax, would decrease loss to stockholders in numerator
Dividing by number of shares including those from conversion would result in lower net loss per share
Only basic net loss per share would be reported

UNOFFICIAL ANSWER

Problem 2 EPS

a. Basic earnings per share is based on income available for common stockholders divided by the weighted-average number of outstanding shares. Income available to common stockholders is net income less preferred dividends declared. Preferred dividends on cumulative preferred stock are deducted whether declared or not.

Diluted earnings per share is basic earnings per share adjusted for the effects of dilutive securities. Dilutive securities include options and warrants and convertible bonds and preferred stock. The adjustments include positive numerator adjustments for bond interest, net of tax, and preferred dividends. The positive denominator adjustments are for dilutive shares that would be issued upon conversion of convertible securities and from applying the treasury stock method for dilutive options and warrants.

b. Columbine's convertible bonds are antidilutive in the diluted EPS calculation because the addition of interest avoided (net of tax) to the numerator and the shares from conversion to the denominator would result in a lower net loss per share than basic net loss per share. Columbine would report only basic net loss per share.

———————

Keep practicing! Wiley's CPA Examination Review Software has over 2,800 questions.

Available at www.wiley.com/cpa

INVESTMENTS

A. Concepts of Accounting and Investment Percentage

1. **Debt securities** are covered by SFAS 115 (see outline), *Accounting for Certain Investments in Debt and Equity Securities*, which defines debt securities as "any security representing a creditor relationship with an enterprise." This includes corporate debt, convertible bonds, US Treasury and municipal securities, redeemable preferred stock, commercial paper, and other secured debt instruments. Excluded are unsecured trade receivables and consumer loans and notes receivable because they are not normally traded on organized exchanges and because of cost/benefit considerations. SFAS 115 requires that investments in debt securities be classified into three categories: trading securities, available-for-sale securities, and held-to-maturity securities. Debt securities are discussed in Section B of this module and also in Module 26, Section B.

2. **Equity securities** include ownership interests (common, preferred, and other capital stock), rights to acquire ownership interests (rights, warrants, call options), and rights to dispose of ownership interests (put options). The accounting rules for investments in the common stock of another corporation are generally based on the percentage of the voting stock obtained.

   a. Investments of less than 20% of the outstanding stock

   In most cases, "small" investments in marketable equity securities are classified into two categories as specified by SFAS 115: trading securities and available-for-sale securities. Discussion of these smaller investments is presented in Section B.

   b. Investments between 20% and 50% of the outstanding stock

   At 20% or more ownership, the investor is presumed to be able to significantly influence the operating or financial decisions of the investee. Most investments in this range will result in significant influence; however, the 20% level is just a guide. FASB Interpretation 35 presents several examples in which an investor owning between 20% and 50% may not be able to exercise influence over the investee. An example of this situation is when the majority ownership is concentrated among a small group of investors who ignore the views of the minority investor. Additional examples are included in the summary of Interpretation 35, page 650. The equity method of accounting is used for investments resulting in significant influence. Investments where significant influence does exist are discussed in Section C.

   c. Investments of more than 50% of the outstanding stock

   At more than 50% ownership, the investor has control because of its majority ownership of the voting stock. Most of these investments will require the preparation of consolidated financial statements. Consolidations are discussed in Module 31.

3. Securities are originally recorded at cost, including any broker's fees, taxes, etc.; this amount is the best estimate of fair value at acquisition. Cost equals the cash paid or, in noncash transactions, the fair value of either the securities received or the resources sacrificed, whichever is more clearly determinable. The fair value of debt securities equals the present value of their future cash inflows. The present value is calculated using the current market rate of interest for similar instruments with similar risk. Any accrued interest is accounted for separately. The fair value of equity securities to be marked to market must be readily determinable from quotes obtainable from a securities exchange registered with the SEC or from the over-the-counter market. Investments which are considered to be nontradeable or investments which do not have determinable market values should be carried at cost and adjusted only for permanent declines in value.

   The exhibit below illustrates the major concepts of accounting for investments in equity securities.

PERCENTAGE OF OUTSTANDING VOTING STOCK ACQUIRED

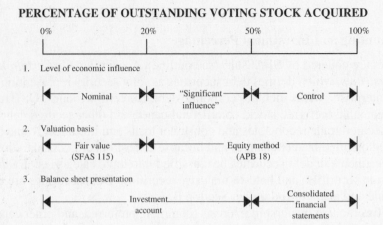

Several exceptions to these general concepts exist. These exceptions are noted in the following discussions.

B. Investments in Which Significant Influence Does *Not* Exist

Investments which do not confer significant influence over the operating or financial decisions of the investee consist of all debt securities and generally all small (less than 20%) investments in equity securities. SFAS 115 dictates that such investments be segregated into held-to-maturity securities (debt securities only), trading securities, and available-for-sale securities; the appropriateness of the classification should be reviewed at each reporting date.

1. Held-to-Maturity Securities (amortized cost)

This category includes only debt securities and requires the positive intent and ability to hold the securities to maturity (not simply an absence of intent to sell). Held-to-maturity securities are carried at amortized cost (acquisition cost adjusted for amortization of premium or discount) using effective interest method; thus, unrealized holding gains and losses are not reported. However, realized gains and losses are included in earnings, as are interest income and premium and discount amortization. These securities are classified on the balance sheet as current or noncurrent on an individual basis, and on the statement of cash flows as investing activities.

In rare instances, the investor company's intent to hold a security to maturity may change without casting doubt on its intent to hold other debt securities to maturity. The circumstances must be nonrecurring and unforeseeable, such as the continuing deterioration of the issuer's credit. Premature sale of held-to-maturity securities may be considered as maturities if either of the following conditions are met:

a. The sale occurs so close to the maturity date that interest rate risk is virtually eliminated, or

b. The sale occurs after at least 85% of the principal has been collected.

Investments in held-to-maturity securities are accounted for under the cost method, which requires that they be carried at amortized cost (acquisition cost adjusted for amortization of premium or discount). Coverage of accounting for these appears under bond investments in Module 26B.

2. Trading Securities (mark-to-market)

Debt and equity securities purchased and held principally for the purpose of generating gains on current resale are classified as trading securities. Trading securities are accounted for according to the cost adjusted for fair value (mark-to-market) method, under which the carrying amount is adjusted at financial statement dates for subsequent changes in fair value (i.e., they are carried at market value). Trading securities are generally held by brokers, bankers, and other financial institutions which engage in active buying and selling activities. Both unrealized and realized gains and losses are included in income. However, to the extent that realized gains/losses have been previously reported as unrealized, only changes in the current period shall be reported as realized in the period of sale. Other components of earnings include dividend and interest revenue. Dividends on equity securities are recognized as income when declared by the investee. However, if dividends received exceed cumulative earnings since acquisition, the excess is accounted for as a liquidating dividend. Trading securities are reported on the balance sheet as current assets and on the statement of cash flows as operating activities.

Debt securities reported at fair value require special accounting treatment. The securities are to be carried at market value while interest and amortization are to be calculated using the effective interest method. Therefore, any unrealized gain or loss is actually the difference between fair value and amortized cost, that is, the adjustment equals the change in fair value during the period, plus premium amortization (decrease in book value) or minus discount amortization (increase in book value). Both the interest revenue and the unrealized holding gain/loss are included in current earnings. An example of accounting for trading debt securities is presented in the comprehensive example at the end of Section B.

3. **Available-for-Sale Securities (mark-to-market)**

Available-for-sale securities include debt and equity securities not categorized as either held-to-maturity securities or trading securities. For example, a company such as a manufacturing firm may purchase securities to make use of idle cash. These securities are not actively traded, nor will they necessarily be held to maturity. Included in earnings are realized gains and losses (which include previously unrealized holding gains and losses) and dividend and interest income. Available-for-sale securities are accounted for according to the cost adjusted for fair value (mark-to-market) method, under which the carrying amount is adjusted at financial statement dates for subsequent changes in fair value (i.e., they are carried at market value).

Unrealized gains and losses on available-for-sale debt and equity securities are calculated in the same manner as those on trading securities. These gains and losses, however, are not recognized in income of the period. Instead, the changes in fair value during a period (unrealized gains/losses) are reported as other comprehensive income (see Module 22D), and the accumulated unrealized gain/loss on marketable securities account is presented as accumulated other comprehensive income in stockholders' equity. The following chart summarizes the three categories of marketable securities and the accounting treatment of each.

ACCOUNTING AND REPORTING OF MARKETABLE DEBT AND EQUITY SECURITIES

Category	*Definition*	*How the security is reported on the balance sheet*	*How unrealized holding gains and losses are reported on the income statement**	*How realized gains and losses are reported on the income statement*
Trading (trading securities)	**Debt and equity** securities bought and held principally for the purpose of selling them in the near term	Reported at fair market value and grouped with current assets on the balance sheet	Unrealized gains and losses are included in earnings in the period they occur	Realized gains and losses not already recognized as unrealized components are recognized
Available-for-sale	**Debt and equity** securities not classified as trading or held-to-maturity	Reported at fair market value and may be classified as current or noncurrent	Unrealized gains and losses for a period are excluded from earnings and reported as other comprehensive income (If decline is "other than temporary" then recognized in earnings)	Realized gains and losses are recognized (which include unrealized holding gains and losses recognized previously as unrealized)
Held-to-maturity	**Debt** securities that the organization has the positive intent and ability to hold to the maturity date	Reported at amortized cost and may be classified as current or noncurrent	Unrealized gains and losses are excluded from earnings (unless decline is "other than temporary")	Realized gains and losses are recognized in accordance with amortized cost method

* *Or on the statement where items of other comprehensive income are reported.*

The fair value of a debt security minus its amortized cost represents the correct unrealized gain or loss for this security in the accumulated other comprehensive income account at year-end. The adjusting entry for this account at the end of the period will equal the difference between the account's balance before adjustment and the cumulative unrealized gain or loss on the debt and equity securities at the end of the period.

Available-for-sale securities are classified on the balance sheet as current or noncurrent on an individual basis based on management's intent concerning the holding period and appear on the statement of cash flows as investing activities.

Comprehensive Example

On 1/01/02, when interest rates were 12%, STC Corporation purchased the following securities:

Security description	Acquisition cost
• Shaner Enterprise ten-year, 10%, $1,000 face value bonds (STC Corp. intends to hold the bond until it matures)	$ 887
• Harmony Corporation five-year, 14%, $5,000 face value bond (STC Corp. expects that interest rates will fall and the bond will be sold at a profit)	$5,360
• 100 shares Keswick Corporation common stock (STC anticipates that the price of the stock will rise 10%, at which time the stock will be sold)	$2,200
• 150 shares Rusell Inc. common stock (STC has no immediate plans to sell this stock)	$5,600

The Shaner bond must be classified as held-to-maturity and carried at amortized cost since management has the ability and intent to hold the investment to the maturity date. The Harmony and Keswick securities are classified as trading securities because STC intends to hold these investments for only a short period of time expressly to realize a quick profit. The Rusell, Inc. stock is classified as available-for-sale because STC has not expressed an intent to hold the stock for current resale. The Harmony, Keswick, and Rusell investments are all carried at fair market value.

At the end of 2002, the fair values of the Keswick and Rusell stock are $2,700 and $5,190, respectively. Interest rates have fallen to 10%, boosting the value of the Harmony bond to $5,634. Interest income, premium amortization, and unrealized gain on this bond are calculated as

Date	14% Cash interest	12% Effective interest	Premium amortization	Carrying value	Fair value	Unrealized gain (loss)
1/01/02				$5,360	$5,360	
12/31/02	$700	$643	$57	5,303	5,634	$331

Note that the unrealized gain ($331) equals the increase in fair value ($274) plus the premium amortization ($57).

Interest income and discount/premium amortization must be recorded for the bonds in any of the three portfolios. Both the Harmony and Shaner bonds were purchased to yield 12%. The adjusting journal entries required at 12/31/02 are

Interest receivable	100	
Investment in Shaner bond—held-to-maturity	6	
Interest income ($887 x 12%)		106
Interest receivable	700	
Investment in Harmony securities—trading		57
Interest income		643

On 12/31/02 after the two adjusting entries above are posted, the carrying values and fair market values are:

	12/31/02 Carrying amount	12/31/02 Fair market value
Held-to-maturity:		
Shaner bond	$ 893	NA
Trading:		
Harmony bond	5,303	$5,634
Keswick stock	2,200	2,700
Available-for-sale:		
Rusell stock	5,600	5,190

At this time, the adjusting journal valuation entries are made for the trading and the available-for-sale portfolios of securities, as follows

Investment in Harmony securities—trading	331	
Unrealized gain on holding debt securities (income statement)		331
Investment in Keswick securities—trading	500	
Unrealized gain on holding equity securities (income statement) ($2,700 FMV – $2,200 CV)		500
Unrealized loss on Rusell securities—available-for-sale (other comprehensive income account)	410	
Investment in Rusell securities—available-for-sale ($5,600 CV – $5,190 FMV)		410

The unrealized holding gain on trading securities is a nominal account which is closed to income at 12/31/02. The unrealized loss on available-for-sale securities is closed out to the "accumulated other comprehensive income" account at year-end, which is presented in the stockholders' equity section of the 12/31/02 balance sheet. **It is important to note that the increases and decreases in market value recorded above may alternatively be recorded in a separate fair value adjustment account (contra asset account).** If a fair value adjustment account is used to carry the holding gains and losses, then the fair value adjustment account and the investment account would be netted for presentation purposes. The carrying amount of the Shaner bond at 12/31/02 is $893 ($887 + $6).

Now assume that in July 2003, 75 of the 150 shares of Rusell stock were sold for $30 per share. The entry to record the sale is

Cash ($30 x 75)	2,250	
Loss on sale of securities	550	
Investment in Rusell securities—available-for-sale*		2,595
Reclassification adjustment of unrealized loss on		
Rusell securities—available-for-sale		205

* *Carrying value = $5,190 ($5,600 – 410) market value on books ÷ 150 shares = $34.60/share.*
  $2,595 = $34.60 x 75 shares

The loss on sale of securities equals the initial acquisition cost of the securities less the sales price. Because the Rusell securities are classified as available-for-sale, the proportionate amount of unrealized holding gains or losses ($205 = ½ x $410) which had accumulated in the stockholders' equity account would be reclassified and becomes part of the realized loss for inclusion in earnings of the period of the sale. Note that the accumulated other comprehensive income account in stockholders' equity is a "holding account" for the difference between the initial acquisition cost of the available-for-sale security and its current fair market value at the balance sheet date. No other holding gains or losses beyond the $410 holding loss recognized on December 31, 2002, had accumulated since December 31, 2002. When the available-for-sale security is sold, the amount of the previously recognized unrealized holding gain or loss is reclassified and becomes part of the realized gain or loss on the sale of available-for-sale securities. The realized gain or loss on the sale is then the difference between the selling price and the initial acquisition cost ($550 = $2,250 – $2,800 acquisition cost of 75 shares).

In September 2003, Keswick Corp. declared a 10% stock dividend. Stock dividends should not be reflected in income. The stock's current carrying value of $2,700 should be allocated to the additional shares received from the dividend. Since STC holds 100 shares, the dividend will be 10 shares, resulting in a total of 110 shares. After the dividend, the 110 shares will each have a carrying value of $24.55 ($2,700 ÷ 110) which will be adjusted to market at the end of the reporting period.

STC Corporation periodically reviews its intent to hold or actively trade its securities. At 12/31/03, when interest rates are 8%, STC decides that it will hold the Harmony bond indefinitely. Because this bond was originally classified as trading, it must be transferred to available-for-sale. Market value on this date is $5,773. The entries to record interest income and to transfer the bond are

Interest receivable	700	
Investment in Harmony securities—trading		64
Interest income		636
Investment in Harmony securities—trading	203	
Unrealized gain on holding debt securities		203
Investment in Harmony securities—available-for-sale	5,773	
Investment in Harmony securities—trading		5,773

The holding gain of $203 ($5,773 FMV 12/03 – $5,634 FMV 12/02 plus premium amortization of $64) is recognized in current earnings, and the value recorded in the available-for-sale portfolio reflects the market value of $5,773 at the transfer date. Note that from this point forward any holding gains or losses should be recognized as other comprehensive income and included in accumulated other comprehensive income in stockholders' equity in accordance with the available-for-sale classification.

Also on 12/31/03, STC sold its held-for-trading Keswick stock for $32 per share. This transaction was recorded as follows:

Cash ($32 x 110 shares)	3,520	
Investment in Keswick securities—trading		2,700
Gain on sale of securities		820

On 12/31/03, STC also recorded the appropriate entries for amortization of the Shaner bond ($7 discount amortization and $107 interest income) and to adjust the Rusell stock to its current fair value of $29 per share.

Finally, on 12/31/03 STC discovered that Shaner Enterprise is experiencing financial difficulty due to mismanagement, and the full amount of the bond will not be collected. This impairment would be considered other than temporary, so the investment in Shaner Enterprise bonds must be reduced to its current fair value of $500. The realized loss of $400 ($900 12/31/03 current carrying value – $500 FMV) is reported in earnings, and no write-up will be allowed if a recovery is made at a later date.

To summarize STC Corporation's marketable securities transactions for 2002 and 2003, T-accounts for each security are shown below, followed by earnings information relating to the investments.

Harmony Bond—Trading			
1/01/02 Acquisition	5,360	57	12/31/02 Amort.
12/31/02 Adj. to FMV	331	64	12/31/03 Amort.
12/31/03 Adj. To FMV	203	5,773	12/31/03 Transfer
Bal. 12/31/03	0		

Harmony Bond—Available-for-Sale		
12/31/03 Transfer	5,773	
Bal. 12/31/03	5,773	

Shaner Bond—Held-to-Maturity			
1/01/02 Acquisition	887		
12/31/02 Amort.	6		
12/31/03 Amort.	7	$400	12/31/03 Write-down
Bal. 12/31/03	500		

Keswick Stock—Trading			
1/01/02 Acquisition			
(100 shares)	2,200		
12/31/02 Adj. to FMV	500		
(9/03 Stock div.—10 shares)		2,700	12/31/03 Sale
Bal. 12/31/03	0		

Rusell Stock—Available-for-Sale			
1/01/02 Acquisition			
(150 shares)	5,600	410	12/31/02 Adj. to FMV
		2,595	7/03 Sale (75 shares)
		420	12/31/03 Adj. to FMV
Bal. 12/31/03	2,175		

Year	Transaction	Income/Gain	Loss	Net earnings	Other comprehensive income
2002	Harmony adj. to FMV	$ 331			
	Keswick adj. to FMV	500			
	Interest on Shaner bond	106			
	Interest on Harmony bond	643			
	Rusell adj. to FMV				$(410)
	2002 total	$1,580		$1,580	(410)
2003	Write-down of Shaner bond		$(400)		
	Sale of one-half of Rusell securities		(550)		$ 205
	Gain on Keswick securities	$ 820			
	Harmony adj. to FMV	203			
	Interest on Shaner bond	107			
	Interest on Harmony bond	636			
	Rusell adj. to FMV				(420)
	2003 total	$1,766	$(950)	$ 816	$(215)

4. **Transfers between Categories**

SFAS 115 requires that the classification of securities be reviewed at each balance sheet date. Although a reclassification should be rare, a company may deem it necessary to transfer a security from one category to another. Such transfers are accounted for at fair value, taking into consideration any unrealized holding gains or losses. For example, when a security is transferred **from** trading securities, any recognized unrealized gain or loss as of the date of transfer should not be reversed. On the other hand, in a transfer **to** trading securities, unrealized holding gains and losses are recognized immediately. Held-to-maturity securities reclassified **to** available-for-sale securities must be restated to fair value; any unrealized holding gain or loss that results is reported as accumulated other comprehensive income in stockholders' equity. However, transfers **from** held-to-maturity should be rare. Unrealized holding gain or loss on securities transferred **to** held-to-maturity from available-for-sale is also reported as accumulated other comprehensive income in stockholders' equity, but this gain or loss is then amortized over the remaining life of the security as an adjustment to yield. The treatment of securities transfers is summarized in the chart below.

	Securities transferred to:		
Securities transferred from:	**Held-to-maturity**	**Available-for-sale**	**Trading**
Held-to-maturity		Report unrealized G/L as accumulated other comprehensive income in SE	Recognize unrealized G/L immediately
Available-for-sale	Report unrealized G/L as accumulated other comprehensive income in SE & amortize the gain or loss over remaining life of security		Recognize unrealized G/L immediately
Trading	Do not reverse unrealized G/L previously recognized in income	Do not reverse unrealized G/L previously recognized in income	

5. **Income Statement Presentation**

Since held-to-maturity and available-for-sale securities are held for some length of time, these securities may become impaired at some point. If the decline in value is other than temporary, then the impaired security must be written down to fair value and the realized loss included in earnings. Any subsequent recovery would not be recognized in earnings unless realized through sale of the security. An other than temporary impairment cannot occur in the context of trading securities because holding gains and losses are recognized in current earnings without limitation.

SFAS 115 does not change the method of recognition of cash dividends or interest income on debt and equity securities. Thus, cash dividends or interest income should be included in the current period's income. The method of recognition for stock dividends is also not affected by SFAS 115; stock dividends should not be reflected in income. Additional shares received from a stock dividend should be added to the original shares and the per share value should be calculated upon the original shares' carrying value. At the end of the period the carrying value of the stock is adjusted to the fair value, and any unrealized holding gain or loss is recorded.

Additionally, SFAS 115 requires that realized and **unrealized** gains and losses on trading securities be included in the current period's earnings. Only realized gains and losses on sales of available-for-sale and held-to-maturity securities should be included in earnings. Unrealized gains (losses) on available-for-sale securities are reported as other comprehensive income in one of three ways (see Module 22D). Finally, amortization of any unrealized holding gain or loss on securities transferred to held-to-maturity from available-for-sale is included in income.

C. **Investments Where Significant Influence *Does* Exist**

APB 18 requires the use of the **equity method** when accounting for investments which give the investor the ability to exercise significant influence over the operating and financial policies of the investee. APB 18 assumes that ownership of 20% or more of the outstanding stock will result in that ability. Exceptions to the use of the equity method (i.e., the cost adjusted for fair value method) are related to an assessment of the investor's level of influence over the investee. The cost adjusted for fair value method in SFAS 115 should be used if an investment of more than 20% is judged to be temporary, if the investment is in a company operating in a foreign country which has severe restrictions on the operations of companies and on the transfer of monies to outside the country, and for other investments of more than 20% that do not result in significant influence. There may be unusual circumstances in which a less than 20% investor may have significant influence over the investee, in which case the equity method must be used to account for the investment.

1. *Cost adjusted for fair value method*—The cost adjusted for fair value and the equity methods differ in the treatment of the investment account and in the recognition of earnings from the investment. The cost adjusted for fair value method first records the cost of the investment in the investment account. Income is recognized for dividends distributed from income of the investee earned since the date the investor acquired the stock. Any dividends distributed by the investee which exceed earnings since the acquisition

date are classified as return of capital and recorded as a reduction of the investment account. Under the cost adjusted for fair value method, equity securities must be adjusted for subsequent changes in market value, and the unrealized holding gain or loss on equity securities for the period equals the current fair value minus the previous period's fair value on the books.

2.   *Equity method*—The equity method also begins with recording the cost of the investment in the investment account but the two methods differ from this point on. A basic concept of the equity method is the reciprocal relationship formed between the investment account on the investor's books and the book values of the net assets on the investee's books. As changes in the investee's net assets occur (e.g., earnings, dividends, etc.), the investor will recognize in the investment account the percentage of ownership share of those changes.

Another aspect of the equity method is the computation and accounting for the difference between the cost of the investment and the book value of the acquired asset share at the investment date. The abundance of advanced accounting texts currently in print use an assortment of terms to describe the characteristics of this concept. For purposes of uniformity, the following boldfaced terms shall be used throughout this module.

Differential: The difference between the cost of the investment and the underlying book value of the net assets of the investee. This difference can be either positive or negative, as follows:

1. **Excess of Cost over Book Value,** which is generally attributable to

    a. **Excess of fair value over book value,** when the fair values of the investee's assets are greater than their book values, and
    b. **Goodwill,** when the investee has high earnings potential for which the investor has paid more than the fair values of the other net assets

2. **Excess of Book Value over Cost,** which is generally attributable to

    a. **Excess of book value over fair value,** when the book values of the net assets of the investee are greater than their fair values, and
    b. **Excess of fair value over cost,** when the cost of the investment is less than even the fair values of the investee's net assets. Some authors term this "negative goodwill."

If the differential is related to assets with finite useful lives, it will be amortized to the investment account. In accordance with SFAS 142, goodwill will not be amortized; it will be written down if the investment is determined to be impaired.

> *EXAMPLE: A Company purchased 20 shares of B Company's 100 shares of common stock outstanding for $25,000. The book value of B's total net worth (i.e., stockholders' equity) at the date of the investment was $120,000. Any excess of cost over book value is due to equipment that has a ten-year remaining useful life.*

Investment cost		*$ 25,000*
Book value of B Company	*$120,000*	
Percentage owned	*20%*	
Investor's share		*24,000*
Excess of cost over book value (due to equipment)		*$ 1,000*

> *Amortization over forty years*
> *$1,000 ÷ 10 years = $100*

Under the equity method, the Income from Investment account is a parallel income statement account to the Investment in Stock balance sheet account. These two accounts should include all the income recognition and amortization resulting from the investment. Note that under the equity method, dividends received from the investee are a reduction in the Investment balance sheet account and are **not** part of the Income from Investment account.

Alternative levels of recording the results of intercompany transactions and amortization in both the investment and investment income accounts are used in accounting practice. The alternatives are presented below.

1. *Cost adjusted for fair value method*—No intercompany transactions or amortization are recognized in either the investment account or investment income account under this method.
2. *"Partial" equity*—Includes recognition of percentage share of income or loss, dividends, and any changes in the investment percentage. This method is often used for investments that will be con-

solidated. Thus, amortization and other adjustments are made on the worksheets, not in the investment account.

3. ***"Full" equity***—In addition to the factors above, this level includes any necessary amortization or write-off of the differential between the investment cost and book value of the investment. This level also recognizes the effects of any intercompany transactions (e.g., inventory, fixed assets, and bonds) between the investor and investee corporations. APB 18 requires that all unconsolidated investments be reported in the financial statements using the "full" equity method.

*EXTENDED EXAMPLE: Assume the same facts for A Company and B Company as stated above. In addition, B Company earned $10,000 income for the year and paid $6,000 in dividends. There were no intercompany transactions. If A Company does **not** have significant influence over B Company, the investment would be accounted for by the cost adjusted for fair value method. If A Company can significantly influence B Company, the equity method is used to account for and report the investment. The appropriate entries are*

	Cost adjusted for fair value method		*Equity method*	
1.	To record purchase of 20% interest			
	Investment in stock of B 25,000		Investment in stock of B 25,000	
	Cash 25,000		Cash 25,000	
2.	To record percentage share of investee's reported income			
	No entry		Investment in stock of B 2,000	
			Income from investment 2,000	
			(20% x $10,000)	
3.	To record percentage share of dividend received as distribution of income			
	Cash 1,200		Cash 1,200	
	Dividend income from		Investment in stock of B 1,200	
	investment (20% x $6,000) 1,200			
4.	To record amortization of equipment in accordance with APB 18.			
	No entry (no differential amortization under this method)		Income from investment 100	
			Investment in stock of B 100	

The differences in the account balances under the equity method vs. the cost adjusted for fair value method reflect the different income recognition processes and underlying asset valuation concepts of the two methods. The investment account balance under the cost adjusted for fair value method remains at the investment cost of $25,000 (although subsequent changes in fair value would require that the investment account be adjusted to market value), while under the equity method, the investment balance increases to $26,700. The $700 difference is the investor's share of the increase in the investee's undistributed earnings less the investor's amortization of the differential (excess of cost over the book value of the investment).

The amount of the investment income to be recognized by the investor also depends upon the length of time during the year the investment is owned. For example, assume that A Company acquired the 20% interest on July 1, 2002, and B Company earned $10,000 of income ratably over the period from January 1 to December 31, 2002. The entry to record A Company's percentage share of B Company's income for the period of July 1 to December 31, 2002, would be

Cost adjusted for fair value method	*Equity method*	
No entry	Investment in stock of B 1,000	
	Income from investment 1,000	
	(20% x $10,000 x 6/12)	

The receipt of the $1,200 dividends after the acquisition date would require additional analysis since the $1,200 dividend received is greater than the investor's share of the investee's income ($1,000) since acquisition. The difference of $200 ($1,200 – $1,000) is a return of capital under the cost adjusted for fair value method, and is recorded as follows:

Cost adjusted for fair value method	*Equity method*	
Cash 1,200	Cash 1,200	
Dividend income	Investment in stock of B 1,200	
from investment 1,000		
Investment in stock		
of B 200		

The amortization of equipment will also be prorated to the time period the investment was held.

3. ***Changes to or from the equity method***—when an investor changes from the cost adjusted for fair value to the equity method, the investment account must be adjusted retroactively and prior years' income

and retained earnings must be retroactively restated. A change to the equity method would be made if an investor made additional purchases of stock and, for the first time, is able to exercise significant influence over the operating and financial decisions of the investee. Remember that APB 18 states that investments of 20% or more of the investee's outstanding stock carry the "presumption" that the investor has the ability to exercise significant influence. Therefore, in most cases, when an investment of less than 20% increases to more than 20%, the investor will retroactively change from the cost adjusted for fair value method to the equity method.

The retroactive change to the equity method requires a prior period adjustment for the difference in the investment account and retained earnings account between the amounts that were recognized in prior periods under the cost adjusted for fair value method and the amounts that would have been recognized if the equity method had been used. In the full-year investment example on the previous page where A Company had a $25,000 balance in its Investment in B account under the cost adjusted for fair value method and $26,700 under the equity method, if A changed from the cost to the equity method because of its increased influence over B, the change entry would be

Investment in B Company	700	
Retained earnings		700
($775 = $2,000 – $1,200 – $25)		

In addition, any balance in the Unrealized holding gain or loss account must be reversed. Assume that the fair value of the B Company stock had increased from $25,000 to $27,000 as of the end of the year of acquisition. The investment account would have been debited for $2,000 and the Unrealized gain on MES account credited for $2,000 to bring the carrying value of the stock up to its market value. Upon retroactive change to the equity method, the following reversing entry would be made:

Unrealized gain on MES	2,000	
Investment in stock of B		2,000

If the change is made at any time point other than the beginning of the fiscal period, the change entry would also include an adjustment to the period's Income from investment account to record the difference between the cost adjusted for fair value and equity methods handling of the investor's share of the investee's income for the current period.

When an investor discontinues using the equity method because of an inability to influence the investee's financial and operating policies, no retroactive restatement is allowed. An example of this would be a disposal of stock resulting in a decrease in the percentage of stock owned from more than 20% to less than 20%. The earnings or losses that relate to the shares retained by the investor that were previously recognized by the investor should remain as a part of the carrying amount. However, if dividends received by the investor in subsequent periods exceed the investor's share of the investee's earnings for such periods, the excess should be accounted for as a return of capital and recorded as a reduction in the investment carrying amount.

A T-account is used to exhibit the major changes in the Investment in stock account under the equity method.

Investment in Stock	
Original cost of investment	Percentage share of investee's losses since acquisition
Percentage share of investee's income since acquisition	Percentage share of dividends received
Amortization of excess of book value over cost	Amortization of excess of cost over book value
Increase above "significant influence" ownership— retroactive adjustment for change to equity	Disposal or sales of investment in stock

In addition to the above, several adjustments may be added if the "full equity" method is used. This method eliminates the effects of intercompany profits from transactions such as sales of inventory between the investor and investee corporations. This method is rarely required on the exam but candidates should briefly review these additions in association with the discussion of the elimination entries required for consolidated working papers presented later in this module.

Investment in Stock (continued)	
Realized portion of intercompany profit from last period confirmed this period	Elimination of unrealized portion of intercompany profit transactions from current period

D. Equity Method and Deferred Income Taxes

Recognition of deferred taxes may be required when the equity method is used. The difference between the income recognized using the equity method and the dividends received from the investee represents a temporary difference for which interperiod allocation is necessary. Note that companies are allowed to exclude 80% of the dividend income from domestic investees. If an investor owns 80% or more of the investee's stock, the dividend exclusion is increased to 100% (i.e., no taxes are due on investee dividend distributions). The dividend exclusion (dividends received deduction) is a permanent difference.

A discussion of deferred income taxes arising from equity method investments and several examples are provided in Module 27, Deferred Taxes.

E. Stock Dividends and Splits

Stock dividends and stock splits are not recorded as income. The recipient continues to own the same proportion of the investee as before the stock split or dividend. The investor should make a memo entry to record the receipt of the additional shares and recompute the per share cost of the stock.

F. Stock Rights

Investors in common stock occasionally receive stock rights to purchase additional common stock below the existing market price. The investee company has probably issued the stock rights to satisfy the investor's preemptive right to maintain an existing level of ownership of the investee. It is possible to waive these preemptive rights in some jurisdictions.

Rights are issued below the existing market price to encourage the exercise of the rights (i.e., the investor's use thereof resulting in acquisitions of additional shares of stock). The rights are separable, having their own markets, and should be accounted for separately from the investment in common stock. The rights represent a possible dilution of investor ownership and should be recorded by allocating the cost of the stock between the market value of the rights and the market value of the stock. This is accomplished by multiplying the following ratio by the cost basis of the stock:

$$\frac{\text{Market value of right}}{\text{Market value of right} + \text{Market value of stock}}$$

The following entry is made to record the receipt of the rights:

Investment in stock rights	xx	
Investment in common stock		xx

The rights can be sold or exercised. The entry for exercise is

Investment in common stock	xx	
Investment in stock rights		xx
Cash		xx

If the stock rights lapse

Loss on expiration of stock rights	xx	
Investment in stock rights		xx

EXAMPLE: A Company acquired 1,000 shares of common stock in B Company for $12,000. A Company subsequently received two stock rights for every share owned in B Company. Four rights and $12 are required to purchase one new share of common stock. At the date of issuance the market value of the stock rights and the common stock is $5 and $20, respectively. The entry to record the receipt of the rights is as follows:

Investment in stock rights	*4,000*	
Investment in common stock		*4,000*

The $4000 above was computed as follows:

Total market value of rights	*2,000 rights*	*x $5 =*	*$10,000*
Total market value of shares	*1,000 shares*	*x $20 =*	*$20,000*
Combined market value			*30,000*

Cost allocated to stock rights $\dfrac{\$10,000}{\$30,000}$ *x $12,000 = $ 4,000*

Cost allocated to common stock $\dfrac{\$20,000}{\$30,000}$ *x $12,000 = $ 8,000*

Note that $2 ($4,000 ÷ 2,000 rights) of cost is assigned to each stock right and $8 ($8,000 ÷ 1,000 shares) of cost to each share of stock.

If A uses 800 rights to purchase 200 additional shares of stock, the following entry would be made to record the transaction.

Investment in common stock	4,000	
Investment in stock rights		1,600*
Cash		2,400**

* *(800 rights x $2/right)*
** *(200 shares x $12/share)*

If 1,000 stock rights are sold outright for $5 per right, the following entry would be made to record the transaction.

Cash	5,000*	
Investment in stock rights		2,000**
Gain on sale of rights		3,000

* *(1,000 rights x $5/right)*
** *(1,000 rights x $2/right)*

If the 200 remaining stock rights are permitted to expire, the following entry would be made:

Loss on expiration of stock rights	400*	
Investment in stock rights		400*

* *(200 rights x $2/right)*

The journal entries above can be summarized as follows:

	Investment in Common Stock				Investment in Stock Rights		
Purchase, 1,000 shares @ $12	12,000	$ 4,000	← Cost allocated to stock rights →		4,000		
						1,600	Exercise of 800 rights
Purchase, 200 shares by exercise of rights	4,000					2,000	Sale of 1,000 rights
						400	Expiration of 200 rights
	12,000					--	

G. Cash Surrender Value of Life Insurance

The cash surrender value of life insurance policies represents a noncurrent investment when the company is the beneficiary (rather than insured employees). The entry to record insurance premiums that increase cash surrender value is

Insurance expense	(plug)
Cash surrender value	(increase in CSV)
Cash	(total premium)

Cash surrender value remains a noncurrent asset unless the company plans to cash in the policy within the next period.

During the first few years of a policy, no cash surrender value may attach to the policy. During this period, the entire insurance premium would be expense. In addition, any dividends received from the life insurance policy are not recorded as revenue, but instead are offset against insurance expense.

MULTIPLE-CHOICE QUESTIONS (1-51)

1. Puff Co. acquired 40% of Straw, Inc.'s voting common stock on January 2, 2003, for $400,000. The carrying amount of Straw's net assets at the purchase date totaled $900,000. Fair values equaled carrying amounts for all items except equipment, for which fair values exceeded carrying amounts by $100.000. The equipment has a five-year life. During 2003, Straw reported net income of $150,000. What amount of income from this investment should Puff report in its 2003 income statement?

   a. $40,000
   b. $52,000
   c. $56,000
   d. $60,000

2. On April 1, 2002, Saxe, Inc. purchased $200,000 face value, 9% US Treasury Notes for $198,500, including accrued interest of $4,500. The notes mature July 1, 2003, and pay interest semiannually on January 1 and July 1. Saxe uses the straight-line method of amortization and intends to hold the notes to maturity. In its October 31, 2002 balance sheet, the carrying amount of this investment should be

   a. $194,000
   b. $196,800
   c. $197,200
   d. $199,000

3. Kale Co. purchased bonds at a discount on the open market as an investment and intends to hold these bonds to maturity. Kale should account for these bonds at

   a.   Cost.
   b.   Amortized cost.
   c.   Fair value.
   d.   Lower of cost or market.

4. For a marketable debt securities portfolio classified as held-to-maturity, which of the following amounts should be included in the period's net income?

  I. Unrealized temporary losses during the period.
  II. Realized gains during the period.
  III. Changes in the valuation allowance during the period.

   a.   III only.
   b.   II only.
   c.   I and II.
   d.   I, II, and III.

Items 5 and 6 are based on the following:

The following data pertains to Tyne Co.'s investments in marketable equity securities:

		Market value	
	Cost	12/31/02	12/31/01
Trading	$150,000	$155,000	$100,000
Available-for-sale	150,000	130,000	120,000

5. What amount should Tyne report as unrealized holding gain in its 2002 income statement?

   a. $50,000
   b. $55,000
   c. $60,000
   d. $65,000

6. What amount should Tyne report as net unrealized loss on marketable equity securities at December 31, 2002, in accumulated other comprehensive income in stockholders' equity?

   a. $0
   b. $10,000
   c. $15,000
   d. $20,000

7. Reed Insurance Co. began operations on January 1, 2002. The following information pertains to Reed's December 31, 2002 portfolio of marketable equity securities:

	Trading securities	Available-for-sale securities
Aggregate cost	$360,000	$550,000
Aggregate market value	320,000	450,000
Aggregate lower of cost or market value applied to each security in the portfolio	304,000	420,000

If the market declines are judged to be temporary, what amounts should Reed report as a loss on these securities in its December 31, 2002 income statement?

	Trading securities	Available-for-sale securities
a.	$40,000	$0
b.	$0	$100,000
c.	$40,000	$100,000
d.	$56,000	$130,000

8. Information regarding Stone Co.'s portfolio of available-for-sale securities is as follows:

Aggregate cost as of 12/31/02	$170,000
Unrealized gains as of 12/31/02	4,000
Unrealized losses as of 12/31/02	26,000
Net realized gains during 2002	30,000

At December 31, 2001, Stone reported an unrealized loss of $1,500 in other comprehensive income to reduce these securities to market. Under the accumulated other comprehensive income in stockholders' equity section of its December 31, 2002 balance sheet, what amount should Stone report?

   a. $26,000
   b. $22,000
   c. $20,500
   d. $0

9. Data regarding Ball Corp.'s available-for-sale securities follow:

	Cost	Market value
December 31, 2001	$150,000	$130,000
December 31, 2002	150,000	160,000

Differences between cost and market values are considered temporary. Ball's 2002 other comprehensive income would be

   a. $30,000
   b. $20,000
   c. $10,000
   d. $0

10. During 2002, Rex Company purchased marketable equity securities as a short-term investment. These securities are classified as available-for-sale. The cost and market value at December 31, 2002, were as follows:

Security	Cost	Market value
A—100 shares	$ 2,800	$ 3,400
B—1,000 shares	17,000	15,300
C—2,000 shares	31,500	29,500
	$51,300	$48,200

Rex sold 1,000 shares of Company B stock on January 31, 2003, for $15 per share, incurring $1,500 in brokerage commission and taxes. On the sale, Rex should report a realized loss of

    a. $ 300
    b. $1,800
    c. $2,000
    d. $3,500

11. Cap Corp. reported accrued investment interest receivable of $38,000 and $46,500 at January 1 and December 31, 2002, respectively. During 2002, cash collections from the investments included the following:

Capital gains distributions	$145,000
Interest	152,000

What amount should Cap report as interest revenue from investments for 2002?

    a. $160,500
    b. $153,500
    c. $152,000
    d. $143,500

12. Nola has a portfolio of marketable equity securities that it does not intend to sell in the near term. How should Nola classify these securities, and how should it report unrealized gains and losses from these securities?

	Classify as	Report as a
a.	Trading securities	Component of income from continuing operations
b.	Available-for-sale securities	Separate component of other comprehensive income
c.	Trading securities	Separate component of other comprehensive income
d.	Available-for-sale securities	Component of income from continuing operations

13. On December 29, 2002, BJ Co. sold a marketable equity security that had been purchased on January 4, 2001. BJ owned no other marketable equity security. An unrealized loss was reported in 2001 as other comprehensive income. A realized gain was reported in the 2002 income statement. Was the marketable equity security classified as available-for-sale and did its 2001 market price decline exceed its 2002 market price recovery?

	Available-for-sale	2001 market price decline exceeded 2002 market recovery
a.	Yes	Yes
b.	Yes	No
c.	No	Yes
d.	No	No

14. On January 10, 2002, Box, Inc. purchased marketable equity securities of Knox, Inc. and Scot, Inc., neither of which Box could significantly influence. Box classified both securities as available-for-sale. At December 31, 2002, the cost of each investment was greater than its fair market value. The loss on the Knox investment was considered other-than-temporary and that on Scot was considered temporary. How should Box report the effects of these investing activities in its 2002 income statement?

  I. Excess of cost of Knox stock over its market value.
 II. Excess of cost of Scot stock over its market value.

    a.   An unrealized loss equal to I plus II.
    b.   An unrealized loss equal to I only.
    c.   A realized loss equal to I only.
    d.   No income statement effect.

15. On both December 31, 2001, and December 31, 2002, Kopp Co.'s only marketable equity security had the same market value, which was below cost. Kopp considered the decline in value to be temporary in 2001 but other than temporary in 2002. At the end of both years the security was classified as a noncurrent asset. Kopp considers the investment to be available-for-sale. What should be the effects of the determination that the decline was other than temporary on Kopp's 2002 net noncurrent assets and net income?

    a.   No effect on both net noncurrent assets and net income.
    b.   No effect on net noncurrent assets and decrease in net income.
    c.   Decrease in net noncurrent assets and **no** effect on net income.
    d.   Decrease in both net noncurrent assets and net income.

16. For the last ten years, Woody Co. has owned cumulative preferred stock issued by Hadley, Inc. During 2002, Hadley declared and paid both the 2002 dividend and the 2001 dividend in arrears. How should Woody report the 2001 dividend in arrears that was received in 2002?

    a.   As a reduction in cumulative preferred dividends receivable.
    b.   As a retroactive change of the prior period financial statements.
    c.   Include, net of income taxes, after 2002 income from continuing operations.
    d.   Include in 2002 income from continuing operations.

Items 17 and 18 are based on the following:

Deed Co. owns 2% of Beck Cosmetic Retailers. A property dividend by Beck consisted of merchandise with a fair value lower than the listed retail price. Deed in turn gave the merchandise to its employees as a holiday bonus.

17. How should Deed report the receipt and distribution of the merchandise in its income statement?

    a.   At fair value for both dividend revenue and employee compensation expense.
    b.   At listed retail price for both dividend revenue and employee compensation expense.
    c.   At fair value for dividend revenue and listed retail price for employee compensation expense.
    d.   By disclosure only.

18. How should Deed report the receipt and distribution of the merchandise in its statement of cash flows?

    a.   As both an inflow and outflow for operating activities.
    b.   As both an inflow and outflow for investing activities.
    c.   As an inflow for investing activities and outflow for operating activities.
    d.   As a noncash activity.

19. Pal Corp.'s 2002 dividend revenue included only part of the dividends received from its Ima Corp. investment. Pal Corp. has an investment in Ima Corp. that it intends to hold indefinitely. The balance of the dividend reduced Pal's carrying amount for its Ima investment. This reflects the fact that Pal accounts for its Ima investment

a. As an available-for-sale investment, and only a portion of Ima's 2002 dividends represent earnings after Pal's acquisition.

b. As an available-for-sale investment and its carrying amount exceeded the proportionate share of Ima's market value.

c. As an equity investment, and Ima incurred a loss in 2002.

d. As an equity investment, and its carrying amount exceeded the proportionate share of Ima's market value.

20. In its financial statements, Pare, Inc. uses the cost method of accounting for its 15% ownership of Sabe Co. At December 31, 2002, Pare has a receivable from Sabe. How should the receivable be reported in Pare's December 31, 2002 balance sheet?

a. The total receivable should be reported separately.

b. The total receivable should be included as part of the investment in Sabe, without separate disclosure.

c. 85% of the receivable should be reported separately, with the balance offset against Sabe's payable to Pare.

d. The total receivable should be offset against Sabe's payable to Pare, without separate disclosure.

Items 21 and 22 are based on the following:

Sun Corp. had investments in marketable debt securities costing $650,000 that were classified as available-for-sale. On June 30, 2002, Sun decided to hold the investments to maturity and accordingly reclassified them from the held-to-maturity category on that date. The investments' market value was $575,000 at December 31, 2001, $530,000 at June 30, 2002, and $490,000 at December 31, 2002.

21. What amount of loss from investments should Sun report in its 2002 income statement?

a. $ 45,000
b. $ 85,000
c. $120,000
d. $0

22. What amount should Sun report as net unrealized loss on marketable debt securities in its 2002 statement of stockholders' equity?

a. $ 40,000
b. $ 45,000
c. $160,000
d. $120,000

23. A marketable debt security is transferred from available-for-sale to held-to-maturity securities. At the transfer date, the security's carrying amount exceeds its market value. What amount is used at the transfer date to record the security in the held-to-maturity portfolio?

a. Market value, regardless of whether the decline in market value below cost is considered permanent or temporary.

b. Market value, only if the decline in market value below cost is considered permanent.

c. Cost, if the decline in market value below cost is considered temporary.

d. Cost, regardless of whether the decline in market value below cost is considered permanent or temporary.

Items 24 through 26 are based on the following:

Grant, Inc. acquired 30% of South Co.'s voting stock for $200,000 on January 2, 2001. Grant's 30% interest in South gave Grant the ability to exercise significant influence over South's operating and financial policies. During 2001, South earned $80,000 and paid dividends of $50,000. South reported earnings of $100,000 for the six months ended June 30, 2002, and $200,000 for the year ended December 31, 2002. On July 1, 2002, Grant sold half of its stock in South for $150,000 cash. South paid dividends of $60,000 on October 1, 2002.

24. Before income taxes, what amount should Grant include in its 2001 income statement as a result of the investment?

a. $15,000
b. $24,000
c. $50,000
d. $80,000

25. In Grant's December 31, 2001 balance sheet, what should be the carrying amount of this investment?

a. $200,000
b. $209,000
c. $224,000
d. $230,000

26. In its 2002 income statement, what amount should Grant report as gain from the sale of half of its investment?

a. $24,500
b. $30,500
c. $35,000
d. $45,500

27. Moss Corp. owns 20% of Dubro Corp.'s preferred stock and 80% of its common stock. Dubro's stock outstanding at December 31, 2002, is as follows:

10% cumulative preferred stock	$100,000
Common stock	700,000

Dubro reported net income of $60,000 for the year ended December 31, 2002. What amount should Moss record as equity in earnings of Dubro for the year ended December 31, 2002?

a. $42,000
b. $48,000
c. $48,400
d. $50,000

28. Sage, Inc. bought 40% of Adams Corp.'s outstanding common stock on January 2, 2002, for $400,000. The carrying amount of Adams' net assets at the purchase date totaled $900,000. Fair values and carrying amounts were the same for all items except for plant and inventory, for which fair values exceeded their carrying amounts by $90,000 and $10,000, respectively. The plant has an eighteen-year life. All inventory was sold during 2002. During 2002, Adams reported net income of $120,000 and paid a $20,000 cash dividend. What amount should Sage report in its income statement from its investment in Adams for the year ended December 31, 2002?

a. $48,000
b. $42,000
c. $36,000
d. $32,000

29. Pear Co.'s income statement for the year ended December 31, 2002, as prepared by Pear's controller, reported income before taxes of $125,000. The auditor questioned the following amounts that had been included in income before taxes:

Unrealized gain on available-for-sale investment	$40,000
Equity in earnings of Cinn Co.	20,000
Dividends received from Cinn	8,000
Adjustments to profits of prior years for arithmetical errors in depreciation	(35,000)

Pear owns 40% of Cinn's common stock. Pear's December 31, 2002 income statement should report income before taxes of

a. $ 85,000
b. $117,000
c. $112,000
d. $152,000

30. On January 2, 2002, Saxe Company purchased 20% of Lex Corporation's common stock for $150,000. Saxe Corporation intends to hold the stock indefinitely. This investment did not give Saxe the ability to exercise significant influence over Lex. During 2002 Lex reported net income of $175,000 and paid cash dividends of $100,000 on its common stock. There was no change in the market value of the common stock during the year. The balance in Saxe's investment in Lex Corporation account at December 31, 2002 should be

a. $130,000
b. $150,000
c. $165,000
d. $185,000

31. On January 2, 2002, Well Co. purchased 10% of Rea, Inc.'s outstanding common shares for $400,000. Well is the largest single shareholder in Rea, and Well's officers are a majority on Rea's board of directors. Rea reported net income of $500,000 for 2002, and paid dividends of $150,000. In its December 31, 2002 balance sheet, what amount should Well report as investment in Rea?

a. $450,000
b. $435,000
c. $400,000
d. $385,000

32. On January 2, 2002, Kean Co. purchased a 30% interest in Pod Co. for $250,000. On this date, Pod's stockholders' equity was $500,000. The carrying amounts of Pod's identifiable net assets approximated their fair values, except for land whose fair value exceeded its carrying amount by $200,000. Pod reported net income of $100,000 for 2002, and paid no dividends. Kean accounts for this investment using the equity method. In its December 31, 2002 balance sheet, what amount should Kean report as investment in subsidiary?

a. $210,000
b. $220,000
c. $270,000
d. $280,000

33. On January 1, 2002, Mega Corp. acquired 10% of the outstanding voting stock of Penny, Inc. On January 2, 2003, Mega gained the ability to exercise significant influence over financial and operating control of Penny by acquiring an additional 20% of Penny's outstanding stock. The two purchases were made at prices proportionate to the value

assigned to Penny's net assets, which equaled their carrying amounts. For the years ended December 31, 2002 and 2003, Penny reported the following:

	2002	2003
Dividends paid	$200,000	$300,000
Net income	600,000	650,000

In 2003, what amounts should Mega report as current year investment income and as an adjustment, before income taxes, to 2002 investment income?

	2003 investment income	Adjustment to 2002 investment income
a.	$195,000	$160,000
b.	$195,000	$100,000
c.	$195,000	$ 40,000
d.	$105,000	$ 40,000

34. Pare, Inc. purchased 10% of Tot Co.'s 100,000 outstanding shares of common stock on January 2, 2002, for $50,000. On December 31, 2002, Pare purchased an additional 20,000 shares of Tot for $150,000. There was no goodwill as a result of either acquisition, and Tot had not issued any additional stock during 2002. Tot reported earnings of $300,000 for 2002. What amount should Pare report in its December 31, 2002 balance sheet as investment in Tot?

a. $170,000
b. $200,000
c. $230,000
d. $290,000

35. When the equity method is used to account for investments in common stock, which of the following affects the investor's reported investment income?

	Equipment amortization related to purchase	Cash dividends from investee
a.	Yes	Yes
b.	No	Yes
c.	No	No
d.	Yes	No

36. Park Co. uses the equity method to account for its January 1, 2002 purchase of Tun Inc.'s common stock. On January 1, 2002, the fair values of Tun's FIFO inventory and land exceeded their carrying amounts. How do these excesses of fair values over carrying amounts affect Park's reported equity in Tun's 2002 earnings?

	Inventory excess	Land excess
a.	Decrease	Decrease
b.	Decrease	No effect
c.	Increase	Increase
d.	Increase	No effect

37. An investor in common stock received dividends in excess of the investor's share of investee's earnings subsequent to the date of the investment. How will the investor's investment account be affected by those dividends for each of the following investments?

	Available-for-sale securities	Equity method investment
a.	No effect	No effect
b.	Decrease	No effect
c.	No effect	Decrease
d.	Decrease	Decrease

38. Peel Co. received a cash dividend from a common stock investment. Should Peel report an increase in the investment account if it has classified the stock as available-for-sale or uses the equity method of accounting?

	Available-for-sale	*Equity*
a.	No	No
b.	Yes	Yes
c.	Yes	No
d.	No	Yes

39. On January 1, 2002, Point, Inc. purchased 10% of Iona Co.'s common stock. Point purchased additional shares bringing its ownership up to 40% of Iona's common stock outstanding on August 1, 2002. During October 2002, Iona declared and paid a cash dividend on all of its outstanding common stock. How much income from the Iona investment should Point's 2002 income statement report?

    a. 10% of Iona's income for January 1 to July 31, 2002, plus 40% of Iona's income for August 1 to December 31, 2002.

    b. 40% of Iona's income for August 1 to December 31, 2002 only.

    c. 40% of Iona's 2002 income.

    d. Amount equal to dividends received from Iona.

40. In its financial statements, Pulham Corp. uses the equity method of accounting for its 30% ownership of Angles Corp. At December 31, 2002, Pulham has a receivable from Angles. How should the receivable be reported in Pulham's 2002 financial statements?

    a. None of the receivable should be reported, but the entire receivable should be offset against Angles' payable to Pulham.

    b. 70% of the receivable should be separately reported, with the balance offset against 30% of Angles' payable to Pulham.

    c. The total receivable should be disclosed separately.

    d. The total receivable should be included as part of the investment in Angles, without separate disclosure.

41. Wood Co. owns 2,000 shares of Arlo, Inc.'s 20,000 shares of $100 par, 6% cumulative, nonparticipating preferred stock and 1,000 shares (2%) of Arlo's common stock. During 2002, Arlo declared and paid dividends of $240,000 on preferred stock. No dividends had been declared or paid during 2001. In addition, Wood received a 5% common stock dividend from Arlo when the quoted market price of Arlo's common stock was $10 per share. What amount should Wood report as dividend income in its 2002 income statement?

    a. $12,000

    b. $12,500

    c. $24,000

    d. $24,500

42. Stock dividends on common stock should be recorded at their fair market value by the investor when the related investment is accounted for under which of the following methods?

	Cost	*Equity*
a.	Yes	Yes
b.	Yes	No
c.	No	Yes
d.	No	No

43. On March 4, 2002, Evan Co. purchased 1,000 shares of LVC common stock at $80 per share. On September 26, 2002, Evan received 1,000 stock rights to purchase an additional 1,000 shares at $90 per share. The stock rights had an expiration date of February 1, 2003. On September 30, 2002, LVC's common stock had a market value, ex-rights, of $95 per share and the stock rights had a market value of $5 each. What amount should Evan report on its September 30, 2002 balance sheet as the cost of its investment in stock rights?

    a. $ 4,000

    b. $ 5,000

    c. $10,000

    d. $15,000

44. On January 3, 2000, Falk Co. purchased 500 shares of Milo Corp. common stock for $36,000. On December 2, 2002, Falk received 500 stock rights from Milo. Each right entitles the holder to acquire one share of stock for $85. The market price of Milo's stock was $100 a share immediately before the rights were issued, and $90 a share immediately after the rights were issued. Falk sold its rights on December 3, 2002, for $10 a right. Falk's gain from the sale of the rights is

    a. $0

    b. $1,000

    c. $1,400

    d. $5,000

45. In 1997, Chain, Inc. purchased a $1,000,000 life insurance policy on its president, of which Chain is the beneficiary. Information regarding the policy for the year ended December 31, 2002, follows:

Cash surrender value, 1/1/02	$ 87,000
Cash surrender value, 12/31/02	108,000
Annual advance premium paid 1/1/02	40,000

During 2002, dividends of $6,000 were applied to increase the cash surrender value of the policy. What amount should Chain report as life insurance expense for 2002?

    a. $40,000

    b. $25,000

    c. $19,000

    d. $13,000

46. An increase in the cash surrender value of a life insurance policy owned by a company would be recorded by

    a. Decreasing annual insurance expense.

    b. Increasing investment income.

    c. Recording a memorandum entry only.

    d. Decreasing a deferred charge.

47. Upon the death of an officer, Jung Co. received the proceeds of a life insurance policy held by Jung on the officer. The proceeds were not taxable. The policy's cash surrender value had been recorded on Jung's books at the time of payment. What amount of revenue should Jung report in its statements?

    a. Proceeds received.

    b. Proceeds received less cash surrender value.

    c. Proceeds received plus cash surrender value.

    d. None.

Items 48 through 50 are based on the following data:

Lake Corporation's accounting records showed the following investments at January 1, 2002:

Common stock:	
Kar Corp. (1,000 shares)	$ 10,000
Aub Corp. (5,000 shares)	100,000
Real estate:	
Parking lot (leased to Day Co.)	300,000
Other:	
Trademark (at cost, less accumulated amortization)	25,000
Total investments	$435,000

Lake owns 1% of Kar and 30% of Aub. Lake's directors constitute a majority of Aub's directors. The Day lease, which commenced on January 1, 2000, is for ten years, at an annual rental of $48,000. In addition, on January 1, 2000, Day paid a nonrefundable deposit of $50,000, as well as a security deposit of $8,000 to be refunded upon expiration of the lease. The trademark was licensed to Barr Co. for royalties of 10% of sales of the trademarked items. Royalties are payable semiannually on March 1 (for sales in July through December of the prior year), and on September 1 (for sales in January through June of the same year).

During the year ended December 31, 2002, Lake received cash dividends of $1,000 from Kar, and $15,000 from Aub, whose 2002 net incomes were $75,000 and $150,000, respectively. Lake also received $48,000 rent from Day in 2002 and the following royalties from Barr:

	March 1	*September 1*
2001	$3,000	$5,000
2002	4,000	7,000

Barr estimated that sales of the trademarked items would total $20,000 for the last half of 2002.

48. In Lake's 2002 income statement, how much should be reported for dividend revenue?
- a. $16,000
- b. $ 2,400
- c. $ 1,000
- d. $ 150

49. In Lake's 2002 income statement, how much should be reported for royalty revenue?
- a. $14,000
- b. $13,000
- c. $11,000
- d. $ 9,000

50. In Lake's 2002 income statement, how much should be reported for rental revenue?
- a. $43,000
- b. $48,000
- c. $53,000
- d. $53,800

51. Band Co. uses the equity method to account for its investment in Guard, Inc. common stock. How should Band record a 2% stock dividend received from Guard?
- a. As dividend revenue at Guard's carrying value of the stock.
- b. As dividend revenue at the market value of the stock.
- c. As a reduction in the total cost of Guard stock owned.
- d. As a memorandum entry reducing the unit cost of all Guard stock owned.

OTHER OBJECTIVE QUESTIONS

Problem 1   (10 to 15 minutes)

The following questions relate to investments in debt securities and in equity securities that do not involve significant influence.

Part a.

Required:

Items 1 through 7. For each item, match the accounting treatment with the appropriate concept. Concepts may be used once, more than once, or not at all.

Accounting treatment	*Concept*
1. Cash flows from purchases and sales of these securities are reported as an operating activity on the statement of cash flows.	A. Available-for-sale securities
	B. Valuation allowance
2. Include unrealized holding gains/losses in earnings of current period.	C. Transfer from trading to available-for-sale
	D. Held-to-maturity securities
3. Amortize unrealized holding gain/loss over life of security.	E. Permanent impairment
	F. Other-than-temporary securities
4. Report at amortized cost.	G. Amortization of differential
	H. Trading securities
5. Report unrealized holding gains/losses as other comprehensive income and close to accumulated other comprehensive income, a separate component of stockholders' equity.	I. Transfer from available-for-sale to held-to-maturity
6. Classify as a current asset.	
7. Subsequent recovery not recognized unless realized.	

Part b.

Required:

Items 8 through 10. Determine whether each statement is true or false.

8. Held-to-maturity securities are classified as current or noncurrent on an individual basis.

9. For trading securities, some realized gains/losses are excluded from earnings.

10. A premature sale of held-to-maturity securities may be considered maturity if at least 80% of the principal has already been collected.

Problem 2   (15 to 25 minutes)

Items 1 through 4 are based on the following:

Camp Co. purchased various securities during 2002 to be classified as held-to-maturity securities, trading securities, or available-for-sale securities.

Required:

Items 1 through 4 describe various securities purchased by Camp. For each item, select from the following list the appropriate category for each security. A category may be used once, more than once, or not at all.

Categories
H. Held-to-maturity.
T. Trading.
A. Available-for-sale.

1. Debt securities bought and held for the purpose of selling in the near term.

2. US Treasury bonds that Camp has both the positive intent and the ability to hold to maturity.

3. $3 million debt security bought and held for the purpose of selling in three years to finance payment of Camp's $2 million long-term note payable when it matures.

4. Convertible preferred stock that Camp does not intend to sell in the near term.

Items 5 through 10 are based on the following:

The following information pertains to Dayle, Inc.'s portfolio of marketable investments for the year ended December 31, 2002:

	Cost	Fair value 12/31/01	2002 activity Purchases	Sales	Fair value 12/31/02
Held-to-maturity securities					
Security ABC			$100,000		$95,000
Trading securities					
Security DEF	$150,000	$160,000			155,000
Available-for-sale securities					
Security GHI	190,000	165,000		$175,000	
Security JKL	170,000	175,000			160,000

Security ABC was purchased at par. All declines in fair value are considered to be temporary.

Required:

Items 5 through 10 describe amounts to be reported in Dayle's 2002 financial statements. For each item, select from the following list the correct numerical response. An amount may be selected once, more than once, or not at all. Ignore income tax considerations.

5. Carrying amount of security ABC at December 31, 2002.

6. Carrying amount of security DEF at December 31, 2002.

7. Carrying amount of security JKL at December 31, 2002.

Items 8 through 10 require a second response. For each item, indicate whether a gain (G) or a loss (L) is to be reported.

8. Recognized gain or loss on sale of security GHI.

9. Unrealized gain or loss to be reported in 2002 net income.

10. Unrealized gain or loss to be reported at December 31, 2002, as a separate component of stockholders' equity entitled "accumulated other comprehensive income."

Answer List

A.	$0	D.	$ 15,000	G.	$100,000	J.	$160,000
B.	$ 5,000	E.	$ 25,000	H.	$150,000	K.	$170,000
C.	$ 10,000	F.	$ 95,000	I.	$155,000		

PROBLEMS

Problem 1   (15 to 25 minutes)

Vane Insurance Company has two portfolios of marketable equity securities. One is classified as available-for-sale and the other is classified as trading securities. Vane does not have the ability to exercise significant influence over any of the companies in either portfolio. Some securities from each portfolio were sold during the year. One of the securities in the trading securities portfolio was reclassified to the available-for-sale securities portfolio when its market value was less than cost. At the beginning and end of the year, the aggregate cost of each portfolio exceeded its aggregate market value by different amounts.

Required:

a.   How should Vane measure and report the income statement effects of the securities sold during the year from each portfolio?

b.   How should Vane account for the security that was reclassified from the trading securities portfolio to the available-for-sale securities portfolio?

c.   How should Vane report the effects of investments in each portfolio in its balance sheet as of the end of the year and its income statement for the year? Why? **Do not discuss the securities sold.**

Problem 2   (40 to 50 minutes)

Johnson, an investor in Acme Co. asked Smith, CPA, for advice on the propriety of Acme's financial reporting for two of its investments. Smith obtained the following information related to the investments from Acme's December 31, 2002 financial statements:

- 20% ownership interest in Kern Co., represented by 200,000 shares of outstanding common stock purchased on January 2, 2002, for $600,000.
- 20% ownership interest in Wand Co., represented by 20,000 shares of outstanding common stock purchased on January 2, 2002, for $300,000.
- On January 2, 2002, the carrying values of the acquired shares of both investments equaled their purchase price.
- Kern reported earnings of $400,000 for the year ended December 31, 2002, and declared and paid dividends of $100,000 during 2002.
- Wand reported earnings of $350,000 for the year ended December 31, 2002, and declared and paid dividends of $60,000 during 2002.
- On December 31, 2002, Kern's and Wand's common stock were trading over-the-counter at $18 and $20 per share, respectively.
- The investment in Kern is accounted for using the equity method.
- The investment in Wand is accounted for as available-for-sale securities.

Smith recalculated the amounts reported in Acme's December 31, 2002 financial statements, and determined that they were correct. Stressing that the information available in the financial statements was limited, Smith advised Johnson that, assuming Acme properly applied generally accepted accounting principles, Acme may have appropriately used two different methods to account for its investments in Kern and Wand, even though the investments represent equal ownership interests.

Smith also informed Johnson that Acme had elected early application of Statement of Financial Accounting Standards 130, *Reporting Comprehensive Income*, beginning with the fiscal year ending December 31, 2002.

Required:

a.   Prepare a detailed memorandum from Smith to Johnson supporting Smith's conclusion that, under generally accepted accounting principles, Acme may have appropriately used two different methods to account for its investments representing equal ownership interests.

b.   Prepare a schedule indicating the amounts Acme should report for the two investments in its December 31, 2002 balance sheet and statement of income and comprehensive income. Show all calculations. Ignore income taxes.

Do not discuss SFAS 115, *Accounting for Investments in Certain Debt and Equity Securities.*

Problem 3   (40 to 50 minutes)

At December 31, 2001, Poe Corp. properly reported as available-for-sale securities the following marketable equity securities:

	Cost	Fair value
Axe Corp., 1,000 shares, $2.40 convertible preferred stock	$ 40,000	$ 42,000
Purl, Inc., 6,000 shares of common stock	60,000	66,000
Day Co., 2,000 shares of common stock	55,000	40,000
Total available-for-sale securities	$155,000	$148,000

On January 2, 2002, Poe purchased 100,000 shares of Scott Corp. common stock for $1,700,000, representing 30% of Scott's outstanding common stock and an underlying equity of $1,400,000 in Scott's net assets on January 2. Poe, which had no other financial transactions with Scott during 2001. As a result of Poe's 30% ownership of Scott, Poe has the ability to exercise significant influence over Scott's financial and operating policies.

During 2002, Poe disposed of the following securities:

- January 18—sold 2,500 shares of Purl for $13 per share.
- June 1—sold 500 shares of Day, after a 10% stock dividend was received, for $21 per share.
- October 1—converted 500 shares of Axe's preferred stock into 1,500 shares of Axe's common stock, when the market price was $60 per share for the preferred stock and $21 per share for the common stock.

The following 2002 dividend information pertains to stock owned by Poe:

- February 14—Day issued a 10% stock dividend, when the market price of Day's common stock was $22 per share.
- April 5 and October 5—Axe paid dividends of $1.20 per share on its $2.40 preferred stock, to stockholders of record on March 9 and September 9, respectively. Axe did not pay dividends on its common stock during 2002.
- June 30—Purl paid a $1.00 per share dividend on its common stock.

• March 1, June 1, September 1, and December 1 —
Scott paid quarterly dividends of $0.50 per share on each of
these dates. Scott's net income for the year ended December 31, 2002 was $1,200,000.

At December 31, 2002, Poe's management intended to
hold Scott's stock on a long-term basis with the remaining
investments considered temporary. Market prices per share
of the marketable equity securities were as follows:

	At December 31,	
	2002	2001
Axe Corp.—preferred	$56	$42
Axe Corp.—common	20	18
Purl, Inc.—common	11	11
Day Co.—common	22	20
Scott Corp.—common	16	18

All of the foregoing stocks are listed on major stock exchanges. Declines in market value from cost would not be
considered permanent.

Required:

a. Prepare a schedule of Poe's available-for-sale securities
at December 31, 2002, including any information necessary
to determine unrealized gains and losses for the current year.

b. Prepare a schedule to show the carrying amount of
Poe's long-term securities accounted for by the equity
method at December 31, 2002.

c. Prepare a schedule showing all revenue, gains, and realized losses relating to Poe's investments for the year ended
December 31, 2002.

MULTIPLE-CHOICE ANSWERS

1. b __ __	12. b __ __	23. a __ __	34. c __ __	45. c __ __
2. b __ __	13. b __ __	24. b __ __	35. d __ __	46. a __ __
3. b __ __	14. c __ __	25. b __ __	36. b __ __	47. b __ __
4. b __ __	15. b __ __	26. b __ __	37. d __ __	48. c __ __
5. b __ __	16. d __ __	27. a __ __	38. a __ __	49. d __ __
6. d __ __	17. a __ __	28. b __ __	39. a __ __	50. c __ __
7. a __ __	18. d __ __	29. c __ __	40. c __ __	51. d __ __
8. b __ __	19. a __ __	30. b __ __	41. c __ __	
9. a __ __	20. a __ __	31. b __ __	42. d __ __	1st: __/51 = __%
10. d __ __	21. d __ __	32. d __ __	43. a __ __	2nd: __/51 = __%
11. a __ __	22. d __ __	33. c __ __	44. c __ __	

MULTIPLE-CHOICE ANSWER EXPLANATIONS

A. Concepts of Accounting and Investment Percentage

1. (b)   The investment should be accounted for on the equity basis and the calculation of Puff's income from the investment is shown below.

Shaw's net income	$150,000
	x 40%
Puff's share of Shaw's net income	$ 60,000
Less: Puff's depreciation of excess value of equipment	
Excess cost	$100,000
	x 40%
Puff's share	$ 40,000
Remaining useful life	÷ 5
Puff's share of excess depreciation for 2003	(8,000)
Income from investment on the equity basis	$ 52,000

B.1. No Significant Influence: Held-to-Maturity

2. (b)   Per SFAS 115, held-to-maturity securities are to be carried at amortized cost. Therefore, the investment is recorded on 4/1/02 at its cost of $194,000 ($198,500 less accrued interest of $4,500). The carrying amount is calculated as cost plus amortized discount, which at 10/31/02 is $196,800 [$194,000 + ($6,000 x 7/15)].

3. (b)   Per SFAS 115, **held-to-maturity** securities, which include only debt securities, are reported on the balance sheet at **amortized cost** without adjustment to fair value. If the investment in bonds had been classified as trading or available-for-sale, answer (c) would be correct. **Trading** securities are reported at **fair value** with holding gains or losses flowing through the income statements. **Available-for-sale** securities are reported at **fair value** with holding gains or losses reported as a component of other comprehensive income. Cost and lower of cost or market are not used as reporting bases for bond investments.

4. (b)   Per SFAS 115, held-to-maturity securities are carried at cost, so unrealized holding gains and losses are not reported. However, realized gains and losses on held-to-maturity securities should always be included in the income statement of the appropriate period. No valuation allowance exists for any marketable debt or equity securities. Realized gains for the period are the only item listed that is included in that period's net income.

B.2. No Significant Influence: Trading

5. (b)   Debt and equity securities that are classified as **trading securities** are reported at fair value with unrealized gains and losses included in earnings. During 2002, Tyne had an unrealized holding gain of $55,000 ($155,000 – $100,000) on its trading securities. The unrealized holding gain on **available-for-sale** securities ($130,000 – $120,000 = $10,000) is excluded from earnings and reported as other comprehensive income.

6. (d)   The requirement is to determine the accumulated other comprehensive income to be reported in the December 31, 2002 statement of stockholders' equity. Unrealized gains and losses on **trading securities** are included in earnings. Unrealized gains and losses on **available-for-sale** securities are excluded from earnings and reported as accumulated other comprehensive income in a separate component of shareholders' equity. This amount is the net unrealized loss on available-for-sale securities at 12/31/02 is $20,000 ($150,000 – $130,000).

7. (a)   SFAS 115 states that unrealized holding gains and losses for trading securities are to be reported in earnings. On the other hand, this statement also states that unrealized gains or losses on available-for-sale securities should be excluded from earnings and reported as other comprehensive income. Therefore, only the $40,000 ($360,000 – $320,000) unrealized loss on trading securities is included in income.

B.3. No Significant Influence: Available-for-Sale

8. (b)   Available-for-sale securities are reported at market value on the balance sheet. At 12/31/02, Stone has incurred gross unrealized gains of $4,000 and gross unrealized losses of $26,000 on its available-for-sale securities. Therefore, at 12/31/02, the net unrealized loss is $22,000 ($26,000 – $4,000). Stone would have to increase the balance in accumulated other comprehensive income from $1,500 to $22,000 at 12/31/02.

9. (a)   SFAS 115, as amended by SFAS 130, dictates that unrealized holding gains and losses on available-for-sale securities be reported as other comprehensive income. At 12/31/01, available-for-sale securities would have been reported in the balance sheet at their fair value of $130,000, with a corresponding unrealized loss of $20,000. At 12/31/02, the fair value of these securities is $160,000. Therefore, an unrealized gain of $30,000 ($160,000 –

$130,000) would result in other comprehensive income of $30,000 as **accumulated** other comprehensive income.

10.   (d)   In accordance with SFAS 115, the securities purchased by Rex are classified as available-for-sale securities and accounted for at fair value. At 12/31/02, the fair value of security B was $15,300; an unrealized loss of $1,700 resulted in other comprehensive income in that amount. At 1/31/03, the stock was sold when its fair value was $15,000 and the following entry would have been made:

Cash (net)	13,500	
Loss on sale of stock	3,500	
Investment in Security B		15,300
Unrealized loss on Sec. B.		1,700

The unrealized loss of $1,700 on Security B is a credit. It would be netted with unrealized gains and/or losses recognized in 2003. The effect is to offset the $1,700 loss recognized in 2002 that was closed to other comprehensive income, net retained earnings, thus avoiding double counting.

11.   (a)   The capital gains distribution ($145,000) would not be reported as interest revenue. The solutions approach is to set up a T-account for interest receivable.

Interest Receivable		
Beg. bal.	38,000	
Int. rev.	?	152,000 Int. collected
End. bal.	46,500	

Beginning and ending balances are given in the question. Interest receivable would be credited for cash collections to reduce the receivable.

Cash	152,000	
Interest receivable		152,000

Interest receivable would be debited for interest revenue.

Interest receivable	xxx	
Interest revenue		xxx

Solve for interest revenue ($46,500 + $152,000 – $38,000 = $160,500).

12.   (b)   In accordance with SFAS 115, marketable equity securities (MES) are classified as either trading (held for current resale) or available-for-sale (if not categorized as trading). Since Nola does not intend to sell these securities in the near term, they should be classified as available-for-sale. SFAS 115 requires MES to be carried at market value. The unrealized gains or losses of available-for-sale MES are reported as a separate component of other comprehensive income. It is important to note that unrealized gains or losses on **trading** securities would be reported as a component of income from continuing operations on the income statement. Thus, answer (b) is correct because the securities would be classified as available-for-sale and unrealized gains and losses from these securities would be reported as other comprehensive income.

13.   (b)   Per SFAS 115, unrealized losses on available-for-sale securities are reported as a separate component of other comprehensive income, while unrealized gains and losses on trading securities are recognized in income and unrealized gains and losses on held-to-maturity securities are ignored. Thus, this security is classified as available-for-sale. A realized gain will be reported only if the security was sold for a price in excess of its cost. Therefore, the 2001 price decline was **less than** the 2002 price recovery.

For example, assume that the investment was purchased for $1,000 on 1/04/01. At 12/31/01, its market value was $800, and on 12/29/02 its market value was $1,200. The following entries would have been made:

1/04/01	Investment	1,000	
	Cash		1,000
12/31/01	Unrealized loss	200	
	Investment		200
12/29/02	Cash	1,200	
	Investment		800
	Unrealized loss		200
	Gain on sale of securities		**200**

14.   (c)   The requirement is to determine how the losses on the securities classified as available-for-sale should be reported. In accordance with SFAS 115, a decline in market value of a security, which is considered to be **other-than-temporary,** should be reported on the income statement in the current period. A decline in market value, which is considered to be **temporary,** would be recorded as an unrealized loss, and recognized as other comprehensive income. Therefore, answer (c) is correct as the loss on the Knox stock is considered to be other-than-temporary and it would be reported on the income statement. Answer (a) is incorrect because the unrealized loss on the Scot stock would be reported as other comprehensive income. Answer (b) is incorrect because the loss on the Knox stock is considered to be a realized loss as it is other-than-temporary. Answer (d) is incorrect because the other-than-temporary decline in Knox stock results in a realized loss that is reported on the income statement.

15.   (b)   Per SFAS 115, the carrying amount of a marketable equity security classified as available-for-sale shall be the fair market value and the unrealized holding gain or loss should be reported as other comprehensive income. In 2001 when the value declined, the portfolio was reported at market with an unrealized holding loss recorded as other comprehensive income. In 2002, the decline is considered to be other than temporary. Thus, the security must be written down to market and a realized loss recognized. However, since there is no actual change in value, in 2002 the security will be reported at the same amount (cost – write-down of asset) as in 2001. Therefore, there is no effect on **net** noncurrent assets in 2002. However, net income will be affected because a realized loss is recorded on the income statement. Note that the unrealized loss account charged to other comprehensive income in 2001 would be credited and the realized loss account would be debited for the same amount. The allowance accounts will be closed against each other because the new basis after the write-down will equal the lower FMV amount. Answer (a) is incorrect because net income is affected. Note that if the decline was merely temporary, there would be no net income effect because temporary declines in value of noncurrent portfolios are reported as other comprehensive income, rather than net income. Answer (c) is incorrect because there is no net decrease in noncurrent assets, but there is a net income effect. Answer (d) is incorrect because only net income decreases.

16.   (d)   Dividends in arrears are not a receivable to the cumulative preferred stockholder until the issuing corporation's board of directors formally declares the dividend. In this case, Hadley, Inc. did not declare the 2001 dividends in arrears until 2002. At the 2002 dividend declaration date, Woody Co. records dividends receivable and dividend income. Dividend income is included in income from continuing operations.

17. **(a)** Per APB 29, a nonmonetary asset (the merchandise in this case) received in a nonreciprocal transfer should be recorded at the fair value of the asset received. Additionally, the transfer of a nonmonetary asset to a stockholder or other entity (Deed's employees in this case) should be recorded at the fair value of the asset received.

18. **(d)** Per SFAS 95, noncash transactions should be excluded from the statement of cash flows to better achieve the statement's objectives. However, SFAS 95 requires that information about noncash investing and financing transactions be reported in related disclosures.

19. **(a)** Per SFAS 115, an investor carries an investment in the stock of an investee at market, and recognizes as income dividends received that are distributed from the net accumulated earnings of the investee **since the date of acquisition** by the investor. Dividends received in excess of earnings subsequent to the date of investment are considered to be return of investment or a liquidating dividend and are recorded as reductions of the cost of the investment. Therefore, Pal Corp.'s accounting treatment of the dividend it received from Ima Corp. indicates that Pal is accounting for the securities under SFAS 115 as an available-for-sale investment in Ima. Answer (b) is incorrect because Ima's market value does not impact Pal's treatment of dividends received. Answers (c) and (d) are incorrect because all dividends received are treated as reductions in an investee's carrying value under the equity method.

20. **(a)** Intercompany receivables and payables are not eliminated unless consolidated financial statements are prepared. Since Pare only has a 15% interest in Sabe, consolidated financial statements would not be prepared. Thus, on the 12/31/02 balance sheet, Pare should separately report the total amount of the receivable.

B.4. No Significant Influence: Transfers

21. **(d)** The requirement is to determine the amount of loss on investments to be reported in Sun's 2002 income statement. SFAS 115 requires this transfer to be accounted for at fair market value and any holding gains or losses on securities that are transferred to held-to-maturity from available-for-sale be reported as accumulated other comprehensive income. This amount is then amortized over the remaining life of the security as an adjustment to yield. Since cost is greater than market value by $75,000 at 12/31/01 ($650,000 cost – $575,000 fair market value), the following entry would be recorded:

Unrealized loss	75,000	
Marketable debt securities		75,000

Then on June 30, 2002, when Sun decides to hold the investments to maturity, an additional $45,000 will be recorded in the valuation account ($575,000 value on books – $530,000 FMV) to reflect the change in FMV. The following entry would be recorded:

Unrealized loss	45,000	
Marketable debt securities		45,000

Each year the unrealized loss would be reported as other comprehensive income that would be closed to "accumulated other comprehensive income."

22. **(d)** Per SFAS 115, when a security is transferred to held-to-maturity from available-for-sale the unrealized holding gain or loss continues to be is reported as a separate component of stockholders' equity. Held-to-maturity securities are carried at amortized cost, and any unrealized holding gains or losses are not reported. Thus, the balance in the "accumulated other comprehensive income" in stockholders' equity on the 2002 statement of stockholders' equity would be $120,000 ($75,000 amount reported at 12/31/01 plus the $45,000 amount reported at June 30, 2002). The $120,000 will be amortized over the remaining life of the security as an adjustment to yield. The additional decline in value from 6/30/02 to 12/31/02 would not be reported, as held-to-maturity securities do not report unrealized losses.

23. **(a)** SFAS 115, states that "the transfer of a security between categories of investments shall be accounted for at fair value." If fair value is less than the security's carrying amount at the date of transfer, it is irrelevant whether the decline is temporary or permanent.

C. Investment Where Significant Influence Does Exist

24. **(b)** This investment should be accounted for using the equity method since Grant owns a 30% interest and can exercise significant influence over South. Grant's share of South's 2000 earnings (30% x $80,000 = $24,000) would be recognized as investment revenue under the equity method. If there was any excess of cost over book value of assets with finite useful lives, resulting from the purchase of the investment, it would be amortized, reducing investment revenue. However, not enough information was given to determine if there was an excess. The dividends received by Grant (30% x $50,000 = $15,000) do not affect investment revenue using the equity method; they are recorded as a reduction of the investment account.

25. **(b)** The equity method is used because Grant owns a 30% interest and can exercise significant influence. Under this method, the investment account is increased by Grant's equity in South's earnings (30% x $80,000 = $24,000) and is decreased by Grant's dividends received from South (30% x $50,000 = $15,000). This results in a 12/31/01 carrying amount for the investment of $209,000, as indicated in the T-account below.

Investment in South			
1/2/01	200,000		
Equity in earnings	24,000	15,000	Dividends
12/31/01	209,000		

26. **(b)** The equity method is used because Grant owns a 30% interest and can exercise significant influence. Under this method, the investment account is increased by Grant's equity in South's earnings (30% x $80,000 = $24,000 in 2001; 30% x $100,000 = $30,000 for first six months of 2002) and is decreased by Grant's dividends received from South (30% x $50,000 = $15,000 in 2002; none in first six months of 2002). This results in a 7/1/02 carrying amount of $239,000, as indicated in the T-account below.

Investment in South			
1/2/01	200,000		
Equity in earnings	24,000	15,000	Dividends
Equity in earnings	30,000		
7/1/02	239,000		

The gain on sale is the excess of the proceeds ($150,000) over the carrying amount of the shares sold (1/2 x $239,000 = $119,500), or $30,500 ($150,000 – $119,500).

27. **(a)** An investor's share of the income of a company in which it holds a 20% or greater investment is referred to as the investor's equity in earnings of the investee. Per APB 18, the investor's share of the investee's earnings should be computed after deducting the investee's cumulative preferred dividends (whether declared or not). In this case, the income available to common stockholders is $50,000 [$60,000 income – (10% x $100,000 total pref. div.)], so Moss Corp.'s equity in earnings is $40,000 (80% ownership x $50,000). Since $40,000 is not one of the answer choices, apparently the candidate is expected to include the preferred dividend revenue of $2,000 [20% ownership x ($100,000 x 10% total pref. div.)] on the income statement in the equity in earnings line item. Although preferred dividends are usually classified separately, answer (a) is the best answer given. The answer, therefore, is $42,000.

Equity in earnings	$40,000
Dividend revenue	2,000
	$42,000

28. **(b)** Sage paid $400,000 for its 40% investment in Adams when Adams' net assets had a carrying amount of $900,000. Therefore, the book value Sage purchased is $360,000 (40% x $900,000), resulting in an excess of cost over book value of $40,000 ($400,000 – $360,000). This excess must be attributed to specific assets of Adams; any amount not attributed to specific assets is attributed to goodwill. In this case, the excess is attributed to plant assets (40% x $90,000 = $36,000) and inventory (40% x $10,000 = $4,000). The portion attributed to plant assets is amortized over eighteen years, while the portion attributed to inventory is expensed immediately (since all inventory was sold during 2002). Therefore, Sage's investment income is $42,000, as computed below.

Share of income (40% x $120,000)	$48,000
Excess amortization [($36,000/18) + $4,000]	(6,000)
	$42,000

29. **(c)** The unrealized gain on the available-for-sale securities is improperly included in Pear's $125,000 income before taxes. Per SFAS 115, unrealized holding gains and losses on available-for-sale securities are reported as a separate component of stockholders' equity. The equity in Cinn's earnings is properly included in Pear Co.'s pretax income. However, the dividends from Cinn are also improperly included in income because under the equity method, dividends received are a reduction of the investment account rather than dividend revenue. The adjustments to profits of prior years for arithmetic errors in depreciation ($35,000) should be recorded as a retroactive adjustment to beginning retained earnings and should **not** have been deducted when computing 2002 income before taxes. Therefore, 2002 income before taxes should be $112,000 as computed below.

Tentative income	$125,000
Unrealized holding gain	(40,000)
Dividends received	(8,000)
Prior period adjustment	35,000
Correct income	$112,000

30. **(b)** The equity method is to be used when the investor owns 20% or more of the investee's voting stock, unless

there is evidence that the investor does **not** have the ability to exercise significant influence over the investee. Since this is the case, Saxe must carry the stock at market in the available-for-sale category. Under this method, dividends received are to be recognized as income to the investor, and the investment account is unaffected. Also, under this method, the investor's share of the investee's net income is not recognized. Any changes in the market value of the stock would be reflected in the book value of the stock with a corresponding amount in a separate account in stockholders' equity. As there has been no change in the market value, the investment account would still have a balance of $150,000 at 12/31/02. Note that the dividends received by Saxe were distributed from Lex's net accumulated earnings since the date of acquisition by Saxe. However, if dividends received had been in excess of earnings subsequent to the investment date, they are considered a return of capital and would be recorded as a reduction in the investment account.

31. **(b)** Ownership of less than 20% leads to the presumption of **no substantial influence** unless evidence to the contrary exists. Well's position as Rea's largest single shareholder and the presence of Well's officers as a **majority** of Rea's board of directors constitute evidence that Well **does have significant influence** despite less than 20% ownership. Therefore, the equity method is used. The investment account had a beginning balance of $400,000 (purchase price). This amount is increased by Well's equity in Rea's earnings (10% ownership x $500,000 income = $50,000) and decreased by Well's dividends received from Rea (10% share x $150,000 total div. = $15,000), resulting in a balance of $435,000 (see T-account below).

	Investment in Rea		
1/2/02	400,000		
Equity in earnings	50,000	15,000	Dividends
12/31/02	435,000		

32. **(d)** The investment should have been originally recorded at the $250,000 purchase price. This amount would be increased by Kean's share of Pod's earnings (30% x $100,000 = $30,000), decreased by the amortization of excess of cost over book value, and decreased by dividends received by Kean (none in this case). The book value Kean purchased is $150,000 (30% x $500,000), resulting in an excess of cost over book value of $100,000 ($250,000 – $150,000). This excess must be attributed to the specific assets of Pod that have a fair value greater than their book value; any amount not attributed to specific assets is attributed to goodwill. In this case, the excess would be attributed first to land (30% x $200,000 = $60,000) and the remainder to goodwill ($100,000 – $60,000 = $40,000). The portion attributed to land and goodwill should not be amortized. Therefore, Kean's 12/31/02 balance of the investment in subsidiary is $280,000 as computed below.

Original cost	$250,000
Share of income (30% x $100,000)	30,000
	$280,000

33. **(c)** APB 18 states that when an investment that has been accounted for using another method qualifies for the use of the equity method due to a change in ownership level (such as from 10% to 30%), the change to the equity method should be reported **retroactively**. At the date of the change (1/2/03), the **investment** account and **retained earnings** are adjusted as if the equity method had been used all along, and the results of operations in prior years are restated to reflect the equity method. In 2003, use of the equity method results in recognition of investment income of $195,000 (30% x $650,000 investee income). 2002 investment income must be restated from the previously reported dividend income (10% x $200,000 = $20,000) to equity method income (10% x $600,000 = $60,000), an adjustment of $40,000 ($60,000 − $20,000 = $40,000).

34.   (c)   The requirement is to determine the balance in the December 31, 2002, investment account. APB 18 states that when an investment that has been accounted for using another method qualifies for the use of the equity method due to a change in ownership level (in this case, from 10% to 30%), the change to the equity method should be applied retroactively. At the date of the change (12/31/02), the accounts are adjusted as if the equity method had been used all along. If the equity method had been used beginning at 1/2/02, Pare would have recorded its share of Tot's earnings (10% x $300,000 = $30,000) as investment revenue and as an increase in the investment account. Therefore, at 12/31/02, Pare's investment in Tot would be reported at $230,000.

Investment in Tot	
1/2/02 purchase	50,000
12/31/02 purchase	150,000
Equity in earnings	30,000
	230,000

35.   (d)   Under the equity method, a reciprocal relationship is formed between the investment account on the investor's books and the book values of the net assets on the investee's books. As changes in the investee's net assets occur (earnings, dividends, etc.), the investor will recognize the percentage of ownership share of that change in the investment account. Therefore, cash dividends from the investee will be recorded in the investment account, not the investment income account. The entry includes a debit to cash and a credit to the investment account. Another aspect of the equity method is the amortization of the equipment related to the purchase. The investment income account and the investment in stock account should include all the income recognitions and amortizations resulting from the investment. The entry to record the equipment amortization is a debit to Investment income and a credit to Investment in stock.

36.   (b)   When the equity method is used, APB 18 requires the investor to amortize any portion of the excess of fair values over carrying amounts (differential) that relates to depreciable or amortizable assets held by the investee. Amortization of the differential results in a reduction of the investment account and a reduction in the equity of the investee's earnings. For inventory, an excess of FMV over cost, FIFO cost in this case, has the same effect on the investment account and equity in investee earnings in the period in which the goods are sold. Therefore, the portion of the differential that relates to inventory would decrease Park's reported equity in Tun's earnings, and answers (c) and (d) are incorrect. Land is not a depreciable asset, so there would be no amortization of the differential related to land, and answer (a) is incorrect.

37.   (d)   Dividends received in excess of earnings subsequent to the date of investment are considered a return of investment and are recorded as reductions of cost of the investment. Additionally, per APB 18, under the equity method, "dividends received from an investee reduce the carrying amount of the investment."

38.   (a)   The requirement is to determine the effects of a cash dividend on an investors investment account, accounted for both as an available-for-sale security, and under the equity method. Dividends received on available-for-sale securities are to be recognized as income to the investor and the investment account is unaffected. If the dividends received are in excess of earnings to date, then they would be considered a return of the investment and would result in a reduction of the investment account. Under the equity method, the receipt of cash dividends reduces the carrying value of the investment. Therefore, answer (a) is correct as the receipt of a cash dividend would not result in an increase in the investment account under either method.

39.   (a)   The requirement is to determine the amount of investment income to be reported in the 2002 income statement. APB 18 states that when an investment which has been accounted for using a different method qualifies for the use of the equity method, due to a change in ownership level (such as 10% to 40%), then the change to the equity method should be reported **retroactively**. At the date of the change, the investment account and the retained earnings account are adjusted as if the equity method had been used all along. Therefore answer (a) is correct as Point owned 10% of Iona's stock from January 1 to July 31, 2002, and 40% of Iona's stock from August 1 to December 31, 2002. Answers (b) and (c) are incorrect because income should be recognized under the equity method according to the percentage of ownership existing during each of the periods. Answer (d) is incorrect because when Iona reports its earnings to Point, Point will record its share of the revenue. When Point receives the dividends, (which may be in a different period than Point recognized its share of Iona's income), the carrying amount of the investment will be reduced by the amount received. Therefore, the income recognized does not usually equal the dividends received.

40.   (c)   APB 18 requires the use of the equity method when accounting for investments in which the investor has the ability to exercise significant influence over the operating and financial policies of the investee. APB 18 generally assumes that ownership of 20% or more of the outstanding common stock demonstrates this ability. In this case, Pulham Corp. owns 30% of Angles and properly uses the equity method. Under the equity method intercompany profits and losses are eliminated. However, receivables and payables are not eliminated as they are in the case of consolidated financial statements. On the December 31, 2002 balance sheet, Pulham should separately disclose the total amount of the receivable. Additionally, this receivable should be shown separately from other receivables.

E. Stock Dividends and Splits

41.   (c)   Arlo's annual preferred stock dividend is $120,000 ($2,000,000 x 6%). The $240,000 dividend paid includes $120,000 dividends in arrears from 2001 and $120,000 for 2002. Therefore, Wood would receive **$24,000 of cash dividends** ($200,000 x 6% x 2) which would be reported as **dividend income** in 2002 (preferred dividends in arrears are not recognized as income until declared). No dividend income is recognized when an investor receives a proportional **stock** dividend, because the investor continues to own the same proportion of the investee as before the stock dividend, and the investee has not distributed any assets to the investor.

42.   (d)   Regardless of the accounting method used, no dividend revenue is recognized when an investor receives a proportional **stock** dividend, because the investor continues to own the same proportion of the investee as before the stock dividend. In addition, the investee has not distributed any assets to the investor. Therefore, **no entry** is prepared to record the receipt of a stock dividend. The investor simply makes a memo entry to record the additional number of shares owned, while leaving the balance in the investment account unchanged. The balance is then spread over the total number of shares (previous holdings + stock dividend) to determine the new per share cost of the stock.

F. Stock Rights

43.   (a)   When stock rights are received, the cost of the investment (1,000 x $80 = $80,000) is allocated between the stock and the rights based on the relative fair market value of each, as calculated below.

FMV of stock	1,000 x $95 =	$ 95,000
FMV of rights	1,000 x $ 5 =	5,000
Total FMV		$100,000

The cost allocated to the stock is $76,000 ($80,000 x 95/100) and the cost allocated to the rights is $4,000 ($80,000 x 5/100).

44.   (c)   When the rights are received, the cost of the investment ($36,000) is allocated between the stock and the rights based on their relative fair market values, calculated below.

FMV of stock	500 x $90	=	$45,000
FMV of rights	500 x $10	=	5,000
Total FMV			$50,000

The cost allocated to the stock is $32,400 ($45,000/ $50,000, or 90%, of $36,000) and to the rights is $3,600 ($5,000/$50,000, or 10%, of $36,000). The net proceeds from the sale of the rights is $5,000 (500 x $10), so the gain on the sale of the rights is $1,400 ($5,000 – $3,600).

G. Cash Surrender Value of Life Insurance

45.   (c)   The cash surrender value (CSV) of the life insurance policy increased by $21,000 during 2001 ($108,000 – $87,000). Therefore, part of the premium paid is not expense but a payment to increase the CSV. The formula to compute insurance expense is

Cash paid — (Ending CSV – Beginning CSV) — Cash divs. received
$40,000 —   ($108,000 – $87,000)   — $0   = $19,000

The dividends in this problem are **not** cash dividends received. They are dividends that the insurance company applied to increase the CSV. They are not separately considered in the formula above because the effect of the dividends is reflected in the increase in CSV, which **is** included in the formula. 2002 journal entries are presented below.

Cash surr. value	$15,000		($21,000 – $6,000)
Ins. expense	25,000		
Cash		$40,000	
Cash surr. value	$ 6,000		
Ins. expense		$ 6,000	

46.   (a)   When a company insures the lives of employees and names itself the beneficiary, the cash surrender value of the policies is considered an asset. During the first few years of a policy, no cash surrender value may accrue. If no increase in cash surrender value (CSV) occurs, the journal entry to record a premium paid would be

Insurance expense	xxx	
Cash		xxx

However, if cash surrender value increases, part of the cash paid is recorded as an increase in the CSV. The entry is

Insurance expense	xx	
Cash surrender value	xx	
Cash		xxx

Therefore, the increase in CSV decreases insurance expense because the same amount of cash paid must be allocated between the two accounts. The increase in CSV does **not** affect investment income or deferred charges.

47.   (b)   When a company insures the lives of employees and names itself as the beneficiary, the cash surrender value (CSV) of the policy is considered an asset. Premiums paid are debited to CSV for the increase in CSV that year and to insurance expense for the excess of cash paid over increase in CSV. Upon the death of the insured employee, the company recognizes a gain for the excess of proceeds received over CSV.

Miscellaneous

48.   (c)   In determining the amount which should be reported in Lake's 2002 income statement as dividend revenue, the first step is to determine what method should be used in accounting for Lake's investments. Per APB 18, the Board concluded that the equity method of accounting for an investment in common stock should be followed by an investor whose investment in common stock gives it the ability to exercise significant influence over the operating and financial policies of an investee even though the investor may hold 50% or less of the voting stock. Ability to exercise that influence may be indicated in several ways, such as representation on the board of directors. Another important consideration is the extent of ownership by an investor. The Board concluded that an investment of 20% or more of the voting stock of an investee should lead to a presumption, in the absence of evidence to the contrary, that an investor has the ability to exercise significant influence over an investee. Conversely, an investment of less than 20% of the voting stock of an investee should lead to a presumption that an investor does **not** have the ability to exercise significant influence unless such ability can be demonstrated. Lake's 30% ownership of Aub and its representation on Aub's board of directors clearly indicate that the investment in Aub should be accounted for using the equity method. Lake's 1% ownership in Kar and lack of evidence in this problem that Lake has "significant influence" over Kar indicate that this investment should be accounted for using the cost adjusted for fair value method, in accordance with SFAS 115. Per APB 18, when the **equity** method is used, dividends received from an investee reduce the carrying amount of the investment (i.e., are **not** reported as dividend revenue). Per APB 18, however, the investor recognizes dividends received from investees as **income** under the **cost adjusted for fair value** method. Therefore, the $1,000 of cash dividends from Kar would be reported as dividend revenue by

Lake, while the $15,000 of cash dividends from Aub would reduce the carrying amount of Lake's investment in Aub.

49.   (d)   Lake's royalty revenue results from the licensing of their trademark to Barr Co. Lake receives royalties of 10% of Barr's sales of trademarked items. To determine royalty revenue for 2002, it must first be realized that the royalty payment on September 1, 2002, is for sales in January through June of 2002. This royalty payment of $7,000 is the first portion of royalty revenue for 2002. The second portion of royalty revenue is for Barr's sales of trademarked items for July through December of 2002. This second portion consists of 10% of Barr's estimated sales of trademarked items for the last half of 2002. Royalty revenue for the second half of 2002 is then $2,000 (10% x $20,000). Therefore, answer (d) is correct because royalty revenue would be $9,000 for 2002 and is comprised of the $7,000 royalty payment received on September 1, 2002, plus 10% of estimated sales for months July through December.

50.   (c)   Lake receives rental revenue from leasing a parking lot to Day Co. The annual rental payment made by Day Co. to Lake is $48,000. However, Day Co. also paid a nonrefundable deposit of $50,000 on January 1, 2000. This $50,000 deposit, since it is nonrefundable, is considered unearned revenue that must be recognized over the life of the lease on a straight-line basis. Therefore, in addition to the $48,000 annual rental payment, $5,000 ($50,000 ÷ 10 years) of the nonrefundable deposit will be recognized as rental revenue in 2002. Thus, answer (c) is correct because $53,000 will be recognized as rental revenue in 2002. Note that the $8,000 security deposit will not be revenue because it is to be refunded at the end of the lease period. It is deferred in its entirety and recorded as a long-term liability. Only a nonrefundable deposit would be recognized as rental revenue over the life of the lease.

51.   (d)   Stock dividends are not income to the recipient, but rather, are an adjustment of the per share basis of the investment. Answer (c) is incorrect because no change in the total investment cost is made when an investor receives stock dividends. Answer (d) is correct because some companies make a memorandum journal entry to note the receipt of the stock dividend and the adjustment of the per share basis of the investment.

OTHER OBJECTIVE ANSWERS AND ANSWER EXPLANATIONS

Problem 1

Part a.

1. **(H)** SFAS 115 dictates that purchases and sales of trading portfolio securities be classified as operating activities on the statement of cash flows due to the short-term, profit-seeking nature of the investment. In contrast, available-for-sale and held-to-maturity securities are classified as investing activities.

2. **(H)** Unrealized holding gains and losses on trading securities are included in income of the period.

3. **(I)** Unrealized holding gains and losses on securities transferred to held-to-maturity from available-for-sale are reported as a separate component of stockholders' equity (accumulated other comprehensive income) and amortized over the remaining life of the security.

4. **(D)** Held-to-maturity securities are carried at amortized cost.

5. **(A)** Unrealized holding gains and losses on available-for-sale securities are reported as other comprehensive income, whereas those on trading securities are included in income and those on held-to-maturity securities are not reported.

6. **(H)** Trading securities appear on the balance sheet as current assets.

7. **(E)** When a decline in value of a security is deemed to be other than temporary, the impaired security is written down to fair value. Any subsequent recovery may not be recognized in earnings unless realized through sale of the security.

Part b.

8. **(T)** Held-to-maturity securities are classified as current or noncurrent according to how soon they will mature, (i.e., a security maturing within one year is classified as current, while one with a more distant maturity date is considered noncurrent).

9. **(T)** Some unrealized holding gains and losses on trading securities could have already been included in income as unrealized components. Thus, to recognize them again upon realization would result in an erroneous doubling of the actual gain/loss.

10. **(F)** Premature sale of held-to-maturity securities are considered at maturity if either (1) the sale occurs so close to maturity that interest rate risk is virtually eliminated, or (2) the sale occurs after at least 85% of the principal has been collected.

Problem 2

1. **(T)** Trading. SFAS 115 states that "securities that are bought and held principally for the purpose of selling them in the near term (thus held for only a short period of time) shall be classified as **trading securities**."

2. **(H)** Held-to-maturity. SFAS 114 states that "investments in debt securities shall be classified as **held-to-maturity** and measured at amortized cost...only if the reporting enterprise has the positive intent and ability to hold those securities to maturity." Both conditions are met in this case. .

3. **(A)** Available-for-sale. The company does not have the "positive intent . . .to hold this debt security to maturity," therefore the security cannot be classified as held-to-maturity. Also, since it will be sold beyond the "near term," it cannot be classified as "trading." SFAS 115 states that "investments not classified as trading (nor as held-to-maturity securities) shall be classified as **available-for-sale securities**."

4. **(A)** Available-for-sale. Since this security is neither a debt security nor a security that will be sold in the near term, it is classified as available-for-sale.

5. **(G; $100,000)** SFAS 115 states that held-to-maturity securities "shall be . . .measured at amortized cost." Since this debt security was purchased at par, there is neither a discount nor a premium to amortize, therefore amortized cost equals par or $100,000. Ignore fair value.

6. **(I; $155,000)** SFAS 115 states "Investments in . . .securities that are not classified as held-to-maturity and that have readily determinable fair values shall be . . .measured at fair value." $155,000 is fair value.

7. **(J; $160,000)** Same answer as question 6. Since security JKL is not a debt security classified as held-to-maturity and since it has a readily determinable fair value it "shall be . . .measured at fair value."

8. **(D, L)** Recognized gains and losses on the sale of available-for-sale securities are measured as the difference between original cost ($190,000) and the selling price of the securities ($175,000). The unrealized loss that existed in accumulated other comprehensive income in the equity section prior to the sale ($25,000) will be reversed as a credit to unrealized loss and that reversal will be reported as other comprehensive income and closed to accumulated other comprehensive income that is reported in the equity section of the balance sheet (see question 10 below). The journal entry to record the sale would be

Cash	175,000	
Realized loss on sale of A-F-S securities	15,000	
A-F-S securities		165,000
Unrealized loss on A-F-S securities		25,000

9. **(B, L)** The only unrealized gains or losses on securities reported in the net income relate to value changes in trading securities. In this case the value of the JKL securities has decreased from $160,000 to $155,000.

10. **(C, L)** The 1/1/02 balance of the unrealized gain or loss on A-F-S securities reported in the equity section was $20,000, the difference between the 1/1/02 $25,000 unrealized loss of GHI ($190,000 – $165,000) and the 1/1/02 $5,000 unrealized gain of JKL ($175,000 – $170,000). The changes during the year were (1) the $25,000 reversal (credit) of the unrealized loss of GHI when it was sold and (2) the $15,000 loss ($175,000 – $160,000) in value during the year of JKL. The Other Comprehensive Income account would appear as follows:

Other Comprehensive Income			
Beg. bal.	--		
12/31/02 JKL	15,000	12/31/02 Reverse GHI	25,000
Close to Accumulated Other Compre-			
hensive Income	10,000		

The Accumulated Other Comprehensive Income account would appear as follows:

Accumulated Other Comprehensive Income		
1/1/02	20,000	
		12/31/02 Close from Other Comprehensive Income
12/31/02 Balance	10,000	

ANSWER OUTLINE

Problem 1   MES: Available-for-Sale and Trading
                Securities Portfolios

a.   Gains or losses should be measured as difference be-
        tween selling prices and carrying amount of securities
        sold
        Differences constitute realized gains and losses
            Recognized in income for trading securities net of
                unrealized gains or losses previously recognized
            Recognize in income for available-for-sale securities

b.   Reclassification of trading security to available-for-sale
        portfolio
            Unrealized losses up to date of transfer, including
                those in the current period, were already recognized
                and are not reversed
            Basis should be fair value at date of reclassification

c.   BS and IS reporting
            Each portfolio is reported at fair value
            Unrealized gains (losses)
                Recognize as income for trading securities
                Report as component of stockholders' equity (ac-
                    cumulated other comprehensive income) for
                    available-for-sale securities
        Reasons portfolios are reported this way
            Relevance—fair value reflects the effects of man-
                agement's decision to buy at a certain time and then
                to hold security for some period of time
            Matching
                Trading securities
                    Estimated loss is reported in period it occurred
                    Indicates expected cash flow consequences from
                        sale of the securities
                Available-for-sale securities
                    Realization of gains (losses) from sale is less
                        certain in near term
                    Market value decline
                        May not be a reasonable estimate
                        Not useful for cash flow projections

UNOFFICIAL ANSWER

Problem 1   MES: Available-for-Sale and Trading
                Securities Portfolios

a.   The differences between the selling prices and the costs
of the available-for-sale securities sold should be reported as
realized gains and losses in the determination of net income.
On the other hand, any realized gains and losses on the
trading securities sold are recognized net of unrealized gains
or losses previously recognized.

b.   The security in the trading securities portfolio should be
reclassified to the available-for-sale portfolio at its fair value
on the date of transfer. Unrealized losses up to the date of
transfer, including those in the current period, were already
recognized in income and should not be reversed.

c.   Each portfolio should be reported on the balance sheet
at fair value. Unrealized gains and losses on the trading
securities portfolio are recognized in earnings on the income
statement. On the other hand, unrealized gains and losses on
the available-for-sale securities portfolio are reported as
other comprehensive income and as a separate component of
stockholders' equity (accumulated other comprehensive
income) on the balance sheet.

Reporting the portfolio at fair value reflects the realizable value of the portfolio at the end of the period. For the
trading securities portfolio, the estimated loss is reported
(matched) in the income statement in the period in which the
change in realizable value occurred. Reporting trading securities at fair value indicates the expected cash flow from the
sale of the securities. Inclusion of the reduction in fair value
in net income assists in cash flow projections by acknowl-
edging the expected impairment in future cash flows as a
consequence of the investment. For the available-for-sale
portfolio, the decline in market value (loss) is less certain of
realization in the near term, and may not be a reasonable
estimate of the cash flow consequence of the investment.
Therefore, changes in market value of the available-for-sale
portfolio are not considered useful for cash flow projections.
Accordingly, these losses are not reported in earnings.

ANSWER OUTLINE

Problem 2   Equity Method Criteria

a.   Despite 20% interest in each, use of different account-
        ing methods may be appropriate under GAAP.
        Must use equity method if ownership interest allows
            significant influence over investee company.
        Significant influence presumed for 20% or more owner-
            ship; not presumed for less than 20% ownership.

        Predominant evidence to the contrary may overcome
        presumptions:

        • Investor's representation on investee's board of di-
          rectors
        • Participation in policymaking activities
        • Extent of ownership compared to investee's other
          stockholders

        Accounting for investment in Kern with equity method
            indicates significant influence.
        Accounting for investment in Wand as available-for-
            sale securities indicates lack of significant influence.

b.   See unofficial answer

UNOFFICIAL ANSWER

Problem 2   Equity Method Criteria

a.

To:	Johnson
From:	Smith, CPA
Re:	Acme Co. Investments in Kern Co. and Wand Co.

        The purpose of this memorandum is to explain to
you that although Acme's investment in Wand and
Kern represents equal ownership interests of 20%, the
use of different accounting methods may be appropriate
under generally accepted accounting principles.

        Under those principles, Acme must use the equity
method to account for an investment if Acme's ownership interest allows it to exercise significant influence
over the investee company.

        Generally, an investor is presumed to be able to
exercise significant influence when it has an ownership
interest of 20% or more, and is presumed to be unable
to exercise significant influence when it has an ownership interest of less than 20%. However, either presumption may be overcome by predominant evidence to

the contrary. The determination of whether an investor can exercise significant influence is not always clear and often requires judgment in light of such factors as an investor's representation on the investee's board of directors, participation in policymaking activities, and/or the extent of ownership as compared to that investee's other shareholders.

Acme used the equity method to account for its investment in Kern that indicates that its 20% ownership

b.   *Kern*

Balance sheet–Acme reported its investment in Kern at a carrying amount of $660,000

Calculations:

Equity in earnings = $80,000 ($400,000 x 20%)

Dividend rec'd = $20,000 ($100,000 x 20%)

Carrying amount = $600,000 + $80,000 – $20,000

Statement of Income and Comprehensive Income

Acme's equity in Kern's earnings $80,000

Calculation:

$400,000 x 20%

interest allowed it to exercise significant influence over Kern's operating and financial policies.

Acme accounted for its investment in Wand as available-for-sale securities. Apparently, despite its 20% ownership interest, there was evidence that Acme could not exercise significant influence over Wand's operating and financial policies. Hence, Acme did not use the equity method to account for its investment in Wand.

Wand

Balance sheet–Acme reported its investment in Wand at a fair value of $400,000

Calculation:

20,000 shares x $20 per share

Statement of Income and Comprehensive Income

Dividend income $12,000

Calculation:

$60,000 x 20%

Unrealized gain $100,000

Calculation:

$400,000 – $300,000

SOLUTION GUIDE

Problem 3   MES & Equity Method Investment

1.   This problem consists of three related requirements concerning a company's investments in marketable equity securities.

1.1   In part a., a schedule of Poe's available-for-sale securities at 12/31/02 must be prepared. This schedule should include columns for cost, market, and unrealized gain or loss.

1.2   A schedule to show the carrying amount of Poe's long-term investments accounted for by the equity method at 12/31/02 is required in part b.

1.3   In part c., a schedule showing all revenues, gains, and losses for 2002 relating to Poe's investments must be prepared.

1.4   The solutions approach for problems of this type in which the requirements are interrelated is to prepare time lines for each security and proceed through the given information making computations and notations on the appropriate time line. Labeling of computations by requirement helps to organize your data. For example, if a computation or number relates to requirement c., it can be labeled "c." Using this approach, the candidate will be solving a part of two to three requirements as each security is covered, but not necessarily in the same order as given on the exam. After working through all the information given, the formal required schedules can be prepared.

2.   At 12/31/01, Poe owned 1,000 shares of Axe preferred with a fair value of $42,000 ($42/share). At 10/1/02, Poe converted 500 shares of Axe preferred into 1,500 shares of Axe common. The preferred fair value is allocated to the common since half of the preferred $21,000 was surrendered to acquire it. The remaining preferred is still carried at $21,000 ($42 x 500 shares). At year-end, the preferred is reported at

$28,000 ($56 FV/sh x 500 sh) and the common stock is reported at $30,000 ($20 FV/sh x 1,500 sh). See time line after 2.1.

2.1   Dividend revenue received on the Axe preferred stock should be included in Poe's income statement. The Axe preferred stock paid a $1.20 dividend on 1,000 shares twice during the year, for a total of $2,400. Note that the second dividend was received on October 5, after 500 shares of preferred were converted. However, the dividend was received for all 1,000 shares, since the date of record was September 9.

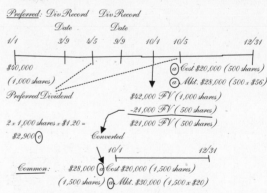

3.   Poe owned 6,000 shares of Purl common that originally cost $60,000 ($10/sh) and had a fair value of $66,000 ($11/sh) at 12/31/01. 2,500 of these shares were sold. The 3,500 still held have a carrying value of $38,500 (3,500 sh x $11). See time line after 3.2.

3.1   On 1/18/02, Poe sold 2,500 shares of Purl common for $32,500 (2,500 sh x $13) when the carrying value (fair value) was $27,500 (2,500 sh x $11). Since unrealized gains/losses on available-for-sale securities are not recognized in income the gain on the sale is $7,500 ($32,500 – $25,000).

3.2   Dividend income received on the Purl common stock should also be included in Poe's income statement. A $1.00 per share dividend was received on the Purl common stock (3,500 shares x $1.00 per share or $3,500).

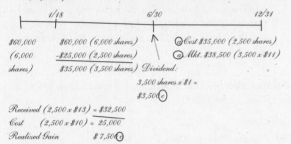

4.   At 1/1/02, Poe owned 2,000 shares of Day common that cost $55,000 and had a fair value of $40,000. Day issued a 10% stock dividend on February 14 when the stock's fair value was $44,000 (2,000 x $22), which gave Poe an additional 200 shares (2,000 x 10%) at no additional cost. Therefore, the 2,200 shares had an adjusted cost of $25 per share ($55,000 ÷ 2,200). The adjusted carrying value per share was $18.18 ($40,000 ÷ 2,200 shs). The stock dividend is not reflected in income. Poe sold 500 shares on June 1. The 1,700 still held have a cost of $42,500 (1,700 x $25), a carrying value of $30,900 (1,700 x $18.18) and a fair value of $37,400 (1,700 x $22). See time line after 4.1.

4.1   The Day stock sold for $10,500 (500 x $21) and had a cost of $12,500 (500 x $25). Thus, a $2,000 loss was realized on the sale of Day common and should be included in Poe's income statement.

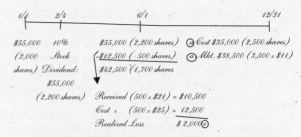

5.   Poe intends to hold the Scott stock as a long-term investment. Since Poe owns 30% of the voting stock and can exercise significant influence over Scott, the use of the equity method is appropriate.

5.1   The original cost of the investment was $1,700,000. The excess of investment cost ($1,700,000) over the book value of the net assets purchased ($1,400,000) is $300,000. This amount is not amortized, in accordance with SFAS 142.

5.2   The investment account is also reduced by dividends received when the equity method is used. Scott paid quarterly dividends of $.50 a share, or a total of $50,000 each quarter to Poe (100,000 x $.50). Therefore, Poe received a total of $200,000 in dividends (4 x $50,000) from Scott. See time line after 5.3.

| Cash | 200,000 | |
| Investment in Scott | | 200,000 |

Note that the dividend received from Scott is not recognized as income under the equity method.

5.3   Using the equity method, the investment account is increased by the investor's share of investee earnings 30% x $1,200,000 = $360,000).

| Investment in Scott | 360,000 | |
| Investment revenue | | 360,000 |

UNOFFICIAL ANSWER

Problem 3   MES & Equity Method Investment

a.

Poe Corp.
**SCHEDULE OF AVAILABLE-FOR-SALE
SECURITIES**
December 31, 2002

	Number of shares	Cost	Beginning carrying amount at market	Ending market price per share	Market value	Cumulative gain or (loss)	Unrealized gain or (loss) in 2002
Axe—preferred	500	$ 20,000	$ 21,000	$56	$ 28,000	$ 8,000	$ 7,000
Axe—common	1,500	20,000	21,000	20	30,000	10,000	9,000
Purl—common	3,500	35,000	38,500	11	38,500	3,500	
Day—common	1,700	42,500	30,900	22	37,400	(5,100)	6,500
		$117,500	$111,400		$133,900	$16,400	$22,500

b.

Poe Corp.
**SCHEDULE OF LONG-TERM MARKETABLE
EQUITY SECURITIES**
December 31, 2002

Scott Corp.—100,000 shares of common stock:

Cost:			
Acquisition price			$1,700,000
Increase in equity during 2002:			
Poe's interest in Scott's income		$360,000	
Less:			
Dividends received		200,000	
Net increase in equity			160,000
Carrying amount of Poe Corp.'s investment in Scott			$1,860,000

c.

Poe Corp.
SCHEDULE OF INVESTMENT INCOME
For the Year Ended December 31, 2002

Dividends:			
Axe Corp.—preferred (1,000 shares x $2.40 per share)		$ 2,400	
Purl, Inc.—common (3,500 shares x $1.00 per share)		3,500	
Total dividend revenue			$ 5,900
Gains on marketable equity securities:	[1]		
Realized gain/(loss) on sale of securities:			
Purl, Inc.—common ($13 – $10 = $3 x 2,500 shares)		$ 7,500	
Day Co.—common ($55,000/2,000 shares x 110%, or cost per share of $25 – $21 selling price per share = $4 loss per share x 500 shares sold)		(2,000)	
Net realized gain on sale of securities			5,500
Equity in income of Scott Corp.:			
Poe's 30% interest in Scott's net income of $1,200,000			360,000
Total investment income			$371,400

Explanation of amount

[1]   Unrealized gains (losses) on available-for-sale securities are excluded from investment income and thus are excluded from Poe's schedule of investment income. They are reported as other comprehensive income.

STATEMENT OF CASH FLOWS

A. Objectives of the Statement of Cash Flows (See outline of SFAS 95 also)

The primary purposes of this statement are to provide information about an entity's cash receipts and cash payments and to disclose information about the financing and investing activities of an entity. This statement should help the users of the statement assess: (1) an entity's ability to generate positive future cash flows; (2) an entity's ability to meet its obligations and pay dividends; (3) the reasons for differences between income and associated cash receipts and payments; and (4) the cash and noncash aspects of an entity's investing and financing transactions.

In order to facilitate the users in making those assessments, a statement of cash flows shall report cash receipts and cash payments of an entity's operations, its investing transactions, and its financing transactions. A separate schedule accompanying the statement should also report the effects of investing and financing transactions that **do not affect cash**.

The statement of cash flows is required to be prepared based on changes during the period in cash and cash equivalents. Cash equivalents include short-term, highly liquid investments that (1) are readily convertible to known amounts of cash and (2) are so near their maturity (original maturity of three months or less from **date of purchase** by the enterprise) that they present negligible risk of changes in value because of changes in interest rates. Treasury bills, commercial paper, and money market funds are all examples of cash equivalents.

B. Statement of Cash Flows Classification

Cash receipts and cash payments are to be classified into operating, financing, and investing activities.

Operating activities include delivering or producing goods for sale and providing services. Operating activities include all transactions that are **not** investing and financing activities. More specifically, cash flows from operations should not include cash flows from transactions whose effects are included in income but are investing and financing activities. For example, a gain (loss) on extinguishment of debt should properly be classified as a financing activity, and a gain (loss) from disposal of property should be classified as an investing activity.

Investing activities include the acquisition and disposition of long-term productive assets or securities that are not considered cash equivalents. Investing activities also include the lending of money and collection on loans.

Financing activities include obtaining resources from owners and returning the investment. Also included is obtaining resources from creditors and repaying the amount borrowed.

The FASB has listed the following as examples of classifications of transactions.

ACTIVITIES REPORTED ON THE STATEMENT OF CASH FLOWS

Description of the activity	Positive cash flow	Negative cash flow
Operating activities (direct method):		
• Cash received from customers	xx	
• Cash received from interest	xx	
• Cash recieved from dividends	xx	
• Cash received from sales of securities classified as trading	xx	
• Cash paid to suppliers		xx
• Cash paid for operating expenses		xx
• Cash paid for interest		xx
• Cash paid for income taxes		xx
• Cash paid for securities classified as trading		xx
Investing activities:		
• Proceeds from sales of property, plant, and equipment	xx	
• Proceeds from sales of investments in stocks (available for sale) and bonds (available for sale)	xx	
• Proceeds from the sale or redemption of investments in bonds classified as held to maturity	xx	
• Proceeds from collection of loans (principal only)	xx	
• Proceeds from selling components of the company	xx	
• Acquisition of property, plant, and equipment (capital expenditures)		xx

Description of the activity	Positive cash flow	Negative cash flow
• Acquisition of investments in stocks and bonds (available for sale or held to maturity)		xx
• Making loans to other entities		xx
• Acquiring other businesses		xx

Financing activities:

	Positive cash flow	Negative cash flow
• Proceeds from issuing common and preferred stock	xx	
• Proceeds from reissuing treasury stock	xx	
• Proceeds from issuing short-term debt	xx	
• Proceeds from issuing long-term debt	xx	
• Paying cash dividends		xx
• Repurchasing common stock (treasury stock)		xx
• Repaying short-term loans (principal only)		xx
• Repaying long-term loans, including capital lease obligations (principal only)		xx

Noncash investing and financing activities

- Acquiring an asset through a capital lease
- Conversion of debt to equity
- Exchange of noncash assets or liabilities for other noncash assets or liabilities
- Issuance of stock to acquire assets

Note that noncash investing and financing activities should be excluded from the statement itself. These transactions involve no cash inflows and outflows, but they have a significant effect on the prospective cash flows of a company. Therefore, they must be distinguished from activities that involved cash receipts and payments and must be reported in a separate schedule or in the footnotes to the financial statements.

In the statement, the inflows and outflows for each category (operating, investing, and financing) should be shown separately, and the **net** cash flows (the difference between the inflows and outflows) should be reported.

C. Direct or Indirect Presentation in Reporting Operating Activities

The FASB decided that the preferable method of presenting net cash flows from operating activities is by **directly** showing major classes of operating cash receipts and payments. However, the **indirect (reconciliation) method** is also permitted. When the direct method is used, it is also necessary to present a separate accompanying schedule showing the indirect method. The **direct method** is discussed first, followed by a discussion of the **indirect method**.

Under the direct approach, cash flow elements of operating activities are derived from the accrual basis components of net income. In converting to the cash basis, accounts that should be analyzed under operating activities are those which are debited or credited when recording transactions that affect the income statement. These transactions include transactions with outsiders and adjusting entries. For example, these accounts include sales, cost of sales, operating expenses, and tax expense, as well as assets and liabilities which are related to them, such as accounts receivable, inventory, accounts payable, accrued expenses, and prepaid expenses. Note that interest expense and interest revenue are included within operating activities. Formulas for conversion of various income statement amounts from the accrual basis to the cash basis are summarized in the following table:

Accrual basis		Additions		Deductions		Cash basis
Net sales	+	Beginning AR	–	$\left(\begin{array}{l}\text{Ending AR}\\\text{AR written off}\end{array}\right)$	=	Cash received from customers
Cost of goods sold	+	$\left(\begin{array}{l}\text{Ending inventory}\\\text{Beginning AP}\end{array}\right)$	–	$\left(\begin{array}{l}\text{Depreciation and amortization}^*\\\text{Beginning inventory}\\\text{Ending AP}\end{array}\right)$	=	Cash paid to suppliers
Operating expenses	+	$\left(\begin{array}{l}\text{Ending prepaid expenses}\\\text{Beginning accrued}\\\quad\text{expenses payable}\end{array}\right)$	–	$\left(\begin{array}{l}\text{Depreciation and amortization}\\\text{Beginning prepaid expenses}\\\text{Ending accrued expenses payable}\end{array}\right)$	=	Cash paid for operating expenses

* *Applies to a manufacturing entity*

A T-account analysis method may be used instead of the above formulas to determine cash received and cash paid. T-account analysis provides a quick, systematic way to accumulate the information needed to prepare the statement.

The direct approach would be presented in the statement of cash flows as follows:

Cash flows from operating activities		
Cash received from dividends	$ 500	
Cash received from interest	1,000	
Cash received from sale of goods	9,000	
Cash provided by operating activities		$10,500
Cash paid to suppliers	5,000	
Cash paid for operating expenses	500	
Cash paid for interest	500	
Cash paid for taxes	500	
Cash disbursed from operating activities		6,500
Net cash flows from operating activities		$ 4,000

The other way of reporting net cash flows from operations is known as the **indirect method**. This is done by starting with income from continuing operations and adjusting for changes in operating related accounts (e.g., inventory and accounts payable) and noncash expenses, revenues, losses, and gains.

Noncash items that were subtracted in determining income must be added back in determining net cash flows from operations. Each of these noncash items is a charge against income but does not decrease cash.

Items to be added back include depreciation, amortization of intangibles, amortization of discount on bonds payable, bad debt expense, and any increase in the deferred tax liability. Note each of these items is charged against income but does not decrease cash.

Noncash items that were added in determining income must be subtracted from net income in determining net cash flows from operations. Each of these noncash items is an increase to income but does not increase cash.

Items to be deducted from income include decreases in the deferred tax liability and amortization of the premium on bonds payable.

Finally, gains (losses) on fixed assets require adjustment, since the cash received is not measured by the gain (loss), that is, a fixed asset with a book value of $10, sold for $15 in cash, provides $15 in cash but is reported as only a $5 gain on the income statement. The $15 is shown as a separate item on the cash flow statement under investing activities and the $5 gain is subtracted from income. Losses on asset disposals are added back to income.

When preparing the cash flows from operating activities section of a Statement of Cash Flows under the indirect method, reconstructing journal entries may help in determining if an item should be added or subtracted to net income.

For example, if accounts receivable increased by $20,000 over the year, the journal entry that would result in an increase to accounts receivable would be

Accounts receivable	xx	
Sales		xx

This entry results in an increase to net income (through sales), but cash is not affected. Therefore, the amount of the increase is deducted from net income in determining cash flows from operating activities.

If accounts payable decreased by $35,000, the entry for a decrease in accounts payable would be

Accounts payable	xx	
Cash		xx

Since the corresponding credit results in a decrease to cash, the amount of this decrease should be deducted from net income in determining cash flows from operating activities.

When the **indirect** method is used, SFAS 95 permits, but does not require, separate disclosure of cash flows related to extraordinary items and discontinued operations. If an entity chooses to disclose this information, disclosure must be consistent for all periods affected. Extraordinary items, if disclosed, should be added to (or subtracted from) operating activities (adjustment to net income) at the gross amount, not the net-of-tax amount. Under either method the extraordinary item should be included in financing or investing activities, whichever is appropriate.

The direct and indirect approaches will both be illustrated throughout the remainder of this module.

ADJUSTMENTS TO NET INCOME FOR INDIRECT METHOD

Add to net income	*Deduct from net income*
Decreases in:	**Increases in:**

Add to net income	Deduct from net income
Accounts receivable (net)	Accounts receivable (net)
Inventories	Inventories
Prepaid expenses	Prepaid expenses
Deferred tax asset	Deferred tax asset

Increases in: **Decreases in:**

Accounts payable	Accounts payable
Income taxes payable	Income taxes payable
Deferred tax liability	Deferred tax liability
Interest payable	Interest payable
Other accrued payables	Other accrued payables
Unearned revenue	Unearned revenue

Other items: **Other items:**

• Losses from disposals of property, plant, and equipment and available-for-sale investments	• Gains from disposals of property, plant and equipment and available-for-sale investments
• Depreciation expense	• Undistributed income from equity method investments (equity income less the cash dividends received during the period)
• Amortization expense related to intangible assets and bond discounts	• Amortization of a bond premium
• Bad debts expense (if adjustment for accounts receivable is based upon the gross, not the net, change in accounts receivable)	• Gains from early extinguishments of debt
• Losses from early extinguishments of debt	

D. Example of Statement of Cash Flows

The following information pertains to the Haner Company at December 31, 2002. Comparative balance sheets for 2001 and 2002 are as follows:

	2002	*2001*	*Net change*
Cash	$ 9,000	$ 8,000	$ 1,000
Treasury bills	4,000	3,000	1,000
Accounts receivable	4,000	5,000	(1,000)
Inventory	1,000	2,000	(1,000)
Prepaid insurance	2,000	3,000	(1,000)
Investment in Simba Co. (held-for-trading)	15,000	15,000	--
Market increase adjustment (trading)	3,000	--	3,000
Investment in ABC Co. (available-for-sale)	15,400	22,000	(6,600)
Market decrease adjustment (available-for-sale)	(3,500)	--	(3,500)
Fixed assets	22,000	17,000	5,000
Accumulated depreciation	(5,000)	(4,000)	(1,000)
Deferred tax asset	1,400	--	1,400
	$68,300	$71,000	$(2,700)
Accounts payable	$ 4,000	$ 7,000	$(3,000)
Income tax payable	3,000	1,000	2,000
Deferred tax liability	6,360	3,000	3,360
Bonds payable	5,000	10,000	(5,000)
Common stock	20,000	20,000	--
Accumulated other comprehensive income Unrealized loss on available-for-sale securities (net of tax)	(2,100)	--	(2,100)
Retained earnings	32,040	30,000	2,040
	$68,300	$71,000	$(2,700)

Income Statement for 2002 is as follows:

Net sales		$50,000
Cost of goods sold		(20,000)
Gross profit		30,000
Operating expenses		(17,000)
Income from operations		13,000
Other revenue and gains	$5,000	
Other expenses and losses	(2,500)	2,500
Income before extraordinary item and income taxes		15,500
Income tax expense:		
Current portion	5,000	
Deferred portion	3,360	8,360
Income before extraordinary item		7,140
Extraordinary loss from early extinguishment of debt, net of income taxes of $40		(60)
Net income		$7,080

Statement of Comprehensive Income for 2002 is as follows:

Net income		$7,080
Other comprehensive income		
Unrealized loss on available-for-sale securities, (net of tax of $2,000)	($3,000)	
Less:		
Reclassification on sale of available-for-sale securities, (net of tax of $600)	(900)	(2,100)
Comprehensive income		$4,980

Additional information includes

- Treasury bills have a maturity of less than three months from date of purchase
- Fixed assets costing $5,000 with a book value of $2,000 were sold for $4,000
- Three-year insurance policy was purchased in 2000
- At 12/31/02, available-for-sale investments with a book value of $6,600 at 12/31/01 and $5,100 at 12/31/02 sold for $5,100.
- Additional bonds were issued on 12/31/02 for $4,000. There was no premium or discount.
- Bonds with a book value of $9,000 were retired on 12/31/02. A $100 loss on the redemption of the bonds ($9,100 FMV – $9,000 BP) was reported on the income statement as an extraordinary item, net of tax of $40.
- Other revenue and gains include a $3,000 unrealized gain recognized for trading securities
- Other expenses and losses consist of $1,000 interest paid and $1,500 realized loss on available-for-sale securities
- Changes in investments:
  - No changes in fair value of the investments occurred prior to 2002
  - There were no sales or purchases of trading securities during 2002
  - The tax rate is 40%

1. **Procedural Steps**

   a. The first step is to calculate the change in cash and cash equivalents.

	2002	2001	*Change*
Cash	$9,000	$8,000	+$1,000
Treasury bills	4,000	3,000	+ 1,000
Net change in cash and cash equivalents			+$2,000

   b. Calculate net cash flows from operating activities

   (1) Indirect approach

Net income	$ 7,080	
Decrease in accounts receivable	1,000	(a)
Decrease in inventory	1,000	(b)
Decrease in prepaid insurance	1,000	(c)
Decrease in accounts payable	(3,000)	(d)
Increase in income tax payable	2,000	(e)
Increase in deferred tax liability	3,360	(f)
Unrealized gain on trading securities	(3,000)	(g)
Realized loss on available-for-sale securities	1,500	(h)
Extraordinary loss from early extinguishment of bonds	100	(i)
Gain on sale of fixed assets	(2,000)	(j)
Depreciation expense	4,000	(k)
Net cash flows from operating activities	$13,040	

   Reconstructing journal entries may serve to explain the effect on net income of an increase or decrease of a particular account.

(a)   **Accounts receivable.** For accounts receivable to decrease, the journal entry must have been

Cash	xx	
Accounts receivable		xx

Cash increased as a result of the collection of accounts receivable. The $1,000 decrease in accounts receivable should be added to net income.

Cost of goods sold	xx	
Inventory		xx

(b)   **Inventory.** For inventory to decrease, the entry must have been

Expenses (CGS) increased without an additional cash outlay for inventory, so the $1,000 decrease is added back to net income.

(c)   **Prepaid insurance.** For prepaid insurance to decrease, the entry must have been

Insurance expense	xx	
Prepaid insurance		xx

Because expenses increased without a corresponding cash outlay, the $1,000 decrease in prepaid insurance should be added to net income.

(d)   **Accounts payable.** For accounts payable to decrease, the entry must have been

Accounts payable	xx	
Cash		xx

The entry involves a cash outlay, so the $3,000 decrease in accounts payable is deducted from net income.

(e)   **Income tax payable.** For income tax payable to increase, the entry must have been

Income tax expense	xx	
Income tax payable		xx

Expenses increased without an actual cash outlay; therefore the $2,000 increase in the liability is added back to net income.

(f)   **Deferred tax liability.** For deferred tax liability to increase, the entry must have been

Income tax expense	xx	
Deferred tax liability		xx

Expenses increased without an actual cash outlay; therefore the $3,360 increase in the liability, which is a noncash expense, is added back to net income.

(g)   **Unrealized gain on trading securities.** The entry to record the unrealized gain on trading securities would have been

Investment in Simba Co.—held-for-trading	3,000	
Unrealized holding gain		3,000

Since unrealized gains on trading securities are recognized as income but do not involve a cash inflow, such gains must be subtracted from net income.

(h)   **Realized loss on available-for-sale securities.** When $5,100 stock in ABC Co. was sold, the previously unrealized loss of $1,500 ($5,100 FMV at 12/31/02 – $6,600 FMV at 12/31/01) which arose in 2002 became realized. The entry to record the sale would have been

Cash	5,100	
Realized loss	1,500	
Available for sale		6,600

Because the realized loss does not involve any cash outflow, it must be added back to net income. Note that a $1,500 unrealized loss would have been recognized in financial statements prepared during 2002. The entry to remove this amount from the other comprehensive income account entitled "Unrealized loss on available-for-sale securities account" and the tax effect is

Adjustment to market (available-for-sale securities)	1,500	
Deferred tax benefit—unrealized loss	600	
Unrealized loss on available-for-sale securities		1,500
Deferred tax asset		600

Since an unrealized loss on AFS securities of $3,500 was recognized during 2002 (from 2001 to 2002), a $5,000 decline in FMV must have occurred in 2002, as shown below. The deferred tax asset of $1,400 came from recognizing the future benefit of the unrealized loss of $3,500. The entry was

Deferred tax asset	1,400	
Deferred tax expense (benefit)		1,400

Available-for-Sale Securities				Market Adjustment (Available-for-Sale Securities)			
2001 Bal.	22,000					--	2001 Bal.
		6,600	Sale	Sale	1,500	5,000	2002 Unreal. loss
2002 Bal.	15,400					3,500	2002 Bal.

Unrealized Loss on AFS Securities				Deferred Tax Benefit— Unrealized Loss			
2001 Bal.	--	1,500	Realized upon	Sale	600	--	
Unreal. Loss recog. during year	5,000		sale	Closing entry	1,400	2,000	2002 adj.
		3,500	Closing entry	2002 Bal.		--	
2002 Bal.	--						

Deferred Tax Asset				Accumulated Other Comprehensive Income			
2001 Bal.	--	600	Sale			--	
2002 Adj.	2,000			Closing entry	3,500	1,400	Closing entry
2002 Bal.	1,400			2002 Bal.	2,100		

Because unrealized gains/losses on available-for-sale securities do not affect cash flows, no adjustment for this change is necessary on the statement of cash flows.

(i) **Loss on redemption of bonds payable.** Since $9,100 in cash was paid to retire $9,000 of bonds payable, a loss of $100 was realized. However, because the loss does not involve a cash outflow, it must be added back to net income.

Bonds payable	9,000	
Loss on redemption	100	
Cash		9,100

(j) **Gain on sale of fixed assets.** The entry to record the sale would have been

Cash	4,000	
Accumulated depreciation	3,000	
Gain on sale		2,000
Asset		5,000

The total amount of cash received in payment for the asset, not just the amount of the gain, represents the cash inflow. Since cash inflow from the sale (including the amount of the gain) appears in the investing section, the gain should be subtracted from net income.

(k) **Depreciation expense.** The entry to record depreciation is

Depreciation expense	4,000	
Accumulated depreciation		4,000

Because expenses increased without a corresponding cash outlay, the amount recorded for depreciation expense should be added to net income. In this case, the increase in accumulated depreciation must take into consideration the accumulated depreciation removed with the sale of the asset.

	AD		
AD of sold asset	3,000*	4,000	Beg. bal.
		4,000	Depreciation (plug)
		5,000	End. bal.

* *$5,000 Cost – $2,000 book value*

(2) Direct approach

Cash received from customers		$51,000 (a)
Cash provided by operating activities		
Cash paid to suppliers	22,000 (b)	
Cash paid for operating expenses	12,000 (c)	
Cash paid for interest	1,000 (d)	
Cash paid for income taxes	2,960 (e)	
Cash disbursed for operating activities		37,960
Net cash flows from operating activities		$13,040

(a) **Cash received from customers.** Net sales + Beginning AR – Ending AR = Cash received from customers ($50,000 + $5,000 – $4,000 = $51,000). Cash received from customers also may be calculated by analyzing T-accounts.

	Accounts Receivable		
Beg. bal.	5,000		
Sales	50,000	51,000	Cash collected
End. bal.	4,000		

(b) **Cash paid to suppliers.** Cost of goods sold + Beginning AP – Ending AP + Ending inventory – Beginning inventory = Cash paid to suppliers ($20,000 + $7,000 – $4,000 + $1,000 – $2,000 = $22,000). This is a two-account analysis. The amount for cash paid to suppliers equals the debit to accounts payable, but to solve for that amount, you must first determine purchases. To calculate purchases you must analyze the inventory account.

Step #1. Calculate purchases

	Inventory		
Beg. bal.	2,000		
Purchases	19,000	20,000	CGS
End. bal.	1,000		

Step #2. Calculate cash payments to suppliers

	Accounts Payable		
Cash paid to suppliers	22,000	7,000	Beg. bal.
		19,000	Purchases
		4,000	End. bal.

Note that the $2,000 difference between the $20,000 CGS (accrual-basis amount) and the $22,000 cash payments made to suppliers (cash-basis amount) equals the difference between the $1,000 decrease in inventory and the $3,000 decrease in accounts payable when the indirect method is used. However, under the indirect method the difference is deducted from net income. This is because when the direct method is used, expenses such as CGS are examined as **outflows** of cash, whereas when the indirect method is used, net income (revenue-expenses, including CGS) is treated as a net cash **inflow**.

(c) **Cash paid for operating expenses.** Operating expenses + Ending prepaid expenses – Beginning prepaid expenses – Depreciation expense (and other noncash operating expenses) = Cash paid for operating expenses ($17,000 + $2,000 – $3,000 – $4,000 = $12,000). The two accounts in this problem that relate to operating expenses are accumulated depreciation and prepaid insurance.

	Prepaid Insurance				Accumulated Depreciation		
Beg. bal.	3,000					4,000	Beg. bal.
		1,000	Insurance expense	AD of sold asset 3,000		4,000	Depreciation expense
End.bal.	2,000					5,000	End. bal.

Since neither the expiration of prepaid insurance nor depreciation expense required a cash outlay, cash basis operating expenses are accrual expenses of $17,000 less depreciation ($4,000) and insurance expense ($1,000), or $12,000.

(d) **Cash paid for interest.** No analysis needed; amount was given in problem

(e) **Cash paid for income taxes.** Current portion of income tax expense + Beginning income tax payable – Ending income tax payable = Cash paid for income taxes ($4,960 + $1,000 – $3,000 = $2,960). The journal entry for income tax expense is

Income tax expense—current	5,000	
Income tax expense—deferred	3,360	
Tax benefit on extraordinary loss		40
Income tax payable (current portion)		4,960*
Deferred tax liability		1,360

* $4,960 is the $5,000 of tax on income before extraordinary item less the $40 tax saving on extraordinary item.

Therefore, taxes paid are $2,960, as shown in the T-account below.

Income Tax Payable

Income taxes paid	2,960	1,000	Beg. bal.
		4,960	Current portion
		3,000	End. bal.

c. Analyze other accounts and determine whether the change is a cash inflow or outflow and whether it is a financing, an investing, or a noncash investing and financing activity.

(1) Investments in ABC Co. decreased by $5,100 when this portion was sold (cash inflow, investing activity). The entry to record the sale was

Cash	5,100	
Investment in ABC Co.— available-for-sale		5,100

(2) Fixed assets increased by $5,000 after $5,000 of assets were sold for $4,000 (cash inflow, investing activity). Thus, $10,000 of fixed assets were purchased (cash outflow, investing activity).

Fixed Assets

Beg. bal.	$17,000		
Purchase of new assets	10,000	5,000	Sold asset
End. bal.	22,000		

(3) Bonds payable increased by $4,000 when additional bonds were issued (cash inflow, financing activity).

(4) Bonds payable decreased by $9,000 when they were retired (cash outflow, financing activity). The entry to record the retirement of debt was

Bonds payable	9,000	
Loss on redemption of bonds	100	
Cash		9,100

The loss on redemption of bonds is included in operating activities as explained in Section D.1.b.(1)(i) above.

(5) Common stock had no change.

(6) Retained earnings increased $2,040 after net income of $7,080, indicating a dividend of $5,040 (cash outflow, financing activity).

Retained Earnings

Cash dividend	5,040	30,000	Beg. bal.
		7,080	Net income
		32,040	End. bal.

d. Prepare formal statement

Haner Company
STATEMENT OF CASH FLOWS
For the Year Ended December 31, 2002

Cash flows from operating activities:		
Cash received from customers	$51,000	
Cash provided by operating activities		$51,000
Cash paid to suppliers	22,000	
Cash paid for operating expenses	12,000	
Cash paid for income taxes	2,960	
Cash paid for interest expense	1,000	
Cash disbursed for operating activities		37,960
Net cash flows from operating activities		$13,040
Cash flows from investing activities:		
Proceeds from sale of investments	$5,100	
Proceeds from sale of fixed assets	4,000	
Acquisition of fixed assets	(10,000)	
Net cash used by investing activities		(900)

Cash flows from financing activities:

Proceeds from sale of bonds	$4,000	
Repayment of long-term debt	(9,100)	
Dividends paid	(5,040)	
Net cash used by financing activities		(10,140)
Net increase in cash and cash equivalents		$ 2,000
Cash and cash equivalents at beginning of year		11,000
Cash and cash equivalents at end of year		$13,000

Reconciliation of net income to cash provided by operating activities:
[This schedule would include the amounts from D.1.b.(1) (near the beginning of this example) starting with "net income" and ending with Net cash flows from operating activities of $13,040.]

Disclosure of accounting policy:
For purposes of the statement of cash flows, the Company considers all highly liquid debt instruments purchased with a maturity of three months or less to be cash equivalents.

Note that if the reconciliation approach for operating activities had been shown in the body of the statement instead of the direct approach, an additional schedule showing interest paid and income taxes paid would be necessary.

E. Capital Leases

In the period an entity enters into a capital lease, a noncash financing and investing activity in the amount of the present value of the minimum lease payments is reported following the cash flow statement. As payments are made by the lessee, the principal reduction component is reported as a cash outflow under financing activities. The interest component is reported in the operating activities section under the direct method. Under the indirect method, interest paid must be disclosed as supplementary information.

MULTIPLE-CHOICE QUESTIONS (1-37)

1. At December 31, 2002, Kale Co. had the following balances in the accounts it maintains at First State Bank:

Checking account #101	$175,000
Checking account #201	(10,000)
Money market account	25,000
90-day certificate of deposit, due 2/28/03	50,000
180-day certificate of deposit, due 3/15/03	80,000

Kale classifies investments with original maturities of three months or less as cash equivalents. In its December 31, 2002 balance sheet, what amount should Kale report as cash and cash equivalents?
     a. $190,000
     b. $200,000
     c. $240,000
     d. $320,000

2. The primary purpose of a statement of cash flows is to provide relevant information about
     a.   Differences between net income and associated cash receipts and disbursements.
     b.   An enterprise's ability to generate future positive net cash flows.
     c.   The cash receipts and cash disbursements of an enterprise during a period.
     d.   An enterprise's ability to meet cash operating needs.

3. Mend Co. purchased a three-month US Treasury bill. Mend's policy is to treat as cash equivalents all highly liquid investments with an original maturity of three months or less when purchased. How should this purchase be reported in Mend's statement of cash flows?
     a.   As an outflow from operating activities.
     b.   As an outflow from investing activities.
     c.   As an outflow from financing activities.
     d.   Not reported.

4. Alp, Inc. had the following activities during 2002:

• Acquired 2,000 shares of stock in Maybel, Inc. for $26,000.
• Sold an investment in Rate Motors for $35,000 when the carrying value was $33,000.
• Acquired a $50,000, four-year certificate of deposit from a bank. (During the year, interest of $3,750 was paid to Alp.)
• Collected dividends of $1,200 on stock investments.

In Alp's 2002 statement of cash flows, net cash used in investing activities should be
     a. $37,250
     b. $38,050
     c. $39,800
     d. $41,000

5. In 2002, a tornado completely destroyed a building belonging to Holland Corp. The building cost $100,000 and had accumulated depreciation of $48,000 at the time of the loss. Holland received a cash settlement from the insurance company and reported an extraordinary loss of $21,000. In Holland's 2002 cash flow statement, the net change reported in the cash flows from investing activities section should be a
     a. $10,000 increase.
     b. $21,000 decrease.

     c. $31,000 increase.
     d. $52,000 decrease.

6. In a statement of cash flows, if used equipment is sold at a gain, the amount shown as a cash inflow from investing activities equals the carrying amount of the equipment
     a.   Plus the gain.
     b.   Plus the gain and less the amount of tax attributable to the gain.
     c.   Plus both the gain and the amount of tax attributable to the gain.
     d.   With **no** addition or subtraction.

7. On September 1, 2002, Canary Co. sold used equipment for a cash amount equaling its carrying amount for both book and tax purposes. On September 15, 2002, Canary replaced the equipment by paying cash and signing a note payable for new equipment. The cash paid for the new equipment exceeded the cash received for the old equipment. How should these equipment transactions be reported in Canary's 2002 statement of cash flows?
     a.   Cash outflow equal to the cash paid less the cash received.
     b.   Cash outflow equal to the cash paid and note payable less the cash received.
     c.   Cash inflow equal to the cash received and a cash outflow equal to the cash paid and note payable.
     d.   Cash inflow equal to the cash received and a cash outflow equal to the cash paid.

Items 8 and 9 are based on the following:

A company acquired a building, paying a portion of the purchase price in cash and issuing a mortgage note payable to the seller for the balance.

8. In a statement of cash flows, what amount is included in investing activities for the above transaction?
     a.   Cash payment.
     b.   Acquisition price.
     c.   Zero.
     d.   Mortgage amount.

9. In a statement of cash flows, what amount is included in financing activities for the above transaction?
     a.   Cash payment.
     b.   Acquisition price.
     c.   Zero.
     d.   Mortgage amount.

10. Fara Co. reported bonds payable of $47,000 at December 31, 2001, and $50,000 at December 31, 2002. During 2002, Fara issued $20,000 of bonds payable in exchange for equipment. There was no amortization of bond premium or discount during the year. What amount should Fara report in its 2002 statement of cash flows for redemption of bonds payable?
     a. $ 3,000
     b. $17,000
     c. $20,000
     d. $23,000

Items 11 and 12 are based on the following:

In preparing its cash flow statement for the year ended December 31, 2002, Reve Co. collected the following data:

Gain on sale of equipment	$ (6,000)
Proceeds from sale of equipment	10,000
Purchase of A.S., Inc. bonds (par value $200,000)	(180,000)
Amortization of bond discount	2,000
Dividends declared	(45,000)
Dividends paid	(38,000)
Proceeds from sale of treasury stock (carrying amount $65,000)	75,000

In its December 31, 2002 statement of cash flows,

11. What amount should Reve report as net cash used in investing activities?
a. $170,000
b. $176,000
c. $188,000
d. $194,000

12. What amount should Reve report as net cash provided by financing activities?
a. $20,000
b. $27,000
c. $30,000
d. $37,000

13. On July 1, 2002, Dewey Co. signed a twenty-year building lease that it reported as a capital lease. Dewey paid the monthly lease payments when due. How should Dewey report the effect of the lease payments in the financing activities section of its 2002 statement of cash flows?
a. An inflow equal to the present value of future lease payments at July 1, 2002, less 2002 principal and interest payments.
b. An outflow equal to the 2002 principal and interest payments on the lease.
c. An outflow equal to the 2002 principal payments only.
d. The lease payments should **not** be reported in the financing activities section.

14. Which of the following should be reported when preparing a statement of cash flows?

	Conversion of long-term debt to common stock	Conversion of preferred stock
a.	No	No
b.	No	Yes
c.	Yes	Yes
d.	Yes	No

15. Which of the following information should be disclosed as supplemental information in the statement of cash flows?

	Cash flow per share	Conversion of debt to equity
a.	Yes	Yes
b.	Yes	No
c.	No	Yes
d.	No	No

16. Which of the following is **not** disclosed on the statement of cash flows when prepared under the direct method, either on the face of the statement or in a separate schedule?
a. The major classes of gross cash receipts and gross cash payments.
b. The amount of income taxes paid.
c. A reconciliation of net income to net cash flow from operations.
d. A reconciliation of ending retained earnings to net cash flow from operations.

Items 17 through 21 are based on the following:

Flax Corp. uses the direct method to prepare its statement of cash flows. Flax's trial balances at December 31, 2003 and 2002, are as follows:

	December 31	
	2003	2002
Debits		
Cash	$ 35,000	$ 32,000
Accounts receivable	33,000	30,000
Inventory	31,000	47,000
Property, plant, & equipment	100,000	95,000
Unamortized bond discount	4,500	5,000
Cost of goods sold	250,000	380,000
Selling expenses	141,500	172,000
General and administrative expenses	137,000	151,300
Interest expense	4,300	2,600
Income tax expense	20,400	61,200
	$756,700	$976,100
Credits		
Allowance for uncollectible accounts	$ 1,300	$ 1,100
Accumulated depreciation	16,500	15,000
Trade accounts payable	25,000	17,500
Income taxes payable	21,000	27,100
Deferred income taxes	5,300	4,600
8% callable bonds payable	45,000	20,000
Common stock	50,000	40,000
Additional paid-in capital	9,100	7,500
Retained earnings	44,700	64,600
Sales	538,800	778,700
	$756,700	$976,100

- Flax purchased $5,000 in equipment during 2003.
- Flax allocated one third of its depreciation expense to selling expenses and the remainder to general and administrative expenses.

What amounts should Flax report in its statement of cash flows for the year ended December 31, 2003, for the following:

17. Cash collected from customers?
a. $541,800
b. $541,600
c. $536,000
d. $535,800

18. Cash paid for goods to be sold?
a. $258,500
b. $257,500
c. $242,500
d. $226,500

19. Cash paid for interest?
a. $4,800
b. $4,300
c. $3,800
d. $1,700

20. Cash paid for income taxes?
a. $25,800
b. $20,400
c. $19,700
d. $15,000

21. Cash paid for selling expenses?
a. $142,000
b. $141,500
c. $141,000
d. $140,000

22. In a statement of cash flows, which of the following would increase reported cash flows from operating activities using the direct method? (Ignore income tax considerations.)

    a.   Dividends received from investments.
    b.   Gain on sale of equipment.
    c.   Gain on early retirement of bonds.
    d.   Change from straight-line to accelerated depreciation.

23. A company's wages payable increased from the beginning to the end of the year. In the company's statement of cash flows in which the operating activities section is prepared under the direct method, the cash paid for wages would be

    a.   Salary expense plus wages payable at the beginning of the year.
    b.   Salary expense plus the increase in wages payable from the beginning to the end of the year.
    c.   Salary expense less the increase in wages payable from the beginning to the end of the year.
    d.   The same as salary expense.

24. Metro, Inc. reported net income of $150,000 for 2002. Changes occurred in several balance sheet accounts during 2002 as follows:

Investment in Videogold, Inc. stock, carried on the equity basis	$5,500 increase
Accumulated depreciation, caused by major repair to projection equipment	2,100 decrease
Premium on bonds payable	1,400 decrease
Deferred income tax liability (long-term)	1,800 increase

In Metro's 2002 cash flow statement, the reported net cash provided by operating activities should be

    a. $150,400
    b. $148,300
    c. $144,900
    d. $142,800

25. Lino Co.'s worksheet for the preparation of its 2002 statement of cash flows included the following:

	December 31	January 1
Accounts receivable	$29,000	$23,000
Allowance for uncollectible accounts	1,000	800
Prepaid rent expense	8,200	12,400
Accounts payable	22,400	19,400

Lino's 2002 net income is $150,000. What amount should Lino include as net cash provided by operating activities in the statement of cash flows?

    a. $151,400
    b. $151,000
    c. $148,600
    d. $145,400

26. In a statement of cash flows (using indirect approach for operating activities) an increase in inventories should be presented as a(n)

    a.   Outflow of cash.
    b.   Inflow and outflow of cash.
    c.   Addition to net income.
    d.   Deduction from net income.

27. How should a gain from the sale of used equipment for cash be reported in a statement of cash flows using the indirect method?

    a.   In investment activities as a reduction of the cash inflow from the sale.
    b.   In investment activities as a cash outflow.

    c.   In operating activities as a deduction from income.
    d.   In operating activities as an addition to income.

28. Would the following be added back to net income when reporting operating activities' cash flows by the indirect method?

	Excess of treasury stock acquisition cost over sales proceeds (cost method)	Bond discount amortization
a.	Yes	Yes
b.	No	No
c.	No	Yes
d.	Yes	No

29. Which of the following should **not** be disclosed in an enterprise's statement of cash flows prepared using the indirect method?

    a.   Interest paid, net of amounts capitalized.
    b.   Income taxes paid.
    c.   Cash flow per share.
    d.   Dividends paid on preferred stock.

Items 30 through 32 are based on the following:

The differences in Beal Inc.'s balance sheet accounts at December 31, 2002 and 2001, are presented below.

	Increase (Decrease)
Assets	
Cash and cash equivalents	$ 120,000
Short-term investments	300,000
Accounts receivable, net	--
Inventory	80,000
Long-term investments	(100,000)
Plant assets	700,000
Accumulated depreciation	--
	$1,100,000
Liabilities and Stockholders' Equity	
Accounts payable and accrued liabilities	$ (5,000)
Dividends payable	160,000
Short-term bank debt	325,000
Long-term debt	110,000
Common stock, $10 par	100,000
Additional paid-in capital	120,000
Retained earnings	290,000
	$1,100,000

The following additional information relates to 2002:

- Net income was $790,000.
- Cash dividends of $500,000 were declared.
- Building costing $600,000 and having a carrying amount of $350,000 was sold for $350,000.
- Equipment costing $110,000 was acquired through issuance of long-term debt.
- A long-term investment was sold for $135,000. There were no other transactions affecting long-term investments.
- 10,000 shares of common stock were issued for $22 a share.

In Beal's 2002 statement of cash flows,

30. Net cash provided by operating activities was

    a. $1,160,000
    b. $1,040,000
    c. $ 920,000
    d. $ 705,000

31. Net cash used in investing activities was

    a. $1,005,000

b. $1,190,000
c. $1,275,000
d. $1,600,000

32. Net cash provided by financing activities was
a. $ 20,000
b. $ 45,000
c. $150,000
d. $205,000

Items 33 through 36 relate to data to be reported in the statement of cash flows of Debbie Dress Shops, Inc. based on the following information:

Debbie Dress Shops, Inc.
BALANCE SHEETS

| | December 31, | |
	2002	2001
Assets		
Current assets:		
Cash	$ 300,000	$ 200,000
Accounts receivable—net	840,000	580,000
Merchandise inventory	660,000	420,000
Prepaid expenses	100,000	50,000
Total current assets	1,900,000	1,250,000
Long-term investments	80,000	--
Land, buildings, and fixtures	1,130,000	600,000
Less accumulated depreciation	110,000	50,000
	1,020,000	550,000
Total assets	$3,000,000	$1,800,000
Equities		
Current liabilities:		
Accounts payable	$ 530,000	$ 440,000
Accrued expenses	140,000	130,000
Dividends payable	70,000	--
Total current liabilities	740,000	570,000
Note payable—due 2004	500,000	--
Stockholders' equity:		
Common stock	1,200,000	900,000
Retained earnings	560,000	330,000
	1,760,000	1,230,000
Total liabilities and stock-holders' equity	$3,000,000	$1,800,000

Debbie Dress Shops, Inc.
INCOME STATEMENTS

| | Year ended December 31, | |
	2002	2001
Net credit sales	$6,400,000	$4,000,000
Cost of goods sold	5,000,000	3,200,000
Gross profit	1,400,000	800,000
Expenses (including income taxes)	1,000,000	520,000
Net income	$ 400,000	$ 280,000

Additional information available included the following:

• All accounts receivable and accounts payable related to trade merchandise. Accounts payable are recorded net and always are paid to take all of the discount allowed. The allowance for doubtful accounts at the end of 2002 was the same as at the end of 2001; no receivables were charged against the allowance during 2002.

• The proceeds from the note payable were used to finance a new store building. Capital stock was sold to provide additional working capital.

33. Cash collected during 2002 from accounts receivable amounted to
a. $5,560,000
b. $5,840,000

c. $6,140,000
d. $6,400,000

34. Cash payments during 2002 on accounts payable to suppliers amounted to
a. $4,670,000
b. $4,910,000
c. $5,000,000
d. $5,150,000

35. Net cash provided by financing activities for 2002 totaled
a. $140,000
b. $300,000
c. $500,000
d. $700,000

36. Net cash used in investing activities during 2002 was
a. $ 80,000
b. $530,000
c. $610,000
d. $660,000

37. Bee Co. uses the direct write-off method to account for uncollectible accounts receivable. During an accounting period, Bee's cash collections from customers equal sales adjusted for the addition or deduction of the following amounts:

	Accounts written off	*Increase in accounts receivable balance*
a.	Deduction	Deduction
b.	Addition	Deduction
c.	Deduction	Addition
d.	Addition	Addition

OTHER OBJECTIVE QUESTIONS

Problem 1   (15 to 25 minutes)

The following condensed trial balance of Probe Co., a publicly held company, has been adjusted except for income tax expense.

Probe Co.
CONDENSED TRIAL BALANCE

	12/31/02 Balances Dr. (Cr.)	12/31/01 Balances Dr. (Cr.)	Net change Dr. (Cr.)
Cash	$ 473,000	$ 817,000	$(344,000)
Accounts receivable, net	670,000	610,000	60,000
Property, plant, and equipment	1,070,000	995,000	75,000
Accumulated depreciation	(345,000)	(280,000)	(65,000)
Dividends payable	(25,000)	(10,000)	(15,000)
Income taxes payable	35,000	(150,000)	185,000
Deferred income tax liability	(42,000)	(42,000)	--
Bonds payable	(500,000)	(1,000,000)	500,000
Unamortized premium on bonds	(71,000)	(150,000)	79,000
Common stock	(350,000)	(150,000)	(200,000)
Additional paid-in capital	(430,000)	(375,000)	(55,000)
Retained earnings	(185,000)	(265,000)	80,000
Sales	(2,420,000)		
Cost of sales	1,863,000		
Selling and administrative expenses	220,000		
Interest income	(14,000)		
Interest expense	46,000		
Depreciation	88,000		
Loss on sale of equipment	7,000		
Gain on extinguishment of bonds	(90,000)		
	$ 0	$ 0	$300,000

Additional information

•   During 2002 equipment with an original cost of $50,000 was sold for cash, and equipment costing $125,000 was purchased.

•   On January 1, 2002, bonds with a par value of $500,000 and related premium of $75,000 were redeemed. The $1,000 face value, 10% par bonds had been issued on January 1, 1993, to yield 8%. Interest is payable annually every December 31 through 2012.

•   Probe's tax payments during 2002 were debited to Income Taxes Payable. Probe recorded a deferred income tax liability of $42,000 based on temporary differences of $120,000 and an enacted tax rate of 35% at December 31, 2001; prior to 2001 there were no temporary differences. Probe's 2002 financial statement income before income taxes was greater than its 2002 taxable income, due entirely to temporary differences, by $60,000. Probe's cumulative net taxable temporary differences at December 31, 2002, were $180,000. Probe's enacted tax rate for the current and future years is 30%.

•   60,000 shares of common stock, $2.50 par, were outstanding on December 31, 2001. Probe issued an additional 80,000 shares on April 1, 2002.

•   There were no changes to retained earnings other than dividends declared.

Required:

For each transaction in **items 1 through 6,** the following two responses are required:

•   Determine the amount to be reported in Probe's 2002 statement of cash flows prepared using the indirect method. On the CPA Exam, candidates are given a list of numeric answers to choose from.

•   Select from the list below where the specific item should be separately reported on the statement of cash flows prepared using the indirect method.

O.   Operating.
I.   Investing.
F.   Financing.
S.   Supplementary information.
N.   Not reported on Probe's statement of cash flows.

1.   Cash paid for income taxes.

2.   Cash paid for interest.

3.   Redemption of bonds payable.

4.   Issuance of common stock.

5. Cash dividends paid.

6. Proceeds from sale of equipment.

NOTE: Problem 4, income statement preparation, on the same exam asked candidates to use the same trial balance and additional information given above. This problem appears as the "Solution Approach Example for Problems" in Chapter 3.

Problem 2   (25 to 30 minutes)

This question appears in Volume 1, Chapter 3 under Other Objective Questions Solution Approach Example—Fill in the Numbers Example.

PROBLEMS

Problem 1　　　(20 to 25 minutes)

The statement of cash flows is normally a required basic financial statement for each period for which an earnings statement is presented.

Required:

a.　What are the objectives of the statement of cash flows?

b.　What are two types of transactions that would be disclosed in a separate schedule in the statement of cash flows although they don't affect cash during the report period?

c.　What effect, if any, would each of the following seven items have upon the preparation of a cash flow statement assuming **direct** presentation is used to present cash flows from operations?

1.　Accounts receivable—trade.
2.　Inventory.
3.　Depreciation.
4.　Deferred tax liability from interperiod allocation.
5.　Issuance of long-term debt in payment for a building.
6.　Payoff of current portion of debt.
7.　Sale of a fixed asset resulting in a loss.

Problem 2　　　　　　　　　　　(45 to 55 minutes)

The following is Omega Corp.'s comparative balance sheet accounts worksheet at December 31, 2002 and 2001, with a column showing the increase (decrease) from 2001 to 2002.

Comparative balance sheet worksheet	2002	2001	Increase (Decrease)
Cash	$ 800,000	$ 700,000	$100,000
Accounts receivable	1,128,000	1,168,000	(40,000)
Inventories	1,850,000	1,715,000	135,000
Property, plant, and equipment	3,307,000	2,967,000	340,000
Accumulated depreciation	(1,165,000)	(1,040,000)	(125,000)
Investment in Belle Co.	305,000	275,000	30,000
Loan receivable	270,000	--	270,000
Total assets	$6,495,000	$5,785,000	$710,000
Accounts payable	$1,015,000	$ 955,000	$ 60,000
Income taxes payable	30,000	50,000	(20,000)
Dividends payable	80,000	90,000	(10,000)
Capital lease obligation	400,000	--	400,000
Capital stock, common, $1 par	500,000	500,000	--
Additional paid-in capital	1,500,000	1,500,000	--
Retained earnings	2,970,000	2,690,000	280,000
Total liabilities and stockholders' equity	$6,495,000	$5,785,000	$710,000

Additional information

•　On December 31, 2001, Omega acquired 25% of Belle Co.'s common stock for $275,000. On that date, the carrying value of Belle's assets and liabilities, which approximated their fair values, was $1,100,000. Belle reported income of $120,000 for the year ended December 31, 2002. No dividend was paid on Belle's common stock during the year.

•　During 2002, Omega loaned $300,000 to Chase Co., an unrelated company. Chase made the first semiannual principal repayment of $30,000, plus interest at 10%, on October 1, 2002.

•　On January 2, 2002, Omega sold equipment costing $60,000, with a carrying amount of $35,000, for $40,000 cash.

•　On December 31, 2002, Omega entered into a capital lease for an office building. The present value of the annual rental payments is $400,000, which equals the fair value of the building. Omega made the first rental payment of $60,000 when due on January 2, 2003.

•　Net income for 2002 was $360,000.

•　Omega declared and paid cash dividends for 2002 and 2001 as follows:

	2002	2001
Declared	December 15, 2002	December 15, 2001
Paid	February 28, 2003	February 28, 2002
Amount	$80,000	$90,000

Required:

Prepare a statement of cash flows for Omega, Inc. for the year ended December 31, 2002, using the indirect method. Supplemental schedules and disclosures are **not** required. A worksheet is **not** required.

Problem 3   (30 to 40 minutes)

Presented below are the condensed statements of financial position of Linden Consulting Associates as of December 31, 2002 and 2001, and the condensed statement of income for the year ended December 31, 2002.

Linden Consulting Associates
CONDENSED STATEMENTS OF FINANCIAL POSITION
December 31, 2002 and 2001

	2002	2001	Net change increase (decrease)
Assets			
Cash	$ 652,000	$ 280,000	$372,000
Accounts receivable, net	446,000	368,000	78,000
Investment in Zach, Inc., at equity	550,000	466,000	84,000
Property and equipment	1,270,000	1,100,000	170,000
Accumulated depreciation	(190,000)	(130,000)	(60,000)
Excess of cost over book value of investment in Zach, Inc. (net)	152,000	156,000	(4,000)
Total assets	$2,880,000	$2,240,000	$640,000
Liabilities and Partners' Equity			
Accounts payable and accrued expenses	$ 320,000	$ 270,000	$ 50,000
Mortgage payable	250,000	270,000	(20,000)
Partners' equity	2,310,000	1,700,000	610,000
Total liabilities and partners' equity	$2,880,000	$2,240,000	$640,000

Linden Consulting Associates
CONDENSED STATEMENT OF INCOME
For the Year Ended December 31, 2002

Fee revenue	$2,664,000
Operating expenses	1,940,000
Operating income	724,000
Equity in earnings of Zach, Inc. (net of $4,000 amortization in excess of cost over book value)	176,000
Net income	$ 900,000

Additional information

- On December 31, 2001, partners' capital and profit sharing percentages were as follows:

	Capital	Profit sharing %
Garr	$1,020,000	60%
Pat	680,000	40%
	$1,700,000	

- On January 1, 2002, Garr and Pat admitted Scott to the partnership for a cash payment of $340,000 to Linden Consulting Associates as the agreed amount of Scott's beginning capital account. In addition, Scott paid a $50,000 cash bonus directly to Garr and Pat. This amount was divided $30,000 to Garr and $20,000 to Pat. The new profit sharing arrangement is as follows:

Garr	50%
Pat	30%
Scott	20%

- On October 1, 2002, Linden purchased and paid for an office computer costing $170,000, including $15,000 for sales tax, delivery, and installation. There were no dispositions of property and equipment during 2002.
- Throughout 2002, Linden owned 25% of Zach, Inc.'s common stock. As a result of this ownership interest, Linden can exercise significant influence over Zach's operating and financial policies. During 2002, Zach paid dividends totaling $384,000 and reported net income of $720,000. Linden's 2002 amortization of excess of cost over book value in Zach was $4,000.
- Partners' drawings for 2002 were as follows:

Garr	$280,000
Pat	200,000
Scott	150,000
	$630,000

Required:

a. Using the direct method, prepare Linden's statement of cash flows for the year ended December 31, 2002.

b. Prepare a reconciliation of net income to net cash provided by operating activities.

MULTIPLE-CHOICE ANSWERS

1. c __ __	9. c __ __	17. d __ __	25. a __ __	33. c __ __
2. c __ __	10. b __ __	18. d __ __	26. d __ __	34. d __ __
3. d __ __	11. a __ __	19. c __ __	27. c __ __	35. d __ __
4. d __ __	12. d __ __	20. a __ __	28. c __ __	36. c __ __
5. c __ __	13. c __ __	21. c __ __	29. c __ __	37. a __ __
6. a __ __	14. d __ __	22. a __ __	30. c __ __	
7. d __ __	15. c __ __	23. c __ __	31. a __ __	1st: __/37 = __%
8. a __ __	16. d __ __	24. c __ __	32. d __ __	2nd: __/37 = __%

MULTIPLE-CHOICE ANSWER EXPLANATIONS

A. Objectives of the Statement of Cash Flows

1. (c) The 12/31/02 cash and cash equivalents balance is $240,000, as computed below.

Checking account #101	$175,000
Checking account #201	(10,000)
Money market account	25,000
90-day CD	50,000
Total cash and cash equivalents	$240,000

Bank overdrafts (like account #201) are normally reported as a current liability. However, when available cash is present in another account **in the same bank,** as in this case, offsetting is required. The money market account of $25,000 and the 90-day CD of $50,000 are considered cash equivalents because they had original maturities of three months or less. The 180-day CD of $80,000 is excluded because its original maturity was more than three months.

2. (c) Per SFAS 95, the **primary** purpose of a statement of cash flows is to provide relevant information about the enterprise's cash receipts and cash payments during a period. Answers (a), (b), and (d) are incorrect because, although they represent uses of the statement of cash flows, they are not the primary use.

3. (d) The statement of cash flows is required to be prepared based on inflows and outflows of cash and cash equivalents during the period. The purchase of a cash equivalent using cash is **not** an outflow of cash and cash equivalents; it is merely a change in the composition of cash and cash equivalents. Cash has decreased and cash equivalents have increased, but total cash and cash equivalents is unchanged. Therefore this purchase is **not** reported in the statement of cash flows.

B. Statement of Cash Flows Classification

4. (d) Investing activities include all cash flows involving **assets,** other than operating items. The investing activities are

Purchase of inv. in stock	$(26,000)
Sale of inv. in stock	35,000
Acquisition of CD	(50,000)
Net cash used	(41,000)

The gain on sale of investment in Rate Motors ($35,000 – $33,000 = $2,000), the interest earned ($3,750), and dividends earned ($1,200) are all operating items. Note that the sale of investment is reported in the investing section at the cash inflow amount ($35,000), not at the carrying value of the investment ($33,000). If the CD had been for three months instead of four years, it would be part of "Cash and Cash equivalents" and would not be shown under investing activities.

5. (c) The building which was destroyed had a book value of $52,000 ($100,000 – $48,000). The cash settlement from the insurance company resulted in a loss of $21,000. Therefore, the cash inflow from this investing activity must be $31,000 as shown below.

Proceeds	–	Book value	=	Loss
?	–	$52,000	=	($21,000)
$31,000	–	$52,000	=	($21,000)

Note that the $21,000 extraordinary loss must be before any income tax effect because SFAS 95 requires that any tax effect be left in operating activities.

6. (a) The cash inflow from the sale of equipment is the carrying amount plus the gain. Answers (b) and (c) are incorrect because the tax attributable to the gain is a cash outflow in the operating activities section of the statement of cash flows. Note that when using the indirect method, the gain is deducted from operating activities, as to not double count the gain.

7. (d) The requirement is to determine how the equipment transactions should be reported in the statement of cash flows. Per SFAS 95, companies are required to report the gross amounts of cash receipts and cash payments, rather than net amounts. Therefore, the gross cash inflow from the sale of equipment and the gross outflow for the payment of new equipment should be reported. Answer (a) is incorrect because both gross inflow and outflow should be reported, rather than reporting the net cash flow from the transaction. Answer (b) is incorrect because gross cash flows, not net, are reported and because a note payable is not reported since the transaction results in no actual inflow or outflow in the period in which the payable occurs. This noncash activity would be reported in a separate schedule or in the footnotes. Noncash transactions commonly recognized in a separate schedule in the financial statements include: conversion of debt to equity and acquisition of assets by assuming liabilities, including lease obligations. Answer (c) is incorrect because the note payable is not reported on the statement of cash flows; rather it is shown in a separate schedule.

8. (a) Per SFAS 95, payments at the time of purchase or soon before or after purchase to acquire property, plant, and equipment and other productive assets are categorized as cash outflows for investing activities. Generally, these payments only include advance payments, down payments, or payments made at the time of purchase or soon before or after purchase. Therefore, only the cash payment is considered a cash outflow for investing activities.

9. (c) Per SFAS 95, noncash investing and financing activities include acquiring assets by assuming directly related liabilities, such as purchasing a building by incurring a mortgage to the seller. This type of transaction does not involve the flow of cash. Therefore, cash flows for financing activities related to this transaction would be zero. Note that the cash down payment would be reported as a cash outflow for **investing** activities.

10. (b) To determine the cash paid for redemption of bonds payable, the solutions approach is to set up a T-account for bonds payable.

		Bonds Payable		
			47,000	12/31/01
Bonds redeemed	?		20,000	Bonds issued
			50,000	12/31/02

The amount of bonds redeemed can be computed as $17,000. ($47,000 + $20,000 − $50,000 = $17,000)

11. (a) Investing activities include all cash flows involving **assets** other than operating items. The investing activities are

Proceeds from sale of equipment	$ 10,000
Purchase of A.S., Inc. bonds	(180,000)
Net cash used in investing activities	$(170,000)

The gain on sale of equipment ($6,000) and amortization of bond discount ($2,000) are net income adjustments in the operating section, while dividends paid ($38,000) and proceeds from sale of treasury stock ($75,000) are financing items. The excess of dividends declared over dividends paid is a noncash financing activity.

12. (d) Financing activities include all cash flows involving **liabilities and owners' equity** other than operating items. The financing activities are

Dividends paid	$(38,000)
Proceeds from sale of treasury stock	75,000
Net cash provided by financing activities	$ 37,000

The excess of dividends declared over dividends paid is a **noncash** financing activity. The gain on sale of equipment ($6,000) and amortization of bond discount ($2,000) are net income adjustments in the operating section, while the proceeds from sale of equipment ($10,000) and purchase of A.S., Inc. bonds ($180,000) are investing items.

13. (c) Financing activities include the repayment of debt principal or, as in this case, the payment of the capital lease obligation. Thus, the cash outflow is equal to the 2002 principal payments only. The interest on the capital lease is classified as an operating cash outflow.

14. (d) According to SFAS 95, information about all investing and financing activities of an enterprise during a period that affect recognized assets and liabilities but that do not affect cash receipts or cash payments in the period should be reported in a supplemental schedule to the financial statements. This schedule includes all noncash investing and financing activities for the period. The conversion of long-term debt into common stock does not have any effect on cash flow, and it also results in a reduction of liabilities and an increase in stockholders' equity. Therefore, the conversion of long-term debt into common stock should be reported as a noncash investing and financing activity in the supplemental schedule. On the other hand, the conversion of preferred stock into common stock would not be reported as a noncash investing and financing activity. The conversion of preferred stock into common does not affect cash flow, but it also does not affect assets or liabilities. The

conversion of preferred stock into common only affects accounts reported in stockholders' equity. Therefore, the conversion of preferred stock into common is not reported as a financing activity in the supplemental note to the financial statements.

15. (c) Noncash investing and financing activities are reported as supplemental information to the statement of cash flows because while they do not affect cash in the current year, they may have a significant effect on the prospective cash flows of the company. Therefore, conversion of debt to equity is disclosed as supplemental information to the statement of cash flows. However, SFAS 95 specifies that cash flow per share should **not** be reported on the statement of cash flows because it may be misleading and may be incorrectly used as a measure of profitability.

C. Direct or Indirect Presentation in Reporting Operating Activities

16. (d) Under either the direct method or indirect method, the major classes of gross cash receipts and gross cash payments must be reported in the statement of cash flows. Under the direct method, the amount of income taxes paid is one of the components of net cash flows from operating activities; under the indirect method, it is a required supplemental disclosure. A reconciliation of net income to net cash flow from operations is a required supplemental disclosure under the direct method, and is included in the body of the statement under the indirect method. Only a reconciliation of ending retained earnings to net cash flow from operations is **not** required under either method.

17. (d) Cash collected from customers can be computed using either a formula or a T-account. The formula is

Sales	−	[End AR	−	(Beg AR	−	Write-offs)]	=	Collections
$538,800	−	[$33,000	−	($30,000	−	$0)]	=	$535,800

In the formula above, sales is adjusted for the **change in AR, exclusive of write-offs,** because write-offs represent sales (and AR) which will never be collected in cash. In this problem, no mention is made of write-offs, so it must be assumed that the change in the allowance account results solely from bad debt expense (no write-offs). Since there are no write-offs, the increase in AR ($33,000 − $30,000 = $3,000) is subtracted from sales because those sales increased AR instead of cash. The T-account solution is below.

	Accounts Receivable		
12/31/02	30,000		
Sales	538,800	0	Write-offs
		?	Collections = 535,800
12/31/03	33,000		

18. (d) Cash paid for goods to be sold can be computed using either a formula or T-accounts. The formula is

CGS	+	(End. inv. − Beg. inv.)	−	(End. AP − Beg AP)	−	Cash paid
$250,000	+	($31,000 − $47,000)	−	($25,000 − $17,500)	−	Cash paid
$250,000	+	$16,000	−	$7,500	−	$226,500

The decrease in inventory ($16,000) is subtracted from CGS because that portion of CGS resulted from a use of inventory purchased in prior years, rather than from a cash payment. The increase in AP is subtracted because that portion of CGS was not paid this year. Using T-accounts, first purchases are computed using the inventory account, then payments are computed using the accounts payable account.

Inventory

12/31/02	47,000		
Purchases	?	250,000	CGS
12/31/03	31,000		

1. Purchases = $234,000

Accounts Payable

		17,500	12/31/02
Payments	?	234,000	Purchases
		25,000	12/31/03

2. Payments = $226,500

19. (c) The trial balance does **not** include prepaid interest or interest payable, both of which would affect the computation of cash paid for interest. In the absence of those accounts, cash paid for interest is equal to interest expense plus (minus) bond premium (discount) amortization.

Interest expense	–	Discount amortization	=	Cash paid
$4,300	–	($5,000 – $4,500)	=	$3,800

Flax's 2002 entry to record interest expense was

Interest expense	4,300	
Cash		3,800
Discount on bonds payable		500

20. (a) Cash paid for income taxes can be computed using the following formula:

$$\text{Inc. tax expense} - \left(\begin{array}{c}\text{End.} \\ \text{inc. tax} \\ \text{payable}\end{array} - \begin{array}{c}\text{Beg.} \\ \text{inc. tax} \\ \text{payable}\end{array}\right) - \left(\begin{array}{c}\text{End.} \\ \text{def. tax} \\ \text{liability}\end{array} - \begin{array}{c}\text{Beg.} \\ \text{def. tax} \\ \text{liability}\end{array}\right) = \begin{array}{c}\text{Cash} \\ \text{paid} \\ \text{for inc. tax}\end{array}$$

$20,400	–	($21,000 – $27,100)	–	($5,300 – $4,600) = Cash paid
$20,400	+	$6,100	–	$700 = $25,800

The decrease in income taxes payable is added to income tax expense because cash was used to decrease the liability as well as to pay tax expense. The increase in the deferred tax liability is deducted from income tax expense because that portion of tax expense was deferred (not paid in cash). Flax's summary journal entry to record income taxes for 2003 is

Inc. tax expense	20,400	
Inc. tax payable	6,100	
Cash		25,800
Deferred taxes		700

21. (c) In general, cash paid for selling expenses is affected by prepaid selling expenses, accrued selling expenses, depreciation and/or amortization expense, and possibly bad debts expense. In this case, there are no prepaid or accrued selling expenses in the trial balances, and bad debts expense is apparently included in general and administrative expenses (see discussion below). Therefore, cash paid for selling expenses is $141,000 ($141,500 selling expenses less $500 depreciation expense). Total depreciation expense can be determined from the change in the accumulated depreciation account ($16,500 – $15,000 = $1,500), and 1/3 of that amount is selling expense (1/3 x $1,500 = $500). Note that bad debt expense ($1,300 – $1,100 = $200) must be included in general and administrative expenses, because the answer obtained by assuming it is part of selling expenses ($141,000 – $200 = $140,800) is not given as one of the four choices.

22. (a) Per SFAS 95, businesses are encouraged to use the direct method of reporting operating activities under which major classes of cash receipts and cash payments are shown. The minimum cash flows to be disclosed under this method are cash collected from customers, interest and divi-

dends received, cash paid to employees and suppliers, income taxes paid, and interest paid.

23. (c) In a statement of cash flows in which the operating activities section is prepared using the direct method, the cash paid for wages would be equal to the accrual-basis salary expense, plus/minus any decrease/increase in the wages payable account. (The logic is essentially the same as an accrual-basis to cash-basis adjustment.)

24. (c) Net income was $150,000. Three of the four items given are net income adjustments (the major repair to projection equipment [$2,100] is a cash outflow under investing activities), resulting in net cash provided by operating activities of $144,900.

Net income	$150,000
Equity method income	(5,500)
Premium amortization	(1,400)
Increase in def. tax liability	1,800
Cash provided by operating activities	$144,900

When equity method income is recorded, the offsetting debit is to the investment account, not cash; when premium on bonds payable is amortized, the credit to interest expense is offset by a debit to the premium account, not cash. Therefore, both of these items **increase** income without increasing cash, and must be **deducted** as a net income adjustment. For the deferred tax items, when income tax expense is debited, the offsetting credit is to deferred tax liability, not cash. Therefore, this item **decreases** net income without decreasing cash, and it must be **added back** as a net income adjustment. Note that there should normally be depreciation expense as a net income adjustment, but it is not given.

25. (a) Based only on the items given, net cash provided by operating activities is $151,400, as computed below.

Net income	$150,000
Increase in net AR	
[($29,000 – 1,000) – ($23,000 – 800)]	(5,800)
Decrease in prepaid rent ($12,400 – $8,200)	4,200
Increase in AP ($22,400 – $19,400)	3,000
Cash provided by ops.	$151,400

The increase in net AR is deducted from net income because it indicates that cash collected is less than sales revenue. The decrease in prepaid rent is added because it reflects rent expense that was **not** a cash payment, but an allocation of previously recorded prepaid rent. Finally, the increase in AP is added because it also represents an expense (cost of goods sold) that was not yet paid.

26. (d) The objective of a statement of cash flows is to explain what caused the change in the cash balance. The first step in this process is to determine cash provided by operations. When presenting cash from operating activities under the indirect approach, net income must be adjusted for changes in current assets other than cash and in current liabilities. These adjustments are required because items that resulted from noncash events must be removed from accrual-based income. For example, when inventory increases during the period, inventory sold is less than inventory purchased. Considering only the increase in the inventory account, cost of goods sold on an accrual basis is less than it would have been if cash basis were being used. In converting to the cash basis, the increase in inventory must be subtracted from net income to arrive at cash from operations. Answer (a) is incorrect because even though an increase in inventories requires an outflow of cash, inventories are shown as adjustments to net income under the indirect method. Answer (b) is incorrect because it describes how a noncash transaction such as the exchange of land for a note would be handled. Answer (c) is incorrect because an increase in an inventory would be a deduction from net income, not an addition.

27. (c)   When using the indirect method for reporting net cash flows from operations, you start with net income from continuing operations and adjust for changes in operating related accounts (i.e., inventory, accounts payable) and non-cash expenses, revenues, gains and losses. The proceeds from the sale of equipment is reported as an inflow in the investing section of the statement of cash flows, at its gross amount. This gross amount includes the gain. Therefore, to avoid double counting and to properly classify cash inflows, the gain is subtracted from net income to show the proper cash balance from operating activities.

28. (c)   Under the indirect method of reporting cash flows from operations, income from continuing operations is adjusted for changes in operating related accounts and non-cash expenses, revenues, losses, and gains. Noncash items that were subtracted in determining income must be added back in. This would include amortization of bond discount, as it is a charge against income but does not decrease cash. The excess of treasury stock acquisition cost over sales proceeds would not be added back to net income. Under the cost method, this loss would not be included in net income but would be charged back to a paid-in capital account or retained earnings. The acquisition and sale of treasury stock, furthermore, would be financing activities.

29. (c)   SFAS 95 specifies that cash flow per share should **not** be reported on the statement of cash flows because it may be misleading and may be incorrectly used as a measure of profitability. Answers (a) and (b) are incorrect because, when the indirect method is used, separate disclosure is required for **interest paid** (net of amounts capitalized) and **income taxes paid**. Answer (d) is incorrect because, regardless of the method used, **dividends paid** on preferred stock are reported as a **financing activity**.

D.   Example of Statement of Cash Flows

30. (c)   Net cash provided by operating activities can be computed by using either the **direct** or **indirect** approach. In this case, there is not enough information to use the direct approach. In the indirect approach, net income is adjusted for noncash items, as shown below.

Net income	$790,000
Gain on sale of LT investment	(35,000)
Increase in inventory	(80,000)
Depreciation expense	250,000
Decrease in AP and accrued liabs.	(5,000)
	$920,000

The additional information indicates that a LT investment was sold for $135,000. The listing of accounts shows a decrease in LT investments of $100,000. The gain on sale ($135,000 – $100,000 = $35,000) is deducted because the total cash effect of this transaction ($135,000) will be reported as an investing activity. Two of the working capital accounts that changed are related to net income. The increase in inventory ($80,000) is deducted because cash was used to increase inventory. The decrease in accounts payable and accrued liabilities is deducted because cash was

used to pay these liabilities. The only other information or account given which affects net income is accumulated depreciation. Although this account did not show any net decrease or increase during 2002, we know it was decreased by $250,000 when the building was sold ($600,000 cost less $350,000 carrying amount equals $250,000 accumulated depreciation). Therefore, depreciation expense of $250,000 must have increased the accumulated depreciation account to result in a net effect for the year of $0. Depreciation expense is added because it is a noncash expense.

An alternative method of computing net cash provided by operating activities is to back into the answer after determining cash used in investing activities and cash provided by financing activities.

Cash provided by Operating Activities	$?
Cash used in Investing Activities	(1,005,000)
Cash provided by Financing Activities	205,000
Net increase in Cash	$ 120,000

The problem tells us that cash and cash equivalents increased by $120,000. Therefore, cash provided by operating activities is $920,000 ($920,000 – $1,005,000 + $205,000 = $120,000).

31. (a)   **Investing** activities include all cash flows involving **assets,** other than operating items. **Financing** activities include all cash flows involving **liabilities and equity,** other than operating items. The common stock issued is a financing activity. In this case, the changes in the inventory and accumulated depreciation accounts are operating items. The cash flows involving the other assets, listed below, are investing activities

Purchase of ST investments	$ (300,000)
Sale of LT investments	135,000
Sale of plant assets	350,000
Purchase of plant assets	(1,190,000)
	$(1,005,000)

The amounts above were given, except for the purchase of plant assets, the amount of which can be determined from the following T-account:

Plant Assets			
Cost of equip. acquired	110,000	600,000	Cost of
Cost of plant assets purchased	?		bldg. sold
Net increase	700,000		

The equipment acquired through issuance of LT debt is a **noncash** investing and financing activity so it does not affect net **cash** used in investing activities.

32. (d)   **Financing** activities include all cash flows involving **liabilities and equity,** other than operating items. **Investing** activities include all cash flows involving **assets,** other than operating items. In this case, the change in the **accounts payable and accrued liabilities** account is an operating item. The part of the change in **retained earnings** caused by net income ($790,000) is also an operating item. The cash flows involving the other liability and equity accounts, listed below, are financing activities.

Payment of dividends ($500,000 – $160,000)	$(340,000)
Issuance of ST debt	325,000
Issuance of common stock (10,000 x $22)	220,000
	$205,000

The problem states that $500,000 of dividends were **declared,** and this is confirmed by the change in the retained earnings account ($790,000 net income – $500,000 dividends declared = $290,000 net increase). However, since dividends payable increased by $160,000, only $340,000 of dividends were **paid** ($500,000 – $160,000). The issuance of common stock (10,000 shares x $22 per share = $220,000) is confirmed by the increases in the **common stock** and **additional paid-in capital** accounts ($100,000 + $120,000 = $220,000). The issuance of LT debt for equipment ($110,000) is a **noncash** financing and investing activity, so it does not affect net **cash** provided by financing activities. Note that the answers to the three related questions can be verified by comparing them to the increase in cash and cash equivalents ($120,000) given in the problem.

Cash provided by oper. acts.	$ 920,000
Cash used in inv. acts.	(1,005,000)
Cash provided by fin. acts.	205,000
Increase in cash and cash equivalents	$ 120,000

33. (c) The requirement is to calculate the amount of cash collected during 2002 from accounts receivable. The solutions approach is to prepare a T-account for accounts receivable. The allowance account has no effect on this analysis, because the problem states that the balance in this account has not changed and no accounts receivable were written off. Net credit sales are the only debit to accounts receivable because all accounts receivable relate to trade merchandise. In the T-account below, you must solve for the missing credit to determine that $6,140,000 was collected on account during 2002.

AR—Net

12/31/01 balance	580,000	?	2001 Collections
2002 net credit sales	6,400,000		
12/31/02 balance	840,000		

NOTE: Based on the information given in this problem, no bad debt expense was recorded during 2002. However unrealistic this assumption might be, it is important to simply work with the information as given.

34. (d) The requirement is to calculate the amount of cash payments during 2002 on accounts payable. The solutions approach is to visualize the accounts payable T-account.

Accounts Payable

		440,000	12/31/01
Payments	?	?	Purchases
		530,000	12/31/02

It is apparent that to determine payments to suppliers, purchases of trade merchandise must first be computed. The cost of goods sold statement can be used to compute purchases.

Beginning inventory	$ 420,000
+ Purchases	+ ?
– Ending inventory	– 660,000
Cost of goods sold	$5,000,000

Purchases = $5,000,000 – ($420,000 – $660,000)
       = $5,240,000

Finally, the purchases are entered into the accounts payable T-account, and payments to suppliers of $5,150,000 can be plugged in.

Accounts Payable

		440,000	12/31/01
Payments	5,150,000	5,240,000	Purchases
		530,000	12/31/02

35. (d) The requirement is to determine net cash flows provided by financing activities in 2002. The solutions approach is to work through the comparative balance sheets noting increases and decreases in liability accounts other than those related to operations and increases or decreases in

stockholders' equity accounts. The additional information given must be considered in connection with these changes. Cash inflows from financing activities include proceeds from long-term borrowing, and issuance of capital stock.

Proceeds from long-term note	$500,000
Proceeds from issuance of common stock	300,000
	$800,000

To determine the amount of dividends paid, it is necessary to analyze both the retained earnings and the dividends payable accounts.

Dividends Payable				Retained Earnings		
		--	12/31/01		330,000	12/31/01
Dividends			Dividends			
paid	?	?	declared	?	400,000	Net income
		70,000	12/31/02		560,000	12/31/02

Dividends declared = $330,000 + 400,000 – 560,000 = $170,000
Dividends paid   = $0 + 170,000 – 70,000 = $100,000

Net cash flows provided by financing activities is $700,000 ($800,000 – $100,000).

36. (c) The requirement is to compute the cash used in investing activities during 2002. The two assets other than those related to operations shown on the balance sheet (long-term investments and land, building, and fixtures) have increased from 12/31/01 to 12/31/02, indicating cash purchases since the additional information does not suggest any other means of acquisition. Therefore, cash outflows from investing activities include $80,000 for long-term investments and $530,000 ($1,130,000 – $600,000) for land, building, and fixtures.

37. (a) The solutions approach is to set up T-accounts for the related accounts.

Sales		AR	
	Sales	Beg. Bal.	Collections
		Sales	Write-offs
		End. Bal.	

Sales are debited to AR and credited to sales; collections are debited to cash and credited to AR. Under the direct write-off method, write-offs of customer accounts are debited to bad debts expense, and credited to AR. To adjust sales to cash collections from customers, Bee must subtract the increase in accounts receivable (because Bee has not yet received cash for the sales remaining in AR). Bee must also subtract the accounts written off, because these sales have not resulted in cash receipts (and probably never will).

OTHER OBJECTIVE ANSWERS AND ANSWER EXPLANATIONS

Problem 1

1. ($185,000, S) The payments for income taxes during the year were debited to the income taxes payable account. To arrive at the amount of payments, a T-account can be used as follows:

```
                    Income Taxes Payable
                                150,000    12/31/01
    Payments      185,000
    12/31/02       35,000
```

Note that the taxes payable for 2002 have not yet been recorded. Therefore, the change in the account is comprised entirely of payments. This amount of cash paid for income taxes would be reported separately as supplementary information for a statement of cash flows prepared using the indirect method.

2. ($ 50,000, S) Interest paid on the bonds in 2002 would be $50,000 ($500,000 x 10%). Alternatively, the $46,000 plus the $4,000 premium amortization (see explanation for the next item below) also results in $50,000 as the amount paid for interest. This amount of cash paid for interest would be reported separately as supplementary information for a statement of cash flows using the indirect method.

3. ($485,000, F) Through the following T-account analyses, a journal entry for the redemption of the bonds payable can be determined:

```
            Bonds Payable                              Unamortized Premium on Bonds
                        1,000,000   12/31/01     Amortization    4,000   150,000   12/31/01
Redemption   500,000                             Redemption     75,000
                          500,000   12/31/02                             71,000   12/31/02

       Gain on Extinguishment of Bonds                         Cash
                           90,000    12/31/02                            ?
```

Journal entry for redemption

```
    Bonds payable                          500,000
    Unamortized premium on bonds            75,000
        Gain on extinguishment of bonds                 90,000
        Cash                                           485,000
```

This amount paid for the redemption of the bonds would be separately reported in the financing section on the statement of cash flows prepared using the indirect method. Financing activities include obtaining resources from owners and returning the investment, as well as obtaining resources from creditors and **repaying the amounts borrowed**.

4. ($255,000, F) An additional 80,000 shares of $2.50 par value common stock were issued during 2002. The following T-accounts depict the changes in the common stock and additional paid-in capital accounts:

```
              Common Stock
                    150,000     12/31/01
                    200,000     Issuance        (80,000 x $2.50)
                    350,000     12/31/02


           Additional Paid-in Capital
                    375,000     12/31/01
                     55,000     Issuance
                    430,000     12/31/02
```

The journal entry for the issuance of the stock would have been

```
    Cash                            255,000
        Common stock                           200,000
        Additional paid-in capital              55,000
```

This amount received for the issuance of the common stock would be reported separately in the financing section of the statement of cash flows prepared using the indirect method. Financing activities include **obtaining resources from owners** and returning the investment, as well as obtaining resources from creditors and repaying the amounts borrowed.

5. ($ 65,000, F) The problem states that there were no changes to retained earnings during the year other than dividends declared. Therefore, the following T-account analyses depict the dividend activity during the year:

```
                    Retained Earnings
                                265,000    12/31/01
    Dividends declared    80,000
                                185,000    12/31/02
```

	Dividends Payable				Cash	
		10,000	12/31/01			?
Dividends paid	?	80,000	Accrual during 2002			
		25,000	12/31/02			

The following journal entry would have been made:

Retained earnings	80,000	
Dividends payable		80,000
Dividends payable	65,000	
Cash		65,000

This amount paid for the dividends would be reported separately in the financing section of the statement of cash flows prepared using the indirect method. Financing activities include obtaining resources from owners and **returning the investment,** as well as obtaining resources from creditors and repaying the amounts borrowed.

6. **($ 20,000, I)** The following T-account analyses depict the sale of the equipment during 2002:

	Property, Plant and Equipment		
12/31/01	995,000		
		50,000	Sale
Purchase	125,000		
12/31/02	1,070,000		

	Accumulated Depreciation		
		280,000	12/31/01
Depreciation on sold asset	23,000	88,000	Depreciation expense
		345,000	12/31/02

	Loss on Sale of Equipment		Cash	
12/31/02	7,000		?	

The following journal entry would have been made for the sale of the equipment:

Cash	20,000	
Accumulated depreciation	23,000	
Loss on sale of equipment	7,000	
Property, plant and equipment		50,000

The proceeds from the sale of equipment would be reported separately in the investing section of the statement of cash flows. Included in the investing section are the acquisition and disposition of long-term productive assets or securities (not considered cash equivalents), as well as the lending of money and collection of loans.

ANSWER OUTLINE

Problem 1   Statement of Cash Flows

a. Objectives of statement
   Information about cash receipts and payments
   Information about investing and financing activities
   Facilitate user assessments

b. Transactions not affecting cash, but reported in separate schedule
   Acquisition of assets with
      Debt
      Other assets
      Equity securities
   Reduction of debt by
      Other debt
      Distribution of assets
      Issuance of equity securities

c. Effect on statement of cash flows when direct presentation used for operating activities
   Change in accounts receivable affects cash received from customers
   Change in inventory affects cash used for CGS
   Depreciation is noncash expense
      Deduct from operating expenses
   Change in deferred tax liability is neither inflow nor outflow of cash
   Long-term debt issued for building does not affect cash
      Noncash financing and investing transaction shown on a separate schedule
   Reduction of current debt is outflow of cash—financing activity
   Proceeds are an inflow of cash—investing activity

UNOFFICIAL ANSWER

Problem 1   Statement of Cash Flows

a.   The objectives of the statement of cash flows are to provide information about cash receipts and payments from operating, investing, and financing activities. This information helps users assess the company's ability to generate future net cash flows and ability to meet obligations and pay dividends. The statement also helps users assess the differences between income and associated cash receipts and payments.

b.   Investing and financing activities that do not involve cash receipts and payments during the period should be excluded from the cash flow statement and reported in a separate schedule. Transactions that would be classified as noncash financing and investing activities would include the following:

1. Purchase of assets by the issuance of capital stock or debt, or a reduction in another asset.
2. Reduction of a liability by the issuance of capital stock or the incurrence of another liability, or a reduction in an asset.

c.   The effects and procedural considerations of the seven account balances (transactions) upon the preparation of a statement of cash flows are as follows:

1.   Accounts receivable—trade are generated as a result of credit sales. A balance in accounts receivable—trade represents sales (a part of operating earnings) not represented by cash. An increase in the accounts receivable—trade balance indicates that the actual cash generated is equal to sales as reported on the earnings statement less the increase in accounts receivable—trade balance. Conversely, a net decrease in the accounts receivable—trade balance would have to be added to sales as reported on the earnings statement to arrive at cash generated from sales. In the preparation of a statement of cash flows the increase (decrease) in this account balance between two periods is subtracted from (or added to) net sales to arrive at cash received from customers for sales.

2.   Inventory is a component part of cost of goods sold. The net change in inventory balances affects the cash used for cost of goods sold. An increase in ending inventory over beginning inventory reduces the cost of goods sold. However, cash was presumed to be used to increase the inventory balance. An increase in the inventory balance represents a use of cash. When there is an increase in inventory balances, the cash used for cost of goods sold is the cost of goods sold as shown in the current earnings statement plus the increase in inventory balance.

A similar analysis leads to the conclusion that a decrease in ending inventory balance with respect to beginning inventory balance gives rise to a net increase in cost of goods sold as shown in the current earnings statement but a reduction in the cash so used.

3.   Depreciation represents a systematic allocation of the cost of a fixed asset to the accounting periods benefited by the asset. The process of recognizing depreciation does not affect cash. Cash paid for operating expenses is determined by deducting depreciation expense from total operating expenses and adjusting the operating expenses for prepaid expenses.

4.   Deferred income taxes are the difference between income taxes matched against earnings and the actual amount paid or payable for the period. If the balance of the deferred tax liability account, for example, increases between two periods, the amount of income taxes paid was less than the indicated income tax expense. Conversely, if deferred liability tax account decreases, the amount paid was greater than the correct income tax expense. Although the change in the deferred tax liability account is included in the indirect approach, the direct approach is not affected by the change. To determine the cash paid for taxes under the direct presentation, the **current** portion of income tax expense is adjusted for the increase or decrease in the income tax payable account.

5.   The purchase of a building by issuing long-term debt obviously does not require a cash outlay. However, this noncash activity should be reported in a separate schedule as a noncash financing and investing activity.

6.   The payment of the current portion of debt represents a cash outflow from financing activities.

7.   The total proceeds from the sale of the fixed asset should be shown as an inflow from investing activities. This transaction would not be reflected under operating activities when the **direct** presentation is used.

SOLUTION GUIDE

Problem 2   Statement of Cash Flows

1.   The problem requires the preparation of a statement of cash flows. The solutions approach is to analyze the net change in each account, using the additional information where applicable, and to identify the cash inflows, cash outflows, and net income adjustments. Journal entries and T-accounts can be used to facilitate the analysis.

1.1   As each item is analyzed, it can be entered into a "skeleton" statement prepared by listing the heading and main categories, such as cash flows from operating activities, investing activities, and financing activities. The individual descriptions and numbers can be filled in as you go through the problem. The first item under operating activities is net income of $360,000, which was given.

2.   Cash increased by $100,000. This should be the net increase in cash reported in the reconciliation of beginning and ending cash shown at the bottom of the statement.

2.1   Accounts receivable decreased by $40,000. This is **added** as a net income adjustment in the operating section because it indicates that cash collections were greater than the sales reported in the income statement.

2.2   Inventories increased by $135,000. This is **deducted** in the operating section as a net income adjustment. An increase in inventory means that cash was used to purchase not only the goods sold, but also additional inventory to increase the amount on hand.

2.3   Property, plant, and equipment increased by $340,000. This is the net result of two transactions described in the additional information. Equipment (cost, $60,000) with a carrying amount of $35,000 was sold for $40,000 cash.

Cash	40,000	
Accum. depr.	25,000	(60,000 – 35,000)
Equipment		60,000
Gain on sale		5,000 (65,000 – 60,000)

The cash received ($40,000) is a **cash inflow** from investing activities. The gain on sale ($5,000) is **deducted** as a net income adjustment in the operating section because there was no cash inflow other than the $40,000 investing inflow. Therefore, the $5,000 gain increased net income without providing an additional $5,000 of cash. The other transaction affecting property, plant, and equipment is a $400,000 purchase of an office building using a capital lease. This transaction does **not** affect cash in 2002, but it is a significant noncash financing and investing activity reported at the bottom of the statement of cash flows. These two transactions explain the $340,000 net increase in the account, as the T-account below illustrates.

	Prop., Plant, and Equip.		
Purchase	400,000	60,000	Sale
Net increase	340,000		

2.4   Accumulated depreciation increased by $125,000. This net change is the result of the sale of equipment (discussed in 2.3) and depreciation expense. The amount of depreciation expense can be determined through T-account analysis.

	Accumulated Depr.		
Sale	25,000	?	Depr. expense
		125,000	Net increase

The missing amount is depreciation expense of $150,000. Depreciation expense is **added** as a net income adjustment in the operating section because, although it decreased net income, it was not a cash outflow.

2.5   The Investment in Belle Co. account increased by $30,000. The additional information indicates that this is due to the recognition of Omega's share of Belle's income (25% x $120,000 = $30,000). Omega uses the equity method due to its 25% ownership interest and would have prepared the following entry in 2002:

Investment in Belle Co.	30,000	
Income from investment		30,000

This entry increases net income, but does not involve a cash inflow. Therefore, it must be **deducted** as a net income adjustment in the operating section. Note that there is no excess of cash over book value on this investment because 25% of $1,100,000 is $275,000.

2.6   The loan receivable increased by $270,000. This is the net result of two transactions described in the additional information. First, Omega loaned $300,000 cash to Chase Co. This is a **cash outflow** from investing activities. Later, Omega collected the first $30,000 principal installment. This is a **cash inflow** from investing activities. These two transactions explain the net change in the account, as the T-account below illustrates.

	Loan Receivable		
Loan to Chase	300,000	30,000	Collection of loan
Net increase	270,000		

3.   Accounts payable increased by $60,000. This is **added** as a net income adjustment in the operating section because some expenses were incurred on account and therefore did not require the use of cash in 2002.

3.1   Income taxes payable decreased by $20,000. This is **deducted** as a net income adjustment in the operating section because cash was used to pay not only 2002 income tax expense, but also to reduce the payable.

3.2   Dividends payable decreased by $10,000. This is the net result of two transactions described in the additional information. On 2/28/02, a cash dividend declared in 2001 was paid. The journal entry was

Dividends payable	90,000	
Cash		90,000

The $90,000 cash paid is a cash **outflow** from financing activities. On 12/15/02, a cash dividend was declared which will not be paid until 2003. The entry was

Retained earnings	80,000	
Dividends payable		80,000

This transaction does **not** affect cash in 2002, but it is a significant noncash financing activity reported at the bottom of the statement of cash flows. These two transactions explain the $10,000 net decrease in the account, as illustrated below.

Dividends Payable			
Div. paid	90,000	80,000	Div. declared
Net decr.	10,000		

3.3   The increase in the capital lease obligation ($400,000) was explained in 2.3.

3.4   There was no change in either the capital stock account or the additional paid-in capital account.

UNOFFICIAL ANSWER

Problem 2   Statement of Cash Flows

3.5   The retained earnings account increased by $280,000. This is the net result of two items described in the additional information: net income of $360,000 (discussed in 1.1) and dividends declared of $80,000 (discussed in 3.2). These two items explain the net increase in retained earnings, as the following T-account illustrates.

Retained Earnings			
Divs. declared	80,000	360,000	Net income
		280,000	Net incr.

Omega Corp.
STATEMENT OF CASH FLOWS
For the Year Ended December 31, 2002

Cash flows from operating activities:			
Net Income			$360,000
Adjustments to reconcile net income to net cash provided by operating activities:			
Depreciation	$150,000	[1]	
Gain on sale of equipment	(5,000)	[2]	
Undistributed earnings of Belle Co.	(30,000)	[3]	
Changes in assets and liabilities:			
Decrease in accounts receivable	40,000		
Increase in inventories	(135,000)		
Increase in accounts payable	60,000		
Decrease in income taxes payable	(20,000)		
			60,000
Net cash provided by operating activities			420,000
Cash flows from investing activities:			
Proceeds from sale of equipment	40,000		
Loan to Chase Co.	(300,000)		
Principal payment of loan receivable	30,000		
Net cash used in investing activities			(230,000)
Cash flows from financing activities:			
Dividends paid	(90,000)		
Net cash used in financing activities			(90,000)
Net increase in cash			100,000
Cash at beginning of year			700,000
Cash at end of year			$800,000

Explanation of Amounts

[1]	Depreciation		
	Net increase in accumulated depreciation for the year ended December 31, 2002		$125,000
	Accumulated depreciation on equipment sold:		
	Cost	$60,000	
	Carrying value	35,000	25,000
	Depreciation for 2002		$150,000
[2]	Gain on sale of equipment		
	Proceeds		$ 40,000
	Carrying value		35,000
	Gain		$ 5,000
[3]	Undistributed earnings of Belle Co.		
	Belle's net income for 2002		$120,000
	Omega's ownership		25%
	Undistributed earnings of Belle Co.		$ 30,000

SOLUTION GUIDE

Problem 3   SCF

1. This problem consists of three related parts. Part a. requires a statement of cash flows using the **direct** method in the operating activities section of the statement, part b. requires a reconciliation of net income to net cash provided by operating activities (**indirect** method), and part c. requires an analysis of changes in partners' capital accounts. Visualize the format of the statement for part a.: operating activities, investing activities, and financing activities.

2. Cash received from fees is an item that should be included under operating activities. Using the **direct** approach, accrual revenues must be adjusted to revenues on a cash basis. To do this, accrual sales must be increased (decreased) by the decrease (increase) in accounts receivable. Accounts receivable increased by $78,000, implying that some revenue has not yet been collected. Therefore, cash received from fees is $2,586,000 ($2,664,000 fee revenue less $78,000 AR increase).

2.1 Dividends received are also an operating activity. Cash received from dividends, not equity in earnings, must be reported in the statement of cash flows. The investee paid dividends of $384,000, and Linden Consulting Associates (LCA) received 25% of those dividends. This resulted in a cash inflow of $96,000 (25% x $384,000). Note that the equity in earnings ($176,000) is **not** a cash inflow; it results in an increase in the investment account, not in the cash account.

2.2 The last item to include under operating activities is operating expenses. Under the direct approach, cash paid for operating expenses must be computed by adjusting operating expenses for noncash expenses, accrued expenses, and prepaid expenses. In this case, operating expenses are $1,940,000. This amount must be adjusted for a noncash expense, depreciation (indicated by the $60,000 increase in accumulated depreciation) and for the increase in accounts payable and accrued expenses ($50,000). This $50,000 increase implies that operating expenses have been recorded for which the cash payment has not been made. Therefore, cash paid for operating expenses (to suppliers and employees) is $1,830,000 ($1,940,000 – $60,000 – $50,000).

2.3 The net cash flow from operating activities is $852,000. It consists of cash received from fees ($2,586,000) and cash received from dividends ($96,000), less cash paid for operating expenses ($1,830,000).

3. Per SFAS 95, an indirect reconciliation of net income to net cash flow from operating activities is required. When the **direct** approach is used in the body of the statement, this reconciliation should be provided in a separate schedule. If the **indirect** approach is used, this reconciliation is included in the body of the statement under operating activities. In this problem, no reconciliation is included with the SCF in part a., since part b. requires a reconciliation.

3.1 The reconciliation starts with net income. Net income in this case is $900,000. Depreciation expense ($60,000) must be added back because it is a noncash expense that reduced net income but did not reduce cash. The excess of equity in earnings over the dividends received from the investment ($176,000 – $96,000 = $80,000) must be subtracted because $80,000 of equity earnings were not received in cash. The increase in accounts receivable ($78,000) is deducted because it implies that $78,000 of revenue was not collected in cash. The increase in accounts payable and accrued expenses ($50,000) is added back to net income because it implies that some recorded expenses were not paid in cash. Therefore, the net cash flow from operating activities under the indirect approach is $852,000 ($900,000 + $60,000 – $80,000 – $78,000 + $50,000), the same as under the direct approach.

4. The other asset accounts must be analyzed to determine the cash flows from investing activities. All the asset accounts except property and equipment were related to operating activities. Property and equipment increased by $170,000 as the result of a July 1 purchase of an office computer. This cash outflow is reported as an investing activity. Note that the portion of the $170,000 cost that was paid for sales tax, delivery, and installation ($15,000) is considered part of the cost of the asset acquired.

5. The other liability and equity accounts must be analyzed to determine the cash flows from financing activities. Only accounts payable and accrued expenses are solely related to operating activities.

5.1 Mortgage payable decreased by $20,000. The cash outflow to reduce the mortgage is reported as a financing activity.

5.2 Partners' equity increased by $610,000. This increase must be analyzed further to determine the related cash flows. The typical items that affect partners' equity are investments, net income, and drawings. These are summarized below.

Partners' equity, 12/31/01	$1,700,000	
1/1/02 investment by Scott	340,000	Financing
Net income	900,000	Operating
Drawings	(630,000)	Financing
Partners' equity, 12/31/02	$2,310,000	

The investment by the new partner ($340,000) is a cash inflow reported as a financing activity, similar to the issuance of common stock by a corporation. The drawings ($630,000) are a cash outflow reported as a financing activity, similar to the payment of dividends by a corporation. Note that the $50,000 cash payment from the new partner directly to the old partners is **not** a cash flow of the partnership.

5.3 Finally, the amounts within each category can be netted to arrive at net cash inflows or outflows in each of the three main sections of the statement, and the beginning and ending balances of cash can be reconciled at the end of the statement.

UNOFFICIAL ANSWER

Problem 3 SCF

a.

Linden Consulting Associates
STATEMENT OF CASH FLOWS
For the Year Ended December 31, 2002
Increase (Decrease) in Cash

Cash flows from operating activities:		
Cash received from customers	$2,586,000 [1]	
Cash paid to suppliers and employees	(1,830,000) [2]	
Dividends received from affiliate	96,000	
Net cash provided by operating activities		$ 852,000
Cash flows from investing activities:		
Purchased property and equipment		(170,000)
Cash flows from financing activities:		
Principal payment of mortgage payable	(20,000)	
Proceeds for admission of new partner	340,000	
Drawings against partners' capital accounts	(630,000)	
Net cash used in financing activities		(310,000)
Net increase in cash		372,000
Cash at beginning of year		280,000
Cash at end of year		$ 652,000

Explanation of amounts		$2,664,000
[1] Fee revenue		
Less ending accounts receivable balance		(446,000)
Add beginning accounts receivable balance		368,000
		$2,586,000
[2] Operating expenses		$1,940,000
Less: Depreciation	$ 60,000	
Ending accounts payable balance	320,000	(380,000)
Add beginning accounts payable balance		270,000
		$1,830,000

b.

Reconciliation of net income to net cash provided by operating activities:		
Net income		$900,000
Adjustments to reconcile net income to net cash provided by operating activities:		
Depreciation and amortization	$ 60,000	
Undistributed earnings of affiliate	(80,000) [1]	
Change in assets and liabilities:		
Increase in accounts receivable	(78,000)	
Increase in accounts payable and accrued expenses	50,000	
Total adjustments		(48,000)
Net cash provided by operating activities		$852,000
[1] Linden's share of Zach, Inc.'s:		
Reported net income for 2002 (25% x $720,000) – $4,000		$176,000
Cash dividends paid for 2002 (25% of $384,000)		96,000
Undistributed earnings for 2002		$ 80,000

Keep practicing! Wiley's CPA Examination Review Software has over 2,800 questions.

Available at www.wiley.com/cpa

BUSINESS COMBINATIONS AND CONSOLIDATIONS

Many companies expand their operations by acquiring other businesses. The acquiring company may be seeking diversification of its business, a more stable supply of raw materials for its production, an increase in the range of products or services it offers, or any one of many other business reasons. The accounting issues of business combinations begin with properly recording and reporting the economic events of the date of business combination. Accounting subsequent to the combination is dependent on the alternatives selected at the combination date. Thus, as you study this section, you should fully understand how the combination is first recorded and reported before proceeding to events occurring after the combination date.

From a legal perspective, business combinations are classified into three categories as follows:

1. **Merger**—One company acquires the assets and liabilities of one or more other companies in exchange for stock, cash, or other consideration. The acquiring company continues to exist as a separate legal entity, but the acquired company ceases to exist as a separate legal entity, its stock is cancelled, and its books are closed. The separate assets and liabilities are recorded on the acquiring firm's books. (A Corp. + B Corp. = A Corp.)

2. **Statutory Consolidation**—A new firm is formed to issue stock in exchange for the stock of two or more combining or consolidating companies. The acquired firms normally cease to continue as separate legal entities; therefore, the new (acquiring) firm will record the separate assets and liabilities of the acquired firms. (A Corp. + B Corp. = C Corp.)

3. **Acquisition**—A company acquires a majority (> 50%) of the common stock of another company and each company continues its legal existence. The acquiring company (parent) will record an "Investment in Acquired Company's Stock" in the combination entry. (A Corp. + B Corp. = Consolidated Financial Statements of A and B)

Mergers and statutory consolidations require 100% ownership of the acquired company but the acquisition business combination requires only a majority ownership of the outstanding stock. In addition, by maintaining the separate legal existence of the acquired company (B Corp.) and not canceling its stock, the parent company (A Corp.) can retain greater flexibility in raising additional capital by using B Corp. shares as collateral for a loan or through the issuance of new shares of B Corp.

Financial statements for combinations which are in the legal forms of mergers and statutory consolidations are prepared in the normal accounting process since all assets and liabilities recorded on just one set of books. Accounting for an **acquisition,** however, results in an investment account on the acquiring company's books while the assets and liabilities are still recorded and shown on the books of the acquired company. Financial reporting for this type of combination generally requires the bringing together, or **accounting consolidation,** of the accounts from these two sets of books to prepare financial reports for the economic entity now formed between the parent and subsidiary companies. This process is explained in detail in Section F. of this module.

A. Accounting for the Combination

Regardless of the legal form (merger, statutory consolidation, acquisition), there is only one accounting method that currently can be applied to any business combination—the purchase method. The FASB in Statement of Financial Accounting Standards 141, *Business Combinations,* eliminated the other method that was used to account for business combinations—pooling of interest accounting. Both methods are described below because combinations that occurred on or before June 30, 2002, and accounted for under the pooling method will continue to be accounted for in that fashion.

1. Purchase Accounting

Purchase accounting for a combination is similar to the accounting treatment used in the acquisition of any asset group. The fair market value of the consideration (cash, stock, debt securities, etc.) given by the acquiring firm is used as the valuation basis of the combination. The assets and liabilities of the acquired firm are revalued to their respective fair market values at the combination date. Any difference between the value of the consideration given and the fair market values of the net assets obtained is normally recorded as goodwill. When the fair market values of the net assets exceed the acquisition cost, the excess first is used to reduce the carrying value of noncurrent, nonfinancial assets. If such assets are reduced to zero, any additional amount is recognized as an extraordinary gain. The financial statements of the acquiring company reflect the combined operations from the date of combination.

2. **The Pooling Method**

The pooling method assumes a combining of stockholders' interests. The basis of valuation in pooling is the book value of the net assets on the books of the acquired company. Therefore, goodwill may **not** be created at the date of combination in a pooling combination. The financial statements of the acquiring company will include a restatement of all prior years presented to include the operations and financial position of the pooled companies for all years presented.

B. A Company and B Company—Date of Combination

A presentation of the date of combination entries for the purchase method will be made in the next two sections of this module. We will be using a comprehensive example for these sections and the remaining parts of the discussion on consolidation accounting. The following balance sheets of A Company and B Company provide the foundation for further discussion. As you study the remainder of this module, be sure you understand where the numbers are being derived from.

A Company and B Company
BALANCE SHEETS 1/1/02
(Immediately Before Combination)

Assets	A Company	B Company
Cash	$ 30,900	$ 37,400
Accounts receivable	34,200	9,100
Inventories	22,900	16,100
Equipment	200,000	50,000
Less: Accumulated depreciation	(21,000)	(10,000)
Patents	--	10,000
Total assets	$267,000	$112,600
Liabilities and Equity		
Accounts payable	$ 4,000	$ 6,600
Bonds payable	100,000	--
Capital stock ($10 par)	100,000	50,000
Additional paid-in capital	15,000	15,000
Retained earnings	48,000	41,000
Total liabilities and equity	$267,000	$112,600

The concept of book value of the investment is a basic principle of accounting for business combinations and will be used in many different computations. Note that the book value of the net assets of B Company may be computed by two different methods.

1. Subtract the book value of the liabilities from the book values of the assets, or

$$\$112,600 - \$6,600 = \$106,000$$

2. Add the book values of the components of B Company stockholders' equity

$$\$50,000 + \$15,000 + \$41,000 = \$106,000$$

C. Date of Combination—Purchase Accounting

Purchase accounting uses fair market values of the net assets as the valuation basis for the combination. The difference between the value of the consideration given by the acquiring firm and the **book value** of the net assets obtained is the excess of cost over book value, or excess of book value over cost (referred to here as differential) of the net assets obtained. As discussed earlier, this differential has two components, as follows:

1. An amount representing an adjustment of the book values of the net assets up (or down) to their respective fair market values, and
2. An amount representing goodwill, or reduction in the carrying value of noncurrent, nonfinancial assets

In determining the components of the assets acquired, intangible assets that arise from contractual or legal rights or can be disposed of separate from the entity should be recognized as assets apart from goodwill. Examples include trademarks, customer contracts. leases, patents, computer software, licensing agreements, and internet domain names.

Assume that our Company A purchased **all** the net assets of B Company. At the date of combination, the fair values of all the assets and liabilities were determined by appraisal, as follows:

B Company item	Book value (BV)	Fair market value (FMV)	Difference between BV and FMV
Cash	$ 37,400	$ 37,400	$ --
Accounts rec. (net)	9,100	9,100	--
Inventories	16,100	17,100	1,000
Equipment (net)	40,000	48,000	8,000
Patents	10,000	13,000	3,000
Accounts payable	(6,600)	(6,600)	--
Totals	$106,000	$118,000	$12,000

The $12,000 is the difference between the book value and fair market values of B Company and is one component of the differential. Goodwill, the other component of the differential, is the difference between the cost of the investment and the FMV of the net assets. Goodwill may be positive or negative.

Four different cases displaying a range of total acquisition costs are presented below. The form of consideration paid to B Company by A Company is assumed to be cash but, under purchase accounting, it could be stock, cash, debentures, or any other form of payment.

The allocation of the difference between cost and book value is a two-step process. First, the assets and liabilities must be valued at their respective fair market values and then any remainder is allocated to goodwill (or a reduction in the carrying value of certain assets). Note that the differential may be positive or negative and that the net assets could have fair market values less than book values.

	Case A	Case B	Case C	Case D
Consideration paid	$134,000	$118,000	$106,000	$100,000
Notes:	(> FMV)	(= FMV)	(< FMV)	(< FMV)
	(> BV)	(> BV)	(= BV)	(< BV)

Step 1. Compute the Differential

Book value	$106,000	$106,000	$106,000	$106,000
Investment cost	134,000	118,000	106,000	100,000
Differential	$ 28,000	$ 12,000	$ --	$ (6,000)

Step 2. Allocation of Differential

a. Revaluation of net assets to fair market value

FMV, net assets	$118,000	$118,000	$118,000	$118,000
Less BV	106,000	106,000	106,000	106,000
Portion to net assets	$ 12,000	$ 12,000	$ 12,000	$ 12,000

b. Remainder (Excess of cost greater than fair value, or fair value greater than cost)

FMV, net assets	$118,000	$118,000	$118,000	$118,000
Less investment cost	134,000	118,000	106,000	100,000
Goodwill	$ 16,000	$ --		
Amount to reduce carrying value of net assets			$ (12,000)	$ (18,000)

Step 3. Accounting for Goodwill and the Excess of Fair Value Greater Than Cost

SFAS 141 assumes the excess of cost greater than fair values of acquired assets and liabilities is goodwill (Case A). Goodwill is accounted for in accordance with SFAS 142. If the fair value of the assets and liabilities is **greater than** the investment cost (Cases C and D), then SFAS 141 requires this excess to be proportionally applied to reduce the assigned values of the noncurrent assets acquired, except financial assets (other than investments accounted for on the equity basis), assets to be disposed of by sale, deferred tax assets, and prepaid assets related to pensions or other postretirement benefit plans. If such assets are reduced to zero value, any remaining excess of fair value over cost should be recognized as an extraordinary gain.

Reallocations are required in Cases C and D because the fair values of the net assets are greater than costs, as follows:

	Item	Assigned values of noncurrent assets acquired	Proportion	Excess of fair value over cost	Reallocation	New assigned value
Case C:	Equipment	$48,000	$48,000/$61,000	($12,000)	$ (9,443)	$38,557
	Patents	$13,000	$13,000/$61,000	($12,000)	$ (2,557)	$10,443
		$61,000			$(12,000)	

Case D:	Equipment	$48,000	$48,000/$61,000	($18,000)	$(14,164)	$33,836
	Patents	$13,000	$13,000/$61,000	($18,000)	$ (3,836)	$ 9,164
		$61,000			$(18,000)	

Date of combination entries on A Company's books for a purchase-merger are

	Case A	Case B	Case C	Case D
Cash	37,400	37,400	37,400	37,400
AR	9,100	9,100	9,100	9,100
Inventories	17,100	17,100	17,100	17,100
Equipment (net)	48,000	48,000	38,557	33,836
Patents	13,000	13,000	10,443	9,164
Goodwill	16,000	--	--	--
AP		6,600	6,600	6,600	6,600
Cash		134,000	118,000	106,000	100,000

B Company would close its books and cease to operate as a separate entity.

If B Company maintained its separate legal status, the combination would be accounted for as a 100% acquisition. The date of combination entries on A Company's books for each of the four cases would be

	Case A	Case B	Case C	Case D
Investment in B Company	134,000	118,000	106,000	100,000
Cash		134,000	118,000	106,000	100,000

Consolidated financial statements would normally be prepared when acquisitions of more than 50% of outstanding stock are made. Consolidated statements are discussed later in this module.

Some candidates find that using value lines to display the features of purchase accounting helps to sort out the various concepts. Value lines are provided below for Cases A and D. You might want to do the value lines for Cases B and C.

CASE A

	Cost		$134,000	(2b)	Remainder (Excess of cost > FMV) Goodwill = $16,000
(1)	Differential = $28,000 (Excess of Cost > BV)	FMV	$118,000		
		BV	$106,000	(2a)	Revalue net assets to FMV $12,000

CASE D

		FMV	$118,000	(2a)	Revalue net assets to FMV		
(1)	Differential = <$6,000> (Excess of BV > Cost)	BV	$106,000		$12,000	(2b)	Remainder (Excess of FMV > Cost) ($18,000)
		Cost	$100,000				

D. Purchase Combination Entries Reviewed

The following table provides a review of the combination entries of the surviving or investing firm for the three legal forms of combination (merger, consolidation, and acquisition) for which stock is given. The legal form is primarily dependent on whether the combined company, Company B in our examples, retains a separate, legal existence or transfers its assets and liabilities to Company A and cancels any remaining stock of Company B. The items in the parentheses are valuation bases or the company source for determining the dollar amount for the entry.

Legal form	*Accounting*
1. Merger (A Co. + B Co. = A Co.)	Assets (FMV of B) Liabilities (FMV of B) Capital stock (Co. A) APIC (Co. A)
2. Statutory Consolidation (A Co. + B Co. = C Co.)	Assets (FMV of both A and B) Liabilities (FMV of A and B) Capital stock (Co. C) APIC (Co. C)
3. Acquisition (A Co. + B Co. = Consolidated statements of A and B)	Investment in B (FMV) Capital stock (Co. A) APIC (Co. A)

E. Consolidated Financial Statements

An acquisition of more than 50% of the outstanding voting stock will normally require the preparation of consolidated financial statements. The complete consolidation process is presented in the next section of this module. The investment account will be eliminated in the consolidation working papers and will be replaced with the specific assets and liabilities of the investee corporation. Consolidation is generally required for investments of more than 50% of the outstanding voting stock except when

1. The control is likely to be temporary.
2. Control is not held by the majority owner.

    a. The investee is in legal reorganization or bankruptcy.
    b. The investee operates in a foreign country which has severe restrictions on the financial transactions of its business firms or is subject to material political or economic uncertainty that casts significant doubt on the parent's ability to control the subsidiary.

In these limited cases, the investment will be reported as a long-term investment in an unconsolidated subsidiary on the investor's balance sheet with its balance determined by using the cost method unless the parent can demonstrate that it has significant influence in which case the equity method shall be used.

The concept of consolidated statements is that the resources of two or more companies are under the control of the parent company. Consolidated statements are prepared as if the group of legal entities were one economic entity group. Consolidated statements are presumed to be more meaningful for management, owners, and creditors of the parent company and they are required for fair presentation of the financially-related companies. Individual company statements should continue to be prepared for minority ownership and creditors of the subsidiary companies.

The accounting principles used to record and report events for a single legal entity are also applicable to a consolidated economic entity of two or more companies. The concept of the reporting entity is expanded to include more than one company, but all other accounting principles are applied in the same way as for an individual company. The consolidation process eliminates reciprocal items that are shown on both the parent's and subsidiary's books. These eliminations are necessary to avoid double-counting the same items which would misstate the financials of the combined economic entity.

Consolidated financial statements are prepared from worksheets which begin with the trial balances of the parent and subsidiary companies. Eliminating worksheet entries are made to reflect the two separate companies' results of operations and financial position as one combined economic entity. The entire consolidation process takes place **only on a worksheet**; no consolidation elimination entries are ever recorded on either the parent's or subsidiary's books.

Consolidated balance sheets are typically prepared at the date of combination to determine the initial financial position of the economic entity. Any intercompany accounts between the parent and subsidiary must be eliminated against each other. In addition, the "Investment in subsidiary's stock" account from the parent's books will be eliminated against the reciprocal accounts of the subsidiary's stockholders' equity. The remaining accounts are then combined to prepare the consolidated balance sheet. The preparation of consolidated statements after the date of combination becomes a little more complex because the parent's and subsidiary's income statements may include reciprocal intercompany accounts which must be eliminated. The next section of the module will present an example of the preparation of a consolidated balance sheet at the date of combination for both purchase and pooling accounting. You should carefully review the date of combination consolidation process before proceeding to the preparation of consolidation statements subsequent to combination.

F. Date of Combination Consolidated Balance Sheet—Purchase Accounting

This example uses the numbers from the A Company and B Company presented at the beginning of Section B of this module. The discussion in the preceding sections assumed a 100% combination in which the parent acquired control of all the subsidiary's stock or net assets. For the remainder of the module, we will assume that the parent company (A Company) acquired a 90% interest in the net assets of the subsidiary company (B Company). The remaining 10% of the outstanding stock is held by third-party investors referred to as the **minority interest**, or noncontrolling interest. In the illustrated problem, you will be able to review the determination of how minority interest is computed and disclosed on the consolidated financial statements. Note that only the "acquisition" legal form leads to the preparation of consolidated statements and includes less than 100% business combinations.

The assumptions for this illustration are

1. On January 1, 2002, A Company acquires a 90% interest in B Company in exchange for 5,400 shares of $10 par value stock having a total market value of $120,600.
2. The purchase method of accounting is used for the combination.

The workpaper for a consolidated balance sheet at the date of acquisition is presented below. The first two columns are the trial balances from the books of A Company and B Company immediately following the acquisition.

1. **Investment Entry on A Company's Books**

    The entry to record the 90% purchase-acquisition on A Company's books was

Investment in Stock of B Company	120,600	
Capital Stock		54,000
Additional Paid-in Capital		66,600

    To record the issuance of 5,400 shares of $10 par value stock to acquire a 90% interest in B Company.

    Although common stock is used for the consideration in our example, A Company could have used debentures, cash, or any other form of consideration acceptable to B Company's stockholders to make the purchase combination.

A COMPANY AND B COMPANY CONSOLIDATED WORKING PAPERS
For Date of Combination - 1/1/02

Purchase accounting
90% Interest

	A Company	B Company	Adjustments and eliminations Debit	Adjustments and eliminations Credit	Minority interest	Consolidated balances
Balance sheet 1/1/02						
Cash	30,900	37,400				68,300
Accounts receivable	34,200	9,100				43,300
Inventories	22,900	16,100	(b) 900			39,900
Equipment	200,000	50,000	(b) 9,000			259,000
Accumulated depreciation	(21,000)	(10,000)		(b) 1,800		(32,800)
Investment in stock of B Company	120,600			(a) 120,600		
Difference between cost and book value			(a) 25,200	(b) 25,200		
Excess of cost over fair value (goodwill)			(b) 14,400			14,400
Patents		10,000	(b) 2,700			12,700
Total assets	387,600	112,600				404,800
Accounts payable	4,000	6,600				10,600
Bonds payable	100,000					100,000
Capital stock	154,000	50,000	(a) 45,000		5,000	154,000
Additional paid-in capital	81,600	15,000	(a) 13,500		1,500	81,600
Retained earnings	48,000	41,000	(a) 36,900		4,100	48,000
Minority interest					10,600	10,600
Total liabilities and equity	387,600	112,600	147,600	147,600		404,800

2. **Difference between Investment Cost and Book Value**

    The difference between the investment cost and the parent company's equity in the net assets of the subsidiary is computed as follows:

Investment cost		$120,600
− Book value % at date of combination		
B Company's:		
Capital stock	$ 50,000	
Additional paid-in capital	15,000	
Retained earnings	41,000	
Total	$106,000	
Parent's share of ownership	x 90%	
Parent's share of book value		95,400
Excess of cost over book value		$ 25,200

    This difference is due to several undervalued assets and to unrecorded goodwill. The allocation procedure is similar to that shown on page 533 for a 100% purchase; however, in this case, the parent company obtained a 90% interest and thus will recognize 90% of the difference between the fair market values and book values of the subsidiary's assets, not 100%. The allocation is presented as

Item	Book value (BV)	Fair market value (FMV)	Difference between BV and FMV	Ownership percentage	Percentage share of difference between BV and FMV
Cash	$ 37,400	$ 37,400	$ --		
Accounts receivable (net)	9,100	9,100	--		
Inventories	16,100	17,100	1,000	90%	$ 900
Equipment	50,000	60,000	10,000	90%	9,000
Accumulated depreciation	(10,000)	(12,000)	(2,000)	90%	(1,800)
Patents	10,000	13,000	3,000	90%	2,700
Accounts payable	(6,600)	(6,600)	--		
Total	$106,000	$118,000	$12,000		$10,800

Amount of difference between cost and book value share allocated to revaluation of net assets	$10,800
Total differential	25,200
Remainder allocated to goodwill	$14,400

The equipment has a book value of $40,000 ($50,000 less 20% depreciation of $10,000). An appraisal concluded with a judgment that the equipment's replacement cost was $60,000 less 20% accumulated depreciation of $12,000 resulting in a net fair value of $48,000.

3. **Elimination Entries on Workpaper**

   The basic reciprocal accounts are the investment in subsidiary account on the parent's books and the subsidiary's stockholder equity accounts. Only the parent's share of the subsidiary's accounts may be eliminated as reciprocal accounts. The remaining 10% portion is allocated to the minority interest. The entries below include documentation showing the company source for the information. Those aids will help you trace the numbers. The workpaper entry to eliminate the basic reciprocal accounts is

(a)	Capital stock—B Co.	45,000	
	Additional paid-in capital—B Co.	13,500	
	Retained earnings—B Co.	36,900*	
	Differential	25,200	
	Investment in stock of B Co.—A Co.		120,600

   * ($36,900 = 90% x $41,000)

   Note that only 90% of B Company's stockholders' equity accounts are eliminated. Also, an account called "Differential" is debited in the workpaper entry. The differential account is a temporary account to record the difference between the cost of the investment in B Company from the parent's books and the book value of the parent's interest (90% in our case) from the subsidiary's books.

   The next step is to allocate the differential to the specific accounts by making the following workpaper entry:

(b)	Inventories	900	
	Equipment	9,000	
	Patents	2,700	
	Goodwill	14,400	
	Accumulated depreciation		1,800
	Differential		25,200

This entry reflects the allocations prepared in Step 2 and recognizes the parent's share of the asset revaluations.

   The minority interest column is the 10% interest of B Company's net assets owned by outside, third parties. Minority interest must be disclosed because 100% of the book values of B Company are included in the consolidated statements although A Company controls only 90% of the net assets. An alternative method to "prove" minority interest is to multiply the net assets of the subsidiary by the minority interest share, as follows:

Stockholders equity of B company		Minority interest %	
$106,000	x	10%	= $10,600

The $10,600 would be reported on the credit side of the consolidated balance sheet between liabilities and stockholders' equity.

   The principle used to prepare the consolidated balance sheet is called the **parent company concept**. This is the method used most often on the CPA exam and also used in virtually all actual cases of consolidations of less than wholly owned subsidiaries. An alternative approach is known as the **entity concept**. The two differ in the amount of the asset revaluations recognized on the consolidated balance sheet. Under the parent company concept, just the parent's share of the revaluation is shown and the minority interest is reported at its share of the subsidiary's book value. If the entity concept were used, the net assets of B Company would be included in the consolidated balance sheet at 100% of their fair values at the date of acquisition and minority interest would be reported at its share of the fair value of the subsidiary. In our example, minority interest under the entity concept would have been

Total fair market value of net assets of B Company   Minority interest
$118,000   x   10%   = $11,800

Our example does not include any other intercompany accounts as of the date of combination. If any existed, they would be eliminated to fairly present the consolidated entity. Several examples of other reciprocal accounts will be shown later in this module for the preparation of consolidated financial statements subsequent to the date of acquisition.

G. Consolidated Financial Statements subsequent to Acquisition

The concepts used to prepare subsequent consolidated statements are essentially the same as used to prepare the consolidated balance sheet at the acquisition date. The income statement and statement of retained earnings are added to reflect the results of operations since the acquisition date for a purchase or from the beginning of the period for a pooling. Furthermore, some additional reciprocal accounts may have to be eliminated because of intercompany transactions between the parent and subsidiary corporations. Please note that the financial statements of a consolidated entity are prepared using the same accounting principles that would be employed by a single, unconsolidated enterprise. The only difference is that some reciprocal accounts appearing on both companies' books must be eliminated against each other before the two corporations may be presented as one consolidated economic entity. Your review should concentrate on the accounts and amounts appearing on the consolidated statements (amounts in the last column of the worksheet). This "end-result" focus will help provide the understanding of why certain elimination entries are necessary.

An expanded version of the consolidated worksheet is necessary if the income statement and retained earnings statement must also be prepared. A comprehensive format often called "the three statement layout" is an integrated vertical array of the income statement, the retained earnings statement, and the balance sheet. The net income of the period is carried to the retained earnings statement and the ending retained earnings are carried down to the balance sheet. If you are required to prepare just the consolidated balance sheet, then eliminating entries involving nominal accounts (income statement accounts and "Dividends declared" account) would be made directly against the ending balance of retained earnings presented on the balance sheet.

The following discussion assumes the parent is using the partial equity method to account for the majority investment. Some firms may use the cost method during the period to record investment income because it requires fewer book adjustments to the investment account. In cases where the cost method is used during the period, one approach is to adjust the investment and investment income accounts to the equity method through an entry on the workpaper and the consolidation process may then be continued. Assuming that an income statement and retained earnings statement are being prepared in addition to the balance sheet, the general form of this restatement from cost to equity entry is made on the workpapers.

Dividend income (for income recognized using cost method)   xx
Investment in sub (% of undistributed income of sub)   xx
    Equity in subsidiary's income (for income recognized using equity method)   xx

Additional workpaper restatement entries would be required to recognize the equity income in prior periods if the investment were owned for more than one period and to recognize the amortizations of any differential for all periods the investment was held. After these entries are made, the investment and equity in subsidiary's income accounts would be stated at equity and the consolidation process may continue. It is important to note that the formal consolidated statements will be the same regardless of the method used by the parent to account for the investment on its books. The concept of measurement used in the preparation of the consolidated statements is equivalent to the full equity method and the elimination process will result in statements presented under that concept.

H. Intercompany Transactions and Profit Confirmation

Three general types of intercompany transactions may occur between the parent and subsidiary companies. Intercompany transactions require special handling because the profit or loss from these events must be properly presented on the consolidated financial statements. The three types of intercompany transactions are: intercompany sales of merchandise, transactions in fixed assets, and intercompany debt/equity transactions. These events may generate "unrealized profit" (also referred to as unconfirmed profit) which is a profit or gain shown in the trial balance from one of the company's books, but should not be shown in the consolidated financial statements. Intercompany bond transactions may require recognition of a gain or loss on the consolidated financials which is not in the trial balances of either the parent or subsidiary companies.

1. **Intercompany Inventory Transactions**

   Unrealized profit in ending inventory arises through intercompany sales above cost that are not resold to third parties prior to year-end. Thus, the profit on the selling corporation's books is overstated, because an arm's-length transaction has not yet taken place. The inventory is overstated on the purchaser's books for the amount of the unrealized intercompany profit. An exhibit of the relationships is shown below.

   Companies A and B are two separate legal entities and will each record the sale or purchase of goods. From a consolidated or economic entity viewpoint, however, the intercompany transaction is a transfer of assets which cannot result in revenue recognition until these goods are sold to a third party. Assuming a sale from Company A to Company B (a "downstream" intercompany sale), the sale income of Company A cannot be recognized until the goods are sold to third parties by Company B. In addition, the ending inventory of Company B is overstated by the amount of profit in the inventory acquired from Company A. Once intercompany sales have been sold to third parties, the earning process has been verified by an arm's-length transaction with third parties. Thus, recognition of previously unrecognized profit must be made at that time.

2. **Intercompany Fixed Asset Transactions**

   Unrealized profits on fixed assets arise through intercompany sales of fixed assets above undepreciated cost. From a consolidated viewpoint, the transaction represents the internal transfer of assets and no gain (loss) should be recognized. Therefore, any gain (loss) must be eliminated and the carrying value of the transferred asset must be returned to its initial book value basis. In subsequent periods, in the case of an intercompany gain, depreciation expense is overstated, because an overvalued asset is being depreciated on the books of the company showing the asset. This overstatement of depreciation must also be eliminated in the consolidation process. In essence, the company that acquired the intercompany asset is including the intercompany gain (loss) in its depreciation expense.

3. **Intercompany Bond Transactions**

   When one consolidated company buys bonds of another consolidated company, there are several reciprocal items to eliminate: investment in bonds and bonds payable, interest income and interest expense, and interest payable and interest receivable. Intercompany gains and losses **cannot** arise from direct intercompany bond purchases. The book value would be the same on both books and the interest accounts would be reciprocal. Note that APB 21 does not require the use of the effective interest method for debt transactions between parent and subsidiary companies. Straight-line amortizations of premiums or discounts are sometimes used in these instances.

   Gains and losses on intercompany bond holdings occur when

   a. Already outstanding bonds of the parent (subsidiary) are purchased by a subsidiary (parent),
   b. From a third party, and
   c. For an amount different from the carrying value of the issuer.

From a consolidated viewpoint, these bonds are viewed as retired. However, the bonds are still recorded as liabilities on the issuer's separate books and as investment in bonds on the purchasing corporation's books. The eliminating entry is to recognize the imputed gain (loss) on the consolidated "retirement of debt" in the year of intercompany bond purchase. This gain (loss) would normally be an extraordinary item in accordance with SFAS 4.

I. Example of Subsequent Consolidated Financial Statements

The following information extends the basic example of A Company and B Company begun earlier in this module. The example illustrates the major consolidation concepts and procedures most likely to appear on the exam.

On January 1, 2002, A Company acquired 90% of the stock of B Company in exchange for 5,400 shares of $10 par value stock having a total market value of $120,600. The purchase method of accounting must be used for the combination.

On January 1, 2002, B Company's assets and liabilities had the following book and fair values.

	Book value	Fair value
Cash	$ 37,400	$ 37,400
Accounts receivable (net)	9,100	9,100
Inventories	16,100	17,100
Equipment	50,000	60,000
Accumulated depreciation	(10,000)	(12,000)
Patents	10,000	13,000
Accounts payable	(6,600)	(6,600)
	$106,000	$118,000

Financial statement data of the two companies as of December 31, 2002 (the end of the first year after combination) are presented below.

During 2002, A Company sold merchandise to B Company that originally cost A Company $15,000 and the sale was made for $20,000. On December 31, 2002, B Company's inventory included merchandise purchased from A Company at a cost to B Company of $12,000.

Also during 2002, A Company acquired $18,000 of merchandise from B Company. B Company uses a normal markup of 25% above its cost. A Company's ending inventory includes $10,000 of the merchandise acquired from B Company.

B Company reduced its intercompany account payable to A Company to a balance of $4,000 as of December 31, 2002, by making a payment of $1,000 on December 30. This $1,000 payment was still in transit on December 31, 2002.

On January 2, 2002, B Company acquired equipment from A Company for $7,000. The equipment was originally purchased by A Company for $5,000 and had a book value of $4,000 at the date of sale to B Company. The equipment had an estimated remaining life of four years as of January 2, 2002.

On December 31, 2002, B Company purchased for $44,000, 50% of the $100,000 of outstanding bonds issued by A Company to third parties. The bonds mature on December 31, 2009 and were originally issued at par. The bonds pay interest annually on December 31 of each year and the interest was paid to the prior investor immediately before B Company's purchase of the bonds.

The consolidated worksheet for the preparation of consolidated financial statements as of December 31, 2002, is presented below.

The investment account balance at the statement date should be reconciled to ensure the parent company made the proper entries under the method of accounting used to account for the investment. As noted earlier, A Company is using the partial equity method, without amortizations. The amortizations of the excess of cost over book value will be recognized only on the worksheets. This method is the one typically followed on the CPA exam; however, be sure you determine the method used in the exam problem—don't assume! The "proof" of the investment account of A Company is

Investment in Stock of B Company			
Original cost	120,600		
% of B Company's income (90% x $9,400)	8,460	3,600	% of B Company's dividends declared (90% x $4,000)
Bal. 12/31/02	125,460		

Any errors will require correcting entries before the consolidation process is continued. Correcting entries will be posted to the books of the appropriate company; eliminating entries are **not** posted to either company's books.

The difference between the investment cost and the book value of the net assets acquired was determined and allocated in the preparation of the date of combination consolidated statements presented on page 536. For purposes of brevity, that process will not be duplicated here since the same computations are used in preparing financial statements for as long as the investment is owned.

A COMPANY AND B COMPANY CONSOLIDATED WORKING PAPERS
Year Ended December 31, 2002

Purchase accounting
90% Owned
Subsequent, partial equity

	A Company	B Company	Adjustments and eliminations Debit	Adjustments and eliminations Credit	Minority interest	Consolidated balances
Income statement for year ended 12/31/02						
Sales	750,000	420,000	(a) 38,000			1,132,000
Cost of sales	581,000	266,000	(b) 5,000	(a) 38,000		814,900
			(i) 900			
Gross margin	169,000	154,000				317,100
Depreciation and interest expense	28,400	16,200	(i) 1,800	(d) 750		45,650
Other operating expenses	117,000	128,400	(i) 270			245,670
Net income from operations	23,600	9,400				25,780
Gain on sale of equipment	3,000		(d) 3,000			
Gain on bonds				(e) 6,000		6,000
Equity in subsidiary's income	8,460		(f) 8,460			
Minority income (.10 x $7,400)					740	(740)
Net income	35,060	9,400	57,430	44,750	740	31,040
Statement of retained earnings for year ended 12/31/02						
1/1/02 Retained earnings						
A Company	48,000					48,000
B Company		41,000	(g) 36,900		4,100	
Add net income (from above)	35,060	9,400	57,430	44,750	740	31,040
Total	83,060	50,400			4,840	79,040
Deduct dividends	15,000	4,000		(f) 3,600	400	15,000
Balance December 31, 2002	68,060	46,400	94,330	48,350	4,440	64,040
Balance sheet 12/31/02						
Cash	45,300	6,400	(l) 1,000			52,700
Accounts receivable (net)	43,700	12,100		(l) 1,000		50,800
				(c) 4,000		
Inventories	38,300	20,750	(h) 900	(b) 5,000		54,050
				(i) 900		
Equipment	195,000	57,000	(h) 9,000	(d) 2,000		259,000
Accumulated depreciation	(35,200)	(18,900)		(d) 250		(57,950)
				(h) 1,800		
				(i) 1,800		
Investment in stock of B Company	125,460			(f) 4,860		
				(g) 120,600		
Differential			(g) 25,200	(h) 25,200		
Goodwill			(h) 14,400			14,400
Investment in bonds of A Company		44,000		(e) 44,000		
Patents		9,000	(h) 2,700	(i) 270		11,430
Total assets	412,560	130,350				384,430
Accounts payable	8,900	18,950	(c) 4,000			23,850
Bonds payable	100,000		(e) 50,000			50,000
Capital stock	154,000	50,000	(g) 45,000		5,000	154,000
Additional paid-in capital	81,600	15,000	(g) 13,500		1,500	81,600
Retained earnings (from above)	68,060	46,400	94,330	48,350	4,440	64,040
Minority interest					10,940	10,940
Total liabilities and equity	412,560	130,350	260,030	260,030		384,430

The following adjusting and eliminating entries will be required to prepare consolidated financials as of December 31, 2002. Note that a consolidated income statement is required and, therefore, the nominal accounts are still "open." The number or letter in parentheses to the left of the entry corresponds to the key used on the worksheet.

Step 1. Complete the transaction for any intercompany items in transit at the end of the year.

(a) Cash	1,000	
Accounts receivable		1,000

This **adjusting** entry will now properly present the financial positions of both companies and the consolidation process may be continued.

Step 2. Prepare the eliminating entries.

(a) Sales   38,000
      Cost of goods sold   38,000

Total intercompany sales of $38,000 include $20,000 in a downstream transaction from A Company to B Company and $18,000 in an upstream transaction from B Company to A Company.

(b) Cost of goods sold   5,000
      Inventories   5,000

The ending inventories are overstated because of the unrealized profit from the intercompany sales. The debit to cost of goods sold is required because a decrease in ending inventory will increase cost of goods sold to be deducted on the income statement. Supporting computations for the entry are

	In ending inventory of	
	A Company	*B Company*
Intercompany sales not resold, at selling price	$10,000	$12,000
Cost basis of remaining intercompany merchandise company merchandise		
From B to A ($\div$125%)	(8,000)	
From A to B ($\div$133 1/3%)	_____	(9,000)
Unrealized profit	$ 2,000	$ 3,000

When preparing consolidated workpapers for 2003 (the next fiscal period), an additional eliminating entry will be required if the goods in 2002's ending inventory are sold to outsiders during 2003. The additional entry will recognize the profit for 2003 that was eliminated as unrealized in 2002. This entry is necessary since the entry at the end of 2002 was made only on the worksheet. The 2003 entry will be

Retained earnings—B Comp. (1/1/03)   200
Retained earnings—A Comp. (1/1/03)   4,800
      Cost of goods sold (2003)   5,000

The $200 debit to B's 1/1/03 retained earnings is for the minority interest's share of the unrealized profit on the 2002 upstream sale.

(c) Accounts payable   4,000
      Accounts receivable   4,000

This eliminates the remaining intercompany receivable/payable owed **by** B Company to A Company. This eliminating entry is necessary to avoid overstating the consolidated entity's balance sheet. The receivable/payable is not extinguished and B Company must still transfer $4,000 to A Company in the future.

(d) Gain on sale of equipment   3,000
      Equipment   2,000
      Accumulated depreciation   250
      Depreciation expense   750

Eliminates the gain on the intercompany sale of the equipment, eliminates the overstatement of equipment, and removes the excess depreciation taken on the gain. Supporting computations for the entry are

	Cost	At date of intercompany sale accum. depr.	2002 depreciation expense	End-of-period accum. depr.
Original basis (to seller-A Co.)	$ 5,000	$(1,000)	$1,000	$(2,000)
New basis (to buyer-B Co.)	7,000	--	1,750	(1,750)
Difference	$(2,000)		$ (750)	$ 250

If the intercompany sale had not occurred, A Company would have depreciated the remaining book value of $4,000 over the estimated remaining life of four years. However, since B Company's acquisition price ($7,000) was more than A Company's basis in the asset ($4,000), the depreciation recorded on the books of B Company will include part of the intercompany unrealized profit. The equipment must be reflected on the consolidated statements at the original cost to the consolidated entity. Therefore, the "write-up" of $2,000 in the equipment, the excess depreciation of $750, and the gain of $3,000 must be eliminated and the ending balance of accumulated depreciation must be shown at what it would have been if the intercompany equipment transaction had not occurred. In future periods, a retained earnings account will be used instead of the gain account; however, the other concepts will be extended to include the additional periods.

(e)	Bonds payable	50,000	
	Investment in bonds of A Company		44,000
	Gain on extinguishment of debt		6,000

This entry eliminates the book value of A Company's debt against the bond investment account of B Company. To the consolidated entity, this transaction must be shown as a retirement of debt even though A Company has the outstanding intercompany debt to B Company. SFAS 4 specifies gains or losses on debt extinguishment, if material, should be shown as an extraordinary item. In future periods, B Company will amortize the discount, thereby bringing the investment account up to par value and a retained earnings account will be used in the eliminating entry instead of the gain account.

(f)	Equity in subsidiary's income—A Co.	8,460	
	Dividends declared—B Co.		3,600
	Investment in stock of B Company		4,860

This elimination entry adjusts the investment account back to its balance at the beginning of the period and also eliminates the income from subsidiary account.

(g)	Capital stock—B Co.	45,000	
	Additional paid-in capital—B Co.	13,500	
	Retained earnings—B Co.	36,900	
	Differential	25,200	
	Investment in stock of B Co.—A Co.		120,600

This entry eliminates 90% of B Company's stockholders' equity at the beginning of the year, 1/1/02. Note that the changes **during** the year were eliminated in entry (f) above. The differential account reflects the excess of investment cost greater than the book value of the assets acquired.

(h)	Inventories	900	
	Equipment	9,000	
	Patents	2,700	
	Goodwill	14,400	
	Accumulated depreciation		1,800
	Differential		25,200

This entry allocates the differential (excess of investment cost over the book values of the assets acquired). Note that this entry is the same as the allocation entry made to prepare consolidated financial statements for January 1, 2002, the date of acquisition.

(i)	Cost of goods sold	900	
	Depreciation expense	1,800	
	Other operating expenses—Patent amortization	270	
	Inventories		900
	Accumulated depreciation		1,800
	Patents		270

This elimination entry amortizes the revaluations to fair market value made in entry (h). The inventory has been sold and therefore becomes part of the cost of goods sold. Other assets including goodwill were evaluated for impairment and determined to be unimpaired. The remaining revaluation will be amortized as follows:

	Amortization revaluation	Annual period	Amortization
Equipment (net)	$ 7,200	4 years	$1,800
Patents	2,700	10 years	270

The amortizations will continue to be made on future worksheets. For example, at the end of the next year (2003), the amortization entry (i) would be as follows:

Retained earnings—A Co. (1/1/03)	2,970	
Depreciation expense	1,800	
Other operating expenses—Patent amortization	270	
Inventories		900
Accumulated depreciation		3,600
Patents		540

The initial debit of $4,410 to retained earnings is an aggregation of the prior period's charges to income statement accounts ($900 + $1,800 + $270). During subsequent years, some authors prefer reducing the allocated amounts in entry (h) for prior period's charges. In this case, the amortization entry in future periods would reflect just that period's amortizations.

This extended example has assumed the purchase method was used to account for the combination of A Company and B Company. As a result, the consolidated financial statements will include the parent company's share of the revaluations to fair market values of the subsidiary's net assets. A pooling, however, is based on book values. No differential exists in pooling accounting and, thus, entry (g) above would be different while entries (h) and (i) would not be made for a pooling. All other eliminating entries would be the same. The basic elimination entry (g) for a pooling, using the equity method of accounting for the investment, would be

Capital stock—B Co.	45,000	
Additional paid-in capital—B Co.	13,500	
Retained earnings—B Co.	36,900	
Investment in stock of B Company		95,400

J. Minority Interest

The parent company often acquires less than 100% (but more than 50%) of the subsidiary's outstanding stock. Under either the purchase or pooling method the consolidated financial statements will include all of the assets, liabilities, revenues, and expenses of these less than wholly owned subsidiaries. The percentage of the stock not owned by the parent company represents the minority interest's share of the net assets of the subsidiary. Minority interest will be a line item deduction on the income statement for its portion of the subsidiary's income and, under the parent company concept, will be shown on the consolidated balance sheet after long-term debt but before stockholders' equity. The following procedures apply to cases of less than wholly owned subsidiaries.

1. Only the parent's share of the subsidiary's shareholders' equity is eliminated in the basic eliminating entry. The minority interest's share is presented separately.
2. The entire amount of intercompany reciprocal items is eliminated. For example, all receivables/payables and sales/cost of sales with a 90% subsidiary are eliminated.
3. For intercompany transactions in inventory and fixed assets, the possible effect on minority interest depends on whether the original transaction affected the subsidiary's income statement. Minority interest is adjusted only for upstream intercompany transactions (i.e., when the subsidiary is the selling entity). In this case, the minority interest is adjusted for its percentage ownership of the common stock of the subsidiary. The minority interest is **not** adjusted for unrealized profits on downstream sales. The effects of downstream transactions are confined solely to the parent's (i.e., controlling) ownership interests.

The minority interest's share of the subsidiary's income is shown as a deduction on the consolidated income statement since 100% of the subsidiary's revenues and expenses are combined although the parent company owns less than a 100% interest. The minority interest receives only its percentage share of the subsidiary's income that has been earned in transactions with external third parties. For our example, the minority interest deduction on the income statement is computed as follows:

B Company's reported income	$ 9,400
Less: Unrealized profit on an upstream inventory sale	(2,000)
B Company's income for consolidated financial purposes	$ 7,400
Minority interest share	10%
Minority interest on income statement	$ 740

The minority interest's share of the net assets of B Company is shown on the consolidated balance sheet between liabilities and controlling interest's equity. The computation for the minority interest shown in the balance sheet for our example is

B Company's capital stock, 12/31/02			$50,000	
Minority interest share			10%	$ 5,000
B Company's additional paid-in capital, 12/31/02			$15,000	
Minority interest share			10%	1,500
B Company's retained earnings, 1/1/02		$41,000		
Minority interest share		10%	4,100	
B Company's 2002 income for consolidated purposes		$ 7,400		
Minority interest share		10%	740	
B Company's dividends during 2002		$ 4,000		
Minority interest share		10%	(400)	4,440
Total minority interest, 12/31/02				$10,940

The remainder of the consolidation process is just worksheet techniques, as follows:

1. Take all income items across horizontally and foot the adjustments, minority interest, and consolidated columns down to the net income line.
2. Take the amounts on the net income line (on income statement) in the adjustments, minority interest, and consolidated balances columns **down to** retained earnings items across the consolidated balances column. Foot and crossfoot the retained earnings statement.
3. Take the amounts of ending retained earnings in each of the four columns down to the ending retained earnings line in the balance sheet. Foot the minority interest column and place its total in the consolidated balances column. Take all the balance sheet items across to consolidated balances column.

K. Subsequent Consolidated Balance Sheet Only

Consolidation exam problems sometimes require only the consolidated balance sheet. In this case, the effects of all the income statement account balances would have been closed to the retained earnings accounts. You should carefully review the adjustments and eliminations that were made noting that the nominal accounts (income statement accounts and dividends declared account) would be replaced with the account "Retained Earnings." Thus, elimination entry (a) would not be required; entry (b) would be

(b)	Retained earnings	5,000	
	Inventories		5,000

Retained earnings would be substituted for the nominal accounts in all other eliminating entries. A shortcut alternative to eliminating entries (f) and (g) is to use the ending balance of B Company's retained earnings as follows.

(f & g)	Capital stock—B Co.	45,000	
	Additional paid-in capital—B Co.	13,500	
	*Retained earnings—B Co.	41,760	
	Differential	25,200	
	Investment in stock of B Co.—A Co.		125,460

      (\$41,760 = 90% x \$46,400 ending balance of B Company's Retained earnings)

A worksheet for just the consolidated balance sheet is presented on the next page. The adjusting and eliminating entries are keyed to the entries and entry explanations for the three-statement layout presented earlier. Several elimination entries have been combined and are shown as (f/g) or (h/i). Note that the final consolidated balance sheet amounts are the same when only the balance sheet is being prepared as well as when all three statements are being prepared.

L. Consolidated Net Income and Consolidated Retained Earnings

In some cases, you may be asked just to determine the Consolidated Net Income (CNI) of the parent and subsidiary companies. A shorter, analytical approach may be used instead of the worksheet method. An analytical definition of CNI is exhibited for our example above.

If the "full" equity method had been used to account for the investment, all the adjustments to the parent company's income (see above) would have been reflected in the "Equity in Subsidiary's Income" account on the parent company's books. Under the "partial" equity method, only the equity accrual of $8,460 is shown in the Equity in Subsidiary's Income account. All other adjustments are made only on the consolidated worksheet.

A COMPANY AND B COMPANY CONSOLIDATED WORKING PAPERS
CONSOLIDATED BALANCE SHEET ONLY
December 31, 2002

Purchase accounting
90% Owned
Subsequent, partial equity

Assets	*A Company*	*B Company*	*Debit*		*Credit*	*Minority interest*	*Consolidated balances*
Cash	45,300	6,400	(l)	1,000			52,700
Accounts receivable (net)	43,700	12,100			(l) 1,000		50,800
					(c) 4,000		
Inventories	38,300	20,750	(h/i)	900	(b) 5,000		54,050
					(h/i) 900		
Equipment	195,000	57,000	(h/i)	9,000	(d) 2,000		259,000
Accumulated depreciation	(35,200)	(18,900)			(d) 250		(57,950)
					(h/i) 3,600		
Investment in stock of B Company	125,460				(f/g) 125,460		
Differential			(f/g)	25,200	(h/i) 25,200		
Goodwill			(h/i)	14,400			14,400
Investment in bonds of A Company		44,000			(e) 44,000		
Patents		9,000	(h/i)	2,430			11,430
Total	412,560	130,350					384,430
Liabilities and Stockholders' Equity							
Accounts payable	8,900	18,950	(c)	4,000			23,850
Bonds payable	100,000		(e)	50,000			50,000
Capital stock	154,000	50,000	(f/g)	45,000		5,000	154,000
Additional paid-in capital	81,600	15,000	(f/g)	13,500		1,500	81,600
Retained earnings	68,060	46,400	(b)	5,000	(e) 6,000	4,400	64,040
			(d)	2,250			
			(f/g)	41,760			
			(h/i)	2,970			
Minority interest						10,940	10,940
Total	412,560	130,350	217,410		217,410		384,430

The computation of CNI for the purchase method is

Parent company's net income from **independent** operations	$26,600
± Parent company's share of subsidiary's equity income (loss) (equity accrual) (90% x $9,400—reported income of B Co.)	+8,460
± Period's amortization of difference between cost and book value ($900—inventories $1,800—equip.; $270—patent)	–2,970
– Parent company's share of **unrealized** profit on intercompany transactions ($3,000—merchandise sale of A to B; $1,800—90% of sale of goods from B to A; $3,000—sale of equipment)	–7,800
+ Parent company's share of **realized** profit on intercompany transactions ($6,000—bonds; $750—from elimination of excessive depr. on equip. sale from A to B)	+ 6,750
CNI (purchase method)	$31,040

Consolidated Retained Earnings (CRE) under the purchase method may be determined once CNI is found. An analytical definition of CRE for our example is

Parent company's beginning retained earnings (1/1/02)	$48,000
+ Consolidated net income for period	+31,040
– Parent company's dividends to its shareholders (NOTE: subsidiary's dividends to outside parties are a component of minority interest, not CRE)	–15,000
CRE (purchase method)	$64,040

Make special note that under the "full" equity method of accounting, consolidated retained earnings will equal the retained earnings of the parent company. This is true because consolidated retained earnings under the full equity method equals beginning of the year consolidated retained earnings plus consolidated net income (which is identical to parent company net income), minus dividends declared during the year by the parent company only.

M. Changes in Ownership

Changes in the level of ownership of subsidiaries frequently occur through purchase or sale of the subsidiary's stock by the parent or changes in the sub's shares outstanding. If the subsidiary changes the number of shares outstanding (for example, through treasury stock transactions), the transaction may require an entry on the parent's books to maintain the parent's reciprocity in the net assets of the subsidiary.

For example, if the subsidiary, through treasury stock transactions, increases the relative book value owned by the parent, the increase must be recorded to maintain reciprocity between the investment account on the parent's accounting records and its equivalent stockholders' equity accounts in the subsidiary's books.

Investment in subsidiary	xx	
Paid-in capital		xx

On the other hand, if the subsidiary's treasury stock transactions decrease the parent's equity

Paid-in capital	xx	
Investment in subsidiary		xx

When the parent's share of ownership increases through a purchase of additional stock, simply debit investment and credit cash for cost. A problem occurs with consolidated income statements when the change in ownership takes place in mid-period. Consolidated statements should be prepared based on the ending ownership level. For example, assume that A Company increased its ownership of B Company from 90% to 95% on October 1, 2002. The investment was acquired at book value of $5,452.50 [5% x ($50,000 CS + $15,000 APIC + $44,050 RE at 10-1-01)]. If the subsidiary earned its income of $9,400 evenly over the year, the consolidated net income should reflect a net of

90%	x	$9,400	x	12/12	=	$8,460.00
+ 5%	x	$9,400	x	3/12	=	117.50
95%						$8,577.50

The interim stock purchase will result in a new account being shown on the consolidated income statement. The account is **Purchased Preacquisition Earnings** which represents the percentage of the subsidiary's earnings earned, in this case, on the 5% stock interest from January 1, 2002, to October 1, 2002. The basic eliminating entries would be based on the 95% ownership as follows:

Equity in subsidiary's income—A Co.	8,577.50	
Dividends declared—B Co.		3,600.00
Investment in stock of B Company		4,977.50
Capital stock—B Co.	47,500.00	
Additional paid-in capital—B Co.	14,250.00	
Retained earnings—B Co.	38,750.00*	
Purchased preacquisition earnings	352.50**	
Differential	25,200.00	
Investment in stock of B Co.—A Co.		126,052.50

* 95% x $41,000 beginning 2001 balance	=	*$38,950*
Less preacquisition dividend of 5% x $4,000	=	*$ (200)*
Retained earnings available, as adjusted	=	*$38,750*
** *$352.50 = 5% x $9,400 x 9/12)*		

Purchased Preacquisition Earnings is shown as a deduction along with Minority Interest to arrive at Consolidated Net Income. You should note that purchased preacquisition earnings are used only with interim acquisitions under the purchase accounting method.

N. Combined Financial Statements

Combined financial statements is the term used to describe financial statements prepared for companies that are owned by the same parent company or individual. These statements are often prepared when several subsidiaries of a common parent are not consolidated. Combined financial statements are prepared by combining all of the separate companies' financial statement classifications. Intercompany transactions, balances, and profit (loss) should be eliminated in the same way as in consolidated statements.

O. Push-Down Accounting

"Push-down accounting" describes the method used to prepare the separate financial statements for significant, very large subsidiaries that are either wholly owned or substantially owned (≥ 90%). For publicly traded companies, the SEC requires a one-time adjustment under the purchase method to revalue the subsidiary's assets and liabilities to fair value, and this entry is made directly on the books of the subsidiary.

Push-down accounting requires the subsidiary to record an entry revaluing all assets and liabilities with a balancing entry to a revaluation capital account. The revaluation capital account will be eliminated in consolidation against the investment in subsidiary account. Push-down accounting will have no effect on the presentation of the consolidated financial statements or the separate financial statements of the parent company. However, the subsidiary's financial statements would be reported at fair value rather than historical cost. Advocates of push-down accounting believe that a change of ownership through a purchase-combination justifies the use of a new basis for the acquired entity. Thus, the new basis should be pushed down or directly recorded on the acquired entity's books.

MULTIPLE-CHOICE QUESTIONS (1-63)

1. On April 1, 2002, Dart Co. paid $620,000 for all the issued and outstanding common stock of Wall Corp. in a transaction properly accounted for as a purchase. The recorded assets and liabilities of Wall Corp. on April 1, 2002, follow:

Cash	$ 60,000
Inventory	180,000
Property and equipment (net of accumulated depreciation of $220,000)	320,000
Goodwill	100,000
Liabilities	(120,000)
Net assets	$ 540,000

On April 1, 2002, Wall's inventory had a fair value of $150,000, and the property and equipment (net) had a fair value of $380,000. What is the amount of goodwill resulting from the business combination?

   a. $150,000
   b. $120,000
   c. $ 50,000
   d. $ 20,000

2. A business combination is accounted for as a purchase. Which of the following expenses related to the business combination should be included, in total, in the determination of net income of the combined corporation for the period in which the expenses are incurred?

	Fees of finders and consultants	*Registration fees for equity securities issued*
a.	Yes	Yes
b.	Yes	No
c.	No	Yes
d.	No	No

3. On August 31, 2002, Wood Corp. issued 100,000 shares of its $20 par value common stock for the net assets of Pine, Inc., in a business combination accounted for by the purchase method. The market value of Wood's common stock on August 31 was $36 per share. Wood paid a fee of $160,000 to the consultant who arranged this acquisition. Costs of registering and issuing the equity securities amounted to $80,000. No goodwill was involved in the purchase. What amount should Wood capitalize as the cost of acquiring Pine's net assets?

   a. $3,600,000
   b. $3,680,000
   c. $3,760,000
   d. $3,840,000

Items 4 and 5 are based on the following:

On December 31, 2002, Saxe Corporation was merged into Poe Corporation. In the business combination, Poe issued 200,000 shares of its $10 par common stock, with a market price of $18 a share, for all of Saxe's common stock. The stockholders' equity section of each company's balance sheet immediately before the combination was

	Poe	*Saxe*
Common stock	3,000,000	$1,500,000
Additional paid-in capital	1,300,000	150,000
Retained earnings	2,500,000	850,000
	$6,800,000	$2,500,000

4. In the December 31, 2002 consolidated balance sheet, additional paid-in capital should be reported at
   a. $ 950,000

   b. $1,300,000
   c. $1,450,000
   d. $2,900,000

5. In the December 31, 2002 consolidated balance sheet, common stock should be reported at
   a. $3,000,000
   b. $3,500,000
   c. $4,000,000
   d. $5,000,000

6. On January 1, 2003, Neal Co. issued 100,000 shares of its $10 par value common stock in exchange for all of Frey Inc.'s outstanding stock. The fair value of Neal's common stock on December 31, 2002, was $19 per share. The carrying amounts and fair values of Frey's assets and liabilities on December 31, 2002, were as follows:

	Carrying amount	*Fair value*
Cash	$ 240,000	$ 240,000
Receivables	270,000	270,000
Inventory	435,000	405,000
Property, plant, and equipment	1,305,000	1,440,000
Liabilities	(525,000)	(525,000)
Net assets	$1,725,000	$1,830,000

What is the amount of goodwill resulting from the business combination?

   a. $175,000
   b. $105,000
   c. $ 70,000
   d. $0

7. Consolidated financial statements are typically prepared when one company has a controlling financial interest in another **unless**
   a. The subsidiary is a finance company.
   b. The fiscal year-ends of the two companies are more than three months apart.
   c. Such control is likely to be temporary.
   d. The two companies are in unrelated industries, such as manufacturing and real estate.

8. With respect to business combinations, SFAS 141 provides that
   a. The pooling of interests method must be used for all combinations.
   b. The pooling of interests method may be used only when specific requirements are met.
   c. The purchase method must be used for all combinations.
   d. The purchase method may be used only when specific requirements are met.

9. A business combination is accounted for appropriately as a purchase. Which of the following should be deducted in determining the combined corporation's net income for the current period?

	Direct costs of acquisition	*General expenses related to acquisition*
a.	Yes	No
b.	Yes	Yes
c.	No	Yes
d.	No	No

10. PDX Corp. acquired 100% of the outstanding common stock of Sea Corp. in a purchase transaction. The cost of the acquisition exceeded the fair value of the identifiable assets and assumed liabilities. The general guidelines for assigning amounts to the inventories acquired provide for

    a.   Raw materials to be valued at original cost.

    b.   Work in process to be valued at the estimated selling prices of finished goods, less both costs to complete and costs of disposal.

    c.   Finished goods to be valued at replacement cost.

    d.   Finished goods to be valued at estimated selling prices, less both costs of disposal and a reasonable profit allowance.

11. In accounting for a business combination, which of the following intangibles should not be recognized as an asset apart from goodwill?

    a.   Trademarks.

    b.   Lease agreements.

    c.   Employee quality.

    d.   Patents.

12. With respect to the allocation of the cost of a business acquisition, SFAS 141 requires

    a.   Cost to be allocated to the assets based on their carrying values.

    b.   Cost to be allocated based on fair values.

    c.   Cost to be allocated based on original costs.

    d.   None of the above.

Items 13 through 17 are based on the following:

On January 1, 2002, Polk Corp. and Strass Corp. had condensed balance sheets as follows:

	Polk	*Strass*
Current assets	$ 70,000	$20,000
Noncurrent assets	90,000	40,000
Total assets	$160,000	$60,000
Current liabilities	$ 30,000	$10,000
Long-term debt	50,000	--
Stockholders' equity	80,000	50,000
Total liabilities and		
stockholders' equity	$160,000	$60,000

On January 2, 2002, Polk borrowed $60,000 and used the proceeds to purchase 90% of the outstanding common shares of Strass. This debt is payable in ten equal annual principal payments, plus interest, beginning December 30, 2002. The excess cost of the investment over Strass' book value of acquired net assets should be allocated 60% to inventory and 40% to goodwill.

On Polk's January 2, 2002 consolidated balance sheet,

13. Current assets should be

    a. $99,000

    b. $96,000

    c. $90,000

    d. $79,000

14. Noncurrent assets should be

    a. $130,000

    b. $134,000

    c. $136,000

    d. $140,000

15. Current liabilities should be

    a. $50,000

    b. $46,000

    c. $40,000

    d. $30,000

16. Noncurrent liabilities including minority interests should be

    a. $115,000

    b. $109,000

    c. $104,000

    d. $ 55,000

17. Stockholders' equity should be

    a. $ 80,000

    b. $ 85,000

    c. $ 90,000

    d. $130,000

18. On November 30, 2002, Parlor, Inc. purchased for cash at $15 per share all 250,000 shares of the outstanding common stock of Shaw Co. At November 30, 2002, Shaw's balance sheet showed a carrying amount of net assets of $3,000,000. At that date, the fair value of Shaw's property, plant and equipment exceeded its carrying amount by $400,000. In its November 30, 2002 consolidated balance sheet, what amount should Parlor report as goodwill?

    a. $750,000

    b. $400,000

    c. $350,000

    d. $0

19. A subsidiary, acquired for cash in a business combination, owned inventories with a market value greater than the book value as of the date of combination. A consolidated balance sheet prepared immediately after the acquisition would include this difference as part of

    a.   Deferred credits.

    b.   Goodwill.

    c.   Inventories.

    d.   Retained earnings.

20. Company J acquired all of the outstanding common stock of Company K in exchange for cash. The acquisition price exceeds the fair value of net assets acquired. How should Company J determine the amounts to be reported for the plant and equipment and long-term debt acquired from Company K?

	Plant and equipment	*Long-term debt*
a.	K's carrying amount	K's carrying amount
b.	K's carrying amount	Fair value
c.	Fair value	K's carrying amount
d.	Fair value	Fair value

21. In a business combination accounted for as a purchase, the appraised values of the identifiable assets acquired exceeded the acquisition price. How should the excess appraised value be reported?

    a.   As negative goodwill.

    b.   As additional paid-in capital.

    c.   As a reduction of the values assigned to certain assets and an extraordinary gain for any unallocated portion.

    d.   As positive goodwill.

22. Wright Corp. has several subsidiaries that are included in its consolidated financial statements. In its December 31, 2002 trial balance, Wright had the following intercompany balances before eliminations:

	Debit	*Credit*
Current receivable due from Main Co.	$ 32,000	
Noncurrent receivable from Main	114,000	
Cash advance to Corn Corp.	6,000	
Cash advance from King Co.		$ 15,000
Intercompany payable to King		101,000

In its December 31, 2002 consolidated balance sheet, what amount should Wright report as intercompany receivables?

- a. $152,000
- b. $146,000
- c. $ 36,000
- d. $0

23. Shep Co. has a receivable from its parent, Pep Co. Should this receivable be separately reported in Shep's balance sheet and in Pep's consolidated balance sheet?

	Shep's balance sheet	Pep's consolidated balance sheet
a.	Yes	No
b.	Yes	Yes
c.	No	No
d.	No	Yes

Items 24 through 27 are based on the following:

Selected information from the separate and consolidated balance sheets and income statements of Pard, Inc. and its subsidiary, Spin Co., as of December 31, 2002, and for the year then ended is as follows:

	Pard	Spin	Consolidated
Balance sheet accounts			
Accounts receivable	$ 26,000	$ 19,000	$ 39,000
Inventory	30,000	25,000	52,000
Investment in Spin	67,000	--	--
Goodwill	--	--	30,000
Minority interest	--	--	10,000
Stockholders' equity	154,000	50,000	154,000
Income statement accounts			
Revenues	$200,000	$140,000	$308,000
Cost of goods sold	150,000	110,000	231,000
Gross profit	50,000	30,000	77,000
Equity in earnings of Spin			
	11,000	--	--
Net income	36,000	20,000	40,000

Additional information

- During 2002, Pard sold goods to Spin at the same markup on cost that Pard uses for all sales. At December 31, 2002, Spin had not paid for all of these goods and still held 37.5% of them in inventory.
- Pard acquired its interest in Spin on January 2, 1999.

24. What was the amount of intercompany sales from Pard to Spin during 2002?

- a. $ 3,000
- b. $ 6,000
- c. $29,000
- d. $32,000

25. At December 31, 2002, what was the amount of Spin's payable to Pard for intercompany sales?

- a. $ 3,000
- b. $ 6,000
- c. $29,000
- d. $32,000

26. In Pard's consolidated balance sheet, what was the carrying amount of the inventory that Spin purchased from Pard?

- a. $ 3,000
- b. $ 6,000
- c. $ 9,000
- d. $12,000

27. What is the percent of minority interest ownership in Spin?

- a. 10%
- b. 20%
- c. 25%
- d. 45%

28. On January 1, 2002, Owen Corp. purchased all of Sharp Corp.'s common stock for $1,200,000. On that date, the fair values of Sharp's assets and liabilities equaled their carrying amounts of $1,320,000 and $320,000, respectively. During 2002, Sharp paid cash dividends of $20,000.

Selected information from the separate balance sheets and income statements of Owen and Sharp as of December 31, 2002, and for the year then ended follows:

	Owen	Sharp
Balance sheet accounts		
Investment in subsidiary	$1,300,000	--
Retained earnings	1,240,000	560,000
Total stockholders' equity	2,620,000	1,120,000
Income statement accounts		
Operating income	420,000	200,000
Equity in earnings of Sharp	120,000	--
Net income	400,000	140,000

In Owen's December 31, 2002 consolidated balance sheet, what amount should be reported as total retained earnings?

- a. $1,240,000
- b. $1,360,000
- c. $1,380,000
- d. $1,800,000

29. When a parent-subsidiary relationship exists, consolidated financial statements are prepared in recognition of the accounting concept of

- a. Reliability.
- b. Materiality.
- c. Legal entity.
- d. Economic entity.

30. A subsidiary was acquired for cash in a business combination on January 1, 2002. The purchase price exceeded the fair value of identifiable net assets. The acquired company owned equipment with a market value in excess of the carrying amount as of the date of combination. A consolidated balance sheet prepared on December 31, 2002, would

- a. Report the unamortized portion of the excess of the market value over the carrying amount of the equipment as part of goodwill.
- b. Report the unamortized portion of the excess of the market value over the carrying amount of the equipment as part of plant and equipment.
- c. Report the excess of the market value over the carrying amount of the equipment as part of plant and equipment.
- d. Not report the excess of the market value over the carrying amount of the equipment because it would be expensed as incurred.

31. Pride, Inc. owns 80% of Simba, Inc.'s outstanding common stock. Simba, in turn, owns 10% of Pride's outstanding common stock. What percentage of the common stock cash dividends declared by the individual companies should be reported as dividends declared in the consolidated financial statements?

	Dividends declared by Pride	Dividends declared by Simba
a.	90%	0%
b.	90%	20%
c.	100%	0%
d.	100%	20%

32. Matt Co. included a foreign subsidiary in its 2002 consolidated financial statements. The subsidiary was acquired in 1996 and was excluded from previous consolidations. The change was caused by the elimination of foreign exchange controls. Including the subsidiary in the 2002 consolidated financial statements results in an accounting change that should be reported

    a. By footnote disclosure only.
    b. Currently and prospectively.
    c. Currently with footnote disclosure of pro forma effects of retroactive application.
    d. By restating the financial statements of all prior periods presented.

33. On June 30, 2002, Purl Corp. issued 150,000 shares of its $20 par common stock for which it received all of Scott Corp.'s common stock. The fair value of the common stock issued is equal to the book value of Scott Corp.'s net assets. Both corporations continued to operate as separate businesses, maintaining accounting records with years ending December 31. Net income from separate company operations and dividends paid were

	Purl	Scott
Net income		
Six months ended 6/30/02	$750,000	$225,000
Six months ended 12/31/02	825,000	375,000
Dividends paid		
March 25, 2002	950,000	--
November 15, 2002	--	300,000

On December 31, 2002, Scott held in its inventory merchandise acquired from Purl on December 1, 2002, for $150,000, which included a $45,000 markup. In the 2002 consolidated income statement, net income should be reported at

    a. $1,650,000
    b. $1,905,000
    c. $1,950,000
    d. $2,130,000

34. On June 30, 2002, Pane Corp. exchanged 150,000 shares of its $20 par value common stock for all of Sky Corp.'s common stock. At that date, the fair value of Pane's common stock issued was equal to the book value of Sky's net assets. Both corporations continued to operate as separate businesses, maintaining accounting records with years ending December 31. Information from separate company operations follows:

	Pane	Sky
Retained earnings— 12/31/01	$3,200,000	$925,000
Net income—six months ended 6/30/02	800,000	275,000
Dividends paid—3/25/02	750,000	--

If the business combination is accounted for as a purchase, what amount of retained earnings would Pane report in its June 30, 2002 consolidated balance sheet?

    a. $5,200,000
    b. $4,450,000
    c. $3,525,000
    d. $3,250,000

Items 35 and 36 are based on the following:

Scroll, Inc., a wholly owned subsidiary of Pirn, Inc., began operations on January 1, 2002. The following information is from the condensed 2002 income statements of Pirn and Scroll:

	Pirn	Scroll
Sales to Scroll	$100,000	$ --
Sales to others	400,000	300,000
	500,000	300,000
Cost of goods sold:		
Acquired from Pirn	--	80,000
Acquired from others	350,000	190,000
Gross profit	150,000	30,000
Depreciation	40,000	10,000
Other expenses	60,000	15,000
Income from operations	50,000	5,000
Gain on sale of equipment to Scroll	12,000	--
Income before income taxes	$ 62,000	$ 5,000

Additional information
   • Sales by Pirn to Scroll are made on the same terms as those made to third parties.
   • Equipment purchased by Scroll from Pirn for $36,000 on January 1, 2002, is depreciated using the straight-line method over four years.

35. In Pirn's December 31, 2002, consolidating worksheet, how much intercompany profit should be eliminated from Scroll's inventory?

    a. $30,000
    b. $20,000
    c. $10,000
    d. $ 6,000

36. What amount should be reported as depreciation expense in Pirn's 2002 consolidated income statement?

    a. $50,000
    b. $47,000
    c. $44,000
    d. $41,000

37. Clark Co. had the following transactions with affiliated parties during 2002:

   • Sales of $60,000 to Dean, Inc., with $20,000 gross profit. Dean had $15,000 of this inventory on hand at year-end. Clark owns a 15% interest in Dean and does not exert significant influence.

   • Purchases of raw materials totaling $240,000 from Kent Corp., a wholly owned subsidiary. Kent's gross profit on the sale was $48,000. Clark had $60,000 of this inventory remaining on December 31, 2002.

Before eliminating entries, Clark had consolidated current assets of $320,000. What amount should Clark report in its December 31, 2002 consolidated balance sheet for current assets?

    a. $320,000
    b. $317,000
    c. $308,000
    d. $303,000

38. Parker Corp. owns 80% of Smith Inc.'s common stock. During 2002, Parker sold Smith $250,000 of inventory on the same terms as sales made to third parties. Smith sold all of the inventory purchased from Parker in 2002. The following information pertains to Smith and Parker's sales for 2002:

	Parker	Smith
Sales	$1,000,000	$700,000
Cost of sales	400,000	350,000
	$ 600,000	$350,000

What amount should Parker report as cost of sales in its 2002 consolidated income statement?

- a. $750,000
- b. $680,000
- c. $500,000
- d. $430,000

39. Selected information from the separate and consolidated balance sheets and income statements of Pare, Inc. and its subsidiary, Shel Co., as of December 31, 2002, and for the year then ended is as follows:

	Pare	Shel	Consolidated
Balance sheet accounts			
Accounts receivable	$ 52,000	$ 38,000	$ 78,000
Inventory	60,000	50,000	104,000
Income statement accounts			
Revenues	$400,000	$280,000	$616,000
Cost of goods sold	300,000	220,000	462,000
Gross profit	$100,000	$ 60,000	$154,000

Additional information:

During 2002, Pare sold goods to Shel at the same markup on cost that Pare uses for all sales.

In Pare's consolidating worksheet, what amount of unrealized intercompany profit was eliminated?

- a. $ 6,000
- b. $12,000
- c. $58,000
- d. $64,000

40. During 2002, Pard Corp. sold goods to its 80%-owned subsidiary, Seed Corp. At December 31, 2002, one-half of these goods were included in Seed's ending inventory. Reported 2002 selling expenses were $1,100,000 and $400,000 for Pard and Seed, respectively. Pard's selling expenses included $50,000 in freight-out costs for goods sold to Seed. What amount of selling expenses should be reported in Pard's 2002 consolidated income statement?

- a. $1,500,000
- b. $1,480,000
- c. $1,475,000
- d. $1,450,000

41. On January 1, 2002, Poe Corp. sold a machine for $900,000 to Saxe Corp., its wholly owned subsidiary. Poe paid $1,100,000 for this machine, which had accumulated depreciation of $250,000. Poe estimated a $100,000 salvage value and depreciated the machine on the straight-line method over twenty years, a policy which Saxe continued. In Poe's December 31, 2002 consolidated balance sheet, this machine should be included in cost and accumulated depreciation as

	Cost	Accumulated depreciation
a.	$1,100,000	$300,000
b.	$1,100,000	$290,000
c.	$ 900,000	$ 40,000
d.	$ 850,000	$ 42,500

42. Wagner, a holder of a $1,000,000 Palmer, Inc. bond, collected the interest due on March 31, 2002, and then sold the bond to Seal, Inc. for $975,000. On that date, Palmer, a 75% owner of Seal, had a $1,075,000 carrying amount for this bond. What was the effect of Seal's purchase of Palmer's bond on the retained earnings and minority interest amounts reported in Palmer's March 31, 2002 consolidated balance sheet?

	Retained earnings	Minority interest
a.	$100,000 increase	$0
b.	$ 75,000 increase	$ 25,000 increase
c.	$0	$ 25,000 increase
d.	$0	$100,000 increase

43. Sun, Inc. is a wholly owned subsidiary of Patton, Inc. On June 1, 2002, Patton declared and paid a $1 per share cash dividend to stockholders of record on May 15, 2002. On May 1, 2002, Sun bought 10,000 shares of Patton's common stock for $700,000 on the open market, when the book value per share was $30. What amount of gain should Patton report from this transaction in its consolidated income statement for the year ended December 31, 2002?

- a. $0
- b. $390,000
- c. $400,000
- d. $410,000

44. Perez, Inc. owns 80% of Senior, Inc. During 2002, Perez sold goods with a 40% gross profit to Senior. Senior sold all of these goods in 2002. For 2002 consolidated financial statements, how should the summation of Perez and Senior income statement items be adjusted?

- a. Sales and cost of goods sold should be reduced by the intercompany sales.
- b. Sales and cost of goods sold should be reduced by 80% of the intercompany sales.
- c. Net income should be reduced by 80% of the gross profit on intercompany sales.
- d. No adjustment is necessary.

45. Water Co. owns 80% of the outstanding common stock of Fire Co. On December 31, 2002, Fire sold equipment to Water at a price in excess of Fire's carrying amount, but less than its original cost. On a consolidated balance sheet at December 31, 2002, the carrying amount of the equipment should be reported at

- a. Water's original cost.
- b. Fire's original cost.
- c. Water's original cost less Fire's recorded gain.
- d. Water's original cost less 80% of Fire's recorded gain.

46. Port, Inc. owns 100% of Salem, Inc. On January 1, 2002, Port sold Salem delivery equipment at a gain. Port had owned the equipment for two years and used a five-year straight-line depreciation rate with no residual value. Salem is using a three-year straight-line depreciation rate with no residual value for the equipment. In the consolidated income statement, Salem's recorded depreciation expense on the equipment for 2002 will be decreased by

- a. 20% of the gain on sale.
- b. 33 1/3% of the gain on sale.
- c. 50% of the gain on sale.
- d. 100% of the gain on sale.

47. P Co. purchased term bonds at a premium on the open market. These bonds represented 20% of the outstanding class of bonds issued at a discount by S Co., P's wholly owned subsidiary. P intends to hold the bonds until maturity. In a consolidated balance sheet, the difference between the bond carrying amounts in the two companies would be

- a. Included as a decrease to retained earnings.

b. Included as an increase to retained earnings.
c. Reported as a deferred debit to be amortized over the remaining life of the bonds.
d. Reported as a deferred credit to be amortized over the remaining life of the bonds.

48. Eltro Company acquired a 70% interest in the Samson Company in 2001. For the years ended December 31, 2002 and 2003, Samson reported net income of $80,000 and $90,000, respectively. During 2002, Samson sold merchandise to Eltro for $10,000 at a profit of $2,000. The merchandise was later resold by Eltro to outsiders for $15,000 during 2003. For consolidation purposes what is the minority interest's share of Samson's net income for 2002 and 2003 respectively?
   a. $23,400 and $27,600.
   b. $24,000 and $27,000.
   c. $24,600 and $26,400.
   d. $26,000 and $25,000.

Items 49 and 50 are based on the following:

On January 1, 2002, Ritt Corp. purchased 80% of Shaw Corp.'s $10 par common stock for $975,000. On this date, the carrying amount of Shaw's net assets was $1,000,000. The fair values of Shaw's identifiable assets and liabilities were the same as their carrying amounts except for plant assets (net) that were $100,000 in excess of the carrying amount. For the year ended December 31, 2002, Shaw had net income of $190,000 and paid cash dividends totaling $125,000.

49. In the January 1, 2002 consolidated balance sheet, goodwill should be reported at
   a. $0
   b. $ 75,000
   c. $ 95,000
   d. $175,000

50. In the December 31, 2002 consolidated balance sheet, minority interest should be reported at
   a. $200,000
   b. $213,000
   c. $220,000
   d. $233,000

Items 51 through 53 are based on the following:

On January 2, 2003, Pare Co. purchased 75% of Kidd Co.'s outstanding common stock. Selected balance sheet data at December 31, 2003, is as follows:

	Pare	Kidd
Total assets	$420,000	$180,000
Liabilities	$120,000	$ 60,000
Common stock	100,000	50,000
Retained earnings	200,000	70,000
	$420,000	$180,000

During 2003 Pare and Kidd paid cash dividends of $25,000 and $5,000, respectively, to their shareholders. There were no other intercompany transactions.

51. In its December 31, 2003 consolidated statement of retained earnings, what amount should Pare report as dividends paid?
   a. $ 5,000
   b. $25,000
   c. $26,250
   d. $30,000

52. In Pare's December 31, 2003 consolidated balance sheet, what amount should be reported as minority interest in net assets?
   a. $0
   b. $ 30,000
   c. $ 45,000
   d. $105,000

53. In its December 31, 2003 consolidated balance sheet, what amount should Pare report as common stock?
   a. $ 50,000
   b. $100,000
   c. $137,500
   d. $150,000

54. On September 1, 2001, Phillips, Inc. issued common stock in exchange for 20% of Sago, Inc.'s outstanding common stock. On July 1, 2002, Phillips issued common stock for an additional 75% of Sago's outstanding common stock. Sago continues in existence as Phillips' subsidiary. How much of Sago's 2002 net income should be reported as accruing to Phillips?
   a. 20% of Sago's net income to June 30 and all of Sago's net income from July 1 to December 31.
   b. 20% of Sago's net income to June 30 and 95% of Sago's net income from July 1 to December 31.
   c. 95% of Sago's net income.
   d. All of Sago's net income.

55. Mr. & Mrs. Dart own a majority of the outstanding capital stock of Wall Corp., Black Co., and West, Inc. During 2002, Wall advanced cash to Black and West in the amount of $50,000 and $80,000, respectively. West advanced $70,000 in cash to Black. At December 31, 2002, none of the advances was repaid. In the combined December 31, 2002 balance sheet of these companies, what amount would be reported as receivables from affiliates?
   a. $200,000
   b. $130,000
   c. $ 60,000
   d. $0

56. Selected data for two subsidiaries of Dunn Corp. taken from December 31, 2002 preclosing trial balances are as follows:

	Banks Co. debit	Lamm Co. credit
Shipments to Banks	$ --	$150,000
Shipments from Lamm	200,000	--
Intercompany inventory profit on total shipments	--	50,000

Additional data relating to the December 31, 2002 inventory are as follows:

Inventory acquired from outside parties	$175,000	$250,000
Inventory acquired from Lamm	60,000	--

At December 31, 2002, the inventory reported on the combined balance sheet of the two subsidiaries should be
   a. $425,000
   b. $435,000
   c. $470,000
   d. $485,000

57. Ahm Corp. owns 90% of Bee Corp.'s common stock and 80% of Cee Corp.'s common stock. The remaining common shares of Bee and Cee are owned by their respective employees. Bee sells exclusively to Cee, Cee buys exclusively from Bee, and Cee sells exclusively to unrelated companies. Selected 2002 information for Bee and Cee follows:

	Bee Corp.	Cee Corp.
Sales	$130,000	$91,000
Cost of sales	100,000	65,000
Beginning inventory	None	None
Ending inventory	None	65,000

What amount should be reported as gross profit in Bee and Cee's combined income statement for the year ended December 31, 2002?

- a. $26,000
- b. $41,000
- c. $47,800
- d. $56,000

58. The following information pertains to shipments of merchandise from Home Office to Branch during 2002:

Home Office's cost of merchandise	$160,000
Intracompany billing	200,000
Sales by Branch	250,000
Unsold merchandise at Branch on December 31, 2002	20,000

In the combined income statement of Home Office and Branch for the year ended December 31, 2002, what amount of the above transactions should be included in sales?

- a. $250,000
- b. $230,000
- c. $200,000
- d. $180,000

59. Mr. and Mrs. Gasson own 100% of the common stock of Able Corp. and 90% of the common stock of Baker Corp. Able previously paid $4,000 for the remaining 10% interest in Baker. The condensed December 31, 2002 balance sheets of Able and Baker are as follows:

	Able	Baker
Assets	$600,000	$60,000
Liabilities	$200,000	$30,000
Common stock	100,000	20,000
Retained earnings	300,000	10,000
	$600,000	$60,000

In a combined balance sheet of the two corporations at December 31, 2002, what amount should be reported as total stockholders' equity?

- a. $430,000
- b. $426,000
- c. $403,000
- d. $400,000

60. Mr. Cord owns four corporations. Combined financial statements are being prepared for these corporations, which have intercompany loans of $200,000 and intercompany profits of $500,000. What amount of these intercompany loans and profits should be included in the combined financial statements?

	Intercompany Loans	Profits
a.	$200,000	$0
b.	$200,000	$500,000
c.	$0	$0
d.	$0	$500,000

61. Combined statements may be used to present the results of operations of

	Companies under common management	Commonly controlled companies
a.	No	Yes
b.	Yes	No
c.	No	No
d.	Yes	Yes

62. Which of the following items should be treated in the same manner in both combined financial statements and consolidated statements?

	Income taxes	Minority interest
a.	No	No
b.	No	Yes
c.	Yes	Yes
d.	Yes	No

63. Which of the following items should be treated in the same manner in both combined financial statements and consolidated statements?

	Different fiscal periods	Foreign operations
a.	No	No
b.	No	Yes
c.	Yes	Yes
d.	Yes	No

OTHER OBJECTIVE QUESTIONS

Problem 1 (45 to 55 minutes)

Presented below are selected amounts from the separate unconsolidated financial statements of Poe Corp. and its 90%-owned subsidiary, Shaw Co., at December 31, 2002. Additional information follows:

	Poe	Shaw
Selected income statement amounts		
Sales	$710,000	$530,000
Cost of goods sold	490,000	370,000
Gain on sale of equipment	--	21,000
Earnings from investment in subsidiary	61,000	--
Interest expense	--	16,000
Depreciation	25,000	20,000
Selected balance sheet amounts		
Cash	$ 50,000	$ 15,000
Inventories	229,000	150,000
Equipment	440,000	360,000
Accumulated depreciation	(200,000)	(120,000)
Investment in Shaw	189,000	--
Investment in bonds	100,000	--
Discount on bonds	(9,000)	--
Bonds payable		(200,000)
Common stock	(100,000)	(10,000)
Additional paid-in capital	(250,000)	(40,000)
Retained earnings	(402,000)	(140,000)
Selected statement of retained earnings amounts		
Beginning balance, December 31, 2001	$272,000	$100,000
Net income	210,000	70,000
Dividends paid	80,000	30,000

Additional information

- On January 2, 2002, Poe, Inc. purchased 90% of Shaw Co.'s 100,000 outstanding common stock for cash of $155,000. On that date, Shaw's stockholders' equity equalled $150,000 and the fair values of Shaw's identifiable assets and liabilities equaled their carrying amounts. Poe has accounted for the acquisition as a purchase.

  - On September 4, 2002, Shaw paid cash dividends of $30,000.
  - On December 31, 2002, Poe recorded its equity in Shaw's earnings.

Required:

a. Items 1 through 3. Items 1 through 3 below represent transactions between Poe and Shaw during 2002. Determine the dollar amount effect of the consolidating adjustment on 2002 consolidated income before considering minority interest. Ignore income tax considerations.

Items to be answered

1. On January 3, 2002, Shaw sold equipment with an original cost of $30,000 and a carrying value of $15,000 to Poe for $36,000. The equipment had a remaining life of three years and was depreciated using the straight-line method by both companies.

2. During 2002, Shaw sold merchandise to Poe for $60,000, which included a profit of $20,000. At December 31, 2002, half of this merchandise remained in Poe's inventory.

3. On December 31, 2002, Poe paid $91,000 to purchase 50% of the outstanding bonds issued by Shaw. The bonds mature on December 31, 2008, and were originally issued at par. The bonds pay interest annually on December 31 of each year, and the interest was paid to the prior investor immediately before Poe's purchase of the bonds.

b. Item 4. Determine the amount of goodwill recorded by Poe.

c. Items 5 through 16. Items 5 through 16 below refer to accounts that may or may not be included in Poe and Shaw's consolidated financial statements. The list on the right refers to the various possibilities of those amounts to be reported in Poe's consolidated financial statements for the year ended December 31, 2002. Consider all transactions stated in items 1 through 4 in determining your answer. Ignore income tax considerations.

Items to be answered	*Responses to be selected*

5. Cash

6. Equipment

7. Investment in subsidiary

8. Bonds payable

9. Minority interest

10. Common stock

11. Beginning retained earnings

12. Dividends paid

13. Gain on retirement of bonds

14. Cost of goods sold

15. Interest expense

16. Depreciation expense

A.   Sum of amounts on Poe and Shaw's separate unconsolidated financial statements

B.   Less than the sum of amounts on Poe and Shaw's separate unconsolidated financial statements but not the same as the amount on either

C.   Same as amount for Poe only

D.   Same as amount for Shaw only

E.   Eliminated entirely in consolidation

F.   Shown in consolidated financial statements but not in separate unconsolidated financial statements

G.   Neither in consolidated nor in separate unconsolidated financial statements

---

Problem 2   (10 to 20 minutes)

On January 2, 2002, Purl Co. purchased 90% of Strand Co.'s outstanding common stock at a purchase price that was in excess of Strand's stockholders' equity. On that date, the fair value of Strand's assets and liabilities equaled their carrying amounts. Purl has accounted for the acquisition as a purchase. Transactions during 2002 were as follows:

•   On February 15, 2002, Strand sold equipment to Purl at a price higher than the equipment's carrying amount. The equipment has a remaining life of three years and was depreciated using the straight-line method by both companies.
•   During 2002, Purl sold merchandise to Strand under the same terms it offered to third parties. At December 31, 2002, one-third of this merchandise remained in Strand's inventory.
•   On November 15, 2002, both Purl and Strand paid cash dividends to their respective stockholders.
•   On December 31, 2002, Purl recorded its equity in Strand's earnings.

Required:

Items 1 through 10 relate to accounts that may or may not be included in Purl and Strand's consolidated financial statements. The list on the right refers to the possible ways those accounts may be reported in Purl's consolidated financial statements for the year ended December 31, 2002. An answer may be selected once, more than once, or not at all.

Items to be answered	*Responses to be selected*

1. Cash

2. Equipment

3. Investment in subsidiary

4. Minority interest

5. Common stock

6. Beginning retained earnings

7. Dividends paid

8. Cost of goods sold

9. Interest expense

10. Depreciation expense

A.   Sum of the amounts on Purl and Strand's separate unconsolidated financial statements

B.   Less than the sum of the amounts on Purl and Strand's separate unconsolidated financial statements, but not the same as the amount on either separate unconsolidated financial statement

C.   Same as the amount for Purl only

D.   Same as the amount for Strand only

E.   Eliminated entirely in consolidation

F.   Shown in the consolidated financial statements but not in the separate unconsolidated financial statements

PROBLEMS

Problem 1   (15 to 25 minutes)

On September 1, 2002, Plains Corp. acquired all of Sox Corp.'s outstanding stock for cash. The fair value of Sox's net assets was less than the purchase price but greater than the net carrying amount. During November 2002, Plains sold goods to Sox at a price that included its normal markup. At December 31, 2002, 20% of these goods remained in Sox's inventory. The separate legal entities were maintained and Sox uses push-down accounting for its separate financial statements.

Required:

Ignore income tax considerations when answering all questions.

a.   1.   Specify three reasons for preparing consolidated financial statements that present operating results, cash flows, and financial position as if a parent company and its subsidiaries were a single entity.

2.   What changes in Plains' September 1, 2002 consolidated balance sheet will result from this acquisition?

3.   In preparing Plains' December 31, 2002 consolidated financial statements, what adjustments or eliminations are required as a consequence of the intercompany sales?

b.   In preparing separate financial statements immediately after acquisition (September 1, 2002), what is the effect of the purchase on the balance sheet of

1.   Plains?
2.   Sox (which uses push-down accounting)?

Problem 2   (10 to 20 minutes)

Flaherty Company acquired all of the voting common stock of Rubin Company in the middle of the year. This combination was accounted for as a purchase and resulted in goodwill. Both companies use the same methods of accounting. Registration fees for the equity securities involved in the combination were incurred. There were no intercompany transactions before or after the combination.

Required:

a.   In the business combination accounted for as a purchase, how should the assets acquired and liabilities assumed be recorded? What is the rationale for accounting for a business combination as a purchase?

b.   In the business combination accounted for as a purchase, how should the registration fees and direct costs related to effecting the business combination be accounted for?

c.   In the business combination accounted for as a purchase, how should the results of operations of the acquired company for the year in which the business combination occurred be reported?

MULTIPLE-CHOICE ANSWERS

1. a __ __	14. c __ __	27. b __ __	40. d __ __	53. b __ __
2. d __ __	15. b __ __	28. a __ __	41. a __ __	54. b __ __
3. c __ __	16. b __ __	29. d __ __	42. a __ __	55. d __ __
4. d __ __	17. a __ __	30. b __ __	43. a __ __	56. c __ __
5. d __ __	18. c __ __	31. a __ __	44. a __ __	57. b __ __
6. c __ __	19. c __ __	32. d __ __	45. c __ __	58. a __ __
7. c __ __	20. d __ __	33. b __ __	46. b __ __	59. b __ __
8. c __ __	21. c __ __	34. d __ __	47. a __ __	60. c __ __
9. c __ __	22. d __ __	35. d __ __	48. a __ __	61. d __ __
10. d __ __	23. a __ __	36. b __ __	49. c __ __	62. c __ __
11. c __ __	24. d __ __	37. c __ __	50. b __ __	63. c __ __
12. c __ __	25. b __ __	38. c __ __	51. b __ __	1st: __/63 = __%
13. a __ __	26. c __ __	39. a __ __	52. b __ __	2nd: __/63 = __%

MULTIPLE-CHOICE ANSWER EXPLANATIONS

A. Accounting for the Combination, and Sections B. - D.

1. (a) In a purchase, the net assets of the acquired firm are recorded at their FMV. The excess of the cost of the investment over the FMV of the net assets acquired is allocated to goodwill. The cost of the investment is $620,000, and the FMV of the net assets acquired, **excluding goodwill,** is $470,000, as computed below.

	FMV
Cash	60,000
Inventory (BV = $180,000)	150,000
Prop. and equip. (BV = $320,000)	380,000
Liabilities	(120,000)
Total FMV	470,000

Therefore, the amount allocated to goodwill is $150,000 ($620,000 – $470,000).

2. (d) Both finders' fees and registration fees are included in the cost of the investment. They are not expensed in the year incurred. Answers (a), (b), and (c) are incorrect because both expenses are included in the cost of the investment and not expensed in the year incurred.

3. (c) In a business combination accounted for as a purchase, the fair market value of the net assets is used as the valuation basis for the combination. In this case, the net assets of the subsidiary have an implied fair market value of $3,600,000 which is the value of the common stock issued to Pine's shareholders (100,000 shares x $36). Also, per SFAS 141, the direct cost of acquisition should be included as part of the cost of a company acquired, and the cost of registering equity securities should be a reduction of the issue price of the securities (i.e., additional paid-in capital) in a business combination accounted for by the purchase method. Thus, the $160,000 paid for a consultant who arranged the acquisition should also be capitalized, and the $80,000 cost for registering and issuing the equity securities should be treated as a reduction of additional paid-in capital. The total amount to be capitalized is $3,760,000 ($3,600,000 + $160,000).

4. (d) In a business combination accounted for as a purchase, the fair market value of the net assets is used as the valuation basis for the combination. In this case, the net assets of the subsidiary have an implied fair market value of $3,600,000 which is the value of the common stock issued to Saxe's shareholders (200,000 x $18). Since $3,600,000 is the basis for recording this purchase, the common stock

issued is recorded at $2,000,000 (200,000 shares x $10 par value per share) and additional paid-in capital is recorded at $1,600,000 ($3,600,000 – $2,000,000). Therefore, in the 12/31/02 consolidated balance sheet, additional paid-in capital should be reported at $2,900,000 ($1,300,000 + $1,600,000).

5. (d) In a business combination, the common stock account of the combined entity is the number of shares outstanding multiplied by the par value of the stock. The total common stock account of the combined entity is equal to $5,000,000, the $3,000,000 originally outstanding plus the total par value of the stock issued, $2,000,000 (200,000 x $10).

6. (c) In a business combination accounted for as a purchase, the fair market value of the net assets is used as the valuation basis for the combination. In this case, Frey's assets have an implied fair market value of $1,900,000 which is the market value of the common stock issue (100,000 shares x $19). The value assigned to goodwill is $70,000, which is the value of the stock minus the fair value of Frey's identifiable assets ($1,900,000 – $1,830,000).

7. (c) Per ARB 51, a subsidiary should not be consolidated when control is likely to be temporary. SFAS 94 requires consolidation of all majority-owned subsidiaries regardless of the industry or business of the subsidiary. ARB 51 states that a difference in fiscal periods of a parent and a subsidiary does not of itself justify the exclusion of the subsidiary from consolidation.

8. (c) SFAS 141 requires the use of the purchase method for all business combinations initiated after June 30, 2002. The pooling of interests method, which was allowed previously under certain circumstances, may no longer be used.

9. (c) Per SFAS 141, the direct costs of acquisition should be included as part of the cost of a company acquired in a business combination accounted for by the purchase method. General expenses related to the acquisition, however, are deducted as incurred in determining the combined corporation's net income for the current period.

10. (d) The requirement is to select the correct general guideline for assigning amounts to inventories under the purchase method. Per SFAS 141, finished goods inventories should be valued at estimated selling prices less the costs of disposal and a reasonable profit allowance for the selling effort of the acquiring corporation. Raw materials should be valued at current replacement costs, not original cost. Work in process should be valued at the estimated selling prices of finished goods less the costs to complete, the costs of disposal, **and** a reasonable profit allowance.

11. **(c)** SFAS 141 requires intangibles to be recognized as assets apart from goodwill if they arise from contractual or legal rights, regardless of whether those rights are transferable or separable from the acquired entity or from other rights and obligations. If an intangible asset does not arise from contractual or other legal rights, it shall be recognized as an asset apart from goodwill only if it is separable (i.e., capable of being sold, transferred, or licensed). Trademarks, lease agreements, and patents all arise from contractual or legal rights. Employee quality does not and is not separable.

12. **(c)** SFAS 141 requires the use of the purchase method for all business combinations. In applying the purchase method, the acquisition cost is allocated to acquired assets and liabilities based on their fair values. Any excess of cost over the fair value of net assets is allocated to goodwill.

F.   Date of Combination Consolidated Balance Sheet—Purchase Accounting

13. **(a)** In the consolidated balance sheet, the parent company's "investment in subsidiary" account should be eliminated and replaced by the net assets of the subsidiary. Under the purchase method, the assets of the acquired firm are recorded at their FMV. The cost of the investment is $60,000 and the book value of the acquired net assets is $45,000 (90% x $50,000), so the excess of cost over book value is $15,000 ($60,000 – $45,000). 60% of this excess is allocated to inventory because its FMV exceeds its cost (60% x $15,000 = $9,000). Therefore, current assets should be reported at $99,000.

Current assets—Polk	$70,000
Current assets—Strass	20,000
Excess allocated to inventory	9,000
Total	$99,000

14. **(c)** In the consolidated balance sheet, the parent company's "investment in subsidiary" account should be eliminated and replaced by the net assets of the subsidiary. Under the purchase method, the assets of the acquired firm are recorded at their FMV. The cost of the investment is $60,000 and the book value of the acquired net assets is $45,000 (90% x $50,000) the excess of cost over book value is $15,000 ($60,000 – $45,000). 40% of this excess is allocated to goodwill (40% x $15,000 = $6,000). Therefore, noncurrent assets should be reported at $136,000.

Noncurrent assets—Polk	$90,000
Noncurrent assets—Strass	40,000
Excess allocated to goodwill	6,000
Total	$136,000

15. **(b)** In the consolidated balance sheet, the parent company's "investment in subsidiary" account should be eliminated and replaced by the assets and liabilities of the subsidiary. Therefore, the consolidated balance sheet should include the current liabilities of both companies, plus the current portion of the debt incurred on 1/2/02 ($60,000 ÷ 10 = $6,000). Thus, current liabilities should be reported at $46,000 as computed below.

Current liabilities—Polk	$30,000
Current liabilities—Strass	10,000
Current portion of new debt	6,000
Total	$46,000

16. **(b)** In the consolidated balance sheet, the parent company's "investment in subsidiary" account should be eliminated and replaced by the assets and liabilities of the subsidiary. Therefore, the consolidated balance sheet should include the noncurrent liabilities of both companies, plus the noncurrent portion of the debt incurred on 1/2/02 ($60,000 – $6,000 = $54,000), plus the minority interest in the subsidiary ($50,000 x 10% = $5,000).

Noncurrent liabilities—Polk	$ 50,000
Noncurrent liabilities—Strass	0
Noncurrent portion of new debt	54,000
Minority interest	5,000
Total	$109,000

17. **(a)** In the consolidated balance sheet, neither the parent company's investment account nor the subsidiary's stockholders' equity is reported. These amounts are eliminated in the same journal entry that records the excess of cost over book value. The portion of the subsidiary's stockholders' equity that is **not** eliminated is reported as minority interest in the noncurrent liabilities section of the consolidated balance sheet. Therefore, the parent's stockholders' equity ($80,000) equals the consolidated stockholders' equity. Note that once the candidate has completed items 14 through 18, the answers can be checked using the balance sheet equation.

Current assets	+	Non-current assets	=	Current liabilities	+	Non-current liabilities	+	Stock-holders' equity
$99,000	+	$136,000	=	$46,000	+	$109,000	+	$80,000

18. **(c)** In a purchase, the net assets of the acquired firm are recorded at their FMV. The excess of the cost of the investment over the FMV of the net assets acquired is allocated to goodwill. The cost of this investment is $3,750,000 (250,000 shares x $15), and the FMV of the net assets acquired, **excluding goodwill** is $3,400,000 ($3,000,000 + $400,000). Therefore, the amount allocated to goodwill is $350,000 ($3,750,000 – $3,400,000).

19. **(c)** The assets acquired would be revalued to their fair market value. The inventory account would then include the difference between the market value and book value. Answer (a) is incorrect because a deferred credit is never recorded. Answer (b) is incorrect because goodwill represents the excess of cost over fair market value. Answer (d) is incorrect because the retained earnings account is not affected by this transaction when purchase accounting is used.

20. **(d)** SFAS 141 states that, in general, all assets and liabilities (including plant and equipment and long-term debt) should be reported at fair value. Answer (a) is incorrect because it describes the treatment accorded to plant and equipment when a combination is accounted for as a pooling of interests.

21. **(c)** When the appraised values of the identifiable assets acquired in a **purchase** combination exceed the acquisition price, the difference is referred to as negative goodwill. APB 16 requires negative goodwill to be allocated against noncurrent assets acquired, excluding marketable securities, in proportion to their fair values. If the noncurrent assets are reduced to zero and some negative goodwill remains unallocated, the excess should be reported on the balance sheet as an extraordinary gain. Subsequently, this amount is amortized over a period not exceeding forty years. Answer (a) is incorrect because the excess is not **reported** as negative goodwill. Answer (b) is incorrect because APIC is not affected by this excess. Answer (d) is incorrect because **positive** goodwill results from an excess of acquisition price over appraised value of identifiable assets, not vice versa.

G. Consolidated Financial Statements subsequent to Acquisition

22. **(d)** Consolidated statements are prepared as if the parent and subsidiaries were one economic entity. From the point of view of the consolidated entity, any intercompany receivables or payables from parent to subsidiary or vice versa are **not** payable to or receivable from any **outside** company. In other words, the consolidated entity does not have a receivable or payable. Therefore, all of Wright's intercompany receivables, payables and advances are eliminated. None are reported as intercompany receivables.

23. **(a)** When a subsidiary prepares separate financial statements, intercompany receivables (and payables) should be reported in the balance sheet as a separate line item. When consolidated financial statements are prepared by the parent company, all intercompany receivables (and payables) should be eliminated to avoid overstating assets and liabilities.

24. **(d)** Pard's separate revenues are $200,000, and Spin's separate revenues are $140,000, resulting in a total of $340,000 ($200,000 + $140,000). Since the consolidated income statement shows sales of only $308,000, intercompany sales of $32,000 ($340,000 – $308,000) from Pard to Spin must have been eliminated during consolidation.

25. **(b)** Pard's separate accounts receivable is $26,000, and Spin's separate accounts receivable is $19,000, resulting in a total of $45,000 ($26,000 + $19,000). Since the consolidated balance sheet shows accounts receivable of only $39,000, intercompany receivables of $6,000 ($45,000 – $39,000) must have been eliminated during consolidation. Since Pard sold goods to Spin that Spin had not fully paid for by 12/31/02, the eliminated receivable must be Pard's receivable from Spin. Therefore, Spin's 12/31/02 payable to Pard is also $6,000.

26. **(c)** Pard's intercompany sales to Spin totaled $32,000 during 2002. Therefore, Spin recorded a purchase of inventory of $32,000. At 12/31/02, Spin still held 37.5% of these goods in inventory; in Spin's books, this inventory was carried at $12,000 (37.5% x $32,000). In the consolidated balance sheet, the intercompany profit would be eliminated, and this inventory would be carried at Pard's original cost. Pard's sales to Spin were at the same markup on cost that Pard uses for all sales. In Pard's income statement, cost of sales is 75% of sales ($150,000 ÷ $200,000). Therefore, Pard's original cost for the $12,000 of goods in Spin's inventory is $9,000 (75% x $12,000).

27. **(b)** The percentage of the subsidiary's stockholders' equity not owned by the parent company represents the minority interest's share of the net assets of the subsidiary. In the 12/31/02 consolidated balance sheet, minority interest is

$10,000. At the same date, Spin's stockholders' equity is $50,000. Therefore, the percent of minority interest ownership is 20% ($10,000 ÷ $50,000).

28. **(a)** When the equity method of accounting is used the parent company's retained earnings will be equal to the consolidated retained earnings balance. It can be determined that the equity method is being followed because the account "Equity in earnings of Sharp" appears in the parent's income statement. In addition it is important to note that the balance sheet accounts presented are dated as of the end of the year; therefore, the parent company's retained earnings of $1,240,000, should already include **all** income statement balance account adjustments. Thus, no additional income amounts will need to be added to the $1,240,000 retained earnings balance, in order to determine the total retained earnings balance.

29. **(d)** The requirement is to determine which accounting concept relates to the preparation of consolidated financial statements. Answer (d) is correct because when a parent-subsidiary relationship exists, the financial statements of each separate entity are brought together, or consolidated. When financial statements represent a consolidated entity, the concept of economic entity applies. Answer (a) is incorrect because reliability is a concept that applies to all financial statements, not just consolidated financial statements. Reliability, as identified in the SFAC 2, is a primary quality that makes accounting information useful for decision making. This quality should be found in all statements. Answer (b) is incorrect because the concept of materiality applies to all financial statements, not just consolidated financial statements. The concept of materiality, as applied to financial statements, deals with the impact an item in the financial statements will have on a users' decision-making process, when studying the financial statements. Answer (c) is incorrect because the concept of legal entity refers to the form or type of combination that takes place between entities (i.e., mergers, consolidations or acquisitions), not the basis on which financial statements are prepared.

30. **(b)** The purchase method is used to account for this situation because the subsidiary was acquired for cash. APB 16 states that, in general, all assets and liabilities (including equipment) should be reported at market value. The excess of the equipment's market value over its carrying amount is allocated to the equipment and amortized over the equipment's useful life. The unamortized portion of the excess of the market value over the carrying amount of the equipment is then reported as part of plant and equipment. Only the unamortized portion of the excess of the acquisition cost over the market value of the net identifiable assets acquired is reported as goodwill. The excess of the market value over the carrying amount of the equipment is capitalized and subsequently amortized over the equipment's useful life, **not** expensed as incurred.

31. **(a)** When two companies own stock in each other, a reciprocal ownership relationship exists. In this case, Pride (the parent) owns 80% of Simba (the sub), and Simba owns 10% of Pride. When Pride declares a cash dividend, 90% of it is distributed to outside parties and 10% goes to Simba. Because Simba is part of the consolidated entity, its 10% share of Pride's dividend is eliminated when determining consolidated dividends declared. Thus, only 90% of dividends declared by Pride will be reported in the consolidated financial statements. When Simba declares a dividend, 80% of the dividend is distributed to Pride (the parent), and 20% is distributed to outside parties (the noncontrolling interest of Simba stock). The 80% share to Pride is eliminated when determining consolidated dividends declared because it represents an intercompany transaction. The remaining 20% to the noncontrolling interest is likewise not included in consolidated dividends declared because, from the parent company's point of view, subsidiary dividends do not represent dividends of the consolidated entity and must be eliminated.

32. (d) APB 20 states that accounting changes that result in financial statements that are, in effect, financial statements of a different reporting entity (such as presenting consolidated statements in place of statements of individual companies) should be reported by restating the financial statements of all prior periods presented so that the resulting restated prior periods' statements on a consolidated basis are the same as if the subsidiary had been consolidated since it was acquired.

33. (b) In a purchase, the consolidated financial statements reflect the combined operations of the parent and subsidiary **from the date of combination**. Earnings of the subsidiary prior to the combination are **not** included with the parent's income. The parent's 2002 income is $1,575,000 ($750,000 + $825,000), while the subsidiary's income after the combination is $375,000 for a total of $1,950,000 ($1,575,000 + $375,000). The unrealized inventory profit of $45,000 must be eliminated, because from a consolidated viewpoint, revenue cannot be recognized until these goods are sold to a third party (i.e., a sale has not yet occurred). Therefore, 2002 consolidated net income is $1,905,000 ($1,950,000 – $45,000). Note that the net income amounts given are from **separate company operations,** so no elimination of equity earnings or dividend income is necessary.

34. (d) In a business combination accounted for as a purchase, the FMV of net assets is used as the valuation basis for the combination. The investment is recorded at the fair value of the net assets, common stock is recorded at par value (150,000 x $20 = $3,000,000), and any difference is recorded as APIC. The subsidiary's retained earnings are **not** recorded in a purchase. Therefore, 6/30/02 consolidated retained earnings is equal to Pane's separate 6/30/02 retained earnings $3,250,000 ($3,200,000 + $800,000 – $750,000).

H. Intercompany Transactions and Profit Confirmation

35. (d) Unrealized profit in ending inventory arises when intercompany sales are made at prices above cost and the merchandise is not resold to third parties prior to year-end. The profit is unrealized because the inventory has not yet been sold outside of the consolidated entity. In this case, Pirn sold goods to Scroll for $100,000, which would become Scroll's cost. However, Scroll's cost of goods sold includes only $80,000 of goods acquired from Pirn. Therefore, $20,000 of original $100,000 remains in Scroll's ending inventory. Since Pirn's gross profit rate is 30% ($150,000 ÷ $500,000), the gross profit Pirn recognized on the original $20,000 sale was $6,000 (30% x $20,000). This intercompany profit must be eliminated on the consolidating worksheet.

36. (b) When computing consolidated income, the objective is to restate the accounts as if the intercompany transactions had not occurred. When Scroll recorded depreciation, it included depreciation on the asset purchased from Pirn for $36,000. Since Pirn recorded a $12,000 gain when it sold the asset to Scroll, Pirn's book value at the time of sale must have been $24,000. Therefore, consolidated depreciation expense should be based on $24,000 rather than on $36,000. Depreciation expense for 2002 must be decreased by $3,000 ($12,000 excess ÷ 4 years). Depreciation expense in Pirn's 2002 consolidated income statement should therefore be $47,000, as computed below.

Pirn's recorded depr.	$40,000
Scroll's recorded depr.	10,000
Less adjustment ($12,000 ÷ 4)	(3,000)
	$47,000

37. (c) Unrealized profit in ending inventory arises when intercompany sales are made at prices above cost and the merchandise is not resold to third parties prior to year-end. The profit is unrealized because the inventory has not yet been sold outside of the consolidated entity. In this case, there is no unrealized profit on the sales to Dean because the consolidated statements would not include Dean, and the equity method is not applicable. (Clark owns only 15% of Dean). However, there is unrealized profit on the materials sold by Kent, a wholly owned subsidiary, to Clark. $60,000 of the $240,000 of materials sold by Kent to Clark remains in ending inventory. The gross profit Kent recognized on this $60,000 of materials at the time of sale was $12,000 ($48,000 ÷ $240,000 = 20% gross profit rate; 20% x $60,000 = $12,000). For the consolidated entity, this $12,000 gross profit has not been earned and must be eliminated. Therefore, consolidated current assets should be $308,000 ($320,000 – $12,000).

38. (c) When preparing the consolidated income statement, the objective is to restate the accounts as if the intercompany transactions had not occurred. As a result of the intercompany sale, Parker has recorded $250,000 of sales and Smith has recorded $250,000 cost of sales which should be eliminated (note that Parker's **cost of sales** on the original sale is the amount left in consolidated cost of sales, and Smith's **sales** when the goods were sold to outside parties is the amount left in consolidated sales). Therefore, Parker should report $500,000 as cost of sales in the 2001 consolidated income statement ($400,000 + $350,000 – $250,000).

39. (a) Pare's separate gross profit is $100,000, and Shel's separate gross profit is $60,000, resulting in a total of $160,000. Since the consolidated income statement shows gross profit of only $154,000, unrealized intercompany profit of $6,000 ($160,000 – $154,000) must have been eliminated.

40. (d) The requirement is to determine the amount of **selling** expenses to be reported in Pard's 2002 consolidated income statement. Pard's selling expenses for 2002 include $50,000 in freight-out costs for goods sold to Seed, its subsidiary. This $50,000 becomes part of Seed's inventory because it is a cost directly associated with bringing the goods to a salable condition. One half of the goods sold to Seed by Pard remained in Seed's inventory at the end of 2002. Therefore, one half of the $50,000 ($25,000) flowed out as part of cost of goods sold, and one half remains in ending inventory. Thus, none of the $50,000 represents a selling expense for the consolidated entity, and $1,450,000 ($1,100,000 + $400,000 – $50,000) should be reported as selling expenses in the consolidated income statement.

41. **(a)** When preparing consolidated financial statements, the objective is to restate the accounts as if the intercompany transactions had not occurred. Therefore, the 2002 gain on sale of machine of $50,000 [$900,000 – ($1,100,000 – $250,000)] must be eliminated, since the consolidated entity has not realized any gain. In effect, the machine must be reflected on the consolidated balance sheet at 1/1/02 at Poe's cost of $1,100,000, and accumulated depreciation of $250,000, instead of at a new "cost" of $900,000. For consolidated statement purposes, 2001 depreciation is based on the original amounts [($1,100,000 – $100,000) x 1/20 = $50,000]. Therefore, in the 12/31/02 **consolidated** balance sheet, the machine is shown at a cost of $1,100,000 less accumulated depreciation of $300,000 ($250,000 + $50,000).

42. **(a)** When Seal purchased the bonds from Wagner, the bonds were viewed as retired from a consolidated viewpoint since there is no longer any obligation to an outside party. Therefore, the consolidated entity would recognize a $100,000 gain ($1,075,000 carrying amount – $975,000 cash paid), which would increase consolidated retained earnings. This transaction has no effect on minority interest, since the subsidiary (Seal) has merely exchanged one asset for another (cash for investment in bonds).

43. **(a)** The requirement is to determine the amount of gain to be reported on the consolidated income statement when a wholly owned subsidiary purchases parent company stock. A parent company reports no gain or loss when a wholly owned subsidiary purchases its common stock. In effect, the consolidated entity is purchasing treasury stock when the purchase is made, and gains are not recognized on treasury stock transactions. The dividends paid by the parent to the subsidiary also do not affect income because such intercompany transactions are eliminated when consolidated financial statements are prepared. Therefore, $0 gain should be reported by the consolidated entity.

44. **(a)** When computing consolidated income, the objective is to restate the accounts as if the intercompany transaction had not occurred. As a result of the intercompany sale, sales and cost of goods sold are overstated and an eliminating entry is needed to reduce these accounts by the intercompany sale. Answer (b) is incorrect because sales and cost of goods sold need to be reduced by the entire amount of the intercompany sale in order to arrive at their proper consolidated amounts. Answer (c) is incorrect because net income is not effected by the intercompany sale. Sales and cost of goods sold are overstated by the same amount; thus, net income is correct for consolidated purposes. Answer (d) is incorrect because an adjustment is necessary.

45. **(c)** The key to this problem is that the equipment must be revalued at Fire's carrying amount (Fire's original cost less accumulated depreciation) in the consolidation process. Assume the following potential scenario:

Fire buys a piece of equipment on 12/31/01 for $1,000. At 12/31/02, the equipment was depreciated $200, and Fire's carrying value is $800 ($1,000 – $200). On 12/31/02, Fire sells the equipment to Water for $900. Water's original cost

is therefore $900, and Fire will record a $100 gain that must be eliminated. After consolidation, the equipment is reported at $800, Fire's carrying value. Fire's carrying value is also equal to Water's original cost ($900) less Fire's recorded gain ($100). Answer (a) is incorrect because Water's original cost includes an unrealized gain that must be eliminated. Answer (b) is incorrect because revaluing the equipment at Fire's original cost would not take into consideration the depreciation already recorded by Fire. Answer (d) is incorrect because the entire gain, not 80% of the gain, must be eliminated.

46. **(b)** The requirement is to determine by how much depreciation will be reduced. Use the solutions approach and set up a simple numerical example.

> Port's original cost = $1,000
> Depreciation per yr = $200
> Selling price = $810

If Port sells equipment for $810, they recognize a $210 gain on the sale (selling price of $810 – carrying value of the equipment $600). Salem, Inc. will now depreciate the equipment on their books at $810, the price that they paid. Because the gain was not realized with an entity outside of the consolidated entity, it must be eliminated. In the consolidated financial statements, equipment will be reported at its original carrying value, the gain on the sale will be removed and depreciation expense must be recorded at Port, Inc. original amount ($200), not the amount of depreciation that Salem, Inc. records. Salem would record depreciation of $270 (810/3). Therefore, depreciation must be reduced by $70 on the consolidated financial statements to reflect the original depreciation recorded by Port. Depreciation is reduced by $70, which as shown by the example, is 33 1/3% of the gain ($70/$210).

47. **(a)** This question is silent as to which year consolidated financial statements are being prepared. However, answer (a) is correct for either the year of acquisition or a subsequent year. If financial statements were being prepared for the current year the loss would be reported as an extraordinary loss on the income statement. P Co. acquired the 20% interest in S Company bonds and incurred a loss on them. This loss would be carried through to the consolidated balance sheet as a decrease in retained earnings. In subsequent years, the unamortized portion of the loss would also decrease retained earnings.

J.   Minority Interest

48. **(a)** Without the intercompany transaction, the minority interest income from Samson in 2002 would be $24,000 (30% of $80,000). In 2003 the minority interest income would be $27,000 (30% of $90,000). On the consolidated statements in 2002 the $2,000 intercompany profit will be eliminated, because from a consolidated viewpoint an arm's-length transaction has not occurred with third parties. The elimination entry will be to credit inventory (which is in effect on the books of Eltro) for $2,000 and debits will be made of $1,400 to majority interest income and $600 to minority interest income. In 2003 when Eltro sells the inventory to outsiders, the $2,000 profit has effectively been earned. In 2003 an entry will be made on the consolidated books to effectively recognize this profit and allocate it to the majority and minority interest. Thus, the

2002 minority interest income will be reduced by $600 and 2003 minority interest income increased by $600.

	2002			2003
MI % of profit	$24,000	MI % of profit		$27,000
Elim. of inter-company profit	– 600	Recognition of profit		600
MI income	$23,400			$27,600

49.   (c)   The cost of this investment is $975,000. Ritt purchased 80% of the identifiable net assets of Shaw, which have a fair value of $1,100,000 ($1,000,000 + $100,000). Thus, Ritt purchased net assets with a fair value of $880,000 (80% x $1,100,000). The excess amount paid ($975,000 – $880,000 = $95,000) is allocated to goodwill.

50.   (b)   The percentage of the subsidiary's stockholders' equity not owned by the parent company represents the minority interest's share of the net assets of the subsidiary. The minority interest is based on **book** value, to remove the minority shareholders' portion of reported equity from the financial statements (parent company concept). At 12/31/02, the subsidiary's stockholders' equity at book value is $1,065,000, as computed below.

1/1/02 net assets (stockholders' equity)	$1,000,000
2002 net income	190,000
2002 dividends	(125,000)
12/31/02 net assets (stockholders' equity)	$1,065,000

Since the parent's share is 80%, the minority interest is 20% of $1,065,000, or $213,000.

51.   (b)   Pare paid cash dividends of $25,000 and Kidd, the 75%-owned subsidiary, paid cash dividends of $5,000. The dividends paid by Pare are all payments to owners of the consolidated company and are reported as dividends paid in the consolidated statement of retained earnings. The $5,000 dividend paid by Kidd is paid 75% to Pare, and 25% to outside parties (the noncontrolling interest in Kidd's stock). The 75% share to Pare is eliminated when determining consolidated dividends declared because it is an intracompany transaction. The remaining 25% to the noncontrolling interest is likewise not included in consolidated dividends declared because, from the parent company's point of view, subsidiary dividends do not represent dividends of the consolidated entity.

52.   (b)   The portion of the subsidiary's stockholders' equity **not** owned by the parent company represents the minority interest's share of the net assets of the subsidiary. At 12/31/03, the subsidiary's stockholders' equity is $120,000 ($50,000 common stock + $70,000 retained earnings). Since the parent's share is 75%, the minority interest is 25% of $120,000, or $30,000.

53.   (b)   In the consolidated balance sheet, neither the parent company's investment account nor the subsidiary's stockholders' equity is reported. These amounts are eliminated in the same journal entry that records the excess of cost over book value. The portion of the subsidiary's stockholders' equity that is **not** eliminated is reported as minority interest. Therefore, the amount reported as common stock in the 12/31/03 consolidated balance sheet consists solely of Pare's common stock ($100,000). Kidd's common stock ($50,000) is eliminated along with the rest of its stockholders' equity.

M.   Changes in Ownership

54.   (b)   The requirement is to determine how much of Sago's 2002 net income should be reported as accruing to Phillips. The key to the problem is to determine if the combination of the two entities should be treated as a purchase or pooling. For treatment as a pooling, APB 16 specifies 12 criteria that must be met before a combination may be accounted for as a pooling. If any one of the criteria are not met, the combination will be treated as a purchase, not a pooling. Consolidated net income, under pooling treatment, will reflect net income for both entities for the entire year, as if they had always been a consolidated entity. Under a purchase, consolidated net income reflects the parent's net income to the date of combination and both entities' income after the combination. In this case, the transaction should be treated as purchase because requirements (1) the combining companies have ownership interests independent of each other and were not recently a subsidiary or division of any other company to the extent that one company was not > 10% owned by another prior to the combination; and, (2) the combination is affected by a single transaction or in accord with a plan lasting not more than one year; are not met. Phillips, Inc. can only recognize the net income of Sago, based on their 20% interest, up to the date of combination. However, after the date of combination they will recognize 95% of Sago's net income, their new ownership interest.

N.   Combined Financial Statements

55.   (d)   **Combined financial statements** are financial statements prepared for companies that are owned by the same parent company or individual. Combined financial statements are prepared by combining all the companies' financial statement classifications. Intercompany transactions and profits should be eliminated in the same way as for consolidated statements (ARB 51). Therefore, **none** of the intercompany receivables should be included in the combined financial statements.

56.   (c)   The inventory reported on the 12/31/02 combined balance sheet should reflect the **original cost** to the companies of any inventory on hand (ARB 51). The inventory on hand that was acquired from outside parties should be reported at its cost ($175,000 + $250,000 = $425,000). The Banks inventory on hand that was acquired from Lamm must be restated back to the cost Lamm originally paid when it was purchased from outside parties. This must be done to eliminate intercompany profits. During 2002, Lamm shipped inventory that originally cost $150,000 to Banks at a billing price of $200,000. Therefore, the original cost is 75% of Banks' carrying amount. Therefore, the correct inventory amount is $470,000 [$175,000 + $250,000 + ($60,000 x 75%)].

57.   (b)   Combined financial statements are prepared for companies that are owned by the same parent company or individual but are not consolidated. These statements are prepared by combining the separate companies' financial statement classifications. Intercompany transactions, balances, and profit (loss) should be eliminated. Therefore, to determine the gross profit in Bee and Cee's combined income statement, the intercompany profit resulting from Bee's sales to Cee should be eliminated. Cee sold to outsiders 50% ($65,000/$130,000) of the inventory purchased from Bee. The cost of sales to the combined entity is thus 50% of the $100,000 cost of sales reported by Bee. Gross profit of the combined entity amounts to $41,000, equal to $91,000 of sales to unrelated companies less $50,000 cost of sales.

58. **(a)** When computing sales to be reported in the combined income statement, the objective is to restate the accounts as if the intercompany transaction had not occurred. Assuming that there were no sales between Home Office and Branch, the correct amount of sales to be included in the combined income statement is the $250,000 sold by Branch to unrelated customers.

59. **(b)** Combined financial statements is the term used to describe financial statements prepared for companies that are owned by the same parent company or individual. Combined financial statements are prepared by combining all of the subsidiaries' financial statement classifications. Intercompany transactions should be eliminated in the same way as for consolidated statements. Combining the stockholders' equity accounts of Able and Baker results in a total of $430,000 ($100,000 + $20,000 + $300,000 + $10,000). The intercompany balances (Investment in Baker, $4,000; and Common Stock, $4,000) must be eliminated, which reduces combined stockholders' equity to $426,000 ($430,000 – $4,000). If these amounts were not eliminated, the combined balance sheet would overstate both assets and equity by $4,000.

60. **(c)** **Combined financial statements** are financial statements prepared for companies that are owned by the same parent company or individual. Combined financial statements are prepared by combining all the companies' financial statement classifications. Intercompany transactions and profits should be eliminated in the same way as for consolidated statements (ARB 51). Therefore, **none** of the intercompany loans or profits should be included in the combined financial statements.

61. **(d)** Per ARB 51, combined statements may be used to present the financial position and results of operations of commonly controlled companies, companies under common management, and of a group of unconsolidated subsidiaries.

62. **(c)** Per ARB 51, where combined statements are prepared for a group of related companies, intercompany transactions and profit and losses should be eliminated. Matters such as minority interests, income taxes, foreign operations, or different fiscal periods should be treated in the same manner for both combined financial statements and consolidated statements.

63. **(c)** Per ARB 51, where combined statements are prepared for a group of related companies, if there are any problems in connection with such matters as minority interests, foreign operations, different fiscal periods, or income taxes, they should be treated in the same manner as in consolidated statements.

OTHER OBJECTIVE ANSWERS AND ANSWER EXPLANATIONS

Problem 1

1. **($14,000)** When preparing consolidated financial statements, the objective is to restate the accounts as if the intercompany transactions had not occurred. Therefore, the 2002 gain on sale of equipment of $21,000 ($36,000 – $15,000) must be eliminated, since the consolidated entity has not realized any gain. In addition, for consolidated statement purposes, 2002 depreciation is based on the original cost of the equipment to Shaw. Therefore, depreciation expense needs to be adjusted by $7,000 ($12,000 depreciation expense after sale to Poe – $5,000 depreciation expense for Shaw if sale never occurred). The net dollar effect of the consolidating adjustments on 2002 consolidated income before minority interest is $14,000 ($21,000 debit to eliminate gain on sale of equipment – $7,000 credit adjustment to depreciation expense).

2. **($10,000)** Unrealized profit in ending inventory arises when intercompany sales are made at prices above cost and the merchandise is not resold to third parties prior to year-end. The profit is unrealized because the inventory has not yet been sold outside the consolidated entity. In this case, one half of the merchandise was left in Poe's inventory at year-end. For the consolidated entity, one half of the $20,000 profit has not been earned and must be eliminated.

3. **($9,000)** When Poe purchased the bonds from an investor outside the consolidated entity, the bonds are viewed as retired from a consolidated viewpoint since there is no longer any obligation to an outside party. Therefore, the consolidated entity would recognize an extraordinary gain of $9,000 ($100,000 carrying value of the bonds – $91,000 purchase price) on the retirement of the debt.

4. **($20,000)** The goodwill from Poe's 90% purchase of Shaw can be determined as follows:

$155,000	Purchase price
135,000	Fair value ($150,000 x 90%)
$ 20,000	Goodwill

5. **(A)** Consolidated statements are prepared as if the parent and subsidiaries are one economic entity. Therefore, cash is included in the consolidated balance sheet at their full amounts regardless of the percentage ownership held by the parent.

6. **(B)** When preparing consolidated financial statements, the objective is to restate the accounts as if the intercompany transaction had not occurred. Therefore, on the consolidated balance sheet the equipment needs to be stated at its original cost to Shaw. The three balance sheets would show the sold equipment at December 31, 2002, as follows:

BALANCE SHEET
12/31/02

	Poe	*Shaw*	*Consolidated*
Equipment	$36,000	$0	$30,000

7. **(E)** In the consolidated balance sheet, the parent company's "Investment in subsidiary" should be eliminated completely and replaced by the net assets of the subsidiary.

8. **(B)** When Poe purchased the bonds from an investor outside the consolidated entity, the bonds are viewed as retired from a consolidated viewpoint since there is no longer any obligation to an outside party. Therefore, the consolidated balance sheet will show the bonds payable at $100,000.

9. **(F)** The percentage of the subsidiary's stockholders' equity not owned by the parent company represents the minority interest's share of the net assets of the subsidiary. This amount is only reported in the consolidated balance sheet in the noncurrent liabilities.

10. **(C)** In the consolidated balance sheet the subsidiary's common stock is not reported. Therefore, the parent's common stock equals the consolidated common stock.

11. **(C)** In the consolidated balance sheet, the subsidiary's beginning retained earnings is not reported. Therefore, the parent's beginning retained earnings equals the consolidated beginning retained earnings.

12. **(C)** The dividends paid by the subsidiary are eliminated in the consolidated financial statements. Ninety percent of the dividends paid are eliminated along with the "Investment in subsidiary" elimination. The remaining 10% is reflected in "Minority Interest." Therefore, only the parent's dividends paid are included on the consolidated financial statements.

13. **(F)** When Poe purchased the bonds from an investor outside the consolidated entity, the bonds are viewed as retired from a consolidated viewpoint since there is no longer any obligation to an outside party. Therefore, the consolidated entity would recognize a gain of $9,000 ($100,000 carrying value of the bonds – $91,000 purchase price) on the retirement of the debt. Since the bonds are still outstanding in relation to Shaw, no gain would be recognized on Shaw's unconsolidated income statement.

14. **(B)** When preparing the consolidated income statement, the objective is to restate the accounts as if the intercompany transactions had not occurred. As a result of the intercompany sale, Poe has recorded cost of sales of $30,000 and Shaw has recorded cost of sales of $40,000. The actual cost of sales to third parties outside the consolidated entity is $20,000 (1/2 of the merchandise Poe sold to third parties at the original cost of the merchandise purchased by Shaw).

15. **(D)** The requirement is to determine how the interest expense is to be reported in Poe's consolidated financial statements for December 31, 2002. As the Shaw bonds were held by an unaffiliated party for the entire period, the entire interest expense amount recorded by Shaw relates to payments outside the consolidated entity. Thus, the entire portion on Shaw's books should be included in the 12/31/02 consolidated financial statements. Therefore, answer (d) is correct.

16.   (**B**) When preparing consolidated financial statements, the objective is to restate the accounts as if the intercompany transactions had not occurred. As a result of the sale of the equipment, Poe recorded depreciation expense of $12,000 ($36,000 ÷ 3 years). For consolidated purposes, depreciation must be computed based on the cost of the asset to the consolidated entity, which is the cost ($30,000) of the asset to Shaw. Therefore, depreciation expense should be $5,000 ($30,000 ÷ 6 yrs.) on the consolidated income statement.

Problem 2

1.   (**A**) The total of cash on each entity's books equals the total for the consolidated entity.

2.   (**B**) The amount shown for equipment on the consolidated balance sheet is less than the sum of the amounts on Purl's and Strand's unconsolidated balance sheets because on an upstream intercompany transaction the parent's share (90%) of the gain would be eliminated. The equipment now on the parent's books would be reduced on the worksheet by subtracting 90% of the gain not realized through depreciation from equipment.

3.   (**E**) The investment in subsidiary would be eliminated in the process of consolidation in the same entry in which the subsidiary's equity accounts are eliminated.

4.   (**F**) Minority interest is presented only in the consolidated balance sheet.

5.   (**C**) Only Purl's common stock would be included in the consolidated balance sheet. All of Strand's common stock would be eliminated. Ten percent would be included in minority interest.

6.   (**C**) Beginning retained earnings would be the same as Purl's. Under the purchase method none of the acquiree's (Strand's) retained earnings is carried forward in recording the business combination.

7.   (**C**) Dividends paid would include only the parent's. The dividends of the subsidiary are all eliminated in consolidation.

8.   (**B**) Cost of goods would be less than the sum of that of Purl and Strand because intercompany profit would be eliminated from cost of goods sold. The amount eliminated would be 100% of the intercompany profit on two thirds of the downstream sale from Purl to Strand.

9.   (**A**) No information is given to indicate that there is any intercompany interest-bearing debt. Thus, the amount included for interest expense in the consolidated financial statements would be the sum of the two entities.

10.   (**B**) Depreciation expense would be less on the consolidated financial statements than the sum of depreciation in each firm's unconsolidated financial statements because the part relating to the intercompany profit on equipment sold upstream would be eliminated in consolidation.

ANSWER OUTLINE

Problem 1 Rationale for and Selected Effects and Adjustments in Preparing Consolidated FS

a. **1.** Consolidated FSs provide information

- Reflecting the status of the companies as a single unit
- Representationally faithful and fair, free of bias
- Comparable with information about other economic entities
- Relevant and complete

2. Changes in consolidated BS upon acquisition

- Include Sox's identifiable assets and liabilities at FV
- Decrease cash by purchase price
- Difference reported as goodwill

3. Effect of intercompany sales is eliminated by reducing the following:

- Sales—intercompany sales
- Ending inventory—markup on goods sold by Plains and held by Sox
- CGS—difference between first two adjustments

b. Effect on BS of

1. Plains

- Establish investment in Sox at purchase price
- Decrease cash by purchase price

2. Sox

- Use push-down accounting
- All assets/liabilities, including goodwill, are restated to fair value at 9/1/02
- Retained earnings eliminated
- APIC adjusted for difference

UNOFFICIAL ANSWER

Problem 1 Rationale for and Selected Effects and Adjustments in Preparing Consolidated FS

a. **1.** Consolidated operating results, cash flows, and financial position are prepared, as if a parent company and its subsidiaries are a single entity, to provide information that

- Reflects the operating results, financial status, and central management ties that bind the companies into a single economic and financial unit.
- Is representationally faithful and fair, without the biases caused by exclusions or netting of data.
- Is comparable with information about other economic entities regardless of the companies' legal framework.
- Is relevant and complete for investors and other parties basing decisions on the data.

2. Plains' September 1, 2002 consolidated balance sheet is changed by including all of Sox's identifiable assets and liabilities at their fair values, and cash is decreased by the purchase price. The excess of purchase price over the fair value of the net assets acquired is reported as goodwill.

3. The effect of the intercompany sales is eliminated from Plains' December 31, 2002 consolidated financial statements by

- Reducing sales by the amount of the intercompany sales.
- Reducing ending inventory by the markup on goods sold by Plains and still held by Sox.

- Reducing cost of goods sold for the difference between the amounts of the two previous adjustments.

b. **1.** The effects on Plains' September 1, 2002 balance sheet, are the establishment of an investment in Sox and a decrease in cash equal to the purchase price.

2. Using push-down accounting, all of Sox's assets and liabilities, including goodwill, are restated to reflect their fair values on September 1, 2002. The retained earnings balance is eliminated. Additional paid-in capital is adjusted for the difference arising from the restatement of the asset and liability balances and the elimination of retained earnings.

ANSWER OUTLINE

Problem 2 Purchase Accounting

a. Accounting for assets and liabilities
Allocate cost of acquired company to assets acquired and liabilities assumed
Identifiable assets acquired and liabilities assumed are recorded at fair values at date of acquisition
Excess of costs over amounts assigned to identifiable assets less liabilities is recorded as goodwill
Regarded as a bargained transaction
Establishes new basis of accounting

b. Accounting for registration fees and direct cost
Registration fees are a reduction of determinable fair value of securities
Direct costs included as part of acquisition cost

c. Reporting in year of combination
Include income of acquired company after date of acquisition
Include revenues and expenses based on cost of acquiring corporation

UNOFFICIAL ANSWER

Problem 2 Purchase Accounting

a. In a purchase, the acquiring corporation should allocate the cost of the acquired company to the assets acquired and liabilities assumed. All identifiable assets acquired and liabilities assumed in the business combination should be recorded at their fair values at date of acquisition. The excess of the cost of the acquired company over the sum of the amounts assigned to identifiable assets acquired less liabilities assumed should be recorded as goodwill. A purchase transaction is regarded as a bargained transaction (i.e., a significant economic event which results from bargaining between independent parties) that establishes a new basis of accounting.

b. In a purchase, the registration fees related to effecting the business combination are a reduction of the otherwise determinable fair value of the securities (usually as a reduction of paid-in capital). The direct costs related to effecting the business combination are included as part of the acquisition cost of the acquired company.

c. In a purchase, the results of operations for the year in which the business combination occurred should include income of the acquired company after the date of acquisition by including the revenues and expenses of the acquired company based on the cost to the acquiring corporation.

DERIVATIVE INSTRUMENTS AND HEDGING ACTIVITIES

A. Foreign Currency Transactions

A foreign currency transaction, according to SFAS 52, is a transaction ". . .denominated in a currency other than the entity's functional currency." Denominated means that the balance is fixed in terms of the number of units of a foreign currency regardless of changes in the exchange rate. When a US company purchases or sells goods or services (or borrows or lends money) to a foreign entity, and the transaction is denominated in foreign currency units, the US company has a foreign currency transaction in which the US dollar is the functional currency. In these situations, the US company has "crossed currencies" and directly assumes the risk of fluctuating foreign exchange rates of the foreign currency units. This exposed foreign currency risk may lead to recognition of foreign exchange transaction gains or losses in the income statement of the US company, as defined in SFAS 52. If the US company pays or receives US dollars in import and export transactions, the risk resulting from fluctuating foreign exchange rates is borne by the foreign supplier or customer, and there is no need to apply the procedures outlined in SFAS 52 to the transaction reported in US dollars on the US company's books.

The following example illustrates the terminology and procedures applicable to the translation of foreign currency transactions. Assume that US Company, an exporter, sells merchandise to a customer in Germany on December 1, 2001, for 10,000 Deutsche Marks (DM). Receipt of DM 10,000 is due on January 31, 2002, and US Company prepares financial statements on December 31, 2001. At the transaction date (December 1, 2001), the spot rate for immediate exchange of foreign currencies indicates that DM 1 is equivalent to $.50. This quotation is referred to as a direct quotation since the exchange rate is stated in terms of a direct translation of the currency in which the debt is measured. To find the US dollar equivalent of this transaction, simply multiply the foreign currency amount, DM 10,000, by $.50 to get $5,000. Occasionally, spot rates are quoted indirectly (e.g., $1 is equivalent to DM 2). In the example used, since $1 is equivalent to DM 2, the foreign currency amount would be divided by 2 to get the US dollar amount of $5,000.

At December 1, 2001, the foreign currency transaction should be recorded by US Company in the following manner:

Accounts receivable (DM)	5,000	
Sales		5,000

The accounts receivable and sales are measured in US dollars at the transaction date using the spot rate at the time of the transaction. While the accounts receivable is measured and reported in US dollars, the receivable is also denominated or fixed in DM. This characteristic can result in foreign exchange transaction gains or losses if the spot rate for DM changes between the transaction date and the date the transaction is settled.

If financial statements are prepared between the transaction date and the settlement date, the FASB requires that receivables and liabilities denominated in a currency other than the functional currency be restated to reflect the spot rates in existence at the balance sheet date. Assume that, on December 31, 2001, the spot rate for DM is DM 1 = $.52. This means that DM 10,000 are worth $5,200, and that the accounts receivable denominated in DM are increased by $200. The following journal entry should be recorded as of December 31, 2001:

Accounts receivable (DM)	200	
Foreign currency transaction gain		200

Note that the sales account, which was credited on the transaction date for $5,000, is not affected by changes in the spot rate. This treatment exemplifies the "two-transaction" viewpoint adopted by the FASB. In other words, making the sale is the result of an operating decision, while bearing the risk of fluctuating spot rates is the result of an investment decision. Therefore, the amount determined as sales revenue at the transaction date should not be altered because of an investment decision to wait until January 31, 2002, for payment of the account. The risk of a foreign exchange transaction loss can be avoided either by demanding immediate payment on December 1 or by entering into a forward exchange contract to hedge the exposed asset (accounts receivable). The fact that US Company in the example did not act in either of these two ways is reflected by the required recognition of foreign currency transaction gains or losses on this type of transaction. These gains or losses are reported on US Company's income statement as financial (nonoperating) items in the period during which the exchange rates changed.

It is also important to note that reporting transaction gains or losses before the transaction is settled results in reporting unrealized gains or losses. This represents an exception to the conventional realization principle which normally applies. This practice also results in a temporary difference between pretax accounting income and taxable income because foreign exchange transaction gains and losses do not enter into the determination of taxable income until the year they are realized. Thus, the recognition of foreign currency transaction gains and losses on unsettled foreign currency transactions results in deferred tax assets/liabilities (depending on whether the temporary differences result in future taxable or future deductible amounts).

To complete the previous illustration, assume that on January 31, 2002, the foreign currency transaction is settled when the spot rate is DM 1 = $.51. Note that the account receivable is still valued at $5,200 at this point. The receipt of DM and their conversion into dollars should be journalized as follows:

Foreign currency (DM)	5,100	
Foreign currency transaction loss	100	
Accounts receivable (DM)		5,200
Cash	5,100	
Foreign currency (DM)		5,100

The net effect of this foreign currency transaction was the receipt of $5,100 from a sale which was measured originally at $5,000. This realized net foreign currency transaction gain of $100 is reported on the income statements of more than one period—a $200 gain in 2001 and a $100 loss in 2002.

The financial statement disclosures required by SFAS 52 include the following:

1. Aggregate transaction gain (loss) that is included in the entity's net income
2. Significant rate changes subsequent to the date of the financial statements including effects on unsettled foreign currency transactions

B. Derivative Instruments and Hedging Activities

Hedging activities and the use of derivative instruments has increased dramatically in the past few years. This increase has raised the concern that inconsistent and/or improper accounting treatment could occur, even in the case of identical hedging/derivative activities. As a result, in June 1998 the FASB issued Statement of Financial Accounting Standards 133, *Accounting for Derivative Instruments and Hedging Activities.* SFAS 137 was issued in June 1999. It delayed the required implementation of SFAS 133 for one year. SFAS 138 was issued in June 2000 and amends several of the specific applications of SFAS 133.

The term "financial instruments and other contracts" is used frequently in SFAS 133. Financial instruments include cash, accounts/notes receivable, accounts/notes payable, bonds, common stock, preferred stock, stock options, foreign currency forward contracts, futures contracts, various financial swaps, etc. Other contracts which are also considered financial instruments meet the following two criteria: (1) the contract imposes a contractual obligation on one party (to the contract) to deliver cash or another financial instrument to the second party, or to exchange financial instruments on potentially unfavorable terms with the second party; (2) the contract conveys a contractual right to the second party to receive cash or another financial instrument from the first party, or to exchange financial instruments on favorable terms with the first party. A glossary of derivative-related terms is presented at the end of this section.

It is from this universe of financial instruments and other contracts that a subset is identified that qualifies as derivative instruments. Derivative instruments are so called because they derive their value as a financial instrument from something outside the instrument itself. For example, a call option to purchase an exchange-traded stock would qualify as a derivative instrument. The value of the call option can only be determined by the market price of the related stock. For example, a call option allows the holder to purchase 1,000 shares of stock at $50 per share, but no determination can be made as to the value of the call option until the stock price is determined. If the market value of the stock is $58 per share, the value of the call option is easily determined to be $8,000 (1,000 shares x [$58 – $50]). In SFAS terminology, the stock price is called the "underlying," the rate or price that exists outside the derivative instrument that is used to determine the value of the derivative instrument. The 1,000 shares of stock is known as the "notional amount," that is the number of units related to the derivative instrument. Both of these terms are important for two reasons: (1) their existence is a necessary condition for determining whether or not a financial instrument or other contract is a derivative instrument; (2) they are determining factors in calculating the "settlement amount" of a derivative instrument. All of these terms are discussed in more detail later in this section, but this basic understanding of derivative instruments may be helpful in working through the remaining definitions, explanations, and examples.

1. **Foundation Principles for SFAS 133**—The basic principles driving the structure of SFAS 133 are

   a. **Fair value measurement.** Derivative instruments meet the definition of assets and liabilities (probable future economic benefits or sacrifices of future economic benefits resulting from past transactions or events). As such they should be reported on an entity's financial statements. The most relevant measure for reporting financial instruments is "fair value." The standard defines fair value as the "current amount at which a financial instrument could be exchanged in a transition between willing parties." As a corollary to this principle, gains and losses that result from the change in the fair value of derivative instruments are **not** assets and liabilities. Therefore, gains and losses should not be reported on the balance sheet but rather should either appear in comprehensive income or be reported in current earnings. The details for reporting gains and losses appear in a subsequent section.

   b. **Hedging.** Certain derivative instruments will qualify under the definition of hedging instruments. Those that qualify will be accounted for using hedge accounting, which generally provides for matching the recognition of gains and losses of the hedging instrument and the hedged asset or liability. (More details about hedge accounting are provided in a later section.) Three kinds of hedges have been defined in the standard.

      (1) Fair value hedge—a hedge of the exposure to changes in the fair value of (a) a recognized asset or liability, or (b) an unrecognized firm commitment.

      (2) Cash flow hedge—a hedge of the exposure to variability in the cash flows of (a) a recognized asset or liability, or (b) a forecasted transaction.

      (3) Foreign currency hedge—a hedge of the foreign currency exposure of (a) an unrecognized firm commitment, (b) an available-for-sale security, (c) a forecasted transaction, or (d) a net investment in a foreign operation.

   If a derivative instrument does not qualify as a hedging instrument under one of the three categories shown above, then its gains or losses must be reported and recognized in current earnings.

2. **Definition of a Derivative Instrument**—SFAS 133 identifies three distinguishing characteristics of a derivative instrument, **all** of which must be present for a financial instrument or other contract to be considered a derivative instrument.

   a. The financial instrument or other contract must contain (a) one or more **underlyings,** and (b) one or more **notional amounts** (or payment provisions or both). An underlying is any financial or physical variable that has either observable changes or objectively verifiable changes. Therefore, underlyings would include traditional financial measures such as commodity prices, interest rates, exchange rates, or indexes related to any of these items. More broadly, measures such as an entity's credit rating, rainfall, or temperature changes would also meet the definition of an underlying.

      Notional amounts are the "number of currency or other units" specified in the financial instrument or other contract. In the case of options, this could include bushels of wheat, shares of stock, etc. The settlement amount of a financial instrument or other contract is calculated using the underlying(s) and notional amount(s) in some combination. Computation of the settlement amount may be as simple as multiplying the fair value of a stock times a specified number of shares. On the other hand, calculation of the settlement amount may require a very complex calculation, involving ratios, stepwise variables, and other leveraging techniques.

      NOTE: The term "notional amount" is sometimes used interchangeably with "settlement amount." Watch to determine if the context in which the term is used is calling for a number of units (notional amount), or a dollar value (settlement amount).

   b. The financial instrument or other contract requires no initial net investment or an initial net investment that is smaller than would be required for other types of contracts that would be expected to have a similar response to changes in market factors. Many derivative instruments require no net investment or simply a premium as compensation for the time value of money. Futures contracts may require the establishment of a margin account with a balance equal to a small percentage (2 - 3%) of the value of the contract. A call option on a foreign currency contract would again only cost a small fraction of the value of the contract. These are typical contracts that would meet this definition and would be included in the definition of derivative instruments.

c. The terms of the financial instrument or other contract do one of the following with regard to settlement:

(1) Require or permit net settlement, either within the contract or by a means outside the contract. Net settlement means that a contract can be settled through the payment of cash rather than the exchange of the specific assets referenced in the contract. This type of settlement typically occurs with a currency swap or an interest rate swap. This definition may have some unanticipated consequences. For example, a contract with a liquidating damages clause for nonperformance, the amount of which is determined by an underlying, would meet this criterion. This is a prime example of the breadth of the definition of a derivative instrument for the purposes of SFAS 133.

(2) Provide for the delivery of an asset that puts the recipient in a position not substantially different from net settlement. This might include a futures contract where one party to the contract delivers an asset, but a "market mechanism" exists (such as an exchange) so that the asset can be readily converted to cash. Convertibility to cash requires an active market and is a determining factor in whether or not a financial instrument or other contract will be treated as a derivative instrument.

3. **Inclusions in and Exclusions from Derivative Instruments**

The following table provides a list of those financial instruments and other contracts that meet the definition of derivative instruments and must be accounted for using SFAS 133, and those that are not required to be accounted for under SFAS 133, either because they do not meet the definition of derivative instruments or because they are specifically excluded from treatment.

Interest rate swaps are one of the most commonly used derivative instruments in business. The following discussion first describes an interest rate swap and then shows how it meets the definition of a derivative instrument. In a common example, two parties may agree to swap interest payments on debt. Usually this occurs when one party (Company F) has issued fixed-rate debt and believes that interest rates are going to drop, while a second party (Company V) has issued variable-rate debt and believes that interest rates are going to rise. In this case, both companies would be interested in exchanging interest payments since both believe that their interest expense would decrease as a result of the swap. Variable-rate interest may be determined by any number of indices (e.g., London Interbank Offered Rate [LIBOR], S&P 500 index, some fixed relationship to T-bill rates, AAA corporate bonds, etc.).

In this example, the notional amount is defined as the principal portion of the debt, which would be the same for both the fixed and variable rate debt. The underlying is the index that determines the variable interest rate, for example, six-month LIBOR. There is no initial net investment required for this contract since the first payment will not occur until the first interest date arrives, and net settlement can be achieved through the payment of interest and principal at the maturity date. Therefore, all three of the criteria for a derivative instrument are present, and SFAS 133 controls the accounting that must be used for this interest rate swap. Similar examples could be developed for the other financial instruments listed in the "included" column below.

Included	*Excluded*
• Options to purchase (call) or sell (put) exchange-traded securities	• Normal purchases and sales (does not exclude "take or pay" contracts with little or no initial net investment and products that are readily convertible to cash)
• Futures contracts	• Equity securities
• Interest rate swaps	• Debt securities
• Currency swaps	• Regular-way (three-day settlement) security trades (this exclusion applies to "to be announced" and "when issued" trades)
• Swaptions (an option on a swap)	• Leases
• Credit indexed contracts	• Mortgage-backed securities
• Interest rate caps/floors/collars	• Employee stock options
	• Royalty agreements and other contracts tied to sales volumes
	• Variable annuity contracts
	• Adjustable rate loans
	• Guaranteed investment contracts
	• Nonexchanged traded contracts tied to physical variables
	• Derivatives that serve as impediments to sales accounting (e.g., guaranteed residual value in a leasing arrangement)

4. **Embedded Derivative Instruments and Bifurcation**

Financial instruments and other contracts may contain features which, if they stood alone, would meet the definition of a derivative instrument. These financial instruments and other contracts are known as "hybrid instruments." This means that there is a basic contract, known as the "host contract," that has an embedded derivative instrument. In these circumstances, the embedded derivative instrument may have to be separated from the host contract, a process known as bifurcation, and treated as if it were a stand-alone instrument. In this case, the host contract (excluding the embedded derivative) would be accounted for in the normal manner (as if it had never contained the embedded derivative), and the now stand-alone derivative instrument would be accounted for using SFAS 133.

Three criteria are used to determine if bifurcation must occur. **All** criteria must be met.

a. The embedded derivative meets the definition of a derivative instrument for the purposes of applying SFAS 133.

b. The hybrid instrument is **not** regularly recorded at fair value, with changes reported in current earnings as they occur under other GAAP. If the hybrid instrument is regularly recorded at fair value, then there is no need to bifurcate the embedded derivative since the same end result is being accomplished already.

c. The economic characteristics and risks of the embedded derivative instrument are **not** "clearly and closely related" to the economic characteristics and risks of the host contract.

Below are listed a number of hybrid instruments that would require bifurcation under SFAS 133.

1. A bond payable with an interest rate based on the S&P 500 index.
2. An equity instrument (stock) with a call option, allowing the issuing company to buy back the stock.
3. An equity instrument with a put option, requiring the issuing company to buy back the stock at the request of the holder.
4. A loan agreement that permits the debtor to pay off the loan prior to its maturity with the loan payoff penalty based on the short-term T-bill rates.
5. Loans with term-extending options whose values are based on the prime rate at the time of the extension.
6. Convertible debt (from the investor's viewpoint)

It should be clear from the brief list shown above that many existing financial instruments that did not require any special accounting treatment prior to SFAS 133 will now be viewed as financial instruments with embedded derivative instruments.

5. **Hedging Instruments—General Criteria**

Two primary criteria must be met in order for a derivative instrument to qualify as a hedging instrument.

a. Sufficient documentation must be provided at the beginning of the process to identify at a minimum (1) the objective and strategy of the hedge, (2) the hedging instrument and the hedged item, and (3) how the effectiveness (see below) of the hedge will be assessed on an ongoing basis.

b. The hedge must be "highly effective" throughout its life. Effectiveness is measured by analyzing the hedging instrument's (the derivative instrument) ability to generate changes in fair value that offset the changes in value of the hedged item. At a minimum, its effectiveness will be measured every three months and whenever earnings or financial statements are reported. A "highly effective" hedge has been interpreted to mean that "the cumulative change in the value of the hedging instrument should be between 80 and 125% of the inverse cumulative changes in the fair value or cash flows of the hedged item." (This is a reuse of the definition of "high correlation" from SFAS 80. SFAS 133 does not provide any specific definition for "highly effective," so this definition has been offered as a surrogate.) The method used to assess effectiveness must be used throughout the hedge period and must be consistent with the approach used for managing risk. Similar hedges should usually be assessed for effectiveness in a similar manner unless a different method can be justified. (Even though a hedging instrument may meet the criterion for being highly effective, it may not eliminate variations in reported earnings, because to the extent that a hedging instrument is not 100% effective, the difference in net loss or gain in each period must be reported in current earnings.)

6. **Fair Value Hedges**

   A fair value hedge is the use of a derivative instrument to hedge the exposure to changes in the fair value of an asset or a liability.

   a. **Specific criteria.** The hedged asset/liability must meet certain criteria in order to qualify as a fair value hedge. The hedged item must be either all or a specific portion (e.g., a percentage, a contractual cash flow) of a recognized asset/liability or an unrecognized firm commitment. Both of these situations arise frequently in foreign currency transactions. For example, a company may enter into a firm commitment with a foreign supplier to purchase a piece of equipment, the price of which is denominated in a foreign currency and both the delivery date and the payment date are in the future. The company may decide to hedge the commitment to pay for the equipment in a foreign currency in order to protect itself from currency fluctuations between the firm commitment date and the payment date. For the period between the firm commitment date and the delivery date, the company will be hedging against an unrecognized firm commitment. For the period between the delivery date and the payment date, the company is hedging against a recognized liability. (See Section 9 of this module for the accounting associated with this example.) For an unrecognized firm commitment to qualify it must be (1) binding on both parties, (2) specific with respect to all significant terms, and (3) contain a nonperformance clause that makes performance probable.

   b. **Accounting for a fair value hedge.** Under SFAS 133, gains and losses on the hedged asset/liability and the hedging instrument will be recognized in current earnings.

   EXAMPLE: On 10/1/01, Dover Corp. purchases 20 shares of Porter, Inc. stock at $40. The securities are classified as available-for-sale. The market price moves to $45 by the end of the year. In order to protect itself from a possible decline in the stock value of its available-for-sale security, Dover purchases an at-the-money put option for $300 on 12/31/01. The put option gives Dover the right, but not the obligation, to sell 200 shares of Porter stock at $45 per share, and the option expires on 12/31/03. Dover designates the hedge as a fair value hedge because it is hedging changes in the security's fair value. The fair value of an option is made up of two components, the time value and the intrinsic value. At the time of purchase, the time value is the purchase price of the options and the intrinsic value is $0 (because the option was purchased at-the-money. Over the life of the option, the time value will drop to $0. This is due to the fact that time value relates to the ability to exercise the option over a specified period of time. As the option moves toward the expiration date, the perceived value of the time value portion of the option will decrease as a function of the time value of money (TVM) issues and other market forces. The time value will generally decrease over the life of the option, but not necessarily in a linear fashion. The intrinsic value will vary based on the difference between the current stock price vs. the stock price on the date the option was purchased. As shown in the table below, the intrinsic value of the option increases from $0 to $200 between 12/31/01 and 12/31/02 because the stock price has dropped by $1 (x 200 shares), and the hedge has been effective for that same amount. As can be seen by analyzing the two components of the put option, the market is the primary driver of the value that should be assigned to the option. As is often the case, the intrinsic value of the option is considered to be a "highly effective" hedge against changes in the stock price, while the time value is ineffective and is reflected in current earnings. Additional information is provided below.

Item	1/1/01	12/31/01	12/31/02	12/31/03
Porter stock price	$40	$ 45	$ 44	$ 42
Put option				
Time value		$300	$160	$0
Intrinsic value		$ 0	$200	$600
			(200 x $1)	(200 x $3)

1/1/01

1. Available-for-sale securities   8,000
       Cash   8,000
   Record the purchase of Porter stock (200 x $40).

12/31/01

2. Available-for-sale securities   1,000
       Other comprehensive income   1,000
   Record the unrealized gain on Porter stock (accounting prior to the hedge in accordance with SFAS 115).
   (200 x $5 valuation increase from holding gain to market value)

3. Put option   300
       Cash   300
   Record the purchase of at-the-money put option.

12/31/02

4. Put option   200
       Gain on hedge activity   200
   Record the increase in the intrinsic value (fair value) of the option.

5. Loss on hedge activity   200
      Available-for-sale securities   200
Record the decrease in the fair value of the securities (accounting after the hedge is established) $200 = 200 shares x $1 holding loss.

Note that the $200 gain on hedge activity from the put option is balanced effectively against the $200 loss on hedge activity from the hedged available-for-sale security. SFAS 133 amends SFAS 115 to require that the portion of the unrealized holding gain or loss on an available-for-sale security that is designated as a hedged item in a fair value hedge be recognized in earnings during the period of the hedge. This is why the $200 holding loss on the available-for-sale securities is recognized in the period's earnings.

6. Loss on hedge activity   140
      Put option   140
Record the loss related to the time value of the option. $140 = $300 – $160

12/31/03

7. Put option   400
      Gain on hedge activity   400
Record the increase in the intrinsic value of the put option.

8. Loss on hedge activity   400
      Available-for-sale securities   400
To record the decrease in the fair value of the securities (accounting after the hedge is established); $400 = 200 shares x $2 holding loss on available-for-sale securities.

9. Loss on hedge activity   160
      Put option   160
Record the loss related to the time value of the option. $140 = $300 – $160

10. Cash   9,000
      Put option   600
      Available-for-sale securities   8,400
Record the exercise of the put option (sell the 200 shares of stock @ $45) and close out the put option investment.

11. Other comprehensive income   1,000
      Gain on Porter stock   1,000
To reclassify the unrealized holding gain recognized in entry 2., from other comprehensive income to earnings, because the securities were sold.

7. Cash Flow Hedges

Cash flow hedges use derivative instruments to hedge the exposure to variability in expected future cash flows.

a. **Specific criteria.** Additional criteria must be met in order to qualify as a cash flow hedge. The primary criterion is that the hedged asset/liability and the hedging instrument must be "linked." Linking is established if the basis (the specified rate or index) for the change in cash flows is the same for the hedged asset/liability and the hedging instrument. Cash flows do not have to be identical, but they must meet the highly effective threshold discussed above. In addition, if the hedged asset/liability is a **forecasted transaction,** it must be considered **probable,** based on appropriate facts and circumstances (i.e., past history). Also, if the forecasted hedged asset/liability is a series of transactions, they must "share the same risk exposure." Purchases of a particular product from the same supplier over a period of time would meet this requirement.

b. **Accounting for a cash flow hedge.** Under SFAS 133, for the hedging instrument (1) the effective portion is reported in other comprehensive income, and (2) the ineffective portion and/or excluded components are reported on a cumulative basis to reflect the lesser of (1) the cumulative gain/loss on the derivative since the creation of the hedge, or (2) the cumulative gain/loss from the change in expected cash flows from the hedged instrument since the creation of the hedge.

The above amounts need to be adjusted to reflect any reclassification of other comprehensive income to current earnings. This will occur when the hedged asset/liability affects earnings (e.g., when hedged inventory is sold and the cost of inventory passes through to cost of goods sold).

EXAMPLE: A commercial bakery believes that wheat prices may increase over the next few months. To protect itself against this risk, the bakery purchases call options on wheat futures to hedge the price risk of their forecasted inventory purchases. If wheat prices increase, the profit on the purchased call options will offset the higher price the bakery must pay for the wheat. If wheat prices decline, the bakery will lose the premium it paid for the call options, but can then buy the wheat at the lower price. On June 1, 2001, the bakery pays a premium of $350 to purchase a September 30, 2001 call for 1,000 bushels of wheat at the futures price of $16.60 per bushel. The call option is considered a cash flow hedge because the designated risk that is being hedged is the risk of changes in the cash flows relating to changes in the purchase price of the wheat. On September 30, the bakery settles its call options and purchases wheat on the open market. Pertinent wheat prices are shown below.

Spot price (June 1)	$16.50
Futures price (as of June 1 for September 30)	$16.60
Spot price (September 30)	$17.30

June 1

1.	Call option	350	
	Cash		350

Record the purchase of the call option.

September 30

2.	Loss on hedge activity	350	
	Call option		350

Record the expiration (change in time value) of the call option.

3.	Call option	700	
	Other comprehensive income		700

Record the increase in intrinsic value of the call option.
$700 = {1,000 bushels x [$17.30 (the spot price per bushel on September 30) – $16.60 (the futures price as of June 1 for September 30)]}

4.	Cash	700	
	Call option		700

Record the cash settlement of the call option.

5.	Inventory	17,300	
	Cash		17,300

Record the purchase of the wheat at the spot price. $17,300 = 1,000 bushels x $17.30

8. **Foreign Currency Hedges**

   Foreign currency denominated assets/liabilities that arise in the course of normal business are often hedged with offsetting forward exchange contracts. This process, in effect, creates a natural hedge. Normal accounting rules (i.e., SFAS 52) apply, and the FASB decided not to change this accounting treatment in the implementation of SFAS 133. SFAS 133 does specify hedge accounting in four areas related to foreign currency hedges. The application of hedge accounting is generally more restrictive under SFAS 133 than it was under SFAS 52. The four foreign currency hedges under SFAS 133 are discussed below.

   a. **Unrecognized firm commitment.** Either a derivative instrument or a nonderivative financial instrument (such as a receivable in a foreign currency) can be designated as a hedge of an unrecognized firm commitment attributable to changes in foreign currency exchange rates. If the requirements for a fair value hedge are met, then this hedging arrangement can be accounted for as a **fair value hedge,** discussed above.

   b. **Available-for-sale securities.** Prior to SFAS 133, a firm commitment to purchase a trading security and several transactions related to held-to-maturity securities were permitted to use hedging accounting under certain conditions. SFAS 133 has eliminated the use of hedge accounting for both trading and held-to-maturity securities (in many cases hedge accounting wasn't required anyway) and limited the use of hedge accounting to transactions for securities designated as available-for-sale. Derivative instruments can be used to hedge debt or equity available-for-sale securities. However, equity securities must meet two additional criteria.

   (1) They cannot be traded on an exchange denominated in the investor's functional currency.
   (2) Dividends must be denominated in the same foreign currency as is expected to be received on the sale of the security.

   If the above criteria are met, hedging instruments related to available-for-sale securities can be accounted for as **fair value hedges,** discussed above.

   c. **Foreign currency denominated forecasted transactions.** This is an expansion in the permitted use of hedge accounting under SFAS 133. Only derivative instruments can be designated as hedges of foreign currency denominated forecasted transactions. A forecasted export sale with the price denominated in a foreign currency might qualify for this type of hedge treatment. Forecasted transactions are distinguished from firm commitments (discussed in a. above) because the timing of the cash flows remains uncertain. This additional complexity results in hedging instruments related to foreign currency denominated forecasted transactions being accounted for as cash flow hedges, discussed above. Hedge accounting is permissible for transactions between unrelated parties, and under special circumstances (not discussed here) for intercompany transactions.

d. **Net investments in foreign operations.** The accounting for net investments in foreign operations has not changed from the SFAS 52 rules, except that the hedging instrument has to meet the new "effective" criterion. The change in the fair value of the hedging derivative is recorded in other comprehensive income which is then closed to the accumulated other comprehensive income account in the equity section of the balance sheet.

Hedge Accounting under SFAS 133

Type of Hedge—SFAS 133

Attribute	*Fair Value*	*Cash Flow*	*Foreign Currency (FC)*
Types of hedging instruments permitted	Derivatives	Derivatives	Derivatives or nonderivatives depending on the type of hedge
Balance sheet valuation of hedging instrument	Fair value	Fair value	Fair value
Recognition of gain or loss on changes in value of hedging instrument	Currently in earnings	Effective portion currently as a component of other comprehensive income (OCI) and reclassified to earnings in future period(s) that forecasted transaction affects earnings Ineffective portion currently in earnings	**FC denominated firm commitment** Currently in earnings **Available-for-sale security (AFS)** Currently in earnings **Forecasted FC transaction** Same as cash flow hedge **Net investment in a foreign operation** OCI as part of the cumulative translation adjustment to the extent it is effective as a hedge

Attribute	*Fair Value*	*Cash Flow*	*Foreign Currency (FC)*
Recognition of gain or loss on changes in the fair value of the hedged item	Currently in earnings	Not applicable; these hedges are not associated with recognized assets or liabilities	**FC denominated firm commitment** Currently in earnings **Available-for-sale security (AFS)** Currently in earnings **Forecasted FC transaction** Not applicable; same as cash flow hedge

9. **Forward Exchange Contracts**

It was stated previously that foreign currency transaction gains and losses on assets and liabilities which are denominated in a currency other than the functional currency can be hedged if a US company enters into a forward exchange contract. The following example shows how a forward exchange contract can be used as a hedge, first against a firm commitment and then, following delivery date, as a hedge against a recognized liability. The general rule for estimating the fair value of forward exchange contracts is to use the forward exchange rate for the remaining term of the contract.

EXAMPLE: Baker Simon, Inc. enters into a firm commitment with Dempsey Ing., Inc. of Germany, on October 1, 2001, to purchase a computerized robotic system for DM 6,000,000. The system will be delivered on March 1, 2002, with payment due sixty days after delivery (April 30, 2002). Baker Simon, Inc. decides to hedge this foreign currency firm commitment and enters into a forward exchange contract on the firm commitment date to receive DM 6,000,000 on the payment date. The applicable exchange rates are shown in the table below.

Date	*Spot rates*	*Forward rates for April 30, 2002*
October 1, 2001	*DM 1 = $.55*	*DM 1 = $ .57*
December 31, 2001	*DM 1 = $.58*	*DM 1 = $.589*
March 1, 2002	*DM 1 = $.58*	*DM 1 = $.585*
April 30, 2002	*DM 1 = $.60*	

The following example separately presents both the forward contract receivable and the dollars payable liability in order to show all aspects of the forward contract. For financial reporting purposes, most companies present just the net fair value of the forward contract, which would be the difference between the current value of the forward contract receivable and the dollars payable accounts.

The transactions which reflect the forward exchange contract, the firm commitment and the acquisition of the asset and retirement of the related liability appear as follows:

Forward contract entries

(1)   10/1/01 (forward rate for 4/30/01 DM 1 = $.57)

Forward contract receivable (DM)	3,420,000	
Dollars payable		3,420,000

This entry recognizes the existence of the forward exchange contract using the gross method. Under the net method, this entry would not appear at all, since the fair value of the forward contract is zero when the contract is initiated. The amount is calculated using the 10/1/01 forward rate for 4/30/02 (DM 6,000,000 x $.57 = $3,420,000). Note that the **net** fair value of the forward exchange contact on 10/1/01 is zero because there is an exact amount offset of the forward contract receivable with the dollars payable liability.

(2)   12/31/01 (forward rate for 4/30/01 DM 1 = $.589)

Forward contract receivable (DM)	114,000	
Gain on hedge activity		114,000

DM 6,000,000 x ($ .589 – $ .57) = $114,000. The dollar values for this entry reflect, among other things, the change in the forward rate from 10/1/01 to 12/31/01. However, the actual amount recorded as gain or loss (gain in this case) will be determined by all market factors.

(4)   3/1/02 (forward rate for 4/30/02 DM 1 = $.585)

Loss on hedge activity	24,000	
Forward contract receivable (DM)		24,000

DM 6,000,000 x ($ .585 – $ .589) = $24,000. These entries again will be driven by market factors, and they are calculated the same way as entries (2) and (3) above. Notice that the decline in the forward rate from 12/31/01 to 3/1/02 resulted in a loss against the forward contract receivable and a gain against the firm commitment.

Hedge against firm commitment entries

(3)   12/31/01

Loss on hedge activity	114,000	
Firm commitment		114,000

The dollar values for this entry are identical to entry (2), reflecting the fact that the hedge is highly effective (100%) and also the fact that the market recognizes the same factors in this transaction as for entry (2). This entry reflects the first use of the firm commitment account, a temporary liability account pending the receipt of the asset against which the firm commitment has been hedged.

(5)   3/1/02

Firm commitment	24,000	
Gain on hedge activity		24,000

Forward contract entries

Hedge against firm commitment entries

(6)   3/1/02 (spot rate DM 1 = $.58)

Equipment	3,390,000	
Firm commitment	90,000	
Accounts payable (DM)		3,480,000

This entry records the receipt of the equipment (recorded at fair value determined on a discounted net present value basis), the elimination of the temporary liability account (firm commitment), and the recognition of the payable, calculated using the spot rate on the date of receipt (DM 6,000,000 x $.58 = $3,480,000).

(7)   4/30/02 (spot rate DM 1 = $.60))

Forward contract receivable (DM)	90,000	
Gain on forward contract		90,000

The gain or loss (gain in this case) on the forward contract is calculated using the change in the forward to the spot rate from 3/1/02 to 4/30/02 [DM 6,000,000 x ($.60 – $.585) = $90,000]

(9)   4/30/02

Dollars payable	3,420,000	
Cash		3,420,000
Foreign currency units (DM)	3,600,000	
Forward contract receivable (DM)		3,600,000

This entry reflects the settlement of the forward contract at the 10/1/01 contracted forward rate (DM 6,000,000 x $.57 = $3,420,000) and the receipt of foreign currency units valued at the spot rate (DM 6,000,000 x $.60 = $3,600,000).

(8)   4/30/02

Transaction loss	120,000	
Accounts payable (DM)		120,000

The transaction loss related to the accounts payable reflects only the change in the spot rates and ignores the accrual of interest. [DM 6,000,000 x ($.60 – $.58) = $120,000]

(10)

Accounts payable (DM)	3,600,000	
Foreign currency units		3,600,000

This entry reflects the use of the foreign currency units to settle the account payable.

In the case of using a forward exchange contract to speculate in a specific foreign currency, the general rule to estimate the fair value of the forward contract is to use the forward exchange rate for the remainder of the term of the forward contract.

10. Disclosures

Disclosures related to financial instruments, both derivative and nonderivative, that are used as hedging instruments must include the following information: (1) objectives and the strategies for achieving them, (2) context to understand the instrument, (3) risk management policies, and (4) a list of hedged instruments. These disclosures have to be separated by type of hedge and reported every time a complete set of financial statements is issued. In addition, disclosure requirements exist for derivative instruments that are not designated as hedging instruments.

11. Fair Value and Concentration of Credit Risk Disclosures of Financial Instruments other than Derivatives

SFAS 107, as amended by SFAS 133, requires disclosure of fair values of financial instruments for which it is practicable to estimate fair value (see outline of SFAS 107). This requirement pertains to both asset and liability financial instruments, whether recognized in the balance sheet or not.

A sample footnote is provided below. Additionally, a summary of SFAS 107 is presented in the following chart.

SFAS 107 requires disclosure of concentrations of credit risk. Credit risk is the risk that a loss will occur because parties to the instrument do not perform as expected. Such concentrations exist when a number of an entity's financial instruments are associated with similar activities and economic characteristics that could be affected by changes in similar conditions (e.g., an entity whose principal activity is to supply parts to one type of industry).

Lenaburg, Inc.
Notes to Financial Statements
FAIR VALUE OF FINANCIAL INSTRUMENTS HELD OR ISSUED FOR PURPOSES OTHER THAN TRADING (in thousands)

December 31, 2001

	Carrying amount	Fair value
Assets		
Cash and cash equivalents	32,656	32,656
Long-term investments	12,719	14,682
Liabilities		
Short-term debt	3,223	3,223
Long-term debt	150,000	182,500

FAIR VALUE OF FINANCIAL INSTRUMENTS HELD FOR TRADING PURPOSES (in thousands)

December 31, 2001

	Carrying amount	Fair value
Assets		
Short-term investments	4,074	4,074

Cash and cash equivalents—The carrying amount of cash and cash equivalents approximates fair value due to their short-term maturities.

Long-term investments—The fair value is estimated based on quoted market prices for these or similar investments.

Short-term investments—The Company holds US Treasury notes and highly liquid investments for trading purposes. The carrying value of these instruments approximates fair value.

Short- and long-term debt—The fair value of short- and long-term debt is estimated using quoted market prices for the same or similar instruments or on the current rates offered to the Company for debt of equivalent remaining maturities.

Summary of Disclosure Standards for Financial Instruments other than Derivatives

SFAS	Pertains to	Required disclosures
107	Financial Instruments (Assets and Liabilities), Whether on Balance Sheet or Not	• Fair value, when practicable to estimate • Information pertinent to estimating fair value (carrying value, effective interest rate, maturity) if not practicable to estimate, and reasons for impracticability of estimation • Distinguish between instruments held or issued for trading purposes and instruments held or issued for purposes other than trading • Do not net or aggregate fair values of derivative financial instruments with fair values of nonderivative financial instruments or with fair values of other derivative financial instruments
	Financial Instruments with Concentrations of Credit Risk	• Information about similar activity, region, or economic characteristics • Maximum potential accounting loss • Information about collateral or security requirements

Glossary

SFAS 133 defines a number of important terms which are used to describe various derivative instruments and hedging relationships. These include the following:

At the money. An at-the-money option is one in which the price of the underlying is equal to the strike or exercise price.

Bifurcation. The process of separating an embedded derivative from its host contract. This process is necessary so that hybrid instruments (a financial instrument or other contract that contains an embedded derivative) can be separated into their component parts, each being accounted for using the appropriate valuation techniques.

Call option. An American call option provides the holder the right to acquire an underlying at an exercise or strike price, anytime during the option term. A premium is paid by the holder for the right to benefit from the appreciation in the underlying.

Derivative instruments. In SFAS 133, derivative instruments are defined by their three distinguishing characteristics. Specifically, derivative instruments are financial instruments or other contracts that have

1. One or more underlyings and one or more notional amounts (or payment provisions or both);
2. No initial net investment or a smaller net investment than required for contracts expected to have a similar response to market changes; and
3. Terms that require or permit

    a. Net settlement
    b. Net settlement by means outside the contract
    c. Delivery of an asset that results in a position substantially the same as net settlement

Discount or premium on a forward contract. The foreign currency amount of the contact multiplied by the difference between the contracted forward rate and the spot rate at the date of inception of the contract.

Embedded derivative. A feature on a financial instrument or other contract, which if the feature stood alone, would meet the definition of a derivative.

Fair value. Defined as the amount at which the asset or liability could be bought or settled in an arm's-length transaction; measured by reference to market prices or estimated by net present value of future cash flows, options pricing models, or by other techniques.

Financial instrument. Financial instruments include cash, accounts/notes receivable, accounts/notes payable, bonds, common stock, preferred stock, stock options, foreign currency forward contracts, futures contracts, various financial swaps, etc. Other contracts which are also considered financial instruments meet the following two criteria: (1) the contract imposes a contractual obligation on one party (to the contract) to deliver cash or another financial instrument to the second party or to exchange potentially unfavorable terms with the second party; (2) the contract conveys a contractual right to the second party to receive cash or another financial instrument from the first party or to exchange financial instruments on favorable terms with the first party.

Firm commitment. An agreement with an unrelated party, binding on both, usually legally enforceable, specifying all significant terms and including a disincentive for nonperformance sufficient to make performance likely.

Forecasted transaction. A transaction expected to occur for which there is no firm commitment, and thus, which gives the entity no present rights or obligations. Under SFAS 133, forecasted transactions can be hedged and special hedge accounting can be applied.

Foreign currency transactions. Transactions whose terms are denominated in a currency other than the entity's functional currency. Foreign currency transactions arise when an enterprise (a) buys or sells on credit goods or services whose prices are denominated in foreign currency, (b) borrows or lends funds and the amounts payable or receivable are denominated in foreign currency, (c) is a party to an unperformed forward exchange contract, or (d) for other reasons, acquires or disposes of assets, or incurs or settles liabilities denominated in foreign currency.

Forward contract. A forward contract is an agreement between two parties to buy and sell a specific quantity of a commodity, foreign currency, or financial instrument at an agreed-upon price, with delivery and/or settlement at a designated future date. Because a forward contract is not formally regulated by an organized exchange, each party to the contract is subject to the default of the other party.

Forward exchange contract. An agreement to exchange at a specified future date currencies of different countries at a specified rate (forward rate).

Futures contract. A futures contract is a forward-based contract to make or take delivery of a designated financial instrument, foreign currency, or commodity during a designated period, at a specified price or yield. The contract frequently has provisions for cash settlement. A futures contract is traded on a regulated exchange and, therefore, involves less credit risk than a forward contract.

In the money. A call option is in the money if the price of the underlying is greater than the strike or exercise price of the underlying.

Initial net investment. A derivative instrument is one where the initial net investment is zero or is less than the notional amount (possibly plus a premium or minus a discount). This characteristic refers to the relative amount of investment. Derivative instruments allow the opportunity to take part in the rate or price change without owning the asset or owing the liability. If an amount approximating the notional amount must be invested or received, it is not a derivative instrument. The two basic forms of derivative instruments are futures contracts and options. The futures contract involves little or no initial net investment. Settlement is usually near the delivery date. Call options, when purchased, require a premium payment that is less than the cost of purchasing the equivalent number of shares. Even though this distinguishing characteristic is the result of only one of the parties, it determines the application for both.

Intrinsic value. With regard to call (put) options, it is the larger of zero or the spread between the stock (exercise) price and the exercise (stock) price.

LIBOR. London Interbank Offer Rate. A widely used measure of average interest rates at a point in time.

Net settlements. To qualify as derivative instruments, one of the following settlement criteria must be met:

1. No delivery of an asset equal to the notional amount is required. For example, an interest rate swap does not involve delivery of the instrument in which the notional amount is expressed.
2. Delivery of an asset equal to the notional amount is required of one of the parties, but an exchange (or other market mechanism, institutional arrangement or side agreement) facilitates net settlement. For example, a call option has this attribute.
3. Delivery by one of the parties of an asset equal to the notional amount is required but the asset is either readily convertible to cash (as with a contract for the delivery of a marketable equity security), or is required but that asset is itself a derivative instrument (as is the case for a swaption [an option on a swap]).

This characteristic means that the derivative instrument can be settled by a net delivery of assets (the medium of exchange does not have to be cash). Contract terms based on changes in the price or rate of the notional that implicitly or explicitly require or permit net settlement qualify. Situations where one of the parties can liquidate their net investment or be relieved of the contract rights or obligations without significant transaction costs because of a market arrangement (broadly interpreted) or where the delivered asset can be readily converted to cash also meet the requirements for net settlement. It is assumed that an exchange traded security is readily converted to cash. Thus, commodity-based contracts for gold, oil, wheat, etc. are now included under this standard. The convertible to cash condition requires an active market and consideration of interchangeability and transaction volume. Determining if delivery of a financial asset or liability equal to the notional amount is a derivative instrument may depend upon whether it is readily convertible into cash. Different accounting will result if the notional is not readily converted to cash. Using the notional as collateral does not necessarily mean it is readily convertible to cash.

Notional amount. The notional amount (or payment provision) is the referenced associated asset or liability. A notional amount is commonly a number of units such as shares of stock, principal amount, face value, stated value, basis points, barrels of oil, etc. It may be that amount plus a premium or minus a discount. The interaction of the price or rate (underlying) with the referenced associated asset or liability (notional amount) determines whether settlement is required and, if so, the amount.

Out of the money. A call option is out of the money if the strike or exercise price is greater than the price of the underlying. A put option is out of the money if the price of the underlying is greater than the strike or exercise price.

Put option. An American put option provides the holder the right to sell the underlying at an exercise or strike price, anytime during the option term. A gain accrues to the holder as the market price of the underlying falls below the strike price.

Swap. A swap is a forward-based contract or agreement generally between two counterparties to exchange streams of cash flows over a specified period in the future.

Swaption. A swaption is an option on a swap that provides the holder with the right to enter into a swap at a specified future date at specified terms (freestanding option on a swap) or to extend or terminate the life of an existing swap (embedded option on a swap). These derivatives have characteristics of an option and an interest rate swap.

Time value. The difference between an option's price and its intrinsic value.

Transaction gain or loss. Transaction gains or losses result from a change in exchange rates between the functional currency and the currency in which a foreign currency transaction is denominated. They represent an increase or decrease in (a) the actual functional currency cash flows realized upon settlement of foreign currency transactions, and (b) the expected functional currency cash flows on unsettled foreign currency transactions.

Underlyings. An underlying is commonly a specified price or rate such as a stock price, interest rate, currency rate, commodity price, or a related index. However, any variable (financial or physical) with (1) observable changes or (2) objectively verifiable changes such as a credit rating, insurance index, climatic or geological condition (temperature, rainfall) qualifies. Unless it is specifically excluded, a contract based on any qualifying variable is accounted for under SFAS 133 if it has the distinguishing characteristics stated above.

MULTIPLE-CHOICE QUESTIONS (1-46)

1. On September 1, 2002, Bain Corp. received an order for equipment from a foreign customer for 300,000 local currency units (LCU) when the US dollar equivalent was $96,000. Bain shipped the equipment on October 15, 2002, and billed the customer for 300,000 LCU when the US dollar equivalent was $100,000. Bain received the customer's remittance in full on November 16, 2002, and sold the 300,000 LCU for $105,000. In its income statement for the year ended December 31, 2002, Bain should report as part of net income a foreign exchange transaction gain of

a. $0
b. $4,000
c. $5,000
d. $9,000

2. On September 1, 2001, Cano & Co., a US corporation, sold merchandise to a foreign firm for 250,000 francs. Terms of the sale require payment in francs on February 1, 2002. On September 1, 2001, the spot exchange rate was $.20 per franc. At December 31, 2001, Cano's year-end, the spot rate was $.19, but the rate increased to $.22 by February 1, 2002, when payment was received. How much should Cano report as foreign exchange transaction gain or loss as part of 2001 income?

a. $0.
b. $2,500 loss.
c. $5,000 gain.
d. $7,500 gain.

3. Lindy, a US corporation, bought inventory items from a supplier in Germany on November 5, 2001, for 100,000 marks, when the spot rate was $.4295. At Lindy's December 31, 2001 year-end, the spot rate was $.4245. On January 15, 2002, Lindy bought 100,000 marks at the spot rate of $.4345 and paid the invoice. How much should Lindy report as part of net income for 2001 and 2002 as foreign exchange transaction gain or loss?

	2001	*2002*
a.	$ 500	$(1,000)
b.	$0	$ (500)
c.	$ (500)	$0
d.	$(1,000)	$ 500

4. Hunt Co. purchased merchandise for £300,000 from a vendor in London on November 30, 2001. Payment in British pounds was due on January 30, 2002. The exchange rates to purchase one pound were as follows:

	November 30, 2001	December 31, 2001
Spot-rate	$1.65	$1.62
30-day rate	1.64	1.59
60-day rate	1.63	1.56

In its December 31, 2001, income statement, what amount should Hunt report as foreign exchange transaction gain as part of net income?

a. $12,000
b. $ 9,000
c. $ 6,000
d. $0

5. Ball Corp. had the following foreign currency transactions during 2002:

• Merchandise was purchased from a foreign supplier on January 20, 2002, for the US dollar equivalent of $90,000. The invoice was paid on March 20, 2002, at the US dollar equivalent of $96,000.

• On July 1, 2002, Ball borrowed the US dollar equivalent of $500,000 evidenced by a note that was payable in the lender's local currency on July 1, 2004. On December 31, 2002, the US dollar equivalents of the principal amount and accrued interest were $520,000 and $26,000, respectively. Interest on the note is 10% per annum.

In Ball's 2002 income statement, what amount should be included as foreign exchange transaction loss as part of net income?

a. $0
b. $ 6,000
c. $21,000
d. $27,000

6. On November 30, 2002, Tyrola Publishing Company, located in Colorado, executed a contract with Ernest Blyton, an author from Canada, providing for payment of 10% royalties on Canadian sales of Blyton's book. Payment is to be made in Canadian dollars each January 10 for the previous year's sales. Canadian sales of the book for the year ended December 31, 2002, totaled $50,000 Canadian. Tyrola paid Blyton his 2002 royalties on January 10, 2003. Tyrola's 2002 financial statements were issued on February 1, 2003. Spot rates for Canadian dollars were as follows:

November 30, 2001	$.87
January 1, 2002	$.88
December 31, 2002	$.89
January 10, 2003	$.90

How much should Tyrola accrue for royalties payable at December 31, 2002?

a. $4,350
b. $4,425
c. $4,450
d. $4,500

7. Shore Co. records its transactions in US dollars. A sale of goods resulted in a receivable denominated in Japanese yen, and a purchase of goods resulted in a payable denominated in French francs. Shore recorded a foreign exchange transaction gain on collection of the receivable and an exchange transaction loss on settlement of the payable. The exchange rates are expressed as so many units of foreign currency to one dollar. Did the number of foreign currency units exchangeable for a dollar increase or decrease between the contract and settlement dates?

	Yen exchangeable for $1	*Francs exchangeable for $1*
a.	Increase	Increase
b.	Decrease	Decrease
c.	Decrease	Increase
d.	Increase	Decrease

8. On October 1, 2002, Mild Co., a US company, purchased machinery from Grund, a German company, with payment due on April 1, 2003. If Mild's 2002 operating income included no foreign exchange transaction gain or loss, then the transaction could have

a. Resulted in an extraordinary gain.
b. Been denominated in US dollars.
c. Caused a foreign currency gain to be reported as a contra account against machinery.
d. Caused a foreign currency translation gain to be reported as other comprehensive income.

9. On October 1, 2002, Velec Co., a US company, contracted to purchase foreign goods requiring payment in francs one month after their receipt at Velec's factory. Title to the goods passed on December 15, 2002. The goods were still in transit on December 31, 2002. Exchange rates were one dollar to twenty-two francs, twenty francs, and twenty-one francs on October 1, December 15, and December 31, 2002, respectively. Velec should account for the exchange rate fluctuation in 2002 as

    a. A loss included in net income before extraordinary items.
    b. A gain included in net income before extraordinary items.
    c. An extraordinary gain.
    d. An extraordinary loss.

10. Derivatives are financial instruments that derive their value from changes in a benchmark based on any of the following except

    a. Stock prices.
    b. Mortgage and currency rates.
    c. Commodity prices.
    d. Discounts on accounts receivable.

11. Derivative instruments are financial instruments or other contracts that must contain

    a. One or more underlyings, **or** one or more notional amounts.
    b. No initial net investment or smaller net investment than required for similar response contacts.
    c. Terms that do not require or permit net settlement or delivery of an asset.
    d. All of the above.

12. The basic purpose of derivative financial instruments is to manage some kind of risk such as all of the following except

    a. Stock price movements.
    b. Interest rate variations.
    c. Currency fluctuations.
    d. Uncollectibility of accounts receivables.

13. Which of the following statements is(are) true regarding derivative financial instruments?

  I. Derivative financial instruments should be measured at fair value and reported in the balance sheet as assets or liabilities.
  II. Gains and losses on derivative instruments not designated as hedging activities should be reported and recognized in earnings in the period of the change in fair value.

    a. I only.
    b. II only.
    c. Both I and II.
    d. Neither I nor II.

14. Which of the following is an underlying, according to SFAS 133?

    a. A credit rating.
    b. A security price.
    c. An average daily temperature.
    d. All of the above could be underlyings.

15. If the price of the underlying is greater than the strike or exercise price of the underlying, the call option is

    a. At the money.
    b. In the money.

    c. On the money.
    d. Out of the money.

16. Which of the following is **not** a distinguishing characteristic of a derivative instrument?

    a. Terms that require or permit net settlement.
    b. Must be "highly effective" throughout its life.
    c. No initial net investment.
    d. One or more underlyings and notional amounts.

17. An example of a notional amount is

    a. Number of barrels of oil.
    b. Interest rates.
    c. Currency swaps.
    d. Stock prices.

18. Disclosures related to financial instruments, both derivative and nonderivative, used as hedging instruments must include

    a. A list of hedged instruments.
    b. Maximum potential accounting loss.
    c. Objectives and strategies for achieving them.
    d. Only a. and c.

19. Which of the following financial instruments or other contracts is not specifically excluded from the definition of derivative instruments in SFAS 133?

    a. Leases.
    b. Call (put) option.
    c. Adjustable rate loans.
    d. Equity securities.

20. Which of the following is **not** a derivative instrument?

    a. Futures contracts.
    b. Credit indexed contracts.
    c. Interest rate swaps.
    d. Variable annuity contracts.

21. Which of the following criteria must be met for bifurcation to occur?

    a. The embedded derivative meets the definition of a derivative instrument.
    b. The hybrid instrument is regularly recorded at fair value.
    c. Economic characteristics and risks of the embedded instrument are "clearly and closely" related to those of the host contract.
    d. All of the above.

22. Financial instruments sometimes contain features that separately meet the definition of a derivative instrument. These features are classified as

    a. Swaptions.
    b. Notional amounts.
    c. Embedded derivative instruments.
    d. Underlyings.

23. The process of bifurcation
    a. Protects an entity from loss by entering into a transaction.
    b. Includes entering into agreements between two counterparties to exchange cash flows over specified period of time in the future.
    c. Is the interaction of the price or rate with an associated asset or liability.
    d. Separates an embedded derivative from its host contract.

24. Hedge accounting is permitted for all of the following types of hedges except
    a. Trading securities.
    b. Unrecognized firm commitments.
    c. Available-for-sale securities.
    d. Net investments in foreign operations.

25. Which of the following is a general criterion for a hedging instrument?
    a. Sufficient documentation must be provided at the beginning of the process.
    b. Must be "highly effective" only in the first year of the hedge's life.
    c. Must contain a nonperformance clause that makes performance probable.
    d. Must contain one or more underlyings.

26. For an unrecognized firm commitment to qualify as a hedged item it must
    a. Be binding on both parties.
    b. Be specific with respect to all significant terms.
    c. Contain a nonperformance clause that makes performance probable.
    d. All of the above.

27. A hedge of the exposure to changes in the fair value of a recognized asset or liability, or an unrecognized firm commitment, is classified as a
    a. Fair value hedge.
    b. Cash flow hedge.
    c. Foreign currency hedge.
    d. Underlying.

28. Gains and losses on the hedged asset/liability and the hedged instrument for a fair value hedge will be recognized
    a. In current earnings.
    b. In other comprehensive income.
    c. On a cumulative basis from the change in expected cash flows from the hedged instrument.
    d. On the balance sheet either as an asset or a liability.

29. Gains and losses of the effective portion of a hedging instrument will be recognized in current earnings in each reporting period for which of the following?

	Fair value hedge	Cash flow hedge
a.	Yes	No
b.	Yes	Yes
c.	No	No
d.	No	Yes

30. Which of the following risks are inherent in an interest rate swap agreement?
    I. The risk of exchanging a lower interest rate for a higher interest rate.
    II. The risk of nonperformance by the counterparty to the agreement.

    a. I only.
    b. II only.
    c. Both I and II.
    d. Neither I nor II.

31. According to SFAS 133, which of the following meet the definition of assets and/or liabilities?

	Derivative instruments	G/L on the fair value of derivatives
a.	Yes	No
b.	No	Yes
c.	Yes	Yes
d.	No	No

32. Which of the following is **not** a type of foreign currency hedge?
    a. A forecasted transaction.
    b. An available-for-sale security.
    c. A recognized asset or liability.
    d. An unrecognized firm commitment.

33. Which of the following foreign currency transactions is not accounted for using hedge accounting?
    a. Available-for-sale securities.
    b. Unrecognized firm commitments.
    c. Net investments in foreign operations.
    d. Foreign currency denominated forecasted transactions.

Items 34 through 37 are based on the following:

On December 12, 2002, Imp Co. entered into three forward exchange contracts, each to purchase 100,000 francs in ninety days. The relevant exchange rates are as follows:

	Spot rate	Forward rate (for March 12, 2003)
November 30, 2002	$.87	$.89
December 12, 2002	.88	.90
December 31, 2002	.92	.93

34. Imp entered into the first forward contract to hedge a purchase of inventory in November 2002, payable in March 2003. At December 31, 2002, what amount of foreign currency transaction gain from this forward contract should Imp include in net income?
    a. $0
    b. $ 3,000
    c. $ 5,000
    d. $10,000

35. At December 31, 2002, what amount of foreign currency transaction loss should Imp include in income from the revaluation of the Accounts Payable of 100,000 francs incurred as a result of the purchase of inventory at November 30, 2002, payable in March 2003?
    a. $0
    b. $3,000
    c. $4,000
    d. $5,000

36. Imp entered into the second forward contract to hedge a commitment to purchase equipment being manufactured to Imp's specifications. The expected delivery date is March 2003 at which time settlement is due to the manufacturer. The hedge qualifies as a fair value hedge. At December 31, 2002, what amount of foreign currency transaction gain from this forward contract should Imp include in net income?
    a. $0
    b. $ 3,000
    c. $ 5,000
    d. $10,000

37. Imp entered into the third forward contract for speculation. At December 31, 2002, what amount of foreign cur-

rency transaction gain from this forward contract should Imp include in net income?

    a. $0
    b. $ 3,000
    c. $ 5,000
    d. $10,000

38. The risk of an accounting loss from a financial instrument due to possible failure of another party to perform according to terms of the contract is known as

    a. Off-balance-sheet risk.
    b. Market risk.
    c. Credit risk.
    d. Investment risk.

39. Examples of financial instruments with off-balance-sheet risk include all of the following except

    a. Outstanding loan commitments written.
    b. Recourse obligations on receivables.
    c. Warranty obligations
    d. Futures contracts.

40. Off-balance-sheet risk of accounting loss does not result from

    a. Financial instruments recognized as assets entailing conditional rights that result in a loss greater than the amount recognized in the balance sheet.
    b. Financial instruments not recognized as either assets or liabilities yet still expose the entity to risk of accounting loss.
    c. Financial instruments recognized as assets or liabilities where the amount recognized reflects the risk of accounting loss to the entity.
    d. Financial instruments recognized as liabilities that result in an ultimate obligation that is greater than the amount recognized in the balance sheet.

41. If it is **not** practicable for an entity to estimate the fair value of a financial instrument, which of the following should be disclosed?

  I. Information pertinent to estimating the fair value of the financial instrument.
  II. The reasons it is not practicable to estimate fair value.

    a. I only.
    b. II only.
    c. Both I and II.
    d. Neither I nor II.

42. Disclosure requirements for financial instruments include

    a. Method(s) and significant assumptions used in estimating fair value.
    b. Distinction between financial instruments held or issued for trading purposes and purposes other than trading.
    c. A note containing a summary table cross-referencing the location of other financial instruments disclosed in another area of the financial statements.
    d. All of the above should be disclosed.

43. Disclosure of credit risk of financial instruments with off-balance-sheet risk does **not** have to include

    a. The amount of accounting loss the entity would incur should any party to the financial instrument fail to perform.
    b. The entity's policy of requiring collateral or security.
    c. The class of financial instruments held.
    d. The specific names of the parties associated with the financial instrument.

44. Disclosure of information about significant concentrations of credit risk is required for

    a. All financial instruments.
    b. Financial instruments with off-balance-sheet credit risk only.
    c. Financial instruments with off-balance-sheet market risk only.
    d. Financial-instruments with off-balance-sheet risk of accounting loss only.

45. Kline Bank has large amounts of notes receivable from companies with high debt-to-equity ratios as a result of buy-out transactions. Kline is contemplating the following disclosures for the notes receivable in its year-end financial statements:

  I. Information about shared activity, region, or economic characteristic.
  II. A brief description of collateral supporting these financial instruments.

Which of the above disclosures are required under GAAP?

    a. I only.
    b. II only.
    c. Neither I nor II.
    d. Both I and II.

46. Whether recognized or unrecognized in an entity's financial statements, disclosure of the fair values of the entity's financial instruments is required when

    a. It is practicable to estimate those values.
    b. The entity maintains accurate cost records.
    c. Aggregated fair values are material to the entity.
    d. Individual fair values are material to the entity.

OTHER OBJECTIVE QUESTIONS

Problem 1   (15 to 25 minutes)

This question consists of 5 items which represent descriptions or definitions from SFAS 133, *Accounting for Derivative Instruments and Hedging Activities.*

Required:

Select the **best** answer for each item from the terms listed in A-E. All terms should be used once.

Answer List

1. Tandem currencies

2. Discount or premium

3. Ineffective portion of a hedge

4. Effective portion of a hedge

5. Forward contract

A. Granted special hedge accounting treatment

B. Resulting gains or losses are taken into current earnings in the period in which they arise.

C. Two currencies other than a functional currency expected to move relative to an entity's functional currency.

D. A hedge against an exposed asset position created by having an account in a denomination other than the functional currency.

E. The difference between the futures rate and the spot rate at the date of a forward contract.

Problem 2   (15 to 25 minutes)

This question consists of ten items which represent descriptions or definitions from SFAS 133, *Accounting for Derivative Instruments and Hedging Activities.*

Required:

Select the **best** answer for each item from the terms listed in A-L. No term should be used more than once.

Answer List

1. Forward contract
2. Forecasted transaction
3. Firm commitment
4. Embedded derivative
5. Intrinsic value
6. Underlying
7. Notional amount
8. Cash flow hedge
9. Fair value hedge
10. Foreign currency hedge

A. A hedge of the exposure to changes in the fair value of a recognized asset or liability or an unrecognized firm commitment.

B. A hedge of the exposure to variability in the cash flows of a forecasted transaction or a recognized asset or liability.

C. A hedge of the foreign currency exposure of an unrecognized firm commitment, an available-for-sale security, a forecasted transaction, or a net investment in a foreign operation.

D. Financial instruments that contain features which, if they stood alone, would meet the definition of a derivative instrument.

E. Two or more separate derivatives traded as a set.

F. Commonly a specified price or rate such as a stock price, interest rate, currency rate, commodity price, or a related index.

G. A legally enforceable, binding agreement with an unrelated party, specifying all significant terms and including a disincentive for nonperformance sufficient to make performance likely.

H. The referenced associated asset or liability, commonly a number of units.

I. The difference between an option's price and its intrinsic value.

J. A transaction expected to occur for which there is no firm commitment, which gives the entity no present rights or obligations.

K. With regard to put options, it is the larger of zero or the spread between the exercise price and the stock price.

L. Agreement between two parties to buy and sell a specific quantity of a commodity, foreign currency, or financial instrument at an agreed-upon price, with delivery and/or settlement at a designated future date.

Problem 3   (15 to 25 minutes)

This question consists of 14 items that represent financial instruments and other contracts that may be included in or excluded from the requirements of SFAS 133, *Accounting for Derivative Instruments and Hedging Activities.*

Required:

For the following items, determine if they are (I) included under the requirement of SFAS 133, or (E) excluded from SFAS 133 treatment.

I.   Item meets the definition of a derivative instrument and must be accounted for using SFAS 133.
E.   Item is not required to be accounted for under SFAS 133, either because it does not meet the definition of derivative instrument or because the item is specifically excluded from SFAS 133 treatment.

1. Leases

2. Guaranteed investment contracts

3. Futures contracts

4. Equity securities

5. Credit indexed contracts

6. Mortgage-backed securities

7. Debt securities

8.   Interest rate caps

9.   Swaptions

10. Employee stock options

11. Options to purchase or sell exchange-traded securities

12. Variable annuity contracts

13. Adjustable rate loans

14. Interest rate swaps

Problem 4   (15 to 25 minutes)

This question consists of 12 items that represent descriptions or definitions from SFAS 133, *Accounting for Derivative Instruments and Hedging Activities.*

Required:

Select the **best** answer for each item from the terms listed in A-O. No answer should be used more than once.

Answer List

1. At the money

2. Bifurcation

3. Call option

4. Embedded derivative

5. Forward contract

6. Futures contract

7. In the money

8. Notional amount

9. Out of the money

10. Put option

11. Swap

12. Underlying

A.   An agreement with an unrelated party, binding on both, usually legally enforceable, specifying all significant terms and including a disincentive for nonperformance sufficient to make performance likely.

B.   A call option where the price of the underlying is greater than the strike or exercise price of the underlying.

C.   A feature on a financial instrument or other contract, which if the feature stood alone, would meet the definition of a derivative.

D.   A forward-based contract or agreement generally between two counterparties to exchange streams of cash flows over a specified period in the future.

E.   With regard to call options, it is the larger of zero or the spread between the stock price and the exercise price.

F.   Provides the holder the right to acquire an underlying at an exercise or stock price, anytime during the option term.

G.   An agreement between the two parties to buy and sell a specific quantity of a commodity, foreign currency, or financial instrument at an agreed-upon price, with delivery and/or settlement at a designated future date.

H.   A call option where the strike or exercise price is greater than the price of the underlying.

I.   The process of separating an embedded derivative from its host contract.

J.   The referenced associated asset or liability, commonly a number of units.

K.   A specified price or rate such as a stock price, interest rate, or commodity price.

L.   An option where the price of the underlying is equal to the strike or exercise price.

M.   The difference between an option's price and its intrinsic value.

N.   Provides the holder the right to sell the underlying at an exercise or strike price, anytime during the option term.

O.   A forward-based contract to make or take delivery of a designated financial instrument, foreign currency, or commodity during a designated period, at a specified price or yield.

PROBLEMS

Problem 1   (15 to 25 minutes)

Kaylee Corporation entered into several derivative contracts to manage its risk exposure and has adopted SFAS 133, *Accounting for Derivative Instruments and Hedging Activities.*

Required:

a. What are the three distinguishing characteristics required for a financial instrument to be considered a derivative instrument?

b. What is the primary specific criterion for defining a derivative instrument to be classified as a fair value hedge? How is the gain or loss on fair value hedges accounted for?

c. What is the primary specific criterion for defining a derivative instrument to be classified as a cash flow hedge? How is the gain or loss on cash flow hedges accounted for?

d. One of Kaylee's foreign currency hedges was the use of a foreign currency receivable contract to hedge an unrecognized firm commitment. At the balance sheet date prior to settlement, describe the accounting for the foreign currency receivable contract and the financial instrument aspect of the firm commitment.

e. How are embedded derivative instruments accounted for?

Problem 2   (15 to 25 minutes)

Coyn, CPA, has been approached by Howe, the chief financial officer of Chatham Co. Howe is aware that the Financial Accounting Standards Board is engaged in an ongoing project to improve disclosure of information about financial instruments and has recently issued two related Statements of Financial Accounting Standards (SFAS): SFAS 107, *Disclosures about Fair Value of Financial Instruments*; and SFAS 133, *Accounting for Derivative Instruments and Hedging Activities.* In accordance with these pronouncements, Howe has prepared the following footnote for Chatham's financial statements:

Note 12: Financial Instruments
The Company is party to financial instruments with off-balance-sheet risk of accounting loss in the normal course of business. The Company uses various financial instruments, including derivative financial instruments, to manage its interest rate and foreign currency exchange rate risks. Other financial instruments that potentially subject the Company to concentrations of credit risk consist principally of trade receivables.

Howe will be meeting with Chatham's board of directors to review the financial statements, and has asked Coyn to prepare a handout for the board explaining some of the terms used in the footnote.

Required:

Prepare the requested handout. Include the following:

a. What is a financial instrument?

b. Define off-balance-sheet risk of accounting loss and give an example of a financial instrument having off-balance-sheet risk of accounting loss.

c. Define credit risk. What is meant by the term concentration of credit risk?

d. Define fair value. Discuss the methods Chatham's management might use to estimate the fair values of its various financial instruments.

Problem 3   (10 to 15 minutes)

Riley Corp. has entered into several derivative contracts in order to manage its risk exposure. Riley Corp. has adopted SFAS 133, *Accounting for Derivative Instruments and Hedging Activities.*

Required:

What disclosures related to financial instruments (SFAS 133) is Riley Corp. required to make?

Problem 4   (15 to 25 minutes)

Alyssa, Inc. is the holder of several hybrid instruments. Alyssa has adopted SFAS 133, *Accounting for Derivative Instruments and Hedging Activities.*

Required:

a. What is a hybrid instrument?

b. What is bifurcation?

c. Identify the three criteria used to determine if bifurcation must occur.

d. List three examples of hybrid instruments that would require bifurcation under SFAS 133.

MULTIPLE-CHOICE ANSWERS

1. c	__ __	11. b	__ __	21. a	__ __	31. a	__ __	41. c	__ __
2. d	__ __	12. d	__ __	22. c	__ __	32. c	__ __	42. d	__ __
3. a	__ __	13. c	__ __	23. d	__ __	33. c	__ __	43. d	__ __
4. b	__ __	14. d	__ __	24. a	__ __	34. b	__ __	44. a	__ __
5. d	__ __	15. b	__ __	25. a	__ __	35. d	__ __	45. d	__ __
6. c	__ __	16. b	__ __	26. d	__ __	36. b	__ __	46. a	__ __
7. b	__ __	17. a	__ __	27. a	__ __	37. b	__ __		
8. b	__ __	18. d	__ __	28. a	__ __	38. c	__ __		
9. b	__ __	19. b	__ __	29. a	__ __	39. c	__ __	1st: __/46 = __%
10. d	__ __	20. d	__ __	30. c	__ __	40. c	__ __	2nd: __/46 = __%

MULTIPLE-CHOICE ANSWER EXPLANATIONS

A.　Foreign Currency Transactions

1.　(c) When the **sale is made** on 10/15/02, Bain would record a receivable and sales at $100,000, the US dollar equivalent on that date.

Accounts receivable	100,000	
Sales		100,000

On 11/16/02, Bain receives foreign currency worth $105,000. Since the receivable was recorded at $100,000, a $5,000 gain must be recorded.

Foreign currency	105,000	
Accounts receivable		100,000
Foreign exchange		
transaction gain		5,000

The US dollar equivalent when the order was received on 9/1/02 ($96,000) is not used to compute the gain because no entry is recorded on this date. The receipt and acceptance of a purchase order from a customer is an executory commitment which is not generally recorded.

2.　(d) On 9/1/01, Cano obtained a receivable which will be collected in a foreign currency. SFAS 52 states that a gain (loss) will result if the exchange rate on the settlement date is different from the rate existing on the transaction date. A gain (loss) must be recognized at any intervening balance sheet dates, if necessary. Therefore, Cano would recognize a $2,500 foreign exchange transaction loss in its **2001** income statement since a change in the exchange rate reduced the receivable (in US dollars) from $50,000 on 9/1/01 (250,000 x $.20) to $47,500 on 12/31/01 (250,000 x $.19). In 2002, a foreign exchange transaction gain of $7,500 is recognized because the receivable (in US dollars) increased from $47,500 on 12/31/01 to $55,000 when received (250,000 x $.22).

3.　(a) A transaction has occurred in which settlement will be made in German marks. Since Lindy's functional currency is the US dollar, a foreign exchange transaction gain (loss) will result if the spot rate on the settlement date is different than the rate on the transaction date (SFAS 52). A provision must be made at any intervening year-end date if there has been a rate change. Thus, in 2001, a $500 foreign exchange transaction gain [100,000 x ($.4295 – $.4245)] would be recognized, while in 2002 a $1,000 foreign exchange transaction loss [100,000 x ($.4245 – $.4345)] would be recognized.

4.　(b) A purchase has been made for which payment will be made in British pounds. A foreign exchange transaction gain or loss will result if the spot rate on the settlement date is different from the rate used on the transaction

date. SFAS 52 states that a gain or loss must also be recorded at any intervening balance sheet date if there has been a rate change. Thus, at 12/31/01 a foreign exchange transaction gain of $9,000 is recognized [300,000 x ($1.65 – $1.62)] as the foreign currency payable is reduced from $495,000 (300,000 x $1.65) to $486,000 (300,000 x $1.62). The thirty-day and sixty-day rates would affect Hunt only if the company had entered into forward contracts.

5.　(d) On 1/20/02, Ball would record purchases and accounts payable at $90,000. When the account was paid, the equivalent of $96,000 was required to liquidate the $90,000 liability, resulting in a foreign exchange transaction loss of $6,000. SFAS 52 requires that foreign exchange transaction gains (losses) also be recognized at intervening balance sheet dates. The note payable originally recorded at $500,000 was equivalent to a liability of $520,000 at the balance sheet date, resulting in a 2002 loss of $20,000. The interest payable of $25,000 ($500,000 x 10% x 6/12) was equivalent to a liability of $26,000 at year-end, resulting in an additional 2002 loss of $1,000. Therefore, the total 2002 foreign exchange transaction loss is $27,000 ($6,000 + $20,000 + $1,000).

6.　(c) The requirement is to determine the amount that Tyrola should accrue for royalties payable, 12/31/02. This situation is a foreign currency transaction in which settlement is denominated in other than a company's functional currency (SFAS 52). In this case the functional currency is the US dollar because it is the currency of the primary economic environment in which the Colorado firm operates. Note that in this royalty agreement, 12/31/02 is the point at which the amount due to the author (50,000 Canadian dollars x 10% = 5,000 Canadian dollars) is determined. Royalty expense is measured and the related liability is denominated at 12/31/02. The year-end accrual would be

.89 (10% x 50,000 Canadian dollars) = $4,450.

On January 10, 2003, Tyrola will have to purchase 5,000 Canadian dollars for payment to the Canadian author. The amount of US dollars required to accomplish this will depend on the spot rate on January 10 ($.90 in this case). The number of US dollars required to satisfy the obligation will be $50 greater [($.90 – .89) x 5,000 Canadian dollars]. This will result in a $50 foreign exchange transaction loss which would be included in 2003 net income.

7.　(b) In the case of the receivable denominated in Japanese yen, a foreign exchange transaction gain was recorded on the collection of the receivable. This means that more yen was received than was recorded in the receivable account. For that to happen the rate of yen exchangeable for a dollar would have had to decrease, requiring more yen to be paid at the settlement date for the same amount of dollars at the contract date. On the other hand, there was a foreign exchange transaction loss on the payable denominated in French francs. This means that at the settlement date Shore Co. had to pay more francs than were recorded in the payable account. For this to occur the rate of francs exchangeable for a dollar would have had to decrease, requiring more francs to be paid at the settlement date for the same amount of dollars at the contract date.

8. (b) Per SFAS 52, a transaction that is denominated in a currency other than the entity's functional currency, which is payable at a fixed amount at a later date, may result in an increased or decreased amount payable because of a change in the exchange rate. This increase/decrease would be classified as a foreign exchange transaction gain/loss, and would be included as a component of income. The gain/loss would not be considered extraordinary.

9. (b) The requirement is to determine how Velec should account for the exchange rate fluctuation in 2002. A foreign currency transaction, according to SFAS 52, is a transaction denominated in a currency other than the entity's functional currency. Denominated means that the balance is fixed in terms of the number of units of a foreign currency, regardless of changes in the exchange rate. When a US company buys or sells to an unrelated foreign company, and the US company agrees either to pay for goods or receive payment for the goods in foreign currency units, this is a foreign currency transaction from the point of view of the US company (the functional currency is the US dollar). In these situations, the US company has "crossed currencies" and directly assumes the risk of fluctuating foreign exchange rates of the foreign currency units. As exchange rates fluctuate, a company will record an ordinary gain or loss on their income statement, **not** an extraordinary gain or loss. Velec has an accounts payable denominated in a foreign currency (francs) as of December 15, the date the title to the goods passes to Velec. As the value of the franc per dollar rises above twenty francs per dollar, Velec Co. will have to come up with less dollars to pay off the payable, as of December 31, 2002, than they would have on December 15, 2002. This creates a foreign exchange transaction gain. As shown numerically, if 4000 francs are assumed as being payable, on December 15 you would need $200 (4000/20) to pay off the payable. However, on December 31, $190 would be needed (4000/21). The difference between $200 and $190 represents the gain. A foreign exchange transaction gain should be included in net income, not a loss.

B.1.-2.   Derivative Instruments and Hedging Activities

10. (d) Derivatives are financial instruments that derive their value from changes in a benchmark based on stock prices, interest rates, mortgage rates, currency rates, commodity prices, or some other agreed-upon base. Discounts on accounts receivable are not the basis of a benchmark for a derivative financial instrument.

11. (b) Derivative instruments must contain one or more underlyings **and** one or more notional amounts. Derivative instruments do contain terms that require or permit net settlement or delivery of an asset.

12. (d) Derivative financial instruments are contracts that are supposed to protect or hedge one or more of the parties from adverse movement in the underlying base. Answer (d) is correct because it does not fit the definition of a financial instrument. Risk of uncollectable accounts can be managed by effective credit policies.

13. (c) Derivative instruments meet the definition of assets and liabilities. As such they should be reported on the entity's financial statements. The most relevant measure for reporting financial instruments is fair value. Thus, statement I is true. If a derivative instrument does not qualify as a hedging instrument, then its gains or losses must be reported and recognized in current earnings. Thus, statement II is also true.

14. (d) All of the above meet the basic definition of an underlying, which is any financial or physical variable that has either observable changes or objectively verifiable changes.

15. (b) A call option is in the money if the price of the underlying is greater than the strike or exercise price of the underlying. An at-the-money option is one in which the price of the underlying is equal to the strike or exercise price. A call option is out of the money if the strike or exercise price is greater than the price of the underlying.

16. (b) Under SFAS 133, derivative instruments contain

1. One or more underlyings and one or more notional amounts
2. No initial net investment or smaller net investment than required for contracts with an expected similar response to market changes, and
3. Terms that require or permit net settlement, net settlement by means outside the contract, and delivery of an asset that is substantially the same as net settlement.

17. (a) Notional amounts are the referenced associated asset or liability that are commonly a number of units such as barrels of oil. Answers (b) and (d) are incorrect because they are examples of underlyings. Answer (c) is incorrect because it is an example of a derivative instrument.

18. (d) Disclosures related to financial instruments that are used as hedging instruments must include the following information:

1. Objectives and strategies for achieving them.
2. Context to understand the instrument.
3. Risk management policies.
4. A list of hedged instruments.

Disclosure of the maximum potential accounting loss is only required for financial instruments with concentrations of credit risk.

B.3.   Inclusions in and Exclusions from Derivative Instruments

19. (b) Only call (put) options are included in the definition of derivative financial instruments. Leases are excluded because they require a payment equal to the value of the right to use the property. Equity securities and adjustable rate loans are excluded because they require an initial net investment equivalent to the fair value.

20. **(d)** Futures contracts, credit indexed contracts, and interest rate swaps are all included in derivative instruments.

B.4. Embedded Derivative Instruments and Bifurcation

21. **(a)** The hybrid instrument is **not** recorded at fair value. Economic characteristics and risks of the embedded instrument are **not** "clearly and closely" related to those of the host contract. For purposes of applying SFAS 133, the embedded derivative must meet the definition of a derivative instrument

22. **(c)** An embedded derivative is a feature of a financial instrument or other contract, which if the feature stood alone, would meet the definition of a derivative.

23. **(d)** Bifurcation is the process of separating an embedded derivative from its host contract. This process is necessary so that hybrid instruments can be separated into their component parts, each being accounted for using the appropriate valuation techniques.

B.5.-8 Hedging Instruments

24. **(a)** According to SFAS 133, hedge accounting is permitted for four types of hedges.

1. Unrecognized firm commitments.
2. Available-for-sale securities.
3. Foreign currency denominated hedge forecasted transactions.
4. Net investments in foreign operations.

Trading securities is not one of the four types.

25. **(a)** The general criteria for a hedging instrument are that sufficient documentation must be provided at the beginning of the process and the hedge must be "highly effective" throughout its life.

26. **(d)** For an unrecognized firm commitment to qualify as a hedged item it must

1. Be binding on both parties.
2. Be specific with respect to all significant items including quantity to be exchanged, the fixed price, and the timing of the transaction.
3. Contain a nonperformance clause that makes performance probable.

27. **(a)** A fair value hedge is a hedge of the exposure to changes in the fair value of a recognized asset or liability or firm commitment. Two other types of hedges are cash flow and foreign currency hedges. An underlying is commonly a specified price or rate.

28. **(a)** Under SFAS 133, gains and losses of a fair value hedge will be recognized in current earnings. The effective portion of a cash flow hedge is reported in other comprehensive income and the ineffective portion is reported on a cumulative basis to reflect the lessor of the cumulative gain/loss on the derivative or the cumulative gain/loss from the change in expected cash flows from the hedged instrument. Gains and losses from a change in the fair value of derivative instruments are not assets and liabilities and should not be reported on the balance sheet.

29. **(a)** Fair value hedges will recognize gains and losses for the effective portion of the hedging instrument in each reporting period. Cash flow hedges will recognize

gains and losses for the effect portion of the hedging instrument in other comprehensive income.

30. **(c)** An interest rate swap agreement involves the exchange of cash flows determined by various interest rates. Fluctuations in interest rates after the agreement is entered into may result in the risk of exchanging a lower interest rate for a higher interest rate. Financial instruments, including swaps, also bear credit risk or the risk that a counterparty to the agreement will not perform as expected.

31. **(a)** One of the basic principles that supports SFAS 133 is that derivatives do meet the definition of assets/liabilities and, therefore, should be recognized and reported as such on the financial statements. In contrast, gains and losses that result from the change in the fair value of derivatives are not assets/liabilities and should either appear in other comprehensive income or be reported in current earnings.

32. **(c)** The four foreign currency hedges under SFAS 133 are an unrecognized firm commitment, an available-for-sale security, a foreign currency denominated forecasted transaction, and a net investment in foreign operations. A hedge of a recognized asset or liability is a fair value hedge or cash flow hedge, not a foreign currency hedge.

33. **(c)** SFAS 52 remains in effect for hedges of net investments in foreign operations. The hedged net investment is viewed as a single asset. The provisions for recognizing the gain or loss on the hedged asset/liability and the hedging instrument in SFAS 133 do not apply to the hedges of net investments in foreign operations.

B.9. Forward Exchange Contracts

34. **(b)** SFAS 133 requires fair market valuation for forward exchange contracts. Each period this is accomplished by marking the forward exchange contract to market using the forward rate at the FS date. At 12/31/02 the forward rate is $.93. The difference between $.93 and $.90, the forward rate on the date the contracts were entered into, times 100,000 francs is $3,000, the forward exchange gain. The entry would be as follows:

Forward contract receivable	3,000	
Forward contract gain		3,000

The $3,000 forward exchange contract gain would be included in 2002 net income.

35. **(d)** The accounting for gains and losses from foreign currency transactions is prescribed by SFAS 52 which requires a revaluation of exposed net assets and liabilities denominated in foreign currency units at the current spot rate. At 12/31/02 there is a foreign exchange transaction loss of $5,000 [($.92 − .87) x 100,000 francs]. Note that accounts payable was created on 11/30/02. The entry to record the loss is as follows:

Foreign exchange loss	5,000	
Accounts payable		5,000

The loss would be reported in 2002 net income.

36. **(b)** Hedges involving firm purchase commitments are treated in the same manner as a forward exchange contract that was entered into to hedge an exposure of a liability.

| Forward contract receivable | 3,000 | |
| Forward contract gain | | 3,000 |

To revalue forward contract using forward rates

| Foreign exchange loss | 3,000 | |
| Firm purchase commitment | | 3,000 |

To recognize loss on firm commitment

Note that this hedge is 100% effective because the gain on the forward contract and the loss on the firm purchase commitment offset each other, net.

37. (b) Using a forward exchange contract to speculate would result in a gain or loss each period FS are prepared. The contract would be revalued each reporting period using the forward rate. The gain or loss calculated would be reported in net income. The journal entry would be as follows:

| Forward contract receivable | 3,000 | |
| Forward contract gain | | 3,000 |

B.11. Fair Value and Credit Risk Disclosures

38. (c) Per SFAS 105, credit risk is the risk of accounting loss from a financial instrument due to possible failure of another party to perform according to the terms of the contract. Off-balance-sheet risk is the possible amount of loss from an instrument that is not reflected on the balance sheet. Market risk is the risk that future changes in market prices may make a financial instrument less valuable.

39. (c) The value of derivative financial instruments is typically derived from the value of an underlying asset or is tied to an index. As the price of the underlying asset changes, the price of the derivative changes. Outstanding loan commitments written, recourse obligations on receivables, and futures contracts are all tied to an asset account. Warranty obligations are the result of the sale of goods.

40. (c) Off-balance-sheet risk is the possible amount of loss from an instrument that is not reflected on the balance sheet because a loss has not yet occurred or because the item is not recognized as an asset or liability. If the amount recognized on the balance sheet reflects the accounting loss to the entity, then there is no off-balance-sheet risk to consider.

41. (c) According to SFAS 107, if it is not practicable for an entity to estimate the fair value of a financial instrument, (1) information pertinent to estimating fair value **and** (2) the reasons why it is not practicable to estimate fair value should be disclosed.

42. (d) SFAS 107 requires the following disclosures:

• Method(s) and significant assumptions used in estimating fair value.

• A distinction between financial instruments held or issued for trading purposes and purposes other than trading.

• Information pertinent to estimating the fair value of a financial instrument if it is not practicable for the entity to estimate and the reason why estimation is not practicable.

• Derivative financial instruments may not be combined, aggregated, or netted with nonderivative or other derivative financial instruments.

• If financial instruments are disclosed in more than one area in the financial statements, one note must contain a summary table cross-referencing the location of the other instruments.

43. (d) SFAS 107 requires the following disclosures about credit risk for financial instruments with off-balance-sheet credit risk:

• The amount of accounting loss the entity would incur should any party to the financial instrument fail to perform according to the terms of the contract and the collateral, if any, is of no value.

• The class of financial instruments held.

• Categorization between instruments held for trading purposes and purposes other than trading.

44. (a) Concentrations of credit risk exist when an entity has a business activity, economic characteristic, or location that is common to most of its financial instruments. SFAS 105 requires disclosure of information about significant concentrations of credit risk for **all** financial instruments.

45. (d) Since many of Kline Bank's debtors have high debt-to-equity ratios, this group of debtors has a similar economic characteristic, and thus, would be considered a concentration of credit risk to Kline Bank. SFAS 107 requires that with concentrations of credit risk, the entity disclose the following:

1. Information about the shared activity, region, or economic characteristic of the group.
2. Amount of accounting loss that the entity would incur as a result of the concentrated parties' failure to perform according to the terms of the contracts.
3. Information regarding entity's policy of requiring collateral.

46. (a) SFAS 107, *Disclosures about Fair Value of Financial Instruments*, requires entities to disclose the fair market value of financial instruments, both assets and liabilities whether recognized or not recognized in the statement of financial position, for which it is practicable to estimate fair value. Pertinent descriptive information as to the fair value of the instrument is to be disclosed if an estimate of fair value cannot be made without incurring excessive costs.

OTHER OBJECTIVE ANSWERS AND ANSWER EXPLANATIONS

Problem 1

1. **(C)** Tandem currencies are two currencies other than a functional currency expected to move in tandem with each other relative to an entity's functional currency.

2. **(E)** A discount or premium is the difference between the futures rate and the spot rate at the date of a forward contract.

3. **(B)** The ineffective portion of a hedge has resulting gains or losses taken into income in the period in which they arise.

4. **(A)** The effective portion of a hedge is given special hedge accounting treatment. The evaluation of effectiveness is done no less than every three months. A highly effective hedge will have a value change ranging from roughly .8 to 1.2 times the variability of the cash flows being hedged.

5. **(D)** A forward contract is a hedge against an exposed asset position created by having an account in a denomination other than the functional currency.

Problem 2

1. **(L)** Agreement for purchase and sale of a specified quantity of a commodity, foreign currency, or financial instrument at an agreed-upon price, with future delivery and/or settlement at a designated future date.

2. **(J)** A transaction expected to occur for which there is no firm commitment, which gives the entity no present rights or obligations.

3. **(G)** A legally enforceable, binding agreement with an unrelated party, specifying all significant terms and including a disincentive for nonperformance sufficient to make performance likely.

4. **(D)** Financial instruments that contain features which, if they stood alone, would meet the definition of a derivative instrument.

5. **(K)** With regard to put options, it is the larger of zero or the spread between the exercise price and the stock price.

6. **(F)** Commonly a specified price or rate such as a stock price, interest rate, currency rate, commodity price, or a related index.

7. **(H)** The referenced associated asset or liability, commonly a number of units.

8. **(B)** A hedge of the exposure to variability in the cash flows of a forecasted transaction or a recognized asset or liability.

9. **(A)** A hedge of the exposure to changes in the fair value of a recognized asset or liability or an unrecognized firm commitment.

10. **(C)** A hedge of the foreign currency exposure of an unrecognized firm commitment, an available-for-sale security, a forecasted transaction, or a net investment in a foreign operation.

Problem 3

1. **(E)** Leases are excluded from SFAS 133 treatment.

2. **(E)** Guaranteed investment contracts are not required to be accounted for under SFAS 133.

3. **(I)** Futures contracts must be accounted for using SFAS 133.

4. **(E)** Equity securities do not fall under the requirements of SFAS 133.

5. **(I)** Credit indexed contracts are required to be accounted for under SFAS 133.

6. **(E)** Mortgage-backed securities are excluded from SFAS 133 treatment.

7. **(E)** Debt securities are not required to be accounted for using SFAS 133.

8. **(I)** Interest rate caps must be accounted for using SFAS 133.

9. **(I)** Swaptions meet the definition of a derivative instrument and must be accounted for using SFAS 133.

10. **(E)** Employee stock options are excluded from SFAS 133 treatment.

11. **(I)** Options to purchase (call) or sell (put) exchange-traded securities are included under SFAS 133 requirements.

12. **(E)** Variable annuity contracts do not fall under the requirements of SFAS 133.

13. **(E)** Adjustable rate loans are not required to be accounted for under SFAS 133.

14. **(I)** Interest rate swaps must be accounted for using SFAS 133.

Problem 4

1.   (**L**)   An at-the-money option is one in which the price of the underlying is equal to the strike or exercise price.

2.   (**I**)   Bifurcation is the process of separating an embedded derivative from its host contract. This process is necessary so that hybrid instruments (a financial instrument or other contract that contains an embedded derivative) can be separated into their component parts, each being accounted for using the appropriate valuation techniques.

3.   (**F**)   An American call option provides the holder the right to acquire an underlying at an exercise or strike price anytime during the option term. A premium is paid by the holder for the right to benefit from the appreciation in the underlying.

4.   (**C**)   An embedded derivative is a feature on a financial instrument or other contract which, if the feature stood alone, would meet the definition of a derivative.

5.   (**G**)   A forward contract is an agreement between two parties to buy and sell a specific quantity of a commodity, foreign currency, or financial instrument at an agreed-upon price, with delivery and/or settlement at a designated future date. Because a forward contract is not formally regulated by an organized exchange, each party to the contract is subject to the default of the other party.

6.   (**O**)   A futures contract is a forward-based contract to make or take delivery of a designated financial instrument, foreign currency, or commodity during a designated period, at a specified price or yield. The contract frequently has provisions for cash settlement. A future contract is traded on a regulated exchange and, therefore, involves less credit risk than a forward contract.

7.   (**B**)   A call option is in the money if the price of the underlying is greater than the strike or exercise price of the underlying.

8.   (**J**)   The notional amount (or payment provision) is the referenced associated asset or liability. A notional amount is commonly a number of units such as shares of stock, principal amount, face value, stated value, basis points, barrels of oil, etc. It may be that amount plus a premium or minus a discount. The interaction of the price or rate (underlying) with the referenced associated asset or liability (notional amount) determines whether settlement is required and, if so, the amount.

9.   (**H**)   A call option is out of the money if the strike or exercise price is greater than the price of the underlying. A put option is out of the money if the price of the underlying is greater than the strike or exercise option.

10.   (**N**)   An American put option provides the holder the right to sell the underlying at an exercise or strike price, anytime during the option term. A gain accrues to the holder as the market price of the underlying falls below the strike price.

11.   (**D**)   A swap is a forward-based contract or agreement generally between two counterparties to exchange streams of cash flows over a specified period in the future.

12.   (**K**)   An underlying is commonly a specified price or rate such as a stock price, interest rate, currency rate, commodity price, or a related index. However, any variable (financial or physical) with (1) observable changes or (2) objectively verifiable changes such as a credit rating, insurance index, climatic or geological condition (temperature, rainfall) qualifies. Unless it is specifically excluded, a contract based on any qualifying variable is accounted for under SFAS 133 if it has the distinguishing characteristics stated above.

ANSWER OUTLINE

Problem 1   Derivative and Hedging Activities

a.   Derivative Financial Instruments (DFI)

- ≥1 underlying + ≥1 notional amount
- No initial investment or one of lesser amount than other contracts having similar market behavior
- Require or allow net settlement, net settlement outside contract, or deliver asset same as net settlement

b.   Fair value hedge criteria

- Hedged item is all or specific portion of asset or liability or unrecognized firm commitment
  - Firm commitments must bind all parties, have detailed terms, and include nonperformance clause
- Report gains (losses) on DFI and hedged asset/liability in earnings

c.   Cash flow hedge criteria

- Hedging instrument must be linked to hedged asset/liability
  - Requires same index for hedging instrument as for hedged asset/liability
- Hedge is highly effective
- Forecasted transaction probable
- Hedged asset/liability that is a series of transactions have same risk exposure
- Reporting gains (losses)
  - Effective portion of hedge in other comprehensive income
  - Ineffective portion of hedge in current earnings

d.   Foreign currency hedge at BS date

- Adjust foreign current receivable contract and firm commitment
- Gain on one should offset loss on the other (i.e., 100% effective)

e.   Embedded DFI separated from host contract if all criteria met

- Embedded DFI's economic characteristics and risks unrelated to host contract
- Hybrid instrument not remeasured at FV under other applicable GAAP
- Separate instrument with same features would meet requirement of DFI

UNOFFICIAL ANSWER

Problem 1   Derivative and Hedging Activities

a.   The three distinguishing characteristics of a derivative financial instrument are

   • The instrument contains one or more underlyings and one or more notional amounts or payment provisions.
   • The instrument requires no initial investment or requires an initial investment that is a lesser amount than contracts expected to have a similar reaction to market changes.
   • The terms allow or require net settlement, can be settled net by means outside the contract, or provide for delivery of an asset resulting in essentially the same as net settlement.

b.   The primary specific criterion for defining a derivative financial instrument to be classified as a fair value hedge is that the hedged item must be all or a specific portion of a recognized asset/liability or an unrecognized firm commitment. In order for a firm purchase commitment to qualify, it must be binding on both parties, detailed with respect to all terms, and include a nonperformance clause that makes performance probable.

Under fair value hedges the gains or loss on the hedged asset/liability and the hedging instrument are recognized in current earnings.

c.   The primary specific criterion for defining a derivative financial instrument to be classified as a cash flow hedge is the hedged asset/liability and the hedging instrument must be linked. Linking means their changes in cash flows are expected to offset each other. This means that the rate or index used for measuring the expected change in cash flows is the same for the hedged asset/liability and the hedging instrument.

Supporting criteria are

   • Cash flows must meet the highly effective threshold.
   • The occurrence of forecasted transactions must be considered probable.
   • If the forecasted hedged asset/liability is a series of transactions, they must share the same risk exposure.

Under a cash flow hedge, the effective portion is reported in other comprehensive income and the ineffective portion is reported in current earnings.

d.   At the balance sheet date, both the foreign currency receivable contract and the firm commitment would be adjusted using changes in the forward exchange rate as the basis of measurement. The hedge of a foreign currency exposure in an unrecognized firm commitment is accounted for as a foreign currency fair value hedge.

If the units of foreign currency to be purchased at a fixed price is the same as the units of foreign currency in which settlement of the obligation is stated, a gain on one should offset the loss on the other. Thus, the forward exchange contract can be 100% effective as a hedge.

e.   Embedded derivative financial instruments must be separated from a host contract and accounted for separately if all of the following criteria are met:

   • Economic characteristics and risks of the embedded instrument are not clearly and closely related to those of the host contract.
   • The hybrid instrument (contract) is not remeasured at fair value according to otherwise applicable generally accepted accounting principles, with changes in value reported in current earnings as they occur.
   • A separate instrument with the same terms as the embedded instrument would meet the requirements for a derivative financial instrument.

ANSWER OUTLINE

Problem 2   Disclosure of Financial Instruments

a.   Financial instruments (FI)
- Cash
- Evidence of ownership interest in entity
- Contractual right to receive or deliver cash or another FI

b. Off-balance-sheet loss
  - Risk that FI's accounting loss > amount recognized on the BS
  - Examples:
    - Noncancelable operating lessees with future minimum lease payments
    - Standby loan commitments
    - Letters of credit
    - Repurchase agreements

c. Credit risk
  - Possibility of loss resulting from other party's lack of contractual nonperformance
  - Example includes receivable having similar characteristics which could affect collection such as customers or geographic region

d. Fair value (FV) of FI
  - Amount at which FI could be exchanged between willing parties
  - Examples: include quoted market price
    - If quoted prices not available, use valuation techniques or use quoted market price of FI with similar characteristics

UNOFFICIAL ANSWER

Problem 2   Disclosure of Financial Instruments

a.   A financial instrument is cash, evidence of an ownership interest in an entity, or a contractual right to receive or deliver cash or another financial instrument.

b.   Off-balance-sheet risk of accounting loss is the risk of accounting loss from a financial instrument that exceeds the amount recognized for the financial instrument in the balance sheet. An example of a financial instrument having off-balance-sheet risk of accounting loss would be a noncancelable operating lease with future minimum lease commitments. Other examples include standby loan commitments written, letters of credit, repurchase agreements, and purchase commitments.

c.   Credit risk is the possibility that a loss may occur from the failure of the other party to perform according to the terms of a contract. Concentrations of credit risk exist when receivables have common characteristics that may affect their collection. One common characteristic might be that the receivables are due from companies in the same industry or in the same region of the country.

d.   The fair value of a financial instrument is the amount at which the instrument could be exchanged in a current transaction between willing parties, other than in a forced or liquidation sale. Quoted market price, if available, is the best evidence of the fair value of a financial instrument. If quoted prices are not available, Chatham's management's best estimate of fair value might be based on valuation techniques or on the quoted market price of a financial instrument with similar characteristics.

ANSWER OUTLINE

Problem 3   Financial Instrument Disclosures

Disclosures for financial statements

  - Objectives and strategies for achieving them
  - Context to understand the instrument

  - Risk management policies
  - List of edged instruments
  - Separated by type of hedge
  - Reported when complete set of financial statements issued

UNOFFICIAL ANSWER

Problem 3   Financial Instrument Disclosures

According to SFAS 133, an entity that holds or issues derivative or nonderivative financial instruments that are used a hedging instruments is required to disclose its objectives for holding or issuing those instruments as well as its strategies for achieving those objectives. The context needed to understand the instruments must also be disclosed. In addition, the entity must disclose its risk management policies and a list of hedged instruments. These disclosures must be separated by type of hedge. Finally, entities must make these financial instrument disclosures for every reporting period for which a complete set of financial statements is issued.

ANSWER OUTLINE

Problem 4   Hybrid Instruments and Bifurcation

a.   Hybrid instrument

  - Financial instrument with feature if stood alone = derivative instrument
  - Feature = embedded derivative instrument
  - Basic contract = host contract

b.   Bifurcation

  - Process to separate embedded derivative instrument from host contract
  - Embedded derivative instrument = stand-alone instrument
  - Host contract treated in normal manner
  - Stand-alone derivative instrument use SFAS 133

c.   Three criteria for bifurcation

  1. Embedded derivative = derivative instrument
  2. Hybrid instrument not recorded at fair value
  3. Economic characteristics and risks of embedded derivative instrument not related to those of host contract

d.   Examples of hybrid instruments requiring bifurcation

  - Bond payable, interest rate - S&P 500
  - Equity instrument with call option
  - Loans with term-extending options - prime rate

UNOFFICIAL ANSWER

Problem 4   Hybrid Instruments and Bifurcation

a.   A hybrid instrument is a financial instrument or other contract containing a feature that, if it stood alone, would meet the definition of a derivative instrument. This feature is known as an embedded derivative instrument. There is a basic contract in a hybrid instrument that is called the host contract that has an embedded derivative instrument.

b.   Bifurcation is the process of separating an embedded derivative instrument from its host contract. The embedded derivative instrument should then be treated as if it were a stand-alone instrument, and accounted for using SFAS 133. The host contract (excluding the embedded derivative) should be accounted for in the normal manner, as if it had never contained the embedded derivative.

c.   Bifurcation must occur if, and only if, all of the following three criteria are met. First, the embedded derivative instrument must meet the definition of a derivative instrument for the purposes of applying SFAS 133. Second, the hybrid instrument must not be regularly reported at fair value, with changes in its fair value being reported in current earnings. Finally, the economic characteristics and risks of

the embedded derivative must not be clearly and closely related to the economic characteristics and risks of the host contract.

d.   Examples of hybrid instruments that would require bifurcation under SFAS 133 include the following:

- A bond payable with an interest rate based on the S&P 500 Index
- An equity instrument with a call option, allowing the issuing company to buy back the stock
- Loans with term-extending options whose values are based on the prime rate at the time of the extension

Keep practicing! Wiley's CPA Examination Review Software has over 2,800 questions.

Available at www.wiley.com/cpa

MISCELLANEOUS

A. Personal Financial Statements[1]

Personal financial statements may be prepared for an individual, husband and wife, or family. Personal financial statements (PFS) consist of

1. Statement of financial condition—presents estimated current values of assets, estimated current amounts of liabilities, estimated income taxes, and net worth at a specified date
2. Statement of changes in net worth—presents main sources of increases (decreases) in net worth over the time period included by the statement of changes in net worth.

Assets and liabilities, including changes therein, should be recognized using the accrual basis of accounting. Assets and liabilities should be listed by order of liquidity and maturity, not a current/noncurrent basis.

In PFS, **assets** should be presented at their estimated current value. This is an amount at which the item could be exchanged assuming both parties are well informed, neither party is compelled to buy or sell, and material disposal costs are deducted to arrive at current values. **Liabilities** should be presented at the lesser of the discounted amount of cash to be paid or the current cash settlement amount. Income taxes payable should include unpaid income taxes as of the date of the statement of financial condition. Also, PFS should include the **estimated income tax** on the difference between the current value (amount) of assets (liabilities) and their respective tax bases as if they had been realized or liquidated. The table below summarizes the methods of determining "estimated current values" for assets and "estimated current amounts" for liabilities.

Business interests which comprise a large portion of a person's total assets should be shown separately from other investments. An investment in a separate entity which is marketable as a going concern (e.g., closely held corporation) should be presented as one amount for its fair value. If the investment is a limited business activity, not conducted in a separate business entity, separate asset and liability amounts should be shown (e.g., investment in real estate and related mortgage). Of course, only the person's beneficial interest in the investment is included in their PFS.

Assets and liabilities	*Discounted cash flow*	*Market price*	*Appraised value*	*Other*
• Receivables	x			
• Marketable securities		x		
• Options		x		
• Investment in life insurance				Cash value less outstanding loans
• Investment in closely held business	x		x	Liquidation value, multiple of earnings, reproduction value, adjustment of book value or cost
• Real estate	x		x	Sales of similar property
• Intangible assets	x			
• Future interests (nonforfeitable rights)	x			
• Payables and other liabilities	x			Discharge amount if lower than discounted amount
• Noncancelable commitments	x			
• Income taxes payable				Unpaid income tax for completed tax years and estimated income tax for elapsed portion of current tax year to date of financial statements
• Estimated income tax on difference between current values of assets and current amounts of liabilities and their respective tax bases				Computed as if current value of assets and liabilities had been respectively realized or liquidated considering applicable tax laws and regulations, recapture provisions and carryovers

---

[1] *The source of GAAP for personal financial statements is AICPA Statement of Position 82-1 which has been summarized in this module. (These are not outlined in this text.)*

MULTIPLE-CHOICE QUESTIONS (1-17)

1. Green, a calendar-year taxpayer, is preparing a personal statement of financial condition as of April 30, 2001. Green's 2000 income tax liability was paid in full on April 15, 2001. Green's tax on income earned between January and April 2001 is estimated at $20,000. In addition, $40,000 is estimated for income tax on the differences between the estimated current values and current amounts of Green's assets and liabilities and their tax bases at April 30, 2001. No withholdings or payments have been made towards the 2001 income tax liability. In Green's April 30, 2001 statement of financial condition, what amount should be reported, between liabilities and net worth, as estimated income taxes?

    a. $0
    b. $20,000
    c. $40,000
    d. $60,000

2. On December 31, 2002, Shane is a fully vested participant in a company-sponsored pension plan. According to the plan's administrator, Shane has at that date the nonforfeitable right to receive a lump sum of $100,000 on December 28, 2003. The discounted amount of $100,000 is $90,000 at December 31, 2002. The right is not contingent on Shane's life expectancy and requires no future performance on Shane's part. In Shane's December 31, 2002, personal statement of financial condition, the vested interest in the pension plan should be reported at

    a. $0
    b. $ 90,000
    c. $ 95,000
    d. $100,000

3. The following information pertains to marketable equity securities owned by Kent:

| | Fair value at December 31, | | Cost in |
Stock	2003	2002	2001
City Mfg., Inc.	$95,500	$93,000	$89,900
Tri Corp.	3,400	5,600	3,600
Zee, Inc.		10,300	15,000

The Zee stock was sold in January 2003 for $10,200. In Kent's personal statement of financial condition at December 31, 2003, what amount should be reported for marketable equity securities?

    a. $93,300
    b. $93,500
    c. $94,100
    d. $98,900

4. Clint owns 50% of Vohl Corp.'s common stock. Clint paid $20,000 for this stock in 1998. At December 31, 2002, Clint's 50% stock ownership in Vohl had a fair value of $180,000. Vohl's cumulative net income and cash dividends declared for the five years ended December 31, 2002, were $300,000 and $40,000, respectively. In Clint's personal statement of financial condition at December 31, 2002, what amount should be shown as the investment in Vohl?

    a. $ 20,000
    b. $150,000
    c. $170,000
    d. $180,000

5. Jen has been employed by Komp, Inc. since February 1, 2000. Jen is covered by Komp's Section 401(k) deferred compensation plan. Jen's contributions have been 10% of salaries. Komp has made matching contributions of 5%. Jen's salaries were $21,000 in 2000, $23,000 in 2001, and $26,000 in 2002. Employer contributions vest after an employee completes three years of continuous employment. The balance in Jen's 401(k) account was $11,900 at December 31, 2002, which included earnings of $1,200 on Jen's contributions. What amount should be reported for Jen's vested interest in the 401(k) plan in Jen's December 31, 2002 personal statement of financial condition?

    a. $11,900
    b. $ 8,200
    c. $ 7,000
    d. $ 1,200

6. The following information pertains to an insurance policy that Barton owns on his life:

Face amount	$100,000
Accumulated premiums paid up to December 31, 2003	8,000
Cash value at December 31, 2003	12,000
Policy loan	3,000

In Barton's personal statement of financial condition at December 31, 2003, what amount should be reported for the investment in life insurance?

    a. $97,000
    b. $12,000
    c. $ 9,000
    d. $ 8,000

7. Ely had the following personal investments at December 31, 2002:

    • Realty held as a limited business activity not conducted in a separate business entity. Mortgage payments were made with funds from sources unrelated to the realty. The cost of this realty was $500,000, and the related mortgage payable was $100,000 at December 31, 2002.

    • Sole proprietorship marketable as a going concern. Its cost was $900,000, and it had related accounts payable of $80,000 at December 31, 2002.

The costs of both investments equal estimated current values. The balances of liabilities equal their estimated current amounts.

How should the foregoing information be reported in Ely's statement of financial condition at December 31, 2002?

		Assets	Liabilities
a.	Investment in real estate	$ 400,000	
	Investment in sole proprietorship	820,000	
b.	Investment in real estate	$ 500,000	
	Investment in sole proprietorship	820,000	
	Mortgage payable		$100,000
c.	Investment in real estate	$ 500,000	
	Investment in sole proprietorship	900,000	
	Mortgage payable		$100,000
	Accounts payable		80,000
d.	Investments	$1,400,000	
	Accounts and mortgage payable		$180,000

8. At December 31, 2002, Ryan had the following noncancelable personal commitments:

Pledge to be paid to County Welfare Home thirty days after volunteers paint the walls and ceiling of the Home's recreation room	$ 5,000
Pledge to be paid to City Hospital on the recovery of Ryan's comatose sister	$25,000

What amount should be included in liabilities in Ryan's personal statement of financial condition at December 31, 2002?

a. $0
b. $ 5,000
c. $25,000
d. $30,000

9. The estimated current values of Lane's personal assets at December 31, 2002, totaled $1,000,000, with tax bases aggregating $600,000. Included in these assets was a vested interest in a deferred profit-sharing plan with a current value of $80,000 and a tax basis of $70,000. The estimated current amounts of Lane's personal liabilities equaled their tax bases at December 31, 2002. Lane's 2001 effective income tax rate was 30%. In Lane's personal statement of financial condition at December 31, 2002, what amount should be provided for estimated income taxes relating to the excess of current values over tax bases?

a. $120,000
b. $117,000
c. $ 3,000
d. $0

10. Shea, a calendar-year taxpayer, is preparing a personal statement of financial condition as of April 30, 2002. Shea's 2001 income tax liability was paid in full on April 15, 2002. Shea's tax on income earned from January through April 2002 is estimated at $30,000. In addition, $25,000 is estimated for income tax on the differences between the estimated current values of Shea's assets and the current amounts of liabilities and their tax bases at April 30, 2002. No withholdings or payments have been made towards the 2002 income tax liability. In Shea's statement of financial condition at April 30, 2002, what is the total of the amount or amounts that should be reported for income taxes?

a. $0
b. $25,000
c. $30,000
d. $55,000

11. The following information pertains to Smith's personal assets and liabilities at December 31, 2002:

	Historical cost	Estimated current values	Estimated current amounts
Assets	$500,000	$900,000	
Liabilities	100,000		$80,000

Smith's 2002 income tax rate was 30%. In Smith's personal statement of financial condition at December 31, 2002, what amount should be reported as Smith's net worth?

a. $294,000
b. $420,000
c. $694,000
d. $820,000

12. Personal financial statements usually consist of
a. A statement of net worth and a statement of changes in net worth.
b. A statement of net worth, an income statement, and a statement of changes in net worth.
c. A statement of financial condition and a statement of changes in net worth.
d. A statement of financial condition, a statement of changes in net worth, and a statement of cash flows.

13. Personal financial statements should report assets and liabilities at
a. Estimated current values at the date of the financial statements and, as additional information, at historical cost.
b. Estimated current values at the date of the financial statements.
c. Historical cost and, as additional information, at estimated current values at the date of the financial statements.
d. Historical cost.

14. A business interest that constitutes a large part of an individual's total assets should be presented in a personal statement of financial condition as
a. A separate listing of the individual assets and liabilities at cost.
b. Separate line items of both total assets and total liabilities at cost.
c. A single amount equal to the proprietorship equity.
d. A single amount equal to the estimated current value of the business interest.

15. Smith owns several works of art. At what amount should these art works be reported in Smith's personal financial statements?
a. Original cost.
b. Insured amount.
c. Smith's estimate.
d. Appraised value.

16. For the purpose of estimating income taxes to be reported in personal financial statements, assets and liabilities measured at their tax bases should be compared to assets and liabilities measured at their

	Assets	*Liabilities*
a.	Estimated current value	Estimated current amount
b.	Historical cost	Historical cost
c.	Estimated current value	Historical cost
d.	Historical cost	Estimated current amount

17. In personal financial statements, how should estimated income taxes on the excess of the estimated current values of assets over their tax bases be reported in the statement of financial condition?
a. As liabilities.
b. As deductions from the related assets.
c. Between liabilities and net worth.
d. In a footnote disclosure only.

MULTIPLE-CHOICE ANSWERS

1. c __ __	5. b __ __	9. a __ __	13. b __ __	17. c __ __
2. b __ __	6. c __ __	10. d __ __	14. d __ __	
3. d __ __	7. b __ __	11. c __ __	15. d __ __	1st: __/17 = __%
4. d __ __	8. a __ __	12. c __ __	16. a __ __	2nd: __/17 = __%

MULTIPLE-CHOICE ANSWER EXPLANATIONS

A. Personal Financial Statements

1. **(c)** Only the estimated amount of income taxes on the differences between the estimated current values and current amounts of assets and liabilities is presented between liabilities and net worth. Answer (a) is incorrect because the $40,000 estimated income taxes on the differences between the estimated current values and current amounts of assets and liabilities is presented between liabilities and net worth. Answer (b) is incorrect because the $20,000 current tax liability would be presented as a liability. Answer (d) is incorrect because the $20,000 current tax liability would be presented as a liability while the $40,000 amount would be presented between liabilities and net worth.

2. **(b)** In a personal statement of financial condition, assets are generally presented at estimated current values. Depending on the nature of the asset, current value can be estimated using fair market value, net realizable value, discounted cash flow, or appraised value. AICPA Statement of Position 82-1 specifies that a future interest that is nonforfeitable should be valued using discounted cash flow. Therefore, the interest in the pension plan should be valued at $90,000.

3. **(d)** Per SOP 82-1, assets are generally presented at their estimated current values on personal financial statements. For Kent's December 31, 2003, personal statement of financial condition, the current values of the marketable equity securities held as of that date should be used. Thus, Kent should report $98,900 ($95,500 + $3,400) for marketable equity securities.

4. **(d)** Per SOP 82-1, assets are generally presented at their estimated current values. Depending on the nature of the asset, current value can be estimated using fair market value (FMV), net realizable value, discounted cash flow, or appraised value. In this problem, the fair value of the stock ($180,000) is known and should be shown as the investment in Vohl. Note that the net income and dividends have nothing to do with the amount shown as the investment in Vohl, and this information is irrelevant.

5. **(b)** This problem requires that we determine Jen's vested interest in the 401(k) plan to be reported in her December 31, 2002 personal statement of financial condition. The problem states that employer contributions vest after an employee completes three years of service. As Jen has not completed three years of service as of December 31, 2002, none of the employer's contributions have vested. Thus, the problem is to determine Jen's contributions and the earnings on **her** contributions as follows:

2000 contributions	2,100
2001 contributions	2,300
2002 contributions	2,600
	7,000
Earnings on above contributions	1,200
Jen's vested interest	8,200

6. **(c)** SOP 82-1 states that assets are generally presented at their estimated current values in personal financial statements. Specifically, investments in life insurance are to be valued at their cash surrender value less outstanding loans on the policy. Therefore, the investment should be reported at $9,000 ($12,000 cash value − $3,000 outstanding loan).

7. **(b)** Per SOP 82-1, when investments in a limited business activity are not conducted in a separate business entity, separate asset and liability amounts of the investment should be shown on the statement of financial condition. Thus, the realty (asset) and the mortgage (liability) should be reported separately at $500,000 and $100,000, respectively (their estimated current values). An investment in a separate entity that is marketable as a going concern (e.g., closely held corporation) should be presented as one amount. Thus, the $80,000 in accounts payable should be netted against the current value of $900,000 to report a net investment of $820,000.

8. **(a)** Per SOP 82-1, noncancelable personal commitments should be reported at their discounted cash flow. A commitment must have all of the following attributes: (1) are for fixed or determinable amounts; (2) are not contingent on others' life expectancies or occurrence of a particular event (e.g., disability/death); and (3) do not require future performance of service by others. As the pledge to County Welfare Home is contingent upon the volunteers painting the walls and ceiling and the pledge to City Hospital is contingent upon the recovery of Ryan's comatose sister, both liabilities should be excluded from Ryan's personal statement of financial condition at December 31, 2002.

9. **(a)** Per SOP 82-1, estimated taxes that would be paid if all the assets were converted to cash and all the liabilities were paid should be included with the liabilities. Thus, $120,000 [($1,000,000 − $600,000) x .30] should be provided for estimated income taxes relating to the excess of current values over tax bases.

10. **(d)** A personal statement of financial condition presents estimated current values of assets and liabilities, estimated income taxes, and estimated net worth at a specified date. Income taxes payable should include unpaid income taxes for completed tax years, the estimated tax for the elapsed portion of the current year, and the estimated income tax on the difference between the current value of assets and the current amounts of liabilities and their respective tax bases. Thus, the amount to be reported on Shea's statement of financial condition for income taxes is $55,000, equal to the sum of $30,000 tax on income earned from January through April and $25,000 estimated income tax on the difference between the current value and tax bases of assets and liabilities.

11. (c)   Per SOP 82-1, assets are generally presented at their estimated current values on personal financial statements. Therefore, the assets should be reported at their fair value of $900,000, rather than at their cost of $500,000. SOP 82-1 also states that liabilities are presented at the lesser of the discounted amount of cash to be paid, or the current cash settlement amount. Therefore, the liabilities should be reported at $80,000. Estimated taxes that would be paid if all the assets were converted to cash and all the liabilities were paid should be included with the liabilities. Thus, 126,000 [(820,000 – 400,000) x .30] should be provided for estimated income taxes relating to the excess of current values over tax bases. Smith's net worth should be reported as $694,000 ($900,000 – $80,000 – $126,000).

12. (c)   Per SOP 82-1, personal financial statements consist of (1) a statement of financial condition and (2) a statement of changes in net worth.

13. (h)   Per SOP 82-1, a personal financial statement presents the estimated current values of assets and liabilities. Additional information at historical cost is not required.

14. (d)   Per SOP 82-1, business interests that constitute a large part of a person's total assets should be shown separately from other investments. The estimated **current value** of an investment in a separate entity, such as a closely held corporation, a partnership, or a sole proprietorship, should be shown in **one amount** as an investment if the entity is marketable as a going concern.

15. (d)   Per SOP 82-1, assets are generally presented at their estimated current values in a personal statement of financial condition. Depending on the nature of the asset, current value can be estimated using fair market value, net realizable value, discounted cash flow, or appraised value. The best estimate of the fair value of art is the appraised value.

16. (a)   In personal financial statements assets should be stated at their estimated current values and liabilities should be stated at the lower of the discounted value of their future cash payments or their current cash settlement amounts in accordance with SOP 82-1. These current amounts will differ from their tax bases and will give rise to **unrealized** tax gains and losses. A provision for estimated income taxes on these unrealized amounts should be incorporated into personal financial statements because when the unrealized gains and losses are realized, the related income taxes will have to be either paid or received.

17. (c)   SOP 82-1 specifically addresses the presentation of estimated income taxes on the excess of the estimated current values of assets over their tax bases in the statement of financial condition. This statement requires that the estimated income taxes should be presented between liabilities and net worth in the statement of financial condition.

B. Interim Reporting

The term interim reporting is used to describe financial reporting for periods of less than one year, generally quarterly financial statements. The primary purposes of interim reporting are to provide information which is more timely than is available in annual reports, and to highlight business turning points which could be "buried" in annual reports.

There are two basic conceptual approaches to interim reporting: the **discrete view** and the **integral view**.

Discrete view—Each interim period is a separate accounting period; interim period must stand on its own; same principles and procedures as for annual reports; no special accruals or deferrals.

Integral view—Each interim period is an integral part of an annual period; expectations for annual period must be reflected in interim reports; special accruals, deferrals, and allocations utilized.

APB 28 (see outline) adopted the **integral view**.

APB 28 consists of two parts. Part one does not require issuance of interim financial statements, but does prescribe accounting standards to be used in preparing such statements. Part two sets forth minimum disclosures to be included in interim financial reports.

The table below summarizes the accounting standards set forth in part one of APB 28.

Income statement item	General rule	Exceptions
Revenues	Same basis as annual reports	None
Cost of goods sold	Same basis as annual reports	1. Gross profit method may be used to estimate CGS and ending inventory for each interim period 2. Liquidation of LIFO base-period inventory, if expected to be replaced by year-end, is changed to CGS at its estimated replacement cost 3. Temporary declines in inventory market value need not be recognized 4. Planned manufacturing variances should be deferred if expected to be absorbed by year-end
All other costs and expenses	Same basis as annual reports	Expenditures which **clearly benefit** more than one interim period may be allocated among periods benefited (e.g., annual repairs, property taxes).
Income taxes	(Year-to-date income x Estimated annual effective tax rate) – (Expense recognized in previous quarters)	None
Discontinued operations	Recognized in interim period as incurred	None
Extraordinary items	Recognized in interim period as incurred. Materiality is evaluated based on expected annual results	None
Change in accounting principle	Retroactive type—same as annual reports; restate all prior periods including those of previous years presented. Cumulative effect type—if change made in first quarter, report cumulative effect in first quarter's results. If change made in second or third quarter, report cumulative effect in first quarter results, and restate previous interim periods as if change had been effective as of the first day of the fiscal year	None

The disclosures required in part two of APB 28 are summarized in the pronouncement outline. A key disclosure item for interim reporting is the seasonal nature of the firm's operations. This disclosure helps prevent misleading inferences and predictions about annual results.

APB 28 as interpreted by FASB Interpretation 18 requires that income tax expense be estimated each period using an estimated annual effective tax rate (see FASB Interpretation 18). The example below illustrates the application of this requirement.

	(a) *Quarterly income before income taxes*	(b) *Year-to-date income before income taxes*	(c) *Estimated annual effective tax rate*	(d) = (b) x (c) *Year-to-date income tax expense*	(e) *Previous quarter's expense*	(f) = (d) – (e) *Current quarter's expense*
Qtr						
1	$100,000	$100,000	30%	$ 30,000	$ 0	$ 30,000
2	150,000	250,000	32%	80,000	30,000	50,000
3	300,000	550,000	36%	198,000	80,000	118,000
4	200,000	750,000	35%	262,500	198,000	64,500

In the above chart, columns (a) and (c) are assumed to be given. Column (b) is obtained by accumulating column (a) figures. Column (e) is either the preceding quarter's entry in column (d) or the **cumulative** total of previous quarters in column (f).

MULTIPLE-CHOICE QUESTIONS (1-16)

1. On January 1, 2002, Builder Associates entered into a $1,000,000 long-term, fixed-price contract to construct a factory building for Manufacturing Company. Builder accounts for this contract under the percentage-of-completion, and estimated costs at completion at the end of each quarter for 2002 were as follows:

Quarter	Estimated percentage-of-completion	Estimated costs at completion
1	10%	$750,000
2*	10%	$750,000
3	25%	$960,000
4*	25%	$960,000

No work performed in the 2nd and 4th quarters.

What amounts should be reported by Builder as "Income on Construction Contract" in its quarterly income statements based on the above information?

	Gain (loss) for the three months ended			
	3/31/02	6/30/02	9/30/02	12/31/02
a.	$0	$0	$0	$10,000
b.	$25,000	$0	$(15,000)	$0
c.	$25,000	$0	$0	$0
d.	$25,000	$0	$ 6,000	$0

2. Kell Corp.'s $95,000 net income for the quarter ended September 30, 2002, included the following after-tax items:

• A $60,000 extraordinary gain, realized on April 30, 2002, was allocated equally to the second, third, and fourth quarters of 2002.

• A $16,000 cumulative-effect loss resulting from a change in inventory valuation method was recognized on August 2, 2001.

In addition, Kell paid $48,000 on February 1, 2002, for 2002 calendar-year property taxes. Of this amount, $12,000 was allocated to the third quarter of 2002.

For the quarter ended September 30, 2002, Kell should report net income of

    a. $ 91,000
    b. $103,000
    c. $111,000
    d. $115,000

3. Vilo Corp. has estimated that total depreciation expense for the year ending December 31, 2002, will amount to $60,000, and that 2002 year-end bonuses to employees will total $120,000. In Vilo's interim income statement for the six months ended June 30, 2002, what is the total amount of expense relating to these two items that should be reported?

    a. $0
    b. $ 30,000
    c. $ 90,000
    d. $180,000

4. On June 30, 2002, Mill Corp. incurred a $100,000 net loss from disposal of a business segment. Also, on June 30, 2002, Mill paid $40,000 for property taxes assessed for the calendar year 2002. What amount of the foregoing items should be included in the determination of Mill's net income or loss for the six-month interim period ended June 30, 2002?

    a. $140,000
    b. $120,000
    c. $ 90,000
    d. $ 70,000

5. During the first quarter of 2002, Tech Co. had income before taxes of $200,000, and its effective income tax rate was 15%. Tech's 2001 effective annual income tax rate was 30%, but Tech expects its 2002 effective annual income tax rate to be 25%. In its first quarter interim income statement, what amount of income tax expense should Tech report?

    a. $0
    b. $30,000
    c. $50,000
    d. $60,000

6. Bailey Company, a calendar-year corporation, has the following income before income tax provision and estimated effective annual income tax rates for the first three quarters of 2002:

Quarter	Income before income tax provision	Estimated effective annual tax rate at end of quarter
First	$60,000	40%
Second	70,000	40%
Third	40,000	45%

Bailey's income tax provision in its interim income statement for the third quarter should be

    a. $18,000
    b. $24,500
    c. $25,500
    d. $76,500

7. Advertising costs may be accrued or deferred to provide an appropriate expense in each period for

	Interim financial reporting	Year-end financial reporting
a.	Yes	No
b.	Yes	Yes
c.	No	No
d.	No	Yes

8. A planned volume variance in the first quarter, which is expected to be absorbed by the end of the fiscal period, ordinarily should be deferred at the end of the first quarter if it is

	Favorable	Unfavorable
a.	Yes	No
b.	No	Yes
c.	No	No
d.	Yes	Yes

9. Due to a decline in market price in the second quarter, Petal Co. incurred an inventory loss. The market price is expected to return to previous levels by the end of the year. At the end of the year the decline had not reversed. When should the loss be reported in Petal's interim income statements?

    a. Ratably over the second, third, and fourth quarters.
    b. Ratably over the third and fourth quarters.
    c. In the second quarter only.
    d. In the fourth quarter only.

10. An inventory loss from a market price decline occurred in the first quarter. The loss was not expected to be restored in the fiscal year. However, in the third quarter the inventory had a market price recovery that exceeded the market decline that occurred in the first quarter. For interim financial reporting, the dollar amount of net inventory should

a. Decrease in the first quarter by the amount of the market price decline and increase in the third quarter by the amount of the market price recovery.

b. Decrease in the first quarter by the amount of the market price decline and increase in the third quarter by the amount of decrease in the first quarter.

c. Not be affected in the first quarter and increase in the third quarter by the amount of the market price recovery that exceeded the amount of the market price decline.

d. Not be affected in either the first quarter or the third quarter.

11. For external reporting purposes, it is appropriate to use estimated gross profit rates to determine the cost of goods sold for

	Interim financial reporting	Year-end financial reporting
a.	Yes	Yes
b.	Yes	No
c.	No	Yes
d.	No	No

12. For interim financial reporting, the computation of a company's second quarter provision for income taxes uses an effective tax rate expected to be applicable for the full fiscal year. The effective tax rate should reflect anticipated

	Foreign tax rates	Available tax planning alternatives
a.	No	Yes
b.	No	No
c.	Yes	No
d.	Yes	Yes

13. For interim financial reporting, a company's income tax provision for the second quarter of 2002 should be determined using the

a. Effective tax rate expected to be applicable for the full year of 2002 as estimated at the end of the first quarter of 2002.

b. Effective tax rate expected to be applicable for the full year of 2002 as estimated at the end of the second quarter of 2002.

c. Effective tax rate expected to be applicable for second quarter of 2002.

d. Statutory tax rate for 2002.

14. APB 28, *Interim Financial Reporting,* concluded that interim financial reporting should be viewed primarily in which of the following ways?

a. As useful only if activity is spread evenly throughout the year.

b. As if the interim period were an annual accounting period.

c. As reporting for an integral part of an annual period.

d. As reporting under a comprehensive basis of accounting other than GAAP.

15. Conceptually, interim financial statements can be described as emphasizing

a. Timeliness over reliability.

b. Reliability over relevance.

c. Relevance over comparability.

d. Comparability over neutrality.

16. Wilson Corp. experienced a $50,000 decline in the market value of its inventory in the first quarter of its fiscal year. Wilson had expected this decline to reverse in the third quarter, and in fact, the third quarter recovery exceeded the previous decline by $10,000. Wilson's inventory did not experience any other declines in market value during the fiscal year. What amounts of loss and/or gain should Wilson report in its interim financial statements for the first and third quarters?

	First quarter	Third quarter
a.	$0	$0
b.	$0	$10,000 gain
c.	$50,000 loss	$50,000 gain
d.	$50,000 loss	$60,000 gain

MULTIPLE-CHOICE ANSWERS

1. b __ __	5. c __ __	9. d __ __	13. b __ __	16. a __ __
2. a __ __	6. b __ __	10. b __ __	14. c __ __	
3. c __ __	7. b __ __	11. b __ __	15. a __ __	1st: __/16 = __%
4. b __ __	8. d __ __	12. d __ __		2nd: __/16 = __%

MULTIPLE-CHOICE ANSWER EXPLANATIONS

B. Interim Reporting

1. (b) The requirement is to compute the income to be recognized in quarterly (interim) financial statements on a construction contract using the percentage-of-completion method. The solutions approach is to compute the income on the contract at the end of each quarter by (1) applying the estimated percentage-of-completion to the total estimated income to be recognized on the contract, and (2) subtracting the income recognized in preceding quarters to arrive at the income for the latest quarter. In the second and fourth quarters there was no work done on the contract and no change in the total estimated cost of completion. In quarter three the estimated costs of completion are revised upward. Since the cumulative income to date is less than income recognized in the first quarter, it is necessary to recognize a loss in the third quarter. The loss is handled as a change in accounting estimate rather than restating the first quarter.

Quarter 1:
10% ($1,000,000 – $750,000) = $25,000 income recognized

Quarter 2:
-0-

Quarter 3:
25% ($1,000,000 – $960,000) = $10,000 income earned to date

$10,000 income to date – $25,000 income recognized
   in previous periods = $(15,000) loss for quarter

Quarter 4:
-0-

2. (a) Per APB 28, extraordinary items, gains or losses from disposal of a segment of a business, and unusual or infrequently occurring items should not be prorated over the balance of the fiscal year. Thus, the $20,000 ($60,000 ÷ 3) extraordinary gain that was allocated to the third quarter should be subtracted from net income as it actually occurred in the second quarter. Consistent with the view that all accounting changes should be made effective as of the beginning of the fiscal period, the cumulative effect of the accounting change on retained earnings is computed at the beginning of the fiscal year and reported in the first interim period's income statement. If a cumulative-effect type change is made during an interim period subsequent to the first one, the prior interim reports must be restated as if the changes had been effective as of the first day of the fiscal year. Thus, the $16,000 cumulative-effect loss should not be recognized in the third quarter. The prior interim reports should be restated and the $16,000 loss should be added back to income of the third quarter to correct the income to be reported for the quarter. Property taxes should be allocated among the applicable quarters. As Kell Corp. properly allocated their property taxes, no adjustment to income is needed. Kell should report $91,000 ($95,000 – $20,000 + $16,000) as net income for the quarter ended September 30, 2002.

3. (c) Per APB 28, a cost charged to expense in an annual period should be allocated among the interim periods which clearly benefit from the expense through the use of accruals and/or deferrals. Both yearly bonuses and the use of an asset (depreciation expense) benefit the entire year. The expense for the **six month** interim statement should be ($60,000 + $120,000) ÷ 2 = $90,000.

4. (b) APB 28 states that revenues and gains should be recognized in interim reports on the same basis as used in annual reports. At June 30, 2002, Mill Corp. would report the entire $100,000 loss on the disposal of its business segment since the loss was incurred during the interim period. APB 28 also states that a cost charged to an expense in an annual period should be allocated among the interim periods that clearly benefit from the expense through the use of accruals and/or deferrals. Since the $40,000 property tax payment relates to the entire 2002 calendar year, $20,000 of the payment would be reported as an expense at June 30, 2002, while the remaining $20,000 would be reported as a prepaid expense.

5. (c) APB 28 states that the tax provision for an interim period is the tax for the year to date (estimated effective rate for the year times year-to-date income) less the total tax provisions reported for previous interim periods. In this case, the requirement is to calculate the tax provision for the first quarter interim income statement. The tax expense is $50,000 ($200,000 x 25%).

6. (b) The requirement is to calculate Bailey's income tax provision (expense) in its interim income statement for the third quarter. APB 28 states that the tax provision for an interim period is the tax for the year-to-date (estimated effective rate for the year times year-to-date income) less the total tax provisions reported for previous interim periods.

Year-to-date tax (45%)($170,000)	$76,500
Previously reported tax (40% x $130,000)	52,000
Third quarter tax provision	$24,500

7. (b) Per APB 28, advertising costs may be deferred within a fiscal year if the benefits clearly extend beyond the interim period that the expense was paid. Also, advertising costs may be accrued and assigned to interim periods in relation to sales. Year-end accruals and deferrals of costs are also considered appropriate accounting treatment. Note, however, that deferral in year-end reporting is permitted only if the advertising has not been run in the media.

8. (d) Per APB 28, a planned volume variance that is expected to be absorbed by the end of the fiscal year should be deferred at interim reporting dates.

9. (d) The requirement is to determine when the inventory loss should be reported. Per APB 28, inventory losses from market declines should not be deferred beyond the interim period in which the loss occurs. However, if the market decline is considered to be **temporary** and will be recovered by year-end, no loss needs to be recognized. A loss will be recognized in the fourth quarter only. In the second quarter the loss is considered temporary, therefore no loss is recognized. However, in the fourth quarter, when the decline does not reverse, it is deemed permanent and recognized in the fourth quarter. Losses are recognized in the period in which they occur, not ratably over several periods. Only expenses that benefit several periods (i.e., repairs and maintenance) are recognized ratably. The loss is not recorded in a period of temporary decline, only when the decline is considered to be permanent.

10. (b) Per APB 28, a decline in inventory market price, expected to be other than temporary, should be recognized in the period of decline. A subsequent recovery of market value should be recognized as a cost recovery in the period of increase, but **never** above original cost. The decline should be recognized when it occurs in the first quarter. The subsequent recovery should be recognized when it occurs in the third quarter. The subsequent recovery cannot exceed the amount of decline. A nontemporary decline should be shown in the quarter of price decrease.

11. (b) The requirement is to determine the appropriateness of estimated gross profit rates in determining cost of goods sold for interim and year-end external financial reporting purposes. The use of estimated gross profit rates to determine the cost of goods sold for an interim period is appropriate per APB 28. The method of estimation used and any significant adjustments that result from reconciliations with the annual physical inventory should be disclosed. An estimation of cost of goods sold is not allowable for year-end financial reporting per APB 43. (The actual cost of the goods sold must be determined by the use of a cost flow assumption that most clearly reflects periodic income.) Thus, an estimated cost of goods sold figure may be used for interim but not year-end statements.

12. (d) Per APB 28, "the effective tax rate should reflect anticipated investment tax credits, foreign tax rates, percentage depletion, capital gains rates, and other available tax planning alternatives."

13. (b) The requirement is to determine what tax rate should be used to calculate the income tax provision for interim reporting. Per APB 28, each interim period is considered to be an integral part of the annual period. Therefore, expectations for the annual period must be reflected in the interim report. The income tax expense should be calculated using the estimated annual effective tax rate. The estimated tax rate should be updated as of the end of each interim period (here, as of the second quarter). The statutory tax rate is only a part of the effective tax. The effective tax rate includes the statutory tax rate and a variety of other items.

14. (c) APB 28 adopted the **integral view,** which holds that each interim period is an integral part of an annual period, must reflect expectations for the annual period, and must utilize special accruals, deferrals, and allocations.

15. (a) The primary purposes of interim reporting are to provide information which is more **timely** than is available in annual reports and to highlight business turning points which could be "buried" in annual reports. This emphasis on timeliness comes at the expense of **reliability**. Accounting information pertaining to shorter periods may require more arbitrary allocations, and may not be as verifiable or representationally faithful as information contained in annual reports. Interim reports are generally more relevant and less reliable. Interim financial statements should not be any more or less comparable than annual reports.

16. (a) According to APB 28, *Interim Financial Reporting*, temporary declines in inventory market values are not recognized. Only declines that are apparently permanent or other than temporary need to be recognized. In this case, Wilson expected the decline to reverse in the third quarter; therefore, the decline is temporary and no loss would be recorded in the first quarter. Because no loss was recorded for the decline, no gain will be recognized in the third quarter for the recovery of the $50,000 decline. Also, assuming that the inventory was valued at cost at the beginning of the fiscal year, no gain will be recorded for the recovery excess of $10,000 since inventory may not be valued at an amount in excess of cost.

C. Segment Reporting

SFAS 131 (see outline) sets forth financial reporting standards for segment reporting, the disclosure of information about different components of an enterprise's operations as well as information related to the enterprise's products and services, its geographic areas, and its major customers.

The purpose of segment disclosure is to assist investors and lenders in assessing the future potential of an enterprise. Consolidated statements give the user the overall view (results of operations, financial position, cash flows). However, trends, opportunities, risk factors, etc., can get lost when data for a diversified company are merged into consolidated statements. Additionally, most intersegment transactions that are eliminated from consolidated financial information are included in segment information.

The approach used in SFAS 131 is a "management approach," meaning it is based on the way management organizes segments internally to make operating decisions and assess performance. Companies can segment their financial information by products or services, by geography, by legal entity, or by type of customer. The management approach facilitates consistent descriptions of an enterprise for both internal and external reporting and, in general, provides that external financial reporting closely conforms to internal reporting.

SFAS 131 does not apply to not-for-profit organizations or nonpublic enterprises.

Operating Segments

In SFAS 131, an **operating segment** is defined as

A component of an enterprise engaged in business activity for which it may earn revenues and incur expenses, about which separate financial information is available that is evaluated regularly by the chief operating decision makers in deciding how to allocate resources and in assessing performance.

A segment is significant (reportable) if it satisfies **at least one** of the following three 10% tests:

Revenues—Segment revenue (including intersegment revenue) is 10% or more of combined segment revenue (including intersegment revenue)

Operating profit or loss—The absolute amount of segment profit or loss is 10% or more of the **greater**, in absolute amount, of combined profit of segments reporting profit, or combined loss of segments reporting loss

Segment assets—Segment assets are 10% or more of total segment assets

Operating profit or loss is unaffiliated revenue and intersegment revenue, less **all** operating expenses as defined by the chief operating decision maker to evaluate the performance of the segments. Since segment revenue includes **intersegment sales, transfer pricing** becomes an issue. FASB requires companies to use the same transfer prices for segment reporting purposes as are used internally. Since most segments are **profit centers,** internal transfer prices generally reflect market prices.

Common costs are operating expenses incurred by the enterprise for the benefit of more than one operating segment. These costs should only be allocated to a segment for external reporting purposes if they are included in the measure of the segments profit or loss that is used internally by the chief operating decision maker.

Similarly, only those assets that are included internally in the measure of the segment's assets used to make operating decisions, shall be reported as assets of the segment in external financial reports.

Interperiod comparability must be considered in conjunction with the results of the 10% tests. If a segment fails to meet the tests, but has satisfied the tests in the past and is expected to in the future, it should be considered reportable in the current year for the sake of comparability. Similarly, if a segment which rarely passes the tests does so in the current year as the result of an unusual event, that segment may be excluded to preserve comparability.

There are some limitations to the number of segments which are to be reported. There must be enough segments separately reported so that at least 75% of unaffiliated revenues is shown by reportable segments (75% test). If the 75% test is not satisfied, additional segments must be designated as reportable until the test is satisfied. Also, the number of reportable segments should not be so large (ten is a rule of thumb) as to make the information less useful.

The following example illustrates the three 10% tests (revenues, operating profit or loss, and identifiable assets) and the 75% test:

Segment	Unaffiliated revenue	Intersegment revenue	Total revenue	Operating profit (loss)	Segment assets
A	$ 90	$ 90	$ 180	$ 20	$ 70
B	120		120	10	50
C	110	20	130	(40)	90
D	200		200	0	140
E	330	110	440	(100)	230
F	380	—	380	60	260
Total	$1,230	$220	$1,450	$(50)	$840

Revenues test: (10%)($1,450) = $145

Reportable segments: A, D, E, F

Operating profit or loss test: (10%)($140) = $14

Reportable segments: A, C, E, F

NOTE: Operating loss ($140) is greater than operating profit, $90

Segment assets test: (10%)($840) = $84

Reportable segments: C, D, E, F

Reportable segments: Those segments which pass **at least one** of the 10% tests. Segments A, C, D, E, and F are reportable in this example.

75% test: (75%)($1,230) = $922.50

Segments A, C, D, E, and F have total unaffiliated revenue of $1,110, which is greater than $922.50. The 75% test is satisfied; no additional segments need be reported.

Certain other factors must be considered when identifying reportable segments. An enterprise may consider aggregating two or more operating segments if they have similar economic characteristics and if the segments are similar in each of the following areas:

1.   The nature of the products and services
2.   The nature of the production processes
3.   The type of customer for their products and services
4.   The methods used to distribute their products or provide their services
5.   The nature of the regulatory environment

Aggregation can occur prior to performing the 10% tests if the enterprise desires.

Additionally, the enterprise may combine information on operating segments that do not meet any of the 10% tests to produce a reportable segment, but only if the segments meet a majority of the aggregation criteria presented above. It should be noted that information about operating segments that do not meet any of the 10% thresholds may still be disclosed separately, rather than as an aggregated total.

Segment Disclosures

SFAS 131 requires several disclosures regarding the enterprise's reportable segments. They include

1.   **General information**—An explanation of how management identified the enterprise's reportable segments, including whether operating segments have been aggregated. Additionally, a description of the types of products and services from which each reportable segment derives its revenues.

2.   **Certain information about reported segment profit and loss, segment assets, and the basis of measurement**—The enterprise shall disclose the following about each reportable segment if the specified amounts are reviewed by the chief operating decision maker:

     a.   Revenues from external customers
     b.   Intrasegment revenues
     c.   Interest revenue and expense (reported separately unless majority of segment's revenues are from interest and management relies primarily on net interest revenue to assess performance)
     d.   Depreciation, depletion, and amortization expense
     e.   Unusual items, extraordinary items
     f.   Equity in the net income of investees accounted for by the equity method
     g.   Income tax expense or benefit
     h.   Significant noncash items

Also, the basis of measurement for these items must be disclosed, including differences in measurement practices between a segment and the complete entity and differences in measurement practices in a segment between periods.

3. **Reconciliations**—The enterprise will need to reconcile the segment amounts disclosed to the corresponding enterprise amounts.

4. **Interim period information**—Although the interim disclosures are not as extensive as in the annual financial report, certain segment disclosures are required in interim financial reports.

Restatement of Previously Reported Segment Information

Segment reporting is required on a comparative basis. Therefore, the information must be restated to preserve comparability whenever the enterprise has changed the structure of its internal organization in a manner that causes a change to its reportable segments. The enterprise must explicitly disclose that it has restated the segment information of earlier periods.

Enterprise-Wide Disclosures about Products and Services, Geographic Areas, and Major Customers

The enterprise-wide disclosures are required for all enterprises, even those that have a single reportable segment. Disclosures need to be provided only if not provided as part of the segment information. Disclosures are required regardless of whether the information is used in making operating decisions.

Products and services. Revenue from external customers for each product and service shall be reported by the enterprise, unless it is impractical to do so.

Geographic areas. An enterprise shall report revenues from external customers and long-lived assets attributable to its domestic operations and **foreign operations,** unless it is impractical to do so. If revenues or assets of an individual foreign country are material, then these amounts should be separately disclosed. In addition, the enterprise's basis for attributing revenue to individual countries shall be disclosed.

Major customers. Certain disclosures are made concerning major customers if the following 10% test is met. If 10% or more of **consolidated revenue** comes from a **single** external customer, the enterprise must disclose this fact in addition to the amount of such revenues, and the identity of the segment or segments making the sales. (A group of customers under common control, such as subsidiaries of a parent, is regarded as a single customer. Similarly the various agencies of a government are considered to be a single customer.)

Flowchart for Identifying Reportable Operating Segments*

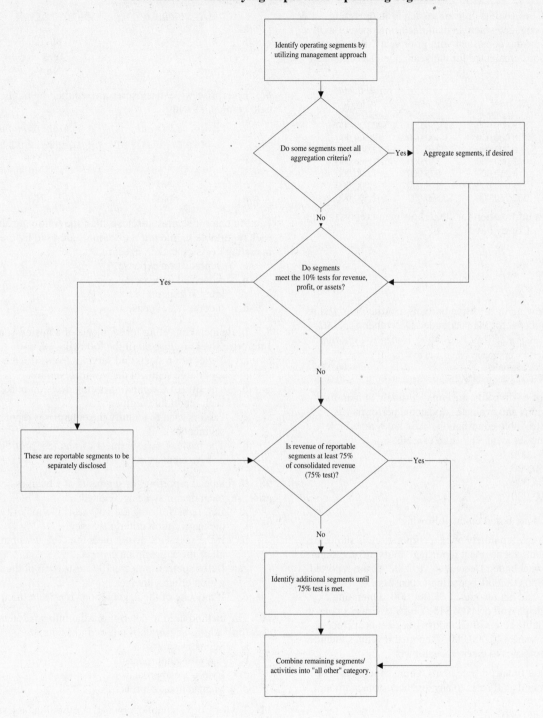

* *Adapted from SFAS 131, Appendix B, p. 47.*

MULTIPLE-CHOICE QUESTIONS (1-11)

1. Correy Corp. and its divisions (each is an operating segment) are engaged solely in manufacturing operations. The following data (consistent with prior years' data) pertain to the operations conducted for the year ended December 31, 2002:

(Industry operating segment)	*Total revenue*	*Operating profit*	*Identifiable assets at 12/31/02*
A	$10,000,000	$1,750,000	$20,000,000
B	8,000,000	1,400,000	17,500,000
C	6,000,000	1,200,000	12,500,000
D	3,000,000	550,000	7,500,000
E	4,250,000	675,000	7,000,000
F	1,500,000	225,000	3,000,000
	$32,750,000	$5,800,000	$67,500,000

In its segment information for 2002, how many reportable segments does Correy have?
    a. Three.
    b. Four.
    c. Five.
    d. Six.

2. The following information pertains to Aria Corp. and its operating segments for the year ended December 31, 2002:

Sales to unaffiliated customers	$2,000,000
Intersegment sales of products similar to those sold to unaffiliated customers	600,000
Interest earned on loans to other industry segments	40,000

Aria and all of its divisions are engaged solely in manufacturing operations and evaluates divisional performance based on controllable contribution. Aria has a reportable segment if that segment's revenue exceeds
    a. $264,000
    b. $260,000
    c. $204,000
    d. $200,000

Items 3 and 4 are based on the following:

Grum Corp., a publicly owned corporation, is subject to the requirements for segment reporting. In its income statement for the year ended December 31, 2002, Grum reported revenues of $50,000,000, operating expenses of $47,000,000, and net income of $3,000,000. Operating expenses include payroll costs of $15,000,000. Grum's combined identifiable assets of all industry segments at December 31, 2002, were $40,000,000. Reported revenues include $30,000,000 of sales to external customers.

3. In its 2002 financial statements, Grum should disclose major customer data if sales to any single customer amount to at least
    a. $ 300,000
    b. $1,500,000
    c. $4,000,000
    d. $5,000,000

4. External revenue reported by operating segments must be at least
    a. $22,500,000
    b. $15,000,000
    c. $12,500,000
    d. $37,500,000

5. Enterprise-wide disclosures include disclosures about

	Geographic areas	*Allocated costs*
a.	Yes	Yes
b.	Yes	No
c.	No	Yes
d.	No	No

6. Enterprise-wide disclosures are required by publicly held companies with

	Only one reportable segment	*More than one reportable segment*
a.	Yes	Yes
b.	Yes	No
c.	No	Yes
d.	No	No

7. An enterprise must disclose all of the following about each reportable segment if the amounts are used by the chief operating decision maker, except
    a. Depreciation expense.
    b. Allocated expenses.
    c. Interest expense.
    d. Income tax expense.

8. In financial reporting for segments of a business, an enterprise shall disclose all of the following except
    a. Types of products and services from which each reportable segment derives its revenues.
    b. The title of the chief operating decision maker of each reportable segment.
    c. Factors used to identify the enterprises reportable segments.
    d. The basis of measurement of segment profit or loss and segment assets.

9. In financial reporting for segments of a business enterprise, segment data may be aggregated
    a. Before performing the 10% tests if a majority of the aggregation criteria are met.
    b. If the segments do not meet the 10% tests but meet all of the aggregation criteria.
    c. Before performing the 10% tests if all of the aggregation criteria are met.
    d. If any one of the aggregation criteria are met.

10. The method used to determine what information to report for business segments is referred to as the
    a. Segment approach.
    b. Operating approach.
    c. Enterprise approach.
    d. Management approach.

11. Taylor Corp., a publicly owned corporation, assesses performance and makes operating decisions using the following information for its reportable segments:

Total revenues	$768,000
Total profit and loss	40,600

Included in the total profit and loss are intersegment profits of $6,100. In addition, Taylor has $500 of common costs for its reportable segments that are not allocated in reports used internally. For purposes of segment reporting, Taylor should report segment profit of
    a. $35,000
    b. $34,500
    c. $41,100
    d. $40,600

PROBLEM

Problem 1   (15 to 25 minutes)

Barnet Co. has several reportable operating segments that account for 90% of its operations. It has no foreign operations, sales, or major individual customers.

Required:

a.   What is the purpose of segment disclosure?

b.   Define operating segments and describe the approach used to identify operating segments.

c.   What tests should Barnet apply in determining its reportable segments?

MULTIPLE-CHOICE ANSWERS

1. c __ __	4. a __ __	7. b __ __	9. c __ __	11. d __ __
2. b __ __	5. b __ __	8. b __ __	10. d __ __	1st: __/11 = __%
3. d __ __	6. a __ __			2nd: __/11 = __%

MULTIPLE-CHOICE ANSWER EXPLANATIONS

C. Segment Reporting

1.   (c)   A division is a reportable segment if it is significant. A division is significant if it satisfies at least **one** of the three 10% tests:

1.   **Revenue** is 10% or more of the combined segment revenue (including intersegment revenue).
2.   **Operating profit** (loss) is 10% or more of the greater of the **absolute** combined segment profit or loss.
3.   **Identifiable assets** are 10% or more of the combined segment identifiable assets.

Industry A, B, C, and E pass the revenue and operating profit tests, but A, B, C, D, and E all pass the identifiable assets test. Since a division only has to pass one of the three 10% tests to be considered a reportable segment, Corey Corp. has five reportable segments.

2.   (b)   SFAS 131 requires that selected data for a segment be reported separately if one of three criteria is met. One of these criteria is met when a segment's revenue is greater than or equal to 10% of the combined revenues of all industry segments. Combined revenue includes sales to unaffiliated customers and intersegment sales or transfers. Thus, Aria has a reportable segment if that segment's revenues exceed $260,000 [($2,000,000 + $600,000) x 10%]. The $40,000 interest would not be included in combined revenue because it is not controllable at the division level.

3.   (d)   Per SFAS 131, if 10% or more of the revenue of an enterprise is derived from sales to any single customer, that fact and the amount of revenue from each customer shall be disclosed. In this problem, Grum reported revenues of $50,000,000 and thus should disclose major customer data if sales to any single customer amount to $5,000,000 ($50,000,000 x 10%).

4.   (a)   Per SFAS 131, there must be enough segments reported so that at least 75% of unaffiliated revenues is shown by reportable segments (75% test). Sales to external customers total $30,000,000 so external revenues reported by operating segments must be at least $22,500,000 ($30,000,000 x 75%).

5.   (b)   Per SFAS 131, enterprise-wide disclosures about products and services, geographic areas, and major customers are required for all enterprises.

6.   (a)   Per SFAS 131, enterprise-wide disclosures are to be reported by all public business enterprises, including those with a single reportable segment because the criteria for splitting the enterprise into reportable segments are not met.

7.   (b)   Per SFAS 131, the enterprise shall disclose the following about each reportable segment if the specified amounts are reviewed by the chief operating decision maker:

a.   Revenues from external customers
b.   Intrasegment revenues
c.   Interest revenue and expense (reported separately unless majority of segment's revenues are from interest and management relies primarily on net interest revenue to assess performance)
d.   Depreciation, depletion, and amortization expense
e.   Unusual items, extraordinary items
f.   Equity in the net income of investees accounted for by the equity method
g.   Income tax expense or benefit
h.   Significant noncash items

Allocated expenses are not specifically included as a required disclosure.

8.   (b)   Per SFAS 131, an enterprise shall disclose general information, including factors used to identify reportable segments and the types of products and services from which each reportable segment derives its revenues. SFAS 131 states that an enterprise shall disclose certain information about reported segment profit and loss, assets, and basis of measurement. SFAS 131 does not require disclosures about the term chief operating decision maker and specifically states that this term identifies a function, not necessarily a manager with a specific title.

9.   (c)   Per SFAS 131, two or more operating segments may be aggregated into a single operating segment if all of the aggregation criteria are met or if after performing the 10% test a majority of the aggregation criteria are met.

10.   (d)   Per SFAS 131, the method chosen for determining what information to report is referred to as the management approach.

11.   (d)   Per SFAS 131, an enterprise shall report a measure of profit and loss based on the measure reported to the chief operating decision maker for purposes of making decisions. The information used by management includes intersegment profits and should be included, but common costs are not allocated to the segments when assessing performance and should not be included.

ANSWER OUTLINE

Problem 1   Segment Reporting: Objectives, Tests, and Discontinued Operations

a.   Purposes of segment disclosures

- Assist in analyzing and understanding FS
- Permit better assessment of past performance and future prospects
- Provide more detail with respect to timing and amount of cash flows
- Show variations in rates of profitability, degrees and types of risk, opportunities for growth, and future capital demands among segments

b.   An operating segment is a component of an enterprise

- Engaged in business activity for which it may earn revenues and incur expenses
- For which separate financial information is available
- Whose operating results are evaluated regularly by the chief operating decision makers in deciding how to allocate resources and assess performance

Management approach

- Based on the way management organizes segments internally to make operating decisions and assess performance
- Facilitates consistent descriptions of an enterprise for both internal and external reporting
- Provides that external financial reporting will more closely conform to internal reporting

c.   Tests applied in determining reportable segments

- Segment revenue (from customers and other segments) is ≥ 10% of combined revenue of all segments
- Segment's absolute operating profit/loss is ≥ 10% of greater in absolute amount of
  - Combined operating profits of all segments with profits, or
  - Combined operating losses of all segments with losses
- Segment's identifiable assets are ≥ 10% of combined identifiable assets of all segments

UNOFFICIAL ANSWER

Problem 1   Segment Reporting: Objectives, Tests, and Discontinued Operations

a.   Segment disclosures assist in analyzing and understanding financial statements by permitting better assessment of past performance and future prospects. Disaggregated information provides more precise details of the uncertainties surrounding the timing and the amount of expected cash flows, because the various segments may have different rates of profitability, degrees and types of risk, opportunities for growth, and future capital demands.

b.   An operating segment is a component of an enterprise engaged in business activity for which it may earn revenues and incur expenses, about which separate financial information is prepared and evaluated by the chief operating decision makers to assess performance and allocate resources.

The approach used to identify segments is referred to as the management approach, meaning it is based on the way management organizes segments internally to make operating decisions and assess performance. The management approach will provide that external descriptions of an enterprise are consistent with internal descriptions and that external reporting will more closely conform to internal reporting used by management.

c.   Barnet should have reported a segment that satisfies one or more of the following tests:

- The segment's revenue, including both sales to unaffiliated customers and intersegment sales or transfers, is 10% or more of the combined revenue of all Barnet's segments.
- The segment's absolute amount of operating profit or loss is 10% or more of the greater in absolute amount of
  - The combined operating profits of all segments with operating profits, or
  - The combined operating losses of all segments with operating losses.
- The segment's identifiable assets are 10% or more of the combined identifiable assets of all segments.

Keep practicing! Wiley's CPA Examination Review Software has over 2,800 questions.

Available at www.wiley.com/cpa

D. Partnership Accounting

There are no authoritative pronouncements concerning the accounting for partnerships; thus, all of the principles described below have evolved through accounting practice.

Partnership accounting typically is tested through a few multiple-choice questions on the Financial Accounting and Reporting Exam. Occasionally, the material is tested through a problem.

1. Partnership Formation

The partnership is a separate **accounting entity** (not to be confused with a separate legal entity), and therefore its assets and liabilities should remain separate and distinct from the individual partner's personal assets and liabilities.

Thus, all assets contributed to the partnership are recorded by the partnership at their **fair market values**. All liabilities assumed by the partnership are recorded at their **present values**.

Upon formation, the amount credited to each partner's capital account is the difference between the fair market value of the assets contributed and the present value of the liabilities assumed from that partner. The capital accounts represent the residual equity of the partnership. The capital account of each partner reflects all of the activity of an individual partner: contributions, withdrawals, and the distributive share of net income (loss). In some cases, a **drawing** account is used as a clearing account for each partner's transactions with only the net effect of each period's activity shown in the capital account.

EXAMPLE: Partnership Formation

A and B form a partnership. A contributes cash of $50,000, while B contributed land with a fair market value of $50,000 and the partnership assumes a liability on the land of $25,000.

The entry to record the formation of the partnership is

Cash	50,000	
Land	50,000	
Liabilities		25,000
A Capital		50,000
B Capital		25,000

2. Allocation of Partnership Income (Loss)

The partners should have a written agreement (articles of copartnership) specifying the manner in which partnership income (loss) is to be distributed. Note that in the absence of a predetermined agreement, the profit and loss (P&L) is divided equally among the partners.

It is important to remember that P&L should **not** be distributed using a ratio based on the partners' capital balances unless this is the ratio specified in the articles of copartnership. A number of issues arise which complicate the allocation of partnership income (loss).

a. Partners may receive interest on their capital balances. If so, it must be determined what will constitute the capital balance (e.g., the year-end amount or some type of weighted-average).

b. Some of the partners may receive a salary.

c. Some of the partners may receive a bonus on distributable net income. If so, you need to determine if the bonus should be computed before or after salary and interest allocations.

d. A formula needs to be determined for allocating the remaining income. The formula agreed upon is usually termed the **residual, remainder**, or **profit (loss) sharing ratio**.

e. Finally, the partners should decide upon how income is to be allocated if net income is insufficient to cover partners' salaries, bonuses, and interest allocations. These allocations are usually made even if the effect is to create a negative remainder. This remainder is usually allocated in accordance with the profit (loss) ratio. However, it is important to note that partners may choose to allocate losses (or a negative remainder) in a different manner than income.

EXAMPLE: Partnership P&L Distribution

Partners receive 5% interest on beginning capital balances
Partner B receives a $6,000 salary
Partner C receives a 10% bonus after interest and salaries
The P&L ratios are A — 50%, B — 30%, C — 20%

Assuming partnership net income of $18,250, the following distribution schedule would be prepared:

	A	B	C	Total
P&L ratio	50%	30%	20%	
Beginning capital balance	30,000	10,000	5,000	45,000
Net income				(18,250)
5% interest	1,500	500	250	2,250
Salary		6,000		6,000
Bonus			1,000*	1,000
Distribution of residual	4,500	2,700	1,800	9,000
Total	6,000	9,200	3,050	--
Ending capital balances	36,000	19,200	8,050	

* ($18,250 - $8,250) x .10 = $1,000

   *Note that if the interest, salary, and bonus allocation had exceeded net income, the excess would have been deducted on the distri-
   bution schedule in the P&L ratio.*

3. **Partnership Dissolution (Changes in Ownership)**

   Partnership dissolution occurs whenever there is a change in ownership (e.g., the addition of a new partner, or the retirement or death of an existing partner). This is not to be confused with partnership liquidation, which is the winding up of partnership affairs and termination of the business. Under dissolution the partnership business continues, but under different ownership.

   When partnership dissolution occurs a new accounting entity results. The partnership should first adjust its records so that all accounts are properly stated at the date of dissolution. After the income (loss) has been properly allocated to the existing partners' capital accounts, all assets and liabilities should be adjusted to their fair market value and their present values, respectively. The latter step is performed because the dissolution results in a new accounting entity.

   After all adjustments have been made, the accounting for dissolution depends on the type of transaction that caused the dissolution. These transactions can be broken down into two types:

   • Transactions between the partnership and a partner (e.g., a new partner contributes assets, or a retiring partner withdraws assets)
   • Transactions between partners (e.g., a new partner purchases an interest from one or more existing partners, or a retiring partner sells his/her interest to one or more existing partners)

   a. **Transactions between a partner and the partnership**

      (1) **Admission of a new partner**

         When a new partner is admitted to the partnership essentially three cases can result. The new partner can invest assets into the partnership and receive a capital balance

         (a) Equal to his/her purchase price
         (b) Greater than his/her purchase price
         (c) Less than his/her purchase price

         If the new partner's capital balance is equal to the assets invested, then the entry debits the asset(s) contributed and credits the new partner's capital account for the fair value of the asset(s) contributed.

         If the new partner's capital balance is not equal to the assets invested [as in situation (b) and (c) above], then either the bonus or goodwill method must be used to account for the difference.

         Bonus method—The old partnership capital plus the new partner's asset contribution is equal to the new partnership capital. The new partner's capital is allocated his purchase share (e.g., 40%) and the old partner's capital accounts are adjusted as if they had been paid (or as if they paid) a bonus. The adjustment to the old partners' capital accounts is made in accordance with their profit (loss) sharing ratio.

         The bonus method implies that the old partners either received a bonus from the new partner, or they paid a bonus to the new partner. As a result the old partners' capital accounts are either debited to reflect a bonus paid, or credited to reflect a bonus received. The new partner's capital account is **never** equal to the amount of assets contributed in a case where the bonus method is used.

         Goodwill method—The old partnership capital plus the new partner's asset contribution is **not** equal to the new partnership capital. This is because goodwill is recorded on the partnership books for the difference between the total identifiable assets of the partnership (not including goodwill) and the deemed value of the partnership entity (which includes goodwill). Under the goodwill method, valuation of the new partnership is the objective.

How the value of the partnership is determined depends on whether the book value acquired is greater or less than the asset(s) invested. If the book value acquired is less than the asset(s) invested, the value is determined based upon the new partner's contribution, and goodwill is allocated to the old partners' accounts. If the book value acquired is greater than the asset(s) contributed, the value is based upon the existing capital accounts, and goodwill is attributed to the new partner.

The decision as to whether the bonus or goodwill method should be used rests with the partners involved. In other words, the bonus and goodwill methods are alternative solutions to the same problem.

EXAMPLE: *Partnership Dissolution—Bonus Method*

Total old capital for ABC Partnership is $60,000.

Partner	A	B	C
Capital	$10,000	$20,000	$30,000
P&L Ratio	40%	40%	20%

Case 1

D is admitted to the partnership and is given a 20% interest in the capital in return for a cash contribution of $30,000.

Cash	30,000	
D Capital		18,000
A Capital		4,800
B Capital		4,800
C Capital		2,400

The total partnership capital to be shown on the books is $90,000 ($60,000 + $30,000) of which D is entitled to a 20% interest, or a capital balance of $18,000. The remaining $12,000 is treated as a bonus to the old partners and is allocated to their capital accounts in accordance with their P&L ratio.

Case 2

D is admitted to the partnership and is given a 20% interest in the capital in return for a cash contribution of $10,000.

Cash	10,000	
A Capital	1,600	
B Capital	1,600	
C Capital	800	
D Capital		14,000

The total partnership capital to be shown on the books is $70,000 ($60,000 + $10,000) of which D is entitled to a 20% interest, or a capital balance of $14,000. The difference of $4,000 ($10,000 – $14,000) is allocated to the old partners' accounts as if they had paid a bonus to the new partner.

EXAMPLE: *Partnership Dissolution—Goodwill Method*

Use the same original data as given above.

Case 1

D is admitted to the partnership and is given a 20% interest in the capital in return for a cash contribution of $20,000. The partners elect to record goodwill. The book value acquired [($60,000 + $20,000) x 20% = $16,000] is less than the asset contributed.

The value of the partnership is determined based upon the contribution of the new partner. In this case it is assumed that the partnership value is $100,000 ($20,000/20%). The resulting goodwill is $20,000 ($100,000 – $80,000). The $80,000 represents the total current capital, exclusive of goodwill, $60,000 of which is attributable to the old partners and $20,000 of which is attributable to the new partner.

Goodwill	20,000	
A Capital		8,000
B Capital		8,000
C Capital		4,000
Cash	20,000	
D Capital		20,000

Goodwill was allocated to the old partners in their P&L ratio. Also note that the capital balance of D represents 20% of the total capital of the partnership.

Case 2

D is admitted to the partnership and is given a 20% interest in the capital in return for a cash contribution of $10,000. The partners elect to record goodwill. The book value acquired [($60,000 + $10,000) x 20% = $14,000] is greater than the asset contributed.

The partnership value is based upon the capital accounts of the existing partners. Because D is entitled to a 20% interest, the $60,000 capital of the old partners must represent 80% of the capital. This means that the total value of the partnership is $75,000 ($60,000/80%). D's total contribution consists of the $10,000 in cash and $5,000 of goodwill. The goodwill is determined as the difference between the cash contribution and the 20% of the partnership capital.

Cash	10,000	
Goodwill	5,000	
D Capital		15,000

Note that in this last case no adjustment is made to the capital accounts of partners A, B, and C.

The table below summarizes the bonus and goodwill situations discussed above:

When to Apply Bonus Method	**When to Apply Goodwill Method**
New Old New Partner's Partnership = Partners' + Asset Capital Capital Investment	New Old New Partner's Partnership > Partners' + Asset Capital Capital Investment
Which Partner(s) Receive Bonus • **New Partner** New Partner's New Partner's Capital Credit > Asset Investment (The difference represents the bonus.)	***Which Partner(s) Goodwill Is Recognized*** • **New Partner's Goodwill** New Partner's New Partner's Capital Credit > Asset Investment (The difference represents goodwill.)
• **Old Partners** New Partner's New Partner's Capital Credit < Asset Investment (The difference represents the bonus allocated to old partners in their P&L Ratio.)	• **Old Partners' Goodwill** New Partner's New Partner's Capital Credit = Asset Investment (Goodwill is allocated to old partners in their P & L Ratio.)

(2) **Partner death or withdrawal**

The death or withdrawal of a partner is treated in much the same manner as the admission of a new partner. However, there is no new capital account to be recorded; we are dealing only with the capital accounts of the original partners. Either the bonus or goodwill method may be used. The key thing to remember in regard to a partner's withdrawal from the partnership is that the withdrawing partner's capital account must be adjusted to the amount that the withdrawing partner is expected to receive.

EXAMPLE: Partner Withdrawal

Assume the same partnership data as given for the ABC partnership earlier.

Case 1

Assume that A withdraws from the partnership after reaching an agreement with partners B & C that would pay him $16,000. The remaining partners elect not to record goodwill.

B Capital	4,000	
C Capital	2,000	
A Capital		6,000
A Capital	16,000	
Cash		16,000

The $6,000 bonus is determined as the difference between the current balance of A's capital account and the amount of his buyout agreement. This "bonus" is then allocated between the remaining partners' capital accounts in proportion to their P&L ratios.

Case 2

Assume again that A withdraws from the partnership pursuant to the same agreement except that this time the partners elect to record goodwill.

The first step is to determine the amount of goodwill to be recorded. In this case we know that A's capital account must have a balance of $16,000, the agreed buyout payment he is to receive. In order to accomplish this, the total partnership assets must be increased by some amount of which $6,000 represents 40%, A's P&L ratio. Therefore, the amount of goodwill to be recorded is $15,000 ($6,000/40%).

Goodwill	15,000	
A Capital		6,000
B Capital		6,000
C Capital		3,000
A Capital	16,000	
Cash		16,000

Note that in this case all of the partners' capital accounts are adjusted to record the goodwill in accordance with their P&L ratios.

b. **Transactions between partners**

The sale of a partnership interest is a transaction only between the partners. Thus, the treatment accorded the transaction is determined by the partners involved.

There are two means of dealing with such a transaction. The first is to simply transfer a portion of the existing partners' capital to a new capital account for the buying partner.

EXAMPLE: Sale of a Partnership Interest—No Goodwill Recorded

Assume the following for the AB partnership:

Partner	A	B
Capital	$50,000	$50,000
P&L Ratio	60%	40%

Case 1

*Assume that C wishes to enter the partnership by buying 50% of the partnership interest from both A and B for a total of $80,000. It is important to note that the $80,000 is being paid to the individual partners and **not** to the partnership. Thus, we are only concerned with the proper adjustment between the capital accounts, **not** the recording of the cash. This approach ignores the price that C paid for the partnership interest.*

A Capital	25,000	
B Capital	25,000	
C Capital		50,000

The other method available for recording a transaction between partners involves the recording of implied goodwill.

EXAMPLE: Sale of Partnership Interest—Recording Goodwill

Assume the same facts presented above for the sale of the partnership interest except that in this case the partners elect to record goodwill.

Case 1

*Assuming that C paid $80,000 for a 50% interest in the partnership the implied value of the partnership assets is $160,000 ($80,000/50%). Because total capital prior to the purchase is only $100,000, the amount of goodwill that must be recorded is $60,000. The goodwill is allocated to the prior partners' accounts in proportion to their P&L ratios. Note that this entry is made **before** an adjustment is made to reflect C's admission to the partnership.*

Goodwill	60,000	
A Capital		36,000
B Capital		24,000

Now we can record the sale of the partnership interest to C. The capital balance of A is now $86,000 ($50,000 + $36,000) while the capital balance of B is $74,000 ($50,000 + $24,000). Recall that C is to receive 50% of each balance.

A Capital	43,000	
B Capital	37,000	
C Capital		80,000

Notice that in this situation the capital balance of C after the purchase is equal to the amount of the purchase price. Again no entry is made to record the receipt of cash because the cash goes directly to the individual partners, A and B.

4. **Partnership Liquidation**

A liquidation is the winding up of the partnership business. That is, it sells all of its noncash assets, pays its liabilities, and makes a final liquidating distribution to the remaining partners.

There are four basic steps to a partnership liquidation.

1. Any operating income or loss up to the date of the liquidation should be computed and allocated to the partners' capital accounts on the basis of their P&L ratio.
2. All noncash assets are sold and converted to cash. The gain (loss) realized on the sale of such assets is allocated to the partners' capital accounts on the basis of their P&L ratio.
3. Any creditors' claims, including liquidation expenses or anticipated future claims, are satisfied through the payment or reserve of cash.
4. The remaining unreserved cash is distributed to the remaining partners in accordance with the balance in their capital accounts. Note that this is **not** necessarily the P&L ratio.

Two factors that may complicate the liquidation process are the existence of loans or advances between the partnership and one or more of the partners, or the creation of a deficit in a partner's capital account because of the allocation of a loss. When loans exist between the partnership and a partner, the capital account and the loan(s) are combined to give a net amount. This is often referred to as the right of offset. When a deficit exists, the amount of the deficit is allocated to the remaining solvent partners' capital accounts on the basis of their relative P&L ratio. Note here that if the partner with the capital deficit is personally solvent, he has a liability to the remaining partners for the amount of the deficit.

There are two topics that appear with regularity on the CPA examination in regard to the liquidation of a partnership. They are the statement of partnership liquidation and the determination of a "safe payment" in an installment liquidation.

a. **Statement of partnership liquidation**

The statement of partnership liquidation shows in detail all of the transactions associated with the liquidation of the partnership. It should be noted here that the liquidation of a partnership can take one of two forms: simple or installment. A simple liquidation (illustrated below) is one in which all of the assets are sold in bulk and all of the creditors' claims are satisfied before a single liquidating distribution is made to the partners. Because the assets are sold in bulk there is a tendency to realize greater losses than if the assets were sold over a period of time. As a result, many partnerships liquidate on an installment basis. In an installment liquidation the assets are sold over a period of time and the cash is distributed to the partners as it becomes available.

EXAMPLE: Statement of Partnership Liquidation—Simple Liquidation

> *Assume the following:*
>
> *The capital balances are as given below.*
> *The P&L ratio is 5:3:2 for A, B, and C, respectively.*

STATEMENT OF PARTNERSHIP LIQUIDATION

	Cash	*Other assets*	*Liabilities*	*A (50%)*	*B (30%)*	*C (20%)*
Balances	5,000	75,000	45,000	12,000	17,000	6,000
Sale of assets ($20,000 loss)	40,000	(60,000)		(10,000)	(6,000)	(4,000)
	45,000	15,000	45,000	2,000	11,000	2,000
Payment of liabilities	(45,000)		(45,000)			
	0	15,000	0	2,000	11,000	2,000
Sale of assets ($5,000 loss)	10,000	(15,000)		(2,500)	(1,500)	(1,000)
	10,000	0	0	(500)	9,500	1,000
Distribution of A's deficit				500	(300)	(200)
	10,000	0	0	0	9,200	800
Final distribution of cash	(10,000)				(9,200)	(800)

> *Notice that after the noncash assets have been sold and the creditors satisfied, a $500 deficit remains in A's capital account. The deficit is allocated to the remaining solvent partners on the basis of their relative P&L ratios, in this case, 3:2. A is liable to the partnership for the $500. If A is personally solvent and repays the $500, then $300 will go to B and $200 will go to C.*

If in the above example there had been liquidation expenses or loans between the partnership and partners, these would have to be recognized in the statement prior to any distribution to partners. A loan receivable from or payable to a partner is simply offset to (closed against) that partner's capital account.

b. **Installment method of cash distribution**

There are two keys to preparing a statement of partnership liquidation under the installment method: the determination of the available cash balance at any given point in time and the determination of which partner(s) is(are) to receive the payment of that cash. The reason that the cash is not distributed in accordance with the P&L ratio is twofold: first, the final cash distribution is based upon the balance in each partner's capital account, **not** the P&L ratio, and second, there will be situations, as illustrated in the previous example, where one or more partners will have deficit balances in their capital accounts. If this is the case, they should **never** receive a cash distribution, even if the deficit does not arise until late in the liquidation process.

The determination of the available cash balance is generally very straightforward. The beginning cash balance (cash on hand at the start of the liquidation process) is adjusted for the cash receipts from receivables, sale of noncash assets, payment to creditors, and liquidation expenses incurred. A situation may occur where a certain amount of cash is to be reserved for payment of future liabilities that may arise. If this is the case, this cash should be treated as an escrowed, or restricted, asset which makes it unavailable for current distribution to the partners.

The determination of which partner(s) is(are) to receive the available cash is somewhat more difficult. There are a number of ways to make this computation, all of which are equally correct in the eyes of the examiners. This determination can be made at the beginning of the liquidation process or at the time of each payment. In making this determination there are two key assumptions that must be made: (1) the individual partners are assumed to be personally insolvent, and (2) the remaining noncash assets are deemed to be worthless (thus creating a maximum possible amount of loss).

One method of determining the amount of the "safe payment" is the use of an Installment Cash Distribution Schedule. This schedule is prepared by determining the amount of loss required to eliminate each partner's capital account. As noted above, all of the remaining noncash assets are to be considered worthless at the time a safe payment is determined. Thus, if we determine the amount of loss required to eliminate each partner's capital balance, we can determine the order in which the partners should receive the cash payments.

When preparing this schedule it is important to make sure that the proper capital balance is used. The capital balance used **must** be inclusive of any loans or advances between the partnership and partners. Thus, the capital balance at the beginning of the liquidation process is increased by any amount owed to the partner by the partnership, and decreased by any amount owed to the partnership by the partner.

EXAMPLE: Schedule of Possible Losses and Installment Cash Distribution

Assume the same data as used for the previous example.

SCHEDULE OF POSSIBLE LOSSES

	Total	*A (50%)*	*B (30%)*	*C (20%)*
Net capital balances	*$35,000*	*$12,000*	*$17,000*	*$6,000*
Loss to eliminate A	*24,000*	*(12,000)*	*(7,200)*	*(4,800)*
		0	*$ 9,800*	*$1,200*
Additional loss to eliminate C	*3,000**		*(1,800)*	*(1,200)*
			8,000	*0*
Additional loss to eliminate B	*8,000*		*(8,000)*	
	$35,000		*0*	

* *Allocated 60:40*

The total capital balance of $35,000 indicates that if the noncash assets are sold for $35,000 less than their book value, then none of the partners will receive a cash distribution. The purpose of this schedule is to determine how much of a loss each partner's capital account can withstand based on that partner's P&L ratio. In this example A's capital would be eliminated if the partnership incurred a $24,000 ($12,000/50%) loss, B's would be eliminated by a $56,667 ($17,000/30%) loss, and C's by a $30,000 ($6,000/20%) loss. A is assumed to be eliminated first because it would take the smallest amount of loss to eliminate his account. Once A is eliminated as a partner, the P&L ratios change to reflect the relative P&L ratio of the remaining partners, in this case B and C. Based on the remaining capital balances and the relative P&L ratio, it would take a $16,333 ($9,800/60%) loss to eliminate B and a $3,000 ($1,200/40%) loss to eliminate C. Now that C is eliminated B will share all of the profits and losses as a sole partner (i.e., 100%). It will now take an $8,000 loss to eliminate B's capital. The resulting installment cash distribution schedule would appear as follows (this schedule assumes that all creditors have already received full payment; thus, the cash amount represents available cash):

INSTALLMENT CASH DISTRIBUTION SCHEDULE

Partner		*A*	*B*	*C*
First	*$ 8,000*		*100%*	
Next	*3,000*		*60%*	*40%*
Next	*24,000*	*50%*	*30%*	*20%*
Any other		*50%*	*30%*	*20%*

While the example shown in section 4.a. was not an installment liquidation, the Installment Cash Distribution Schedule shown above could still be used to determine how the available cash of $10,000 is to be distributed. This is illustrated below.

Partner		*A*	*B*	*C*
First	*$ 8,000*		*$8,000*	
Next	*$ 2,000*		*$1,200*	*$800*
Total	*$10,000*	*--*	*$9,200*	*$800*

It is important to note that this method is acceptable for most purposes; however, a CPA exam problem may require the "safe payment" approach where the amount of the safe payment is computed at a specific point in time.

5. **Incorporation of a Partnership**

The incorporation of a partnership results in the formation of a new accounting (and legal) entity. This means that the partnership must adjust its records up to the date of incorporation. First, the partnership closes its books and recognizes any income or loss up to the date of incorporation. Second, the books of the partnership are adjusted to reflect the fair market value of the partnership assets and the present value of partnership liabilities. A corresponding adjustment is made to the capital accounts in accordance with the partners' P&L ratio. Third, common stock is distributed to the partners in accordance with the amounts in their capital accounts. Note that the entries to record the receipt of stock by the corporation are different depending upon whether the corporation retains the partnership books or establishes new books.

Retention of the partnership books means that the issuance of common stock results in the closing of the partners' capital accounts with credits going to common stock and additional paid-in capital.

Establishing new books means that the assets and liabilities are closed out and the difference between their net value and the value of the corporate stock is debited to an asset "capital stock from corporation." This account is then credited and the partners' capital accounts debited to record the distribution of stock.

MULTIPLE-CHOICE QUESTIONS (1-23)

1. Roberts and Smith drafted a partnership agreement that lists the following assets contributed at the partnership's formation:

| | Contributed by | |
	Roberts	Smith
Cash	$20,000	$30,000
Inventory	--	15,000
Building	--	40,000
Furniture & equipment	15,000	--

The building is subject to a mortgage of $10,000, which the partnership has assumed. The partnership agreement also specifies that profits and losses are to be distributed evenly. What amounts should be recorded as capital for Roberts and Smith at the formation of the partnership?

	Roberts	Smith
a.	$35,000	$85,000
b.	$35,000	$75,000
c.	$55,000	$55,000
d.	$60,000	$60,000

2. On April 30, 2002, Algee, Belger, and Ceda formed a partnership by combining their separate business proprietorships. Algee contributed cash of $50,000. Belger contributed property with a $36,000 carrying amount, a $40,000 original cost, and $80,000 fair value. The partnership accepted responsibility for the $35,000 mortgage attached to the property. Ceda contributed equipment with a $30,000 carrying amount, a $75,000 original cost, and $55,000 fair value. The partnership agreement specifies that profits and losses are to be shared equally but is silent regarding capital contributions. Which partner has the largest April 30, 2002 capital account balance?

    a.   Algee.
    b.   Belger.
    c.   Ceda.
    d.   All capital account balances are equal.

3. Abel and Carr formed a partnership and agreed to divide initial capital equally, even though Abel contributed $100,000 and Carr contributed $84,000 in identifiable assets. Under the bonus approach to adjust the capital accounts, Carr's unidentifiable asset should be debited for

    a. $46,000
    b. $16,000
    c. $ 8,000
    d. $0

4. When property other than cash is invested in a partnership, at what amount should the noncash property be credited to the contributing partner's capital account?

    a.   Fair value at the date of contribution.
    b.   Contributing partner's original cost.
    c.   Assessed valuation for property tax purposes.
    d.   Contributing partner's tax basis.

5. Red and White formed a partnership in 2002. The partnership agreement provides for annual salary allowances of $55,000 for Red and $45,000 for White. The partners share profits equally and losses in a 60/40 ratio. The partnership had earnings of $80,000 for 2002 before any allowance to partners. What amount of these earnings should be credited to each partner's capital account?

	Red	White
a.	$40,000	$40,000
b.	$43,000	$37,000
c.	$44,000	$36,000
d.	$45,000	$35,000

6. Fox, Greg, and Howe are partners with average capital balances during 2001 of $120,000, $60,000, and $40,000, respectively. Partners receive 10% interest on their average capital balances. After deducting salaries of $30,000 to Fox and $20,000 to Howe, the residual profit or loss is divided equally. In 2002 the partnership sustained a $33,000 loss before interest and salaries to partners. By what amount should Fox's capital account change?

    a. $ 7,000 increase.
    b. $11,000 decrease.
    c. $35,000 decrease.
    d. $42,000 increase.

7. The partnership agreement of Axel, Berg & Cobb provides for the year-end allocation of net income in the following order:

    •   First, Axel is to receive 10% of net income up to $100,000 and 20% over $100,000.
    •   Second, Berg and Cobb each are to receive 5% of the remaining income over $150,000.
    •   The balance of income is to be allocated equally among the three partners.

The partnership's 2002 net income was $250,000 before any allocations to partners. What amount should be allocated to Axel?

    a. $101,000
    b. $103,000
    c. $108,000
    d. $110,000

8. The partnership agreement of Reid and Simm provides that interest at 10% per year is to be credited to each partner on the basis of weighted-average capital balances. A summary of Simm's capital account for the year ended December 31, 2002, is as follows:

Balance, January 1	$140,000
Additional investment, July 1	40,000
Withdrawal, August 1	(15,000)
Balance, December 31	165,000

What amount of interest should be credited to Simm's capital account for 2002?

    a. $15,250
    b. $15,375
    c. $16,500
    d. $17,250

9. The Flat and Iron partnership agreement provides for Flat to receive a 20% bonus on profits before the bonus. Remaining profits and losses are divided between Flat and Iron in the ratio of 2:3, respectively. Which partner has a greater advantage when the partnership has a profit or when it has a loss?

	Profit	Loss
a.	Flat	Iron
b.	Flat	Flat
c.	Iron	Flat
d.	Iron	Iron

10. Blau and Rubi are partners who share profits and losses in the ratio of 6:4, respectively. On May 1, 2002, their respective capital accounts were as follows:

Blau	$60,000
Rubi	50,000

On that date, Lind was admitted as a partner with a one-third interest in capital and profits for an investment of $40,000. The new partnership began with total capital of $150,000. Immediately after Lind's admission, Blau's capital should be

- a. $50,000
- b. $54,000
- c. $56,667
- d. $60,000

11. Kern and Pate are partners with capital balances of $60,000 and $20,000, respectively. Profits and losses are divided in the ratio of 60:40. Kern and Pate decided to form a new partnership with Grant, who invested land valued at $15,000 for a 20% capital interest in the new partnership. Grant's cost of the land was $12,000. The partnership elected to use the bonus method to record the admission of Grant into the partnership. Grant's capital account should be credited for

- a. $12,000
- b. $15,000
- c. $16,000
- d. $19,000

12. Dunn and Grey are partners with capital account balances of $60,000 and $90,000, respectively. They agree to admit Zorn as a partner with a one-third interest in capital and profits, for an investment of $100,000, after revaluing the assets of Dunn and Grey. Goodwill to the original partners should be

- a. $0
- b. $33,333
- c. $50,000
- d. $66,667

Items 13 and 14 are based on the following:

The following condensed balance sheet is presented for the partnership of Alfa and Beda, who share profits and losses in the ratio of 60:40, respectively:

Cash	$ 45,000
Other assets	625,000
Beda, loan	30,000
	$700,000
Accounts payable	$120,000
Alfa, capital	348,000
Beda, capital	232,000
	$700,000

13. The assets and liabilities are fairly valued on the balance sheet. Alfa and Beda decide to admit Capp as a new partner with 20% interest. No goodwill or bonus is to be recorded. What amount should Capp contribute in cash or other assets?

- a. $110,000
- b. $116,000
- c. $140,000
- d. $145,000

14. Instead of admitting a new partner, Alfa and Beda decide to liquidate the partnership. If the other assets are sold for $500,000, what amount of the available cash should be distributed to Alfa?

- a. $255,000
- b. $273,000
- c. $327,000
- d. $348,000

15. In the Adel-Brick partnership, Adel and Brick had a capital ratio of 3:1 and a profit and loss ratio of 2:1, respectively. The bonus method was used to record Colter's admittance as a new partner. What ratio would be used to allocate, to Adel and Brick, the excess of Colter's contribution over the amount credited to Colter's capital account?

- a. Adel and Brick's new relative capital ratio.
- b. Adel and Brick's new relative profit and loss ratio.
- c. Adel and Brick's old capital ratio.
- d. Adel and Brick's old profit and loss ratio.

Items 16 and 17 are based on the following:

On June 30, 2002, the condensed balance sheet for the partnership of Eddy, Fox, and Grimm, together with their respective profit and loss sharing percentages were as follows:

Assets, net of liabilities	$320,000
Eddy, capital (50%)	$160,000
Fox, capital (30%)	96,000
Grimm, capital (20%)	64,000
	$320,000

16. Eddy decided to retire from the partnership and by mutual agreement is to be paid $180,000 out of partnership funds for his interest. Total goodwill implicit in the agreement is to be recorded. After Eddy's retirement, what are the capital balances of the other partners?

	Fox	*Grimm*
a.	$ 84,000	$56,000
b.	$102,000	$68,000
c.	$108,000	$72,000
d.	$120,000	$80,000

17. Assume instead that Eddy remains in the partnership and that Hamm is admitted as a new partner with a 25% interest in the capital of the new partnership for a cash payment of $140,000. Total goodwill implicit in the transaction is to be recorded. Immediately after admission of Hamm, Eddy's capital account balance should be

- a. $280,000
- b. $210,000
- c. $160,000
- d. $140,000

18. On June 30, 2002, the balance sheet for the partnership of Coll, Maduro, and Prieto, together with their respective profit and loss ratios, were as follows:

Assets, at cost	$180,000
Coll, loan	$ 9,000
Coll, capital (20%)	42,000
Maduro, capital (20%)	39,000
Prieto, capital (60%)	90,000
Total	$180,000

Coll has decided to retire from the partnership. By mutual agreement, the assets are to be adjusted to their fair value of $216,000 at June 30, 2002. It was agreed that the partnership would pay Coll $61,200 cash for Coll's partnership interest, including Coll's loan which is to be repaid in full. No goodwill is to be recorded. After Coll's retirement, what is the balance of Maduro's capital account?

- a. $36,450
- b. $39,000

c. $45,450
d. $46,200

19. Allen retired from the partnership of Allen, Beck, and Chale. Allen's cash settlement from the partnership was based on new goodwill determined at the date of retirement plus the carrying amount of the other net assets. As a consequence of the settlement, the capital accounts of Beck and Chale were decreased. In accounting for Allen's withdrawal, the partnership could have used the

	Bonus method	Goodwill method
a.	No	Yes
b.	No	No
c.	Yes	Yes
d.	Yes	No

20. When Mill retired from the partnership of Mill, Yale, and Lear, the final settlement of Mill's interest exceeded Mill's capital balance. Under the bonus method, the excess
   a.   Was recorded as goodwill.
   b.   Was recorded as an expense.
   c.   Reduced the capital balances of Yale and Lear.
   d.   Had **no** effect on the capital balances of Yale and Lear.

21. The following condensed balance sheet is presented for the partnership of Smith and Jones, who share profits and losses in the ratio of 60:40, respectively:

Other assets	$450,000
Smith, loan	20,000
	$470,000
Accounts payable	$120,000
Smith, capital	195,000
Jones, capital	155,000
	$470,000

The partners have decided to liquidate the partnership. If the other assets are sold for $385,000, what amount of the available cash should be distributed to Smith?
   a. $136,000
   b. $156,000
   c. $159,000
   d. $195,000

22. On January 1, 2002, the partners of Cobb, Davis, and Eddy, who share profits and losses in the ratio of 5:3:2, respectively, decided to liquidate their partnership. On this date the partnership condensed balance sheet was as follows:

Assets	
Cash	$ 50,000
Other assets	250,000
	$300,000

Liabilities and Capital	
Liabilities	$ 60,000
Cobb, capital	80,000
Davis, capital	90,000
Eddy, capital	70,000
	$300,000

On January 15, 2002, the first cash sale of other assets with a carrying amount of $150,000 realized $120,000. Safe installment payments to the partners were made the same date. How much cash should be distributed to each partner?

	Cobb	Davis	Eddy
a.	$15,000	$51,000	$44,000
b.	$40,000	$45,000	$35,000
c.	$55,000	$33,000	$22,000
d.	$60,000	$36,000	$24,000

23. Jay & Kay partnership's balance sheet at December 31, 2002, reported the following:

Total assets	$100,000
Total liabilities	20,000
Jay, capital	40,000
Kay, capital	40,000

On January 2, 2003, Jay and Kay dissolved their partnership and transferred all assets and liabilities to a newly formed corporation. At the date of incorporation, the fair value of the net assets was $12,000 more than the carrying amount on the partnership's books, of which $7,000 was assigned to tangible assets and $5,000 was assigned to goodwill. Jay and Kay were each issued 5,000 shares of the corporation's $1 par value common stock. Immediately following incorporation, additional paid-in capital in excess of par should be credited for
   a. $68,000
   b. $70,000
   c. $77,000
   d. $82,000

MULTIPLE-CHOICE ANSWERS

1. b __ __	6. a __ __	11. d __ __	16. c __ __	21. a __ __	
2. c __ __	7. c __ __	12. c __ __	17. b __ __	22. a __ __	
3. d __ __	8. b __ __	13. d __ __	18. c __ __	23. d __ __	
4. a __ __	9. b __ __	14. b __ __	19. d __ __	1st: __/23 = __%	
5. b __ __	10. b __ __	15. d __ __	20. c __ __	2nd: __/23 = __%	

MULTIPLE-CHOICE ANSWER EXPLANATIONS

D.1. Partnership Formation

1. (b) The requirement is to determine the amounts to be recorded as capital for Roberts and Smith at the formation of the partnership. Unless otherwise agreed upon by the partners, individual capital accounts should be credited for the fair market value (on the date of contribution) of the net assets contributed by that partner. It is necessary to assume that the amounts listed are fair market values. The amount of net assets that Roberts contributed is $35,000 ($20,000 + $15,000). The fair market value of the net assets Smith contributed is $75,000 ($30,000 + $15,000 + $40,000 – $10,000). The partners' profit and loss sharing ratio does not affect the initial recording of the capital accounts.

2. (c) The requirement is to determine which partner has the largest capital account balance. Use the solutions approach to solve the problem.

	Algee	Belger	Ceda
Partner contribution	50,000	80,000	55,000
Less: Liabilities assumed by the partnership	0	(35,000)	0
Ending capital balance	$50,000	$45,000	$55,000

Each partner values his contribution to the partnership at its fair market value. The fair market value becomes the partner's balance in his capital account and is basis to the partnership under generally accepted accounting principles. Any liabilities assumed by the partnership, reduces the partners' capital balance by the amount assumed.

3. (d) Under the bonus method, unidentifiable assets (i.e., goodwill) are not recognized. The total resulting capital is the FMV of the tangible investments of the partners. Thus, there would be no unidentifiable assets recognized by the creation of this new partnership.

4. (a) Noncash assets contributed to an entity should be recorded at fair market value at the date of contribution. The creation of a new entity creates a new accountability for these assets. The partner's original cost relates to a previous accountability. The assessed valuation and the tax basis may differ from fair market value.

D.2. Allocation of Partnership Income (Loss)

5. (b) Credits to partners' capital accounts are based upon earnings after allowance for interest, salary and bonus. The earnings before any allowance of $80,000 is reduced by the salary allowances of $100,000 and results in a loss of $20,000. The $20,000 loss is then distributed to the partners in relation to their profit and loss ratios as follows:

	Red	White	Total
Profit before allowance			$ 80,000
Salary allowances	$55,000	$45,000	(100,000)
Loss after allowances 60/40	(12,000)	(8,000)	(20,000)
Earnings credited to partners	$43,000	$37,000	$ 80,000

It is important to note that the losses are distributed 60/40 while profits are shared equally.

6. (a) When dividing the partnership loss of $33,000, first interest and salaries are allocated to the partners, **increasing** their capital balances. This allocation of interest and salaries will also increase the amount of loss. This increased loss amount would then be allocated to the partners, **decreasing** their capital accounts. The computations are shown below.

	Fox	Greg	Howe
Interest allowance (10% of avg. cap. balances)	$12,000	$ 6,000	$ 4,000
Salaries	30,000		20,000
Residual* ($105,000 ÷ 3)	(35,000)	(35,000)	(35,000)
Increase (decrease) in cap. account	$ 7,000	$(29,000)	$(11,000)

Thus, Fox's account increases by $7,000.

*The residual loss of $105,000 is the loss resulting after the interest and salary allowances are deducted [$33,000 loss – ($12,000 + $6,000 + $4,000) – ($30,000 + $20,000)].

7. (c) The distribution of the partnership net income of $250,000 occurs in three steps as follows:

	Axel	Berg	Cobb
a) Axel: 10% of first $100,000, 20% over $100,000	$ 10,000 30,000		
b) Berg & Cobb: 5% of remaining income over $150,000 [($250,000 – $10,000 – $30,000 – $150,000) x .05]		$ 3,000	$ 3,000
c) Remaining allocated equally: [($250,000 – $10,000 – $30,000 – $3,000 – $3,000) x 1/3]	68,000	68,000	68,000
Totals	$108,000	$71,000	$71,000

Thus, $108,000 would be distributed to Axel.

8. (b) We must first determine Simm's weighted-average capital balance for 2002 as follows:

Capital bal.	x	# of months/12	=	Weighted-avg.
140,000	x	6/12	=	$ 70,000
180,000	x	1/12	=	15,000
165,000	x	5/12	=	68,750
				$153,750

The problem states that interest of 10% per year is to be credited to each partner's capital account, and 10% of Simm's weighted-average capital balance of $153,750 is $15,375.

9. (b) In both the case of a profit or a loss, Flat will have a greater advantage. When there is a profit, Flat will obtain a 20% bonus on profits before the bonus, and also take 40% of the profit after the bonus. Iron on the other hand, will only receive 60% of the profit after the bonus. The following example illustrates this:

	Flat	*Iron*	*Profit*
P & L ratio	40%	60%	1,000
20% Bonus	200	0	(200)
			800
Share in profit	320	480	
Total distribution	520	480	

In the case of a loss, it can easily be seen that since Flat has a smaller percentage share in the loss that he has a greater advantage.

D.3.a.(1) Admission of a New Partner

10.   (b)   The requirement is to calculate the balances in the capital accounts of a partnership after the admission of a new partner. In this case, the new partner is investing $40,000 for a 1/3 interest in the new total capital of $150,000. No goodwill is recorded because the new capital ($150,000) equals the total of the old capital ($110,000) and Carter's investment ($40,000). However, a bonus of $10,000 is being credited to the new partner's capital account because his interest (1/3 of $150,000, or $50,000) exceeds his investment ($40,000). The bonus to the new partner is charged to the old partners in their profit and loss ratios as shown below.

Blau [60,000 – 3/5 (10,000)]	$54,000
Rubi [50,000 – 2/5 (10,000)]	46,000
Lind (150,000 ÷ 3)	50,000
	$150,000

11.   (d)   The requirement is to determine the balance in the new partner's capital account after admission using the bonus method. In this case, Grant is investing land with a FMV of $15,000 for a 1/5 interest in the new total capital of $95,000. Using the bonus method, the new capital $95,000 equals the total of the old capital plus Grant's investment ($60,000 + $20,000 + $15,000). Thus, a bonus of $4,000 is being credited to Grant's capital account because his interest (1/5 of $95,000, or $19,000) exceeds his investment ($15,000). The bonus to the new partner is charged to the old partners' capital accounts in their profit and loss ratios.

12.   (c)   The requirement is to determine the amount of goodwill implied by Zorn's investment. Zorn is investing $100,000 for a 1/3 interest in the partnership. Therefore, $100,000 represents 1/3 of the value of the equity of the new partnership ($100,000 ÷ 1/3 = $300,000). The tangible portion of the equity is $250,000 ($60,000 + $90,000 + $100,000). Thus, the total implied goodwill is $50,000 ($300,000 – $250,000).

13.   (d)   If no goodwill or bonus is to be recorded, the formula to determine the necessary contribution is

$$
\begin{array}{l}
\text{Partnership} \\
\text{interest of} \\
\text{new partner}
\end{array}
\times
\left(
\begin{array}{l}
\text{Capital bal.} \quad \text{Amount} \\
\text{of existing} + \text{to be} \\
\text{partners} \quad \text{contributed}
\end{array}
\right)
=
\begin{array}{l}
\text{Amount} \\
\text{to be} \\
\text{contributed}
\end{array}
$$

20% x ($580,000 + x)	=	x
$116,000 + .2x	=	x
$116,000	=	.8x
$145,000	=	x

An alternative computation is to divide the old partner's capital ($580,000) by their interest after the new partner's admission. The result is the total capital after admission ($580,000 ÷ 80% = $725,000). To compute the new partner's contribution, the old partners' capital can be subtracted

from total capital ($725,000 – $580,000 = $145,000), or total capital can be multiplied by 20% (20% x $725,000 = $145,000).

14.   (b)   To determine the amount of cash distributed during liquidation, the solutions approach is to prepare an abbreviated statement of partnership liquidation. In a partnership liquidation, cash is distributed based on the capital balances of the partners **after** adjusting them for any income (loss) to the date of liquidation and any loans or advances between the partners and the partnership. The abbreviated statement follows:

	Alfa	*Beda*	*Total*
Beg. capital balance	$348,000	$232,000	$580,000
Adj. for loans		(30,000)	(30,000)
Adj. for loss on sale of assets* (60-40)	(75,000)	(50,000)	(125,000)
Adj. capital balance	$273,000	152,000	$425,000

*($500,000 – $625,000)

Note that the total cash available also equals $425,000.

Beginning cash	$ 45,000
Proceeds from sale	500,000
Payment of AP	(120,000)
	$425,000

Therefore, Alfa can receive $273,000 in cash in full liquidation of his capital balance.

15.   (d)   The bonus method implies that the old partners either received a bonus from the new partner, or they paid a bonus to the new partner. In this case, Colter, the new partner, contributed an amount in excess of the amount credited to Colter's capital account. Accordingly, the excess should be treated as a bonus to Adel and Brick. This bonus should be treated as an adjustment to the old partners' capital accounts and should be allocated by using Adel and Brick's old profit and loss ratio.

D.3.a.(2) Partner Death or Withdrawal

16.   (c)   Eddy is to be paid $180,000 for his 50% interest in the partnership. This implies that the net assets of the partnership are worth $360,000 ($180,000 ÷ 50%). Since the net assets are currently reported at $320,000, implied goodwill is $40,000 ($360,000 – $320,000). When goodwill is recorded, the goodwill account is debited and the partners' capital accounts are credited for their share of the goodwill. Therefore, the capital balances of Fox and Grimm are $108,000 and $72,000, as computed below.

	Fox	*Grimm*
Previous capital balance	$96,000	$64,000
Share of goodwill		
Fox (30% x $40,000)	12,000	
Grimm (20% x $40,000)		8,000
New capital balance	$108,000	$72,000

17.   (b)   Hamm will pay $140,000 for a 25% interest in the partnership. This implies that the net assets of the partnership, including the new investment, are worth $560,000 ($140,000 ÷ 25%). Net assets are currently reported at $320,000, and Hamm's cash payment of $140,000 brings that total up to $460,000. Therefore, implied goodwill is $100,000 [$560,000 – ($320,000 + $140,000)]. When goodwill is recorded, the goodwill account is debited and the partners' capital accounts are credited for their share of goodwill. Therefore, Eddy's capital balance ($160,000) is increased by his share of the goodwill (50% x $100,000 = $50,000), to result in a balance of $210,000 ($160,000 + $50,000).

18.   (c)   The requirement is to determine the balance in Maduro's capital account after Coll's retirement. When a partner withdraws from a partnership a determination of the fair market value of the entity must be made. Since it is stated in the problem that the withdrawing partner is selling his interest to the partnership and that no goodwill is to be recorded, the bonus method must be employed after restatement of assets to FMV. The capital accounts after restatement to FMV would be

Coll
[$42,000 + 20%($216,000 – $180,000)] = $ 49,200

Maduro
[$39,000 + 20%($216,000 – $180,000)] = $ 46,200

Prieto
[$90,000 + 60%($216,000 – $180,000)] = $111,600

The bonus paid to Coll is the difference between the cash paid to him for his partnership interest and the balance of that interest plus his loan balance.

Bonus = [$61,200 – ($49,200 + $9,000)] = $3,000

Maduro's capital account would be reduced by his proportionate share of the bonus, based on the profit and loss ratio of the remaining partners [20%/(20% + 60%) = 25%].

Maduro's capital [$46,200 – 25% ($3,000)] = $45,450.

19.   (d)   Under both the bonus and goodwill methods, the assets of the partnership must first be restated to their fair market value. Then, the withdrawing partner's capital account must be adjusted to the amount that the withdrawing partner is expected to receive. When the bonus method is used, no new goodwill is recorded. Instead, the existing partners' capital accounts are reduced by the amount necessary to increase the withdrawing partner's capital to the amount s/he is to be paid. When the goodwill method is used, new goodwill is recorded, and each partner's capital account is increased accordingly. Therefore, the bonus method results in a **decrease** of existing partners' capital accounts, while the goodwill method results in an **increase** of existing partners' capital accounts.

20.   (c)   Under the bonus method, adjustments are made only among partner's capital accounts (no goodwill is recorded on the partnership books). Since Mill's partnership interest exceeded the amount of Mill's capital balance, the excess interest would reduce the capital balances of Yale and Lear. Only under the goodwill method can the excess interest be recorded as goodwill. Under no circumstances should the excess partnership interest be recorded as an expense.

D.4.   Partnership Liquidation

21.   (a)   This situation represents a simple liquidation since all assets are distributed at one point in time rather than in installments. In a simple liquidation all of the noncash assets are sold and the proceeds from their sale are compared to their book value to compute the gain or loss. The gain or loss on the assets is then distributed to the partners' accounts before any of the cash is distributed. The

partner loan should not be considered a noncash asset for the purpose of determining gain or loss, thus, Smith is responsible to the partnership for the repayment of the entire amount of the loan. The repayment of the loan reduces that partner's (Smith) distribution as follows:

Partner balances before liquidation	*Smith*	*Jones*	*Total*
Loan (debit)	$(20,000)		$(20,000)
Capital (credit)	195,000	$155,000	350,000
Net balances	$175,000	$155,000	$330,000
Loss on sale of other assets (450 – 385)	39,000	26,000	(65,000)
Cash available for partners	$136,000	$129,000	$265,000
Cash available for credits			120,000
Total cash from sale of noncash assets			$385,000

22.   (a)   A schedule of safe payments must be prepared to determine the amount of cash to be distributed to each partner at January 15, 2001. The first cash sale of other assets with a total book value of $150,000 realized $120,000 in cash, resulting in a $30,000 loss. This loss is allocated among the partners based upon their profit and loss ratios. The schedule is completed based upon the assumption that the remaining other assets are totally worthless, and their book values are distributed to the partners as losses, based upon the partners' profit and loss ratios. The cash payments to each partner can be found at the bottom of the schedule.

	Cash	*O/A*	*Liab.*
Beginning	$ 50	$ 250	$ 60
Sale of assets	+120	–150	
	170	100	60
Dist. to creditors	–60		–60
	110	100	-0-
Disposal of other assets		–100	
Dist. to partners	–110		
	-0-	-0-	-0-

	Capital		
	C	*D*	*E*
Beginning	$ 80,000	$ 90,000	$ 70,000
Sale of assets	–15,000	– 9,000	– 6,000
	65,000	81,000	64,000
Disposal of other assets	–50,000	–30,000	–20,000
	15,000	51,000	44,000
Dist. to partners	–15,000	–51,000	–44,000
	0	0	0

Thus, the cash should be distributed as follows: $15,000 to Cobb, $51,000 to Davis, and $44,000 to Eddy.

D.5.   Incorporation of a Partnership

23.   (d)   When a partnership incorporates, assets and liabilities must be revalued to their fair market values on the date of incorporation. In this case, the net assets have a fair market value of $92,000 ($80,000 + $12,000) and the amount to be credited to Additional Paid-in Capital is $82,000 ($92,000 – $10,000 par value).

Keep practicing!   Wiley's CPA Examination Review Software has over 2,800 questions.

Available at www.wiley.com/cpa

E. Foreign Currency Translation

1. **Objective of Foreign Currency Translation**

   The rules for the translation of foreign currency into US dollars apply to two major areas.

   a. Foreign currency transactions which are denominated in other than a company's functional currency (e.g., exports, imports, loans), and
   b. Foreign currency financial statements of branches, divisions, subsidiaries, and other investees which are incorporated with the financial statements of a US company by combination, consolidation, or the equity method

   The objectives of translation are

   a. To provide information relative to the expected economic effects of rate changes on an enterprise's cash flows and equity, and
   b. To provide information in consolidated statements relative to the financial results and relationships of each individual foreign consolidated entity as reflected by the functional currency of each reporting entity

   The first objective influences the rules for the translation of foreign currency transactions, while both objectives influence the rules for the translation of foreign currency financial statements. After working through this module, read through the outline of SFAS 52.

2. **Translation of Foreign Currency Statements**

   Assume that a US company has a 100% owned subsidiary in Germany. The subsidiary's operations consist of leasing space in an office building. Its balance sheet at December 31, 2002, and its income statement for 2002 are presented below.

German Company
BALANCE SHEET
December 31, 2002

Assets	*Deutsche Marks*	*Liabilities and Owners' Equity*	*Deutsche Marks*
Cash	60	Accounts payable	100
Accounts receivable (net)	100	Mortgage payable	200
Land	200	Common stock	100
Building	500	Retained earnings	360
Less accumulated depr.	(100)	Total liabilities and	
Total assets	DM 760	Owners' equity	DM 760

German Company
INCOME STATEMENT
For Year Ended December 31, 2002

Revenues	DM 260
Operating Expenses (includes depreciation expense of DM 20)	160
Net Income	DM 100

In addition to the information above, the following data are also needed for the translation process:

1. Transactions involving land, building, mortgage payable, and common stock all occurred in 1997.
2. No dividends were paid during the period 1997-2002.
3. Exchange rates for various dates follow.

   DM 1 = $.30 in 1997
   DM 1 = $.50 at beginning of 2002
   DM 1 = $.55 at end of 2002
   DM 1 = $.53 weighted-average for 2002

If the US company wants to present consolidated financial statements which include the results of its German subsidiary, the financial statements of the German company must be translated into US dollars. However, before this can be accomplished, the management of the US company must determine the functional currency of its German subsidiary. SFAS 52 defines an entity's functional currency as ". . .the currency of the primary economic environment in which the entity operates; normally, that is the currency of the environment in which an entity primarily generates and expends cash." The decision concerning the functional currency is important because, once determined, it should be used consistently, unless it is clear that economic facts and circumstances have changed. The selection of the functional currency depends upon an evaluation of several factors. These factors include the following:

1. Cash flows (Do the foreign entity's cash flows directly affect the parent's cash flows and are they immediately available for remittance to the parent?)
2. Sales prices (Are the foreign entity's sales prices responsive to exchange rate changes and to international competition?)
3. Sales markets (Is the foreign entity's sales market the parent's country or are sales denominated in the parent's currency?)
4. Expenses (Are the foreign entity's expenses incurred in the parent's country?)
5. Financing (Is the foreign entity's financing primarily from the parent or is it denominated in the parent's currency?)
6. Intercompany transactions (Is there a high volume of intercompany transactions between the parent and foreign entity?)

If the answers to the questions above are predominantly yes, the functional currency would be the reporting currency of the parent (i.e., the US dollar). On the other hand, if the answers to the questions were predominantly no, the functional currency would be the foreign currency. In the example described previously, the DM would be the functional currency if the answers were no. Note that the functional currency does not necessarily have to be the local currency of the foreign country when the answers to the questions are negative. In other words, it is possible for a foreign currency other than deutsche marks to be the functional currency of our German company. For example, Swiss francs or Italian lira could be the functional currency for the German company if one of these currencies is the currency of the primary economic environment in which the entity operates. However, assume these other possibilities are not alternatives in the example mentioned previously.

If the circumstances indicate the DM to be the functional currency, SFAS 52 mandates that the current rate method be used for translation of the foreign currency financial statements. This technique is illustrated below for the German financial statements shown previously.

BALANCE SHEET
(Deutsche Mark is Functional Currency)

	DM	Exchange rates	US dollars
Assets			
Cash	60	.55	33
Accounts receivable (net)	100	.55	55
Land	200	.55	110
Building (net)	400	.55	220
Totals	DM 760		$418
Liabilities and Owners' Equity			
Accounts payable	100	.55	55
Mortgage payable	200	.55	110
Common stock	100	.30	30
Retained earnings	360 see income statement		157
Translation adjustment	—		66
Totals	DM 760		$418

COMBINED INCOME AND RETAINED EARNINGS STATEMENT

	DM	Exchange rates	US dollars
Revenues	260	.53	$ 137.80
Operating expenses (including DM 20 of depreciation expense)	160	.53	84.80
Net income	100		53.00
Retained earnings at 1/1/02	260		104.00*
Retained earnings at 12/31/02	DM 360		$157.00

*   *The US dollar amount of retained earnings results from applying weighted-average exchange rates to translate revenues and expenses during the period 1997 through 2001. Retained earnings cannot be translated using a single exchange rate. The beginning retained earnings would be taken from the prior period's translated financial statements.*

The following points should be noted from the illustration of the translation process:

1. All assets and liabilities are translated using the current rate at the balance sheet date. All revenues and expenses are translated at the rates in effect when these items are recognized during the period. Due to practical considerations, however, weighted-average rates can be used to translate revenues and expenses which were incurred throughout the year.

2. Owners' equity accounts are translated using historical exchange rates. Common stock was issued in 1997 when the exchange rate was DM 1 = $.30. The beginning balance of retained earnings for 2002 was accumulated during the period 1997 through 2001.

3. Translation adjustments result from translating all assets and liabilities at the current rate, while owners' equity is translated using historical rates and income statement items are translated using weighted-average rates. The translation adjustment for the period is reported as other comprehensive income under one of several acceptable reporting alternatives and the parent company's share of the accumulated amount is reported as accumulated other comprehensive income in the stockholders' equity section of the consolidated balance sheet.

This illustration of the current rate technique assumed the DM to be the functional currency. Assume, however, that the circumstances were evaluated by the US company, and the US dollar was chosen as the functional currency. Under this alternative, SFAS 52 requires the foreign currency financial statements to be remeasured into US dollars. According to SFAS 52, the " . . .remeasurement process is intended to produce the same result as if the entity's books of record had been maintained in the functional currency." If the US dollar is the functional currency, the remeasurement of foreign currency financial statements into US dollars results in a remeasurement gain or loss that is included in the subsidiary's income for the period. The remeasurement process is illustrated below for the German subsidiary.

BALANCE SHEET
(Deutsche Mark is Functional Currency)

	DM	Exchange rates	US dollars
Assets			
Cash	60	.55	33
Accounts receivable (net)	100	.55	55
Land	200	.30	60
Building (net)	400	.30	120
Totals	DM 760		$268
Liabilities and Owners' Equity			
Accounts payable	100	.55	55
Mortgage payable	200	.55	110
Common stock	100	.30	30
Retained earnings	360	see income statement	73
Totals	DM 760		$268

COMBINED INCOME AND RETAINED EARNINGS STATEMENT

	DM	Exchange rates	US dollars
Revenues	260	.53	137.80
Expenses (exclusive of depreciation)	140	.53	74.20
Depreciation	20	.30	6.00
Total expenses	160		80.20
Remeasurement loss	--	--	10.60
Total expenses and loss	160	--	90.80
Net income (loss)	100		47.00
Retained earnings at 1/1/02	260		26.00*
Retained earnings at 12/31/02	DM 360		$ 73.00

* *Retained earnings of $26 includes remeasured income from the period 1997 through 2001, which includes remeasurement losses applicable to those years due to the strengthening of the DM compared to the US dollar. Beginning retained earnings were taken from the prior period's financial statements.*

The following observations should be noted about the remeasurement process:

1. Nonmonetary assets and liabilities (e.g., land, building) which have historical cost balances are remeasured using historical exchange rates at the date the item entered the subsidiary. Monetary assets and monetary liabilities, on the other hand, are remeasured using the current rate at the balance sheet date.

2. Revenues and most expenses that occur during a period are remeasured, for practical purposes, using the weighted-average exchange rate for the period. Revenues and expenses, however, that represent allocations of historical balances (e.g., depreciation) are remeasured using the same historical exchange rates as used for those items on the balance sheet.

3. The remeasurement loss of $10.60 is reported on the consolidated income statement. The loss is the result of a remeasurement process which assumes that the US dollar is the functional currency.

4. The calculation of the remeasurement loss is the result of the rules employed in the remeasurement process. In mechanical terms, the remeasurement loss is the amount needed to make the debits equal the credits in the German company's US dollar trial balance. Note this technique below.

	DM			US dollars	
	DR	*CR*	*Exchange rates*	*DR*	*CR*
Cash	60		.55	33	
Accounts rec. (net)	100		.55	55	
Land	200		.30	60	
Building (net)	400		.30	120	
Accounts payable		100	.55		55
Mortgage payable		200	.55		110
Common stock		100	.30		30
Retained earnings 1/1/01		260			26
Revenues		260	.53		137.80
Expenses	140		.53	74.20	
Depreciation exp.	20		.30	6	
Totals	DM 920	DM 920		$348.20	$358.80
Remeasurement loss				10.60	
Totals				$358.80	$358.80

The significant points to remember about the German illustration are summarized below.

1. Before foreign currency financial statements can be translated into US dollars, a decision must be made regarding the functional currency.

2. If the functional currency is the foreign currency, the current rate method is used to translate to US dollars. All assets and liabilities are translated using the current rate at the balance sheet date. Owners' equity is translated using historical rates while revenues (and gains) and expenses (and losses) are translated at the rates in existence during the period when the transactions occurred. A weighted-average rate can be used for items occurring numerous times throughout the period. The translation adjustments (debit or credit) which result from the application of these rules are reported as a separate item in owners' equity in the consolidated balance sheet of the US parent.

3. If the functional currency is the reporting currency (the US dollar), the foreign currency financial statements are remeasured into US dollars. All foreign currency balances are restated to US dollars using either historical or current exchange rates. Foreign currency balances which reflect prices from past transactions (e.g., inventories carried at cost, prepaid insurance, property, plant, and equipment, etc.) are remeasured using historical rates while foreign currency balances which reflect prices from current transactions (e.g., inventories and trading and available-for-sale securities carried at market, etc.) are remeasured using the current rate. Monetary assets and liabilities are remeasured using the current rate. (Deferred taxes are remeasured using the current rate.) Remeasurement gains/losses that result from the remeasurement process are reported on the consolidated income statement under "Other Income (Expense)."

The above summary can be arranged in tabular form as shown below.

Functional currency	*Functional currency determinants*	*Translation method*	*Reporting*
Local currency of foreign company	a. Operations not integrated with parent's operations b. Buying and selling activities primarily in local currency c. Cash flows not immediately available for remittance to parent	Current Rate (All assets/ liabilities translated using current rate; revenues/expenses use weighted-average rate; equity accounts use historical rates)	Translation adjustments are reported as other comprehensive income under one of several acceptable reporting alternatives and as accumulated other comprehensive income in the equity section of consolidated balance sheet. Analysis of changes in accumulated translation adjustments disclosed via footnote
US Dollar	a. Operations integrated with parent's operations b. Buying and selling activities primarily in US and/or US dollars c. Cash flows immediately available for remittance to parent	Remeasurement (Monetary assets/ liabilities use current rate; historical cost balances use historical rates; revenues/ expenses use weighted-average rates and historical rates, the latter for allocations such as depr. exp.).	Remeasurement gain/loss is reported on the consolidated income statement.

A few comments concerning the translation of foreign currency financial statements in highly inflationary economies should be made. If the cumulative inflation rate is $\geq 100\%$ over a three-year period in a foreign country, the foreign currency statements of a company located in that country are remeasured into the reporting currency (i.e., the US dollar). In other words, it is assumed the US dollar is the functional currency. The following flowchart summarizes the requirements of SFAS 52 with respect to foreign currency financial statements.

FOREIGN CURRENCY FINANCIAL STATEMENTS

Functional Currency = Local Currency	Functional Currency = Reporting Currency	Functional Currency ≠ Local Currency **or** Reporting Currency

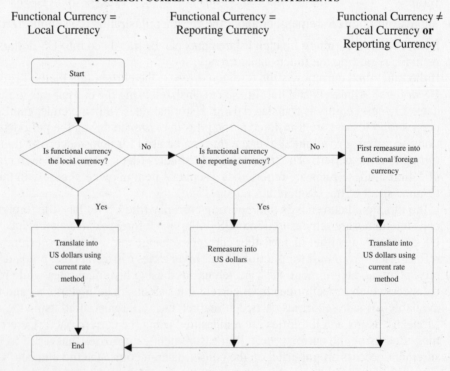

3. **Glossary**

Foreign Currency Statements

Financial statements that employ as the unit of measure a functional currency that is not the reporting currency of the enterprise.

Foreign Currency Translation

The process of expressing in the reporting currency of the enterprise those amounts that are denominated or measured in a different currency.

Functional Currency

An entity's functional currency is the currency of the primary economic environment in which the entity operates; normally, that is the currency of the environment in which an entity primarily generates and expends cash.

Local Currency

The currency of a particular country being referred to.

Remeasurement

If an entity's books and records are not kept in its functional currency, remeasurement into the functional currency is required. Monetary balances are translated using the current exchange rate and nonmonetary balances are translated using historical exchange rates. If the US dollar is the functional currency, remeasurement into the reporting currency (the US dollar) makes translation unnecessary.

Reporting Currency

The currency in which an enterprise prepares its financial statements.

Translation Adjustments

Translation adjustments result from the process of translating financial statements from the entity's functional currency into the reporting currency.

MULTIPLE-CHOICE QUESTIONS (1-9)

1. Certain balance sheet accounts of a foreign subsidiary of Rowan, Inc., at December 31, 2002, have been translated into US dollars as follows:

	Translated at	
	Current rates	*Historical rates*
Note receivable, long-term	$240,000	$200,000
Prepaid rent	85,000	80,000
Patent	150,000	170,000
	$475,000	$450,000

The subsidiary's functional currency is the currency of the country in which it is located. What total amount should be included in Rowan's December 31, 2002 consolidated balance sheet for the above accounts?

- a. $450,000
- b. $455,000
- c. $475,000
- d. $495,000

2. A wholly owned subsidiary of Ward, Inc. has certain expense accounts for the year ended December 31, 2002, stated in local currency units (LCU) as follows:

	LCU
Depreciation of equipment (related assets were purchased January 1, 2000)	120,000
Provision for doubtful accounts	80,000
Rent	200,000

The exchange rates at various dates are as follows:

	Dollar equivalent of 1 LCU
December 31, 2002	$.40
Average for year ended 12/31/02	.44
January 1, 2000	.50

Assume that the LCU is the subsidiary's functional currency and that the charges to the expense accounts occurred approximately evenly during the year. What total dollar amount should be included in Ward's 2002 consolidated income statement to reflect these expenses?

- a. $160,000
- b. $168,000
- c. $176,000
- d. $183,200

3. Which of the following should be reported as a stockholders' equity account?

- a. Discount on convertible bonds.
- b. Premium on convertible bonds.
- c. Cumulative foreign exchange translation loss.
- d. Organization costs.

4. A foreign subsidiary's functional currency is its local currency, which has not experienced significant inflation. The weighted-average exchange rate for the current year would be the appropriate exchange rate for translating

	Sales to customers	*Wages expense*
a.	No	No
b.	Yes	Yes
c.	No	Yes
d.	Yes	No

5. The functional currency of Nash, Inc.'s subsidiary is the French franc. Nash borrowed French francs as a partial hedge of its investment in the subsidiary. In preparing consolidated financial statements, Nash's translation loss on its investment in the subsidiary exceeded its exchange gain on the borrowing. How should the effects of the loss and gain be reported in Nash's consolidated financial statements?

- a. The translation loss less the exchange gain is reported as other comprehensive income.
- b. The translation loss less the exchange gain is reported in net income.
- c. The translation loss is reported as other comprehensive income and the exchange gain is reported in net income.
- d. The translation loss is reported in net income and the exchange gain is reported as other comprehensive income.

6. A balance arising from the translation or remeasurement of a subsidiary's foreign currency financial statements is reported in the consolidated income statement when the subsidiary's functional currency is the

	Foreign currency	*US dollar*
a.	No	No
b.	No	Yes
c.	Yes	No
d.	Yes	Yes

7. When remeasuring foreign currency financial statements into the functional currency, which of the following items would be remeasured using historical exchange rate?

- a. Inventories carried at cost.
- b. Marketable equity securities reported at market values.
- c. Bonds payable.
- d. Accrued liabilities.

8. Park Co.'s wholly owned subsidiary, Schnell Corp., maintains its accounting records in German marks. Because all of Schnell's branch offices are in Switzerland, its functional currency is the Swiss franc. Remeasurement of Schnell's 2002 financial statements resulted in a $7,600 gain, and translation of its financial statements resulted in an $8,100 gain. What amount should Park report as a foreign exchange gain as net income in its income statement for the year ended December 31, 2002?

- a. $0
- b. $ 7,600
- c. $ 8,100
- d. $15,700

9. In preparing consolidated financial statements of a US parent company with a foreign subsidiary, the foreign subsidiary's functional currency is the currency

- a. In which the subsidiary maintains its accounting records.
- b. Of the country in which the subsidiary is located.
- c. Of the country in which the parent is located.
- d. Of the environment in which the subsidiary primarily generates and expends cash.

OTHER OBJECTIVE QUESTIONS

Problem 1 (15 to 25 minutes)

This question consists of 9 items that relate to foreign currency translation.

Required:

Items 1 through 9 are based on the following:

A foreign subsidiary's trial balance is translated from its functional currency to the functional currency of the parent. For each item determine which date the exchange rate from table A should be used for the translation. The subsidiary's functional currency is its **local** currency.

TABLE A

	Event	Date
a.	Company begins	12/31/99
b.	Beginning of current year	1/1/02
c.	1st quarter	4/1/02
d.	2nd quarter	7/1/02
e.	3rd quarter	10/1/02
f.	Year-end	12/31/02
g.	1st quarter	4/1/03
h.	Year average	
i.	Average since acquisition	
j.	No translation rate used	

1. Cash

2. Inventory that had been purchased evenly through the year

3. Account payable for equipment purchased on 4/1/02

4. Cost of goods sold

5. Sales

6. Dividends declared on 10/1/02

7. Dividends declared in **6.** above were paid 1/2/03

8. Retained earnings

9. Common stock

PROBLEM

Problem 1   (15 to 25 minutes)

Jay Co.'s 2002 consolidated financial statements include two wholly owned subsidiaries, Jay Co. of Australia (Jay A) and Jay Co. of France (Jay F). Functional currencies are the US dollar for Jay A and the franc for Jay F.

Required:

a.   What are the objectives of translating a foreign subsidiary's financial statements?

b.   How are gains and losses arising from translating or remeasuring of each subsidiary's financial statements measured and reported in Jay's consolidated financial statements?

c.   SFAS 52 identifies several economic indicators that are to be considered both individually and collectively in determining the functional currency for a consolidated subsidiary. List three of those indicators.

d.   What exchange rate is used to incorporate each subsidiary's equipment cost, accumulated depreciation, and depreciation expense in Jay's consolidated financial statements?

MULTIPLE-CHOICE ANSWERS

1. c	__ __	4. b	__ __	6. b	__ __	8. b	__ __	1st:	__/9 = __%
2. c	__ __	5. a	__ __	7. a	__ __	9. d	__ __	2nd:	__/9 = __%
3. c	__ __								

MULTIPLE-CHOICE ANSWER EXPLANATIONS

E.2. Translation of Foreign Currency Statements

1.   (c)   When the **functional currency** of a foreign subsidiary is the **foreign currency,** asset and liability accounts are **translated** using the **current** exchange rate (the rate of translation in effect at the balance sheet date). Therefore, these accounts should be included in the balance sheet at $475,000. Note that if the **functional currency** was the **US dollar,** balance sheet accounts would be **remeasured** using a combination of **historical and current rates**.

2.   (c)   The requirement is to determine the total amount of various expenses incurred by a foreign subsidiary which should be reported in the 2002 consolidated income statement. SFAS 52 states that if the foreign currency is the functional currency of the subsidiary, the **current rate** method should be used to translate the financial statements. In this method, revenues and expenses are translated at the rates in effect at the time these items were recognized during the period. Because translation at the date the revenues and expenses were recognized is generally deemed impractical, SFAS 52 allows that an appropriate weighted-average rate may be used to translate these items. This results in a translated expense of $176,000 [($120,000 + $80,000 + $200,000) x .44].

3.   (c)   The requirement is to determine which item is reported in the stockholders' equity section. According to SFAS 52 and 130, accumulated gains and losses on certain foreign currency transactions should be reported as a component of stockholders' equity entitled other comprehensive income. Answers (a), (b), and (d) are incorrect because these items are reported on the balance sheet in the assets and liabilities sections and are amortized over their respective lives.

4.   (b)   SFAS 52 mandates the current rate method for the translation of foreign currency financial statements when a foreign subsidiary's functional currency is its local currency. Using the current rate method, revenue and expenses should be translated into US dollars at the weighted-average rate for the current year. Thus, both sales to customers and wages expense should be translated at the weighted-average rate.

5.   (a)   According to SFAS 52 and SFAS 130, translation adjustments resulting from the translation of foreign currency statements should be reported separately as components of other comprehensive income, accumulated other comprehensive income, and stockholders' equity. Additionally, gains and losses on certain foreign currency transactions should also be reported similarly. Those gains and losses which should be excluded from net income and instead reported as components of other comprehensive income and of accumulated other comprehensive income in stockholders' equity include foreign currency transactions designated as economic hedges of a net investment in a foreign entity. Thus, both the translation loss and the exchange gain are to be reported as other comprehensive income and

accumulated other comprehensive income in the stockholders' equity section of the balance sheet. Because the translation loss on the investment exceeds the exchange gain on the borrowing, the translation loss less the exchange gain is the amount to be reported as separate components of other comprehensive income and accumulated other comprehensive income equity in the consolidated financial statements.

6.   (b)   Per SFAS 12, **translation** adjustments result from translating an entity's financial statements into the reporting currency. Such adjustments, which result when the entity's functional currency is the **foreign currency,** should not be included in net income. Instead, such adjustments should be reported as other comprehensive income and accumulated other comprehensive income in the stockholders' equity section of the balance sheet. If the functional currency is the **reporting currency** (US dollar), a **remeasurement** process takes place, with the resulting gain or loss included in net income.

7.   (a)   The requirement is to determine which item would be remeasured using historical exchange rates when foreign currency financial statements are being remeasured into the functional currency. Per SFAS 52, when an entity's books are not maintained in the functional currency, it is necessary to use historical exchange rates in the remeasurement process of certain accounts. Among the accounts listed is inventories carried at cost. Only marketable equity securities reported at **cost** would be remeasured using historical exchange rates. Bonds payable and accrued liabilities would be remeasured at the current rate.

8.   (b)   Schnell's accounting records are kept in German marks, and its functional currency is the Swiss franc. Before Schnell's financial statements can be consolidated with Park's financial statements, they must be remeasured from German marks to Swiss francs, and then translated from Swiss francs to US dollars. As a result of these restatements, there is a remeasurement gain of $7,600, and a credit translation adjustment of $8,100. SFAS 52 states that a remeasurement gain or loss is included in net income, but a translation adjustment is **not**. Therefore, Park would report a foreign exchange gain of $7,600 in its 2002 income statement.

9.   (d)   SFAS 52, *Foreign Currency Translation*, defines an entity's functional currency as the currency of the primary economic environment in which the entity operates; normally, that is the currency of the environment in which an entity primarily generates and expends cash.

OTHER OBJECTIVE ANSWER EXPLANATIONS

Problem 1

1. **(F)** Assets are valued at the current rate at year-end.

2. **(F)** Assets are valued at the current rate at year-end.

3. **(F)** Liabilities are valued at the current rate at year-end.

4. **(H)** Expense accounts are valued at the average rate for the current year of business.

5. **(H)** Revenue accounts are valued at the average rate for the current year of business.

6. **(E)** Dividends are valued at the rate of the date of declaration.

7. **(F)** Liabilities (dividends payable) are valued at the current rate at year-end.

8. **(J)** The retained earnings are carried over from 1/1/02 with the translated net income added and translated dividends subtracted.

9. **(A)** Common stock is valued at the historical rate when it was issued.

ANSWER OUTLINE

Problem 1   Foreign Currency Remeasurement and Translation

a.   Objectives of translating foreign sub's FS
   Provide information compatible with economic effects of rate change on sub's cash flows and equity
   Reflect sub's financial results and relationships in consolidated FS
      Measured in its functional currency
         In conformity with GAAP

b.   Gain (loss) is amount required to bring restated FS into balance
   Gain (loss) from **remeasuring** Jay A's FS reported in consolidated IS
   Gain (loss) from **translating** Jay F's FS reported as other comprehensive income and in BS as accumulated other comprehensive income under SE

c.   Economic indicators used to determine functional currency
      Cash flow indicators
      Sales price indicators
      Sales market indicators
      Expense indicators
      Financing indicators
      Intercompany transactions and arrangement indicators

d.   Jay A's equipment and related accounts
      Remeasured by exchange rate prevailing between US and Australian dollars on date equipment purchased
      Jay F's equipment and related accounts
      Translated using current exchange rates prevailing between US dollar and French franc
         For equipment cost and AD, use exchange rate at 12/31/01
         For depreciation expense, use rate on date expense recognized or use average rate for 2002

UNOFFICIAL ANSWER

Problem 1   Foreign Currency Remeasurement and Translation

a.   The objectives of translating a foreign subsidiary's financial statements are to

   •   Provide information that is generally compatible with the expected economic effects of a rate change on a subsidiary's cash flows and equity.
   •   Reflect the subsidiary's financial results and relationships in single currency consolidated financial statements, as measured in its functional currency and in conformity with GAAP.

b.   Applying different exchange rates to the various financial statement accounts causes the restated statements to be unbalanced. The amount required to bring the restated statements into balance is termed the gain or loss from the translation or remeasurement. The gain or loss arising from remeasuring Jay A's financial statements is reported in the consolidated income statement. The gain or loss arising from translating Jay F's financial statements is reported as other comprehensive income and in the balance sheet as accumulated other comprehensive income under stockholders' equity.

c.   The functional currency is the foreign currency or parent's currency that most closely correlates with the following economic indicators:

   •   Cash flow indicators
   •   Sales price indicators
   •   Sales market indicators
   •   Expense indicators
   •   Financing indicators
   •   Intercompany transactions and arrangement indicators

d.   All accounts relating to Jay A's equipment are remeasured by the exchange rate prevailing between the US and Australian dollars at the time equipment was purchased.

   All accounts relating to Jay F's equipment are translated by the current exchange rates prevailing between the US dollar and French franc. For the equipment cost and accumulated depreciation this is the current exchange rate at December 31, 2002. Depreciation expense is translated at the rate prevailing on the date the depreciation expense was recognized or an appropriate weighted-average exchange rate for 2002.

Keep practicing! Wiley's CPA Examination Review Software has over 2,800 questions.

Available at www.wiley.com/cpa

ARB, APB, AND FASB PRONOUNCEMENTS

Study Program for the Accounting Pronouncements

Outlines of the unsuperseded official accounting pronouncements are presented in chronological order in this chapter. Effective dates of pronouncements are omitted unless they are a current implementation problem. You should

1. Study through the outlines as you are referred to them in the modules in this chapter
   a. On the exam it is not necessary to know the pronouncement numbers
   b. The outlines presume some prior study of the topics covered by the pronouncements
   c. Note that additional comments have been added to some outlines, relating to the rationale or justification for these standards
2. **Required disclosures.** It is not necessary to memorize all the required disclosures. A good approach is to take the position of a financial analyst: What data would you want to know? Utilizing this approach, you only have to memorize any exceptions (i.e., items you would not normally think a financial analyst would be interested in).

References to FASB Materials

Each of the outlines in the last part of this chapter is referenced to the section where it is found in the FASB *Accounting Standards—Current Texts: General/Industry Standards*, John Wiley & Sons, Inc. These references appear in parentheses right after the original pronouncement reference in the heading of each pronouncement outlined. When using either the FASB's Current Text or Original Pronouncements to supplement your study, be sure you have a recent edition (not more than two years old). If your study of intermediate accounting has been recent (within the last two years) or, if longer and you purchase a new intermediate text, it is not likely that you will need them.

In studying the outlines, you might notice that parts of some pronouncements have not been outlined. The reason some sections of the pronouncements are excluded from the outlines is that they have never been tested on the exam. Also, outlines for very specialized pronouncements (e.g., SFAS 50, *Financial Reporting in the Record and Music Industry*) are not included in this manual. Several others are outlined more generally. Only those FASB Interpretations and Technical Bulletins having widespread applicability are included in this chapter. They are set apart with solid lines **only** to distinguish them from the SFAS.

ACCOUNTING RESEARCH BULLETINS

ARB 43—Chapter 1A (A31, B50, C08, C23, R36, R70, R75)[1] Rules Adopted by Membership

Four rules recommended by the Committee on Cooperation with Stock Exchanges in 1934. The last rule is from another 1934 Institute committee.

1. Profit is realized at the point of sale unless collection is not reasonably assured.
2. Capital (paid-in) surplus should not be charged with losses or expenses, except in quasi reorganizations.
3. Receivables from officers, employees, and affiliates must be separately disclosed.
4. Par value of stock issued for assets cannot be used to value the assets if some of the stock is subsequently donated back to the corporation.

Chapter 1B (C23) Profits or Losses on Treasury Stock (Revised by APB 6)

Profits on treasury stock are not income and should be reflected in capital surplus.

Chapter 2A (F43) Comparative Financial Statements (Cross-referenced to APB 20)

Comparative statements enhance the usefulness of financial statements and should be presented.

Chapter 3A (B05, I78) Current Assets and Current Liabilities

(Amended by APB 6, 21 and SFAS 6)

Chapter 3A contains the definitions and examples of current assets and liabilities.

A. **Current assets** are "cash and other assets or resources commonly identified as those which are reasonably expected to be (1) realized in cash, (2) sold, or (3) consumed during the ordinary operating cycle of the business."
   1. Cash available for current operations
   2. Inventories
   3. Trade receivables

---

[1] *The references in parentheses are from the **FASB Accounting Standards—Current Texts: Volumes 1 and 2**, John Wiley & Sons, Inc. These are included only for facilitating the use of the Current Texts for candidates who have access to them.*

    4. Other receivables collectible in one year

    5. Installment, deferred accounts, and notes receivable

    6. Prepaid expenses

B. **Current liabilities** are "obligations whose liquidation is reasonably expected to require the use of existing resources properly classifiable as current assets or the creation of other current liabilities during the ordinary operating cycle of the business."

    1. Trade payables

    2. Collections received in advance of services

    3. Accruals of expenses

    4. Other liabilities coming due in one year

    5. Note that liabilities not using current assets for liquidation are not current liabilities (e.g., bonds being repaid from a sinking fund)

C. **Operating cycle** is "average time intervening between the acquisition of materials or services entering this process and the final cash realization."

Chapter 4 (I78) Inventory Pricing

Contains 10 statements outlining inventory valuation

    1. Inventory consists of tangible personal property

       a. Held for sale in ordinary course of business

       b. In process of production for such sale

       c. To be currently consumed in the production of such goods

    2. Major objective of inventory valuation is proper income determination

       a. Matching of costs and revenues

    3. Primary basis is cost. Cost includes all reasonable and necessary costs of preparing inventory for sale. These costs would include expenditures to bring inventory to existing condition and location.

       a. Direct or variable costing is not acceptable (use absorption costing)

    4. Cost may be determined under any flow assumption. Use method which most clearly reflects income.

    5. Departure from cost to market required when utility of goods, in their disposal in the ordinary course of business, is not as great as cost.

       a. Write-down recognized as a loss of the current period

       b. Use of lower of cost or market method more fairly reflects income of the period than would the cost method

       c. Results in a more realistic estimate of future cash flows to be realized from the assets

       d. Supported by doctrine of conservatism

    6. Market means current replacement cost subject to

       a. Market should not exceed net realizable value (sales price less selling and completion costs)

       b. Market should not be less than net realizable value less normal profit

    7. Lower of cost or market may be applied to individual items or the inventory as a whole. Use method that most clearly reflects income.

    8. Basis for stating inventories and changes therein should be consistent and disclosed.

    9. Inventories may be stated above cost in exceptional cases

       a. No basis for cost allocation (e.g., meatpacking)

       b. Disposal assured and price known (e.g., precious metals)

  10. Purchase commitment loss should be recognized in the same manner as inventory losses.

Chapter 7A (Q15) Quasi Reorganization

Describes what is permitted before and after quasi reorganization.

A. Procedure in readjustment

    1. A clear report should be made to shareholders to obtain consent for the proposed restatements of assets and shareholders' equity.

    2. Write-down of assets should not go below fair value.

    3. If potential losses exist, provide for maximum probable loss.

    4. When determined, amounts should be written off first to retained earnings and then to capital surplus.

B. Procedure after readjustment

    1. After readjustment, accounting should be similar to that appropriate for a new company

    2. A new, dated retained earnings account should be created

       a. Dated for ten years to indicate when the reorganization occurred.

Chapter 7B (C20, Q15) Stock Dividends and Stock Splits

A. **Dividend**—evidence given to shareholders of their share of accumulated earnings that are going to be retained in the business

B. **Split**—stock issued to increase number of outstanding shares to reduce market price and/or to obtain a wider distribution of ownership

C. To the recipient, splits and dividends are not income. Dividends and splits take nothing from the property of the corporation and add nothing to the property of the recipient.

    1. Upon receipt of stock dividend or split, recipient should reallocate cost of shares previously held to all shares held.

D. Issuer of a stock dividend (issuance is small in relation to shares outstanding and consequently has no apparent effect on market price) should capitalize retained earnings equal to the fair market value of shares issued.

    1. Unless retained earnings are capitalized, retained earnings thought to be distributed by the recipient will be available for subsequent distribution.

    2. Issuances less than 20-25% of previously outstanding shares are dividends. Issuances greater than 20-25% of previously outstanding shares are splits.

    3. Where stock dividend is so large it may materially affect price (a split effected in the form of a dividend), no capitalization is necessary other than that required by law.

        a. Some jurisdictions require that the par value of splits be capitalized (i.e., changes in par value are not permitted).

    4. For closely held corporations, there is no need to capitalize retained earnings other than to meet legal requirements.

Chapter 10A (T10) Real and Personal Property Taxes

Accounting for personal and real property taxes which vary in time of determination and collection from state to state

A. In practice, the dates below have been used to apportion taxes between accounting periods.

    1. Assessment date

    2. Beginning of fiscal period of taxing authority

    3. End of fiscal period of taxing authority

    4. Lien date

    5. Date of tax levy

    6. Date tax is payable

    7. Date tax is delinquent

    8. Period appearing on tax bill

B. The most acceptable basis is a monthly accrual on the taxpayer's books during the fiscal period of the taxing authority.

    1. At year-end, the books will show the appropriate prepayment or accrual.

    2. An accrued liability, whether known or estimated, should be shown as a current liability.

    3. On income statement, property taxes may be charged to operating expense, deducted separately from income, prorated among accounts to which they apply, or combined with other taxes (but not with income taxes).

Chapter 13B (C47) Stock Option Compensation Plans (Also see APB 25 and SFAS 123)

Cost of services received for compensation paid in stock options should be included in operations.

A. Compensation may arise when the corporation agrees to issue common stock to an employee at a stated price.

    1. Other options may result in employee obligations such as continued employment.

B. Stock options do not result in compensation if

    1. Stock options are offered at a reasonable amount to raise capital

    2. Stock options are offered at a reasonable amount to induce wider holdings by employees

C. Date of grant should be used for measurement

    1. Considering the date of grant as a contract, it is the date value is determined

    2. Date of grant is date corporation foregoes alternative use

    3. Adoption date and grantee's disposition date are not relevant

D. Per APB 25, compensation is excess of quoted market price **over option price**. SFAS 123 uses an option pricing model to determine fair value.

E. Compensation cost should be spread over the period of service covered by the option contract.
1. Cash and compensation are equal to consideration for the stock when exercised (amount credited stock and paid-in capital).
F. Disclosure should be made annually of
1. Number of shares under option
2. Option price
3. Number of shares exercisable
4. Number of shares and price of options exercised

ARB 45 (Co4) Long-Term Construction Contracts
Discusses accounting for multiple-period projects
A. The percentage-of-completion method recognizes income as work progresses.
1. Recognized income based upon a percentage of estimated total income
a. (Incurred costs to date)/(Total expected costs) known as cost-to-cost measure
b. Other measure of progress based on work performed (e.g., engineering or architectural estimate)
2. Costs, for percentage-of-completion estimate, might exclude materials and subcontracts, especially in the early stages of a contract.
a. Avoids overstating the percentage-of-completion
3. If a loss is estimated on the contract, the **entire loss** should be recognized currently.
4. Contracts should be separated into net assets and net liabilities.
a. Current assets include costs and income (loss) in excess of billings.
b. Current liabilities include billings in excess of costs and income (loss).
c. Contracts should not be offset on the balance sheet.
5. Advantages of percentage-of-completion are periodic recognition of income and reflection of the status of the contract.
a. Results in appropriate matching of costs and revenues
b. Avoids distortions in income from year to year and thus provides more relevant information to financial statement users.
6. The principal disadvantage is the reliance on estimates.
7. The percentage-of-completion method is required when total costs and percent of completion can be reasonably estimated.
B. The completed-contract method recognizes income when the contract is complete.
1. General and administrative expenses can be allocated to contracts.
a. Not necessary if many projects are in process
b. No excessive deferring of costs
2. Provision should be made for **entire amount of any expected loss** prior to job completion.
a. That is, losses are recognized immediately in their entirety—conservative treatment
3. An excess of accumulated costs over related billings is a current asset. An excess of accumulated billings over related costs is a liability (current in most cases).
a. Balance sheet accounts are determined as in A.4., except no income is included
b. Recognized losses in B.2. reduce accumulated costs.
4. The advantage of the completed-contract method is that it is based on final results, and its primary disadvantage is that it does not reflect current performance.
a. Overall, the completed-contract method represents a conservative approach.

ARB 51 (B50, C20, C51, R70) Consolidated Financial Statements (Also see APB 16)
(Amended by SFAS 94)
A. Consolidated statements present financial statements of a parent and subsidiaries, as if the group were a single company for the benefit of the parent's stockholders and creditors.
1. **Substance** (effectively a single entity) takes precedence over **legal form** (legally separate entities).
2. Consolidated financial statements result in **more meaningful presentation of financial position and operating results** than if separate statements were presented for the parent and subsidiary.
B. The general condition for consolidation is over 50% ownership of subsidiaries.
1. Theoretical condition is **control** of the subsidiaries.
a. This is generally implicit in greater than 50% ownership.

...t are a temporary investment (in reorganization, in bankruptcy, etc.) should not be con-

...ness to bondholders should not preclude consolidation.

...al periods should not preclude consolidation.

...three months are acceptable if one discloses material intervening events.

...excess of three months should be consolidated on the basis of interim statements of the

...cy should be disclosed by headings or footnotes.

...nces and transactions should be eliminated in consolidated statements.

    1. Intercompany gains and losses on assets remaining in the group should be eliminated (eliminate entire gross profit or loss even on transactions with minority interest subsidiaries).

F. Retained earnings of subsidiaries at the acquisition date should not appear in the consolidated statements.

G. When a parent purchases a subsidiary in several blocks of stock, the subsidiary's retained earnings should be determined by the step method (apply equity method to subsidiary retroactively).

H. When a subsidiary is purchased in midyear, subsidiary operations may be included in the consolidated income statement for the year and then the operating results prior to acquisition would be deducted.

    1. As an alternative for a subsidiary purchased in midyear, postacquisition operations can be included in the consolidated income statement.

    2. For midyear disposals, omit operations from the consolidated income statement and include equity in subsidiary's operations up to disposal date as a separate item in the income statement.

NOTE: F. through H. pertain only to acquisitions accounted for as purchases per APB 16.

I. Sometimes combined, as distinguished from consolidated, financial statements are appropriate for commonly owned companies and are prepared when consolidated statements are not appropriate.

ACCOUNTING PRINCIPLES BOARD OPINIONS

APB 6 (B05, C23, D40, I60) Status of Accounting Research Bulletins

A. ARB 43, Chapter 1B Treasury Stock

    1. An excess of purchase price of treasury stock, purchased for retirement or constructive retirement, over par or stated value may be allocated between paid-in capital and retained earnings.

        a. The charge to paid-in capital is limited to all paid-in capital from treasury stock transactions and retirements of the same issue and a pro rata portion of all other paid-in capital of that issue.

        b. Also, paid-in capital applicable to fully retired issues may be charged.

    2. Alternatively, losses may be charged entirely to retained earnings.

    3. All gains on retirement of treasury stock go to paid-in capital.

    4. When the decision to retire treasury stock has not been made, the cost of such is a contra shareholders' equity item. Losses may only be charged to paid-in capital from treasury transactions and retirements of the same issue.

    5. Some state laws prescribe accounting for treasury stock. The laws are to be followed where they are at variance with this APB. Disclose all statutory requirements concerning treasury stock such as dividend restrictions.

B. ARB 43, Chapter 3A Current Assets and Liabilities

Unearned interest, finance charges, etc. included in receivables should be deducted from the related receivable.

C. ARB 43, Chapter 7B Stock Dividends and Splits

States "the shareholder has no income solely as a result of the fact that the corporation has income," but does not preclude use of the equity method.

APB 9 (I17, C08) Reporting the Results of Operations

A. Designates a new format for income statement in which all normal operating items would be presented at the top of the income statement resulting in "net income before extraordinary items."

    1. "Net income before extraordinary items" is followed by extraordinary items resulting in "net income."

B. "Prior period adjustments" are excluded from the income statement and constitute adjustments of beginning retained earnings disclosed at the top of the retained earnings statement. (See SFAS 16.)

    1. Beginning retained earnings are adjusted by "prior period adjustments" resulting in "restated beginning retained earnings."

2. "Restated retained earnings" is then adjusted for net income and dividends which results in ending retained earnings.

C. Prior period adjustments should be disclosed in the period of adjustment.
1. The effect on each prior period presented should be disclosed including restated income taxes.
2. Disclosure in subsequent periods is not normally required.
3. Historical summary data should also be restated and disclosed in the period of adjustment.

D. The APB also reaffirmed earlier positions that the following should not affect determination of net income:
1. Transactions in the company's own stock
2. Transfers to or from retained earnings
3. Quasi reorganization adjustments

APB 10 (A35, B10, C16, I24, I25, I28, R75) Omnibus Opinion—1966

A. ARB 43, Chapter 3B Working Capital
1. Offsetting of liabilities and assets in the balance sheet is not acceptable unless a right of offset exists.
2. Most government securities are not designed to be prepayment of taxes and thus may not be offset against tax liabilities. Only where an explicit prepayment exists may an offset be used.

B. Installment method of accounting
Revenues should be recognized at the point of sale unless receivables are in doubt. The installment or cost recovery method may be used.

APB 12 (C08, C38, D40, I69, V18) Omnibus Opinion—1967

A. Allowance or contra accounts (allowance for bad debts, accumulated depreciation, etc.) should be deducted from assets or groups of assets with appropriate disclosure.

B. Disclosure of depreciable assets should include
1. Depreciation expense for the period
2. Balances of major classes of depreciable assets by nature or function
3. Accumulated depreciation either by major class or in total
4. Description of method(s) of depreciation by major classes of assets

C. Changes in the separate shareholder equity accounts in addition to retained earnings and changes in number of equity securities must be disclosed in the year of change
1. In separate statements
2. Or the financial statements
3. Or the notes

APB 14 (D10, C08) Convertible Debt and Debt Issued with Stock Warrants

A. Convertible debt constitutes securities which are convertible into common stock of the user or affiliate. Terms generally include
1. Lower interest rate than on ordinary debt
2. Initial conversion price greater than the common price at time of issuance
3. A conversion price which does not decrease except to protect against dilution

B. While there are arguments to account for the debt and equity characteristics separately, the APB has concluded no proceeds of a convertible issue should be attributed to the conversion factor.
1. Primary **reasons** are
   a. The inseparability of the debt and conversion features
   b. The practical difficulties of valuing the conversion feature

C. When debt is issued with detachable purchase warrants, the debt and warrants generally trade separately and should be treated separately.
1. The allocation of proceeds should be based on relative market value at date of issuance.
2. Any resulting debt discount or premium should be accounted for as such.

D. Separate valuation of debt and warrants is applicable where the debt may be used as consideration when exercising the warrants. Separate valuation is **not** acceptable where the debt must be tendered to exercise the warrants (i.e., the warrants are, in essence, nondetachable).

APB 18 (I82) The Equity Method for Investments

A. The equity method should be used for corporate joint ventures.

B. The equity method should be applied to investments where less than 50% ownership is held but the investor **can exercise significant influence over operating and financing policies of the investee**.
1. Twenty percent (20%) or more ownership should lead to presumption of substantial influence, unless there is evidence to the contrary.
2. Conversely, less than 20% ownership leads to the presumption of no substantial influence unless there is evidence to the contrary.
3. The 20% test should be based on voting stock outstanding and disregard common stock equivalents.
4. The following procedures should be used in applying the equity method:
   a. Intercompany profits should be eliminated.
   b. Difference between cost and book value of net assets acquired should be accounted for per SFAS 141 and 142.
   c. The investment account and investor's share of investee income should be presented as single amounts in investor statements with the exception of d. below.
   d. Investor's share of discontinued operations, extraordinary items, cumulative effects of accounting changes, and prior period adjustments of investee should be so presented in statements of investor.
   e. Investee capital transactions should be accounted for as are subsidiary capital transactions in consolidated statements.
   f. Gains on sale of investment are the difference between selling price and carrying value of investment.
   g. When investee and investor fiscal periods do not coincide, use most recent investee statement and have consistent time lag.
   h. Losses, not temporary in nature, of investment value should be recognized by investor.
   i. Investor's share of investee loss should not be recorded once investment account is written to zero. Subsequent income should be recognized after losses not recognized are made up.
   j. Investor's share of investee's earnings should be computed after deducting investee's cumulative preferred dividends whether declared or not.
   k. If an investor's holding falls below 20%, discontinue applying the equity method but make no retroactive adjustment.
   l. When an investor's holding increases from a level less than 20% to a level equal to or greater than 20%, the investment account and retained earnings of the investor should be adjusted retroactively to reflect balances as if the equity account had been used. This is accounted for like a prior period adjustment.
5. Statements of investors applying the equity method should disclose
   a. Investees and percentages held
      (1) Accounting policies followed
      (2) Treatment of goodwill, if any
   b. Aggregate market value of investment (not for subsidiaries)
   c. When investments are material to investor, summarized information of assets, liabilities, and results of operations of investee may be necessary
   d. Conversion of securities, exercise of warrants, or issuances of investee's common stock which significantly affects investor's share of investee's income

FASB INTERPRETATION NO. 35 CRITERIA FOR APPLYING THE EQUITY METHOD OF ACCOUNTING FOR INVESTMENTS IN COMMON STOCK. Interprets APB 18.

Investors owning between 20 and 50 percent of an investee may **not** be able to exercise significant influence over the investee's operating and financial policies. The presumption of significant influence stands until overcome by evidence to the contrary, such as: (1) opposition by the investee, (2) agreements under which the investor surrenders shareholder rights, (3) majority ownership by a small group of shareholders, (4) inability to obtain desired information from the investee, (5) inability to obtain representation on investee board of directors, etc. Whether contrary evidence is sufficient to negate the presumption of significant influence is a matter of judgment requiring a careful evaluation of all pertinent facts and circumstances, in some cases over an extended period of time. Application of this interpretation resulting in changes to or from the equity method shall be treated per APB 18, paras 19l and 19m.

APB 20 (A06, A35) Accounting Changes

Prescribes accounting for three types of accounting changes and correction of an error in prior periods' financial statements. Both should be reported to facilitate analysis and understanding of the financial statements.

A. Changes in principle
   1. Changes of principles should not be made unless to a preferable principle.
      a. When the APB expresses a preference or rejects a principle, this is a justification for change.
      b. Burden of justification for other changes rests on entity proposing change.
   2. Special changes require recognition of cumulative effect on beginning retained earnings as a prior period adjustment, as if new principle had always been followed, and retroactive adjustment of prior period statements.
      a. Special changes include
         (1) **From** LIFO to any other inventory method
         (2) Change in accounting for long-term contracts
         (3) Change to or from full cost method in extractive industries
      b. Nature and justification for change should be disclosed. Also, disclose effect on income before extraordinary items, net income, and per share amounts for all periods presented. The purpose of the disclosure is to avoid misleading financial statement users.
   3. For **all other changes** do not retroactively adjust prior periods.
      a. Apply new method to current year
      b. The cumulative effect of the change on beginning retained earnings, as if the new principle had always been followed, should be presented on the income statement between extraordinary items and net income.
         (1) The cumulative effect should be net of tax effects.
      c. The effect of the change in principle, on income before extraordinary items and net income, should be disclosed for the period of change.
      d. The pro forma effect of retroactive application of the change should be shown on the face of the income statement as a separate section.
      e. If pro forma amounts cannot be calculated, disclose reasons.
      f. If the cumulative effect cannot be computed, disclose reasons and effect of change on current year's income figures.
   4. Exception for a change in amortization (depreciation) method of assets applied to new assets only (existing assets depreciated using old method).
      a. No cumulative effect involved in this exception
      b. Disclose change and effect on income figures in year of change
B. Changes in estimate
   1. A change in estimate should be disclosed in the period of change if it affects that period only.
      a. Disclosure should be made in year of change if it affects future periods (e.g., change in useful life of depreciable assets).
      b. A change in estimate that is recognized by a change in principle should be accounted for as a change in estimate.
         (1) For example, change from capitalizing a cost to immediately expensing it
   2. Disclosure of changes in estimates should include effect on
      a. Income before extraordinary items
      b. Net income
      c. Related per share amounts
C. Change in accounting entity (e.g., a business combination accounted for as a pooling)
   1. Financial statements should be restated for all prior periods.
   2. The nature and reasons of change should be explained in year of change.
   3. Effect of changes on income figures and per share amounts should be disclosed for all periods presented.
D. Correction of an error in prior statements
   1. Prior period adjustment
   2. Nature of error and effect on the income figures and per share amounts should be disclosed in the period the error is discovered.

E. Methods of accounting for and disclosing accounting changes and error correction are designed to facilitate **consistency** in reporting by the entity from period to period, and **comparability** of reporting with that of other entities.

FASB INTERPRETATION NO. 1 ACCOUNTING CHANGES RELATED TO THE COST OF INVENTORY

  Changes in the cost composition of inventory is an accounting change and must conform to APB 20, including justification for the change. Preferably should be based on financial reporting objectives rather than tax-related benefits.

APB 21 (I69) Interest on Receivables and Payables

Accounting for receivables and payables whose face value does not approximate their present value

A. Applies to receivables and payables except
1. Normal course of business receivables and payables maturing in less than one year
2. Amounts not requiring repayment in the future (will be applied to future purchases or sales)
3. Security deposits and retainages
4. Customary transactions of those whose primary business is lending money
5. Transactions where interest rates are tax affected or legally prescribed (e.g., municipal bonds and tax settlements)
6. Parent-subsidiary transactions
7. Estimates of contractual obligations such as warranties

B. Notes exchanged for cash are recorded at their present value. Present value equals the cash paid/received. If face value of note ≠ cash paid/received, difference is a discount/premium.
1. If **unstated rights or privileges** are exchanged in issuance of note for cash, adjust cash payment to obtain present value of the note and unstated rights.

C. Notes exchanged for **goods or services** in arm's-length transaction are recorded at face amount (presumption that face amount = present value).
1. Presumption not valid if note is
   a. Noninterest-bearing
   b. Stated interest rate is unreasonable
   c. Face amount of the note differs materially from sales price of goods or services
2. When presumption not valid, record note at fair value of goods or services
   a. Compute **implicit** rate (rate that discounts the future value [face of note plus cash interest, if any] to fair value of goods and services) for interest expense/revenue recognition
3. When no established market price for goods and services exists, record note at its fair market value.
   a. Compute **implicit** rate (rate that discounts the future value [face of note plus cash interest, if any] to fair [present] value of note) for interest expense/revenue recognition
4. When no fair market value exists for either the goods and services or the note, record note at approximation of market value.
   a. Use **imputed** rate to compute present value of (and discount on) note.
   b. Imputed rate should approximate the rate an independent borrower and lender would negotiate in a similar transaction. Consider
      (1) Credit standing of issuer
      (2) Restrictive covenants
      (3) Collateral
      (4) Payment and other terms
      (5) Tax consequences to buyer and seller
      (6) Market rate for sale or assignment
      (7) Prime rate
      (8) Published rates of similar bonds
      (9) Current rates charged for mortgages on similar property

D. Discount or premium should be amortized by the interest method (constant rate of interest on the amount outstanding).
1. Other methods (e.g., straight-line) may be used if the results are not materially different from those of the interest method.

E. Discount or premium should be netted with the related asset or liability and **not** shown as separate asset or liability.
   1. Issue costs should be reported as deferred charges.

APB 22 (A10) Disclosure of Accounting Policies

A. Accounting policies can affect reported results significantly and the usefulness of the financial statements depends on the user's understanding of the accounting policies adopted by the reporting entity. Disclosure of accounting policies are
   1. Essential to users
   2. Integral part of financial statements
   3. Required for one or more financial statements
   4. Required for not-for-profit entities
   5. Not required for unaudited interim statements
      a. If no change in accounting policy has occurred
B. Disclosure should include accounting principles and methods of applying them if material to reported amounts.
   1. Generally, disclosure pertinent to principles involving recognition of revenue and expense
   2. Specifically, disclosure pertinent to
      a. Selection from existing alternatives
      b. Principles peculiar to a particular industry
      c. Unusual or innovative applications
   3. Examples
      a. Consolidation method
      b. Depreciation method
      c. Amortization of intangibles
      d. Inventory pricing
      e. R&D references amended by SFAS 2
      f. Translation of foreign currencies
      g. Long-term contract accounting
      h. Franchising and leasing activities
   4. Accounting policy disclosure should not duplicate disclosures elsewhere in the statements.
C. Particularly useful is a separate **Summary of Significant Accounting Policies** either preceding or as the initial note.

APB 23 (I25, I42, and B17) Accounting for Income Taxes—Special Areas
(Amended by SFAS 109)
A. Undistributed earnings of domestic subsidiaries
   1. Inclusion of undistributed earnings in pretax accounting income of parent (either through consolidation or equity method) results in temporary difference.
      a. Tax effect may be based on assumptions such as
         (1) Earnings would be distributed currently as dividends or
         (2) Earnings would be distributed in form of capital gain.
B. Foreign subsidiaries are not required to accrue deferred taxes for undistributed earnings if sufficient evidence exists that subsidiary would reinvest the undistributed earnings indefinitely or remit them tax free.

APB 25 (C47) Accounting for Stock Issued to Employees
Redefines "measure of compensation" in ARB 43, Chapter 13B and prescribes accounting for "variable factor" plans and tax benefits related to stock issue plans (also see SFAS 123)
A. No compensation is recognized for noncompensatory plans. Four noncompensation characteristics must be present.
   1. Substantially all full-time employees may participate.
   2. Stock is offered to employees equally or based on salary.
   3. Time permitted for exercise of option is reasonable.
   4. Discount from market is not greater than would be in an offer to sell stock to shareholders.
B. All other plans are compensatory.
   1. Compensation is the quoted market price less the amount the employee is required to pay.
      a. If unavailable, use best estimate of market value.

2. The measurement date for determining compensation is the first date on which **both** of the following are known:
   a. Number of shares the individual may receive
   b. Option price, if any
3. Note that the corporation recognizes compensation cost unless the employee must pay at least the market price (at measurement date).

C. Special rules in applying the measurement principle
1. Cost of treasury stock distributed in an option plan does not determine compensation cost. Use market value unless
   a. Treasury stock is acquired during period, and
   b. Is awarded to employees shortly thereafter
2. Measurement date is not changed because of provision that termination of employment reduces shares available.
3. Measurement date may be year-end rather than date of individual award if
   a. Award is provided by formal plan, and
   b. Plan designates factors to determine award, and
   c. Award pertains to current service
4. Measurement date for convertible securities is date the ratio of conversion is known.
   a. Compensation is based on the higher value of
      (1) Original security, or
      (2) Security into which original is convertible
5. If option plans are combination of more than one plan, compensation should be measured for each of the parts.
   a. If employee has a selection of alternatives, compensation on cost should be measured for the alternative most likely to be chosen.

D. Compensation expense should be recognized as an expense in periods employee performs services.
1. If an employee performs services for several periods prior to stock issuance, compensation expense should be accrued.
   a. If the measurement date is after the grant date, the compensation should be accrued based on the current market price of stock.
2. If stock is issued prior to when some of the services are performed, compensation expense should be deferred to those periods as a contra shareholder's equity item.
3. Any adjustments of estimates regarding option plans should be done currently and prospectively.
   a. If an employee fails to exercise an option, compensation expense recognized in earlier periods should reduce compensation expense of the present period.

FASB INTERPRETATION NO. 28 ACCOUNTING FOR STOCK APPRECIATION RIGHTS AND OTHER VARIABLE STOCK OPTION OR AWARD PLANS

Changes in the market value of stock between the date of the grant and the measurement date (the date both the number of shares and the option price are known) are adjustments to compensation expense in the period the market value of the stock changes.

APB 26 (D14) Early Extinguishment of Debt
(Amended by SFAS 84)

A. Definitions
1. **Net carrying amount.** "Amount due at maturity, adjusted for unamortized premium, discount, and cost of issuance."
2. **Reacquisition price.** "Amount paid on extinguishment, including a call premium and miscellaneous costs of reacquisition."
3. **Refunding.** Replacement of debt with other debt

B. Retirement is usually achieved by use of liquid assets.
1. Currently in existence
2. From sale of equity securities
3. From sale of debt securities

C. A **difference** between **reacquisition price** and **net carrying amount** of the extinguished debt should be recognized in the year of extinguishment as a separate item.

    1. Gains and losses should not be amortized to future years.

    2. Gains and losses are extraordinary (except on purchases to satisfy sinking fund requirements that an enterprise would have to meet within one year of extinguishment date). See SFAS 4 and 64.

APB 28 (I73) Interim Financial Reporting
(Amended by SFAS 3, FASB Interpretation 18)

PART I Application of GAAP to Interim Periods

A. APB faced basic question about interim periods

    1. Are interim periods basic accounting periods?

    2. Are interim periods integral parts of the annual period?

B. The APB decided interim periods are an **integral part of an annual period**.

    1. Certain GAAP must be modified for interim reporting to better relate the interim period to the annual period.

C. Revenue should be recognized on the same basis as for the annual period.

D. Costs directly associated with revenue should be reported as in annual periods with the following **exceptions:**

    1. Estimated gross profit rates may be used to estimate inventory. Disclose method used and significant adjustments to reconcile to later physical inventory.

    2. When LIFO base period inventories are liquidated during the interim period but are expected to be replaced by the end of the annual period, cost of sales should be priced at replacement costs rather than at base period costs.

    3. Declines in inventory market values, unless temporary, should be recognized. Subsequent recovery of market value should be recognized as a cost recovery in the subsequent period.

    4. Unanticipated and unplanned standard cost variances should be recognized in the respective interim period.

E. The objective of reporting all other costs is to obtain fair measure of operations for the annual period. These expenses include

    1. Direct expenditures—salaries

    2. Accruals—vacation pay

    3. Amortization of deferrals—insurance

F. These costs should be applied in interim statements as follows:

    1. Charge to income as incurred, or based on time expiration, benefit received, etc. Follow procedures used in annual reports.

    2. Items not identified with specific period are charged as incurred.

    3. No arbitrary assignment.

    4. Gains and losses of any interim period that would not be deferred at year-end cannot be deferred in the interim period.

    5. Costs frequently subjected to year-end adjustments should be anticipated in the interim periods.

        a. Inventory shrinkage

        b. Allowance for uncollectibles, quantity discounts

        c. Discretionary year-end bonuses

G. Seasonal variations in above items require disclosure and one may add twelve-month reports ending at the interim date for current and preceding years.

H. The best estimate of the annual tax rate should be used to provide taxes on a year-to-date basis.

    1. The best estimate should take investment credits, capital gains, etc. into account, but not extraordinary items.

    2. Tax effects of losses in early portion of the year should not be recognized unless realization in subsequent interim periods is assured beyond a reasonable doubt (e.g., an established pattern of loss in early periods).

        a. When tax effects of losses in early periods are not recognized, no taxes should be accrued in later periods until loss credit has been used.

I. Extraordinary items should be disclosed separately and recognized in the interim period in which they occur.

    1. The materiality of extraordinary items should be determined in relation to expected annual income.

2. Effects of disposals of a component of a business are not extraordinary items, but should be disclosed separately.
3. Extraordinary items should **not** be prorated over remainder of the year.
4. Contingencies should be disclosed in the same manner as required in annual reports.

J. Each interim report should disclose any change in accounting principle from
1. Comparable period of prior year
2. Preceding periods of current year
3. Prior annual report

K. Reporting these changes
1. APB 20 should be complied with, including restatement provisions.
2. A change in accounting estimate (including effect on estimated tax rate) should be accounted for in period of change and disclosed in subsequent periods if material.
3. Changes in principle, requiring cumulative effect, should be calculated for the effect on beginning annual retained earnings.
   a. The cumulative effect should be reported in the first interim period.
   b. Previously reported interim information should be restated.
   c. Changes should be made in first period whenever possible.
   d. Items not material to annual results, but material to interim results, should be disclosed separately in the interim reports.

PART II Required Interim Disclosures by Publicly Traded Companies

A. Minimum disclosure includes
1. Sales, provision for taxes, extraordinary items, cumulative effect of principle changes, and net income
2. BEPS and DEPS
3. Seasonal revenue, costs, and expenses
4. Significant changes in estimates of taxes
5. Disposal of a business component and extraordinary items
6. Contingent items
7. Changes in accounting principles and estimates
8. Significant changes in financial position
9. Reportable operating segments
   a. External revenues
   b. Intersegment revenues
   c. Segment profit/loss
   d. Total assets (if material change from last annual report)
   e. Description of changes from last annual report in method of determining segments or measurement of segment profit/loss
   f. Reconciliation of total of reportable segments' profit/loss to corresponding enterprise amount

B. When **summarized interim data** are reported regularly, the above should be reported for the
1. Current quarter
2. Current year-to-date or last twelve months with comparable data for the preceding year

C. If fourth quarter data are not separately reported, disclose in annual report
1. Disposal of business component
2. Extraordinary, unusual, and infrequent items
3. Aggregate year-end adjustments

D. The APB encourages interim disclosure of financial position and funds flow data.
1. If not disclosed, significant changes therein should be disclosed.

FASB INTERPRETATION NO. 18 ACCOUNTING FOR INCOME TAXES IN INTERIM PERIODS
    Tax on income from continuing operations for an interim period is based on estimated annual effective rate, which reflects anticipated tax planning alternatives. Expense of interim period is (Year-to-date income) x (Estimated rate) less (Expense recognized in prior interim periods). Tax effect of special items (below continuing operations) computed as they occur.

APB 29 (N35, C11) Accounting for Nonmonetary Transactions
A. Definitions

1. **Monetary assets and liabilities.** "Assets and liabilities whose amounts are fixed in terms of units of currency by contract or otherwise. Examples are cash, short- or long-term accounts and notes receivable in cash, and short- or long-term accounts and notes payable in cash."
2. **Nonmonetary assets and liabilities.** "Assets and liabilities other than monetary ones. Examples are inventories; investments in common stocks; property, plant and equipment; and liabilities for rent collected in advance."
3. **Exchange.** "A reciprocal transfer between an enterprise and another entity that results in the enterprise's acquiring assets or services or satisfying liabilities by surrendering other assets or services or incurring other obligations."
4. **Nonreciprocal transfer.** "Transfer of assets or services in one direction, either from an enterprise to its owners (whether or not in exchange for their ownership interests) or another entity or from owners or another entity to enterprise. An entity's reacquisition of its outstanding stock is an example of a nonreciprocal transfer."
5. **Productive assets.** "Assets held for or used in the production of goods or services by the enterprise. Productive assets include an investment in another entity if the investment is accounted for by the equity method but exclude an investment not accounted for by that method. **Similar productive assets** are productive assets that are of the same general type, that perform the same function or that are employed in the same line of business."

B. APB 29 does **not** apply to
1. Business combinations
2. Transfer of nonmonetary assets between companies under common control
3. Acquisition of nonmonetary assets with capital stock of an enterprise
4. Stock dividends and splits, issued or received

C. APB 29 does apply to
1. Nonreciprocal transfers with owners. Examples are distributions to stockholders
   a. Dividends
   b. To redeem capital stock
   c. In liquidation
   d. To settle rescission of a business combination
2. Nonreciprocal transfer with other than owners. Examples are
   a. Contribution to charitable institutions
   b. Contribution of land by governmental unit to a business
3. Nonmonetary exchange. Examples are exchanges of
   a. Property exchanged for dissimilar property
   b. Property exchanged for similar property

D. Nonmonetary transactions should generally be accounted for as are monetary transactions.
1. Cost of a nonmonetary asset is the fair value of the asset surrendered to obtain it.
   a. The difference between fair value and book value is a gain or loss.
   b. Fair value of asset received, if clearer than that of asset given, should value transaction.
2. Fair value should **not** be used to recognize gains unless fair value is determinable within reasonable limits.
3. Fair value should **not** be used to recognize gains when exchange is not the culmination of an earnings process; for example
   a. Exchange of property held for sale for similar property
   b. Exchange of similar productive assets

E. If a nonmonetary exchange, which is not a culmination of the earnings process, contains boot received, the portion of the gain recognized should be limited to the ratio [Boot ÷ (Boot received + FMV of asset received)] times the gain (Boot + FMV received minus total book value given).
1. Firm paying boot should **not** recognize any gain.

F. Liquidation distributions to owners should **not** be accounted for at fair value if a gain results (loss may be recognized).
1. Use historical cost
2. Other nonreciprocal distributions to owners should be accounted for at fair value if fair value
   a. Is objectively measurable
   b. Would be clearly realizable if sold

G. Fair value should be determined in reference to
1. Estimated realizable values in cash transactions of similar assets
2. Quoted market prices
3. Independent appraisals
4. Estimated fair value of that received in exchange
5. Other evidence
H. Nonmonetary transaction disclosures should include
1. Nature of the transactions
2. Basis of accounting
3. Gains and losses recognized

FASB INTERPRETATION NO. 30 ACCOUNTING FOR INVOLUNTARY CONVERSIONS OF NONMONETARY ASSETS TO MONETARY ASSETS

When involuntary conversions of nonmonetary assets (e.g., fixed assets) to monetary assets (e.g., insurance proceeds) occur, the difference between the assets' cost and the monetary assets received should be reported as a gain or loss. If an unknown amount of monetary assets are to be received in a later period, gain (loss) is estimated per SFAS 5. Could be extraordinary per APB 30.

APB 30 (E09, I13, I17, I22) Reporting the Results of Operations
(Amended by SFAS 4 and SFAS 144)
A. Extraordinary items are **both** unusual and infrequent.
1. **Unusual nature.** "The underlying event or transaction should possess a high degree of abnormality and be of a type clearly unrelated to, or only incidentally related to, the ordinary and typical activities of the entity, taking into account the environment in which the entity operates."
   a. Special characteristics of the entity
      (1) Type and scope of operations
      (2) Lines of business
      (3) Operating policies
2. **Infrequency of occurrence.** "The underlying event or transaction should be of a type that would not reasonably be expected to recur in the foreseeable future, taking into account the environment in which the entity operates."
3. Example of extraordinary presentation

Income before extraordinary items..	$xxx
Extraordinary items (less applicable income taxes of $__) (Note __).	xxx
Net income	$xxx

4. Examples of gains and losses that are **not** generally extraordinary
   a. Write-downs or write-offs of receivables, inventories, R&D, etc.
   b. Translation of foreign exchange including major devaluations
   c. Disposal of a segment of a business
   d. Sale of productive assets
   e. Effects of strikes
   f. Accruals on long-term contracts
5. Extraordinary items should be classified separately if material on an individual basis.
6. Gains or losses that are unusual **or** infrequent but not both should be disclosed separately (but not net of tax) in the income statement or notes.

STATEMENTS OF FINANCIAL ACCOUNTING STANDARDS

SFAS 2 (Co2, R50) Accounting for Research and Development Costs (R&D)
A. Establishes accounting standards for R&D costs with objective of reducing alternative practices. In summary, all R&D costs are expensed except intangible assets purchased from others and tangible assets that have alternative future uses (which are capitalized and depreciated or amortized as R&D expense).
1. SFAS 2 specifies
   a. R&D activities
   b. Elements of R&D costs
   c. Accounting for R&D costs

      d. Required disclosures for R&D
   2. SFAS 2 does not cover
      a. R&D conducted for others under contract
      b. Activities unique to extractive industries

B. R&D activities
   1. Research is "planned search or critical investigation aimed at discovery of new knowledge with the hope that such knowledge will be useful in developing a new product or service or a new process or technique in bringing about a significant improvement to an existing product or process."
   2. Development is "the translation of research findings or other knowledge into a plan or design for a new product or process or for a significant improvement to an existing product or process whether intended for sale or use."
   3. R&D examples
      a. Laboratory research to discover new knowledge
         (1) Seeking applications for new research findings
      b. Formulation and design of product alternatives
         (1) Testing for product alternatives
         (2) Modification of products or processes
      c. Preproduction prototypes and models
         (1) Tools, dies, etc. for new technology
         (2) Pilot plants not capable of commercial production
      d. Engineering activity until product is ready for manufacture
   4. Exclusions from R&D
      a. Engineering during an early phase of commercial production
      b. Quality control for commercial production
      c. Troubleshooting during commercial production breakdowns
      d. Routine, ongoing efforts to improve products
      e. Adaptation of existing capability for a specific customer or other requirements
      f. Seasonal design changes to products
      g. Routine design of tools, dies, etc.
      h. Design, construction, startup, etc. of equipment except that used solely for R&D
      i. Legal work for patents or litigation
      j. Items a. - h. above are normally expensed but not as R&D; i. is capitalized

C. Elements of R&D costs
   1. Materials, equipment, and facilities
      a. If acquired for a specific R&D project and have no alternative use
      b. If there are alternative uses, costs should be capitalized
         (1) Charge to R&D as these materials, etc., are used
   2. Salaries, wages, and related costs
   3. Intangibles purchased from others are treated as materials, etc. in 1. above
      a. If capitalized, amortization is covered by APB 17
   4. R&D services **performed by others**
   5. A reasonable allocation of indirect costs
      a. Exclude general and administrative costs not clearly related to R&D

D. Accounting for R&D
   1. Expense R&D as incurred

E. Disclosure required on face of IS or notes
   1. Total R&D expensed per period

SFAS 5 (C59, I50, In6, R70) Accounting for Contingencies (Supersedes Chapter 6, ARB 43, ARB 50)

A. Contingency is "an existing condition, situation, or set of circumstances involving uncertainty as to possible gain (loss) to an enterprise that will ultimately be resolved when one or more future events occur or fail to occur."
   1. Definitions
      a. Probable—future events are likely to occur
      b. Reasonably possible—chance of occurrence is more than remote, but less than likely
      c. Remote—chance of occurrence is slight

2. Loss contingency examples
    a. Receivable collection
    b. Product warranty obligations
    c. Risk of property losses by fire, explosion, etc.
    d. Asset expropriation threat
    e. Pending, threatened, etc., litigation
    f. Actual or possible claims and assessments
    g. Catastrophe losses faced by insurance companies
    h. Guarantees of indebtedness of others
    i. Banks' obligations under "standby letters of credit"
    j. Agreements to repurchase receivables, related property, etc. that have been sold
B. Estimated loss from contingencies shall be accrued and charged to income when
1. It is probable (at balance sheet date) that an asset has been impaired or liability incurred
2. **And** the amount of loss can be reasonably estimated
    a. Difference between estimate recorded and actual amount determined in subsequent period is a change in accounting estimate
C. Loss contingency disclosures
1. Nature and amount of material items
2. Nonaccrued loss contingencies for which a reasonable possibility of loss exists
    a. Disclose nature of contingency
    b. Estimate possible range of loss
        (1) Or state estimate cannot be made
3. If a loss contingency develops after year-end, but before statements are issued, disclosure of the nature of the contingency and amount may be necessary.
    a. If a year-end contingency results in a loss before issuance of the statements, disclosure (possibly pro forma amounts) may be necessary.
4. Disclose nature and amount of the following loss contingencies (even if remote)
    a. Guarantees of others' debts
    b. Standby letters of credit by banks
    c. Agreements to repurchase receivables
D. General, unspecified risks are not contingencies.
E. Appropriation of RE for contingencies shown within shareholders' equity is not prohibited.
1. Cannot be shown outside shareholders' equity
2. Contingency costs and losses cannot be charged to appropriation.
F. Gain contingency accounting
1. Normally not reflected in accounts until realized.
2. Adequate disclosure should be made without misleading implications of likelihood of realization.
G. Rationale for accounting for contingencies per SFAS 5
1. Reflects **conservatism**—recognize losses immediately (if probable and reasonably estimable), but recognize gains only when realized.
2. Results in better matching—contingent losses are recognized in time period of origin.

FASB INTERPRETATION NO. 14 REASONABLE ESTIMATION OF THE AMOUNT OF LOSS

A range of the amount of a loss is sufficient to meet the criteria of SFAS 5 that the amount of loss be "subject to reasonable estimate." When one amount in the range is a better estimate, use it; otherwise, use the minimum of the range and disclose range.

STATEMENTS OF POSITION NO. 96-1 ENVIRONMENTAL REMEDIATION LIABILITIES

This SOP includes accounting guidance, preceded by a very detailed description of relevant laws, remediation laws, remediation provisions and other pertinent information, useful to auditors as well as clients. Auditing guidance is limited to recitation of SFAS 5 concerns about reasonable estimation of loss accruals.

Accounting guidance includes the following provisions:

A. Interprets SFAS 5 in the context of environmental obligations (e.g., threshold for accrual of liability, etc.) and sets "benchmarks" for recognition.

B. Benchmarks for accrual and evaluation of estimated liability (stages which are deemed to be important to ascertaining the existence and amount of the liability) are
1. Identification and verification of an entity as a potentially responsible party (PRP), since the proposal stipulated that accrual should be based on premise that expected costs will be borne by only the "participating potentially responsible parties" and that the "recalcitrant, unproven and unidentified" PRP will not contribute to costs of remediation
2. Receipt of unilateral administrative order
3. Participation, as a PRP, in the remedial investigation/feasibility study (RI/FS)
4. Completion of the feasibility study
5. Issuance of the Record of Decision (ROD)
6. Remedial design through operation and maintenance, including postremediation monitoring
C. The amount of liability is affected by
1. The entity's allocable share of liability for a specified site; and
2. Its share of the amounts related to the site that will not be paid by the other PRP or the government
D. Costs to be included in the accrued liability are
1. Incremental direct costs of the remediation effort itself; and
   a. Fees to outside law firms for work related to the remediation effort
   b. Costs relating to completing the RI/FS
   c. Fees to outside consulting and engineering firms for site investigations and development of remedial action plans and remedial actions
   d. Costs of contractors performing remedial actions
   e. Government oversight costs and past costs
   f. Cost of machinery and equipment dedicated to the remedial actions that do not have an alternative use
   g. Assessments by a PRP group covering costs incurred by the group in dealing with a site
   h. Costs of operation and maintenance of the remedial action, including costs of postremediation monitoring required by the remedial action plan
2. Costs of compensation and benefits for employees directly involved in the remediation effort
3. Costs are to be estimated based on existing laws and technologies, and not discounted to present value unless timing of cash payments is fixed or reliably determinable

---

SFAS 6 (B05) Classification of Short-Term Obligations Expected to Be Refinanced
(Modifies para 8 of Chapter 3A, ARB 43)
A. Short-term obligations shall be classified as a current liability unless
1. Enterprise intends to refinance the obligation on a long-term basis
2. AND the intent is supported by ability to refinance
   a. Post-balance-sheet issuance of long-term debt or equity securities, or
   b. Financing agreement that clearly permits refinancing on a long-term basis
      (1) Does not expire or is not callable for one year
      (2) No violation of the agreement exists at the balance sheet date or has occurred to date
3. The amount of the short-term obligation excluded from current liability status should not exceed the
   a. Net proceeds of debt or securities issued
   b. Net amounts available under refinancing agreements
      (1) The enterprise must intend to exercise the financing agreement when the short-term obligation becomes due.
4. Refinancing of short-term obligations is a FS **classification** issue, **not** a **recognition** and **measurement** issue.

FASB INTERPRETATION NO. 8 CLASSIFICATION OF A SHORT-TERM OBLIGATION REPAID PRIOR TO BEING REPLACED BY A LONG-TERM SECURITY
Short-term obligations that are repaid after the balance sheet date but **before** funds are obtained from long-term financing are to be classified as current liabilities at the balance sheet date.
EXAMPLES:
*In situation 1 below, the obligation will be classified as a noncurrent liability at the balance sheet date. Why? Proceeds from refinancing were obtained **prior** to the due date of the obligation.*

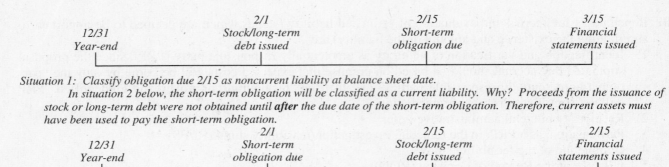

Situation 1: Classify obligation due 2/15 as noncurrent liability at balance sheet date.

> *In situation 2 below, the short-term obligation will be classified as a current liability. Why? Proceeds from the issuance of stock or long-term debt were not obtained until **after** the due date of the short-term obligation. Therefore, current assets must have been used to pay the short-term obligation.*

	2/1	2/15	2/15
12/31	*Short-term*	*Stock/long-term*	*Financial*
Year-end	*obligation due*	*debt issued*	*statements issued*

Situation 2: Classify obligation due 2/1 as current liability at balance sheet date

---

SFAS 7 (De4) Accounting and Reporting by Development Stage Companies

A. A company, division, component, etc., is in the development stage if
  1. Substantially all efforts are devoted toward establishing the business, or
  2. Principal operations are underway but have not produced significant revenues

B. Example activities of development stage companies
  1. Financial planning
  2. Raising capital
  3. Exploring or developing natural resources
  4. R&D
  5. Establishing sources of supply
  6. Acquiring property, plant, equipment, etc.
  7. Personnel recruitment and training
  8. Developing markets
  9. Production start-up

C. No special accounting standards apply to development stage companies.
  1. Report revenue in the income statement as in normal operations
  2. Expense costs as one would for a company in normal operations
  3. Capitalize costs as one would for a company in normal operations
      a. Determine cost recoverability within entity for which statements are being prepared

D. Development stage company statements include
  1. A balance sheet with cumulative net losses termed "deficit accumulated during development stage"
  2. An income statement with revenues and expenses for both current period and cumulative expenses and revenues from the inception of the development stage
  3. A statement of cash flows for both current period and cumulative amounts from inception
  4. Statement of owner's investment including
      a. Dates of issuance and number of shares, warrants, etc.
      b. Dollar amounts must be assigned to each issuance
          (1) Dollar amounts must be assigned for noncash consideration
      c. Dollar amounts received for each issuance or basis for valuing noncash consideration
  5. Identification of statements as those of a development stage company
  6. During the first period of normal operations, notes to statements should disclose that company was, but is no longer, in the development stage

SFAS 13 (L10, C51) Accounting for Leases

(Supersedes APB 5, 7, 27, 31, and para 15 of APB 18; paras 18 and 23 amended by SFAS 91)
(The outline below is based on the comprehensive restatement as of January 1990 which includes SFAS 17 [rescinded by SFAS 91], 22, 23, 26, 27, 28, and 29 and Interpretations 19, 21, 23, 24, 26, and 27.)

Applies to agreements for use of property, plant, and equipment, but not natural resources and not for licensing agreements such as patents and copyrights.

The major issue in accounting for leases is whether the benefits and risks incident to ownership have been transferred from lessor to lessee. If so, the lessor treats the lease as a sale or financing transaction and the lessee treats it as a purchase. Otherwise, the lease is accounted for as a rental agreement. These different treatments recognize the **substance** of a transaction rather than its **form;** that is, what is legally a lease may be effectively the same as or similar to an installment purchase by the lessee and a sale or financing transaction by the lessor.

The following terms are given specific definitions for the purpose of SFAS 13:

Bargain purchase option—A provision allowing the lessee the option of purchasing the leased property for an amount that is sufficiently lower than the expected fair value of the property at the date the option becomes exercisable. Exercise of the option must appear reasonably assured at the inception of the lease.

Contingent rentals—Rentals that represent the increases or decreases in lease payments which result from changes in the factors on which the lease payments are based occurring subsequent to the inception of the lease.

Estimated economic life of lease property—The estimated remaining time which the property is expected to be economically usable by one or more users, with normal maintenance and repairs, for its intended purpose at the inception of the lease. This estimated time period should not be limited by the lease term.

Estimated residual value of leased property—The estimated fair value of the leased property at the end of the lease term.

Executory costs—Those costs such as insurance, maintenance, and taxes incurred for leased property, whether paid by the lessor or lessee. Amounts paid by a lessee in consideration for a guarantee from an unrelated third party of the residual value are also executory costs. If executory costs are paid by the lessor, any lessor's profit on those costs is considered the same as executory costs.

Fair value of leased property—The property's selling price in an arm's-length transaction between unrelated parties.

When the lessor is a **manufacturer or dealer,** the fair value of the property at the inception of the lease will ordinarily be its normal selling price net of volume or trade discounts.

When the lessor is not a **manufacturer or dealer,** the fair value of the property at the inception of the lease will ordinarily be its costs net of volume or trade discounts.

Implicit interest rate—The discount rate that, when applied to the minimum lease payments, excluding that portion of the payments representing executory costs to be paid by the lessor, together with any profit thereon, and the unguaranteed residual value accruing to the benefit of the lessor, causes the aggregate present value at the beginning of the lease term to be equal to the fair value of the leased property to the lessor at the inception of the lease.

Inception of the lease—The date of the written lease agreement or commitment (if earlier) wherein all principal provisions are fixed and no principal provisions remain to be negotiated.

Incremental borrowing rate—The rate that, at the inception of the lease, the lessee would have incurred to borrow over a similar term (i.e., a loan term equal to the lease term) the funds necessary to purchase the leased asset

Initial direct costs—(See outline of SFAS 91)

Lease term—The fixed, noncancelable term of the lease plus all renewal terms when renewal is reasonably assured.

NOTE: The lease term should not extend beyond the date of a bargain purchase option.

Minimum lease payments—For the **lessee:** The payments that the lessee is or can be required to make in connection with the leased property. Contingent rental guarantees by the lessee of the lessor's debt, and the lessee's obligation to pay executory costs are excluded from minimum lease payments. If the lease contains a bargain purchase option, only the minimum rental payments over the lease term and the payment called for in the bargain purchase option are included in minimum lease payments. Otherwise, minimum lease payments include the following:

1. The minimum rental payments called for by the lease over the lease term
2. Any guarantee of residual value at the expiration of the lease term made by the lessee (or any party related to the lessee), whether or not the guarantee payment constitutes a purchase of the leased property. When the lessor has the right to require the lessee to purchase the property at termination of the lease for a certain or determinable amount, that amount shall be considered a lessee guarantee. When the lessee agrees to make up any deficiency below a stated amount in the lessor's realization of the residual value, the guarantee to be included in the MLP is the stated amount rather than an estimate of the deficiency to be made up.
3. Any payment that the lessee must or can be required to make upon **failure to renew or extend** the lease at the expiration of the lease term, whether or not the payment would constitute a purchase of the leased property

For the **lessor:** The payments described above plus any guarantee of the residual value or of the rental payments beyond the lease term by a third party unrelated to either the lessee or lessor (provided the third party is financially capable of discharging the guaranteed obligation).

Unguaranteed residual value—the estimated residual value of the leased property exclusive of any portion guaranteed by the lessee, by any party related to the lessee, or any party unrelated to the lessee. If the guarantor is related to the lessor, the residual value shall be considered as unguaranteed.

A. Classification of leases by lessees. Leases that meet one or more of the following criteria are accounted for as capital leases; all other leases are accounted for as operating leases:

1. Lease transfers ownership (title) to lessee during lease term.
2. Lease contains a bargain purchase option.
3. Lease term is 75% or more of economic useful life of property.
4. Present value of minimum lease payments equals 90% or more of FMV of the leased property.
   a. Present value is computed with lessee's incremental borrowing rate, unless lessor's implicit rate is known and is less than lessee's incremental rate (then use lessor's implicit rate).
   b. FMV is cash selling price for sales-type lease; lessor's cost for direct financing of lease. (If not recently purchased, estimate FMV)

      NOTE: 3. and 4. do not apply if lease begins in last 25% of asset's life.

B. Classification of leases by lessors
1. Sales-type leases provide for a manufacturer or dealer profit (i.e., FMV of leased property is greater than lessor cost or carrying value).
   a. Sales-type leases must meet one of the four criteria for lessee capital leases (A.1. to A.4. above) and **both** of the following two criteria:
      (1) Collectibility is reasonably predictable, and
      (2) No important uncertainties regarding costs to be incurred by lessor exist, such as unusual guarantees of performance. Note estimation of executory expense such as insurance, maintenance, etc., is not considered.
2. Direct financing leases must meet same criteria as sales-type leases (just above) but do not include a manufacturer's or dealer's profit.
3. Operating leases are all other leases that have not been classified as sales-type, direct financing, or leveraged.

C. Lease classification is determined at the inception of the lease.
1. If changes in the lease are subsequently made which change the classification, the lease generally should be considered a new agreement and reclassified and accounted for as a new lease. Exercise of renewal options, etc., are not changes in the lease. However, if the terms of a capital lease are modified such that it should be reclassified as an operating lease, the lessee should account for it under the sale-leaseback provisions of SFAS 98
2. Changes in estimates (e.g., economic life or residual value) or other circumstances (e.g., default) do not result in a new agreement but accounts should be adjusted and gains or losses recognized.
3. An important goal of SFAS 13 was to achieve **symmetry** in lease accounting (i.e., an operating lease for the lessee will be an operating lease for the lessor) and likewise for capital leases.

D. Accounting and reporting by lessees
1. Record capital leases as an asset and liability
   a. Leased asset shall not be recorded in excess of FMV. If the present value of the lease payments is greater than the FMV, the leased asset and related liability are recorded at FMV and the effective interest rate is thereby increased.
   b. Recognize interest expense using the effective interest method.
   c. If there is a transfer of ownership or a bargain purchase option, the asset's depreciation/amortization period is its economic life. Otherwise, depreciate/amortize assets to the expected residual value at the end of the lease term.
2. Rent on operating leases should be expensed on a straight-line basis unless another method is better suited to the particular benefits and costs associated with the lease.
3. Contingent rentals are reported as rent expense in the period incurred.
4. Disclosures by lessees include
   a. General description of leasing arrangement including
      (1) Basis of computing contingent payments

       (2) Existence and terms of renewal or purchase options and escalation clauses

       (3) Restrictions imposed by the lease agreement such as limitations on dividends and further leasing arrangements

   b. Capital lease requirements

       (1) Usual current/noncurrent classifications

       (2) Depreciation/amortization should be separately disclosed

       (3) Future minimum lease payments in the aggregate and for each of the five succeeding fiscal years with separate deductions being made to show the amounts representing executory cost and interest

       (4) Total minimum sublease rentals to be received in the future under noncancelable subleases

       (5) Total contingent rental actually incurred for each period for which an income statement is presented

   c. Operating leases which have initial or remaining noncancelable term > 1 year

       (1) Future minimum lease payments in the aggregate and for each of the five succeeding fiscal years

       (2) Total minimum sublease rentals to be received in the future under noncancelable subleases

       (3) All operating leases—rent expense of each IS period

          (a) Present separate amounts for minimum rentals, contingent rentals, and sublease rentals

          (b) Rental payments for leases with a term of a month or less may be excluded

E. Accounting and reporting by lessors

  1. Sales-type leases

   a. Lease receivable is charged for the gross investment in the lease (the total net minimum lease payments plus the unguaranteed residual value). Sales is credited for the present value of the minimum lease payments.

   b. Cost of sales is the carrying value of the leased asset plus any initial direct costs less the present value of the unguaranteed residual value. Note that in a sales-type lease, initial direct costs are deducted in full in the period when the sale is recorded. Unearned Interest Income is credited for the difference between the gross investment and the sales price.

   c. Recognize interest revenue using the effective interest method

   d. At the end of the lease term, the balance in the receivable account should equal the amount of residual value guaranteed, if any.

   e. Contingent rental payments are reported as income in the period earned.

  2. Direct financing leases

   a. Accounting is similar to sales-type lease except that no manufacturer's or dealer's profit is recognized.

   b. Lease receivable is charged for the gross investment in the lease, the asset account is credited for the net investment in the lease (cost to be acquired for purpose of leasing) and the difference is recorded as unearned income.

   c. Initial direct costs are recorded in a separate account. A new effective interest rate is computed that equates the minimum lease payments and any unguaranteed residual value with the combined outlay for the leased asset and initial direct costs. The initial direct costs and unearned lease revenue are both amortized so as to produce a constant rate of return over the life of the lease.

   d. The remaining requirements are the same as those for the sales-type lease.

  3. Operating leases

   a. Leased property is to be included with or near PP&E on the BS, and lessor's normal depreciation policies should be applied.

   b. Rental revenue should be recognized on a straight-line basis unless another method is better suited to the particular benefits and costs associated with the lease.

   c. Initial direct costs should be deferred and allocated over the lease term in proportion to the recognition of rental revenue.

F. Related-party leases shall be accounted for as unrelated-party leases except when terms have been significantly affected by relationship.

G. Sale-leasebacks

  1. Legally two separate transactions

  2. Lessee (seller) accounts for the gain (loss) as follows:

    a. Loss (when FMV < Book value) on the sale should be recognized immediately.

    b. Gain treatment

        (1) Seller relinquishes the right to substantially all of the remaining use of the property sold (PV of reasonable rentals ≤ 10% of fair value of asset sold)—then separate transactions, and entire gain is recognized.

        (2) Seller retains more than a minor part, but less than substantially all of the remaining use (PV of reasonable rentals are > 10% but < 90% of fair value of asset sold)—then gain on sale is recognized to the extent of the excess of gain over the present value of minimum lease payments (operating) or the recorded amount of the leased asset (capital).

        (3) Seller retains right to substantially all of the remaining use—then entire gain on sale is deferred.

    c. If the gain is deferred and lease is accounted for as

        (1) Capital lease—defer and amortize gain over lease term using same method and life used for depreciating/amortizing cost of leased asset

            (a) Deferral and amortization of the gain are required because the sale and leaseback are components of a single transaction and are interdependent.

        (2) Operating lease—recognize gain on straight-line basis

            (a) Treat as a reduction of rent expense.

  3. Lessor records as a purchase of asset to be leased and as a direct financing or operating lease

---

FASB TECHNICAL BULLETIN 85-3 ACCOUNTING FOR OPERATING LEASES WITH SCHEDULED RENT INCREASES

    SFAS 13 requires lessees or lessors to recognize rent expense or rental income for an operating lease on a straight-line basis. Certain operating lease agreements specify scheduled rent increases over the lease term. The effects of these scheduled rent increases, which are included in minimum lease payments under SFAS 13, should also be recognized by lessors and lessees on a straight-line basis over the lease term.

SFAS 15 (D22) Accounting by Debtors and Creditors for Troubled Debt Restructurings
(Superseded by SFAS 114 with regard to creditors)

A. Troubled debt restructurings occur when a creditor is compelled to grant relief to a debtor due to the debtor's inability to service the debt. This SFAS prescribes accounting for such debt restructurings if

  1. By creditor-debtor agreement

  2. Imposed by a court

  3. Result of repossessions and foreclosures

  4. But not changes in lease agreements

    a. Nor legal actions to collect receivables

    b. Nor quasi reorganizations

B. If a **debtor** transfers assets to settle fully a payable, recognize a gain on restructuring equal to the book value of the payable less FMV of assets transferred.

  1. Estimate asset value by cash flows and risk if FMV cannot be determined.

  2. The difference between set FMV and carrying value of the assets transferred is a gain or loss in disposition of assets per APB 30.

C. If a **debtor** issues an equity interest to settle fully a payable, account for equity issued at FMV.

  1. Excess of carrying value of payable over equity FMV is a gain on restructuring.

D. A **debtor** having the terms of troubled debt modified should account for the restructure prospectively (i.e., no adjustment of the payable).

  1. Recompute the new effective rate of interest based on the new terms

    a. Total cash payments to be paid, less carrying value of payable is the interest

    b. Amortize the payable by the interest method (APB 21) using the new interest rate

  2. Exception is if restructured terms require total cash payments (including interest) which are less than the carrying value of the payable, write down the payable to the total cash to be paid

    a. Include contingent payments in calculation; this precludes recognizing a gain currently and interest expense later

    b. Recognize gain on the write-down

    c. All future cash payments reduce the payable (i.e., no interest expense is recognized)

E. If restructured by partial settlement (assets and/or equity issuance) and modified terms
   1. First account for asset and/or equity issuance per above
   2. Then account for modified terms per above
F. Related matters
   1. A repossession or foreclosure is accounted for per the above.
   2. Contingent payments on restructured debt shall be recognized per SFAS 5 (i.e., its payment is probable and subject to reasonable estimate).
   3. Legal fees on debt restructuring involving equity issuance reduce the amounts credited to the equity accounts.
      a. All other direct costs of debt restructuring reduce gain or are expenses of the period if there is no gain.
G. Disclosures by **debtors**
   1. Description of major changes in debt of each restructuring
   2. Aggregate gain on debt restructuring and related tax effect
   3. Aggregate net gain (loss) on asset transfers due to restructuring
   4. EPS amount of aggregate gain on restructuring net of tax effect

SFAS 16 (A35, C59, I16, I17, and I73) Prior Period Adjustments
(Supersedes paras 23 and 24 of APB 9)
(Amends inconsistent references to APB 9 in APB 20, 30, and SFAS 5)
A. All P&L items are included in the determination of net income except the correction of an error in statements of a prior period.
   1. Account for and report as a prior period adjustment to beginning retained earnings
B. An exception exists for interim reporting regarding certain adjustments relating to prior interim periods of the current year.
   1. These "adjustments" (affecting prior interim periods of the current fiscal year) are settlements or adjustments of
      a. Litigation or similar claims
      b. Income taxes
      c. Renegotiation proceedings
      d. Utility revenue per the rate-making process
   2. These "adjustments" must also
      a. Be material to operating income, trends in income, etc.
      b. All or part of the adjustment is specifically identified with specified prior interim periods of the current fiscal year.
      c. Not subject to reasonable estimation prior to the current interim period (e.g., new retroactive tax legislation)

SFAS 34 (I67, I69) Capitalization of Interest Cost
(Paras 8 and 9 amended by SFAS 42) (Paras 9, 10, and 20 amended by SFAS 58)
A. Interest costs, when material, incurred in acquiring the following types of assets, shall be capitalized:
   1. Assets constructed or produced for a firm's own use
      a. Including construction by others requiring progress payments
   2. Assets intended for lease or sale that are produced as discrete projects
      a. For example, ships and real estate developments
   3. But not on
      a. Routinely produced inventories
      b. Assets ready for their intended use
      c. Assets not being used nor being readied for use
      d. Land, unless it is being developed (e.g., as a plant site, real estate development, etc.)
   4. The objective of interest capitalization is to
      a. Reflect the acquisition cost of assets
      b. Match costs to revenues in the period benefited
   5. Capitalized interest shall be treated as any other asset cost for depreciation and other purposes.
   6. Required interest cost disclosures
      a. Total interest cost incurred

    b.   Interest capitalized, if any

B. Amount of interest to be capitalized

    1.   Conceptually, the interest that would have been avoided if the expenditures had not been made

    2.   Based on the average accumulated expenditures on the asset for the period

        a.   Includes payment of cash, transfer of other assets, and incurring interest-bearing liabilities

        b.   Reasonable approximations are permitted

    3.   Use the interest rates incurred during period

        a.   First, the rates on specific new borrowings for the asset

        b.   Second, a weighted-average of other borrowings

           (1) Use judgment to identify borrowings

    4.   Interest cost capitalized in any period cannot exceed interest cost incurred in that period.

        a.   On a consolidated basis for consolidated statements

        b.   On an individual company basis for individual company statements

    5.   Capitalized interest should be compounded.

C. Interest capitalization period

    1.   Begins when all the following three conditions are present:

        a.   Asset expenditures have been made

        b.   Activities to ready asset for intended use are in progress

           (1) Includes planning stages

        c.   Interest cost is being incurred

    2.   If activities to ready asset for intended use cease, interest capitalization ceases

        a.   Not for brief interruptions that are externally imposed

    3.   Capitalization period ends when asset is substantially complete

        a.   For assets completed in parts, interest capitalization on a part of the asset ends when that part is complete

        b.   Capitalize all interest on assets required to be completed in entirety until entire project is finished

    4.   Interest capitalization continues if capitalized interest raises cost above market values

        a.   Apply impairment accounting per SFAS 144

SFAS 43 (C44) Accounting for Compensated Absences

A. This statement addresses the accounting for future sick pay benefits, holidays, vacation benefits, and other like compensated absences.

B. Accrual of a liability for future compensated absences is required if **all** of the conditions listed below exist.

    1.   Obligation of employer to compensate employees arises from services already performed

    2.   Obligation arises from vesting or accumulation of rights

    3.   Probable payment of compensation

    4.   Amount can be reasonably estimated

C. Above criteria require accrual of a liability for vacation benefits; however, other compensated absences typically may not require accrual of a liability.

    1.   In spite of the above criteria, accrual of a liability is not required for accumulating nonvesting rights to receive sick pay benefits because amounts are typically not large enough to justify cost.

SFAS 45 (Fr3) Accounting for Franchise Fee Revenue

A. Definitions

    1.   **Franchisee**—Party who has been granted business rights

    2.   **Franchisor**—Party who grants business rights

    3.   **Area franchise**—Agreement transferring franchise rights within a geographical area permitting the opening of a number of franchise outlets

    4.   **Continuing franchise fee**—Consideration for continuing rights granted by the agreement (general or specific) during its life

    5.   **Franchise agreement**—Essential criteria

        a.   Contractual relation between franchisee and franchisor

        b.   Purpose is distribution of a product, service, or entire business concept

        c.   Resources contributed by both franchisor and franchisee in establishing and maintaining the franchise

        d.   Outline of specific marketing practices to be followed

    e.   Creation of an establishment that will require and support the full-time business activity of the franchisee

    f.   Both franchisee and franchisor have a common public identity

  6. **Initial franchise fee**—Consideration for establishing the relationship and providing some initial services

  7. **Initial services**—Variety of services and advice (e.g., site selection, financing and engineering services, advertising assistance, training of personnel, manuals for operations, administration and recordkeeping, bookkeeping and advisory services, quality control programs)

B. Franchise fee revenue from individual sales shall be recognized when all material services or conditions relating to the sale have been substantially performed or satisfied by the franchisor.

  1. Substantial performance means

    a.   Franchisor has no remaining obligation or intent to refund money or forgive unpaid debt

    b.   Substantially all initial services have been performed

    c.   No other material conditions or obligations exist

  2. If large initial franchise fee is required and continuing franchise fees are small in relation to future services, then portion of initial franchise fee shall be deferred and amortized over life of franchise.

C. Continuing franchise fees shall be reported as revenue as fees are earned and become receivable from the franchise. Related costs shall be expensed as incurred.

D. Direct franchise costs shall be deferred until related revenue is recognized.

  1. These costs should not exceed anticipated revenue less estimated additional related costs.

E. Disclosure of all significant commitments and obligations that have not yet been substantially performed are required

  1. Notes to the FS should disclose whether the installment or cost recovery method is used.

  2. Initial franchise fees shall be segregated from other franchise fee revenue if significant.

SFAS 47 (C32) Disclosure of Long-Term Obligations

A. This statement requires that firm disclose

  1. Commitments under unconditional purchase obligations that are associated with suppliers (financing arrangements)

  2. Future payments on long-term borrowings

B. **Unconditional purchase obligations** are obligations to transfer funds in the future for fixed or minimum amounts of goods or services at fixed or minimum prices.

C. Unconditional purchase obligations that have all the following characteristics must be disclosed; they are not recorded on the balance sheet.

  1. Is noncancelable or cancelable only

    a.   Upon occurrence of a remote contingency, or

    b.   With permission of another party, or

    c.   If a replacement agreement is signed between same parties, or

    d.   Upon penalty payment such that continuation appears reasonably assured

  2. Was negotiated as part of arranging financing for the facilities that will provide the contracted goods

  3. Has a remaining term greater than one year

D. Disclosure of those unconditional purchase obligations **not recorded** on the balance sheet shall include

  1. Nature and term of obligation

  2. Amount of fixed and determinable portion of obligation as of most recent BS in aggregate and if determinable for each of next five years

  3. Description of any variable elements of the obligation

  4. Amounts purchased under the obligation(s) for each year an income statement is presented

  5. Encourages disclosing imputed interest to reduce the obligation to present value using

    a.   Effective interest rate, or if unknown

    b.   Purchaser's incremental borrowing rate at date obligation was entered into

E. This statement **does not change** the accounting for obligations that **are recorded on the balance sheet,** nor does it suggest that disclosure is a substitute for accounting recognition. For **recorded** obligations, the following information should be disclosed for each of the next five years:

  1. Aggregate amount of payments for unconditional obligations that meet criteria for balance sheet recognition

  2. Combined aggregate amount of maturities and sinking fund requirements for all long-term borrowings

SFAS 48 (R75) Revenue Recognition When Right of Return Exists
(Extracts from AICPA Statement of Position [SOP] 75-1)

A. Specifies accounting for sales in which a product may be returned for refund, credit applied to amounts owed, or in exchange for other products.
1. Right is specified by contract or is a matter of existing practice.
2. Right may be exercised by ultimate customer or party who resells product to others.
3. Not applicable to service revenue, real estate or lease transactions, or return of defective goods

B. Recognize revenue from right of return sales only if all of the following conditions are met:
1. Price is substantially fixed or determinable at date of sale.
2. Buyer has paid or is unconditionally obligated to pay.
3. Obligation is not changed by theft, destruction, or damage of product.
4. Buyer has "economic substance" apart from seller (i.e., sale is not with a party established mainly for purpose of recognizing sales revenue).
5. Seller has no significant obligation for performance to directly cause resale of product.
6. Amount of future returns can be reasonably estimated.

C. If all of the conditions in B. above are met, record sales and cost of sales **and**
1. Reduce sales revenue and cost of sales to reflect estimated returns
2. Accrue expected costs or losses in accordance with SFAS 5

D. If any condition in B. above is not met, do not recognize sales and cost of sales until either
1. All conditions are subsequently met, or
2. Return privilege has substantially expired

E. Factors which may impair ability to make a reasonable estimate of returns include
1. Susceptibility of product to significant external factors (e.g., obsolescence or changes in demand)
2. Long period of return privilege
3. Absence of experience with similar products or inability to apply such experience due to changing circumstances (e.g., marketing policies or customer relationships)
4. Absence of large volume of similar transactions

SFAS 52 (F60) Foreign Currency Translation
(Supersedes SFAS 8, SFAS 20, and FASB Interpretations 15 and 17)

A. Primary objectives of foreign currency translation
1. Should provide information disclosing effects of rate changes on enterprise cash flows and equity
2. Should also provide information in consolidated statements as to financial results and relationships of individual consolidated entities measured in their respective functional currencies in accordance with US GAAP

B. **Functional currency** is the currency of the primary economic environment in which a foreign entity operates (i.e., the environment in which the entity generates and spends cash).
1. A foreign entity's assets, liabilities, revenues, expenses, gains, and losses shall be measured in that entity's functional currency.
2. The functional currency could be the currency of the country in which the entity operates if the entity is a self-contained unit operating in a foreign country.

   EXAMPLE: An entity (1) whose operations are not integrated with those of the parent, (2) whose buying and selling activities are primarily local, and (3) whose cash flows are primarily in the foreign currency.

3. There may be several functional currencies if there are many self-contained entities operating in different countries.
4. The functional currency might be the US dollar if the foreign entity's operations are considered to be a direct and integral part of the US parent's operations.

   EXAMPLE: An entity (1) whose operations are integrated with those of the parent, (2) whose buying and selling activities are primarily in the parent's country and/or the parent's currency, and (3) whose cash flows are available for remittance to the parent.

5. Functional currency for a foreign entity, once determined, shall be used consistently unless it is clear that economic facts and circumstances have changed.
   a. If a change is made, do not restate previously issued financial statements
6. If a foreign entity's bookkeeping is not done in the functional currency, the process of converting from the currency used for the books and records to the functional currency is called remeasurement.

a. Remeasurement is intended to produce the same result (e.g., balances for assets, expenses, liabilities, etc.) as if the functional currency had been used for bookkeeping purposes.

b. In highly inflationary economies (cumulative inflation over a 3-year period is $\geq 100\%$), the remeasurement of a foreign entity's financial statements shall be done as if the functional currency were the reporting currency (i.e., the US dollar).

7. The functional currency (if not the US dollar) is translated to the reporting currency (assumed to be the US dollar) by using appropriate exchange rates (see item C. below).

a. If the functional currency is the US dollar, there is no need to translate (if the books and records are maintained in US dollars).

C. The translation of foreign currency FS (those incorporated in the FS of a reporting enterprise by consolidation, combination, or the equity method of accounting) should use a current exchange rate if the foreign currency is the functional currency.

1. Assets and liabilities—exchange rate at the balance sheet date is used to translate the functional currency to the reporting currency

2. Revenues (expenses) and gains (losses)—exchange rates when the transactions were recorded shall be used to translate from the functional currency to the reporting currency

a. Weighted averages for exchange rates may be used for items occurring numerous times during the period.

3. Translation adjustments will result from the translation process if the functional currency is a foreign currency.

a. Translation adjustments are not an element of net income of the reporting entity.

b. Effects of current translation adjustments are reported in other comprehensive income for the period with the accumulated amount reported as part of the reporting entity's owners' equity and labeled accumulated other comprehensive income.

c. Accumulated translation adjustments remain part of the owners' equity until the reporting entity disposes of the foreign entity.

(1) In period of disposal, these adjustments are reported as part of the gain (loss) on sale or liquidation.

D. **Foreign currency transactions** are those which are denominated (fixed) in other than the entity's functional currency.

1. Receivables and/or payables, which are fixed in a currency other than the functional currency, may result in transaction gains (losses) due to changes in exchange rates after the transaction date.

2. Transaction gains or losses generally are reported on the income statement in the period during which the exchange rates change.

3. Deferred taxes may have to be provided for transaction gains or losses that are realized for income tax purposes in a time period different than that for financial reporting.

E. **A forward exchange contract** represents an agreement to exchange different currencies at a specified future rate and at a specified future date. (Accounting and reporting now specified by SFAS 133)

F. FS disclosures required

1. Aggregate transaction gain (loss) that is included in the entity's net income

2. Analysis of changes in accumulated translation adjustments which are reported as part of other comprehensive income

3. Significant rate changes subsequent to the date of the financial statements including effects on unsettled foreign currency transactions

---

FASB INTERPRETATION NO. 37 ACCOUNTING FOR TRANSLATION ADJUSTMENTS UPON SALE OF PART OF AN INVESTMENT IN A FOREIGN ENTITY

If an enterprise sells part of its ownership interest in a foreign entity, a pro rata portion of the accumulated translation adjustment component of equity attributable to that investment shall be recognized in measuring the gain (loss) on the sale.

SFAS 57 (R36) Related-Party Disclosures

A. Definitions

1. **Affiliate**—Party is controlled by another enterprise that controls, or is under common control with another enterprise, directly or indirectly

2. **Control**—Power to direct or cause direction of management through ownerships contract, or other means
3. **Immediate family**—Family members whom principal owners or management might control/influence or be controlled/influenced by
4. **Management**—Persons responsible for enterprise objectives who have policy-making and decision-making authority
    a. For example, board of directors, chief executive and operating officers, and vice-presidents
    b. Includes persons without formal titles
5. **Principal owners**—Owners of more than 10% of a firm's voting interests
    a. Includes known beneficial owners
6. **Related parties**—Affiliates, equity method investees, employee benefit trusts, principal owners, management or any party that can significantly influence a transaction

B. FS shall include disclosures of material transactions between related parties except
1. Compensation agreements, expense allowances, and other similar items in the ordinary course of business
2. Transactions which are eliminated in the preparation of consolidated/combined FS

C. Disclosures of material transactions shall include
1. Nature of relationship(s)
2. Description of transaction(s), including those assigned zero or nominal amounts
3. Dollar amounts of transactions for each income statement period and effect of any change in method of establishing terms
4. Amounts due to/from related parties, including terms and manner of settlement

D. Representations concerning related-party transactions shall not imply that terms were equivalent to those resulting in arm's-length bargaining unless such statement can be substantiated.

E. When a **control** relationship exists, disclose such relationship even though no transactions have occurred.

SFAS 66 (Re1, R10) Accounting for Sales of Real Estate

A. Other than retail land sales
1. Use the full accrual method if the following criteria are satisfied:
    a. Sale is consummated
    b. Buyer's initial and continuing investments demonstrate a commitment to pay for the property
    c. Seller's receivable is not subject to future subordination
    d. Risks and rewards of ownership have been transferred
2. When the criteria are not met and dependent upon the particular circumstance, use one of the following methods:
    a. Installment method
    b. Cost recovery method
    c. Deposit method
    d. Reduced profit method
    e. Percentage-of-completion

B. Retail land sales (not outlined due to specialized nature)

SFAS 78 (B05) Classification of Obligations That Are Callable by the Creditor
(Amends ARB 43, Chapter 3A)

A. Statement specifies that the current liability classification is also intended to include
1. Obligations that, by their terms, are due on demand or will be due on demand within one year (or operating cycle, if longer) from balance sheet date, even though liquidation may not be expected within that period
2. Long-term obligations that are or will be callable by creditor either because
    a. Debtor's violation of debt agreement provision at balance sheet date makes obligation callable **or**
    b. Violation, if not cured within grace period, will make obligation callable

B. Callable obligations in A.2. should be classified current unless one of the following conditions is met:
1. Creditor has waived or subsequently lost the right to demand repayment for more than one year (or operating cycle, if longer) from balance sheet date
2. For long-term obligations containing grace period within which debtor may cure violation, it is probable violation will be cured within that period

       a.   If obligation meets this condition, the circumstances shall be disclosed

C. This statement does **not** modify SFAS 6 or 47

SFAS 84 (D10, D14) Induced Conversions of Convertible Debt
(Amends APB 26, para 2)

A. Establishes accounting and reporting standards for conversion of convertible debt to equity securities when debtor induces conversion of the debt

    1. Applies only to conversions that both

       a.   Occur pursuant to changed conversion privileges exercisable only for limited period of time

       b.   Include issuance of all of the equity securities issuable pursuant to the original conversion privileges for each instrument that is converted

    2. Examples of changed terms to induce conversion

       a.   Reduction of original conversion price

       b.   Issuance of warrants or other securities not included in original conversion terms

       c.   Payment of cash or other consideration to debt holders who convert during the specified time period

B. Debtor enterprise shall recognize expense equal to excess of fair value of all securities and other consideration transferred in the transaction over fair value of securities issuable pursuant to the original conversion terms.

    1. Expense is not an extraordinary item.

    2. Fair value of securities/other consideration measured as of inducement date

       a.   Typically date converted by debt holder or binding agreement entered into

SFAS 86 (Co2) Accounting for the Costs of Computer Software to Be Sold, Leased, or Otherwise Marketed

A. Establishes standards of financial accounting and reporting for the costs of computer software to be sold, leased, or otherwise marketed as a separate product or as part of a product or process, whether internally developed and produced or purchased.

B. Research and development costs consist of all costs to establish technological feasibility.

    1. Evidence of technological feasibility

       a.   Process of creating the computer software product includes a detailed program design **or**

       b.   Process of creating the computer software product includes a product design and a completed working model.

C. Capitalization costs include costs incurred subsequent to establishing technological feasibility.

    1. Capitalization shall cease when product is available for general release to customers.

D. Amortization of capitalized software costs is performed on a product-by-product basis.

    1. Annual amortization is the greater of

       a.   The amount computed using the ratio current gross product revenues to total current and anticipated future gross product revenues **or**

       b.   S-L method using the estimated economic life of the software product

    2. Amortization begins when product is available for general release to customers.

    3. Unamortized capitalized costs cannot exceed the net realizable value (NRV) of that software product. Any excess shall be written off at the end of the year.

E. Inventory costs include costs incurred for duplicating software materials and for physically packaging the product.

    1. Costs of maintenance and customer support are charged to expense.

F. FS disclosures shall include

    1. Unamortized computer software costs

    2. Total amount charged to amortization expense and amounts written down to NRV

SFAS 87 (C59, I67, P16, Re6) Employers' Accounting for Pensions
(Supersedes ARB 8 and SFAS 36, Amended by SFAS 132)

    Applies to any arrangement that is similar in substance to pension plan regardless of form or means of financing. Applies to written plan and to plan whose existence may be implied from well-defined, although perhaps unwritten, practice of paying postretirement benefits. Does not apply to plan that provides only life insurance benefits or health insurance benefits, or both, to retirees. Does not apply to postemployment health care benefits.

The following terms are given specific definitions for the purposes of SFAS 87:

Accumulated benefit obligation—Actuarial present value of benefits (whether vested or nonvested) attributed by the pension benefit formula to employee service rendered before a specified date and based on employee service and compensation (if applicable) prior to that date. The accumulated benefit obligation differs from the projected benefit obligation in that it includes no assumption about future compensation levels. For plans with flat-benefit or non-pay-related pension benefit formulas, the accumulated benefit obligation and the projected benefit obligation are the same.

Actual return on plan assets component (of net periodic pension cost)—Difference between fair value of plan assets at the end of the period and the fair value at the beginning of the period, adjusted for contributions and payments of benefits during the period.

Actuarial present value—Value, as of a specified date, of an amount or series of amounts payable or receivable thereafter, with each amount adjusted to reflect (a) the time value of money (through discounts for interest) and (b) the probability of payment (by means of decrements for events such as death, disability, withdrawal, or retirement) between the specified date and the expected date of payment.

Amortization—Usually refers to the process of reducing a recognized liability systematically by recognizing revenues or reducing a recognized asset systematically by recognizing expenses or costs. In pension accounting, amortization is also used to refer to the systematic recognition in net pension cost over several periods of previously **unrecognized** amounts, including unrecognized prior service cost and unrecognized net gain or loss.

Defined contribution pension plan—Plan that provides pension benefits in return for services rendered, provides an individual account for each participant, and specifies how contributions to the individual's account are to be determined instead of specifying the amount of benefits the individual is to receive. Under a defined contribution pension plan, the benefits a participant will receive depend solely on the amount contributed to the participant's account, the returns earned on investments of those contributions, and forfeitures of other participants' benefits that may be allocated to such participant's account.

Gain or loss—Change in the value of either the projected benefit obligation or the plan assets resulting from experience different from that assumed or from a change in an actuarial assumption. See also **Unrecognized net gain or loss**.

Gain or loss component (of net periodic pension cost)—The gain or loss component is the net effect of delayed recognition of gains and losses (the net change in the unrecognized net gain or loss) except that it does not include changes in the projected benefit obligation occurring during the period and deferred for later recognition.

Interest cost component (of net periodic pension cost)—Increase in the projected benefit obligation due to passage of time.

Market-related value of plan assets—Balance used to calculate the expected return on plan assets. Market-related value can be either fair market value or a calculated value that recognizes changes in fair value in a systematic and rational manner over not more than five years. Different ways of calculating market-related value may be used for different classes of assets, but the manner of determining market-related value shall be applied consistently from year to year for each asset class.

Net periodic pension cost—Amount recognized in an employer's financial statements as the cost of a pension plan for a period. Components of net periodic pension cost are service cost, interest cost, actual return on plan assets, gain or loss, amortization of unrecognized prior service cost, and amortization of the unrecognized net obligation or asset existing at the date of initial application of SFAS 87. SFAS 87 uses the term **net periodic pension cost** instead of **net pension expense** because part of the cost recognized in a period may be capitalized along with other costs as part of an asset such as inventory.

Prepaid pension cost—Cumulative employer contributions in excess of accrued net pension cost.

Prior service cost—Cost of retroactive benefits granted in a plan amendment. See also **Unrecognized prior service cost**.

Projected benefit obligation—Actuarial present value as of a date of all benefits attributed by the pension benefit formula to employee service rendered prior to that date. The projected benefit obligation is measured using assumptions as to future compensation levels if the pension benefit formula is based on those future compensation levels (pay-related, final-pay, final-average-pay, or career-average-pay plans).

Service cost component (of net periodic pension cost)—Actuarial present value of benefits attributed by the pension benefit formula to services rendered by employees during the period. The service cost component is a portion of the projected benefit obligation and is unaffected by the funded status of the plan.

Unfunded accrued pension cost—Cumulative net pension cost accrued in excess of the employer's contributions (usually used without word "unfunded").

Unfunded accumulated benefit obligation—Excess of the accumulated benefit obligation over plan assets.

Unrecognized net gain or loss—Cumulative net gain (loss) that has not been recognized as a part of net periodic pension cost. See **Gain or loss**.

Unrecognized prior service cost—Portion of prior service cost that has not been recognized as a part of net periodic pension cost.

A. Single-Employer Defined Benefit Plans
  1. Pension benefits are part of compensation paid to employees for services
    a. Amount of benefits to be paid depends on a number of future events specified in the **plan's benefit formula**.
  2. Any method of pension accounting that recognizes cost before payment of benefits to retirees must deal with two problems
    a. Assumptions must be made concerning future events that will determine amount and timing of benefits
    b. Approach to attributing cost of pension benefits to individual years of service must be selected
B. Basic Elements of Pension Accounting
  1. Prior service cost
    a. Except as specified otherwise, prior service cost shall be amortized by assigning an equal amount to each future service period of each employee active at the date of a plan amendment who is expected to receive benefits under plan.
    b. If all/almost all of plan's participants are inactive, cost of retroactive plan benefits should be amortized over remaining life expectancy of those participants.
    c. Consistent use of alternative amortization approach that more rapidly reduces unrecognized cost of retroactive amendments is acceptable.
      (1) Alternative method used should be disclosed.
    d. When period during which employer expects to realize economic benefits from amendment granting retroactive benefits is shorter than entire remaining service period of active employees, amortization of prior service cost should be accelerated.
    e. Plan amendment can reduce, rather than increase, the projected benefit obligation.
      (1) Reduction should be used to reduce any existing unrecognized prior service cost.
      (2) Excess should be amortized on same basis as cost of benefit increases.
  2. Gains and losses
    a. Gains (losses)
      (1) Result from changes in amount of either projected benefit obligation or plan assets due to experience different than assumed and changes in assumptions
      (2) Include both **realized** and **unrealized** amounts
    b. Asset gains (losses) include both changes reflected in the market-related value of assets and changes not yet reflected in the market-related value.
      (1) Asset gains (losses) not yet reflected in market-related value are not required to be amortized as B.2.c. below.
    c. As a minimum, amortization of unrecognized net gain (loss) should be included as a component of net pension cost for a year if, as of the beginning of the year, that unrecognized net gain (loss) $\geq$ .10 of the larger of the projected benefit obligation or the market-related value of plan assets.
      (1) Minimum amortization should be the excess divided by the average remaining service period of active employees expected to receive benefits under the plan.
        (a) Amortization must always reduce beginning-of-the-year balance.
        (b) Amortization of a net unrecognized gain (loss) results in a decrease (increase) in net periodic pension cost.
      (2) If all or almost all of plan's participants are inactive, average remaining life expectancy of inactive participants should be used instead of average remaining service.
    d. Any systematic method of amortization of unrecognized gains (losses) may be used in lieu of the minimum specified above provided that
      (1) Minimum is used in any period in which minimum amortization is greater (reduces the net balance by more)

(2) Method is applied consistently and disclosed
3. Recognition of liabilities and assets
    a. Liability (asset) is recognized if net periodic pension cost recognized exceeds (is less than) amounts the employer has contributed to the plan.
    b. Recognition of "additional minimum liability" is required if accumulated benefit obligation is greater than the fair market value of plan assets and
        (1) An asset has been recognized as prepaid pension cost,
        (2) The liability already recognized as unfunded accrued pension cost is less than the unfunded accumulated benefit obligation, or
        (3) No accrued or prepaid pension cost has been recognized
    c. If "additional minimum liability" must be recognized, recognize an equal amount as an "intangible asset," provided that asset recognized should not exceed amount of unrecognized prior service cost.
        (1) If "additional liability" required to be recognized exceeds unrecognized prior service cost, excess should be reported as other comprehensive income and a separate component (a reduction) of equity labeled accumulated other comprehensive income.
        (2) Each time a new determination of required additional liability is made, related intangible asset and accumulated other comprehensive income should be eliminated or adjusted as necessary.
C. Attribution
  1. Pension benefits should be attributed to periods of employee service based on plan's benefit formula.
  2. When employer has a present commitment to make future amendments, and substance of plan is to provide benefits attributable to prior service that are greater than benefits defined by written terms of the plan.
    a. The substantive commitment should be basis for accounting, and
    b. Existence and nature of the commitment to make future amendments should be disclosed
  3. Assumptions
    a. Assumed discount rates reflect rates at which pension benefits could be effectively settled
        (1) Used in measurements of projected and accumulated benefit obligations and the service and interest cost components of net periodic pension cost
    b. Assumed compensation levels (when measuring service cost and the projected benefit obligation) should reflect an estimate of the actual future compensation levels of employees involved, including future changes attributed to general price levels, productivity, seniority, promotion, and other factors.
    c. Accumulated benefit obligation shall be measured based on employees' history of service and compensation without estimate of future compensation levels.
    d. Automatic benefit increases specified by plan that are expected to occur should be included in measurements of projected and accumulated benefit obligations and the service cost component.
    e. Retroactive plan amendments should be included in computations of projected and accumulated benefit obligations.
        (1) Once they have been contractually agreed to
        (2) Even if some provisions take effect only in future periods
D. Measurement of Plan Assets
  1. For purposes of measuring minimum liability and required disclosures, plan investments, whether equity or debt securities, real estate, or other, should be measured at their fair value as of measurement date.
  2. Market-related asset value is used for purposes of determining the expected return on plan assets and accounting for asset gains and losses.
E. Acceptable Measurement Dates
  1. As of date of financial statements, or
  2. If used consistently from year to year, as of a date $\leq$ 3 months prior to that date
  3. Measurement date is not intended to require that all procedures be performed after that date.
  4. Information for items requiring estimates can be prepared as of an earlier date and projected forward to account for subsequent events (e.g., employee service).
  5. The "additional minimum liability" reported in interim financial statements should be the same "additional minimum liability" recognized in previous year-end balance sheet.

    a. Adjusted for subsequent accruals and contributions unless measures of both the obligation and plan assets are available as of a current date or a significant event occurs, such as plan amendment, that would call for such measurements

6. Measurements of net periodic pension cost for both interim and annual financial statements should be based on assumptions used for previous year-end measurements.

    a. If more recent measurements are available or a significant event occurs, use these more recent measurements.

F. Disclosures (Amended by SFAS 132)

SFAS 88 (P16) Employers' Accounting for Settlements and Curtailments of Defined Benefit Pension Plans and for Termination Benefits (Supersedes SFAS 74, Amended by SFAS 132)

Statement applies to an employer that sponsors a defined benefit pension plan accounted for under the provisions of SFAS 87 if all or part of the plan's pension benefit obligation is settled or the plan is curtailed. It also applies to an employer that offers benefits to employees in connection with their termination of employment.

The following terms are given specific definitions for the purposes of SFAS 88:

Settlement—Transaction that (a) is an irrevocable action, (b) relieves the employer (or the plan) of primary responsibility for a pension benefit obligation, and (c) eliminates significant risks related to the obligation and the assets used to effect the settlement.

Annuity contract—Irrevocable contract in which an insurance company[2] unconditionally undertakes a legal obligation to provide specified benefits to specific individuals in return for a fixed consideration or premium. It involves the transfer of significant risk from the employer to the insurance company.

Curtailment—Event that significantly reduces the expected years of future service of present employees or eliminates for a significant number of employees the accrual of defined benefits for some or all of their future services.

A. Relationship of Settlements and Curtailments to Other Events

  1. Settlement and curtailment may occur separately or together.

B. Accounting for Settlement of Pension Obligation

  1. For purposes of this statement, when a pension obligation is settled, the maximum gain or loss subject to recognition is the unrecognized gain or loss defined in SFAS 87 plus any remaining unrecognized net asset existing at the date of initial application of SFAS 87.

  2. If the purchase of a participating annuity contract constitutes a settlement, the maximum gain (but not the maximum loss) should be reduced by the cost of the participation right before determining the amount to be recognized in earnings.

  3. If the cost of all settlements in a year is less than or equal to the sum of the service cost and interest cost components of net periodic pension cost for the plan for the year, gain or loss recognition is permitted but not required for those settlements.

C. Accounting for Plan Curtailment

  1. Unrecognized prior service cost is a loss.

  2. The projected benefit obligation may be decreased (a gain) or increased (a loss) by a curtailment.

D. Termination Benefits

  1. Employer may provide benefits to employees in connection with their termination of employment.

  2. Termination benefits may take many forms consisting of

    a. Lump-sum payments

    b. Periodic future payments

  3. The cost of termination benefits recognized as a liability and a loss shall include the amount of any lump-sum payments and present value of any expected future payments.

SFAS 89 (C28) Financial Reporting and Changing Prices

This statement **encourages** but does not require a business enterprise that prepares its financial statements in US dollars and in accordance with US generally accepted accounting principles to disclose supplementary information on changing prices.

A. Measurement

  1. Inventory

---

[2] *If the insurance company is controlled by the employer or there is any reasonable doubt that the insurance company will meet its obligation under the contract, the purchase of the contract does not constitute a settlement for purposes of this statement.*

a. Current cost is the current cost of purchasing or manufacturing, whichever is applicable
  (1) Or recoverable amount if lower
2. Property, plant, and equipment
  a. Current cost is current cost of acquiring same service potential (or recoverable amount if lower)
    (1) That is, the same operating costs and output
    (2) Three valuation methods
      (a) Current cost of new asset less depreciation
      (b) Cost of comparable used asset
      (c) Adjusting new asset cost for differences in
        1] Useful life
        2] Output capacity
        3] Nature of service
        4] Operating costs
3. Recoverable amount
  a. Current worth of net amount of cash expected to be recoverable from the use or sale of an asset
4. Increase or decrease in current cost amount of inventory and PP&E, net of inflation
  a. Differences between current cost at entry dates and exit dates
    (1) Entry dates are the later of the beginning of the year or date of acquisition
    (2) Exit dates are the earlier of date of use, sale, etc., or year-end

SFAS 91 (Bt7, D22, Fi4, In6, I89, L10, L20, Mo4) Accounting for Nonrefundable Fees and Costs Associated with Originating or Acquiring Loans and Initial Direct Costs of Leases
(Rescinds SFAS 17, Amends SFAS 13, 60, and 65)

Establishes the accounting for nonrefundable fees and costs associated with lending, committing to lend, or purchasing a loan or group of loans. Applies to all types of loans.

A. Loan origination fees shall be recognized over life of related loan as adjustment of yield.
B. Certain direct loan origination costs shall be deferred over the life of the related loan as a reduction of the loan's yield.
C. All loan commitment fees shall be deferred except for certain retrospectively determined fees.
  1. Those commitment fees meeting specified criteria shall be recognized over the loan commitment period.
  2. All other commitment fees shall be recognized as an adjustment of yield over the related loan's life.
  3. If commitment expires unexercised, then recognize in income upon expiration of the commitment.
D. Loan fees, certain direct loan origination costs, and purchase premiums and discounts on loans shall be recognized as an adjustment of yield generally by the interest method based on contractual terms of the loan.
  1. Prepayments by debtors may be anticipated in certain specified circumstances.

SFAS 94 (C51) Consolidation of All Majority-Owned Subsidiaries (Amends ARB 51 with related amendment of ARB 43, Chapter 12, and APB 18)

A. Precludes use of parent company FS prepared for issuance to stockholders as FS of primary reporting entity
B. Requires consolidation of all majority-owned (ownerships, directly or indirectly, of more than 50% of outstanding voting shares of another company) subsidiaries
  1. Unless control
    a. Temporary
    b. Not held by majority owner (e.g., subsidiary)
      (1) Is in legal reorganization or bankruptcy
      (2) Operates under foreign exchange restrictions, controls, or other governmentally imposed uncertainties
  2. Even if
    a. Subsidiary's operations nonhomogeneous
    b. Large minority interest exists
    c. Subsidiary located in foreign country

SFAS 95 (C25) Statement of Cash Flows
A. Statement of Cash Flows in General

1. Required for each period results of operation (income statement) are provided
2. Objectives
   a. Provide information about cash receipts and cash payments
   b. Provide information about operating, investing, and financing activities
   c. Helps users to assess
      (1) Ability to generate future net cash flows
      (2) Ability to meet obligations and pay dividends
      (3) Reasons for differences between income and associated cash receipts and payments
      (4) Both cash and noncash aspects of entity's investing and financing activities
3. Shall report
   a. Cash effects during a period from
      (1) Operating activities
      (2) Investing activities
      (3) Financing activities
   b. Noncash financing and investing activities in supplemental schedule
B. Gross and Net Cash Flows
   1. Gross amount of cash receipts and payments is relevant.
      a. For example, must show issuance of bonds and retirement of bonds separately
   2. Statement should explain change during the period in **cash and cash equivalents**.
      a. Cash equivalents
         (1) Short-term, highly liquid investments that are
            (a) Readily convertible into known amounts of cash
            (b) Near maturity (original maturity of three months or less from **date of purchase** by the enterprise) and present negligible risk of changes in value
         (2) Examples
            (a) Treasury bills
            (b) Commercial paper
            (c) Money market funds
C. Classification
   1. Investing activities
      a. Include
         (1) Lending money and collecting on those loans
         (2) Acquiring and selling, or disposing
            (a) Securities that are neither cash equivalents nor held in a trading portfolio
            (b) Productive assets expected to generate revenue over long periods of time
         (3) Cash inflows
            (a) Receipts from loans by
               1] Principal repayments
               2] Sale of loans made by the entity
            (b) Receipts from sale of
               1] Securities of other entities carried in held-to-maturity (debt only) or available-for-sale portfolios (debt or equity)
               2] Property, plant, and equipment
         (4) Cash outflows
            (a) Loans made or purchased by the entity
            (b) Payments to acquire assets
               1] Securities of other entities carried in held-to-maturity (debt only) or available-for-sale portfolios (debt or equity)
               2] Property, plant, and equipment
   2. Financing activities
      a. Include
         (1) Obtaining resources from owners and providing them with a return on, and a return of, their investment
         (2) Obtaining resources from creditors and repaying the amounts borrowed
      b. Cash inflows

        (1) Proceeds from the issuance of
            (a) Equity securities
            (b) Bonds
            (c) Mortgages
            (d) Notes
            (e) Other short- or long-term borrowing
    c. Cash outflows
        (1) Payments of dividends
        (2) Outlays to repurchase entity's shares
        (3) Repayments of amounts borrowed
  3. Operating activities
    a. Include
        (1) All transactions and other events that are not investing and financing
        (2) Delivering or producing goods for sale and providing services
        (3) Cash effects of transactions and other events that enter into the determination of income
    b. Cash inflows
        (1) Cash receipts from sale of goods or services
        (2) Interest and dividends received
        (3) Other operating cash receipts
        (4) Sales of "trading portfolio" securities
    c. Cash outflows
        (1) Payments to employees and other suppliers of goods or services
        (2) Income taxes paid
        (3) Interest paid
        (4) Other operating cash payments
        (5) Purchases of "trading portfolio" securities

D. Exchange Rate Effects
  1. Report the reporting currency equivalent of foreign currency cash flows using exchange rates in effect at time of cash flows
    a. Weighted-average exchange rate may be used, if result substantially same.

E. Content and Form
  1. Report net cash provided or used by operating, investing, and financing activities
  2. At end of statement, reconcile beginning and ending cash and cash equivalents by showing net increase or decrease for period as addition to beginning balance to obtain ending balance
  3. Cash flow from operating activities
    a. Direct presentation (encouraged by FASB)
        (1) Report major classes of operating receipts and payments (C.3.b.-c. above)
        (2) Difference between cash receipts and payments—net cash flow from operating activities
        (3) Supplemental schedule using indirect presentation must be presented when direct method used in body of statement
    b. Indirect presentation (acceptable format)
        (1) Shall separately report all major classes of reconciling items
            (a) Deferrals of past operating cash receipts and cash payments such as depreciation and changes during the period in inventory and unearned revenue
            (b) Accruals of expected future operating cash receipts and cash payments such as changes during the period in receivables and payables
        (2) Interest paid (net of amounts capitalized) and income taxes paid must appear in related disclosures
    c. Does not include cash flows from transactions or events whose effects are included in income, but which are not operating activities; for example,
        (1) Gain or loss on extinguishment of debt—financing activities
        (2) Gain or loss on sale of assets or from disposal of discontinued operations—investing activities
  4. Inflows and outflows of cash from investing and financing activities
    a. Noncash aspects should be clearly identified in separate schedule; for example,
        (1) Conversion of debt to equity
        (2) Acquisition of assets by assuming liabilities

        (a) Includes capital lease obligations
      (3) Exchanges of assets or of liabilities
  5. Enterprise shall disclose policy for determining items included in cash equivalent.
    a. Change in policy is change in accounting principle requiring restatement of comparative FS.
F. Cash flow per share shall not be reported.

SFAS 98 (L10) Accounting for Leases (Amends SFAS 13, 66, and 91. Rescinds SFAS 26 and Technical Bulletin 79-11)

NOTE: The outline below includes those changes that relate to all leases. The remainder of SFAS 98 deals with real estate leases that are not outlined since they are not expected to be tested on the exam.

A. Lease term, as redefined, includes
  1. All periods covered by bargain renewal options
  2. All periods for which failure to renew the lease imposes a penalty
  3. All periods during which a loan, directly or indirectly related to the leased property, is outstanding
  4. All periods covered by ordinary renewal options preceding the exercisable date of a bargain purchase option
  5. All periods representing renewals or extensions of the lease at the lessor's option

SFAS 106 (P40) Employers' Accounting for Postretirement Benefits other than Pensions
(Supersedes SFAS 81; amends APB 12, SFAS 87, APB 16; Amended by SFAS 132)

    Standard applies to all forms of postretirement benefits, particularly postretirement health care benefits. Applies to written plan and to a plan whose existence may be implied from well-defined, although perhaps unwritten, practice of paying postretirement benefits (called the substantive plan). Does not apply to pensions.
    The following terms are given specific definitions for purposes of SFAS 106:

Attribution period—The period of an employee's service to which the expected postretirement benefit obligation for that employee is assigned. The beginning of the attribution period is the employee's date of hire unless the plan's benefit formula grants credit only for service from a later date, in which case the beginning of the attribution period is generally the beginning of that credited service period. The end of the attribution period is the full eligibility date.

Benefit formula—The basis for determining benefits to which participants may be entitled under a postretirement benefit plan. A plan's benefit formula specifies the years of service to be rendered, age to be attained while in service, or a combination of both that must be met for an employee to be eligible to receive benefits under the plan.

Full eligibility date—The date at which an employee has rendered all of the service necessary to have earned the right to receive all of the benefits expected to be received by that employee (including any beneficiaries and dependents expected to receive benefits).

Health care cost trend rates—An assumption about the annual rate(s) of change in the cost of health care benefits currently provided by the postretirement benefit plan, due to factors other than changes in the composition of the plan population by age and dependency status, for each year from the measurement date until the end of the period in which benefits are expected to be paid.

Incurred claims cost (by age)—The cost of providing the postretirement health care benefits covered by the plan to a plan participant, after adjusting for reimbursements from Medicare and other providers of health care benefits and for deductibles, coinsurance provisions, and other specific claims costs borne by the retiree.

Net periodic postretirement benefit cost—The amount recognized in an employer's financial statements as the cost of a postretirement benefit plan for a period. Components of net periodic postretirement benefit cost include service cost, interest cost, actual return on plan assets, gain or loss, amortization of unrecognized prior service cost, and amortization of the unrecognized transition obligation or asset.

Plan amendment—A change in the existing terms of a plan. A plan amendment may increase or decrease benefits, including those attributed to years of service already rendered.

Transition asset—The unrecognized amount, as of the date this statement is initially applied, of (a) the fair value of plan assets plus any recognized accrued postretirement benefit cost or less any recognized prepaid postretirement benefit cost in excess of (b) the accumulated postretirement benefit obligation.

Transition obligation—The unrecognized amount, as of the date this statement is initially applied, of (a) the accumulated postretirement benefit obligation in excess of (b) the fair value of plan assets plus any recognized accrued postretirement benefit cost or less any recognized prepaid postretirement benefit cost.

Unrecognized transition asset—The portion of the transition asset that has not been recognized either immediately as the effect of a change in accounting or on a delayed basis as a part of net periodic postretirement benefit cost, as an offset to certain losses, or as a part of accounting for the effects of a settlement or a curtailment.

Unrecognized transition obligation—The portion of the transition obligation that has not been recognized either immediately as the effect of a change in accounting or on a delayed basis as a part of net periodic postretirement benefit cost, as an offset to certain gains, or as a part of accounting for the effects of a settlement or a curtailment.

A. Single Employer Defined Benefit Plans
 1. Postretirement benefits are part of compensation paid to employees for services
  a. Amount of benefits to be paid depends on future events specified in plan's benefit formula
 2. Postretirement benefits formerly were accounted for on a pay-as-you-go (cash) basis. SFAS 106 changes this practice by requiring accrual, during the years that the employee renders necessary service, of **expected** cost of providing those benefits to an employee. Any method of postretirement benefits accounting that recognizes cost before payment of benefits to retirees must deal with two problems.
  a. Assumptions must be made concerning future events that will determine amount and timing of benefits.
  b. Approach to attributing cost of postretirement benefits to individual years of service must be selected.

B. Basic Elements of Postretirement Benefits Accounting
 1. Prior service cost
  a. Except as specified otherwise, prior service cost shall be amortized by assigning an equal amount to each future service period of each employee active at the date of a plan amendment who was not yet fully eligible for benefits at that date.
  b. If all or almost all of a plan's participants are fully eligible for benefits, prior service cost shall be amortized over remaining life expectancy of those participants.
  c. Consistent use of alternative amortization approach that more rapidly reduces unrecognized cost of retroactive amendments is acceptable.
   (1) Alternative method used should be disclosed.
  d. When period during which employer expects to realize economic benefits from amendment granting increased benefits is shorter than entire remaining service period of active employees, amortization of prior service cost shall be accelerated.
  e. Plan amendment can reduce, rather than increase, accumulated postretirement benefit obligation
   (1) Reduction should be used to reduce any existing unrecognized prior service cost
   (2) Then to reduce any remaining unrecognized transition obligation
   (3) Excess, if any, shall be amortized on same basis as specified for prior service cost
 2. Gains and losses
  a. Gains (losses)
   (1) Result from changes in amount of either accumulated postretirement benefit obligation or plan assets due to experience different than assumed and changes in assumptions
   (2) Include both **realized** and **unrealized** amounts
  b. Asset gains (losses) include both (a) changes reflected in market-related value of assets and (b) changes not yet reflected in market-related value.
   (1) Asset gains (losses) not yet reflected in market-related value are not required to be amortized as c. below.
  c. As a minimum, amortization of unrecognized net gain (loss) should be included as a component of net postretirement benefit cost for a year if, as of the beginning of the year, that unrecognized net gain (loss) > .10 of the larger of the accumulated postretirement benefit obligation or the market-related value of plan assets.
   (1) Minimum amortization should be the excess divided by the average remaining service period of active employees expected to receive benefits under the plan
    (a) Amortization must always reduce beginning of the year balance
    (b) Amortization of a net unrecognized gain (loss) results in a decrease (increase) in net periodic pension cost

       (2) If all or almost all of plan's participants are inactive, average remaining life expectancy of inactive participants should be used instead of average remaining service.

   d. Any systematic method of amortization of unrecognized gains (losses) may be used in lieu of the minimum specified above provided that

       (1) Minimum is used in any period in which minimum amortization is greater (reduces the net balance by more)

       (2) Method is applied consistently and disclosed

3. Recognition of liabilities and assets

   a. SFAS 106 requires an employer's obligation for postretirement benefits expected to be provided to an employee be **fully** accrued by the full eligibility date of employee, even if employee is to render additional service beyond that date

   b. Transition obligations

       (1) SFAS 106 measures the transition obligation as the unfunded and unrecognized accumulated postretirement benefit obligation for all plan participants. Two options are provided for recognizing that transition obligation.

          (a) **Immediate** recognition of the transition obligation as the effect of an accounting change (i.e., include all of the obligation as part of the net periodic postretirement benefit cost)

          (b) Recognize the transition obligation in the balance sheet and income statement on a delayed basis over the plan participants' future service periods, with proper disclosure of the remaining unrecognized amount. Note that delayed recognition **cannot** result in less rapid recognition than accounting for the transition obligation on a pay-as-you-go basis

C. Attribution

1. The expected postretirement benefit obligation shall be attributed, in equal amounts, to each year of service in the attribution period.

2. However, if a benefit plan contains a benefit formula that attributes a disproportionate share of the expected postretirement benefit obligation to employees' early years of service, the postretirement benefits should be attributed based on the plan's benefit formula.

3. Assumptions

   a. Assumed discount rates shall reflect time value of money in determining present value of future cash outflows currently expected to be required to satisfy postretirement benefit obligation

       (1) Used in measurements of expected and accumulated postretirement benefit obligations and service and interest cost components of net periodic postretirement benefit cost

   b. Assumed compensation levels (when measuring service cost and expected and accumulated postretirement benefit obligations) shall reflect estimate of actual future compensation levels of employees involved, including future changes attributed to general price levels, productivity, seniority, promotion, and other factors.

   c. Accumulated postretirement benefit obligation shall be measured based on employees' history of service and compensation without estimate of future compensation levels.

   d. Automatic benefit changes specified by plan that are expected to occur should be included in measurements of projected and accumulated benefit obligations and the service cost component.

   e. Plan amendments should be included in computations of projected and accumulated benefit obligations.

       (1) Once they have been contractually agreed to

       (2) Even if some provisions take effect only in future periods

D. Measurement of Plan Assets

1. For purposes of required disclosures, plan investments, whether equity or debt securities, real estate, or other, shall be measured at FMV as of measurement date.

2. Market-related asset value is used for purposes of determining the expected return on plan assets and accounting for asset gains and losses.

E. Acceptable Measurement Dates

1. As of date of financial statements, or

2. If used consistently from year to year, as of a date $\leq$ 3 months prior to that date

3. Measurement date is not intended to require that all procedures be performed after that date

4. Information for items requiring estimates can be prepared as of an earlier date and projected forward to account for subsequent events (e.g., employee service)

5. Measurements of net periodic postretirement benefit cost for both interim and annual financial statements shall be based on assumptions used for previous year-end measurements
    a. If more recent measurements are available or a significant event occurs, use more recent measurements

F. Disclosures (amended by SFAS 132)

SFAS 107 (F25) Disclosures about Fair Value of Financial Instruments

A. Statement requires entities to disclose the fair value of financial instruments, both assets and liabilities whether recognized or not recognized in the statement of financial position, for which it is practicable to estimate fair value.
1. Applies to all entities
2. Does not change any recognition, measurement, or classification requirements for financial instruments in financial statements
3. Fair value disclosures of financial instruments previously prescribed by GAAP meet the requirements of this statement.

B. Financial Instruments include
1. Cash
2. Evidence of ownership interest in an entity, or
3. A contract that both
    a. Imposes contractual obligation on one entity to deliver cash or another financial instrument to second entity or to exchange financial instruments on potentially unfavorable terms with second entity, and
    b. Conveys contractual right to second entity to receive cash or another financial instrument from first entity or to exchange financial instruments on potentially favorable terms with first entity

C. Fair value of a financial instrument is the current amount at which a financial instrument could be exchanged in a transaction between willing parties.

D. Standard lists a number of areas for which the disclosure requirements are not applicable, including pensions and other deferred compensation arrangements and leases.

E. Disclosure Requirements
1. When practicable (i.e., without incurring excessive costs), an entity must disclose the fair value of financial instruments in either the body of the financial statements or in the accompanying notes.
    a. Disclosure must include the method(s) and significant assumptions used in estimating fair value
        (1) Quoted market price is generally the best estimate of fair value.
        (2) If quoted market price is not available, management must estimate fair value based upon similar financial instruments or valuation techniques.
        (3) No disclosure is required for trade receivables and payables when carrying amount approximates fair value.
    b. Disclosure must distinguish between financial instruments held or issued for
        (1) Trading purposes
        (2) Purposes other than trading
2. If estimation of the fair value of financial instruments is not practicable, entity must disclose
    a. Information pertinent to estimating the fair value (i.e., the carrying amount, effective interest rate, and maturity), and
    b. The reason why estimation of fair value is not practicable.
3. Derivative financial instruments may not be combined, aggregated or netted with nonderivative or other derivative financial instruments.
4. If financial instruments disclosed in more than one area in FS, one note must contain a summary table cross-referencing the location of the other instruments.
5. Disclosure of concentrations of credit risk of all financial instruments
    a. Disclose all significant concentrations of credit risk from **all** financial instruments, whether from an individual counterparty or groups of counterparties.
    b. Group concentrations exist if a number of counterparties are engaged in similar activities and have similar economic characteristics such that they would be similarly affected by changes in conditions.
    c. Disclose for each significant concentration
        (1) Information about the (shared) activity, region, or economic characteristics

(2) The amount of accounting loss the entity would incur should any party to the financial instrument fail to perform according to the terms of the contract and the collateral or security, if any, is of no value.

(3) The entity's policy of requiring collateral or security, the entity's access to that collateral or security, and the nature and brief description of the collateral or security.

SFAS 109 (I27) Accounting for Income Taxes
(Supercedes SFAS 96, 100, 103, and 108)

A. Establishes financial accounting and reporting requirements for income taxes resulting from an entity's activities during the current and preceding years.
   1. Continues BS oriented asset and liability approach consistent with SFAC 6.
   2. Objectives
      a. Recognize taxes payable or refundable for current year.
      b. Recognize deferred tax liabilities and assets for future tax consequences of events previously recognized in financial statements or tax returns.

B. Basic principles
   1. Recognize current tax liability or asset for estimated taxes payable or refundable on tax returns for current year
   2. Measure and recognize deferred tax liability or asset using enacted tax rate(s) expected to apply to taxable income in periods in which the deferred tax assets and liabilities are expected to be realized or settled
   3. Adjust measurement of deferred tax assets so as to not recognize tax benefits not expected to be realized
   4. Deferred tax assets and liabilities are **not** discounted to reflect their present value

C. Measurement of Deferred Taxes
   1. Temporary differences
      a. Difference between tax basis of asset or liability and its reported amount for financial accounting which results in taxable or deductible amounts in future years
         (1) Includes all timing differences
         (2) Includes tax-book differences in asset's bases
      b. Future effects
         (1) **Taxable amounts** are from temporary differences that will result in lower amounts of expense or higher amounts of revenue being reported on the tax return than are reported on the books in the future period.
         (2) **Deductible amounts** are from temporary differences that will result in higher amounts of expense or lower amounts of revenue being reported on the tax return than are reported on the books in the future period.
   2. Deferred tax liability or asset measured each BS date
      a. Identify types and amounts of existing temporary differences **and** nature of each type of operating loss and tax credit carryforward and the remaining length of the carryforward period
      b. Measure total deferred tax liability for taxable temporary differences using the enacted applicable tax rate
      c. Measure total deferred tax asset for deductible temporary differences and operating loss carryforwards using the enacted applicable tax rate
      d. Measure deferred tax assets for each type of tax credit carryforward
      e. Reduce deferred tax assets by a valuation allowance, **if more likely than not** (a likelihood of more than 50%) that some or all of deferred tax asset will not be realized
         (1) All available evidence (positive and negative) should be considered to determine whether valuation allowance is needed.

D. Changes in Tax Rates
   1. Change in rates
      a. Change previously recorded amounts of deferred tax liabilities or assets
      b. Net adjustments shall be reflected in tax expense on continuing operations in period that includes enactment date.

E. Business Combinations
    1. Recognize deferred tax asset or liability for differences between assigned values and tax basis of assets and liabilities recognized in a purchase combination

F. Intraperiod Tax Allocation
    1. Allocate income tax expense or benefit for the period among continuing operations, extraordinary items, other comprehensive income, and items charged or credited to stockholders' equity
        a. In cases where there is only one item after continuing operations, portion of income tax expense (benefit) remaining after allocation to continuing operations is amount allocated to that item.
        b. In cases where there are two or more items after continuing operations, portion left after allocation to continuing operations is allocated among other items in proportion to their individual effects on income tax expense (benefit).

G. Financial Statement Presentation and Disclosure
    1. Balance sheet
        a. Report deferred tax liabilities and assets as current or noncurrent based on classification of related asset or liability
        b. Classify deferred tax liabilities or assets not related to an asset or liability (i.e., one related to a carryforward) according to the expected reversal date of the temporary difference
        c. For a taxpaying component of an enterprise and within a particular tax jurisdiction
            (1) All current deferred tax liabilities and assets should be offset and reported as a single amount
            (2) All noncurrent deferred tax liabilities and assets should be offset and reported as a single amount
    2. Must disclose the following components of the net deferred tax liability or asset:
        a. The total of all deferred tax liabilities
        b. The total of all deferred tax assets
        c. The total valuation allowance for deferred tax assets
    3. Additional disclosures
        a. Disclose any net change in the total valuation allowance
        b. Disclose the types of temporary differences, carryforwards, and carrybacks
    4. Income statement
        a. Components of tax expense attributable to continuing operations shall be disclosed in financial statements or notes. For example
            (1) Current tax expense or benefit
            (2) Deferred tax expense or benefit (exclusive of other components listed below)
            (3) Investment tax credits
            (4) Government grants (to the extent recognized as a reduction of income tax expense)
            (5) Benefits of operating loss carryforwards
            (6) Tax expense resulting from allocation of certain tax benefits either directly to contributed capital or to reduce goodwill or other noncurrent intangible assets of an acquired entity
            (7) Adjustments of a deferred tax liability or asset resulting from enacted changes in tax laws, rates, or status
        b. Variances between statutory and effective tax rates must be disclosed.
            (1) Public entities should disclose reconciliation using percentages or dollar amounts.
            (2) Nonpublic entities must disclose nature of significant reconciling items.
        c. Disclose amounts and expiration dates of operating loss and tax credit carryforwards **and** any portion of the deferred tax asset valuation allowance for which subsequently recognized tax benefits will be allocated to reduce intangible assets or directly reduce accumulated other comprehensive income.

SFAS 112 (C44) Employers' Accounting for Postemployment Benefits

A. Statement sets forth accounting standards for employers providing post**employment** benefits to former/inactive employees, **after employment but before** retirement.
    1. Applies to any postemployment benefits provided to former employers and their beneficiaries and dependents except
        a. Special or contractual termination benefits addressed by SFAS 88 and 106.
        b. Postemployment benefits derived from post**retirement** benefit or pension plans.
        c. Stock compensation plans covered by APB 25.

     d.   Deferred compensation plans for individual employees that are covered by APB 12.
   2. Postemployment benefits may
     a.   Result from death, disability, layoff, etc.
     b.   Be paid in cash or in kind
     c.   Be paid upon assumption of inactive status or over a period of time

B. Applicable postemployment benefits must be accounted for according to SFAS 43, which states:
   1. Liability for future compensated absences must be accrued if
     a.   Obligation relates to services already provided by the employee,
     b.   Rights to compensation vest or accumulate,
     c.   Payment of obligation is probable, **and**
     d.   Amount to be paid is reasonably estimable.

C. If conditions listed above are not met but the benefits are within scope of SFAS 43, they are accounted for according to SFAS 5, which states:
   1. Estimated loss contingency accrued if
     a.   It is known before FS are issued that it is probable that asset has been impaired or a liability incurred and that future events will probably confirm the loss, **and**
     b.   Amount of loss is reasonably estimable.

D. Disclosure required if liability for postemployment benefits not accrued solely because amount not reasonably estimable.

SFAS 114 (D22) Accounting by Creditors for Impairment of a Loan (Amends SFAS 5 and 15; amended by SFAS 118)

A. Scope of SFAS 114
   1. Applies to all creditors and to all loans except for those specified in A.3 (a.-d.)
   2. Applies to all loans (including A.3.a.) that are restructured in a troubled debt restructuring involving a modification of terms
   3. Exceptions
     a.   Large groups of smaller-balance homogeneous loans collectively evaluated for impairment
     b.   Loans that are measured at fair value or at the lower of cost or fair value
     c.   Leases
     d.   Debt securities
   4. Does not specify how a creditor should identify loans that are to be evaluated for collectibility

B. Recognition of Impairment
   1. A loan is impaired when it is probable that a creditor will be unable to collect all amounts due according to the contractual terms.
     a.   Probable—future event or events are likely to occur
     b.   All amounts due according to the contractual terms include both interest and principal payments collected as scheduled in loan agreement.
   2. If a loan qualifies as exception A.3.a., the creditor may not apply the provisions of SFAS 114 until the debt is restructured.
   3. Instances when a loan is not impaired
     a.   Insignificant delays or shortfalls
     b.   A delay in which creditor expects to collect all amounts due including interest accrued for the period of delay

C. Measurement of Impairment
   1. Creditor measures impairment based on present value of expected future cash flows discounted at the loan's effective interest rate
     a.   Effective interest rate—rate implicit in loan at time of origination
     b.   If effective interest rate varies (based on an independent index or rate)
       (1) May be calculated based on the index or rate as it changes over life of loan
       (2) Or may be fixed at rate in effect at date the loan meets impairment criterion
     c.   Expected future cash flows determined as creditor's best estimate based on reasonable and supportable assumptions and projections (including estimated costs to sell)
   2. Loans with common risk characteristics may be aggregated and impairment measured using historical statistics and a composite effective interest rate.
   3. Alternative measures of impairment

      a.   Loan's observable market price
      b.   Fair value of collateral if loan is collateral dependent
         (1) Collateral dependent means repayment provided solely by the underlying collateral
         (2) This method must be used when foreclosure is probable (and loan is collateral dependent)
    4.   When measure of impaired loan is less than recorded investment in loan
      a.   Create valuation allowance with charge to bad debt expense
      b.   Or adjust existing valuation allowance with charge to bad debt expense
    5.   Significant changes (increases or decreases) subsequent to initial measure of impairment
      a.   Recalculate impairment
      b.   Adjust valuation allowance
      c.   Net carrying amount of loan may never exceed recorded investment in loan
D. Income Recognition
    1.   The present value of an impaired loan changes over time and also changes because of revised estimates in the amount or timing of cash flows.
    2.   Recognition and measurement methods to reflect changes in present value are not specified in this statement as amended.
E. Disclosures
    1.   The recorded investment in impaired loans, total allowance for credit losses related to impaired loans, and amount for which no allowance for credit losses
    2.   The creditor's income recognition method, including cash receipts
    3.   For each period presented which relates to the impaired loans
      a.   Average recorded investment
      b.   Interest revenue recognized
      c.   If practicable, interest revenue recognized on a cash basis

SFAS 115 (I80) Accounting for Certain Investments in Debt and Equity Securities
(Supersedes SFAS 12)

A. Establishes financial accounting and reporting requirements for all investments in debt securities and for small investments in equity securities with readily determinable fair values
    1.   "Small" investments are those not accounted for by the equity method or involving consolidated subsidiaries
B. Segregates debt and equity securities into three categories
    1.   Held-to-maturity securities
      a.   Applies only to debt securities
      b.   Requires intent and ability to hold to maturity
         (1) Will **not** sell in response to changes in
           (a) Funding terms and sources
           (b) Interest rates and prepayment risk
           (c) Foreign currency risk
           (d) Attractiveness of alternative investments
           (e) Liquidity needs
         (2) In rare cases, intent may change due to nonrecurring and unforeseeable circumstances.
           (a) Continuing deterioration of issuer's credit
           (b) Elimination of tax-exempt status of interest
           (c) Business combination or disposition that increases interest rate risk or credit risk
           (d) Regulatory change in permissible investments
           (e) Downsizing to meet industry capital requirements
           (f) Increased risk weight of debt securities held as regulatory risk-based capital
         (3) Considered maturity if
           (a) Sale occurs so close to maturity that interest rate risk is virtually eliminated
           (b) Sale occurs after at least 85% of the principal has been collected
      c.   Balance sheet
         (1) Report at amortized cost
         (2) Classify as current or noncurrent on an individual basis
      d.   Income statement
         (1) Do not report unrealized holding gains and losses

           (2) Include realized G(L) in earnings

           (3) Include interest income and premium/discount amortization in earnings

    e. Statement of cash flows

           (1) Classify cash inflows from sales and outflows from purchases gross (not netted) as investing activities

  2. Trading securities

    a. Applies to debt and equity securities held for current resale

    b. Balance sheet

           (1) Report at fair value

           (2) Classify as current assets, generally

    c. Income statement

           (1) Include unrealized holding G(L) in earnings

           (2) Exclude previously recognized realized G(L) from earnings

           (3) Include dividend and interest revenue

    d. Statement of cash flows

           (1) Classify purchases and sales as operating activity

  3. Available-for-sale securities

    a. Applies to debt and equity securities not categorized as held-to-maturity or trading securities

    b. Balance sheet

           (1) Report at fair value

           (2) Classify as current or noncurrent on an individual basis

           (3) Report net unrealized holding G(L) in other comprehensive income and accumulated other comprehensive income as separate component of stockholders' equity

    c. Income statement

           (1) Include realized G(L) in earnings

           (2) Include dividend and interest revenue and premium/discount amortization in earnings

    d. Statement of cash flows

           (1) Classify sales and purchases gross (not netted) as investing activity

C. Transfers between categories are accounted for at fair value

  1. From trading

    a. Do not reverse recognized unrealized holding G(L) at date of transfer

  2. To trading

    a. Recognize unrealized holding G(L) immediately

  3. To available-for-sale from held-to-maturity

    a. Report unrealized holding G(L) as other comprehensive income

    b. Transfers from held-to-maturity should be rare

  4. To held-to-maturity from available-for-sale

    a. Report unrealized holding G(L) as other comprehensive income

    b. Amortize G(L) over remaining life of security as adjustment to yield

D. Impairment of securities

  1. Applies to held-to-maturity and available-for-sale securities

  2. If permanent decline

    a. Write down to fair value

    b. Include realized loss in earnings

  3. No write-up for subsequent recoveries

E. Disclosures

  1. Only held-to-maturity and available-for-sale securities

  2. By major security type

    a. Aggregate fair value

    b. Gross unrealized holding gains and losses

    c. Amortized cost basis

  3. By maturity of debt securities

    a. All enterprises disclose contractual information.

    b. Financial institutions disclose fair value and amortized cost for four or more groups of maturities

           (1) Up to one year

        (2) Over one through five years
        (3) Over five through ten years
        (4) Over ten years
    c. Securities maturing at multiple dates
        (1) May disclose separately
        (2) May allocate over groupings

4. Available-for-sale securities
    a. Proceeds from sales
    b. Gross realized G(L)
    c. Cost basis for determining G(L)
    d. Change in net unrealized holding G(L) reported as comprehensive income in stockholders' equity

5. Trading securities
    a. Change in net unrealized holding G(L) reported in earnings

6. Transfers
    a. Gross G(L) on transfer from available-for-sale to trading
    b. Of held-to-maturity securities
        (1) Amortized cost
        (2) Realized or unrealized G(L)
        (3) Reason for sale

SFAS 116 (C67) Accounting for Contributions Received and Contributions Made[3]

Establishes accounting standards for contributions received or made for all types of entities, not-for-profit, and business enterprises.

A. Contributions—defined

    Contributions can be defined as an unconditional promise to give cash or other assets to an entity. A cancellation of a liability is also considered a contribution.

B. Contributions received (donee accounting)

1. Shall be capitalized by the donee at FMV of the item and recognized as revenue in period received.

C. Contributions made (donor accounting) shall be recognized at FMV as expense in period the item is donated

1. Donation expense should be classified under other expense on the income statement.
2. If difference exists between the FMV and book value of the item, then gain or loss on disposal will be recognized.

SFAS 123 (C36) Accounting for Stock-Based Compensation

A. Provides a fair value based method of accounting for stock-based compensation plans

1. Encourages entities to adopt provisions of this standard rather than those of APB 25
2. Applies to all transactions between an entity and its "suppliers" (whether employees or nonemployees) in which the entity acquires goods or services through issuance of equity instruments or incurrence of liabilities based on fair value of the entity's common stock or other equity instruments
3. Examples include stock purchase plans, stock options, restricted stock, and stock appreciation rights

B. Transactions with Nonemployees—Accounted for based on fair value of consideration received or fair value of equity instruments given, whichever is more readily determinable.

C. Transactions with Employees—Utilize the intrinsic value based method (i.e., difference between market price and exercise price) outlined in APB 25 or the fair value based method (use of estimates to value compensation cost) per SFAS 123; however, both require disclosures as specified in SFAS 123.

D. Measurement Methods

1. Settlement by equity instrument
    a. Nonvested stock is measured at market price of a share of the same stock as if it were vested and issued at grant date.
    b. Stock options are measured via use of an option pricing model which considers, as of grant date, exercise price and expected life of the option, current price of underlying stock and its anticipated volatility, expected dividends on the stock, and risk-free interest rate for expected term of the option.

---

[3] *This standard and SFAS 117 are discussed in more detail in Module 39, Not-for-Profit Accounting, because most of the exam questions from this standard are likely to appear on the Accounting and Reporting Exam.*

c. If fair value cannot be determined as of grant date, final measure shall be based on stock price and any other pertinent factors when it becomes reasonably possible to estimate that value. Current intrinsic value shall be used as a measure until a final determination of fair value can be made.

2. Settlement by cash requires the recording of liability based on current stock price at end of each period. Changes in stock price during service period are recognized as compensation cost over service period. A change in stock price subsequent to service period is recognized as compensation cost of that period.

E. Recognition of Compensation Cost
1. Total compensation cost is based on the number of instruments that eventually vest
    a. Vesting is defined as moment when employee's right to receive or retain such instruments or cash is no longer contingent on performance of additional services
    b. No compensation cost shall be recognized for employees that forfeit eligibility due to failure either to achieve service requirement or performance condition
    c. Compensation cost shall not be reversed if vested employee's stock option expires unexercised
2. Acceptable accrual methods
    a. As of grant date, base accruals of compensation cost on best available estimate of the number of options or instruments expected to vest, with necessary adjustments made if additional information indicates that actual forfeitures vary from initial estimates made.
    b. As of grant date, accrue compensation cost as if all options or instruments that are subject only to a service requirement will vest. Recognize actual forfeitures as they occur.

F. Tax consequences of stock-based compensation transactions shall be accounted for pursuant to SFAS 109.

G. Disclosures
1. APB 25 and SFAS 123 require disclosures listed under 3-7 below
2. Additionally, when APB 25 used for recognition and measurement SFAS 123 requires that pro forma net income and earnings per share shall be presented for the intrinsic value based method as if fair value based method had been used. Pro forma amounts should reflect
    a. Difference in compensation cost under APB 25 and SFAS 123
    b. Related tax effect of using SFAS 123 vs. APB 25
3. Vesting requirements, maximum term of options granted, and number of shares authorized for grants of options or other equity instruments
4. The number and weighted-average exercise prices of each group of options
5. The weighted-average grant-date fair value of options granted during the year, classified according to whether exercise price equals, exceeds, or is less than fair value of stock at date of grant
6. A description of methods used and assumptions made in determining fair values of the options
7. Total compensation cost recognized for the year
8. For options still outstanding, range of exercise prices and weighted-average remaining contractual life

SFAS 128 (E11) Earnings Per Share
A. Presentation on Financial Statements
1. Entities with publicly held common stock and simple capital structures (no potential common shares) need only present basic per share amounts. All other entities must present basic and diluted per share amounts with equal prominence.
2. Must present EPS on face of income statement for
    a. Income from continuing operations
    b. Net income
3. May present on face of income statement or in notes
    a. Discontinued operations
    b. Extraordinary items
    c. Cumulative effect of change in accounting principle
B. Basic EPS—Measures entity performance over a period of time
1. Computed as net income minus preferred dividends divided by the weighted-average number of common shares outstanding. The claims of senior securities (nonconvertible preferred dividends) should be deducted from income prior to computing EPS to properly determine net income available to **common** shareholders. Therefore, dividends on cumulative preferred are deducted whether or not declared, while dividends on noncumulative preferred are deducted only if declared.

2. EPS figures should be based upon consolidated income figures after consolidating adjustments and eliminations.
3. To compute the weighted-average of common shares outstanding, treasury shares should be excluded as of date of repurchase.
4. EPS data for all periods presented should be retroactively adjusted for all splits and dividends, even those subsequent to the period being presented.
5. For stock issued in purchase combinations, use weighted-average from date of combination. For pooling combination, shares assumed outstanding the entire period regardless of when issued.

C. For Diluted EPS, these additional procedures apply
1. The "if-converted" method is used to adjust EPS on outstanding common shares for dilutive convertible securities.
    a. The convertible securities are considered to have been converted at the beginning of the period (or at issuance if later) increasing the denominator of EPS.
    b. For convertible bonds, the interest savings net of tax is added to the numerator of EPS.
    c. For convertible preferred, the preferred dividends deducted in arriving at EPS are not deducted, thereby increasing the numerator. There is no tax effect because dividends are not an expense.
2. The "treasury stock" method is used to adjust EPS on outstanding common shares for dilutive options and warrants (i.e., those for which the exercise price is below the market price).
    a. The options and warrants are assumed to be exercised at the beginning of the period (or the date the options and warrants were issued if later). The shares assumed issued increase the denominator of EPS.
    b. The hypothetical proceeds are used to purchase treasury stock at the average price over the year.
    c. No retroactive adjustment should be made to EPS figures for options and warrants as a result of market price changes.
3. When convertible securities require payment of cash at conversion, they are considered the equivalent of warrants. The "if-converted" method is used for the conversion and the "treasury stock" method is applied to the cash proceeds.
4. Fixed awards and nonvested stock to be issued to an employee under a stock-based compensation arrangement are considered options and are considered to be outstanding as of the grant date even though their exercise may be contingent upon vesting.
5. Contingently issuable shares are shares whose issuance is contingent upon the satisfaction of certain conditions and shall be considered outstanding and included in the diluted EPS computation as follows:
    a. If all necessary conditions have been satisfied by the end of the period, the shares should be included as of the beginning of the period in which the conditions were satisfied (or as of the date of the contingent stock agreement, if later).
    b. If all necessary conditions have not been satisfied, the number of contingently issuable shares shall be based on the number of shares (if any) that would be issuable if the end of the reporting period were the end of the contingency period and if the result would be dilutive. These shares shall be included in the diluted EPS denominator as of the beginning of the period (or as of the date of the contingent stock agreement if later).
6. Antidilutive securities shall not be included in diluted EPS computations.

D. Additional Disclosure Requirements
1. A reconciliation of the numerators and denominators of the basic and diluted per share computations for income from continuing operations, including the individual income and share amount effects of all securities that affect earnings per share.
2. The effect that has been given to preferred dividends in arriving at income available to common shareholders in computing basic EPS.
3. Securities that are antidilutive for the period(s) presented but could potentially dilute basic EPS in the future.
4. A description of any transaction that occurs after the end of the most recent period but before issuance of the financial statements that would materially change the number of shares outstanding at the end of the period if the transaction had occurred before the end of the period.

SFAS 129 (C24) Disclosure of Information about Capital Structure
A. Information to Be Disclosed about Securities within the Financial Statements

1. The rights and privileges of the various securities outstanding; for example
   a. Dividend and liquidation preferences
   b. Participation rights
   c. Call prices and dates
   d. Conversion/exercise prices/rates and dates
   e. Sinking fund requirements
   f. Unusual voting rights
   g. Significant terms of contracts to issue additional shares
2. The number of shares issued upon conversion, exercise, or satisfaction of required conditions during at least the most recent annual fiscal period and any subsequent interim period presented.

B. Disclosure of Liquidation Preference of Preferred Stock within the Financial Statements
1. Relationship between the preference in liquidation and the par/stated value of the shares when preferred stock (or other senior stock) has a preference in involuntary liquidation considerably in excess of the par/stated value of the shares. This disclosure should be made in the equity section of the balance sheet in the aggregate, either parenthetically or "in short."
2. Aggregate or per share amounts at which preferred stock may be called or is subject to redemption through sinking fund operations or otherwise.
3. Aggregate and per share amount of arrearages in cumulative preferred dividends.

C. Disclosure of Redeemable Stock within the Financial Statements
1. The amount of redemption requirements, separately by issue or combined, for all issues of capital stock that are redeemable at fixed or determinable prices on fixed or determinable dates in each of the five years following the date of the latest balance sheet presented.

SFAS 130 (C49) Reporting Comprehensive Income

A. Establishes standards for reporting and display of comprehensive income (net income plus **other comprehensive income**) in a full set of general-purpose FS
B. Items, and changes therein, to be included as part of and separately classified in **other comprehensive income**
1. Foreign currency items
2. Unrealized gains (losses) on certain investments in debt and equity securities
3. Minimum pension liability adjustments
C. Presentation of comprehensive income
1. Alternative display options
   a. At the bottom of IS, continue from net income to arrive at a **comprehensive income** figure (equals net income plus other comprehensive income), or
   b. In a separate statement that starts with net income, or
   c. In the statement of changes in stockholders' equity; FASB prefers a. or b.
2. Components of other comprehensive income may be displayed net of related tax effects or before related tax effects with one amount shown for the aggregate income tax effect (with detail shown in notes)
3. Reclassification (recycling) adjustments
   a. Made to avoid double counting of items included in other comprehensive income in a prior year or current year that are included in net income (earnings) for the period
   b. Display separately from the balance of each item adjusted (B.1. and B.2. above) (gross display)
      (1) For reclassification adjustments related to the minimum pension liability, a single amount shall be displayed (net display)
D. Separate EPS numbers are not required for other comprehensive income or comprehensive income

SFAS 131 (S30) Disclosures about Segments of an Enterprise and Related Information[4]

A. Requires disclosures about
   Operating segments of an enterprise, products and services, geographic areas, major customers
1. Disclosures are required for **public** companies in complete annual FS per GAAP and in condensed FS of interim periods including comparative presentations
2. Purpose of disclosures is to better assist statement users in appraising past and future performance of the enterprise and assessing prospects for future net cash flows.

---

[4] *Refer to the flowchart on page 613 as you study this outline.*

B. Definitions
   1. **Management approach.** Method chosen by the FASB to determine what information should be reported; it is based on the way that management organizes segments internally for making operating decisions and assessing performance.
   2. **Operating segment.** Component of an enterprise that may earn revenues and incur expenses, about which separate financial information is available that is evaluated regularly by the chief operating decision maker in deciding how to allocate resources and in assessing performance.
   3. **Chief operating decision maker.** Person whose general function (not specific title) is to allocate resources to, and assess the performance of, the segments of an enterprise.
   4. **Segment revenue.** Includes revenue from unaffiliated customers and intersegment sales (use company transfer prices to determine intersegment sales).
   5. **Segment operating profit (loss).** Segment revenue less all operating expenses, including any allocated revenues or expenses.
   6. **Segment assets.** Tangible and intangible assets directly associable or used by the segment, including any allocated portion of assets used jointly by more than one segment
C. To determine reportable segments
   1. Identify operating segments under management approach
   2. Determine if aggregation of operating segments is appropriate.
   3. Perform quantitative threshold tests (10% tests).
D. Operating segments may be aggregated by management if they have similar economic characteristics and if segments are similar in each of the following areas:
   1. Nature of products and services
   2. Nature of production processes
   3. Type of customer for their products and services
   4. Methods used to distribute their products or provide their services
   5. Nature of regulatory environment; for example, banking
E. Operating segments that meet any of the three quantitative thresholds (10% tests) are immediately deemed reportable segments.
   1. Segment revenue is ≥ 10% of combined revenue (revenue includes intersegment revenue).
   2. Segment operating profit or loss is ≥ 10% of the greater of, in absolute amount
      a. Combined operating profit of all operating segments with profit, or
      b. Combined operating loss of all operating segments with loss
   3. Segment assets are ≥ 10% of combined assets of all segments.
F. Additional considerations when determining reportable segments
   1. Management may combine information about operating segments that do not meet the 10% tests with information on other operating segments that do meet the 10% tests to produce reportable segment only if majority of the aggregation criteria exists.
   2. Segment that was reported previously should continue to be reported if judged to be of continuing significance by management even if it does not meet the 10% tests in current period.
   3. Combined sales to nonaffiliated customers of segments reporting separately must be at least 75% of total consolidated sales
      a. If not, additional segments must be identified as reportable segments
   4. All other operating segments which are not reportable shall be combined with any other business activities (e.g., corporate headquarters) and disclosed in "all other" category.
   5. Number of reportable segments probably should not exceed ten.
      a. Combine closely related segments if number of segments becomes impracticable
G. Information is to be presented for each reportable segment and in aggregate for remaining segments not reported separately
   1. General information, including
      a. Explanation of factors used to identify the enterprise's reportable segments
      b. Types of products and services from which revenue is derived
   2. An enterprise shall report a measure of profit or loss and total assets for each reportable segment. To the extent the following is included in the measure of profit or loss or assets it shall also be disclosed:
      a. Revenues from external customers
      b. Revenues from transactions with other operating segments of the same enterprise

    c.   Interest revenue

    d.   Interest expense

    e.   Depreciation, depletion, and amortization expense

    f.   Unusual items not qualifying as extraordinary items

    g.   Equity in net income of investees accounted for by equity method

    h.   Income tax expense or benefit

    i.   Extraordinary items

    j.   Significant noncash items other than depreciation, depletion, and amortization expense

3. For segment assets

    a.   Total expenditures for additions to long-lived assets

    b.   Amount of investment in equity method investees

4. Enterprise shall provide an explanation of the measurements of segment profit or loss and assets, including

    a.   Basis of accounting

    b.   Nature of any differences between measurement of profit and loss or assets for the segment and that of the consolidated enterprise

    c.   Nature of any changes from prior periods

    d.   Nature and effect of asymmetrical allocations (e.g., allocating depreciation, but not related assets to segment)

5. Enterprise will need to provide reconciliations for the segment amounts disclosed to the corresponding enterprise amounts.

6. Although not as extensive as in the annual report, certain disclosures are required in the interim reports.

H. Previously issued segment information must be restated (unless impractical to do so) if any enterprise changes structure of internal organization that causes composition of reportable segments to change

I. Information about products and services

1. Enterprise-wide disclosure required even if only one and segment disclosures required.

2. Revenue from external customers for each product and service shall be reported by the enterprise.

J. Information about geographic areas (individual countries)

1. Enterprise-wide disclosure required even if only one and segment disclosures required.

2. Enterprise shall report revenues from external customers and long-lived assets attributable to its domestic operations and foreign operations.

3. If enterprise functions in two or more foreign geographic areas, to the extent revenues or assets of an individual foreign geographic area are material, then these amounts should be separately disclosed.

K. Major customers

1. Enterprise-wide disclosure required even if segment disclosures are not required

2. Disclose amount of revenue to each customer accounting for $\geq$ 10% of revenue

3. Disclose similarly if $\geq$ 10% of revenue derived from sales to domestic government agencies or foreign governments

4. Identify segment making sales

SFAS 132 (P16) Employers' Disclosures about Pensions and Other Postretirement Benefits (Amends SFAS 87, 88, and 106)

A. Disclosures for defined benefit pensions plans and defined benefit postretirement plans

1. A reconciliation of beginning and ending balances of the benefit obligation with the effects of the following shown separately:

    a.   Service cost

    b.   Interest cost

    c.   Contributions by plan participants

    d.   Actuarial gains and losses

    e.   Foreign currency exchange rate changes

    f.   Benefits paid

    g.   Plan amendments

    h.   Business combinations

    i.   Divestitures

    j.   Curtailments

    k. Settlements
    l. Special termination benefits
2. A reconciliation of beginning and ending balances of the fair value of plan assets with the effects of
    the following shown separately:
    a. Actual return on plan assets
    b. Foreign currency exchange rate changes
    c. Contributions by the employer
    d. Contributions by plan participants
    e. Benefits paid
    f. Business combinations
    g. Divestitures
    h. Settlements
3. The funded status of the plans
4. The amounts recognized and the amounts not recognized in the statement of financial position such as
    a. Any unamortized service cost
    b. Any unrecognized net gain or loss
    c. Any unamortized net obligation or net asset existing at the initial date of prior SFAS 87 or 106
        that are still unrecognized
    d. Prepaid assets or accrued liabilities of the net pension or other postretirement benefits
    e. Any intangible asset
    f. The amount of other comprehensive income recognized
5. The recognized amount of the net periodic benefit cost with the components shown separately
6. The amount caused from a change in the additional minimum pension liability that was included in
    other comprehensive income
7. Rates for
    a. Assumed discount rate
    b. Rate of compensation increase
    c. Expected long-term rate of return on plan assets
8. Trend rates assumed for health care cost for the next year and thereafter
9. The effects of a one-percentage-point increase or decrease of the trend rates for health care costs on
    a. The aggregate of the service and interest cost components
    b. The accumulated postretirement benefit obligation
10. If applicable
    a. The amounts and types of securities of the employer or a related party in plan assets
    b. The amount of future benefits covered by insurance contracts issued by the employer or a related
        party
    c. Any significant transactions between the plan and the employer or a related party
    d. Any substantive commitment used as the basis for accounting for the benefit obligation
    e. The cost of special or contractual termination benefits recognized during the period with a descrip-
        tion of the event
11. An explanation of significant changes in the benefit obligation or plan assets that is not apparent in the
    other disclosures required
B. Disclosures for employers with more than one plan
    1. Disclosures required in this statement may be disclosed in aggregate for an employer's defined benefit
        pension plans and in aggregate for an employer's defined benefit postretirement plans but must still
        present separately prepaid benefit costs and accrued benefit liabilities recognized in the statement of
        financial position.
    2. An employer may not combine the disclosures of plans outside the US and plans in the US if the bene-
        fit obligation of the plans outside the US represent a significant portion of the total benefit obligation
        and significant differences exist in the assumptions used.
C. Disclosure requirements for nonpublic entities
    1. Nonpublic entities may choose to disclose the following instead of the disclosures stated in A.:
        a. Benefit obligation
        b. Fair value of plan assets
        c. Funded status of the plan
        d. Contributions by the employer and the participant

    e. Amounts recognized in the statement of financial position of
      (1) Prepaid assets or accrued liabilities
      (2) Any intangible asset
    f. Amount of accumulated other comprehensive income recognized and the amount resulting from a change in the minimum pension liability recognized
    g. Net periodic benefit cost recognized
    h. Rates for
      (1) Assumed discount rate
      (2) Rate of compensation increase
      (3) Expected long-term rate of return on plan assets
    i. Trend rates assumed for health care cost for the next year and thereafter
    j. If applicable
      (1) Amounts and types of securities of the employer or a related party
      (2) Future annual benefits covered by insurance contracts issued by the employer or a related party
      (3) Any significant transactions between the plan and the employer or a related party
    k. Nature and effect of significant nonroutine events

D. Disclosures for defined contribution plans
  1. Amount of cost recognized for pension or postretirement benefit plans must be separate from the cost recognized for defined benefit plans
  2. Nature and effect of any significant changes that affect comparability must be disclosed

E. Disclosures for multiemployer plans
  1. Amount of contributions to multiemployer plans
  2. Nature and effect of changes which affect comparability
  3. If withdrawals made by an employer from a multiemployer plan will result in an obligation for a portion of the unfunded benefit obligation or the unfunded accumulated postretirement benefit obligation, follow the provision of SFAS 5, *Accounting for Contingencies*

SFAS 133 (D50) Accounting for Derivative Instruments and Hedging Activities

A. Foundation principles for SFAS 133
  1. Financial instruments should be measured at fair value
  2. Changes in fair value, or gains and losses, should be reported in comprehensive income or in current earnings
  3. Hedging instrument criteria
    a. Fair value hedge
      (1) Recognized asset or liability
      (2) Unrecognized firm commitment
    b. Cash flow hedge
      (1) Recognized asset or liability
      (2) Forecasted transaction
    c. Foreign currency hedge
      (1) Unrecognized firm commitment
      (2) Available-for-sale security
      (3) Forecasted transaction
      (4) Net investment in foreign operations

B. Definition of derivative instrument
  1. Contract must contain one or more underlyings and one or more notional amounts
  2. Contract requires no initial net investment, or a smaller initial net investment than required for contracts with an expected similar response to market changes
  3. Terms that require or permit net settlement, net settlement by means outside the contract, or delivery of an asset that results in a position no substantially different from net settlement

C. Embedded derivative instruments
  1. Financial instruments which contain features which separately meet the definition of a derivative instrument
  2. Three criteria used to determine whether the instrument should be separated from the host contract
    a. The embedded derivative instrument meets the definition of a derivative instrument (e.g. strips)

        b.   The hybrid instrument is not regularly recorded at fair value
        c.   The economic characteristics and risks of the embedded instrument are not clearly and closely related to the economic characteristics of the host contract

D. Hedging instruments criteria
    1.   Sufficient documentation must be provided at the beginning of the process
        a.   Identify the objective and strategy of the hedge
        b.   Identify the hedging instrument and the hedged item
        c.   Identify how the effectiveness of the hedge will be assessed on an ongoing basis
    2.   The hedge must be highly effective throughout its life
        a.   Measured every three months and whenever earnings or financial statements are reported

E. Fair value hedges
    1.   Specific criteria
        a.   Hedged item must be a specific portion of a recognized asset/liability or an unrecognized firm commitment
        b.   An unrecognized firm commitment must be binding on both parties, specific with respect to all significant terms, and contain a nonperformance clause that makes performance probable.
    2.   Gains and losses will be recognized in current earnings

F. Cash flow hedges
    1.   Specific hedges
        a.   The change in cash flows must be the same, or linked, for the hedge's asset/liability and the hedging instrument
        b.   A forecasted transaction's cash flows must be considered probable
        c.   A forecasted series of transactions must share the same risk exposure
    2.   Accounting for
        a.   Effective portion reported in other comprehensive income
        b.   Ineffective portion reported in earnings

G. Foreign currency hedge
    1.   Unrecognized firm commitment
        a.   Accounted for as fair value hedge if requirements met
    2.   Available-for-sale securities
        a.   Accounted for as fair value hedge if requirements met and
            (1) Cannot be traded on exchange denominated in investor's functional currency
            (2) Dividends must be denominated in same foreign currency as expected sale proceeds
    3.   Foreign currency denominated forecasted transactions
        a.   Accounted for as cash flow hedges
    4.   Net investments in foreign operations
        a.   Must meet hedge effectiveness criterion
        b.   Change in fair value recorded in other comprehensive income

H. Forward exchange contracts
    1.   Mark to market using the forward exchange rate at each reporting date
    2.   Recognize changes in fair value in current earnings

I. Disclosures
    1.   Objectives and strategies for achieving financial instruments
    2.   Context to understand the instrument
    3.   Risk management policies
    4.   A list of hedged instruments
    5.   Disclosure of fair value of financial instruments required when practicable to estimate fair value

SFAS 134 (I80, Mo4) Accounting for Mortgage-Backed Securities Retained after the Securitization of Mortgage Loans Held for Sale by a Mortgage Banking Enterprise
(The authors believe that this topic is too specialized for the CPA exam.)

SFAS 135 (P16) Rescission of FASB Statement No. 75 and Technical Corrections
(The SFAS 75 rescission deals with pension plan requirements that is covered in Module 38. The technical corrections have been made throughout this volume.)

SFAS 136 (C67, No5) Transfers of Assets to a Not-for-Profit Organization or a Charitable Trust That Raises or Holds Contributions for Others
(This statement deals with a topic covered on the Accounting and Reporting Examination; it is included in Module 39.)

SFAS 137 Accounting for Derivative Instruments and Hedging Activities—Deferral of the Effective Date of FASB Statement No. 133.
In June 1999, the FASB issued this statement which delays the effective date of SFAS 133 for one year.

SFAS 138 (D50) Accounting Certain Derivative Instruments and Certain Hedging Activities: An Amendment of FASB Statement No. 133
A. Amended four specific items in SFAS 133
   1. Normal purchases and sales exception extended
      a. Applies to contracts that require delivery of nonfinancial assets to be used in the normal operations of an entity
      b. These contracts need not be accounted for as derivative instruments unless the contracts require net settlements of gains or losses
   2. Redefined the interest rate risk
      a. Permits a benchmark interest rate to be designated as the hedged risk in a hedge of interest rate risk
      b. This benchmark presents the risk-free rate and is the interest rate on direct Treasury obligations of the US government, or the London Interbank Offered Rate (LIBOR)
      c. A company's actual interest rate above the benchmark interest rate reflects that company's credit risk which is separate from the risk-free rate of interest
   3. Hedging recognized foreign currency denominated assets or liabilities
      a. Permits a recognized foreign currency denominated asset or liability, for which a foreign currency transaction gain or loss is recognized in earnings under the provisions of SFAS 52, to be the hedged item in a fair value or cash flow hedge.
      b. The foreign currency denominated asset or liability continues to be remeasured using the spot exchange rates to compute the transaction gain or loss for the period
      c. In the case of cash flow hedges, the transaction gain or loss would be offset by an equal amount of reclassified from other comprehensive income. In the case of fair market value hedges, the hedging instrument would be a hedge of both interest rate risk and foreign exchange rate risk. The foreign currency denominated asset or liability would be adjusted for changes in fair value attributable to changes in foreign interest rates before remeasurement at the spot exchange rate. This eliminates the differences on earnings related to the use of different measurement criteria for the hedged item and the hedging instrument
   4. Hedging with intercompany derivatives
      a. Permits derivative instruments entered into with another member of the consolidated group to qualify as hedging instruments in the consolidated financial statements if those internal derivatives are offset by unrelated third-party contracts on a net basis
      b. Previously, the internal derivative had to be offset on an individual derivative contract basis with a third party

SFAS 140 (F35 and L35) Accounting for Transfers and Servicing of Financial Assets and Extinguishment of Liabilities
A. Provides accounting and reporting standards for transfers and servicing of financial assets and extinguishment of liabilities
B. Transfer of Assets
   1. Necessary conditions to qualify as a sale
      a. Transferred assets have been isolated from the transferor or its creditors,
      b. Transferee has the unconstrained right to pledge or exchange the transferred assets, and
      c. Transferor does not maintain effective control over the transferred assets through
         (1) An agreement that obligates the transferor to repurchase or redeem them before their maturity, or
         (2) The ability to unilaterally cause the holder to return specific assets
   2. Upon any transfer of assets the transferor shall

      a.   Continue to carry in its balance sheet any retained interest in the transferred assets

      b.   Allocate the previous carrying amount between the assets sold and the retained interest based on their relative fair values

   3. Upon any completion of a transfer of assets which satisfies the conditions of a sale, the transferor shall

      a.   Derecognize all assets sold

      b.   Recognize all assets obtained and liabilities incurred in consideration as sale proceeds

      c.   Initially measure at fair value assets obtained and liabilities incurred in a sale

      d.   Recognize in earnings any gain (loss) on sale

   4. Upon any completion of a transfer of assets which satisfies the conditions of a sale, the transferee shall

      a.   Recognize all assets obtained and liabilities incurred at fair value

   5. If transfer of assets does not meet the criteria for a sale, the transfer shall be accounted for as a secured borrowing with pledge of collateral

C. Servicing Assets and Liabilities

   1. Under an obligation to service financial assets, an entity recognizes either a service asset or service liability unless it

      a.   Transfers assets to a qualifying Special Purpose Entity in a guaranteed mortgage securitization

      b.   Retains all resulting securities

      c.   Classifies them as held-to-maturity

   2. Servicing assets purchased or assumed

      a.   Measured at fair value

      b.   Amortized in proportion to and over the period of estimated net servicing income or net servicing loss

      c.   Assessed for impairment or increased obligation based on fair value

D. Financial Assets Subject to Prepayment

   1. Shall be measured like investments in debt securities classified as available-for-sale or trading

E. Secured Borrowing and Collateral

   1. Pledge

      a.   Debtor grants a security interest in certain assets

      b.   Collateral is transferred to the secured party

   2. Accounting for noncash collateral

      a.   Debtor to separate asset on balance sheet into an encumbered asset section if secured party has right to sell or repledge collateral

      b.   Secured party recognizes the proceeds from sale and obligation to return collateral if it sells collateral pledged to it

      c.   Debtor defaults under terms of agreement and is no longer entitled to redeem the pledged asset

         (1) Derecognize the pledged asset

         (2) Secured party recognizes collateral as an asset at fair value

         (3) If collateral already sold, secured party derecognizes its obligation to return collateral.

F. Extinguishment of Liabilities

   1. Debtor shall derecognize a liability when it has been extinguished

      a.   Debtor pays the creditor and is relieved of its obligation for the liability

      b.   Debtor is legally released from being obligor under the liability, either judicially or by the creditor.

G. Required Disclosures

   1. Collateral

      a.   Policy for requiring collateral or other security due to repurchase agreements or securities lending transactions

      b.   Carrying amount and classification of pledged assets as collateral that are not reclassified and separately reported in the balance sheet

      c.   The fair value of collateral that can be sold or repledged and information about the sources and uses of that collateral

   2. Extinguished debt

      a.   General description of transaction

      b.   Amount of debt that was considered extinguished at end of period

   3. Description of assets set aside for satisfying scheduled payments of a specific obligation

   4. Nonestimable fair value of assets

a. Description of the assets or liabilities
b. The reasons why it is not practicable to estimate the assets or liabilities
5. Servicing assets and servicing liabilities
   a. Amounts of servicing assets or liabilities recognized and amortized during the period
   b. Fair value on recognized servicing assets and liabilities and the method used to estimate the fair value
   c. Risk characteristics of the underlying financial assets used to stratify recognized servicing assets
   d. Activity in any valuation allowance for impairment of recognized servicing assets
6. Transfer of securitized financial assets accounted for as a sale
   a. Accounting policies for measuring the retained interest
   b. Characteristics of securitizations and the gain (loss) from sale
   c. Key assumptions used in measuring the fair value of retained interests at time of securitization
   d. Cash flows between the securitization SPE and the transferor
7. Retained interests in secured financial assets
   a. Accounting policies for subsequently measuring retained interests
   b. Key assumptions used in subsequently measuring fair value of retained interests
   c. Sensitivity analysis or stress test showing hypothetical effect of unfavorable variations on the retained interest's fair value, including limitations of analysis
   d. Securitized assets
      (1) Total principal outstanding, portion derecognized, and portion that continues to be recognized
      (2) Delinquencies at end of period
      (3) Credit losses, net of recoveries

SFAS 141 (B51) Business Combinations

The purchase method of accounting is required for all business combinations initiated after June 30, 2001.
A. Application of the **purchase method**
   1. Identifying the acquiring entity. In identifying which entity is the acquiring entity that will continue into the future, the following facts and circumstances shall be considered:
      a. The relative voting rights in the combined entity after the combinations
      b. The existence of a large minority voting interest in the combined entity when no other owner or organized group of owners has a significant voting interest
      c. The composition of the governing body of the combined entity
      d. The composition of the senior management of the combined entity
      e. The terms of the exchange of equity securities
   2. The standard historical cost principle is applied in purchase accounting.
      a. Assets and liabilities are recorded using the fair value of the property given or fair value of property received, whichever is more clearly evident
   3. The cost of a company includes direct costs of acquisition but not indirect general expenses
   4. Additional payments to be made, contingent on future earnings and/or security prices, should be disclosed but not recorded as a liability
      a. If contingent payments are made because of attainment of specified earnings levels, the additional payment is considered an increase in the cost of the subsidiary (usually results in an increase in goodwill)
      b. If contingent payments are made due to attainment of specified security price levels, the cost of the acquired company is not affected. Rather the amount originally recorded as consideration in acquisition should be reduced by the contingency payment (usually results in decreasing paid-in capital).
      c. If contingent payments are based on both security prices and earnings, the payments should be separated and accounted for as in a. and b. above
   5. The acquiring entity should allocate the cost of the acquired company to assets and liabilities acquired (determining their revised values). Independent appraisals may be used based on the following principles:
      a. Marketable securities—fair value
      b. Receivables—present value after allowance and collection costs
      c. Finished inventories and work in process inventories—net realizable value less normal profit
      d. Raw materials—replacement cost

    e.   Plant and equipment to be used—replacement cost for similar capacity

    f.   Plant and equipment to be sold—fair value less costs to sell

    g.   Intangible assets that arise from contractual or legal rights or are separable from the entity—fair value

    h.   Other assets—appraised value

    i.   Payables—present value

    j.   Pensions and other postretirement obligations—in accordance with SFAS 87 or SFAS 106

    k.   Liabilities and accruals—present value

    l.   Preacquisition contingencies—fair value, if determinable

6. Previously recorded goodwill of the acquired company should not be recorded by the acquiring company

7. A deferred tax liability or asset shall be recognized for differences between the assigned values and the tax bases of the recognized assets and liabilities acquired

8. The value assigned to net assets should not exceed cost

    a.   If the cost of the net assets acquired exceeds the net revised asset values, the excess should be recorded as goodwill

    b.   If the net revised asset value exceeds cost, the excess should be credited, pro rata, to all noncurrent assets except marketable securities, assets to be disposed of, deferred tax assets, and prepaid assets relating to pension or other postretirements benefit plans

    c.   If any excess remains after reducing to zero the amounts that otherwise would have been assigned to those assets, the remaining excess shall be recognized as an extraordinary gain

9. Goodwill should be allocated to individual reporting units which are equivalent to the operating segments or one level below. (See the outline of SFAS 142.)

10. The date of acquisition is the date assets are received and securities issued

11. The notes of the acquiring company in the year of purchase should include

    a.   Name and description of acquired company

    b.   The primary reasons for the acquisition, including a description of the factors that contributed to the purchase price that results in recognition of goodwill

    c.   The periods for which the results of operations of the acquired entity are included in the income statement of the combined entity

    d.   The costs of the acquired entity and, if applicable, the number of shares of equity interests issued or issuable

    e.   A condensed balance sheet disclosing the amount assigned to each major asset and liability caption on the date of acquisition

    f.   Contingent payments, options, or commitments and the related proposed accounting

    g.   The amount of purchased research and development costs written off in the period

    h.   For any purchase price allocation not finalized, that fact and the reasons therefor

12. If the amounts assigned to goodwill or other intangibles are significant in relation to the total cost, disclosure should include

    a.   For intangible assets subject to amortization

        (1) The total amount assigned to each major class of asset

        (2) The amount of any residual value, in total and by major asset category

        (3) The weighted-average amortization period, in total and by major asset category

    b.   For intangible assets not subject to amortization, the amount assigned, in total and by major asset category

    c.   For goodwill

        (1) The total amount assigned and the amount expected to be tax deductible

        (2) The amount of goodwill by reportable unit

13. Pro forma results of operations of the current and immediate prior period (no other prior periods) of public business enterprises should reflect operations of the combination including

    a.   Revenue

    b.   Income before extraordinary items

    c.   Net income

    d.   EPS

14. Accounting for intangible assets, including goodwill—see outline of SFAS 142

SFAS 142 (G40) Goodwill and Other Intangible Assets

This standard provides guidance on accounting for intangible assets including goodwill.

A. Initial Recognition and Measurement of Intangible Assets
  1. Intangible assets not acquired in a business combination
    a. An intangible asset that is acquired either individually or with a group of other assets shall be initially recognized at its fair value
    b. The cost of assets acquired as a group should be allocated to the individual assets based on their relative fair values and shall not give rise to goodwill
  2. Intangible assets (including goodwill) acquired in a business combination shall be recognized in accordance with SFAS 141
  3. Costs of internally developing, maintaining, or restoring intangible assets that are not specifically identifiable, that have indeterminate lives, or that are inherent in a continuing business and related to an entity as a whole, shall be recognized as an expense when incurred

B. Accounting for Intangible Assets
  1. The cost of an intangible asset with a finite useful life is amortized over its estimated useful life
    a. The useful life of an intangible asset should be estimated by considering factors such as
      (1) Expected use
      (2) Expected useful life of assets related to the intangible asset
      (3) Legal, regulatory, and contractual provisions that may limit or extend the useful life
      (4) The effects of obsolescence, demand, competition, and other economic factors
      (5) The level of expenditures expected to be required to maintain the asset
    b. The method of amortization shall reflect the pattern in which the economic benefits of the intangible assets are consumed; if the pattern cannot be reliable determined, a straight-line amortization method shall be used
    c. The residual value of the intangible asset will be presumed to be zero unless there is a commitment from a third party to purchase the asset at the end of its useful life, or the residual value can be determined by reference to an exchange transaction in an existing market
    d. The remaining useful life of the intangible asset should be reevaluated each reporting period—if it is no longer appropriate the carrying amount should be amortized prospectively over the revised remaining useful life
    e. Intangible assets with finite useful lives should be reviewed for impairment in accordance with SFAS 144
  2. An intangible asset that is determined to have an indefinite useful life should not be amortized until its useful life is determined to be no longer indefinite
    a. An intangible asset that is not subject to amortization should be tested for impairment annually, or more frequently if events or changes in circumstances indicate that the asset might be impaired
    b. The impairment test involves comparison of the carrying amount of the asset to its fair value
  3. Goodwill should not be amortized
    a. Goodwill should be tested for impairment at the level of reporting referred to as a reporting unit (an operating segment or one level below). See the outline of SFAS 131
    b. A two-step test for impairment is required
      (1) The first step involves a comparison of the fair value of the reporting unit with its carrying amount. If the carrying amount of the unit exceeds its fair value, the second step is performed. In estimating the fair value of a reporting unit, a valuation technique based on multiples of earnings or revenue or other performance measure may be used.
      (2) The second step involves a comparison of the implied fair value of goodwill of the reporting unit with the carrying amount of that goodwill
      (3) The implied fair value of goodwill is determined in the same manner as the amount of goodwill recognized in a business combination—see outline of SFAS 141. That is, all assets in the segment are valued in accordance with SFAS 141 and the excess of the fair value of the reporting unit as a whole over the amounts assigned to its recorded assets and liabilities is the implied goodwill. If the implied value of goodwill is less than the carrying amount, goodwill is written down to its implied value and an impairment loss is recognized.
    c. Goodwill should be tested for impairment on an annual basis and between annual dates if one or more of the following events occur:

       (1) A significant adverse change in legal factors or in the business climate

       (2) An adverse action or assessment by a regulator

       (3) Unanticipated competition

       (4) A loss of key personnel

       (5) A more-likely-than-not expectation that a reporting unit or a significant portion of a reporting unit will be sold or otherwise disposed of

       (6) The test for recoverability under SFAS 144 within a reporting unit reveals that a significant group of assets are recorded at amounts above their recoverable values

       (7) Recognition of a goodwill impairment loss in the financial statements of a subsidiary that is a component of a reporting unit

   d. A reporting unit may be tested at any time during the fiscal year as long as it is tested at the same time each year. Different reporting units may be tested at different times during the year.

   e. Initially goodwill is allocated to reporting units. Then the assets and liabilities of the reporting units are valued individually with goodwill being measured as the difference between the cost assigned to the reporting unit and the fair value of the individual assets and liabilities.

C. Disclosures

  1. In the period of acquisition

    a. For intangible assets subject to amortization

      (1) The amount assigned in total and by major intangible asset class

      (2) Significant residual value, in total and by major intangible asset class

      (3) The weighted-average amortization period, in total and by major intangible asset class

    b. For intangible assets not subject to amortization, the amount assigned in total and by major intangible asset class

    c. The amount of research and development assets acquired and written off and in which financial statement line items the amounts are included

  2. Continuing disclosures

    a. For intangible assets subject to amortization

      (1) The gross carrying amount and accumulated amortization, in total and by major intangible asset class

      (2) The aggregate amortization expense for the period

      (3) The estimated aggregate amortization expense for each of the five succeeding fiscal years

    b. For intangible assets not subject to amortization, the carrying amount in total and by each major intangible asset class

    c. The changes in the carrying amount of goodwill during the period including

      (1) The aggregate amount of goodwill acquired

      (2) The aggregate amount of impairment losses recognized

      (3) The amount of goodwill included in the gain or loss on disposal of all or a portion of a reporting unit

    d. For each other-than-goodwill impairment loss recognized (other than for goodwill)

      (1) A description of the impaired intangible asset and the facts and circumstances leading to the impairment

      (2) The amount of the impairment loss and the method of determining fair value

      (3) The caption in the income statement or the statement of activities in which the impairment loss is aggregated

      (4) If applicable, the segment in which the impaired intangible asset is reported under SFAS 131

    e. For each goodwill impairment loss recognized

      (1) A description of the facts and circumstances leading to the impairment

      (2) The amount of the impairment loss and the method of determining the fair value of the associated reporting unit

      (3) If a recognized impairment loss is an estimate that has not yet been finalized, the facts and circumstances and the amount of subsequent adjustments

SFAS 143 (A50) Accounting for Asset Retirement Obligations

This standard provides guidance on accounting for obligations associated with the retirement of tangible long-lived assets.

A. The guidance applies to legal obligations associated with the retirement of long-lived assets that result from the acquisition, construction, development and/or normal operation of a long-lived asset, except for certain obligations of lessees. Examples include

   1. Costs to decommission a nuclear utility plant at the end of its useful life

   2. Costs to dismantle and remove an offshore oil platform at the end of its useful life

B. Such legal obligation may arise from

   1. Existing or enacted law, statute, ordinance

   2. Written or oral contract

   3. Legal construction of a contract under the doctrine of promissory estoppel (inferred legal obligation)

C. An asset retirement obligation is recognized at its fair value in the period in which it is incurred providing that a reasonable estimate of fair value can be made

D. Upon initial recognition of a liability, the entity shall increase the carrying amount of the related long-lived asset by the same amount as that recognized for the liability

E. The cost shall be subsequently expensed using a systematic and rational method over periods no longer than that for which the related asset is expected to provide benefits

F. Initial measurement of the liability

   1. The best source of fair value of the liability would be provided by market-determined values but they will seldom be available

   2. In the absence of a market, expected present value of future cash flows should be used. In determining the expected present value, the entity should

     a. Use probability-weighted present values in a range of the estimated cash flows

     b. The amounts should be discounted to present value using a credit-adjusted risk-free rate

G. Subsequent to the initial measurement of the liability the obligation should be adjusted for

   1. The passage of time, and

   2. Revisions in estimates of timing or amounts of future cash flows

H. Adjustments to the liability for revisions in estimates of timing or amounts of cash flows should also be reflected in the carrying value of the related asset

I. Disclosures related to asset retirement obligations should include

   1. Description of the obligation and related asset

   2. Description of how fair value was determined

   3. The funding policy, if any

   4. A reconciliation of the beginning and ending aggregate carrying value

SFAS 144 (D60 and I08) Accounting for the Impairment or Disposal of Long-Lived Assets

A. Establishes financial and reporting requirements for the impairment or disposal of long-lived assets. In addition to property, plant, equipment, and intangible assets being amortized, SFAS 144 applies to capital leases of lessees, long-lived assets of lessors subject to operating leases, proved oil and gas properties that are being accounted for using the successful efforts method of accounting, and long-term prepaid assets.

B. If a long-lived asset (or assets) is part of a group that includes other assets and liabilities not covered by SFAS 144, the statement applies to the group.

C. Assets to be held and used

   1. Reviewed for impairment when circumstances indicate that the carrying amount of a long-term asset (or group) is not recoverable and exceeds its fair value. The carrying amount of a long-lived asset (asset group) is not recoverable it if exceeds the sum of the undiscounted cash flows expected to result from its use and eventual disposal.

   2. A long-lived asset (asset group) shall be tested for recoverability whenever events or changes in circumstances indicate that its carrying amount may not be recoverable. Examples of such events include

     a. Significant decrease in market value

     b. Change in way asset used or physical change in asset

     c. Legal factors or change in business climate that might affect asset's fair value or adverse action or assessment by regulator

     d. Asset costs incurred greater than planned

     e. Current-period operating or cash flow loss combined with historical or projection of such amounts demonstrates continuing losses from the asset

     f.   A current expectation that, more likely than not a long-lived asset will be disposed of significantly before the end of its previously estimated useful life

  3. Impaired if the expected total future cash flows are less than the carrying amount of the asset (asset group)

     a.   Assets should be grouped at lowest level for which there are identifiable cash flows independent of other groupings

     b.   Expected future cash flows are future cash inflows to be generated by the asset (asset group) less the future cash outflows expected to be necessary to obtain those inflows

     c.   Expected future cash flows are **not** discounted and do not consider interest charges

     d.   If the management has alternative courses of action to recover the carrying amount, or if a range of possible cash flows are associated with a particular course of action, a probability-weighted approach may be useful

  4. Written down to fair value and loss recognized upon impairment

     a.   Fair value is the amount at which the asset can be bought or sold in a current transaction between willing parties

     b.   If quoted market price in active market is not available, the estimate of fair value should be based on best information available

  5. An impairment loss for an asset group shall reduce only the carrying amounts of the long-lived assets. Impairment of other assets in the group should be accounted for in accordance with other applicable accounting standards

  6. If an impairment loss is recognized, the adjusted carrying amount becomes it new cost basis

  7. Fair value increases on assets previously written down for impairment losses may not be recognized

  8. Disclosures

     a.   Description of impaired asset (asset group) and circumstances which led to impairment

     b.   Amount of impairment and manner in which fair value was determined

     c.   Caption in income statement in which impairment loss is aggregated, if it is not presented separately thereon

     d.   Business segment(s) affected (if applicable)

D. Long-lived assets to be disposed of other than by sale

  1. Long-lived assets to be abandoned are disposed of when they cease to be used

  2. Long-lived assets to be exchanged for similar assets or to be distributed to owners are disposed of when they are exchanged or distributed

E. Long-lived assets to be disposed of by sale

  1. Long-lived assets to be sold shall be classified as "held-for-sale" in the period in which all of the following criteria are met:

     a.   Management commits to a plan of disposal

     b.   The assets are available for sale

     c.   An active program to locate a buyer has been initiated

     d.   The sale is probable

     e.   The asset is being actively marketed for sale at a fair price

     f.   It is unlikely that the disposal plan will significantly change

  2. Reported at lesser of the carrying amount or fair value less cost to sell

     a.   Cost to sell includes broker commissions, legal and title transfer fees, and closing costs prior to legal title transfer

  3. In future periods, adjusted carrying amount of asset shall be revised down or up to extent of changes in estimate of fair value less cost to sell, provided that the adjusted carrying amount does not exceed the carrying amount of the asset prior to the adjustment reflecting the decision to dispose of the asset

     a.   Thus, recoveries may be recognized when assets are to be **disposed of** but not on impaired assets that continue to be used

F. Reporting long-lived assets and disposal groups to be disposed of

  1. Discontinued operations of a component of an entity

     a.   A component of an entity comprises operations and cash flows that can be clearly distinguished, operationally and for financial reporting purposes

     b.   The results of a component of an entity that either has been disposed of or is classified as held for sale shall be reported as discontinued operations if both of the following conditions are met:

(1) The operations and cash flows of the component have been (will be) eliminated from ongoing operations

(2) The entity will not have any significant continuing involvement in the operations of the component after disposal

   c. In reporting discontinued operations, the income statement should present the results of discontinued operations separately after income from continuing operations and before extraordinary items as shown below

Income from continuing operations before income taxes	$xxxxx	
Income taxes	xxx	
Income from continuing operations		$xxxx
Discontinued operations (Note X)		
Loss from operations of discontinued Component Z (including loss		
on disposal of $xxx)		xxxx
Income tax benefit		xxxx
Loss on discontinued operations		xxxx
Net income		$xxxx

2. A gain or loss recognized for long-term asset (group) classified for sale that is not a component of an entity shall be included in income from continuing operations before income taxes
3. Disclosures
   a. Description of assets to be disposed of, reasons for disposal, expected disposal date, and carrying amount of those assets
   b. Gain or loss, if any, resulting from changes in carrying amount due to further changes in market value
   c. If applicable, amounts of revenue and pretax profit or loss reported in discontinued operations
   d. If applicable, the segment of the business affected (see outline of SFAS 131)

SFAS 145 (I17, L10, and L35) Rescission of FASB Statements No. 4, 44, and 64, Amendment of FASB Statement No. 13, and Technical Corrections (Rescinds SFAS 4, 44, and 64 and amends SFAS 13)

A. Rescinds SFAS 4, 44, and 64 to no longer allow treatment of extinguishment of debt as an extraordinary item in the statement of income

B. Amends SFAS 13 to require that when a modification of a capital lease terms gives rise to a new agreement classified as an operating lease, the lessee should account for the new agreement under the sale-leaseback requirements of SFAS 98 (see outline)

SFAS 146 (Not available) Accounting for Costs Associated with Exit or Disposal Activities

A. A liability for cost associated with an exit or disposal shall be recognized and measured initially at its fair value in the period in which the liability is incurred
  1. There is an exception for a liability for one-time termination benefits that involves employees providing future services
  2. When fair value cannot be reasonably estimated, the liability shall be recognized initially in the period in which fair value can be reasonably estimated

B. An exit activity includes but is not limited to restructurings which are programs that are planned and controlled by management, and materially changes either
  1. The scope of a business undertaken by the company, or
  2. The manner in which that business is conducted
  3. Examples include
     a. Sale or termination of line of business
     b. Closure of business activities at a particular location
     c. Relocation of business activities from one location to another
     d. Changes in management structure
     e. Fundamental reorganization of the business

C. Exit or disposal activities covered by this statement do not include those that involve an entity acquired in a business combination, nor do they include disposals covered by SFAS 144. It also does not apply to costs associated with the retirement of a long-lived asset covered by SFAS 143. Examples of exit or disposal activities covered by this statement include
  1. Termination benefits provided to involuntarily terminated employees (other than ongoing arrangements and deferred compensation agreements)

2. Costs to terminate a contract that is not a capital lease

3. Costs to consolidate facilities or relocate employees

D. A liability for a cost associated with an exit or disposal activity shall be recognized and measured initially at fair value in the period in which the liability is incurred

   1. This typically is measured by determining the present value of the liability by discounting it using the entity's credit-adjusted risk-free interest rate

E. In the unusual circumstance in which fair value cannot be reasonably estimated, the liability shall be recognized initially in the period in which fair value can be reasonably estimated

F. Subsequent to initial recognition, the liability is adjusted over time by using the discount rate used to initially determine the liability

G. Measurement of one-time termination benefits

   1. A onetime termination agreement exists when the plan of termination meets the following criteria and has been communicated to the employees:

      a. Management commits to the plan

      b. The plan identifies the number of employees to be terminated, their job classifications and locations, and the expected completion date

      c. The plan establishes the terms of the benefit arrangement

      d. It is unlikely that significant changes in the plan will be made

   2. The liability is recognized and measured at the communication date if

      a. The employees are not required to perform additional services to receive termination benefits, or

      b. The employees will not be retained to render services beyond the minimum retention period (not to exceed the legal notification period)

   3. If the employees are required to render service until they are terminated in order to receive termination benefits and will render service beyond the minimum retention period

      a. The liability for termination benefits shall be initially measured at the communication date based on the fair value of the liability as of the termination date, and

      b. The liability shall be recognized ratably over the future service period

H. Measurement of contract termination costs

   1. Costs to terminate the contract before term end

      a. Recognized and measured when the contract is terminated

   2. Costs that will be incurred for the remaining term without benefit to the entity

      a. Recognized and measured when the entity ceases to use the rights conveyed by the contract (e.g., when the entity returns the leased assets)

I. Disclosure

   1. A description of the exit or disposal activity

   2. For each major type of cost associated with the activity

      a. The total amount expected to be incurred

      b. A reconciliation of the beginning and ending liability amounts

   3. The line items in the income statements in which the costs are included

   4. For each reportable segment, the total amount of costs expected to be incurred in connection with the activity

   5. If a liability cannot be reasonably estimated, the reasons therefor

STATEMENTS OF FINANCIAL ACCOUNTING CONCEPTS (SFAC)

Statements of Financial Accounting Concepts (SFAC) set forth financial accounting and reporting objectives and fundamentals that will be used by the FASB in developing standards. While practitioners may also use SFAC in areas where promulgated GAAP does not exist, it is important to note that the SFAC do not constitute authoritative GAAP.

SFAC 1 Objectives of Financial Reporting by Business Enterprises

A. Financial accounting concepts are fundamentals on which standards of financial accounting and reporting are based.

   1. That is, do not establish GAAP

      a. And do not come under AICPA Ethics Rule 203

   2. Defines financial accounting concepts broader than financial statements and other data

B. Environmental context of objectives
1. Financial reporting provides information for making business and economic decisions.
2. The United States is a market economy
   a. Dominated by investor-owned enterprises
   b. Even though the government generates economic statistics

C. Characteristics and limitations of information
1. Primarily financial (quantitative) in nature
2. Limited to individual business enterprises
3. Based on approximated measures (i.e., estimates)
4. Largely limited to past transactions (i.e., historically based)
5. Just one source of users' data base
6. Must conform to cost-benefit rationale

D. Potential users and their interests
1. "Owners, lenders, potential investors, suppliers, creditors, employees, management, directors, customers, financial analysts and advisors, brokers, underwriters, stock exchanges, lawyers, economists, taxing authorities, regulatory authorities, legislators, financial press and reporting agencies, labor unions, trade associations, business researchers, teachers and students, and the public."
2. Users are generally interested in cash flow generation.
   a. Amounts, timing, and uncertainties
3. Many external users lack authority to prescribe information.
   a. For example, absentee owners, customers, etc.

E. General-purpose external financial reporting
1. To satisfy informational needs of external users who lack authority to prescribe data they desire
2. Focuses on external users
   a. Management may prescribe data for their needs
3. Directed primarily at investors and creditors
   a. Which results in data of likely usefulness to others

F. Objectives of financial reporting
1. "Financial reporting should provide information that is useful to present and potential investors and creditors and other users in making rational investment, credit, and similar decisions."
2. "Financial reporting should provide information to help present and potential investors and creditors and other users in assessing the amounts, timing, and uncertainty of prospective cash receipts from dividends or interest and the proceeds from the sale, redemption, or maturity of securities or loans."
3. "Financial reporting should provide information about the economic resources of an enterprise, the claims to those resources (obligations of the enterprise to transfer resources to other entities and owner's equity), and the effects of transactions, events, and circumstances that change resources and claims to those resources."
   a. Economic resource, obligation, and owners' equity data permit assessment of
      (1) Liquidity and solvency
      (2) Financial strength
   b. Funds flow data is important
   c. Earnings performance data permit assessment of future performance
      (1) Thus, primary focus of reporting is on earnings
   d. Management stewardship and performance are reported on
   e. Management explanation and interpretation are important

SFAC 2 Qualitative Characteristics of Accounting Information
(Para 4 superseded by SFAC 6)

A. Purpose is to examine the characteristics that make accounting information useful and establish criteria for selecting and evaluating accounting alternatives.
1. Guidance needed by both FASB and individual accountants
2. The usefulness of accounting information must be evaluated in relation to decision making.
3. Based on objectives of financial reporting (SFAC 1)
4. Applies to financial information reported by business enterprises and not-for-profit organizations

B. The hierarchy of accounting qualities
1. User-specific qualities (not inherent in information)

      a. Understandability

      b. Decision usefulness

  2. Decision-specific qualities (necessary for usefulness)

      a. **Relevance**—"capacity" of information to "make a difference" in a decision

         (1) **Timeliness**—being available while able to influence decisions

         (2) **Predictive value**—improves decision makers' capacity to predict

         (3) **Feedback value**—enables users to confirm or correct prior expectations

      b. **Reliability**—freedom from error and bias and faithful representation of what is claimed to be represented

         (1) **Verifiability**—secures a high degree of consensus among independent measurers

         (2) **Representative faithfulness**—agreement between data and resources or events represented (validity)

         (3) **Neutrality**—freedom from bias toward a predetermined result

  3. Secondary and interactive qualities

      a. Comparability between enterprises

      b. Consistency in application over time

  4. Constraints

      a. **Materiality**—information should not be provided if below the user's threshold for recognition

      b. **Costs and benefits**—benefits derived from disclosure must exceed associated costs

SFAC 5 Recognition and Measurement in Financial Statements of Business Enterprises

A. Statement addresses principal items that a full set of FS should show and provides fundamental recognition criteria to use in deciding which items to include in FS.

  1. Recognition criteria presented are not radical change from current practice.

  2. Only applies to business enterprises

B. FS

  1. A principal means of communicating financial information to those outside an entity

  2. Some useful information is better provided by other means of financial reporting, such as notes to the statements or supplementary information (SFAC 1).

  3. Objectives of financial reporting (which encompasses FS) are detailed in SFAC 1.

  4. Full set of FS should show

      a. Financial position at end of period

      b. Earnings for period

      c. Comprehensive income for period

      d. Cash flows for period

      e. Investments by and distributions to owners during period

  5. Are intended as "general-purpose" statements and, therefore, do not necessarily satisfy all users equally well

  6. Simplifications, condensations, and aggregations are necessary and useful, but focusing on one figure (i.e., "the bottom line") exclusively should be avoided.

  7. FS interrelate and complement each other.

  8. Information detailed in 4. above is provided by the following individual financial statements:

      a. **Statement of Financial Position**

         (1) Provides information about entity's assets, liabilities, and equity and their relationships to each other at a particular point in time

         (2) Does not purport to show the value of an entity

      b. **Statement of Earnings and Comprehensive Income**

         (1) Shows how the equity of an entity increased or decreased from all sources (other than from transactions with owners) during period

         (2) Item "earnings" is similar to present net income term but does not include certain accounting adjustments recognized in current period (i.e., change in accounting principle).

         (3) Earnings is a performance measure concerned primarily with cash-to-cash cycles.

         (4) Comprehensive income includes all recognized changes in equity except those from transactions with owners (SFAC 6).

         (5) The terms "gains" and "losses" are used for those items included in earnings.

(6) The terms "cumulative accounting adjustments" and "other nonowner changes in equity" are used for those items excluded from earnings but included in comprehensive income.

  c. **Statement of Cash Flows**

    (1) Shows entity's cash flows from operating, investing, and financing activities during a period

  d. **Statement of Investments by and Distributions to Owners**

    (1) Shows capital transactions of entity which are increases and decreases in equity from transactions with owners during period

9. FS help users assess entity's liquidity, financial flexibility, profitability, and risk.

10. Full set of FS based on concept of financial capital maintenance—a return is achieved only after capital has been maintained or recovered.

C. Recognition criteria

1. Recognition is presentation of item in both words and numbers that is included in the totals of the financial statements (SFAC 6).

2. Item should meet four fundamental recognition criteria to be recognized

  a. **Definitions**—item is element of FS as defined by SFAC 6

  b. **Measurability**—item has a relevant attribute that is measurable with sufficient reliability

    (1) Five measurement attributes are used in current practice

      (a) Historical cost (historical proceeds)

      (b) Current (replacement) cost

      (c) Current market value

      (d) Net realizable (settlement) value

      (e) Present (discounted) value of future cash flows

    (2) Statement suggests that use of different attributes will continue

    (3) The monetary unit of measurement of nominal units of money is expected to continue to be used

  c. **Relevance**—item has capacity to make a difference in users' decisions (SFAC 2)

  d. **Reliability**—item is representationally faithful, verifiable, and neutral (SFAC 2)

    (1) Reliability may affect timing of recognition due to excessive uncertainties

    (2) A trade-off may sometimes be needed between relevance and reliability because waiting for complete reliability may make information untimely

D. Guidance in applying recognition criteria

1. Need to identify which cash-to-cash cycles are substantially complete

2. Degree of skepticism is needed (SFAC 2)

3. **Revenues and gains**

  a. Generally not recognized until realizable (SFAC 6)

    (1) Realizable means assets received or held are readily convertible to known amounts of cash or claims to cash

  b. Not recognized until earned (APB 4, SFAC 6)

4. **Expenses and losses**

  a. Generally recognized when economic benefits are consumed or assets lose future benefits

  b. Some expenses are recognized when associated revenues are recognized (e.g., cost of goods sold).

  c. Some expenses are recognized when cash is spent or liability incurred (e.g., selling and administrative salaries).

  d. Some expenses are allocated by systematic and rational procedures to periods benefited (e.g., depreciation and insurance).

E. Recognition of changes in assets and liabilities

1. Initial recognition generally based on current exchange prices at date of recognition

2. Changes can result from two types of events

  a. Inflows and outflows

  b. Changes in amounts which can be a change in utility or substance (e.g., depreciation) or changes in price

3. Current price information may only be used if it is reliable, cost justified, and more relevant than alternative information.

SFAC 6 Elements of Financial Statements
(Replaces SFAC 3)
A. Statement contains definitions of FS elements
    1. Definitions provide a significant first screen in determining content of FS.
        a. Possessing characteristics of a definition of an element is necessary but not sufficient condition for including an item in FS
        b. To qualify for inclusion in FS an item must
            (1) Meet recognition criteria (e.g., revenue recognition tests)
            (2) Possess a relevant attribute which can be measured reliably (e.g., historical cost/historical proceeds)
B. Elements of FS of both business enterprises and not-for-profit organizations
    1. **Assets** are probable future economic benefits controlled by a particular entity as a result of past transactions or events.
        a. Characteristics of assets
            (1) Probable future benefit by contribution to future net cash inflows
            (2) Entity can obtain and control access to benefit
            (3) Transaction or event leading to control has already occurred
        b. Asset continues as an asset until collected, transferred, used, or destroyed.
        c. Valuation accounts are part of related asset.
    2. **Liabilities** are probable future sacrifices of economic benefits, arising from present obligations of a particular entity that result from past transactions or events.
        a. Characteristics of liabilities
            (1) Legal, equitable, or constructive duty to transfer assets in future
            (2) Little or no discretion to avoid future sacrifice
            (3) Transaction or event obligating enterprise has already occurred
        b. Liability remains a liability until settled or discharged.
        c. Valuation accounts are part of related liability.
    3. **Equity** (net assets) is the owner's residual interest in the assets of an entity that remains after deducting liabilities.
        a. Business enterprises
            (1) Characteristics of equity
                (a) The source of distributions by enterprise to its owners
                (b) No unconditional right to receive future transfer of assets; depends on future profitability
                (c) Inevitably affected by enterprise's operations and circumstances affecting enterprise
            (2) Transactions or events that change owners' equity include revenues and expenses; gains and losses; investments by owners; distributions to owners; and changes within owners' equity (does not change total amount)
        b. Not-for-profit organizations
            (1) Characteristics of net assets (equity)
                (a) Absence of ownership interest
                (b) Operating purposes not centered on profit
                (c) Significant receipt of contributions, many involving donor-imposed restrictions
            (2) Classes of net assets
                (a) **Permanently restricted net assets** is the part of net assets of a not-for-profit organization resulting from
                    1] Contributions and other inflows of assets whose use by the organization is limited by donor-imposed stipulations that neither expire by passage of time nor can be fulfilled or otherwise removed by actions of the organization
                    2] Other asset enhancements and diminishments subject to same kinds of stipulations
                    3] Reclassifications from (or to) other classes of net assets as a consequence of donor-imposed stipulations
                (b) **Temporarily restricted net assets** is the part of net assets of a not-for-profit organization resulting from

        1] Contribution and other inflows of assets whose use by the organization is limited by donor-imposed stipulations that either expire by passage of time or can be fulfilled and removed by actions of the organization pursuant to those stipulations

        2] Other asset enhancements and diminishments subject to same kinds of stipulations

        3] Reclassifications to (or from) other classes of net assets as a consequence of donor-imposed stipulations, their expiration by passage of time, or their fulfillment and removal by actions of the organization pursuant to those stipulations

  (c) **Unrestricted net assets** is the part of net assets of a not-for-profit organization that is neither permanently restricted nor temporarily restricted by donor-imposed stipulations. They result from

        1] All revenues, expenses, gains, and losses that are not changes in permanently or temporarily restricted net assets and

        2] Reclassifications from (or to) other classes of net assets as a consequence of donor-imposed stipulations, their expiration by passage of time, or their fulfillment and removal by actions of the organization pursuant to those stipulations

  (3) Transactions and events that change net assets include revenues and expenses, gains and losses, and changes within net assets that do not affect assets or liabilities (including reclassifications between classes of net assets).

  (4) Changes in classes of net assets of not-for-profit organizations may be significant because donor-imposed restrictions may affect the types and levels of services that a not-for-profit organization can provide.

    (a) Characteristics of change in permanently restricted net assets

        1] Most increases in permanently restricted net assets are from accepting contributions of assets that donors stipulate must be maintained in perpetuity. Only assets that are not by their nature used up in carrying out the organization's activities are capable of providing economic benefits indefinitely. Gifts of cash, securities, and nonexhaustible property are examples.

    (b) Characteristics of change in temporarily restricted net assets

        1] Most increases in temporarily restricted net assets are from accepting contributions of assets that donors limit to use after specified future time or for specified purpose. Temporary restrictions pertain to contributions with donor stipulations that expire or can be fulfilled and removed by using assets as specified.

    (c) Characteristics of change in unrestricted net assets

        1] Change in unrestricted net assets for a period indicates whether organization has maintained the part of its net assets that is fully available (free of donor-imposed restrictions) to support the organization's services to beneficiaries in the next period.

4. **Revenues** are increases in assets or decreases in liabilities during a period from delivering goods, rendering services, or other activities constituting the entity's major or central operations.

  a. Characteristics of revenues

    (1) Accomplishments of the earning process

    (2) Actual or expected cash inflows resulting from central operations

    (3) Inflows reported gross

5. **Expenses** are decreases in assets or increases in liabilities during a period from delivery of goods, rendering of services, or other activities constituting the entity's major or central operations.

  a. Characteristics of expenses

    (1) Sacrifices involved in carrying out earnings process

    (2) Actual or expected cash outflows resulting from central operations

    (3) Outflows reported gross

6. **Gains (losses)** are increases (decreases) in equity from peripheral transactions of entity excluding revenues (expenses) and investment by owners (distribution to owners).

  a. Characteristics of gains and losses

    (1) Result from peripheral transactions and circumstances that may be beyond control

    (2) May be classified according to sources or as operating and nonoperating

    (3) Change in equity reported net

7. **Accrual accounting** and **related concepts** include

a. **Transaction**—external event involving transfer of something of value between two or more entities

b. **Event**—a happening of consequence to an entity (internal or external)

c. **Circumstances**—a set of conditions developed from events which may occur imperceptibly and create possibly unanticipated situations

d. **Accrual accounting**—recording "cash consequence" transactions as they occur rather than with movement of cash; deals with process of cash movement instead of beginning or end of process (per SFAC 1)

   (1) Based on cash and credit transactions, exchanges, price changes, changes in form of assets and liabilities

e. **Accrual**—recognizing revenues and related asset increases and expenses and related liability increases as they occur; expected future cash receipt or payment follows recognition of revenue (expense)

f. **Deferral**—recognizing liability for cash receipt with expected future revenue or recognizing asset for cash payment with expected future expense; cash receipt (payment) precedes recognition of revenues (expenses)

g. **Allocation**—process of assigning or distributing an amount according to a plan or formula

   (1) Includes amortization

h. **Amortization**—process of systematically reducing an amount by periodic payments or write-downs

i. **Realization**—process of converting noncash resources and rights into money; refers to sales of assets for cash or claims to cash

   (1) Realized—identifies revenues or gains or losses on assets sold

   (2) Unrealized—identifies revenues or gains or losses on assets unsold

j. **Recognition**—process of formally recording an item in financial statements

   (1) Major differences between accrual and cash basis accounting is timing of recognition of income items

k. **Matching**—simultaneous recognition of revenues with expenses which are related directly or jointly to the same transaction or events

C. Elements of FS exclusive to business enterprises

  1. **Investments by owners** are increases in net assets resulting from transfers by other entities of something of value to obtain ownership.

  2. **Distributions to owners** are decreases in net assets resulting from transferring assets, rendering services, or incurring liabilities by the enterprise to owners.

  3. **Comprehensive income** is the change in equity of an entity during a period from transactions and other events of nonowner sources (i.e., all equity amount changes except investment and distributions).

    a. Term "comprehensive" income is used instead of net earnings (net income) because the board is reserving "earnings" for a component part of comprehensive income yet to be determined.[5]

    b. Concept of capital maintenance or recovery of cost is needed in order to separate return **on** capital from return **of** capital.

    c. Financial capital maintenance concept vs. physical capital maintenance concept

      (1) Financial capital maintenance—objective is to maintain purchasing power

      (2) Physical capital maintenance—objective is to maintain operating capacity

    d. Comprehensive income is return on financial capital.

    e. Characteristics, sources, and components of comprehensive income include

      (1) Cash receipts (excluding owner investments) less cash outlays (excluding distributions to owners) over life of enterprise

        (a) Recognition criteria and choice of attributes to be measured affect timing, not amount.

      (2) Specific sources of income are

        (a) Transactions between enterprise and nonowners

        (b) Enterprise's productive efforts

---

[5] *Although SFAS 130 has defined comprehensive income as including net income plus other comprehensive income, it has not yet changed the components that comprise net income. Additionally, prior period adjustments are still reported in the retained earnings statement, not as comprehensive income.*

(c) Price changes, casualties, and other interactions with environment

 (3) **Earnings process** is the production and distribution of goods or services so firm can pay for goods and services it uses and provide return to owners.

 (4) Peripheral activities may also provide income.

 (5) Components of comprehensive income

  (a) Basic components—revenues, expenses, gains and losses

  (b) Intermediate components result from combining basic components

 (6) Display considerations (e.g., items included in operating income) are the subject of another SFAC.

SFAC 7 Using Cash Flow Information and Present Value in Accounting Measurements

A. Statement provides

 1. A framework for using future cash flows as the basis for accounting measurements

  a. At initial recognition

  b. In **fresh-start measurements**—measurements in period following initial recognition that establish a new carrying amount unrelated to previous amounts and accounting conventions.

  c. For the **interest method of allocation**—reporting conventions that use present value techniques in the absence of a fresh-start measurement to compute changes in the carrying amount of an asset or liability from one period to the next. Like depreciation and amortization conventions, interest methods are grounded in notion of historical cost.

 2. General principles that govern the use of present value

  a. Especially when uncertainties exist in

   (1) The amount of future cash flows

   (2) The timing of future cash flows, or

   (3) Both (1) and (2)

 3. Common understanding of objective of present value in accounting measurements

 4. **Guidance on measurement issues only—recognition issues are not addressed by SFAS 7.**

B. Statement does not specify when fresh-start measurements are appropriate

 1. FASB expects to decide whether a particular situation requires a fresh-start measurement (or some other accounting response) on a project-by-project basis.

C. Objective of present value in an accounting measurement is to capture, to the extent possible, the economic difference between sets of estimated cash flows

 1. Without present value, a $3,000 cash flow due tomorrow and a $3,000 cash flow due in fifteen years appear the same.

 2. Because present value distinguishes between cash flows that might otherwise appear similar, a measurement based on the present value of estimated future cash flows provides more relevant information than a measurement based on the undiscounted sum of those cash flows.

 3. A present value measurement that fully captures the economic differences between various sets of future cash flows would necessarily include the following elements:

  a. An estimate of the future cash flow (or in more complex cases, series of future cash flows at different times)

  b. Expectations about possible variations in the amount or timing of those cash flows

  c. The time value of money, represented by the risk-free rate of interest.

  d. The price for bearing the uncertainty inherent in the asset or liability.

  e. Other sometimes unidentifiable factors, including liquidity and market imperfections

D. To provide relevant information in financial reporting, present value must represent some observable measurement attribute of assets or liabilities.

 1. In the absence of observed transaction prices, accounting measurements at initial recognition and fresh-start measurements should attempt to capture the elements that taken together would comprise a market price if one existed, that is, fair value.

  a. The **fair value** of an asset (or liability) is the amount at which that asset or liability could be bought (or incurred) or sold (or settled) in a current transaction between willing parties.

 2. While the expectations of an entity's management are often useful and informative, the marketplace is the final arbiter of asset and liability values.

 3. The entity must pay the market's price when it acquires an asset or settles a liability in a current transaction, regardless of its intentions or expectations.

    4. For some assets and liabilities, management's estimates may be the only available information.

        a. In this case, the objective is to estimate the price likely to exist in the marketplace, if there were a marketplace.

E. The techniques used to estimate future cash flows and interest rates will vary from one situation to another depending on the circumstances surrounding the asset or liability in question. Certain general principles govern any application of present value techniques in measuring assets or liabilities.

    1. To the extent possible, estimated cash flows and interest rates should reflect assumptions about the future events and uncertainties that would be considered in deciding whether to acquire an asset or group of assets in an arm's-length transaction for cash.

    2. Interest rates used to discount cash flows should reflect assumptions that are consistent with those inherent in the estimated cash flows. Otherwise, the effect of some assumptions will be double-counted or ignored. For example, an interest rate of 12% might be applied to contractual cash flows of a loan. That rate reflects expectations about future defaults from loans with particular characteristics. That same 12% rate should not be used to discount expected cash flows because those cash flows already reflect assumptions about future defaults.

    3. Estimated cash flows and interest rates should be free from both bias and factors unrelated to the asset, liability, or group of assets or liabilities in question. For example, deliberately understating estimated net cash flows to enhance the apparent future profitability of an asset introduces bias into the measurement.

    4. Estimated cash flows or interest rates should reflect the range of possible outcomes rather than a single most-likely, minimum, or maximum possible amount.

F. An accounting measurement that uses present value should reflect the uncertainties inherent in the estimated cash flows. Otherwise items with different risks may appear similar.

G. Accounting applications of present value have typically used a single set of estimated cash flows and a single interest rate. SFAC 7 introduces the expected cash flow approach.

    1. The expected cash flow approach focuses on explicit assumptions about the range of possible estimated cash flows and their respective possibilities.

    2. The traditional approach treats those uncertainties implicitly in the selection of an interest rate.

    3. By incorporating a range of possible outcomes, the expected cash flow approach accommodates the use of present value techniques when the timing of cash flows is uncertain.

H. The measurement of liabilities involves different problems from the measurement of assets.

    1. The most relevant measurement of an entity's liabilities at initial recognition and fresh-start measurements should always reflect the credit standing of the entity.

I. Interest method of allocation

    1. Present value techniques are also used in periodic reporting conventions known collectively as **interest methods of allocation**.

    2. Financial statements usually attempt to represent the changes in assets and liabilities from one period to the next. By using current information and assumptions, fresh-start measurements capture all the factors that create change, including

        a. Physical consumption of assets (or reduction of liabilities)

        b. Changes in estimates, and

        c. Holding gains and losses that result from price changes

    3. Accounting allocations are planned approaches designed to represent only consumption or reduction.

    4. Changes in estimates may receive some recognition, but the effects of a change often have been spread over future periods.

    5. Holding gains and losses are generally excluded from allocation systems.

    6. In principle, the purpose of all accounting allocations is to report changes in the value, utility, or substance of assets and liabilities over time.

    7. Accounting allocations attempt to relate the change in an asset or liability to some observable real-world phenomenon.

        a. An interest method of allocation relates changes in the reported amount with changes in present value of a set of future cash flows.

    8. Allocation methods are only representations (not measurements) of an asset or liability.

9. While an interest method could be applied to any asset or liability, it is generally considered more relevant than other methods when applied to assets and liabilities that exhibit one or more of the following characteristics:
    a. The transaction giving rise to the asset or liability is commonly viewed as a borrowing or lending
    b. Period-to-period allocation of similar assets or liabilities employs an interest method
    c. A particular set of estimated future cash flows is closely associated with the asset or liability
    d. The measurement at initial recognition was based on present value
10. Like all allocation systems, the manner in which an interest method of allocation is applied can greatly affect the pattern of income or expense. In particular, the interest method requires a careful description of the following:
    a. The cash flows to be used (promised cash flows, expected cash flows, or some other estimate)
    b. The convention that governs the choice of an interest rate (effective rate or some other rate)
    c. How the rate is applied (constant effective rate or a series of annual rates)
    d. How changes in the amount or timing of estimated cash flows are reported
11. In most situations, the interest is based on contractual cash flows and assumes a constant effective interest rate over the life of those cash flows.
    a. That is, the method uses promised cash flows (rather than expected cash flows) and bases the interest rate on the single rate that equates the present value of the promised cash flows with the initial price of the asset or liability.
12. In reality, actual cash flows often occur sooner or later in greater or lesser amounts than expected. Changes from the original estimate of cash flows, in either timing or amount, can be accommodated in the interest amortization scheme or included in a fresh-start measurement of the asset or liability.
    a. Presently, the FASB doesn't address the conditions that might govern the choice between those two approaches.
13. If a change occurs in the amount or timing of estimated cash flows and the item is not remeasured, the interest amortization scheme must be altered to incorporate the new estimate of cash flows.
    a. The following techniques have been used to address the changes in estimated cash flows:
        (1) A prospective approach computes a new effective interest rate based on the carrying amount and remaining cash flows.
        (2) A catch-up approach adjusts the carrying amount to the present value of the revised estimated cash flows, discounted at the original effective interest rate.
        (3) A retrospective approach computes a new effective interest rate based on the original carrying amount, actual cash flows to date, and remaining estimated cash flows. The new effective interest rate is then used to adjust the carrying amount to the present value of the revised estimated cash flows, discounted at the new effective interest rate.
    b. The FASB considers the catch-up approach to be preferable to other techniques for reporting changes in estimated cash flows because
        (1) It is consistent with the present value relationships portrayed by the interest method, and
        (2) It can be implemented at a reasonable cost
        Under the catch-up approach, the recorded amount of an asset or liability (assuming estimated cash flows do not change) is the present value of the estimated future cash flows discounted at the original effective interest rate. If a change in estimate is effected through the catch-up approach, the measurement basis after the change will be the same as the measurement basis for the same asset or liability before the change in estimate (estimated cash flows discounted at the original effective rate).
    c. The prospective approach obscures the impact of changes in estimated cash flows and, as a result, produces information that is both less useful and less relevant. The interest rate that is derived under the prospective approach is unrelated to the rate at initial recognition or to current market rates for similar assets and liabilities. The amount that remains on the balance sheet can be described as "the unamortized amount," but no more.
    d. In some pronouncements, the retrospective approach has been used. Some consider it the most precise and complete of the three techniques listed above. However, the retrospective approach requires that entities retain a detailed record of all past cash flows. The costs of maintaining these detailed records usually outweigh any advantage provided by this approach.

EXAMINATION IN FINANCIAL ACCOUNTING AND REPORTING
(Business Enterprises)

NOTE TO CANDIDATES: *Information for Uniform CPA Examination Candidates*, published by the AICPA, states that candidates should allocate the total time for each examination section to the questions for that section in proportion to the point value given for the question. Thus, candidates should begin each examination session by calculating the estimated time to be spent on each question.

		Point *Value*
All questions are required:		
No. 1	....	60
No. 2	....	10
No. 3	....	10
No. 4	....	10
No. 5	....	10
	Total	100

Number 1

Select the **best** answer for each of the following items relating to a **variety of issues** in financial **accounting**.

1. Which of the following is considered a pervasive constraint by Statement of Financial Accounting Concepts 2?
- a. Benefits/costs.
- b. Conservatism.
- c. Timeliness.
- d. Verifiability.

2. Which of the following is **not** a comprehensive basis of accounting other than generally accepted accounting principles?
- a. Cash receipts and disbursements basis of accounting.
- b. Basis of accounting used by an entity to file its income tax return.
- c. Basis of accounting used by an entity to comply with the financial reporting requirements of a government regulatory agency.
- d. Basis of accounting used by an entity to comply with the financial reporting requirements of a lending institution.

3. How is compensation expense measured by public entities under SFAS 123?
- a. Measure the fair value of options using an option-pricing model.
- b. Measure the intrinsic value of options difference between market price and exercise price at measurement date.
- c. Use the normal hourly rate of the employees.
- d. Measure the difference between the market price and the fair value of the options.

4. Bear Co., which began operations on January 2, 2001, appropriately uses the installment method of accounting. The following information is available for 2001:

Installment sales	$4,400,000
Realized gross profit on installment sales	240,000
Gross profit percentage on sales	40%

For the year ended December 31, 2001, what amounts should Bear report as accounts receivable and deferred gross profit?

	Accounts receivable	*Deferred gross profit*
a.	$600,000	$320,000
b.	$600,000	$360,000
c.	$800,000	$320,000
d.	$800,000	$560,000

5. A temporary difference that could result in a deferred tax asset is
- a. Excess of tax depreciation over financial accounting depreciation.
- b. Excess of tax goodwill amortization over financial accounting write-off.
- c. Subscriptions received in advance.
- d. Interest revenue on municipal bonds.

6. When an investor accounts for investments in common stock at fair value, dividends received by the investor from the investee should normally be recorded as
- a. Dividend income.
- b. An addition to the investor's share of the investee profit.
- c. A deduction from the investor's share of the investee's profit.
- d. A deduction from the investment account.

7. Which of the following is not a derivative financial instrument?
- a. Interest rate and foreign currency swaps.
- b. Outstanding loan commitments written.
- c. Option contract.
- d. Trade accounts receivable.

8. Zap Company had three equity securities that it included in its trading portfolio on December 31, 2001. The market value of these securities was $125,000, and their acquisition cost was $115,000. What effect would there have been on Zap's total assets and total stockholders' equity on December 31, 2001, if these securities had been in Zap's available-for-sale portfolio instead of its trading portfolio?

	Total assets	*Total stockholders' equity*
a.	No effect	No effect
b.	No effect	Decrease
c.	Decrease	No effect
d.	No effect	Increase

9. How should the cash proceeds from convertible bonds sold at issue date at par be recorded?
- a. As additional paid-in capital for the portion of the proceeds attributable to the conversion feature and as a liability for the portion of the proceeds attributable to the debt.
- b. As retained earnings for the portion of the proceeds attributable to the conversion feature and as a liability for the portion of the proceeds attributable to the debt.
- c. As a liability for the entire proceeds.

d.   As additional paid-in capital for the portion of the proceeds attributable to the conversion feature and as retained earnings for the portion of the proceeds attributable to the debt.

10. A company's accounts receivable decreased from the beginning to the end of the year. In the company's statement of cash flows (operating activities shown using direct approach), the cash collected from customers would be

a.   Sales revenues plus accounts receivable at the beginning of the year.

b.   Sales revenues plus the decrease in accounts receivable from the beginning to the end of the year.

c.   Sales revenues less the decrease in accounts receivable from the beginning to the end of the year.

d.   The same as sales revenue.

11. During June 2001, Maxwell Corporation determined that actual costs incurred associated with the equipment used in its assembly line significantly exceeded original expected costs. At June 30, 2001, Maxwell had compiled the following information:

Original cost of the equipment	$800,000
Accumulated depreciation	$300,000
Expected net future cash inflows (undiscounted) related to the continued use and eventual disposal of the equipment	$450,000
Fair value of the equipment	$375,000

What is the amount of impairment loss that should be reported on Maxwell's income statement prepared for the period ended June 30, 2001?

a. $125,000
b. $350,000
c. $375,000
d. $50,000

12. Darnell Company reported a loss of $40,000 on its 2000 income statement related to long-lived assets that it expected to dispose of. On Darnell's December 31, 2000 balance sheet, these long-lived assets were reported at $200,000. During 2001, Darnell did not sell any of these long-lived assets, and at December 31, 2001, Darnell compiled the following information related to these assets that it still expects to dispose of:

Fair value	$220,000
Cost to sell	15,000

On Darnell's December 31, 2001 balance sheet, what amount should be reported for the long-lived assets expected to be disposed of?

a. $200,000.
b. $220,000.
c. $240,000.
d. $205,000.

13. An investor purchased a bond that is to be held to maturity between interest dates at a discount. At the purchase date, the carrying amount of the bond is more than the

	Cash paid to seller	Face amount of bond
a.	Yes	No
b.	Yes	Yes
c.	No	Yes
d.	No	No

Items 14 and 15 are based on the following:

A company buys ten shares of securities at $2,000 each on December 31, 1998. The securities are classified as available for sale. The fair value of the securities increases to $2,500 per share on December 31, 1999, and to $2,750 per share on December 31, 2000. On January 2, 2001, the company sells the securities. Assume no dividends are paid and that the company has a tax rate of 30%.

14. What is the amount of the unrealized holding gain arising during the period that is classified in other comprehensive income for the period ending December 31, 2000?

a. $0
b. $7,500
c. $2,500
d. $1,750

15. In 2000, what is the amount of the reclassification adjustment for other comprehensive income?

a. $ 7,500
b. $(7,500)
c. $ 5,250
d. $(5,250)

16. Huskie Corp. accounts for its compensatory stock option plan under APB 25. If the stock is issued before some or all of the services are performed, a part of the consideration recorded for the stock issued is unearned compensation and should be shown in the balance sheet as a line item in

a.   Noncurrent liabilities.
b.   Stockholders' equity.
c.   Current assets.
d.   Noncurrent assets.

17. On September 1, 2000, a company borrowed cash and signed a one-year interest-bearing note on which both the principal and interest are payable on September 1, 2001. How will the note payable and the related interest be classified in the December 31, 2000 balance sheet?

	Note payable	Accrued interest
a.	Current liability	Noncurrent liability
b.	Noncurrent liability	Current liability
c.	Current liability	Current liability
d.	Noncurrent liability	No entry

18. Smith Corp. owns only 25% of the voting stock of Jones Corp. but exercises significant influence over its operating and financial policies. The tax effect of differences between taxable income and the portion of pretax accounting income attributable to undistributed earnings of Jones Corp. that will be taxable in the future should be

a.   Accounted for as a temporary difference.
b.   Accounted for as a permanent difference.
c.   Ignored because it must be based on estimates and assumptions.
d.   Ignored because Smith holds less than 51% of the voting stock of Jones.

19. Barrett Co. maintains a defined benefit pension plan for its employees. At each balance sheet date, Barrett should report a minimum liability at least equal to the

a.   Accumulated benefit obligation.
b.   Projected benefit obligation.
c.   Unfunded accumulated benefit obligation.
d.   Unfunded projected benefit obligation.

20. In 2001, Wallace Corporation purchased marketable securities, and at December 31, 2001, had the following marketable equity securities:

		Cost	Market	Unrealized gain(loss)
Trading				
Security	X	$ 80,000	$ 50,000	$(30,000)
	Y	15,000	20,000	5,000
Totals		$ 95,000	$ 70,000	$(25,000)
Available-for-sale				
Security	Q	$ 60,000	$ 70,000	$ 10,000
	R	90,000	45,000	(45,000)
Totals		$150,000	$115,000	$(35,000)

As of December 31, 2001, the following amounts should be charged against

	Income	Other comprehensive income
a.	$0	$60,000
b.	$15,000	$0
c.	$25,000	$35,000
d.	$60,000	$0

21. Doe Corporation owned 1,000 shares of Spun Corporation. These shares were purchased in 1997 for $9,000. On September 15, 2001, Doe declared a property dividend of one share of Spun for every ten shares of Doe held by a stockholder. On that date, when the market price of Spun was $14 per share, there were 9,000 shares of Doe outstanding. What gain and net reduction in retained earnings would result from this property dividend?

	Gain	Net reduction in retained earnings
a.	$0	$ 8,100
b.	$0	$12,600
c.	$4,500	$ 3,600
d.	$4,500	$ 8,100

22. The Chance Company, a holding company, has two operating subsidiaries; one manufacturing wheelbarrows and the other manufacturing toothbrushes. The wheelbarrow subsidiary has been unprofitable, and in late December 2000, Chance contracted to sell that subsidiary to another company for $60,000. The sale will be effective on April 1, 2001. Chance will continue to operate the wheelbarrow subsidiary during the first three months of 2001, even though those operations are expected to result in a $10,000 loss (before income taxes) during that period.

At December 31, 2000, the carrying amount of Chance's investment in the wheelbarrow subsidiary is $100,000. Both the $40,000 loss on the sale of the investment and the $10,000 operating loss will be deductible on Chance's 2001 income tax return, resulting in an anticipated tax savings of $15,000 at an assumed 30% tax rate.

Chance's statement of income for its year ended December 31, 2000, should include a "loss on disposal of wheelbarrow subsidiary, net of applicable income tax benefit" in the amount of
- a. $0
- b. $28,000
- c. $35,000
- d. $ 7,000

23. The balance in Reed Company's accounts payable account at December 31, 2000, was $1,225,000 before the following information was considered:

- Goods shipped FOB destination on December 21, 2000, from a vendor to Reed were lost in transit. The invoice cost of $45,000 was not recorded by Reed. On December 28, 2000, Reed notified the vendor of the lost shipment.

- Goods were in transit from a vendor to Reed on December 31, 2000. The invoice cost was $60,000, and the goods were shipped FOB shipping point on December 28, 2000. Reed received the goods on January 6, 2001.

What amount should Reed report as accounts payable in its December 31, 2000 balance sheet?
- a. $1,330,000
- b. $1,285,000
- c. $1,270,000
- d. $1,225,000

24. Dee's inventory and accounts payable balances at December 31, 2000, increased over their December 31, 1999 balances. Should these increases be added to or deducted from cash payments to suppliers to arrive at 2000 cost of goods sold?

	Increase in inventory	Increase in accounts payable
a.	Added to	Deducted from
b.	Added to	Added to
c.	Deducted from	Deducted from
d.	Deducted from	Added to

25. The Ackley Company exchanged 100 shares of Burke Company common stock, which Ackley was holding as an investment, for a piece of equipment from the Flynn Company. The Burke Company common stock, which had been purchased by Ackley for $30 per share, had a quoted market value of $34 per share at the date of exchange. The piece of equipment had a recorded amount on Flynn's books of $3,100. What journal entry should Ackley have made to record this exchange?

		Debit	Credit
a.	Equipment	3,000	
	Investment in Burke Co. com. stk.		3,000
b.	Equipment	3,100	
	Investment in Burke Co. com. stk.		3,000
	Other income		100
c.	Equipment	3,100	
	Other expense	300	
	Investment in Burke Co. com. stk.		3,400
d.	Equipment	3,400	
	Investment in Burke Co. com. stk.		3,000
	Other income		400

26. Graf Corp.'s 2000 income statement showed pretax accounting income of $200,000. To compute the federal income tax liability, the following 2000 data are provided:

Income from exempt municipal bonds	$10,000
Depreciation deducted for tax purposes in excess of depreciation deducted for financial statement purposes	$20,000
Estimated federal income tax payments made	$40,000
Enacted corporate income tax rate	30%

If the alternate minimum tax provisions are ignored, what amount of current federal income tax liability should be included in Graf's December 31, 2000 balance sheet?
- a. $11,000
- b. $20,000
- c. $39,000
- d. $51,000

27. Haft Construction Co. has consistently used the percentage-of-completion method. On January 10, 1999, Haft began work on a $3,000,000 construction contract. At the inception date, the estimated cost of construction was $2,250,000. The following data relate to the progress of the contract:

Income recognized at 12/31/99	$ 300,000
Costs incurred 1/10/98 through 12/31/00	1,800,000
Estimated cost to complete at 12/31/00	600,000

In its income statement for the year ended December 31, 2000, what amount of gross profit should Haft report?

- a. $450,000
- b. $300,000
- c. $262,500
- d. $150,000

28. Howe Corporation bought a cola franchise from Pennington, Inc. on January 2, 2001, for $100,000. A highly regarded independent research company estimated that the remaining useful life of the franchise was fifty years. Its unamortized cost on Pennington's books at January 1, 2001, was $15,000. Howe has decided to write off the franchise over the longest possible period. How much should be amortized for the year ended December 31, 2001?

- a. $ 375
- b. $ 2,000
- c. $ 2,500
- d. $15,000

29. Fore Company had a $30,000 translation adjustment debit (the foreign currency is the functional currency) resulting from the translation of the accounts of its wholly owned foreign subsidiary for the year ended December 31, 2001. Fore also had a receivable from a foreign customer which was payable in the local currency of the foreign customer. On December 31, 2000, this receivable for 500,000 local currency units (LCU) was appropriately included in the accounts receivable section of Fore's balance sheet at $245,000. When the receivable was collected on February 5, 2001, the exchange rate was 2 LCU to $1. What amount should be included as an exchange gain or loss in the 2001 consolidated income statement of Fore Company and its wholly owned foreign subsidiary as a result of the above?

- a. $ 5,000 exchange gain.
- b. $20,000 exchange loss.
- c. $25,000 exchange loss.
- d. $30,000 exchange loss.

30. Orr Company had the following bank reconciliation at March 31, 2001:

Balance per bank statement, 3/31/01	$46,500
Add: Deposit in transit	10,300
	56,800
Less: Outstanding checks	12,600
Balance per books, 3/31/01	$44,200

Data per bank statement for the month of April 2001 follow:

Deposits	$58,400
Disbursements	49,700

All reconciliation items at March 31, 2001, cleared through the bank in April. Outstanding checks at April 30, 2001, totaled $7,500. What is the amount of cash disbursements per books in April?

- a. $44,600
- b. $49,700
- c. $54,800

- d. $57,200

31. Bell, Inc. owns 60% of Dart Corporation's common stock. On December 31, 2000, Dart is indebted to Bell for a $200,000 cash advance. In preparing the consolidated balance sheet at that date, what amount of the advance should be eliminated?

- a. $0
- b. $ 80,000
- c. $120,000
- d. $200,000

32. On October 1, 2000, Dean Company leased office space at a monthly rental of $30,000 for ten years expiring September 30, 2010. As an inducement for Dean to enter into the lease, the lessor permitted Dean to occupy the premises rent-free from October 1 to December 31, 2000. For the year ended December 31, 2000, Dean should record rent expense of

- a. $0
- b. $29,250
- c. $87,750
- d. $90,000

33. The following information pertains to Hay Corp. and its divisions for the year ended December 31, 2001:

Sales to unaffiliated customers	$1,000,000
Intersegment sales of products similar to those sold to unaffiliated customers	300,000
Interest earned on loans to other industry segments	20,000

Hay and all of its divisions are engaged solely in manufacturing operations. Hay has a reportable segment if that segment's revenue exceeds

- a. $100,000
- b. $102,000
- c. $130,000
- d. $132,000

34. On January 2, 2001, Amadeo Corporation entered into a ten-year noncancelable lease requiring year-end payments of $100,000. Amadeo's incremental borrowing rate is 12%, while the lessor's implicit interest rate, known to Amadeo, is 10%. Present value factors for an ordinary annuity for 10 periods are 6.14457 at 10% and 5.65022 at 12%. Ownership of the property remains with the lessor at expiration of the lease. There is no bargain purchase option. The leased property has an estimated economic life of twelve years. How much should be capitalized by Amadeo for this leased property?

- a. $0
- b. $ 565,022
- c. $ 614,457
- d. $1,000,000

35. On January 1, 1996, Darby Company purchased, at par, 500 of the $1,000 face value, 8% bonds of Clark Corporation as a held-to-maturity investment. The bonds mature on January 1, 2006, and pay interest semiannually on July 1 and January 1. Clark incurred heavy losses from operations for several years and defaulted on the July 1, 2000 and January 1, 2001 interest payments. Because of the permanent decline in market value of Clark's bonds, Darby wrote down its investment to $400,000 at December 31, 2000. Pursuant to Clark's plan of reorganization effected on July 1, 1995, Darby received 5,000 shares of $100 par value, 8% cumulative preferred stock of Clark in exchange for the $500,000 face value bond investment. The quoted market value of the preferred stock was $70 per share on July 1, 2001. What amount of loss should be included in the determination of Darby's net income for 2001?

a. $0
b. $ 50,000
c. $100,000
d. $150,000

Items 36 through 38 are based on the following:

Karl Corp.'s trial balance of income statement accounts for the year ended December 31, 2001, included the following:

	Debit	Credit
Sales		$150,000
Cost of sales	$ 60,000	
Administrative expenses	15,000	
Loss on sale of equipment	9,000	
Commissions to salespersons	10,000	
Interest revenue		5,000
Freight-out	3,000	
Loss on earthquake (unusual and infrequent)	10,000	
Bad debt expense	3,000	
Totals	$110,000	$155,000

Other information

Finished goods inventory:	
January 1, 2001	$100,000
December 31, 2001	$ 90,000

Karl's income tax rate is 30%.

On Karl's multiple-step income statement for 2001

36. Cost of goods manufactured is
a. $73,000
b. $70,000
c. $53,000
d. $50,000

37. Income before extraordinary item is
a. $55,000
b. $45,000
c. $38,500
d. $31,500

38. Extraordinary loss is
a. $ 7,000
b. $10,000
c. $13,300
d. $19,000

39. On the December 31, 2001 balance sheet of the Stat Company, the current assets were comprised of the following items:

Cash	$ 70,000
Accounts receivable	120,000
Inventories	60,000
	$250,000

An examination of the accounts revealed that the accounts receivable were composed of the following items:

Accounts receivable	
Trade accounts	$ 93,000
Allowance for uncollectible accounts	(2,000)
Claim against shipper for goods lost in transit (November 2001)	3,000
Selling price of unsold goods sent by Stat on consignment at 130% of cost (and not included in Stat's ending inventory)	26,000
	$120,000

What is the correct amount of current assets as of December 31, 2001?

a. $221,000
b. $224,000

c. $244,000
d. $250,000

40. On April 1, 2001, the Jack Company paid $800,000 for all the issued and outstanding common stock of Ann Corporation in a transaction properly accounted for as a purchase. The recorded assets and liabilities of Ann Corporation on April 1, 2001, follow:

Cash	$ 80,000
Inventory	240,000
Property and equipment (net of accumulated depreciation of $320,000)	480,000
Liabilities	(180,000)

On April 1, 2001, it was determined that the inventory of Ann had a fair value of $190,000, and the property and equipment (net) had a fair value of $560,000. What is the amount of goodwill resulting from the business combination?

a. $0
b. $ 50,000
c. $150,000
d. $180,000

41. Aprile Company had the following information for its noncontributory defined benefit pension plan on December 31, 2001:

Long-term expected rate of return	.08
Settlement basis discount rate	.08
Service cost	$ 60,000
Projected benefit obligation (1/1/01)	650,000
Fair value of plan assets (1/1/01)	300,000
Actual return on plan assets	60,000
Unamortized prior service cost	350,000
Average remaining service period	16 years

What is pension expense for December 31, 2001?

a. $ 72,000
b. $109,875
c. $111,333
d. $156,000

42. The following information is available from Sand Corp.'s accounting records for the year ended December 31, 2001:

Cash received from customers	$870,000
Rent received	10,000
Cash paid to suppliers and employees	510,000
Taxes paid	110,000
Cash dividends paid	30,000

Net cash flow provided by operations for 2001 was

a. $220,000
b. $230,000
c. $250,000
d. $260,000

43. On August 1, 2001, Winston Company reacquired 4,000 shares of its $15 par value common stock for $18 per share. Winston uses the cost method to account for treasury stock. What journal entry should Winston make to record the acquisition of treasury stock?

		Debit	Credit
a.	Treasury stock	60,000	
	Additional paid-in capital	12,000	
	Cash		72,000
b.	Treasury stock	60,000	
	Retained earnings	12,000	
	Cash		72,000

c.	Retained earnings	72,000	
	·Cash		72,000
d.	Treasury stock	72,000	
	Cash		72,000

44. If an enacted US income tax rate changes during the current period that affects future deductible and future taxable temporary differences that were tax-effected using a prior enacted rate, the effect of the rate change shall be recognized as a

   a. Prior period adjustment reported in retained earnings.
   b. Adjustment of deferred tax expense in the current period.
   c. Cumulative effect reported in net income.
   d. Adjustment of the current portion of income tax expense.

45. During 2001, Beck Co. purchased equipment for cash of $47,000, and sold equipment with a $10,000 carrying value for a gain of $5,000. How should these transactions be reported in Beck's 2001 statement of cash flows?

   a. Cash outflow of $32,000.
   b. Cash outflow of $42,000.
   c. Cash inflow of $5,000 and cash outflow of $47,000.
   d. Cash inflow of $15,000 and cash outflow of $47,000.

46. Redford Corporation's capital structure at December 31, 2000, was as follows:

Shares issued and outstanding
Common stock	100,000
Nonconvertible preferred stock	20,000

On July 1, 2001, Redford issued a 10% stock dividend on its common stock, and paid a cash dividend of $2.00 per share on its preferred stock. Net income for the year ended December 31, 2001, was $780,000. What should be Redford's 2001 earnings per common share?

   a. $6.73
   b. $7.05
   c. $7.09
   d. $7.80

47. Marshall Company prepared an aging of its accounts receivable at December 31, 2001, and determined that the net realizable value of the receivables at that date is $50,000. Additional information is available as follows:

Accounts receivable at December 31, 2000	$48,000
Accounts receivable at December 31, 2001	54,000
Allowance for doubtful accounts at December 31, 2000–credit balance	6,000
Accounts written off as uncollectible during 2001	5,000

Marshall's bad debt expense for the year ended December 31, 2001, was

   a. $3,000
   b. $4,000
   c. $5,000
   d. $7,000

48. How should the effect of a change in accounting principle that is inseparable from the effect of a change in accounting estimate be reported?

   a. As a component of income from continuing operations.

   b. By restating the financial statements of all prior periods presented.
   c. As a correction of an error.
   d. By footnote disclosure only.

49. On January 1, 2000, Purl Corp. purchased as a long-term investment $500,000 face value of Shaw, Inc.'s 8% bonds for $456,200. The bonds were purchased to yield 10% interest. The bonds mature on January 1, 2006, and pay interest annually on January 1. Purl uses the interest method of amortization. These bonds are to be held until maturity. What amount (rounded to nearest $100) should Purl report on its December 31, 2001 balance sheet for this long-term investment?

   a. $468,000
   b. $466,200
   c. $461,800
   d. $456,200

50. Bronson Apparel, Inc. operates a retail store and must determine the proper December 31, 2001 year-end accrual for the following expenses:

   • The store lease calls for fixed rent of $1,000 per month, payable at the beginning of the month, and additional rent equal to 6% of net sales over $200,000 per calendar year, payable on January 31 of the following year. Net sales for 2001 are $800,000.

   • Bronson has personal property subject to a city property tax. The city's fiscal year runs from July 1 to June 30 and the tax, assessed at 3% of personal property on hand at April 30, is payable on June 30. Bronson estimates that is personal property tax will amount to $6,000 for the city's. fiscal year ending June 30, 2002.

In its December 31, 2001 balance sheet, Bronson should report accrued expenses of

   a. $39,000
   b. $39,600
   c. $51,000
   d. $51,600

51. Denso Corporation reports on a calendar-year basis. Its December 31, 2001 financial statements were issued on February 3, 2002. The auditor's report was dated January 22, 2002. The following information pertains to an investment in Company Z carried as the sole available-for-sale security:

Cost	$500,000
Market value, 12/31/01	400,000
Market value, 1/22/02	350,000
Market value, 2/3/02	300,000

How much should be reported on Denso's balance sheet at December 31, 2001, for available-for-sale marketable equity securities?

   a. $500,000
   b. $400,000
   c. $350,000
   d. $300,000

52. On June 30, 2001, Rickert Corporation declared and issued a 10% common stock dividend. Prior to this dividend, Rickert had 10,000 shares of $5 par value common stock issued and outstanding. The market price of Rickert's common stock on June 30 was $12 per share. As a result of this stock dividend, by what amount should Rickert's total stockholders' equity increase (decrease)?

   a. $0
   b. $ 5,000

c. $ 7,000
d. $(12,000)

53. On January 1, 2001, Jaffe Corporation issued at 95, 500 of its 9%, $1,000 bonds. Interest is payable semiannually on July 1 and January 1, and the bonds mature on January 1, 2011. Jaffe paid bond issue costs of $20,000, which are appropriately recorded as a deferred charge. Jaffe uses the straight-line method of amortizing bond discount and bond issue costs. On Jaffe's December 31, 2001 balance sheet, the bonds payable should be reported at their carrying value of

   a. $459,500
   b. $477,500
   c. $495,500
   d. $522,500

54. On June 30, 2001, Gulch Corporation sold equipment to an unaffiliated company for $550,000. The equipment had a book value of $500,000 and a remaining useful life of ten years. That same day, Gulch leased back the equipment at $1,500 per month for two years with no option to renew the lease or repurchase the equipment. The present value of the lease payments using the appropriate rate of interest was $31,865 on June 30. Gulch's equipment rent expense for this equipment for the year ended December 31, 2001, should be

   a. $ 4,000
   b. $ 5,000
   c. $ 9,000
   d. $11,000

55. When a loan receivable is impaired but foreclosure is **not** probable, which of the following may the creditor use to measure the impairment?

  I. The loan's observable market price.
  II. The fair value of the collateral if the loan is collateral dependent.

   a.   I only.
   b.   II only.
   c.   Either I or II.
   d.   Neither I nor II.

56. Pacter Co., which makes some sales on an installment basis, earns a $300 pretax gross profit on each installment sale. For financial reporting purposes the entire $300 is recognized at the time of sale, but for income tax purposes the installment method of accounting is appropriately used.

    Assume Pacter makes one sale in 1999, another sale in 2000, and a third sale in 2001. In each case, one-third of the gross sales price is collected in the year of sale, one-third in the next year, and the final installment in the next year.

    Assuming an enacted income tax rate of 30% for 2001 and 35% for all subsequent years, the amount that should be shown on Pacter's December 31, 2001 balance sheet as a current deferred tax liability is

   a. $ 90
   b. $ 70
   c. $150
   d. $ 60

Items 57 and 58 are based on the following:

The following balance sheet is for the partnership of Able, Boyer, and Cain:

Cash	$ 20,000
Other assets	180,000
	$200,000
Liabilities	$ 50,000
Able, capital (40%)	37,000
Boyer, capital (40%)	65,000
Cain, capital (20%)	48,000
	$200,000

Figures shown parenthetically reflect agreed profit and loss sharing percentages.

57. If the assets are fairly valued on the above balance sheet and the partnership wishes to admit Day as a new one-sixth partner without recording goodwill or bonus, Day should contribute cash or other assets of

   a. $40,000
   b. $36,000
   c. $33,333
   d. $30,000

58. If assets on the initial balance sheet are fairly valued, Able and Boyer consent and Day pays Cain $51,000 for his interest; the revised capital balances of the partners would be

   a.   Able, $38,500; Boyer, $66,500; Day, $51,000.
   b.   Able, $38,500; Boyer, $66,500; Day, $48,000.
   c.   Able, $37,000; Boyer, $65,000; Day, $51,000.
   d.   Able, $37,000; Boyer, $65,000; Day, $48,000.

59. On July 1, 1999, Apgar Publishing, Inc. acquired the copyright to a book owned by Seaford Company for royalties of 20% of future sales. Royalties are payable semiannually on March 31 for sales in July through December of the preceding year, and on September 30 for sales in January through June of the same year. During 2000 and 2001, Apgar remitted the following royalty checks to Seaford:

	March 31	*September 30*
2000	$18,000	$21,000
2001	15,000	19,000

Apgar estimated that sales of the Seaford book would total $110,000 for the last half of 2001. How much royalty expense for this book should Apgar report in its 2001 income statement?

   a. $34,000
   b. $35,000
   c. $36,000
   d. $41,000

60. A company sold bonds on July 1, 2001, with a face value of $100,000 and due in ten years. The stated annual interest rate is 6%, payable semiannually on June 30 and December 31. These bonds were sold to yield 8%. The present value of $1 for 20 periods at 4% is 0.4563. The present value of an annuity of $1 in arrears for 20 periods at 4% is 13.5903. For how much did these bonds sell on July 1, 2001 (rounded to the nearest dollar)?

   a. $ 86,401
   b. $ 91,452
   c. $100,000
   d. $127,172

Number 2

Information pertaining to Blake Corporation's property, plant, and equipment for 2001 is presented below.

Account balances at January 1, 2001

	Debit	Credit
Land	$450,000	
Building	900,000	
Accumulated depreciation		$250,000
Machinery and equipment	900,000	
Accumulated depreciation		300,000
Automotive equipment	115,000	
Accumulated depreciation		85,000

Depreciation method and useful life

Building—150% declining balance; twenty-five years.
Machinery and equipment—Straight-line; ten years.
Automotive equipment—Sum-of-the-years' digits; four years.
Leasehold improvements—Straight-line.
The salvage value of the depreciable assets is immaterial.
Depreciation is computed to the nearest month.

Transactions during 2001 and other information

• On March 1, 2001, Blake purchased a new car for $8,000 cash and trade-in of a one-year-old car with a cost of $10,000 and a book value of $6,000. The new car has a cash price of $12,000; the market value of the trade-in is not known.

• Also, on March 1, 2001, a machine purchased for $24,000 on March 1, 1996, was destroyed by fire. Blake recovered $16,000 from its insurance company.

• On May 1, 2001, costs of $170,000 were incurred to improve leased office premises. The leasehold improvements have a useful life of eight years. The related lease, which terminates on December 31, 2007, is renewable for an additional six-year term. The decision to renew will be made in 2007 based on office space needs at that time.

• On July 1, 2001, machinery and equipment were purchased at a total invoice cost of $280,000; additional costs of $5,000 for freight and $15,000 for installation were incurred.

• Blake determined that the automotive equipment comprising the $115,000 balance at January 1, 2001, would have been depreciated at a total amount of $17,500 for the year ended December 31, 2001.

Required:

Items 101 through 110 require the computation of numerical answers.

101. Implied fair market value of the old car traded in.

102. Gain (loss) on the March 1, 2001 trade-in of automotive equipment.

103. Gain (loss) on the insurance recovery for the machine destroyed by fire on March 1, 2001.

104. Amortization expense for the year ended December 31, 2001, for leasehold improvements.

105. Machinery and equipment additions during the year ended December 31, 2001.

106. Balance of Automotive equipment account at December 31, 2001.

107. Depreciation expense for the year ended December 31, 2001, for new equipment purchases.

108. Balance of the Building account at December 31, 2001.

109. Balance of the Accumulated depreciation on building account at December 31, 2001.

110. Balance of the Accumulated depreciation on machinery and equipment at December 31, 2001.

Number 3

Question number 3 consists of 10 items to be reported on Chem Co.'s 2001 financial statements. **Answer all items.** Your grade will be based on the total number of correct answers.

Items 111 through 118 are based on the following:

• Accounts receivable at December 31, 2000, were $100,000 before allowance for uncollectible accounts of $10,000. Sales to customers on account (excluding credit card sales) during 2001 were $1,810,000, and collections from customers, excluding recoveries, totaled $1,795,000. During 2001 accounts receivable of $45,000 were written off and $17,000 were recovered. An aging of the accounts receivable at December 31, 2001, indicated that $15,000 may be uncollectible.

• Chem accepts credit cards for payments of sales, and deposits the credit card slips in the bank, which credits Chem's account with the amount of the sale less a 4% commission. For 2001 credit card sales, Chem received proceeds of $600,000, net of commission.

• During 2001 Chem was involved in a tax dispute with the IRS. At December 31, 2001, Chem's tax advisor believed that an unfavorable outcome was probable. A reasonable estimate of additional tax payments was between $45,000 and $95,000, but $60,000 was the best estimate in that range.

• During 2001 Chem transferred $50,000 of accounts receivable to Jones Bank for $45,500. The factor's holdback is $1,500, the financing fee is $3,000, and the recourse obligation is $2,000. Control over the receivables was surrendered by Chem.

    • On July 1, 2001, Chem issued an 8%, $1,000,000 bond at a discount of $160,000 to yield 10%. The bond is due on June 30, 2016, and pays interest annually on June 30. Chem applies the effective interest method on an annual basis to amortize the discount.

    • On September 1, 2001, Chem entered into a foreign exchange contract for speculative purposes by purchasing 50,000 deutsche marks for delivery in sixty days. The rates to exchange $1 for one deutsche mark follow:

	9/1/01	9/30/01
Spot rate	.75	.70
30-day forward rate	.73	.72
60-day forward rate	.74	.73

Required:

    Items 111 through 118, determine the amount to be reported in Chem's 2001 financial statements.

111. Accounts receivable (excluding credit card sales).

112. Allowance for uncollectible accounts.

113. Uncollectible accounts expense.

114. Credit card commission expense.

115. Estimated liability for tax assessment.

116. Gain or loss on transfer of accounts receivable.

117. Bond interest payable.

118. Forward exchange contract loss.

Number 4

The following trial balance of Garr Corporation at December 31, 2001, has been adjusted except for income tax expense.

Garr Corporation
TRIAL BALANCE
December 31, 2001

	Dr.	Cr.
Cash	$ 635,000	
Accounts receivable, (net)	1,697,000	
Inventory	2,185,000	
Property, plant, and equipment (net)	8,660,000	
Accounts payable and accrued liabilities		$ 1,897,000
Income tax payable		360,000
Deferred income tax		285,000
Common stock		2,300,000
Additional paid-in capital		3,675,000
Retained earnings, 1/1/01		3,350,000
Net sales		10,750,000
Cost of sales	5,920,000	
Selling and administrative expenses	2,600,000	
Interest income		65,000
Gain on litigation settlement		200,000
Depreciation adjustment from accounting change	350,000	
Income tax expense	835,000	
	$22,882,000	$22,882,000

Other financial data for the year ended December 31, 2001:

Income tax expense

Estimated tax payments	$475,000
Accrued	360,000
Total charged to income tax expense (estimated)	$835,000
Tax rate on all types of income	40%

Gain from litigation settlement is a taxable gain and is not considered infrequent.

The $835,000 does not properly reflect current or deferred income tax expense or intraperiod income tax allocation for financial statement purposes.

Temporary differences

Depreciation per tax return	$750,000
Depreciation per financial statements (excluding cumulative effect of accounting change)	$575,000

Change in depreciation method

On January 1, 2001, Garr changed to the 150% declining balance method from the straight-line method of depreciation for certain of its plant assets. The pretax cumulative effect of this accounting change was determined to be a charge of $350,000. There was no change in depreciation method for income tax purposes.

Capital structure

Common stock, $10 par, traded on a national exchange

	Shares
Outstanding at 1/1/01	200,000
Issued on 7/1/01 at a 15% stock dividend	30,000
	230,000

Required:

Using the multiple-step format, prepare a formal income statement for Garr for the year ended December 31, 2001. All components of income tax expense should be appropriately shown.

Number 5

Hanlon Company purchased a significant amount of raw materials inventory for a new product that it is manufacturing. Hanlon purchased insurance on these raw materials while they were in transit from the supplier.

Hanlon uses the lower of cost or market rule for these raw materials. The replacement cost of the raw materials is above the net realizable value and both are below the original cost.

Hanlon uses the average cost inventory method for these raw materials. In the last two years, each purchase has been at a lower price than the previous purchase, and the ending inventory quantity for each period has been higher than the beginning inventory quantity for that period.

Required:

a. What is the theoretically appropriate method that Hanlon should use to account for the insurance costs on the raw materials while they were in transit from the supplier? Why?

b. 1. At which amount should Hanlon's raw materials inventory be reported on the balance sheet? Why?
2. In general, why is the lower of cost or market rule used to report inventory?

c. What would have been the effect on ending inventory and cost of goods sold had Hanlon used the LIFO inventory method instead of the average cost inventory method for the raw materials? Why?

ANSWERS TO SAMPLE EXAMINATION
FINANCIAL ACCOUNTING AND REPORTING
(Business Enterprises)

Answer 1

1. a	11. a	21. d	31. b	41. b	51. b
2. d	12. d	22. c	32. c	42. d	52. a
3. a	13. d	23. b	33. c	43. d	53. b
4. c	14. d	24. d	34. c	44. b	54. c
5. c	15. d	25. d	35. b	45. d	55. c
6. a	16. b	26. a	36. d	46. a	56. c
7. d	17. c	27. d	37. c	47. a	57. d
8. a	18. a	28. d	38. a	48. a	58. d
9. c	19. c	29. a	39. c	49. a	59. d
10. b	20. c	30. a	40. c	50. a	60. a

Hints for Multiple-Choice Questions

1. This constraint allows an efficient allocation of resources within society.

2. What is the significance of an individual lender?

3. No tricks on this one.

4. What was total gross profit on 2001 sales?

5. A deferred tax asset is defined as an increase in taxes refundable in future years as a result of deductible **temporary** differences existing at the end of the current year.

6. As the investments are accounted for at fair value, the investor has a holding of less than 20% in the entity.

7. Derivatives derive value from an underlying asset or are tied to an index.

8. For a trading portfolio, where does the amount recognized in income end up on the balance sheet?

9. The conversion feature does not change the nature of the bond.

10. The direct method adjusts each income statement item from the accrual to the cash basis.

11. No tricks on this one.

12. What was the carrying value before recognizing the loss?

13. A discount decreases the carrying amount of a bond that is held to maturity.

14. The required amount is a single year change.

15. The reclassification adjustment is a cumulative amount.

16. The amount representing deferred compensation expense is a contra account.

17. Current liabilities mature within one year or within the operating cycle, whichever is longer. Long-term liabilities are all other liabilities that are not current.

18. Compare the net income ramifications to Smith Corp. of the equity method as applied to accounting income and the appropriate recognition criteria as applied to taxable income.

19. The fair value of plan assets is compared to the accumulated benefit obligation to determine whether a plan is properly funded.

20. Holding gains and losses are treated differently for trading and available-for-sale securities.

21. Nonreciprocal transfers of nonmonetary assets between an enterprise and its owners require gain or loss recognition.

22. Apply a conservative position in loss recognition.

23. Liabilities are recorded at time of title passage.

24. More goods were purchased than sold, and payments to suppliers were less than purchases.

25. The exchange of nonmonetary assets is accounted for through use of the fair value of the asset given up or the fair value of the asset received, whichever is more clearly evident.

26. Accounting income is reconciled to taxable income by adjusting the effects of temporary and permanent differences.

27. Income calculated using the cost-to-cost ratio is a cumulative amount.

28. Amortization of the cost of a franchise should be over its estimated useful life.

29. Consider the difference between transaction and translation gains and losses and where they are reported.

30. Determine to which period each cash disbursement belongs.

31. In consolidation the two entities are treated as one; the assets and liabilities are added together.

32. Divide the rent paid over the entire lease period.

33. Segment revenue includes both sales to unaffiliated customers and intersegment sales of products.

34. The key is that the lessor's implicit interest rate is known.

35. Use the fair value of the cumulative preferred stock to compute the loss in 2001.

36. Cost of goods manufactured is a subcomponent of cost of goods sold.

37. Income before extraordinary item includes income tax expense for 2001.

38. Extraordinary items are presented under net income before extraordinary items, which has accounted for income tax expense.

39. Consider where the consignment goods should be classified and at what value.

40. In a purchase transaction, assets acquired are properly recorded at their FMV.

41. Amortization of PSC, service cost (current year), interest on liability, actual return on plan assets, and gain/loss are all components of pension expense.

42. Operating activities involve the cash effects of transactions that enter into the determination of net income.

43. View this acquisition as the first step of a two-part transaction.

44. What does the rate change relate to?

45. No tricks here.

46. Compute the weighted-average of common shares outstanding for the year.

47. Use T-accounts to follow the transactions affecting accounts receivable and allowance for doubtful accounts.

48. No tricks here.

49. Must do amortization for two years.

50. Accrue the expenses in the year in which they occur, not in the year in which cash is paid.

51. Market value for available-for-sale securities is properly measured at the balance sheet date.

52. A dividend is a distribution of retained earnings.

53. Treat the bond issue costs as a deferred charge.

54. Review the criteria for the three categories of sales-leaseback transactions. Then record rent expense in 2001.

55. What makes sense?

56. The current deferred tax liability represents the amount of the temporary difference that will reverse in 2002.

57. Consider the existing partners' capital balances (book value) and disregard the fair value of the assets.

58. This is a personal transaction between two individuals.

59. Consider when the expense is incurred rather than when it is paid.

60. Use the actual interest payments rather than the effective yield in calculating the present value of the bonds.

Answer 2

101.	$ 4,000	106.	$117,000
102.	$ (2,000); Loss	107.	$ 15,000
103.	$ 4,000; Gain	108.	$900,000
104.	$ 17,000	109.	$289,000
105.	$300,000	110.	$391,000

Hints for Other Objective Answer Format Questions

101. Disregard the old car's BV in determining its FV.

102. Compare the FMV and BV of the old car to determine the gain (loss).

103. Compute the BV of the machine as of the date of destruction.

104. Leasehold improvements are amortized over the remaining life of the lease or the useful life of the improvements, whichever is shorter.

105. Historical cost for machinery and equipment is measured by the cash or cash equivalent price of obtaining an asset and readying it for its intended use.

106. Record the impacts of the similar asset exchange at the beginning of the year.

107. Calculate depreciation from the **acquisition** date.

108. No tricks here.

109. Apply the 150% declining balance method.

110. Calculate the depreciation effects for the machinery added and subtracted from the account and for the remaining balance of the asset account.

Answer Explanations

101. (**$4,000**) The exchange of cars on March 1, 2001, resulted in a loss on disposal. Per APB 29, this loss should be recognized even though the exchange involves similar productive assets. The gain or loss is the difference between the FMV of the old car and its BV. The old auto was traded with $8,000 cash for a new auto with a cash value of $12,000, so the implied FMV of the old car is $4,000 ($12,000 – $8,000).

102. (**[$2,000]; Loss**) The old auto was one year old (i.e., purchased 3/1/00). Accumulated depreciation on this car at the time of sale was $4,000 ($10,000 cost – ? Accumulated depreciation = $6,000 Book value). Therefore, the exchange results in a loss on disposal of $2,000.

	1-Year-old car		
FMV		BV	Gain/(loss)
$12,000		$10,000	
(8,000)		(4,000)	
$ 4,000	–	$ 6,000	= $(2,000)

The journal entry is

Loss on disposal	2,000	
Car (new)	12,000	
Accumulated depreciation	4,000	
Car (old)		10,000
Cash		8,000

103. (**$4,000; Gain**) The insurance proceeds from the destroyed machine total $16,000. The machine was in service for five years (3/1/96 – 3/1/01) of its ten-year useful life. Using the straight-line method with no salvage value, the book value of the machine at the time of the fire was $12,000 (5/10 x $24,000). Therefore, the gain on disposal is $4,000 ($16,000 – $12,000).

104. (**$17,000**) The leasehold improvement costs were incurred on 5/1/01. These costs should be amortized over the **shorter** of the remaining lease life (eighty months) or the useful life of the improvements (eight years or ninety-six months). The lease term should **not** include the option period unless renewal is relatively certain. Therefore, 2001 amortization expense is 8/80 of $170,000, or $17,000.

105. (**$300,000**) The machinery and equipment account was increased by $300,000 on July 1 from the purchase. This cost includes all expenditures necessary to acquire the equipment and prepare it for use: invoice cost ($280,000), freight costs ($5,000), and installation costs ($15,000), for a total of $300,000.

106. (**$117,000**) The automotive equipment was reported at $115,000 at 1/1/01. This amount must be reduced by the cost of the car traded in ($10,000) and increased by the cost of the new car acquired ($12,000), resulting in a 12/31/01 balance of $117,000.

107. (**$15,000**) As discussed in item 65 above, the additions to Machinery and equipment during 2001 were $300,000. 2001 depreciation expense is computed using the straight-line method for 1/2 year (the assets were purchased July 1, 2001). $300,000 x 6/12 x 1/10 = $15,000.

108. (**$900,000**) No 2001 transactions affected the building account; it will still be reported at $900,000 on 12/31/01.

109. (**$289,000**) The 1/1/01 balance of accumulated depreciation (building) is $250,000. Depreciation is computed using the 150% declining balance method. Using this method, depreciation expense is computed by multiplying the beginning of the year book value ($900,000 – 250,000 = $650,000) by 150% of the straight-line rate (1/25 x 150% = 6%). This results in 2001 depreciation expense of $39,000 and 12/31/01 accumulated depreciation of $289,000 ($250,000 + $39,000).

110. (**$391,000**) The 1/1/01 balance of accumulated depreciation (machinery and equipment) is $300,000. 2001 depreciation (straight-line method) must be computed in three parts: on the machine destroyed by fire ($24,000 x 1/10 x 2/12 = $400), on the remainder of the equipment owned at 1/1/01 [($900,000 – $24,000) x 1/10 = $87,600], and on the new equipment purchased [($280,000 + $5,000 + $15,000) x 1/10 x 6/12 = $15,000]. The 12/31/01 balance of accumulated depreciation is $391,000. This is computed by taking the beginning balance ($300,000), adding 2001 depreciation expense ($400 + $87,600 + $15,000 = $103,000), and subtracting the accumulated depreciation taken off the books for the destroyed machine ($24,000 x 5/10 = $12,000).

Answer 3

111. $20,000	115. $60,000
112. $15,000	116. $ 6,500
113. $33,000	117. $40,000
114. $25,000	118. $ 1,000

Hints for Other Objective Answer Format Questions

111. Set up a T-account for AR.

112. What are the differences between the percentage of sales method and the aging method of determining uncollectible accounts expense?

113. What are the differences between the percentage of sales method and the aging method of determining uncollectible accounts expense?

114. No tricks here.

115. No tricks here.

116. What are the two components of the loss?

117. Which rate is used to calculate interest payments?

118. No tricks here.

Answer Explanations

111. (**$20,000**) The accounts receivable balance Chem Co. will report is $20,000. There is a beginning debit balance of $100,000. Recoveries would result in a debit to accounts receivable and a credit to the allowance account followed by a debit to cash and a credit to accounts receivable. During the year, sales on account would be recorded by debiting accounts receivable and crediting sales for $1,810,000. When payments are received on account, Chem Co. will debit cash and credit accounts receivable for $1,795,000. Proper write-off of accounts receivable is done under the allowance method. The proper entry to record the write-off is as follows:

Allowance for doubtful accounts	45,000	
Accounts receivable		45,000

Finally, Chem transferred $50,000 of accounts receivable during 2001. $20,000 is calculated by subtracting the total credits ($17,000 + $1,795,000 + $45,000 + $50,000 = $1,907,000) from the total debits ($100,000 + $17,000 + $1,810,000 = $1,927,000).

	Accounts receivable		
1/1/01	100,000	17,000	recoveries
reinstatements	17,000	1,795,000	collections
of sales	1,810,000	45,000	write-offs
		50,000	transferred receivables
12/31/01	20,000		

112. ($15,000) An aging for accounts receivable at year-end calculates the required amount in the allowance account by applying different percentages based on past experience to various age categories. In this case, Chem Co. has calculated that $15,000 may be uncollectible. This should be the balance in the allowance account after adjustment.

113. ($33,000) Uncollectible accounts expense is calculated in a two-step approach. The first step is to calculate the preadjustment balance of the allowance for doubtful accounts. This is done by adding the beginning balance of the allowance account to any recoveries less the write-offs ($10,000 + $17,000 – $45,000 = –$18,000). Next, uncollectible accounts expense is calculated as the difference between the desired ending allowance for uncollectible accounts balance and the preadjustment balance [$15,000 – (–$18,000) = $33,000].

	Allowance		
		10,000	1/1/01
write-offs	45,000	17,000	2001 recoveries
12/31/01 before adjustment	18,000		
		33,000	Uncollectible accounts expense
	20,000	15,000	

114. ($25,000) $25,000 is the credit card commission expense. Chem Co. receives $600,000 net of the 4% commissions. To calculate the total commissions, divide $600,000 by one minus the commission rate ($600,000 ÷ $.96 = $625,000). The amount of commission expense is $25,000 ($625,000 – $600,000).

115. ($60,000) Chem Co.'s contingent liability for tax assessment is both probable and reasonably estimable. The amount to accrue is the best estimate within the range, $60,000.

116. ($6,500) The transfer should be recognized as a sale because control was surrendered. The loss on the sale of accounts receivable is $6,500 [($50,000 – $45,500) + $2,000]. The sale would be recorded as follows:

Cash	44,000	
Factor's holdback	1,500	
Loss	6,500	
Accounts receivable		50,000
Recourse obligation		2,000

117. ($40,000) Bond interest payable should be recorded as interest due from the bond date (7/1/01) to the year-end (12/31/01). This amount is one-half of the cash interest to be paid 6/30/02. Interest payable is calculated as the face value ($1,000,000 multiplied by the stated (cash) rate (8%) times the time period (6/12 months). Therefore, bond interest payable is $40,000 ($1,000,000 x 8% x 6/12).

118. ($1,000) When speculating in foreign currency, both the fixed liability/receivable and the foreign currency receivable/payable are recorded in dollars using the **forward rate** rather than the spot rate. At 9/1/01, the sixty-day forward rate is $.74, so the transaction is recorded at $37,000 (50,000 x $.74). At an intervening balance sheet date, the foreign currency receivable/payable is adjusted to reflect the new forward rate and any resulting gain or loss is included in the income statement. At 9/30/01, thirty days have gone by, so the thirty-day forward rate is used rather than the sixty-day rate, so the foreign currency receivable is adjusted to $36,000 (50,000 x $.72) and a loss of $1,000 is recognized ($37,000 – $36,000). The entries are

9/1	FC receivable	37,000	
	Liability to FC dealer		37,000
9/30	Forward contract loss	1,000	
	FC receivable		1,000

Answer 4

Garr Corporation
INCOME STATEMENT
For the Year Ended December 31, 2001

Net sales			$10,750,000
Cost of sales			5,920,000
Gross profit			4,830,000
Selling and administrative expenses			2,600,000
Operating income			2,230,000
Other income or gain			
Interest income	65,000		
Gain on litigation settlement	200,000		265,000
Income before income tax and cumulative effect of a change in accounting principle			2,495,000
Income tax			
Current	$928,000	[1]	
Deferred	70,000	[2]	998,000
Income before cumulative effect of a change in accounting principle			1,497,000
Cumulative effect on prior years of changing to a different depreciation method (less applicable deferred income tax of $140,000)			(210,000) [3]
Net income			$ 1,287,000
Basic earnings per share			
Income before cumulative effect			$6.51 [4]
Cumulative effect on prior years of changing to a different depreciation method			(0.91) [5]
Net income			$5.60 [6]

Explanations of amounts:

[1] Total income tax for 2001 excluding cumulative effect of accounting change

Income before income tax and accounting change	$2,495,000
Less:	
Excess tax depreciation	175,000
(See [2])	$2,320,000
Income tax rate	x 40%
Current portion of income taxes	$ 928,000

[2] Deferred income tax expense for 2001

Depreciation per tax return	$750,000
Less depreciation per books	575,000
Temporary difference	175,000
Income tax rate	x 40%
Deferred income tax expense	$ 70,000

[3] Cumulative effect of changing to a different depreciation method

Depreciation adjustment–accounting change	$ 350,000
Reduction in deferred income tax ($350,000 x 40%)	140,000
Net of income tax	$ 210,000

[4] Basic earnings per share–income before cumulative effect

Income before cumulative effect	$1,497,000
Weighted-average number of shares outstanding for 2001 (200,000 + 30,000)	230,000
Earnings per share ($1,497,000 ÷ 230,000)	$6.51

[5] Basic earnings per share–cumulative effect on prior years of changing to a different depreciation method

Cumulative effect	$ (210,000)
Weighted-average number shares	230,000
Earnings per share	$(0.91)

[6] Basic earnings per share–Net income

Net income	$1,287,000
Weighted-average number of shares	230,000
Earnings per share	$5.60

Answer 5

a. The insurance costs on the raw materials while they were in transit from the supplier should be accounted for as part of inventory. Theoretically, insurance cost on raw materials in transit is a cost associated with readying the goods for sale.

b. 1. Hanlon's inventory should be reported at net realizable value. According to the lower of cost or market rule, market is defined as replacement cost. However, market cannot exceed net realizable value. In this instance, net realizable value is below original cost.

    2. The lower of cost or market rule is used to report the inventory in the balance sheet at its future utility value. It also recognizes a decline in the utility of inventory in the income statement in the period in which the decline occurs.

c. Generally, ending inventory would have been higher and cost of goods sold would have been lower had Hanlon used the LIFO inventory method. Inventory quantities increased and LIFO associates the oldest purchase prices with inventory. However, in this instance, there would have been no effect on ending inventory or cost of goods sold had Hanlon used the LIFO inventory method, because Hanlon's ending inventory would have been reported at net realizable value according to the lower of cost or market rule. Net realizable value of the inventory is less than either its average cost or LIFO cost.

APPENDIX B

AICPA Summary of Exam Coverage (Last 6 Exams) from the Financial Accounting and Reporting (FARE) Section of the Uniform CPA Examination[1]

Summary of Exam Coverage—May 1999 through November 2001 Uniform CPA Examinations

The following summary of coverage provides an analysis of the Content Specification Outline coverage for the May 1999 through November 2001 FARE section of the Uniform CPA Examinations. This summary is intended only as a study aid and should not be used to predict the content of future Examinations.

How to interpret this table

The percentages on the third line of the table indicate the percentage points allocated to each type of question on these Examinations. For example, on the May 1999 Financial Accounting and Reporting section (FARE), 60% of the examination points were allocated to multiple-choice questions, 20% of the points were allocated to other objective answer format (OOAF), and 20% of the points were allocated to the essays.

The AICPA has also provided the **actual number** of multiple-choice questions asked for each area (identified with a roman numeral) and topic (identified with an uppercase letter) of the content specification outlines; (e.g., for the May 1999 Examination, there were seven multiple-choice questions asked in Area I that were distributed among topics A-D). In addition, the AICPA has indicated the **percentage** of OOAF and essay questions asked by area and topic.

---

[1] These Content Specification Outlines were published in *Selected Questions and Unofficial Answers Supplement Indexed to Content Specification Outlines* (2001 Edition); reprinted with permission of the AICPA.

Financial Accounting and Reporting	Multiple-Choice						OOAFs						Essays					
	N01	M01	N00	M00	N99	M99	N01	M01	N00	M00	N99	M99	N01	M01	N00	M00	N99	M99
	60 (60%)	60 (60%)	60 (60%)	60 (60%)	60 (60%)	60 (60%)	20%	20%	20%	20%	20%	20%	20%	20%	20%	20%	20%	20%
I. Concepts and Standards for Financial Statements	20	10	5	13	5	7			10%	2%	10%	5%		10%	5%	5%	5%	8%
A. Financial Accounting Concepts					1	0												4%
B. Financial Accounting Standards for Presentation and Disclosure in General-Purpose Financial Statements					0	5					10%	5%					5%	4%
C. Other Presentations of Financial Data					4	2												
D. Financial Statement Analysis					0	0												
II. Recognition, Measurement, Valuation, and Presentation of Typical Items in Financial Statements in Conformity with Generally Accepted Accounting Principles	20	20	25	22	25	22	10%	10%	0%	8%	10%	10%	10%	10%	15%	0%	5%	8%
A. Cash, Cash Equivalents, and Marketable Securities					2	2												
B. Receivables					0	2					5%							
C. Inventories					3	1						5%						
D. Property, Plant, and Equipment					3	2												
E. Investments					2	1												
F. Intangibles and Other Assets					0	1											5%	
G. Payables and Accruals					2	1												
H. Deferred Revenues					2	1												
I. Notes and Bonds Payable					2	2												
J. Other Liabilities					2	3												
K. Equity Accounts					3	2						5%						
L. Revenue, Cost, and Expense Accounts					4	4					5%							8%

Financial Accounting and Reporting	Multiple-Choice						OOAFs						Essays					
	N01	M01	N00	M00	N99	M99	N01	M01	N00	M00	N99	M99	N01	M01	N00	M00	N99	M99
III. Recognition, Measurement, Valuation, and Presentation of Specific Types of Transactions and Events in Financial Statements in Conformity with Generally Accepted Accounting Principles	20	30	30	25	30	31	10%	10%	10%	10%	0%	5%	10%		0%	15%	10%	4%
A. Accounting Changes and Corrections of Errors					2	2												1%
B. Business Combinations					3	2												
C. Cash Flow Components—Financing, Investing, and Operating					0	2												
D. Contingent Liabilities and Commitments					2	1												
E. Discontinued Operations					1	2						5%					3%	
F. Earnings Per Share					2	0												2%
G. Employee Benefits					2	3												
H. Extraordinary Items					1	2											1%	1%
I. Financial Instruments					2	3												
J. Foreign Currency Transactions and Translation					3	2												
K. Income Taxes					2	1												2%
L. Interest Costs					2	1												
M. Interim Financial Reporting					2	2												
N. Leases					2	1												
O. Nonmonetary Transactions					1	2												
P. Quasi Reorganizations, Reorganizations, and Changes in Entity					1	1												
Q. Related Parties					2	2												
R. Research and Development Costs					0	1											3%	
S. Segment Reporting					0	1											3%	